WileyPLUS with ORION

A personalized, adaptive learning experience.

WileyPLUS with ORION delivers easy-to-use analytics that help educators and students see strengths and weaknesses to give learners the best chance of succeeding in the course.

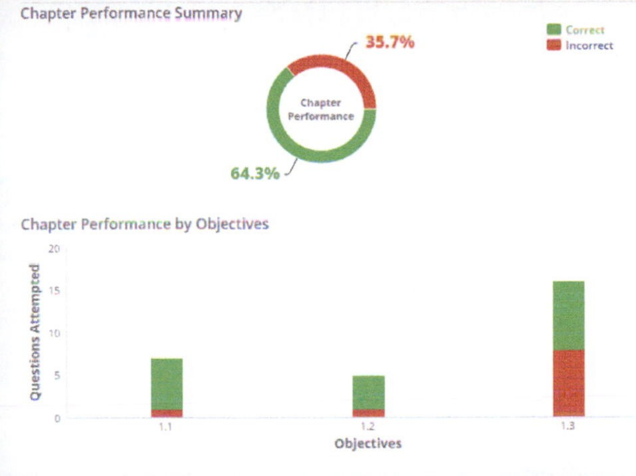

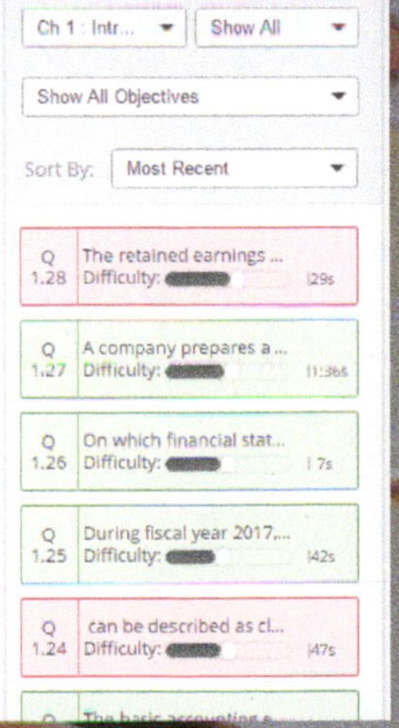

Identify which students are struggling early in the semester.

Educators assess the real-time engagement and performance of each student to inform teaching decisions. Students always know what they need to work on.

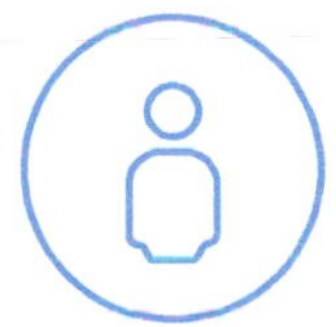

Help students organize their learning and get the practice they need.

With ORION's adaptive practice, students quickly understand what they know and don't know. They can then decide to study or practice based on their proficiency.

Measure outcomes to promote continuous improvement.

With visual reports, it's easy for both students and educators to gauge problem areas and act on what's most important.

www.ORION.wileyplus.com

Operations and Supply Chain Management

Ninth Edition

ROBERTA S. RUSSELL
Professor
Virginia Polytechnic Institute and State University

BERNARD W. TAYLOR III
R. B. Pamplin Professor
Virginia Polytechnic Institute and State University

WILEY

In memory of my parents, with appreciation for their love and support throughout the years.

To my mother, Jean V. Taylor, and in memory of my father, Bernard W. Taylor Jr., with love and appreciation.

VICE PRESIDENT & DIRECTOR	George Hoffman
EDITORIAL DIRECTOR	Veronica Visentin
EXECUTIVE EDITOR	Darren LaLonde
SPONSORING EDITOR	Jennifer Manias
PRODUCT DESIGN ASSOCIATE	Rebecca Costantini
EXECUTIVE MARKETING MANAGER	Christopher DeJohn
SENIOR CONTENT MANAGER	Dorothy Sinclair
SENIOR PRODUCTION EDITOR	Sandra Rigby
SENIOR PHOTO EDITOR	Billy Ray
SENIOR DESIGNER	Thomas Nery
COVER PHOTO	Disassembled smartphone © Yomka, Disassembled smartphone memory card © Oleksandr Lysenko, Assembling electronic device © ArtWell, Production of smartphones © Emiel de Lange, Cargo plane © gerenme, New mobile smartphones in showroom © Michael Dechev

This book was set in Stix Regular 10/12 by Aptara, Inc. India and printed and bound by Quad/Graphics-Versailles. The cover was printed by Quad/Graphics-Versailles.

This book is printed on acid free paper. ∞

Founded in 1807, John Wiley & Sons, Inc. has been a valued source of knowledge and understanding for more than 200 years, helping people around the world meet their needs and fulfill their aspirations. Our company is built on a foundation of principles that include responsibility to the communities we serve and where we live and work. In 2008, we launched a Corporate Citizenship Initiative, a global effort to address the environmental, social, economic, and ethical challenges we face in our business. Among the issues we are addressing are carbon impact, paper specifications and procurement, ethical conduct within our business and among our vendors, and community and charitable support. For more information, please visit our website: www.wiley.com/go/citizenship.

ISBN 13: 978-1-119-32097-5

The inside back cover will contain printing identification and country of origin if omitted from this page. In addition, if the ISBN on the back cover differs from the ISBN on this page, the one on the back cover is correct.

Printed in the United States of America.

V10003049_073118

About the Authors

Bernard W. Taylor III and Roberta S. Russell

BERNARD W. TAYLOR III is the Pamplin Professor of Management Science and Head of the Department of Business Information Technology in the Pamplin College of Business at Virginia Polytechnic Institute and State University. He received a Ph.D. and an M.B.A. from the University of Georgia and a B.I.E. from the Georgia Institute of Technology. He is the author of the book *Introduction to Management Science* (12th ed.) and co-author of *Management Science* (4th ed.), both published by Pearson. Dr. Taylor has published over 80 articles in such journals as *Operations Research*, *Management Science*, *Decision Sciences*, *IIE Transactions*, *Journal of the Operational Research Society*, *Computers and Operations Research*, *Omega*, and the *International Journal of Production Research*, among others. His paper in *Decision Sciences* (with P. Y. Huang and L. P. Rees) on the Japanese kanban production system received the Stanley T. Hardy Award for its contribution to the field of production and operations management. He has served as President of the Decision Sciences Institute (DSI) as well as Program Chair, Council Member, Vice President, Treasurer, and as the Editor of *Decision Line*, the newsletter of DSI. He is a Fellow of DSI and a recipient of their Distinguished Service Award. He is a former President, Vice-President, and Program Chair of the Southeast Decision Sciences Institute and a recipient of their Distinguished Service Award. He teaches management science and production and operations management courses at both the undergraduate and graduate level. He has received the University Certificate of Teaching Excellence on four occasions, the Pamplin College of Business Certificate of Teaching Excellence Award, and the Pamplin College of Business Ph.D. Teaching Excellence Award at Virginia Tech.

ROBERTA S. RUSSELL is a Professor of Business Information Technology in the Pamplin College of Business at Virginia Polytechnic Institute and State University. She received a Ph.D and a B.S. from Virginia Polytechnic Institute and State University and an M.B.A. from Old Dominion University. Dr. Russell's primary research and teaching interests are in the areas of operations and supply chain management, with special emphasis on humanitarian and healthcare operations. She has published in *Journal of Operations Management*, *Decision Sciences*, *IIE Transactions*, *International Journal of Production Research*, *IEEE Transactions*, *Annals of Operations Research*, and many others. She is also co-author of the text *Service Management and Operations*. In 2016, she received the Gyrna Award from the American Society of Quality (ASQ) for research that has made "the largest single contribution to the extension of understanding and knowledge in the philosophy, principles, or methods of quality management." Dr. Russell is a member of DSI, ASQ, POMS, and IIE. She is past President of the APICS Foundation, past Co-Chair of the Supply Chain Academic Talent Initiative (SCTAI), a Certified Fellow in Production and Inventory Management (CFPIM) and a Certified Supply Chain Management Professional (CSCP). She is past Vice President of POMS, past President of the Southwest Virginia Chapter of APICS and has held numerous offices in Southeast DSI. Her consulting experience with IBM, AT&T, Dupont, Courtaulds, Xaloy, Newport News Shipbuilding and others brings a practical perspective into the classroom. She has received the Pamplin College of Business Certificate of Teaching Excellence on two occasions, the University Certificate of Teaching Excellence, the Excellence in Diversity Award, and the MBA Association's Outstanding Professor Award. Dr. Russell teaches both undergraduate and graduate students in the classroom and online. She is frequently called upon to give workshops on teaching with technology, and has incorporated her experiences into the ancillary material that accompanies this text.

Preface

Changes in the Ninth Edition

This new ninth edition is organized around the important and prevalent topic of operations as the creation of value along the supply chain. We describe how every chapter topic fits within a supply chain framework in a company or organization in an increasingly global operating environment. Two chapters deal directly with supply chain management: Chapter 10, Supply Chain Management Strategy and Design, and Chapter 11, Global Supply Chain Procurement and Distribution. However, every chapter includes material relating the chapter topics to supply chain management in a global operating environment. In addition, Chapter 5, Service Design, reflects the expanding presence and importance of the service sector in operations management. We have also added new material throughout the book on the increasingly important OM topics of sustainability, corporate social responsibility, and risk and resilience. To help us show how the OM topics in this new edition fit together within a supply chain framework, we open each chapter with a specific example about one product group, electronics, and in particular, smartphones. Electronics and smartphones are ideal to use as examples to introduce all the various operations and supply chain management topics in this text because they are familiar and popular products to our readers, their supply chain is global, and their production process is complex and interesting.

In addition to opening each chapter with an electronics example, this new edition also includes 86 "Along the Supply Chain" boxes, 45 of which are new, that describe real-world business applications of OM topics at companies around the world. Many of these boxes focus on the increasingly important topics of sustainability and global supply chains. The boxes conclude with critical thinking questions that can be used for assignments and in-class or online discussion.

Chapter 1 focuses on examples of excellence in operations management, current issues in operations and supply chain management, and the strategic design of operations and supply chain management. Chapter 2, Quality Management, emphasizes the necessity and use of quality management systems throughout the supply chain, and includes an expanded section on ISO and its most recent updates. Chapter 3 introduces statistical process control as essential to ensuring quality along the supply chain.

Chapter 4 has sections on Design for the Environment and Collaborative Product Design Systems. Chapter 5 incorporates new statistics on the service economy, the blending of products and services, and expanded tools for service design. A streamlined waiting line analysis section is also included in the chapter. Chapter 6 emphasizes process analysis skills and includes revised material on the Internet of Things, 3D printing, and other new technologies. Chapter 7 incorporates strategies for capacity management, facility selection and design, green facilities, and examples of various service layouts.

Chapter 8, Human Resources, has an increased emphasis on sustainability in the workplace, especially among global suppliers of U.S. companies, as well as increased attention to employee cultural and diversity issues. Chapter 9, Project Management, has an increased focus on cultural and diversity issues in the management of global projects, plus sections on project risk and how to manage it. Chapter 10, Supply Chain Management Strategy and Design, has a section on risk and resilience in global supply chains, increased attention to global sustainability issues and an updated section on SCOR. Chapter 11, Global Supply Chain Procurement and Distribution, addresses spend analysis, global logistics, and additional issues in sustainability. Chapter 12, Forecasting, includes a section on the increasingly important IT topic of data mining, and Chapter 13, Inventory Management, emphasizes its important role in controlling costs along a global supply chain.

Chapter 14 emphasizes the need for effective Sales and Operations Planning, and includes a section on Revenue Management. Chapter 15, Resource Planning, updates resource planning with discussions of cloud computing, in-memory computing, big data, and analytics. Chapter 16 expands Lean Systems to lean services, including lean supply chain and lean and the environment. Chapter 17 incorporates employee scheduling, artificial intelligence, and theory of constraints, along with traditional scheduling methods.

Major Text Themes

Operations Strategy: Creating Value Along the Supply Chain

A company's plan for being competitive is its strategy. The success of a strategic plan is largely determined by how well a company coordinates all of its internal processes, including operations, with its suppliers and customers to produce products and services that provide value. Throughout this book, we try to show how the functions and processes described in each chapter fit into a company's strategic design for the creation of value. In each chapter, we emphasize the need for considering the overall strategic implications of particular operating decisions.

One way in which companies can gain a competitive edge is by deploying the basic functions of operations management in a more effective manner than their rivals, e.g., building a better supply chain. Therefore, we give literally dozens of examples that explain how companies deploy specific operations functions along their supply chain to provide value and make them successful. Throughout the book, "Along the Supply Chain" boxes describe how successful companies have gained a competitive edge through operations.

Focusing on Electronics Every edition of this text has focused on one product group as a continuing story for the introduction to each chapter topic. These introductory product themes for previous editions have included rice, coffee, chocolate, and denim jeans (and thus textiles and apparel). They all have a global supply chain in common. For this ninth edition, we focus on smartphones and the electronics industry that supports it. Electronics is an interesting, diverse industry that includes highly automated advanced manufacturing, low-tech manual assembly operations and a global supply chain. Product life is short and new technology makes previous product versions obsolete within the span of six months to two years. The pace is fast moving and challenging – the type of energy and environment that college students enjoy.

Global Operations

Companies and organizations today must increasingly compete in a global marketplace. The establishment of new trade agreements between countries, innovations in information technology, and improvements in transport and shipping are just a few of the factors that have enabled companies to develop global supply chains. The opening of the global marketplace has only served to introduce more competitors and make competition tougher, thus making strategic supply chain design even more important for achieving success. In this edition, we introduce this global aspect of operations into every chapter. In each chapter, we include examples that touch on the impact of global operations relative to the topic under discussion, and we discuss how globalization affects supply chain management.

Sustainability

Environmental concerns are changing every aspect of operations and supply chain management from product and service design, to supplier sourcing, to manufacture and delivery. In virtually every chapter of this text we address the impact of "sustainability" (i.e., meeting present needs without sacrificing future resources) and give examples of "green practices." For example, in Chapter 4 on product design, we discuss the design for environment lifecycle, eco-labeling, recycling and reuse, and sustainable operations. In Chapter 6 on processes we discuss green manufacturing; and in Chapter 7 on facilities we discuss LEED certified green buildings. In Chapter 8 we discuss how companies achieve a sustainable work place when they have suppliers around the world. In Chapter 10 on supply chain management we discuss sustainable sourcing in a global environment; and in Chapter 16 on lean systems we discuss lean and the environment.

Services and Manufacturing

We have attempted to strike a balance between manufacturing and service operations in this book. Traditionally, operations and supply chain management was thought of almost exclusively in a manufacturing context. However, in the United States and other industrialized nations, there has been a dramatic shift toward service industries. Thus, managing service operations is an important area of study. In many cases, operations and supply chain management processes and techniques are indistinguishable between service and manufacturing. However, in many other instances, service operations present unique situations and problems that require focused attention and unique solutions. We have tried to reflect the uniqueness of service operations by providing focused discussions on service operations throughout the text. For example, in Chapter 2 on quality management we specifically address the importance of quality management in service companies, in Chapter 5 on Service Design we emphasize the differences in design considerations between manufacturing and services, and in Chapter 14 we discuss aggregate planning in services. One type of service examined in virtually every chapter in the book is health care.

Qualitative and Quantitative Processes

We have also attempted to strike a balance between the qualitative (or managerial) aspects of operations management and the quantitative aspects. In the contemporary world of operations management, the quantitative and technological aspects are probably more important than ever. The ability to manage people and resources effectively, to motivate, organize, control, evaluate, and adapt to change, have become critical to competing in today's global markets. Thus, throughout this book we seek to explain and clearly demonstrate how the successful operations manager manages, and how to use quantitative techniques and technology when they are applicable.

However, we attempt to present these quantitative topics in a way that's not overly complex or mathematically intimidating. Above all, we want to show how the quantitative topics fit in with, and complement, the qualitative aspects of operations management. We want you to be able to see both "the forest and the trees."

Teaching and Learning Support Features

Russell & Taylor, 9th Edition, is supported by a comprehensive learning package that assists the instructor in creating a motivating and enthusiastic environment.

Pedagogy in the Textbook

"Along the Supply Chain" Boxes These boxes are located in every chapter in the text. They describe the application of operations in a real-world company, organization, or agency related to specific topics in each chapter. They emphasize how companies effectively compete with operations management in the global marketplace. The descriptions of operations at actual companies in these boxes help the student understand how specific OM techniques and concepts are used by companies, which also make the topics and concepts easier to understand. In addition, we have added discussion questions to these boxes to help students and teachers "connect" the example to the chapter topics.

OM Dialogue Boxes These boxes include dialogues with recent college business school graduates who are working in operations management in the real world. They describe how they apply various OM topics in the text in their own jobs and the value of their own OM training in college. This provides students with a perspective on the benefit of studying operations management now and its future benefit.

Examples The primary means of teaching the various quantitative topics in this text is through examples. These examples are liberally distributed throughout the text to demonstrate how problems are solved in a clear, straightforward approach to make them easier to understand.

Solved Problems At the end of each chapter, just prior to the homework questions and problems, there is a section with solved examples to serve as a guide for working the homework problems. These examples are solved in a detailed, step-by-step manner.

Summary of Key Formulas These summaries at the end of each chapter and supplement include all of the key quantitative formulas introduced in the chapter in one location for easy reference.

Summary of Key Terms Located at the end of each chapter, these summaries provide a list of key terms introduced in that chapter and their definitions in one convenient location for quick and easy reference.

Homework Problems, Questions, and Cases Our text contains a large number of end-of-chapter exercises for student assignments. There are almost 700 homework problems and 56 more advanced case problems. There are also 500 discussion questions including new questions. Answers to selected odd-numbered homework problems are included in the back of the book. As we mention in the following "Online Resources for Instructors" section, Excel spreadsheet solution files are available to the instructor for the majority of the end-of-chapter problems and cases.

Online Resources for Students

www.wiley.com/college/Russell

No other innovation has affected operations management in the past few years as much as digital technology and the Internet, and this is no less true in education. Therefore, we make full use of technology as a learning and teaching medium in the courses we teach and in our text. Students can link to the text website or WileyPLUS where an exciting set of Internet resources has been compiled.

Dynamic resources include animated demo problems, interactive applications and exercises, and direct links to other sources on the Internet. These various resources and learning tools are organized by chapter and are flagged in the textbook with a web icon. Here are some of the items available to students:

- ***Web links*** for companies and concepts discussed in each chapter can be accessed online. These provide enrichment for those students who want to learn more about a topic, and serve as a valuable resource for student assignments and papers.
- ***Virtual Tours*** provided for each chapter bring operations management to life. Selected tours are accompanied by a set of questions directly related to concepts discussed in the chapter.
- ***Internet Exercises*** provide up-to-date access to current issues in operations. These add immediacy to classroom discussions and ensure that operations management topics remain relevant to the student.
- ***Practice Quizzes*** are provided online where students can get immediate feedback on their progress.

Excel Files of Exhibits Excel is used extensively throughout the text to solve various quantitative problems and many Excel illustrations are provided throughout the text.

Every Excel spreadsheet used to prepare the examples in the text is available on the text website for students and instructors. They are organized by chapter and are listed by their exhibit number. Below is an example of Exhibit 1.1 from Chapter 1. Notice the file name is simply the exhibit number plus the topic

EXHIBIT 1.1

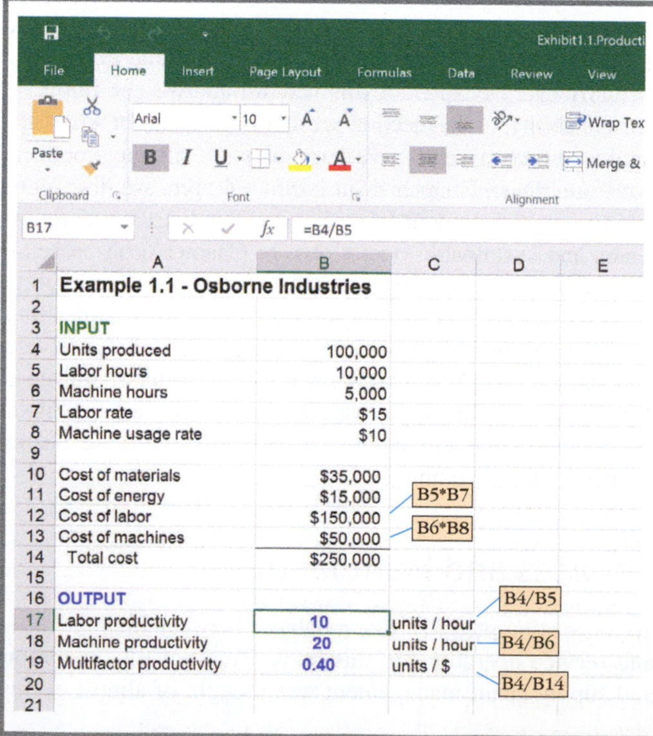

(i.e., Exhibit 1.1. Productivity). Please look in each file carefully. In many cases, several sheets in one file have been used to display different parts of a problem, such as a graphical solution as well as a numerical solution. Example files are also available for MS Project files in Chapter 9.

Online Resources for Instructors

www.wiley.com/college/russell

Instructor's Manual The Instructor's Manual, updated by the authors, features chapter outlines, teaching notes, experiential exercises, alternate examples to those provided in the text, pause and reflect questions for classroom discussion, and suggested online videos to use in class or assign for homework.

Test Bank Fully revised from the previous edition, this test bank consists of true/false, multiple-choice, short answer, and essay questions. All questions have been carefully accuracy-checked to ensure the highest quality of materials for our customers. The questions are also available electronically on the textbook support site. The Computerized Test Bank, for use on a PC running Windows, is from a test-generating program that allows instructors to modify and add questions in order to customize their exams.

PowerPoint Presentation Slides The PowerPoint presentation slides, revised by Lance Matheson of Virginia Tech, include outlines for every chapter, exhibits from the text, and additional examples, providing instructors with a number of learning opportunities for students. The PowerPoint slides can be accessed on the instructor's portion of the 9th edition website. Lecture notes accompany each slide.

Solutions Manual The Solutions Manual, updated by the authors, features detailed answers to end-of-chapter questions, homework problems, and case problems.

Excel Homework Solutions and Excel Exhibit Files This new edition includes almost 700 homework problems and 56 case problems. Excel solution files for the instructor are provided on the website for the majority of these problems. In addition, Microsoft Project solution files are provided for most of the homework problems in Chapter 9 (Project Management). Excel worksheets for class handouts or homework assignments are provided for QFD, process flow charts, MRP matrices, and others. Excel exhibit files for every example in the text solved with Excel are provided as templates for solving similar problems for both student and instructor and are available on the text website.

Web Quizzes These online quizzes, revised by Scott Hedin of Gonzaga University, vary in level of difficulty and are designed to help your students evaluate their individual progress through a chapter. Web quizzes are available on the student portion of the website. Here students will have the ability to test themselves with 15–20 questions per chapter that include true-false and multiple choice questions.

OM Tools OM Tools is an Excel add-in designed to accompany the Russell/Taylor, *Operations and Supply Chain Management*, 9th edition text. The software consists of 18 modules with over 60 problem types. OM Tools is easy to use and interpret, and is accompanied by a help file with text references. A new and updated version of OM Tools is available for this edition of the text.

Virtual Tours are online tours of service and production facilities. Selected tours are made available to students on the student portion of the website, along with questions that help students apply the concepts they've learned in the text to real-world companies. A Virtual Tours Master List, organized by industry, contains links to over 200 online tours that instructors may use for assignments or classroom presentation.

OM Student Videos Offered on the instructor companion website, we offer a collection of videos done by students that provide excellent examples of the concepts illustrated in the text. These videos can be accessed on the instructor companion website. Please go to www.wiley.com/college/russell, for more information.

Darden Business Cases Darden Business Publishing Cases delivered through the Wiley Custom Select website www.customselect.wiley.com.

Littlefield Technologies Operations Management Simulation Empowers students to make real world decisions and apply what they learn in the classroom. www.wileydifferenceinbusiness.com

WileyPLUS

WileyPLUS is a research-based online environment for effective teaching and learning.

WileyPLUS builds students' confidence because it takes the guess-work out of studying by providing students with a clear roadmap: what to do, how to do it, if they did it right. Students will take more initiative so you'll have greater impact on their achievement in the classroom and beyond.

Now with ORION, An Adaptive Learning Experience Based on cognitive science, *WileyPLUS* with ORION provides students with a personal, adaptive learning experience so they can build their proficiency on topics and use their study time most effectively.

ORION helps students learn by learning about them.

- Students BEGIN by taking a quick diagnostic for any chapter. This will determine their baseline proficiency on each topic in the chapter. A diagnostic report helps students decide what to do next.
- Students can either STUDY or PRACTICE. Study directs students to the specific topic they choose in *WileyPLUS*, where they can read from the e-textbook or use the variety of relevant resources. Student can also practice, using questions and feedback powered by ORION's adaptive learning engine.
- A number of reports and ongoing recommendations help students MAINTAIN their proficiency over time for each topic.

For more information, go to: www.wiley.com/college/sc/oriondemo.

WileyPLUS for Instructors WileyPLUS enables you to:

- Assign automatically graded homework, practice, and quizzes from the end of chapter and test bank.
- Track your students' progress in an instructor's grade book.

- Access all teaching and learning resources, including an online version of the text, and student and instructor supplements, in one easy-to-use website. These include full colour PowerPoint slides, teaching videos, case files, and answers and animations.
- Create class presentations using Wiley-provided resources, with the ability to customize and add your own materials.

WileyPLUS for Students In WileyPLUS, students will find various helpful tools, such as an ebook, the students, study manual, videos with tutorials by the author applets, Decision Dilemma and Decision Dilemma Solved animations, learning activities, flash cards for key terms, demonstration problems, databases in both Excel and Minitab, case data in both Excel and Minitab, and problem data in both Excel and Minitab.

Acknowledgments

The writing and revision of a textbook, like any large project, requires the help and creative energy of many people, and this is certainly not the exception. We especially appreciate the confidence, support, help, and friendship of our editor at Wiley. We also thank the Wiley staff members who helped with our book including:

Jennifer Manias, Sponsoring Editor; Darren LaLonde, Executive Editor; Rebecca Costantini, Product Design Associate; Chris DeJohn, Executive Marketing Manager; Sandra Rigby, Production Editor; and, numerous other people who work behind the scenes to whom we never saw or spoke. We are indebted to the reviewers of the text including: Robert Donnelly; Robert Aboolian, California State University San Marcos; Ajay Aggarwal, Millsaps College; Fred Anderson, Indiana University of Pennsylvania; Beni Asllani, University of Tennessee Chattanooga; Anteneh Ayanso, University of Connecticut, Storrs; Brent Bandy, University of Wisconsin, Oshkosh; Joe Biggs, California Polytechnic State University; Tom Bramorski, University of Wisconsin, Whitewater; Kimball Bullington, Middle Tennessee State University; Cem Canel, University of North Carolina, Wilmington; Janice Cerveny, Florida Atlantic University; Robert Clark, SUNY Stony Brook; Ajay Das, Baruch College CUNY; Kathy Dhanda, University of Portland; Susan Emens, Kent State University; Yee Fok, University of New Orleans; Phillip Fry, Boise State University; Mark Gershon, Temple University; Robert Greve, Oklahoma State University; Robert Frese, Maryville University; Jay Jayaram, University of South Carolina, Columbia; Vaidy Jayaraman, University of Miami; Serge Karalli, DePaul University; William Kime, University of New Mexico; Peter Klein, Ohio University; Howard Kraye, University of New Mexico, Albuquerque; John Kros, East Carolina University; Gopalan Kutty, Mansfield University; Bingguang Li, Albany State University; Royce Lorentz, Slippery Rock University; Sheldon Lou, California State University, San Marcos; Ken Mannino, Milwaukee School of Engineering; Lance Matheson, Virgina Tech; Duncan McDougall, Plymouth State University; Jaideep Motwani, Grand Valley State University; Hilary Moyes, University of Pittsburgh; Barin Nag, Towson University; Ozgur Ozluk, San Francisco State University; Amer Qureshi, University of Texas Arlington; Jim Robison, Sonoma State University; Raj Selladurai, Indiana University Northwest; Robert Setaputro, University of Wisconsin, Milwaukee; Jacob Simons, Georgia Southern University; Marilyn Smith, Winthrop University; Donna Stewart, University of Wisconsin, Stout; Donald Stout, St. Martin's College; Dothang Truong, Fayetteville State University; Elizabeth Trybus, California State University, Northridge; Ray Vankataraman, Pennsylvania State University, Erie; Timothy Vaughan, University of Wisconsin, Eau Claire; Mark Vrobelfski, University of Arizona; Gustavo Vulcano, New York University; Kevin Watson, University of New Orleans; Michel Whittenberg, University of Texas, Arlington; Hulya Yazici, University of Wisconsin, La Crosse; Jinfeng Yue, Middle Tennessee State University; and Xiaoqun Zhang, Pennsylvania State University, Harrisburg. We also thank the reviewers of the sixth edition including: Ajay Aggarwal, Millsaps College; Binguang Li, Albany State University; Christina McCart, Roanoke College; Cuneyt Altinoz, East Carolina University; Dana Johnson, Michigan Technical University; David Frantz, Indiana University; Donald Stout, St. Martin's University; Doug Hales, University of Rhode Island; Drew Stapleton, University of Wisconsin, LaCrosse; Fataneh Taghaboni-Dutta, University of Michigan, Flint; Ike Ehie, Kansas State University; John Hebert, University of Akron; John Kros, East Carolina University; Kaushik Sengupta, Hofstra University; Larry White, Eastern Illinois University; Lewis Coopersmith, Rider University; Mohammad Sedaghat, Fairleigh Dickinson University; Morgan Henrie, University of Alaska, Anchorage; Phil Fry, Boise State University; Robert Aboolian, California State University, San Marcos; Robert Clark, SUNY, Stony Brook; Scott Hedin, Gonzaga University; Susan Emens, Kent State University, Trumbull; Tom Wilder, California State University, Chico; Zhiwei Zhu, University of Louisiana, Lafayette.

They contributed numerous suggestions, comments, and ideas that dramatically improved and changed this book over several editions. We offer our sincere thanks to these colleagues and hope that they can take some satisfaction in their contribution to our final product. We wish to thank our students who have class-tested, critiqued, and contributed to the first eight editions and this ninth edition from a consumer's point of view. We thank colleagues Michelle Seref, Virginia Tech, for creating a new version of OM Tools; Laura Clark, Virginia Tech, for her help with WileyPLUS; Ronny Richardson, Southern Polytechnic State University, who accuracy checked all of the supplements for this text; and graduate student Yuhong Li for her assistance in numerous capacities. We are especially grateful to Tracy McCoy and Sylvia Seavey at Virginia Tech for their unstinting help, hard work, and patience.

R.S.R and B.W.T

Brief Contents

Contents

5 Service Design 189

6 Processes and Technology 224

7 Capacity and Facilities Design 254

S7 Operational Decision-Making Tools: Facility Location Models 292

8 Human Resources 312

S8 Operational Decision-Making Tools: Work Measurement 343

11 Global Supply Chain Procurement and Distribution 440

S11 Operational Decision-Making Tools: Transportation and Transshipment Models 466

12 Forecasting 487

CHAPTER 1

Introduction to Operations and Supply Chain Management

Christopher Futcher/Getty Images

LEARNING OBJECTIVES

After reading this chapter, you will be able to:

- Describe what the operations function is and how it relates to other business functions.
- Discuss the key factors that have contributed to the evolution of operations and supply chain management.
- Discuss how and why businesses operate globally, and the importance of globalization in supply chain management.
- Calculate and interpret productivity measures used for measuring competitiveness.
- Discuss the importance of operations and supply chain management to a firm's strategy, and the process of developing, aligning, and deploying strategy.

The Cell Is the Thing

What is the most important product in your life? I'm betting most of you would say your smartphone. Smartphones (see photo) allow us to communicate with our friends, our family, and the world. They organize our lives and tell us where to go and what to do. They connect us to each other and share what is important, what is trending, who is who, and how we can participate. We will be following the design, manufacture, use and re-use of cell phones in this book as background for decisions in operations and supply chain management. Our journey will take us from the desert sands, through the most advanced and automated factories on the planet, across oceans to massive assembly lines of workers, and through high-tech design centers and logistics hubs. We will crisscross the world several times before landing in a retail store or website and arriving at your door. And when the next latest and greatest technology is available and you opt for an upgrade, we'll follow the disposal, recycling, and reuse of your old unit and muse about what might be next on the horizon.

Operations management designs, operates, and improves productive systems—systems for getting work done. Operations managers are found in banks, hospitals, factories, and government. They design systems, ensure quality, produce products, and deliver services. They work with customers and suppliers, the latest technology, and global partners. They solve problems, reengineer processes, innovate, and integrate. Operations is more than planning and controlling; it's doing. Whether it's superior quality, speed-to-market, customization, or low cost, excellence in operations is critical to a firm's success.

Operations management The design, operation, and improvement of productive systems.

Along the Supply Chain

What Do Operations and Supply Chain Managers Do?

Operations and supply chain managers are the *improvement people*, the realistic, hard-nosed, make-it-work, get-it-done people; the planners, coordinators, and negotiators. They perform a variety of tasks in many different types of businesses and organizations.

Jim Craigmyle/Getty Images

SUZANNE DECHILLO/The New York Times

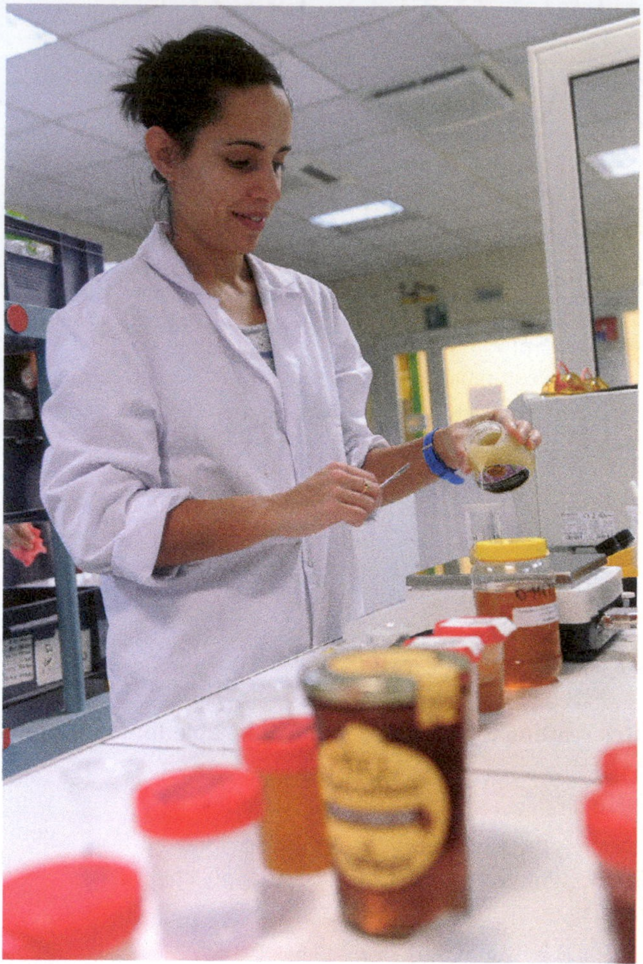

GAIZKA IROZ/Getty Images, Inc.

Let's meet Claire Thielen, director of informatics for a healthcare system; Ada Liu, division manager for Li & Fung Trading Company; and Erin Hiller, food technologist at a major branded food manufacturer.

Claire Thielen is a healthcare professional who specializes in decision support, process improvement, and organizational performance. She facilitates interdisciplinary teams as they pursue continuous quality improvement projects and analyzes methods and systems for managing information. Her projects include determining staffing patterns and workflow for computerized scheduling systems; consolidating policies, procedures, and practices for hospital mergers; developing and implementing balanced scorecards and benchmarking reports; designing clinical studies of new medication effectiveness; and conducting training sessions on process mapping and analysis (see photo). Claire Thielen improves quality, productivity, and information in the healthcare industry.

Ada Liu is a division manager for Li & Fung, a global sourcing company. She coordinates global production and distribution for major players in the garment industry (see photo). For one particular trouser order, she had the fabric woven in China (for their unique dyeing process), chose fasteners from Hong Kong and Korea (for their durability), and sent the raw materials to Guatemala for sewing (for their basic skills, low cost, and proximity to the United States). If problems should arise, Liu can reroute the order to one of its 7500 suppliers in 37 countries. Ada Liu is a supply chain expert for Li & Fung.

Erin Hiller is a food technologist at a major branded food manufacturer. She works in research and development (R&D) devising, developing, and testing new products, as shown in the photo. For part of her job, she travels to manufacturing plants across the country to monitor the ramp-up of production for consumer food products with new formulas or ingredients. She verifies that correct procedures are being followed, samples and tests output for quality and consistency, and revises formulaic recipes as required. She also evaluates new and emerging technologies and determines whether they would be beneficial to the product lines and manufacturing operations. Erin Hiller brings fresh designs to the market, keeps operations up to date, and ensures the safety and quality of the foods you eat every day.

Sources: Claire Theilen, LinkedIn, accessed January 10, 2010; Joanne Lee-Young, "Furiously Fast Fashions," *The Industry Standard Magazine*, (June 22, 2001); Interview with Erin Hiller (January 3, 2013).

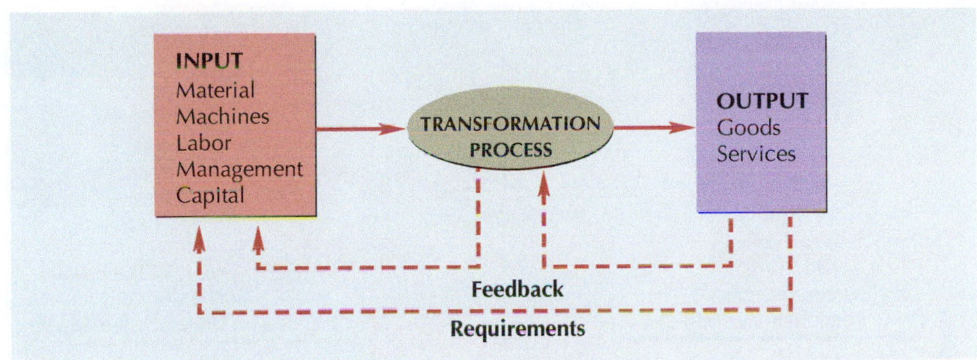

FIGURE 1.1 **Operations as a Transformation Process**

Operations is often defined as a transformation process. As shown in **Figure 1.1**, inputs (such as material, machines, labor, management, and capital) are transformed into outputs (goods and services). Requirements and feedback from customers are used to adjust factors in the transformation process, which may in turn alter inputs. In operations management, we try to ensure that the transformation process is performed efficiently and that the output is of greater *value* than the sum of the inputs. Thus, the role of operations is to create value. The transformation process itself can be viewed as a series of activities along a **value chain** extending from supplier to customer.

Operations A function or system that transforms inputs into outputs of greater value.

Value chain A series of activities from supplier to customer that add value to a product or service.

The input–transformation–output process is characteristic of a wide variety of operating systems. In an automobile factory, sheet steel is formed into different shapes, painted and finished, and then assembled with thousands of component parts to produce a working automobile. In an aluminum factory, various grades of bauxite are mixed, heated, and cast into ingots of different sizes. In a hospital, patients are helped to become healthier individuals through special care, meals, medication, lab work, and surgical procedures. Obviously, "operations" can take many different forms. The transformation process can be

physical,	as in manufacturing operations;
locational,	as in transportation or warehouse operations;
exchange,	as in retail operations;
physiological,	as in healthcare;
psychological,	as in entertainment; or
informational,	as in communication.

The Operations Function

Activities in operations management (OM) include organizing work, selecting processes, arranging layouts, locating facilities, designing jobs, measuring performance, controlling quality, scheduling work, managing inventory, and planning production. Operations managers deal with people, technology, and deadlines. These managers need good technical, conceptual, and behavioral skills. Their activities are closely intertwined with other functional areas of a firm.

The four primary functional areas of a firm are marketing, finance, operations, and human resources. As shown in **Figure 1.2**, for most firms, operations is the technical core or "hub" of the organization, interacting with the other functional areas and suppliers to produce goods and provide services for customers. For example, to obtain monetary resources for production, operations provides finance and accounting with production and inventory data, capital budgeting requests, and capacity expansion and technology plans. Finance pays workers and suppliers, performs cost analyses, approves capital investments, and communicates requirements of shareholders and financial markets. Marketing provides operations with sales forecasts, customer orders, customer feedback, and information on promotions and product development. Operations, in turn, provides marketing with information on product or service availability, lead-time estimates, order status, and delivery schedules. For personnel needs, operations relies on human resources to recruit, train, evaluate, and compensate workers and to assist with legal issues, job design, and union activities. Outside the organization operations interacts with suppliers to order materials or services, communicate production and delivery requirements, certify quality, negotiate contracts, and finalize design specifications.

FIGURE 1.2 **Operations as the Technical Core**

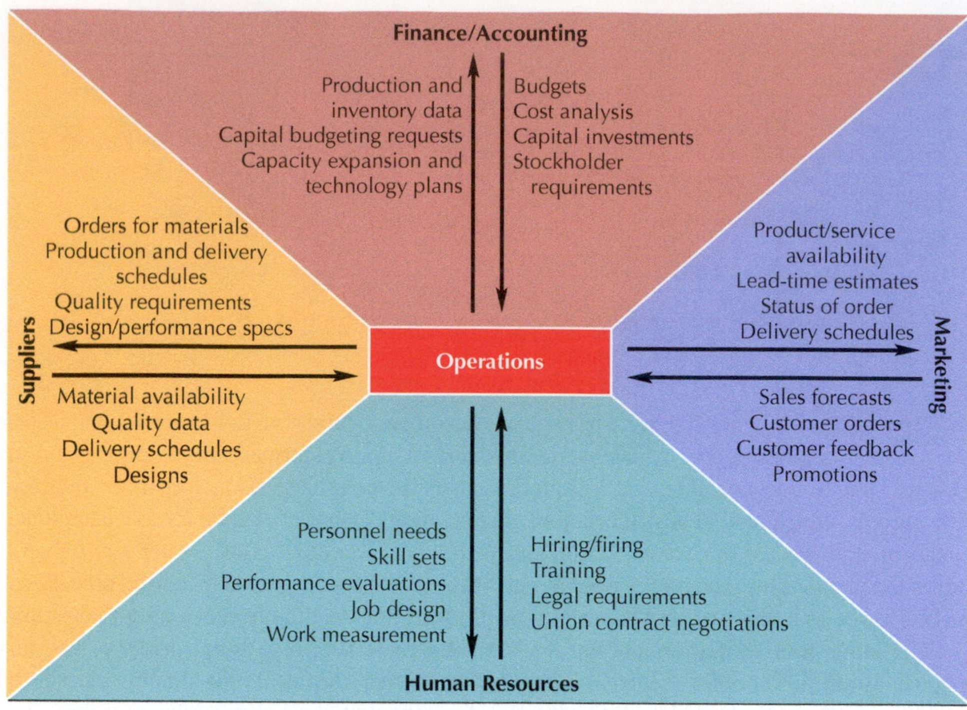

As a field of study, operations brings together many disciplines and provides an integrated view of business organizations. Operations managers are in demand in business, industry, and government. Chief operating officers (COOs) run major corporations as shown in **Figure 1.3**, Vice-presidents of Operations and Supply Chain Management oversee scores of departments, facilities, and employees. Typical jobs for new college graduates include business process analyst, inventory analyst, project coordinator, unit supervisor, supply chain analyst, materials manager, quality assurance specialist, production scheduler, and logistics planner. Even if you do not pursue a career in operations and supply chain management, you'll be able to use the ideas you learn in this course to organize work, ensure quality, and manage processes. Regardless of your major, you can apply some aspect of operations and supply chain management to your future career—as did Mark, Nicole, John, Vignesh, Margie, and Anastasia, who tell their stories in **Figure 1.4** and the OM Dialogues dispersed throughout the text.

FIGURE 1.3 **Sample Organizational Structure**

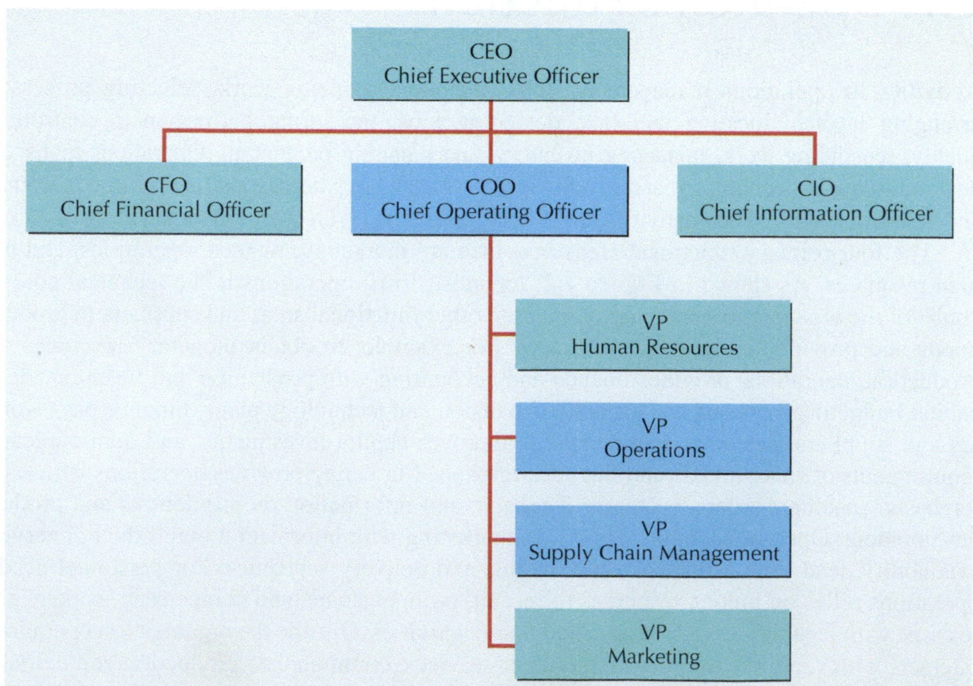

Mark Jackson

Marketing Manager for Pizza Hut

Roberta Russell

As regional marketing manager for Pizza Hut, I'm responsible for 21 stores. It's my job to make sure each store is operating properly and, when new products come out, to see that they are given the attention they deserve. I also coach managers and employees about their job and their relationship with the customer.

You would think that a marketing manager's job would be concerned solely with advertising, special promotions, store signage, customer service, and the like. But we also deal with quality, forecasting, logistics, and other operational issues. Marketing and operations are almost inseparable in services. We can come out with a new product and spend megabucks advertising it, but if the product is not made or delivered properly, all is lost.

The most important aspect of quality is consistency—so that the customer gets the same pizza at any Pizza Hut from whichever cook happens to be on shift. We have exact standards and specifications for our products, and it's important that operating procedures be followed.

Scheduling is somewhat of a headache because of staff turnover and individual limitations on working hours. Some of that is alleviated in our new system where we allow employees to request days off up to six months in advance. They can put requests into the system when they clock in each day, and they can view upcoming schedules.

Our forecasting system keeps historical data on sales by hour and day of the week five years back. Forecasts are weighted averages of past demand—usually 60% of the past two weeks' sales and 40% of the past six weeks' sales. A manager can *freeze* the forecast and make manual adjustments, such as increasing demand during a home football game weekend or when a local festival is under way. Managers can also enter notes into the system when unusual occurrences affect demand, like a snowstorm. When the forecast is set, it generates a labor plan for the week, along with prep plans for salad, dough, breadsticks, and so forth. The labor plan just specifies the number of workers needed; it is up to the manager to do the detailed scheduling of individuals.

After quality, it's all about speed of delivery—whether to the customer's table or to the customer's home. We have initiatives such as *Ready for Revenue* where we pre-sauce and pre-cheese in anticipation of customer orders, and *Aces in Their Places* where we make sure the best people are scheduled and ready to go for peak demand periods. As for delivery, we keep track of percent of deliveries under 39 minutes and percent of deliveries to promise. We found we could significantly reduce the number of drivers needed (and keep the same customer satisfaction numbers) by promising delivery within 39 minutes rather than 30. We also are more efficient now that dispatching divides our delivery areas into delivery pods and uses computerized estimates of transit time.

MARKETING
Mark: "How can you do a good job marketing a product if you're unsure of its quality or delivery status?"

MANAGEMENT
Margie: "We use so many things you learn in an operations class—scheduling, lean production, theory of constraints, and tons of quality tools."

ACCOUNTING
Vignesh: "As an auditor you must understand the fundamentals of operations management."

INFORMATION TECHNOLOGY
Nicole: "IT is a tool, and there's no better place to apply it than in operations."

FINANCE
John: "Most of our capital budgeting requests are from operations, and most of our cost savings, too."

ECONOMICS
Anastasia: "It's all about processes. I live by flowcharts and Pareto analysis."

Roberta Russell

FIGURE 1.4 How Is Operations Relevant to My Major?

Now that you are aware of how operations might relate to your interests, let's take a brief look at how the field of operations and supply chain management (OSM) has evolved to its present state.

The Evolution of Operations and Supply Chain Management

Although history is full of amazing production feats—the pyramids of Egypt, the Great Wall of China, the roads and aqueducts of Rome—the widespread production of consumer goods—and thus, operations management—did not begin until the Industrial Revolution in the 1700s. Prior to that time, skilled craftspersons and their apprentices fashioned goods for individual customers from studios in their own homes. Every piece was unique, hand-fitted, and made entirely by one person, a process known as **craft production**. Although *craft production* still exists today, the availability of coal, iron ore, and steam power set into motion a series of industrial inventions that revolutionized the way work was performed. Great mechanically powered machines replaced the laborer as the primary factor of production and brought workers to a central location to perform tasks under the direction of an "overseer" in a place called a "factory." The revolution first took hold in textile mills, grain mills, metalworking, and machine-making facilities.

Craft production The process of handcrafting products or services for individual customers.

Around the same time, Adam Smith's *Wealth of Nations* (1776) proposed the **division of labor**, in which the production process was broken down into a series of small tasks, each performed by a different worker. The specialization of the workers on limited, repetitive tasks allowed them to become very proficient at those tasks and further encouraged the development of specialized machinery.

Division of labor Dividing a job into a series of small tasks each performed by a different worker.

The introduction of **interchangeable parts** by Eli Whitney (1790s) allowed the manufacture of firearms, clocks, watches, sewing machines, and other goods to shift from customized one-at-a-time production to volume production of standardized parts. This meant the factory needed a system of measurements and inspection, a standard method of production, and supervisors to check the quality of the worker's production.

Interchangeable parts The standardization of parts initially as replacement parts enabled mass production.

Advances in technology continued through the 1800s. Cost accounting and other control systems were developed, but management theory and practice were virtually nonexistent.

In the early 1900s an enterprising laborer (and later chief engineer) at Midvale Steel Works named Frederick W. Taylor approached the management of work as a science. Based on observation, measurement, and analysis, he identified the best method for performing each job. Once determined, the methods were standardized for all workers, and economic incentives were established to encourage workers to follow the standards. Taylor's philosophy became known as **scientific management**. His ideas were embraced and extended by efficiency experts Frank and Lillian Gilbreth, Henry Gantt, and others. One of Taylor's biggest advocates was Henry Ford.

Scientific management The systematic analysis of work methods.

Henry Ford applied scientific management to the production of the Model T in 1913 and reduced the time required to assemble a car from a high of 728 hours to 1½ hours. A Model T chassis moved slowly down a conveyor belt with six workers walking alongside it, picking up parts from carefully spaced piles on the floor and fitting them to the chassis.[1] The short assembly time per car allowed the Model T to be produced in high volumes, or "en masse," yielding the name **mass production**.

Mass production The high-volume production of a standardized product for a mass market.

American manufacturers became adept at mass production over the next 50 years and easily dominated manufacturing worldwide. The human relations movement of the 1930s, led by Elton Mayo and the Hawthorne studies, introduced the idea that worker motivation, as well as the technical aspects of work, affected productivity. Theories of motivation were developed by Frederick Herzberg, Abraham Maslow, Douglas McGregor, and others. Quantitative models and techniques spawned by the operations research groups of World War II continued to develop and were applied successfully to manufacturing and services. Computers and automation led still another upsurge in technological advancements applied to operations. These events are summarized in Table 1.1.

[1]David Halberstam, *The Reckoning* (New York: William Morrow, 1986), pp. 79–81.

TABLE 1.1 Historical Events in Operations Management

ERA	EVENTS/CONCEPTS	DATES	ORIGINATOR
Industrial Revolution	Steam engine	1769	James Walt
	Division of labor	1776	Adam Smith
	Interchangeable parts	1790	Eli Whitney
Scientific Management	Principles of scientific management	1911	Frederick W. Taylor
	Time and motion studies	1911	Frank and Lillian Gilbreth
	Activity scheduling chart	1912	Henry Gantt
	Moving assembly line	1913	Henry Ford
Human Relations	Hawthorne studies	1930	Elton Mayo
	Motivation theories	1940s	Abraham Maslow
		1950s	Frederick Herzberg
		1960s	Douglas McGregor
Operations Research	Linear programming	1947	George Dantzig
	Digital computer	1951	Remington Rand
	Simulation, waiting line theory, decision theory, PERT/CPM	1950s	Operations research groups
	MRP	1960s	Joseph Orlicky, IBM, and others
	EDI, CIM	1970s	Auto industry, DARPA
Quality Revolution	JIT (just-in-time)	1970s	Taiichi Ohno (Toyota)
	TQM (total quality management)	1980s	W. Edwards Deming, Joseph Juran
	Strategy and operations		Wickham Skinner, Robert Hayes
	Reengineering	1990s	Michael Hammer, James Champy
	Six Sigma	1990s	GE, Motorola
Internet Revolution	Internet, WWW	1990s	ARPANET, Tim Berners-Lee
	ERP, supply chain management,		SAP, Oracle, Dell, Apple
	E-commerce, social networking	2000s	Amazon, Yahoo, eBay, Google, Facebook, YouTube, Twitter, etc.
Globalization	World Trade Organization	1990s	GATT
	European Union		Europe
	Global supply chains	2000s	China, India
	Outsourcing		Emerging economies
Sustainability	Global warming	2010s, Today	Numerous companies, scientists, statesmen and governments
	Carbon footprint		
	Green products		
	Corporate social responsibility (CSR)		World Economic Forum, Kyoto Protocol
	UN Global Compact		United Nations
Digital Revolution	Big data, Internet of Things (IoT), 3D printing, Smart cities, Autonomous vehicles, Drones	Today	Google, Apache, P&G, MIT, NSF, Amazon, and others

Along the Supply Chain

Feeding America

Each year, the Feeding America network helps provide food to more than 46 million people facing hunger in the United States, including 12 million children and 7 million seniors. Through 61,000 food pantries, 200 food banks, and innumerable community meal programs, the Feeding America network provides more than 3.7 billion meals to individuals and families in need. The non-profit accomplishes its goals by working closely with manufacturers, retailers, communities and farmers across the nation. The logistics of collecting, sorting and distributing donated food (with limited shelf life) to a widespread base of needy customers is challenging. To respond to this challenge, Feeding America has created several online connection tools to match donors and recipients, such as Produce MatchMakers and Online Marketplace (funded by Google), and has partnered with the Food Waste Reduction Alliance to divert 2.6 billion pounds of food headed to landfills to more than 2 billion meals for people in need. Feeding America has further partnered with organizations and government programs such as Kids Café and Summer Food Service Programs, School Backpack programs, the Rural Child Hunger Capacity Institute, and the Child Hunger Corps to distribute food to children in need. A peer-to-peer benchmarking report prepared by a store chain spurred a 14% increase in retail donations over the previous year.

Feeding America also provides monetary grants to local food pantries to support storing and distributing food, processing applicants, and educating recipients on how to prepare and serve the food in healthy ways. The group seeks to build the capacity of food banks to prepare for and respond to natural disasters and to aid in stabilizing communities post-disaster. For example, thousands of pounds of supplies were positioned along Hurricane Sandy's path to provide immediate access to food and water at food pantries, emergency shelters, and soup kitchens. Feeding America operates a high-volume, sophisticated food distribution network through its food banks with advanced technology and food distribution software from eSoftware Professionals. Even so, donor and recipient operations are staffed by more than 2 million volunteers in communities across the nation.

Feeding America excels on both the supply and demand side—exploring new food sourcing models and finding innovative ways to distribute the food where and when it is needed. The organization works with professional staff, volunteers, corporations, and community centers to source and deliver a better life to its constituents. This is an example of how operations and supply chain management tools can be used to alleviate major societal problems.

1. Is there a food bank for students in your community? Find out what challenges the group faces, and how food is collected and distributed.
2. What is difficult about balancing supply and demand for this non-profit? Looking at the range of topics covered in the textbook, what skills in operations and supply chain management would be useful?
3. Explore the software available for the food distribution industry. What kinds of data are kept on the warehoused food and food in transit? Why?
4. Explore how other organizations fight hunger across the globe. What is the scope of their efforts? How do they connect supply and demand? What innovative methods are used for food distribution? How is success measured?

Source: Feeding America Annual Report, 2015, www.feedingamerica.org (accessed January 4, 2016); "Feeding America Harnesses Food Distribution Software to Help Victims of Hurricane Sandy," http://www.erpsoftwareblog.com, November 1, 2012 (accessed January 5, 2016).

From the Industrial Revolution through the 1960s, the United States was the world's greatest producer of goods and services, as well as the major source of managerial and technical expertise. But in the 1970s and 1980s, industry by industry, U.S. manufacturing superiority was challenged by lower costs and higher quality from foreign manufacturers, led by Japan. Several studies published during those years confirmed what the consumer already knew—U.S.-made products of that era were inferior and could not compete on the world market. Early rationalizations that the Japanese success in manufacturing was a cultural phenomenon were disproved by the successes of Japanese-owned plants in the United States, such as the Matsushita purchase of a failing Quasar television plant in Chicago from Motorola. Part of the purchase contract specified that Matsushita had to retain the entire hourly workforce of 1000 persons. After only two years, with the identical workers, half the management staff, and little or no capital investment, Matsushita doubled production, cut assembly repairs from 130% to 6%, and reduced warranty costs from $16 million a year to $2 million a year. You can bet Motorola took notice, as did the rest of U.S. industry.

Quality revolution An emphasis on quality and the strategic role of operations.

The **quality revolution** brought with it a realization that production should be tied to consumer demand. Product proliferation, shortened product lifecycles, shortened product development times, changes in technology, more customized products, and segmented markets did not fit mass production assumptions. Using a concept known as just-in-time, Toyota changed the rules of production from mass production to **lean production**, a system that prizes flexibility (rather than efficiency) and quality (rather than quantity).

Lean production An adaptation of mass production that prizes quality and flexibility.

The renewed emphasis on quality and the *strategic importance* of operations made some U.S. companies competitive again. Others continued to stagnate, buoyed temporarily by the expanding economies of the Internet era and globalization. Productivity soared as return on investment in information technology finally came to fruition. New types of businesses and business models emerged, such as Amazon, Google, and eBay, and companies used the Internet to connect with customers and suppliers around the world. The inflated expectations of the dot-com era came to an end and, coupled with the terrorist attacks of 9/11 and their aftermath, brought many companies back to reality, searching for ways to cut costs and survive in a global economy. They found relief in the emerging economies of China and India, and began accelerating the outsourcing of not only goods production, but services, such as information technology, call centers, and other business processes. The outsourcing of business processes brought with it a new awareness of business-to-business (B2B) services.

With more and more activities taking place outside the enterprise in factories, distribution centers, offices and stores overseas, managers needed to develop skills in coordinating operations across a global supply chain. The field of **supply chain management** was born to manage the flow of information, products, and services across a network of customers, enterprises, and supply chain partners. In Figure 1.1, we depicted operations as a transformation process. Extending that analogy in **Figure 1.5**, supply chain management concentrates on the input and output sides of transformation processes. Increasingly, however, as the transformation process is performed by suppliers who may be located around the world, the supply chain manager is also concerned with the timeliness, quality, and legalities of the supplier's operations.

Supply chain management Managing the flow of information, products, and services across a network of customers, enterprises, and suppliers.

The era of globalization was in full swing in 2008 when a financial crisis brought on by risky loans, inflated expectations, and unsavory financial practices brought the global economy to a standstill. Operations and supply chain management practices based on assumptions of growth had to be reevaluated for declining markets and resources. Companies began to reassess the value of their business, their customers, and their suppliers with an eye toward focusing on the most critical factors to sustain their business through the downturn.

Thus began the *era of sustainability*, in which countries, companies, and industries evaluate what it takes to sustain the health of their enterprise or people in the long term. This is especially important in light of climate change, natural and man-made disasters, scarcity of resources, and the competitive landscape. Nike CEO Mark Parker calls sustainability the "defining issue for our generation."

A concept related to sustainability is **resilience**, the ability to bounce back, change, or adapt in response to a disaster, failure, or disruption. Globalization has increased the risk of

Resilience The ability to bounce back, change, or adapt in response to a disaster, failure, or disruption.

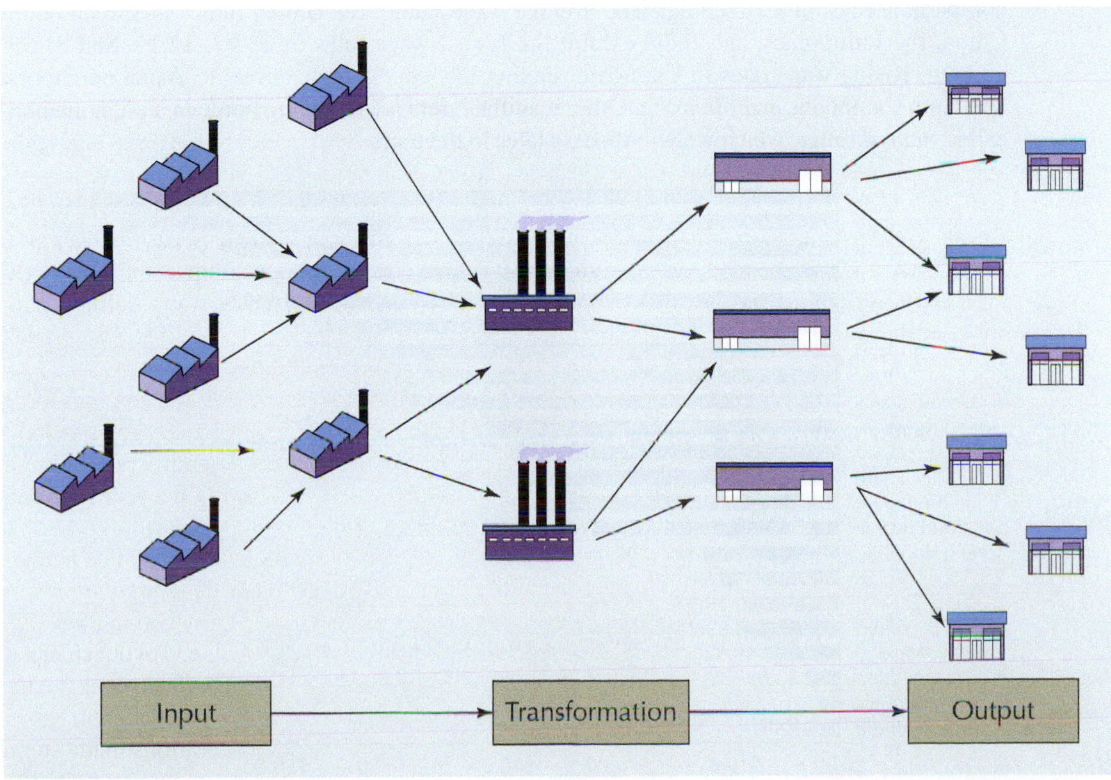

FIGURE 1.5 **Supply Chain Management**

disruptions in operations and supply chain activities, but it has also provided more flexibility in responding to disruptions. Building resilient systems is key to achieving sustainability.

In the midst of a global concern about sustainability comes dramatic new technology ushering in a *digital revolution.* Smart materials, smartphones, smart appliances, smart cars, even smart cities contain sensors that collect data, connect with networks, and have the ability to control processes and affect behavior. This explosion of the Internet of Things (IoT) is accompanied by new platforms for consuming products and services, the immediacy of which raises expectations and amps up innovation. Wearable technology, 3D printing, the sharing economy, and autonomous vehicles are just some of the results. This is indeed an exciting time for innovation and technology.

We discuss technology at length later in the text. In the next section, we delve more deeply into the effect of globalization on operations and supply chain management.

Globalization

Two thirds of today's businesses operate globally through global markets, global operations, global financing, and global supply chains. Globalization can take the form of selling in foreign markets, producing in foreign lands, purchasing from foreign suppliers, or partnering with foreign firms. Companies "go global" to take advantage of favorable costs, to gain access to international markets, to be more responsive to changes in demand, to build reliable sources of supply, and to keep abreast of the latest trends and technologies.

Falling trade barriers and the Internet paved the way for globalization. The World Trade Organization (WTO) has opened up the heavily protected industries of agriculture, textiles, and telecommunications, and extended the scope of international trade rules to cover services, as well as goods. The European Union (EU) requires that strict quality and environmental standards be met before companies can do business with member countries. Strategic alliances, joint ventures, licensing arrangements, research consortia, supplier partnerships, and direct marketing agreements among global partners have proliferated.

Figure 1.6 shows the hourly wage rates (including benefits) in U.S. dollars for production workers in 15 selected countries. Wage rates in Norway are the highest at $66 an hour, with comparable rates in Switzerland. The average wage rate in the United States is $36 an hour. China, the Philippines, and India exhibit the lowest wage rates of $3.07, $2.12, and $1.59 an hour. Rising wage rates in China are sending low-cost manufacturers to Asian neighbors Vietnam, Cambodia, and Malaysia. Other manufacturers are returning home in a phenomenon called *near shoring*, which we will discuss later in the text.

FIGURE 1.6 Hourly Compensation Costs for Production Workers (in U.S. Dollars)

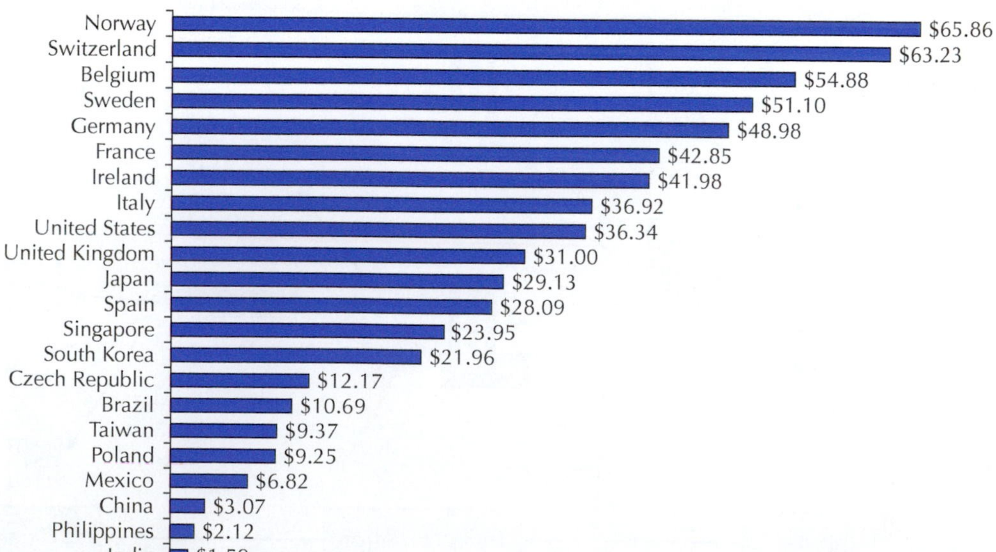

Source: The Conference Board, "International Comparisons of Hourly Compensation Costs in Manufacturing, 2013," New York: December 2014.

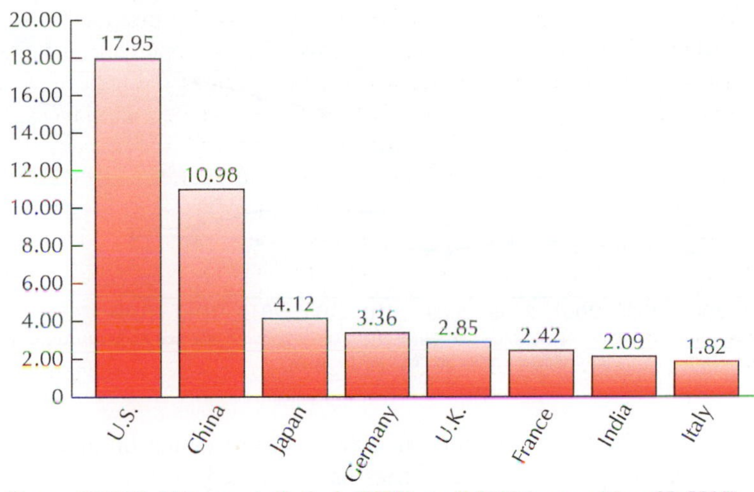

FIGURE 1.7 GDP, current prices (in $US trillions), 2015

Source: IMF World Economic Outlook (WEO), April 2015 (accessed June 22, 2016), http://knoema.com/nwnfkne/world-gdp-ranking-2015-data-and-charts.

China accounts for 20% of the world's population and is the world's largest manufacturer, employing more production workers than the United States, United Kingdom, Germany, Japan, Italy, Canada, and France combined. Its 1.3 billion people represent not only an immense labor market, but a huge consumer market as well. As China's industrial base multiplies, so does its need for machinery and basic materials, and as more companies move to China, so do their suppliers and their supplier's suppliers. Although initially the preferred location for the production of low-tech goods such as toys, textiles, and furniture, China has become a strategic manufacturing base for nearly every industry worldwide.

The scale of manufacturing in China is mind-boggling. For example, Foxconn (the trade name of Taiwan's Hon Hai Precision Industry Company) has several enormous industrial complexes in mainland China. The Guangdong Province site employs and houses approximately 270,000 workers, with its own dormitories, restaurants, hospital, police force, chicken farm, and soccer stadium. There are 40 separate production facilities "on campus," each dedicated to one of its major customers such as Apple, Dell, Motorola, Sony, Nintendo, and HP. Foxconn is the world's largest electronics manufacturer and China's largest exporter. It also represents a shorter supply chain because it *makes* components as well as *assembles* final products. Currently, Foxconn is expanding production into Mexico and Brazil to better serve the Americas.

Let's take a look at the health of the global economy in terms of GDP, trade in goods as a percent of GDP, and percentage manufacturing output by country. **Figure 1.7** shows the gross domestic product (GDP) for the largest economies in 2014. Note that China's GDP is more than twice that of Germany. However, Germany and Mexico beat out both China and the United States in trade as a percentage of GDP, as shown in **Figure 1.8**. The United States, Brazil, and to some extent, Japan, are producing goods and services for their own markets, rather than exporting them.

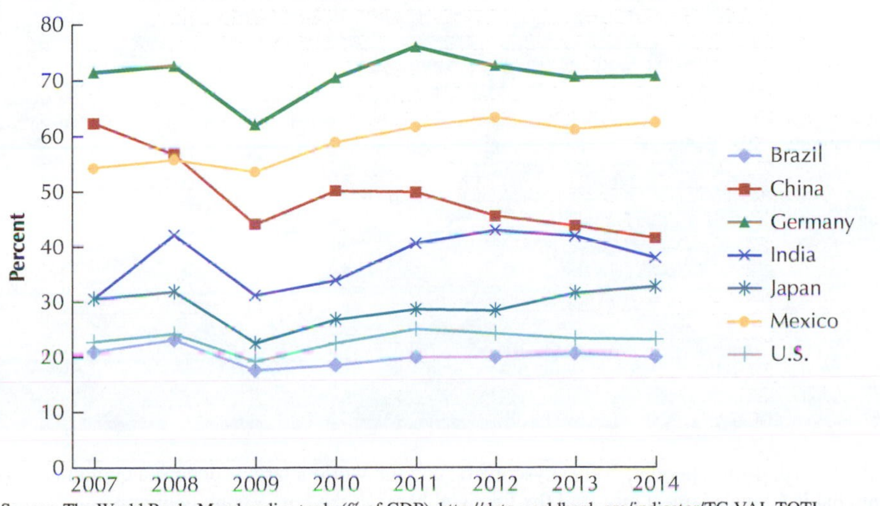

FIGURE 1.8 Trade in Goods as a Percent of GDP

Source: The World Bank, Merchandise trade (% of GDP), http://data.worldbank.org/indicator/TG.VAL.TOTL.GD.ZS, accessed January 18, 2016.

FIGURE 1.9 Manufacturing Output (in $US trillions)

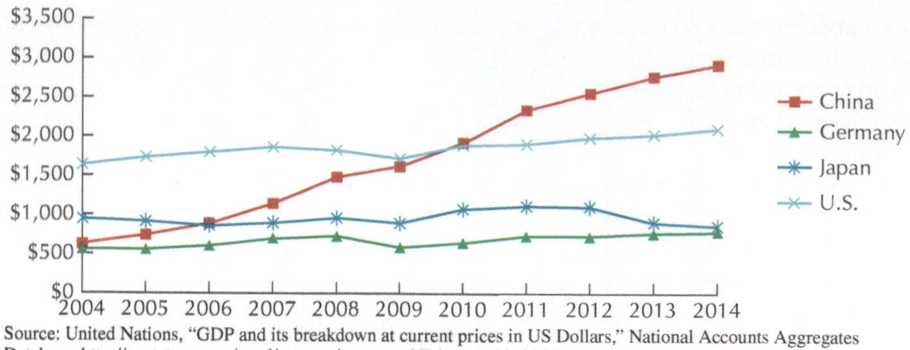

Source: United Nations, "GDP and its breakdown at current prices in US Dollars," National Accounts Aggregates Database, http://unstats.un.org/unsd/snaama/, accessed February 10, 2016.

Trade dropped in all of the economies in 2009 as the recession hit and stores were no longer placing orders for goods. Most countries have returned to their pre-recession trade, with Germany and Mexico gaining orders, most likely from an increase in near-shoring at the expense of China. India has also recovered well. China's slowdown in trade could be attributed to a higher percent of its factory output filling domestic demand for goods. The predominance of global supply chains means that intermediate goods cross borders many more times than they did when products and their components were manufactured in one country. That explains why the volume of trade declines more sharply than GDP during downturns and why trade accelerates faster than GDP when the global economy picks up.

Finally, let's examine production output from 2004 to 2014 for the world's largest manufacturing economies, as shown in **Figure 1.9**. In 2004, China held a slight edge over Germany as the world's third largest manufacturing economy. By 2006, China had surpassed Germany and was tied with Japan as the second largest manufacturer. Thus began a dramatic rise until 2010, where China edged ahead of the United States, producing 19.8% of the world's goods as compared to the United States' 19.4%. Then from 2011, China's manufacturing output soared. Prior to 2010, the United States had led world output in manufacturing since the 1930s. Prior to 2010, China's last number one ranking came in 1830, when it accounted for 30% of the world's production of goods. In 2014, China accounted for 24% of global manufacturing.

Paul Souders/Photodisc/Getty Images

With over 18 million people, 5000 skyscrapers, and the world's largest deep sea container port, Shanghai is China's largest city, and the financial heart of the burgeoning economy.

Low labor costs, economies of scale, and a strong infrastructure have drawn goods production to China. But while China's manufacturing prowess may seem unbeatable, its aging workforce and increased standard of living are causing labor costs to rise and low-cost manufacturing to move to such countries as India, Bangladesh, Indonesia, Vietnam, and Eastern Europe. Because of its proximity to the United States, Mexico and several Central American countries are seeing a resurgence in orders, as well. Quality, reliability, and security problems present additional challenges to managing global operations, as do questions of worker rights and environmental concerns. Physical distance and different mores, laws, and legal systems in other countries can make it harder to maintain control over a global supply chain.

Productivity and Competitiveness

A global marketplace for products and services means more customers and more intense competition. In the broadest terms, we speak of competitiveness in reference to other *countries* rather than to other companies. That's because how effectively a nation competes in the global marketplace affects the economic success of the nation and the quality of life for its citizens. The OECD (Organisation for Economic Co-operation and Development) defines **competitiveness** as "the degree to which a nation can produce goods and services that meet the test of international markets while simultaneously maintaining or expanding the real incomes of its citizens." The most common measure of competitiveness is productivity. Increases in productivity allow wages to grow without producing inflation, thus raising the standard of living. Productivity growth also represents how quickly an economy can expand its capacity to supply goods and services.

Competitiveness The degree to which a nation can produce goods and services that meet the test of international markets.

Productivity is calculated by dividing units of output by units of input.

Productivity The ratio of output to input.

$$\text{Productivity} = \frac{\text{Output}}{\text{Input}}$$

Output can be expressed in units or dollars in a variety of scenarios, such as sales made, products produced, customers served, meals delivered, or calls answered. *Single-factor productivity* compares output to individual inputs, such as labor hours, investment in equipment, material usage, or square footage. *Multifactor productivity* relates output to a combination of inputs, such as (labor + capital) or (labor + capital + energy + materials). Capital can include the value of equipment, facilities, inventory, and land. *Total factor productivity* compares the total quantity of goods and services produced with all the inputs used to produce them. These productivity formulas are summarized in Table 1.2. Note when several factors are included in a formula, they should be expressed in common terms, such as dollars.

TABLE 1.2 Measures of Productivity

Single-Factor Productivity		
$\frac{\text{Output}}{\text{Labor}}$	$\frac{\text{Output}}{\text{Materials}}$	$\frac{\text{Output}}{\text{Capital}}$
Multifactor Productivity		
$\frac{\text{Output}}{\text{Labor + Materials + Overhead}}$		$\frac{\text{Output}}{\text{Labor + Energy + Capital}}$
Total Factor Productivity		
$\frac{\text{Goods and services produced}}{\text{All inputs used to produce them}}$		

EXAMPLE 1.1 | Calculating Productivity

Osborne Industries is compiling the monthly productivity report for its board of directors. From the following data, calculate (a) labor productivity, (b) machine productivity, and (c) the multifactor productivity of output per dollars spent on labor, machine, materials, and energy. The average labor rate is $15 an hour, and the average machine usage rate is $10 an hour.

Units produced	100,000
Labor hours	10,000
Machine hours	5,000
Cost of materials	$35,000
Cost of energy	$15,000

Solution

(a) $\text{Labor productivity} = \dfrac{\text{Output}}{\text{Labor hours}} = \dfrac{100{,}000}{10{,}000} = 10 \text{ units/hour}$

(b) $\text{Machine productivity} = \dfrac{\text{Output}}{\text{Machine hours}} = \dfrac{100{,}000}{5{,}000} = 20 \text{ units/hour}$

(c) Multifactor productivity =

$$\frac{\text{Output}}{(\text{Labor costs} + \text{Machine costs} + \text{Material costs} + \text{Energy costs})}$$

$$= \frac{100{,}000}{(10{,}000 \times \$15) + (5{,}000 \times \$10) + \$35{,}000 + \$15{,}000}$$

$$= \frac{100{,}000}{\$250{,}000} = 0.4 \text{ units per dollar spent}$$

The Excel solution to this problem is shown in Exhibit 1.1.

The most common input in productivity calculations is labor hours. Labor is an easily identified input to virtually every production process. If labor is used as the basis for productivity calculations consistently over time, changes in other factors of production will be reflected in the changes in labor.

There are many ways in which productivity statistics can be misleading. Examining the formula for productivity, *output/input,* it becomes apparent that productivity can be increased in different ways. For example, a country or firm may increase productivity by decreasing input faster than output. Thus, although a country or firm may be retrenching, its productivity is increasing. Seldom is this avenue for increasing productivity sustainable. Let's look at some recent global productivity statistics.

Figure 1.10 shows productivity per hour of labor in U.S. dollars for select countries in 2014. Norway is the most productive, with $89 worth of goods produced with one hour of labor. The United States and Belgium are next, producing $67 worth of goods for each hour of labor. China is the least productive, using one hour of labor to produce $10 of output. This makes sense considering that fully developed nations are more invested in automation and thus use fewer labor hours in the production process. Productivity expressed in labor hours (which is the norm) can be misleading since it does not include the cost of the labor.

EXHIBIT 1.1 | Osborne Industries

Excel File

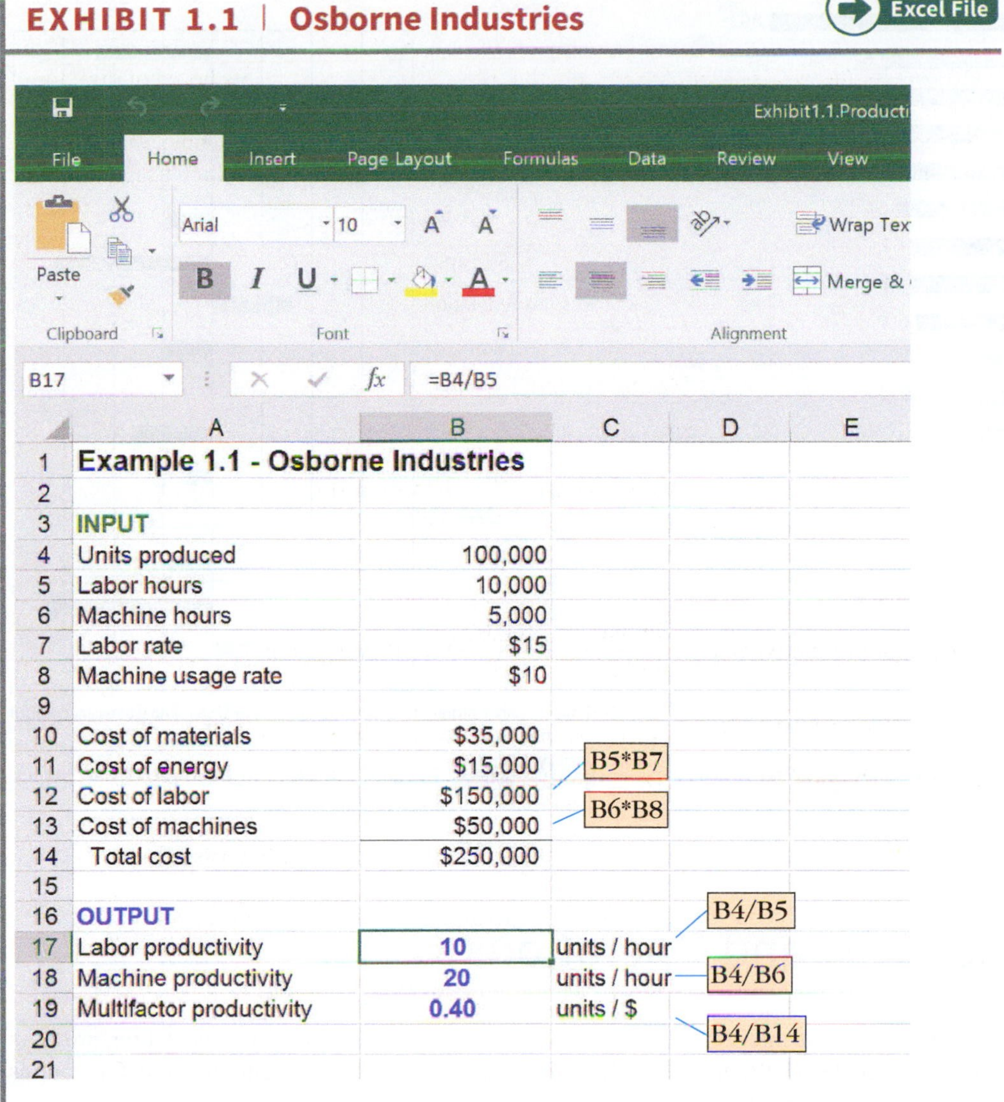

B17 | =B4/B5

	A	B	C	D
1	**Example 1.1 - Osborne Industries**			
2				
3	**INPUT**			
4	Units produced	100,000		
5	Labor hours	10,000		
6	Machine hours	5,000		
7	Labor rate	$15		
8	Machine usage rate	$10		
9				
10	Cost of materials	$35,000		
11	Cost of energy	$15,000	B5*B7	
12	Cost of labor	$150,000		
13	Cost of machines	$50,000	B6*B8	
14	Total cost	$250,000		
15				
16	**OUTPUT**			B4/B5
17	Labor productivity	**10**	units / hour	
18	Machine productivity	**20**	units / hour	B4/B6
19	Multifactor productivity	**0.40**	units / $	
20				B4/B14
21				

Productivity statistics also assume that if more input were available, output would increase at the same rate. This may not necessarily be true, as there are limits to output in addition to those on which the productivity calculations are based. Furthermore, productivity emphasizes *output produced,* not *output sold*. If products produced are not sold, inventories pile up and increases in output can actually accelerate a company's decline.

Finally, productivity is a relative measure, which is why statistics provided in government reports typically measure percent *changes* in productivity from month to month, quarter to quarter, year to year, or over a number of years. Thus, **Figure 1.11**, showing percent changes in productivity from 2014 to 2015, paints quite a different picture than Figure 1.10. Here the 6.7%, 6.3%, and 4.7% increases in productivity by China, Sri Lanka, and Vietnam are excellent; while the 6.7%, 3.2% and 2% decreases in productivity in Venezuela, the Russian Federation, and Brazil are discouraging. The United States shows a very small increase in productivity at 0.4%.

As the business world becomes more competitive, firms must find their own path to sustainable competitive advantage. Effectively managed operations are important to a firm's competitiveness. How a firm chooses to compete in the marketplace is the subject of the next section: *Strategy and Operations*.

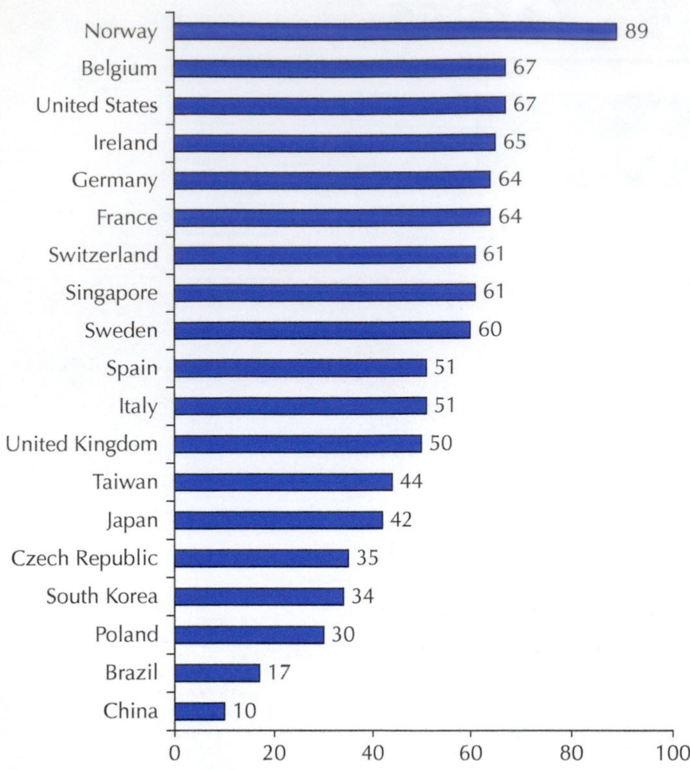

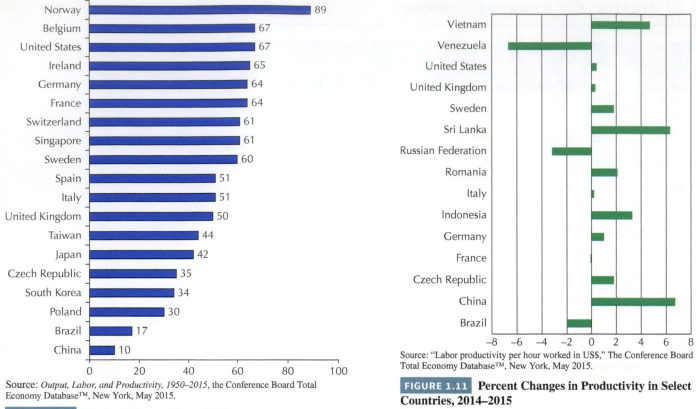

Source: *Output, Labor, and Productivity, 1950–2015*, the Conference Board Total Economy Database™, New York, May 2015.

FIGURE 1.10 Productivity per Hour ($US)

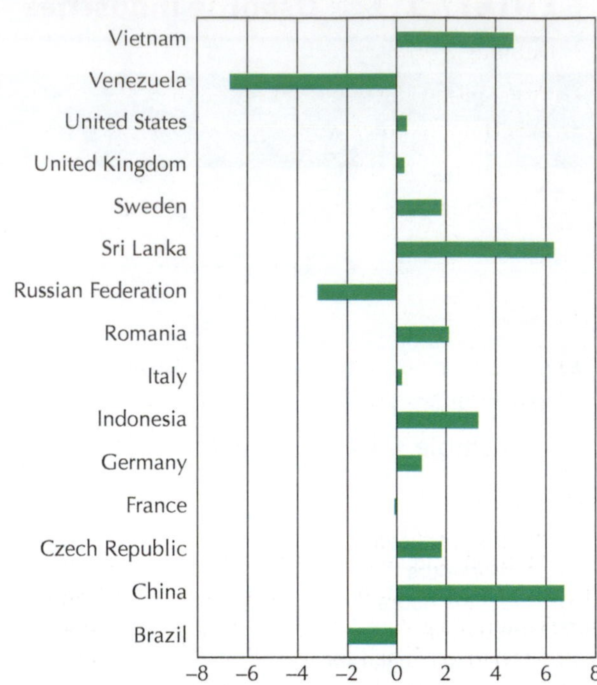

Source: "Labor productivity per hour worked in US$," The Conference Board Total Economy Database™, New York, May 2015.

FIGURE 1.11 Percent Changes in Productivity in Select Countries, 2014–2015

Strategy and Operations

Strategy Provides direction for achieving a mission.

Strategy is how the mission of a company is accomplished. It unites an organization, provides consistency in decisions, and keeps the organization moving in the right direction. Operations and supply chain management play an important role in corporate strategy.

As shown in **Figure 1.12**, the strategic planning process involves a hierarchy of decisions. Senior management, with input and participation from different levels of the organization, develops a corporate strategic plan in concurrence with the firm's mission and vision, customer requirements (voice of the customer), and business conditions (voice of the business). The strategic plan focuses on the gap between the firm's vision and its current position. It identifies and prioritizes what needs to be done to close the gap, and it provides direction for formulating strategies in the functional areas of the firm, such as marketing, operations, and finance. It is important that strategy in each of the functional areas be internally consistent as well as consistent with the firm's overall strategy.

FIGURE 1.12 Strategic Planning

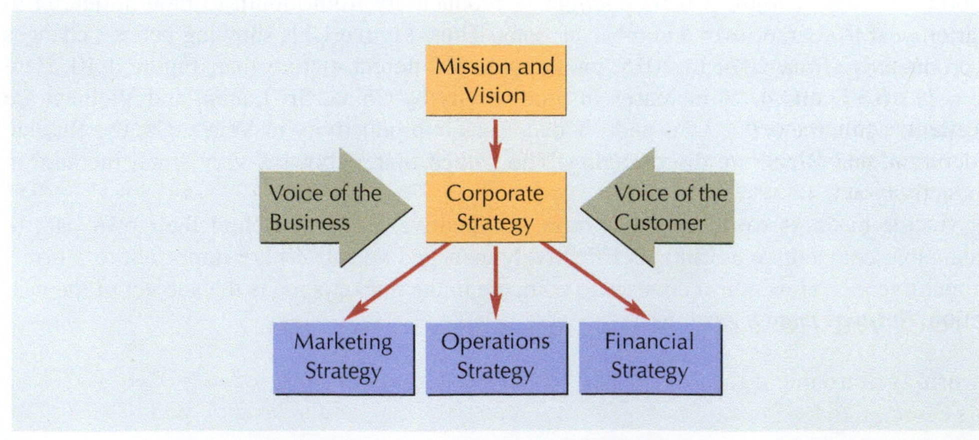

Strategy formulation consists of five basic steps:

1. Defining a primary task.
2. Assessing core competencies.
3. Determining order winners and order qualifiers.
4. Positioning the firm.
5. Deploying the strategy.

Primary Task

Primary task What the firm is in the business of doing.

The **primary task** represents the purpose of a firm—what the firm is in the business of doing. It also determines the competitive arena. As such, the primary task should not be defined too narrowly. For example, Norfolk Southern Railway is in the business of transportation, not railroads. Paramount is in the business of communication, not making movies. Amazon's business is providing the fastest, easiest, and most enjoyable shopping experience, while Disney's is making people happy! The primary task is usually expressed in a firm's *mission* statement.

Mission statements clarify what business a company is in—for Google, it's "organizing the world's information"; for Hallmark, it's creating a "more emotionally connected world"; for Twitter, it's giving "everyone the power to create and share ideas and information instantly, without barriers"; and for Merck it's "saving and improving human life." Mission statements are the "constitution" for an organization, the corporate directive, but they are no good unless they are supported by strategy and converted into action. Thus, the next step in strategy formulation is assessing the core competencies of a firm.

Core Competencies

Core competency What the firm does better than anyone else.

Core competency is what a firm does better than anyone else, its *distinctive competence*. A firm's core competence can be exceptional service, higher quality, faster delivery, or lower cost. One company may strive to be first to the market with innovative designs, whereas another may look for success arriving later but with better quality.

Based on experience, knowledge, and know-how, core competencies represent *sustainable competitive advantages*. For this reason, products and technologies are seldom core competencies. The advantage they provide is short-lived, and other companies can readily purchase, emulate, or improve on them. Core competencies are more likely to be *processes*, a company's ability to *do* certain things better than a competitor. Thus, while a particular product is not a core competence, the process of developing new products is. For example, while the iPod was a breakthrough product, it is Apple's ability to turn out hit product after hit product (e.g., iPhone, iPad, MacBook, iWatch, etc.) that gives it that competitive advantage.

Core competencies are not static. They should be nurtured, enhanced, and developed over time. Close contact with the customer is essential to ensuring that a competence does not become obsolete. Core competencies that do not evolve and are not aligned with customer needs can become *core rigidities* for a firm. Walmart and Dell, seemingly unstoppable companies in their field, went astray when they failed to update their competencies to match changes in customer desires. For Dell, the low cost and mail-order delivery of computers did not match the customer's desire to see and test computers before purchase, or to receive personalized after-purchase customer service. For Walmart, their big-box retail model is being challenged by Amazon's online shopping model. Walmart tried smaller stores with little success, and may now convert some of their larger stores into warehouses for shipping out customer orders. To avoid these problems, companies need to continually evaluate the characteristics of their products or services that prompt customer purchase; that is, the order qualifiers and order winners.

Order Winners and Order Qualifiers

A firm is in trouble if the things it does best are not important to the customer. That's why it's essential to look toward customers to determine what influences their purchase decision.

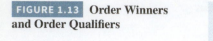

FIGURE 1.13 Order Winners and Order Qualifiers

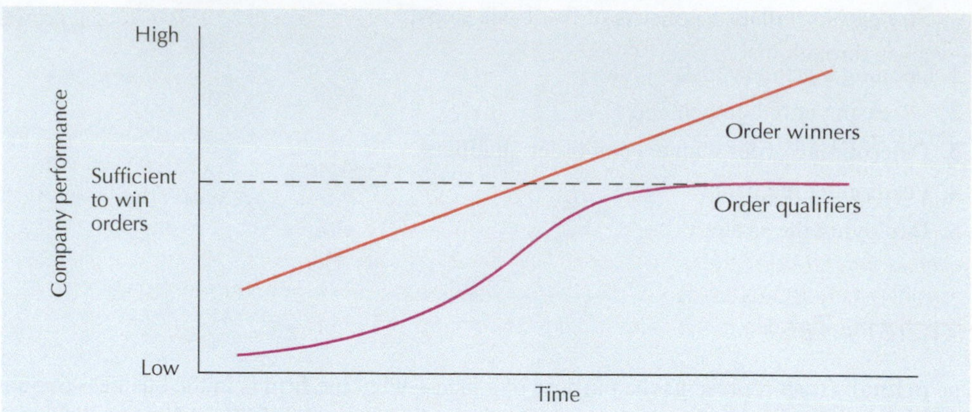

Source: Adapted from *Operations and Process Management,* Nigel Slack, Stuart Chambers, Robert Johnston, and Alan Betts, ©*2006 Prentice Hall. Reproduced with permission of Pearson Education, Inc.*

Order qualifiers What qualifies an item to be considered for purchase.

Order winner What wins the order.

Order qualifiers are the characteristics of a product or service that qualify it to be considered for purchase by a customer. An **order winner** is the characteristic of a product or service that wins orders in the marketplace—the final factor in the purchasing decision. For example, when purchasing a 4K TV, customers may determine a price range (order qualifier) and then choose the product with the most features (order winner) within that price range. Or they may have a set of features in mind (order qualifiers) and then select the least expensive player (order winner) that has all the required features.

Order winners and order qualifiers can evolve over time, just as competencies can be gained and lost. Japanese and Korean automakers initially competed on price but had to ensure certain levels of quality before the U.S. consumer would consider their product. Over time, the consumer was willing to pay a higher price for the assurance of a superior-quality Japanese car. Price became a qualifier, but quality won the orders. Today, high quality, as a standard of the automotive industry, has become an order qualifier, and innovative design or superior gas mileage wins the orders.

As shown in Figure 1.13, order qualifiers will only take a firm so far. The customer expects the qualifiers, but is not "wowed" by them. For example, a low price might be a qualifier, but reducing the price further may not win orders if the features or design are not adequate. At a minimum, a firm should meet the qualifiers. To excel, the firm needs to develop competencies that are in tune with the order winners. Marketing helps to identify these qualifiers and winners. Oftentimes, these characteristics are in the purview of operations and supply chain management, such as cost, speed to the market, speed of delivery, or customization. Other characteristics such as product or service design are supported by operations and supply chain management, but are not completely under their control.

Positioning the Firm

Positioning How the firm chooses to compete.

No firm can be all things to all people. Strategic **positioning** involves making choices—choosing one or two important things on which to concentrate and doing them extremely well. A firm's positioning strategy defines how it will compete in the marketplace—what unique value it will deliver to the customer. An effective positioning strategy considers the strengths and weaknesses of the organization, the needs of the marketplace, and the positions of competitors.[2]

Let's look at firms that have positioned themselves to compete on cost, speed, quality, and flexibility.

Competing on Cost

Companies that compete on cost relentlessly pursue the elimination of all waste. In the past, companies in this category produced standardized products for large markets. They improved yield by stabilizing the production process, tightening productivity standards, and investing in automation. Today, the entire cost structure is examined for reduction potential, not just direct labor costs. High-volume production and automation

[2]These factors can be depicted in a SWOT matrix, which lists the current strengths (S) and weaknesses (W) internal to the company, and the opportunities (O) and threats (T) external to the company.

may or may not provide the most cost-effective alternative. A lean production system provides low costs through disciplined operations.

Competing on Speed More than ever before, speed has become a source of competitive advantage. The Internet has conditioned customers to expect immediate response and rapid product shipment. Service organizations such as McDonald's, LensCrafters, and FedEx have always competed on speed. Now manufacturers are discovering the advantages of *time-based competition*, with build-to-order production and efficient supply chains. In the fashion industry where trends are temporary, Gap's six-month time-to-market can no longer compete with the nine-day design-to-rack lead time of Spanish retailer Zara.

Competing on Quality Most companies approach quality in a defensive or reactive mode; quality is confined to minimizing defect rates or conforming to design specifications. To compete on quality, companies must view it as an opportunity to please the customer, not just a way to avoid problems or reduce rework costs.

To please the customer, one must first understand customer attitudes toward and expectations of quality. One good source is the American Customer Satisfaction Index compiled each year by the American Society for Quality and the National Quality Research Center. Examining recent winners of the Malcolm Baldrige National Quality Award and the criteria on which the award are based also provides insight into companies that compete on quality.

The Ritz-Carlton Hotel Company is a Baldrige Award winner and a recognized symbol of quality. The entire service system is designed to understand the individual expectations of more than 500,000 customers and to "move heaven and earth" to satisfy them. Every employee is empowered to take immediate action to satisfy a guest's wish or resolve a problem. Processes are uniform and well defined. Teams of workers at all levels set objectives and devise quality action plans. Each hotel has a quality leader who serves as a resource and advocate for the development and implementation of those plans.

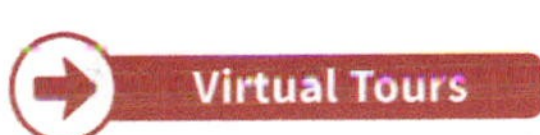

Competing on Flexibility Marketing always wants more variety to offer its customers. Manufacturing resists this trend because variety upsets the stability (and efficiency) of a production system and increases costs. The ability of manufacturing to respond to variation has opened up a new level of competition. **Flexibility** has become a competitive weapon. It includes the ability to produce a wide variety of products, to introduce new products and modify existing ones quickly, and to respond to customer needs.

Flexibility Adjust to changes in product mix, production volume, or design.

Shoes, bicycles, and suits are examples of standard products that can be built or "tailored" to individual customers. Republic Bikes, Villy Customs (a shark tank winner), and Mission Bikes are but a few of the customized biking shops that fit bicycles to exact customer measurements and encourage customized colors, handlebars, frames, and other design options. Bicycle manufacturers typically offer customers a choice among 20 or 30 different models. Handcrafted customer designed bicycles can be configured in thousands of different ways. Computer-aided design (CAD) and computer-aided manufacturing (CAM) allow customized products to be essentially mass produced. The popular term for this phenomenon is **mass customization**.

Mass customization The mass production of customized products.

Competing on Innovation Companies that compete on innovation establish a corporate culture that encourages risk taking, challenges the status quo, accepts failure as part of the learning process, and celebrates successes. Three such companies are Apple, Google, and 3M. Apple *thinks different* to create incredibly fresh, beautiful game-changing designs. Google's open culture has produced such innovations as Google Street View, Google Fiber, Google People Finder (for disasters), Google Driverless Vehicles, and Google Glass. 3M defines itself as a global innovation company that never stops inventing. Ranging from Post-It notes to micro-needle skin patches designed to replace hypodermic needles, 3M produces hundreds of small innovations each year that improve how products or services operate. Like Google, 3M sets aside 20% of its engineers' time to be spent on projects of their own choosing. 3M also gives out $100,000 genius grants to its employees and has its own venture capitalist program that supports disruptive, early-stage innovations outside of the company's existing portfolio.

Innovation is exciting; however, it is not a competitive advantage if it cannot be transformed into marketable and profitable products or services (read about Xaiomi and its competitor OPPO in the "Along the Supply Chain" box). That's where operations and supply chain management come into play. We'll discuss their role more directly in Chapter 4 on Product Design.

Strategy Deployment

Implementing strategy can be more difficult than formulating strategy. Strategies unveiled with much fanfare may never be followed because they are hard to understand, too general, or unrealistic. Strategies that aim for results five years or so down the road mean very little to the worker who is evaluated on his or her daily performance. Different departments or functional areas in a firm may interpret the same strategy in different ways. If their efforts are not coordinated, the results can be disastrous.

Consider Schlitz Brewing Company, whose strategy called for reduced costs and increased efficiency. Operations achieved its goals by dramatically shortening its brewing cycle—and, in the process, lost 6 of every 10 customers when the clarity and taste of the beer suffered. The efficiency move that was to make the company the most profitable in its industry instead caused its stock value to plummet from $69 per share to $5 per share. Schiltz has since been sold to Pabst Brewing Company, who combed through company documents and interviewed retired Schlitz brewmasters and taste-testers to derive and reintroduce the original 1960s "with gusto" formula.

Strategy deployment converts a firm's positioning strategy and resultant order winners and order qualifiers into specific performance requirements. Companies struggling to align day-to-day decisions with corporate strategy have found success with two types of planning systems—policy deployment and the balanced scorecard.

Policy Deployment Policy deployment, also known as hoshin planning, is adapted from Japan's system of *hoshin kanri*, which is roughly translated from Japanese as "shining metal pointing direction"—a compass.

Policy deployment Translates corporate strategy into measurable objectives.

Policy deployment tries to focus everyone in an organization on common goals and priorities by translating corporate strategy into measurable objectives throughout the various functions and levels of the organization. As a result, everyone in the organization should understand the strategic plan, be able to derive several goals from the plan, and determine how each goal ties into their own daily activities.

Suppose the corporate strategic plan of competing on speed called for a reduction of 50% in the length of the supply chain cycle. Senior management from each functional area would assess how their activities contribute to the cycle, confer on the feasibility of reducing the cycle by 50%, and agree on each person's particular role in achieving the reduction. Marketing might decide that creating strategic alliances with its distributors would shorten the average time to release a new product. Operations might try to reduce its purchasing and production cycles by reducing its supplier base, certifying suppliers, using e-procurement, and implementing a just-in-time (JIT) system. Finance might decide to eliminate unnecessary approval loops for expenditures, begin prequalifying sales prospects, and explore the use of electronic funds transfer (EFT) in conjunction with operations' lean strategy.

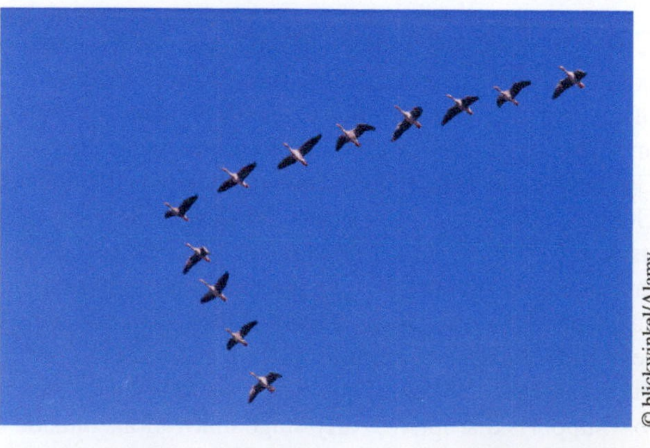

Is your company pointed in one direction? AT&T uses the analogy of migrating geese to explain the concept of policy deployment. Naturalists believe the instinctive V-formation allows the geese to follow one leader and migrate in a cohesive unit toward their destination. Policy deployment does the same thing—it enables business leaders to mobilize the organization toward a common destination, aligning all employees behind a common goal and a collective wisdom.

Along the Supply Chain

New Players Disrupt with Innovation

New companies entering an established market often disrupt how products are perceived, made, or delivered. Apple and Samsung are still the world's leading smartphone manufacturers, but as the market for smartphones matures, look out for high performers in emerging markets, such as Huawei, OPPO, and Xiaomi (see photo). Business is, after all, played out on a global landscape. So what do these newcomers bring to the table?

Bloomberg/Contributor/Getty Images, Inc.

For one thing, Xiaomi, an Android-based product, updates its operating system once a week, and each week the batch of phones shipped by Xiaomi are "incrementally better" than the last batch. Yes, every Friday, Xiaomi delivers unmatched responsiveness to an expanding base of loyal customers who provide input in online forums and company-sponsored community engagements. Online sales account for 70% of Xiaomi's orders. These pre-orders allow the company to purchase materials only after orders are placed and basically build each phone to order. The reduced risk of forecast errors and surplus material saves costs and lets the company look for other ways to add value. For example, the phone's platform is now available in more than 20 languages. Retail prices have been kept very close to manufacturing costs.

OPPO has a different strategy, focusing on Southeast Asia, South Asia, Africa, and the Middle East. In India alone, OPPO has 35,000 sales outlets and close to 200 service centers. Branding its products the "OPPO Camera Phone" and "Selfie Expert," the company knows that a superior camera is the most important feature for India's market and that experiencing the phone is the key to building market share. OPPO designs, develops, manufactures, markets, and sells its products with full control over the entire supply chain. It's also the number-three producer of wearables, behind Fitbit and Apple.

Notice in each case, finding a gap, choosing a strategy and supporting it through a corresponding operations and supply chain strategy can lead to results.

Source: John Hagel, John Brown, Duleesha Kulasooriyam, Craig Giffi, and Menmend Chen, "The Future of Manufacturing: Making things happen in a changing world," Deloitte University Press, 2015, p. 32; "OPPO Launches F1 'Selfie Expert' in India," *Indian News and Times*, January 29, 2016; Company website, www.oppo.com (accessed February 8, 2016).

The process for forming objectives would continue in a similar manner down the organization with the *means* of achieving objectives for one level of management becoming the *target*, or objectives, for the next level. The outcome of the process is a cascade of action plans (or **hoshins**) aligned to complete each functional objective, which will, in turn, combine to achieve the strategic plan.

Hoshins The action plans generated from the policy deployment process.

Figure 1.14 shows an abbreviated operations action plan for reducing supply chain cycle time. Policy deployment has become more popular as organizations become more geographically dispersed and culturally diverse.

Balanced Scorecard

The **balanced scorecard**, developed by Robert Kaplan and David Norton,[3] examines a firm's performance in four critical areas:

Balanced scorecard A performance assessment that includes metrics related to customers, processes, and learning and growing, as well as financials.

1. *Finances*—How should we look to our shareholders?
2. *Customers*—How should we look to our customers?
3. *Processes*—At which business processes must we excel?
4. *Learning and Growing*—How will we sustain our ability to change and improve?

It's called a *balanced* scorecard because more than financial measures are used to assess performance. Operational excellence is important in all four areas. How efficiently a firm's assets are managed, products produced, and services provided affect the financial health of the firm. Identifying and understanding targeted customers helps determine the processes and

[3]See Robert S. Kaplan and David P. Norton, "Transforming the Balanced Scorecard from Performance Measurement to Strategic Management." *Accounting Horizons* (March 2001), pp. 87–104; and Robert S. Kaplan and David P. Norton, "Having Trouble with Your Strategy? Then Map It," *Harvard Business Review* (September/October 2000), pp. 167–176.

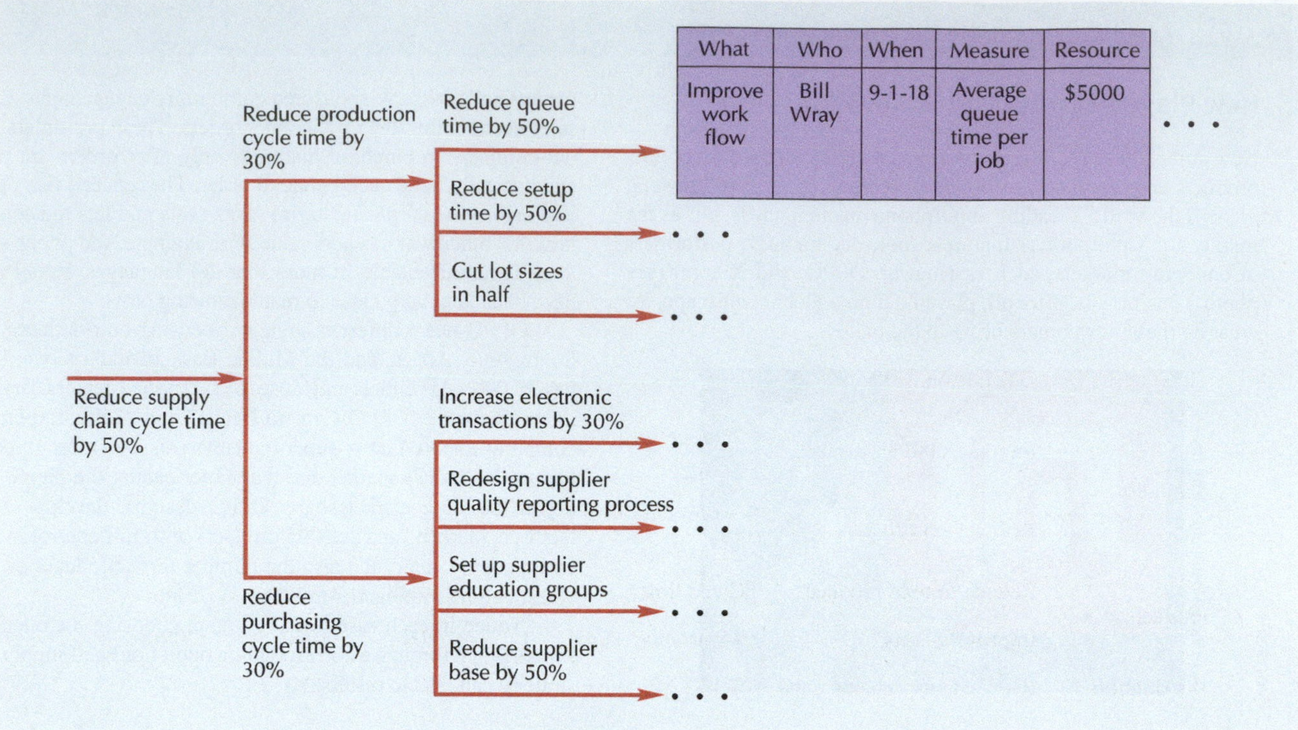

FIGURE 1.14 **Derivation of an Action Plan Using Policy Deployment**

capabilities the organization must concentrate on to deliver value to the customer. The firm's ability to improve those processes and develop competencies in new areas is critical to sustaining competitive advantage.

Key performance indicators (KPI) A set of measures that help managers evaluate performance in critical areas.

Table 1.3 is a balanced scorecard worksheet. The worksheet selects areas of the strategy map to incorporate in annual objectives for the company. The objectives are then operationalized with **key performance indicators (KPI)**. The goals for the year are given, and the KPI results are recorded. The score converts the different performance measures into percentage completed. For example, if the goal is to achieve 12 inventory turns a year and the company manages only 6, then the goal is 50% achieved. The mean performance column averages the score for each dimension. The scorecard performance can be visualized in many ways, two of which are illustrated in Figures 1.15 and 1.16.

Figure 1.15 is a radar chart of the balanced scorecard. Goals 0% to 40% achieved appear in the red "danger" zone, 40% to 80% achieved are in the yellow "cautionary" zone, and 80%

FIGURE 1.15 **A Radar Chart of the Balanced Scorecard**

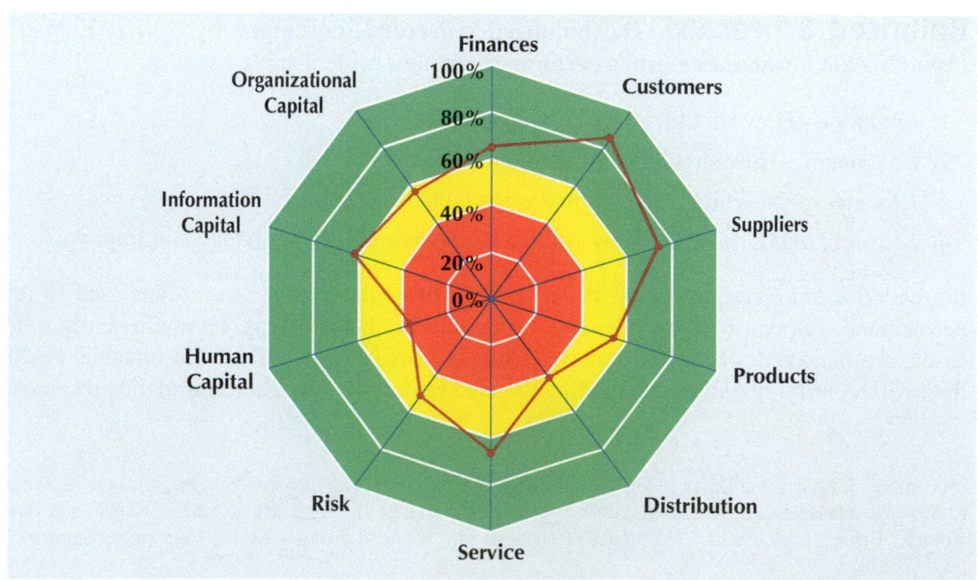

TABLE 1.3 The Balanced Scorecard Worksheet

	DIMENSION	OBJECTIVES	KEY PERFORMANCE INDICATOR	GOAL FOR 2015	KPI RESULTS TO DATE	SCORE	MEAN PERFORMANCE
Finances	Productivity	Become industry cost leader	% reduction in cost per unit	20%	10%	50%	65%
	Growth	Increase market share	Market share	50%	40%	80%	
Customers	Quality	Zero defects	% good quality first pass	100%	80%	80%	87%
	Timeliness	On-time delivery	% on-time deliveries	95%	90%	95%	
Processes	Suppliers	Integrate into production	% orders delivered to assembly	50%	40%	80%	73%
		Reduce inspections	% suppliers ISO 9000 certified	90%	60%	67%	
	Products	Reduce time to produce	Cycle time	10 mins.	12 mins.	83%	52%
		Improve quality	# warranty claims	200	1000	20%	
	Distribution	Reduce transportation costs	% FTL shipments	75%	30%	40%	40%
	Service	Improve response to customer inquiries	% queries satisfied on first pass	90%	60%	67%	67%
	Risk	Reduce inventory obsolescence	Inventory turnover	12	6	50%	50%
		Reduce customer backlog	% orders backlogged	10%	20%	50%	
Learning & Growing	Human capital	Develop quality improvement skills	# of Six Sigma Black Belts	25	2	8%	35%
			% trained in SPC	80%	50%	63%	
	Information capital	Provide technology to improve processes	% customers who can track orders	100%	60%	60%	61%
			% suppliers who use EDI	80%	50%	63%	
	Organizational capital	Create innovative culture	# of employee suggestions	100	60	60%	55%
			% products new this year	20%	10%	50%	

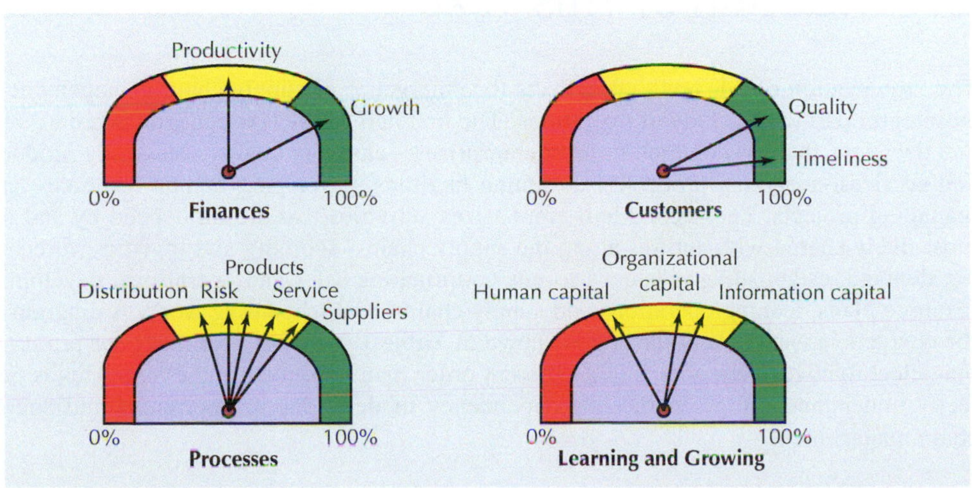

FIGURE 1.16 A Dashboard for the Balanced Scorecard

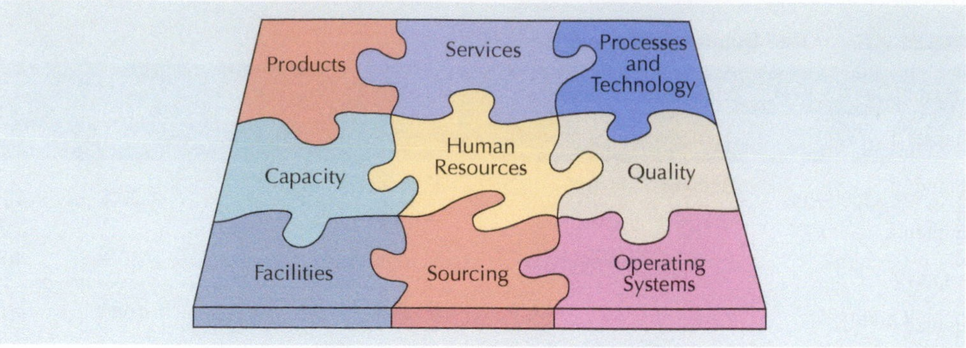

FIGURE 1.17 An Integrated Operations Strategy

to 100% achieved are in the green "moving ahead" zone. In this example, the company is in the danger zone for human capital and distribution, but is doing well with growth, quality, timeliness, and service. Figure 1.16 shows the same information in an alternative format. The dashboard presents each scorecard perspective in a different graphic. The red zone is set at 25% or less goal achievement, yellow from 25% to 75%, and green in excess of 75%, although different limits can be set for each perspective. The company excels in growth, quality, and timeliness, and is not in danger on any measure. Note that in addition to setting different limits for each gauge measures other than percentages can be used. Dashboards are popular ways for managers to quickly interpret the massive amounts of data collected each day and in some cases can be updated in real time. They often consist of graphs and other visual representations of performance.

Operations Strategy

The operations function helps strategy evolve by creating new and better ways of delivering a firm's competitive priorities to the customer. Once a firm's competitive priorities have been established, its operating system must be configured and managed to provide for those priorities. This involves a whole series of interrelated decisions on products and services, processes and technology, capacity and facilities, human resources, quality, sourcing, and operating systems. As shown in **Figure 1.17**, all these decisions should "fit" like pieces in a puzzle. A tight strategic fit means competitors must replicate the entire system to obtain its advantages. Thus, the competitive advantage from an integrated operating system is more sustainable than short-lived products or technologies. Beginning with quality, the remaining chapters in Part I put together the pieces of the operations strategy puzzle.

Organization of This Text

The organization of this textbook reflects the emergence of supply chain management as an integral part of the study of operations. The first half of the text concentrates on issues and decisions that are common to most enterprises—ensuring quality, designing products and services, analyzing processes, designing facilities, developing human resources, and managing projects. The second half emphasizes activities that are influenced by and are most likely shared with entities along the supply chain—sourcing and logistics, forecasting demand, establishing inventory levels, coordinating sales and operations, developing resource plans, leaning operations and supply chains, and scheduling work. A diagram of the chapters in each half of the text is shown in **Table 1.4**. Please note that your professor may elect to cover these topics in a different order than presented in the text. This is perfectly understandable given the interdependency of decisions in operations and supply chain management.

TABLE 1.4 Organization of the Text

PART I—OPERATIONS MANAGEMENT	
Chapter 1	Introduction to Operations and Supply Chain Management
Chapter 2	Quality Management
Chapter 3	Statistical Process Control
Chapter 4	Product Design
Chapter 5	Service Design
Chapter 6	Processes and Technology
Chapter 7	Capacity and Facilities Design
Chapter 8	Human Resources
Chapter 9	Project Management
PART II—SUPPLY CHAIN MANAGEMENT	
Chapter 10	Supply Chain Strategy and Design
Chapter 11	Global Supply Chain Procurement and Distribution
Chapter 12	Forecasting
Chapter 13	Inventory Management
Chapter 14	Sales and Operations Planning
Chapter 15	Resource Planning
Chapter 16	Lean Systems
Chapter 17	Scheduling

Learning Objectives of This Course

The learning objectives of this course are threefold:

1. ***To gain an appreciation of the strategic importance of operations and supply chain management in a global business environment and to understand how operations relates to other business functions.*** Regardless of your major, as you pursue a career in business you will need to understand the basic issues, capabilities, and limitations of operations and supply chains. By the conclusion of this course, you will be able to describe the impact of operations and supply chain management on other functions within a firm, as well as on the competitive position of the firm. You will also be more aware of the global nature of operations and the complexity of supply chains.
2. ***To develop a working knowledge of the concepts and methods related to designing and managing operations and creating value along the supply chain.*** In this course, you will learn the basic steps involved in bringing a product to market from its design through production and delivery. You will also learn such skills as how to forecast demand, lay out a facility, manage a project, work with suppliers, and schedule work.
3. ***To develop a skill set for continuous improvement.*** From this course, you will gain the ability to conceptualize how systems are interrelated, to organize activities effectively, to analyze processes critically, to make decisions based on data, and to push for continual process improvement. These skills will serve you well in whatever career you choose.

Summary

Operations can be viewed as a transformation process that converts inputs into outputs of greater value.

Operations management is the study of processes directly related to the creation and distribution of goods and services. Increasingly, these operations are taking place outside of the boundaries of a traditional enterprise. Thus, while today's managers need to understand how to manage operations efficiently within their own firm, they also need to develop skills in coordinating operations across a global supply chain. This text teaches students how to analyze processes, ensure quality, create value, and manage the flow of information, products, and services across a network of customers, enterprises, and supply chain partners.

Firms choose to compete in different ways. A firm's *strategy* defines how it will compete in the marketplace—its own best way. Strategy formulation involves defining the primary task, assessing core competencies, determining order winners and order qualifiers, and positioning the firm. An effective strategy meets the order qualifiers and excels on the order winners. A competitive position is not sustainable unless the operating system that supports it is configured and managed effectively.

Policy deployment is a planning system that helps align day-to-day operating decisions with the company's overall strategy. The *balanced scorecard* reinforces a firm's strategy by providing customer-oriented and process-oriented measures of performance, in addition to traditional financial measures.

Decision making for the future can be scary at best. Fortunately, there are quantitative tools available for making decisions under uncertain conditions. The supplement to this chapter reviews several of them for us.

Key Terms

balanced scorecard A performance assessment that includes metrics related to customers, processes, and learning and growing, as well as financials.

competitiveness The degree to which a nation can produce goods and services that meet the test of international markets.

core competencies The essential capabilities that create a firm's sustainable competitive advantage.

craft production The process of handcrafting products or services for individual customers.

division of labor Dividing a job into a series of small tasks each performed by a different worker.

flexibility In operations, the ability to adjust to changes in product mix, production volume, or product and process design.

hoshins The action plans generated from a policy deployment process.

interchangeable parts The standardization of parts initially as replacement parts; enabled mass production.

key performance indicators (KPI) A set of measures that help managers evaluate performance in critical areas.

lean production An adaptation of mass production that prizes quality and flexibility.

mass customization The mass production of customized products.

mass production The high-volume production of a standardized product for a mass market.

operations A function or system that transforms inputs into outputs of greater value.

operations management The design and operation of productive systems.

order qualifiers The characteristics of a product or service that qualify it to be considered for purchase.

order winner The characteristic of a product or service that wins orders in the marketplace.

policy deployment A planning system for converting strategy to measurable objectives throughout all levels of an organization.

positioning Determining how a firm will compete in the marketplace.

primary task The task that is most central to the operation of a firm; it defines the business that a firm is in and is often expressed in a mission statement.

productivity The ratio of output to input.

quality revolution An emphasis on quality and the strategic role of operations.

resilience The ability to bounce back, change, or adapt in response to a disaster, failure, or disruption.

scientific management The systematic analysis of work methods proposed by Frederick Taylor in the early 1900s.

strategy A common vision that unites an organization, provides consistency in decisions, and keeps the organization moving in the right direction.

supply chain management Managing the flow of information, products, and services across a network of customers, enterprises, and supply chain partners.

value chain A series of activities from supplier to customer that add value to a product or service.

Questions

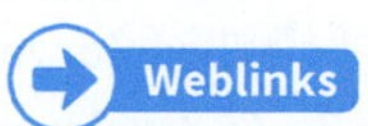

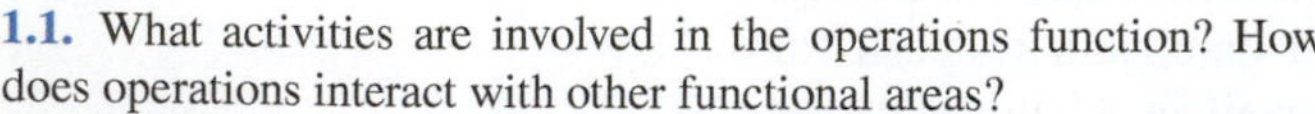

1.1. What activities are involved in the operations function? How does operations interact with other functional areas?

1.2. What constitutes "operations" at (a) a bank, (b) a retail store, (c) a hospital, (d) a cable TV company?

1.3. Briefly describe how operations has evolved from the Industrial Revolution to the Digital Revolution.

1.4. What is competitiveness? How is it measured? How has the Internet affected competitiveness?

1.5. Read about the Smart Cities Initiative and other smart technologies. Write a thought piece on the impact of new digital technologies on business operations, supply chains, and consumers.

1.6. Describe the global activities of a corporation of your choice. How many foreign plants or suppliers do they have? Where are they located? How much of their business is foreign? Are any global strategies evident?

1.7. Choose an industry on which you will be the class "expert" for the duration of this course. Write an initial profile of major players, customers, structure, and competitive issues.

1.8. Find an interesting website related to the operations function in a firm with which you are familiar. Write a summary of what you find.

1.9. Look for articles related to supply chains online or at *Fortune*, *Bloomberg Businessweek*, or CNN. How do they relate to the primary topics discussed in this chapter? If your university has access to Bloomberg terminals, map out the supply chain for a company of your choosing.

1.10. The World Bank ranks countries in terms of globalization. Go to the research section of *www.worldbank.org* and choose four countries to compare.

1.11. The World Trade Organization has its advocates and its adversaries. Find out more about the organization by visiting its website at *www.wto.org*. What kinds of activities does the organization support? What rules and regulations does it enforce? Who are its member states, and how is membership achieved?

1.12. Cultural differences can make it difficult to do business in other countries. Go to *www.worldbusinessculture.com* and choose a country to explore. Share your discoveries with your professor and classmates in a one- to two-page write-up.

1.13. Much of the negotiation in trade agreements centers on ethical/legal issues such as intellectual property protection, bribery and payoffs, and copyright and patent infringement. Transparency International at *www.transparency.org* publishes a bribe payers by country. Report on which countries and industries are most susceptible to bribery.

1.14. Ethics is easier when there are laws to fall back on. Search the Internet for information on the Foreign Corrupt Practices Act. Briefly describe what it entails. Then find two companies that explicitly state a code of conduct on their website and, in particular, reference the Foreign Corrupt Practices Act. How does each company approach the issue?

1.15. Gather mission or vision statements from four different companies. What do they tell you about the organizations? Is their mission or vision reflected in the way they do business?

1.16. List and explain the five steps of strategy formulation. Follow the steps to outline a strategy for a company or organization with which you are familiar.

1.17. Explain the concept of core competencies in your own words. Provide examples of a core competency for a bank, a retail store, and an auto manufacturer.

1.18. What is your core competency? Make a list of the core competencies you will need to compete successfully in the job market. Design a strategy for developing the competencies that you do not have and capitalizing on the competencies that you do have.

1.19. What is the difference between an order winner and an order qualifier? Tell how you have used the two concepts in a purchasing decision.

1.20. Discuss the requirements from an operations perspective of competing on (a) quality, (b) cost, (c) flexibility, (d) speed, (e) innovation, and (f) service. Give examples of manufacturing or service firms that successfully compete on each of the criteria listed.

1.21. What role should operations play in corporate strategy?

1.22. Name several strategic decisions that involve operations and supply chain management.

1.23. Why do companies need policy deployment? What does it do?

1.24. What is the balanced scorecard? How does it relate to operations?

1.25. Examine the annual reports of a company of your choosing over three years. Use quotes from the reports to describe the company's overall strategy and its specific goals each year. Pay special attention to global, digital, or big data strategies. How well do you think the company deploys its strategy?

1.26. Use either policy deployment or a balanced scorecard to map out a personal strategy for your future.

Problems

WileyPLUS

1.1. Tried and True Clothing has opened four new stores in college towns across the state. Data on monthly sales volume and labor hours are given below. Which store location has the highest labor productivity?

STORE	ANNANDALE	BLACKSBURG	CHARLOTTESVILLE	DANVILLE
Sales volume	$40,000	$12,000	$60,000	$25,000
Labor hours	250	60	500	200

1.2. Tried and True's accountant (from Problem 1.1) suggests that monthly rent and hourly wage rate also be factored into the productivity calculations. Annandale pays the highest average wage at $10 an hour. Blacksburg pays $7.25 an hour, Charlottesville $8, and Danville $7.50. The cost to rent store space is $2800 a month in Annandale, $1200 a month in Blacksburg, $2000 a month in Charlottesville, and $800 a month in Danville.

a. Which store is most productive?

b. Tried and True is not sure it can keep all four stores open. Based on multifactor productivity, which store would you close? What other factors should be considered?

1.3. At last year's bass tournament, Jim caught 12 bass in a four-hour period. This year he caught 15 in a six-hour period. In which year was he most productive? If the average size of the bass last year was 20 lb and the average size this year was 25 lb, would your decision change?

1.4. It is time for the annual performance review of Go-Com's account executives. Account values and hours spent each week acquiring and servicing accounts are shown below. Each agent works approximately 45 weeks out of the year, but the time spent on accounts each week differs considerably. How would you rate the performance of each individual? Which agent is most productive? Which agents show the most potential?

AGENTS	ALBERT	BATES	CRESSEY	DUONG
New accounts	$100,000	$40,000	$80,000	$200,000
Existing accounts	$40,000	$40,000	$150,000	$100,000
Labor hours	40	20	60	80

1.5. The Bureau of Labor Statistics collects input and output data from various countries for comparison purposes. Labor hours are the standard measure of input. Calculate the output per hour from the following data. Which country is most productive?

	LABOR HOURS	UNITS OF OUTPUT
United States	89.5	136
Germany	83.6	100
Japan	72.7	102

1.6. Omar Industries maintains production facilities in several locations around the globe. Average monthly cost data and output levels are given in the following tables.

a. Calculate the labor productivity of each facility.
b. Calculate the multifactor productivity of each facility.
c. If Omar needed to close one of the plants, which one would you choose?

UNITS (IN 000S)	CINCINNATI	FRANKFURT	GUADALAJARA	BEIJING
Finished goods	10,000	12,000	5,000	8,000
Work-in-process	1,000	2,200	3,000	6,000

COSTS (IN 000S)	CINCINNATI	FRANKFURT	GUADALAJARA	BEIJING
Labor costs	$3,500	$4,200	$2,500	$800
Material costs	$3,500	$3,000	$2,000	$2,500
Energy costs	$1,000	$1,500	$1,200	$800
Transportation costs	$250	$2,500	$2,000	$5,000
Overhead costs	$1,200	$3,000	$2,500	$500

1.7. Rushing yardage for three Heisman Trophy candidates is given below. Which candidate is the most productive running back? How did you measure productivity?

CANDIDATES	HENRY	McCAFFREY	FOURNETTE
Rushing yards	2110	3623	6925
No. of carries	105	875	1186
No. of touchdowns	15	20	70

1.8. Carpet City recorded the following data on carpet installations over the past week. Use the data to calculate the average rate (in yards per hour) at which carpet can be installed.

INSTALLATION	1	2	3
Square yards	1225	1435	2500
No. of workers	4	3	5
No. of hours per worker	3	5	6

1.9. Merrifield Post Office is evaluating the productivity of its mail processing centers. The centers differ in the degree of automation, the type of work that can be performed, and the skill of the workers.

CENTER	1	2	3
Pieces processed/hr	1000	2000	3000
No. of workers/hr	10	5	2
Hourly wage rate	$5.50	$10	$12
Overhead rate/hr	$10	$25	$50

a. Calculate the multifactor productivity for each center.
b. Workers in Center 1 are scheduled to receive a 10% pay raise next month. How will that affect productivity?
c. A new processing machine is available for Center 3 that would increase the output to 5000 pieces an hour at an additional overhead rate of $30 an hour. Should Merrifield install the new processing machine?

1.10. Posey Ceramics makes ceramic vases for a chain of department stores. The output and cost figures over the past four weeks are shown here. Labor costs $10 an hour, and materials are $4 a pound. Calculate the (a) labor productivity (in hrs), (b) material productivity (in lbs), and (c) multifactor productivity for each week. Comment on the results.

WEEK	1	2	3	4
Units of output	2000	4000	5000	7000
No. of workers	4	4	5	6
Hours per week per worker	40	48	56	70
Material (lbs)	286	570	720	1000

1.11. Jake and his friends sell newspaper ads for the *Campus Times* to supplement their income each year. From the data below, determine which person is the most productive.

	JAKE	JOSH	JENNIFER	JOHN
No. ads sold	100	50	200	35
No. hours spent	40	15	85	10

1.12. Nicholas is the facilities manager for Green Market Groceries. The store is remodeling and wants to determine which brand of freezer to use for its frozen goods section. The freezers vary by size, cabinet type, accessibility, refrigerant, and interliner. These variables affect both the purchase cost and the operating cost (e.g., energy consumption) of each freezer. Currently, the cost of energy per kilowatt hour (kwh) is $0.10. Green Market expenses capital purchases over a three-year period. Given the cost and capacity data below, calculate the "productivity" (i.e., the cubic feet of freezer space per dollar) for each freezer alternative. Which freezer brand would you recommend to Nicholas?

	ALASKAN SEAL	BRR FROST	COLD CASE	DEEP FREEZE
Purchase cost	$3270	$4000	$4452	$5450
Daily energy consumption (kwh)	3.61	3.88	6.68	29.07
Volume (cu ft)	25	35	49	72

1.13. Sweet Tooth Inc., a leading chocolatier, can produce 100 lbs of chocolate powder from 1000 lbs of cocoa beans in 10 hours of processing. Not satisfied with this output, the company is contemplating switching to a more automated process that would yield 200 lbs of chocolate powder per 1800 lbs of cocoa beans and take 15 hours to process. The cost of processing is $25 per hour. Cocoa beans cost $6.80 per lb. Calculate:

a. The labor productivity of the current process
b. The labor productivity of the proposed process
c. The multifactor productivity of the current process
d. The multifactor productivity of the proposed process
e. Should Sweet Tooth Inc. continue with the existing process or switch to the new process?

1.14. True Value Jeans currently produces 60 pairs of jeans in an 8-hour day. The costs of production include:

Raw material	$10.00/pair
Labor	3 workers, $20/hour
Energy	$1/hour of machine time
Machines	3 machines, $10/hour

a. Calculate the labor productivity for True Value, i.e., the number of jeans that can be produced with one hour of labor.
b. What is the per unit cost of manufacturing True Value jeans? What is the multifactor productivity for True Value? Explain in your own words what the multifactor productivity means.

1.15. Use the data contained in Figure 1.6 and Figure 1.10 to calculate productivity in terms of output per $ spent on labor for the countries listed in both figures. Which five countries are the most productive by this measure? Which five countries are the least productive?

Case Problems

Case Problem 1.1 Visualize This

Visualize This (VT) is a small start-up company specializing in virtual reality and computer visualizations. Located in the research park of a major university, the company was founded by Isaac Trice, a university professor, and staffed with the brightest of his former students. By all accounts the technology is cutting edge. Facilities include a lab of 14 high-end computer workstations adjacent to a CAVE (computer-aided virtual environment) and a small office. A conference room and central lobby are shared with other tenants in the building. Originally the company had partnered with the Swedish firm Salvania to create virtual environments for medical and industrial design. Trice and his staff would develop the software for each application, create a visual database supported with engineering or medical data, and run design sessions for their clients in the CAVE. Salvania provided the capital, generated the clients, and handled the business end of the operations.

In its first two years of business, VT completed four projects. With each project, VT advanced its skills in visualization and developed customized tools to help its clients design intricate products. The clients were pleased but did not anticipate repeating the intensive design process for several years. Unfortunately, Salvania was unable to remain solvent and dissolved its partnership with VT. VT was able to keep its workstations (whose salvage value was low), but gave up its rights to the CAVE and furloughed all but three employees. To stay afloat, VT needed new clients and a steady stream of income. Trice hit the streets and came back with the following possibilities:

- Designing computer-based training sessions for bank tellers of an international finance institution
- Conducting software certification for the sales staff of a large software vendor
- Designing virtual reality tours through history for a major museum
- Developing Web-based virtual models for a women's clothing retailer
- Creating virtual catalogs in which a customer can enlarge, rotate, and dissect a product online.

"This isn't what I had in mind for my company," Trice lamented as he shared the list with his employees. "I wanted to be developing the next generation of visualization tools in concert with the brightest minds in industry, not digitizing pictures of products and making them turn around, or teaching people to use software that's not even our own!"

That said, Trice and his staff of three began going through the list analyzing the pros and cons of each alternative.

1. Help Professor Trice formulate a strategy for his company by going through the steps of strategy formulation. For ideas, search the Internet for other companies that provide visualization solutions.
2. What capabilities does VT need to develop in order to pursue the strategy developed in question 1?
3. How can Trice reconcile his goals for the organization with the needs of the marketplace?
4. Compare the processes required to satisfy each customer on Trice's client list. Consider the mix of equipment and personnel, the length and scope of each project, and the potential for future business. How do the requirements differ from the projects already completed by VT?
5. Which projects would you recommend to VT? Why?

Case Problem 1.2 Whither an MBA at Strutledge?

Strutledge is a small private liberal arts school located within 50 miles of a major urban area in the southeast United States. As with most institutions of higher education, Strutledge's costs are rising and its enrollments are decreasing. In an effort to expand its student base, build valuable ties with area businesses, and simply survive, the Board of Regents is considering establishing an MBA program.

Currently no undergraduate degree is given in business, although business courses are taught. The dean of the school visualizes the MBA as an interdisciplinary program emphasizing problem solving, communication, and global awareness. Faculty expertise would be supplemented by instructors from local industry. The use of local faculty would better connect the university with the business community and provide opportunities for employment of the program's graduates.

In terms of competition, a major state-funded university that offers an MBA is located in the adjacent urban area. Strutledge hopes that state budget cutbacks and perceptions of overcrowded classrooms and overworked professors at public institutions will open the door for a new entrant into the market. The Board of Regents also feels that the school's small size will allow Strutledge to tailor the MBA program more closely to area business needs.

Several members of the Board are concerned about recent reports of the dwindling value of an MBA and are wondering if a better niche could be found with another graduate degree, perhaps a master of science in business analytics or something in the education or healthcare field.

1. What action would you recommend to the Board of Regents?
2. How should Strutledge go about making a strategic decision such as this?

Case Problem 1.3 Weighing Options at the Weight Club

The Weight Club started out as a student organization of 25 individuals who gathered together to discuss fitness goals and lift weights in the campus gym. When budget cutbacks cut gym hours and equipment availability, the students began to look elsewhere for a facility they could organize and control as they wished. They found an empty store in a small, abandoned strip mall, rented it for next to nothing, asked its members to pay dues, and began sponsoring weight-lifting contests to raise money for equipment. Off-campus now, they could recruit members from the town as well as the university. Their members had many talents, and they began sponsoring cheerleading training and other specialized training programs for athletes.

Growth of the student-run organization was phenomenal. Within six years the club had more than 4000 members from inside and outside of the university community. The facility itself extended over three additional storefronts in the now bustling mall, housing more than 50 pieces of aerobic equipment, two complete sets of Nautilus equipment for circuit training, an entire floor of free weights, a separate room for heavy weights, and a large exercise room for a full range of aerobic, step, kick boxing, and stretch and tone classes. Graduate students found the facility an excellent source of subjects for projects ranging from nutrition to exercise to lifestyle changes (after heart attacks, for instance). Members were often able to take advantage of these additional services free of charge.

The Weight Club clientele began to change as more nonuniversity students joined (from moms in the morning hours to teenagers after school and businesspersons after work). This diversity brought with it numerous requests for additional services such as child care, personal trainers, children's classes, massages, swimming and running facilities, locker rooms and showers, food and drink, sportswear, gymnastics, hotel and corporate memberships, meetings, and sponsored events.

Currently, all members pay the same $25 monthly usage fee with no other membership fees or assessments for additional services (like exercise classes). The staff consists predominantly of student members, many of whom have financed their way through school by working at the Weight Club. The organization is run by a founding member of the original weight club, who will finally graduate this year. Two other founding members have already graduated but work full time in the area and help administer the club whenever they can, serving as an informal "board of directors." In general, this arrangement has worked well, although decisions are made by whoever is behind the desk at the time, and there is no long-range planning.

The Weight Club has no significant competition. The three remaining "administrators" wonder if they need to make any changes.

Help the Weight Club get a handle on its operations and plan for the future by creating a balanced scorecard. Make a list of possible objectives for the Weight Club in terms of finance, customers, processes, and development (i.e., learning and growing). Add key performance measures and set goals for the year. Visit an exercise facility near you for ideas as you complete this assignment.

References

AT&T Quality Steering Committee. *Policy Deployment: Setting the Direction for Change.* Indianapolis: AT&T Technical Publications Center, 1992.

Christensen, Clayton. *The Innovator's Dilemma.* New York: Harper Business, 2003.

Engardio, Pete, and Dexter Roberts, "The China Price." *Business Week* (December 6, 2004).

Friedman, Thomas. *Hot, Flat, and Crowded*, New York: Farrar, Straus, and Giroux, 2008.

Friedman, Thomas. *The World Is Flat.* New York: Farrar, Straus and Giroux, 2005.

Friedman, Thomas, and Michael Mandelbaum, *That Used to Be Us.* New York: Picador, 2012.

Hammer, Michael. *Beyond Reengineering.* New York: HarperCollins, 1996.

Hayes, Robert, Gary Pisano, David Upton, and Steven Wheelwright. *Operations Strategy and Technology: Pursuing the Competitive Edge.* Hoboken, NJ: John Wiley, 2005.

Hill, Terry. *Manufacturing Strategy: Test and Cases*, 3rd ed. Homewood, IL: Irwin, 2000.

Jones, Patricia, and Larry Kahaner. *Say It and Live It: The 50 Corporate Mission Statements That Hit the Mark.* New York: Currency Doubleday, 1995.

Kaplan, Robert, and David Norton. *Strategy Maps: Converting Intangible Assets into Tangible Outcomes.* Boston: Harvard Business School Press, 2004.

King, Bob. *Hoshin Planning: The Developmental Approach.* Springfield, MA: GOAL/QPC, 1989.

Leonard-Barton, Dorothy. *Wellsprings of Knowledge: Building and Sustaining the Sources of Innovation.* Boston: Harvard Business School Press, 1995.

Manufacturing Studies Board. *Towards a New Era in Manufacturing: The Need for a National Vision.* Washington, DC: National Academy Press, 1986.

Midler, Paul. *Poorly Made in China.* Hoboken, NJ: John Wiley and Sons, Inc., 2011.

Peters, Tom. *Thriving on Chaos.* New York: Alfred A. Knopf, 1987.

Porter, Michael. *On Competition.* Boston: Harvard Business School Publishing, 2008.

Quade, Walter. "Beginner's Guide to the Asian Supply Chain." *Inside Supply Management* (March 2004), pp. 8–9.

Schwab, Klaus. "The Fourth Industrial Revolution: What it Means, How to Respond," *Foreign Affairs*, December 12, 2015.

Skinner, Wickham. *Manufacturing: The Formidable Competitive Weapon.* New York: John Wiley, 1985.

Skinner, Wickham. "Three Yards and a Cloud of Dust: Industrial Management at Century End." *Production and Operations Management* 5(1; Spring 1996):15–24.

Voss, Christopher. "Operations Management—from Taylor to Toyota—and Beyond." *British Journal of Management* 6 (December 1995), S17–S29.

Womack, James, Daniel Jones, and Daniel Roos. *The Machine that Changed the World.* New York: Macmillan, 1990.

SUPPLEMENT TO CHAPTER 1

Operational Decision-Making Tools: Decision Analysis

IN THIS SUPPLEMENT, YOU WILL LEARN ABOUT . . .

- Decision Analysis (With and Without Probabilities)

At the operational level hundreds of decisions are made in order to achieve local outcomes that contribute to the achievement of a company's overall strategic goal. These local outcomes are usually not measured directly in terms of profit, but instead are measured in terms of quality, cost-effectiveness, efficiency, productivity, and so forth. Achieving good results for local outcomes is an important objective for individual operational units and individual operations managers. However, all these decisions are interrelated and must be coordinated for the purpose of attaining the overall company goals. Decision making is analogous to a great stage play or opera, in which all the actors, the costumes, the props, the music, the orchestra, and the script must be choreographed and staged by the director, the stage managers, the author, and the conductor so that everything comes together for the performance.

For many topics in operations management, there are quantitative models and techniques available that help managers make decisions. Some techniques simply provide information that the operations manager might use to help make a decision; other techniques recommend a decision to the manager. Some techniques are specific to a particular aspect of operations management; others are more generic and can be applied to a variety of decision-making categories. These different models and techniques are the "tools" of the operations manager. Simply having these tools does not make someone an effective operations manager, just as owning a saw and a hammer does not make someone a carpenter. An operations manager must know how to use decision-making tools. How these tools are used in the decision-making process is an important and necessary part of the study of operations management. In this supplement and others throughout this book, we examine several different aspects of operational decision making using these tools.

Decision Analysis With and Without Probabilities

In this supplement we demonstrate a quantitative technique called **decision analysis** for decision-making situations in which uncertainty exists. Decision analysis is a generic technique that can be applied to a number of different types of operational decision-making areas.

Decision analysis A set of quantitative decision-making techniques for decision situations in which uncertainty exists.

Many decision-making situations occur under conditions of uncertainty. For example, the demand for a product may not be 100 units next week but may vary between 0 and 200 units, depending on the state of the market, which is uncertain. Decision analysis is a set of quantitative decision-making techniques to aid the decision maker in dealing with a decision situation in which there is uncertainty. However, the usefulness of decision analysis for decision making is also a beneficial topic to study because it reflects a structured, systematic approach to decision making that many decision makers follow intuitively without ever consciously thinking about it. Decision analysis represents not only a collection of decision-making techniques but also an analysis of logic underlying decision making.

Decision Making Without Probabilities

A decision-making situation includes several components—the decisions themselves and the events that may occur in the future, known as *states of nature*. Future states of nature may be high or low demand for a product or good or bad economic conditions. At the time a decision is made, the decision maker is uncertain which state of nature will occur in the future and has no control over these states of nature.

When probabilities can be assigned to the occurrence of states of nature in the future, the situation is referred to as *decision making under risk*. When probabilities cannot be assigned to the occurrence of future events, the situation is called *decision making under uncertainty*. We discuss the latter case next.

To facilitate the analysis of decision situations, they are organized into **payoff tables**. A payoff table is a means of organizing and illustrating the payoffs from the different decisions, given the various states of nature, and has the general form shown in Table S1.1.

Payoff table A method for organizing and illustrating the payoffs from different decisions given various states of nature.

Payoff The outcome of the decision.

Each decision, 1 or 2, in Table S1.1 will result in an outcome, or **payoff**, for each state of nature that will occur in the future. Payoffs are typically expressed in terms of profit, revenues, or cost (although they may be expressed in terms of a variety of quantities). For example, if decision 1 is to expand a production facility and state of nature *a* is good economic conditions, payoff 1a could be $100,000 in profit.

Once the decision situation has been organized into a payoff table, several criteria are available to reflect how the decision maker arrives at a decision, including maximax, maximin, minimax regret, Hurwicz, and equal likelihood. These criteria reflect different degrees of decision-maker conservatism or liberalism. On occasion they result in the same decision; however, they often yield different results. These decision-making criteria are demonstrated by the following example.

TABLE S1.1 Payoff Table

	STATES OF NATURE	
DECISION	*a*	*b*
1	Payoff 1a	Payoff 1b
2	Payoff 2a	Payoff 2b

EXAMPLE S1.1 | Decision-Making Criteria Under Uncertainty

The Southern Textile Company is contemplating the future of one of its plants located in South Carolina. Three alternative decisions are being considered: (1) Expand the plant and produce lightweight, durable materials for possible sale to the military, a market with little foreign competition; (2) maintain the status quo at the plant, continuing production of textile goods that are subject to heavy foreign competition; or (3) sell the plant now. If one of the first two alternatives is chosen, the plant will still be sold at the end of the year. The amount of profit that could be earned by selling the plant in a year depends on foreign market conditions, including the status of a trade embargo bill in Congress. The following payoff table describes this decision situation.

	STATES OF NATURE	
DECISION	*GOOD FOREIGN COMPETITIVE CONDITIONS*	*POOR FOREIGN COMPETITIVE CONDITIONS*
Expand	$800,000	$500,000
Maintain status quo	1,300,000	−150,000
Sell now	320,000	320,000

Determine the best decision using each of the decision criteria.

1. Maximax
2. Maximin
3. Minimax regret
4. Hurwicz
5. Equal likelihood

Solution:

1. Maximax

The decision is selected that will result in the maximum of the maximum payoffs. This is how this criterion derives its name—the maximum of the maxima. The **maximax criterion** is very optimistic. The decision maker assumes that the most favorable state of nature for each decision alternative will occur. Thus, for this example, the company would optimistically assume that good competitive conditions will prevail in the future, resulting in the following maximum payoffs and decisions:

Maximax criterion A decision criterion that results in the maximum of the maximum payoffs.

Expand:	$800,000	
Status quo:	1,300,000	← Maximum
Sell:	320,000	

Decision: Maintain status quo

2. Maximin

The **maximin criterion** is pessimistic. With the maximin criterion, the decision maker selects the decision that will reflect the maximum of the minimum payoffs. For each decision alternative, the decision maker assumes that the minimum payoff will occur; of these, the maximum is selected as follows:

Maximin criterion A decision criterion that results in the maximum of the minimum payoffs.

Expand:	$500,000	← Maximum
Status quo:	−150,000	
Sell:	320,000	

Decision: Expand

3. **Minimax Regret Criterion**
   The decision maker attempts to avoid regret by selecting the decision alternative that minimizes the maximum regret. A decision maker first selects the maximum payoff under each state of nature; then all other payoffs under the respective states of nature are subtracted from these amounts, as follows:

GOOD COMPETITIVE CONDITIONS	POOR COMPETITIVE CONDITIONS
\$1,300,000 − 800,000 = 500,000	\$500,000 − 500,000 = 0
1,300,000 − 1,300,000 = 0	500,000 − (−150,000) = 650,000
1,300,000 − 320,000 = 980,000	500,000 − 320,000 = 180,000

These values represent the regret for each decision that would be experienced by the decision maker if a decision were made that resulted in less than the maximum payoff. The maximum regret for *each decision* must be determined, and the decision corresponding to the minimum of these regret values is selected as follows:

Expand: \$500,000 ← Minimum
Status quo: 650,000
Sell: 980,000

Decision: Expand

Minimax regret criterion A decision criterion that results in the minimum of the maximum regrets for each alternative.

4. Hurwicz
   A compromise is made between the maximax and maximin criteria. The decision maker is neither totally optimistic (as the maximax criterion assumes) nor totally pessimistic (as the maximin criterion assumes). With the **Hurwicz criterion**, the decision payoffs are weighted by a **coefficient of optimism**, a measure of the decision maker's optimism. The coefficient of optimism, defined as α, is between 0 and 1 (i.e., $0 < \alpha < 1.0$). If $\alpha = 1.0$, the decision maker is completely optimistic; if $\alpha = 0$, the decision maker is completely pessimistic. (Given this definition, $1 - \alpha$ is the *coefficient of pessimism.*) For each decision alternative, the maximum payoff is multiplied by α and the minimum payoff is multiplied by $1 - \alpha$. For our investment example, if α equals .3 (i.e., the company is slightly optimistic) and $1 - \alpha = .7$, the following decision will result:

Expand: \$800,000(0.3) + 500,000(0.7) = \$590,000 ← Maximum
Status quo: 1,300,000(0.3) − 150,000(0.7) = 285,000
Sell: 320,000(0.3) + 320,000(0.7) = 320,000

Decision: Expand

Hurwicz criterion A decision criterion in which the decision payoffs are weighted by a coefficient of optimism, α.

Coefficient of optimism (α) A measure of a decision maker's optimism, from 0 (completely pessimistic) to 1 (completely optimistic).

5. Equal Likelihood
   The **equal likelihood** (or **Laplace**) **criterion** weights each state of nature equally, thus assuming that the states of nature are equally likely to occur. Since there are two states of nature in our example, we assign a weight of 0.50 to each one. Next, we multiply these weights by each payoff for each decision and select the alternative with the maximum of these weighted values.

Expand: \$800,000(0.50) + 500,000(0.50) = \$650,000 ← Maximum
Status quo: 1,300,000(0.50) − 150,000(0.50) = 575,000
Sell: 320,000(0.50) + 320,000(0.50) = 320,000

Decision: Expand

Equal likelihood (Laplace) criterion Decision criterion in which each state of nature is weighted equally.

The decision to expand the plant was designated most often by four of the five decision criteria. The decision to sell was never indicated by any criterion. This is because the payoffs for expansion, under either set of future economic conditions, are always better than the payoffs for selling. Given any situation with these two alternatives, the decision to expand will always be made over the decision to sell. The sell decision alternative could have been eliminated from consideration under each of our criteria. The alternative of selling is said to be *dominated* by the alternative of expanding. In general, dominated decision alternatives can be removed from the payoff table and not considered when the various decision-making criteria are applied, which reduces the complexity of the decision analysis.

Different decision criteria often result in a mix of decisions. The criteria used and the resulting decisions depend on the decision maker. For example, the extremely optimistic decision maker might disregard the preceding results and make the decision to maintain the status quo, because the maximax criterion reflects his or her personal decision-making philosophy.

Decision Analysis With Excel

Throughout this book we will demonstrate how to solve quantitative models using the computer with Microsoft Excel spreadsheets. **Exhibit S1.1** shows the Excel spreadsheet solutions for the different decision-making criteria in Example S1.1. The call-out boxes displayed on and around the spreadsheet define the cell formulas used to compute the criteria values. For example, the spreadsheet formula used to compute the maximum payoff value for the decision to "Expand," **=MAX(C6:D6)**, is embedded in cell E6 and is also shown on the toolbar at the top of the spreadsheet. The formula for the Maximax decision, **=MAX(E6:E8)**, is embedded in cell C10.

The Excel file for Exhibit S1.1 and the Excel files for all of the exhibits in the subsequent chapters in this text are contained on the text website. Students and instructors can download this file to see how the spreadsheet was constructed as well as the individual cell formulas. This spreadsheet can also be used as a guideline or template to solve the homework problems at the end of the chapter using Excel.

EXHIBIT S1.1

ExhibitS1.1.Decision Analysis [Compatibility Mode] - Excel

File Home Insert Page Layout Formulas Data Review View Tell me what you want to do...

E6 =MAX(C6:D6)

	A	B	C	D	E	F	G	H
1	**Example S1.1: Decision-Making Criteria Under Uncertainty**							
2								
3								
4			*States of Nature*				*Regret*	
5		*Decision*	Good Conditions	Poor Conditions	*Maximum*	*Minimum*	Good	Poor
6		Expand	800,000	500,000	800,000	500,000	500,000	-
7		Maintain status quo	1,300,000	(150,000)	1,300,000	(150,000)	-	650,000
8		Sell now	320,000	320,000	320,000	320,000	980,000	180,000
9								
10	(1)	Maximax decision =	1,300,000	*Status quo*				
11	(2)	Maximin decision =	500,000	*Expand*				
12								
13	(3)	*Minimax Regret:*						
14		Expand =	500,000	*Select*				
15		Maintain status quo =	650,000					
16		Sell now =	980,000					
17								
18	(4)	*Hurwicz:*						
19		Alpha =	0.30					
20		1 - Alpha =	0.70					
21		Expand =	590,000	*Select*				
22		Maintain status quo =	285,000					
23		Sell now =	320,000					
24								
25	(5)	*Equal Likelihood:*						
26		Expand =	650,000	*Select*				
27		Maintain status quo =	575,000					
28		Sell now =	320,000					
29								

=MIN(C8:D8)

=MAX(F6:F8)

=MAX(G7:H7)

=C19*E7+C20*F7

=.5*E8+.5*F8

EXHIBIT S1.2 | Excel File

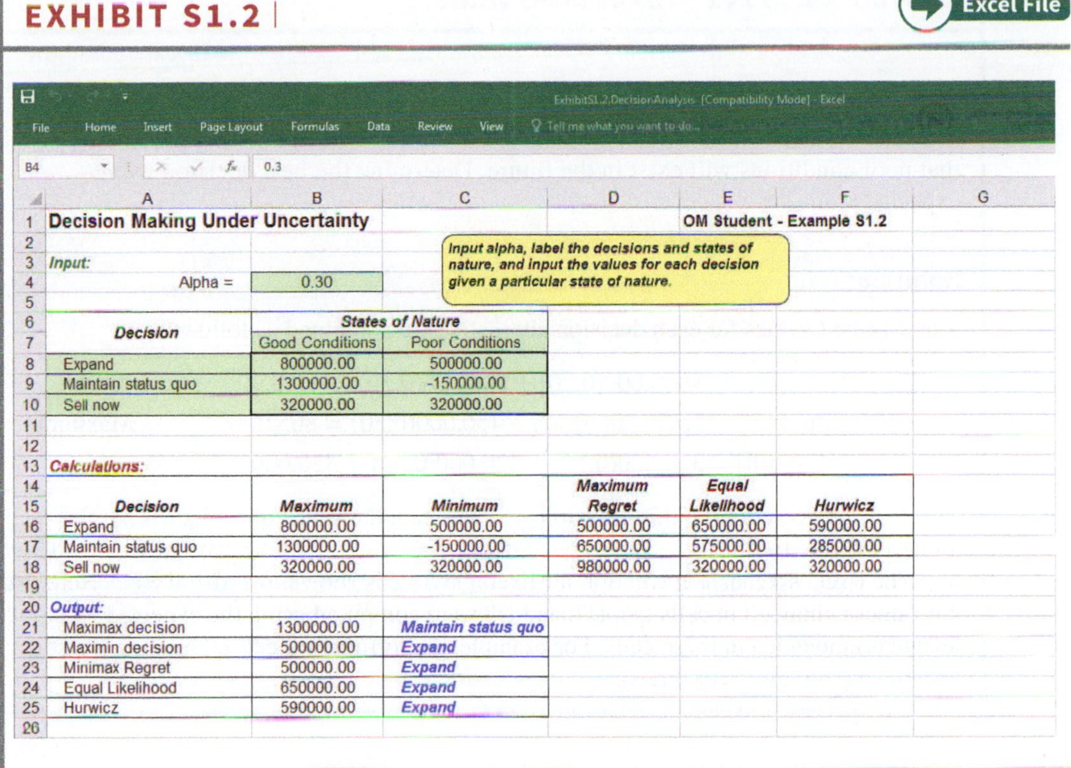

Decision Making Under Uncertainty — OM Student - Example S1.2

Input:

Alpha = 0.30

Input alpha, label the decisions and states of nature, and input the values for each decision given a particular state of nature.

Decision	States of Nature	
	Good Conditions	Poor Conditions
Expand	800000.00	500000.00
Maintain status quo	1300000.00	-150000.00
Sell now	320000.00	320000.00

Calculations:

Decision	Maximum	Minimum	Maximum Regret	Equal Likelihood	Hurwicz
Expand	800000.00	500000.00	500000.00	650000.00	590000.00
Maintain status quo	1300000.00	-150000.00	650000.00	575000.00	285000.00
Sell now	320000.00	320000.00	980000.00	320000.00	320000.00

Output:

Maximax decision	1300000.00	*Maintain status quo*
Maximin decision	500000.00	*Expand*
Minimax Regret	500000.00	*Expand*
Equal Likelihood	650000.00	*Expand*
Hurwicz	590000.00	*Expand*

Decision Analysis with OM Tools

OM Tools is an Excel-based software package published by Wiley that was specifically designed for use with this text. It includes solution modules for most of the quantitative techniques in this text. After downloading OM Tools, modules can be selected by clicking on the "OM Tools" button on the tool bar at the top of the page, which provides a drop-down list of modules, and then clicking on the specific module you want to use. In this case we want to use the "Decision Analysis" module with "Decision Making Under Uncertainty." A window for providing the initial problem data, including the problem name and the number of decision alternatives and states of nature, will then be displayed. Exhibit S1.2 shows the OM Tools Excel spreadsheet for Example S1.1 with all of the problem data input into the cells. Notice that the difference between this spreadsheet and the one in Exhibit S1.1 is that the spreadsheet has already been set up with all of the Excel formulas for the various decision criteria in the cells. Thus, all you have to do to solve the problem is type in the problem data.

Decision Making With Probabilities

For the decision-making criteria we just used we assumed no available information regarding the probability of the states of nature. However, it is often possible for the decision maker to know enough about the future states of nature to assign probabilities that each will occur, which is decision making under conditions of *risk*. The most widely used decision-making criterion under risk is **expected value**, computed by multiplying each outcome by the probability of its occurrence and then summing these products according to the following formula:

Expected value A weighted average of decision outcomes in which each future state of nature is assigned a probability of occurrence.

$$\text{EV}(x) = \sum_{i=1}^{n} p(x_i)x_i$$

where

$$x_i = \text{outcome } i$$
$$p(x_i) = \text{probability of outcome } i$$

EXAMPLE S1.2 | Expected Value

Assume that it is now possible for the Southern Textile Company to estimate a probability of .70 that good foreign competitive conditions will exist and a probability of .30 that poor conditions will exist in the future. Determine the best decision using expected value.

Solution:

The expected values for each decision alternative are computed as follows.

$$\text{EV(expand)} = \$800{,}000(0.70) + 500{,}000(0.30) = \$710{,}000$$
$$\text{EV(status quo)} = 1{,}300{,}000(0.70) - 150{,}000(0.30) = 865{,}000 \qquad \leftarrow \text{Maximum}$$
$$\text{EV(sell)} = 320{,}000(0.70) + 320{,}000(0.30) = 320{,}000$$

The decision according to this criterion is to maintain the status quo, since it has the highest expected value.

The Excel spreadsheet solution for Example S1.2 is shown in Exhibit S1.3. Note that the values contained in cells D6, D7, and D8 were computed using the expected value formulas embedded in these cells. For example, the formula for cell D6 is shown on the formula bar on the Excel screen.

EXHIBIT S1.3 |

Excel File

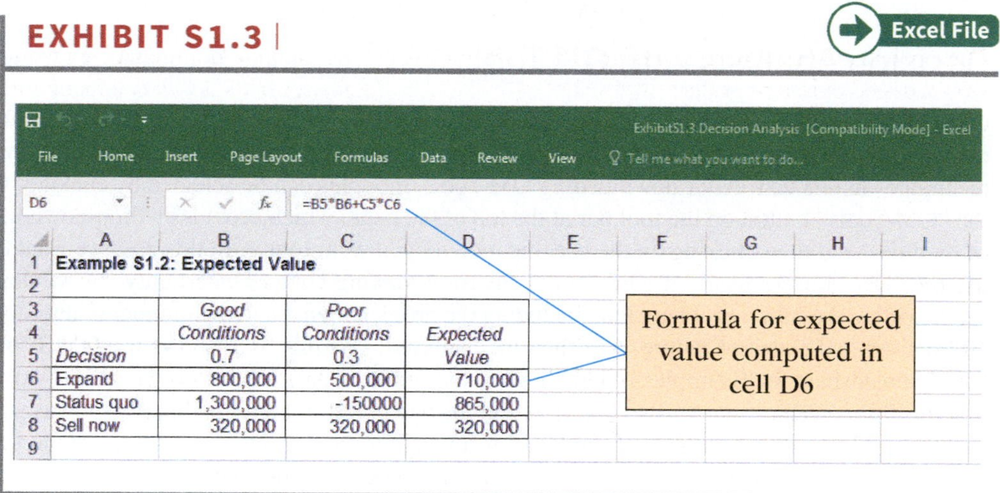

Example S1.2: Expected Value

Decision	Good Conditions 0.7	Poor Conditions 0.3	Expected Value
Expand	800,000	500,000	710,000
Status quo	1,300,000	-150000	865,000
Sell now	320,000	320,000	320,000

Expected Value of Perfect Information

Expected value of perfect information (EVPI) The maximum value of perfect information to the decision maker.

Occasionally, additional information is available, or can be purchased, regarding future events, enabling the decision maker to make a better decision. For example, a company could hire an economic forecaster to determine more accurately the economic conditions that will occur in the future. However, it would be foolish to pay more for this information than it stands to gain in extra profit from having the information. The information has some maximum value that is the limit of what the decision maker would be willing to spend. This value of information can be computed as an expected value—hence its name, the **expected value of perfect information (EVPI)**.

To compute the expected value of perfect information, first look at the decisions under each state of nature. If information that assured us which state of nature was going to occur (i.e., perfect information) could be obtained, the best decision for that state of nature could be selected. For example, in the textile company example, if the company executives knew for sure that good competitive conditions would prevail, they would maintain the status quo. If they knew for sure that poor competitive conditions will occur, then they would expand.

The probabilities of each state of nature (i.e., .70 and .30) indicate that good competitive conditions will prevail 70% of the time and poor competitive conditions will prevail 30% of the time (if this decision situation is repeated many times). In other words, even though perfect information enables the investor to make the right decision, each state of nature will occur only a certain portion of the time. Thus, each of the decision outcomes obtained using perfect information must be weighted by its respective probability:

$$\$1{,}300{,}000(0.70) + (500{,}000)(0.30) = \$1{,}060{,}000$$

The amount of $1,060,000 is the expected value of the decision *given perfect information*, not the expected value of perfect information. The expected value of perfect information is the maximum amount that would be paid to gain information that would result in a decision better than the one made without perfect information. Recall from Example S1.2 that the expected-value decision without perfect information was to maintain the status quo and the expected value was $865,000.

The expected value of perfect information is computed by subtracting the expected value without perfect information from the expected value given perfect information:

$$\text{EVPI} = \text{expected value given perfect information} - \text{expected value without perfect information}$$

For our example, the EVPI is computed as

$$\text{EVPI} = \$1{,}060{,}000 - 865{,}000 = \$195{,}000$$

The expected value of perfect information, $195,000, is the maximum amount that the investor would pay to purchase perfect information from some other source, such as an economic forecaster. Of course, perfect information is rare and is usually unobtainable. Typically, the decision maker would be willing to pay some smaller amount, depending on how accurate (i.e., close to perfection) the information is believed to be.

Sequential Decision Trees

A payoff table is limited to a single decision situation. If a decision requires a series of decisions, a payoff table cannot be created, and a **sequential decision tree** must be used. We demonstrate the use of a decision tree in the following example.

Sequential decision tree A graphical method for analyzing decision situations that require a sequence of decisions over time.

EXAMPLE S1.3 | A Sequential Decision Tree

The Southern Textile Company is considering two alternatives: to expand its existing production operation to manufacture a new line of lightweight material, or to purchase land on which to construct a new facility in the future. Each of these decisions has outcomes based on product market growth in the future that result in another set of decisions (during a 10-year planning horizon), as shown in the following figure of a sequential decision tree. In this figure the square nodes represent decisions, and the circle nodes reflect different states of nature and their probabilities.

The first decision facing the company is whether to expand or buy land. If the company expands, two states of nature are possible. Either the market will grow (with a probability of .60) or it will not grow (with a probability of .40). Either state of nature will result in a payoff. On the other hand, if the company chooses to purchase land, three years in the future another decision will have to be made regarding the development of the land.

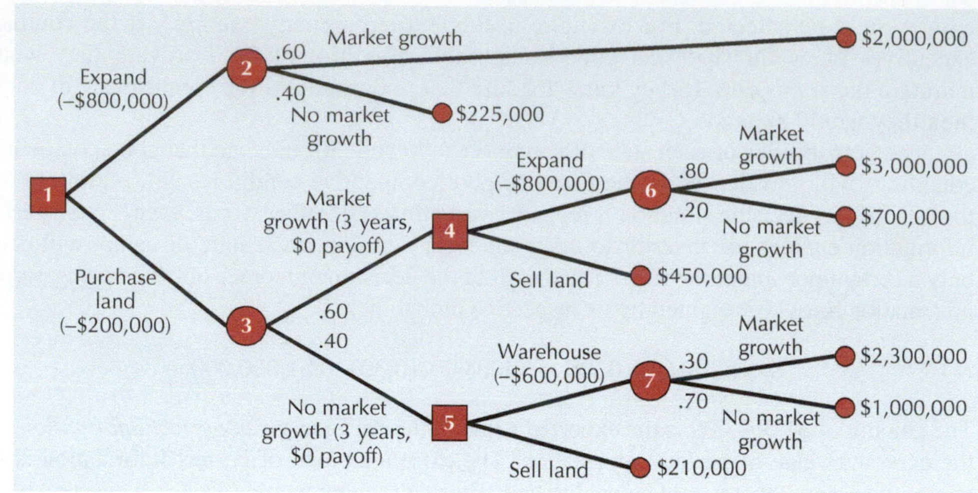

At decision node 1, the decision choices are to expand or to purchase land. Notice that the costs of the ventures ($800,000 and $200,000, respectively) are shown in parentheses. If the plant is expanded, two states of nature are possible at probability node 2: The market will grow, with a probability of .60, or it will not grow or will decline, with a probability of .40. If the market grows, the company will achieve a payoff of $2,000,000 over a 10-year period. However, if no growth occurs, a payoff of only $225,000 will result.

If the decision is to purchase land, two states of nature are possible at probability node 3. These two states of nature and their probabilities are identical to those at node 2; however, the payoffs are different. If market growth occurs for a three-year period, no payoff will occur, but the company will make another decision at node 4 regarding development of the land. At that point, either the plant will be expanded at a cost of $800,000 or the land will be sold, with a payoff of $450,000. The decision situation at node 4 can occur only if market growth occurs first. If no market growth occurs at node 3, there is no payoff, and another decision situation becomes necessary at node 5: A warehouse can be constructed at a cost of $600,000 or the land can be sold for $210,000. (Notice that the sale of the land results in less profit if there is no market growth than if there is growth.)

If the decision at decision node 4 is to expand, two states of nature are possible: The market may grow, with a probability of .80, or it may not grow, with a probability of .20. The probability of market growth is higher (and the probability of no growth is lower) than before because there has already been growth for the first three years, as shown by the branch from node 3 to node 4. The payoffs for these two states of nature at the end of the 10-year period are $3,000,000 and $700,000, respectively.

If the company decides to build a warehouse at node 5, two states of nature can occur: Market growth can occur, with a probability of .30 and an eventual payoff of $2,300,000, or no growth can occur, with a probability of .70 and a payoff of $1,000,000. The probability of market growth is low (i.e., .30) because there has already been no market growth, as shown by the branch from node 3 to node 5.

Solution:

We start the decision analysis process at the end of the decision tree and work backward toward a decision at node 1.

First, we must compute the expected values at nodes 6 and 7:

$$\begin{aligned}\text{EV(node 6)} &= 0.80(\$3{,}000{,}000) + 0.20(\$700{,}000) = \$2{,}540{,}000\\ \text{EV(node 7)} &= 0.30(2{,}300{,}000) + 0.70(\$1{,}000{,}000) = \$1{,}390{,}000\end{aligned}$$

These expected values (as well as all other nodal values) are shown in boxes in the figure.

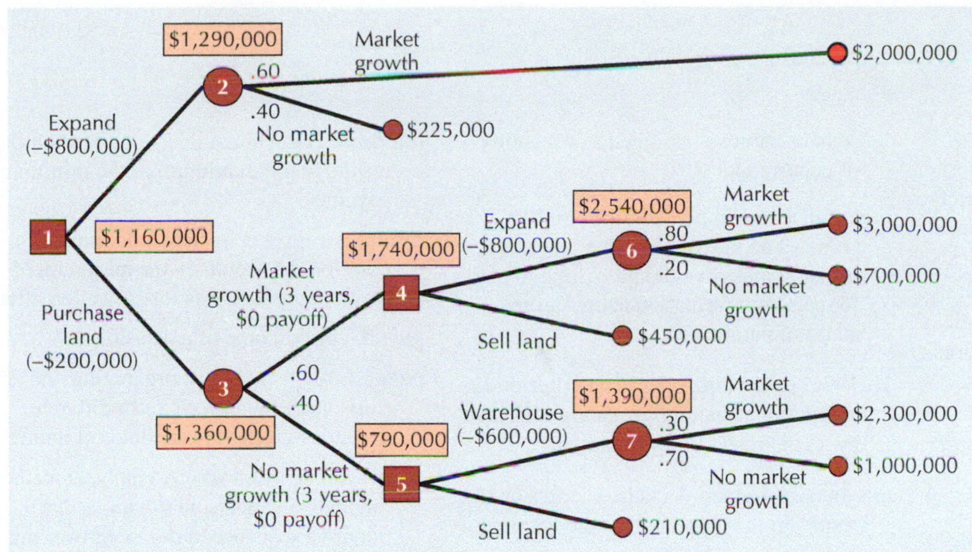

At decision nodes 4 and 5, a decision must be made. As with a normal payoff table, the decision is made that results in the greatest expected value. At node 4 the choice is between two values: $1,740,000, the value derived by subtracting the cost of expanding ($800,000) from the expected payoff of $2,540,000, and $450,000, the expected value of selling the land computed with a probability of 1.0. The decision is to expand, and the value at node 4 is $1,740,000.

The same process is repeated at node 5. The decisions at node 5 result in payoffs of $790,000 (i.e., $1,390,000 – 600,000 = $790,000) and $210,000. Since the value $790,000 is higher, the decision is to build a warehouse.

Next, the expected values at nodes 2 and 3 are computed:

$$\text{EV(node 2)} = 0.60(\$2{,}000{,}000) + 0.40(\$225{,}000) = \$1{,}290{,}000$$
$$\text{EV(node 3)} = 0.60(\$1{,}740{,}000) + 0.40(\$790{,}000) = \$1{,}360{,}000$$

(Note that the expected value for node 3 is computed from the decision values previously determined at nodes 4 and 5.)

Now the final decision at node 1 must be made. As before, we select the decision with the greatest expected value after the cost of each decision is subtracted.

$$\text{Expand: } \$1{,}290{,}000 - 800{,}000 = \$490{,}000$$
$$\text{Land: } \$1{,}360{,}000 - 200{,}000 = \$1{,}160{,}000$$

Since the highest *net* expected value is $1,160,000, the decision is to purchase land, and the payoff of the decision is $1,160,000.

Decision trees allow the decision maker to see the logic of decision making by providing a picture of the decision process. Decision trees can be used for problems more complex than this example without too much difficulty.

Summary

In this supplement we have provided a general overview of decision analysis. To a limited extent, we have also shown that the logic of such operational decisions throughout the organization is interrelated to achieve strategic goals.

Key Terms

coefficient of optimism (α) A measure of a decision maker's optimism, from 0 (completely pessimistic) to 1 (completely optimistic), used in the Hurwicz decision criterion.

decision analysis A set of quantitative decision-making techniques to aid the decision maker in dealing with decision situations in which uncertainty exists.

equal likelihood (Laplace) criterion A decision criterion in which each state of nature is weighted equally.

expected value A weighted average of decision outcomes in which each future state of nature is assigned a probability of occurrence.

expected value of perfect information (EVP) The maximum value that a decision maker would be willing to pay for perfect information about future states of nature.

Hurwicz criterion A decision criterion in which the decision payoffs are weighted by a coefficient of optimism, α.

maximax criterion A decision criterion that results in the maximum of the maximum payoffs.

maximin criterion A decision criterion that results in the maximum of the minimum payoffs.

minimax regret criterion A decision criterion that results in the minimum of the maximum regrets for each alternative.

payoff The outcome of a decision.

payoff table A means of organizing and illustrating the payoffs from different decisions given various states of nature.

sequential decision tree A graphical method for analyzing decision situations that require a sequence of decisions over time.

Key Formulas

Expected Value

$$\text{EV}(x) = \sum_{i=1}^{n} p(x_i)x_i$$

Expected Value of Perfect Information

EVPI = expected value given perfect information − expected value without perfect information

Solved Problems

Consider the following payoff table for three product decisions (A, B, and C) and three future market conditions (payoffs = $ millions).

	MARKET CONDITIONS		
DECISION	1	2	3
A	$1.0	$2.0	$0.5
B	0.8	1.2	0.9
C	0.7	0.9	1.7

Determine the best decision using the following decision criteria.

1. Maximax
2. Maximin

Solution

Step 1. Maximax criterion

	MAXIMUM PAYOFFS	
A	$2.0	← Maximum
B	1.2	
C	1.7	

Decision: Product A

Step 2. Maximin criterion

	MAXIMUM PAYOFFS	
A	0.5	
B	0.8	← Maximum
C	0.7	

Decision: Product B

Problems

WileyPLUS

S1.1. Telecomp is a U.S.-based manufacturer of cellular telephones. It is planning to build a new manufacturing and distribution facility in either South Korea, China, Taiwan, Poland, or Mexico. The cost of the facility will differ between countries and will even vary within countries depending on the economic and political climate, including monetary exchange rates. The company has estimated the facility cost (in $ millions) in each country under three different future economic/political climates as follows.

	ECONOMIC/POLITICAL CLIMATE		
COUNTRY	DECLINE	SAME	IMPROVE
South Korea	21.7	19.1	15.2
China	19.0	18.5	17.6
Taiwan	19.2	17.1	14.9
Poland	22.5	16.8	13.8
Mexico	25.0	21.2	12.5

Determine the best decision using the following decision criteria. (Note that since the payoff is cost, the maximax criteria becomes minimin and maximin becomes minimax.)

a. Minimin
b. Minimax
c. Hurwicz ($\alpha = .40$)
d. Equal likelihood

S1.2. A global economist hired by Telecomp, the U.S.-based computer manufacturer in Problem S1-1, estimates that the probability that the economic and political climate overseas and in Mexico will decline during the next five years is .30, the probability that it will remain approximately the same is .40, and the probability that it will improve is .30. Determine the best country to construct the new facility in and the expected value of perfect information.

S1.3. Landloc, a real estate development firm, is considering several alternative development projects. These include building and leasing an office building, purchasing a parcel of land and building a parking lot, buying and leasing a warehouse, building a shopping mall, and building and selling condominiums. The financial success of these projects depends on interest rate movement in the next five years. The various development projects and their five-year financial return ($ millions) given that interest rates will decline, remain stable, or increase are shown in the following payoff table.

Determine the best investment using the following decision criteria.

a. Maximax
b. Maximin
c. Equal likelihood
d. Hurwicz ($\alpha = .3$)

	INTEREST RATES		
PROJECT	DECLINE	STABLE	INCREASE
Office building	0.5	1.7	4.5
Parking lot	1.5	1.9	2.4
Warehouse	1.7	1.4	1.0
Shopping mall	0.7	2.4	3.6
Condominiums	3.2	1.5	0.6

S1.4. In Problem S1-3 the Landloc real estate development firm has hired an economist to assign a probability to each direction interest rates may take over the next five years. The economist has determined that there is a .50 probability that interest rates will decline, a .40 probability that rates will remain stable, and a .10 probability that rates will increase.

a. Using expected value, determine the best project.
b. Determine the expected value of perfect information.

S1.5. Nicole Nelson has come into an inheritance from her grandparents. She is attempting to decide among several investment alternatives. The return after one year is dependent primarily on the interest rate during the next year. The rate is currently 7%, and she anticipates it will stay the same or go up or down by at most 2 points. The various investment alternatives plus their returns ($10,000s) given the interest rate changes are shown in the following table.

	INTEREST RATES				
INVESTMENTS	5%	6%	7%	8%	9%
Money market fund	1.7	2.8	3.0	3.6	4.5
Stock growth fund	−5	−3	3.5	5	7.5
Bond fund	5	4	3.5	3	2
Government fund	4	3.6	3.2	2.8	2.1
Risk fund	−12	−7	4.2	9.3	16.7
Savings bonds	3	3	3.2	3.4	3.5

Determine the best investment using the following decision criteria.

a. Maximax
b. Maximin
c. Equal likelihood

S1.6. In Problem S1-5 assume that Nicole, with the help of a financial newsletter and some library research, has been able to assign probabilities to each of the possible interest rates during the next year as follows:

Interest Rate	5%	6%	7%	8%	9%
Probability	.1	.2	.4	.2	.1

a. Using expected value, determine her best investment decision.
b. Nicole is considering hiring a financial analyst to help her determine the best investment. What is the maximum amount she should pay an analyst?

S1.7. Leevi Starch, an apparel company with a global supply chain, is adding a new supplier for several new styles of its denim jeans, and the suppliers it's considering are in China, India, the Philippines, Brazil, and Mexico. A major factor in the company's decision is transportation and shipping costs, which are dependent on future oil prices. The following payoff table summarizes the total monthly costs (in $100,000s), including manufacturing and shipping costs for the suppliers in each of the countries given the future state of oil prices.

	OIL PRICES		
SUPPLIER	DECREASE	SAME	INCREASE
China	$2.7	$3.9	$6.3
India	2.1	3.8	6.5
Philippines	1.7	4.3	6.1
Brazil	3.5	4.5	5.7
Mexico	4.1	5.1	5.4

Determine the best decision using each of the following criteria.

a. Minimin
b. Minimax
c. Equal likelihood
d. Minimax regret

S1.8. Leevi Starch in Problem S1-7 estimates that the probabilities of future global changes in oil prices are .09 that they will decrease, .27 that they will remain the same, and .64 that they will decrease.

a. Determine the best supplier for the company using expected value.
b. If the company wants to hire an energy analyst to help it determine more accurately what future oil prices will do, what is the maximum amount it should pay the analyst?

S1.9. Telecomp, a computer manufacturer with a global supply chain, is adding a new supplier for some of its component parts, and the suppliers it's considering are in China, India, Thailand, and the Philippines. As part of its risk management program Telecomp wants to assess the possible impact of a supplier shutdown in the event of a natural disaster, such as a flood, fire, or an earthquake. The following payoff table summarizes Telecomp's losses (in millions of dollars) for supplier shutdowns given different levels of event severity.

	EVENT SEVERITY		
SUPPLIER COUNTRY	LOW	MODERATE	HIGH
China	$8	$11	$21
India	6	7	14
Thailand	3	12	17
Philippines	5	9	15

Determine the best decision using each of the following criteria.

a. Minimin
b. Minimax
c. Equal likelihood
d. Minimax regret

S1.10. Telecomp in Problem S1-9 estimates that the probabilities of the severity of events in each of the countries are as follows:

	EVENT SEVERITY		
SUPPLIER COUNTRY	LOW	MODERATE	HIGH
China	.43	.45	.12
India	.56	.33	.11
Thailand	.37	.41	.22
Philippines	.47	.46	.07

Determine the best decision for Telecomp using expected value.

S1.11. The Dynamax Company is going to introduce one of three new products: a widget, a hummer, or a nimnot. The market conditions (favorable, stable, or unfavorable) will determine the profit or loss the company realizes, as shown in the following payoff table.

	MARKET CONDITIONS		
PRODUCT	FAVORABLE .2	STABLE .5	UNFAVORABLE .3
Widget	$160,000	$90,000	−$50,000
Hummer	70,000	40,000	20,000
Nimnot	45,000	35,000	30,000

a. Compute the expected value for each decision and select the best one.
b. Determine how much the firm would be willing to pay to a market research firm to gain better information about future market conditions.
c. Assume that probabilities cannot be assigned to future market conditions, and determine the best decision using the maximax, maximin, minimax regret, and equal likelihood criteria.

S1.12. John Wiley & Sons, Inc. publishes an operations management textbook that is scheduled for a revision. The book has been moderately successful, but each year more new books enter the market, some existing books are dropped by publishers, and various innovative pedagogical approaches are introduced by authors and publishers, so that the competitive market is always highly uncertain. In addition, the role that the Internet will play in future textbook publishing is an unknown. As a result, Wiley is trying to decide whether to publish the next edition of the OM book as a smaller paperback, publish a new edition very similar in size and content to the current edition, significantly revise the book with an emphasis on services and processes, or make a major revision with significant physical changes including adding color and more graphics. The following payoff table summarizes the possible revision decisions with profits (or losses) for the three-year lifecycle of the new edition, and the future states of nature relative to the competitive market.

	COMPETITIVE MARKET		
PUBLICATION DECISION	UNFAVORABLE	SAME	FAVORABLE
Paperback	$68,000	$170,000	$395,000
Similar revision	24,000	375,000	672,000
Major content revision	31,000	515,000	725,000
Major physical revision	−105,000	280,000	972,000

Determine the best decision for the publisher using the following criteria.

a. Maximax
b. Minimax
c. Equal likelihood
d. Hurwicz ($\alpha = .35$)

S1.13. In Problem S1-12, if Wiley is able to assign probabilities of occurrence of .23 to unfavorable market conditions, .46 for the same market conditions, and .31 for favorable market conditions, what is the best decision using expected value? Based on the results in Problem S1-12 and the expected value result in this problem, does there appear to be an overall "best" decision? Compute the expected value of perfect information, and explain its meaning.

S1.14. Amtrex International is a major U.S.-based electronics firm that manufactures a number of electronic components for domestic and global consumer electronics companies. It imports most of its materials and the components used in its products to the United States from overseas suppliers. Amtrex is in the process of trying to improve its global supply chain operations, and as part of this process the company wants to determine a single supplier located at one of the major ports around the world to contract with for the majority of its business. The company is considering six suppliers, each located at one of the following ports: Hong Kong, Singapore, Shanghai, Busan, and Kaohsiung. The company has estimated the possible profit (or loss) it might achieve with each of the potential suppliers depending on a variety or possible future company and port conditions, including IT capability, port growth and expansion, ship and container availability, security, regional market and political environment, and transport to the port from the supplier's suppliers. Depending on these various factors, further supplier and port conditions could decline, grow and expand, or remain the same. The following payoff table summarizes the increased outcomes (in $ millions) for the potential suppliers and the possible future states of nature for a specific time frame.

	STATES OF NATURE		
DECISION	DECLINING CONDITIONS	SAME CONDITIONS	GROWTH CONDITIONS
Hong Kong	−$31	$28	$67
Singapore	−24	33	71
Shanghai	−28	35	55
Busan	−17	25	49
Kaohsiung	−15	41	59

Determine the best decision using each of the following criteria.

a. Maximax
b. Maximin
c. Equal likelihood
d. Hurwicz ($\alpha = .65$)
e. Minimax regret

S1.15. In Problem S1-14, suppose Amtrex is able to assign probabilities to each of the states of nature for each of the suppliers/ports as follows:

	STATES OF NATURE		
DECISION	DECLINING CONDITIONS	SAME CONDITIONS	GROWTH CONDITIONS
Hong Kong	.27	.45	.28
Singapore	.18	.51	.31
Shanghai	.22	.61	.17
Busan	.15	.45	.40
Kaohsiung	.25	.38	.37

a. Using expected value, determine the port/supplier Amtrex should use.
b. Based on the results from Problem S1-14, and the result from part a, is there a best overall decision?

S1.16. The Willow Café is located in an open-air mall. Its lease expires this year and the restaurant owner has the option of signing a 1-, 2-, 3-, 4-, or 5-year lease. However, the owner is concerned about recent energy price increases (including the price of gasoline), which affect virtually every aspect of the restaurant operation including the price of food items and materials, delivery costs, and its own utilities. The restaurant was very profitable when energy prices were lower, and the owner believes if prices remain at approximately their current level profits will still be satisfactory; however, if prices continue to rise he believes that he might be forced to close. In these latter circumstances a longer-term lease could be a financial disaster, but with a shorter-term lease the mall landlord could always rent the restaurant's space out from under it when the lease expires. Thus, the restaurant owner's estimates of future profits must also reflect the possibility that the lease will not be renewable. The following payoff table summarizes the owner's profit (and loss) estimates for each future state of nature of energy prices (over a five-year period).

	ENERGY PRICES		
LEASE DECISION	DECREASE .17	SAME .34	INCREASE .49
1-year	$156,000	$93,000	$16,000
2-year	427,000	150,000	−42,000
3-year	642,000	319,000	−171,000
4-year	933,000	473,000	−337,000
5-year	1,228,000	516,000	−551,000

Determine the best decision using expected value.

S1.17. Compute the expected value of perfect information for the Willow Café in Problem S1-16. Explain what this value means and how such information might be obtained.

S1.18. The Weight Club (see Case Problem 1.3) is considering adding a new service facility among several possible alternatives including a child care center, a swimming pool, new locker rooms and showers, a health-oriented food court, and a spa. The success of each alternative depends on their demand (i.e., new members who would join because of the new facility), which is uncertain. The following payoff table summarizes the returns (based on costs and increased enrollments) for each alternative service facility given three future levels of demand.

	DEMAND		
SERVICE FACILITY	POOR	MODERATE	HIGH
Child care center	$17,000	$27,000	$41,000
Swimming pool	−75,000	26,000	71,000
New lockers and showers	12,000	37,000	57,000
Food court	−31,000	19,000	87,000
Spa	6,000	25,000	32,000

Determine the best decision for the club using the following criteria.

a. Maximax
b. Minimax
c. Hurwicz ($\alpha = .45$)
d. Equal likelihood

S1.19. In Problem S1-18, assume the Weight Club is able to estimate probabilities of occurrence for each possible future demand state, as follows:

	DEMAND		
SERVICE FACILITY	POOR	MODERATE	HIGH
Child care center	.12	.54	.34
Swimming pool	.24	.63	.13
New lockers and showers	.09	.44	.47
Food court	.18	.74	.08
Spa	.31	.48	.21

Determine the best decision using expected value.

S1.20. The Midtown Market purchases apples from a local grower. The apples are purchased on Monday at $2.00 per pound, and the market sells them for $3.00 per pound. Any apples left over at the end of the week are sold to a local zoo for $0.50 per pound. The possible demands for apples and the probability for each are as follows.

DEMAND (LB)	PROBABILITY
20	.10
21	.20
22	.30
23	.30
24	.10
	1.00

a. The market must decide how many apples to order in a week. Construct a payoff table for this decision situation and determine the amount of apples that should be ordered using expected value.

b. Assuming that probabilities cannot be assigned to the demand values, what would the best decision be using the maximax and maximin criteria?

S1.21. The manager of the greeting card section of Harvey's Department Store is considering her order for a particular line of holiday cards. The cost of each box of cards is $3; each box will be sold for $5 during the holiday season. After the holiday season, the cards will be sold for $2 a box. The card section manager believes that all leftover cards can be sold at that price. The estimated demand during the holiday season for the cards, with associated probabilities, is as follows:

DEMAND (BOXES)	PROBABILITY
25	.10
26	.15
27	.30
28	.20
29	.15
30	.10

a. Develop the payoff table for this decision situation and compute the expected value for each alternative and identify the best decision.

b. Compute the expected value of perfect information.

S1.22. Assume that the probabilities of demand in Problem S1-21 are no longer valid; the decision situation is now one without probabilities. Determine the best number of cards to stock using the following decision criteria.

a. Maximin

b. Maximax

c. Hurwicz ($\alpha = .4$)

d. Minimax regret

S1.23. Zarax, a global apparel company, is adding a new supplier for denim fabric that it uses to manufacture denim jeans, and the suppliers it's considering are located near the ports of Shanghai, Mumbai, Manila, Santos, and Veracruz. A major factor in the company's decision is transportation and shipping costs, which are dependent on several factors including port traffic, container costs, and future oil prices. The following payoff table summarizes the total monthly shipping costs (in $1 millions) for the suppliers in each of the ports given the future state of related logistics costs.

	LOGISTICS COSTS		
PORT	DECREASE	SAME	INCREASE
Shanghai	$2.7	$3.9	$6.3
Mumbai	2.1	3.8	6.5
Manila	1.7	4.3	6.1
Santos	3.5	4.5	5.7
Veracruz	4.1	5.1	5.4

Determine the best decision using each of the following criteria.

a. Minimin

b. Minimax

c. Equal likelihood

d. Minimax regret

S1.24. Zarax in problem S1-23 estimates that the probabilities of future changes in global logistics are .09 that they will decrease, .27 that they will remain the same, and .64 that they will increase. Determine the best supplier for the company using expected value.

S1.25. If Zarax in problems S1-23 and S1-24 wants to hire a supply chain analyst to help it determine more accurately what future logistics costs will be, what is the maximum amount they should pay the analyst?

S1.26. A machine shop owner is attempting to decide whether to purchase a new drill press, a lathe, or a grinder. The return from each will be determined by whether the company succeeds in getting a government military contract. The profit or loss from each purchase and the probabilities associated with each contract outcome are shown in the following payoff table. Compute the expected value for each purchase and select the best one.

PURCHASE	CONTRACT .40	NO CONTRACT .60
Drill press	$40,000	$28,000
Lathe	20,000	4,000
Grinder	12,000	10,000

S1.27. The Extron Oil Company is considering making a bid for a shale oil development contract to be awarded by the federal government. The company has decided to bid $110 million. The company estimates that it has a 60% chance of winning the contract with this bid. If the firm wins the contract, it can choose one of three methods for getting the oil from the shale: It can develop a new method for oil extraction, use an existing (inefficient) process, or subcontract the processing out to a number of smaller companies once the shale has been excavated. The results from these alternatives are given as follows.

DEVELOP NEW PROCESS		
OUTCOMES	PROBABILITY	PROFIT (MILLIONS)
Great success	.30	$600
Moderate success	.60	300
Failure	.10	−100

USE PRESENT PROCESS		
OUTCOMES	PROBABILITY	PROFIT (MILLIONS)
Great success	.50	$300
Moderate success	.30	200
Failure	.20	−40

SUBCONTRACT		
OUTCOMES	PROBABILITY	PROFIT (MILLIONS)
Moderate success	1	$250

The cost of preparing the contract proposal is $2,000,000. If the company does not make a bid, it will invest in an alternative venture with a guaranteed profit of $30 million. Construct a sequential decision tree for this decision situation and determine whether the company should make a bid.

S1.28. The New England Bombers professional basketball team just missed making the playoffs last season and believes it only needs to sign one very good free agent to make the playoffs next season. The team is considering four players: Jamelle Morris, Rayneal O'Neal, Marvin Jackson, and Michael Gordon. Each player differs according to position, ability, and attractiveness to fans. The payoffs (in $ millions) to the team for each player based on their contract, profits from attendance, and team product sales for several different seasonal outcomes are provided in the following table.

	SEASON OUTCOME		
PLAYER	LOSER	COMPETITIVE	PLAYOFFS
Morris	$−3.2	$1.3	$4.4
O'Neal	−5.1	1.8	6.3
Jackson	−2.7	0.7	5.8
Gordon	−6.3	−1.6	9.6

Determine the best decision using the following decision criteria.

a. Maximax
b. Maximin
c. Hurwicz ($\alpha = .25$)
d. Equal likelihood
e. The Bombers' management has determined the following probabilities of the occurrence of each future seasonal outcome for each player.

	PROBABILITY		
PLAYER	LOSER	COMPETITIVE	PLAYOFFS
Morris	.15	.55	.30
O'Neal	.18	.26	.56
Jackson	.21	.32	.47
Gordon	.30	.25	.45

Compute the expected value for each player and indicate which player the team should try to sign.

S1.29. The director of career advising at Grand Valley Community College wants to use decision analysis to provide information to help students decide which two-year degree program they should pursue. The director has set up the following payoff table for six of the most popular and successful degree programs at GVCC that shows the estimated five-year gross income ($) from each degree for four future economic conditions:

	ECONOMIC CONDITIONS			
DEGREE PROGRAM	RECESSION	AVERAGE	GOOD	ROBUST
Graphic Design	$115,000	$155,000	$190,000	$220,000
Nursing	140,000	175,000	210,000	225,000
Real Estate	95,000	135,000	230,000	350,000
Medical Technology	120,000	180,000	210,000	270,000
Culinary Technology	85,000	125,000	180,000	290,000
Computer Information Technology	125,000	160,000	200,000	260,000

Determine the best degree program in terms of projected income, using the following decision criteria:

a. Maximax
b. Maximin
c. Equal likelihood
d. Hurwicz ($\alpha = .25$)

S1.30. In Problem S1-29 the director of career advising at Grand Valley Community College has paid a local economic forecasting firm to indicate a probability for each future economic condition over the next five years. The firm estimates that there is a .15 probability of a recession, a .50 probability that the economy will be average, a .25 probability that the economy will be good, and a .10 probability that it will be robust. Using expected value determine the best degree program in terms of projected income. If you were the director of career advising which degree program would you recommend?

S1.31. The Sharks major league baseball team is going to enter the free agent market over the winter to sign a new starting pitcher. They have five prospects that will enter the free agent market that they are considering. All five pitchers are in their mid-twenties, have been in the major leagues for approximately five years, and have been relatively successful. The team's general manager has compiled a lot of information about the pitchers from scouting reports and their playing histories since high school. He has developed a chart projecting how many wins each pitcher will likely have during the next 10 years given three possible future states of nature—that the pitchers will be relatively injury free, they will have a normal career with injuries, or that they will have excessive injuries, as shown in the following payoff table:

	PHYSICAL CONDITION		
PITCHER	NO INJURIES	NORMAL	EXCESSIVE INJURIES
Miguel Garcia	142	117	65
Juan Ramon	164	140	58
Fred Terry	129	108	76
Alan Rodriguez	112	92	87
Jared Washburn	124	94	63

Determine the best pitcher to sign, using the following decision criteria:

a. Maximax
b. Maximin
c. Equal likelihood
d. Hurwicz ($\alpha = .35$)

S1.32. In Problem S1-31 the Sharks general manager has asked a super scout to assign a probability to each of the three states of nature that may occur for the pitchers during the next 10 years. The scout estimates that there is a .08 probability that these pitchers at this stage of their careers will have no injuries, a .56 probability that they will have a career with the normal amount of injuries, and a .36 probability that they will have excessive injuries.

(a) Using expected value, determine the best pitcher to sign.
(b) Given the following 10-year contract price for each pitcher (in $ millions), which would you recommend signing?

Miguel Garcia	$96.2
Juan Ramon	$118.4
Fred Terry	$81.6
Alan Rodriguez	$102.8
Jared Washburn	$75.7

(c) Suppose that the general manager asked the super scout to determine the probabilities of each state of nature for each individual pitcher, as follows:

	PHYSICAL CONDITION		
PITCHER	NO INJURIES	NORMAL	EXCESSIVE INJURIES
Miguel Garcia	.27	.46	.27
Juan Ramon	.14	.45	.41
Fred Terry	.37	.35	.28
Alan Rodriguez	.43	.45	.12
Jared Washburn	.21	.57	.22

Determine the expected number of wins for each pitcher, and combined with the contract price in part (b), indicate which pitcher you would recommend signing.

S1.33. Federated Electronics, Ltd., manufactures display screens and monitors for computers and televisions, which it sells to companies around the world. It wants to construct a new warehouse and distribution center in Asia to serve emerging markets there. It has identified potential sites in the port cities of Shanghai, Singapore, Pusan, Kaohsiung, and Hong Kong and has estimated the possible revenues for each (minus construction costs, which are higher in some cities like Hong Kong). At each site the projected revenues are primarily based on these factors: (1) the economic conditions at the port including the projected traffic, infrastructure, labor rates and availability, and expansion and modernization; and (2) the future government situation, which includes the political stability, fees, tariffs, duties, and trade regulations. Following is a payoff table that shows the projected revenues (in $ billions) for six years given the four possible combinations for positive and negative port and government conditions:

PORT	PORT NEGATIVE/ GOVERNMENT NEGATIVE	PORT NEGATIVE/ GOVERNMENT POSITIVE	PORT POSITIVE/ GOVERNMENT NEGATIVE	PORT POSITIVE/ GOVERNMENT POSITIVE
Shanghai	−$0.271	$0.437	$0.523	$1.08
Singapore	−0.164	0.329	0.441	0.873
Pusan	0.119	0.526	0.337	0.732
Kaoshiung	−0.235	0.522	0.226	1.116
Hong Kong	−0.317	0.256	0.285	1.653

Determine the port city Federated should select for its new distribution center using the following decision criteria:

a. Maximax
b. Maximin
c. Equal likelihood
d. Hurwicz ($\alpha = .55$)

S1.34. In Problem S1-33 Federated Electronics, Ltd. has hired a Washington, D.C.-based global trade research firm to assess the probabilities of each combination of port and government conditions for the five ports. The research firm probability estimates for the five ports are as follows:

PORT	PORT NEGATIVE/ GOVERNMENT NEGATIVE	PORT NEGATIVE/ GOVERNMENT POSITIVE	PORT POSITIVE/ GOVERNMENT NEGATIVE	PORT POSITIVE/ GOVERNMENT POSITIVE
Shanghai	.09	.27	.32	.32
Singapore	.05	.22	.22	.51
Pusan	.08	.36	.27	.29
Kaoshiung	.11	.12	.46	.31
Hong Kong	.10	.23	.30	.37

(a) Using expected value, determine the best port to construct the distribution center.
(b) Using any decision criterion, determine the port you think would be the best location for the distribution center, and justify your answer.

S1.35. Alex Mason has a wide-curving, uphill driveway leading to his garage. When there is a heavy snow, Alex hires a local carpenter, who shovels snow on the side in the winter, to shovel his driveway. The snow shoveler charges $30 to shovel the driveway. Following is a probability distribution of the number of heavy snows each winter.

HEAVY SNOWS	PROBABILITY
1	.12
2	.19
3	.24
4	.22
5	.13
6	.08
7	.02
	1.00

Alex is considering the purchase of a new self-propelled snowblower for $575 that would allow him, his wife, or his children to clear the driveway after a snow. Discuss what you think Alex's decision should be and why.

S1.36. The management of State Union Bank was concerned about the potential loss that might occur in the event of a physical catastrophe such as a power failure or a fire. The bank estimated that the loss from one of these incidents could be as much as $100 million, including losses due to interrupted service and customer relations. One project the bank is considering is the installation of an emergency power generator at its operations headquarters. The cost of the emergency generator is $900,000, and if it is installed no losses from this type of incident will be incurred. However, if the generator is not installed, there is a 10% chance that a power outage will occur during the next year. If there is an outage, there is a .04 probability that the resulting losses will be very large, or approximately $90 million in lost earnings. Alternatively, it is estimated that there is a .96 probability of only slight losses of around $2 million. Using decision tree analysis, determine whether the bank should install the new power generator.

S1.37. Allegheny Mountain Power and Light is an electric utility company with a large fleet of vehicles including automobiles, light trucks, and construction equipment. The company is evaluating four alternative strategies for maintaining its vehicles at the lowest cost: (1) including take no preventive maintenance at all and repair vehicle components when they fail; (2) take oil samples at regular intervals and perform whatever preventive maintenance is indicated by the oil analysis; (3) change the vehicle oil on a regular basis and perform repairs when needed; and (4) change the oil at regular intervals and take oil samples regularly, performing maintenance repairs as indicated by the sample analysis.

For autos and light trucks, strategy 1 (no preventive maintenance) costs nothing to implement and results in two possible outcomes: There is a .08 probability that a defective component will occur, requiring emergency maintenance at a cost of $1600, or there is .92 probability that no defects will occur and no maintenance will be necessary.

Strategy 2 (take oil samples) costs $40 to implement (i.e., take a sample), and there is a .08 probability that there will be a defective part and .92 probability that there will not be a defect. If there is actually a defective part, there is a .70 probability the sample will correctly identify it, resulting in preventive maintenance at a cost of $500. However, there is a .30 probability that the sample will not identify the defect and indicate everything is okay, resulting in emergency maintenance later at a cost of $1600. On the other hand, if there are actually no defects, there is a .20 probability that the sample will erroneously indicate that there is a defect, resulting in unnecessary maintenance at a cost of $250. There is a .80 probability that the sample will correctly indicate there are no defects, resulting in no maintenance and no costs.

Strategy 3 (changing the oil regularly) costs $34.80 to implement and has two outcomes: a .04 probability of a defective component, which will require emergency maintenance at a cost of $1600, and a .96 probability that no defects will occur, resulting in no maintenance and no cost.

Strategy 4 (changing the oil and sampling) costs $54.80 to implement and results in the same probabilities of defects and no defects as strategy 3. If there is a defective component, there is a .70 probability that the sample will detect it and $500 in preventive maintenance costs will be incurred. Alternatively, there is a .30 probability that the sample will not detect the defect, resulting in emergency maintenance at a cost of $1600. If there is no defect, there is a .20 probability the sample will indicate there is a defect, resulting in an unnecessary maintenance cost of $250, and a .80 probability that the sample will correctly indicate no defects, resulting in no cost.

Develop a decision strategy for Allegheny Mountain Power and Light and indicate the expected value of this strategy.[1]

S1.38. In Problem S1-37, the decision analysis is for automobiles and light trucks. Allegheny Mountain Power and Light would like to reformulate the problem for its heavy construction equipment. Emergency maintenance is much more expensive for heavy equipment, costing $15,000. Required preventive maintenance costs $2000 and unnecessary maintenance costs $1200. The cost of an oil change is $200 and the cost of taking an oil sample and analyzing it is $50. All the probabilities remain the same. Determine the strategy the company should use for its heavy equipment.

S1.39. Tech is playing State in the last conference game of the season. Tech is trailing State 21 to 14 with 7 seconds left in the game, when they score a touchdown. Still trailing 21 to 20, Tech can either go for two points and win or go for one point to send the game into overtime. The conference championship will be determined by the outcome of this game. If Tech wins they will go to the Sugar Bowl, with a payoff of $9.2 million; if they lose they will go to the Gator Bowl, with a payoff of $1.5 million. If Tech goes for two points there is a 30% chance they will be successful and win (and a 70% chance they will fail and lose). If they go for one point there is a .98 probability of success and a tie and a .02 probability of failure. If they tie they will play overtime, in which Tech believes they have only a 20% chance of winning because of fatigue.

a. Use decision-tree analysis to determine if Tech should go for one point or two points.

b. What would Tech's probability of winning the game in overtime have to be to make Tech indifferent between going for one point or two points?

S1.40. Mary Decker is suing the manufacturer of her car because of a defect that she believes caused her to have an accident, and kept her out of work for a year. She is suing the company for $3.5 million. The company has offered her a settlement of $700,000, of which Mary would receive $600,000 after attorneys' fees. Her attorney has advised her that she has a 50% chance of winning her case. If she loses she will incur attorneys' fees and court costs of $75,000. If she wins she is not guaranteed her full requested settlement. Her attorney believes that if she wins, there is a 50% chance she could receive the full settlement, in which case Mary would get $2 million after her attorney takes his cut, and a 50% chance that the jury will award her a lesser amount of $1,000,000, of which Mary would get $500,000.

Using decision-tree analysis, decide if Mary should sue the manufacturer.

S1.41. State University has three healthcare plans for its faculty and staff to choose from, as follows.

[1]This problem is based on J. Mellichamp, D. Miller, and O-J. Kwon, "The Southern Company Uses a Probability Model for Cost Justification of Oil Sample Analysis," *Interfaces* 23 (3; May-June 1993), pp. 118–124.

Plan 1—monthly cost of $32 with a $500 deductible; the participants pay the first $500 of medical payments for the year, the insurer pays 90% of all remaining expenses.
Plan 2—monthly cost of $5 but a deductible of $1200, with the insurer paying 90% of medical expenses after the insured pays the first $1200 in a year.
Plan 3—monthly cost of $24 with no deductible, the participants pay 30% of all expenses with the remainder paid by the insurer.

Tracy McCoy, an administrative assistant in the management department, estimates that her annual medical expenses are defined by the following probability distribution.

ANNUAL MEDICAL EXPENSES	PROBABILITY
$100	.15
500	.30
1,500	.35
3,000	.10
5,000	.05
10,000	.05

Determine which medical plan Tracy should select.

S1.42. The Orchard Wine Company purchases grapes from one of two nearby growers each season to produce a particular red wine. It purchases enough grapes to produce 3000 bottles of the wine. Each grower supplies a certain portion of poor-quality grapes that will result in a percentage of bottles being used as fillers for cheaper table wines according to the following probability distribution.

	PROBABILITY OF % DEFECTIVE	
PERCENTAGE DEFECTIVE	GROWER A	GROWER B
2	.12	.26
4	.21	.34
6	.26	.22
8	.31	.10
10	.10	.08

The two growers charge a different price for their grapes and because of differences in taste, the company charges different prices for their wine depending on which grapes they use. The annual profit from the wine produced from each grower's grapes for each percentage defective is as follows.

	PROFIT	
DEFECTIVE	GROWER A	GROWER B
2%	$44,200	$42,600
4	40,200	40,300
6	36,200	38,000
8	32,200	35,700
10	28,200	33,400

Use decision-tree analysis to determine from which grower the company should purchase grapes.

S1.43. Huntz Food Products is attempting to decide if it should introduce a new line of salad dressings called Special Choices. The company can test market the salad dressings in selected geographic areas or bypass the test market and introduce the product nationally. The cost of the test market is $150,000. If the company conducts the test market, it must wait to see the results before deciding whether or not to introduce the salad dressings nationally. The probability of a positive test market result is estimated to be .6. Alternatively, the company cannot conduct the test market and make the decision to introduce the dressings or not. If the salad dressings are introduced nationally and are a success, the company estimates it will realize an annual profit of $1,600,000 while if the dressings fail it will incur a loss of $700,000. The company believes the probability of success for the salad dressings is .50 if it is introduced without the test market. If the company does conduct the test market and it is positive, the probability of successfully introducing the salad dressings increases to .8. If the test market is negative and the company introduces the salad dressings anyway, the probability of success drops to .30.

Using decision-tree analysis, determine if the company should conduct the test market.

Case Problems

Case Problem S1.1 Whither an MBA at Strutledge?

Strutledge (see Case Problem 1.3) is a small liberal arts college faced with rising costs and decreasing enrollments. It would like to increase revenues (including tuition, donations, and grants) by expanding its student base and building ties with businesses in the surrounding area. To do so, it is considering establishing a new graduate program—an MBA, a master's in computer science, a master's in information technology, a master's in nursing (affiliated with a major hospital in a nearby urban area), or a master's in healthcare administration. In addition to generating additional enrollments within a new program, administrators also believe that a new graduate program could increase exposure and visibility for the school and enhance its reputation, as a whole, which could also result in increased enrollments and revenue sources. The cost to establish and maintain each new program differs according to faculty salaries, facilities, and the support necessary to attract new students, which, in turn, affects revenues. The degree of success that each new graduate program might achieve is affected by competition from other colleges and universities, and the ability of a program to attract new faculty and students. The following payoff table summarizes the possible gains (i.e., revenues less costs) the college might realize with each new program under different future success scenarios.

GRADUATE PROGRAM	PROGRAM SUCCESS			
	UNSUCCESSFUL	MODERATE SUCCESS	SUCCESSFUL	VERY SUCCESSFUL
MBA	−$316,000	−$57,000	$231,000	$424,000
Computer Science	−210,000	−35,000	190,000	375,000
Information Technology	−472,000	−75,000	305,000	517,000
Nursing	−135,000	81,000	205,000	307,000
Health Administration	−75,000	55,000	180,000	245,000

Determine the best decision for the college using the following criteria.

a. Maximax

b. Maximin

c. Equal likelihood

d. Hurwicz ($\alpha = .50$)

e. If Strutledge administrators use the Hurwicz criterion to make their decision, explain what this might mean about their decision-making strategy.

f. Strutledge has estimated probabilities of occurrence for the different states of program success as shown in the following table. What is the best decision using expected value?

g. Based on these decision analysis results, what would you recommend that Strutledge College's decision be?

h. What decision would you recommend to Strutledge? Explain your reasons.

GRADUATE PROGRAM	PROGRAM SUCCESS			
	UNSUCCESSFUL	MODERATE SUCCESS	SUCCESSFUL	VERY SUCCESSFUL
MBA	.32	.35	.24	.09
Computer Science	.38	.41	.16	.05
Information Technology	.25	.33	.30	.12
Nursing	.17	.28	.41	.14
Health Administration	.08	.34	.47	.11

Case Problem S1.2 Transformer Replacement at Mountain States Electric Service

Mountain States Electric Service is an electrical utility company serving several states in the Rocky Mountain region. It is considering replacing some of its equipment at a generating substation and is attempting to decide whether it should replace an older, existing PCB transformer. (PCB is a toxic chemical known formally as polychlorinated biphenyl.) Even though the PCB generator meets all current regulations, if an incident occurred, such as a fire, and PCB contamination caused harm either to neighboring businesses or farms or to the environment, the company would be liable for damages. Recent court cases have shown that simply meeting utility regulations does not relieve a utility of liability if an incident causes harm to others. Also, courts have been awarding large damages to individuals and businesses harmed by hazardous incidents.

If the utility replaces the PCB transformer, no PCB incidents will occur, and the only cost will be that of the transformer, $85,000. Alternatively, if the company decides to keep the existing PCB transformer, then management estimates there is a 50-50 chance of there being a high likelihood of an incident or a low likelihood of an incident. For the case in which there is a high likelihood that an incident will occur, there is a .004 probability that a fire will occur sometime during the remaining life of the transformer and a .996 probability that no fire will occur. If a fire occurs, there is a .20 probability that it will be bad and the utility will incur a very high cost of approximately $90 million for the cleanup, whereas there is a .80 probability that the fire will be minor and a cleanup can be accomplished at a low cost of approximately $8 million. If no fire occurs, then no cleanup costs will occur. For the case in which there is a low likelihood of an incident occurring, there is a .001 probability that a fire will occur during the life of the existing transformer and a .999 probability that a fire will not occur. If a fire does occur, then the same probabilities exist for the incidence of high and low cleanup costs, as well as the same cleanup costs, as indicated for the previous case. Similarly, if no fire occurs, there is no cleanup cost.

Perform a decision-tree analysis of this problem for Mountain States Electric Service and indicate the recommended solution. Is this the decision you believe the company should make? Explain your reasons.

Source: This case was adapted from W. Balson, J. Welsh, and D. Wilson, "Using Decision Analysis and Risk Analysis to Manage Utility Environmental Risk," *Interfaces* 22 (6) (November–December 1992), pp. 126–139.

Case Problem S1.3 Evaluating Projects at Nexcom Systems

Nexcom Systems develops information technology systems for commercial sale. Each year it considers and evaluates a number of different projects to undertake. It develops a road map for each project in the form of a decision tree that identifies the different decision points in the development process from the initial decision to invest in a project's development through the actual commercialization of the final product.

The first decision point in the development process is whether or not to fund a proposed project for one year. If the decision is no, then there is no resulting cost; if the decision is yes, then the project proceeds at an incremental cost to the company. The company establishes specific short-term, early technical milestones for its projects after one year. If the early milestones are achieved, the project proceeds to the next phase of project development; if the milestones are not achieved, the project is abandoned. In its planning process, the company develops probability estimates of achieving and not achieving the early milestones. If the early milestones are achieved, then the project is funded for further development during an extended time frame specific to a project. At the end of this time frame, a project is evaluated according to a second set of (later) technical milestones. Again the company attaches probability estimates for achieving and not achieving these later milestones. If the late milestones are not achieved, the project is abandoned.

If the late milestones are achieved, this means that technical uncertainties and problems have been overcome and the company next assesses the project's ability to meet its strategic business objectives. At this stage the company wants to know if the eventual product coincides with the company's competencies, and if there appears to be an eventual clear market for the product. It invests in a product "prelaunch" to ascertain the answers to these questions. The outcomes of the prelaunch are that either there is a strategic fit or there is not, and the company assigns probability estimates to each of these two possible outcomes. If there is not a strategic fit at this point, the project is abandoned and the company loses its investment in the prelaunch process. If it is determined that there is a strategic fit, then three possible decisions result. (1) The company can invest in the product's launch and a successful or unsuccessful outcome will result, each with an estimated probability of occurrence. (2) The company can delay the product's launch and at a later date decide whether to launch or abandon. (3) If it launches later, then the outcomes are success or failure, each with an estimated probability of occurrence. Also, if the product launch is delayed, there is always a likelihood that the technology will become obsolete or dated in the near future, which tends to reduce the expected return.

The table provides the various costs, event probabilities, and investment outcomes for five projects the company is considering.

Determine the expected value for each project and then rank the projects accordingly for the company to consider.

Source: This case was adapted from R. K. Perdue, W. J. McAllister, P. V. King, and B. G. Berkey, "Valuation of R and D Projects Using Options Pricing and Decision Analysis Models," *Interfaces* 29, (6) (November–December 1999), pp. 57–74.

	PROJECT				
DECISION OUTCOMES/EVENT	1	2	3	4	5
Fund—1 year	$200,000	380,000	270,000	230,000	400,000
P(Early milestones—yes)	.72	.64	.84	.56	.77
P(Early milestones—no)	.28	.36	.16	.44	.23
Long-term funding	$690,000	730,000	430,000	270,000	350,000
P(Late milestones—yes)	.60	.56	.65	.70	.72
P(Late milestones—no)	.40	.44	.35	.30	.28
Prelaunch funding	$315,000	420,000	390,000	410,000	270,000
P(Strategic fit—yes)	.80	.75	.83	.67	.65
P(Strategic fit—no)	.20	.25	.17	.33	.35
P(Invest—success)	.60	.65	.70	.75	.83
P(Invest—failure)	.40	.35	.30	.25	.17
P(Delay—success)	.80	.70	.65	.80	.85
P(Delay—failure)	.20	.30	.35	.20	.15
Invest—success	$7,300,000	8,200,000	4,700,000	5,200,000	3,800,000
Invest—failure	−2.000,000	−3,500,000	−1,500,000	−2,100,000	−900,000
Delay—success	4,500,000	6,000,000	3,300,000	2,500,000	2,700,000
Delay—failure	−1,300,000	−4,000,000	−800,000	−1,100,000	−900,000

References

Holloway, C. A. *Decision Making Under Uncertainty*. Englewood Cliffs, NJ: Prentice Hall, 1979.

Howard, R. A. "An Assessment of Decision Analysis." *Operations Research* 28 (1; January–February 1980), pp. 4–27.

Keeney, R. L. "Decision Analysis: An Overview." *Operations Research* 30 (5; September–October 1982), pp. 803–838.

Luce, R. D., and H. Raiffa. *Games and Decisions*. New York: John Wiley, 1957.

Von Neumann, J., and O. Morgenstern. *Theory of Games and Economic Behavior*, 3rd ed. Princeton, NJ: Princeton University Press, 1953.

Williams, J. D. *The Complete Strategist*, rev. ed. New York: McGraw-Hill, 1966.

Quality Management

Echo/Getty Images

LEARNING OBJECTIVES

After reading this chapter, you will be able to:

- Discuss and define the dimensions of quality.
- Articulate the benefits and costs of good quality, and the costs of poor quality.
- Understand how quality management systems have evolved and be able to assess the stage of quality evolution a particular company exhibits.
- Utilize quality tools and the DMAIC methodology in problem solving.
- Explain the philosophy and magnitude of Six Sigma quality.
- Recognize quality awards and ISO certifications.

Quality and Value in Smartphones

Global sales of smartphones approach 1.3 billion annually. Apple and Samsung are by far the largest players in this market, with the two rivals together holding over 40% of the market, followed by Lenovo, LG, and Huawei, each with approximately a 5% market share. Perceived quality is likely the most prominent purchasing factor among smartphone consumers in this ultra-competitive global market. Smartphone quality can be considered along a number of product dimensions such as performance and reliability, but there are also service dimensions such as the cell-phone service provider and the operating system (OS or Android) that to the consumer reflect on a smartphone's quality. Quality has long been at the core of Apple's corporate culture. Apple has a history of using the highest quality materials, offering innovative design, and providing seamless, easy-to-use software, attributes that other companies have emulated, most prominently and effectively Samsung.

J.D. Power is a global marketing information services company that conducts surveys of customer satisfaction and product quality for a variety of industries and products. Its annual survey of smartphone customer satisfaction is based on four factors (in order of importance): performance, features, physical design, and ease of operation. In their surveys, J.D. Power has found that brands must work extremely well to help differentiate their products from their competitors. When a smartphone performs well, by meeting or exceeding the customer's expectations for features like battery life, camera quality, speaker and screen clarity, touch screen ease of operation, etc., the likelihood of brand loyalty and customer satisfaction increases. Across all cell phone service providers, Apple and Samsung smartphones are consistently rated as the top two and the only smartphone brands that achieve the maximum J.D. Power consumer "Power Circle Score" of 5. In another well-recognized survey of consumer satisfaction with product and service quality, the American Customer Satisfaction Index (ACSI), Apple and Samsung consistently achieve the highest ACSI scores for cell phones, and, in general, the survey shows overall customer satisfaction with product quality for all cell phone companies.

For companies like Apple and Samsung, as well as for other cell phone competitors, to be successful in the highly competitive global smartphone market requires product quality to be central to their corporate strategy. These companies must focus on well-conceived, pervasive, and all-encompassing quality management programs throughout every part of their supply chains to ensure that they are able to meet their customers' expectations for product quality. In this chapter we will discuss what quality is and how companies develop effective quality management programs using well-defined and established quality management tools and systems.

What is Quality?

Asked "What is quality?" one of our students replied, "getting what you pay for." Another student added that to her, quality was "getting *more* than you paid for!" The *Oxford American Dictionary* defines quality as "a degree or level of excellence."

The American Society for Quality (ASQ) defines quality as "a subjective term for which each person has his or her own definition. In technical usage, quality can have two meanings: (1) The characteristics of a product or service that bear on its ability to satisfy stated or implied needs and (2) A product or service free of deficiencies." Obviously, quality can be defined in many ways, depending on who is defining it and the product or service it refers to. In this section we provide a perspective on what quality means to customers and companies.

Quality from the Customer's Perspective

A business organization produces goods and services to meet its customers' needs. Customers want value and quality has become a major factor in the value of products and service. Customers know that certain companies produce better-quality products than others, and they buy accordingly. That means a firm must consider how the consumer defines quality. The

Along the Supply Chain

Defining Quality

In the 1930s, Walter A. Shewhart, a pioneer in quality management known as the "father of modern quality control," defined quality as satisfying the wants of the customer by converting the customer's subjective wants and values into measurable objective characteristics that could be achieved with minimal variation. More recently, the American Society for Quality (ASQ) published a report, the *Global State of Quality Research*, which provided survey findings about the practices used by organizations around the world to manage and measure quality. The survey results were gathered from almost 2000 respondents from manufacturing and service organizations from 15 countries around the world. One of the first questions in the survey asked respondents to define quality; following are the ten most common responses:

1. Efficiently providing products and services that meet or exceed customer expectations.
2. Adding value for the customer.
3. Continuously measuring the improvement of processes and service for the customers.
4. Acting as promised and reporting failures.
5. Doing the right thing at the right time in the right way with the right people.
6. Ensuring customers come back and products do not.
7. Providing the best value to customers by improving everyday activities and processes.
8. Beyond delivering what the customer wants, anticipating what the customer will want when he/she knows the possibilities.
9. Delivering customer value across the company through best-in-class products, services, and support.
10. Meeting and exceeding the expectations of clients, employees, and relevant constituencies in the community.

However, the ASQ also reported that there appears to be no official definition of quality that serves all purposes, and, fifty percent say there is no single definition of quality. What is clear is that how an individual, company, or organization defines quality is determined within their own system context.

Visit the ASQ website at http://asq.org/ and read about Walter A. Shewhart, and the "ASQ Global State of Quality: Discoveries 2016" research report. What are some of the measures the report cites that organizations commonly use to measure quality?

Source: "The ASQ Global State of Quality Research: Discoveries 2013," at http://asq.org/.

customer can be a manufacturer purchasing raw materials or parts, a store owner or retailer purchasing products to sell, or someone who purchases retail products or services over the Internet. W. Edwards Deming, author and consultant on quality, said that "The consumer is the most important part of the production line. Quality should be aimed at the needs of the consumer, present and future." From this perspective, product and service quality is determined by what the customer wants and is willing to pay for. Since customers have different product needs, they will have different quality expectations. This results in a commonly used definition of quality as a service's or product's *fitness for its intended use*, or **fitness for use**: how well does it do what the customer or user thinks it is supposed to do and wants it to do?

Fitness for use Is how well the product or service does what it is supposed to.

Products and services are designed with intentional differences in quality to meet the different wants and needs of individual consumers. A Mercedes and a Ford truck are equally "fit for use," in the sense that they both provide automobile transportation for the consumer, and each may meet the quality standards of its individual purchaser. However, the two products have obviously been designed differently for different types of consumers. This is commonly referred to as the **quality of design**—the degree to which quality characteristics are designed into the product. Although designed for the same use, the Mercedes and Ford differ in their performance, features, size, and various other quality characteristics.

Quality of design Involves designing quality characteristics into a product or service.

Dimensions of Quality for Manufactured Products

The *dimensions of quality* for manufactured products that a consumer looks for include the following[1]:

1. ***Performance:*** The basic operating characteristics of a product; for example, how well a car handles or its gas mileage.
2. ***Features:*** The "extra" items added to the basic features, such as a stereo CD or a leather interior in a car.
3. ***Reliability:*** The probability that a product will operate properly within an expected time frame; that is, that a TV will work without repair for about seven years.
4. ***Conformance:*** The degree to which a product meets preestablished standards.
5. ***Durability:*** How long the product lasts; its life span before replacement. A pair of L.L. Bean boots, with care, might be expected to last a lifetime.
6. ***Serviceability:*** The ease of getting repairs, the speed of repairs, and the courtesy and competence of the repair person.
7. ***Aesthetics:*** How a product looks, feels, sounds, smells, or tastes.
8. ***Safety:*** Assurance that the customer will not suffer injury or harm from a product; an especially important consideration for automobiles.
9. ***Other perceptions:*** Subjective perceptions based on brand name, advertising, and the like.

These quality characteristics are weighed by the customer relative to the cost of the product. In general, customers will pay for the level of quality they can afford. If they feel they are getting what they paid for (or more), then they tend to be satisfied with the quality of the product.

Dimensions of Quality for Services

The dimensions of quality for a service differ somewhat from those of a manufactured product. Service quality is more directly related to time and the interaction between employees and the customer. Evans and Lindsay[2] identify the following dimensions of service quality.

1. ***Time and timeliness:*** How long must a customer wait for service, and is it completed on time? For example, is an overnight package delivered overnight?
2. ***Completeness:*** Is everything the customer asked for provided? For example, is a mail order from a catalog company complete when delivered?

[1]Adapted from D. A. Garvin, "What Does Quality Really Mean?" *Sloan Management Review* 26(1; 1984), pp. 25–43.
[2]J. R. Evans and W. M. Lindsay, *The Management and Control of Quality*, 3rd ed. (St. Paul, MN: West, 1996).

In the J.D. Power 2015 *Initial Quality Study (IQS)*, the Ford F-Series Super Duty was the highest-ranked model in the Large Heavy Duty Pickup segment. In the 2015 *IQS*, the Lexus LS was not only the highest-ranked model in the Large Premium Car segment, it also achieved the best overall score in the study.

Toyota Motor Corporation

The Ford Motor Company

J.D. Power

3. ***Courtesy:*** How are customers treated by employees? For example, are catalog phone operators at L.L. Bean nice and are their voices pleasant?
4. ***Consistency:*** Is the same level of service provided to each customer each time? Is your newspaper delivered on time every morning?
5. ***Accessibility and convenience:*** How easy is it to obtain the service? For example, when you call L.L. Bean does the service representative answer quickly?
6. ***Accuracy:*** Is the service performed right every time? Is your bank or credit card statement correct every month?
7. ***Responsiveness:*** How well does the company react to unusual situations, which can happen frequently in a service company? For example, how well is a telephone operator at L.L. Bean able to respond to a customer's questions about a catalog item not fully described in the catalog?

Quality from the Producer's Perspective

Now we need to look at quality the way a producer or service provider sees it: how value is created. We already know that product development is a function of the quality characteristics (i.e., the product's fitness for use) the customer wants, needs, and can afford. Product or service design results in design specifications that should achieve the desired quality. However, once the product design has been determined, the producer perceives quality to be how effectively the production process is able to conform to the specifications required by the design, referred to as the **quality of conformance**. What this means is quality during production focuses on making sure that the product meets the specifications required by the design.

Quality of conformance Is making sure the product or service is produced according to design.

Examples of the quality of conformance: If new tires do not conform to specifications, they wobble. If a hotel room is not clean when a guest checks in, the hotel is not functioning according to the specifications of its design; it is a faulty service. From the producer's

Joel Page/©AP/Wide World Photos

L.L. Bean's first product was the Maine Hunting shoe, developed in 1912 by company founder Leon Leonwood Bean, a Maine outdoorsman. He initially sold 100 pairs to fellow sportsmen through the mail, but 90 pairs were sent back when the stitching gave way. However, true to his word, L.L. Bean returned their money and started over with an improved boot. In years to come L.L. Bean operated his business according to the following belief: "Sell good merchandise at a reasonable profit, treat your customers like human beings, and they will always come back for more." L.L. Bean also guarantees their products to "give 100% satisfaction in every way." If they don't, L.L. Bean will replace the item or refund the purchase price "at any time."

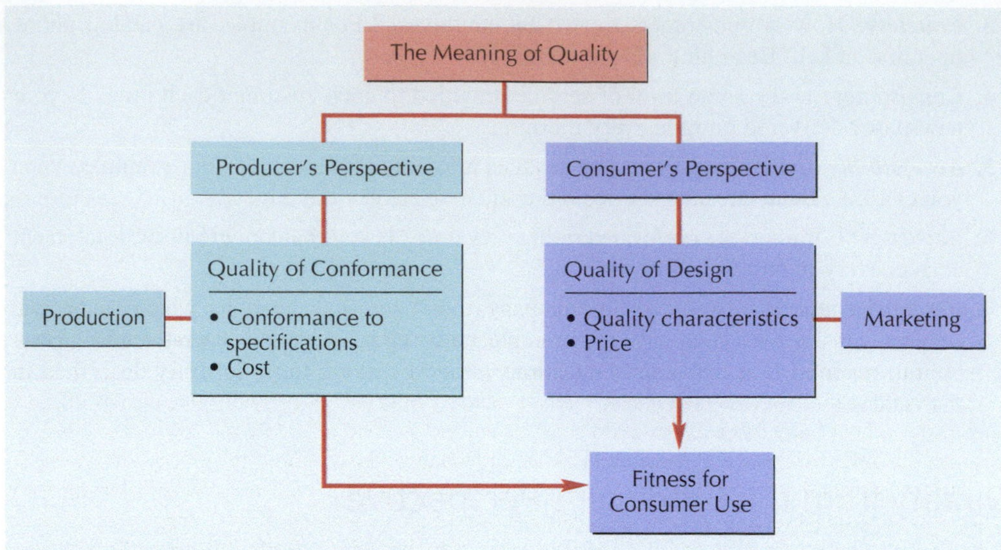

FIGURE 2.1 The Meaning of Quality

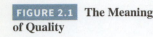

perspective, good-quality products conform to specifications—they are well made; poor-quality products are not made well—they do not conform to specifications.

Achieving quality of conformance depends on a number of factors, including the design of the production process (distinct from product design), the performance level of machinery, equipment and technology, the materials used, the training and supervision of employees, and the degree to which statistical quality-control techniques are used. When equipment fails or is maladjusted, when employees make mistakes, when material and parts are defective, and when supervision is lax, design specifications are generally not met. Key personnel in achieving conformance to specifications include the engineering staff, supervisors and managers, and, most importantly, employees.

An important consideration from the customer's perspective of product quality is product or service price. From the producer's perspective, an important consideration is achieving quality of conformance at an acceptable cost. Product cost is also an important design specification. If products or services cannot be produced at a cost that results in a competitive price, then the final product will not have acceptable value—the price is more than the consumer is willing to pay given the product's quality characteristics. Thus, the quality characteristics included in the product design must be balanced against production costs.

A Final Perspective on Quality

We approached quality from two perspectives, the customer's and the producer's. These two perspectives are dependent on each other, as shown in **Figure 2.1**. Although product design is customer-motivated, it cannot be achieved without the coordination and participation of the production process. When a product or service is designed without considering how it will be produced, it may be impossible for the production process to meet design specifications or it may be so costly to do so that the product or service must be priced prohibitively high.

Figure 2.1 depicts the meaning of quality from the producer's and consumer's perspectives. The final determination of quality is fitness for use, which is the customer's view of quality. It is the consumer who makes the final judgment regarding quality, and so it is the customer's view that must dominate.

Quality Management System

To make sure that products and services have the quality they have been designed for, strategy to achieve quality throughout the organization is required. This approach to the management of quality throughout the entire organization and supply chain has evolved into what is generally referred to as a quality management system (QMS).

Along the Supply Chain

Quality vs. Value in Denim Jeans

Denim jeans are a global wardrobe staple with about 2 billion pairs of jeans worth nearly $55 billion sold worldwide each year (70% in the United States, European Union, and China). About 780 million pairs of jeans are sold annually in the United States; virtually all U.S. consumers own at least one pair of denim jeans, and, on average, seven pairs. However, regardless of the price of their jeans, which generally average a little less than $40, but can approach $500, American consumers expect them to last longer and be more durable than any other piece of clothing in their closets. U.S. jeans retailers generally acknowledge that while price is the top factor for most consumer clothing decisions, it is less of a factor when buying denim jeans; consumers see the *value* in paying a little more for jeans that have "better" quality, i.e., a better fit and will last longer. Among women jeans buyers, price is the fourth most important factor behind other quality attributes, and among men less than half view price as important when buying jeans. As such, quality is perhaps the most important factor to the various companies up and down the global denim jeans supply chain that grow cotton, manufacture denim cloth, produce denim jeans, and sell jeans to consumers.

How the customer perceives "value" in denim jeans is a key factor that drives the quality management (QM) programs of most major denim jeans companies like Levi Strauss and VF Corporation (Lee and Wrangler Jeans). There are a number of attributes that affect the feel, look, and fit of denim jeans, and thus distinguish their quality. For example, jeans buyers have historically been willing to pay more for jeans with a higher cotton content (resulting in a better "feel"), and apparel consumers, in general, believe better quality clothing is made from natural fibers (like cotton). Different fabric qualities are determined not only by the quality of the cotton used, but by the manufacturing process used to make it; more expensive processes that spin the cotton into fabric unevenly give the fabric more character and depth. How the fabric is cut and sewn; how it is dyed; how it is ultimately washed in the finishing process (which can sometimes exceed all of the other production costs combined); the various trim items such as rivets and buttons, zippers, etc.; and, last but not least, fit, are distinguishing quality attributes. To be successful in the highly competitive global denim jeans market companies must rely on well-conceived and managed quality management programs throughout their supply chains to ensure that they are able to provide the value their customers demand.

What are the quality attributes that affect your purchasing decisions for denim jeans?

The Evolution of Quality Management

A handful of prominent individuals, summarized in Table 2.1, have had a profound impact on the importance of quality in the United States, Japan, and other countries. Of these "quality gurus" W. Edwards Deming has been the most prominent.

In the 1940s Deming worked at the Census Bureau, where he introduced the use of statistical process control to monitor the mammoth operation of key-punching data from census questionnaires onto millions of punch cards. During World War II, Deming, who is shown in the photo, developed a national program of 8- and 10-day courses to teach statistical quality-control techniques to over 10,000 engineers at companies that were suppliers to the military during the war. By the end of World War II he had an international reputation.

© Catherine Karnow/©Corbis

W. E. Deming is the most famous of all "quality gurus." He introduced statistical quality control to the Japanese, which served as the catalyst for a worldwide quality movement. His "14 points" were the foundation for modern QMS processes.

In 1950 Deming began teaching statistical quality control to Japanese companies. As a consultant to Japanese industries and as a teacher, he was able to convince them of the benefits of statistical quality control. He is a major figure in the Japanese quality movement, and in Japan he is frequently referred to as the father of quality control.

Deming's approach to quality management advocated continuous improvement of the production process to achieve conformance to specifications and reduce variability. He identified two primary sources of process improvement: eliminating common causes of quality problems, such as poor product design and insufficient employee training, and eliminating special causes, such as specific equipment or an operator. Deming emphasized the use of statistical quality-control techniques to reduce variability in the production process. He dismissed the then widely used approach of final product inspection as a means of ensuring good quality as coming too late to reduce product defects. Primary responsibility for quality improvement, he said, was employees' and management's. He promoted extensive employee involvement in a quality improvement program, and he recommended training for workers in quality-control techniques and methods.

Deming's overall philosophy for achieving improvement is embodied in his 14 points, summarized in Table 2.2.

Deming is also credited with the development of the *Deming Wheel*, although it was originally formulated by Walter Shewart, and later recast and renamed by the Japanese as the *plan-do-check-act (PDCA) cycle.* The PDCA cycle is a four-stage process for continuous

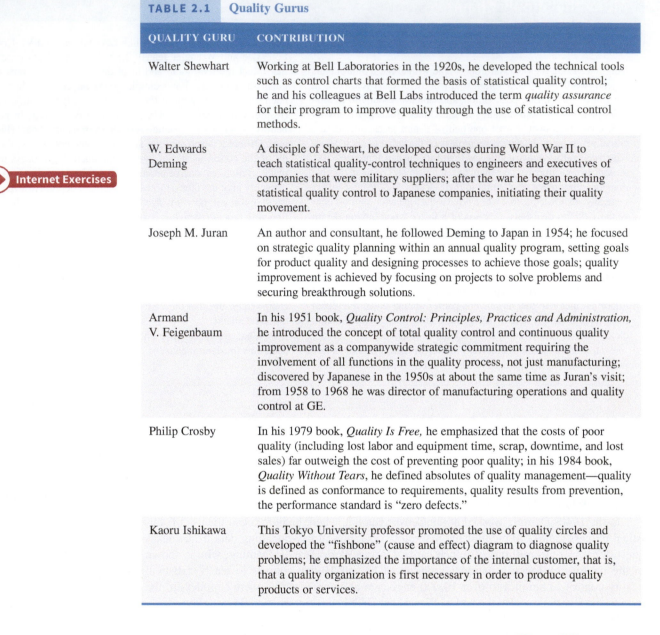

TABLE 2.1 Quality Gurus

QUALITY GURU	CONTRIBUTION
Walter Shewhart	Working at Bell Laboratories in the 1920s, he developed the technical tools such as control charts that formed the basis of statistical quality control; he and his colleagues at Bell Labs introduced the term *quality assurance* for their program to improve quality through the use of statistical control methods.
W. Edwards Deming	A disciple of Shewart, he developed courses during World War II to teach statistical quality-control techniques to engineers and executives of companies that were military suppliers; after the war he began teaching statistical quality control to Japanese companies, initiating their quality movement.
Joseph M. Juran	An author and consultant, he followed Deming to Japan in 1954; he focused on strategic quality planning within an annual quality program, setting goals for product quality and designing processes to achieve those goals; quality improvement is achieved by focusing on projects to solve problems and securing breakthrough solutions.
Armand V. Feigenbaum	In his 1951 book, *Quality Control: Principles, Practices and Administration,* he introduced the concept of total quality control and continuous quality improvement as a companywide strategic commitment requiring the involvement of all functions in the quality process, not just manufacturing; discovered by Japanese in the 1950s at about the same time as Juran's visit; from 1958 to 1968 he was director of manufacturing operations and quality control at GE.
Philip Crosby	In his 1979 book, *Quality Is Free,* he emphasized that the costs of poor quality (including lost labor and equipment time, scrap, downtime, and lost sales) far outweigh the cost of preventing poor quality; in his 1984 book, *Quality Without Tears*, he defined absolutes of quality management—quality is defined as conformance to requirements, quality results from prevention, the performance standard is "zero defects."
Kaoru Ishikawa	This Tokyo University professor promoted the use of quality circles and developed the "fishbone" (cause and effect) diagram to diagnose quality problems; he emphasized the importance of the internal customer, that is, that a quality organization is first necessary in order to produce quality products or services.

quality improvement that complements Deming's 14 points, as shown in Figure 2.2. Years later, Deming once again modified the original Shewart cycle as a circle flow diagram for learning and improvement of a product and process that he called the *plan-do-study-act (PDSA) cycle* (also shown in Figure 2.2). The PDCA cycle later formed the basis for the Six Sigma five-step DMAIC breakthrough strategy (we'll talk about this in the "Six Sigma" section later in this chapter).

Deming's approach to quality embodied in his 14 points and PDCA cycle are the foundation for today's quality management systems employed by many successful companies.

TQM and QMS

Total Quality Management (TQM) Customer-oriented, leadership, strategic planning, employee responsibility, continuous improvement, cooperation, statistical methods, and training and education.

Total quality management (TQM) has been the most prominent and visible approach to quality to evolve from the work of Deming and the early quality gurus. TQM originated in the 1980s as a Japanese-style management approach to quality improvement, and became very popular during the 1990s, being adopted by thousands of companies. Although it has taken on many meanings, it was (and still is) a philosophy for managing an organization centered on quality and customer satisfaction as "the" strategy for achieving long-term success. It requires the active involvement, participation, and cooperation of everyone in the organization, and encompasses

TABLE 2.2 W. E. Deming's 14 Points

1. Create a constancy of purpose toward product improvement to achieve long-term organizational goals.
2. Adopt a philosophy of preventing poor-quality products instead of acceptable levels of poor quality as necessary to compete internationally.
3. Eliminate the need for inspection to achieve quality by relying instead on statistical quality control to improve product and process design.
4. Select a few suppliers or vendors based on quality commitment rather than competitive prices.
5. Constantly improve the production process by focusing on the two primary sources of quality problems, the system and employees, thus increasing productivity and reducing costs.
6. Institute worker training that focuses on the prevention of quality problems and the use of statistical quality-control techniques.
7. Instill leadership among supervisors to help employees perform better.
8. Encourage employee involvement by eliminating the fear of reprisal for asking questions or identifying quality problems.
9. Eliminate barriers between departments, and promote cooperation and a team approach for working together.
10. Eliminate slogans and numerical targets that urge employees to achieve higher performance levels without first showing them how to do it.
11. Eliminate numerical quotas that employees attempt to meet at any cost without regard for quality.
12. Enhance worker pride, artisanry, and self-esteem by improving supervision and the production process so that employees can perform to their capabilities.
13. Institute vigorous education and training programs in methods of quality improvement throughout the organization, from top management down, so that continuous improvement can occur.
14. Develop a commitment from top management to implement the previous 13 points.

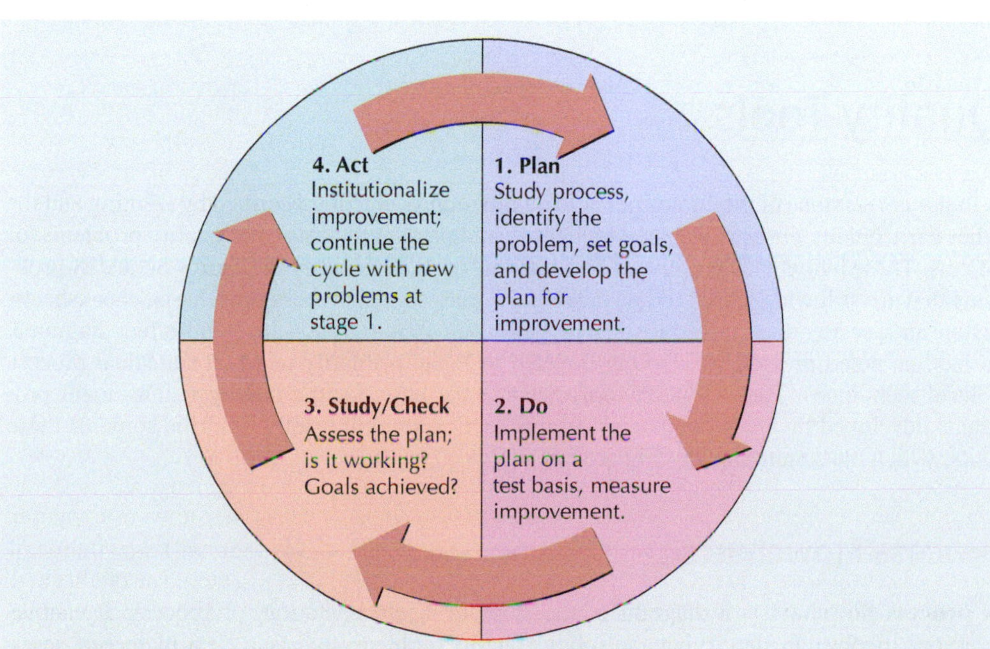

FIGURE 2.2 The Deming Wheel (PDCA Cycle)

virtually all of its activities and processes. To achieve and sustain this pervasive focus on quality requires a significant long-term commitment on the part of the organization's leadership. Deming's 14 points and the philosophies and teachings of the early quality gurus are clearly embodied in the basic principles of TQM:

1. Quality can and must be *managed*.
2. The *customer* defines quality, and customer satisfaction is the top goal; it is a requirement and is not negotiable.
3. Management must be involved and provide *leadership*.
4. Continuous quality improvement is "the" *strategic* goal, which requires planning and organization.
5. Quality improvement is the responsibility of every *employee*; all employees must be trained and educated to achieve quality improvement.
6. Quality problems are found in *processes*, and problems must be prevented, not solved.
7. The quality *standard* is "no defects."
8. Quality must be *measured*; improvement requires the use of *quality tools*, and especially statistical process control.

Quality Management System (QMS) A system to achieve customer satisfaction that complements other company systems.

TQM has been supplanted to a large extent by what is most commonly referred to as a **quality management system (QMS)**. This approach (or term) has evolved out of the ISO:9001 certification process that many companies around the world have gone through; essentially ISO certifies a company's "quality management system," and much of the ISO's written materials refer directly to "quality management systems." (ISO certification is discussed in greater detail in a separate section later in this chapter.) A QMS is not as much of a philosophy as TQM; rather, it is a system that complements a company's other systems and functions. It is a systematic approach to achieving quality and hence customer satisfaction, and while it suggests no less commitment to that goal than TQM, it maintains less of a core strategic focus than TQM. Further, since a QMS is not a "philosophy," it more naturally is designed to meet the individual needs and circumstances of a particular company. It outlines the policies and procedures necessary to improve and control specific (but not all) processes that will lead to improved business performance. A QMS tends to focus more on individual projects that have a quantifiable impact (i.e., increased profitability). Some companies have adopted the Malcolm Baldrige National Quality Award criteria as its QMS; another well-known QMS is Six Sigma (discussed in detail in a later section).

Regardless of the term a company uses to identify its approach to achieving quality improvement, and the possible differences between TQM and a QMS or other approaches, there are certain common characteristics of companywide approaches to quality improvement, such as customer satisfaction and employee involvement, topics we will talk about later in the chapter.

Quality Tools

A major cornerstone of the commitment to quality improvement prescribed by Deming and the other early quality gurus is the need to identify and prevent the causes of quality problems, or defects. These individuals prescribed a number of "tools" to identify the causes of quality problems that are still widely used today, including Pareto charts, process flowcharts, checksheets, histograms, scatter diagrams, statistical process control charts, and cause-and-effect diagrams. In fact, as noted previously, Deming traveled to Japan primarily to teach statistical process control techniques. These popular tools became the basis for the quality management programs developed by many companies. In this section we will briefly describe some of these tools, which are summarized in **Figure 2.3**.

Process Flowcharts

Process flowchart A diagram of the steps in a job, operation, or process.

A **process flowchart** is a diagram of the steps in a job, operation, or process. It enables everyone involved in identifying and solving quality problems to have a clear picture of how a

FIGURE 2.3 **Quality Tools**

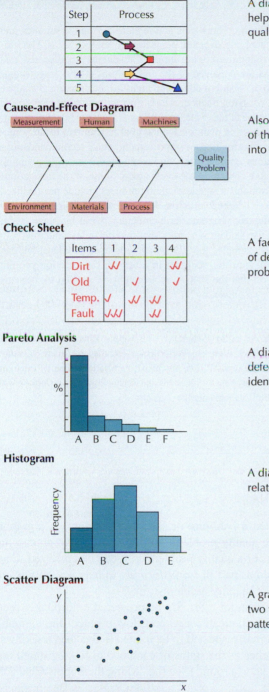

Process Flowchart

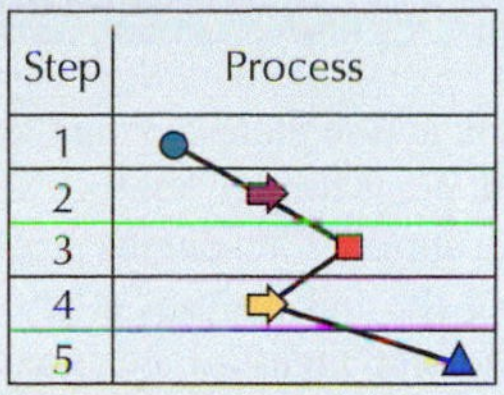

Step	Process
1	
2	
3	
4	
5	

A diagram of the steps in a process; helps focus on where in a process a quality problem might exist.

Cause-and-Effect Diagram

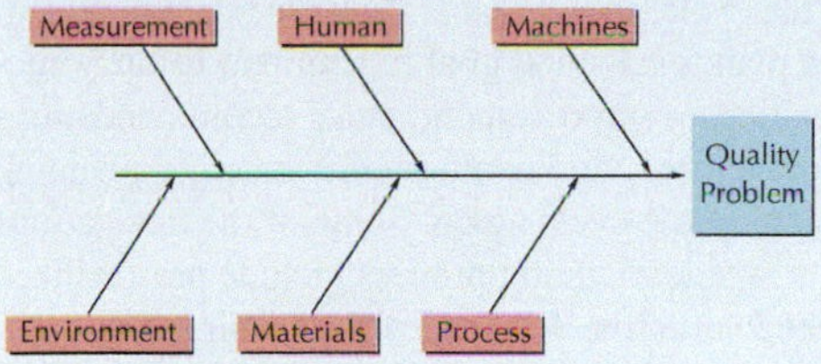

Also called a "fishbone" diagram; a graph of the causes of a quality problem divided into categories.

Check Sheet

Items	1	2	3	4
Dirt	✓✓			✓✓
Old		✓		✓
Temp.	✓	✓✓	✓✓	
Fault	✓✓✓		✓✓	

A fact-finding tool for tallying the number of defects for a list of previously identified problem causes.

Pareto Analysis

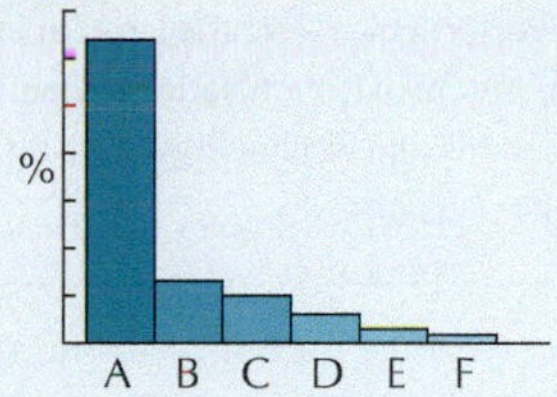

A diagram for tallying the percentage of defects resulting from different causes to identify major quality problems.

Histogram

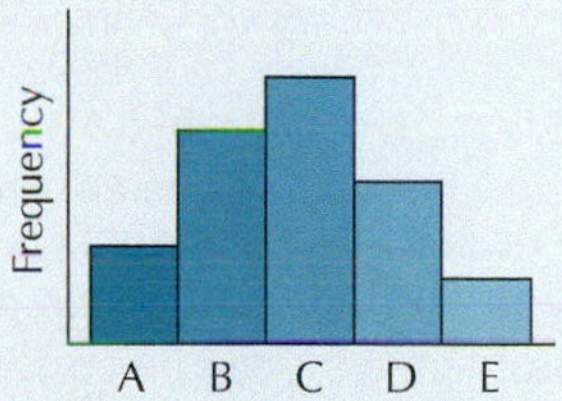

A diagram showing the frequency of data related to a quality problem.

Scatter Diagram

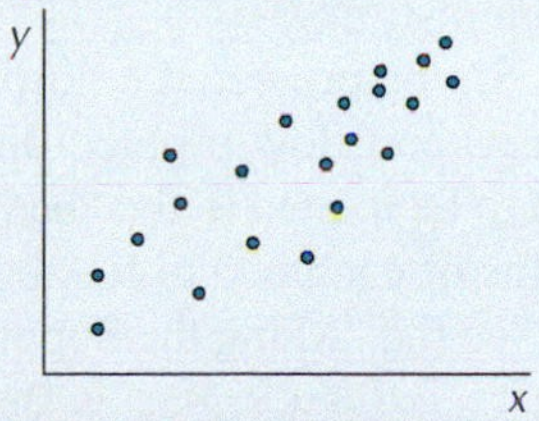

A graph showing the relationship between two variables in a process; identifies a pattern that may cause a quality problem.

Statistical Process Control Chart

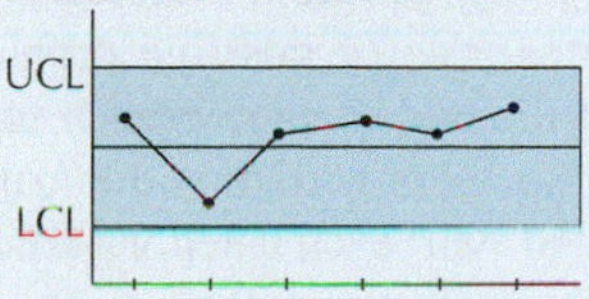

A chart with statistical upper and lower limits; if the process stays between these limits over time, it is in control and a problem does not exist.

specific operation works and a common frame of reference. It also enables a process improvement team to understand the interrelationship of the departments and functions that constitute a process. This helps focus on where problems might occur and if the process itself needs fixing. Development of the flowchart can help identify quality problems by helping the problem solvers better understand the process. Flowcharts are described in greater detail in Chapter 6 ("Processes and Technology") and Chapter 8 ("Human Resources").

Along the Supply Chain

Applying Deming's PDCA Cycle in Education

The Pewaukee School District (PSD), located in Waukesha County, Wisconsin (just west of Milwaukee), with 2760 K–12 students and 296 employees in four schools (two elementary, one middle, and one high school) was a 2013 Baldrige National Quality Award Winner. Despite having one of the state's most rigorous graduation requirements (28 credits), it has had a higher graduation rate and percentage of graduates attending college than other county, state, and nearby high-performing districts. Its AP exam pass rate (76%) was higher than the county and state and its ACT composite score (23.4) was better than both state and national averages. Parent surveys showed satisfaction with communication was 20% higher than the national average, and satisfaction with education quality was over 93%. PSD also significantly outperformed county and state districts in dropout and truancy rates and in student volunteering. PSD has been named one of "Wisconsin's Top 100 Workplaces" by the *Milwaukee Journal Sentinel* and staff satisfaction ratings for salaries, benefits, and engagement/involvement greatly exceed national averages.

PSD's strategic planning process is based on Deming's PDCA cycle. In the "plan" stage of the cycle a large stakeholder group assembled in the spring clarifies purpose and direction by assessing performance and reviewing progress on goals and action plans, and validates missions and strategies. In the "do" stage, administrative, school, and department teams align action by updating plan goal measures, creating short-term action plans during the summer, and creating school improvement plans for five strategy areas. The strategic plan is approved in the summer, resources are allocated, and action plans are deployed in the fall. In the "study" stage senior leaders and the board of education measure plan goals and analyze the results of action plans quarterly during the school year. In the final "act" stage of the cycle, senior leaders and the board of education evaluate action plan results and goal attainment, identify successes and opportunities for improvement, make recommendations for continuous improvement, and evaluate the strategic planning process before beginning the cycle again. Some of the innovations resulting from this strategic planning process include personalized learning, a 1:1 laptop initiative for grades 5 and higher, a community volunteer program, an elementary world language study, and innovative student schedules that maximize learning time.

In this examples the PDCA cycle is used in education; can you think of specific processes in a service organization you are familiar with that the PDCA cycle might be applied to, perhaps even your own university?

Sources: Based on M. Schmidt, "The Ripple Effect, Education and Healthcare Makes Waves in Performance Excellence Circles," *Quality Progress* 47, (8: August 2014), pp. 32–41; and National Quality Program at the National Institute of Standards and Technology website http://www.nist.gov/baldrige/about/baldrige_faqs.cfm.

Cause-and-Effect Diagrams

Cause-and-effect diagram or fishbone diagram A chart showing the different categories of problem causes.

A **cause-and-effect diagram**, also called a **fishbone** or Ishikawa diagram, is a graphical description of the elements of a specific quality problem and the relationship among those elements. It is used to identify the causes of a quality problem so it can be corrected. Cause-and-effect diagrams are usually developed as part of *brainstorming* to help a quality team of employees and managers identify causes of quality problems.

Figure 2.4 is a cause-and-effect diagram for a Six Sigma project at a hospital to reduce delays in patient bed turnaround time, which creates a patient flow problem throughout the hospital. The primary cause of the problem is suspected to be related to the "bed tracking system" (BTS), an electronic system that indicates the status of each bed to the registered nurse (RN) who admits patients and assigns them to a room. (See the "Along the Supply Chain" box for the North Shore University Hospital.)

The "effect" box at the end of the diagram is the quality problem that needs correction. A center line connects the effect box to the major categories of possible problem causes, displayed as branches off of the center line. The box at the end of each branch (or fishbone) describes the cause category. The diagram starts out in this form with only the major categories at the end of each branch. Individual causes associated with each category are attached as separate lines along the length of the branch during the brainstorming process. Sometimes the causes are rank-ordered along the branches in order to identify those that are most likely to affect the problem. The cause-and-effect diagram is a means for thinking through a problem and recording the possible causes in an organized and easily interpretable manner.

Cause-and-effect matrix A grid used to prioritize causes of quality problems.

A complementary tool related to the fishbone diagram is the **cause-and-effect matrix**, which is used to prioritize the potential causes of quality problems in a process that might first be identified using a cause-and-effect diagram. The output (or *Y*) variables are listed along the top of the matrix. These are also referred to as CTQs or CTQCs, (i.e., "critical-to-quality characteristics") and they are measurable characteristics that express the key requirements

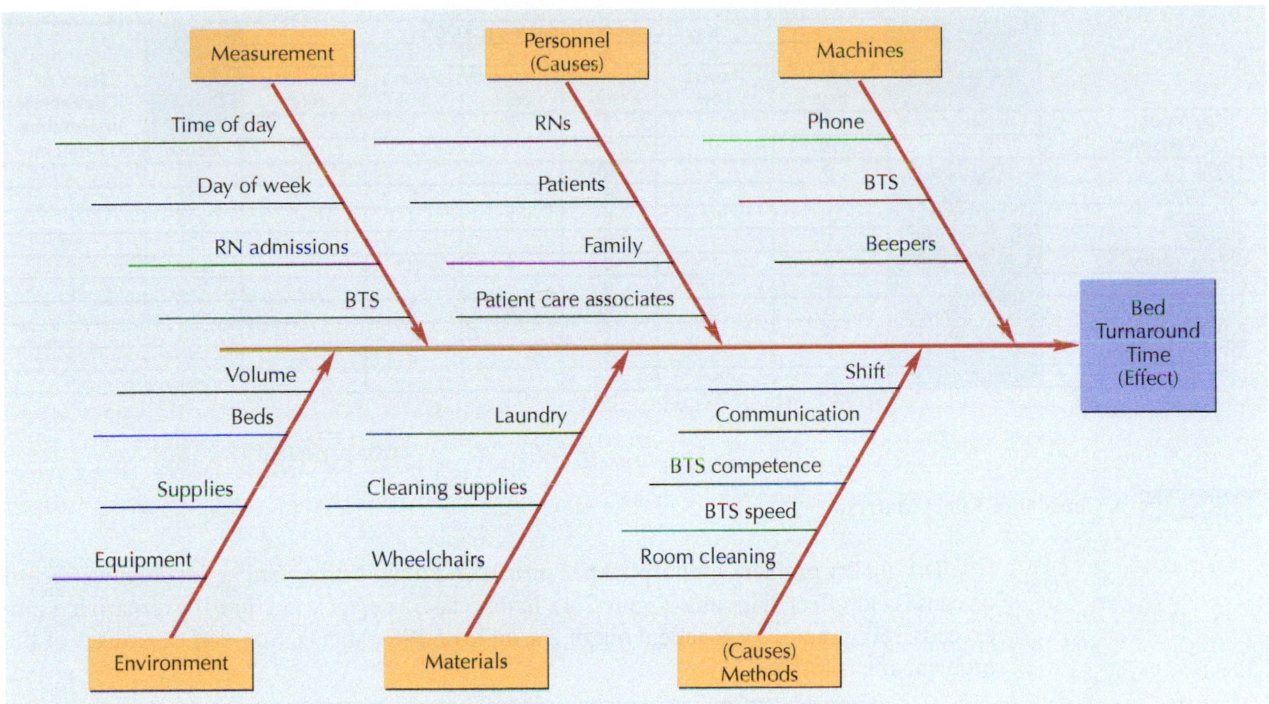

FIGURE 2.4 **A Cause-and-Effect Diagram**

defined by a customer. CTQCs are what the customer expects from a product, and accordingly they have a significant impact on customer satisfaction. The input (or *X*) variables that might affect the outcome of process (i.e., the potential causes of an outcome) are listed along the left side of the matrix (or grid). The CTQCs are ranked or weighted in terms of importance to the customer; then, the relationship between causes and effects (CTQs) are weighted or ranked; and finally, an overall score is calculated for the causes (or *X* variables). The causes with the highest score should be addressed first in improvement efforts because they will have the largest impact on customer satisfaction. Figure 2.5 shows a cause-and-effect matrix for the hospital bed turnaround time example. Note that staff communication has the highest score, and thus, the greatest impact on how satisfied the customers are with the overall process.

Checksheets and Histograms

Checksheets are frequently used in conjunction with histograms, as well as with Pareto diagrams. A *checksheet* is a fact-finding tool used to collect data about quality problems. A typical check sheet for quality defects tallies the number of defects for a variety of previously identified problem causes. When the check sheet is completed, the total tally of defects for each cause can be used to create a *histogram* or a Pareto chart, as shown in Figure 2.6.

Pareto Analysis

Pareto analysis is a method of identifying the causes of poor quality. It was devised in the early 1950s by the quality expert Joseph Juran. He named this method after a nineteenth-century Italian economist, Vilfredo Pareto, who determined that a small percentage of the people accounted for most of the wealth. Pareto analysis is based on Juran's finding that most quality problems and costs result from only a few causes. For example, he discovered in a textile mill that almost 75% of all defective cloth was caused by only a few weavers, and in a paper mill he studied, more than 60% of the cost of poor quality was attributable to a single category of defects. Correcting the few major causes of most of the quality problems will result in the greatest cost impact.

Pareto analysis Most quality problems result from a few causes.

Pareto analysis can be applied by tallying the number of defects for each of the different possible causes of poor quality in a product or service and then developing a frequency distribution from the data. This frequency distribution, referred to as a *Pareto diagram*, is a useful visual aid for focusing on major quality problems.

	Key Input (X) Variables		Key Output (Y) Variables (CTQC's)							Rank of X Variables/ Importance to Customer
			1	2	3	4	5	6		
			Turnaround time	Patient flow	Physician time	Emergency dept.	Patient time	Operating room		
		Customer rank	1	3	2	5	6	4		
		Weight	*10*	*9*	*9*	*7*	*7*	*8*	Score	
1	BTS		9	8	10	8		5	348	3
2	Beepers		7	5	8		5		222	7
3	Volume		7	10	6	7	5	5	338	4
4	Beds		4		9				121	10
5	Time of day		3	4	5	4	10		209	8
6	Day of week		9	10	6			6	282	5
7	Communication		9	8	10	8	7	9	429	1
8	BTS competence		10	9	7		7	7	349	2
9	Room cleaning		7	5	3		8	4	230	6
10	Supplies		8	9					161	9

(8)(10) + (9)(9) = 161

FIGURE 2.5 A Cause-and-Effect Matrix

The quality problem for hospital bed turnaround time is described in the previous section on cause-and-effect diagrams (Figure 2.4). In this case, a defect is anytime the turnaround time exceeds 150 minutes for a patient out of a sample of 195 patients. Some of the causes of this problem are as follows.

CAUSE	NUMBER OF DEFECTS	PERCENTAGE
Staff communication	83	64%
BTS system	17	13
Room cleaning	13	10
Beepers	7	6
Laundry	4	3
Patients	3	2
Family	3	2
	130	100%

For each cause of poor quality, the number of defects attributed to that cause has been tallied. This information is then converted into the Pareto chart shown in Figure 2.6.

FIGURE 2.6 Pareto Chart

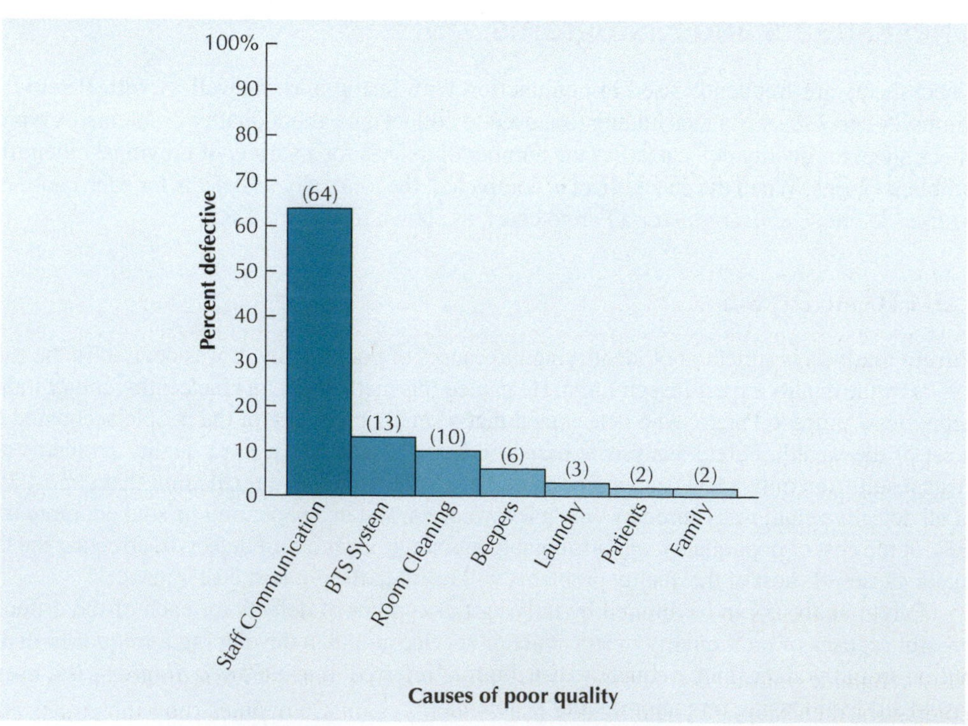

This Pareto chart identifies the major cause of poor quality to be poor staff communication. Correcting the problem will result in the greatest quality improvement. However, the other problems should not be ignored. Continual quality improvement is the long-term goal. The Pareto diagram simply identifies the quality problems that will result in the greatest immediate impact on quality improvement.

Scatter Diagrams

Scatter diagrams graphically show the relationship between two variables, such as the brittleness of a piece of material and the temperature at which it is processed. One temperature reading should result in a specific degree of brittleness representing one point on the diagram. Many such points on the diagram visually show a pattern between the two variables and a relationship or lack of one. This diagram could be used to identify a particular quality problem associated with the baking process.

Process Control Charts and Statistical Quality Control

We discuss control charts and other statistical quality-control methods in Chapter 3, "Statistical Process Control." For now, it is sufficient to say that a control chart is a means for measuring if a process is doing what it is supposed to do, like a thermostat monitoring room temperature. It is constructed with a horizontal line through the middle of a chart representing the process average or norm. It also has a line below this center line representing a lower control limit and a line above it for the upper control limit. Samples from the process are taken over time and measured according to some attribute. In its simplest form, if the measurement is within the upper and lower control limits, the process is said to be in control and there is no quality problem, but if the measurement is outside the limits, then a problem probably exists and should be investigated and corrected.

Statistical quality-control methods such as the process control chart are important tools for quality improvement. Employees who are provided with extensive training in statistical quality-control methods are able to identify quality problems and their causes and to make suggestions for improvement. (See the "Along the Supply Chain" box to see how a control chart is used to monitor hospital bed turnaround times.)

Customers and Employees in Quality Management

The main focus of Deming's 14 points, TQM, and all QMSs is to achieve customer satisfaction, and most of Deming's 14 points refer to employees. The reasons are simple. Customers who are very happy and delighted are less likely to switch to a competitor, which translates to profits. Employees have the most direct influence on quality.

A high level of satisfaction creates an emotional bond instead of simply a rational preference. Research by companies has shown that there is a direct link between customer satisfaction and attrition rates, indicating that delighted customers are less likely to defect than dissatisfied customers. Figure 2.7 highlights some of the "facts" that are generally known to exist about customer satisfaction.

Quality Management in the Supply Chain

Most companies not only have customers they want to satisfy, but they are also customers of other companies, their *suppliers*, within a company's supply chain. Companies know that to satisfy its customers requires not only their own commitment to quality, but also the support and resources of its suppliers. This is especially true of companies that outsource many of their activities to suppliers. Companies and their suppliers joined together in a supply chain must work together to meet the needs of the company's customers. A partnership exists between the supplier and its customer wherein the supplier is expected to manage its own quality effectively so that the company it supplies can count on the quality of the materials, parts, and services it receives.

Many companies reduce their number of suppliers in order to have more direct influence over their suppliers' quality and delivery performance, which was one of Deming's 14 points. It is based on the notion that if a company has a major portion of a supplier's business, then the supplier is more willing to meet the customer's quality standards. The company and supplier enter into a business relationship referred to as **partnering**, in which the supplier agrees to meet the company's quality standards, and in return the company enters into a long-term purchasing agreement with the supplier that includes a stable order and delivery schedule.

Partnering A relationship between a company and its supplier based on mutual quality standards.

In order to ensure that its supplier meets its quality standards, a company will often insist that the supplier adopt a QMS similar to its own, or a company's QMS will include its suppliers. Still other companies require that their suppliers achieve ISO 9001 certification, an international quality standard that ensures a high industry standard of quality as its QMS; some companies require their suppliers to follow Baldrige National Quality Award guidelines or even enter the Baldrige Award competition as their QMS.

At the other end of a company's spectrum from its suppliers is its direct relationship with its own customers. An important component of any QMS is the company's ability to measure customer satisfaction; to "hear" what the customer wants. The company needs to know if its QMS is effective. Is the company meeting customer expectations? Are its products or services meeting their fitness for use definition? Is it what the customer wants, does the customer like it, does the customer need it, would the customer like it changed? A QMS requires that some form of measurement system be in place to answer these questions and provide data about the customer's level of satisfaction. It is a well-established fact of consumer behavior that unhappy customers will tell almost twice as many others about their quality problems as they will about satisfactory products or services.

Along the Supply Chain

Achieving Quality in Target's Supply Chain

Target, a *Fortune 500* company headquartered in Minneapolis, Minnesota, is one of the largest and best known retail chains in the United States, with over 900 stores in 49 states, over 365,000 employees, and revenues over $70 billion. Target's supply chain includes 37 distribution centers across the United States and four warehouse centers near U.S. coastal ports that receive overseas shipments from suppliers around the world. For its hard good (nonfabric) products such as toys, furniture, electronics, sporting goods, and kitchen goods, Target works with over 3000 factories around the world, and because of its large network of suppliers and factories, realizing its commitment to total quality requires constant diligence.

Quality is an essential component of Target's global sourcing process so that quality is achieved while products are moving through the supply chain before they reach store shelves. The ultimate goal is to drive variability out of the supply chain. However, with an enormous number of hard good products coming from those 3000 factories, the opportunities for variability to enter the supply chain are substantial. Suppliers are required to sign a "standards of supplier engagement" agreement that clearly spells out Target's quality requirements. When a factory enters the Target supply chain, it is subjected to a thorough evaluation with a rating system that includes an assessment of product quality, which determines if a supplier can use the factory. Also, every factory must meet Target's global social compliance requirements regarding worker treatment, which are nonnegotiable and are the most important part of Target's partnering relationship with its suppliers.

Target works with existing factories and suppliers that experience failures to improve performance. However, repeated failures result in an end to the relationship. Target uses various statistical quality control tools in its evaluations, plus it also employs Six Sigma throughout its supply chain and business processes, in formal project management, problem solving, and process improvement.

Research how other large companies with a global supply chain might use formal rating systems to evaluate suppliers.

Sources: Based on William H. Murphy, "Bull's Eye: An Inside Look at How Target Ensures Quality in a Complex Supply Chain," *Quality Progress* (June 2010), pp. 22–29; and the Target website at www.target.com.

- It costs 5 or 6 times more to attract a new customer than it does to keep an existing one.
- Between 94 and 96 percent of dissatisfied customers don't complain, they just walk away and about 91 percent of them don't come back.
- Between 54 and 70 percent of customers who complain will do business with the company again if their complaints are resolved satisfactorily; this number increases to around 95 percent if the complaint is resolved quickly.
- A typical dissatisfied customer will tell 8 to 10 people about their problem; one in five will tell 20 (and the Internet now makes it possible to tell thousands). A satisfied complainer will tell an average of five people about how a problem was resolved to their satisfaction.
- It takes about 12 positive service encounters to make up for a single negative one.
- Only about five percent of customers who cannot buy a product because it's out of stock return to make the originally planned purchase.
- Around 68 percent of customers stop doing business with suppliers because they perceive an attitude of indifference toward them; only 14 percent leave because they are dissatisfied with a product, and only 9 percent leave for competitive reasons.
- Between 80 and 90 percent of customers who defect say they are "satisfied;" but "very satisfied" customers are four to seven times more likely to repeat their purchase within the next 18 months than those who were merely "satisfied."
- An increase of as little as five percent in customer retention can result in an 80 to 100 percent increase in profits.
- Businesses with low quality service average only one percent return on sales and lose market share at a rate of two percent annually; businesses with high-quality service average a 12 percent return on sales and gain market share at the rate of 6 percent annually (and charge significantly higher prices).

Source: The British Quality Foundation, "Back to Basics," *Quality World* 32 (5; May 2006), p. 37.

FIGURE 2.7 The Impact of Customer Satisfaction

Measuring Customer Satisfaction

For most companies, figuring out what satisfies customers (i.e., what they want and need) is easier said than done. It requires that a company somehow gather information on what the customer wants and needs, disseminate that information throughout the company, use that information to improve its products and processes and develop new products, and then monitor customer satisfaction to ensure that the customer's needs are being met.

Along the Supply Chain

Measuring Customer Satisfaction with Customer Feedback and Voice of the Customer (VoC) at JetBlue

JetBlue Airways is a recipient of multiple J.D. Power and Associates Awards for leading all airlines in customer satisfaction, and has a place on *Bloomberg Businessweek*'s list of top 25 Customer Service Champs. JetBlue believes its success in distinguishing itself from its competitors is due in large part to customer feedback, which shows that more travelers choose JetBlue for its superior quality service than for its low fares. JetBlue receives direct feedback from its customers from passenger surveys, ad hoc surveys, interviews, and an online customer panel. On average, JetBlue receives more than 40,000 survey responses every month plus online customer surveys from its over 15,000 "TrueBlue" members. These surveys provide feedback in a structured format. JetBlue also receives, on average, around 500 emails each day plus customer comments from posts on its website, other websites, forums, and blogs. However, this feedback is provided in an unstructured text format that is time-consuming and expensive to individually read and analyze, especially when events occur that spike emails (such as a 2007 ice storm that canceled almost 1000 flights, resulting in 30,000 emails in two days).

To accommodate valuable email correspondence from its customers, JetBlue implemented *text analytics* software that breaks down sentences linguistically to identify facts, which can then be searched and analyzed in a structured format with survey data. Text analytics automatically extracts relevant data from customer text communications, including emails and web forums, that identifies facts, opinions, requests, trends and trouble spots and provides JetBlue with insights into customer satisfaction, sentiment and loyalty. JetBlue also uses Voice of the Customer (VoC) software to search the Internet for customer conversations about competitors, including service, products, and price issues.

Examples were given of how JetBlue used survey and VoC tools to assess customer satisfaction. What other tools do you think they (or other organizations) might employ to get customer feedback?

Sources: Based on B. Jeppsen, "Safe Landing, Thanks to Text Analytics, JetBlue Ensures Customers Are Heard," *Quality Progress* 43 (2); (February 2010), pp. 19–23.

FIGURE 2.8 VoC on the Internet

- Over 80% of consumers consult online reviews prior to their holiday purchases.
- 90% of consumers trust peer recommendations, and only 14% trust advertisements.
- On average, satisfied customers will tell over 40 people on social media about their experiences, while an unsatisfied customer will tell over 50.
- The average Facebook user has about 130 "friends" to share their product opinions with.
- A happy customer who uses social media will tell more than four times as many people about good experiences than will someone who does not use social media.
- Customers who "like" Wal-Mart on Facebook are four times more likely to buy there than the average person.

Source: S. Liu, "Like Abilities: Engaging Customers through Social Media is a Key to Earning Trust," *Quality Progress* (June 2015), pp. 25–29.

The primary means for garnering information from customers, and measuring customer satisfaction is the customer survey. The customer survey is a means for companies to listen to what is often referred to as the "voice of the customer (VoC)." Applicants for the Malcolm Baldrige National Quality Award are expected to provide measures of customer satisfaction typically through customer surveys. Motorola, a two-time Baldrige Award winner, contracts with an independent survey firm to conduct regularly scheduled surveys with its customers around the world to help Motorola determine how well it's meeting its customers' needs.

Increasingly prevalent VoC sources are the Internet and social media. Customers can easily post reviews of products and services in a matter of seconds on company websites like Amazon, Best Buy, and Target, and share opinions about products and services on social media sites like Facebook and Twitter. These sources are easy for customers to access and use, and fast, which results in feedback to companies about what their customers are thinking virtually every second. This can result in a huge amount of information, which is referred to as "big data," that companies can store and analyze mathematically to not only fix quality problems, but also to understand and predict its customers' needs and wants (i.e., fitness for use).

J.D. Power and Associates, as mentioned in the chapter introduction, is an independent, third-party company that provides companies in the automotive, energy/communications, travel, financial, and home-building industries with feedback from their customers based on surveys that they conduct. They also annually present awards to companies that have excelled in their industry based on independently financed consumer opinion studies. Award-winning companies are allowed to license the use of J.D. Power and Associates awards in advertising. For example, for 2015 Lexus was the highest ranked automobile brand for dependability. For 2014, Holiday Inn had the highest "guest satisfaction" for mid-scale hotels (with full service).

The *American Customer Satisfaction Index (ACSI)* was established in 1994 through a partnership of the University of Michigan Business School, the American Society for Quality (ASQ), and the international consulting firm CFI Group. The ACSI is funded in part by corporate subscribers who receive industry benchmarking data and company-specific information about financial returns from improving customer satisfaction.

ACSI measures customer satisfaction with the goods and services of 7 economic sectors, 39 industries (including e-commerce and e-business), and more than 200 companies and 70 federal and local government agencies. The ACSI reports scores on a 0 to 100 scale, which are based on econometric modeling of data obtained from telephone interviews with customers. From random-digit-dial (RDD) telephone samples (and Internet samples for e-commerce and e-business), more than 65,000 consumers are identified and interviewed annually.

ACSI scores are posted on their website at www.theacsi.org. For example, Amazon has been the highest ranked in the "Internet retail" category with an ACSI score of 86, one of the highest scores ever recorded in any service industry. In the automobile category, Lexus has been the highest ranked. Samsung has been ranked first in cell phones; Chick-fil-A has been ranked first in customer service for fast food restaurants; while in wireless telephone service Verizon has been ranked first.

The Role of Employees in Quality Improvement

Job training and employee development are major features of a successful quality management program. Increased training in job skills results in improved processes that improve product quality. Training in quality tools and skills such as statistical process control enables employees to diagnose and correct day-to-day problems related to their job. This provides employees with greater responsibility for product quality and greater satisfaction for doing their part to achieve quality. When achievement is reinforced through rewards and recognition, it further increases employee satisfaction. At Ritz-Carlton, employees receive over 100 hours of training annually. Marriott employees are trained to view breakdowns in service as opportunities for satisfying customers; for example, they may send a gift and note of apology to customers who have experienced a problem in the hotel.

In our previous discussions, the importance of customer satisfaction as an overriding company objective was stressed. However, another important aspect of a successful QMS is internal customer (e.g., employee) satisfaction. It is unlikely that a company will be able to make its customers happy if its employees are not happy. For that reason, many successful companies conduct employee satisfaction surveys just as they conduct customer surveys.

When employees are directly involved in the quality management process, it is referred to as **participative problem solving**. Employee participation in identifying and solving quality problems has been shown to be effective in improving quality, increasing employee satisfaction and morale, improving job skills, reducing job turnover and absenteeism, and increasing productivity.

Participative problem solving Employees are directly involved in the quality management process.

Participative problem solving is usually within an *employee-involvement (EI)* program, with a team approach. We will look at some of these programs for involving employees in quality management, including kaizen, quality circles, and process improvement teams.

Kaizen and Continuous Improvement

Kaizen is the Japanese term for *continuous improvement*, not only in the workplace but also in one's personal life, home life, and social life. In the workplace, kaizen means involving everyone in a process of gradual, organized, and continuous improvement. Every employee within an organization should be involved in working together to make improvements. If an improvement is not part of a continuous, ongoing process, it is not considered kaizen. Kaizen is most closely associated with *lean systems,* an approach to continuous improvement throughout the organization that is the subject of Chapter 16.

kaizen Involves everyone in a process of continuous improvement.

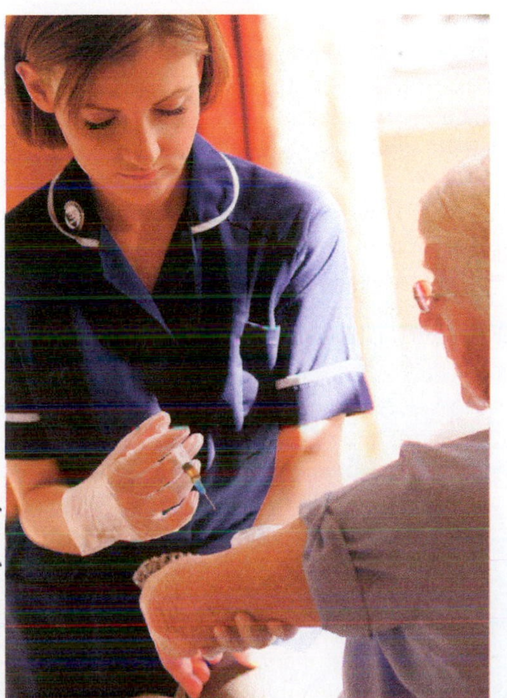

With today's focus on healthcare costs, quality in healthcare is a major issue in the service sector. Its importance is signified by the fact that it is one of five categories in which the Baldrige National Quality Award is annually given.

Employees are most directly involved in kaizen when they are determining solutions to their own problems. Employees are the real experts in their immediate workspace. In its most basic form, kaizen is a system in which employees identify many small improvements on a continual basis and implement these improvements themselves. This is actually the application of the steps in the Deming Wheel (Figure 2.2) at its most basic, individual level. Employees identify a problem, come up with a solution, check with their supervisor, and then implement it. This works to involve all employees in the improvement process and gives them a feeling that they are really participating in quality improvement, which in turn keeps them excited about their jobs. Nothing motivates someone more than when they come up with a solution to their own problem. Small individual changes have a cumulative effect in improving entire processes, and with this level of participation improvement occurs across the entire organization. No companywide quality management program can succeed without this level of total employee involvement in continuous improvement.

Employees at Dana Corporation's Spicer Driveshaft Division, North America's largest independent manufacturer of driveshafts and a 2000 Malcolm Baldrige National Quality Award winner, participate in a kaizen-type program. On average, each employee submits three suggestions for improvements per month and almost 80 percent of these ideas are implemented. The company also makes use of kaizen "blitzes" in which teams brainstorm, identify, and implement ideas for improvement, sometimes as often as every three or four weeks. Companywide, Dana Corporation employees implemented almost 2 million ideas in one year alone.

Quality Circles

Quality circle A group of workers and supervisors from the same area who address quality problems.

One of the first team-based approaches to quality improvement was quality circles. Called quality-control circles in Japan when they originated during the 1960s, they were introduced in the United States in the 1970s, and they are still used today. A **quality circle** is a small, voluntary group of employees and their supervisor(s), comprising a team of about 8 to 10 members from the same work area or department. The supervisor is typically the circle moderator, promoting group discussion but not directing the group or making decisions; decisions result from group consensus. A circle meets about once a week during company time in a room designated especially for that purpose, where the team works on problems and projects of their own choice. These problems may not always relate to quality issues; instead, they focus on productivity, costs, safety, or other work-related issues in the circle's area. Quality circles follow an established procedure for identifying, analyzing, and solving quality-related (or other) problems. Figure 2.9 is a graphical representation of the quality circle process.

FIGURE 2.9 The Quality Circle Process

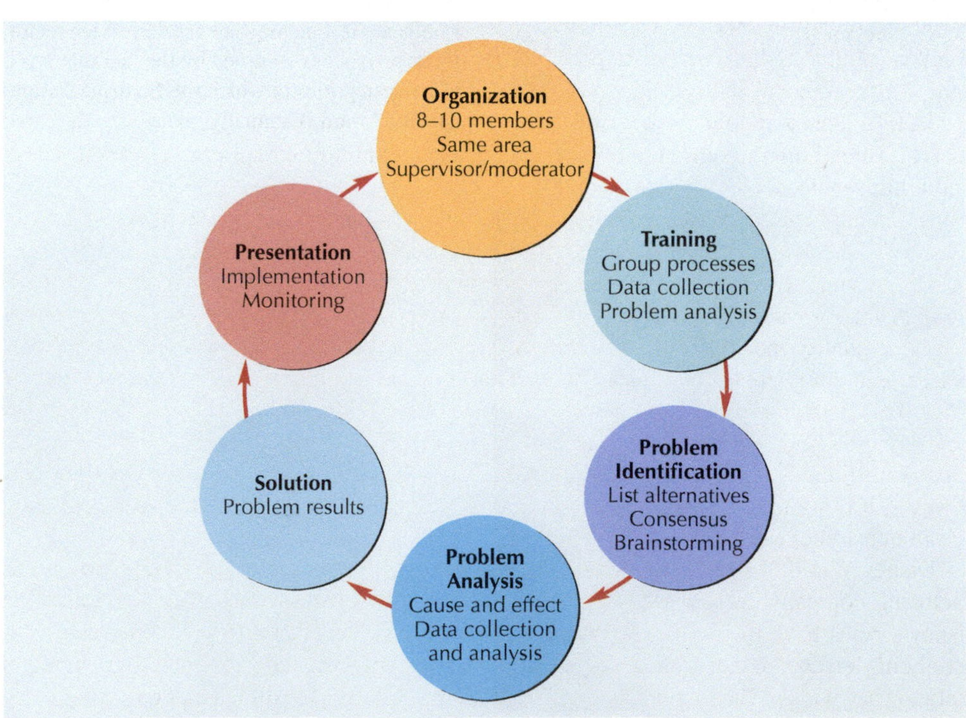

Process Improvement Teams

Process improvement teams, also called quality improvement teams (QIT), focus attention on business processes rather than separate company functions. It was noted previously that quality circles are generally comprised of employees and supervisors from the same work area or department, whereas process improvement teams tend to be cross-functional or even cross-business between suppliers and their customers. A process improvement team would include members from the various interrelated functions or departments that constitute a process. For example, a process improvement team for customer service might include members from distribution, packaging, manufacturing, and human resources. A key objective of a process improvement team is to understand the process the team is addressing in terms of how all the parts (functions and departments) work together. The process is then measured and evaluated, with the goal of improving the process to make it more efficient and the product or service better. A key tool in helping the team understand how the process works is a *process flowchart*, a quality tool we discussed in greater detail in the section on "Quality Tools."

Quality in Services

From our discussion so far it is clear that most quality management approaches evolved in manufacturing companies like Toyota, GE, and Motorola. However, toward the end of the last century service companies began to embrace quality management. This was important because the service sector is the largest segment of the U.S. economy, employing almost three times as many people as manufacturing industries.

Service organizations and manufacturing companies both convert inputs into outputs—products or services—through a productive process. Both manufacturing and services use the same kinds of inputs—resources such as physical facilities, capital, materials, equipment, and people. In some instances the processes and products are similar. For example, both Toyota and McDonald's produce a tangible, physical product (cars and hamburgers) assembled from component parts. However, in pure service industries such as law, hotels, entertainment, communication, engineering, education, clubs, real estate, banks, retail, healthcare (see photo), and airlines, the processes are less similar and the products are not as tangible. The "products" provided by these organizations are not typically a physical item that can be held or stored. The customer of a manufacturer tends to interact only at the output end of the production process. The customer of a service often interacts directly with the production process, consuming services like legal advice, a classroom lecture, or an airline flight as they are being produced. Services tend to be customized and provided at the convenience of the customer; for example, doctors prescribe individually to patients. In addition, services tend to be labor intensive, while manufacturing is more capital-intensive. Thus, human contact and its ramifications are an important part of the process of producing services.

If a manufactured item is defective, the defect can usually be felt or seen, and counted or measured. The improvement (or deterioration) in a product's quality can likewise be measured. It's not the same for service. A service cannot be held, felt, stored, and used again. A service output is not always tangible; thus, it is not as easy to measure service defects. The dimensions of service quality include timeliness, courtesy, consistency, accuracy, convenience, responsiveness, and completeness—all hard to measure beyond a subjective assessment by the customer. This does not mean that the potential for quality improvement is any less in services. Each day thousands of travelers check into and out of Ritz-Carlton Hotels, UPS handles and delivers millions of packages, and Visa processes millions of credit transactions worldwide. However, it is sometimes more difficult to assess defects in service and thus more difficult to measure customer satisfaction.

Disney World, for example, has had to develop a "different" view of quality from a manufacturing company. In some ways, a theme park is similar to an assembly line except that Disney's rides have to work flawlessly all the time. However, the Disney experience is not just about defect-free rides. It is also about customer emotions and expectations, which are likely to vary widely. Customers have different tolerance levels for things that go wrong. When there is a long line at a ride, the issue is not just the length of the wait, but how a customer feels about waiting. Disney addresses this problem by being innovative; costumed characters entertain customers waiting in line.

Quality Attributes in Services

Timeliness, or how quickly a service is provided, is an important dimension of service quality, and it is not difficult to measure. The difficulty is determining what is "quick" service and what is "slow" service. How long must a caller wait to place a phone catalog order before it is considered poor service? The answer, to a large extent, depends on the caller's expectations: "too long" is not the same for everyone. Varying expectations make it difficult to determine an exact specification.

Quality management in services must focus also on employee performance related to intangible, difficult-to-measure quality dimensions. The most important quality dimensions may be how correctly and pleasantly employees are able to provide service. That is why service companies such as Federal Express, Starbucks, Avis, Disney, and Ritz-Carlton Hotels have well-developed quality management programs that focus on employee performance, behavior,

Along the Supply Chain

Two-Time Baldrige National Quality Award Winner, Ritz-Carlton Hotels

The Ritz-Carlton Hotel Company is one of only two two-time recipients of the Malcolm Baldrige National Quality Award, having won in 1992 and 1999, and the only hotel company ever to receive the award. An independently operated division of Marriott International, Inc., it manages 87 luxury hotels in 29 countries around the world.

The Ritz-Carlton's commitment to its total quality management program comes from the top down; approximately a quarter of each senior executive's time is devoted to quality-related matters, and top executives and the senior quality-management team meet weekly to review quality measures and guest satisfaction. The hotel motto, "We are ladies and gentlemen, serving ladies and gentlemen," and its three service steps—a warm and sincere greeting using the guest's name, anticipation of and fulfillment of each guest's needs, and a fond farewell and warm goodbye using the guest's name—reflect the company's commitment to guest satisfaction through its employees.

Ritz-Carlton (shown in photo) is recognized as an industry and corporate leader in employee training. Employees are carefully selected; for every employee selected ten others applied. New employees attend a two-day corporate orientation that's followed by extensive training that results in job certification. In their first year employees receive an average of 300 hours of training, and 100 hours of training every year thereafter. The company spends around 10% of its total payroll expenses on training. Training is reinforced by routine skills testing for more than 75% of its employees, and each hotel has a daily lineup at which employees reaffirm their commitment to quality.

To help it meet its goal of total elimination of problems and defects, the Ritz-Carlton gathers and tracks data on a daily basis for quality-related parameters such as annual guest-room preventive maintenance cycles, percentage of check-ins with no wait lines, time spent to achieve industry best clean-room appearance, and time to service an occupied guest room. To cultivate customer loyalty Ritz-Carlton uses a companywide, cross-functional guest recognition database called "Mystique;" a tool created to meet and anticipate returning customers' preferences and requirements. Information gathered during various types of customer contacts, such as check-in requests, responses to service requests by overnight guests, or post-event reviews with meeting planners, are systematically entered into the database, which holds over a million files. A system called CARE (Clean and Repair Everything) that coordinates housekeeping with the preventive maintenance schedule ensures that all guestrooms are guaranteed to be defect-free every 90 days, the most defect-free guestrooms in the industry. Daily quality reports derived from data submitted from each of 720 hotel working areas help to identify problems before a guest does. Employees armed with quality processes and tools ranging from nine-step quality improvement teams to guest surveys examine every hotel process. To ensure that guests' problems are resolved quickly, employees are required to act immediately. Any employee can spend up to $2000 and demand assistance from other employees to immediately correct a guest's problem or respond to a complaint, and a manager can spend an additional $5,000.

The Ritz-Carlton Company has became known for its influence on service in a wide range of industries, through the creation of The Ritz-Carlton Learning Institute and The Ritz-Carlton Leadership Center, where nearly 50,000 executives from other companies worldwide have come to learn, and be trained in, the Ritz-Carlton principles of quality service.

In independent customer surveys, between 92% and 97% of guests leave the hotel with a positive impression, and 99% said they were satisfied with their overall Ritz-Carlton experience, compared with under 70% for their nearest luxury hotel competitor. As a result, hotel revenue per available room (the industry's measure of market share) has exceeded the industry average by more than 300%.

The Ritz-Carlton is an expensive luxury hotel chain. Do you think this enables it to have an approach to quality that less-expensive, economy-class hotel chains cannot afford? Is revenue a factor in implementing a successful QMS, or is it a result?

Source: National Quality Program at the National Institute of Standards and Technology, http://www.nist.gov/baldrige/.

AFP PHOTO/TOSHIFUMI KITAMURA/NewsCom

The "Ladies and Gentlemen of the Ritz-Carlton" are the key factor in Ritz-Carlton's receipt of two Malcolm Baldrige National Quality Awards and the highest guest satisfaction level in the luxury hotel industry.

and training, and serve as "**benchmarks**" for other companies. Service companies lose more customers because either their service is poor or their competitor's is better, than for any other reason, including price.

Benchmark "Best" level of quality achievement in one company that other companies seek to achieve.

McDonald's has a reputation for high-quality service resulting from its application of established quality management principles. It provides fresh food promptly on demand. Restaurant managers meet with customer groups on a regular basis and use questionnaires to identify quality "defects" in its operation. It monitors all phases of its process continuously from purchasing to restrooms to restaurant decor and maintenance. It empowers all employees to make spot decisions to dispose of unfresh food or to speed service. The McDonald's workforce is flexible so that changes in customer traffic and demand can be met promptly by moving employees to different tasks. Food is sampled regularly for taste and freshness. Extensive use is made of information technology for scheduling, cash register operation, food inventory, cooking procedures, and food assembly processes—all with the objective of faster service. All of these quality improvement procedures are standard and similar to approaches to quality improvement that could be found in a manufacturing firm.

Six Sigma

Six Sigma was first developed at Motorola, and they and other companies have had a great deal of success with it as reported in the "Along the Supply Chain" boxes. A number of companies have credited Six Sigma with billions of dollars in cost savings and increased profits, and these reported successes have led many other large and small companies to adopt all or some of the Six Sigma methodology. As a result Six Sigma is currently one of the most popular quality management systems in the world.

Basically, Six Sigma is a project-oriented methodology (or system) that provides businesses with the tools and expertise to improve their processes. This increase in performance through a decrease in process variation leads to defect reduction (to near zero) and an increase in product and service quality and increased profits. In its simplest form, Six Sigma is based on Deming's PDCA cycle and Joseph Juran's assertion that "all quality improvement occurs on a project-by-project" basis, with elements of kaizen-type employee involvement. In this section we will provide a more detailed description of the elements and components of Six Sigma. Figure 2.10 illustrates the primary elements of a Six Sigma program.

FIGURE 2.10 The Six Sigma DMAIC Approach

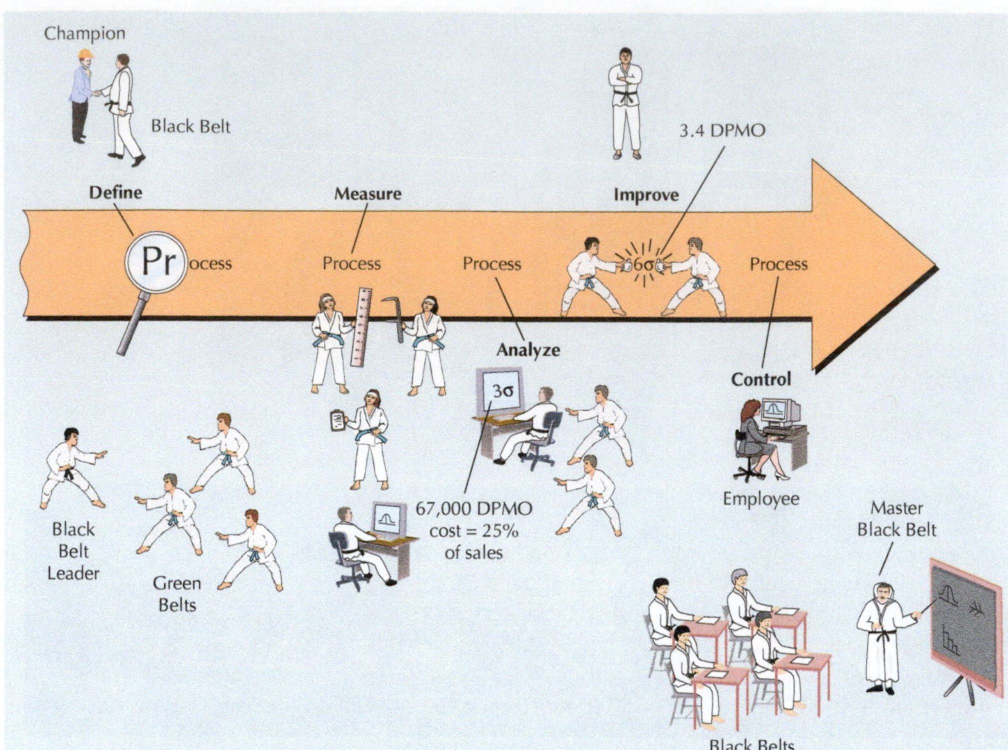

The Six Sigma Goal—3.4 DPMO

Six Sigma Measure of how much a process deviates from perfection.

Six Sigma is a process for developing and delivering virtually perfect products and services. The word "sigma" is a familiar statistical term for the standard deviation, a measure of variability around the mean of a normal distribution. In Six Sigma it is a measure of how much a given product or process deviates from perfection, or zero defects. The main idea behind Six Sigma is that if the number of "defects" in a process can be measured, then it can be systematically determined how to eliminate them and get as close to zero defects as possible. In Six Sigma "as close to zero defects as possible" translates into a statistically based numerical goal of *3.4 defects per million opportunities* (DPMO), which is the near elimination of defects from a process, product, or service. This is a goal far beyond the quality level at which most companies have traditionally operated. Through the reduction of variation in all processes (i.e., achieving the Six Sigma goal), the overall performance of the company will be improved and significant overall cost savings will be realized.

The Six Sigma Process

As implemented by Motorola, Six Sigma follows four basic steps—*align*, *mobilize*, *accelerate*, and *govern*. In the first step, "align," senior executives create a *balanced scorecard* (see Chapter 1) of strategic goals, metrics, and initiatives to identify the areas of improvement that will have the greatest impact on the company's bottom line. Process owners (i.e, the senior executives who supervise the processes) "champion" the creation of high-impact improvement projects that will achieve the strategic goals.

In the second step, "mobilize," project teams are formed and empowered to act. The process owners select "Black Belts" to lead well-defined improvement projects. The teams follow a step-by-step, problem-solving approach referred to as *DMAIC*.

In the third step, "accelerate," improvement teams made up of Black Belt and Green Belt team members with appropriate expertise use an action-learning approach to build their capability and execute the project. This approach combines training and education with project work and coaching. Ongoing reviews with project champions ensure that projects progress according to an aggressive timeline.

Along the Supply Chain

Motorola's Six Sigma Quality

Motorola began in the late 1920s as a small manufacturer of car radios (hence the name *Motorola*). It has grown to a $30 billion corporation with more than 68,000 employees at 320 facilities in 73 countries around the world, manufacturing such products as semiconductors, integrated circuits, paging systems, cellular telephones, computers, and wireless communications systems. Motorola was an engineering-oriented company that focused on product development to create new markets. In the mid-1970s it changed its focus from products to customers, with an objective of total customer satisfaction. Motorola is now recognized as having one of the best quality management systems in the world. In 1988 it was among the first group of winners of the prestigious Malcolm Baldrige National Quality Award and in 2002 it was one of very few companies to win the Baldrige Award a second time.

In 1986 it invented Six Sigma and in 1987 Motorola announced its goal of "Six Sigma" quality. This goal effectively changed the focus of quality in the United States, where quality levels had traditionally been measured in terms of percentages or parts per hundred. Motorola's Six Sigma has since become a benchmark standard that many other companies have adopted. Six Sigma has evolved from a metric (or standard) achieved through the application of various methodologies into a complete quality management system (QMS). GE, Ford, Coors, Boeing, Xerox, Bank of America, Honeywell, Kraft Foods, Intel, Microsoft, NASA, Dannon, UPS, Sony, and Texaco are just a few of the companies that have adopted Six Sigma as their quality management system. Motorola has reported over $17 billion in savings with Six Sigma. The companies that have adopted Six Sigma see it as the basis for a "best-in-class" philosophy and a long-term business strategy to achieve overall business improvement. The fundamental objective of Six Sigma is to focus on improvement in key processes and transactions within a company. In this way, waste and cost are driven out as quality and processes improve, and customer satisfaction and loyalty, and thus profits, are increased through continuous business improvement.

All of the companies cited above are large, well-known, national or international firms. What do you think some of the obstacles might be for a smaller company to implement a Six Sigma program? Are certain features and components of Six Sigma more applicable than others to a small company?

In the final step, "govern," executive process owners monitor and review the status of improvement projects to make sure the system is functioning as expected. Leaders share the knowledge gained from the improvement projects with other parts of the organization to maximize benefit.

In the next few sections we describe some components of the Six Sigma process in greater detail.

Improvement Projects

The first step in the Six Sigma process is the identification of improvement projects. These projects are selected according to business objectives and the goals of the company. As such, they normally have a significant financial impact. These projects are not one-time, unique activities as projects are typically thought of, but team-based activities directed at the continuing improvement of a process.

Once projects are identified, they are assigned a **champion** from upper management who is responsible for project success, providing resources and overcoming organizational barriers. Champions are typically paid a bonus tied to the successful achievement of Six Sigma goals.

Champion An executive responsible for project success.

The Breakthrough Strategy: DMAIC

At the heart of Six Sigma is the **breakthrough strategy**, a five-step process applied to improvement projects. The five steps in the breakthrough strategy are very similar to Deming's four-stage PDCA cycle (Figure 2.2), although more specific and detailed. The breakthrough strategy steps are *define, measure, analyze, improve*, and *control* (DMAIC), shown in Figure 2.10.

Breakthrough strategy Define, measure, analyze, improve, control.

Define: The problem is defined, including who the customers are and what they want, to determine what needs to improve. It is important to know which quality attributes are most important to the customer, what the defects are, and what the improved process can deliver.

Measure: The process is measured; data are collected and compared to the desired state.

Analyze: The data are analyzed in order to determine the cause of the problem.

Improve: The team brainstorms to develop solutions to problems; changes are made to the process, and the results are measured to see if the problems have been eliminated. If not, more changes may be necessary.

Along the Supply Chain

Six Sigma Highlights

- A Six Sigma team at North Carolina Baptist Hospital reduced the time for getting heart attack patients from the emergency room into the cardiac catheterization lab for treatment by an average of 41 minutes.
- A Bechtel project team working on the Channel Tunnel Rail Link in the United Kingdom used Six Sigma to save hundreds of hours on different tunneling jobs.
- A Six Sigma project for truck modification at Volvo's North American Truck Division resulted in cost savings of over $1 million; other projects improved forecasting processes and reduced fuel tank replacement down time.
- A Six Sigma team at Ford fixed a body-side molding problem and the resulting process improvements saved $100,000 annually in waste elimination and eliminated customer complaints about the body-side molding lifting off of the car.
- A Six Sigma project at HSBC Securities (USA) to improve the bottom line performance of its U.S. futures business increased net income from $1.9 million to $7.1 million, a 274% increase, with a 10% reduction in staff.
- Since implementing Six Sigma in 1999, Ford experienced a 27% decrease in warranty spending in a two-year period and credits Six Sigma with savings of over $2 billion.
- A six sigma project in Denver for its E-470 toll road reduced deer kills by 56%, preventing accidents and saving wildlife.
- Royal Mail, one of the United Kingdom's largest employers with over 196,000 employees, used Six Sigma for one project to centralize a key process and halved the process workforce from 450 to 220.
- Since implementing Six Sigma on a corporatewide basis in 1997, Citibank has seen five- and ten-time defect reductions; examples include decreased response times for credit card applications and fewer errors in customer statements.
- Houston's Memorial Hermann Hospital used Six Sigma to increase its reimbursement percentage from Medicare services, resulting in savings of $62 million, an almost 50% improvement.
- Six Sigma projects at Bank of America saved the company in excess of $2 billion in 2005 and over $1 billion in 2009; the company completes thousands of Six Sigma projects each year.
- A Six Sigma project at Telefonica (Argentina) to eliminate broadband Internet outages saved the company $400,000 annually and won the Gold Award at ASQ International Team Excellence Award competition.
- A Six Sigma continuous improvement model at Honeywell Federal Manufacturing & Technologies resulted in annual savings from increased productivity and innovations of $27 million, a 20 percent improvement in energy conservation, and $65 million in supply chain savings, and won the company the 2009 Baldrige Award.

CONTROL: If the process is operating at the desired level of performance, it is monitored to make sure the improvement is sustained and no unexpected and undesirable changes occur.

Black Belts and Green Belts

Black Belt The project leader.

The project leader who implements the DMAIC steps is called a **Black Belt**. Black Belts hold full-time positions and are extensively trained in the use of statistics and quality-control tools, as well as project and team management. A Black Belt assignment normally lasts two years during which the Black Belt will lead 8 to 12 projects from different areas in the company, each lasting about one quarter. A Black Belt is certified after two successful projects. Black Belts are typically very focused change agents who are on the fast track to company advancement. Figure 2.11 describes some of the most important tools used by Black Belts at Motorola.

Master Black Belt A teacher and mentor for Black Belts.

Master Black Belts monitor, review, and mentor Black Belts across all projects. They are primarily teachers who are selected based on their quantitative skills, and on their teaching and mentoring ability. As such, they are a resource for project teams and Black Belts. They also hold full-time positions and are usually certified after participating in about 20 successful projects, half while a Black Belt and half as a Master Black Belt.

Green Belts Project team members.

Project team members are **Green Belts**, which is not a full-time position; they do not spend all of their time on projects. Green Belts receive similar training to Black Belts but somewhat less of it.

At General Electric employees are not considered for promotion to any management position without Black Belt or Green Belt training. It is part of the Six Sigma overall strategy that as Black Belts and Green Belts move into management positions they will continue to promote and advance Six Sigma in the company. A generally held perception is that companies that have successfully implemented Six Sigma have one Black Belt for every 100 employees and one Master Black Belt for every 100 Black Belts. This will vary according to the size of the company and the number of projects regularly undertaken. At GE, Black Belt projects typically save $250,000 or more and Green Belt projects frequently yield savings in the $50,000 to $75,000 range.

Quality Function Deployment (QFD)

Developed by the Japanese and first used in the United States by the auto industry in 1983, QFD is a system and set of procedures for understanding customer needs, what "value" means to a customer, and how customers are satisfied, and then translating that information into the design and development process for a product or service. Six Sigma teams use QFD to focus on what means most to the customer. (QFD is described in detail in Chapter 4, "Product Design.)"

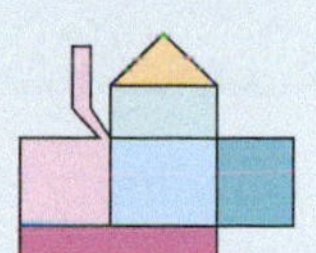

Cause and Effect (C&E) Matrix

The C&E Matrix is primarily used in the "measure" step of the five-step DMAIC process. It helps Six Sigma teams working on an improvement project to identify and prioritize causes of a problem found in a process. It is described in more detail earlier in this chapter.

	Output (y)			
Input (x)				Score
1	10	5		50
2	8		8	30
3		9	7	40

Failure Modes and Effects Analysis (FMEA)

FMEA is a tool for analyzing potential reliability problems and weaknesses in a product or process during the development stage, before they actually occur, when they are easier to fix. Six Sigma teams use FMEA to identify how new products, processes, or services might fail and then identify actions to prevent the failures. There are different types of FMEAs for systems, design, process, service, and software. FMEA is also discussed in Chapter 4, "Product Design."

Failure Mode	Cause	Effect	Action

t-Test

The t-test is a statistical measure used to determine if there is a statistical (and not a random) difference in the means between two groups of data. It is used in Six Sigma to validate test results from small sample sizes. It was first developed at the Guinness brewery to help select the best barley for Guinness beer.

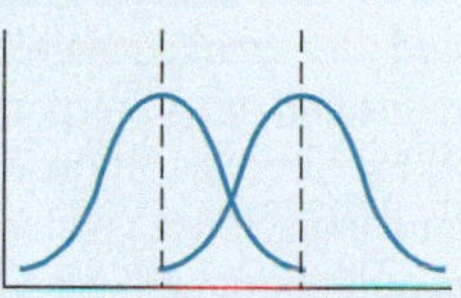

Statistical Process Control (SPC) Chart

SPC charts are used to monitor a process over time to determine if any variation in the process is the result of a cause or problem. They are constructed with a centerline representing an average, and lines above and below the centerline representing statistical upper and lower control limits. The SPC chart is one of the key tools for monitoring and improving quality specifically identified by Deming and the other quality gurus. A more detailed discussion of SPC charts is presented in this chapter and it is the subject of Chapter 3 on "Statistical Process Control."

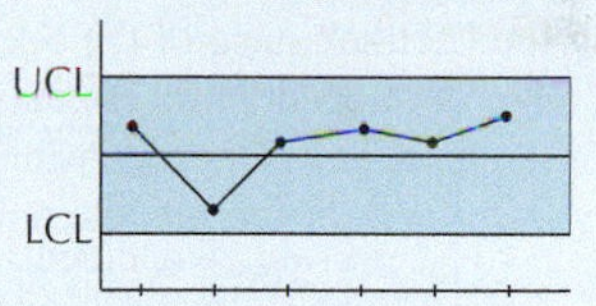

Design of Experiments (DOE)

A statistical technique that is used in Six Sigma to collect, analyze and interpret data. A DOE is a structured, organized method for determining the relationship between factors (Xs) affecting a process and the output of that process (Y). In this method one or more input variables are controlled at two or more levels to determine if and how one or more output variables change.

Main Effects	Level 1	Level 2
A	10	20
B	30	50
C		
D		
E		

Source: Motorola University, "Six Tools Every Six Sigma Black Belt Loves," http//mu.motorola.com/six_sigma_lessons/(2004).

FIGURE 2.11 Six Sigma Tools

In Six Sigma all employees receive training in the Six Sigma breakthrough strategy, statistical tools, and quality-improvement techniques. Employees are trained to participate in Six Sigma project teams. Because quality is considered to be the responsibility of every employee, every employee must be involved in, motivated by, and knowledgeable about Six Sigma.

Design for Six Sigma

An important element of the Six Sigma system is **Design for Six Sigma (DFSS)**, a systematic project methodology for designing products and processes that meet customer expectations and can be produced at Six Sigma quality levels. Also known as **DMADV**, it follows the same basic five-step approach as the DMAIC breakthrough strategy with Master Black Belts, Black Belts, and Green Belts, and makes extensive use of statistical tools and design techniques, training, and measurement. The five DMADV steps are *define* design goals consistent with customer demand; *measure* and identify characteristics that are "critical to quality" (CTQs), product capabilities, process capabilities, and risks: *analyze* design alternatives and select the best design; *design* details and optimize the design; and *verify* the design and implement the production process. However, it employs this strategy earlier, up front in the design phase and developmental stages. This is a more effective and less expensive way to achieve the Six Sigma goal than fixing problems after the product or process is already developed and in place.

Design for Six Sigma (DFSS) A systematic approach to designing products and processes that will achieve Six Sigma.

DMADV Define, measure, analyze, design, and verify.

Along the Supply Chain

North Shore University Hospital: A Six Sigma Project Example

North Shore University Hospital in Manhasset, New York, is part of the North Shore-Long Island Jewish Health System, the third largest nonsectarian health system in the United States with 14 hospitals. The hospital used Six Sigma on a project to reduce delays in bed assignment turnaround time. The problem analysis showed that delays in the post-anesthesia care unit and the emergency department resulted in the hospital not always having the staff or beds available to accept additional patients, which resulted in delays in start times in the operating room and a decrease in patient and physician satisfaction. It was subsequently realized that staff were incorrectly using the bed tracking system (BTS), the electronic system that indicates the status of each bed. Delays in bed turnaround time resulted in delayed notification of a ready bed to the RN (registered nurse) responsible for the patient admission process. This led to delays in the operating room and emergency department and impacted the patient flow throughout the hospital. The bed turnaround time project focused on one surgical nursing unit that had 2578 discharged patients in one year.

During the "define" stage of the Six Sigma DMAIC process the project team developed a process map of the steps in the discharge–admission process. The admissions RNs were identified as the primary customers of the process and they were surveyed to establish process targets. These "voice of the customer (VoC)" responses helped establish a target turnaround time of 120 minutes with an upper limit of 150 minutes. In the "measure" stage of DMAIC a defect was defined as any time the turnaround time exceeded 150 minutes. The team measured the process by having a team member on the surgical unit monitor the process for one week, which yielded data on 195 patients. Based on the data (which showed 130 defects), the team calculated a DPMO of 672,725, which translated to a score of 1 sigma. The average turnaround time was 226 minutes. The team then developed a cause and effect diagram to help identify all the variables that affected the turnaround time.

During the "analyze" step of the DMAIC process the variables that impacted the turnaround time process were discussed, targeted for statistical analysis, and prioritized. The team investigations at this stage showed that a communication failure and a technical failure at two key steps in the process caused significant delays. The team realized that the staff lacked proficiency in the use of the BTS. The lack of communication between the admission RNs and other patient care team members was identified as a priority, as was the lack of timely notification of a ready bed to the admission RN. Several solutions were developed to resolve these problems, including staff training and the use of improved documentation about discharge patients, laminated bedside cards, and reformatted beepers for RNs to accelerate the process. In the "improve" step, the turnaround time was reduced from a mean of 226 minutes to 90 minutes, which resulted in a metric of 2.3 sigma by the time the project ended. In the "control" step moving range and SPC charts were used to monitor turnaround times, and the turnaround time continued to improve to 69 minutes.

The results of this project were subsequently applied to all nursing units in the hospital. Patient satisfaction scores improved in two categories related to readiness for discharge and speed of the discharge process. Since initiating its Six Sigma program, the health system has completed over 60 Six Sigma projects and trained 24 Black Belts, 70 Green Belts, and two master Black Belts.

Identify a process in a hospital, restaurant, school, or other service that you think might be improved by the Six Sigma DMAIC process, and discuss how you would apply it, including the specific DMAIC stages.

Source: A. Pellicone and M. Martocci, "Faster Turnaround Time," *Quality Progress* 39 (3: March 2006), pp. 31–36.

Lean Six Sigma

Lean Six Sigma Integrating Six Sigma and lean systems.

A recent trend in quality management is **Lean Six Sigma** (also known as Lean Sigma), which integrates Six Sigma and "lean systems." Lean systems are the subject of Chapter 16 so we do not offer a detailed presentation of it at this point; rather we will discuss lean systems in general terms and how they relate to Six Sigma.

Lean is a systematic method for reducing the complexity of a process and making it more efficient by identifying and eliminating sources of waste in a process (such as materials, labor, and time) that hinder flow. Lean basically seeks to optimize process flows through the organization in order to create more value for the customer with less work; i.e., get the product through the process faster. The lean process management philosophy was derived mainly from the Toyota Production System (including push and pull production, JIT, and kanbans; see Chapter 16) that has been very effective in manufacturing. As in the case of TPS, lean is basically a more sophisticated extension of earlier efforts to achieve efficiency (i.e., speed) in a manufacturing process by OM pioneers like Henry Ford and Frederick R. Taylor.

The lean approach to process improvement includes five steps. First it is determined what creates value for the customer, i.e., quality from the customer's perspective discussed earlier in this chapter. Second, the sequence of activities (in the process) that create value, called the "value stream," is identified, and those activities that do not add value are eliminated from the production process. Third, waste (such as inventory or long process times) along the value stream is removed through process improvements. Fourth, the process is made responsive to the customer's needs; i.e., making the product or service available when the customer needs it.

Along the Supply Chain

Six Sigma Success at Telefonica Group

Telefonica Group, headquartered in Spain, is the world's third largest telecommunications company, providing cell phone and landline communications, broadband, and paid TV services in Europe, the United States, and Latin America. Worldwide it has over 265 million customers, three-quarters of whom are cell phone users. Telefonica's Argentine mobile cell phone communication subsidiary, Movistar, with 16 million customers and 4000 employees, has been a company leader in quality deployment throughout Telefonica. Movistar first deployed Six Sigma and lean philosophy in 2002 and through 2011 had undertaken more than 200 improvement projects with goals of cost reduction, productivity improvement, service-level increases, process redesign, and quality assurance, resulting in cumulative savings of $245 million. In this same period over 165 Champions, 200 Black Belts, and over 900 Green Belts have been trained. Projects are developed according to three key practices—an improvement community, workshops, and an inheritance stage.

The improvement community is made up of Master Black Belts and Black Belts that deliver training in quality improvement, act as facilitators in workshops, and mentor Champions, Blacks Belts, and Green Belts in the correct use of quality improvement tools, providing examples of best practices, helping with team formation, and problem solving. The improvement community facilitates workshops where projects are developed and where team members from similar process improvement projects share their experiences, analyses, and conclusions. After a project team completes the DMAIC stages, quality leaders, together with the team's Champion and Black Belt, conduct a team performance evaluation, which is followed by a one-year inheritance period. The team's best-performing Green Belt is deemed the project heir whose responsibility it is to make sure the "improve" and "control" actions of the DMAIC are correctly implemented.

The success of the Movistar quality improvement program using Six Sigma has resulted in Telefonica replicating it throughout its organization, and joining with key suppliers in training and quality project ventures.

Search the Internet and identify another global company that has successfully implemented Six Sigma and discuss its experiences.

Source: Based on Matias G. Thompson and Veronica Rosano, "A Decade of Distinction," *Quality Progress* 44 (11); (November 2011), pp. 30–35.

Finally, lean continually repeats the attempt to remove waste (nonvalue activity) and improve flow; it seeks perfection. As such, lean is more of a philosophical approach to continuous improvement by eliminating waste throughout the organization everywhere along the value stream by involving everyone in the organization.

Lean Six Sigma attempts to combine the best features of lean and Six Sigma. As we have discussed, Six Sigma is a disciplined and very organized approach for improving processes and preventing defects. It employs a specific program (DMAIC) to identify and eliminate waste and achieve perfection (no defects). By focusing on reducing and controlling variation in targeted processes in an organization (via projects), Six Sigma improves the organization's performance. Through process improvement methods lean attempts to eliminate waste and accelerate process efficiency and flow times, thus increasing value to the customer. Lean improvements cause products to flow through processes faster while Six Sigma improves quality and prevents defects by reducing variation through individual projects. Six Sigma identifies the key factors in the performance of a process and sets them at their best level. Lean reduces the complexity of processes everywhere by eliminating waste that can slow down process flow. Lean focuses on what should not be done in a process and removes it; Six Sigma considers what should be done and how to get it right for all time.

The common link between the two is that they both seek to improve processes and provide value to the customer; however, they go about it in different ways. The proponents of Lean Six Sigma believe the two approaches complement each other, and that combining them can result in greater benefits than implementing them separately. However, others consider lean and Six Sigma to be mostly incompatible; Six Sigma is considered to be more of a management tool (i.e., a program), whereas lean is a philosophical approach to process improvement that, like the Toyota Production System, is most effective in a mass manufacturing setting.

The Bottom Line—Profitability

The criterion for selecting Six Sigma projects by executives is typically based on the financial impact of the improvement expected from the project—how it will affect the bottom line. This focus on profitability for initiating quality improvement projects is one of the factors that distinguishes Six Sigma from TQM.

In *Quality Is Free*, Philip Crosby states that, "Quality is not only free, it is an honest-to-everything profit maker." Gary L. Tooker, former CEO and vice chairman of Motorola, in response to the question, "Is there a link between quality and profitability?" responded that "We've saved several billion dollars over the last year because of our focus on quality improvement and the Six Sigma initiative . . . . there is no doubt about the fact that it has enhanced our bottom line."

This is only the tip of a mountain of conclusive evidence that quality improvement and profitability are closely related. As quality improves, the costs associated with poor quality decline. Quality improvements result in increased productivity. As the quality of a company's products or services improve, it becomes more competitive and its market share increases. Customers' perception of a company's products as being of high quality and its competitive posture enables the company to charge higher prices. Taken together, these things result in higher profitability.

Example 2.1 describes a scenario illustrating the impact of profitability that can result from a Six Sigma project.

EXAMPLE 2.1 | The Impact of Six Sigma on Profit

The Medtek Company produces parts for an electronic bed tracking system (BTS) it sells to medical suppliers and hospitals. It contracted for and sold 1000 units of one of its products during the past quarter for $1000 each resulting in total sales of $1,000,000. During the quarter the company incurred variable costs (e.g., direct labor, materials, and energy) of $600,000, so that the unit variable cost was $600. The company also incurred fixed costs of $350,000 (for items such as plant and equipment, and management salaries) during the quarter. This resulted in a (before-tax) profit of $50,000, as shown in the following income statement:

Sales	$1,000,000
Variable costs	600,000
Fixed costs	350,000
Profit	$50,000

However, now let's consider another factor—the company currently operates with a 10% defects rate and the defective products cannot be reworked. Since the company sold 1000 products it actually had to produce 1111 units (i.e., 1,000/0.90 = 1111), or 111 extra units to compensate for the scrapped units. The variable cost includes this cost of making scrap so the unit variable cost is really $540.05 (i.e., $600,000/1111 = $540.05). The company has paid a "quality tax" (sometimes called the "hidden factory") of $59,946 (i.e., 111 scrap units × $540.05 per unit = $59,946).

Now let's assume that the company implements a successful Six Sigma improvement project and it achieves a defect level of 3.4 DPMO, or virtually zero defects. The elimination of defects will (at a minimum) erase the variable costs consumed by making those 111 scrap units. The effect of the elimination of this "quality tax" is shown in the following revised income statement:

Sales	$1,000,000
Variable costs	540,054
Fixed costs	350,000
Profit	$109,946

The company's profit has more than doubled! An approximate 10% reduction in variable costs because of Six Sigma has resulted in a 120% increase in profit. And, the company has actually increased its capacity to 1111 units without spending more on plant and equipment.

Next assume that the company spent $120,000 on the Six Sigma project to eliminate defects. If the project was completed in one quarter and the company expects to benefit from the project for 3 years, or 12 quarters, the company should add $10,000 to fixed costs on its income statement:

Sales	$1,000,000
Variable costs	540,054
Fixed costs	360,000
Profit	$99,946

The increase in profit is $49,946 (i.e., $99,946 − 50,000 = $49,946), which is still almost double the profit before Six Sigma. Ignoring interest rates, this represents a 41.6% return per quarter on the company's investment in the Six Sigma project:

$$\text{Return} = \frac{100(49{,}946)}{120{,}000}$$
$$= 41.6\%$$

Source: S. Bisgaard and J. Freiesleben, "Six Sigma and the Bottom Line," *Quality Progress* 39 (9: September 2004), pp. 57–62.

Quality Costs and Productivity

According to legendary quality guru Armand Feigenbaum, "Quality costs are the foundation for quality systems economics." Quality costs have traditionally served as the basis for evaluating investments in quality programs. The costs of quality are those incurred to achieve good quality and to satisfy the customer, as well as costs incurred when quality fails to satisfy the customer. Thus, quality costs fall into two categories: the cost of achieving good quality, also known as the *cost of quality assurance*, and the cost associated with poor-quality products, also referred to as the *cost of not conforming* to specifications.

Two recent trends are driving a renewed interest within organizations for measuring quality costs. First, the most recent version of ISO 9000 emphasizes measurements and requires that quality improvement be quantifiably demonstrated. Maintaining quality cost data can provide ISO auditors with evidence of improvement in an organization applying for ISO certification. Second, the popularity and proliferation of Six Sigma, which emphasizes the financial impact of projects as a measure of improvement, has created a need in organizations for quality cost data in order to determine project success.

The Cost of Achieving Good Quality

The costs of a quality management program are *prevention costs* and *appraisal costs*. **Prevention costs** are the costs of trying to prevent poor-quality products from reaching the customer. Prevention reflects the quality philosophy of "do it right the first time," the goal of a quality management program. Examples of prevention costs include:

Prevention costs Costs incurred during product design.

QUALITY PLANNING COSTS: The costs of developing and implementing the quality management program.

PRODUCT-DESIGN COSTS: The costs of designing products with quality characteristics.

PROCESS COSTS: The costs expended to make sure the productive process conforms to quality specifications.

TRAINING COSTS: The costs of developing and putting on quality training programs for employees and management.

INFORMATION COSTS: The costs of acquiring and maintaining (typically on computers) data related to quality, and the development and analysis of reports on quality performance.

Appraisal costs Costs of measuring, testing, and analyzing.

Appraisal costs are the costs of measuring, testing, and analyzing materials, parts, products, and the productive process to ensure that product-quality specifications are being met. Examples of appraisal costs include:

Inspection and testing: The costs of testing and inspecting materials, parts, and the product at various stages and at the end of the process.

Test equipment costs: The costs of maintaining equipment used in testing the quality characteristics of products.

Operator costs: The costs of the time spent by operators to gather data for testing product quality, to make equipment adjustments to maintain quality, and to stop work to assess quality.

Appraisal costs tend to be higher in a service organization than in a manufacturing company and, therefore, are a greater proportion of total quality costs. Quality in services is related primarily to the interaction between an employee and a customer, which makes the cost of appraising quality more difficult. Quality appraisal in a manufacturing operation can take place almost exclusively in-house; appraisal of service quality usually requires customer interviews, surveys, questionnaires, and the like.

The Cost of Poor Quality

The cost of poor quality (COPQ) is the difference between what it actually costs to produce a product or deliver a service and what it would cost if there were no defects. Most companies find that defects, rework, and other unnecessary activities related to quality problems significantly inflate costs; estimates range as high as 20% to 30% of total revenues. This is generally the largest quality cost category in a company, frequently accounting for 70% to 90% of total quality costs. This is also where the greatest cost improvement is possible.

Internal failure costs Include scrap, rework, process failure, downtime, and price reductions.

The cost of poor quality can be categorized as *internal failure costs* or *external failure costs*. **Internal failure costs** are incurred when poor-quality products are discovered before they are delivered to the customer. Examples of internal failure costs include:

Scrap costs: The costs of poor-quality products that must be discarded, including labor, material, and indirect costs.

Rework costs: The costs of fixing defective products to conform to quality specifications.

Process failure costs: The costs of determining why the production process is producing poor-quality products.

Process downtime costs: The costs of shutting down the productive process to fix the problem.

Price-downgrading costs: The costs of discounting poor-quality products—that is, selling products as "seconds."

External failure costs Include complaints, returns, warranty claims, liability, and lost sales.

External failure costs are incurred after the customer has received a poor-quality product and are primarily related to customer service. Examples of external failure costs include:

Customer complaint costs: The costs of investigating and satisfactorily responding to a customer complaint resulting from a poor-quality product.

Product return costs: The costs of handling and replacing poor-quality products returned by the customer. In the United States it is estimated that product returns reduce company profitability by an average of 4% annually.

Warranty claims costs: The costs of complying with product warranties.

Product liability costs: The litigation costs resulting from product liability and customer injury.

Lost sales costs: The costs incurred because customers are dissatisfied with poor-quality products and do not make additional purchases.

Internal failure costs tend to be low for a service, whereas external failure costs can be quite high. A service organization has little opportunity to examine and correct a defective internal process, usually an employee–customer interaction, before it actually happens. At that point it becomes an external failure. External failures typically result in an increase in service time or inconvenience for the customer. Examples of external failures include a customer waiting too long to place a catalog phone order; a catalog order that arrives with the wrong item, requiring the customer to repackage and send it back; an error in a charge card billing statement, requiring the customer to make phone calls or write letters to correct it; sending a customer's orders or statements to the wrong address; or an overnight mail package that does not arrive overnight.

Measuring and Reporting Quality Costs

Collecting data on quality costs can be difficult. The costs of lost sales, of responding to customer complaints, of process downtime, of operator testing, of quality information, and of quality planning and product design are all costs that may be difficult to measure. These costs must be estimated by management. Training costs, inspection and testing costs, scrap costs, the cost of product downgrading, product return costs, warranty claims, and liability costs can usually be measured. Many of these costs are collected as part of normal accounting procedures.

Management wants quality costs reported in a manner that can be easily interpreted and is meaningful. One format for reporting quality costs is with **index numbers**, or indices. Index numbers are ratios that measure quality costs relative to some base value, such as the ratio of quality costs to total sales revenue or the ratio of quality costs to units of final product. These index numbers are used to compare quality management efforts between time periods or between departments or functions. Index numbers themselves do not provide very much information about the effectiveness of a quality management program. They usually will not show directly that a company is producing good- or poor-quality products. These measures are informative only when they are compared to some standard or other index. Some common index measures are:

Index numbers Ratios that measure quality costs against a base value.

LABOR INDEX: The ratio of quality cost to direct labor hours; it has the advantage of being easily computed (from accounting records) and easily understood, but it is not always effective for long-term comparative analysis when technological advances reduce labor usage.

COST INDEX: The ratio of quality cost to manufacturing cost (direct and indirect cost); it is easy to compute from accounting records and is not affected by technological change.

SALES INDEX: The ratio of quality cost to sales; it is easily computed, but it can be distorted by changes in selling price and costs.

PRODUCTION INDEX: The ratio of quality cost to units of final product; it is easy to compute from accounting records but is not effective if a number of different products exist.

Labor index The ratio of quality cost to labor hours.

Cost index The ratio of quality cost to manufacturing cost.

Sales index The ratio of quality cost to sales.

Production index The ratio of quality cost to units of final product.

Example 2.2 illustrates several of these index numbers.

EXAMPLE 2.2 | An Evaluation of Quality Costs and Quality Index Numbers

The H&S Motor Company produces small motors (e.g., 3 hp) for use in lawnmowers and garden equipment. The company instituted a quality management program in 2013 and has recorded the following quality cost data and accounting measures for four years.

	YEAR			
	2013	2014	2015	2016
Quality Costs				
Prevention	$27,000	41,500	74,600	112,300
Appraisal	155,000	122,500	113,400	107,000
Internal failure	386,400	469,200	347,800	219,100
External failure	242,000	196,000	103,500	106,000
Total	$810,400	829,200	639,300	544,400
Accounting Measures				
Sales	$4,360,000	4,450,000	5,050,000	5,190,000
Manufacturing costs	1,760,000	1,810,000	1,880,000	1,890,000

The company wants to assess its quality management program and develop quality index numbers using sales and manufacturing cost bases for the four-year period.

Solution

The H&S Company experienced many of the typical outcomes when its quality management program was instituted. Approximately 78% of H&S's total quality costs are a result of internal and external failures, not unlike many companies. Failure costs frequently contribute 50 to 90% of overall quality costs. The typical reaction to high failure costs is to increase product monitoring and inspection to eliminate poor-quality products, resulting in high appraisal costs. This appeared to be the strategy employed by H&S when its quality management program was initiated in 2013. In 2014, H&S was able to identify more defective items, resulting in an apparent increase in internal failure costs and lower external failure costs (as fewer defective products reached the customer).

During 2013 and 2014, prevention costs were modest. However, prevention is critical in reducing both internal and external failures. By instituting quality training programs, redesigning the production process, and planning how to build in product quality, companies are able to reduce poor-quality products within the production process and prevent them from reaching the customer. This was the case at H&S, because prevention costs increased by more than 300% during the four-year period. Since fewer poor-quality products are being made, less monitoring and inspection is necessary, and appraisal costs thus decline. Internal and external failure costs are also reduced because of a reduction in defective products. In general, an increase in expenditures for prevention will result in a decrease in all other quality-cost categories. It is also not uncommon for a quality management program to isolate one or two specific quality problems that, when prevented, have a large impact on overall quality cost reduction. Quality problems are not usually evenly distributed throughout the product process; a few isolated problems tend to result in the majority of poor-quality products.

The H&S Company also desired to develop index numbers using quality costs as a proportion of sales and manufacturing costs, generally two of the more popular quality indexes. The general formula for these index numbers is

$$\text{Quality index} = \frac{\text{total quality costs}}{\text{base}}(100)$$

For example, the index number for 2013 sales is

$$\begin{aligned}\text{Quality cost per sale} &= \frac{\$810{,}400(100)}{4{,}360{,}000} \\ &= 18.58\end{aligned}$$

The quality index numbers for sales and manufacturing costs for the four-year period are given in the following table.

YEAR	QUALITY SALES INDEX	QUALITY MANUFACTURING COST INDEX
2013	18.58	46.04
2014	18.63	45.18
2015	12.66	34.00
2016	10.49	28.80

These index numbers alone provide little insight into the effectiveness of the quality management program; however, as a standard to make comparisons over time they can be useful. The H&S Company quality index numbers reflect dramatically improved quality during the four-year period. Quality costs as a proportion of both sales and manufacturing costs improved significantly. Quality index numbers do not provide information that will enable the company to diagnose and correct quality problems in the production process. They are useful in showing trends in product quality over time and reflecting the impact of product quality relative to accounting measures with which managers are usually familiar.

The Quality–Cost Relationship

In Example 2.2 we showed that when the sum of prevention and appraisal costs increased, internal and external failure costs decreased. Recall that prevention and appraisal costs are the costs of achieving good quality, and internal and external failure costs are the costs of poor quality. In general, when the cost of achieving good quality increases, the cost of poor quality declines.

Philip Crosby's fourth absolute from his 1984 book *Quality Without Tears* explains that the dollar *cost of quality* is the difference between the price of nonconformance, the cost of doing things wrong (i.e., the cost of poor quality), and the price of conformance, the cost of doing things right (i.e., the cost of achieving good quality). He estimates that the cost of doing things wrong can account for 20% to 35% of revenues, while the cost of doing things right is typically 3% to 4%. As such, managers should determine where the cost of quality is occurring and find out what causes it.

Companies committed to quality improvement know that the increase in sales and market share resulting from increased customer satisfaction offsets the costs of achieving good quality. Furthermore, as a company focuses on good quality, the cost of achieving good quality will be less because of the improvements in technologies and processes that will result from the quality improvement effort. These companies are frequently the ones that seek to achieve *zero defects*, the goal of Six Sigma.

The Japanese first recognized that the costs of poor quality had been traditionally underestimated. These costs did not take into account the customer losses that can be attributed to a reputation for poor quality. The Japanese viewed the cost associated with a reputation for poor quality to be quite high. A General Accounting Office report on companies that have been Baldrige Quality Award finalists has shown that corporate-wide quality improvement programs result in higher worker motivation, improved employee relations, increased productivity, higher customer satisfaction, and increased market share and profitability.

In the previous section we saw how an effective quality management program can help to reduce quality-related costs and improve market share and profitability. Quality management can also improve productivity—the number of units produced from available resources.

Productivity

Productivity is a measure of a company's effectiveness in converting inputs into outputs. It is broadly defined as

Productivity The ratio of output to input.

$$\text{Productivity} = \frac{\text{output}}{\text{input}}$$

An output is the final product from a service or production process, such as an automobile, a hamburger, a sale, or a catalog order. Inputs are the parts, material, labor, capital, and so on that go into the productive process. Productivity measures, depending on the outputs and inputs used, are labor productivity (output per labor-hour) and machine productivity (output per machine-hour).

Improving quality by reducing defects will increase good output and reduce inputs. In fact, virtually all aspects of quality improvement have a favorable impact on different measures of productivity. Improving product design and production processes, improving the quality of materials and parts, and improving job designs and work activity will all increase productivity.

Measuring Product Yield and Productivity

Product **yield** is a measure of output used as an indicator of productivity. It can be computed for the entire production process (or for one stage in the process) as follows:

Yield A measure of productivity.

$$\begin{aligned}\text{Yield} = {} & (\text{total input})(\%\ \text{good units}) \\ & + (\text{total input})(1 - \%\ \text{good units})(\%\ \text{reworked})\end{aligned}$$

or

$$Y = (I)(\%G) + (I)(1 - \%G)(\%R)$$

where

I = planned number of units of product started in the production process
$\%G$ = percentage of good units produced
$\%R$ = percentage of defective units that are successfully reworked

In this formula, yield is the sum of the percentage of products started in the process (or at a stage) that will turn out to be good quality plus the percentage of the defective (rejected) products that are reworked. Any increase in the percentage of good products through improved quality will increase product yield.

EXAMPLE 2.3 | Computing Product Yield

The H&S Motor Company starts production for a particular type of motor with a steel motor housing. The production process begins with 100 motors each day. The percentage of good motors produced each day averages 80% and the percentage of poor-quality motors that can be reworked is 50%. The company wants to know the daily product yield and the effect on productivity if the daily percentage of good-quality motors is increased to 90%.

Solution

$$\begin{aligned} \text{Yield} &= (I)(\%G) + (I)(1 - \%G)(\%R) \\ Y &= 100(0.80) + 100(1 - 0.80)(0.50) \\ &= 90 \text{ motors} \end{aligned}$$

If product quality is increased to 90% good motors, the yield will be

$$\begin{aligned} Y &= 100(0.90) + 100(1 - 0.90)(0.50) \\ &= 95 \text{ motors} \end{aligned}$$

A 10 percentage-point increase in quality products results in a 5.5% increase in productivity output.

Now we will expand our discussion of productivity to include product manufacturing cost. The manufacturing cost per (good) product is computed by dividing the sum of total direct manufacturing cost and total cost for all reworked units by the yield, as follows:

$$\text{Product cost} = \frac{\begin{array}{c}(\text{direct manufacturing cost per unit})(\text{input}) \\ +(\text{rework cost per unit})(\text{reworked units})\end{array}}{\text{yield}}$$

or

$$\text{Product cost} = \frac{(K_d)(I) + (K_r)(R)}{Y}$$

where

K_d = direct manufacturing cost per unit
I = input
K_r = rework cost per unit
R = reworked units
Y = yield

EXAMPLE 2.4 | Computing Product Cost per Unit

The H&S Motor Company has a direct manufacturing cost per unit of $30, and motors that are of inferior quality can be reworked for $12 per unit. From Example 2.3, 100 motors are produced daily, 80% (on average) are of good quality and 20% are defective. Of the defective motors, half can be reworked to yield good-quality products. Through its quality management program, the company has discovered a problem in its production process that, when corrected (at a minimum cost), will increase the good-quality products to 90%. The company wants to assess the impact on the direct cost per unit of improvement in product quality.

Solution

The original manufacturing cost per motor is

$$\text{Product cost} = \frac{(K_d)(I) + (K_r)(R)}{Y}$$

$$\text{Product cost} = \frac{(\$30)(100) + (\$12)(10)}{90 \text{ motors}}$$

$$= \$34.67 \text{ per motor}$$

The manufacturing cost per motor with the quality improvement is

$$\text{Product cost} = \frac{(\$30)(100) + (\$12)(10)}{95 \text{ motors}}$$

$$\text{Product cost} = 32.21 \text{ per motor}$$

The improvement in the production process as a result of the quality management program will result in a decrease of $2.46 per unit, or 7.1%, in direct manufacturing cost per unit as well as a 5.5% increase in product yield (computed in Example 2.3), with a minimal investment in labor, plant, or equipment.

In Examples 2.3 and 2.4 we determined productivity measures for a single production process. However, it is more likely that product quality would be monitored throughout the production process at various stages. Each stage would result in a portion of good-quality, "work-in-process" products. For a production process with n stages, the yield, Y (without reworking), is

$$Y = (I)(\%g_1)(\%g_2) \cdots (\%g_n)$$

where

I = input of items to the production process that will result in finished products

g_i = good-quality, work-in-process products at stage i

EXAMPLE 2.5 | Computing Product Yield for a Multistage Process

At the H&S Motor Company, motors are produced in a four-stage process. Motors are inspected following each stage, with percentage yields (on average) of good-quality, work-in-process units as follows.

STAGE	AVERAGE PERCENTAGE GOOD QUALITY
1	0.93
2	0.95
3	0.97
4	0.92

The company wants to know the daily product yield for product input of 100 units per day. Furthermore, it would like to know how many input units it would have to start with each day to result in a final daily yield of 100 good-quality units.

Solution

$$\begin{aligned} Y &= (I)(\%g_1)(\%g_2)(\%g_3)(\%g_4) \\ &= (100)(0.93)(0.95)(0.97)(0.92) \\ Y &= 78.8 \text{ motors} \end{aligned}$$

Thus, the production process has a daily good-quality product yield of 78.8 motors.

To determine the product input that would be required to achieve a product yield of 100 motors, I is treated as a decision variable when Y equals 100:

$$I = \frac{Y}{(\%g_1)(\%g_2)(\%g_3)(\%g_4)}$$

$$I = \frac{100}{(0.93)(0.95)(0.97)(0.92)}$$

$$= 126.8 \text{ motors}$$

To achieve output of 100 good-quality motors, the production process must start with approximately 127 motors.

The Quality–Productivity Ratio

Quality–productivity ratio (QPR) A productivity index that includes productivity and quality costs.

Another measure of the effect of quality on productivity combines the concepts of quality index numbers and product yield. Called the **quality–productivity ratio (QPR)**,[3] it is computed as follows:

$$\text{QPR} = \frac{\text{good quality units}}{(\text{input units})(\text{unit processing cost}) + (\text{reworked units})(\text{rework cost})}(100)$$

This is actually a quality index number that includes productivity and quality costs. The QPR increases if either processing cost or rework costs or both decrease. It increases if more good-quality units are produced relative to total product input (i.e., the number of units that begin the production process).

EXAMPLE 2.6 | Computing the Quality Productivity Ratio (QPR)

The H&S Motor Company produces small motors at a processing cost of $30 per unit. Defective motors can be reworked at a cost of $12 each. The company produces 100 motors per day and averages 80% good-quality motors, resulting in 20% defects, 50% of which can be reworked prior to shipping to customers. The company wants to examine the effects of (1) increasing the production rate to 200 motors per day; (2) reducing the processing cost to $26 and the rework cost to $10; (3) increasing, through quality improvement, the product yield of good-quality products to 95%; and (4) the combination of 2 and 3.

[3]E. E. Adam, J. E. Hershauer, and W. A. Ruch, *Productivity and Quality: Measurement as a Basis of Improvement*, 2nd ed. Columbia, MO: Research Center, College of Business and Public Administration, University of Missouri, 1986.

Solution

The QPR for the base case is computed as follows.

$$\begin{aligned} QPR &= \frac{80 + 10}{(100)(\$30) + (10)(\$12)}(100) \\ &= 2.89 \end{aligned}$$

Case 1. Increase input to production capacity of 200 units.

$$\begin{aligned} QPR &= \frac{160 + 20}{(200)(\$30) + (20)(\$12)}(100) \\ &= 2.89 \end{aligned}$$

Increasing production capacity alone has no effect on the QPR; it remains the same as the base case.

Case 2. Reduce processing cost to \$26 and rework cost to \$10.

$$\begin{aligned} QPR &= \frac{80 + 10}{(100)(\$26) + (10)(\$10)}(100) \\ &= 3.33 \end{aligned}$$

These cost decreases cause the QPR to increase.

Case 3. Increase initial good-quality units to 95 percent.

$$\begin{aligned} QPR &= \frac{95 + 2.5}{(100)(\$30) + (2.5)(\$12)}(100) \\ &= 3.22 \end{aligned}$$

Again, the QPR increases as product quality improves.

Case 4. Decrease costs and increase initial good-quality units.

$$\begin{aligned} QPR &= \frac{95 + 2.5}{(100)(\$26) + (2.5)(\$10)}(100) \\ &= 3.71 \end{aligned}$$

The largest increase in the QPR results from decreasing costs and increasing initial good-quality product through improved quality.

Quality Awards

The Baldrige Award, Deming Prize, and other award competitions have become valuable and coveted prizes for U.S. companies eager to benefit from the aura and reputation for quality that awaits the winners, and the decreased costs and increased profits that award participants and winners have experienced. They have also provided widely used sets of guidelines to help companies implement an effective quality management system (QMS), and winners provide quality standards, or "benchmarks," for other companies to emulate.

The Malcolm Baldrige Award

The Malcolm Baldrige National Quality Award is given annually to up to 18 organizations in six categories: manufacturing, services, small businesses, nonprofits (with less than 500 full-time employees), healthcare, and education. It was created by law in 1987 (named after former Secretary

Along the Supply Chain

K&N Management, Baldrige National Quality Award Winner in Small Business

Courtesy of Mighty Fine Burger

K&N Management, the second foodservice recipient of the Baldrige Award, is an Austin, Texas, developer for Rudy's Country Store and Bar-B-Q restaurants, and the creator of Mighty Fine Burgers, Fries and Shakes restaurants, both fast-casual food concepts with a limited menu and walk-up counter service. The company has more than 450 employees referred to as "team members," and the company culture is based on quality and excellence, strong relationships with its "guests," and a vision to become "world famous by delighting one guest at a time." In sales the restaurants significantly outperform local competitors and national chains earning K&N revenues of around $50 million, and gross profits significantly exceed industry standards. Guest feedback is collected with an iPad that administers short surveys around main meal times and takeout guests are directed to web-based surveys. Restaurant "leaders" carry PDAs that alert them to guest comments and complaints and to daily performance results. Guests rate their satisfaction with food quality, hospitality, cleanliness, speed of service, and value on a 5-point scale with an overall guest rating of 4.7 compared to a rating of 4 for their best competitor. For all worker categories K&N's turnover rate is lower than industry averages, and absenteeism is a little more than 1% compared to 5% for its best competitor. The *Austin American-Statesman* named K&N "the best place to work in Austin."

Many of the Baldrige principles K&N Management implemented and employs were learned at Pal's Business Excellence Institute (Pal's BEI). Pal's Sudden Service was the first foodservice operation to win the Baldrige Award in 2001, and their BEI derived from that commitment. All Baldrige winners must agree to share their secrets to success with other businesses. K&N Management has subsequently created educational courses in their key business practices that provide training to others to drive continuous quality improvement.

Visit the Baldrige Award website at http://www.nist.gov/baldrige/ to read more about Pal's Sudden Service and K&N Management and identify and discuss some of the common quality-motivated characteristics they share.

Source: National Quality Program at the National Institute of Standards and Technology web site, http://www.quality.nist.gov, and Pal's Business Excellence Institute, http://www.palsbei.com/.

Courtesy National Institute of Standards and Measures

The Malcolm Baldrige National Quality Award is given each year to companies in six categories—manufacturing, services, small businesses, nonprofits, health care, and education. The award criteria and guidelines have become a template for a successful quality management system.

of Commerce Malcolm Baldrige, who died in 1987) to (1) stimulate U.S. companies to improve quality, (2) establish criteria for businesses to use to evaluate their individual quality-improvement efforts, (3) set as examples those companies that were successful in improving quality, and (4) help other U.S. organizations learn how to manage quality by disseminating information about the award winners' programs.

The award criteria focus on the soundness of the approach to quality improvement, the overall quality management program as it is implemented throughout the organization, and customer satisfaction. The seven major categories of criteria by which companies are examined are leadership; strategic planning; customer focus; measurement, analysis, and knowledge management; workforce focus; operations focus; and results.

The Baldrige Award, which is pictured in the photo, has had a major influence on U.S. companies, thousands of which request applications from the government each year to obtain a copy of the award guidelines and criteria for internal use in establishing a quality management system. Many companies have made the Baldrige criteria for quality their own, and have also demanded that their suppliers submit applications for the Malcolm Baldrige National Quality Award. Since its inception in 1987, it has been estimated that the economic benefits of the Baldrige Program as a ratio compared to its costs is 820 to 1. Companies that have won the Baldrige Quality Award and have become known as leaders in quality include Motorola, Xerox, Cadillac, Federal Express, Ritz Carlton, and IBM. These and other Baldrige Award winners have become models or benchmarks for other companies to emulate in establishing their own quality management systems.

Other Awards for Quality

The creation and subsequent success of the Baldrige Award has spawned a proliferation of national, international, government, industry, state, and individual quality awards. The American Society for Quality (ASQ) sponsors a number of national individual awards, including,

Along the Supply Chain

Baldrige National Quality Award Winners in Healthcare: What It Takes

Since the first Baldrige National Quality Award in the healthcare category in 2002, a third of the subsequent 57 Baldrige Awards have gone to healthcare facilities. This is no doubt due to the increased emphasis on healthcare quality in the United States, increased competition among hospitals and HMOs, a nationwide desire to see healthcare costs decrease, and the very visible successes of the healthcare facilities that have won the award. Three recent Baldrige Award winners in the healthcare category include Hill Country Memorial Hospital (2014), Sutter Davis Hospital (2014), and North Mississippi Health Services, a two-time winner (2006 and 2012).

Hill Country Memorial (HCM) is an 86-bed nonprofit community hospital with a workforce of over 800 employees that serves 10 counties in the heart of Texas Hill Country (west of Austin and San Antonio). Strategically, HCM focuses on four areas—finance and growth, service, quality, and people—within its "Remarkable Always" culture. It has been named a top-100 hospital in the nation by several healthcare-related organizations, and has consistently graded in the top 10 nationally for patient safety, general surgery, gastrointestinal care, and joint replacement. HCM outperformed every hospital in Texas and ranked 57th nationally for "value-based purchasing," a program that ranks hospitals on quality health care performance. In rankings based on various financial measures, HCM was ahead of the top 25% of hospitals nationally. HCM has also consistently ranked in the top 10 nationally for employee satisfaction and engagement.

Sutter Davis Hospital (SDH) is a 48-bed nonprofit acute care hospital with 385 employees and 394 medical staff members in Davis, California. It offers care in four primary areas—medical-surgical and intensive care, birthing, emergency care, and surgical services. SDH's performance for various specific patient groups, such as congestive heart failure and pneumonia, rank in the top 10 nationally. Its average emergency door-to-doctor time has been 22 minutes compared to the California benchmark of 58 minutes. Its employee satisfaction and engagement survey scores exceed the national top 10% level.

North Mississippi Health Services (NMHS) is a nonprofit, community-owned health service that includes four hospitals, four nursing homes, and 34 clinics with over 6200 employees and 490 physicians, serving 24 rural counties in northeast Mississippi and northwest Alabama. Its flagship hospital, North Mississippi Medical Center, was a 2006 Baldrige Award winner. Its mission is "to continuously improve the health of the people of our region" and it uses five critical success factors—people, service, quality, financial, and growth—in conjunction with the Baldrige Criteria to drive all parts of its operation. As with Hill Country Memorial and Sutter Davis Hospital, its patient and employee satisfaction scores rank in the top 10% nationally. Despite its location in what has been called "the nation's epicenter of poverty," NMHS is the only healthcare organization in Mississippi or Alabama with an S&P AA credit rating.

Visit the Baldrige Award website at http://www.nist.gov/baldrige/ to read more about these and other award recipients, and identify and discuss the common quality-motivated characteristics they share.

Source: National Quality Program at the National Institute of Standards and Technology website, http://www.nist.gov/baldrige/.

among others, the Armand V. Feigenbaum Medal, the Deming Medal, the E. Jack Lancaster Medal, the Edwards Medal, the Shewart Medal, and the Ishikawa Medal.

Prominent international awards include the EFQM (formerly the European Foundation for Quality Management) Excellence Award that recognizes outstanding businesses in European countries, with similar scope and criteria to the Baldrige Award, the UK Excellence Award, the Canada Awards for Excellence, the Deming Prize (Japan), and the Japan Quality Award.

ISO 9000

The International Organization for Standardization (ISO), headquartered in Geneva, Switzerland, has as its members the national standards organizations for more than 163 countries. The ISO member for the United States is the American National Standards Institute (ANSI). The purpose of ISO is to facilitate global consensus agreements on international quality standards. It has resulted in a system for certifying suppliers to make sure they meet internationally accepted standards for quality management. It is a nongovernment organization and is not a part of the United Nations.

During the 1970s it was generally acknowledged that the word *quality* had different meanings within and among industries and countries and around the world. In 1979 the ISO member representing the United Kingdom, the British Standard Institute (BSI), recognizing the need for standardization for quality management and assurance, submitted a formal proposal to ISO to develop international standards for quality assurance techniques and practices. Using standards that already existed in the United Kingdom and Canada as a basis, ISO established generic quality standards, primarily for manufacturing firms, that could be used worldwide.

Standards

A standard is a document that provides requirements, specifications, guidelines, or other precise criteria that can be used consistently to ensure that materials, products, processes, and services are fit for their purpose. ISO has over 19,500 published standards covering almost all aspects of technology and business. For example, the format for credit cards was derived from ISO standards that specify such physical features as the cards' thickness so that they can be used worldwide. Standards, in general, increase the safety, quality, reliability, and effectiveness of goods and services around the world and as a result make life easier for everyone. For a business they can be strategic tools that reduce costs by minimizing waste and errors and facilitate global trade.

The ISO 9000 family of standards address various aspects of quality management and are the best-known ISO standards. The ISO 9000 quality management standards, guidelines, and technical reports were first published in 1987. ISO 9000 includes a number of supporting documents and publications that provide detailed guidance to a company for developing and continual improvement of its quality management system in order to achieve and sustain customer satisfaction. The recently revised standard ISO 9001:2015 establishes the requirements of a quality management system and it is the only standard in the ISO 9000 family that can be certified. ISO 9001:2015 is based on a number of quality management principles including customer focus, the involvement of top management, a process approach, and continuous improvement.

All ISO standards are reviewed every five years to keep them current and relevant. A significant change in the recently revised ISO 9001:2015 standard was an increased emphasis on "risk." Risk is defined as the "effect of uncertainty on an expected result." While the evolving global economy has provided organizations with new opportunities, it has also presented them with new risks created by extended global supply chains and outsourcing. Risks can be anything that impacts the customer adversely such as a defective or late order, a shortage of shipping containers, a transportation breakdown, a supplier bankruptcy, or natural disasters such as hurricanes, tsunamis, volcanic eruptions, or earthquakes. For the first time, ISO 9001:2015 requires an organization to address its potential risks so that undesirable outcomes can be planned for, prevented, or reduced; intended results can be achieved; and continual improvement sustained. Organizations must take a risk-based management approach as part of their quality management system, where they understand their possible risks and develop methods to identify, manage, and mitigate these risks so that customer satisfaction is maintained.

In addition to this change regarding risk in the ISO 9001:2015 standard, ISO has introduced a number of new certifications in recent years dealing with "sustainability" (defined by the United Nations as "meeting present needs without compromising the ability of future generation to meet their needs") and social responsibility. These concepts and initiatives are increasingly becoming part of many company's and organization's quality management systems, which ISO recognizes and is addressing. (See the "Along the Supply Chain" box).

Certification

Many companies around the world require that companies they do business with (e.g., suppliers) have ISO 9001 certification, as shown in the photo. In that way, despite possible language, technology, and cultural differences, a company can be sure that the company it's doing business with meets uniform standards—that is, they are "on the same page." ISO 9001:2015 is the only standard in the ISO 9000 family that carries third-party *certification* (referred to as *registration* in the United States). A third-party company called a registrar is the only authorized entity that can award ISO 9001 certification. Registrars are accredited by an authoritative national body and are contracted by companies to evaluate their quality management system to see if it meets the ISO 9001 standards; if the company does, it is issued an ISO 9001 certification, which is recognized around the world. Over a million organizations around the world have been certified.

ISO 9001:2015 primarily serves as a basis for benchmarking a company's quality-management system. Quality management, in ISO terms, measures how effectively

Thousands of businesses have improved their operations by fully implementing a quality system based on the international standards known as ISO 9001:2015. When a company has met all the requirements of the standards, a registrar will certify/register it. This status is represented by a certificate, such as this sample.

management determines the company's overall quality policy, its objectives, and its responsibilities, as well as its quality policy implementation. A company has to fulfill all of the requirements in ISO 9001:2015 to be certified (except for activities and functions it does not perform at all). Customer satisfaction is an explicit requirement. Thus, to be certified a company must identify and review customer requirements, ensure that customer requirements are met, and be able to measure and monitor customer satisfaction. The company

Along the Supply Chain

ISO Certifications for Sustainability and Social Responsibility

The International Organization for Standardization (ISO) has various certifications for sustainability and social responsibility standards. For example, the ISO 14000 family of standards provides tools for companies and organizations of all kinds seeking to manage their environmental responsibilities. ISO 14001 sets out a framework that any organization can use to set up an effective environmental management system. Surveys show that users found this certification valuable for meeting legal requirements, achieving management commitment and employee engagement, for meeting stakeholder requirements, and improving public image, giving them a competitive advantage and gaining a financial benefit. Denver was the first U.S. city to achieve ISO 14001 certification for its Environmental Management System (EMS), which was developed to guide its sustainability initiatives. The EMS's achievements include increased energy efficiency, reduction of hazardous waste and increased safety, a reduction in water usage in its parks, LEED certifications for city facilities, and a commitment to alternative energy sources.

ISO 37120 is a certification for cities that provides common standards for urban areas that measure a city's quality of life, focusing on the environment and the local government's provision of services. Cities that have been awarded ISO 37120 certification include London, Boston, Amsterdam, Dubai, Toronto, and Manila. Benefits of this certification can include more effective government and delivery of services, international benchmarks and sharing of best practices, informed decision making and planning, leverage for funding, a model for sustainability planning, and data to support city investment attractiveness. ISO 50001 is a standard for energy management through the development of energy management systems that optimize energy efficiency. Certification demonstrates a company's commitment to improving energy performance and reducing greenhouse gas emissions. Arvind Mills, the first denim company in India to achieve ISO 50001 certification, launched a range of denim products that have zero discharge of dye, thus reducing fresh water consumption.

Using the Internet, identify and discuss additional examples of organizations that are using ISO certifications for sustainability and social responsibility initiatives.

Source: The International Organization for Standardization (ISO) website at http://www.iso.org.

must also be able to show that measuring and monitoring customer satisfaction leads to corrective and preventive actions when nonconformance (to the standards) is found—that is, continual improvement. This type of analysis of customer satisfaction requires a large amount of data collection and processing.

Implications of ISO 9000 for U.S. Companies

Originally, ISO 9000 was adopted by the 12 countries of the European Community (EC)—Belgium, Denmark, France, Germany, Greece, Ireland, Italy, Luxembourg, the Netherlands, Portugal, Spain, and the United Kingdom. The governments of the EC countries adopted ISO 9000 as a uniform quality standard for cross-border transactions within the EC and for international transactions. The EC has since evolved into the European Union (EU) with 28 member countries.

These EU countries and many others are specifically acknowledging that they prefer suppliers with ISO 9000 certification. To remain competitive in international markets, U.S. companies must comply with the standards in the ISO 9000 series. Some products in the EU, for example, are "regulated" to the extent that the products must be certified to be in ISO 9000 compliance by an EU-recognized accreditation registrar. Most of these products have health and safety considerations. However, companies discovered that to remain competitive and satisfy customer preferences, their products had to be in compliance with ISO 9000 requirements even if these products were not specifically regulated.

The United States exports more than $270 billion annually to the EU market, much of it to France, Germany, Italy, Spain, and the United Kingdom. Most of these exports are affected in some way by ISO 9000 standards.

Companies are also pressured within the United States to comply with ISO 9000 by more and more customers. They recognize the value of these standards for helping to ensure top-quality products and services, and require that their suppliers comply with ISO 9000.

Along the Supply Chain

Orkin Uses ISO Certification to Improve Service Quality

Orkin, Inc., headquartered in Atlanta, with 8000 employees and more than 400 U.S. locations, is a leader in pest control services for residential and commercial customers. Approximately a third of Orkin's revenue is from its commercial business, which provides pest control for hospitals, hotels, food processing plants, and similar business facilities that have a very low tolerance for pests.

In the 1990s, as a number of Orkin's commercial customers achieved ISO certification, they wanted to partner with suppliers that subscribed to the same quality management standards, while at the same time Orkin wanted to achieve a higher level of consistency of quality service across its branches. Over time the company developed a quality assurance (QA) team that was responsible for developing a companywide quality management process that would eventually earn Orkin ISO 9001 certification in 2005.

Orkin's QA team is composed of experienced quality professionals who have worked at Orkin for an average of 30 years, and who have completed ISO technical courses and audit coursework. The team conducts approximately 200 commercial branch internal audits each year. A typical audit takes one QA member four days and consists of nine administrative reviews, four vehicle inspections, and ten on-site customer inspections. Auditors document their findings in a two-page summary and each branch receives a score on administration, employee training, and on-site service evaluations. In accordance with ISO 9001:2008, if a branch fails any part of an audit, a formal corrective process is required and the QA team performs a follow-up audit within 90 to 120 days. However, even branches that receive very high scores are given areas of improvement to work on. Since achieving ISO certification, Orkin decreased its commercial business cancellation rate, saving approximately $600,000 per year, established companywide consistency in the quality of its service, and improved customer satisfaction from 95.8% to 97.7% for customers who rated Orkin's service as excellent or good.

Although Orkin franchises branches overseas, its ISO certification was directed at U.S. customers; why do you think it believed it had a need to meet international standards for quality?

Source: Based on Mark Udell and Mike Buffingtion, "Eradicating Inconsistency," *Quality Progress* 45 (3); (March 2012), pp. 38–44.

In the EU registration system, the third-party assessors of quality are referred to as *notified bodies*; that is, the 28 EU governments *notify* one another as to which organization in their country is the officially designated government-approved quality assessor. The notified bodies ultimately certify a company with a European Conformity (CE) mark. The CE mark must be on any product exported from the United States that is ISO 9000-regulated. It is illegal to sell a regulated product in a store in the EU without the CE mark. For a supplier in the United States to export regulated products to an EU country, it must be accredited by European registrars—notified bodies within the EU. However, more and more EU companies are requiring ISO 9000 certification for suppliers of products that fall in the unregulated categories, and eventually all products exported to the EU will probably require certification. It is also important that U.S. companies obtain accreditation with a notified body that has widespread positive recognition in the EU so that they will have broad access to markets in the EU.

The U.S. member of the ISO, the American National Standards Institute (ANSI) designated the American Society for Quality (ASQ), as the sponsoring organization for ISO 9000 in the United States. ASQ and ANSI created the Registrar Accreditation Board (RAB) to act as an accrediter of third-party registrars in the United States.

ISO Registrars

A registrar is an organization that conducts audits by individual auditors. Auditors are skilled in quality systems and the manufacturing and service environments in which an audit will be performed. The registrar develops an audit team of one or more auditors to evaluate a company's quality program and then report back to the registrar. An organization that wants to become a registrar must be accredited by the Registrar Accreditation Board (RAB) founded by the American Society for Quality Control, which links the U.S. with ISO 9000 standards. Once RAB accredits a registrar, the registrar can then authorize its registered suppliers to use the RAB certificate in advertising, indicating compliance with ISO 9000.

ISO certification, or registration as it is called in the United States, is accomplished by a registrar through a series of document reviews and facility visits and audits. The registrar's auditors review a company's procedures, processes, and operations to see if the company conforms to the ISO quality management system standards. The registrar looks at a variety of things, including the company's administrative, design, and production processes; quality system documentation; personnel training records; management reviews; and internal audit processes. The registration process might typically include an initial document review that describes the company's quality management system, followed by the development of an audit plan and then the audit itself. This is usually followed by semiannual or annual surveillance audits to make sure the quality system is being maintained. The registration process can take from several weeks up to a year, depending on how ready the company is for registration. A RAB accredited registrar does not "help" the company attain certification either by giving advice or consulting.

Summary

In our discussion of quality management in this chapter, certain consistencies or commonalities have surfaced. The most important perspective of quality is the customer's; products and services must be designed to meet customer expectations and needs for quality. A total commitment to quality is necessary throughout an organization for it to be successful in improving and managing product quality. This commitment must start at the top and filter down through all levels of the organization and across all areas and departments. Employees need to be active participants in the quality-improvement process and must feel a responsibility for quality. Employees must feel free to make suggestions to improve product quality, and a systematic procedure is necessary to involve workers and solicit their input. Improving product quality is cost-effective; the cost of poor quality greatly exceeds the cost of attaining good quality. Quality can be improved with the effective use of statistical quality-control methods. In fact, the use of statistical quality control has been a pervasive part of our discussions on quality management, and it has been identified as an important part of any quality-management program. In the following chapter we concentrate on statistical quality-control methods and principles.

Key Terms

appraisal costs Costs of measuring, testing, and analyzing materials, parts, products, and the productive process to make sure they conform to design specifications.

benchmark A level of quality achievement established by one company that other companies seek to achieve (i.e., a goal).

Black Belt In a Six Sigma program, the leader of a quality improvement project; a full-time position.

breakthrough strategy In Six Sigma, a five-step process for improvement projects: define, measure, analyze, improve, and control.

cause-and-effect diagram or fishbone diagram A graphical description of the elements of a specific quality problem.

cause-and-effect matrix A grid used to prioritize causes of quality problems.

champion A member of top management who is responsible for project success in a Six Sigma program.

cost index The ratio of quality cost to manufacturing cost.

design for Six Sigma (DFSS) A systematic methodology to design products and processes that meet customer expectations and can be produced at Six Sigma quality levels.

DMADV Define, measure, analyze, design, and verify.

external failure costs Costs of poor quality incurred after the product gets to the customer; that is, customer service, lost sales, and so on.

fitness for use A measure of how well a product or service does what the consumer thinks it is supposed to do and wants it to do.

Green Belt In a Six Sigma program, a project team member, a part-time position.

index numbers Ratios that measure quality costs relative to some base accounting values such as sales or product units.

internal failure costs Costs of poor-quality products discovered during the production process—that is, scrap, rework, and the like.

kaizen Involving everyone in the workplace in a process of gradual, organized, and continuous improvement.

labor index The ratio of quality cost to direct labor hours.

Lean Six Sigma Integrating Six Sigma and lean systems.

Master Black Belt In a Six Sigma program, a teacher and mentor for Black Belts; a full-time position.

Pareto analysis A method for identifying the causes of poor quality, which usually shows that most quality problems result from only a few causes.

participative problem solving Involving employees directly in the quality-management process to identify and solve problems.

partnering A relationship between a company and its supplier based on mutual quality standards.

prevention costs Costs incurred during product design and manufacturing that prevent nonconformance to specifications.

process flowchart A diagram of the steps in a job, operation, or process.

production index The ratio of quality cost to final product units.

productivity A measure of effectiveness in converting resources into products, generally computed as output divided by input.

quality circles A small, voluntary group (team) of workers and supervisors formed to address quality problems in their area.

quality impact on productivity Fewer defects increase output and quality improvement reduces inputs.

quality management system (QMS) A system to achieve customer satisfaction that complements other company systems.

quality of conformance The degree to which the product or service meets the specifications required by design during the production process.

quality of design The degree to which quality characteristics are designed into a product or service.

quality–productivity ratio (QPR) A productivity index that includes productivity and quality costs.

sales index The ratio of quality cost to sales.

Six Sigma A measure of how much a given product or process deviates from perfection, or zero defects; the basis of a quality-improvement program.

total quality management (TQM) The management of quality throughout the organization at all management levels and across all areas.

yield A measure of productivity; the sum of good-quality and reworked units.

Key Formulas

Quality Index Numbers

$$\text{Quality index} = \frac{\text{total quality costs}}{\text{base}}(100)$$

Product Yield

$$Y = (I)(\%G) + (I)(1 - \%G)(\%R)$$

Manufacturing Cost per Product

$$\text{Product cost} = \frac{(K_d)(I) + (K_r)(R)}{Y}$$

Multistage Product Yield

$$Y = (I)(\%g_1)(\%g_2)\cdots(\%g_n)$$

Quality-Productivity Ratio

$$\text{QPR} = \frac{\text{good quality units}}{(\text{input units})(\text{processing cost}) + (\text{reworked units})(\text{rework cost})}(100)$$

Solved Problems

1. Product Yield

A manufacturing company has a weekly product input of 1700 units. The average percentage of good-quality products is 83%. Of the poor-quality products, 60% can be reworked and sold as good-quality products. Determine the weekly product yield and the product yield if the good-product quality is increased to 92%.

WileyPLUS

Solution

Step 1. Compute yield according to the following formula:

$$Y = (I)(G\%) + (I)(1 - \%G)(\%R)$$
$$Y = (1700)(0.83) + (1700)(0.17)(0.60)$$
$$= 1584.4 \text{ units}$$

Step 2. Increase %G to 92%:

$$Y = (1700)(0.92) + (1700)(0.08)(0.60)$$
$$= 1645.6 \text{ units}$$

2. Quality–Productivity Ratio

A retail telephone catalog company takes catalog orders from customers and then sends the completed orders to the warehouses to be filled. An operator processes an average of 45 orders per day. The cost of processing an order is \$1.15, and it costs \$0.65 to correct an order that has been filled out incorrectly by the operator. An operator averages 7% bad orders per day, all of which are reworked prior to filling the customer order. Determine the quality–productivity ratio for an operator.

Solution

Compute the quality–productivity ratio according to the following formulas:

$$\text{QPR} = \frac{\text{good quality units}}{(\text{input})(\text{processing cost}) + (\text{defective units})(\text{rework cost})}(100)$$

$$\text{QPR} = \frac{45}{(45)(\$1.15) + (3.15)(\$0.65)}(100)$$
$$= 83.65$$

Questions

2.1. How does the consumer's perspective of quality differ from the producer's?

2.2. Briefly describe the *dimensions of quality* for which a consumer looks in a product, and apply them to a specific product.

2.3. How does *quality of design* differ from *quality of conformance*?

2.4. Define the two major categories of quality cost and how they relate to each other.

2.5. What is the difference between internal and external failure costs?

2.6. A defense contractor manufactures rifles for the military. The military has exacting quality standards that the contractor must meet. The military is very pleased with the quality of the products provided by the contractor and rarely has to return products or has reason for complaint. However, the contractor is experiencing extremely high quality-related costs. Speculate on the reasons for the contractor's high quality-related costs.

2.7. Consider your school (university or college) as a production system in which the final product is a graduate. For this system:

- **a.** Define quality from the producer's and customer's perspectives.
- **b.** Develop a fitness-for-use description for final product quality.
- **c.** Give examples of the cost of poor quality (internal and external failure costs) and the cost of quality assurance (prevention and appraisal) costs.
- **d.** Describe how quality circles might be implemented in a university setting. Do you think they would be effective?

2.8. Discuss how a quality management program can affect productivity.

2.9. The Aurora Electronics Company has been receiving a lot of customer complaints and returns of a DVD player that it manufactures. When a DVD is pushed into the loading mechanism, it can stick inside and it is difficult to get the DVD out. Consumers will try to pull the DVD drawer out with their fingers or pry it out with an object such as a knife, pencil, or screwdriver, frequently damaging the DVD or hurting themselves. What are the different costs of poor quality and costs of quality assurance that might be associated with this quality problem?

2.10. What are the different quality characteristics you (as a consumer) would expect to find in the following three products: a DVD player, a pizza, running shoes?

2.11. AMERICARD, a national credit card company, has a toll-free, 24-hour customer service number. Describe the input for this system function and the final product. What quality-related costs might be associated with this function? What impact might a quality management program have on this area?

2.12. A number of quality management philosophies hold that prevention costs are the most critical quality-related costs. Explain the logic behind this premise.

2.13. Why is it important for companies to measure and report quality costs?

2.14. Describe the primary contribution to quality management of each of the following: W. E. Deming, Joseph Juran, Phillip Crosby, Armand Feigenbaum, and Kaoru Ishikawa.

2.15. Describe the impact that the creation of the Malcolm Baldrige Award has had on quality improvement in the United States.

2.16. Write a one- to two-page summary of an article from *Quality Progress* about quality management in a company or organization.

2.17. More companies probably fail at implementing quality-management programs than succeed. Discuss the reasons why a quality-management program might fail.

2.18. Select a service provider and discuss the dimensions of quality on which a customer might evaluate it.

2.19. Select two competing service providers that you are familiar with or can visit, such as fast-food restaurants, banks, or retail stores, and compare how they interact with customers in terms of quality.

2.20. Develop a hypothetical quality-improvement program for the class in which you are using this textbook. Evaluate the class according to the dimensions of quality for a service. Include goals for quality improvement and ways to measure success.

2.21. Identify a company or organization from which you have received poor-quality products or services, describe the nature of the defects, and suggest ways in which you might improve quality.

2.22. Identify a company or organization from which you have received high-quality products and describe the characteristics that make them high-quality.

2.23. Explain why strategic planning might benefit from a QMS program.

2.24. Why has ISO 9000 become so important to U.S. firms that do business overseas?

2.25. Go to the Baldrige Award website, http://www.nist.gov/baldrige/, and research several companies that have won the Malcolm Baldrige Award. Describe any common characteristics that the quality-management programs in those companies have.

2.26. The discussion in this chapter has focused on the benefits of implementing a quality management program; however, many companies do not have such a program. Discuss the reasons why you think a company would not adopt a quality management program.

2.27. Access a website of a company that sells products to the general public on the Internet. Discuss the quality attributes of the site, and evaluate the quality of the website.

2.28. For an airline you have flown on list all of the quality "defects" you can recall. Discuss whether you think the airline exhibited overall good or poor quality. If it exhibited good quality, explain what made it so; if it exhibited poor quality, what actions do you think could be taken by the airline to improve quality?

2.29. Identify three websites that you think are poor quality and three that are good quality. What common characteristics are exhibited by the group of poor-quality sites? the group of good-quality sites? Compare the two groups.

2.30. The production and home delivery of a pizza is a relatively straightforward and simple process. Develop a fishbone diagram to identify potential defects and opportunities for poor quality in this process.

2.31. Most students live in a dormitory or apartment that they rent. Discuss whether this type of living accommodation is a product or service. Assess the quality of your living accommodation according to your previous response.

2.32. Amazon operates what is considered to be an "open market" wherein it provides space and opportunity on its website for independent, competing companies to sell products. Discuss the type of quality problems that this arrangement might pose for Amazon, and how it might deal with quality problems in this kind of open marketplace environment.

2.33. Describe, in general, how the J.D. Power "Circle Ratings" are calculated.

2.34. Select a product that you own (like a cell phone, tablet, laptop, auto, etc.), and a service that you have used (like a hotel, restaurant, airline, Internet site, retail store, etc.) that are rated on the J.D. Power website, and indicate how they are rated and how this rating compares with your own experiences and perceptions about the product and service you selected.

2.35. K&N Management is a 2010 Malcolm Baldrige Award winner in the small business category. Compare the quality of K&N's restaurants with a similar type of fast food restaurant you have visited before. The restaurant you select does not have to be one with necessarily good quality or poor quality, just one that it is similar that you have visited. Be mindful of the "dimensions of quality" for both products and services. (Use the Internet to research both K&N and the restaurant you select to find out more about its performance, both financially and in terms of customer satisfaction.)

2.36. Identify a service provider that you have experienced more than normal quality problems with, list the type of quality problems you have experienced, and suggest ways to correct these problems.

2.37. Successful "sit-down" restaurant companies such as the Cheesecake Factory, Red Lobster, Red Robin, and Outback Steakhouse are known for providing quality food and service at reasonable prices, thus providing customer "value." Identify the common quality characteristics among these and similar restaurant chains.

2.38. In recent years, a large number of the Malcolm Baldrige Award winners have been from the healthcare industry. Discuss why you think this is.

2.39. Discuss how you think sustainability issues are related to quality issues in a company.

2.40. Some companies, like Target and Amazon, are known for outstanding quality. Discuss why you think the processes and systems they use have not, or cannot, be applied to companies that are sometimes known for poor quality, like airlines.

2.41. Many companies have outsourced their customer service activity to overseas providers, most visibly computer, credit card, and airline companies. The quality issues this kind of outsourcing has created have become known to such a large extent that they are often parodied in the media. Discuss why you think companies persist in outsourcing such an important quality-related process as customer service, and what steps these companies might employ to improve the quality of their customer service if they continue to outsource it.

2.42. When Apple introduces new products, it is speculated that it markets first-generation versions of the product without first correcting all of the possible quality problems that might exist, preferring instead to let their customers do their product testing for them and discover any problems. This is a cost-effective process that doesn't seem to hurt Apple's reputation for high quality or sales. Why do you think this is?

2.43. One of the difficult aspects of global supply chain management is ensuring quality across a number of different suppliers. Discuss how a company can ensure quality along its supply chain.

2.44. Within a company's supply chain, identify and discuss some of the different supply chain processes where quality issues might arise.

2.45. Research the companies on the annual Gartner Supply Chain "Top 25" (at www.gartner.com) and identify some of the quality management characteristics they share.

2.46. Find an article from *Quality Progress* about a specific company's supply chain quality and write a brief report similar to the "Along the Supply Chain" about Target's supply chain in this chapter.

2.47. Research the website of a company that is known to be a leading user and proponent of Six Sigma (like some of those identified in this chapter), and discuss what they say about their use of Six Sigma.

2.48. Develop a fishbone diagram for the possible causes of flight delays.

2.49. Observe a business with which you are familiar and interact with frequently, such as a restaurant or food service, a laundry service, your bank, or the college bookstore. Develop a Pareto chart that encompasses the major service defects of the business, identify the most significant service problems and suggest how quality could be improved.

2.50. County school buses are inspected every month for "defects." In a recent monthly inspection, 27 worn or torn seats were found, 22 buses had dirty floors, there were 14 cases of exterior scratches and chipped paint, there were 8 cracked or broken windows, the engines on 4 buses had trouble starting or were not running smoothly, and 2 buses had faulty brakes. Develop a Pareto chart for the bus inspections and indicate the most significant quality-problem categories. What does this tell you about the limitations of applying Pareto chart analysis? How might these limitations be overcome in Pareto chart analysis?

2.51. Joseph Juran created a "quality spiral" showing that each element of the business process, each function, not just the end product, is important. Describe how each of the following business process areas might impact quality: marketing, engineering, purchasing/sourcing, human resources, and distribution.

2.52. Using the Internet, research the winner of an international quality award at one of the award websites and write a brief report.

2.53. Go to the Malcolm Baldrige Award website, http://www.nist.gov/baldrige/, and write a brief report on one of the most recent years' Baldrige Award winners similar to the "Along the Supply Chain" boxes in this chapter.

2.54. Write a brief summary on how a company relates quality management to sustainability by researching *Quality Progress* or the Internet.

2.55. Develop a fishbone diagram for the possible causes of your car not starting.

2.56. Describe the differences among Black Belts, Green Belts, and Master Black Belts in a Six Sigma program.

2.57. Describe the steps in the Six Sigma breakthrough strategy for quality improvement.

2.58. Develop a quality-improvement project in a situation you are familiar with such as a current or former job, a part-time job, a restaurant, your college bookstore, your dorm or apartment, a local business, and so on, and describe how you would apply the steps of the Six Sigma breakthrough strategy.

2.59. Reference the website for the American Customer Satisfaction Index (ACSI) at www.theacsi.org and write a brief summary describing how the numerical ACSI value is determined. Also, select an industry or service sector and pick two companies, one with a high ACSI and one with a relatively low ACSI; using your own knowledge and research about the companies, explain why you think they have different ACSI values.

2.60. Develop a Six Sigma-type quality improvement project employing the DMAIC steps for your own personal health such as losing weight, improving your diet, exercise, etc.

2.61. Develop a Six Sigma-type project employing the DMAIC steps for improving any phase of your personal life that you feel may be "defective."

2.62. Visit your university infirmary and study the process inpatients follow to see a doctor and describe a quality improvement project to improve this process.

2.63. At most universities course registration for future semesters typically involves some type of computerized online process possibly combined with some personal consultation with an academic advisor. Describe the registration process in your academic college or at your university and suggest ways the process could be improved.

2.64. The Japanese are generally credited with starting the global quality revolution that in the 1970s became an integral part of corporate culture, and eventually led to the development of quality improvement programs systems like TQM and Six Sigma. Research and write a report about what Japan did to initiate the quality movement and why it differed from what was being done in the United States.

2.65. Describe the general steps a company must go through to obtain ISO 9001:2015 certification.

2.66. Select a retail store you are familiar with such as a grocery store, J. Crew, Macy's, Best Buy, Target, etc., and identify what might be considered as "defects" in their processes and how improvement might be measured.

2.67. ISO 9000 and the Malcolm Baldrige Award competition are both programs that seek to achieve recognition for outstanding quality, one in the form of a certificate and the other in the form of an award. Discuss how the two are similar and different, and how they might complement each other.

2.68. Explain how you would determine customer satisfaction with a bank, your university, a football game, an airline, a car, a cell phone, and a television. Describe the tools and processes you would use to measure customer satisfaction.

2.69. In the ongoing national debate about healthcare that is likely to continue for years, one view holds that quality improvement (and corresponding cost reduction) across the industry is fundamentally not possible because the direct consumer (i.e., the patient) is not who pays the bill; for most people the insurance company is. Since insurance companies do not directly receive the service provided, they cannot assess how well "value" is being delivered, and neither the customer nor the insurance company are motivated to reduce costs. Discuss this phenomenon of the healthcare industry and make a case for why you think it is accurate or inaccurate. Also address in your discussion how healthcare insurance differs from other forms of personal insurance.

Problems

WileyPLUS

2.1. Backwoods American, Inc., produces expensive water-repellent, down-filled parkas. The company implemented a total quality-management program in 2011. Following are quality-related accounting data that have been accumulated for the five-year period after the program's start.

	YEAR				
	2012	2013	2014	2015	2016
Quality Costs (000s)					
Prevention	$3.2	10.7	28.3	42.6	50.0
Appraisal	26.3	29.2	30.6	24.1	19.6
Internal failure	39.1	51.3	48.4	35.9	32.1
External failure	118.6	110.5	105.2	91.3	65.2
Accounting Measures (000s)					
Sales	$2,700.6	2,690.1	2,705.3	2,310.2	2,880.7
Manufacturing cost	420.9	423.4	424.7	436.1	435.5

a. Compute the company's total failure costs as a percentage of total quality costs for each of the five years. Does there appear to be a trend to this result? If so, speculate on what might have caused the trend.

b. Compute prevention costs and appraisal costs, each as a percentage of total costs, during each of the five years. Speculate on what the company's quality strategy appears to be.

c. Compute quality-sales indices and quality-cost indices for each of the five years. Is it possible to assess the effectiveness of the company's quality-management program from these index values?

d. List several examples of each quality-related cost—that is, prevention, appraisal, and internal and external failure—that might result from the production of parkas.

2.2. The Backwoods American company in Problem 2-1 produces approximately 20,000 parkas annually. The quality management program the company implemented was able to improve the average percentage of good parkas produced by 2% each year, beginning with 83% good-quality parkas in 2012. Only about 20% of poor-quality parkas can be reworked.

a. Compute the product yield for each of the five years.

b. Using a rework cost of $12 per parka, determine the manufacturing cost per good parka for each of the five years. What do these results imply about the company's quality management program?

2.3. The Colonial House Furniture Company manufactures two-drawer oak file cabinets that are sold unassembled through catalogs. The company initiates production of 150 cabinet packages each week. The percentage of good-quality cabinets averages 83% per week, and the percentage of poor-quality cabinets that can be reworked is 60%.

a. Determine the weekly product yield of file cabinets.

b. If the company desires a product yield of 145 units per week, what increase in the percentage of good-quality products must result?

2.4. In Problem 2-3, if the direct manufacturing cost for cabinets is $27 and the rework cost is $8, compute the manufacturing cost per good product. Determine the manufacturing cost per product if the percentage of good-quality file cabinets is increased from 83% to 90%.

2.5. The Omega Shoe Company manufactures a number of different styles of athletic shoes. Its biggest seller is the X-Pacer running shoe. In 2014 Omega implemented a quality-management program. The company's shoe production for the past three years and manufacturing costs are as follows.

	YEAR		
	2014	2015	2016
Units produced/input	32,000	34,600	35,500
Manufacturing cost	$278,000	291,000	305,000
Percent good quality	78%	83%	90%

Only one-quarter of the defective shoes can be reworked, at a cost of $2 apiece. Compute the manufacturing cost per good product for each of the three years and indicate the annual percentage increase or decrease resulting from the quality-management program.

2.6. The Colonial House Furniture Company manufactures four-drawer oak filing cabinets in six stages. In the first stage, the boards forming the walls of the cabinet are cut; in the second stage, the front drawer panels are woodworked; in the third stage, the boards are sanded and finished; in the fourth stage, the boards are cleaned, stained, and painted with a clear finish; in the fifth stage, the hardware for pulls, runners, and fittings is installed; and in the final stage, the cabinets are assembled. Inspection occurs at each stage of the process, and the average percentages of good-quality units are as follows.

STAGE	AVERAGE PERCENTAGE GOOD QUALITY
1	87%
2	91%
3	94%
4	93%
5	93%
6	96%

The cabinets are produced in weekly production runs with a product input for 300 units.

a. Determine the weekly product yield of good-quality cabinets.

b. What would weekly product input have to be in order to achieve a final weekly product yield of 300 cabinets?

2.7. In Problem 2-6, the Colonial House Furniture Company has investigated the manufacturing process to identify potential improvements that would improve quality. The company has identified four alternatives, each costing $15,000, as follows.

ALTERNATIVE	QUALITY IMPROVEMENT
1	Stage 1: 93%
2	Stage 2: 96%. Stage 4: 97%
3	Stage 5: 97%, Stage 6: 98%
4	Stage 2: 97%

a. Which alternative would result in the greatest increase in product yield?

b. Which alternative would be the most cost effective?

2.8. The Backwoods American company operates a telephone order system for a catalog of its outdoor clothing products. The catalog orders are processed in three stages. In the first stage, the telephone operator enters the order into the computer; in the second stage, the items are secured and batched in the warehouse; and in the final stage, the ordered products are packaged. Errors can be made in orders at any of these stages, and the average percentage of errors that occurs at each stage are as follows.

STAGE	% ERRORS
1	12%
2	8%
3	4%

If an average of 320 telephone orders are processed each day, how many errorless orders will result?

2.9. The total processing cost for producing the X-Pacer running shoe in Problem 2-5 is $18. The Omega Shoe Company starts production of 650 pairs of the shoes weekly, and the average weekly yield is 90%, with 10% defective shoes. One quarter of the defective shoes can be reworked at a cost of $3.75.

a. Compute the quality-productivity ratio (QPR).

b. Compute the QPR if the production rate is increased to 800 pairs of shoes per week.

c. Compute the QPR if the processing cost is reduced to $16.50 and the rework cost to $3.20.

d. Compute the QPR if the product yield is increased to 93% good quality.

2.10. Airphone, Inc., manufactures cellular telephones at a processing cost of $47 per unit. The company produces an average of 250 phones per week and has a yield of 87% good-quality phones, resulting in 13% defective phones, all of which can be reworked. The cost of reworking a defective telephone is $16.

a. Compute the quality-productivity ratio (QPR).

b. Compute the QPR if the company increased the production rate to 320 phones per week while reducing the processing cost to $42, reducing the rework cost to $12, and increasing the product yield of good-quality telephones to 94%.

2.11. Burger Doodle is a fast-food restaurant that processes an average of 680 food orders each day. The average cost of each order is $6.15. Four percent of the orders are incorrect, and only 10% of the defective orders can be corrected with additional food items at an average cost of $1.75. The remaining defective orders have to be thrown out.

a. Compute the average product cost.

b. In order to reduce the number of wrong orders, Burger Doodle is going to invest in a computerized ordering and cash register system. The cost of the system will increase the average order cost by $0.05 and will reduce defective orders to 1%. What is the annual net cost effect of this quality-improvement initiative?

c. What other indirect effects on quality might be realized by the new computerized order system?

2.12. Compute the quality–productivity ratio (QPR) for the Burger Doodle restaurant in parts (a) and (b) in Problem 2-11.

2.13. For the Medtek Company in Example 2.1, determine the break-even point (in sales) and draw the break-even diagram for both cases described in the example—with defects and without. (Refer to Chapter 6, "Processes and Technology," for a description of break-even analysis.) Discuss the significance of the difference between the two break-even points.

2.14. The Blue Parrot is an expensive restaurant in midtown open only for dinner. Entrees are set at a fixed price of $42. In a typical month the restaurant will serve 3600 entrees. Monthly variable costs are $61,200, and fixed costs are $31,000 per month. Customers or waiters send back 8% of the entrees because of a defect, and they must be prepared again; they cannot be reworked. The restaurant owners hired a qualified Black Belt to undertake a Six Sigma project at the restaurant to eliminate all defects in the preparation of the entrees (i.e., 3.4 DPMO). Compare the profit in both situations, with and without defects, and indicate both the percentage decrease in variable costs and the percentage increase in profits following the Six Sigma project. Assuming that the restaurant paid the Black Belt $25,000 to achieve zero defects, and the restaurant owners plan to amortize this payment over a three-year period (as a fixed cost), what is the restaurant return on its investment (without applying an interest rate)? Discuss some other aspects of quality improvement at the restaurant that might result from the Six Sigma project.

2.15. A Black Belt has identified the following key input (X) and output (Y) variables for the process of laundering your clothes in your washing machine at home:

INPUT (X) VARIABLES	OUTPUT (Y) VARIABLES
Sort laundry	Clothes clean
Cycle	Clothes not damaged
Wash temperature	Colors okay
Rinse temperature	Lint free
Stain treatment	Stains removed
Load size	Smell fresh/no odors
Fabric softener	
Detergent	
Bleach	
Type of washer	

Develop a cause-and-effect diagram for this process of washing clothes. Next develop a cause-and-effect matrix and use your own insight and judgment about the process to rank and weight the output (Y) variables, assign a numerical score to each X-Y combination, develop overall scores for each X variable, and then rank the X variables in terms of importance.

2.16. A retail website sells a variety of products including clothes, electronics, furniture, sporting goods, books, video games, CDs and DVDs, among other items. An average customer order is $47. Weekly total variable costs are $365,000 and weekly fixed costs are $85,000. The company averages 18,400 orders per week and 12% of all orders are returned for a variety of reasons besides the customer not liking the product, including product misinformation on the website, errors in fulfilling the order, incomplete orders, defective product, breakage, etc. Thirty percent of all returned orders are turned around and refilled correctly per the customer's desire, but at a cost (for handling, packaging, and mailing) of $8 per order, while the remaining 70% of returned orders are lost. In addition, it is estimated that half of the customers associated with lost orders will not return to the website at a cost of $15 per order. Determine the weekly cost of poor quality for the website. The company can implement a quality improvement program for $800,000 a year that will reduce the percentage of returned orders to 2%; should the company invest in the program? How should the company address its quality problem, i.e., what processes does it likely need to improve? Why would zero defects not eliminate returned orders?

Case Problems

Case Problem 2.1 Designing a Quality-Management Program for the Internet at D4Q

Design for Quality (D4Q) is a consulting firm that specializes in the design and implementation of quality management programs for service companies and organizations. It has had success designing quality programs for retail stores and catalog order services. Recently D4Q was approached by a catalog order company, BookTek Media, Inc., with the offer of a job. BookTek sells books, CDs, DVDs, and videos through its mail-order catalog operation. BookTek has decided to expand its service to the Internet. BookTek is experienced in catalog telephone sales and has a successful quality-management program in place. Thus, the company is confident that it can process orders and make deliveries on time with virtually no errors.

A key characteristic of BookTek's quality management program is the company's helpful, courteous, and informative phone representatives. These operators can answer virtually any customer question about BookTek's products, with the help of an information system. Their demeanor toward customers is constantly monitored and graded. Their telephone system is so quick that customers rarely have to wait for a representative to assist them. However, the proposed Internet ordering system virtually eliminates direct human contact with the customer. Since there will be no human contact, BookTek is concerned about how it will be able to make customers feel that they are receiving high-quality service. Furthermore, the company is unsure how its employees can monitor and evaluate the service to know if the customer thinks it is good or poor. The primary concern is how to make customers feel good about the company in such an impersonal, segregated environment. At this point BookTek is unconcerned with costs; management simply wants to develop the highest-quality, friendliest website possible.

D4Q indicated that it would like to take on the job, but while it is familiar with BookTek's type of catalog order system, it is relatively unfamiliar with how things are ordered on the Internet for this kind of retail book business. It suggested that its first order of business might be to investigate what other companies were doing on the Internet.

Help D4Q develop a quality management plan for BookTek. Include in your plan the quality dimensions and characteristics of an Internet ordering system specifically for BookTek's products, suggestions for achieving customer satisfaction, ways to measure defective service, and how to evaluate the success of the order system in terms of quality.

Case Problem 2.2 Quality Management at State University

As a result of several years of severe cuts to its operating budget by the state legislature, the administration at State University has raised tuition annually for the past five years. Five years ago getting an education at State was a bargain for both in-state and out-of-state students; now it is one of the more expensive state universities. An immediate repercussion has been a decline in applications for admission. Since a portion of state funding is tied to enrollments, State has kept its enrollments up at a constant level by going deeper into its pool of applications, taking some less-qualified students.

The increase in the cost of a State degree has also caused legislators, parents, and students to be more conscious of the value of a State education—that is, the value parents and students are receiving for their money. This increased scrutiny has been fueled by numerous media reports about the decreased emphasis on teaching in universities, low teaching loads by faculty, and the large number of courses taught by graduate students. This, in turn, has led the state legislature committee on higher education to call for an "outcomes assessment program" to determine how well State University is achieving its mission of producing high-quality graduates.

On top of those problems, a substantial increase in the college-age population is expected this decade, resulting from a "baby boom" during the 1990s. Key members of the state legislature have told the university administration that they will be expected to absorb their share of the additional students during the next decade. However, because of the budget situation, they should not expect any funding increases for additional facilities, classrooms, dormitory rooms, or faculty. In effect, they will be expected to do more with their existing resources. State already faces a classroom deficit, and faculty have teaching loads above the average of its peer institutions. Legislators are fond of citing a study that shows that if the university simply gets all the students to graduate within a four-year period or reduces the number of hours required for graduation, they can accommodate the extra students.

This entire scenario has made the university president, Fred McMahan, consider retirement. He has summarized the problems to his administration staff as "having to do more, better, with less." One of the first things he did to address these problems was to set up a number of task forces made up of faculty and administrators to brainstorm a variety of topics. Among the topics and problems these task forces addressed were quality in education, educational success, graduation rates, success rates in courses (i.e., the percentage of students passing), teaching, the time to graduation, faculty issues, student issues, facilities, class scheduling, admissions, and classroom space.

Several of the task forces included faculty from engineering and business. These individuals noted that many of the problems the university faced would benefit from the principles and practices of a quality management approach. This recommendation appealed to Fred McMahan and the academic vice president, Anne Baker.

Discuss in general terms how a quality philosophy and practices might be instituted at State University.

Case Problem 2.3 Quality Problems at the Tech Bookstores

Tech is a major state university located in a small, rural college town. Tech Services is an incorporated university entity that operates two bookstores, one on campus and one off campus at a nearby mall. The on-campus store sells school supplies, textbooks, and school-licensed apparel and gifts and it has a large computer department. The off-campus store sells textbooks, school supplies, and licensed apparel and gifts and it has a large trade book department. The on-campus store has very limited parking, but it is within easy walking distance of the downtown area, all dormitories, and the football stadium and basketball arena. The off-campus store has plenty of parking, but it is not within walking distance of campus, although it is on the town bus line. Both stores compete with several other independent and national chain college bookstores in the town plus several school supply stores, apparel stores, computer stores, and trade bookstores. The town and university have been growing steadily over the past decade, and the football team has been highly ranked and gone to a bowl for eight straight seasons.

The Tech bookstores have a long-standing policy of selling textbooks with a very small markup (just above cost), which causes

	CAMPUS STORE				OFF-CAMPUS STORE			
	STUDENT		NONSTUDENT		STUDENT		NONSTUDENT	
	YES	NO	YES	NO	YES	NO	YES	NO
Were employees courteous and friendly?	572	93	286	147	341	114	172	156
Were employees knowledgeable and helpful?	522	143	231	212	350	105	135	193
Was the overall service good?	569	96	278	165	322	133	180	148
Did you have to wait long for service?	74	591	200	243	51	404	150	178
Did you have to wait long to check out?	81	584	203	240	72	383	147	181
Was the item you wanted available?	602	63	371	72	407	48	296	32
Was the cost of your purchase(s) reasonable?	385	280	398	45	275	180	301	27
Have you visited the store's website?	335	330	52	391	262	193	17	311

competing stores to follow suit. However, because textbooks are so expensive anyway most students believe the Tech bookstores gouge them on textbook prices. In order to offset the lack of profit on textbooks, the Tech bookstores sell all other products at a relatively high price. All "profits" from the stores are used to fund student-related projects such as new athletic fields and student center enhancements.

Tech Services has a board of directors made up of faculty, administrators, and students. The executive director, Mr. David Watson, reports to the board of directors and oversees the operation of the bookstores (plus all on-campus vending and athletic event vending). His office is in the on-campus store. Both bookstores have a store manager and an assistant store manager. There is one textbook manager for both stores, a trade book manager, a single school supplies and apparel manager, and a computer department manager, as well as a number of staff people, including a computer director and staff, a marketing director, a finance staff, a personnel director, a warehouse manager and secretaries. Almost all of the floor employees, including cash register operators, sales clerks, stock people, delivery truck drivers, and warehouse workers, are part-time Tech students. Hiring Tech students has been a long-standing university policy in order to provide students with employment opportunities. The bookstores have a high rate of turnover among the student employees, as would be expected.

Several incidents have occurred at the off-campus store that have caused the Tech Services board of directors concern. In one incident a student employee was arrested for drug possession. In another incident a faculty customer and student employee got into a shouting match when the employee could not locate a well-known book on the bookstore computer system and the faculty member got frustrated over the time it was taking. In still another incident an alumnus who had visited the store after a football game sent a letter to the university president indicating that a student employee had been rude to him when he asked a question about the return policy for an apparel item he had purchased on the bookstore's website. When the student did not know the return policy, he told the customer in a condescending manner to come back later. The last incident was an offhand remark made by a local town resident to a board member at a party about the difficulty she had completing a purchase at the mall store because the registers were unmanned, although she could see several employees talking together in the store.

Although sales and profits at the bookstore have been satisfactory and steady over the past few years, the board of directors is extremely sensitive to criticism about anything that might have the potential to embarrass the university. The board of directors suggested to Mr. Watson that he might consider some type of assessment of the service at the bookstores to see if there was a problem. Mr. Watson initially attempted to make random, surprise visits to the bookstores to see if he could detect any problems; however, there seemed to be a jungle telegraph system that alerted his employees whenever he entered a store, so he abandoned that idea. Next he decided to try two other things. First he conducted a customer survey during a two-week period in the middle of the semester at both stores. As customers left the store, he had employees ask them to respond to a brief questionnaire. Second, he hired several graduate students to pose as customers and make purchases and ask specific questions of sales clerks, and report on their experiences.

Selected results from the customer survey are in the table above.

The only consistent responses from the graduate students posing as customers were that the student employees were sometimes not that familiar with store policies, how to operate the store computer systems, what products were available, and where products were located in the stores. When they didn't know something they sometimes got defensive. A few also said that students sometimes appeared lackadaisical and bored.

Using observations of the operation of your own college bookstores to assist you, answer the following questions.

a. Why do you think Mr. Watson organized the customer survey the way he did? What other things do you think he might have done to analyze the stores' quality problems?

b. Develop Pareto charts to help analyze the survey results.

c. How would you define quality at the bookstores?

d. Discuss what you believe are the quality problems the bookstores have.

e. What are the bookstores' costs of poor quality?

f. What actions or programs would you propose to improve quality at the bookstores?

g. What obstacles do you perceive might exist to hinder changes at the bookstores and quality improvement?

h. What benefits do you think would result from quality improvement at the bookstores?

Case Problem 2.4 Product Yield at Continental Luggage Company

The Continental Luggage Company manufactures several different styles of soft- and hardcover luggage, briefcases, hanging bags, and purses. Its best-selling item is a line of hardcover luggage called the Trotter. It is produced in a basic five-stage assembly process that can accommodate several different outer coverings and colors. The assembly process includes constructing a heavy-duty plastic and metal frame; attaching the outer covering; joining the top and bottom and attaching the hinge mechanism; attaching the latches, lock, and handle; and doing the finishing work, including the luggage lining.

ASSEMBLY STAGE	AVERAGE PERCENTAGE GOOD QUALITY	AVERAGE PERCENTAGE REWORKED
1	0.94	0.23
2	0.96	0.91
3	0.95	0.67
4	0.97	0.89
5	0.98	0.72

The market for luggage is extremely competitive, and product quality is a very important component in product sales and market share. Customers normally expect luggage to be able to withstand rough handling while retaining its shape and an attractive appearance and protecting the clothing and personal items inside the bag. They also prefer the bag to be lightweight and not cumbersome. Furthermore, customers expect the latches and locks to work properly over an extended period of time. Another key factor in sales is that the luggage must be stylish and visually appealing.

Because of the importance of quality, company management has established a process control procedure that includes inspection at each stage of the five major stages of the assembly process. The table at left shows the percentage of good-quality units yielded at each stage of the assembly process and the percentage of bad units that can be reworked, on average.

The first stage of the process is construction of the frame, and it is very difficult to rework the frame if an item is defective, which is reflected in the low percentage of reworked items.

Five hundred new pieces of luggage of a particular style and color are initiated through the assembly process each week. The company would like to know the weekly product yield and the number of input units that would be required to achieve a weekly yield of 500 units. Furthermore, the company would like to know the impact on product yield (given 500 initial starting units) if a quality-improvement program were introduced that would increase the average percentage of good-quality units at each stage by 1%.

References

Crosby, P. B. *Quality is Free*. New York: McGraw-Hill, 1979.

Deming, W. E. *Out of the Crisis*. Cambridge, MA: MIT Center for Advanced Engineering Study, 1986.

Evans, J. R., and W. M. Lindsay. *The Management and Control of Quality*. 3rd ed. St. Paul, MN: West, 1996.

Feigenbaum, A. V. *Total Quality Control*. 3rd ed. New York: McGraw-Hill, 1983.

Garvin, D. A. *Managing Quality*. New York: Free Press/Macmillan, 1988.

Ishikawa, K. *Guide to Quality Control*. 2nd ed. White Plains, NY: Kraus International Publications, 1986.

Juran, J. M. *Juran on Planning for Quality*. New York: Free Press/Macmillan, 1988.

Juran, J. M., and F. M. Gryna, Jr. *Quality Planning and Analysis*. 2nd ed. New York: McGraw-Hill, 1980.

Montgomery, D. C. *Introduction to Statistical Quality Control*. 2nd ed. New York: John Wiley, 1991.

Taguchi, G. *Introduction to Quality Engineering*. Tokyo: Asian Productivity Organization, 1986.

CHAPTER 3

Statistical Process Control

Bloomberg/Contributor/Getty Images, Inc.

LEARNING OBJECTIVES

After reading this chapter, you will be able to:

- Explain when and how to use statistical process control to ensure the quality of products and services.
- Discuss the rationale and procedure for constructing control charts.
- Utilize attribute control charts to determine if a process is in control.
- Utilize variable control charts to determine if a process is in control.
- Identify control chart patterns and describe appropriate data collection.
- Develop control charts using Excel and OM Tools.
- Assess the process capability of a process.

Quality Control in Smartphone Manufacturing

Because of the importance of quality to smartphone purchasers—often more important than price—process control techniques are employed throughout the smartphone supply chain. All smartphone manufacturers, and especially Samsung and Apple, have well-developed and extensive quality management systems that make use of a host of quantitative techniques and tools, including, very prominently, statistical process control (SPC), to monitor and improve manufacturing processes in order to remove and prevent defects.

The key physical part of every cell phone is its electronics, which controls everything, from the way the phone displays information, places calls, sends location information, takes pictures, and more. For most smartphones, there are three key components: a printed circuit that controls the keypad and signal reception, a battery, and a screen. First, the casing for the phone is made, usually from simple plastic using a process known as injection molding, and sometimes from metal. Next, a printed circuit board with the necessary electronic components including chips and a software/operating system is placed into the casing using a series of eyeglass screws. Finally, the other key components of the phone are added, including the display screen, keypad, antenna, microphone, and speaker. After the phone is assembled, it is tested. During the testing phase, the battery for the phone is added and a worker checks the phone for power, button functionality, and reception. All the different component parts that go into an assembled smartphone are typically made by different suppliers from around the globe. Apple manufactures few of its own components; it has over 800 suppliers around the world, nearly half in China where final manufacture takes place, and all are subject to Apple's very stringent quality standards. Some of Apple's major competitors are also its major suppliers. For example, Samsung produces chips for Apple smartphones and LG is the leading supplier of Apple display panels. To maintain the quality Apple requires, its suppliers make extensive and pervasive use of statistical process control, among other quality control tools, to make sure there is little-to-no variation in complex smartphone component manufacturing processes, to prevent defects, and to continually improve processes. At Samsung, for example, statistical process control is a key method used in its chip and smartphone manufacturing processes to ensure that its products will have excellent unfailing quality and to guarantee customer satisfaction.

In this chapter we will learn about the fundamentals of statistical process control (SPC) that companies and organizations use to monitor and test processes so that they won't produce defective products or services, and so customers will be satisfied.

After World War II, W. E. Deming, the quality expert and consultant, was invited to Japan by the Japanese government to give a series of lectures on improving product reliability. This was probably the single most important event that started the Japanese toward a global quality revolution. These lectures were based on statistical quality control, and they became a cornerstone of the Japanese commitment to quality management.

Statistical process control (SPC) Involves monitoring the production process to detect and prevent poor quality.

A major topic in statistical quality control is *statistical process control*. **Statistical process control (SPC)** is a statistical procedure using control charts to see if any part of a production process is not functioning properly and could cause poor quality. SPC is used to inspect and measure the production process to see if it is varying from what it is supposed to be doing. If there is unusual or undesirable variability, the process is corrected so that defects will not occur. In this way, statistical process control is used to prevent poor quality before it occurs. It is such an important part of quality management that nearly all workers at all levels in companies committed to quality management are given extensive and continual training in SPC. Conversely, in many companies the reason cited for failure to achieve high quality is the lack of comprehensive training for employees in SPC methods. U.S. companies successful in quality management train employees in SPC methods and make extensive use of SPC for continuous process improvement.

The Basics of Statistical Process Control

Sample A subset of the items produced to use for inspection.

Process control is achieved by taking periodic **samples** from the process and plotting these sample points on a chart, to see if the process is within statistical control limits. A sample can be a single item or a group of items. If a sample point is outside the limits, the process may be out of control, and the cause is sought so that the problem can be corrected. If the sample is within the control limits, the process continues without interference but with continued monitoring. In this way, SPC prevents quality problems by correcting the process before it starts producing defects.

No production process produces exactly identical items, one after the other. All processes contain a certain amount of variability that makes some variation between units inevitable. There are two reasons why a process might vary. The first is the inherent random variability of the process, which depends on the equipment and machinery, engineering, the operator, and the system used for measurement. This kind of variability is a result of natural occurrences. The other reason for variability is unique or special causes that are identifiable and can be corrected. These causes tend to be nonrandom and, if left unattended, will cause poor quality. These might include equipment that is out of adjustment, defective materials, changes in parts or materials, broken machinery or equipment, operator fatigue or poor work methods, or errors due to lack of training.

SPC in Quality Management

Companies use SPC to see if their processes are in control—working properly. This requires that companies provide SPC training on a continuing basis that stresses that SPC is a tool

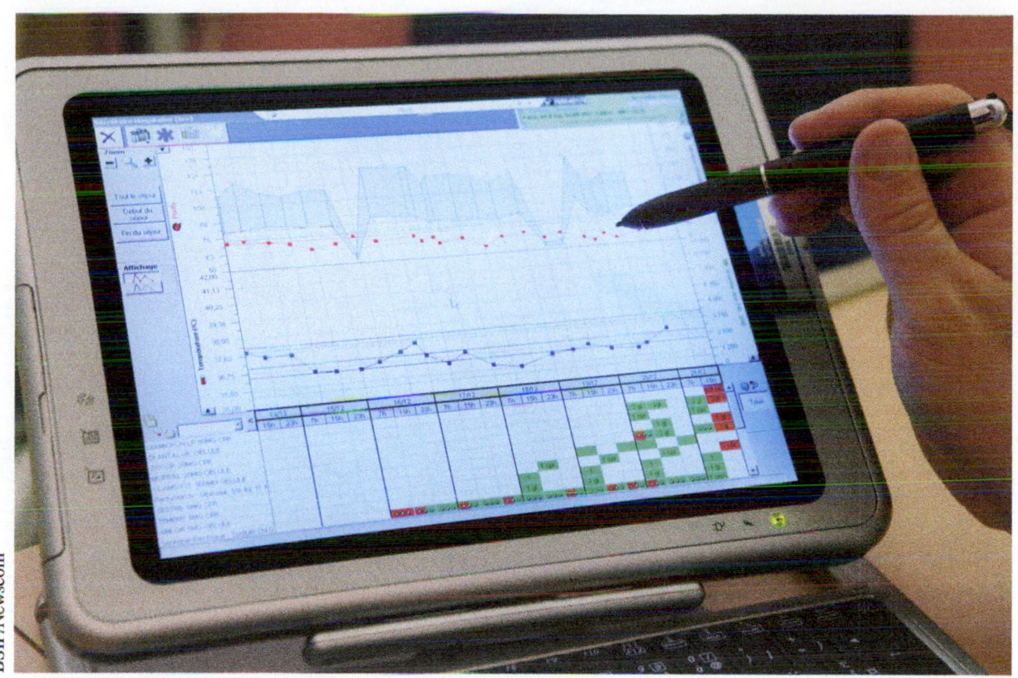

BSIP/Newscom

A statistical control chart is a graph to monitor a production process. By monitoring a process with a control chart, the employee and management can detect problems quickly and prevent poor-quality items from proceeding through the remainder of the process and ending up as defective products that must be thrown away or reworked, thus wasting time and resources.

individuals can use to monitor production or service process *for the purpose of making improvements*. Through the use of statistical process control, employees can be made responsible for quality in their area: to identify problems and either correct them or seek help in correcting them. By continually monitoring the production process and making improvements, the employee contributes to the goal of continuous improvement and few or no defects.

The first step in correcting the problem is identifying the causes. In Chapter 2 we described several quality-control tools used for identifying causes of problems, including brainstorming, Pareto charts, histograms, checksheets, quality circles, and fishbone (cause-and-effect) diagrams.

When an employee is unable to correct a problem, management typically initiates problem solving. This problem-solving activity may be within a group like a quality circle, or it

Along the Supply Chain

Using Sampling and Statistics to Analyze MillerCoors Distribution Network Performance

MillerCoors is a U.S. manufacturer of beer brands including Miller, Coors, Molson, and Blue Moon, operating 10 breweries with a network of over 500 distributors servicing over 700,000 retail accounts, including supermarkets, bars, and restaurants. All U.S. breweries are required by law (emanating from the repeal of prohibition) to use a three-tier distribution system with a wholesaler/distributor layer between the brewery and the retail customer. An advantage of this system is that the distributor has direct local contact with retailers, which can help them develop a locally engaged market strategy. However, the distribution network must also be efficient and cost effective in order to deliver the brewer's products to retailers fresh, in a timely manner, and damage free.

MillerCoors collects data from its distributors for seven attributes, weighted according to business considerations—expired products, processes, product damage, in-house audits, incorrect product staging, quality certifications, and consumer complaints. Data are collected using facility inspections and retail account audits; the latter collected by visiting a sample of 15, 20, or 25 random retailers based on the size of the distributor. This results in over 6000 of the brewer's national retail accounts being audited each year. These data are used to develop a performance ranking of distributors based on a scaled score of each of the seven quality attributes (computed by using the z value for a normal distribution). The final rankings are developed by multiplying each distributor's score by the weighting factors, and adding the seven attribute scores for each distributor, and then "curving" (like grades are curved in a class) the summed distributor scores to develop a systemwide comparison based on performance. One direct outcome of the evaluation process was discovering (using a process flow diagram) that there was excessive and inefficient package handling in the distribution system.

Identify another company with a national distribution network and discuss how it might use a similar sampling process to evaluate distributor's performance.

Source: Based on Tony Gojanovic and Ernie Jiminez, "Brewed Awakening, Beer Maker Uses Statistical Methods to Improve How Its Products Are Distributed," *Quality Progress* 43 (4); (April 2010), pp. 38–44.

Housekeepers at luxury hotels like the Ritz-Carlton strive to achieve the hotel's goal of a totally defect-free guest experience. Housekeeping processes are closely monitored for defects using statistical process control techniques.

Larry Lilac/Alamy

may be less formal, including other employees, engineers, quality experts, and management. This group will brainstorm the problem to seek out possible causes. Alternatively, quality problems can be corrected through Six Sigma projects.

Quality Measures: Attributes and Variables

Attribute A product characteristic that can be evaluated with a discrete response (good/bad, yes/no).

Variable measure A product characteristic that is continuous and can be measured (weight, length).

The quality of a product or service can be evaluated using either an *attribute* of the product or service or a *variable measure*. An **attribute** is a product characteristic such as color, surface texture, cleanliness, or perhaps smell or taste. Attributes can be evaluated quickly with a discrete response such as good or bad, acceptable or not, or yes or no. Even if quality specifications are complex and extensive, a simple attribute test might be used to determine whether or not a product or service is defective. For example, an operator might test a light bulb by simply turning it on and seeing if it lights. If it does not, it can be examined to find out the exact technical cause for failure, but for SPC purposes, the fact that it is defective has been determined.

A **variable measure** is a product characteristic that is measured on a continuous scale such as length, weight, temperature, or time. For example, the amount of liquid detergent in a plastic container can be measured to see if it conforms to the company's product specifications. Or the time it takes to serve a customer at McDonald's can be measured to see if it is quick enough. Since a variable evaluation is the result of some form of measurement, it is sometimes referred to as a *quantitative* classification method. An attribute evaluation is sometimes referred to as a *qualitative* classification, since the response is not measured. Because it is a measurement, a variable classification typically provides more information about the product—the weight of a product is more informative than simply saying the product is good or bad.

SPC Applied to Services

Control charts have historically been used to monitor the quality of manufacturing processes. However, SPC is just as useful for monitoring quality in services as shown in photo. The difference is the nature of the "defect" being measured and monitored. Using Motorola's definition—*a failure to meet customer requirements in any product or service*—a defect can be an empty soap dispenser in a restroom or an error with a phone catalog order, as well as a blemish on a piece of cloth or a faulty tray on a DVD player. Control charts for service processes tend to use quality characteristics and measurements such as time and customer satisfaction (determined by surveys, questionnaires, or inspections). Following is a list of several different services and the quality characteristics for each that can be measured and monitored with control charts.

Hospitals: Timeliness and quickness of care, staff responses to requests, accuracy of lab tests, cleanliness, courtesy, accuracy of paperwork, speed of admittance and checkouts.

Grocery stores: Waiting time to check out, frequency of out-of-stock items, quality of food items, cleanliness, customer complaints, checkout register errors.

Airlines: Flight delays, lost luggage and luggage handling, waiting time at ticket counters and check-in, agent and flight attendant courtesy, accurate flight information, passenger cabin cleanliness and maintenance.

Fast-food restaurants: Waiting time for service, customer complaints, cleanliness, food quality, order accuracy, employee courtesy.

Catalog-order companies: Order accuracy, operator knowledge and courtesy, packaging, delivery time, phone order waiting time.

Insurance companies: Billing accuracy, timeliness of claims processing, agent availability and response time.

Where to Use Control Charts

Most companies do not use control charts for every step in a process. Although that might be the most effective way to ensure the highest quality, it is costly and time consuming. In most manufacturing and service processes, there are clearly identifiable points where control charts should be used. In general, control charts are used at critical points in the process where historically the process has shown a tendency to go out of control, and at points where if the process goes out of control it is particularly harmful and costly. For example, control charts are frequently used at the beginning of a process to check the quality of raw materials and parts, or supplies and deliveries for a service operation. If material and parts are bad to begin with, it is a waste of time and money to begin the production process with them. Control charts are also used before a costly or irreversible point in the process, after which the product is difficult to rework or correct; before and after assembly or painting operations that might cover defects; and before the outgoing final product or service is shipped or delivered.

Along the Supply Chain

Quality Food and Service at the Cheesecake Factory

The Cheesecake Factory, with over 150 restaurants across the United States, serves more than 80 million customers per year. The restaurant's extensive menu includes over 300 items, served in a clean, friendly, and efficient environment that has gained the Cheesecake Factory a reputation for quality food and service at reasonable prices. One thing that helps chain restaurants such as the Cheesecake Factory thrive is their size, which gives them buying power. This allows them to centralize common supply chain functions, and adopt innovations quicker than smaller restaurants. These basic factors have made Walmart the most successful retail firm on the planet.

Almost all Cheesecake Factory menu items are made from scratch—except, ironically, the cheesecake, which is made at a company bakery in California. The kitchen design is the same for all Cheesecake Factory restaurants, laid out like a manufacturing assembly line with raw materials coming in at the back of the facility and finished items rolling out the front. Along the restaurant's back wall are walk-in refrigerators and prep stations where food is chopped, stirred, and mixed. In the next food preparation area there are two parallel lines of 40-foot countertops, a hot side with stovetops and grills, and an opposite cold side neatly laid out with bins of fixings.

The highly trained prep staff handles parts, stocking pullout drawers with the food items (i.e., meats, fishes, rice, potatoes, etc.), while cooks assemble the final products. Overhead computer monitors located every few feet along the assembly line include touch-screen tabs for the precise recipe for each order with photos of how the preparation should look. A timer on the screen counts down a target time for completion and the screen background turns from green to yellow as the order target time is getting close, and to red when the target time is reached.

As each order comes off the assembly line, a kitchen manager inspects the food for defects, including appearance, and rates the food on a scale from 1 to 10, with 9 as near–perfect. An 8 requires one or two corrections while a 7 requires three corrections, and 6 is unacceptable and must be redone. Any consistent pattern of defects causes the kitchen manager to address the responsible station.

The managers also monitor the processing time, looking for instances where red screens are accumulating, indicating that "late" orders are stacking up. They also watch for food waste plus wasted effort and time. The company's target for food use efficiency is 97.5%, with only 2.5% of groceries thrown away without running out of food. The company achieves this high level of material efficiency by using forecasting models based on six-week and annual historical trend data, adjusted for factors like weather and sporting events, to gain a very high level of sales predictability.

Do you think the Cheesecake Factory's order processing system is likely unique to itself, or would it be similar to what other sit-down restaurant chains, and individual independent restaurants, might use?

Source: Based on Atul Gawande, "Big Med," The *New Yorker* (August 13 and 20, 2012), pp. 53–63.

FIGURE 3.1 **Process Control Chart**

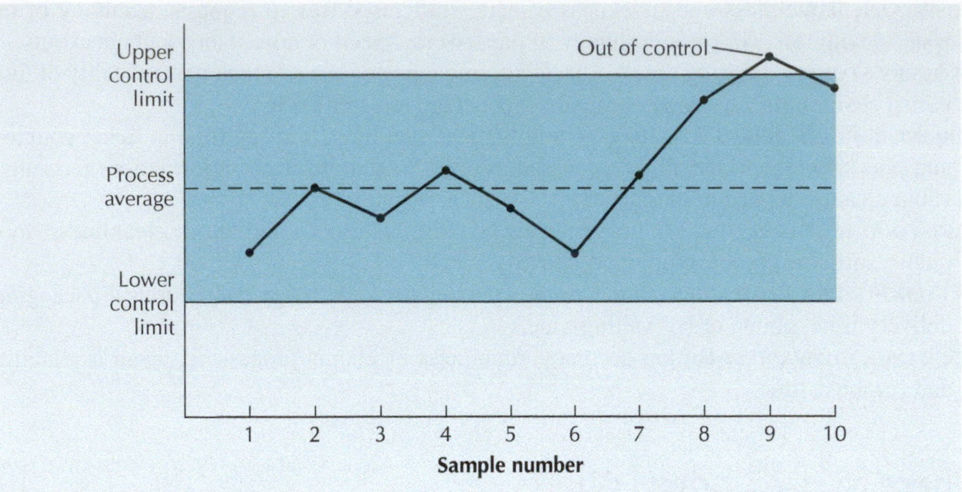

Control Charts

Control chart A graph that establishes the control limits of a process.

Control limits The upper and lower bands of a control chart.

Control charts are graphs that visually show if a sample is within statistical **control limits.** They have two basic purposes: to establish the control limits for a process and then to monitor the process to indicate when it is out of control. Control charts exist for attributes and variables; within each category there are several different types of control charts. We will present four commonly used control charts, two in each category: *p*-charts and *c*-charts for attributes and *mean* ($\bar{x}$) and *range* (R) control charts for variables. Even though these control charts differ in how they measure process control, they all have certain similar characteristics. They all look alike, with a line through the center of a graph that indicates the process average and lines above and below the center line that represent the upper and lower limits of the process, as shown in Figure 3.1.

The formulas for conducting upper and lower limits in control charts are based on a number of standard deviations, z, from the process average (e.g., center line) according to a normal distribution. Occasionally, z is equal to 2.00 but most frequently is 3.00. A z value of 2.00 corresponds to an overall normal probability of 95%, and $z = 3.00$ corresponds to a normal probability of 99.73%.

The normal distribution in Figure 3.2 below shows the probabilities corresponding to z values equal to 2.00 and 3.00 standard deviations (σ).

The smaller the value of z, the more narrow the control limits are and the more sensitive the chart is to changes in the production process. Control charts using $z = 2.00$ are often referred to as having 2-sigma (2σ) limits (referring to two standard deviations), whereas $z = 3.00$ means 3-sigma (3σ) limits.

Management usually selects $z = 3.00$ because if the process is in control it wants a high probability that the sample values will fall within the control limits. In other words, with wider limits management is less likely to (erroneously) conclude that the process is out of control when points outside the control limits are due to normal, random variations. Alternatively, wider limits make it harder to detect changes in the process that are not random and have an assignable cause. A process might change because of a nonrandom, assignable cause and be detectable with the narrower limits but not with the wider limits. However, companies traditionally use the wider control limits.

FIGURE 3.2 **The Normal Distribution**

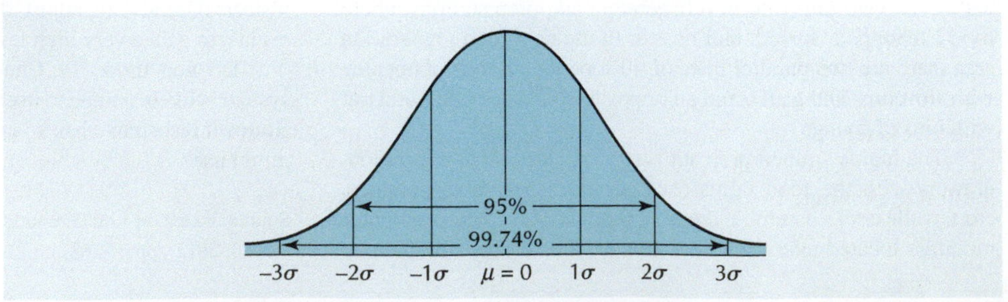

Each time a sample is taken, the mathematical average of the sample is plotted as a point on the control chart as shown in Figure 3.1. A process is generally considered to be in control if, for example,

1. There are no sample points outside the control limits.
2. Most points are near the process average (i.e., the center line), without too many close to the control limits.
3. Approximately equal numbers of sample points occur above and below the center line.
4. The points appear to be randomly distributed around the center line (i.e., no discernible pattern).

If any of these conditions are violated, the process may be *out of control*. The reason must be determined, and if the cause is not random, the problem must be corrected.

Sample 9 in Figure 3.1 is above the upper control limit, suggesting the process is out of control (i.e., something unusual has happened). The cause is not likely to be random since the sample points have been moving toward the upper limit, so management should attempt to find out what is wrong with the process and bring it back in control. Perhaps the employee was simply interrupted. Although the other samples display some degree of variation from the process average, they are usually considered to be caused by normal, random variability in the process and are thus in control. However, it is possible for sample observations to be within the control limits and the process to be out of control anyway, if the observations display a discernible, abnormal pattern of movement. We discuss such patterns in a later section.

After a control chart is established, it is used to determine when a process goes out of control and corrections need to be made. As such, a process control chart should be based only on sample observations from when the process is in control so that the control chart reflects a true benchmark for an in-control process. However, it is not known whether the process is in control until the control chart is first constructed. Therefore, when a control chart is first developed if the process is found to be out of control, the process should be examined and corrections made. A new center line and control limits should then be determined from a new set of sample observations. This "corrected" control chart is then used to monitor the process. It may not be possible to discover the cause(s) for the out-of-control sample observations. In this case, a new set of samples is taken, and a completely new control chart constructed. Or it may be decided simply to use the initial control chart, assuming that it accurately reflects the process variation.

Control Charts for Attributes

The quality measures used in *attribute control charts* are discrete values reflecting a simple decision criterion such as good or bad. A ***p*-chart** uses the proportion of defective items in a sample as the sample statistic; a **c-chart** uses the actual number of defects per item in a sample. A *p*-chart can be used when it is possible to distinguish between defective and non-defective items and to state the number of defectives as a percentage of the whole. In some processes, the proportion defective cannot be determined. For example, when counting the number of blemishes on a roll of upholstery material (at periodic intervals), it is not possible to compute a proportion. In this case a *c*-chart is required.

***p*-chart** Uses the proportion defective in a sample.

***c*-chart** Uses the number of defects in a sample.

p-Chart

With a *p*-chart a sample of n items is taken periodically from the production or service process, and the proportion of defective items in the sample is determined to see if the proportion falls within the control limits on the chart. Although a *p*-chart employs a discrete attribute measure (i.e., number of defective items) and thus is not continuous, it is assumed that as the sample size (n) gets larger, the normal distribution can be used to approximate the distribution of the proportion defective. This enables us to use the following formulas based on the normal distribution to compute the upper control limit (UCL) and lower control limit (LCL) of a *p*-chart:

$$\text{UCL} = \bar{p} + z\sigma_p$$

$$\text{LCL} = \bar{p} - z\sigma_p$$

where

z = the number of standard deviations from the process average

$\bar{p}$ = the sample proportion defective; an estimate of the process average

σ_p = the standard deviation of the sample proportion

The sample standard deviation is computed as

$$\sigma_p = \sqrt{\frac{\bar{p}(1-\bar{p})}{n}}$$

where n is the sample size.

Example 3.1 demonstrates how a p-chart is constructed.

EXAMPLE 3.1 | Construction of a *p*-Chart

The Western Jeans Company produces denim jeans. The company wants to establish a p-chart to monitor the production process and maintain high quality. Western believes that approximately 99.74% of the variability in the production process (corresponding to 3-sigma limits, or $z = 3.00$) is random and thus should be within control limits, whereas 0.26% of the process variability is not random and suggests that the process is out of control.

The company has taken 20 samples (one per day for 20 days), each containing 100 pairs of jeans ($n = 100$), and inspected them for defects, the results of which are as follows.

SAMPLE	NUMBER OF DEFECTIVES	PROPORTION DEFECTIVES
1	6	.06
2	0	.00
3	4	.04
4	10	.10
5	6	.06
6	4	.04
7	12	.12
8	10	.10
9	8	.08
10	10	.10
11	12	.12
12	10	.10
13	14	.14
14	8	.08
15	6	.06
16	16	.16
17	12	.12
18	14	.14
19	20	.20
20	18	.18
	200	

The proportion defective for the population is not known. The company wants to construct a p-chart to determine when the production process might be out of control.

Solution: Since p is not known, it can be estimated from the total sample:

$$\bar{p} = \frac{\text{total defectives}}{\text{total sample observations}} = \frac{200}{20(100)} = 0.10$$

The control limits are computed as follows:

$$\text{UCL} = \bar{p} + z\sqrt{\frac{\bar{p}(1-\bar{p})}{n}}$$

$$= 0.10 + 3.00\sqrt{\frac{0.10(1-0.10)}{100}} = 0.190$$

$$\text{LCL} = \bar{p} - z\sqrt{\frac{\bar{p}(1-\bar{p})}{n}}$$

$$= 0.10 - 3.00\sqrt{\frac{0.10(1-0.10)}{100}} = 0.010$$

The p-chart, including sample points, is shown in the following figure.

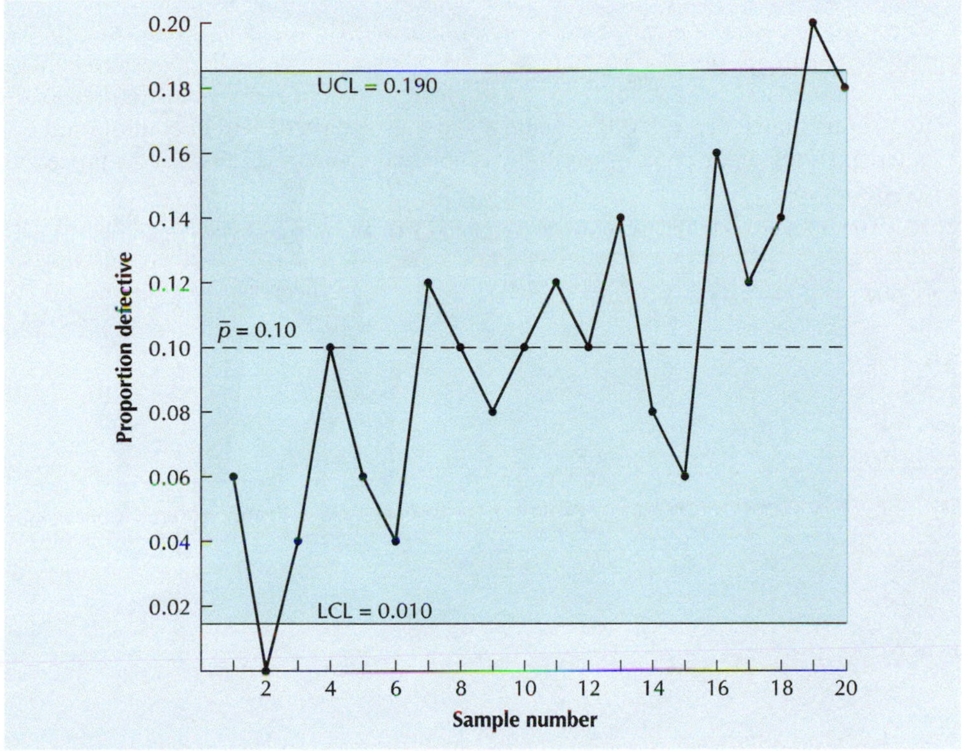

The process was below the lower control limits for sample 2 (i.e., during day 2). Although this could be perceived as a "good" result since it means there were very few defects, it might also suggest that something was wrong with the inspection process during that week that should be checked out. If there is no problem with the inspection process, then management would want to know what caused the quality of the process to improve. Perhaps "better" denim material came from a new supplier that week or a different operator was working.

The process was above the upper limit during day 19. This suggests that the process may not be in control and the cause should be investigated. The cause could be defective or maladjusted machinery, a problem with an operator, defective materials (i.e., denim cloth), or a number of other correctable problems. In fact, there is an upward trend in the number of defectives throughout the 20-day test period. The process was consistently moving toward an out-of-control situation. This trend represents a pattern in the observations, which suggests a nonrandom cause. If this was the actual control chart used to monitor the process (and not the initial chart), it is likely this pattern would have indicated an out-of-control situation before day 19, which would have alerted the operator to make corrections. Patterns are discussed in a separate section later in this chapter.

This initial control chart shows two out-of-control observations and a distinct pattern of increasing defects. Management would probably want to discard this set of samples and develop a new center line and control limits from a different set of sample values after the process has been corrected. If the pattern had not existed and only the two out-of-control observations were present, these two observations could be discarded, and a control chart could be developed from the remaining sample values.

Once a control chart is established based solely on natural, random variation in the process, it is used to monitor the process. Samples are taken periodically, and the observations are checked on the control chart to see if the process is in control.

Marta Sarlo/contrasto/Redux

A quality inspector at a jeans manufacturer tests the quality attributes (i.e., shrinkage) of a new pair of jeans.

c-Chart

A *c*-chart is used when it is not possible to compute a proportion defective and the actual number of defects must be used. For example, when automobiles are inspected, the number of blemishes (i.e., defects) in the paint job can be counted for each car, but a proportion cannot be computed, since the total number of possible blemishes is not known. In this case a single car is the sample. Since the number of defects per sample is assumed to derive from some extremely large population, the probability of a single defect is very small. As with the *p*-chart, the normal distribution can be used to approximate the distribution of defects. The process average for the *c*-chart is the mean number of defects per item, $\bar{c}$, computed by dividing the total number of defects by the number of samples. The sample standard deviation, σ_c, is $\sqrt{\bar{c}}$. The following formulas for the control limits are used:

$$\text{UCL} = \bar{c} + z\sigma_c$$

$$\text{LCL} = \bar{c} - z\sigma_c$$

EXAMPLE 3.2 | Construction of a *c*-Chart

The Ritz Hotel has 240 rooms. The hotel's housekeeping department is responsible for maintaining the quality of the rooms' appearance and cleanliness. Each individual housekeeper is responsible for an area encompassing 20 rooms. Every room in use is thoroughly cleaned and its supplies, toiletries, and so on are restocked each day. Any defects that the housekeeping staff notice that are not part of the normal housekeeping service are supposed to be reported to hotel maintenance. Every room is briefly inspected each day by a housekeeping supervisor. However, hotel management also conducts inspection tours at random for a detailed, thorough inspection for quality-control purposes. The management inspectors not only check for normal housekeeping service defects like clean sheets, dust, room supplies, room literature, or towels, but also for defects like an inoperative or missing TV remote, poor TV picture quality or reception, defective lamps, a malfunctioning clock, tears or stains in the bedcovers or curtains, or a malfunctioning curtain pull. An inspection sample includes 12 rooms, that is, one room selected at random from each of the twelve 20-room blocks serviced by a housekeeper. Following are the results from 15 inspection samples conducted at random during a one-month period:

SAMPLE	NUMBER OF DEFECTS
1	12
2	8
3	16
4	14
5	10
6	11
7	9
8	14
9	13
10	15
11	12
12	10
13	14
14	17
15	15
	190

The hotel believes that approximately 99% of the defects (corresponding to 3-sigma limits) are caused by natural, random variations in the housekeeping and room maintenance service, with 1% caused by nonrandom variability. It wants to construct a *c*-chart to monitor the housekeeping service.

Solution: Because c, the population process average, is not known, the sample estimate, $\bar{c}$, can be used instead:

$$\bar{c} = \frac{190}{15} = 12.67$$

The control limits are computed using $z = 3.00$, as follows:

$$\text{UCL} = \bar{c} + z\sqrt{\bar{c}} = 12.67 + 3\sqrt{12.67} = 23.35$$
$$\text{LCL} = \bar{c} - z\sqrt{\bar{c}} = 12.67 - 3\sqrt{12.67} = 1.99$$

The resulting c-chart, with the sample points, is shown in the following figure:

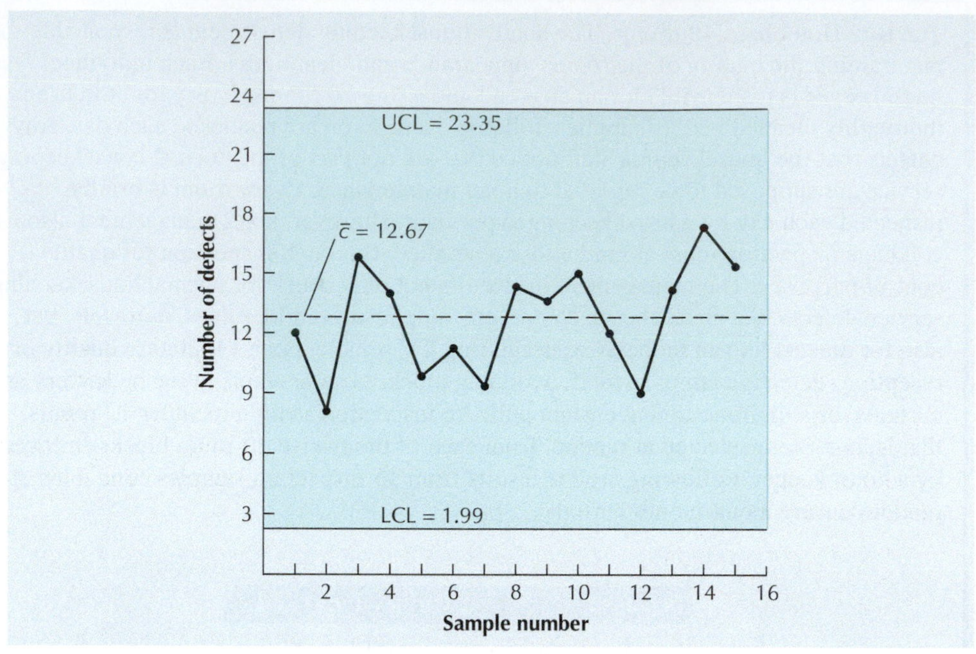

All the sample observations are within the control limits, suggesting that the room quality is in control. This chart would be considered reliable for monitoring the room quality in the future.

Control Charts for Variables

Range (R-) chart Uses the amount of dispersion in a sample.

Mean ($\bar{x}$-) chart Uses the process average of a sample.

Variable control charts are used for continuous variables that can be measured, such as weight or volume. Two commonly used variable control charts are the range chart, or R-chart, and the mean chart, or $\bar{x}$-chart. A **range (R-) chart** reflects the amount of dispersion present in each sample; a **mean ($\bar{x}$-) chart** indicates how sample results relate to the process average or mean. These charts are normally used together to determine whether a process is in control.

Mean ($\bar{x}$-) Chart

In a mean (or $\bar{x}$-) control chart, each time a sample of a group of items is taken from the process, the mean of the sample is computed and plotted on the chart. Each sample mean ($\bar{x}$) is a point on the control chart. The samples taken tend to be small, usually around 4 or 5. The center line of the control chart is the overall process average, that is, the mean of the sample means.

The $\bar{x}$-chart is based on the normal distribution. It can be constructed in two ways depending on the information that is available about the distribution. If the standard deviation of the distribution is known from past experience or historical data, then formulas using the standard deviation can be used to compute the upper and lower control limits. If the standard deviation is not known, then a table of values based on sample ranges is available to develop the upper and lower control limits. We will first look at how to construct an $\bar{x}$-chart when the standard deviation is known.

The formulas for computing the upper control limit (UCL) and lower control limit (LCL) are

$$\text{UCL} = \bar{\bar{x}} + z\sigma_{\bar{x}}$$
$$\text{LCL} = \bar{\bar{x}} - z\sigma_{\bar{x}}$$

where

$$\bar{\bar{x}} = \text{process average} = \frac{\bar{x}_1 + \bar{x}_2 + \cdots + \bar{x}_n}{k}$$

σ = process standard deviation

$\sigma_{\bar{x}}$ = standard deviation of sample means = $\sigma/\sqrt{n}$

k = number of samples

n = sample size (i.e., number of observations in each sample)

Example 3.3 illustrates how to develop an $\bar{x}$-chart using these formulas.

EXAMPLE 3.3 | Constructing an $\bar{x}$-Chart

The Goliath Tool Company produces slip-ring bearings, which look like flat doughnuts or washers. They fit around shafts or rods, such as drive shafts in machinery or motors. At an early stage in the production process for a particular slip-ring bearing, the outside diameter of the bearing is measured. Employees have taken 10 samples (during a 10-day period) of 5 slip-ring bearings and measured the diameter of the bearings. The individual observations from each sample (or subgroup) are as follows:

	OBSERVATIONS (SLIP-RING DIAMETER, CM), x					
SAMPLE k	1	2	3	4	5	$\bar{x}$
1	5.02	5.01	4.94	4.99	4.96	4.98
2	5.01	5.03	5.07	4.95	4.96	5.00
3	4.99	5.00	4.93	4.92	4.99	4.97
4	5.03	4.91	5.01	4.98	4.89	4.96
5	4.95	4.92	5.03	5.05	5.01	4.99
6	4.97	5.06	5.06	4.96	5.03	5.01
7	5.05	5.01	5.10	4.96	4.99	5.02
8	5.09	5.10	5.00	4.99	5.08	5.05
9	5.14	5.10	4.99	5.08	5.09	5.08
10	5.01	4.98	5.08	5.07	4.99	5.03
						50.09

From past historical data it is known that the process standard deviation is 0.08. The company wants to develop a control chart with 3-sigma limits to monitor this process in the future.

The process average is computed as

$$\bar{\bar{x}} = \frac{50.09}{10} = 5.01$$

The control limits are

$$\begin{aligned} \text{UCL} &= \bar{\bar{x}} + z\sigma_{\bar{x}} \\ &= 5.01 + 3(0.08/\sqrt{5}) \\ &= 5.12 \end{aligned}$$

$$\begin{aligned} \text{LCL} &= \bar{\bar{x}} - z\sigma_{\bar{x}} \\ &= 5.01 - 3(0.08/\sqrt{5}) \\ &= 4.90 \end{aligned}$$

None of the sample means ($\bar{x}$) falls outside these control limits, which indicates that the process is *in control* and this is an accurate control chart.

In the second approach to developing an $\bar{x}$-chart, the following formulas are used to compute the control limits:

$$\text{UCL} = \bar{\bar{x}} + A_2\bar{R}$$

$$\text{LCL} = \bar{\bar{x}} - A_2\bar{R}$$

TABLE 3.1 Factors for Determining Control Limits for $\bar{x}$- and R-Charts

SAMPLE SIZE	FACTOR FOR $\bar{x}$ CHART	FACTORS FOR R-CHART	
n	A_2	D_3	D_4
2	1.88	0	3.27
3	1.02	0	2.57
4	0.73	0	2.28
5	0.58	0	2.11
6	0.48	0	2.00
7	0.42	0.08	1.92
8	0.37	0.14	1.86
9	0.34	0.18	1.82
10	0.31	0.22	1.78
11	0.29	0.26	1.74
12	0.27	0.28	1.72
13	0.25	0.31	1.69
14	0.24	0.33	1.67
15	0.22	0.35	1.65
16	0.21	0.36	1.64
17	0.20	0.38	1.62
18	0.19	0.39	1.61
19	0.19	0.40	1.60
20	0.18	0.41	1.59
21	0.17	0.43	1.58
22	0.17	0.43	1.57
23	0.16	0.44	1.56
24	0.16	0.45	1.55
25	0.15	0.46	1.54

where $\bar{\bar{x}}$ is the average of the sample means and $\bar{R}$ is the average range value. A_2 is a tabular value that is used to establish the control limits. Values of A_2 are included in Table 3.1. They were developed specifically for determining the control limits for $\bar{x}$-charts and are comparable to three-standard deviation (3σ) limits. These table values are frequently used to develop control charts.

EXAMPLE 3.4 | An $\bar{x}$-Chart

The Goliath Tool Company desires to develop an $\bar{x}$-chart using table values. The sample data collected for this process with ranges is shown in the following table.

	OBSERVATIONS (SLIP-RING DIAMETER, CM), X						
SAMPLE k	1	2	3	4	5	$\bar{x}$	R
1	5.02	5.01	4.94	4.99	4.96	4.98	0.08
2	5.01	5.03	5.07	4.95	4.96	5.00	0.12
3	4.99	5.00	4.93	4.92	4.99	4.97	0.08
4	5.03	4.91	5.01	4.98	4.89	4.96	0.14
5	4.95	4.92	5.03	5.05	5.01	4.99	0.13

6	4.97	5.06	5.06	4.96	5.03	5.01	0.10
7	5.05	5.01	5.10	4.96	4.99	5.02	0.14
8	5.09	5.10	5.00	4.99	5.08	5.05	0.11
9	5.14	5.10	4.99	5.08	5.09	5.08	0.15
10	5.01	4.98	5.08	5.07	4.99	5.03	0.10
						50.09	1.15

The company wants to develop an $\bar{x}$-chart to monitor the process.

Solution: $\bar{R}$ is computed by first determining the range for each sample by computing the difference between the highest and lowest values as shown in the last column in our table of sample observations. These ranges are summed and then divided by the number of samples, ***k***, as follows:

$$\bar{R} = \frac{\Sigma R}{k} = \frac{1.15}{10} = 0.115$$

$\bar{\bar{x}}$ is computed as follows:

$$\bar{\bar{x}} = \frac{\Sigma \bar{x}}{k} = \frac{50.09}{10} = 5.01 \text{ cm}$$

Using the value of $A_2 = 0.58$ for $n = 5$ from Table 3.1 and $\bar{R} = 0.115$, we compute the control limits as

$$\begin{aligned} \text{UCL} &= \bar{\bar{x}} + A_2\bar{R} \\ &= 5.01 + (0.58)(0.115) = 5.08 \\ \text{LCL} &= \bar{\bar{x}} - A_2\bar{R} \\ &= 5.01 - (0.58)(0.115) + 4.94 \end{aligned}$$

The $\bar{x}$-chart defined by these control limits is shown in the following figure. Notice that the process is on the UCL for sample 9; in fact, samples 4 to 9 show an upward trend. This would suggest that the process variability is subject to nonrandom causes and should be investigated.

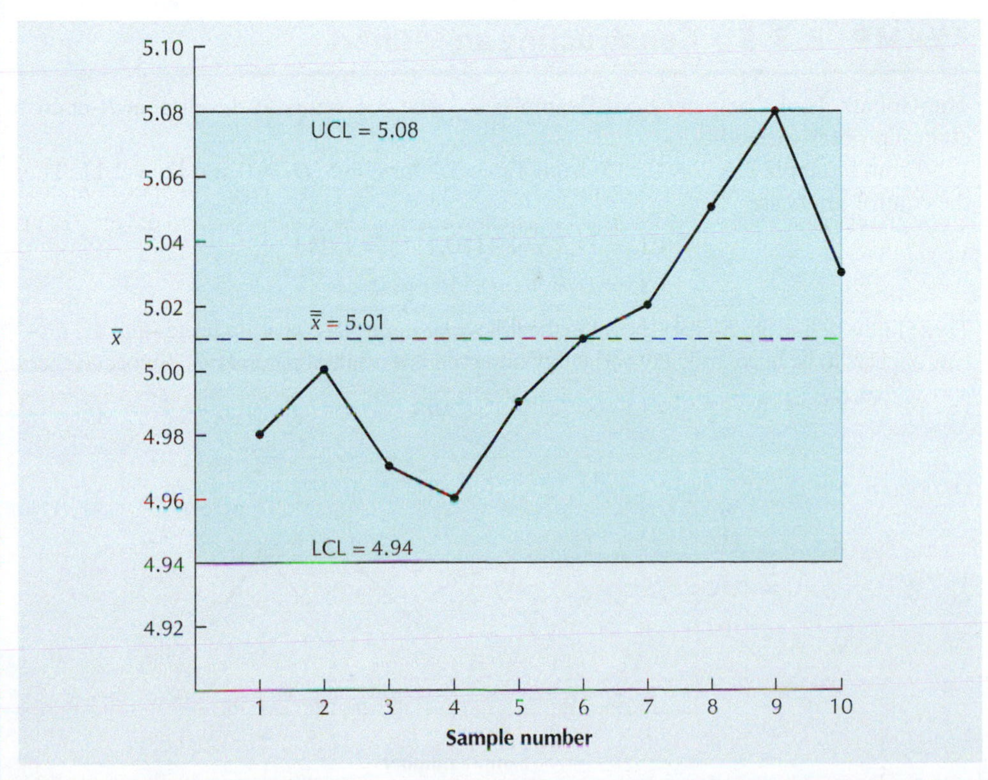

A quality control inspector tests samples of chocolate candy. The sample results can be plotted on a control chart to see if the production process is in control. If not, it will be corrected before a large number of defective candies are produced, thereby preventing costly waste.

Vincent Mundy/Bloomberg via Getty Images

Range (*R*-) Chart

Range The difference between the smallest and largest values in a sample.

In an *R*-chart, the **range** is the difference between the smallest and largest values in a sample. This range reflects the process variability instead of the tendency toward a mean value. The formulas for determining control limits are

$$\text{UCL} = D_4\overline{R}$$
$$\text{LCL} = D_3\overline{R}$$

$\overline{R}$ is the average range (and center line) for the samples,

$$\overline{R} = \frac{\Sigma R}{k}$$

where

R = range of each sample
k = number of samples (subgroups)

D_3 and D_4 are table values like A_2 for determining control limits that have been developed based on range values rather than standard deviations. Table 3.1 also includes values for D_3 and D_4 for sample sizes up to 25.

EXAMPLE 3.5 | Constructing an *R*-Chart

The Goliath Tool Company from Examples 3.3 and 3.4 wants to develop an *R*-chart to control process variability.

From Example 3.4, $\overline{R} = 0.115$; from Table 3.1 for $n = 5$, $D_3 = 0$ and $D_4 = 2.11$. Thus, the control limits are

$$\text{UCL} = D_4\overline{R} = 2.11(0.115) = 0.243$$
$$\text{LCL} = D_3\overline{R} = 0(0.115) = 0$$

These limits define the *R*-chart shown in the following figure. The chart indicates that the process appears to be in control; any variability observed is a result of natural random occurrences.

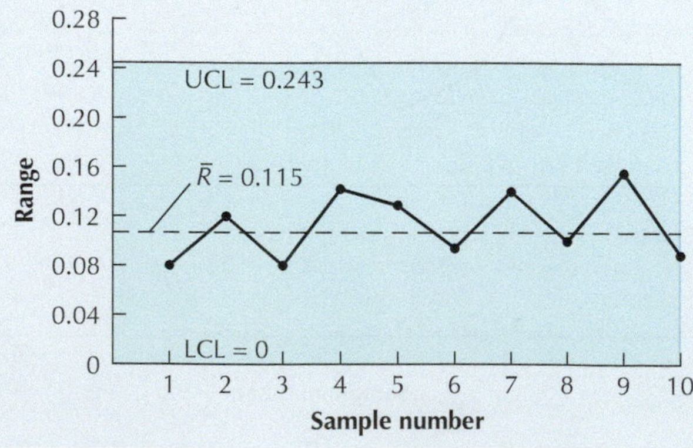

This example illustrates the need to employ the R-chart and the $\bar{x}$-chart together. The R-chart in this example suggests that the process is in control, since none of the ranges for the samples are close to the control limits. However, the $\bar{x}$-chart in Example 3.4 suggests that the process is not in control. In fact, the ranges for samples 8 and 10 were relatively narrow, whereas the means for these samples were relatively high. The use of both charts together provided a more complete picture of the overall process variability.

Using $\bar{X}$- and R-Charts Together

The $\bar{x}$-chart is used with the R-chart under the premise that both the process average and variability must be in control for the process to be in control. This is logical. The two charts measure the process differently. It is possible for samples to have very narrow ranges, suggesting little process variability, but the sample averages might be beyond the control limits.

For example, consider two samples, the first having low and high values of 4.95 and 5.05 centimeters, and the second having low and high values of 5.10 and 5.20 centimeters. The range of both is 0.10 centimeters, but $\bar{x}$ for the first is 5.00 centimeters and $\bar{x}$ for the second is 5.15 centimeters. The two sample ranges might indicate the process is in control and $\bar{x} = 5.00$ might be okay, but $\bar{x} = 5.15$ could be outside the control limit.

Conversely, it is possible for the sample averages to be in control, but the ranges might be very large. For example, two samples could both have $\bar{x} = 5.00$ centimeters, but sample 1 could have a range between 4.95 and 5.05 ($R = 0.10$ centimeter) and sample 2 could have a range between 4.80 and 5.20 ($R = 0.40$ centimeter). Sample 2 suggests the process is out of control.

Along the Supply Chain

Using Control Charts for Improving Healthcare Quality

The National Health Service (NHS) in the United Kingdom makes extensive use of SPC charts to improve service delivery to patients. SPC charts are frequently developed using Excel spreadsheets. Employees throughout NHS attend a two-day training course where they learn about X- and R-charts and their application. They also learn about Deming's 14 points and principles of quality management and how to improve processes in their own operation.

The number of possible applications of SPC charts for a healthcare facility is very high, with many applications relating to waiting times (as is the case with many service organizations); for example, the time to see a doctor, nurse, or other medical staff member, or to get medical results. One specific example in the NHS is "door to needle" times, which is the time it takes after a heart attack patient is registered into the hospital to receive an appropriate injection. The systemwide goverment-mandated target value for this process is that 75% of heart patients receive treatment within 20 minutes of being received into the hospital. Control charts are also used to monitor administrative errors.

Bellin Health System is as an integrated healthcare organization serving Green Bay, Wisconsin, and the surrounding region. It specializes in cardiac care and its 167-bed hospital is known as the regon's heart center. In addition it operates a psychiatric center, 20 regional clinics, and a college of nursing. Bellin's quality management program is based on improving processes by identifying measures of success, setting goals for improvement that can be measured, applying Deming's PDCA cycle (see Chapter 2) for improving processes, and using statistical process control charts to monitor processes for stability and to see if improvement efforts are successful. Bellin has over 1250 quality indicators reported monthly, quarterly, or annually, and over 90% are monitored with SPC charts. For example, one such quality indicator is for compliance with the Centers for Disease Control guidelines on healthcare hand hygiene, which Bellin measures across its entire system. The lack of hand hygiene is a leading cause of fatal hospital-borne infections, and thus a very important quality indicator. The quality resource department (QRD) at Bellin uses a p-chart to monitor hand hygiene for system nursing care, where the control measure is the portion of hand opportunities that meet the criteria divided by the total number of opportunities available to meet the criteria. Using SPC charts, Bellin was able to improve the hand hygiene process such that a 90% target level was acheived. Throughout the Bellin Health System, control charts are employed to identify special cause variations outside the norm in processes that require improvement. SPC has become an essential part of the continuous quality improvement program at Bellin used by all members of the organization to improve service and healthcare, and reduce costs.

Identify and discuss other applications of SPC charts in a healthcare facility that you think might improve processes.

Sources: Based on M. Owen, "From Sickness to Health," *Qualityworld* 29 (8: August 2003), pp. 18–22; and C. O'Brien and S. Jennings, *Quality Progress* 41 (3; March 2008), pp. 36–43.

It is also possible for an *R*-chart to exhibit a distinct downward trend in the range values, indicating that the ranges are getting narrower and there is less variation. This would be reflected on the $\bar{x}$-chart by mean values closer to the center line. Although this occurrence does not indicate that the process is out of control, it does suggest that some nonrandom cause is reducing process variation. This cause must be investigated to see if it is sustainable. If so, new control limits would need to be developed. Sometimes an $\bar{x}$-chart is used alone to see if a process is improving, perhaps toward a specific performance goal.

In other situations, a company might have studied and collected data for a process for a long time and already knows what the mean and standard deviation of the process are; all it wants to do is monitor the process average by taking periodic samples. In this case it would be appropriate to use the mean chart where the process standard deviation is already known, as shown in Example 3.3.

Control Chart Patterns

Even if a control chart indicates that a process is in control, it is possible that the sample variations within the control limits are not random. If the sample values display a consistent pattern, even within the control limits, it suggests that this pattern has a nonrandom cause that might warrant investigation. We expect the sample values to "bounce around" above and below the center line, reflecting the natural random variation in the process that will be present. However, if the sample values are consistently above (or below) the center line for an extended number of samples or if they move consistently up or down, there is probably a reason for this behavior; that is, it is not random. Examples of nonrandom patterns are shown in Figure 3.3.

FIGURE 3.3 Control Chart Patterns

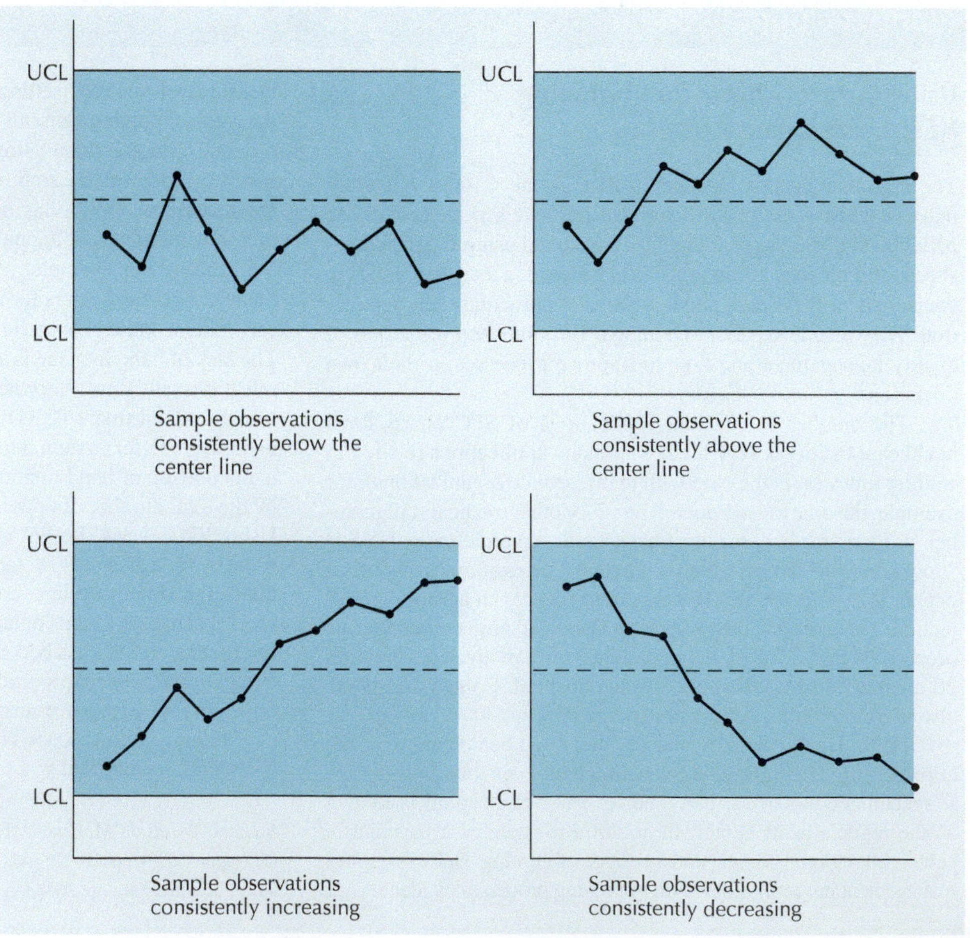

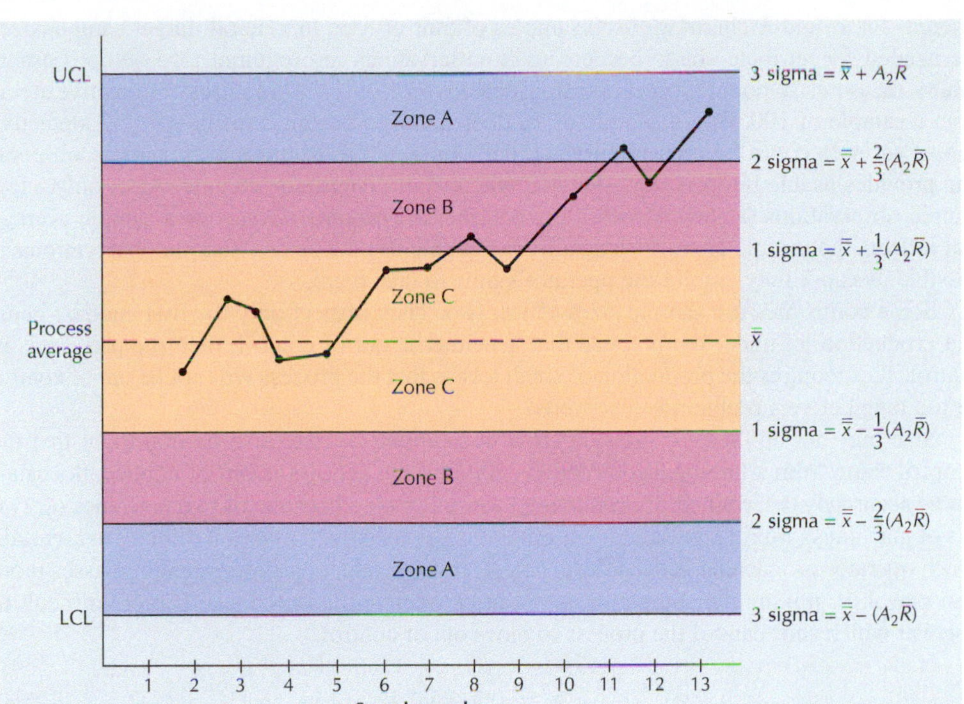

FIGURE 3.4 Zones for Pattern Tests

A pattern in a control chart is characterized by a sequence of sample observations that display the same characteristics—also called a **run**. One type of pattern is a sequence of observations either above or below the center line. For example, three values above the center line followed by two values below the line represent two runs of a pattern. Another type of pattern is a sequence of sample values that consistently go up or go down within the control limits. Several tests are available to determine if a pattern is nonrandom or random.

Run A sequence of sample values that display the same characteristic.

One type of **pattern test** divides the control chart into three "zones" on each side of the center line, where each zone is one standard deviation wide. These are often referred to as 1-sigma, 2-sigma, and 3-sigma limits. The pattern of sample observations in these zones is then used to determine if any nonrandom patterns exist. Recall that the formula for computing an $\bar{x}$-chart uses A_2 from Table 3.1, which assumes 3 standard deviation control limits (or 3-sigma limits). Thus, to compute the dividing lines between each of the three zones for an $\bar{x}$-chart, we use $^1/_3 A_2$. The formulas to compute these zone boundaries are shown in Figure 3.4.

Pattern test Determines if the observations within the limits of a control chart display a nonrandom pattern.

There are five general guidelines associated with the zones for identifying patterns in a control chart where none of the observations are beyond the control limits:

1. Eight consecutive points on one side of the center line
2. Eight consecutive points up or down
3. Fourteen points alternating up or down
4. Two out of three consecutive points in zone A (on one side of the center line)
5. Four out of five consecutive points in zone A or B on one side of the center line

If any of these guidelines applied to the sample observations in a control chart, it would imply that a nonrandom pattern exists and the cause should be investigated. In Figure 3.4, rules 1, 4, and 5 are violated. Example 3.6 on the next page demonstrates how a pattern test is performed.

Sample Size Determination

In our examples of control charts, sample sizes varied significantly. For p-charts, we used sample sizes in the hundreds and for c-charts sample sizes can be as small as one item, whereas for $\bar{x}$- and R-charts we used samples of four or five. In general, larger sample sizes are needed for attribute charts because more observations are required to develop a usable quality measure. A population proportion defective of only 5% requires 5 defective items from a sample of 100. But, a sample of 10 does not even permit a result with 5% defective items. Variable control charts require smaller sample sizes because each sample observation provides usable information—for example, weight, length, or volume. After only a few sample observations (as few as two), it is possible to compute a range or a sample average that reflects the sample characteristics. It is desirable to take as few sample observations as possible, because they require the operator's time to take them.

Some companies use sample sizes of just two. They inspect only the first and last items in a production lot under the premise that if neither is out of control, then the process is in control. This requires the production of small lots so that the process will not be out of control for too long before a problem is discovered.

Size may not be the only consideration in sampling. It may also be important that the samples come from a homogeneous source so that if the process is out of control, the cause can be accurately determined. If production takes place on either one of two machines (or two sets of machines), mixing the sample observations between them makes it difficult to ascertain which operator or machine caused the problem. If the production process encompasses more than one shift, mixing the sample observation between shifts may make it more difficult to discover which shift caused the process to move out of control.

EXAMPLE 3.6 | Performing a Pattern Test

The Goliath Tool Company $\bar{x}$-chart shown in Example 3.4 indicates that the process might not be in control. The company wants to perform a pattern test to see if there is a pattern of nonrandomness exhibited within the control limits.

Solution: In order to perform the pattern test, we must identify the runs that exist in the sample data for Example 3.4, as follows. Recall that $\bar{\bar{x}} = 5.01$ cm.

SAMPLE	$\bar{x}$	ABOVE/BELOW	UP/DOWN	ZONE
1	4.98	B	—	B
2	5.00	B	U	C
3	4.97	B	D	B
4	4.96	B	D	A
5	4.99	B	U	C
6	5.01	—	U	C
7	5.02	A	U	C
8	5.05	A	U	B
9	5.08	A	U	A
10	5.03	A	D	B

No pattern rules appear to be violated.

SPC with Excel and OM Tools

Computer software and spreadsheet packages are available that perform statistical quality control analysis, including the development of process control charts. We will demonstrate how to develop a statistical process control chart on the computer using Excel and OM Tools. The Excel spreadsheet in Exhibit 3.1 shows the data for Example 3.1 in which we constructed a p-chart to monitor the production process for denim jeans at the Western Jeans Company.

EXHIBIT 3.1

Excel File

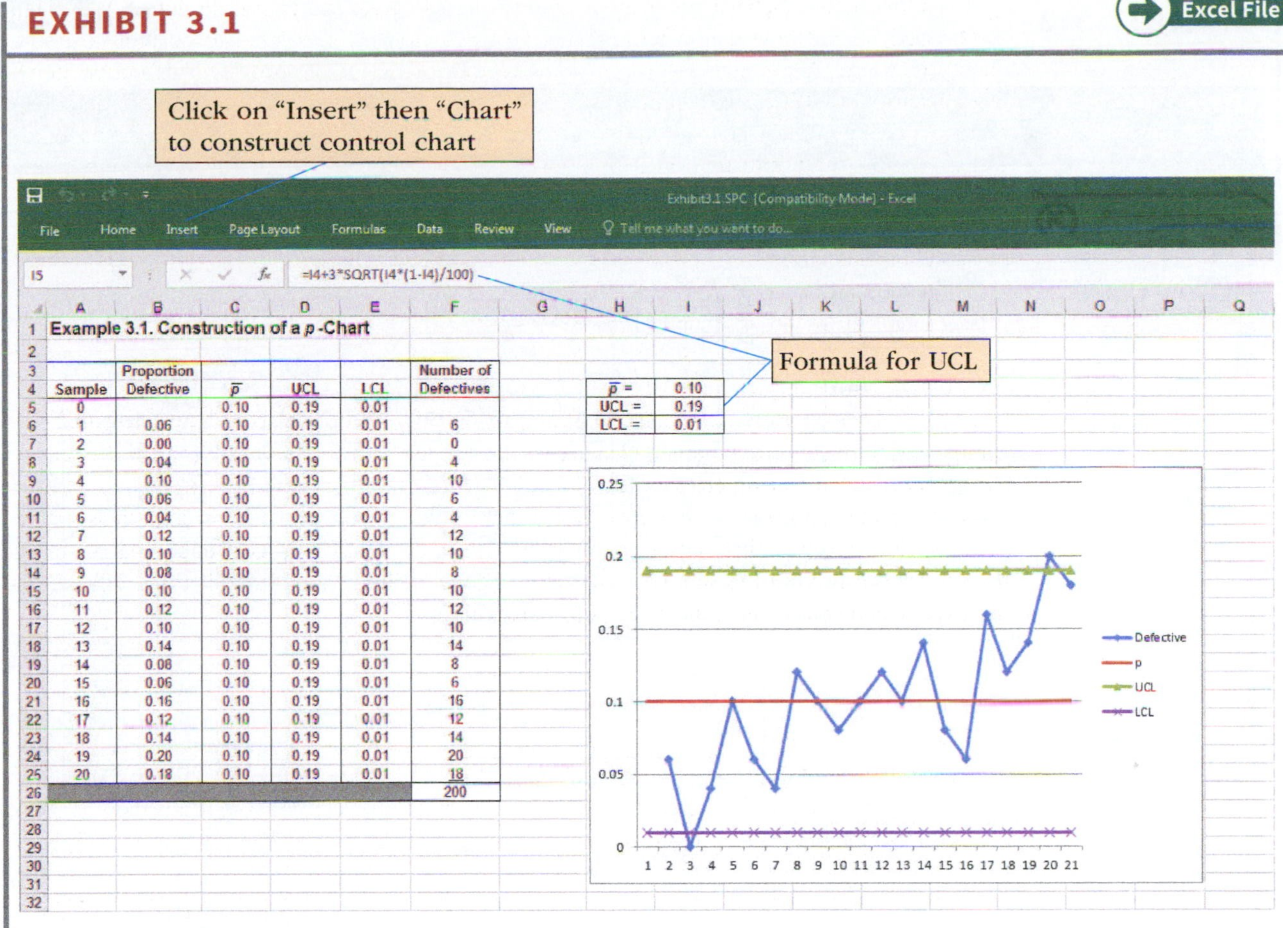

Sample	Proportion Defective	$\overline{p}$	UCL	LCL	Number of Defectives
0		0.10	0.19	0.01	
1	0.06	0.10	0.19	0.01	6
2	0.00	0.10	0.19	0.01	0
3	0.04	0.10	0.19	0.01	4
4	0.10	0.10	0.19	0.01	10
5	0.06	0.10	0.19	0.01	6
6	0.04	0.10	0.19	0.01	4
7	0.12	0.10	0.19	0.01	12
8	0.10	0.10	0.19	0.01	10
9	0.08	0.10	0.19	0.01	8
10	0.10	0.10	0.19	0.01	10
11	0.12	0.10	0.19	0.01	12
12	0.10	0.10	0.19	0.01	10
13	0.14	0.10	0.19	0.01	14
14	0.08	0.10	0.19	0.01	8
15	0.06	0.10	0.19	0.01	6
16	0.16	0.10	0.19	0.01	16
17	0.12	0.10	0.19	0.01	12
18	0.14	0.10	0.19	0.01	14
19	0.20	0.10	0.19	0.01	20
20	0.18	0.10	0.19	0.01	18
					200

The values for $\overline{p}$, UCL, and LCL have been computed using formulas embedded in cells I4, I5, and I6. To construct our control chart, it is necessary to enter the values for the control chart mean ($\overline{p}$) and upper and lower control limits (UCL and LCL) in columns B, C, D, and E for all 20 sample points. This will provide the data points to construct UCL and LCL lines on the control chart.

The Excel file for the example problem spreadsheet shown in Exhibit 3.1 is provided on the text website, as are all Excel exhibits in the text. These files can be easily accessed and downloaded for use. The exhibit spreadsheets can often be used as templates for solving end-of-chapter homework problems.

The control chart shown in the lower-right-hand corner of Exhibit 3.1 was constructed by clicking on the "Insert" tab on the toolbar at the top of the spreadsheet, then covering the data points **B4:E25**. The next step was to click on the "Charts" tab and select a line chart, then after clicking "OK," the chart in Exhibit 3.1 appeared.

Exhibit 3.2 shows the $\overline{x}$-chart and R-chart developed in Examples 3.4 and 3.5 using the "quality control" module from the OM Tools software. Notice that it is only necessary to input the sample data from the $\overline{x}$-chart example in order to develop both control charts.

Process Capability

Control limits are occasionally mistaken for tolerances; however, they are quite different things. Control limits provide a means for determining natural variation in a production process. They are statistical results based on sampling. **Tolerances** are design specifications reflecting customer requirements for a product. They specify a range of values above and

Tolerances Design specifications reflecting product requirements.

EXHIBIT 3.2

Excel File

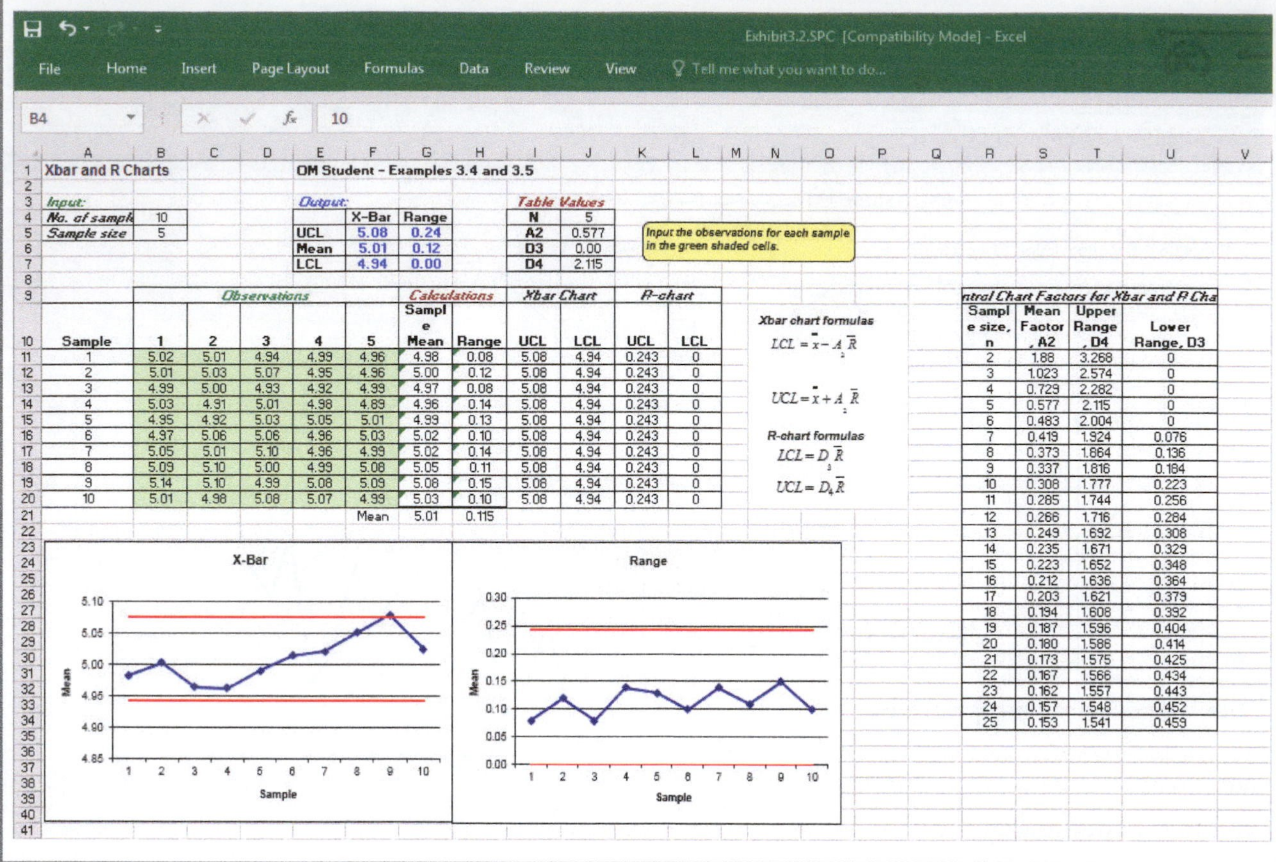

below a designed target value (also referred to as the *nominal value*) within which product units must fall to be acceptable. For example, a bag of potato chips might be designed to have a net weight of 9.0 oz of chips with a tolerance of ±0.5 oz. The design tolerances are thus between 9.5 oz (the *upper specification limit*) and 8.5 oz (the *lower specification limit*). The packaging process must be capable of performing within these design tolerances or a certain portion of the bags will be defective, that is, underweight or overweight. Tolerances are not determined from the production process; they are externally imposed by the designers of the product or service. Control limits, on the other hand, are based on the production process, and they reflect process variability. They are a statistical measure determined from the process. It is possible for a process in an instance to be statistically "in control" according to control charts, yet the process may not conform to the design specifications. To avoid such a situation, the process must be evaluated to see if it can meet product specifications before the process is initiated, or the product or service must be redesigned.

Process capability The range of natural variability in a process—what we measure with control charts.

Process capability refers to the natural variation of a process relative to the variation allowed by the design specifications. In other words, how capable is the process of producing acceptable units according to the design specifications? Process control charts are used for process capability to determine if an existing process is capable of meeting design specifications.

The three main elements associated with process capability are process variability (the natural range of variation of the process), the process center (mean), and the design specifications. Figure 3.5 shows four possible situations with different configurations of these elements that can occur when we consider process capability.

Figure 3.5*a* depicts the natural variation of a process, which is greater than the design specification limits. The process is not capable of meeting these specification limits. This situation will result in a large proportion of defective parts or products. If the limits of a control chart measuring natural variation exceed the specification limits or designed tolerances of a

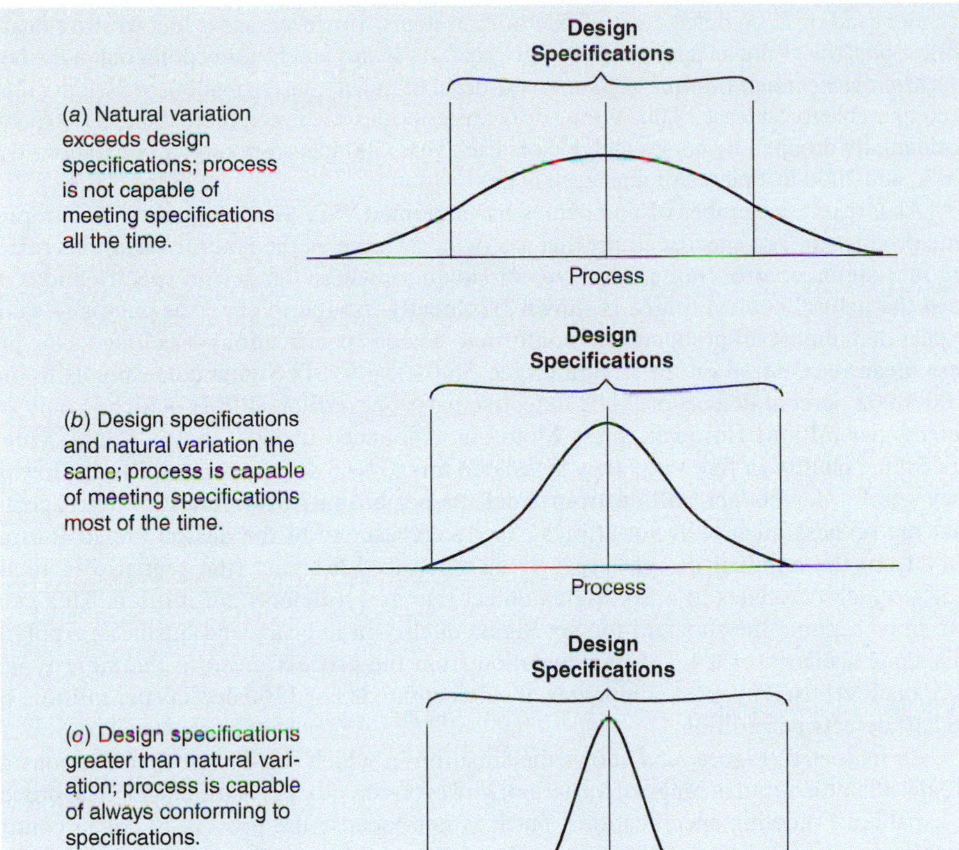

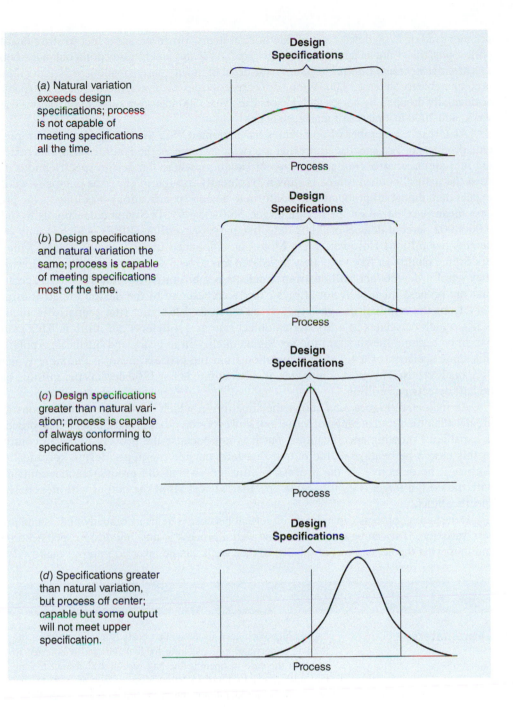

FIGURE 3.5 **Process Capability**

product, the process cannot produce the product according to specifications. The variation that will occur naturally, at random, is greater than the designed variation.

Parts that are within the control limits but outside the design specification must be scrapped or reworked. This can be very costly and wasteful. Alternatives include improving the process or redesigning the product. However, these solutions can also be costly. As such, it is important that process capability studies be done during product design, and before contracts for new parts or products are entered into.

Figure 3.5*b* shows the situation in which the natural control limits and specification limits are the same. This will result in a small number of defective items, the few that will fall outside the natural control limits due to random causes. For many companies, this is a reasonable quality goal. If the process distribution is normally distributed and the natural control limits are three standard deviations from the process mean—that is, they are 3-sigma limits—then the probability between the limits is 0.9973. This is the probability of a good item. This means the area, or probability, outside the limits is 0.0027, which translates to 2.7 defects per thousand or 2700 defects out of one million items. However, according to strict quality philosophy, this is not an appropriate quality goal. As Evans and Lindsay point out in the book *The Management and Control of Quality*, this level of quality corresponding to 3-sigma limits is comparable to "at least 20,000 wrong drug prescriptions each year, more than 15,000 babies accidentally dropped by nurses and doctors each year, 500 incorrect surgical operations each week, and 2000 lost pieces of mail each hour."[1]

As a result, a number of companies have adopted "Six Sigma" quality. This represents product-design specifications that are twice as large as the natural variations reflected in 3-sigma control limits. This type of situation, where the design specifications exceed the natural control limits, is shown graphically in Figure 3.5*c*. The company would expect that almost all products will conform to design specifications—as long as the process mean is centered on the design target. Statistically, Six Sigma corresponds to only 0.0000002 percent defects or 0.002 defective parts per million (PPM), which is only two defects per billion! However, when Motorola announced in 1989 that it would achieve Six Sigma quality in five years they translated this to be 3.4 defects per million. How did they get 3.4 defects per million from 2 defects per billion? Motorola took into account that the process mean will not always exactly correspond to the design target; it might vary from the nominal design target by as much as 1.5 sigma (the scenario in Figure 3.5*d*), which translates to a Six Sigma defect rate of 3.4 defects per million. This value has since become the standard for Six Sigma quality in industry and business. Applying this same scenario of a 1.5-sigma deviation from the process mean to the more typical 3-sigma level used by most companies, the defect rate is not 2700 defects per million, but 66,810 defects per million.

As indicated, Figure 3.5*d* shows the situation in which the design specifications are greater than the process range of variation; however, the process is off center. The process is capable of meeting specifications, but it is not because the process is not in control. In this case a percentage of the output that falls outside the upper design specification limit will be defective. If the process is adjusted so that the process center coincides with the design target (i.e., it is centered), then almost all of the output will meet design specifications.

Determining process capability is important because it helps a company understand process variation. If it can be determined how well a process is meeting design specifications, and thus what the actual level of quality is, then steps can be taken to improve quality. Two

Along the Supply Chain

Determining Quality Process Parameters for Starbucks Coffee Bags

Starbucks, headquartered in Seattle, is the largest coffeehouse chain in the world with over 17,000 retail stores in more than 55 countries. Starbucks sells its packaged whole bean and ground coffees in its coffeehouses and in stores. When voice-of-customer (VoC) data indicated quality issues with the packaging of its one-pound coffee products, Starbucks engineers embarked on a project to learn the effects of process parameters on key packaging quality characteristics.

The airtight seal on a coffee bag is critical to coffee quality, but the ability to open a bag easily is an important factor in providing a great customer experience. Starbucks used a sophisticated mathematical modeling approach (called response surface methodology) to determine the settings for the production process to produce an airtight seal that would be easy to open without damaging the top of the coffee bag. After a bag is sealed with bag-sealing machinery, its airtight property is tested by pressuring the bag underwater and checking for leakage, and it is tested to measure the ease in opening the bag repeatedly without tearing the inner freshness liner. In initial experiments, an airtight seal was easily achieved, but not one that could be easily opened.

The mathematical modeling analysis and bag testing produced feasible process settings that were well within the process capability range, and the new process settings were implemented across the Starbucks manufacturing facility. After several months of operation, defect levels for bag leakage were at the benchmark of 0%, and tear levels were less than one-tenth of their benchmark levels, with an overall defect reduction of 90%.

What are some examples of other product packaging and their critical quality characteristics?

Source: Based on Louis Johnson and Sarah Burrows, "For Starbucks It's in the Bag: How the Java Giant Fine-Tuned Its Sealing Process and Improved Product Quality," *Quality Progress* 44 (3); (March 2011), pp. 18–23.

[1]J. R. Evans and W. M. Lindsay, *The Management and Control of Quality*, 3rd ed. (Minneapolis: West, 1993), p. 602.

measures used to quantify the capability of a process, that is, how well the process is capable of producing according to design specifications, are the capability ratio (C_p) and the capability index (C_{pk}).

Process Capability Measures

One measure of the capability of a process to meet design specifications is the *process capability ratio* (C_p). It is defined as the ratio of the range of the design specifications (the tolerance range) to the range of the process variation, which for most firms is typically $\pm 3\sigma$ or 6σ.

$$C_p = \frac{\text{tolerance range}}{\text{process range}}$$
$$= \frac{\text{upper specification limit} - \text{lower specification limit}}{6\sigma}$$

If C_p is less than 1.0, the process range is greater than the tolerance range, and the process is not capable of producing within the design specifications all the time. This is the situation depicted in Figure 3.5*a*. If C_p equals 1.0, the tolerance range and the process range are virtually the same—the situation shown in Figure 3.5*b*. If C_p is greater than 1.0, the tolerance range is greater than the process range—the situation depicted in Figure 3.5*c*. Thus, companies would logically desire a C_p equal to 1.0 or greater, since this would indicate that the process is capable of meeting specifications.

A second measure of process capability is the *process capability index* (C_{pk}). The C_{pk} differs from the C_p in that it indicates if the process mean has shifted away from the design target, and in which direction it has shifted—that is, if it is off center. This is the situation depicted in Figure 3.5*d*. The process capability index specifically measures the capability of the process relative to the upper and lower specifications.

$$C_{pk} = \text{minimum}\left[\frac{\bar{\bar{x}} - \text{lower specification}}{3\sigma}, \frac{\text{upper specification} - \bar{\bar{x}}}{3\sigma}\right]$$

If the C_{pk} index is greater than 1.00, then the process is capable of meeting design specifications. If C_{pk} is less than 1.00, then the process mean has moved closer to one of the upper or lower design specifications, and it will generate defects. When C_{pk} equals C_p, this indicates that the process mean is centered on the design (nominal) target.

EXAMPLE 3.7 | Computing C_p

The Munchies Snack Food Company packages potato chips in bags. The net weight of the chips in each bag is designed to be 9.0 oz, with a tolerance of ±0.5 oz. The packaging process results in bags with an average net weight of 8.80 oz and a standard deviation of 0.12 oz. The company wants to determine if the process is capable of meeting design specifications.

Solution:

$$C_p = \frac{\text{upper specification limit} - \text{lower specification limit}}{6\sigma}$$
$$= \frac{9.5 - 8.5}{6(0.12)}$$
$$= 1.39$$

Thus, according to this process capability ratio of 1.39, the process is capable of being within design specifications.

EXAMPLE 3.8 | Computing C_{pk}

Recall that the Munchies Snack Food Company packaged potato chips in a process designed for 9.0 oz of chips with a tolerance of ±0.5 oz. The packaging process had a process mean ($\bar{\bar{x}}$) of 8.80 oz and a standard deviation of 0.12 oz. The company wants to determine if the process is capable, and if the process mean is on or off center.

$$C_{pk} = \text{minimum}\left[\frac{\bar{\bar{x}} - \text{lower specification}}{3\sigma}, \frac{\text{upper specification} - \bar{\bar{x}}}{3\sigma}\right]$$

$$= \text{minimum}\left[\frac{8.80 - 8.50}{3(0.12)}, \frac{9.5 - 8.80}{3(0.12)}\right]$$

$$= \text{minimum}[0.83, 1.94]$$

$$= 0.83$$

Although the C_p of 1.39 computed in Example 3.7 indicated that the process is capable (it is within the design specifications), the C_{pk} value of 0.83 indicates the process mean is off center. It has shifted toward the lower specifications limit; that means underweight packages of chips will be produced. Thus, the company needs to take action to correct the process and bring the process mean back toward the design target.

Process Capability with Excel and OM Tools

Exhibit 3.3 shows the Excel solution screen for the computation of the process capability ratio and the process capability index for Examples 3.7 and 3.8. The formula for the process capability index in cell D16 is shown on the formula bar at the top of the screen.

Exhibit 3.4 shows the computation of the process capability ratio and the process capability index for Example 3.7 and 3.8 using the "quality control" module from the OM Tools software.

Along the Supply Chain

Design Tolerances at Harley-Davidson Company

Harley-Davidson, once at the brink of going out of business, is now a successful company known for high quality. It has achieved this comeback by combining the classic styling and traditional features of its motorcycles with advanced engineering technology and a commitment to continuous improvement. Harley-Davidson's manufacturing process incorporates computer-integrated manufacturing (CIM) techniques with state-of-the-art computerized numerical control (CNC) machining stations. These CNC stations are capable of performing dozens of machining operations and provide the operator with computerized data for statistical process control.

Harley-Davidson uses a statistical operator control (SOC) quality-improvement program to reduce parts variability to only a fraction of design tolerances. SOC ensures precise tolerances during each manufacturing step and predicts out-of-control components before they occur. SOC is especially important when dealing with complex components such as transmission gears.

The tolerances for Harley-Davidson cam gears are extremely close, and the machinery is especially complex. CNC machinery allows the manufacturing of gear centers time after time with tolerances as close as 0.0005 inch. SOC ensures the quality necessary to turn the famous Harley-Davidson Evolution engine shift after shift, mile after mile, year after year.

Discuss how reducing "parts variability to only a fraction of design tolerances" is related to a goal of achieving Six Sigma quality.

EXHIBIT 3.3

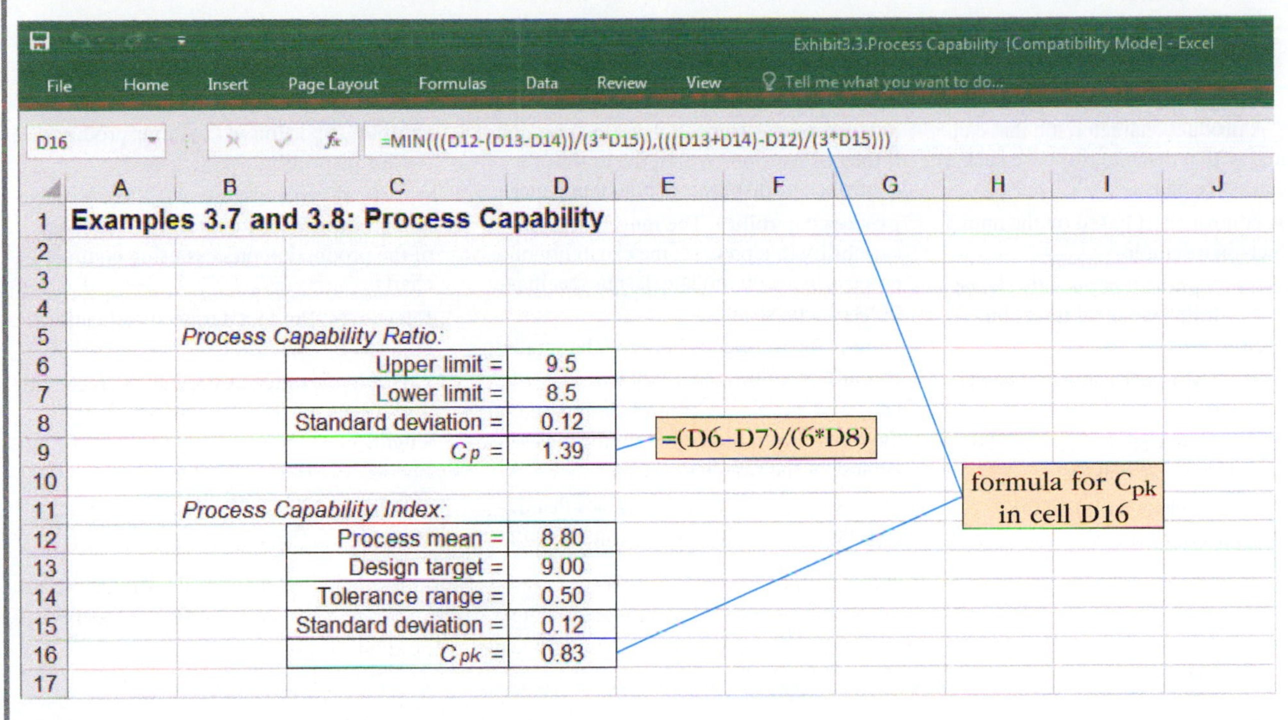

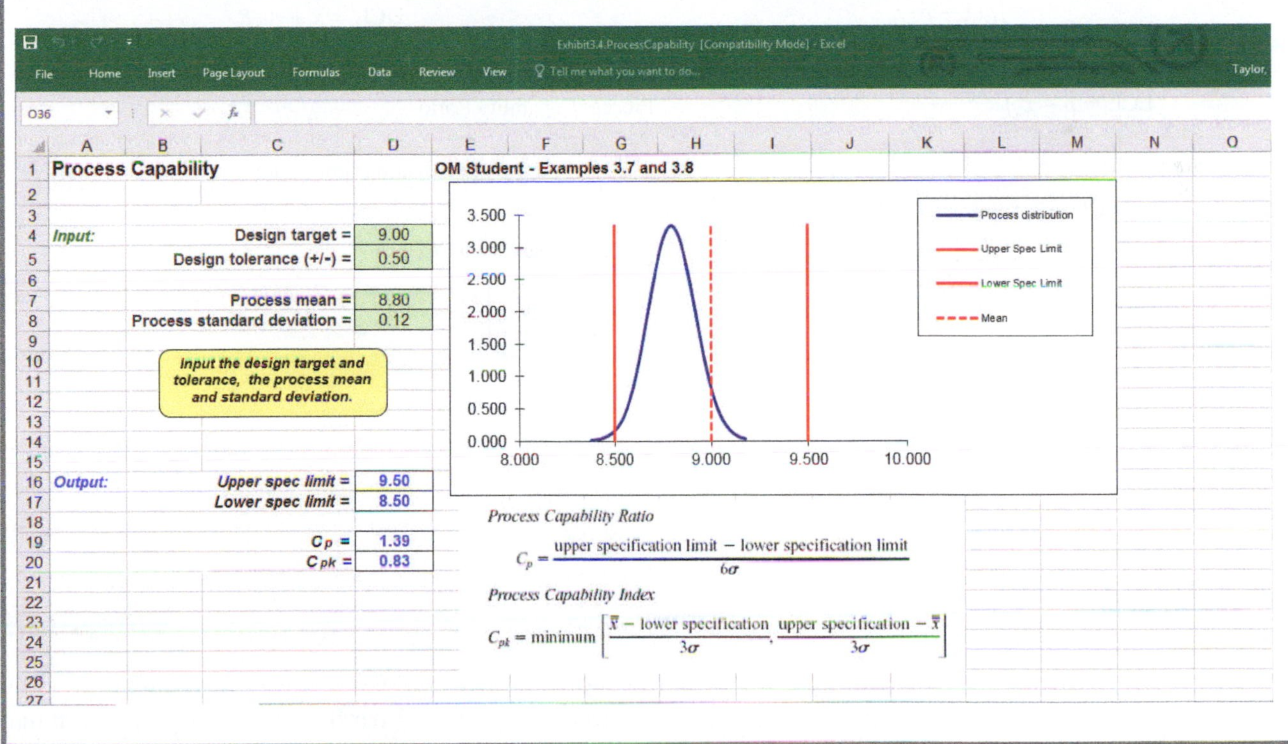

Summary

Statistical process control is one of the main quantitative tools used in most quality management systems. Quality-focused companies provide extensive training in SPC methods for all employees at all levels. In this environment employees have more responsibility for their own operation or process. Employees recognize the need for SPC for accomplishing a major part of their job, product quality. When employees are provided with adequate training and understand what is expected of them, they have little difficulty using statistical process control methods.

Key Terms

attribute A product characteristic that can be evaluated with a discrete response such as yes or no, good or bad.

***c*-chart** A control chart based on the number of defects in a sample.

control chart A graph that visually shows if a sample is within statistical limits for defective items.

control limits The upper and lower bands of a control chart.

mean ($\bar{x}$-) chart A control chart based on the means of the samples taken.

***p*-chart** A control chart based on the proportion defective of the samples taken.

pattern test A statistical test to determine if the observations within the limits of a control chart display a nonrandom pattern.

process capability The range of natural variability in a process; the capability of a process to accommodate design specifications of a product.

range The difference between the smallest and largest values in a sample.

range (*R*-) chart A control chart based on the range (from the highest to the lowest values) of the samples taken.

run A sequence of sample values that display the same tendency in a control chart.

sample A portion of the items produced to use for inspection.

statistical process control (SPC) A statistical procedure for monitoring the quality of the production process using control charts.

tolerances Product design specifications required by the customer.

variable measure A product characteristic that can be measured, such as weight or length.

Key Formulas

Control Limits for *p*-Charts

$$\text{UCL} = \bar{p} + z\sqrt{\frac{\bar{p}(1-\bar{p})}{n}}$$

$$\text{LCL} = \bar{p} - z\sqrt{\frac{\bar{p}(1-\bar{p})}{n}}$$

Control Limits for *c*-Charts

$$\text{UCL} = \bar{c} + z\sqrt{\bar{c}}$$

$$\text{LCL} = \bar{c} - z\sqrt{\bar{c}}$$

Control Limits for *R*-Charts

$$\text{UCL} = D_4\bar{R}$$

$$\text{LCL} = D_3\bar{R}$$

Control Limits for $\bar{x}$-Charts

$$\text{UCL} = \bar{\bar{x}} + A_2\bar{R}$$

$$\text{LCL} = \bar{\bar{x}} - A_2\bar{R}$$

Process Capability Ratio

$$C_p = \frac{\text{upper specification limit} - \text{lower specification limit}}{6\sigma}$$

Process Capability Index

$$C_{pk} = \text{minimum}\left[\frac{\bar{\bar{x}} - \text{lower specification}}{3\sigma}, \frac{\text{upper specification} - \bar{\bar{x}}}{3\sigma}\right]$$

Solved Problems

WileyPLUS

1. *p*-Charts

Twenty samples of $n = 200$ were taken by an operator at a workstation in a production process. The number of defective items in each sample were recorded as follows.

SAMPLE	NUMBER OF DEFECTIVES	*p*	SAMPLE	NUMBER OF DEFECTIVES	*p*
1	12	0.060	5	16	0.080
2	18	0.090	6	19	0.095
3	10	0.050	7	17	0.085
4	14	0.070	8	12	0.060
9	11	0.055	15	18	0.090
10	14	0.070	16	20	0.100
11	16	0.080	17	18	0.090
12	14	0.070	18	20	0.100
13	12	0.060	19	21	0.105
14	16	0.080	20	22	0.110

Management wants to develop a *p*-chart using 3-sigma limits. Set up the *p*-chart and plot the observations to determine if the process was out of control at any point.

Solution

Step 1. Compute $\overline{p}$:

$$\overline{p} = \frac{\text{total number of defectives}}{\text{total number of observations}} = \frac{320}{(20)(200)} = 0.08$$

Step 2. Determine the control limits:

$$\text{UCL} = \overline{p} + z\sqrt{\frac{\overline{p}(1-\overline{p})}{n}} = 0.08 + (3.00)(0.019) = 0.137$$

$$\text{LCL} = \overline{p} - z\sqrt{\frac{\overline{p}(1-\overline{p})}{n}} = 0.08 - (3.00)(0.019) = 0.023$$

Step 3. Construct the $\overline{p}$-chart with $\overline{p} = 0.08$, UCL = 0.137, and LCL = 0.023. The process does not appear to be out of control.

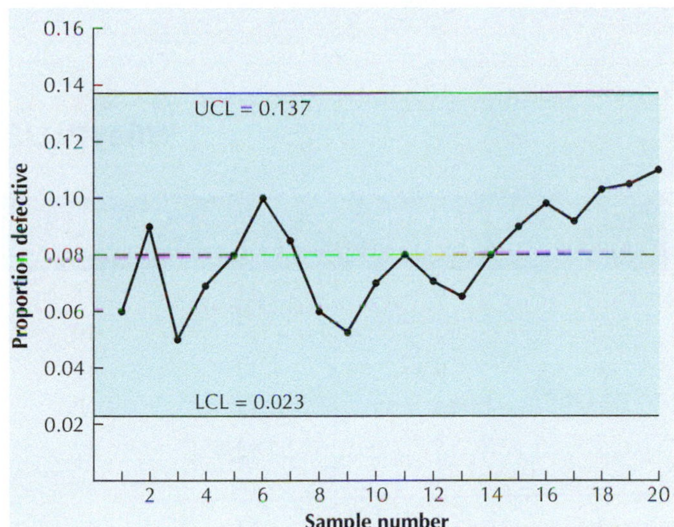

2. Pattern Tests

In the preceding problem, even though the control chart indicates that the process is in control, management wants to use pattern tests to further determine if the process is in control.

Solution

Step 1. Determine the "up-and-down" and "above-and-below" runs and zone observations. Construct the zone boundaries on the control chart as follows.

SAMPLE	ABOVE/BELOW $\overline{p} = 0.08$	UP/DOWN	ZONE
1	B	—	B
2	A	U	C
3	B	D	B
4	B	U	C
5	A	U	C
6	A	U	B
7	A	D	C
8	B	D	B
9	B	D	B
10	B	U	C
11	A	U	C
12	B	D	C
13	B	D	C
14	A	U	C
15	A	U	C
16	A	U	B
17	A	D	C
18	A	U	B
19	A	U	B
20	A	U	B

(*Note*: Ties are broken in favor of A and U.)

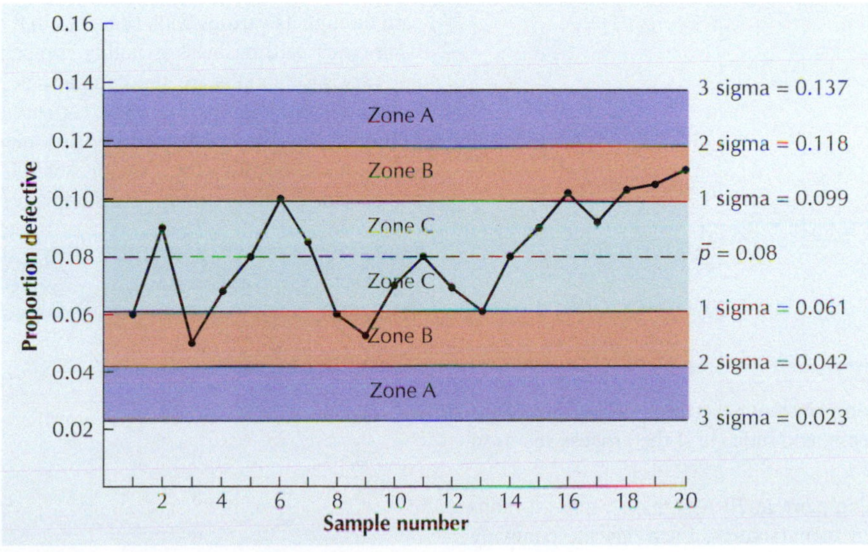

Because four of five consecutive points are in Zone B (i.e., points 16 to 20), it suggests that nonrandom patterns may exist and that the process may not be in control.

Questions

3.1. Explain the difference between attribute control charts and variable control charts.

3.2. How are mean ($\bar{x}$-) and range (R-) charts used together?

3.3. What is the purpose of a pattern test?

3.4. What determines the width of the control limits in a process chart?

3.5. Under what circumstances should a c-chart be used instead of a p-chart?

3.6. What is the difference between tolerances and control limits?

3.7. Why have companies traditionally used control charts with 3-sigma limits instead of 2-sigma limits?

3.8. Select three service companies or organizations you are familiar with and indicate how process control charts could be used in each.

3.9. Visit a local fast-food restaurant, retail store, grocery store, or bank, and identify the different processes that control charts could be used to monitor.

3.10. Explain the different information provided by the process capability ratio and the process capability index.

3.11. For the Goliath Tool Company in Example 3.4, if the design tolerances are ±0.07 cm, is the process capable of meeting tolerances of ±0.08 cm for the slip-ring bearings?

Problems

WileyPLUS

3.1. The Great North Woods Clothing Company sells specialty outdoor clothing through its catalog. A quality problem that generates customer complaints occurs when a warehouse employee fills an order with the wrong items. The company has decided to implement a process control plan by inspecting the ordered items after they have been obtained from the warehouse and before they have been packaged. The company has taken 30 samples (during a 30-day period), each for 100 orders, and recorded the number of defective orders in each sample, as follows:

SAMPLE	NUMBER OF DEFECTIVES	SAMPLE	NUMBER OF DEFECTIVES
1	12	16	6
2	14	17	3
3	10	18	7
4	16	19	10
5	18	20	14
6	19	21	18
7	14	22	22
8	20	23	26
9	18	24	20
10	17	25	24
11	9	26	18
12	11	27	19
13	14	28	20
14	12	29	17
15	7	30	18

Construct a p-chart for the company that describes 99.74% (3σ) of the random variation in the process, and indicate if the process seems to be out of control at any time.

3.2. The Road King Tire Company in Birmingham wants to monitor the quality of the tires it manufactures. Each day the company quality-control manager takes a sample of 100 tires, tests them, and determines the number of defective tires. The results of 20 samples have been recorded as follows:

SAMPLE	NUMBER OF DEFECTIVES	SAMPLE	NUMBER OF DEFECTIVES
1	14	11	18
2	12	12	10
3	9	13	19
4	10	14	20
5	11	15	17
6	7	16	18
7	8	17	18
8	14	18	22
9	16	19	24
10	17	20	23

Construct a p-chart for this process using 2σ limits and describe the variation in the process.

3.3. The Commonwealth Banking Corporation issues a national credit card through its various bank branches in five southeastern states. The bank credit card business is highly competitive and interest rates do not vary substantially, so the company decided to attempt to retain its customers by improving customer service through a reduction in billing errors. The credit card division monitored its billing department process by taking daily samples of 200 customer bills for 30 days and checking their accuracy. The sample results are as follows:

SAMPLE	NUMBER OF DEFECTIVES	SAMPLE	NUMBER OF DEFECTIVES
1	7	9	14
2	12	10	10
3	9	11	9
4	6	12	6
5	5	13	3
6	8	14	2
7	10	15	8
8	11	16	10

17	12	24	12
18	14	25	15
19	16	26	14
20	15	27	16
21	13	28	12
22	9	29	15
23	10	30	14

Develop a *p*-chart for the billing process using 3σ control limits and indicate if the process is out of control.

3.4. In the assembly process for automobile engines, at one stage in the process a gasket is placed between the two sections of the engine block before they are joined. If the gasket is damaged (e.g., bent, crimped), oil can leak from the cylinder chambers and foul the spark plugs, in which case the entire engine has to be disassembled and a new gasket inserted. The company wants to develop a *p*-chart with 2σ limits to monitor the quality of the gaskets prior to the assembly stage. Historically, 2% of the gaskets have been defective, and management does not want the upper control limit to exceed 3% defective. What sample size will be required to achieve this control chart?

3.5. The Great North Woods Clothing Company is a mail-order company that processes thousands of mail and telephone orders each week. It has a customer service number to handle customer order problems, inquiries, and complaints. The company wants to monitor the number of customer calls that can be classified as complaints. The total number of complaint calls the customer service department has received for each of the last 30 weekdays are shown as follows:

DAY	COMPLAINT CALLS	DAY	COMPLAINT CALLS
1	27	16	19
2	15	17	12
3	38	18	17
4	41	19	18
5	19	20	26
6	23	21	31
7	21	22	14
8	16	23	18
9	33	24	26
10	35	25	27
11	26	26	35
12	42	27	20
13	40	28	12
14	35	29	16
15	25	30	15

a. Construct a *c*-chart for this process with 3σ control limits and indicate if the process was out of control at any time.

b. What nonrandom (i.e., assignable) causes might result in the process being out of control?

3.6. One of the stages in the process of making denim cloth at the Southern Mills Company is to spin cotton yarn onto spindles for subsequent use in the weaving process. Occasionally the yarn breaks during the spinning process, and an operator ties it back together. Some number of breaks is considered normal; however, too many breaks might mean that the yarn is of poor quality. In order to monitor this process, the quality-control manager randomly selects a spinning machine each hour and checks the number of breaks during a 15-minute period. Following is a summary of the observations for the past 20 hours:

SAMPLE	NUMBER OF BREAKS	SAMPLE	NUMBER OF BREAKS
1	3	11	3
2	2	12	4
3	4	13	6
4	1	14	7
5	5	15	8
6	3	16	6
7	2	17	5
8	4	18	7
9	0	19	8
10	2	20	6

Construct a *c*-chart using 3σ limits for this process and indicate if the process was out of control at any time.

3.7. At the Venice Garden restaurant chain, when orders come into the kitchen via a touchscreen computer system, the order is given a processing time. When the order preparation exceeds this time, computer screens positioned every few feet along the order assembly line turn red. The restaurant manager monitored the number of "late" orders by randomly visiting the kitchen during its busiest times between 6 P.M. and 10 P.M. on Friday and Saturday evenings for 12 weekends, and counted the number of red screens, collecting the following sample results for the number of orders that exceeded their projected processing times.

MANAGER INSPECTION	LATE ORDERS	MANAGER INSPECTION	LATE ORDERS
1	3	13	6
2	2	14	2
3	6	15	2
4	4	16	4
5	8	17	5
6	5	18	6
7	9	19	3
8	3	20	1
9	3	21	7
10	4	22	3
11	1	23	4
12	5	24	2

Construct a *c*-chart with 2σ limits for this process and indicate if the process was out of control at any time.

3.8. Telecom manufactures electronic components for computers. One measure it uses to monitor the quality of its distribution process is the number of customer invoice errors. The distribution center manager monitored the company's order processing and distribution by recording the number of invoice errors for 30 days. The sample results are as follows:

DAY	NUMBER OF ERRORS	DAY	NUMBER OF ERRORS
1	4	16	6
2	6	17	9
3	2	18	12
4	5	19	10
5	1	20	11
6	3	21	8
7	4	22	8
8	7	23	7
9	6	24	3
10	5	25	4
11	10	26	7
12	8	27	10
13	9	28	12
14	9	29	12
15	7	30	14

Construct a *c*-chart with 3σ limits for invoice errors and indicate if the process was out of control at any time.

3.9. The National Bread Company delivers multiple orders daily by truck from its regional distribution center to stores in the Wayman's Supermarket chain. One measure of its supply chain performance is the number of late deliveries. The company's goal is to make all deliveries within one day, so a delivery is late if it exceeds one day. The late deliveries for each of the past 20 days are as follows:

DAY	LATE DELIVERIES	DAY	LATE DELIVERIES
1	7	11	6
2	16	12	12
3	14	13	15
4	8	14	10
5	19	15	17
6	12	16	16
7	10	17	14
8	14	18	12
9	8	19	18
10	7	20	20

Construct a *c*-chart for late deliveries with 3σ control limits and indicate if the delivery process was out of control at any time.

3.10. BooksCDs.com sells books, videos, DVDs, and CDs through its website. The company ships thousands of orders each day from seven national distribution centers. BooksCDs.com wants to establish a *p*-chart to monitor the quality of its distribution process, specifically the number of "problem" orders. A problem order is one that is delivered to a customer late (i.e., after five days), incorrect, or incomplete. The company sampled 500 orders every other day for 20 samples and tracked them to final customer delivery, the results of which are as follows:

SAMPLE	NUMBER OF PROBLEMS ORDERS	SAMPLE	NUMBER OF PROBLEMS ORDERS
1	14	11	38
2	22	12	24
3	36	13	15
4	17	14	12
5	25	15	10
6	41	16	16
7	18	17	9
8	19	18	21
9	26	19	18
10	28	20	12

Construct a *p*-chart for this process using 3σ limits and indicate if the process was out of control.

3.11. Valtec Electronics fills orders for its electronic components and parts by truck to customers through several distribution centers. A measure of its supply chain responsiveness is order fulfillment lead time, which is the number of days from when a company receives an order to when it is delivered to the customer. A distribution center manager has taken 20 samples of five orders each during the month and recorded the lead time for each as follows:

SAMPLES	LOAD TIME (DAYS)				
1	1.3	2.4	0.7	3.0	1.8
2	2.1	1.2	1.0	2.5	3.6
3	4.2	3.3	2.6	1.5	3.0
4	1.6	2.1	2.8	0.9	1.5
5	2.6	3.0	1.4	4.6	1.9
6	0.8	2.7	5.8	3.7	4.5
7	2.6	3.5	3.1	3.6	1.4
8	3.4	6.1	1.5	2.5	2.8
9	3.1	2.5	2.2	2.9	1.8
10	2.4	4.8	5.9	3.2	4.4
11	1.9	2.7	3.4	2.2	0.4
12	6.1	4.9	2.1	3.6	5.2
13	1.2	3.4	2.8	2.3	4.5
14	2.4	2.9	3.4	2.3	2.5
15	3.7	7.0	1.4	2.4	3.3
16	3.6	2.7	4.8	2.0	1.7
17	0.4	1.8	6.5	3.2	4.8
18	5.3	2.9	3.4	4.8	4.4
19	2.7	3.6	2.9	4.1	5.2
20	4.7	2.0	2.0	3.1	1.8

Construct an $\bar{x}$-chart to be used in conjunction with an *R*-chart using 3σ limits for these data and indicate if the process is in control.

3.12. The Startrac Coffee Company is a national coffeehouse chain. The company has a contract with a Mexican supplier for paper cups, lids, and insulated sleeves. Startrac management has found that the paper cups sometimes leak around the lid, dripping the contained beverage on their customers. The leaks can be caused by several factors, including defective manufacturing, damage during shipping and handling, and even how the lids are placed on the cups by employees. The company has sampled 1000 filled cups each week for 20 weeks from a number of different randomly selected store locations around the country, with the following number of cups that leak.

SAMPLE	DEFECTIVE CUPS	SAMPLE	DEFECTIVE CUPS
1	78	11	123
2	116	12	71
3	49	13	87
4	51	14	43
5	37	15	91
6	63	16	63
7	77	17	107
8	106	18	54
9	31	19	73
10	28	20	65

Construct a *p*-chart for the cups using 3σ limits and indicate if the process was out of control, and if the control chart is reliable to monitor cup quality in the future. Visit your favorite coffee shop and see if your beverage cup leaks, and if so, try to determine what the cause might be.

3.13. The Southern Mills Company produces denim cloth. During the weaving process, dyed yarn on large, round beams is fed into looms where it is woven into cloth. During this weaving process the yarns are stretched beyond their natural length. As a result, the woven fabric can shrink as much as 15 percent; however, shrinkage of only as much as 3 percent is the acceptable limit for Southern's customers. To prevent shrinkage, the fabric is put through a chemical process, but beams of fabric can still exceed the shrinkage limit. The Southern quality management team has taken a sample of 100 finished fabric beams each day for one month (i.e., 30 days) and tested them for shrinkage. The results of this inspection process showing the number of fabric beams that exceed the 3 percent shrinkage limit are as follows.

SAMPLE	DEFECTIVE BEAMS	SAMPLE	DEFECTIVE BEAMS
1	6	16	12
2	9	17	15
3	11	18	6
4	3	19	3
5	10	20	4
6	14	21	8
7	8	22	14
8	6	23	17
9	6	24	22
10	12	25	13
11	7	26	16
12	10	27	12
13	6	28	10
14	5	29	9
15	9	30	9

Develop a *p*-chart for fabric shrinkage using 3σ control limits and indicate if the process is out of control.

3.14. The town of Blakesburg has a customer service hotline that town residents can call and leave phone messages with complaints about town services including such things as garbage pickup, recreation facilities, taxes, bills, etc. As part of a quality improvement process the town manager wants to develop a control chart to monitor resident complaints. During the past year the town had a total of 370 complaints and it wants to use this data to construct a *c*-chart with 3σ control limits to monitor weekly complaints. Over the past three months the town has recorded the number of weekly complaints it received as follows:

WEEK	COMPLAINTS	WEEK	COMPLAINTS
1	7	7	3
2	5	8	6
3	9	9	6
4	3	10	7
5	10	11	9
6	8	12	4

a. Using the data above and pattern tests determine if the process is out of control.

b. Reconstruct the control chart using 2σ control limits and indicate if there is any difference from the results in part (a).

3.15. Historically, student advising in the College of Business at Tech was done by faculty in the individual departments that housed a student's major. However, the College received poor advising ratings on national student surveys that rank business schools, which caused the College to have a low ranking. In order to remedy this problem the College centralized its advising activity in the Dean's office using full-time, trained advisors. After a transition period the advising office sampled 50 students every week during a semester using a brief in-class survey in classes selected randomly. Any survey that indicated an advising problem was considered one defect. The semester-long survey resulted in 68 total defects.

a. Using this result develop a *p*-chart for advising defects using 3σ control limits.

b. Given the following survey results for a subsequent semester, indicate if the process is in control.

WEEK	NUMBER OF DEFECTS	WEEK	NUMBER OF DEFECTS
1	7	9	4
2	5	10	6
3	4	11	9
4	8	12	3
5	10	13	8
6	6	14	7
7	9	15	7
8	3		

3.16. The Tech Athletic Department has developed a reseating plan for its football stadium. Football season-ticket holders can pick their seats using a computerized system according to their rank in a point system based on cumulative contributions over the years plus their current annual contribution giving level to the athletic fund. In order to determine when (i.e., what day and time) contributors can select their seats, their contribution data are manually entered into a computer program that computes their points and ranking by Tech students hired on a part-time basis. As this information is determined, it is mailed to the contributors, who can check it for accuracy. During the first several weeks of this process, the athletic department received a number of phone calls and visits from upset contributors who found errors in their points and ranking, so the athletic department staff went back and determined how many errors were made for each of the first 14 days of the process, shown as follows.

DAY	NUMBER OF ERRORS	DAY	NUMBER OF ERRORS
1	19	8	37
2	26	9	22
3	14	10	19
4	17	11	23
5	32	12	41
6	16	13	27
7	15	14	30

Construct a *c*-chart with 3σ limits for the number of errors, and indicate if this chart would be reliable to monitor the quality of the data input process in the future.

3.17. A machine at the Pacific Fruit Company fills boxes with raisins. The labeled weight of the boxes is 9 oz. The company wants to construct an *R*-chart to monitor the filling process and make sure the box weights are in control. The quality-control department for the company sampled five boxes every two hours for three consecutive working days. The sample observations are as follows:

SAMPLES	BOX WEIGHTS (OZ)				
1	9.06	9.13	8.97	8.85	8.46
2	8.52	8.61	9.09	9.21	8.95
3	9.35	8.95	9.20	9.03	8.42
4	9.17	9.21	9.05	9.01	9.53
5	9.21	8.87	8.71	9.05	9.35
6	8.74	8.35	8.50	9.06	8.89
7	9.00	9.21	9.05	9.23	8.78
8	9.15	9.20	9.23	9.15	9.06
9	9.98	8.90	8.81	9.05	9.13
10	9.03	9.10	9.26	9.46	8.47
11	9.53	9.02	9.11	8.88	8.92
12	8.95	9.10	9.00	9.06	8.95

Construct an *R*-chart from these data with 3σ control limits, plot the sample range values, and comment on process control.

3.18. The City Square Grocery and Meat Market has a large meat locker in which a constant temperature of approximately 40° F should be maintained. The market manager has decided to construct an *R*-chart to monitor the temperature inside the locker. The manager had one of the market employees take sample temperature readings randomly five times each day for 20 days in order to gather data for the control chart. Following are the temperature sample observations:

SAMPLES	TEMPERATURE (°F)				
1	46.3	48.1	42.5	43.1	39.6
2	41.2	40.5	37.8	36.5	42.3
3	40.1	41.3	34.5	33.2	36.7
4	42.3	44.1	39.5	37.7	38.6
5	35.2	38.1	40.5	39.1	42.3
6	40.6	41.7	38.6	43.5	44.6
7	33.2	38.6	41.5	40.7	43.1
8	41.8	40.0	41.6	40.7	39.3
9	42.4	41.6	40.8	40.9	42.3
10	44.7	36.5	37.3	35.3	41.1
11	42.6	43.5	35.4	36.1	38.2
12	40.5	40.4	39.1	37.2	41.6
13	45.3	42.0	43.1	44.7	39.5
14	36.4	37.5	36.2	38.9	40.1
15	40.5	34.3	36.2	35.1	36.8
16	39.5	38.2	37.6	34.1	38.7
17	37.6	40.6	40.3	39.7	41.2
18	41.0	34.3	39.1	45.2	43.7
19	40.9	42.3	37.6	35.4	34.8
20	37.6	39.2	39.3	41.2	37.6

a. Construct an *R*-chart based on these data using 3σ limits, and plot the 20 sample range values.

b. Does it appear that the temperature is in control according to the criteria established by management?

3.19. The Oceanside Apparel Company manufactures expensive, polo-style men's and women's short-sleeve knit shirts at its plant in Jamaica. The production process requires that material be cut into large patterned squares by operators, which are then sewn together at another stage of the process. If the squares are not of a correct length, the final shirt will be either too large or too small. In order to monitor the cutting process, management takes a sample of four squares of cloth every other hour and measures the length. The length of a cloth square should be 36 inches, and historically, the company has found the length to vary across an acceptable average of 2 inches.

a. Construct an *R*-chart for the cutting process using 3σ limits.

b. The company has taken 10 additional samples with the following results:

SAMPLES	MEASUREMENTS (IN.)			
1	37.3	36.5	38.2	36.1
2	33.4	35.8	37.9	36.2
3	32.1	34.8	39.1	35.3
4	36.1	37.2	36.7	34.2
5	35.1	38.6	37.2	33.6
6	33.4	34.5	36.7	32.4
7	38.1	39.2	35.3	32.7
8	35.4	36.2	36.3	34.3
9	37.1	39.4	38.1	36.2
10	32.1	34.0	35.6	36.1

Plot the new sample data on the control chart constructed in part (a) and comment on the process variability.

3.20. For the sample data provided in Problem 3-17, construct an $\bar{x}$-chart in conjunction with the R-chart, plot the sample observations, and, using both $\bar{x}$- and R-charts, comment on the process control.

3.21. For the sample data provided in Problem 3-18, construct an $\bar{x}$-chart in conjunction with the R-chart, plot the sample observations, and, using both $\bar{x}$- and R-charts, comment on the process control.

3.22. Using the process information provided in Problem 3-19, construct an $\bar{x}$-chart in conjunction with the R-chart, plot the sample observations provided in part (b), and, using both $\bar{x}$- and R-charts, comment on the process control.

3.23. Use pattern tests to determine if the sample observations used in the $\bar{x}$-chart in Problem 3-20 reflect any nonrandom patterns.

3.24. Use pattern tests to determine if the sample observations in Problem 3-5 reflect any nonrandom patterns.

3.25. Use pattern tests to determine if the sample observations in Problem 3-18 reflect any nonrandom patterns.

3.26. Use pattern tests to determine if the sample observations used in the $\bar{x}$-chart in Problem 3-21 reflect any nonrandom patterns.

3.27. Use pattern tests to determine if the sample observations used in the p-chart in Problem 3-1 reflect any nonrandom patterns.

3.28. Dave's Restaurant is a chain that employs independent evaluators to visit its restaurants as customers and assess the quality of the service by filling out a questionnaire. The company evaluates restaurants in two categories, products (the food) and service (e.g., promptness, order accuracy, courtesy, friendliness). The evaluator considers not only his or her order experiences but also observations throughout the restaurant. Following are the results of an evaluator's 20 visits to one particular restaurant during a month showing the number of "defects" noted in the service category:

SAMPLE	NUMBER OF DEFECTS	SAMPLE	NUMBER OF DEFECTS
1	4	11	9
2	6	12	4
3	10	13	3
4	3	14	4
5	6	15	13
6	7	16	9
7	8	17	10
8	5	18	11
9	2	19	15
10	5	20	12

Construct a control chart for this restaurant using 3σ limits to monitor quality service and indicate if the process is in control.

3.29. The National Bank of Warwick is concerned with complaints from customers about its drive-through window operation. Customers complain that it sometimes takes too long to be served and since there are often cars in front and back of a customer, they cannot leave if the service is taking a long time. To correct this problem the bank installed an intercom system so the drive-through window teller can call for assistance if the line backs up or a customer has an unusually long transaction. The bank's objective is an average customer's waiting and service time of approximately three minutes. The bank's operations manager wants to monitor the new drive-through window system with SPC. The manager has timed five customers' waiting and service times at random for 12 days as follows:

	OBSERVATION TIMES (MIN)				
SAMPLE	1	2	3	4	5
1	3.05	6.27	1.35	2.56	1.05
2	7.21	1.50	2.66	3.45	3.78
3	3.12	5.11	1.37	5.20	2.65
4	2.96	3.81	4.15	5.01	2.15
5	3.25	3.11	1.63	1.29	3.74
6	2.47	2.98	2.15	1.88	4.95
7	6.05	2.03	3.17	3.18	2.34
8	1.87	2.65	1.98	2.74	3.63
9	3.33	4.15	8.06	2.98	3.05
10	2.61	2.15	3.80	3.05	3.16
11	3.52	5.66	1.18	3.45	2.07
12	3.18	7.73	2.06	1.15	3.11

Develop an $\bar{x}$-chart to be used in conjunction with an R-chart to monitor this drive-through window process and indicate if the process is in control using these charts.

3.30. The Great Outdoors Clothing Company is a mail-order catalog operation. Whenever a customer returns an item for a refund, credit, or exchange, he or she is asked to complete a return form. For each item returned the customer is asked to insert a code indicating the reason for the return. The company does not consider the returns related to style, size, or "feel" of the material to be a defect. However, it does consider returns because the item "was not as described in the catalog," "didn't look like what was in the catalog," or "the color was different than shown in the catalog," to be defects in the catalog. The company has randomly checked 100 customer return forms for 20 days and collected the following data for catalog defects:

SAMPLE	NUMBER OF CATALOG DEFECTS	SAMPLE	NUMBER OF CATALOG DEFECTS
1	18	11	54
2	26	12	37
3	43	13	26
4	27	14	29
5	14	15	37
6	36	16	65
7	42	17	54
8	28	18	31
9	61	19	28
10	37	20	25

Construct a control chart using 3σ limits to monitor catalog defects and indicate if the process is in control. Use pattern tests to verify an in-control situation.

3.31. The dean of the College of Business at State University wants to monitor the quality of the work performed by the college's secretarial staff. Each completed assignment is returned to the faculty with a check sheet on which the faculty member is asked to list the errors made on the assignment. The assistant dean has randomly collected the following set of observations from 20 three-day work periods:

SAMPLE	NUMBER OF ERRORS	SAMPLE	NUMBER OF ERRORS
1	17	11	12
2	9	12	17
3	12	13	16
4	15	14	23
5	26	15	24
6	11	16	18
7	18	17	14
8	15	18	12
9	21	19	20
10	10	20	16

Construct a process control chart for secretarial work quality using 3σ limits and determine if the process was out of control at any point. Use pattern tests to determine if any nonrandom patterns exist.

3.32. Metro Food Products is a food produce distributor that serves a number of restaurants, grocery stores, and schools from a central distribution center and warehouse. Poor forecasting, late deliveries from its suppliers, food mishandling, and order cancellations can result in food spoilage in its warehouse. It has collected the following daily dollar value of spoiled food in its warehouse for four randomly selected days each month for a year.

	WASTE VALUE ($)/DAY			
MONTH	1	2	3	4
1	1,126	784	1,996	1,175
2	2,705	906	2,775	408
3	3,836	1,037	771	1,562
4	720	2,063	690	3,558
5	2,458	1,558	1,806	2,003
6	1,406	3,698	1,729	1,529
7	3,338	2,706	2,885	1,781
8	917	1,380	5,433	1,004
9	2,415	788	1,193	753
10	2,604	611	764	1,761
11	937	2,756	1,308	3,407
12	327	3,055	2,005	1,107

Construct a control chart for Metro using 3σ limits to monitor the dollar value food produce waste and indicate if the process is in control, and if the control chart would be reliable to monitor the process in the future.

3.33. Martha's Wonderful Cookie Company makes a special super-chocolate-chip peanut butter cookie. The company would like the cookies to average approximately eight chocolate chips apiece. Too few or too many chips distort the desired cookie taste. Twenty samples of five cookies each during a week have been taken and the chocolate chips counted. The sample observations are as follows:

SAMPLES	CHIPS PER COOKIE				
1	7	6	9	8	5
2	7	7	8	8	10
3	5	5	7	6	8
4	4	5	9	9	7
5	8	8	5	10	8
6	7	6	9	8	4
7	9	8	10	8	8
8	7	6	5	4	5
9	9	10	8	9	7
10	11	9	9	10	6
11	5	5	9	8	8
12	6	8	8	5	9
13	7	3	7	8	8
14	6	9	9	8	8
15	10	8	7	8	6
16	5	6	9	9	7
17	6	10	10	7	3
18	11	4	6	8	8
19	9	5	5	7	7
20	8	8	6	7	3

Construct an $\bar{x}$-chart in conjunction with an R-chart using 3σ limits for these data and comment on the cookie-production process.

3.34. Thirty patients who check out of the Rock Creek County Regional Hospital each week are asked to complete a questionnaire about hospital service. Since patients do not feel well when they are in the hospital, they typically are very critical of the service. The number of patients who indicated dissatisfaction of any kind with the service for each 30-patient sample for a 16-week period is as follows:

SAMPLE	NUMBER OF DISSATISFIED PATIENTS	SAMPLE	NUMBER OF DISSATISFIED PATIENTS
1	6	9	6
2	3	10	6
3	10	11	5
4	7	12	3
5	2	13	2
6	9	14	8
7	11	15	12
8	7	16	8

Construct a control chart to monitor customer satisfaction at the hospital using 3σ limits and determine if the process is in control.

3.35. An important aspect of customer service and satisfaction at the Big Country theme park is the maintenance of the restrooms throughout the park. Customers expect the restrooms to be clean; odorless; well stocked with soap, paper towels, and toilet paper; and to have a comfortable temperature. In order to maintain quality, park quality-control inspectors randomly inspect restrooms daily (during the day and evening) and record the number of defects (incidences of poor maintenance). The goal of park management is approximately 10 defects per inspection period. Following is a summary of the observations taken by these inspectors for 20 consecutive inspection periods:

SAMPLE	NUMBER OF DEFECTS	SAMPLE	NUMBER OF DEFECTS
1	7	11	14
2	14	12	10
3	6	13	11
4	9	14	12
5	12	15	9
6	3	16	13
7	11	17	7
8	7	18	15
9	7	19	11
10	8	20	16

Construct the appropriate control chart for this maintenance process using 3σ limits and indicate if the process was out of control at any time. If the process is in control, use pattern tests to determine if any nonrandom patterns exist.

3.36. The Great Outdoors Clothing Company, a mail-order catalog operation, contracts with the Federal Parcel Service to deliver all of its orders to customers. As such, Great Outdoors considers Federal Parcel to be part of its QMS program. Great Outdoors processes orders rapidly and requires Federal Parcel to pick them up and deliver them rapidly. Great Outdoors has tracked the delivery time for five randomly selected orders for 12 samples during a two-week period as follows:

SAMPLE	DELIVERY TIME (DAYS)				
1	2	3	3	4	3
2	5	3	6	2	1
3	4	3	3	2	2
4	6	1	5	3	3
5	2	4	1	4	4
6	5	1	3	3	3
7	2	3	3	2	1
8	1	1	3	1	2
9	6	3	3	3	3
10	6	7	5	5	6
11	6	1	1	3	2
12	5	5	3	1	3

Construct an $\bar{x}$-chart in conjunction with an R-chart using 3σ limits for the delivery process.

3.37. The Great Outdoors Clothing Company in Problem 3-36 has designed its packaging and delivery process to deliver orders to a customer within 3 business days ±1 day, which it tells customers. Using the process mean and control limits developed in Problem 3-36, compute the process capability ratio and index, and comment on the capability of the process to meet the company's delivery commitment.

3.38. Martha's Wonderful Cookie Company in Problem 3-33 has designed its special super-chocolate-chip peanut butter cookies to have 8 chocolate chips with tolerances of ±2 chips. Using the process mean and control limits developed in Problem 3-33, determine the process capability ratio and index, and comment on the capability of the cookie production process.

3.39. The Pacific Fruit Company in Problem 3-17 has designed its packaging process for boxes to hold a net weight (nominal value) of 9.0 oz. of raisins with tolerances of ±0.5 oz. Using the process mean and control limits developed in Problem 3-17, compute the process capability ratio and index, and comment on the capability of the process to meet the company's box weight specifications.

3.40. Sam's Long Life 75-watt light bulbs are designed to have a life of 1125 hours with tolerances of ±210 hours. The process that makes light bulbs has a mean of 1050 hours, with a standard deviation of 55 hours. Compute the process capability ratio and the process capability index, and comment on the overall capability of the process.

3.41. Elon Corporation manufactures parts for an aircraft company. It uses a computerized numerical controlled (CNC) machining center to produce a specific part that has a design (nominal) target of 1.275 inches with tolerances of ±0.024 inch. The CNC process that manufactures these parts has a mean of 1.281 inches and a standard deviation of 0.008 inch. Compute the process capability ratio and process capability index, and comment on the overall capability of the process to meet the design specifications.

3.42. Explain to what extent the process for producing Sam's Long Life bulbs in Problem 3-40 would have to be improved in order to achieve Six Sigma quality.

3.43. The Elon Company manufactures parts for an aircraft company using three computerized numerical controlled (CNC) turning centers. The company wants to decide which machines are capable of producing a specific part with design specifications of 0.0970 inch ±0.015 inch. The machines have the following process parameters—machine 1 ($\bar{\bar{x}} = 0.0995$, $\sigma = 0.004$); machine 2 ($\bar{\bar{x}} = 0.1002$, $\sigma = 0.009$); machine 3 ($\bar{\bar{x}} = 0.095$, $\sigma = 0.005$). Determine which machines (if any) are capable of producing the products within the design specifications.

3.44. The emergency medical response (EMR) team in Brookville has instituted a quality improvement program and it makes extensive use of SPC charts. It wants to monitor the response times for emergency calls to make sure they stay around nine minutes on average. The EMR administration staff has randomly timed five emergency calls each month during a 12-month period and collected the following data.

MONTH	RESPONSE TIMES (MINS)				
1	8.6	4.5	6.2	5.7	10.1
2	10.1	8.9	7.3	8.1	6.4
3	5.3	9.4	10.2	10.2	5.8
4	6.1	11.5	9.3	9.4	9.6
5	12.4	8.3	12.4	10.1	8.4
6	9.7	10.4	7.5	8.5	11.6
7	6.5	5.9	5.6	7.7	9.1
8	15.6	6.6	10.7	11.5	7.5
9	12.5	3.6	8.5	6.4	9.6
10	9.3	7.4	9.9	10.4	14.3
11	14.5	8.6	9.3	5.3	10.6
12	10.3	9.6	11.2	7.5	6.9

Develop a $\bar{x}$-chart in conjunction with an R-chart to monitor the response times and indicate if the process appears to be in control. If the

EMR team cannot consistently meet its target, what kind of actions (i.e., improvements) might it need to make to achieve its target?

3.45. The Balston Healthcare System uses SPC charts extensively to monitor various quality indicators and improve processes at its hospitals. One of the hospitals has discovered a potential problem in hand hygiene among its nursing staff. Lack of hand hygiene can be a major cause of fatal hospital-borne infections. The Centers for Disease Control has established criteria for hand hygiene in hospitals and the hospital suspects it is not meeting these criteria. When the CDC published the criteria for hand hygiene the first of January the hospital began collecting data—it sampled 150 opportunities for hand hygiene each week and recorded how many times hand hygiene was actually practiced according to the CDC criteria. The data showed a deficiency in hand hygiene among the nurses in the first six weeks. In week 7, a program to improve hand hygiene among the nurses was implemented with a goal of consistently reaching a target value of meeting 90% of all hand hygiene opportunities. Following is a table showing the data for the year.

WEEK	NURSES PRACTICING HAND HYGIENE
1	68
2	83
3	82
4	84
5	51
6	58
7	45
8	46
9	104
10	74
11	70
12	95

Develop a control chart based on these data (using 3σ control limits) and explain what the chart means and the steps in a quality improvement process the SPC chart results would lead the quality management staff to take.

3.46. The Rollins Sporting Goods Company manufactures baseballs for the professional minor and major leagues at its plants in Costa Rica. According to the rules of major league baseball, a baseball must weigh between 142 and 149 grams. The company has taken 20 samples of five baseballs each and weighed the baseballs as follows:

SAMPLE	WEIGHT (GM)				
1	143.1	142.5	148.1	149.4	146.3
2	145.8	144.0	149.8	141.2	143.5
3	140.3	144.5	146.2	140.4	149.7
4	143.4	145.2	147.8	144.1	148.6
5	142.5	141.7	139.6	145.4	146.3
6	147.4	145.2	145.0	150.3	151.2
7	144.7	145.0	145.2	140.6	139.7
8	141.4	138.5	140.3	142.6	144.4
9	151.3	149.7	145.4	148.2	149.0
10	137.3	144.6	145.8	141.9	144.5
11	142.3	144.7	141.6	145.8	148.3
12	143.6	145.4	145.0	144.3	149.1
13	148.4	147.3	149.1	140.6	140.9
14	151.3	150.6	147.2	148.3	146.5
15	145.2	146.3	141.2	142.5	142.7
16	146.3	147.4	148.2	145.4	145.1
17	143.9	144.6	145.2	146.1	146.3
18	145.6	145.3	142.1	146.7	144.3
19	142.8	141.7	140.9	145.6	146.3
20	145.4	142.3	147.5	145.0	149.4

Construct an $\bar{x}$-chart in conjunction with an R-chart to monitor the baseball-making process, and comment on the capability of the process.

3.47. Explain to what extent the process for manufacturing baseballs in Problem 3-46 must be improved in order to achieve 6σ quality.

3.48. At Samantha's Super Store, the customer service area processes customer returns, answers customer questions and provides information, addresses customer complaints, and sells gift certificates. The manager believes that if customers must wait longer than 8 minutes to see a customer service representative they get very irritated. The customer service process has been designed to achieve a customer wait time of between 6 and 12 minutes. The store manager has conducted 10 samples of five observations each of customer waiting time over a two-week period as follows:

SAMPLE	WAIT TIME (MIN)				
1	8.3	9.6	10.2	7.4	3.1
2	2.8	5.9	6.7	8.3	9.2
3	11.3	7.4	16.2	20.1	9.5
4	10.7	7.5	9.8	11.3	4.5
5	4.3	12.4	10.6	16.7	11.3
6	5.3	9.7	10.8	11.3	7.4
7	18.2	12.1	3.6	9.5	14.2
8	8.1	10.3	8.9	7.2	5.6
9	9.3	12.4	13.7	7.3	5.2
10	6.7	8.5	8.0	10.1	12.3

Construct an $\bar{x}$-chart in conjunction with an R-chart to monitor customer service wait time, and comment on the capability of the service area to meet its designated goal.

3.49. Metropolitan General Hospital is a city-owned and -operated public hospital. Its emergency room is the largest and most prominent in the city. Approximately 70% of emergency cases in the city come or are sent to Metro General's emergency room. As a result, the emergency room is often crowded and the staff is overworked, causing concern among hospital administrators and city officials about the quality of service and healthcare the emergency room is able to provide. One of the key quality attributes administrators focus on is patient waiting time—that is, the time between when a patient checks in and registers and when the patient first sees an appropriate medical staff member. Hospital administration wants to monitor patient waiting time using statistical process control charts. At different times of the day over a period of several days, patient waiting times were recorded at random with the following results:

SAMPLE	WAITING TIMES (MIN) 1	2	3	4	5
1	27	18	20	23	19
2	22	25	31	40	17
3	16	15	22	19	23
4	35	27	16	20	24
5	21	33	45	12	22
6	17	15	22	20	30
7	25	21	26	33	19
8	15	38	23	25	31
9	31	26	24	35	32
10	28	23	29	20	27

a. Develop an $\bar{x}$-chart to be used in conjunction with an R-chart to monitor patient waiting time and indicate if the process appears to be in control.

b. The city has established a requirement that emergency room patients have a waiting time of 25 minutes ±5 minutes. Based on the results in part (a), is the emergency room capable of meeting this requirement with its current process?

3.50. The three most important quality attributes at Mike's Super Service fast-food restaurant are considered to be good food, fast service, and a clean environment. The restaurant manager uses a combination of customer surveys and statistical measurement tools to monitor these quality attributes. A national marketing and research firm has developed data showing that when customers are in line up to five minutes, their perception of that waiting time is only a few minutes; however, after five minutes customer perception of their waiting time increases exponentially. Furthermore, a five-minute average waiting time results in only 2% of customers leaving. The manager wants to monitor speed of service using a statistical process control chart. At six different times during the day over a period of 15 days the manager had an employee time customers' waiting times (from the time they entered an order line to the time they received their order) at random, with the following results:

SAMPLE	WAITING TIMES (MIN) 1	2	3	4	5	6
1	6.3	2.7	4.5	3.9	5.7	5.9
2	3.8	6.2	7.1	5.4	5.1	4.7
3	5.3	5.6	6.2	5.0	5.3	4.9
4	3.9	7.2	6.4	5.7	4.2	7.1
5	4.6	3.9	5.1	4.8	5.6	6.0
6	5.5	6.3	5.2	7.4	8.1	5.9
7	6.1	7.3	6.5	5.9	5.7	8.4
8	2.2	3.6	5.7	5.3	5.6	5.0
9	6.5	4.7	5.1	9.3	6.2	5.3
10	4.7	5.8	5.4	5.1	5.0	5.9
11	3.4	2.9	1.6	4.8	6.1	5.3
12	4.5	6.3	5.4	5.7	2.1	3.4
13	7.4	3.9	4.2	4.9	5.6	3.7
14	5.7	5.3	4.1	3.7	5.8	5.7
15	6.0	3.6	2.4	5.4	5.5	3.9

a. Develop an $\bar{x}$-chart to be used in conjunction with an R-chart to monitor speed of service and indicate if the process is in control using this chart.

b. Management at Mike's Super Service restaurant wants customers to receive their orders within 5 minutes ±1 minute, and it has designed its ordering and food preparation process to meet that goal. Using the process mean and control limits developed in part (a), compute the process capability ratio and index, and indicate if the process appears to be capable of meeting the restaurant's goal for speed of service.

3.51. The family of a patient at County General Hospital complained when the patient fell in the hospital and broke her hip. The family was threatening a lawsuit, and there had been some negative publicity about the hospital in the local media suggesting that patient falls might be common. The hospital administration decided to investigate this potential problem by developing a control chart based on two years of monthly data for the number of patient falls each month as follows:

MONTH	FALLS	MONTH	FALLS
1	3	13	1
2	2	14	1
3	4	15	4
4	3.5	16	3
5	0	17	6
6	2	18	3
7	2	19	5
8	4	20	2
9	4	21	1
10	2.5	22	2.5
11	1.5	23	2.5
12	3	24	1.5

Develop a control chart with 3σ limits to monitor patient falls, and discuss if you think there appears to be a quality problem at the hospital.

3.52. The Shuler Motor Mile is a high-volume discount car dealership that stocks several different makes of cars. It also has a large service department. The dealership telephones six randomly selected customers each week and conducts a survey to determine their satisfaction with the service they received. Each survey results in a customer satisfaction score based on a 100-point scale, where 100 is perfect (and what the dealership ultimately aspires to). Following are the survey results for three months:

WEEK	CUSTOMER SATISFACTION SCORES 1	2	3	4	5	6
1	87	94	91	76	89	93
2	97	100	88	93	91	91
3	90	78	87	65	93	82
4	93	89	77	94	99	94
5	91	94	90	90	81	93
6	95	86	88	91	82	80
7	81	84	93	90	94	96
8	100	95	66	78	94	83

WEEK	CUSTOMER SATISFACTION SCORES 1	2	3	4	5	6
9	94	63	89	91	88	79
10	95	85	100	98	91	93
11	93	100	92	99	87	86
12	78	91	82	86	85	91

a. Develop an x-chart to be used in conjunction with an R-chart using 3σ limits to monitor the level of customer satisfaction at the dealership and indicate if customer satisfaction is being accomplished on a continuing basis.

b. The dealership would like to achieve an average customer satisfaction score of 95 (± 3); is the service department capable of this?

3.53. The time from when a patient is discharged from North Shore Hospital to the time the discharged patient's bed is ready to be assigned to a new patient is referred to as the bed assignment turnaround time. If the bed turnaround time is excessive, it can cause problems with patient flow and delay medical procedures throughout the hospital. This can cause long waiting times for physicians and patients, thus creating customer dissatisfaction. The admissions RN has assigned a patient care associate to measure the bed turnaround time for a randomly selected bed each morning, afternoon, and evening for 30 days. Following are the bed turnaround time sample observations:

DAY	BED TURNAROUND TIMES (MIN)		
1	127	135	167
2	140	155	122
3	112	128	97
4	223	135	154
5	181	155	160
6	103	158	145
7	146	135	167
8	104	122	115
9	136	158	137
10	145	163	106
11	84	146	125
12	169	152	208
13	216	124	163
14	190	178	103
15	148	205	144
16	157	151	126
17	142	102	95
18	166	178	159
19	177	211	204
20	98	91	158
21	133	160	152
22	212	131	138
23	180	165	134
24	88	126	108
25	95	156	138
26	156	202	177
27	144	157	165
28	184	171	106
29	138	142	155
30	150	99	148

a. Develop an x-chart to be used in conjunction with an R-chart using 3σ limits to monitor the bed turnaround times and indicate if the process is in control using these charts.

b. Is the hospital capable of consistently achieving bed turnaround times of 120 minutes ± 15 minutes without improving the process?

Case Problems

Case Problem 3.1 Quality Control at Rainwater Brewery

Bob Raines and Megan Waters own and operate the Rainwater Brewery, a microbrewery that grew out of their shared hobby of making home-brew. The brewery is located in Whitesville, the home of State University where Bob and Megan went to college.

Whitesville has a number of bars and restaurants that are patronized by students at State and the local resident population. In fact, Whitesville has the highest per capita beer consumption in the state. In setting up their small brewery, Bob and Megan decided that they would target their sales toward individuals who would pick up their orders directly from the brewery and toward restaurants and bars, where they would deliver orders on a daily or weekly basis.

The brewery process essentially occurs in three stages. First, the mixture is cooked in a vat according to a recipe; then it is placed in a stainless-steel container, where it is fermented for several weeks. During the fermentation process the specific gravity, temperature, and pH must be monitored on a daily basis. The specific gravity starts out at about 1.006 to 1.008 and decreases to around 1.002, and the temperature must be between 50° and 60°F. After the brew ferments, it is filtered into another stainless-steel pressurized container, where it is carbonated and the beer ages for about a week (with the temperature monitored), after which it is bottled and is ready for distribution. Megan and Bob brew a batch of beer each day, which will result in about 1000 bottles for distribution after the approximately three-week fermentation and aging process.

In the process of setting up their brewery, Megan and Bob agreed they had already developed a proven product with a taste that was appealing, so the most important factor in the success of their new venture would be maintaining high quality. Thus, they spent a lot of time discussing what kind of quality-control techniques they should employ. They agreed that the chance of brewing a "bad," or "spoiled," batch of beer was extremely remote, plus they could not financially afford to reject a whole batch of 1000 bottles of beer if the taste or color was a little "off" the norm. So they felt as if they needed to focus more on process control methods to identify quality problems that would enable them to adjust their equipment, recipe, or process parameters rather than rejecting the entire batch.

Describe the different quality-control methods that Rainwater Brewery might use to ensure good-quality beer and how these methods might fit into an overall quality management program.

Case Problem 3.2 Quality Control at Grass, Unlimited

Mark Sumansky owns and manages the Grass, Unlimited, lawn-care service in Middleton. His customers include individual homeowners and businesses that subscribe to his service for lawn care beginning in the spring and ending in the fall with leaf raking and disposal. Thus, when he begins his service in April he generally has a full list of customers and does not take on additional customers unless he has an opening. However, if he loses a customer any time after the first of June, it is difficult to find new customers, since most people make lawn-service arrangements for the entire summer.

Mark employs five crews, with three to five workers each, to cut grass during the spring and summer months. A crew normally works 10-hour days and can average cutting about 25 normal-size lawns of less than a half-acre each day. A crew will normally have one heavy-duty, wide-cut riding mower, a regular power mower, and trimming equipment. When a crew descends on a lawn, the normal procedure is for one person to mow the main part of the lawn with the riding mower, one or two people to trim, and one person to use the smaller mower to cut areas the riding mower cannot reach. Crews move very fast, and they can often cut a lawn in 15 minutes.

Unfortunately, although speed is an essential component in the profitability of Grass, Unlimited, it can also contribute to quality problems. In his or her haste, a mower might cut flowers, shrubs, or border plants, nick and scrape trees, "skin" spots on the lawn creating bare spots, trim too close, scrape house paint, cut or disfigure house trim, and destroy toys and lawn furniture, among other things. When these problems occur on a too-frequent basis, a customer cancels service, and Mark has a difficult time getting a replacement customer. In addition, he gets most of his subscriptions based on word-of-mouth recommendations and retention of previous customers who are satisfied with his service. As such, quality is a very important factor in his business.

In order to improve the quality of his lawn-care service, Mark has decided to use a process control chart to monitor defects. He has hired Lisa Anderson to follow the teams and check lawns for defects after the mowers have left. A defect is any abnormal or abusive condition created by the crew, including those items just mentioned. It is not possible for Lisa to inspect the more than 100 lawns the service cuts daily, so she randomly picks a sample of 20 lawns each day and counts the number of defects she sees at each lawn. She also makes a note of each defect, so that if there is a problem, the cause can easily be determined. In most cases the defects are caused by haste, but some defects can be caused by faulty equipment or by a crew member using a poor technique or not being attentive.

Over a three-day period Lisa accumulated the following data on defects:

DAY 1		DAY 2		DAY 3	
SAMPLE	NUMBER OF DEFECTS	SAMPLE	NUMBER OF DEFECTS	SAMPLE	NUMBER OF DEFECTS
1	6	1	2	1	5
2	4	2	5	2	5
3	5	3	1	3	3
4	9	4	4	4	2
5	3	5	5	5	6
6	8	6	3	6	5
7	6	7	2	7	4
8	1	8	2	3	3
9	5	9	2	9	2
10	6	10	6	10	2
11	4	11	4	11	2
12	7	12	3	12	4
13	6	13	8	13	1
14	5	14	5	14	5
15	8	15	6	15	9
16	3	16	3	16	4
17	5	17	4	17	4
18	4	18	3	18	4
19	3	19	3	19	1
20	2	20	4	20	3

Develop a process control chart for Grass, Unlimited, to monitor the quality of its lawn service using 2-sigma limits. Describe any other quality-control or quality-management procedures you think Grass, Unlimited, might employ to improve the quality of its service.

Case Problem 3.3 Improving Service Time at Dave's Burgers

Dave's Burgers is a fast-food restaurant franchise in Georgia, South Carolina, and North Carolina. Recently, Dave's Burgers has followed the lead of larger franchise restaurants like Burger King, McDonald's, and Wendy's and constructed drive-through windows at all its locations. However, instead of making Dave's Burgers more competitive, the drive-through windows have been a source of continual problems and it has lost market share to its larger competitors in almost all locations. To identify and correct the problems, top management has selected three of its restaurants (one in each state) as test sites and has implemented a quality management program at each of them. At the Charlotte, North Carolina, test restaurant, a quality team made up of employees, managers, and quality specialists from company headquarters, using traditional quality tools like Pareto charts, checksheets, fishbone diagrams, and process flowcharts, have determined that the primary problem is slow, erratic service at the drive-through window. Studies show that the time a customer arrives at the window to the time the order is received averages 2.6 minutes. To be competitive, management believes service time should be reduced to at least 2.0 minutes and ideally 1.5 minutes.

The Charlotte Dave's Burgers franchise implemented a number of production process changes to improve service time at the drive-through window. It provided all employees with more training across all restaurant functions, improved the headset system, improved the equipment layout, developed clearer signs for customers, streamlined the menu, and initiated even-dollar (tax-inclusive) pricing to speed the payment process. Most importantly, the restaurant installed large, visible electronic timers that showed how long a customer was at the window. This not only allowed the quality team to measure service speed but also provided employees with a constant reminder that a customer was waiting.

These quality improvements were implemented over several months, and their effect was immediate. Service speed was obviously improved, and market share at the Charlotte restaurant increased by 5%. To maintain quality service, make sure the service time remained fast, and continue to improve service, the quality team decided to use a statistical process control chart on a continuing basis. They collected six service time observations daily over a 15-day period, as follows:

	OBSERVATIONS OF SERVICE TIME (MIN)					
SAMPLE	1	2	3	4	5	6
1	1.62	1.54	1.38	1.75	2.50	1.32
2	1.25	1.96	1.55	1.66	1.38	2.01
3	1.85	1.01	0.95	1.79	1.66	1.94
4	3.10	1.18	1.25	1.45	1.09	2.11
5	1.95	0.76	1.34	2.12	1.45	1.03
6	0.88	2.50	1.07	1.50	1.33	1.62
7	1.55	1.41	1.95	1.14	1.86	1.02
8	2.78	1.56	1.87	2.03	0.79	1.14
9	1.31	1.05	0.94	1.53	1.71	1.15
10	1.67	1.85	2.03	1.12	1.50	1.36
11	0.95	1.73	1.12	1.67	2.05	1.42
12	3.21	4.16	1.67	1.75	2.87	3.76
13	1.65	1.78	2.63	1.05	1.21	2.09
14	2.36	3.55	1.92	1.45	3.64	2.30
15	1.07	0.96	1.13	2.05	0.91	1.66

Construct a control chart to monitor the service at the drive-through window. Determine if your control chart can be implemented on a continuing basis or if additional observations need to be collected. Explain why the chart you developed can or cannot be used. Also discuss what other statistical process control charts Dave's Burgers might use in its overall quality-management program.

References

Charbonneau, H. C., and G. L. Webster. *Industrial Quality Control.* Englewood Cliffs, NJ: Prentice Hall, 1978.

Dodge, H. F., and H. G. Romig. *Sampling Inspection Tables—Single and Double Sampling*. 2nd ed. New York: Wiley.

Duncan, A. J. *Quality Control and Industrial Statistics.* 4th ed. Homewood, IL: Irwin, 1974.

Evans, James R., and William M. Lindsay. *The Management and Control of Quality.* 3rd ed. St. Paul, MN: West, 1993.

Fetter, R. B. *The Quality Control System.* Homewood, IL: Irwin, 1967.

Grant, E. L., and R. S. Leavenworth. *Statistical Quality Control.* 5th ed. New York: McGraw-Hill, 1980.

Montgomery, D. C. *Introduction to Statistical Quality Control.* 2nd ed. New York: Wiley, 1991.

SUPPLEMENT TO CHAPTER 3

Operational Decision-Making Tools: Acceptance Sampling

- Utilizing appropriately the basic tools of acceptance sampling including sampling plans, operating characteristic curves, and average outgoing quality curves

Acceptance sampling Accepting or rejecting a production lot based on the number of defects in a sample.

In **acceptance sampling,** a random sample of the units produced is inspected, and the quality of this sample is assumed to reflect the overall quality of all items or a particular group of items, called a *lot*. Acceptance sampling is a statistical method, so if a sample is random, it ensures that each item has an equal chance of being selected and inspected. This enables statistical inferences to be made about the population—the lot—as a whole. If a sample has an acceptable number or percentage of defective items, the lot is accepted, but if it has an unacceptable number of defects, it is rejected.

Acceptance sampling is a historical approach to quality control based on the premise that some acceptable number of defective items will result from the production process. The producer and customer agree on the number of acceptable defects, normally measured as a percentage. However, the notion of a producer or customer agreeing to any defects at all is anathema to the adherents of quality management. The goal of these companies is to achieve zero defects. Acceptance sampling identifies defective items after the product is already finished, whereas quality-focused companies desire the prevention of defects altogether. Acceptance sampling is simply a means of identifying products to throw away or rework. It does nothing to prevent poor quality and to ensure good quality in the future.

Six Sigma companies do not even report the number of defective parts in terms of a percentage because the fraction of defective items they expect to produce is so small that a percentage is meaningless. The international measure for reporting defects has become defective parts per million, or PPM. For example, a defect rate of 2%, used in acceptance sampling, was once considered a high-quality standard: 20,000 defective parts per million! This is a totally unacceptable level of quality for companies continuously trying to achieve zero defects. Three or four defects per million would be a more acceptable level of quality for these companies.

Nevertheless, acceptance sampling is still used as a statistical quality control method by many companies that either have not yet adopted a QMS or are required by customer demands or government regulations to use acceptance sampling. Since this method still has wide application, it is necessary for it to be studied.

Sampling plan Provides the guidelines for accepting a lot.

When a sample is taken and inspected for quality, the items in the sample are being checked to see if they conform to some predetermined specification. A **sampling plan** establishes the guidelines for taking a sample and the criteria for making a decision regarding the quality of the lot from which the sample was taken. The simplest form of sampling plan is a single-sample attribute plan.

Single-Sample Attribute Plan

A single-sample attribute plan has as its basis an attribute that can be evaluated with a simple, discrete decision, such as defective or not defective or good or bad. The plan includes the following elements:

N = the lot size

n = the sample size (selected randomly)

c = the acceptable number of defective items in a sample

d = the actual number of defective items in a sample

A single sample of size n is selected randomly from a larger lot, and each of the n items is inspected. If the sample contains $d \leq c$ defective items, the entire lot is accepted; if $d > c$, the lot is rejected.

Management must decide the values of these components that will result in the most effective sampling plan, as well as determine what constitutes an effective plan. These are design considerations. The design of a sampling plan includes both the structural components (n, the decision criteria, and so on) and performance measures. These performance measures include the *producer's* and *consumer's risks*, the *acceptable quality level*, and the *lot tolerance percent defective*.

Producer's and Consumer's Risks

When a sample is drawn from a production lot and the items in the sample are inspected, management hopes that if the actual number of defective items exceeds the predetermined acceptable number of defective items ($d > c$) and the entire lot is rejected, then the sample results have accurately portrayed the quality of the entire lot. Management would hate to think that the sample results were not indicative of the overall quality of the lot and a lot that was actually acceptable was erroneously rejected and wasted. Conversely, management hopes that an actual bad lot of items is not erroneously accepted if $d \leq c$. An effective sampling plan attempts to minimize the possibility of wrongly rejecting good items or wrongly accepting bad items.

Acceptable quality level (AQL) An acceptable proportion of defects in a lot to the consumer.

When an acceptance-sampling plan is designed, management specifies a quality standard commonly referred to as the **acceptable quality level (AQL)**. The AQL reflects the consumer's willingness to accept lots with a small proportion of defective items. The AQL is the fraction of defective items in a lot that is deemed acceptable. For example, the AQL might be two defective items in a lot of 500, or .004. The AQL may be determined by management to be the level that is generally acceptable in the marketplace and will not result in a loss of customers. Or, it may be dictated by an individual customer as the quality level it will accept. In other words, the AQL is negotiated.

Producer's risk The probability of rejecting a lot that has an AQL.

The probability of rejecting a production lot that has an acceptable quality level is referred to as the **producer's risk**, commonly designated by the Greek symbol α. In statistical jargon, α is the probability of committing a type I error.

Lot tolerance percent defective (LTPD) The maximum number of defective items a consumer will accept in a lot.

There will be instances in which the sample will not accurately reflect the quality of a lot and a lot that does not meet the AQL will pass on to the customer. Although the customer expects to receive some of these lots, there is a limit to the number of defective items the customer will accept. This upper limit is known as the **lot tolerance percent defective**, or **LTPD** (LTPD is also generally negotiated between the producer and consumer). The probability of accepting a lot in which the fraction of defective items exceeds the LTPD is referred to as the

consumer's risk, designated by the Greek symbol β. In statistical jargon, β is the probability of committing a type II error.

Consumer's risk The probability of accepting a lot in which the fraction of defective items exceeds LTPD.

In general, the customer would like the quality of a lot to be as good as or better than the AQL but is willing to accept some lots with quality levels no worse than the LTPD. Frequently, sampling plans are designed with the producer's risk (α) about 5% and the consumer's risk (β) around 10%. Be careful not to confuse α with the AQL or β with the LTPD. If α equals 5% and β equals 10%, then management expects to reject lots that are as good as or better than the AQL about 5% of the time, whereas the customer expects to accept lots that exceed the LTPD about 10% of the time.

The Operating Characteristic Curve

The performance measures we described in the previous section for a sampling plan can be represented graphically with an **operating characteristic (OC) curve**. The OC curve measures the probability of accepting a lot for different quality (proportion defective) levels given a specific sample size (n) and acceptance level (c). Management can use such a graph to determine if their sampling plan meets the performance measures they have established for AQL, LTPD, α, and β. Thus, the OC curve indicates to management how effective the sampling plan is in distinguishing (more commonly known as *discriminating*) between good and bad lots. The shape of a typical OC curve for a single-sample plan is shown in **Figure S3.1**.

Operating characteristic (OC) curve A graph that shows the probability of accepting a lot for different quality levels with a specific sampling plan.

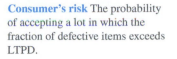

In Figure S3.1 the percentage defective in a lot is shown along the horizontal axis, whereas the probability of accepting a lot is measured along the vertical axis. The exact shape and location of the curve is defined by the sample size (n) and acceptance level (c) for the sampling plan.

In Figure S3.1, if a lot has 3% defective items, the probability of accepting the lot (based on the sampling plan defined by the OC curve) is .95. If management defines the AQL as 3%, then the probability that an acceptable lot will be rejected (α) is 1 minus the probability of accepting

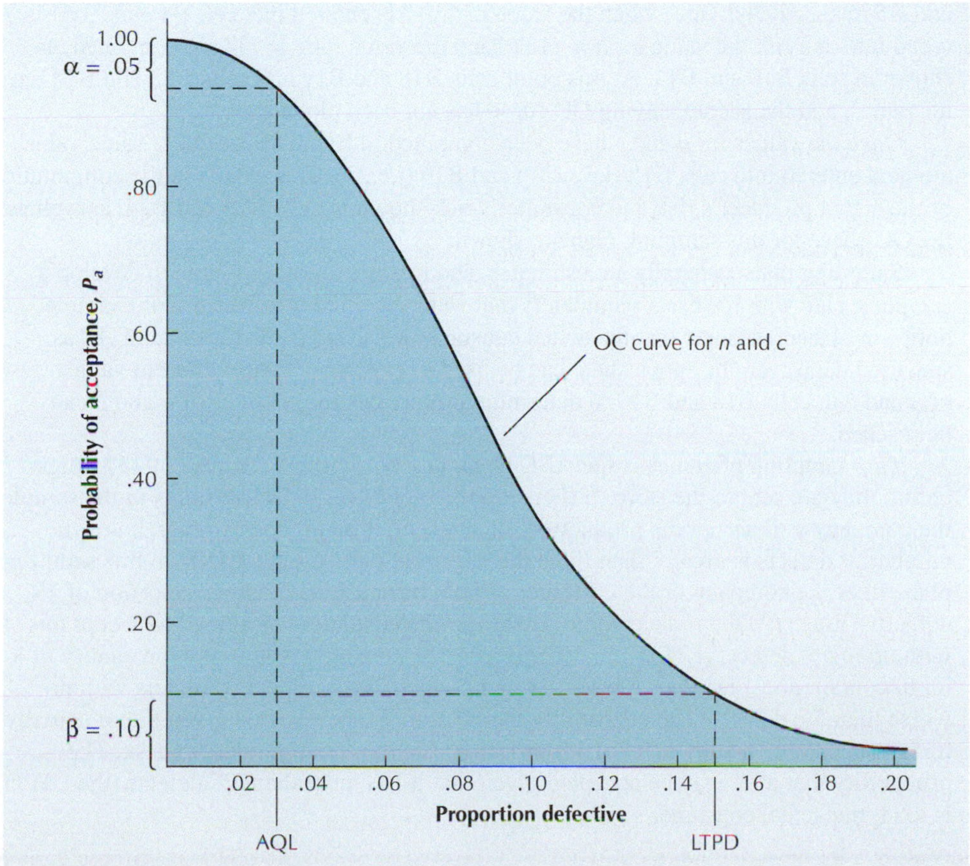

FIGURE S3.1 **An Operating Characteristic Curve**

a lot, or $1 - .95 = .05$. If management is willing to accept lots with a percentage defective up to 15% (i.e., the LTPD), this corresponds to a probability that the lot will be accepted (β) of .10. A frequently used set of performance measures is $\alpha = .05$ and $\beta = .10$.

Developing a Sampling Plan with OM Tools

Developing a sampling plan manually requires a tedious trial-and-error approach using statistical analysis. n and c are progressively changed until an approximate sampling plan is obtained that meets the specified performance measures. A more practical alternative is to use OM Tools. Example S3.1 demonstrates the use of OM Tools to develop a sampling plan.

EXAMPLE S3.1 Developing a Sampling Plan and Operating Characteristic Curve

The Anderson Bottle and China (ABC) Company produces a style of solid-colored blue china exclusively for a large department store chain. The china includes a number of different items that are sold in open stock in the stores, including coffee mugs. Mugs are produced in lots of 10,000. Performance measures for the quality of mugs sent to the stores call for a producer's risk (α) of .05 with an AQL of 1% defective and a consumer's risk (β) of .10 with a LTPD of 5% defective. The ABC Company wants to know what size sample, n, to take and what the acceptance number, c, should be to achieve the performance measures called for in the sampling plan.

Solution:

The OM Tools spreadsheet shown in Exhibit S3.1 is set up to determine an estimated sampling plan, n and c, based on the AQL and LTPD values initially input into cells B4 and B5, respectively. Thus, when the value of ".01" is entered into cell B4 and ".05" is typed into cell B5, the value for n = "137" and the value for c = "3" are computed, as shown in cells B10 and B11. At this point cells B18 and B19 and cells B23 and B24 have no values, and the accompanying OC curve has not been plotted yet.

Once the values for n and c have been computed in Exhibit S3.1, these same values are next entered into cells B18 (i.e., 137) and B19 (i.e., 3). This results in the computation of the actual producer's risk and consumer's risk shown in cells B23 and B24, as well as the OC curve for this sampling plan are shown.

Sampling plans generally are estimates, and it is not always possible to develop a sampling plan with the exact parameters that were specified in advance. For example, notice on the spreadsheet that the actual consumer's risk (β) is .084 instead of .10 as specified. However, the spreadsheet can be used to experiment with different values of n and c in cells B18 and B19 to determine if more desirable values of α and β can be reached.

This sampling plan means the ABC Company will inspect samples of 137 mugs before they are sent to the store. If there are three or fewer defective mugs in the sample, the company will accept the production lot and send it on to the customer, but if the number of defects is greater than three the entire lot will be rejected. With this sampling plan either the company or the customer or both have decided that a proportion of 1% defective mugs (AQL) is acceptable. However, the customer has agreed to accept lots with up to 5% defects (LTPD). In other words, the customer would like the quality of a lot to contain no worse than 1% defects, but it is willing to accept some lots with no worse than 5% defects. The probability that a lot might be rejected given that it actually has an acceptable quality level of 1% or less is .05, the actual producer's risk. The probability that a lot may be accepted given that it has more than 5% defects (the LTPD) is .084, the actual consumer's risk.

EXHIBIT S3.1

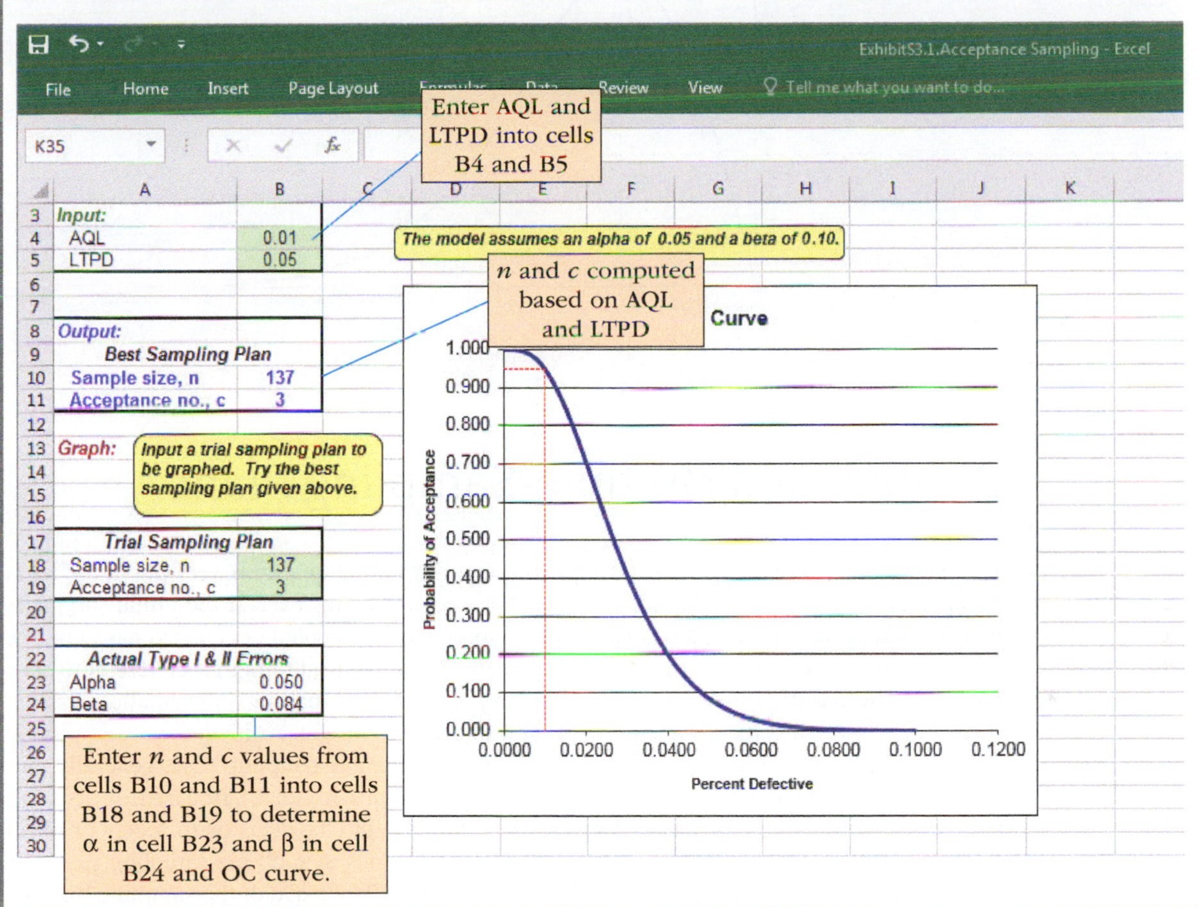

Average Outgoing Quality

The shape of the operating characteristic curve shows that lots with a low percentage of defects have a high probability of being accepted, and lots with a high percentage of defects have a low probability of being accepted, as one would expect. For example, using the OC curve for the sampling plan in Example S3.1 ($n = 137$, $c \leq 3$) for a percentage of defects = 0.01, the probability the lot will be accepted is approximately 0.95, whereas for 0.05, the probability of accepting a lot is relatively small. However, all lots, whether or not they are accepted, will pass on some defective items to the customer. The **average outgoing quality (AOQ)** is a measure of the expected number of defective items that will pass on to the customer with the sampling plan selected.

Average outgoing quality (AOQ) The expected number of defective items that will pass on to the customer with a sampling plan.

When a lot is rejected as a result of the sampling plan, it is assumed that it will be subjected to a complete inspection, and all defective items will be replaced with good ones. Also, even when a lot is accepted, the defective items found in the sample will be replaced. Thus, some portion of all the defective items contained in all the lots produced will be replaced before they are passed on to the customer. The remaining defective items that make their way to the customer are contained in lots that are accepted. Figure S3.2 shows the average outgoing quality curve for Example S3.1.

The maximum point on the curve is referred to as the *average outgoing quality limit* (AOQL). For our example, the AOQL is 1.42% defective when the actual proportion defective of the lot is 2%. This is the worst level of outgoing quality that management can expect on average, and if this level is acceptable, then the sampling plan is deemed acceptable. Notice that as the percentage of defects increases and the quality of the lots deteriorates, the AOQ improves. This occurs because as the quality of the lots becomes poorer, it is more likely that bad lots will be identified and rejected, and any defective items in these lots will be replaced with good ones.

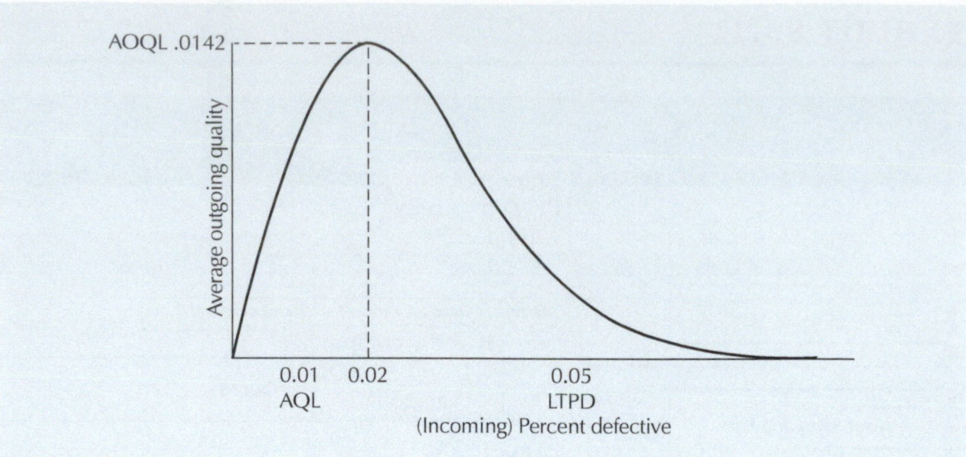

FIGURE S3.2 An Average Outgoing Quality Curve

Double- and Multiple-Sampling Plans

In a *double-sampling plan*, a small sample is taken first; if the quality is very good, the lot is accepted, and if the sample is very poor, the lot is rejected. However, if the initial sample is inconclusive, a second sample is taken and the lot is either accepted or rejected based on the combined results of the two samples. The objective of such a sampling procedure is to save costs relative to a single-sampling plan. For very good or very bad lots, the smaller, less expensive sample will suffice and a larger, more expensive sample is avoided.

A *multiple-sampling plan*, also referred to as a sequential-sampling plan, generally employs the smallest sample size of any of the sampling plans we have discussed. In its most extreme form, individual items are inspected sequentially, and the decision to accept or reject a lot is based on the cumulative number of defective items. A multiple-sampling plan can result in small samples and, consequently, can be the least expensive of the sampling plans.

The steps of a multiple-sampling plan are similar to those for a double-sampling plan. An initial sample (which can be as small as one unit) is taken. If the number of defective items is less than or equal to a lower limit, the lot is accepted, whereas if it exceeds a specified upper limit, the lot is rejected. If the number of defective items falls between the two limits, a second sample is obtained. The cumulative number of defects is then compared with an increased set of upper and lower limits, and the decision rule used in the first sample is applied. If the lot is neither accepted nor rejected with the second sample, a third sample is taken, with the acceptance/rejection limits revised upward. These steps are repeated for subsequent samples until the lot is either accepted or rejected.

Choosing among single-, double-, or multiple-sampling plans is an economic decision. When the cost of obtaining a sample is very high compared with the inspection cost, a single-sampling plan is preferred. For example, if a petroleum company is analyzing soil samples from various locales around the globe, it is probably more economical to take a single, large sample in Brazil than to return for additional samples if the initial sample is inconclusive. Alternatively, if the cost of sampling is low relative to inspection costs, a double- or multiple-sampling plan may be preferred. For example, if a winery is sampling bottles of wine, it may be more economical to use a sequential sampling plan, tasting individual bottles, than to test a large single sample containing a number of bottles, since each bottle sampled is, in effect, destroyed. In most cases in which quality control requires destructive testing, the inspection costs are high compared with sampling costs.

Summary

Five decades ago acceptance sampling constituted the primary means of quality control in many U.S. companies. However, it is the exception now, as most quality-conscious firms in the United States and abroad have either adopted or moved toward a quality-management program such as a QMS or Six Sigma. The cost of inspection, the cost of sending lots back, and the cost of scrap and waste are costs that most companies cannot tolerate and remain competitive in today's global market. Still, acceptance sampling is used by some companies and government agencies, and thus it is a relevant topic for study.

Key Terms

acceptable quality level (AQL) The fraction of defective items deemed acceptable in a lot.

acceptance sampling A statistical procedure for taking a random sample in order to determine whether a lot should be accepted or rejected.

average outgoing quality (AOQ) The expected number of defective items that will pass on to the customer with a sampling plan.

consumer's risk (β) The profitability of accepting a lot in which the fraction of defective items exceeds the LTPD the consumer is willing to accept.

lot tolerance percent defective (LTPD) The maximum percentage defective items in a lot that the consumer will knowingly accept.

operating characteristic (OC) curve A graph that measures the probability of accepting a lot for different proportions of defective items.

producer's risk (α) The probability of rejecting a lot that has an acceptable quality level (AQL).

sampling plan A plan that provides guidelines for accepting a lot.

Solved Problems

Single-Sample, Attribute Plan

Problem Statement

A product lot of 2000 items is inspected at a station at the end of the production process. Management and the product's customer have agreed to a quality-control program whereby lots that contain no more than 2% defectives are deemed acceptable, whereas lots with 6% or more defectives are not acceptable. Furthermore, management desires to limit the probability that a good lot will be rejected to 5%, and the customer wants to limit the probability that a bad lot will be accepted to 10%. Using OM Tools, develop a sampling plan that will achieve the quality-performance criteria.

Solution

The OM Tools solution is shown as follows:

OM Tools

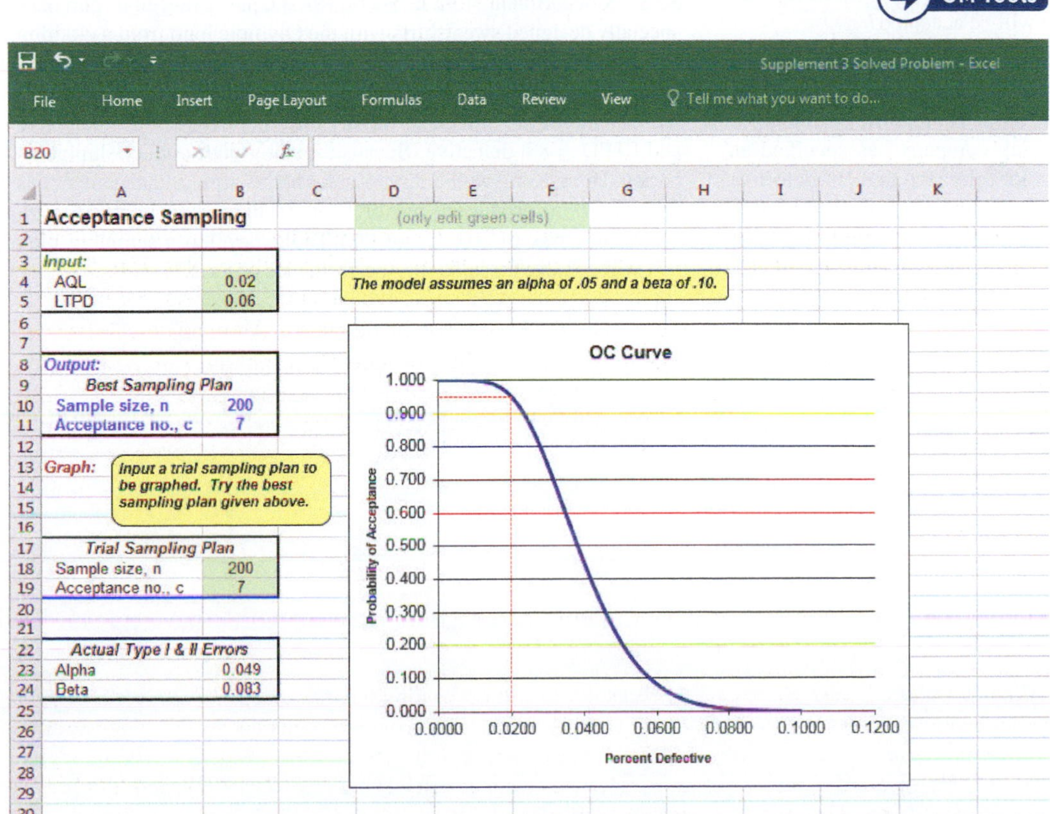

Questions

S3.1. What is the difference between acceptance sampling and process control?

S3.2. Why are sample sizes for attributes necessarily larger than sample sizes for variables?

S3.3. How is the sample size determined in a single-sample attribute plan?

S3.4. How does the AQL relate to producer's risk (α) and the LTPD relate to consumer's risk (β)?

S3.5. Explain the difference between single-, double-, and multiple-sampling plans.

S3.6. Why is the traditional view of quality control reflected in the use of acceptance sampling unacceptable to adherents of quality management and continuous improvement?

S3.7. Under what circumstances is the total inspection of final products necessary?

Problems

WileyPLUS

S3.1. The Great Lakes Company, a grocery store chain, purchases apples from a produce distributor in Virginia. The grocery company has an agreement with the distributor that it desires shipments of 10,000 apples with no more than 2% defectives (i.e., severely blemished apples), although it will accept shipments with up to a maximum of 8% defective. The probability of rejecting a good lot is set at .05, whereas the probability of accepting a bad-quality lot is .10. Determine a sampling plan that will approximately achieve these quality performance criteria and the operating characteristic curve.

S3.2. The Academic House Publishing Company sends out the textbooks it publishes to an independent book binder. When the bound books come back, they are inspected for defective bindings (e.g., warped boards, ripples, cuts, poor adhesion). The publishing company has an acceptable quality level of 4% defectives but will tolerate lots of up to 10% defective. What (approximate) sample size and acceptance level would result in a probability of .05 that a good lot will be rejected and a probability of .10 that a bad lot will be accepted?

S3.3. The Metro Packaging Company in Richmond produces clear plastic bottles for the Kooler Cola Company, a soft-drink manufacturer. Metro inspects each lot of 5000 bottles before they are shipped to the Kooler Company. The soft-drink company has specified an acceptable quality level of .06 and a lot tolerance percent defective of .12. Metro currently has a sampling plan with $n = 150$ and $c \leq 4$. The two companies have recently agreed that the sampling plan should have a producer's risk of .05 and a consumer's risk of .10. Will the current sampling plan used by Metro achieve these levels of α and β?

S3.4. The Fast Break Computer Company assembles personal computers and sells them to retail outlets. It purchases keyboards for its PCs from a manufacturer in the Orient. The keyboards are shipped in lots of 1000 units, and when they arrive at the Fast Break Company samples are inspected. Fast Break's contract with the overseas manufacturer specifies that the quality level that they will accept is 4% defective. The personal computer company wants to avoid sending a shipment back because the distance involved would delay and disrupt the assembly process; thus, it wants only a 1% probability of sending a good lot back. The worst level of quality the Fast Break Company will accept is 10% defective items. Using OM Tools, develop a sampling plan that will achieve these quality-performance criteria.

S3.5. A department store in Sochi, Russia, has arranged to purchase specially designed sweatshirts with the Olympic logo from a clothing manufacturer in Hong Kong. When the sweatshirts arrive in Sochi in lots of 2000 units, they are inspected. The store's management and manufacturer have agreed on quality criteria of AQL = 2% defective and LTPD = 8% defective. Because sending poor-quality shipments back to Hong Kong would disrupt sales at the stores, management has specified a low producer's risk of .01 and will accept a relatively high consumer's risk of .10. Using OM Tools, develop a sampling plan that will achieve these quality-performance criteria.

CHAPTER 4

Product Design

VCG/Getty Images, Inc.

LEARNING OBJECTIVES

After reading this chapter, you will be able to:

- Explain the importance of the product design process and provide an overview of each step of the process.
- Calculate the reliability and availability of a product or service.
- Understand the technologies involved in designing new products and their related production processes.
- Utilize techniques for analyzing design failures and eliminating unnecessary design features.
- Explain why and how each step of the product lifecycle can be changed for improved environmental stewardship, and provide examples of programs that support green efforts.
- Use quality function deployment as a design tool.

Apple's Fastidious Design Process

It would be difficult to write a chapter on product design and not include Apple and its iPhone. At Apple, design is part of every conversation from the big picture to infinitesimal details. We hear accolades for Apple designs (and design process), such as "emotionally warm modernism," "effortless elegance," "technological advancements made approachable," "huge degree of care," and "fastidious attention to detail." Chief Design Officer (CDO) Jony Ives has put together a small, eclectic team of 20 designers from around the world who regularly work 12-hour days until a design is "inevitable" and customers wonder how it could be any other way.

Speed of design is not a particular virtue at Apple, which spent more than five years developing the 3D touch feature for the iPhone 6s. Hardware and software design worked together with the hardware "measuring force" and the software "measuring intent." The touch feature involves 96 sensors and a special pliable glass cover that requires precise manufacturing skills, which Apple makes sure its suppliers acquire.

In most companies, designers decide what they want, then pass it along to engineers who build what they think the designers want, and the back and forth commences. At Apple, the designers work directly with the machines that will fabricate the product to test its producibility during the important early phases of design. And when the design has reached its "inevitable" stage, the designers work with manufacturing on site and at their supply sites to supervise initial production runs and issue precise manufacturing instructions (down to the type and make of CNC milling machine and cutting tools to be used, and the tool's exact cutting path, its speed and how much lubricant to apply). From innovative ideas to "real-world, fail-safe, supply-chainable products," Apple knows design. Now, how about that Apple car?

In this chapter we talk about the product design process and the importance of building and testing product prototypes, not just with the customer but, like Apple, with those who will be manufacturing the product as well.

Sources: Josh Tyrangiel, "How Apple Built the 3d touch iPhone," *Bloomberg Businessweek*, (September 9, 2015); Ian Parker, "The Shape of Things to Come," *The New Yorker*, (February 23, 2015); Leaner Kahney, "How Apple's Super-Secret Industrial Design Team Really Works," *The Cult of Mac*, (December 19, 2015).

New products and services are the lifeblood of an organization. Designs can provide a competitive edge by bringing new ideas to the market quickly, doing a better job of satisfying customer needs, or being easier to manufacture, use, and repair.

Design is a critical process for a firm. Strategically, it defines a firm's customers, as well as its competitors. It capitalizes on a firm's core competencies and determines what new competencies need to be developed. It is also the most obvious driver of change—new products and services can rejuvenate an organization, define new markets, and inspire new technologies.

The design process itself is beneficial because it encourages companies to look outside their boundaries, bring in new ideas, challenge conventional thinking, and experiment. Product and service design provide a natural venue for learning, breaking down barriers, working in teams, and integrating across functions.

The Design Process

Design has a tremendous impact on the quality of a product or service. Poor designs may not meet customer needs or may be so difficult to make that quality suffers. Costly designs can result in overpriced products that lose market share. If the design process is too lengthy, a competitor may capture the market by being the first to introduce new products, services, or features. However, rushing to be first to the market can result in design flaws and poor performance, which totally negate first-mover advantages. Design may be an art, but the design process must be managed effectively.

An effective design process:

- Matches product or service characteristics with customer requirements,
- Ensures that customer requirements are met in the simplest and least costly manner,
- Reduces the time required to design a new product or service, and
- Minimizes the revisions necessary to make a design workable.

Product design defines the appearance of the product, sets standards for performance, specifies which materials are to be used, and determines dimensions and tolerances. Figure 4.1 outlines the design process from idea generation to product launch. Let's examine each step in detail.

Idea Generation

The design process begins with understanding the customer and actively identifying customer needs. Ideas for new products or improvements to existing products can be generated from many sources, including a company's own R&D department, customer complaints or suggestions, marketing research, suppliers, salespersons in the field, factory workers, and new technological developments. Competitors are also a source of ideas for new products or services. Perceptual maps, benchmarking, and reverse engineering can help companies learn from their competitors.

Perceptual map Visual method of comparing customer perceptions of different products or services.

Perceptual maps compare customer perceptions of a company's products with competitors' products. Consider the perceptual map of breakfast cereals in terms of taste and nutrition shown in Figure 4.2. The lack of an entry in the good-taste, high-nutrition category suggests there are opportunities for this kind of cereal in the market. This is why Cheerios introduced honey-nut and apple-cinnamon versions while promoting its "oat" base. Fruit bits and nuts were added to wheat flakes to make them more tasty and nutritious. Shredded Wheat opted

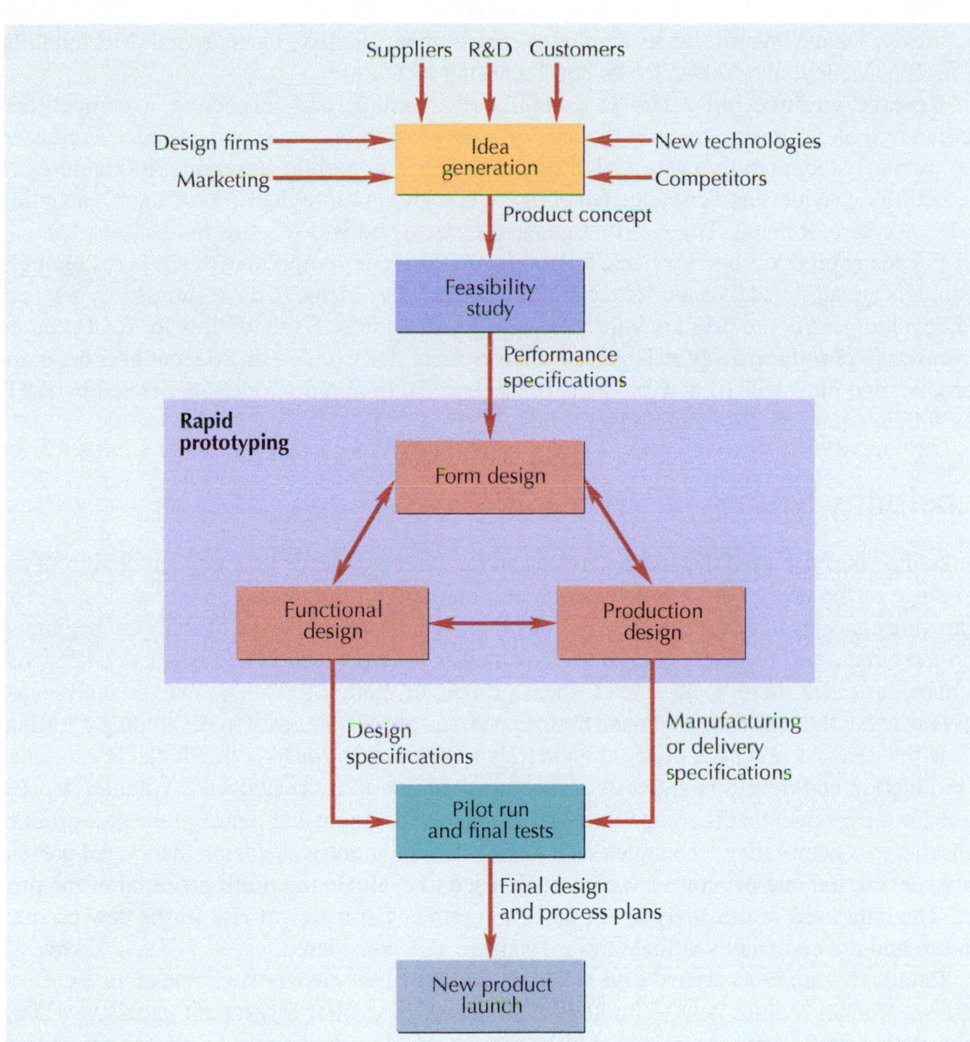

FIGURE 4.1 **The Design Process**

for more taste by reducing its size and adding a sugar frosting or berry filling. Rice Krispies, on the other hand, sought to challenge Cocoa Puffs in the "more tasty" market quadrant with marshmallow and fruit-flavored versions.

Benchmarking refers to finding the best-in-class product or process, measuring the performance of your product or process against it, and making recommendations for improvement based on the results. The benchmarked company may be in an entirely different line of business. For example, American Express is well known for its ability to get customers to pay

Benchmarking Comparing a product or process against the best-in-class product.

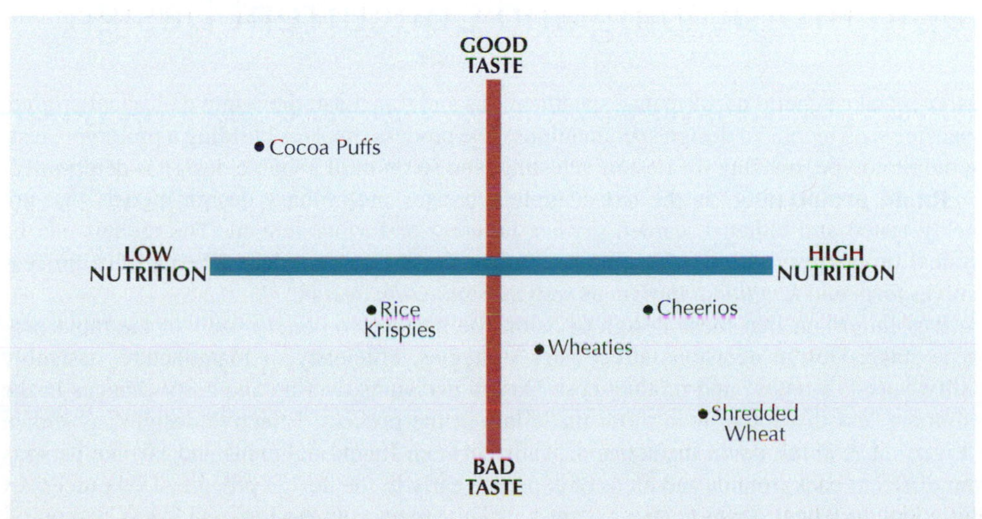

FIGURE 4.2 **A Perceptual Map of Breakfast Cereals**

up quickly; Disney World, for its employee commitment; FedEx, for its speed; McDonald's, for its consistency; and Xerox, for its benchmarking techniques.

Reverse engineering Carefully dismantling a competitor's product to improve your own product.

Reverse engineering refers to carefully dismantling and inspecting a competitor's product to look for design features that can be incorporated into your own product. Ford used this approach successfully in its design of the Taurus automobile, assessing 400 features of competitors' products and copying, adapting, or enhancing more than 300 of them, including Audi's accelerator pedal, Toyota's fuel-gauge accuracy, and BMW's tire and jack storage.

For many products and services, following consumer or competitors' leads is not enough; customers are attracted by superior technology and creative ideas. In these industries, research and development is the primary source of new product ideas. Expenditures for R&D can be enormous ($27 million a day at Toyota) and investment risky (only 1 in 20 ideas ever becomes a product and only 1 in 10 new products is successful). In addition, ideas generated by R&D may follow a long path to commercialization.

Feasibility Study

Marketing takes the ideas that are generated and the customer needs that are identified from the first stage of the design process and formulates alternative product and service concepts. The promising concepts undergo a feasibility study that includes several types of analyses, beginning with a ***market analysis***. Most companies have staffs of market researchers who can design and evaluate customer surveys, interviews, focus groups, or market tests. The market analysis assesses whether there's enough demand for the proposed product to invest in developing it further.

If the demand potential exists, then there's an ***economic analysis*** that looks at estimates of production and development costs and compares them to estimated sales volume. A price range for the product that is compatible with the market segment and image of the new product is discussed. Quantitative techniques such as cost/benefit analysis, decision theory, net present value, or internal rate of return are commonly used to evaluate the profit potential of the project. The data used in the analysis are far from certain. Estimates of risk in the new product venture and the company's attitude toward risk are also considered.

Finally, there are ***technical* and *strategic analyses*** that answer such questions as: Does the new product require new technology? Is the risk or capital investment excessive? Does the company have sufficient labor and management skills to support the required technology? Is sufficient capacity available for production? Does the new product provide a competitive advantage for the company? Does it draw on corporate strengths? Is it compatible with the core business of the firm?

Performance specifications are written for product concepts that pass the feasibility study and are approved for development. They describe the function of the product—that is, what the product should do to satisfy customer needs.

The next step in the process is rapid prototyping.

Rapid Prototyping and Concurrent Design

Designers take general performance specifications and transform them into a physical product or service with technical design specifications. The process involves building a prototype, testing the prototype, revising the design, retesting, and so on until a viable design is determined.

Rapid prototyping Creating preliminary design models that are quickly tested and refined.

Rapid prototyping, as the name implies, creates preliminary design models that are quickly tested and either discarded (as fast failures) or further refined. The models can be physical or electronic, rough facsimiles or full-scale working models. The iterative process involves *form* and *functional design*, as well as *production design*.

Concurrent design A new approach to design that involves the simultaneous design of products and processes by design teams.

It is important that these design decisions be performed *concurrently* at the rapid prototype stage. Design decisions affect sales strategies, efficiency of manufacture, assembly quality, speed of repair, and product cost. Design decisions overlap and early changes in the design are less disruptive than those made late in the process. Effective designs, as shown in **Figure 4.3**, break down the series of walls between functional areas and involve persons from different backgrounds and areas of expertise early in the design process. This process of jointly and iteratively developing a design is called **concurrent design**.

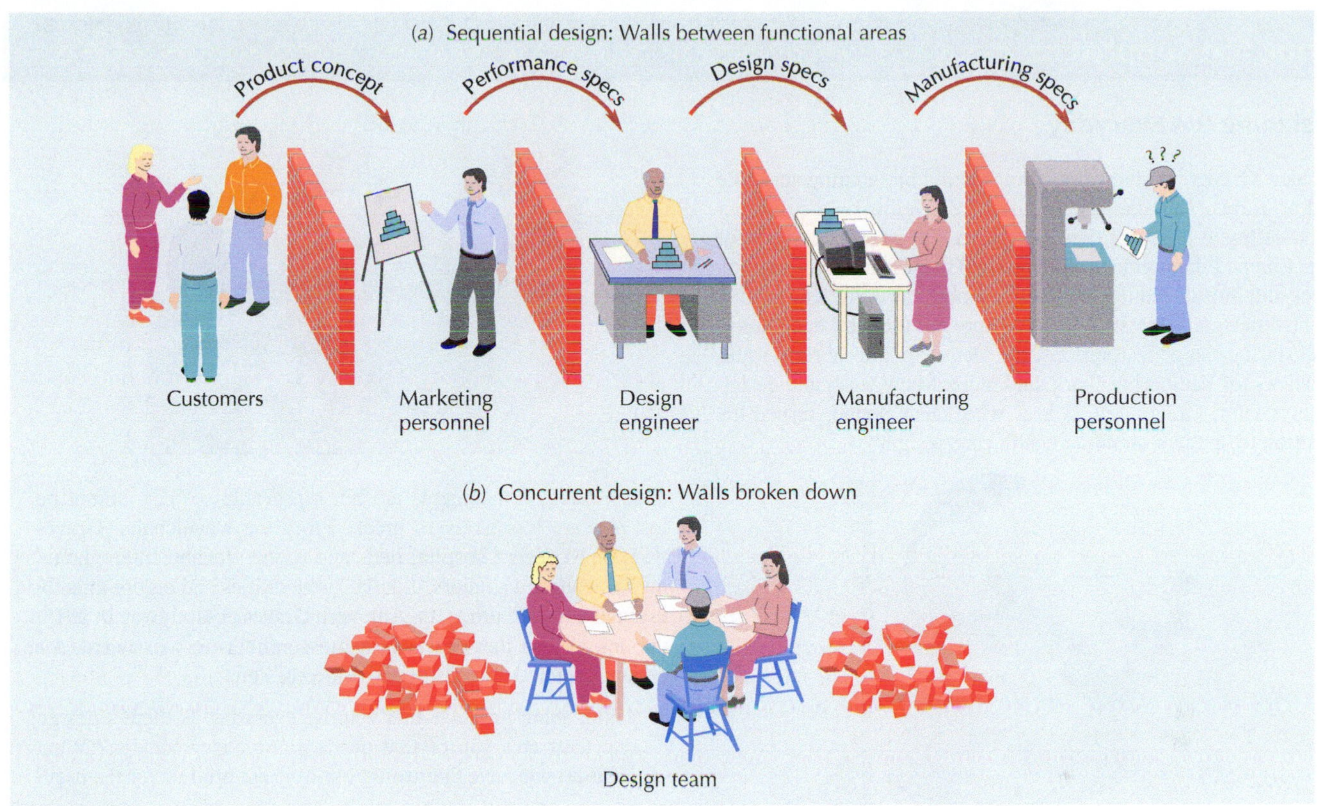

FIGURE 4.3 **Concurrent Design, Breaking Down Barriers**

Concurrent design improves both the quality of the design and the time-to-market. This is especially true with the design of component parts to be completed by a supplier. Rather than designing the parts and giving the design specs to a supplier to complete, concurrent design involves the supplier in the design process. For example, a company may share with a potential supplier the performance specs and ask the supplier to complete the design so that the part performs properly and fits within space, weight, and cost parameters.

In the next sections, we discuss the three types of concurrent designs: form, functional, and production design.

Form Design

Form design refers to the physical appearance of a product—its shape, color, size, and style. Aesthetics such as image, market appeal, and personal identification are also part of form design. In many cases, functional design must be adjusted to make the product look or feel right. For example, the form design of Mazda's Miata sports car went further than looks—the exhaust had to have a certain "sound," the gearshift lever a certain "feel," and the seat and window arrangement the proper dimensions to encourage passengers to ride with their elbows out. Both form and functional design are important to the customer. Read about the re-design of everyday things in the "Along the Supply Chain" box.

Form design How the product will look.

Functional Design

Functional design is concerned with how the product performs. It seeks to meet the performance specifications of fitness for use by the customer. Three performance characteristics considered during this phase of design are *reliability*, *maintainability*, and *usability*.

Functional design How the product will perform.

Reliability

Reliability is the probability that a given part or product will perform its intended function for a specified length of time under normal conditions of use. You may be familiar with reliability information from product warranties. A hair dryer might be guaranteed to function

Reliability The probability that a product will perform its intended function for a specified period of time.

Along the Supply Chain

Designing the Everyday

Michael Graves Architecture and Design

Michael Graves, probably best known for his singing teakettle sold at Target, was the first architect to have his own consumer brand of home products. His more than 800 product designs for Target helped the company differentiate itself from other big box stores and introduced the value of design to the American public. He also designed the scaffolding to protect the National Monument during major restorations, the Denver public library, walking sticks for Kimberley Clark, and more. Many years and design projects later, Graves fell ill and, wheelchair bound, turned his attention to "patient-centered health care design."

Michael Graves Architecture and Design

When you think about it, the traditional wheelchair has a horrendous design. It is uncomfortable, difficult to get in and out of, hard to push and maneuver, and most egregiously, patients actually put their hands on the wheels that have been picking up debris and germs from the hospital floors to self-propel themselves. As seen in the photo, Graves' design, produced by Stryker, has a more comfortable and cleanable molded seat with multi-formed armrests to aid entering and exiting the chair, smaller solid wheels located in the back out of reach of the patient, elevated handles and foot-operated brakes to alleviate back strain for the care provider, and a smaller footprint so multiple chairs can be stacked until needed. Attachments are not removable so they cannot be lost and are less likely to break. From the wheelchairs, Graves went on to design hospital beds and rooms, rehab centers, housing for wounded soldiers, elderly care facilities and ergonomically useful healthcare products. Although Graves passed away in 2015, the design firm that bears his name continues to win awards for patient-centered and customer-centric design.

1. Think about products that you use everyday. Is there a design that frustrates you or that needs a complete redesign? What ideas do you have that would improve the product for the user?
2. Identify the different "customers" the new wheelchair design considered. How did Graves incorporate the process of using a wheelchair in his design?
3. Ever wonder how some designs came to be? Read a selection from the *Design of Everyday Things* by Don Norman and share with the class.

Source: Kristin Hohenadel, "From Teakettles to Libraries, the Wide-Ranging Career of Architect Michael Graves," *Slate*, (March 13, 2015); Barbara Sadick, "Famed architect Michael Graves, in a wheelchair, widens his design focus," *The Washington Post*, (July 14, 2014); Company website, http://michaelgraves.com (accessed January 25, 2016).

(i.e., blow air with a certain force at a certain temperature) for one year under normal conditions of use (defined to be 300 hours of operation). A car warranty might extend for three years or 50,000 miles. Normal conditions of use would include regularly scheduled oil changes and other minor maintenance activities. A missed oil change or mileage in excess of 50,000 miles in a three-year period would not be considered "normal" and would nullify the warranty.

A product or system's reliability is a function of the reliabilities of its component parts and how the parts are arranged. If all parts must function for the product or system to operate, then the system reliability is the *product* of the component part reliabilities.

$$R_s = (R_1)(R_2) \ldots (R_n), \text{ where } R_n \text{ is the reliability of the } n\text{th component.}$$

For example, if two component parts are required and each has a reliability of 0.90, the reliability of the system is 0.90 × 0.90 = 0.81, or 81%. The system can be visualized as a *series* of components as follows:

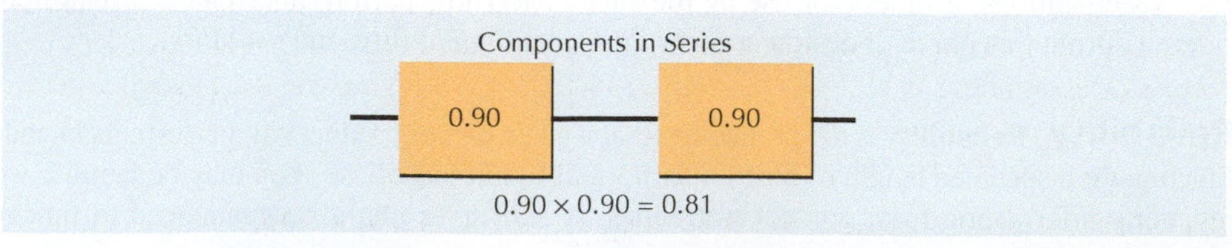

Note that the system reliability of 0.81 is considerably less than the component reliabilities of 0.90. As the number of serial components increases, system reliability will continue to deteriorate. This makes a good argument for simple designs with fewer components!

Failure of some components in a system is more critical than others—the brakes on a car, for instance. To increase the reliability of individual parts (and thus the system as a whole), *redundant* parts can be built in to back up a failure. Providing emergency brakes for a car is an example. Consider the following redundant design with R_1 representing the reliability of the original component and R_2 the reliability of the backup component.

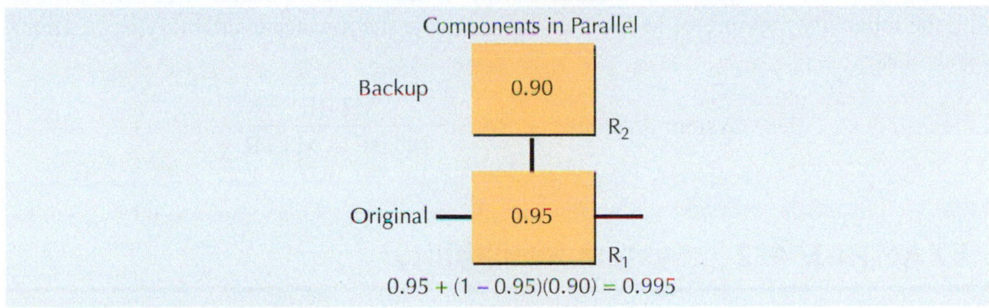

These components are said to operate in *parallel*. If the original component fails (a 5% chance), the backup component will automatically kick in to take its place—but only 90% of the time. Thus, the reliability of the system is[1]

$$\begin{aligned} R_s &= R_1 + (1 - R_1)(R_2) \\ &= 0.95 + (1 - 0.95)(0.90) = 0.995 \end{aligned}$$

EXAMPLE 4.1 | Reliability

Determine the reliability of the system of components shown below.

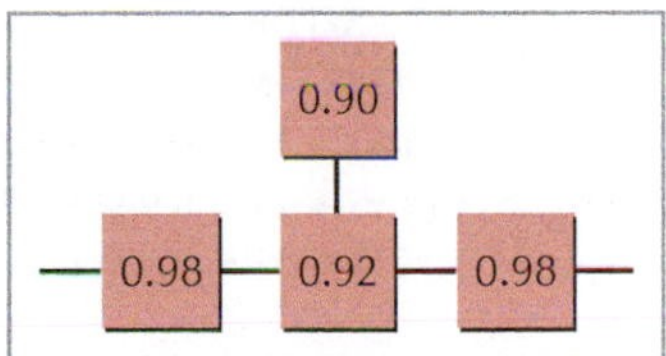

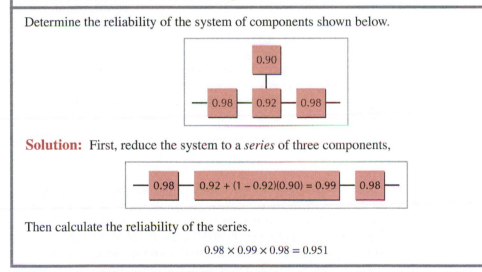

Solution: First, reduce the system to a *series* of three components,

0.98 — 0.92 + (1 − 0.92)(0.90) = 0.99 — 0.98

Then calculate the reliability of the series.

$$0.98 \times 0.99 \times 0.98 = 0.951$$

Reliability can also be expressed as the length of time a product or service is in operation before it fails, called the *mean time between failures* (MTBF). In this case, we are concerned with the distribution of failures over time, or the *failure rate*. The MTBF is the reciprocal of the failure rate (MTBF = 1/failure rate). For example, if your laptop battery fails four times in 20 hours of operation, its failure rate would be 4/20 = 0.20, and its MTBF = 1/0.20 = 5 hours.

Reliability can be improved by simplifying product design, improving the reliability of individual components, or adding redundant components. Products that are easier to manufacture or assemble, are well maintained, and have users who are trained in proper use have higher reliability.

[1]The reliability of parallel components can also be calculated as $R_s = 1 - [(1 - R_1)(1 - R_2)\ldots]$.

Maintainability The ease with which a product is maintained or repaired.

Maintainability **Maintainability** (also called *serviceability*) refers to the ease and/or cost with which a product or service is maintained or repaired. Products can be made easier to maintain by assembling them in modules, like computers, so that entire control panels, cards, or disk drives can be replaced when they malfunction. The location of critical parts or parts subject to failure affects the ease of disassembly and, thus, repair. Instructions that teach consumers how to anticipate malfunctions and correct them themselves can be included with the product. Specifying regular maintenance schedules is part of maintainability, as is proper planning for the availability of critical replacement parts.

One quantitative measure of maintainability is mean time to repair (MTTR). Combined with the reliability measure of MTBF, we can calculate the average availability or "uptime" of a system as

$$\text{System Availability, SA} = \frac{\text{MTBF}}{\text{MTBF} + \text{MTTR}}$$

EXAMPLE 4.2 | System Availability

Amy Russell must choose a service provider for her company's e-commerce site. Other factors being equal, she will base her decision on server availability. Given the following server performance data, which provider should she choose?

PROVIDER	MTBF (hr)	MTTR (hr)
A	60	4.0
B	36	2.0
C	24	1.0

Solution:

$$\text{SA} = \frac{\text{MTBF}}{\text{MTBF} + \text{MTTR}}$$

$$\text{SA}_A = 60/(60+4) = 0.9375 \text{ or } 94\%$$

$$\text{SA}_B = 36/(36+2) = 0.9473 \text{ or } 95\%$$

$$\text{SA}_C = 24/(24+1) = 0.96 \text{ or } 96\%$$

Amy should choose Provider C.

Usability All of us have encountered products or services that are difficult or cumbersome to use. Consider:

- Cup holders in cars that, when in use, hide the radio buttons or interfere with the stick shift.
- Salt shakers that must be turned upside down to fill (thereby losing their contents).
- Speakers in laptop computers that are covered by your wrists as you type.
- Doors that you can't tell whether to pull or push.
- Remote controls with more and more buttons of smaller and smaller size for multiple products.
- Levers for popping the trunk of a car and unlocking the gas cap located too close together.

Usability Ease of use of a product or service.

These are usability issues in design. **Usability** is what makes a product or service easy to use and a good fit for its targeted customer. It is a combination of factors that affect the user's experience with a product, including: ease of learning, ease of use and ease of remembering how to use, frequency and severity of errors, and user satisfaction with the experience.

Although usability engineers have long been a part of the design process, their use has skyrocketed with electronics, computer software, and website design. Forrester Research estimates that 50% of potential sales from websites are lost from customers who cannot locate what they need. Researchers have found that Internet users have a particularly low tolerance for poorly designed sites and cumbersome navigation.

Apple revolutionized the computer industry with its intuitive, easy-to-use designs and continues to do so with its sleek and functional iPods, iPads, and iPhones. Microsoft employs over 140 usability engineers. Before a design is deemed functional, it must go through usability testing. Simpler, more standardized designs are usually easier to use. They are also easier to produce, as we'll see in the next section.

Production Design

Production design How the product will be made.

Production design is concerned with how the product will be made. Designs that are difficult to make often result in poor-quality products. Engineers tend to overdesign products, with too many features, options, and parts. Lack of knowledge of manufacturing capabilities can result in designs that are impossible to make or require skills and resources not currently available. Many times, production personnel find themselves redesigning products on the factory floor. Late changes in design are both costly and disruptive. An adjustment in one part may necessitate an adjustment in other parts, "unraveling" the entire product design. That's why production design is considered in the preliminary design phase. Recommended approaches to production design include *simplification*, *standardization*, *modularity*, *design for manufacture*, and *design for supply chain*.

Simplification Reduces the number of parts, assemblies, or options in a product.

Design **simplification** attempts to reduce the number of parts, subassemblies, and options in a product. It also means avoiding tools, separate fasteners, and adjustments. We'll illustrate simplification with an example. Consider the case of the toolbox shown in Figure 4.4. The company wants to increase productivity by using automated assembly. The initial design in Figure 4.4*a* contains 24 common parts (mostly nuts and bolts fasteners) and requires 84 seconds to assemble. The design does not appear to be complex for manual assembly but can be quite complicated for a robot to assemble.

As shown in Figure 4.4*b*, the team assigned to revise the design simplified the toolbox by molding the base as one piece and eliminating the fasteners. Plastic inserts snap over the spindle to hold it in place. The number of parts was reduced to four, and the assembly time cut to 12 seconds. This represents a significant gain in productivity, from 43 assemblies per hour to 300 assemblies per hour.

Figure 4.4*c* shows an even simpler design, consisting of only two parts, a base and spindle. The spindle is made of flexible material, allowing it to be snapped downward into place in a quick, one-motion assembly. Assembly time is reduced to four seconds, increasing production

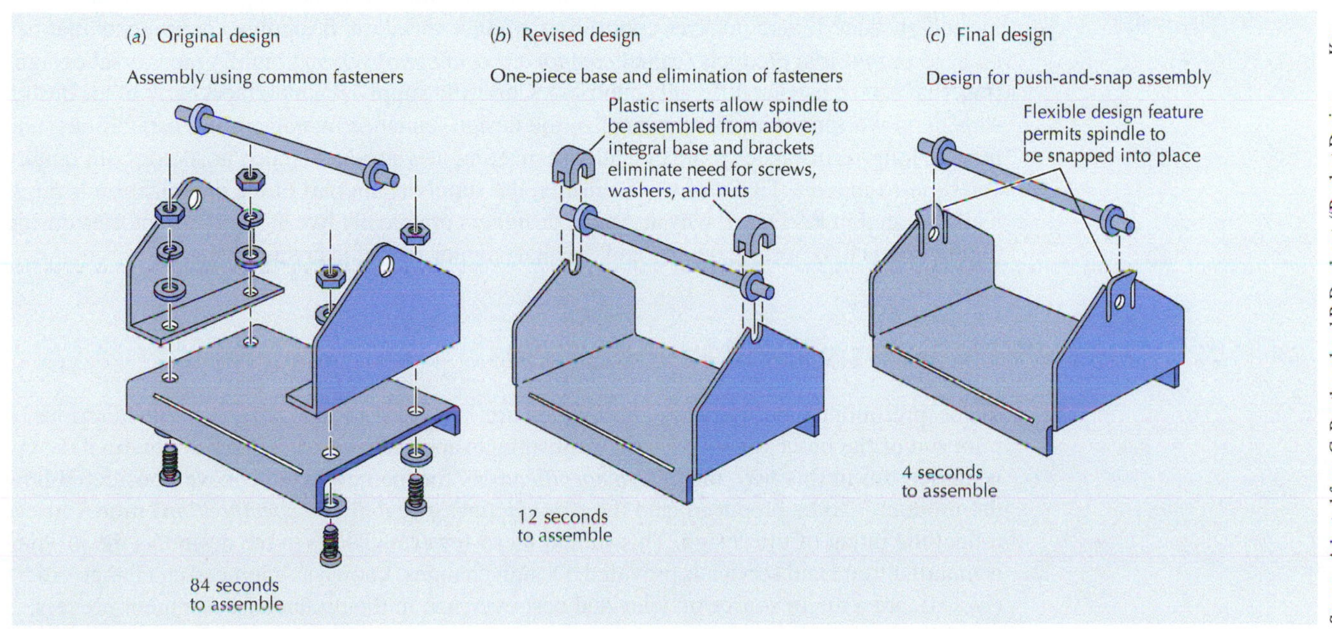

Source: Adapted from G. Boothroyd and P. Dewhurst, "Product Design. . . . Key to Successful Robotic Assembly," *Assembly Engineering* (September 1986), pp. 90–93.

FIGURE 4.4 Design Simplification

to 900 assemblies an hour. With this final design, the team agreed that the assembly task was too simple for a robot. Indeed, many manufacturers have followed this process in rediscovering the virtues of simplification—in redesigning a product for automation, they find that automation isn't necessary!

Standardization When commonly available and interchangeable parts are used.

Using standard parts in a product or throughout many products saves design time, tooling costs, and production worries. **Standardization** makes possible the interchangeability of parts among products, resulting in higher-volume production and purchasing, lower investment in inventory, easier purchasing and material handling, fewer quality inspections, and fewer difficulties in production. Some products, such as light bulbs, batteries, and DVDs, benefit from being totally standardized. For others, being different is a competitive advantage. The question becomes how to gain the cost benefits of standardization without losing the market advantage of variety and uniqueness.

Modular design Combines standardized building blocks, or modules, to create unique finished products.

One solution is **modular design**. Modular design consists of combining standardized building blocks, or *modules*, in a variety of ways to create unique finished products. Modular design is common in the electronics industry and the automobile industry. Toyota's Camry, Corolla, and Lexus share the same body chassis. Even Campbell's Soup Company practices modular design by producing large volumes of four basic broths (beef, chicken, tomato, and seafood bisque) and then adding special ingredients to produce 125 varieties of final soup products.

Design for manufacture (DFM) Designing a product so that it can be produced easily and economically.

Design for manufacture (DFM) is the process of designing a product so that it can be produced easily and economically. The term was coined in an effort to emphasize the importance of incorporating production design early in the design process. When successful, DFM not only improves the quality of product design but also reduces both the time and cost of product design and manufacture.

Specific DFM software can recommend materials and processes appropriate for a design and provide manufacturing cost estimates throughout the design process. More generally, DFM guidelines promote good design practice, such as:

1. Minimize the number of parts and subassemblies.
2. Avoid tools, separate fasteners, and adjustments.
3. Use standard parts when possible and repeatable, well-understood processes.
4. Design parts for many uses, and modules that can be combined in different ways.
5. Design for ease of assembly, minimal handling, and proper presentation.
6. Allow for efficient and adequate testing and replacement of parts.

Design for supply chain (DFSC) Considering supply chain capabilities in product design.

With much of today's manufacturing outsourced to suppliers, one of the key aspects of production design is designing for the supply chain. **Design for the supply chain (DFSC)** means considering the capabilities of suppliers at each level of the supply chain when designing the product. It also involves controlling product variation, designing components that can be used in multiple products (called *component commonality*), and building universal designs (i.e., that can be used in different countries). Choosing supply chain partners early in the design stage, and working with them to finalize the design, enhance manufacturing capabilities, and reserve long-term capacity, are essential to meeting new product launch goals for both quality and time-to-market. That's why at Samsung, the supply chain part of the organization is physically located in R&D, and why at Apple, designers practically live at supplier factories during product launch to oversee quality and tweak design or manufacture as needed.

Final Design and Process Plans

In the preliminary design stage, prototypes are built and tested. After several iterations, a pilot run of the process is conducted. Adjustments are made as needed before the final design is agreed on. In this way, the *design specifications* for the new product have considered how the product is to be produced, and the *manufacturing* or *delivery specifications* more closely reflect the intent of the design. This should mean fewer revisions in the design as the product is manufactured and service is provided. Design changes, known as engineering change orders (ECOs), are a major source of delay and cost overruns in the product development process.

The *final design* consists of detailed drawings and specifications for the new product or service. The accompanying *process plans* are workable instructions for manufacture, including necessary equipment and tooling, component sourcing recommendations, job descriptions and procedures for workers, and computer programs for automated machines. We discuss process planning in more detail in Chapter 6.

Good design is aided by the use of technology. The next section describes technology in design.

Technology in Design

New products for more segmented markets have proliferated over the past decade. Changes in product design are more frequent, and product lifecycles are shorter. IBM estimates the average life of its new product offerings is about six months. The ability to get new products to the market quickly has revolutionized the competitive environment and changed the nature of manufacturing.

Courtesy of Titleist and FootJoy Worldwide

Computer-aided design (CAD) is used to design everything from pencils to submarines. Some of our everyday products are more difficult to design than you may think. Potato chips with ridges, the top of a soda can, a two-liter bottle of soft drink, a car door, and golf balls are examples of simple products that require the sophistication of CAD for effective design and testing. Shown here are two examples of dimple design on Titleist golf balls. The number, size, and patterns of dimples on a golf ball can affect the distance, trajectory, and accuracy of play. The advent of CAD has allowed many more designs to be tested. Today, more than 200 different dimple patterns are used by golf-ball manufacturers. Golf clubs and golf courses are also designed using CAD.

Part of the impetus for the deluge of new products is the advancement of technology available for designing products. It begins with computer-aided design (CAD) and includes related technologies such as computer-aided engineering (CAE), computer-aided manufacturing (CAM), and collaborative product design (CPD).

Computer-aided design (CAD) is a software system that uses computer graphics to assist in the creation, modification, and analysis of a design. A geometric design is generated that includes not only the dimensions of the product but also tolerance information and material specifications. The ability to sort, classify, and retrieve similar designs from a CAD database facilitates standardization of parts, prompts ideas, and eliminates building a design from scratch.

Computer-aided design (CAD) Assists in the creation, modification, and analysis of a design.

CAD-generated products can also be tested more quickly. Engineering analysis, performed with a CAD system, is called **computer-aided engineering (CAE)**. CAE retrieves the description and geometry of a part from a CAD database and subjects it to testing and analysis on the computer screen without physically building a prototype. CAE can maximize the storage space in a car trunk, detect whether plastic parts are cooling evenly, and determine how much stress will cause a bridge to crack. With CAE, design teams can watch a car bump along a rough road, the pistons of an engine move up and down, a golf ball soar through the air (see photos), or the effect of new drugs on virtual DNA molecules. Advances in virtual reality and motion capturing technology allow designers and users to experience the design without building a physical prototype.

Computer-aided engineering (CAE) A software system that tests and analyzes designs on the computer screen.

Computer-aided design/computer-aided manufacturing (CAD/CAM) The ultimate design-to-manufacture connection.

The ultimate design-to-manufacture connection is a **computer-aided design/computer-aided manufacturing (CAD/CAM)** system. CAM is the acronym for *computer-aided manufacturing*. CAD/CAM involves the automatic conversion of CAD design data into processing instructions for computer-controlled equipment and the subsequent manufacture of the part as it was designed. This integration of design and manufacture can save enormous amounts of time, ensure that parts and products are produced *precisely* as intended, and facilitate revisions in design or customized production.

Besides the time savings, CAD and its related technologies have also improved the *quality* of designs and the products manufactured from them. The communications capabilities of CAD may be more important than its processing capabilities in terms of design quality. CAD systems enhance communication and promote innovation in multifunctional design teams by providing a visual, interactive focus for discussion. Watching a vehicle strain its wheels over mud and ice prompts ideas on product design and customer use better than stacks of consumer surveys or engineering reports. New ideas can be suggested and tested immediately, allowing more alternatives to be evaluated. To facilitate discussion or clarify a design, CAD data can be sent electronically between designer and supplier or viewed simultaneously on computer screens by different designers in physically separate locations. Rapid prototypes can be tested more thoroughly with CAD/CAE. More prototypes can be tested as well. CAD improves every stage of product design and is especially useful as a means of integrating design and manufacture.

Product lifecycle management (PLM) Managing the entire lifecycle of a product.

With so many new designs and changes in existing designs, a system is needed to keep track of design revisions. Such a system is called **product lifecycle management (PLM)**. PLM stores, retrieves, and updates design data from the product concept, through manufacturing, revision, service, and retirement of the product.

Collaborative Product Design Systems

The benefits of CAD-designed products are magnified when combined with the ability to share product-design files and work on them in real time from physically separate locations. Collaborative design can take place between designers in the same company, between manufacturers and suppliers, or between manufacturers and customers. Manufacturers can send out product designs electronically with request for quotes (RFQ) from potential component suppliers. Or performance specs can be posted to a website from which suppliers can create and transmit their own designs. Designs can receive final approval from customers before expensive processing takes place. A complex design can involve hundreds of suppliers. The Web allows them to work together throughout the design and manufacturing processes, not just at the beginning and the end.

Collaborative product design (CPD) A software system for collaborative design and development among trading partners.

Software systems for collaborative design are loosely referred to as **collaborative product design (CPD)**. These systems provide the interconnectivity and translation capabilities necessary for collaborative work across platforms, departments, and companies. In conjunction with PLM systems, they also manage product data, set up project workspaces, and follow product development through the entire product lifecycle.

Collaborative design accelerates product development, helps to resolve product launch issues, and improves the quality of the design. Designers can conduct virtual review sessions, test "what if" scenarios, assign and track design issues, communicate with multiple tiers of suppliers, and create, store, and manage project documents.

These virtual review sessions often include the design review tools presented in the next section.

Design Quality Reviews

Before finalizing a design, formal procedures for analyzing possible failures and rigorously assessing the value of every part and component should be followed. Three such techniques are failure mode and effects analysis, fault tree analysis, and value analysis.

Failure mode and effects analysis (FMEA) A systematic method of analyzing product failures.

Failure mode and effects analysis (FMEA) is a systematic approach to analyzing the causes and effects of product failures. It begins with listing the functions of the product and each of its parts. Failure modes are then defined and ranked in order of their seriousness and likelihood of failure. Failures are addressed one by one (beginning with the most catastrophic),

TABLE 4.1 Failure Mode and Effects Analysis for Potato Chips

FAILURE MODE	CAUSE OF FAILURE	EFFECT OF FAILURE	CORRECTIVE ACTION
Stale	Low moisture content, expired shelf life, poor packaging	Tastes bad, won't crunch, thrown out, lost sales	Add moisture, cure longer, better package seal, shorter shelf life
Broken	Too thin, too brittle, rough handling, rough use, poor packaging	Can't dip, poor display, injures mouth, choking, perceived as old, lost sales	Change recipe, change process, change packaging
Too Salty	Outdated recipe, process not in control, uneven distribution of salt	Eat less, drink more, health hazard, lost sales	Experiment with recipe, experiment with process, introduce low-salt version

causes are hypothesized, and design changes are made to reduce the chance of failure. The objective of FMEA is to anticipate failures and prevent them from occurring. Table 4.1 shows a partial FMEA for potato chips.

Fault tree analysis (FTA) A visual method for analyzing the interrelationships among failures.

Fault tree analysis (FTA) is a visual method of analyzing the *interrelationship* among failures. FTA lists failures and their causes in a tree format using two hatlike symbols, one with a straight line on the bottom representing *and*, and one with a curved line on the bottom for *or*. Figure 4.5 shows a partial FTA for a food manufacturer who has a problem with potato chip breakage. In this analysis, potato chips break because they are too thin *or* because they are too brittle. The options for fixing the problem of too-thin chips—increasing thickness or reducing size—are undesirable, as indicated by the Xs. The problem of too-brittle chips can be alleviated by adding more moisture *or* having fewer ridges *or* adjusting the frying procedure. We choose to adjust the frying procedure, which leads to the question of how hot the oil should be *and* how long to fry the chips. Once these values are determined, the issue of too-brittle chips (and thus chip breakage) is solved, as indicated.

Value analysis (VA) A procedure for eliminating unnecessary features and functions.

Value analysis (VA) (also known as value engineering) was developed by General Electric in 1947 to eliminate unnecessary features and functions in product designs. It has reemerged as a technique for use by multifunctional design teams. The design team defines the essential functions of a component, assembly, or product using a verb and a noun. For example, the function of a container might be described as *holds fluid*. Then the team assigns a value to each function and determines the cost of providing the function. With that information, a ratio of value to cost can be calculated for each item. The team attempts to improve the ratio by either reducing the cost of the item or increasing its worth. Updated versions of value analysis also assess the environmental impact of materials, parts, and operations. This leads us to the next section on design for environment.

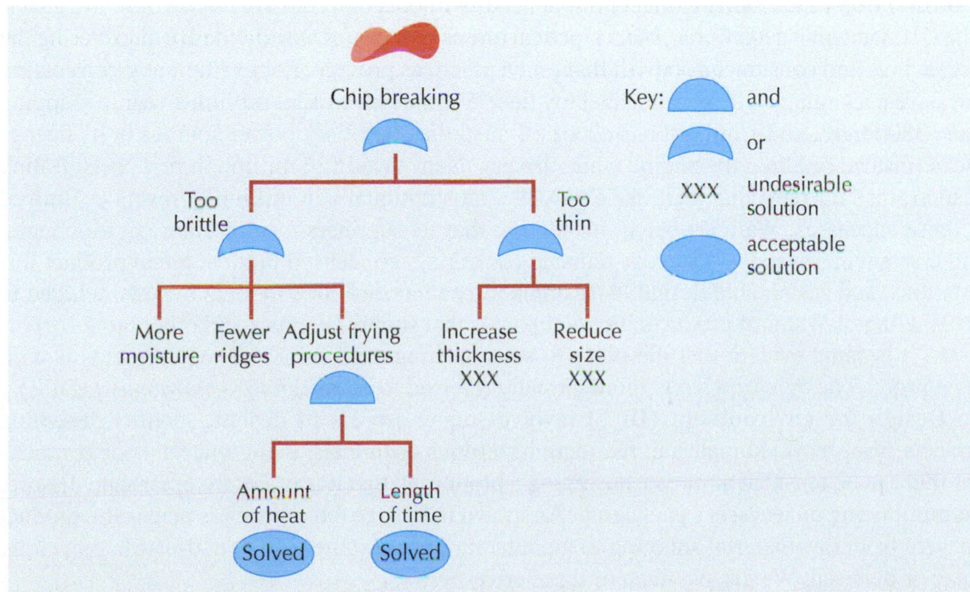

FIGURE 4.5 Fault Tree Analysis for Potato Chips

Along the Supply Chain

Jugaad, Design for the Times

India has a Hindi slang word that describes their mode of innovation, *jugaad* (pronounced "joo-gaardh"). Roughly translated, it means "invention on the fly," an improvisational style of innovation based on the immediate and affordable needs of customers. It works well in environments of scarce resources where workable options that are inexpensive and quick to implement are valued. Tata, Infosys, and other Indian corporations have used jugaad for years. Now Best Buy, Cisco Systems, and Oracle, among others, are following suit.

One example of jugaad, which is shown in the photo, is Tata Motor's Nano mini-car, a bare-bones product that sells for $2800 to consumers who had heretofore been priced out of the automobile market. Best Buy holds jugaad workshops to generate new product ideas that can be added easily and inexpensively to existing stores (e.g., home healthcare equipment). Cisco likes the Indian approach of affordability and scale. Repurposing existing ideas and technologies in simple ways helps to reduce R&D spending and adds to high-margin products.

This is similar to the micro-financing success in third-world countries, where small loans applied to basic needs can make a big difference. In fact, there is a reversal in the trend in design from multinationals who would typically "trickle down" ideas and products from affluent Western nations, to "trickling up" ideas and solutions from third-world countries. GE, Procter & Gamble, Nokia, and others are watching how Asian and African consumers handle medical equipment, foods, and cell phones. Designing for these markets gives insight for home markets that respond favorably to reduced size, cost, and complexity, and increased sharing and connectivity.

For example, in healthcare, GE offers a portable baby warmer that uses hot water and costs 99% less than traditional infant incubators. Johnson & Johnson sponsors a Text4baby messaging

JTB/UIG via Getty Images

service for new mothers where they can get advice on caring for their babies. Philips offers hospital beds with fewer adjustment options, which are actually easier to use, at half the price.

Frugal innovation and low-priced no-frills products are right for the times, and they are changing the very process of design.

1. What products do you own that perform their function simply and inexpensively? What products or services would you like to see redesigned by a jugaad process?
2. Are there any products or services that you prefer to be designed more carefully and more futuristically and thus would not be good candidates for jugaad?
3. Get in the jugaad mindset by visiting *http://www.frugalsolutions.org/* and discussing the best ideas.

Sources: Reena Jana "India's Next Export—Innovation," *BusinessWeek* (December 2, 2009); Reena Jana, "Innovation Trickles Down," *BusinessWeek* (March 11, 2009); Navi Radjou, Jaideep Prabhu and Simone Ahuja, "Finding the Jugaad for U.S. Health Care," *CNN Global* (November 9, 2012); http://globalpublicsquare.blogs.cnn.com/2012/11/09/finding-the-jugaad-for-u-s-healthcare/; Philip McClellan, "Is Jugaad Going Global?" *The New York Times* (October 11, 2012); Peter Hesseldahl, "Jugaad Innovation," *Innovation Management* (December 12, 2012).

Design for Environment

Sustainability Meeting present needs without compromising future generations.

Sustainability is the ability to meet present needs without compromising those of future generations. It is not only a lofty goal, but a practical one as companies worldwide are discovering the cost savings and consumer goodwill that green practices provide. For example, by eliminating excessive packaging on its private label toy line, Walmart saved $2.4 million a year in shipping costs, 3800 trees, and 1 million barrels of oil. Installing auxiliary power sources in its fleet of trucks (instead of idling the engine while drivers sleep) saved $26 million in fuel costs. Baling plastic refuse for recycling and resale provided an additional $28 million in revenue. Buoyed by these successes, Walmart began mandating that its suppliers meet certain environmental (and cost-saving) standards such as reduced packaging, condensed liquids, green product formulations, and sustainable design. A sustainability scorecard for suppliers is now included in eco-labeling of Walmart products. For companies that supply Walmart and other large corporations, it became evident that the place to start meeting environmental requirements is with green product design, or what is more globally referred to as *design for environment* (DFE).

Design for environment (DFE) Designing a product from material that can be recycled or easily repaired rather than discarded.

Design for environment (DFE) involves many aspects of design, such as designing products from recycled material, reducing hazardous chemicals, using materials or components that can be recycled after use, designing a product so that it is easier to repair than discard, and minimizing unnecessary packaging. As shown in Figure 4.6, it extends across the product lifecycle from raw material sourcing to manufacture to consumer use to end-of-life recycling, reuse, or disposal. We discuss each of these areas below.

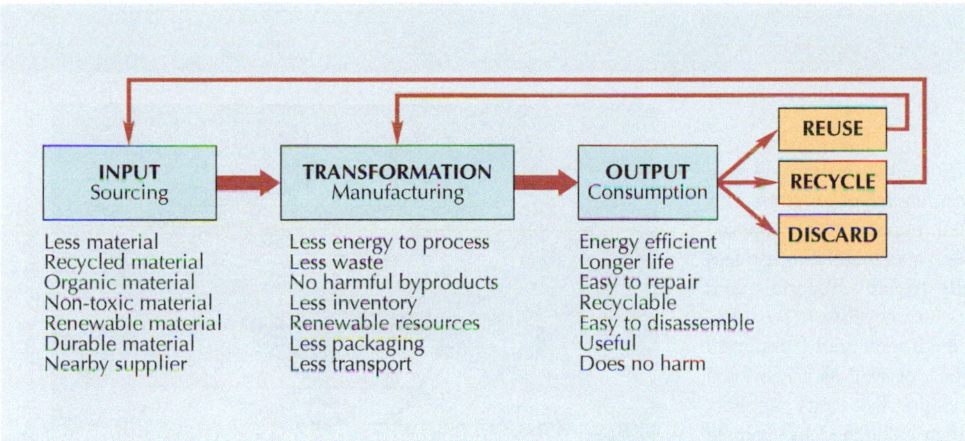

FIGURE 4.6 Design for Environment Lifecycle

Green Sourcing

Design for environment begins with using less material, and, where possible, using recycled material, organic material (e.g., that has not been treated with chemicals), nontoxic material, and conflict-free material. The material should also be renewable, not endangered or scarce, and durable, so that the product will last. Suppliers should be vetted to ensure that their processes are environmentally sound, and should be located nearby so that greenhouse gases are minimized in transportation. Finally, the design should be rationalized so that only the needed features (and thus material) are included, and so that the product is saleable and will not end up, unused, in landfills. Standard procurement practices focus on meeting design specifications, without considering how this occurs. Strictly written requests for quotes or proposals (RFQs or RFPs) make it difficult for potential suppliers to suggest alternate materials, methods, or technologies. In green sourcing, suppliers are encouraged to suggest more environmentally friendly materials, methods, and processes, especially if these also reduce cost. Suppliers and designers may brainstorm to develop new materials or methods. Sustainability becomes part of the strategic sourcing process. Greening the supply chain is discussed more thoroughly in Chapter 10 on Supply Chain Strategy and Design. Nike's CEO Mark Parker calls sustainability our generation's defining issue. Read about Nike's green sourcing and design in the "Along the Supply Chain" box that follows.

Green Manufacture

In the manufacturing process, green design is concerned with the energy needed to produce the product, whether that energy is renewable, how much waste or harmful byproducts are generated from the process, and if that waste can be recycled or byproduct disposed of safely. Production should be carefully planned so that inventory is minimized, and the manufacturing plant should be located in close proximity to customers to minimize transportation and its effect on greenhouse gas emissions. The product should have minimal packaging and the boxes or bins used for transportation should be reusable.

Carbon footprints measure the amount of carbon dioxide (CO_2) and other greenhouse gases that contribute to global warming and climate change. A product's carbon footprint is calculated by estimating the greenhouse gas emissions from the energy used in manufacturing and transporting the product along its supply chain, the energy used in stocking and selling the product, the energy used by the consumer in using the product, and the energy used to recycle and dispose of the product at the end of its useful life. Carbon footprints are part of a more comprehensive lifecycle assessment initiative supported by ISO 14000 environmental standards. ISO 14000 standards provide guidelines and certifications for environmental requirements of doing business in certain countries, and are often used to qualify for foreign aid, business loans, and reduced insurance premiums.

Carbon footprint A measure of greenhouse gases.

A manufacturing plant's carbon footprint can be determined from the processing, waste, and transport that takes place across the products it produces. Recycling, renewable resources, clean energy, efficient operations, and proper waste disposal can help mitigate the environmental impact of manufacturing.

Along the Supply Chain

Consider Nike's Flyknit Design

© Rodrigo Reyes Marin/AFLO/Nippon News/Corbis

Nike has been aggressively pursuing sustainable design and production for more than a decade. Its *Considered Design* ethos asks designers to consider the environmental impact of a proposed product at the early stages of development; specifically, to use less toxins, less waste, more environmentally friendly materials, and more life cycle assessments (which promote recycling). To aid in that pursuit, Nike provides a list of environmentally preferred materials (EPM) and sustainable materials, as well as a restricted substances list (RSL) and restricted packaging list, to its suppliers and designers. A *Considered Index* is then calculated to evaluate the proposed design. Products or designs are scored on the use of solvents, waste, materials, treatments (such as fading or distressing), and innovation. Only those products that score significantly higher than the Nike average are designated as "Considered."

The company has also developed a *Sourcing & Manufacturing Sustainability Index* (SMSI) that assesses contract factory performance on sustainability measures such as lean production, environmental performance (water, energy, carbon, waste), health and safety, and labor management factors. The company's recycling program, called *Reuse-A-Shoe*, has recycled more than 21 million pairs of athletic shoes to create public basketball courts, athletic tracks, and playground surfaces around the world. Sustainability is now one of Nike's core values, as noted in its recent annual report.

How appropriate, then, that one of Nike's biggest commercial successes is also an environmental success—a 5.6 ounce running shoe called the Flyknit, which is shown in the photo. The Flyknit design changes the look, feel, performance, and manufacture of Nike's biggest sales category, running shoes. The upper portion of these shoes are "knitted" on a custom-made 15-foot-long machine that weaves together colored polyester yarn and adds tiny synthetic cables into the weave around the midfoot for support. The cables loosen and contract with the runner's foot, for form-fitting comfort and performance. For more stretch in the toe, Lycra-infused thread can be used; for added strength in the heel, multiple layers of yarn of varying thickness can be added. The warp and weft of the weaving process opens up interesting color combinations for the shoes as well. In the future, a shoe might be knitted to fit the particular needs of a customer's feet (even if that means a different knit pattern for the left foot than the right).

The Flyknit has 35 fewer pieces to assemble than a traditional shoe and produces very little waste. Since there is no cutting, sewing, stitching, or gluing, the labor requirements and cost of manufacture are considerably less, too.

Nike has made great strides in apparel manufacturing, as well, with its ColorDry dyeing process. The new technology uses CO_2 instead of water to dye material, eliminating wastewater pollution and avoiding depletion of a resource that is becoming increasingly scarce. Since it takes 30 liters of water to dye just one T-shirt and 5.8 trillion liters of water to dye apparel each year across the industry, using zero water makes a huge difference. The new process is 40% faster, too; it uses a quarter of the space and reduces energy consumption by 63%. Further, the color is more saturated, intense, and consistent.

Nike's environmental actions promise to be a game-changer both for the company and the industry, and the resulting increase in profit is not bad either.

1. Why do you think Nike is so concerned about sustainability and the environment?
2. It's not often that a design totally changes an industry. Can you think of other designs that have played that role? Comment on the competitive landscape for both the Flyknit and the example you find.
3. The ColorDry technology will have a huge impact on sustainability for the textile industry. Find examples of environmental "pain points" in other industries and what is being done about them.

Sources: Nike corporate website, http://www.nikeresponsibility.com/ (accessed January 24, 2016); Matt Townsend, "Is Nike's Flyknit the Swoosh of the Future?" *Business Week*, (March 15, 2012); "Nike ColorDry adds water-free dyed fabric to sustainable materials menu," *The Guardian*, (December 18, 2013).

Green Consumption

Images of overflowing landfills, toxic streams, and global warming have prompted governments worldwide to enact laws and regulations protecting the environment and rewarding environmental stewardship.

Extended producer responsibility (EPR) When companies are held responsible for their product even after its useful life.

Extended producer responsibility (EPR) is a concept that holds companies responsible for their product even after its useful life. German law mandates the collection, recycling, and safe disposal of computers and household appliances, including stereos, televisions, washing machines, dishwashers, and refrigerators. Some manufacturers pay a tax for recycling; others include the cost of disposal in a product's price. Norwegian law requires producers and importers of electronic equipment to recycle or reuse 80% of the product. Twenty-five U.S. states now have ***takeback*** laws that require the return and recycling of batteries, appliances, and other electronics. Brazil considers all packaging that cannot be recycled hazardous waste. The European Union requires that 80% of the weight of discarded cars must be reused or recycled. Companies responsible for disposing of their own products are more conscious of the design decisions that generated the excess and the toxic waste that can be expensive to process.

Once purchased, green design affects how efficiently the product uses energy, how long the product will last (i.e., reliability), if the product can be repaired instead of discarded (i.e., maintainability) and whether it can be recycled at the end of its useful life. If recyclable, the product should be easy to disassemble. Finally, the product should not cause harm to the customer or the environment (e.g., lead in toys or toxic fumes), and it should serve a useful purpose.

It's in the company mission statement, "Build the best product, cause no unnecessary harm, use business to inspire and implement solutions to the environmental crisis," but few would expect even outdoors retailer Patagonia to begin a "don't buy" campaign. "Don't buy this jacket, don't buy this shirt . . . unless you really need it," said the ad appearing on Black Friday in *The New York Times*. Limiting consumption is part of sustainability, even if it seems ill-fitted for an economy based on growth and consumer spending. Companies can also design a product that has a longer useful life, is easier to repair than discard, can be recycled into other products, or is more environmentally friendly to use.

Recycling and Reuse

When a product reaches the end of its useful life, it can be recycled, reused, or discarded (usually to a landfill). Recycling and reuse close the design loop, and are the ideal for sustainability. Unfortunately, that rarely happens for electronic products, less than 20% of which are recycled. Read more about the implications of an environmentally conscious smartphone in the "Along the Supply Chain" box that follows.

Increased consumption of electronic products has skyrocketed in recent years, producing 30 to 50 million metric tons of e-waste annually worldwide. In the United States alone, almost half a million mobile devices are discarded every day. To complicate matters, electronics contain lead, cadmium, mercury, and other hazardous wastes, which can leech into groundwater and create severe health and environmental problems.

Along the Supply Chain

Creating Fairphones

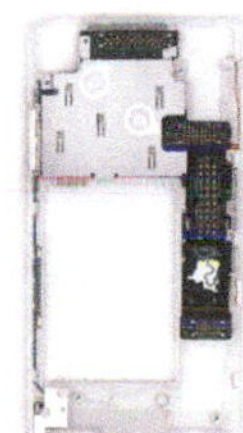

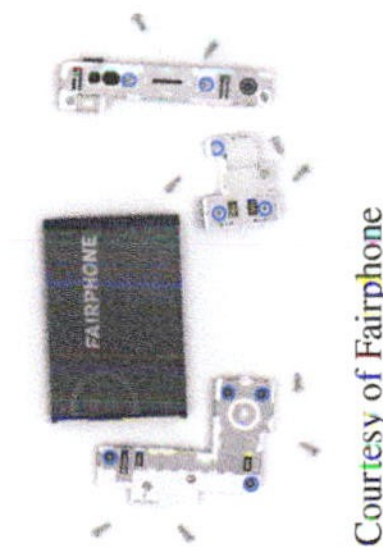

Courtesy of Fairphone

Fairphone launched its first crowd-funded, ethically-sourced, and environmentally conscious smart phone in 2013. Built with many conflict-free materials in factories concerned about worker welfare, and designed for recyclability, the Fairphone sold more than 100,000 units worldwide. The Fairphone 2, which is shown in the photo, improves upon the first model with a modular design that allows users to disassemble, maintain, repair and eventually upgrade parts of the phone to extend its useful life; hopefully, well beyond the current two-year replacement cycle of smartphones. Replacing batteries is simple and the "yours to open, yours to keep" message is a refreshing change from "opening your phone will void your warranty" message of current smartphones. The ability to upgrade the camera, add a SIM card (two slots are available), or expand memory is also appealing.The rubberized back with reinforced corners doubles as a case, eliminating the need for extra accessories. Spare parts are available for purchase, and accessories can be 'printed' with a 3D printer. iFixit rates the repairability of the phone a 10 out of 10. And when the customer is ready to upgrade to a new phone, the company's Take Back program ensures safe and reliable reuse or recycling.

The Fairphone's software is standard Android with a few differences. An App Life Cycle keeps track of how much an app is being used and puts less-often-used apps in the idle section after a certain amount of time. An extra layer is added to privacy control that rates the "Privacy Impact" of an app as low, medium, or high before a user downloads it. Most importantly, unlike most Android devices, unlocking the software does not violate the phone's warranty; Fairphone 2 has superuser access built into the operating system. In fact, the company has released the complete build environment and full open source code for developers to build their own Fairphone operating system.

The Fairphone project began with hopes to open up the supply chain and increase the transparency of worker treatment and materials sourcing within the consumer electronics industry.

It has evolved into the ethically-sourced production of a viable smartphone with innovative design ideas. Who knows how that will change the industry?

1. Fairphone designers imagined a 5-year replacement cycle for smartphones. What challenges does this create for the designer and the user?
2. How do you think Fairphone's ethical sourcing and design ideas will affect other cell phone manufacturers?
3. Google's Ara project with its modular design might overshadow Fairphone's sleekest design feature. Compare the two products and their price. Is there a market for ethically sourced design otherwise?
4. Fairphone's goal is to change behavior rather than sell more phones. What kind of balance between design and commercialization is needed to accomplish its goal?
5. Explore one of the following topics on the Web and report your findings to class: a) conflict materials, b) electronic waste.

Sources: Jo Best, "The Gadget with a Conscience: How Fairphone Crowdfunded its Way to an Industry-Changing Smart Phone," *Tech Republic*, (May 2014); Caroline Winter, "Why It's Hard to Make an Ethically Sourced Smartphone," *Bloomberg Business*, 9/20/13; Andy Boxall, "Hands on: Fairphone 2," *Digital Trends*, 9/28/15; "The Fairphone 2, Free Software and Alternative Operating Systems, "http://libre-software.net (accessed January 30, 2016).

Design factors such as product life, recoverable value, ease of repair, and disposal cost affect the consumer's decision to recycle, discard, or continue to use. Many products are discarded because they are difficult or expensive to repair. Materials from discarded products may not be recycled if the product is difficult to disassemble. That's why companies like Hewlett-Packard and Xerox design their products for disassembly. As a result, HP has been able to disassemble and refurbish 12,000 tons of equipment annually with less than 1% waste.

Remanufacturing Making new products from recycled parts.

Xerox, a leader in **remanufacturing**, designs its copiers for multiple lifecycles. Old models can be refurbished or upgraded with new controls, software, and features because the basic form (i.e., rack or frame) and design layout of the machine remains the same. In a discarded copier with 8000 parts, over 90% can typically be reused. Disassembly is easier because parts are labeled and those that are likely to default or become obsolete at the same time are clustered together. The remanufacturing process involves disassembling and sorting the parts, inspecting them, cleaning them, reprocessing them, then reassembly, final inspection, and testing.

One of the more amazing recycled products on the market is polar fleece, made from recycled soda bottles, as shown in the photo. But that is not where the journey ends. Patagonia, which makes garments from polar fleece, accepts worn-out fleece, wool, and other garments from its customers and completely recycles them. Discarded garments are cut into bits, pulverized into small pellets, purified, polymerized, melted, and spun into new fabric for new

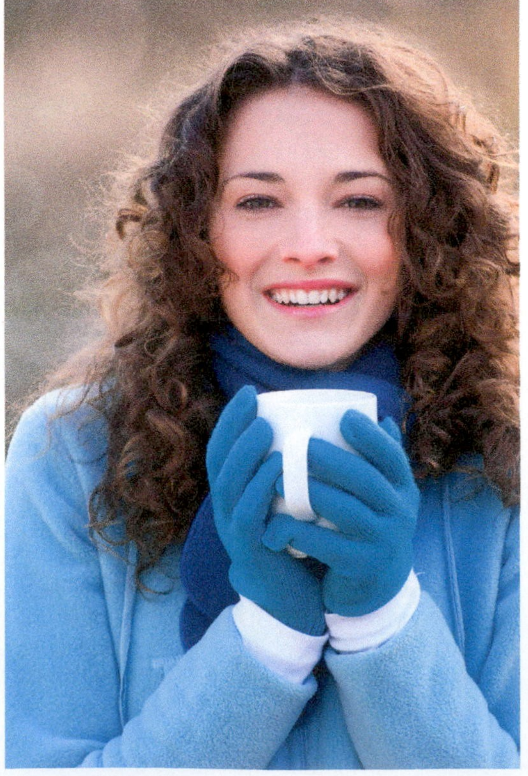

Did you know that polar fleece can be made from recycled soda bottles? Patagonia estimates that they have saved 86 million soda bottles from landfills by using them to make polar fleece. The company also takes back worn-out garments from customers and recycles the fibers into new products. And their Common Threads storefront on eBay helps customers find new homes for garments they no longer want. Read about Patagonia's responsible supply chain in the Footprint Chronicles online.

garments, thus completing the cycle in a cradle-to-cradle design. Through its Common Threads recycling program, Patagonia saves 38 million pounds of carbon dioxide emissions each year and creates 20% of its products from post-consumer waste.

Whether it's greening a design or making other design changes to please the customer, companies need a procedure for ensuring that the myriad of design decisions are consistent and reflective of customer needs. Such a technique, *quality function deployment*, is discussed in the next section.

Quality Function Deployment

Imagine that two engineers are working on two different components of a car sunroof simultaneously but separately.[2] The "insulation and sealing" engineer develops a new seal that will keep out rain, even during a blinding rainstorm. The "handles, knobs, and levers" engineer is working on a simpler lever that will make the roof easier to open. The new lever is tested and works well with the old seal. Neither engineer is aware of the activities of the other. As it turns out, the combination of heavier roof (due to the increased insulation) and lighter lever means that the driver can no longer open the sunroof with one hand! Hopefully, the problem will be detected in prototype testing before the car is put into production. At that point, one or both components will need to be redesigned. Otherwise, cars already produced will need to be reworked and cars already sold will have to be recalled. None of these alternatives is pleasant, and they all involve considerable cost.

Could such problems be avoided if engineers worked in teams and shared information? Not entirely. Even in design teams, there is no guarantee that all decisions will be coordinated. Ford and Firestone have worked together for over 75 years. But teamwork did not prevent Firestone tires designed to fit the Ford Explorer from failing when inflated to Ford specifications. A formal method is needed for making sure that everyone working on a design project knows the design objectives and is aware of the interrelationships of the various parts of the design. Similar communications are needed to translate the voice of the customer to technical design requirements. Such a process is called quality function deployment (QFD).

Quality functional deployment (QFD) uses a series of matrix diagrams that resemble connected houses. The first matrix, dubbed the *house of quality*, converts customer requirements into product design characteristics. As shown in Figure 4.7, the house of quality has six sections: a customer requirements section, a competitive assessment section, a design characteristics section, a relationship matrix, a tradeoff matrix, and a target values section. Let's see how these sections interrelate by building a house of quality for a steam iron.

Quality functional deployment (QFD) A structured process that translates the customer's voice into technical design.

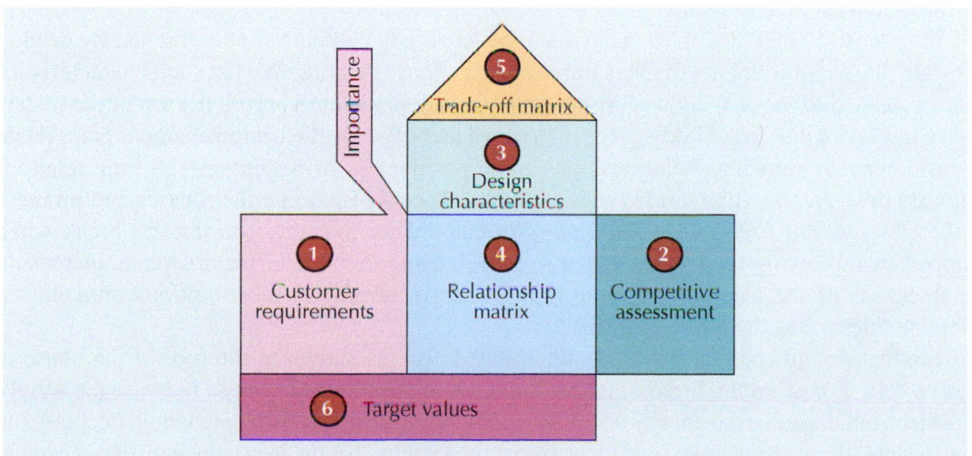

FIGURE 4.7 Outline of the House of Quality

[2]Adapted from Bob King, *Better Designs in Half the Time* (Methuen, MA: GOAL/QPC, 1989), pp. 1.1–1.3.

FIGURE 4.8 **A Competitive Assessment of Customer Requirements**

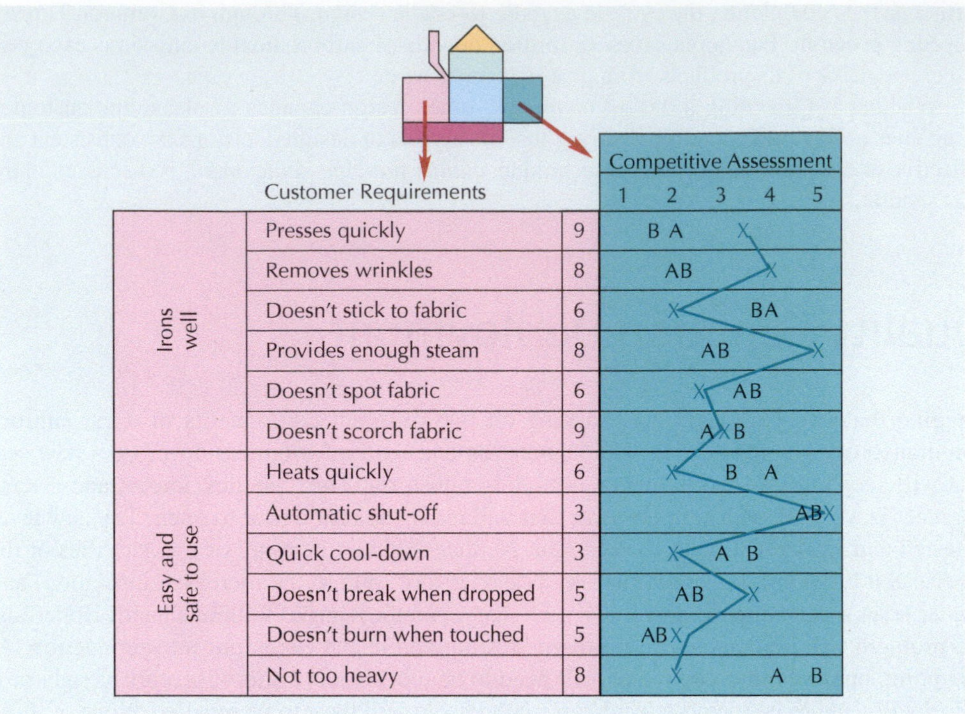

Competitive Assessment
1 2 3 4 5
Customer Requirements
Irons well
Easy and safe to use
Presses quickly 9 B A X
Removes wrinkles 8 AB X
Doesn't stick to fabric 6 X BA
Provides enough steam 8 AB X
Doesn't spot fabric 6 X AB
Doesn't scorch fabric 9 AXB
Heats quickly 6 X B A
Automatic shut-off 3 ABX
Quick cool-down 3 X A B
Doesn't break when dropped 5 AB X
Doesn't burn when touched 5 ABX
Not too heavy 8 X A B

Our customers tell us they want an iron that presses quickly, removes wrinkles, doesn't stick to fabric, provides enough steam, doesn't spot fabric, and doesn't scorch fabric (see Figure 4.8). We enter those attributes into the *customer requirements* section of the house. For easier reference, we can group them into a category called "Irons well." Next we ask our customers to rate the list of requirements on a scale of 1 to 10, with 10 being the most important. Our customers rate presses quickly and doesn't scorch fabric as the most important attributes, with a score of 9. A second group of attributes, called "Easy and safe to use" is constructed in a similar manner.

Next, we conduct a *competitive assessment*. On a scale of 1 to 5 (with 5 being the highest), customers evaluate our iron (we'll call it "X") against competitor irons, A and B. We see that our iron excels on the customer attributes of presses quickly, removes wrinkles, provides enough steam, automatic shutoff, and doesn't break when dropped. So there is no critical need to improve those factors. However, we are rated poorly on doesn't stick, doesn't spot, heats quickly, quick cool-down, and not too heavy. These are order qualifiers. We need to improve these factors just to be considered for purchase by customers. None of the irons perform well on doesn't scorch fabric, or doesn't burn when touched. Perhaps we could win some orders if we satisfied these requirements.

In order to change the product design to better satisfy customer requirements, we need to translate those requirements to measurable *design characteristics*. We list such characteristics (energy needed to press, weight of iron, size of the soleplate, etc.) across the top of the matrix shown in Figure 4.9. In the body of the matrix, we identify *how* the design characteristics relate to customer requirements. Relationships can be positive, +, or negative, −. Strong relationships are designated with a circled plus or minus, ⊕ or ⊖. Examine the plusses and minuses in the row *Doesn't break when dropped*. We can ensure that the iron doesn't break when dropped by increasing the weight of the iron, increasing the size of the soleplate, increasing the thickness of the soleplate, or adding a protective cover. Of those options, making the soleplate thicker has the strongest impact.

Product design characteristics are interrelated also, as shown in the roof of the house in Figure 4.10. For example, increasing the thickness of the soleplate would increase the weight of the iron but decrease the energy needed to press. Also, a thicker soleplate would decrease the flow of water through the holes, and increase the time it takes for the iron to heat up or cool down. Designers must take all these factors into account when determining a final design.

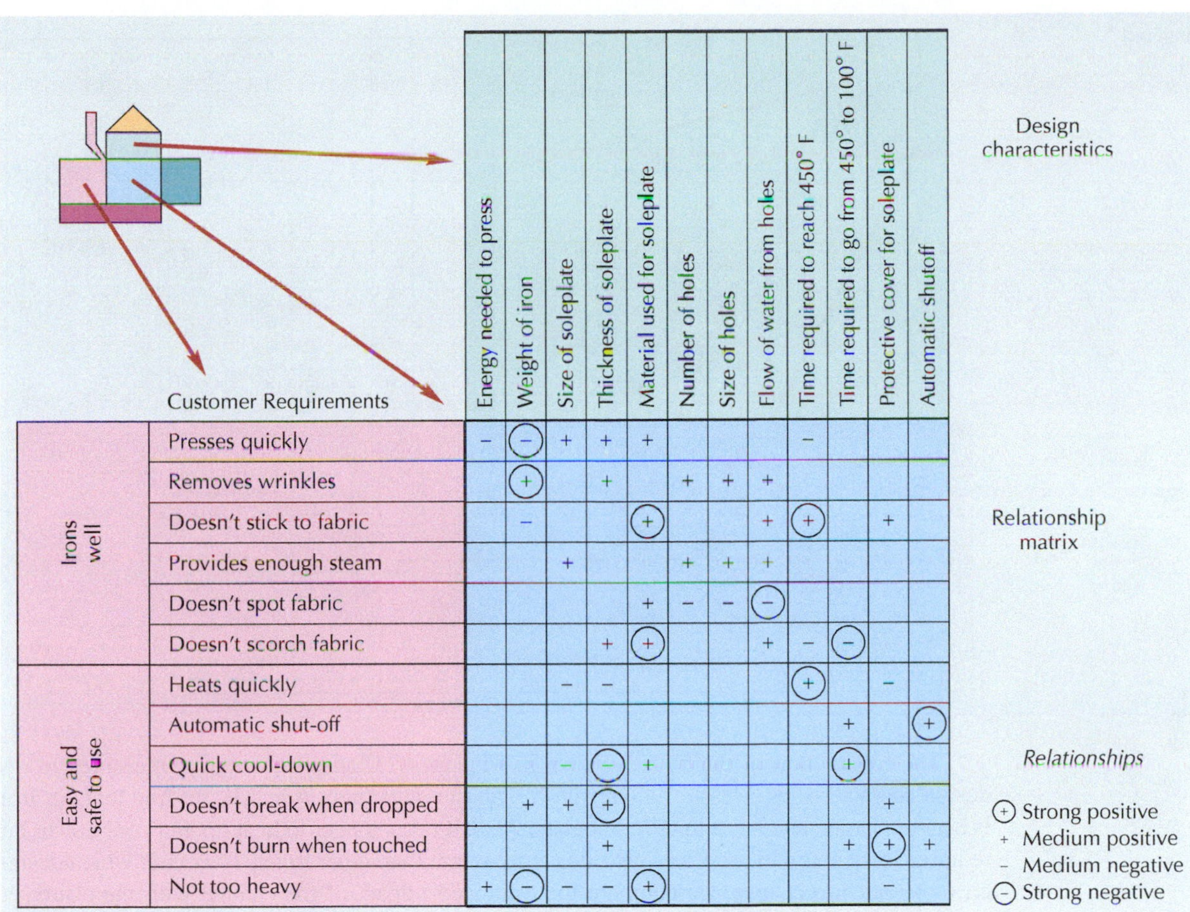

FIGURE 4.9 Converting Customer Requirements to Design Characteristics

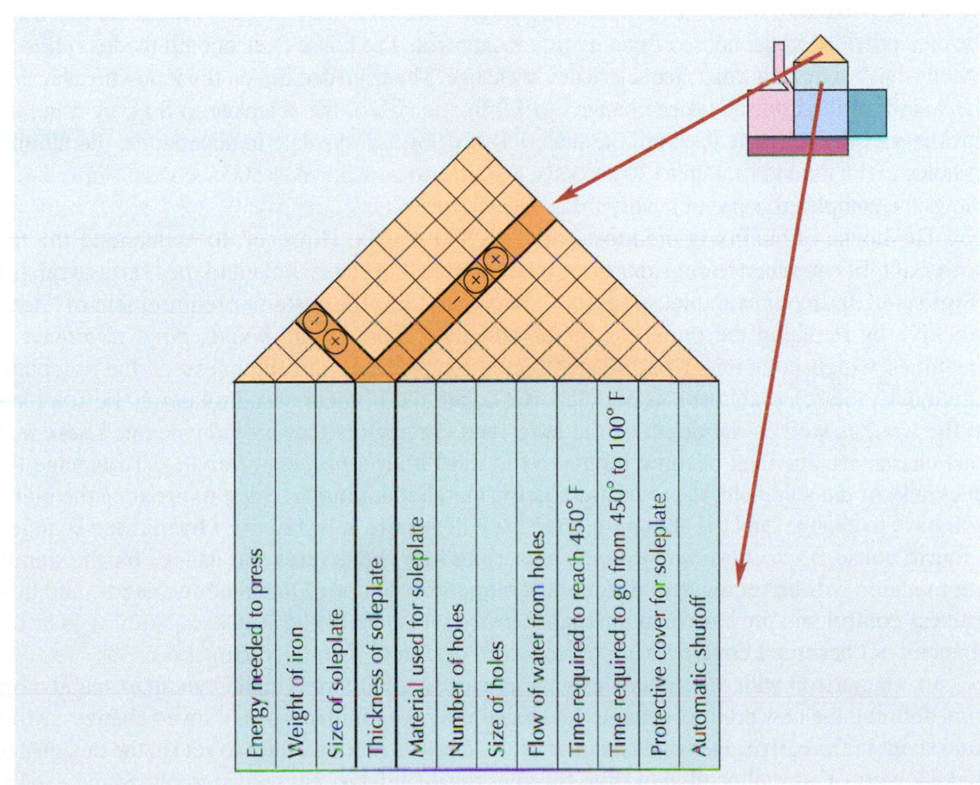

FIGURE 4.10 The Tradeoff Matrix: Effects of Increasing Soleplate Thickness

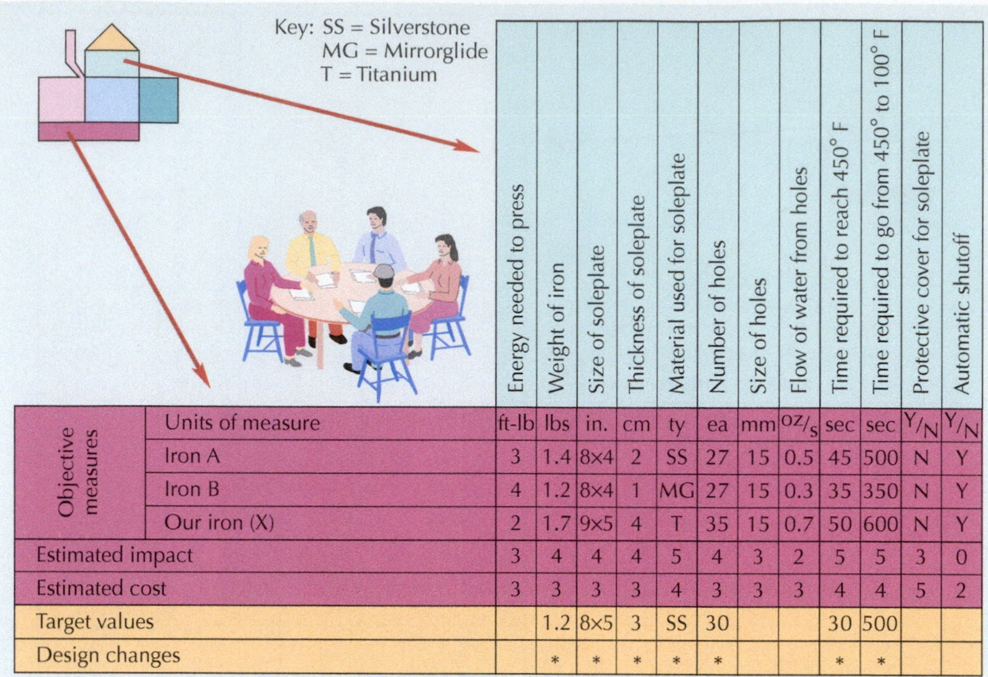

		Energy needed to press	Weight of iron	Size of soleplate	Thickness of soleplate	Material used for soleplate	Number of holes	Size of holes	Flow of water from holes	Time required to reach 450° F	Time required to go from 450° to 100° F	Protective cover for soleplate	Automatic shutoff
Objective measures	Units of measure	ft-lb	lbs	in.	cm	ty	ea	mm	oz/s	sec	sec	Y/N	Y/N
	Iron A	3	1.4	8x4	2	SS	27	15	0.5	45	500	N	Y
	Iron B	4	1.2	8x4	1	MG	27	15	0.3	35	350	N	Y
	Our iron (X)	2	1.7	9x5	4	T	35	15	0.7	50	600	N	Y
Estimated impact		3	4	4	4	5	4	3	2	5	5	3	0
Estimated cost		3	3	3	3	4	3	3	3	4	4	5	2
Target values			1.2	8x5	3	SS	30			30	500		
Design changes			*	*	*	*	*			*	*		

FIGURE 4.11 Targeted Changes in Design

The last section of the house, shown in Figure 4.11, adds quantitative measures to our design characteristics. Measuring our iron X against competitors A and B, we find that our iron is heavier, larger, and has a thicker soleplate. Also, it takes longer to heat up and cool down, but requires less energy to press and provides more steam than other irons. To decide which design characteristics to change, we compare the estimated impact of the change with the estimated cost. We rate these factors on a common scale, from 1 to 5, with 5 being the most. As long as the estimated impact exceeds the estimated cost, we should make a change. Thus, we need to change several product characteristics in our new design, such as weight of the iron, size of the soleplate, thickness of the soleplate, material used for the soleplate, number of holes, time required to heat up, and time required to cool down.

Now visualize a design team discussing target values for these product characteristics using the data provided in the house of quality as a focal point. The house does not tell the team how to change the design, only what characteristics to change. The team decides on the following changes: the weight of the iron should be changed to 1.2 lb, the size of the soleplate to 8 in. by 5 in., the thickness of the soleplate to 3 cm, the material used for the soleplate to silverstone, the number of holes to 30, time to heat up to 30 seconds, and time to cool down to 500 seconds. Figure 4.12 shows the completed house of quality for the steam iron.

The house of quality is the most popular QFD matrix. However, to understand the full power of QFD, we need to consider three other houses that can be linked to the house of quality (Figure 4.13). In our example, suppose we decide to meet the customer requirement of "heats quickly" by reducing the thickness of the soleplate. The second house, *parts deployment*, examines which component parts are affected by reducing the thickness of the soleplate. Obviously, the soleplate itself is affected, but so are the fasteners used to attach the soleplate to the iron, as well as the depth of the holes and connectors that provide steam. These new part characteristics then become inputs to the third house, *process planning*. To change the thickness of the soleplate, the dyes used by the metal-stamping machine to produce the plates will have to change, and the stamping machine will require adjustments. Given these changes, a fourth house, *operating requirements*, prescribes how the fixtures and gauges for the stamping machine will be set, what additional training the operator of the machine needs, and how process control and preventive maintenance procedures need to be adjusted. Nothing is left to chance—all bases are covered from customer to design to manufacturing.

In comparison with traditional design approaches, QFD forces management to spend more time defining the new product changes and examining the ramifications of those changes. More time spent in the early stages of design means less time is required later to revise the design and make it work. This reallocation of time shortens the design process considerably. Some experts suggest that QFD can produce better product designs in *half* the time of conventional design

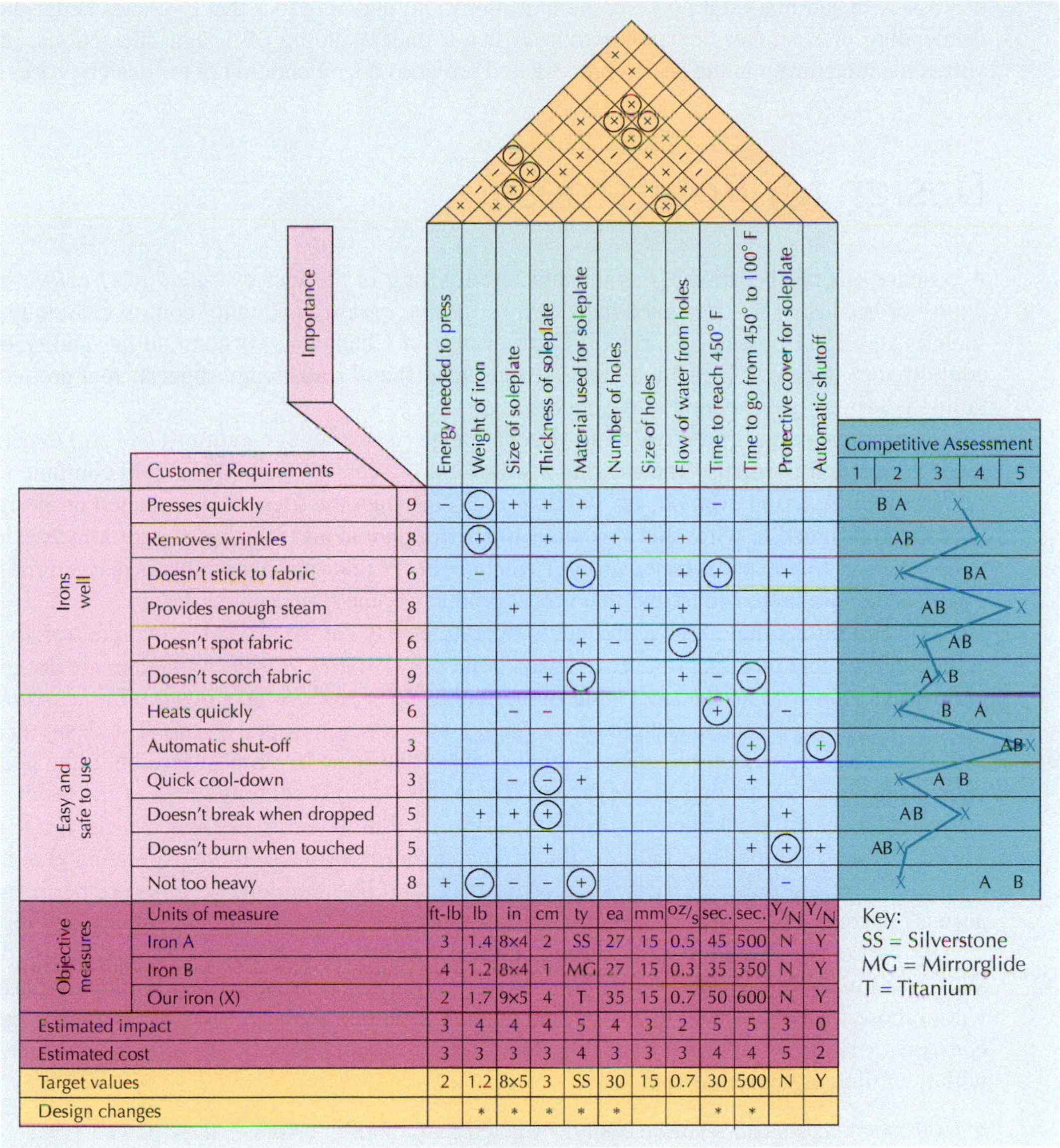

	Customer Requirements	Importance	Energy needed to press	Weight of iron	Size of soleplate	Thickness of soleplate	Material used for soleplate	Number of holes	Size of holes	Flow of water from holes	Time to reach 450° F	Time to go from 450° to 100° F	Protective cover for soleplate	Automatic shutoff	Competitive Assessment (1 2 3 4 5)
Irons well	Presses quickly	9	–	⊖	+	+	+				–				B A X
	Removes wrinkles	8		⊕		+		+	+	+					AB X
	Doesn't stick to fabric	6		–			⊕			+	⊕		+		X BA
	Provides enough steam	8			+			+	+	+					AB X
	Doesn't spot fabric	6					+	–	–	⊖					X AB
	Doesn't scorch fabric	9				+	⊕			+	–	⊖			A X B
Easy and safe to use	Heats quickly	6			–	–					⊕		–		X B A
	Automatic shut-off	3										⊕		⊕	AB X
	Quick cool-down	3			–	⊖	+					+			X A B
	Doesn't break when dropped	5		+	+	⊕							+		AB X
	Doesn't burn when touched	5				+						+	⊕	+	AB X
	Not too heavy	8	+	⊖	–	–	⊕						–		X A B
Objective measures	Units of measure		ft-lb	lb	in	cm	ty	ea	mm	oz/s	sec.	sec.	Y/N	Y/N	
	Iron A		3	1.4	8×4	2	SS	27	15	0.5	45	500	N	Y	
	Iron B		4	1.2	8×4	1	MG	27	15	0.3	35	350	N	Y	
	Our iron (X)		2	1.7	9×5	4	T	35	15	0.7	50	600	N	Y	
Estimated impact			3	4	4	4	5	4	3	2	5	5	3	0	
Estimated cost			3	3	3	3	4	3	3	3	4	4	5	2	
Target values			2	1.2	8×5	3	SS	30	15	0.7	30	500	N	Y	
Design changes				*	*	*	*	*			*	*			

Key:
SS = Silverstone
MG = Mirrorglide
T = Titanium

FIGURE 4.12 The Completed House of Quality for a Steam Iron

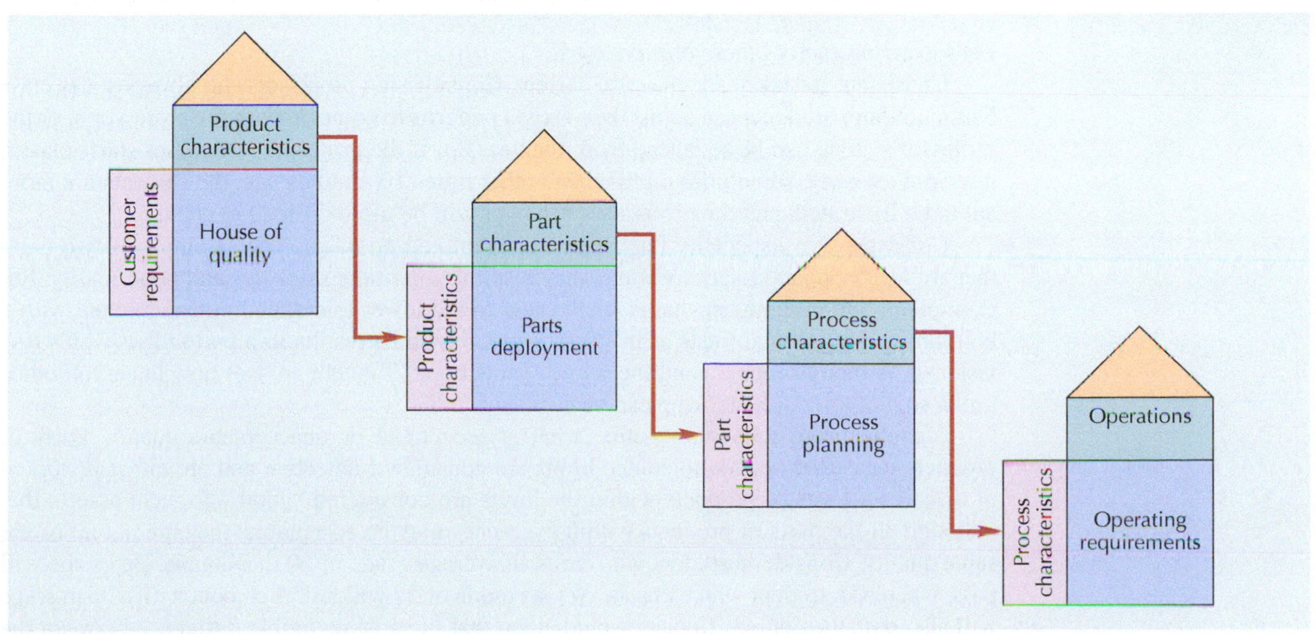

FIGURE 4.13 A Series of Connected QFD Houses

processes. In summary, QFD is a communications and planning tool that promotes better understanding of customer demands, produces better understanding of design interactions, involves manufacturing in the design process, and provides documentation of the design process.

Design for Robustness

A product can fail because it was manufactured wrong in the factory—*quality of conformance*—or because it was designed incorrectly—*quality of design*. Quality-control techniques, such as statistical process control (SPC) discussed in Chapter 3, concentrate on quality of conformance. Genichi Taguchi, a Japanese industrialist and statistician, suggests that product failure is primarily a function of design quality.

Consumers subject products to an extreme range of operating conditions and still expect them to function normally. The steering and brakes of a car, for example, should continue to perform their function even on wet, winding roads or when the tires are not inflated properly. A product designed to withstand variations in environmental and operating conditions is said to be *robust* or to possess *robust quality*. Taguchi believes that superior quality is derived from products that are more robust and that robust products come from **robust design**.

Robust design Yields a product or service designed to withstand variations.

The conditions that cause a product to operate poorly can be separated into controllable and uncontrollable factors. From a designer's point of view, the *controllable factors* are design parameters such as material used, dimensions, and form of processing. *Uncontrollable factors* are under the user's control (length of use, maintenance, settings, and so on). The designer's job is to choose values for the controllable variables that react in a robust fashion to the possible occurrences of uncontrollable factors. To do this, various configurations of the product are tested under different operating conditions specified in the *design of experiments* (DOE). The experiment is replicated multiple times. The *mean* performance of an experimental configuration over a number of trials is called the "signal." The *standard deviation* of performance is referred to as "noise." The most robust design exhibits the highest signal-to-noise ratio.

Tolerances Allowable ranges of variation.

As part of the design process, design engineers must also specify certain **tolerances**, or allowable ranges of variation in the dimension of a part. It is assumed that producing parts within those tolerance limits will result in a quality product. Taguchi, however, suggests that *consistency* is more important to quality than being within tolerances. He supports this view with the following observations.

- Consistent errors can be more easily corrected than random errors,
- *Parts* within tolerance limits may produce *assemblies* that are not within limits, and
- Consumers have a strong preference for product characteristics near their ideal values.

Let's examine each of these observations.

Consistent mistakes are easier to correct. Consider the professor who always starts class 5 minutes late. Students can adjust their arrival patterns to coincide with the professor's, or the professor's clock can be set ahead by 5 minutes. But if the professor sometimes starts class a few minutes early, sometimes on time, and other times 10 minutes late, the students are more apt to be frustrated, and the professor's behavior will be more difficult to change.

Consistency is especially important for assembled products. The assembly of two parts that are near opposite tolerance limits may result in *tolerance stack-ups* and poor quality. For example, a button diameter that is small (near to the lower tolerance limit) combined with a buttonhole that is large (near to its upper tolerance limit) results in a button that won't stay fastened. Although it is beyond the scope of this book, Taguchi advises how to set tolerance limits so that tolerance stack-up can be avoided.

Manufacturing tolerances define what is acceptable or unacceptable quality. Parts or products measured outside tolerance limits are considered defective and are either reworked or discarded. Parts or products within the limits are considered "good." Taguchi asserts that although all the parts or products within tolerances may be acceptable, they are not all of the same quality. Consider a student who earns an average grade of 60 in a course. He or she will pass, whereas a student who earns an average grade of 59 will fail. A student with a 95 average will also pass the course. Taguchi would claim that there is negligible difference between the quality of the students with averages of 59 and 60, even though one was "rejected" and the

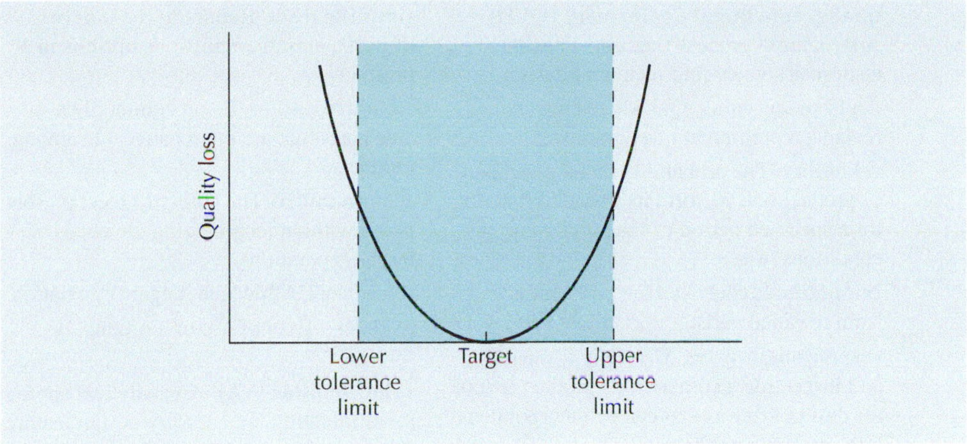

FIGURE 4.14 Taguchi's Quality Loss Function

other was not. There is, however, a great deal of difference in the quality of the student with an average of 60 and the student with an average of 95. Furthermore, a professor in a subsequent class or a prospective employer will be able to detect the difference in quality and will overwhelmingly prefer the student who passed the course with a 95 average. Quality near the target value is preferable to quality that simply conforms to specifications.

Taguchi quantified customer preferences toward on-target quality in the *quality loss function* (QLF). The quadratic function, graphed in Figure 4.14, implies that a customer's dissatisfaction (or quality loss) increases geometrically as the actual value deviates from the target value. The quality loss function is used to emphasize that customer preferences are strongly oriented toward *consistently* meeting quality expectations. *Design for Six Sigma* (DFSS) uses the Taguchi method to reduce variability in design.

Summary

New products and services enhance a company's image, invigorate employees, and help a firm to grow and prosper. The design process begins with ideas formulated into a product concept. Once a product concept passes a feasibility study, performance specs are given to designers who develop and test prototype designs. For selected prototypes, design and manufacturing specs are taken through a pilot run where the design is finalized and the planning for product launch begins.

Time-to-market can be accelerated by using design teams, concurrent design, design for manufacture concepts, and CAD/CAM systems. The quality of design can be improved through design reviews, design for environment, quality function deployment, and robust design.

Key Terms

benchmarking Finding the best-in-class product or process, measuring one's performance against it, and making recommendations for improvements based on the results.

carbon footprint A measure of the greenhouse gases produced by an activity, product or company.

collaborative product design (CPD) Software system for collaborative design and development among trading partners.

computer-aided design (CAD) A software system that uses computer graphics to assist in the creation, modification, and analysis of a design.

computer-aided design/computer-aided manufacturing (CAD/CAM) The ultimate design-to-manufacture connection.

computer-aided engineering (CAE) Engineering analysis performed at a computer terminal with information from a CAD database.

concurrent design A new approach to design that involves the simultaneous design of products and processes by design teams.

design for environment (DFE) Designing a product from material that can be recycled or easily repaired rather than discarded.

design for manufacture (DFM) Designing a product so that it can be produced easily and economically.

design for supply chain (DFSC) Considering supply chain capabilities during product design.

extended producer responsibility (EPR) Holding a company responsible for its product even after its useful life.

failure mode and effects analysis (FMEA) A systematic approach to analyzing the causes and effects of product failures.

fault tree analysis (FTA) A visual method for analyzing the interrelationships among failures.

form design The phase of product design concerned with how the product looks.

functional design The phase of product design concerned with how the product performs.

maintainability The ease with which a product is maintained or repaired.

modular design Combining standardized building blocks, or modules, in a variety of ways to create unique finished products.

perceptual map Visual method for comparing customer perceptions of different products or services.

production design The phase of product design concerned with how the product will be produced.

product lifecycle management (PLM) Software for managing the entire lifecycle of a product.

quality functional deployment (QFD) A structured process that translates the customer's voice into technical design.

rapid prototyping Quickly testing and revising a preliminary design model.

reliability The probability that a given part or product will perform its intended function for a specified period of time under normal conditions of use.

remanufacturing Making new products from recycled parts.

reverse engineering Carefully dismantling and inspecting a competitor's product to look for design features that can be incorporated into your own product.

robust design The design of a product or a service that can withstand variations in environmental and operating conditions.

simplification Reducing the number of parts, subassemblies, or options in a product.

standardization Using commonly available parts that are interchangeable among products.

sustainability The ability to meet present needs without jeopardizing the needs of future generations.

tolerances Allowable ranges of variation.

usability Ease of use of a product or service.

value analysis (VA) An analytical approach for eliminating unnecessary design features and functions.

Key Formulas

Reliability in series

$$R_s = (R_1)(R_2)\ldots(R_n)$$

Reliability in parallel

$$R_s = R_1 + (1 - R_1)R_2$$

or

$$R_s = 1 - [(1 - R_1)(1 - R_2)\ldots(1 - R_n)]$$

Mean time between failures

$$\text{MTBF} = \frac{\text{time}}{\text{\# failures}}$$

System availability

$$\text{SA} = \frac{\text{MTBF}}{\text{MTBF} + \text{MTTR}}$$

Solved Problems

1. Reliability

Jack McPhee, a production supervisor for McCormick, Inc., is committed to the company's new quality efforts. Part of the program encourages making product components in-house to ensure higher quality levels and instill worker pride. The system seems to be working well. One assembly, which requires a reliability of 0.95, is normally purchased from a local supplier. Now it is being assembled in-house from three components that each boast a reliability of 0.96.

a. Customer complaints have risen in the three months since McCormick started doing its own assembly work. Can you explain why?

b. What level of component reliability is necessary to restore the product to its former level of quality?

c. Jack can't increase the reliability of the individual components; however, he can add a backup with a reliability of 0.90 to each component. If the backups have a reliability of 0.90, how many will be needed to achieve a 0.95 reliability for the assembly?

Solution

a.

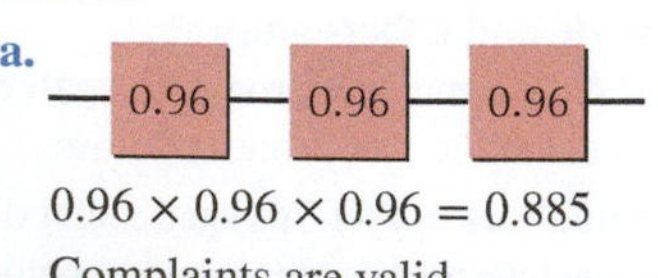

$0.96 \times 0.96 \times 0.96 = 0.885$

Complaints are valid

b. $\sqrt[3]{0.95} = 0.983$

Each component would need a reliability of 0.983 to guarantee an assembly reliability of 0.95

c.

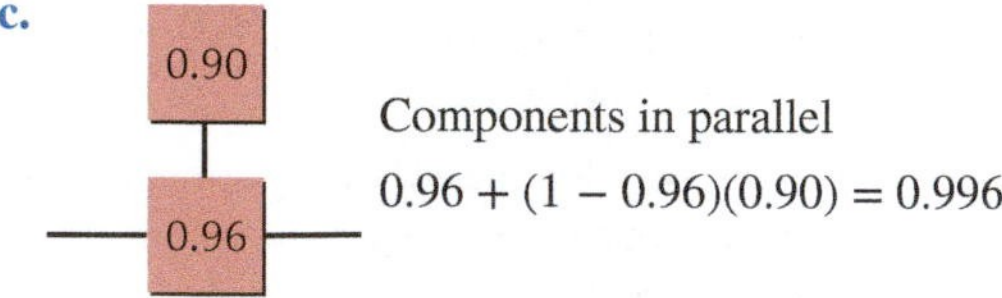

One backup

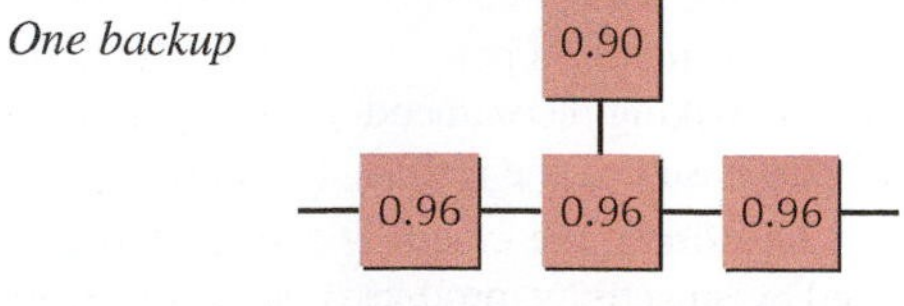

$0.96 \times 0.996 \times 0.96 = 0.918$

Two backups

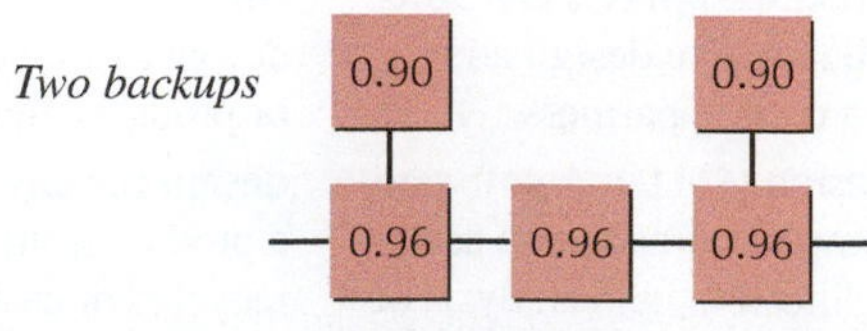

$0.996 \times 0.96 \times 0.996 = 0.952$

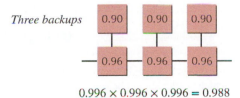

Three backups

0.90	0.90	0.90
0.96	0.96	0.96

$0.996 \times 0.996 \times 0.996 = 0.988$

For a system reliability of 0.95, choose two backups.

2. System Availability

Amanda is trying to decide which Internet service provider to use. Her friends are always complaining about service interruptions and how long it takes to get the service up and running again. Amanda is a conscientious student and wants reliable access to the Internet. With that goal in mind, she has collected data on mean time between failures (MTBF) and mean time to repair (MTTR) for three Internet service providers. Given that cost and speed are comparable among the three options, which provider would you recommend?

PROVIDER	MTBF	MTTR
MostTel	20	1
Star	40	4
CableX	80	6

Solution

PROVIDER	MTBF	MTTR	SYSTEM AVAILABILITY
MostTel	20	1	$20/(20 + 1) = 0.952$
Star	40	4	$40/(40 + 1) = 0.909$
CableX	80	6	$80/(80 + 6) = 0.930$

Choose MostTel

Questions

4.1. Describe the strategic significance of design. How can organizations gain a competitive edge with product or service design?

4.2. Look around your classroom and make a list of items that impede your ability to learn. Classify them as problems in *quality of design* or *quality of conformance*.

4.3. Give an example of a product or service you have encountered that was poorly designed. Read about more bad designs at the bad designs website *http://www.baddesigns.com*. Make a list of the factors that make a design unworkable.

4.4. Sometimes failures provide the best opportunities for new products and services. Search for the Post-It Note story on the web, and at least one other failure-to-success story. What do these stories tell you about the process of design?

4.5. *BusinessWeek* sponsors a best design competition each year. Read about this year's winners and write a brief summary about what makes these designs special.

4.6. Automakers often post concept cars on their websites. Find out how the design process for these cars differs. Which cars do you think will be commercially successful? Why?

4.7. Construct a perceptual map for the following products or services: (a) business schools in your state or region, (b) software packages, and (c) car rental/car sharing services. Label the axes with the dimensions you feel are most relevant. Explain how perceptual maps are used.

4.8. Read about benchmarking at the American Productivity and Quality Center *http://www.apqc.org* and the Benchmarking Exchange *http://www.benchnet.com*. What is benchmarking? What types of things do these organizations benchmark? How are the studies conducted? If possible, access one of the free benchmarking reports and summarize its findings.

4.9. Find out if your university benchmarks itself against other universities. If so, write a summary of the characteristics that are considered, the measures that are used, and the results. Do the data support your views as a customer?

4.10. What kinds of analyses are conducted in a feasibility study for new products?

4.11. Differentiate between performance specifications, design specifications, and manufacturing specifications. Write sample specifications for a product or service of your choosing.

4.12. How are reliability and maintainability related? Give an example for a product or service you have experienced.

4.13. Explain how simplification and standardization can improve designs. How does modular design differ from standardization?

4.14. How can design teams improve the quality of design? Relate your experiences in working in teams. What were the advantages and disadvantages?

4.15. Discuss the concept of concurrent design. What are the advantages of this approach? How would you apply concurrent design to a group project?

4.16. What does design for manufacture entail? List several techniques that can facilitate the DFM process. How do DFM and DFSC differ?

4.17. Describe the objectives of failure mode and effect analysis, fault tree analysis, and value analysis. Apply one of the techniques to a project, computer assignment, or writing assignment you have recently completed.

4.18. Access the Environmental Protection Agency *http://www.epa.gov/* to read about the U.S. government's commitment to environmental product design. Compare the U.S. approach to that of other countries.

4.19. Search the Internet for two or more companies that publish sustainability reports. What are the main components of each company's green initiatives? How do their approaches differ?

4.20. Link to the International Standards Organization *http://www.iso.org* and explore ISO 14000. What do these standards entail? How were they developed? How does a company attain ISO 14001 certification? Why would it want to?

4.21. What is the purpose of QFD? Find out if companies really use QFD by visiting the QFD Institute *http://www.qfdi.org* and summarizing one of their case studies.

4.22. Discuss the concept of robust design. Give an example of a robust product or service.

4.23. How does CAD relate to CAE and CAM? How do CAD and the Internet promote collaborative design?

Problems

WileyPLUS

4.1. Use the following instructions to construct and test a prototype paper airplane. Are the instructions clear? How would you improve the design of the airplane or the manner in which the design is communicated?

- Begin with an 8½ in. by 11 in. sheet of paper.
- Fold the paper together lengthwise to make a center line.
- Open the paper and fold the top corners to the center line.
- Fold the two top sides to the center line.
- Fold the airplane in half.
- Fold back the wings to meet the center line.
- Hold the plane by the center line and let it fly.

4.2. An alternative airplane design is given here. Follow the assembly instructions and test the airplane. Are the instructions clear? Compare the performance of this airplane design with the one described in Problem 4.1. Which plane was easier to construct? How would you improve the design of this plane or the manner in which the design is communicated?

- Begin with an 8½ in. by 11 in. sheet of paper.
- Fold it lengthwise in alternating directions. The folds should be about 1 in. wide.
- Hold the top of the folded paper in one hand and fan out the back portion with the other hand.
- Make a small fold in the nose of the plane to hold it together, and let it fly.

4.3. Calculate the reliability of the following system.

4.4. A broadcasting station has five major subsystems that must all be operational before a show can go on the air. If each subsystem has the same reliability, what reliability would be required to be 95% certain of broadcast success? 98% certain? 99% certain?

4.5. Competition for a new generation of computers is so intense that MicroTech has funded three separate design teams to create the new systems. Due to varying capabilities of the team members, it is estimated that team A has a 90% probability of coming up with an acceptable design before the competition, team B has an 80% chance, and team C has a 70% chance. What is the probability that MicroTech will beat the competition with its new computers?

4.6. MagTech assembles Blu-ray players from four major components arranged as follows:

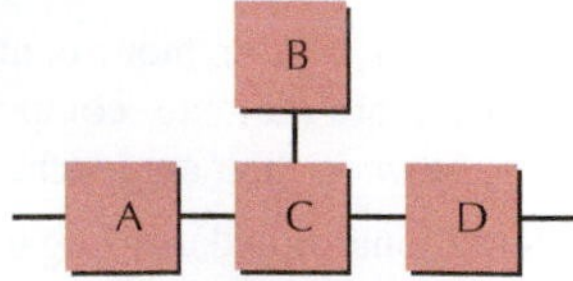

The components can be purchased from three different vendors, who have supplied the following reliability data:

COMPONENT	VENDOR 1	VENDOR 2	VENDOR 3
A	0.94	0.85	0.92
B	0.86	0.88	0.90
C	0.90	0.93	0.95
D	0.93	0.95	0.90

a. If MagTech has decided to use only one vendor to supply all four components, which vendor should be selected?
b. Would your decision change if all the components were assembled in series?

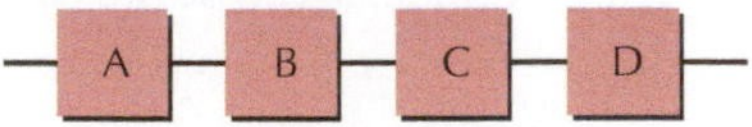

4.7. Glen Evans is an emergency medical technician for a local rescue team and is routinely called on to render emergency care to citizens facing crisis situations. Although Glen has received extensive training, he also relies heavily on his equipment for support. During a normal call, Glen uses five essential pieces of equipment, whose individual reliabilities are 0.98, 0.97, 0.95, 0.96, and 0.99, respectively.

a. Glen claims his equipment has maximum probability of failure of 5%. Is he correct?
b. What individual equipment reliabilities would guarantee an overall reliability of 96%?

4.8. Examine the systems given below. Which system is more reliable, a or b? c or d? Now calculate the reliability of each system. Were your perceptions correct?

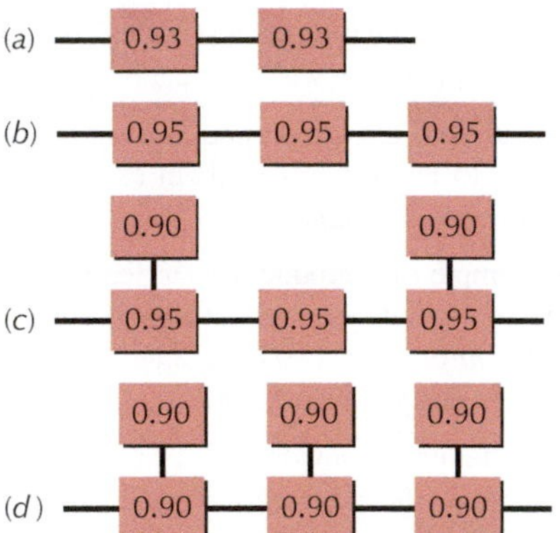

If it costs $1000 for each 90% reliable component, $1500 for each 93% component, $2000 for each 95% reliable component, and $10,000 to replace a failed system, which system would you choose, a or b? c or d?

4.9. Omar Marquez is the audio engineer for Summer Musical Enterprises. The group is considering the purchase of a new sound system consisting of five separate components. The components are arranged in series with identical reliabilities. The Basic system with component reliabilities of 80% costs $1000, the Standard system with component reliabilities of 90% costs $2000, and the Professional system with component reliabilities of 99% costs $5000. The cost of a failure during a performance is $50,000.

a. Calculate the reliability of each system. Which system would you recommend?
b. Omar has learned that each system described above can also be purchased in a Plus configuration, where each component has an identical backup, for double the original cost. Which system would you recommend now?

4.10. Dfinity promises its customers that network services are 90% reliability. The network consists of three serial nodes, each of which must work for the network to be operational. Consistent with its customer guarantee, the reliability of each node is 90%; however, the company has been receiving complaints about its service.

a. Calculate the reliability of the network. Are customer complaints justified?
b. Dfinity is considering adding nodes to its network structure so that each of the current nodes is "backed up" by a lesser node

with a reliability of 80%. What is the reliability of this revised network?

4.11. Identify, Inc. guarantees that it can correctly identify individuals from three pieces of information—date of birth, place of birth, and profession. In reality, whether Identify can keep that guarantee is dependent on the reliability of the information provided. Calculate the probability of correctly identifying an individual if:

a. The three pieces of information each have a 75% chance of being correct.

b. The date of birth is 99% correct, the profession is 50% correct, and the place of birth is 70% correct.

c. The date of birth is found in two publications, each with a 60% chance of being correct, the profession is from an association membership with an 80% accuracy, and the place of birth is self-reported on one site with a 50% chance of veracity and confirmed by a tabloid with a 40% reliability.

d. Which of the scenarios above has the highest reliability?

4.12. You have won two tickets to a Lady Gaga concert in Atlantic City. The concert is three days from now and you have to make travel arrangements. Calculate the reliability of each of the following options:

a. Take the bus from campus to Washington, DC, and from DC to Atlantic City. The bus from campus to DC has a reliability of 90%, and from DC to Atlantic City has a reliability of 93%.

b. Fly directly from the local airport to Atlantic City. The chance that the flight will leave on time and thus arrive in time for the concert is 90%, but there is also a 50% chance that you will be able to beg or borrow enough money to pay for the flight.

c. Drive to Atlantic City. Your car has a 70% chance of making the entire trip without breaking down. Although not recommended, if your car breaks down, you could hitchhike with a 40% chance of getting to Atlantic City unscathed and in time for the concert.

d. Drive to Washington, DC, and take the bus to Atlantic City from there. Your car has a 79% chance of making it to DC. If it doesn't make it to DC, you can hitchhike there with a 40% chance of success.

4.13. Lisa Garrett has been a shift scheduler at a local fast-food chain for the past three years. Although the restaurant's patronage is relatively stable, employee attendance is not. For the most part the restaurant employs students from a nearby high school. Experience has taught Lisa that both the age of the employee and the season of the year affect the reliability of employee attendance. During the school year, seniors are the most responsible and report to work 97% of the time, whereas juniors report only 95% of the time, and sophomores report 90% of the time. After graduation, however, students' thoughts turn to fun and freedom, and everyone's attendance drops to 90%.

a. If a shift consists of two seniors, one junior, and one sophomore, what is the probability that Lisa will be able to operate with a full shift during the school year? During the summer months?

b. Suppose during the summer months, Lisa can find replacement workers 90% of the time. However, during the school year, she is successful only 80% of the time. How do replacement workers improve shift reliability during the summer months? During the school year?

c. Restaurant management recognizes supervisors with a Super Fry award if shifts are completely staffed over 95% of the time. Does Lisa qualify for a Super Fry?

4.14. La Pied manufactures high-quality orthopedic shoes. Over the past five years, the general public has "found" La Pied products, and sales have skyrocketed. One unanticipated result has been a sharp increase in factory returns for repair, since local shoe repair shops do not have the materials or expertise to fix La Pied products. The popular walking sandal has been targeted for redesign. Currently, the leather pieces are glued together, then stitched. There is a 70% chance that the glue will last for the life of the sandal, and a 50% chance that the stitching will remain intact. Determine the sandal's reliability. How would the reliability of the sandal increase if the company adds two more rows of stitching?

4.15. As manager of *The Fitness Center*, Dana is constantly trying new initiatives to keep her clients fit. Recent studies show that using several different cardio regimens for short periods of time is more effective than an extended period of time on one type of equipment. Dana has taken some of the existing cardio equipment and arranged them in a line as follows: stationary bike, treadmill, stair stepper. Clients would select this part of the gym for cardio "circuit training," spending 15 minutes at each piece of equipment for a total cardio workout time of 45 minutes.

a. If the reliability of the bike is 96%, the treadmill is 95%, and the stair stepper is 92%, what is the probability that a client can complete his or her workout uninterrupted by faulty equipment?

b. Dana has added a second cardio "line" for circuit training with the same type of equipment as the first line. This equipment, however, is older with reliabilities of 80% each. If only one client were using the cardio circuit training section of the gym, the second line could be used as a backup for faulty equipment. What is the revised probability of completing a workout uninterrupted?

4.16. The Management Department recently purchased a small copier for faculty use. Although the workload of the office staff has improved somewhat, the secretaries are still making too many trips to the Dean's office when the departmental copier is out of service. Sylvia, the departmental secretary, has been keeping track of failure rates and service times. With a mean time between failures of 100 hours and a mean time to repair of 24 hours, how much of the time is the new copier available for faculty use?

4.17. Karen Perez runs an office supply store that also performs simple office services, such as copying. It is time to purchase a new high-speed copier and Karen has learned that machine uptime is a critical factor in selection. She has gathered the following data on reliability and maintainability for the three copiers she is considering. Given that all other factors are equal, which machine should Karen purchase?

COPIER	MEAN TIME BETWEEN FAILURES (HOURS)	MEAN TIME TO REPAIR (HOURS)
Able Copy	40	1
Business Mate	80	4
Copy Whiz	240	8

4.18. As a regional sales manager, Nora Burke travels frequently and relies on her cell phone to keep up to date with clients. She has tried three different service providers, Airway, Bellular, and CyCom, with varying degrees of success. The number of failures in a typical eight-hour day and the average time to regain service are shown below. Nora's contract is up for renewal. Which cellular service should she use?

CELLULAR CO.	NUMBER OF FAILURES	TIME TO REGAIN SERVICE
Airway	10	2 minutes
Bellular	8	4 minutes
CyCom	3	10 minutes

4.19. Nadia Algar is the overworked IT resource person for her department. In the next round of computer purchases, she is determined to recommend a vendor who does a better job of documenting possible errors in the system and whose customer service line is more responsive to the needs of her colleagues. Nadia compiled the following data over an eight-week observation period. Assuming 40 hours per week, which computer vendor should Nadia pursue?

COMPUTER VENDOR	NUMBER OF PROBLEMS	MEAN TIME TO REACH CUSTOMER SERVICE (HOURS)	MEAN TIME TO FIX PROBLEM (HOURS)
JCN	50	3.0	2.0
Bell	100	2.0	1.0
Comtron	250	1.0	0.5

4.20. Derek is disappointed in his high-speed Internet service. Although the Internet is seldom down, it kicks into slow mode quite often, which Derek considers to be a failure. He has tried three service providers with varying degrees of success. The number of failures in a typical eight-hour day and the average time to regain high-speed service are shown below. Derek must choose one of the following options. Calculate the system availability for each option. Which service would you recommend?

ISP	NUMBER OF FAILURES	TIME TO REGAIN SERVICE
Xceptional	12	2 minutes
Yourizon	4	4 minutes
Zelltell	3	10 minutes

4.21. The PlayBetter Golf Company has experienced a steady decline in sales of golf bags over the past five years. The basic golf bag design has not changed over that period, and PlayBetter's CEO, Jack Palmer, has decided that the time has come for a customer-focused overhaul of the product. Jack read about a new design method called QFD in one of his professional magazines (it was used to design golf balls), and he commissioned a customer survey to provide data for the design process. Customers considered the following requirements essential for any golf bag they would purchase and rated PlayBetter's bag (X) against two competitor bags (A and B) on those requirements.

Construct a house of quality for golf bags. Then write a brief report to Mr. Palmer recommending revisions to the current golf bag design and explaining how those recommendations were determined.

Customer Requirements	Competitive Assessment 1	2	3	4	5
Lightweight		B	A		X
Comfortable carrying strap				XBA	
Stands upright					XBA
Sturdy handle			XBA		
Easy to remove/replace clubs		X		B	A
Easy to identify clubs		X			BA
Protects clubs		B	X	A	
Plenty of compartments		B	X		A
Place for towel			BAX		
Place for scorecard/pencil		XBA			
Easy to clean		X	B		A
Attractive	X		A	B	

4.22. Students often complain that the requirements of assignments or projects are unclear. From the student's perspective, whoever can guess what the professor wants wins the highest grade. Thus, grades appear to be assigned somewhat arbitrarily. If you have ever felt that way, here is your chance to clarify that next project or assignment.

Construct a house of quality for a paper or project. View the professor as the customer. For the perceptual map, have your professor compare one of your papers with typical A, B, or C papers. When you have completed the exercise, give your opinion on the usefulness of QFD for this application.

4.23. Create a house of quality for a computer. Develop customer requirements related to ease of use, cost, capabilities, and connectivity. Make sure the customer requirements are a "wish list" stated in nontechnical terms.

4.24. Create a QFD example from your own experience. Describe the product or service to be designed and then complete a house of quality using representative data. Explain the entries in the house and how target values were reached. Also, describe how other houses might flow from the initial house you built. Finally, relate how QFD improves the design process for the example you chose.

Excel File

Case Problems

Case Problem 4.1 Not My Fault

The online reviews had a familiar ring, and it was not pleasant.

> *"Great book, too many errors."*
>
> *"The errors distracted from the story."*
>
> *"Was I missing something? Like spelcheck?"*
>
> *"Who published this? A bunch of pre-schoolers?"*
>
> *"I think you are missing a line on page 123, or else it belongs on page 231."*
>
> *"itt wuz VeRy harrd to reaed..."*
>
> *"Yikes, takes me back to my days as an English teacher!"*

"Okay," Stephane said, to the project team assembled, "I guess we shouldn't have used a compositor from Russia for this one."

"I personally think it's the copy editor," Chris replied.

"But doesn't the author have some responsibility for submitting a readable manuscript?" piped up Yuhong.

"It's the number of steps in the process, and lack of accountability," George said as he paced back and forth.

Milad was making a list of all the stages and people along the way who handled the manuscript, and thinking about reliability and redundancy. Where were errors introduced? Where were errors caught?

1-Author: 70%—more concerned about content
2-Copy editor: 90% —usually does a good job
3-Compositor: 60%—can introduce errors
4-Proofreader: 80%—works with both copies
5-Author proof: 75%—mostly answers queries from proofreader
6-Production: 80%—could ignore/misplace corrections
7-Final proof: 50%—time-constrained; skims

a. Assume that each step in Milad's list is performed in sequence. What is the reliability of the process?

b. Assume steps 1, 3, and 6 are the components of the process, and 2, 4, 5, and 7 are backups to catch errors. What is the reliability of the process?

c. What suggestions do you have for improving the reliability of the publishing process and final product?

Case Problem 4.2 Greening Product Design

Hal Parker was not convinced that customers cared about green design. "Sure, if it reduces their power consumption, they care, but using less resources to produce the product or using recycled raw materials to begin with? I think our efforts are wasted there."

"But doesn't that save us money in the long run?" commented Sasha Minolta, the finance director.

"If we're in business that long to reap the benefits," Hal retorted. "A recession is not the time to go green."

"Why are you fighting this?" Alex Verera, the CEO, questioned. "Just redesign us a sustainable product and be done with it!"

"That's my point," Hal replied. "Just change the product platform, the basic materials used, the tooling, the operating requirements, the power source, the supplier specs, the quality standards, the production runs, the warranties and take-back conditions, and toss in untested new technology with a product that won't have the feel and performance of the previous version . . . all to say we are green, too. Let's make sure this is really what we want to do. I need some guidance here."

1. Do you think Hal's concerns have merit?
2. How would you present the case that a green design will help the company in the future?
3. Should a company engage in green design if it is not required by law? Under what circumstances? Is a recession an appropriate time to go green?
4. As a consumer, do you select products for their sustainability? What types of products are you more likely to buy green?

Case Problem 4.3 Lean and Mean

Megan McNeil, product manager for Lean and Mean (L&M) weight reduction company, is considering offering its own brand of prepared dinners to its clients. Clients would order the dinners, usually a month's supply at a time, from L&M's website and have them delivered to their home address. The dinners would, of course, encourage weight loss, but would also be more nutritious, tastier, and easier to prepare than current grocery store offerings. The price would most likely be on the high end of the scale.

The product design team has constructed the framework for a house of quality from initial customer interviews. Now the team is set to perform a competitive assessment by selecting three popular grocery store brands and measuring the design characteristics. As the team works on the house, it is anticipated that additional design characteristics may emerge. The target values section of the house would represent L&M's new brand.

Complete the house of quality in Figure 4.15 Lean & Mean House of Quality, and write a report to Megan containing your recommendations for the new product development. Be sure to explain how you arrived at your conclusions.

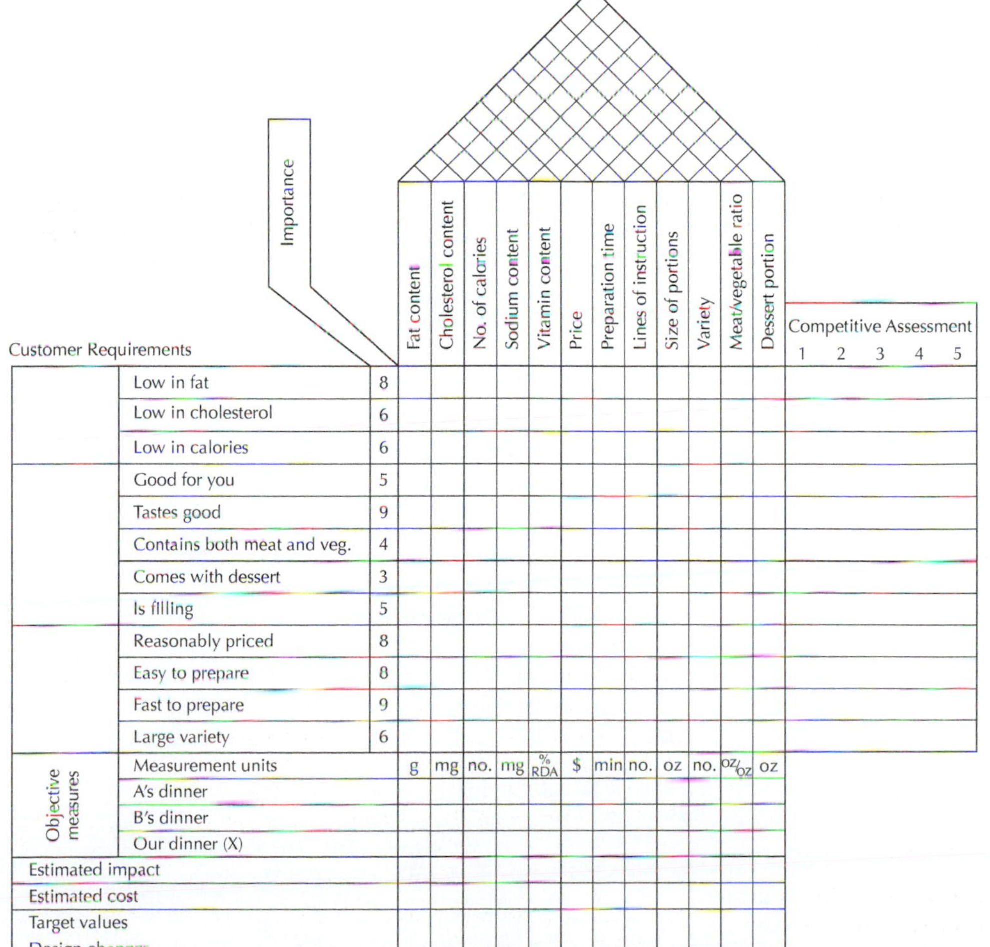

FIGURE 4.15 Lean & Mean House of Quality

References

Atasu, Atalay, and Luk Wassenhove. "Getting to Grips with Take-back Laws." *IESE Insight* (July/August 2011), pp. 29–35.

Baldwin, C., and K. Clark. *Design Rules: The Power of Modularity*. Boston: MIT Press, 2000.

Blackburn, J. (ed.). *Time-Based Competition: The Next Battleground*. Homewood, IL: Irwin, 1991.

Bowen, H. K., K. Clark, and C. Holloway. *The Perpetual Enterprise Machine*. New York: Oxford University Press, 1994.

Goleman, Daniel. *Ecological Intelligence*. New York: Broadway Books, 2009.

Hawkens, Paul. *The Ecology of Commerce*. New York: Harper Collins, 1994.

Hauser, J. R., and D. Clausing. "The House of Quality." *Harvard Business Review* (May–June 1988), pp. 63–73.

Hegarty, S. "How Jeans Conquered the World." BBC World Service (January 28, 2012).

Kelley, T., Jonathan Littman, and Tom Peters, *The Art of Innovation: Lessons in Creativity from IDEO*. New York: Currency/ Doubleday, 2001.

King, B. *Better Designs in Half the Time*. Methuen, MA: GOAL/ QPC, 1989.

Leonard-Barton, D. *Wellsprings of Knowledge: Building and Sustaining the Sources of Innovation*. Boston: Harvard Business School Press, 1995.

McDonough, William, and Michael Braungart, *Cradle to Cradle*, New York: North Point Press. 2002.

Miller, Reed, Jeremy Gregory, Huabo Duan, and Randoph Kirchain. "Characterizing Transboundary Flows of Used Electronics: Summary Report." Materials System Laboratory, MIT (January 2012).

Nidumolu, Ram, C. K. Prahlad, and M. R. Rangaswami, "Why Sustainability Is Now the Key Driver for Innovation." *Harvard Business Review* (September 2009).

Norman, Don. *The Design of Everyday Things*. New York: Hatchett, 2013 (revised version).

Snyder, R. *Fugitive Denim: A Moving Story of People and Pants in the Borderless World of Global Trade*. New York: Norton, 2009.

Stoll, H. "Design for Manufacture." *Manufacturing Engineering* (January 1988), pp. 67–73.

Sullivan, L. P. "Quality Function Deployment." *Quality Progress* 19 (6; 1986), p. 39.

Taguchi, G., and D. Clausing. "Robust Quality." *Harvard Business Review* (January–February 1990), pp. 65–75.

Unruh, Gregory. "The Biosphere Rules," *Harvard Business Review* (February 2008).

Whitney, D. "Manufacturing by Design." *Harvard Business Review* (July–August 1988), pp. 83–91.

Womack, J. P., D. T. Jones, and D. Roos. *The Machine that Changed the World*. New York: Macmillan, 1990.

CHAPTER 5

Service Design

Bloomberg/Getty Images, Inc.

LEARNING OBJECTIVES

After reading this chapter, you will be able to:

- Evaluate the impact of services on jobs and the economy.
- Appreciate and articulate the differences between products and services.
- Utilize tools for envisioning and designing quality services.
- Map out service processes and suggest process improvements.
- Model waiting lines and evaluate their performance for service improvement.

Keep the Music Coming

Innovations in service design can happen more rapidly than in product design, and those innovations can be imitated more readily as well. Take digital music services, for example. From personalizing Internet radio with Pandora (2000), to downloading songs on iTunes (2003), to music subscription services at Spotify (2011), what once was a novelty has become more of a commodity business (see photo). A recent attempt by *The Verge* to compare the top 8 (out of 30+) music streaming services failed to reach a conclusion because virtually all of them offered a library of 30 million songs for about $10 a month. The competition is fierce, with numerous acquisitions and the closing of ten streaming services in 2015 alone. All the major technology players, including Google, Apple, Amazon, and Microsoft, have music streaming sites, not to mention artist-funded sites like Tidal, specialty sites such as Deezer, or Qobuz, or the many new entries that will certainly appear in the coming months.

So what can be done to set one streaming service apart from another? Pandora's algorithmic-fueled Music Genome Project is still the best at matching user preferences to new artists. To capitalize on this "music discovery" skill, Pandora is offering its analytics services to artists and getting into concert promotions and sales. Spotify gives users the best overall capability to connect with friends and share favorite songs, playlists, and artists on a variety of platforms. Spotify, too, wants to share its fan insights data with artists, and is creating more ways to share and promote user-identified trends in music. As for iTunes, its business model is better than the others and the introduction of Apple Music promises to bring more customer-focused and device-specific extras to streaming music.

What will future innovation look like in the music industry? Look for better sound quality, exclusive contracts with artists, more shared and premium services, and maybe (down the road) replacing music labels with an integrated model of music distribution and monetization that includes artist development, audience research, marketing, and live concert promotions.

In this chapter we talk about what sets services apart, what service design entails, and how to make the service process more efficient and customer-focused.

Sources: Rick Stella, "With Grooveshark out of the picture, we pit Spotify against Pandora," *Digital Trends*, (May 8, 2015); Jacob Kastrenakes and Frank Bi, "Here's how Apple Music compares to Spotify, Tidal, and other streaming services," *The Verge*, (June 30, 2015); Ben Popper, "The new reality for the streaming music industry: go big or go home," *The Verge*, (November 17, 2015); J.P. Titlow, "Five Ways Streaming Music Will Change in 2016," *Fast Company*, (December 30, 2015).

The Service Economy

Services are the predominant force in our society. In the United States, services account for 85% of the labor force, 94% of job growth, and 78% of GDP. The rise of the service sector is not just a U.S. phenomenon. Globally, as shown in Figure 5.1, services account for more than 50% of the economies of every nation listed, except China. The impact of supporting services on product success has turned product-producing companies into service providers. Increased outsourcing of business services demands more in-depth understanding of the service product and standards for quality. Service computing has prompted a new level of understanding of customer requirements and design theory. Major societal problems, such as education, healthcare, disaster relief, and government services, depend on complex customer-focused processes and benefit significantly from an innovative and interdisciplinary approach to their study and analysis. This unprecedented shift in customer, corporate, and societal demand for services and the management of corresponding resources has created a critical need for the study, analysis, and design of service systems.

Services represent the fastest-growing sector of the global economy, accounting for two-thirds of global output and nearly 20% of global trade. Services also account for a large percentage of employment worldwide. Figure 5.2 shows U.S. figures on percent of employment by industry sector. The three slices pulled out from the pie are agriculture, which accounts for 1.4% of employment, mining and construction at 4.7% of employment, and manufacturing at 8.1%. The remainder, over 80% of employment, takes place in the service sector. Financial services, government, professional services, and retail, each employ more workers than manufacturing.

The leading service exporters are the United States, United Kingdom, Germany, China, and France. The United States accounts for more trade in commercial services than the United Kingdom and Germany combined, and three times more than China.

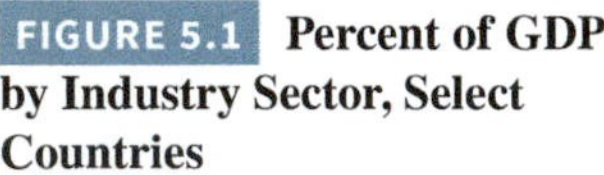

FIGURE 5.1 Percent of GDP by Industry Sector, Select Countries

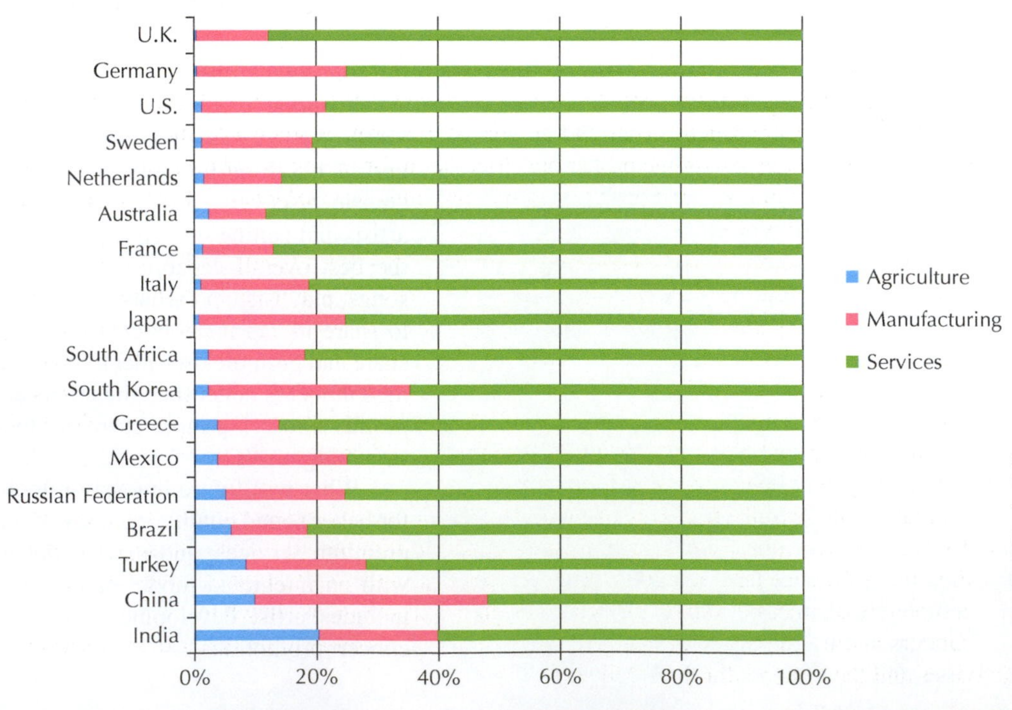

Source: The World Bank, 2015.

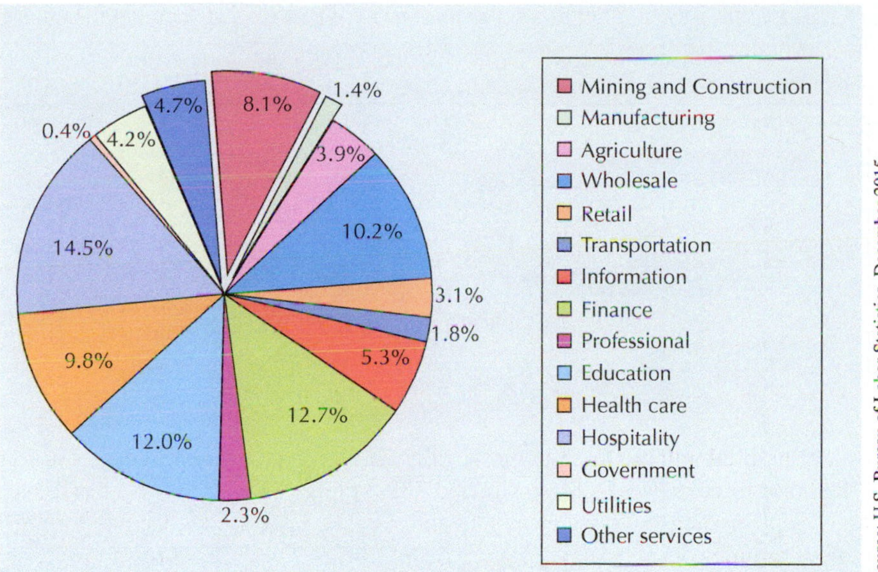

FIGURE 5.2 Percent of Employment by Industry Sector, U.S.

Innovations is services include the popularity of a "sharing economy," that in many ways forgoes ownership. In turn, many goods-producing companies consider their products as conduits for providing services to the customer. Increased outsourcing of business and professional services has prompted a more in-depth understanding of the service "product" and how standards for quality should be set. Similarly, the business model of software as a service (SaaS) has necessitated a new level of understanding of customer requirements and design theory. Major societal problems, such as education, healthcare, disaster relief, and government services, depend on complex customer-focused processes that can benefit significantly from an innovative and interdisciplinary approach to their study and analysis. This unprecedented shift in customer, corporate, and societal demand for services and the management of corresponding resources has created a critical need for the study, analysis, and design of service systems. We do so in this chapter by first defining the characteristics of services and then exploring various aspects of service design.

Characteristics of Services

Services are acts, deeds, performances, or relationships that produce time, place, form, or psychological utilities for customers. A cleaning service saves the customer *time* from doing the chores himself. Department stores and grocery stores provide many commodities for sale in one convenient *place*. An online broker puts together information in a *form* more usable for the investor. A night out at a restaurant or movie provides *psychological* refreshment in the middle of a busy workweek.

Services Acts, deeds, or performances.

Services can also be defined in contrast to goods. A **good** is a tangible object that can be created and sold or used later. A service is intangible and perishable. It is created and consumed simultaneously. Although these definitions may seem straightforward, the distinction between goods and services is not always clear-cut. For example, when we purchase a car, are we purchasing a good or the service of transportation? A flat-screen TV is a manufactured good, but what use is it without the service of television broadcasting? When we go to a fast-food restaurant, are we buying the service of having our food prepared for us, or are we buying goods that happen to be ready-to-eat food items?

Goods Tangible objects.

In reality, almost all purchases of goods are accompanied by *facilitating services*, and almost every service purchase is accompanied by *facilitating goods*. Thus, the key to understanding the difference between goods and services lies in the realization that these items are not completely distinct but rather are two poles on a continuum, as shown in **Figure 5.3**.

Understanding the different characteristics of services can help us better design service activities and the systems for their delivery.

FIGURE 5.3 **A Continuum from Goods to Services**

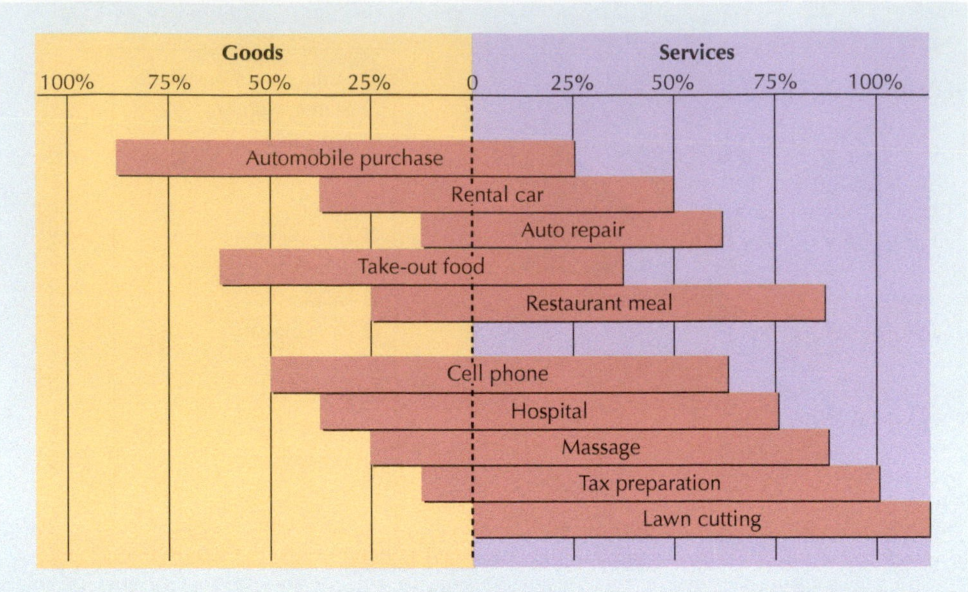

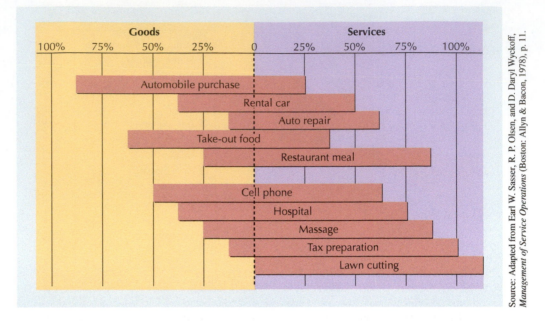

Source: Adapted from Earl W. Sasser, R. P. Olsen, and D. Daryl Wyckoff, *Management of Service Operations* (Boston: Allyn & Bacon, 1978), p. 11.

Services can be distinguished from manufacturing by the following eight characteristics. Although not all services possess each of these characteristics, they do exhibit at least some of them to some degree.

1. ***Services are intangible.*** It is difficult to design something you cannot see, touch, store on a shelf, or try on for size. Services are *experienced*, and that experience may be different for each individual customer. Designing a service involves describing what the customer is supposed to "experience," which can be a difficult task. Designers begin by compiling information on the way people think, feel, and behave (called *psychographics*).

   Because of its intangibility, consumers perceive a service to be more risky to purchase than a product. Cues (such as physical surroundings, server's demeanor, and service guarantees) need to be included in service design to help form or reinforce accurate perceptions of the service experience and reduce the consumer's risk.

   The quality of a service experience depends largely on the customer's service *expectations*. Expectations can differ according to a customer's knowledge, experience, and self-confidence.

   Customers also have different expectations of different types of service providers. You probably expect more from a department store than from a discount store, or from a car dealer's service center than from an independent repair shop. Understanding the customer and his or her expectations is essential in designing good service.

2. ***Service output is variable.*** This is true because of the various service providers employed and the variety of customers they serve, each with his or her own special needs. Even though customer demands vary, the service experience is expected to remain consistent. According to a recent survey, the most important measures of service quality to the customer are reliability and consistency. Service design, then, must strive for predictability or robustness. Examples of services known for their consistency include McDonald's, Marriott, and ServiceMaster. Extensive employee training, set operating procedures, and standardized materials, equipment, and physical environments are used by these companies to increase consistency.

3. ***Services have higher customer contact.*** The service "encounter" between service provider and customer *is* the service in many cases. Making sure the encounter is a positive one is part of service design. This involves giving the service provider the skills and authority necessary to complete a customer transaction successfully. Studies show a direct link between service provider motivation and customer satisfaction. Moreover, service providers are not motivated primarily by compensation but rather by concurrence with the firm's "service concept" and being able to perform their job competently.

   High customer contact can interfere with the efficiency of a service and make it difficult to control its quality (i.e., there is no opportunity for testing and rework). However, direct contact with customers can also be an advantage for services. Observing

Along the Supply Chain

Uber and the Sharing Economy

QUIQUE GARCIA/Getty Images, Inc.

First there was Zipcar and BikeShare, where customers could conveniently rent a vehicle or bike near their home or place of work; then came Airbnb, Uber, and Snapgoods, where ordinary people could use their assets (homes, cars, household goods) to bring in extra cash. Now a full-blown sharing economy exists that supplies income to providers and new functionality to users (e.g., Dogvacy, TaskRabbit, Getaround, Lyft, LendingClub, Fon, and Turo).

Take Uber, for example, with its easy-to-use apps, quick service, and affordable prices. Uber acts as a broker, connecting people who need rides with people who can provide them. Add cool cars (UberBLACK and UberLUX), larger vehicles (UberSUV and UberHAUL), ride sharing (UberPOOL), and new modes of transportation (UberTAXI and UberCOPTER). Look for new logistical opportunities to deliver packages (UberRUSH), groceries (UberFRESH), and restaurant meals (UberEATS). Use Uber data to recommend services or activities, send messages or predict behavior, and when technology allows, send out an autonomous vehicle coordinated to a customer's daily schedule. That's Uber's plan.

Innovations such as shared services are transforming industries. It may seem simple for a company like Uber to establish an online marketplace where providers and customers match needs, but it can actually be quite complex. Companies that run this type of business are data- and technology-driven, and they are constantly looking for ways to use data to improve their services or gain a competitive edge. Operating in 330 cities and 59 countries, Uber's one million active drivers transport millions of customers each day. Uber maintains a vast database on its drivers, wherever they are located, so that passengers can be matched quickly with available drivers. Data about passenger preferences is collected, too, for future use. And both the driver and the passenger can submit reviews of the service encounter.

Fares are calculated automatically, using GPS, street data and, of course, Uber's own algorithms that make adjustments based on trip time (because time, not distance, drives fares) and other factors. "Surge pricing" kicks in during busy or difficult times to incentivize drivers to become active. Sometimes the results are extreme, as when one passenger paid $137 a mile on New Year's Eve in New York City, or when a Washington, DC, passenger paid $640 for a $50 trip during a snowstorm. New York City has since negotiated a cap on surge pricing during inclement weather at 3.5 times the normal rate. In the meantime, Uber has applied for a patent on its special surge-pricing model.

1. How far do you think the shared economy can go? Give examples of services that you would be willing to use or host peer-to-peer. What new shared services are on the horizon?
2. Compare Uber and Airbnb. What kind of support (and tools) does each company give to its providers? What is different about the types of customers, service, company culture, and expectations for service?
3. Explore how big data is used at Uber. What benefits does it produce? What are possible drawbacks from the collection and use of passenger and driver data?
4. The Uber phenomenon is changing the world of work. Discuss.

Source: Emily Badger, "Why Uber is joining the race to dominate urban logistics," *The Washington Post*, (April 8, 2014); Max Chafkin, "What Makes Uber Run," *Fast Company*, Issue 199 (October 2015); "The Rise of the Sharing Economy," *The Economist*, (March 9, 2013); Bernard Marr, "The Amazing Ways Uber is using Big Data," *Data Science Central*, (May 7, 2015).

customers experiencing a service generates new service ideas and facilitates feedback for improvements to existing services.

4. ***Services are perishable.*** Because services can't be inventoried, the timing and location of delivery are important. Service design should define not only *what* is to be delivered but also *where* and *when*.
5. ***The service and the service delivery are inseparable.*** That means service design and process design must occur concurrently. (This is one area in which services have an advantage over manufacturing—it has taken manufacturing a number of years to realize the benefits of concurrent design.) In addition to deciding what, where, and when, service design also specifies *how* the service should be provided. "How" decisions include the degree of customer participation in the service process, which tasks should be done in the presence of the customer (called front-room activities) and which should be done out of the customer's sight (back-room activities), the role and authority of the service provider in delivering the service, and the balance of "touch" versus "tech" (i.e., how automated the service should be).
6. ***Services tend to be decentralized and geographically dispersed.*** Many service employees are on own to make decisions. Although this can present problems, careful service design

will help employees deal successfully with contingencies. Multiple service outlets can be a plus in terms of rapid prototyping. New ideas can be field-tested with a minimum disturbance to operations. McDonald's considers each of its outlets a "laboratory" for new ideas.

7. ***Services are consumed more often than products***, so there are more opportunities to succeed or fail with the customer. Jan Carlzon, former president of SAS Airlines, calls these opportunities "moments of truth." Services are confronted with thousands of moments of truth each day. Careful design and redesign of the service encounter can help make each moment of truth a positive experience. In a sense, the service environment lends itself more readily to continuous improvement than does the manufacturing environment.
8. ***Services can be easily emulated.*** Competitors can copy new or improved services quickly. New ideas are constantly needed to stay ahead of the competition. As a result, new service introductions and service improvements occur even more rapidly than new product introductions.

The Service Design Process

Services that are allowed to just happen rarely meet customer needs. World-class services that come to mind—Amazon, Nordstrom, UPS, and Disney World—are all characterized by impeccable design. Amazon is constantly updating its website to make searching and purchasing easier, and creates a profile of each customer that is pretty savvy at recommending what to purchase next; Nordstrom creates a pleasurable shopping environment with well-stocked shelves, live music, fresh flowers in the dressing rooms, and legendary salespersons; UPS is relentless at designing an efficient and responsive delivery process; and Disney World plans every aspect of its magical kingdom to please that special guest.

Service design is more comprehensive and occurs more often than product design. The inherent variability of service processes requires that the service system be carefully designed. **Figure 5.4** shows the service design process beginning with a service concept and ending with service delivery.

FIGURE 5.4 The Service Design Process

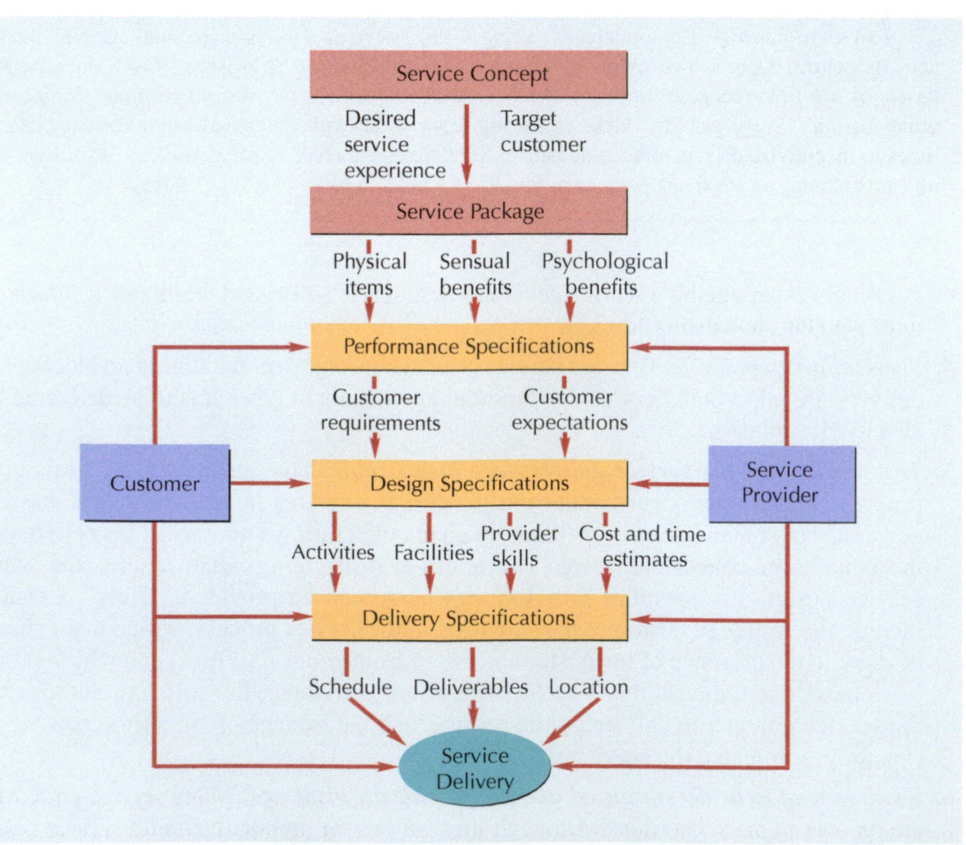

Along the Supply Chain

Warby-Parker Game Changer

Warby Parker, rated the #1 most innovative company by *Fast Company* magazine, designs and sells eyeglasses primarily over the Internet. Why the Internet? Because it's easier, quicker, cheaper, and the market reach is larger. Why eyeglasses? Because the cost of glasses is astronomical ($400–$700 a pair), the process of buying new glasses is slow and laborious, and customer service is terrible.

The founders of Warby Parker, four Wharton students, wondered why eyeglasses were so expensive and why the process took so long. After some investigation into the business landscape of the industry, they found that one company, the Italian frame-maker Luxottica, controls 80% of the eyewear market. Luxottica designs and manufactures over 30 different brands of eyeglasses (including Ray-Ban, Oakley, Prada, Ralph Lauren, Tiffany, and more), serves as wholesaler and distributor for each brand, sells the glasses through its 20 different retail store chains (LensCrafters, Pearle Vision, Sunglass Hut, Sears Optical, Glasses.com, etc.), and manages the largest vision insurance plan in the United States (EyeMed Vision Care) which serves over 3400 corporations. With that much control over the industry, it is no surprise that the markup on frames alone is 20 times the cost of manufacture.

Enter Warby with cool designs, a $95 price tag (for frames and prescription lenses), a 7–10 day turnaround, and a "buy one, give one" promise. As shown in the photo, the product is made of good quality materials with precision processing and sought-after features (such as UV coating, ultra thin lens, etc.). Frames are designed internally and sourced directly from the manufacturer—no middleman. Glasses are sold directly to the customer online (with no need for insurance subsidies) in a fun, easy, and quick manner. To help select a pair, Warby offers a five pair/five days try-on program, #warbyhometryon feedback, a virtual online model, and easy measuring tools. Uploading a prescription is as simple as snapping a photo. Warby has physical stores in urban areas, too. Or you could wait for the Warby Class Trip school bus (outfitted as an optical store) to visit your location.

Rob Kim/Getty Images, Inc.

1. Visit Luxottica's website and note the number of brands and retail chains it owns. Comment on the degree of vertical integration at Luxottica and its control over the competitive landscape. What does the managed vision care plan add to its portfolio? How vertically integrated is Warby Parker?
2. Would you shop online at Warby Parker? Why or why not? What features or services does Warby *not* provide that you would find in traditional optical centers? How does it make up for the absence of those services?
3. In the eyeglass industry, was it the product design or the service design that was most in need of revision? Describe how both designs support the Warby Parker vision (no pun intended).
4. What other kinds of businesses can you think of that need major overhauls? Why?

Sources: Max Chafkin, "Warby Parker Sees the Future of Retail," *Fast Company*, March 2015; Neal Blumenthal, "How We took on Goliath and Won," *Inc. Magazine*, May 2015; Dean Crutchfield. "Luxottica sees itself as king, raising questions about brand authenticity," *Forbes*, (November 27, 2012).

The **service concept** defines the target customer and the desired customer experience. It also defines how the service is different from others and how it will compete in the marketplace. Sometimes services are successful because their service concept fills a previously unoccupied niche or differs from the generally accepted mode of operation. Uber, Airbnb, Netflix, and all manner of social networking sites are good examples of innovative service concepts. Even product designers, such as Warby Parker, are creating new service concepts to accompany their products.

Service concept The purpose of a service; it defines the target market and the customer experience.

From the service concept, a **service package** is created to meet customer needs. The package consists of a mixture of physical items, sensual benefits, and psychological benefits. For a restaurant the physical items consist of the facility, food, drinks, tableware, napkins, and other touchable commodities. The sensual benefits include the taste and aroma of the food and the sights and sounds of the people. Psychological benefits are rest and relaxation, comfort, status, and a sense of well-being.

Service package The mixture of physical items, sensual benefits, and psychological benefits.

Effective service design recognizes and defines *all* the components of a service package. Finding the appropriate mix of physical items and sensual and psychological benefits, and designing them to be consistent with each other and the service concept, are also important. A fast-food restaurant promises nourishment with speed. The customer is served quickly and is expected to consume the food quickly. Thus, the tables, chairs, and booths are not designed to be comfortable, nor does their arrangement encourage lengthy or personal conversations. The service package is consistent. This is not the case for an upscale restaurant located in a renovated train station. The food is excellent, but it is difficult to enjoy a full-course meal sitting on wooden benches in a drafty facility, where conversations echo and tables shake when the trains pass by. In the hospitality industry, Marriott Corporation is known for its careful design of specialty hotels. From its Courtyard Marriott to Fairfield Inn to residential centers, each facility "fits" its clientele with a well-researched service package.

Performance specifications Outline expectations and requirements.

Design specifications Describe the service in enough detail to be replicated.

Delivery specifications Specify schedules, deliverables, location.

From the service package, service specifications are developed for performance, design, and delivery. **Performance specifications** outline expectations and requirements for general and specific customers. Performance specifications are converted into design specifications and, finally, delivery specifications (in lieu of manufacturing specifications).

Design specifications must describe the service in sufficient detail for the desired service experience to be replicated for different individuals at numerous locations. The specifications typically consist of activities to be performed, skill requirements and guidelines for service providers, and cost and time estimates. Facility size, location, and layout, as well as equipment needs, are also included. **Delivery specifications** outline the steps required in the work process, including the work schedule, deliverables, and the locations at which the work is to be performed.

The Service-Process Matrix

Notice in Figure 5.4 that both customers and service providers may be involved in determining performance, design, and delivery specifications. Service processes can be classified according to the degree of customization (involvement of the customer in service design and delivery) and labor intensity (involvement of the service provider in service design and delivery).

Figure 5.5 shows a service-process matrix based on these two service characteristics. A *professional service*, such as accountant, lawyer, or doctor, is highly customized and very labor intensive. A *service shop*, such as schools and hospitals, is less customized and labor intensive but still attentive to individual customers. A *mass service*, such as

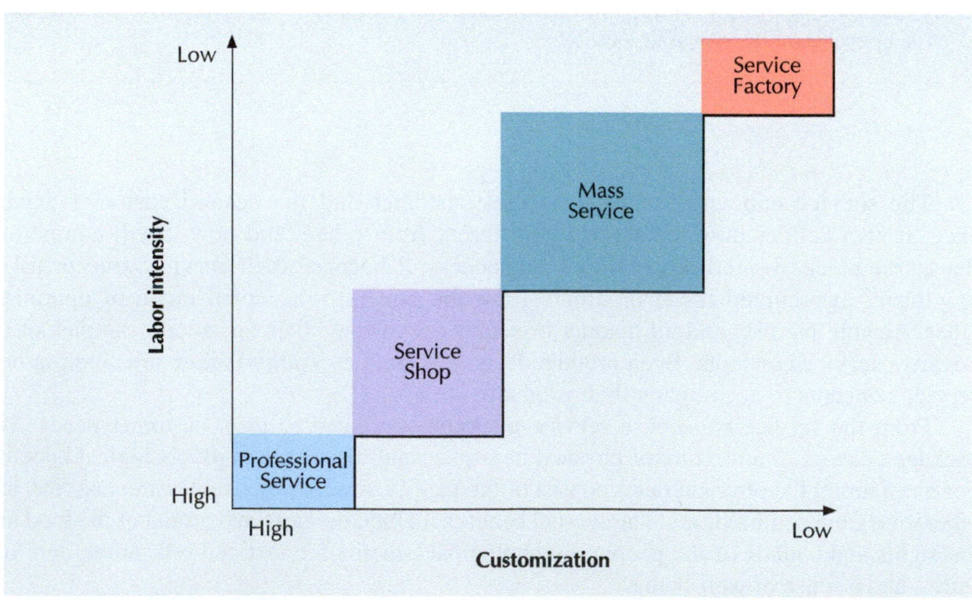

Source: Adapted from Roger Schmenner, "How Can Service Businesses Survive and Prosper?" *Sloan Management Review* 27(3), 29.

FIGURE 5.5 The Service-Process Matrix

TABLE 5.1 Differences in Design for High-Contact and Low-Contact Services

DESIGN DECISION	HIGH-CONTACT SERVICE	LOW-CONTACT SERVICE
Facility location	Convenient to customer	Near labor or transportation source
Facility layout	Must look presentable, accommodate customer needs, and facilitate interaction with customer	Designed for efficiency
Quality control	More variable since customer is involved in process; customer expectations and perceptions of quality may differ; customer present when defects occur	Measured against established standards; testing and rework possible to correct defects
Capacity	Excess capacity required to handle peaks in demand	Planned for average demand
Worker skills	Must be able to interact well with customers and use judgment in decision making	Technical skills
Scheduling	Must accommodate customer schedule	Customer concerned only with completion date
Service process	Mostly front-room activities; service may change during delivery in response to customer	Mostly back-room activities; planned and executed with minimal interference
Service package	Varies with customer; includes environment as well as actual service	Fixed, less extensive

Source: Adapted from R. Chase, N. Aquilano, and R. Jacobs, *Operations Management for Compensative Advantage* (New York: McGraw-Hill, 2001), p. 210.

retailing and banking, offers the same basic services to all customers and allows less interaction with the service provider. Services with the least degree of customization and labor intensity, such as airlines and trucking, are most like manufactured products and are thus best processed by a *service factory*. Examples of each kind of service are shown in the photos on the next page.

The degree of contact between the customer and service provider has an impact on how individual services are designed and delivered. A large lecture class is taught differently from a senior-level seminar class. Charter airline flights entail more customer and provider participation than a commercial flight. Commissioning a work of art or custom building a home can involve the customer throughout the design and delivery process. Table 5.1 describes the design decisions involved in high-contact versus low-contact services. Think about how these decisions affect the operations and supply chain system.

Tools for Service Design

There are many different tools for designing services. Quality function deployment (QFD), discussed in the previous chapter, has wide application in services. Other common tools are service blueprints, scripting, servicescapes, and waiting line analysis.

Service Blueprinting

Service operations involve several different players (the customer, other customers in the system, the primary service provider, other service providers), both front and back room operations, and different opportunities for interaction among the players during the service process. **Service blueprinting** is the process of recording in graphical form the activities and interactions in a service process. The term *blueprinting* is used to reinforce the idea that services need to be as carefully designed as a physical product and documented with a blueprint of their own.

Service blueprinting A specialized flow chart used for service processes.

Less Labor Intensive, Less Customized

Service Factory. *Electricity is a commodity available continuously to customers.*

Alamy Images

© Alan King/Alamy

Mass Service. *A retail store provides a standard array of products from which customers may choose.*

Gary Conner/PhotoEdit

Service Shop. *A professor interacts with a classroom of students. Although a lecture may be prepared in advance, its delivery is affected by the students in each class, and the students chosen to demonstrate a problem.*

SuperStock, Inc.

Professional Service. *A doctor provides personal service to each patient based on extensive training in medicine.*

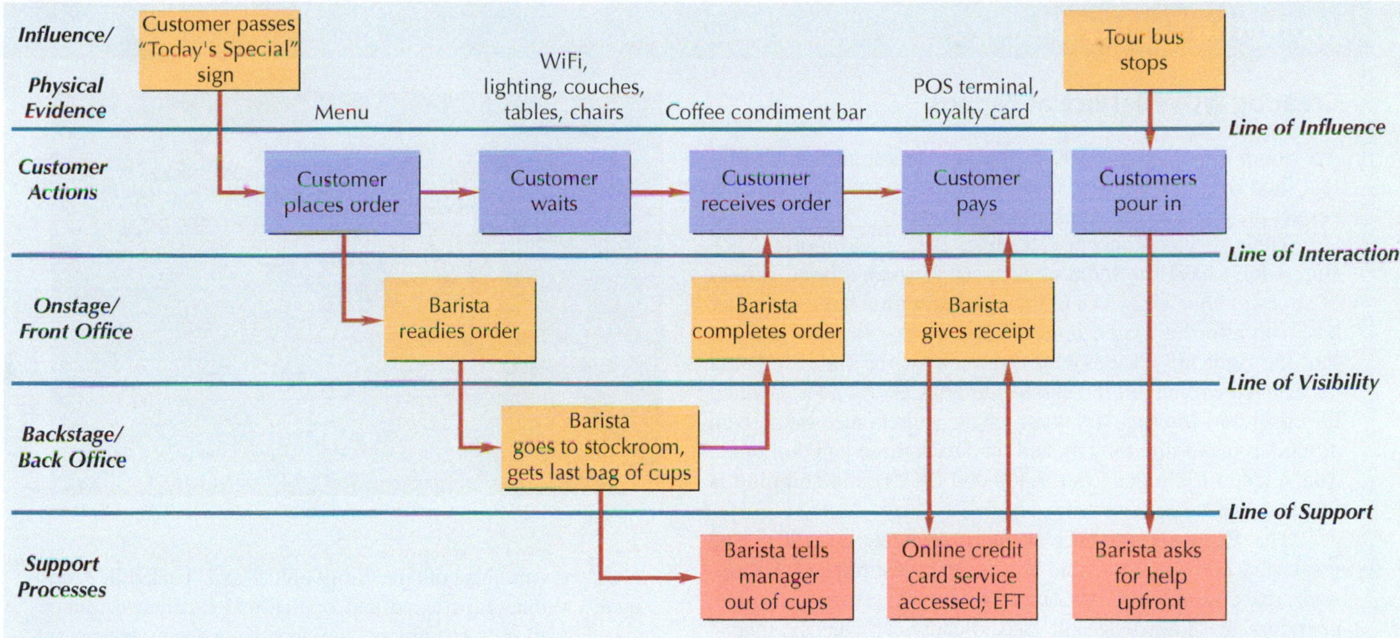

FIGURE 5.6 **A Service Blueprint for a Coffee Shop**

Figure 5.6 shows a sample service blueprint for a coffee shop operation. The blueprint consists of five components or lanes: (1) influence and physical evidence; (2) customer actions; (3) onstage provider actions (i.e., front office); (4) backstage provider actions (i.e., back office); and (5) support processes. Lines separate these components of the service encounter. The **line of influence** shows activities designed to influence the customer to enter the service facility, and the physical evidence to take action throughout the service process. The **line of interaction** is where the customer interacts with the service provider face-to-face. The **line of visibility** separates front-office (or onstage) activities from back-office (or backstage) activities. In this example, the barista prepares the coffee in front of the customer, but must go backstage to retrieve cups from the stockroom. The **line of support** is where the service provider interacts with backstage support personnel to complete their tasks. Moving these various lines on the service blueprint allows the designer to experiment with expanding or decreasing the activities in each area. For example, the barista could disappear behind a curtain to prepare the coffee, or the customer could serve the coffee herself and interact with the service provider only when paying.

line of influence Signs or activities that influences a customer to seek a service.

line of interaction Point where a customer and service provider interact.

line of visibility Point that separates front-office and back-office activities.

line of support Point where service provider interacts with support personnel.

In services there are constant tradeoffs between customer service and efficiency. Starbucks has redesigned the role of its barista several times, at one point reducing the number of baristas and thus requiring them to prepare several customer orders at a time, and more recently, increasing quality by asking baristas to prepare no more than two orders at a time, starting the second order while the first is being readied. A service blueprint can specify the exact process for serving a customer (including whether a barista rings up an order or simply prepares the order) and can codify rules (such as when to call in additional baristas). The consistency with which a service is provided is an important measure of service quality and customer satisfaction.

Front-Office and Back-Office Activities

In manufacturing firms, the focus of activities is on the back office (i.e., producing products efficiently), whereas in service firms, the focus is on the front office, interacting with the customer. Every firm needs both a front and back office, but firms may structure these in different ways.

In the front office, the customer interface can be an individual, the service provider, or a self-service kiosk or machine. The interactions in the front office influence the customer's

Along the Supply Chain

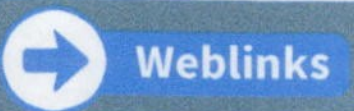

Creating WOW Service at Zappos

James Leynse/Getty Images, Inc.

Are you a Zappos customer? If you love shoes, have a hard-to-find shoe size, or hate to go from store to store trying to find that perfect fit, you'll be a Zappos customer soon.

Their service concept is simple. Bricks-and-mortar shoe stores don't have the room or finances to stock a large variety of shoes or shoe sizes. An online retailer with a large customer base can afford a larger, more diverse stock—but how do you find the right fit? Zappos seeks to replicate the shoe shopping experience without all the hassle. Order as many shoes as you'd like over the Internet, try them on in your home, wear them around to make sure they fit, and send back those you don't like. The selection is huge (over 2,500,000 SKUs) and shipping is fast and free.

The Zappos experience includes free returns, a fast and responsive website, top-name brands, elaborate product descriptions, real customer reviews, and a 24-hour call center. Call center operators are knowledgeable and friendly, answer the phone within 20 seconds, have the authority to resolve disputes and spend as much time as necessary with each customer (longest recorded customer call—10 hours). Most orders are updated to next-day delivery, and customers have 365 days to return unwanted merchandise. Collectively, these deliver WOW service, one of Zappos' ten core values.

So how does Zappos do it? To compensate for free shipping and call center expenses, the company has to be very cost conscious. There are no fancy headquarters or separate offices for executives. The West Coast and East Coast locations are smart and low-cost. Programming is coded in-house using open source software. Warehousing and distribution are handled at its own fulfillment center. The fulfillment center is located near UPS's worldwide air hub (Worldport) at the Louisville, Kentucky, airport where hourly pickups from UPS allow overnight delivery to more locations. Returns are sent by ground. Zappos trucks pick up merchandise from its suppliers at the docks to save time and freight costs. At the warehouse, state-of-the-art robots (from Kiva) transport shelves stocked with needed items to workers who *pick* a customer's order. Lights and heat are provided only in the picking area of the warehouse, thus saving energy costs. Supplier visibility into Zappos' on-hand inventory, sales, prices, and margins encourages collaborative ordering strategies and lower inventory levels. Data on consumer buying habits improve forecasts of demand. Shoes are sold at retail, seldom discounted. Excess inventory is sent to Zappo-owned 6pm.com, rather than marked down.

Zappos masters both the "front office" and "back office" with a quality online experience and operational excellence. Zappos knows how to treat customers, how to run a website, how to fulfill orders quickly and efficiently, and how to manage inventory. And now it does that for other companies, too. Look for "Powered by Zappos" on your favorite website. As CEO Tony Hsieh says, "Zappos is a service company that just happens to sell shoes," and now other merchandise, too.

1. Zappos has an interesting corporate culture. Go to the company website and read about the company and its management. What advantage does this culture provide?
2. Amazon now owns Zappos. What are the similarities and differences between the two companies? What changes would you anticipate at each company as a result of the merger?
3. Read about UPS Worldport on the web and watch a video about the facility on National Geographic's Ultimate Factories. How does the strategic partnership with UPS enhance Zappos' customer service model?

Sources: Based on Tony Hsieh, "Why I Sold Zappos," *Inc.* (June 6, 2010); "Zappos.com: Developing a Supply Chain to Deliver WOW," Stanford School of Business, Case GS-65, 2009; Jessie Scanlon, "How Kiva Robots Help Zappos and Walgreens," *Business Week* (April 15, 2009); Christopher Palmeri, "Zappos Retails Its Culture," *Business Week* (December 30, 2009); Martha White, "Zappos Service Call Lasts 10 Hours," NBC News.com, (October 31, 2012); National Geographic Ultimate Factories, http://channel.nationalgeographic.com/channel/ultimate-factories/videos/ups-worldport/.

perception of the service and thus are critical to a successful design. Typical front office goals are courtesy, transparency, responsiveness, usability, and fun.

The back-office processes material or information to support the front-office needs. Typical goals of the back office are efficiency, productivity, standardization, and scalability.

Obvious conflicts exist between front and back offices. Connecting the front and back offices in a meaningful way and encouraging the flow of information and support are two of the challenges of service design. Designing the service with an eye to the entire system will help alleviate some of the tensions. Mass customization is an example of a front/back compromise. Instead of giving customers the freedom to order anything they want, present a menu of options from which the customer may choose. This provides some stability to the back office, while also being responsive to the customer.

Servicescapes

It is precisely because services are so intangible that physical cues to service quality are needed. **Servicescapes** design: (1) the space and function where the service takes places; (2) the ambient conditions, such as music, temperature, décor, and noise; and (3) signs, symbols, and artifacts. It is important that the servicescape be consistent with the service concept, and that all the elements be consistent with each other.

Servicescapes The design of the physical environment (including signs, symbols, and artifacts) in which a service takes place.

Servicescapes have proved to be extremely important to customer perceptions of service quality and to their satisfaction with the service.

Quantitative Techniques

There are many quantitative techniques for improving the service process. One of the most common and powerful is waiting line analysis, covered in the next several sections.

Waiting Line Analysis for Service Improvement

Anyone who goes shopping, to the post office, or to a movie experiences the inconvenience of waiting in line. Not only do people spend time waiting in lines, but machinery waits in line to be serviced or repaired, trucks line up to be loaded or unloaded at a shipping terminal, and planes wait to take off and land. Waiting takes place in virtually every productive process or service. Since the time spent by people and things waiting in line is a valuable resource, the reduction of waiting time is an important aspect of operations management.

Companies are able to reduce waiting time and provide faster service by increasing their service capacity, which usually means adding more servers—that is, more tellers, more mechanics, or more checkout clerks. However, increasing service capacity has a monetary cost, and therein lies the basis of waiting line analysis: the tradeoff between the cost of improved service and the cost of making customers wait.

Waiting lines are analyzed with a set of mathematical formulas that comprise a field of study called *queuing theory*. Different queuing models and mathematical formulas exist to deal with different types of waiting line systems. Although we discuss several of the most common types of queuing systems, we do not investigate the mathematical derivation of the queuing formulas. They are generally complex and not really pertinent to our understanding of the use of waiting line analysis to improve service.

Elements of Waiting Line Analysis

Waiting lines form because people or things arrive at a server faster than they can be served. This does not mean that the service operation is understaffed or does not have the capacity to handle the influx of customers. Most businesses and organizations have sufficient serving capacity available to handle their customers *in the long run*. Waiting lines result because customers do not arrive at a constant, evenly paced rate, nor are they all served in an equal amount of time. Customers arrive at random times, and the time required to serve each individual is not the same. A waiting line is continually increasing and decreasing in length (and is sometimes empty) but in the long run approaches an average length and waiting time. For example, your local bank may have enough tellers to serve an average of 100 customers in an hour, and in a particular hour only 60 customers might arrive. However, at specific points in time during the hour, waiting lines may form because more than an average number of customers arrive and they have transactions that require more than the average amount of time.

Decisions about waiting lines and the management of waiting lines are based on these averages for customer arrivals and service times. They are used in queuing formulas or models to compute **operating characteristics** such as the average number of customers waiting in

Operating characteristics Average values for characteristics that describe the performance of a waiting line system.

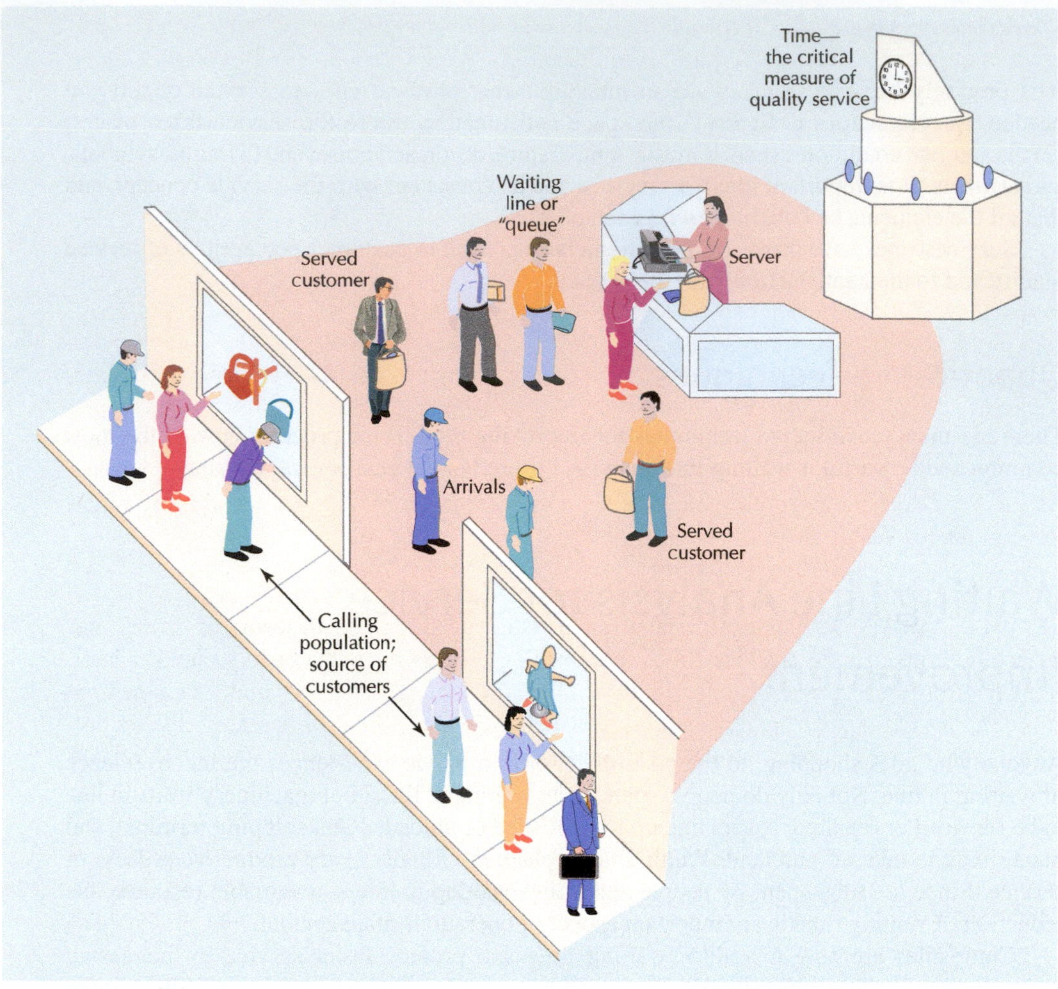

FIGURE 5.7 **Elements of a Waiting Line System**

line and the average time a customer must wait in line. Different sets of formulas are used, depending on the type of waiting line system being investigated. A bank drive-up teller window at which one bank clerk serves a single line of customers in cars is different from a single line of passengers at an airline ticket counter that are served by three or four airline agents. In this section, we present the elements that make up waiting lines before looking at waiting line formulas.

Queue A single waiting line.

The Waiting Line The basic elements of a waiting line are the calling population, arrivals, servers, and the waiting line or **queue**. The relationship between these elements is shown in Figure 5.7 for the simplest type of *waiting line system*, a single server with a single queue. Following is a brief description of each of these waiting line elements.

Calling population The source of customers; infinite or finite.

The Calling Population In our discussions of waiting lines, a customer is a person or thing that wants service from an operation. The **calling population** is the source of the customers to the waiting line system, and it can be either *infinite* or *finite*. An infinite calling population assumes such a large number of potential customers that it is always possible for one more customer to arrive to be served. For example, for the department store in Figure 5.7, we assume the calling population is infinite; to have, that is, the whole town or geographic area.

A finite calling population has a specific, countable number of potential customers. Examples of a finite calling population are a repair person in a shop who is responsible for a fixed number of machines to work on, a trucking terminal that services a fleet of ten trucks, or a nurse assigned to attend to only 12 patients.

The Arrival Rate The **arrival rate** is the rate at which customers arrive at the service facility during a specified period. This rate can be estimated from empirical data derived from studying the system or a similar system, or it can be an average of these empirical data. For example, if 100 customers arrive at a store checkout counter during a 10-hour day, we could say the arrival rate averages 10 customers per hour. However, it might be that no customers would arrive during one hour and 20 customers would arrive during another hour. Arrivals are assumed to be independent of each other and to vary randomly over time.

Arrival rate The frequency at which customers arrive at a waiting line; most frequently described by a Poisson distribution and indicated by λ.

The variability of arrivals at a service facility often conform to a probability distribution. Arrivals could be described by many distributions, but it has been determined (through years of research and the practical experience of people in the field of queuing) that the number of arrivals per unit of time at a service facility can frequently be described by a *Poisson distribution*. In queuing, the average arrival rate, or how many customers arrive during a period of time, is signified by λ.

For the models presented in this chapter, we assume there is no *balking* (refusing to join a line), *reneging* (leaving a line), or *jockeying* (changing lines) by customers in the waiting line system. We also assume that the arrival rate is less than the service rate (or else the line would grow infinitely long).

Service Times In waiting line analysis arrivals are described in terms of a *rate*, and service in terms of *time*. **Service times** in a queuing process may also be any one of a large number of different probability distributions. The distribution most commonly assumed for service times is the negative *exponential distribution*. Although this probability distribution is for service *times*, service must be expressed as a *rate* to be compatible with the arrival rate. The average service rate, or how many customers can be served in a period of time, is expressed as μ.

Service time The time required to serve a customer, most frequently described by the negative exponential distribution; the service rate, μ, is total time/service time.

Empirical research has shown that the assumption of negative exponentially distributed service times is not valid as often as is the assumption of Poisson-distributed arrivals. For actual applications of queuing analysis, the assumptions for both arrival rate and service time distribution would have to be verified.

Interestingly, if service times are exponentially distributed, then the service rate is Poisson distributed. For example, if the average time to serve a customer is three minutes (and exponentially distributed), then the average service rate is 20 customers per hour (and Poisson distributed). The converse holds true for Poisson arrivals. If the arrival rate is Poisson distributed, then the time between arrivals is exponentially distributed.

Queue Discipline and Length The **queue discipline** is the order in which waiting customers are served. The most common type of queue discipline is *first come, first served*—the first person or item waiting in line is served first. Other disciplines are possible. For example, a machine operator might stack parts to be worked on beside a machine so that the last part is on top of the stack and will be selected first. This queue discipline is *last in, first out*. Or the machine operator might reach into a box full of parts and select one at random. This queue discipline is *random*. Often customers are scheduled for service according to a predetermined appointment, such as patients at a dentist's office or diners at a restaurant where reservations are required. These customers are taken according to a prearranged schedule regardless of when they arrive at the facility. Another example of the many types of queue disciplines is when customers are processed alphabetically according to their last names, such as at school registration or at job interviews.

Queue discipline The order in which customers are served; most commonly first come, first served.

In manufacturing operations, sometimes jobs with the shortest expected processing times are selected first in order to get the most jobs processed in the shortest time period. In emergency services like emergency rooms at hospitals, the most critical problem is typically served first.

Queues can be of an infinite or finite size or length. An **infinite queue** can be of any size, with no upper limit, and is the most common queue structure. For example, it is assumed that the waiting line at a movie theater could stretch through the lobby and out the door if necessary. A **finite queue** is limited in size. An example is the driveway at a bank teller window that can accommodate only a limited number of cars before it backs up to the street.

Infinite queue Can be of any length.

Finite queue The length is limited.

(a) Single-server waiting line

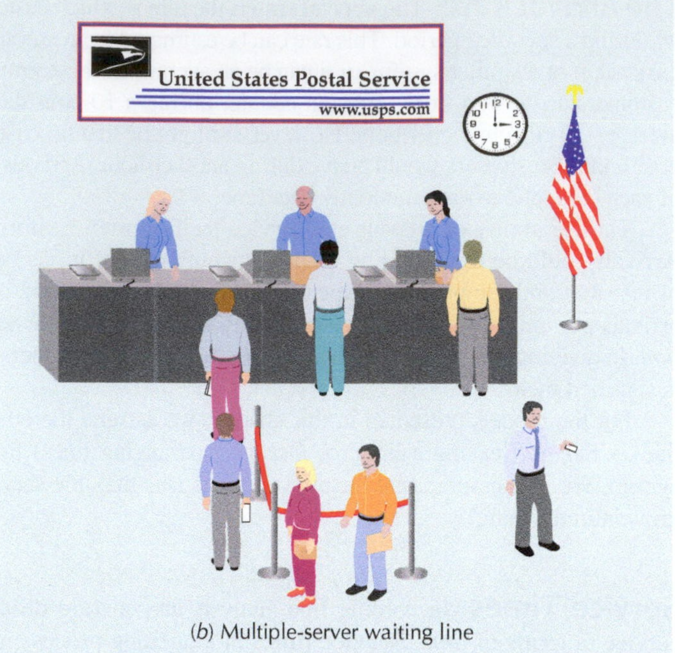

(b) Multiple-server waiting line

FIGURE 5.8 **Basic Waiting Line Structures**

Basic Waiting Line Structures Waiting line processes are generally categorized into four basic structures, according to the nature of the service facilities. In technical terminology they are called single-channel, single-phase; single-channel, multiple-phase; multiple-channel, single-phase; and multiple-channel, multiple-phase processes.

Channels The number of parallel servers for servicing customers.

Phases The number of servers in sequence that a customer must go through.

The number of **channels** in a queuing process is the number of parallel servers available. The number of **phases**, on the other hand, denotes the number of sequential servers each customer must go through to complete service. An example of a *single-channel, single-phase* queuing operation is a post office with only one postal clerk waiting on a single line of customers. This is more commonly called simply a *single-server* waiting line, and it is illustrated in **Figure 5.8*a***. A post office with several postal clerks waiting on a single line of customers is an example of a *multiple-channel, single-phase* process or simply a *multiple-server* waiting line. It is illustrated in **Figure 5.8*b***. These are the two basic waiting line structures we will focus on in this chapter.

The other two waiting line structures we mentioned have multiple phases; that is, they have a sequence of servers, one following another. For example, when patients go to a clinic for treatment or check into a hospital, they first wait in a reception room, then they may go to an office to fill out some paperwork. When they get to the treatment room, the patients receive an initial checkup or treatment from a nurse, followed by treatment from a doctor. This arrangement constitutes a *single-channel, multiple-phase* queuing process. If there are several doctors and nurses, the process is a *multiple-channel, multiple-phase process*. Another example of a multiple-phase system is a manufacturing assembly line in which a product is worked on at several sequential machines or by several sequential operators at workstations. These are more complex structures and are beyond the scope of this text.

You may quickly visualize a familiar waiting situation that fits none of these categories of waiting line structures. The four waiting line structures we have described are simply the four basic general categories; but there are many variations, which often require very complex mathematical formulas to analyze. In some cases they can only be analyzed using simulation (the topic of Supplement 13). However, the basic fundamentals of waiting line analysis for the simpler queuing models that we will discuss in this chapter are relevant to the analysis of all queuing problems, regardless of their complexity.

Operating Characteristics

The mathematics used in waiting line analysis do not provide an optimal, or "best," solution. Instead they generate measures referred to as *operating characteristics* that describe the performance of

TABLE 5.2 Queuing System Operating Characteristics

NOTATION	OPERATING CHARACTERISTIC
L	Average number of customers in the system (waiting and being served)
L_q	Average number of customers in the waiting line
W	Average time a customer spends in the system (waiting and being served)
W_q	Average time a customer spends waiting in line
P_o	Probability of no (i.e., zero) customers in the system
P_n	Probability of n customers in the system
ρ	Utilization rate; the proportion of the time the system is in use

the waiting line system and that management uses to evaluate the system and make decisions. It is assumed these operating characteristics will approach constant, average values after the system has been in operation for a long time, which is referred to as a *steady state*. These basic operating characteristics used in a waiting line analysis are defined in Table 5.2.

Traditional Cost Relationships in Waiting Line Analysis

There is generally an inverse relationship between the cost of providing service and the cost of making customers wait, as reflected in the cost curves in Figure 5.9. As the level of service, reflected by the number of servers, goes up, the cost of service increases, whereas waiting cost decreases. In the traditional view of waiting line analysis, the level of service should coincide with the minimum point on the total cost curve.

The cost of providing the service is usually reflected in the cost of the servers, such as the cost of the tellers at a bank, postal workers at a post office counter, or the repair crew in a plant or shop. As the number of servers is increased to reduce waiting time, service cost goes up. Service cost is normally direct and easy to compute. The cost of waiting is not as easy to determine. The major determinant of waiting cost is the loss of business that might result because customers get tired of waiting or frustrated and leave. This business loss can be temporary (a single event) or permanent (the customer never comes back). The cost due to a loss of business is especially difficult to determine, since it is not part of normal accounting records, although some trade organizations for businesses and industries occasionally provide such data. Other types of waiting costs include the loss of production time and salary for employees waiting to use machinery or load and unload vehicles.

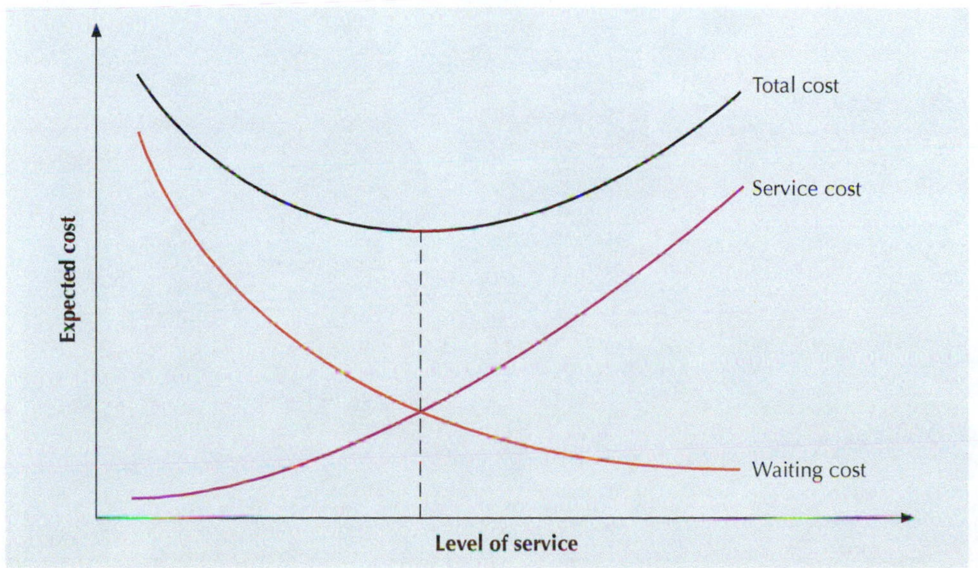

FIGURE 5.9 The Cost Relationship in Waiting Line Analysis

Most companies and organizations that have waiting as an integral part of their service process usually establish a goal for customer waiting time that corresponds to a level of service they want to achieve. For example, Taco Bell has determined that a three-minute average waiting time will result in only 2.5% of customers leaving, which they consider to be an acceptable service goal. Bank of America has a similar waiting time goal for serving its bank customers. The U.S. Postal Service has a goal of five minutes to serve its retail customers.

The Psychology of Waiting

In some instances, it is not possible to reduce waiting times, or other important issues besides cost may be involved. When these situations occur, the problem of providing quality service often depends more on psychological solutions. In other words, the organization will try to make waiting more palatable. For example, long lines are fairly common at Disney World, especially at certain peak times during the day. Although it is unlikely that any company has analyzed the technical aspects of waiting more than Disney, customers must still wait for long periods of time at certain shows, exhibits, and rides. Given the limited physical capacity of some attractions, the time required for a customer to complete them, and the large flow of customers, it is simply not possible to make the lines shorter or the service quicker without letting fewer people into the park. In these cases Disney management attempts to improve service in other ways to reduce customer dissatisfaction. As shown in the photo, costumed characters are used to entertain customers waiting in line and distract them from the long waits. Mobile vendors sell food, drinks, and souvenirs to people in line. Disney provides accurate wait times, which are more tolerable than vague ones, and provides frequent updates. For customers who are particularly annoyed by long waits, Disney sells special passes that allow customers to go to the front of the line for some attractions and to get into the park early before its normally scheduled opening.

Joe Raedle/Getty Images

Disney uses costumed characters like Minnie Mouse to entertain customers waiting in line to distract them from their long wait.

Waiting rooms, such as at a doctor's office, provide magazines and newspapers for customers to read while waiting. Televisions are occasionally available in auto repair waiting areas, in airport terminals, or in bars and lounges of restaurants where customers wait. Mirrors are purposely located near elevators to distract people while they wait. Supermarkets locate magazines, candy bars, and other "impulse-purchase" items at the checkout counter, not only as a diversion while waiting but as potential purchases. All these tactics are designed to improve the quality of service that requires waiting without actually incurring the cost of reducing waiting time.

Some service companies attempt to handle customer arrivals in a "smarter" way, by providing selective preferential treatment to certain types of customers in order to reduce their waiting time. For example, grocery stores have express lanes for customers with only a few purchases. Airlines and car rental agencies issue special cards to frequent-use customers or customers who pay an additional fee that allows them to join special waiting lines at their check-in counters. Online retailers check a customer's sales history and route the call or inquiry to more experienced or specialized customer service reps.

For some critical service providers, waiting times of any duration are simply not allowable. A police or fire department must provide sufficient service capacity so that calls for assistance can have quick response. This often results in long periods of underutilization where police officers or firefighters are basically idle. In these cases, cost takes a back seat to service.

Waiting Line Models

The simplest, most basic waiting line structure illustrated in Figure 5.8 is the *single-server* model. We run into this type of waiting line every day. When you buy a cup of coffee at your local Starbucks, when you go to a professor's office, when you use the copier in the library, and when you buy a ticket to see a movie, you wait in line to be served by one server.

The Basic Single-Server Model There are several variations of the single-server waiting line system; however, in the basic single-server model we assume the following:

- Poisson arrival rate
- Exponential service times
- First-come, first-served queue discipline
- Infinite queue length
- Infinite calling population

The basic operating characteristics of this single-server model are computed using the following formulas, where λ = mean arrival rate, μ = mean service rate, and n = the number of customers in the waiting line system, including the customer being served (if any).

The probability that no customers are in the queuing system (either in the queue or being served) is

$$P_0 = \left(1 - \frac{\lambda}{\mu}\right)$$

The probability of exactly n customers in the queuing system is

$$P_n = \left(\frac{\lambda}{\mu}\right)^n \cdot P_0 = \left(\frac{\lambda}{\mu}\right)^n \left(1 - \frac{\lambda}{\mu}\right)$$

The average number of customers in the queuing system (i.e., the customers being serviced and in the waiting line) is

$$L = \frac{\lambda}{\mu - \lambda}$$

The average number of customers in the waiting line is

$$L_q = \frac{\lambda^2}{\mu(\mu - \lambda)}$$

The average time a customer spends in the queuing system (i.e., waiting and being served) is

$$W = \frac{1}{\mu - \lambda} = \frac{L}{\lambda}$$

The average time a customer spends waiting in line to be served is

$$W_q = \frac{\lambda}{\mu(\mu - \lambda)}$$

Utilization factor (ρ) The probability the server is busy and the customer must wait.

The probability that the server is busy and a customer has to wait, known as the **utilization factor**, is

$$\rho = \frac{\lambda}{\mu}$$

The probability that the server is idle and a customer can be served is

$$I = 1 - \rho = 1 - \frac{\lambda}{\mu} = P_0$$

Remember that these operating characteristics are averages that result over a period of time; they are not absolutes. In other words, customers who arrive at the bookstore checkout counter will not find 3.2 customers in line. There could be no customers or 1, 2, 3, or 4 customers. The value 3.2 is simply an average over time, as are the other operating characteristics. Notice that there are four customers in the system ($L = 4$) and 3.2 customers in line ($L_q = 3.2$). The difference is only 0.8 customer being served because 20% of the time there is no customer being served ($I = .20$). Also note that the total time in the system of 10 minutes ($W = 10$) is exactly equal to the waiting time of 8 minutes ($W_q = 8$) plus the service time of 2 minutes (i.e., 60/30).

Service Improvement Analysis The operating characteristics developed from the queuing formulas in Example 5.1 indicate the quality of service at the Tech auxiliary bookstore. The average waiting time of eight minutes is excessive and would likely cause customers to become frustrated and leave without making a purchase. Normally, a waiting time of two to three minutes is the most a customer will comfortably tolerate at a store like this. Thus, the bookstore management could use the operating characteristics to formulate new strategies to improve service and then test these strategies.

For example, the bookstore might consider adding another employee to assist the present operator. This would enable more customers to be served in less time, thus increasing the service rate. If the service rate were increased from 30 customers per hour to 40 customers per hour, the waiting time would be reduced to only 2.25 minutes. Management would then have to decide whether the cost of the new employee is worth the reduction in waiting time. Alternatively, the bookstore could be redesigned to add an additional cash register as well as another employee to operate it. This would have the effect of reducing the arrival rate. If exiting customers split evenly between the two cash registers, then the arrival rate at each register would decrease from 24 per hour to 12 per hour with a resulting customer waiting time of 1.33 minutes. Again, management would have to determine whether the reduction in waiting time is worth the cost of a new cash register and employee. This is the crux of waiting line analysis: determining whether the improvement in service is worth the cost to achieve it.

EXAMPLE 5.1 | A Single-Server Model

The auxiliary bookstore in the student center at Tech is a small facility that sells school supplies and snacks. It has one checkout counter where one employee operates the cash register. The cash register and operator represent the server in this waiting line system; the customers who line up at the counter to pay for their selections form the waiting line.

Customers arrive at a rate of 24 per hour according to a Poisson distribution ($\lambda = 24$), and service times are exponentially distributed, with a mean rate of 30 customers per hour ($\mu = 30$). The bookstore manager wants to determine the operating characteristics for this waiting line system.

Solution: The operating characteristics are computed using the queuing formulas for the single-server model as follows:

$$P_0 = \left(1 - \frac{\lambda}{\mu}\right) = \left(1 - \frac{24}{30}\right)$$

$= 0.20$ probability of no customers in the system

$$L = \frac{\lambda}{\mu - \lambda} = \frac{24}{30 - 24}$$

$= 4$ customers on the average in the queuing system

$$L_q = \frac{\lambda^2}{\mu(\mu - \lambda)} = \frac{(24)^2}{30(30 - 24)}$$

$= 3.2$ customers on the average in the waiting line

$$W = \frac{1}{\mu - \lambda} = \frac{1}{30 - 24}$$

$= 0.167$ hour (10 minutes) average time in the system per customer

$$W_q = \frac{\lambda}{\mu(\mu - \lambda)} = \frac{24}{30(30 - 24)}$$

$= 0.133$ hour (8 minutes) average time in the waiting line per customer

$$\rho = \frac{\lambda}{\mu} = \frac{24}{30}$$

$= 0.80$ probability that the server will be busy and the customer must wait

$$I = 1 - \rho = 1 - 0.80$$

$= 0.20$ probability that the server will be idle and a customer can be served

Solution of the Single-Server Model with Excel Excel can be used to solve all of the queuing models in this chapter. The Excel solution screen for the single-server model for the auxiliary bookstore at Tech in Example 5.1 is shown in **Exhibit 5.1**. Excel files for this exhibit and all other exhibits in this chapter can be downloaded from the text website.

EXHIBIT 5.1 | Single Server

Excel File

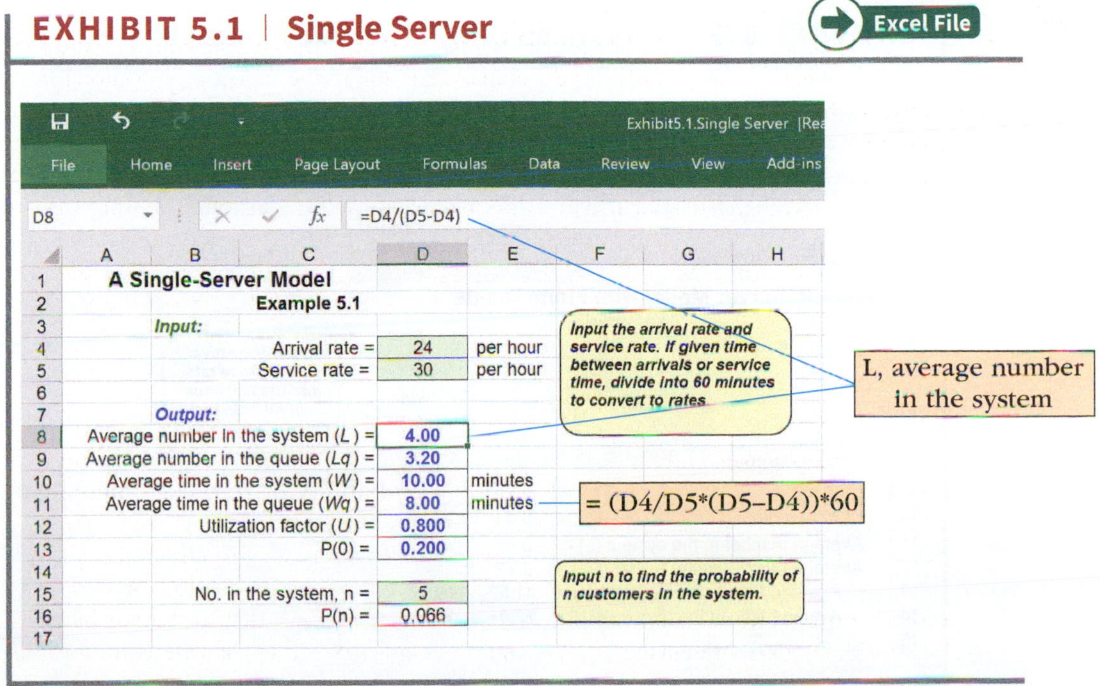

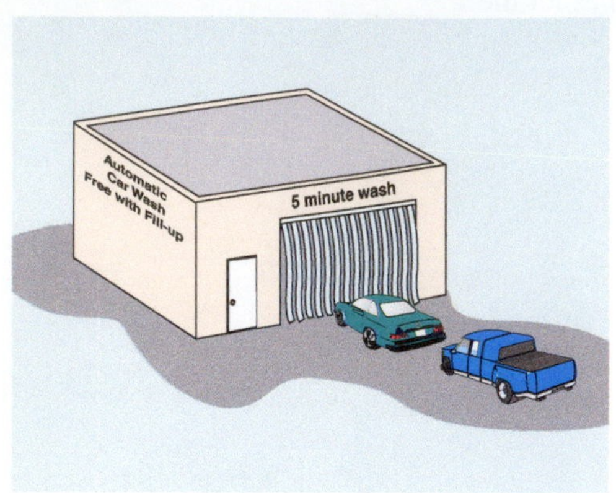

(a) Single-Server, Constant Time

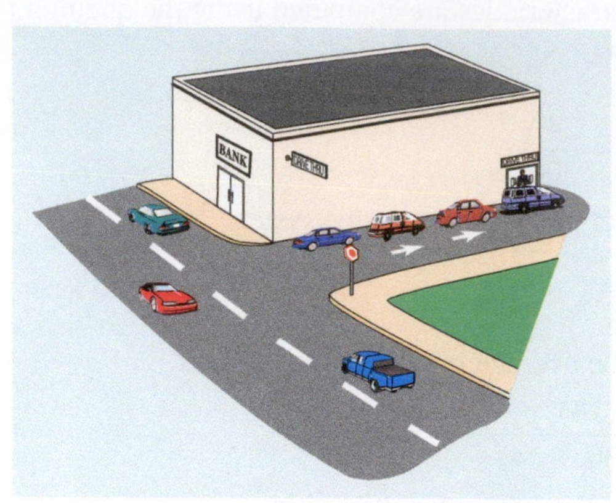

(b) Single-Server, Finite Queue

(c) Single-Server, Finite Calling Population

FIGURE 5.10 Advanced Single-Server Models

Advanced Single-Server Models There are many variations of the single-server model, as shown in Figure 5.10. The most common are: constant service times, finite queue length, and finite calling populations.

Constant service times occur most often when automated equipment or machinery performs the service. Examples are vending machines, car washes, and many manufacturing operations.

Finite queue lengths occur when there is a physical limitation to the length of the waiting line. For example, this can occur when cars waiting at a bank for an ATM machine are prohibited from extending into the street.

A *finite calling population refers* to a situation when the number of "customers" that can arrive to a system is limited, such as invitation-only events, student advisees, or maintenance for a fleet of rental cars.

The formulas for these models, included in the *Summary of Key Formulas* at the end of the chapter, can be quite involved. For that reason, all of these models, along with the single-server model and the multiple-server model discussed in the next section, can be solved with the Excel add-in that accompanies this book, *OM Tools*. Exhibit 5.2 shows the OM Tools solution to a single-server finite queue problem.

EXHIBIT 5.2 | Advanced Single-Server Models

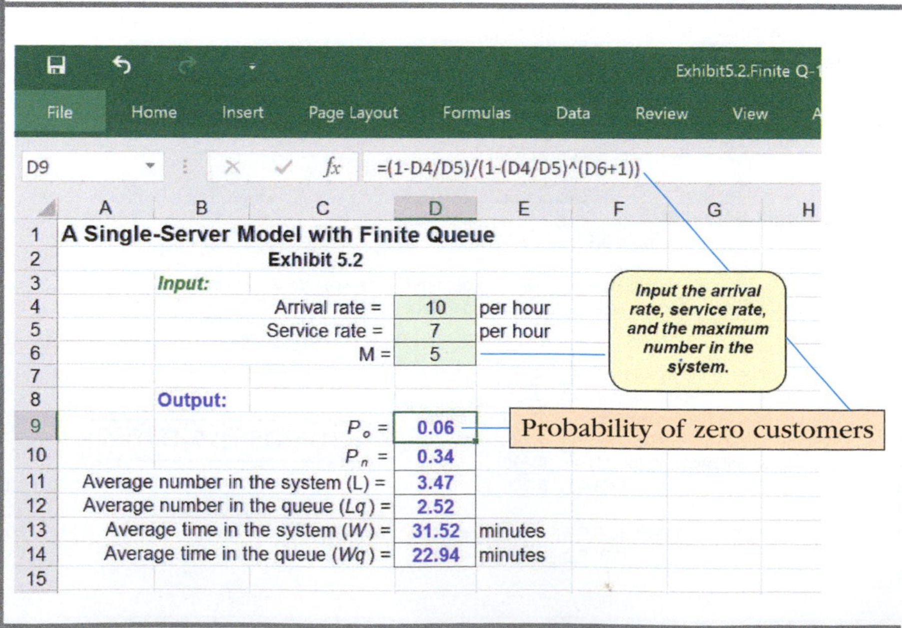

	A	B	C	D	E
1	A Single-Server Model with Finite Queue				
2			Exhibit 5.2		
3		Input:			
4			Arrival rate =	10	per hour
5			Service rate =	7	per hour
6			M =	5	
7					
8		Output:			
9			P_o =	0.06	
10			P_n =	0.34	
11			Average number in the system (L) =	3.47	
12			Average number in the queue (Lq) =	2.52	
13			Average time in the system (W) =	31.52	minutes
14			Average time in the queue (Wq) =	22.94	minutes
15					

Multiple-Server Model

A large number of operational waiting line systems include multiple servers. These models can be very complex, so in this section we present only the most basic multiple-server (or channel) waiting line structure. This system includes a single waiting line and a service facility with several independent servers in parallel, as shown in Figure 5.8*b*. An example of a multiple-server system is an airline ticket and check-in counter, where passengers line up in a roped-off single line waiting for one of several agents for service, as seen in the photo. The same waiting line structure is found at the post office, where customers in a single line wait for service from several postal clerks, or at a multiplex theater where customers typically line up in a single line to buy movie tickets from one of several ticket sellers.

Kevork Djansezian/Getty Images Inc.

These passengers waiting in line to purchase tickets or check baggage and get a boarding pass at LAX are part of a waiting line system with multiple servers. Passengers are cordoned into a single line to wait for one of several airline agents to serve them. The number of agents scheduled for duty at the check-in counter is determined by waiting line operating characteristics based on different passenger arrival rates during the day and for different days.

The Basic Multiple-Server Model The formulas for determining the operating characteristics for the multiple-server model are based on the same assumptions as the single-server model—Poisson arrival rate, exponential service times, infinite calling population and queue length, and FIFO queue discipline. Also, recall that in the single-server model, $\mu > \lambda$; however, in the multiple-server model, $s\mu > \lambda$, where s is the number of servers. The operating characteristics formulas are as follows.

The probability that there are no customers in the system (all servers are idle) is

$$P_0 = \frac{1}{\left[\sum_{n=0}^{n=s-1} \frac{1}{n!}\left(\frac{\lambda}{\mu}\right)^n\right] + \frac{1}{s!}\left(\frac{\lambda}{\mu}\right)^s\left(\frac{s\mu}{s\mu - \lambda}\right)}$$

The probability of n customers in the queuing system is

$$P_n = \begin{cases} \frac{1}{s!s^{n-s}}\left(\frac{\lambda}{\mu}\right)^n P_0, & \text{for } n > s \\ \frac{1}{n!}\left(\frac{\lambda}{\mu}\right)^n P_0, & \text{for } n \leq s \end{cases}$$

The probability that a customer arriving in the system must wait for service (i.e., the probability that all the servers are busy) is

$$P_w = \frac{1}{s!}\left(\frac{\lambda}{\mu}\right)^s \frac{s\mu}{s\mu - \lambda} P_0$$

$$\text{Avg. no. in system} = L = \frac{\lambda\mu(\lambda/\mu)^s}{(s-1)!(s\mu - \lambda)^2} P_0 + \frac{\lambda}{\mu}$$

$$\text{Avg. time in system} = W = \frac{L}{\lambda}$$

$$\text{Avg. no. in queue} = L_q = L - \frac{\lambda}{\mu}$$

$$\text{Avg. time in queue} = W_q = W - \frac{1}{\mu} = \frac{L_q}{\lambda}$$

$$\text{Utilization} = \rho = \frac{\lambda}{s\mu}$$

EXAMPLE 5.2 | A Multiple-Server Waiting Line System

The student health service at Tech has a waiting room in which chairs are placed along a wall, forming a single waiting line. Some students have health problems that only require a nurse. The students are served by three nurses, each located in a separate room. Students are treated on a first-come, first-served basis.

The health service administrator wants to analyze this queuing system because excessive waiting times can make students angry and they complain. Students have a medical problem and thus are impatient anyway. Waiting increases their impatience.

A study of the health service for a six-month period shows that an average of 10 students arrive per hour (according to a Poisson distribution), and an average of four students can be served per hour by a nurse (Poisson distributed). Compare a three-server versus four-server system.

Solution:

$$\lambda = 10 \text{ students per hour}$$

$$\mu = 4 \text{ students per hour per service representative}$$

$$s = 3 \text{ service representatives}$$

$$s\mu = (3)(4) = 12\ (>\lambda = 10)$$

Three-server system

$$P_0 = \frac{1}{\left[\sum_{n=0}^{n=s-1} \frac{1}{n!}\left(\frac{\lambda}{\mu}\right)^n\right] + \frac{1}{s!}\left(\frac{\lambda}{\mu}\right)^s\left(\frac{s\mu}{s\mu - \lambda}\right)}$$

$$= \frac{1}{\left[\frac{1}{0!}\left(\frac{10}{4}\right)^0 + \frac{1}{1!}\left(\frac{10}{4}\right)^1 + \frac{1}{2!}\left(\frac{10}{4}\right)^2\right] + \frac{1}{3!}\left(\frac{10}{4}\right)^3 \frac{3(4)}{3(4) - 10}}$$

$$= 0.045 \text{ probability that no customers are in the health service.}$$

$$L = \frac{\lambda\mu(\lambda/\mu)^s}{(s-1)!(s\mu - \lambda)^2} P_0 + \frac{\lambda}{\mu}$$

$$= \frac{(10)(4)(10/4)^3}{(3-1)!(3(4) - 10)^2}(0.045) + \frac{10}{4}$$

$$= 6 \text{ students in the health service}$$

$$W = \frac{L}{\lambda} = \frac{6}{10}$$

$$= 0.60 \text{ hour or 36 minutes in the health service}$$

$$L_q = L - \frac{\lambda}{\mu} = 6 - \frac{10}{4}$$

$$= 3.5 \text{ students waiting to be served}$$

$$W_q = \frac{L_q}{\lambda} = \frac{3.5}{10}$$

$$= 0.35 \text{ hour, or 21 minutes waiting in line}$$

$$P_w = \frac{1}{s!}\left(\frac{\lambda}{\mu}\right)^s \frac{s\mu}{s\mu - \lambda} P_0$$

$$= \frac{1}{3!}\left(\frac{10}{4}\right)^3 \frac{3(4)}{3(4) - (10)}(0.045)$$

$$= 0.703 \text{ probability that a student must wait for service}$$

(i.e., that there are three or more students in the system)

The health service administrator has observed that students are frustrated by the waiting time of 21 minutes and the 0.703 probability of waiting. To try to improve matters, the administrator is considering adding another nurse. The operating characteristics for this system must be recomputed with $s = 4$ nurses.

Four-server system

Substituting $s = 4$ along with λ and μ in the queuing formulas results in the following operating characteristics:

P_0 = 0.073 probability that no students are in the health service

L = 3.0 students in the health service

W = 0.30 hour, or 18 minutes, in the health service

L_q = 0.5 students waiting to be served

W_q = 0.05 hour, or 3 minutes, waiting in line

P_w = 0.31 probability that a student must wait for service

These results are significantly better: waiting time is reduced from 21 minutes to 3 minutes. This improvement in the quality of the service would have to be compared to the cost of adding an extra nurse.

EXHIBIT 5.3 | Multiple-Server Waiting Line in Excel

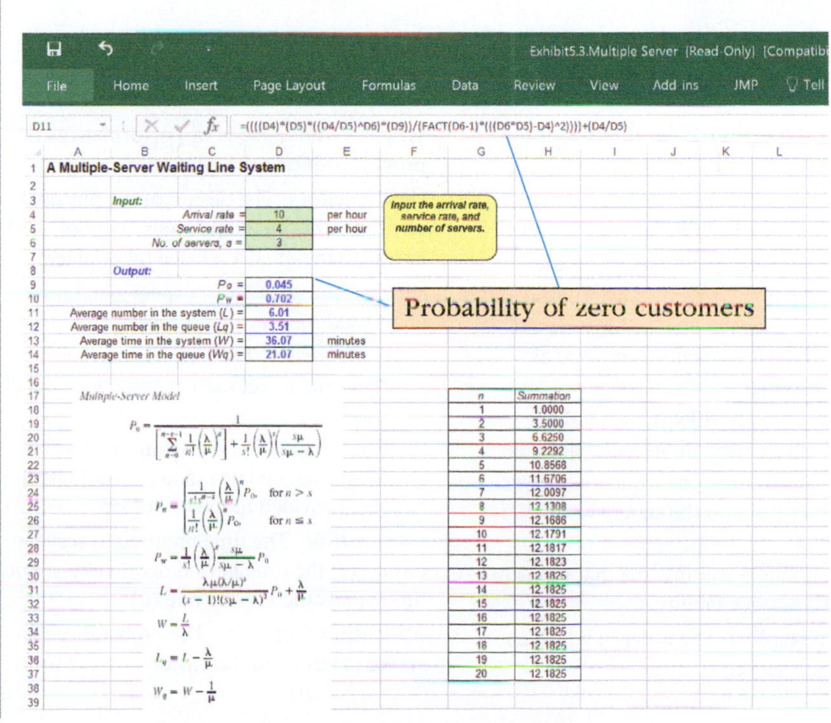

Explanation of Excel functions used in Exhibit 5.3

FACT (number)

A factorial is a count of the number of ways a group of items can be arranged (also called a permutation). The mathematical symbol for factorial is !. For example, 5! = 5 * 4 * 3 * 2 * 1 = 120. In Excel, FACT (5) = 120.

VLOOKUP (lookup value, table array, column number that contains the value to be returned).

VLOOKUP searches for a value in the first column of a table array and returns a value in the same row from another column in the table array. In this example, VLOOKUP(D6,G18:H36,2) looks up the number of servers, *s*, in the first column of the table and returns the value from the second column, which calculates the summation portion of the P_0 formula.

Summary

Services represent the fastest-growing sector of the global economy and account for two thirds of global output, one third of global employment, and nearly 20% of global trade. The world's most industrialized nations are predominantly service economies.

Service design and operations present unique challenges due to the intangible nature of services, the inherent variability in service delivery, and the co-production of value by the customer and service provider. The design process involves developing a service concept, defining the service package, and determining performance, design, and delivery specifications. Design tools such as service blueprints, servicescapes, service scripts, and waiting line analysis facilitate the design process.

Since waiting is an integral part of many service-related operations, it is an important area of analysis. The mathematical formulas presented in this chapter for modeling various waiting line structures provide the basis for designing and improving service systems.

Key Terms

arrival rate The rate (λ) at which customers arrive at a service facility during a specified period.

calling population The source of customers to a waiting line.

channels The number of parallel servers.

delivery specifications Specify schedules, deliverables, location.

design specifications Describe the service in enough detail to be replicated.

finite queue A waiting line whose length is limited.

goods Tangible objects that can be created and sold at a later date.

infinite queue A waiting line that grows to any length.

line of influence Signs or activities that influences a customer to seek a service.

line of interaction Point where a customer and service provider interact.

line of support Point where a service provider interacts with support personnel.

line of visibility Point that separates front-office and back-office activities.

operating characteristics Measures of waiting line performance expressed as averages.

performance specifications Outline performance expectations and requirements.

phases The number of sequential servers a customer must go through to receive service.

queue A single waiting line that forms in front of a service facility.

queue discipline The order in which customers are served.

services Acts, deeds or performances that provide value to the customer.

servicescapes The design of the physical environment (including signs, symbols and, artifacts) in which a service takes place.

service blueprinting A specialized flow chart used for service processes.

service concept The purpose of a service; it defines the target market and the customer experience.

service package The mixture of physical items, sensual benefits, and psychological benefits provided to the customer.

service time The time required to serve a customer; the time period divided by service time yields the service rate (μ).

utilization factor (ρ) The probability the server is busy and the customer must wait.

Key Formulas

Single-Server Model

$$P_0 = 1 - \frac{\lambda}{\mu}$$

$$P_n = \left(\frac{\lambda}{\mu}\right)^n\left(1 - \frac{\lambda}{\mu}\right)$$

$$L = \frac{\lambda}{\mu - \lambda}$$

$$L_q = \frac{\lambda^2}{\mu(\mu - \lambda)}$$

$$W = \frac{1}{\mu - \lambda}$$

$$W_q = \frac{\lambda}{\mu(\mu - \lambda)}$$

$$\rho = \frac{\lambda}{\mu}$$

$$I = 1 - \frac{\lambda}{\mu}$$

where λ *= arrival rate*
μ *= service rate*

Single-Server Model with Finite Calling Population

$$P_0 = \frac{1}{\sum_{n=0}^{N} \frac{N!}{(N-n)!}\left(\frac{\lambda}{\mu}\right)^n}$$

$$W_q = \frac{L_q}{(N - L)\lambda}$$

$$L_q = N - \left(\frac{\lambda + \mu}{\lambda}\right)(1 - P_0)$$

$$W = W_q + \frac{1}{\mu}$$

$$L = L_q + (1 - P_0)$$

$$P_n = \frac{N!}{(N-n)!}\left(\frac{\lambda}{\mu}\right)^n P_0$$

where N = population size

Single-Server Model with Finite Queue

$$P_0 = \frac{1 - \lambda/\mu}{1 - (\lambda/\mu)^{M+1}}$$

$$W = \frac{L}{\lambda(1 - P_M)}$$

$$P_n = (P_0)(\lambda/\mu)^n, n \le M$$

$$W_q = W - \frac{1}{\mu}$$

$$L = \frac{\lambda/\mu}{1 - \lambda/\mu} - \frac{(M+1)(\lambda/\mu)^{M+1}}{1 - (\lambda/\mu)^{M+1}}$$

$$L_q = L - \frac{\lambda(1 - P_M)}{\mu}$$

where M = maximum number allowed in the system

Single-Server Model with Constant Service Times

$$P_0 = 1 - \frac{\lambda}{\mu}$$

$$L_q = \frac{\lambda^2}{2\mu(\mu - \lambda)}$$

$$L = L_q + \frac{\lambda}{\mu}$$

$$W_q = \frac{L_q}{\lambda}$$

$$W = W_q + \frac{1}{\mu}$$

$$\rho = \frac{\lambda}{\mu}$$

Multiple-Server Model

$$P_0 = \frac{1}{\left[\sum_{n=0}^{n=s-1} \frac{1}{n!}\left(\frac{\lambda}{\mu}\right)^n\right] + \frac{1}{s!}\left(\frac{\lambda}{\mu}\right)^s\left(\frac{s\mu}{s\mu - \lambda}\right)}$$

$$P_n = \begin{cases} \frac{1}{s!s^{n-s}}\left(\frac{\lambda}{\mu}\right)^n P_0, & \text{for } n > s \\ \frac{1}{n!}\left(\frac{\lambda}{\mu}\right)^n P_0, & \text{for } n \le s \end{cases}$$

$$P_w = \frac{1}{s!}\left(\frac{\lambda}{\mu}\right)^s \frac{s\mu}{s\mu - \lambda} P_0$$

$$L = \frac{\lambda\mu(\lambda/\mu)^s}{(s-1)!(s\mu - \lambda)^2} P_0 + \frac{\lambda}{\mu}$$

$$W = \frac{L}{\lambda}$$

$$L_q = L - \frac{\lambda}{\mu}$$

$$W_q = W - \frac{1}{\mu}$$

where s = number of servers

Solved Problems

1. Single-Server Model

The new-accounts officer at the Citizens Northern Savings Bank enrolls all new customers in checking accounts. During the three-week period in August encompassing the beginning of the new school year at State University, the bank opens a lot of new accounts for students. The bank estimates that the arrival rate during this period will be Poisson distributed with an average of four customers per hour. The service time is exponentially distributed with an average of 12 minutes per customer to set up a new account. The bank wants to determine the operating characteristics for this system to determine if the current person is sufficient to handle the increased traffic.

Solution

Determine operating characteristics for the single-server system:

λ = 4 customers per hour arrive

μ = 5 customers per hour are served

$$P_0 = \left(1 - \frac{\lambda}{\mu}\right) = \left(1 - \frac{4}{5}\right)$$

= 0.20 probability of no customers in the system

$$L = \frac{\lambda}{\mu - \lambda} = \frac{4}{5 - 4}$$

= 4 customers on average in the queuing system

$$L_q = \frac{\lambda^2}{\mu(\mu - \lambda)} = \frac{4^2}{5(5-4)}$$

$= 3.2$ customers on average waiting

$$W = \frac{1}{\mu - \lambda} = \frac{1}{5-4}$$

$= 1$ hour average time in the system

$$W_q = \frac{\lambda}{\mu(\mu - \lambda)} = \frac{4}{5(5-4)}$$

$= 0.80$ hour (48 minutes) average time waiting

$$P_w = \frac{\lambda}{\mu} = \frac{4}{5}$$

$= 0.80$ probability that the new-accounts officer will be busy and that a customer must wait

The average waiting time of 48 minutes and the average time in the system are excessive, and the bank needs to add an extra employee during the busy period.

2. Multiple-Server Model

The Citizens Northern Bank wants to compute the operating characteristics if an extra employee were added to assist with new-accounts enrollments.

Solution

Determine the operating characteristics for the multiple-server system:

$\lambda = 4$ customers per hour arrive

$\mu = 5$ customers per hour are served

$s = 2$ servers

$$P_0 = \frac{1}{\left[\sum_{n=0}^{n=s-1} \frac{1}{n!}\left(\frac{\lambda}{\mu}\right)^n\right] + \frac{1}{s!}\left(\frac{\lambda}{\mu}\right)^s \left(\frac{s\mu}{s\mu - \lambda}\right)}$$

$$= \frac{1}{\left[\frac{1}{0!}\left(\frac{4}{5}\right)^0 + \frac{1}{1!}\left(\frac{4}{5}\right)^1\right] + \frac{1}{2!}\left(\frac{4}{5}\right)^2 \frac{(2)(5)}{(2)(5) - 4}}$$

$= 0.429$ probability that no customers are in the system

$$L = \frac{\lambda\mu(\lambda/\mu)^s}{(s-1)!(s\mu - \lambda)^2} P_0 + \frac{\lambda}{\mu}$$

$$= \frac{(4)(5)(4/5)^2}{1![(2)(5) - 4]^2}(0.429) + \frac{4}{5}$$

$= 0.952$ customer on average in the system

$$L_q = L - \frac{\lambda}{\mu} = 0.952 - \frac{4}{5}$$

$= 0.152$ customer on average waiting to be served

$$W = \frac{L}{\lambda} = \frac{0.952}{4}$$

$= 0.238$ hour (14.3 minutes) average time in the system

$$W_q = \frac{L_q}{\lambda} = \frac{0.152}{4}$$

$= 0.038$ hour (2.3 minutes) average time in line

$$P_w = \frac{1}{s!}\left(\frac{\lambda}{\mu}\right)^s \frac{s\mu}{s\mu - l} P_0$$

$$= \frac{1}{2!}\left(\frac{4}{5}\right)^2 \frac{(2)(5)}{(2)(5) - 4}(0.429)$$

$= 0.229$ probability that a customer must wait

The waiting time with the multiple-server model is 2.3 minutes, which is a significant improvement over the previous system; thus, the bank should add the second new-accounts officer.

Questions

5.1. How would you define a service? What services blur the distinction between a product and a service?

5.2. List eight characteristics of services and explain what impact each characteristic has on the design process.

5.3. Describe the service package for (a) a bank, (b) an airline, and (c) a lawn service.

5.4. Generate as many ideas as you can for additional services or improvements in service delivery for (a) banking, (b) higher education, and (c) healthcare.

5.5. Explain the components of a service blueprint.

5.6. Identify 10 real-life examples of queuing systems with which you are familiar.

5.7. Why must the utilization factor in a single-server model be less than one?

5.8. Give five examples of real-world queuing systems with finite calling populations.

5.9. List the elements that define a queuing system.

5.10. How can the results of queuing analysis be used by a decision maker for making decisions?

5.11. What is the mean effective service rate in a multiple-server model, and what must be its relationship to the arrival rate?

5.12. For each of the following queuing systems, indicate if it is a single- or multiple-server model, the queue discipline, and if its calling population is infinite or finite:

- **a.** Hair salon
- **b.** Bank
- **c.** Laundromat
- **d.** Doctor's office
- **e.** Adviser's office
- **f.** Airport runway
- **g.** Service station
- **h.** Copy center
- **i.** Team trainer
- **j.** Mainframe computer

5.13. For Example 5.1 in this chapter, discuss why the multiple-server model would or would not be appropriate as an alternative to reduce waiting time.

5.14. Discuss briefly the relationship between waiting line analysis and quality improvement.

5.15. Define the four basic waiting line structures and give an example of each.

5.16. Describe the traditional cost relationship in waiting line analysis.

5.17. a. Is the following statement true or false? The single-phase, single-channel model with Poisson arrivals and undefined service times will always have larger (i.e., greater) operating characteristic values (i.e., W, W_q, L, L_q) than the same model with exponentially distributed service times. Explain your answer.

b. Is the following statement true or false? The single-phase, single-channel model with Poisson arrivals and constant service times will always have smaller (i.e., lower) operating characteristic values (i.e., W, W_q, L, L_q) than the same model with exponentially distributed service times. Explain your answer.

5.18. Under what conditions can the basic single-server and multiple-server models be used to analyze a multiple-phase waiting line system?

5.19. Why do waiting lines form at a service facility even though there may be more than enough service capacity to meet normal demand in the long run?

5.20. Provide an example of when a first-in, first-out (FIFO) rule for queue discipline would not be appropriate.

5.21. Under what conditions will the single-channel, single-phase queuing model with Poisson arrivals and undefined service times provide the same operating characteristics as the basic model with exponentially distributed service times?

5.22. What types of waiting line systems have constant service times?

5.23. Compare traditional car rental services with Zipcar and Uber. Each of these has a different service concept. Explain.

5.24. Track your waiting line experience over a week's time. What was the longest time you waited in line? What was the longest length of a line? What kind of line behavior did you observe (balking, reneging, cutting in line, queue priority)?

Problems

5.1. McBurger's fast-food restaurant has a drive-through window with a single server who takes orders from an intercom and is also the cashier. The window operator is assisted by other employees who prepare the orders. Customers arrive at the ordering station prior to the drive-through window every 3.6 minutes (exponentially distributed) and the service time is 2.4 minutes (exponentially distributed). Determine the average length of the waiting line and the waiting time. Discuss the quality implications of your results. If you decide that the quality of the service could be improved, indicate what things you might do to improve quality.

5.2. The ticket booth on the Tech campus is operated by one person, who is selling tickets for the annual Tech versus State football game on Saturday. The ticket seller can serve an average of 12 customers per hour (Poisson distributed); on average, 8 customers arrive to purchase tickets each hour (Poisson distributed). Determine the average time a ticket buyer must wait and the portion of time the ticket seller is busy.

5.3. The Minute Stop Market has one pump for gasoline, which can service 10 customers per hour (Poisson distributed). Cars arrive at the pump at a rate of 5 per hour (Poisson distributed).

a. Determine the average queue length, the average time a car is in the system, and the average time a car must wait.

b. If, during the period from 4:00 P.M. to 5:00 P.M., the arrival rate increases to 12 cars per hour, what will be the effect on the average queue length?

5.4. The Universal Manufacturing Company produces a particular product in an assembly-line operation. One of the machines on the line is a drill press that has a single assembly line feeding into it. A partially completed unit arrives at the press to be worked on every 8 minutes, on average, according to an exponential distribution. The machine operator can process an average of 10 parts per hour (Poisson distributed). Determine the average number of parts waiting to be worked on, the percentage of time the operator is working, and the percentage of time the machine is idle.

5.5. The management of Universal Manufacturing Company (Problem 5-4) likes to have its operators working 90% of the time. What must the assembly line arrival rate be in order for the operators to be as busy as management would like?

5.6. The Peachtree Airport in Atlanta serves light aircraft. It has a single runway and one air traffic controller to land planes. It takes an airplane 8 minutes to land and clear the runway (exponentially distributed). Planes arrive at the airport at the rate of 5 per hour (Poisson distributed).

a. Determine the average number of planes that will stack up waiting to land.

b. Find the average time a plane must wait in line before it can land.

c. Calculate the average time it takes a plane to clear the runway once it has notified the airport that it is in the vicinity and wants to land.

d. The FAA has a rule that an air traffic controller can, on the average, land planes a maximum of 45 minutes out of every hour. There must be 15 minutes of idle time available to relieve the tension. Will this airport have to hire an extra air traffic controller?

5.7. The National Bank of Union City currently has one outside drive-up teller. It takes the teller an average of three minutes (exponentially distributed) to serve a bank customer. Customers arrive at the drive-up window at the rate of 12 per hour (Poisson distributed). The bank operations officer is currently analyzing the possibility of adding a second drive-up window at an annual cost of $20,000. It is assumed that arriving cars would be equally divided between both windows. The operations officer estimates that each minute's reduction in customer waiting time would increase the bank's revenue by $2000 annually. Should the second drive-up window be installed? What other factors should be considered in the decision besides cost?

5.8. During registration at Tech every quarter, students in the Department of Management must have their courses approved by the departmental advisor. It takes the advisor an average of five minutes (exponentially distributed) to approve each schedule, and students arrive at the advisor's office at the rate of 10 per hour (Poisson distributed). Compute L, L_q, W, W_q, and ρ. What do you think about this system? How would you change it?

5.9. All trucks traveling on Interstate 40 between Albuquerque and Amarillo are required to stop at a weigh station. Trucks arrive at the weigh station at a rate of 120 per eight-hour day (Poisson distributed), and the station can weigh, on the average, 140 trucks per day (Poisson distributed).

a. Determine the average number of trucks waiting, the average time spent at the weigh station by each truck, and the average waiting time before being weighed for each truck.

b. If the truck drivers find out they must remain at the weigh station longer than 15 minutes on the average, they will start taking a different route or traveling at night, thus depriving the state of taxes. The state of New Mexico estimates it loses $10,000 in taxes per year for each extra minute (over 15) that trucks must remain at the weigh station. A new set of scales would have the same service capacity as the present set of scales, and it is assumed that arriving trucks would line up equally behind the two sets of scales. It would cost $50,000 per year to operate the new scales. Should the state install the new set of scales?

5.10. In Problem 5.9(a), suppose arriving truck drivers look to see how many trucks are waiting to be weighed at the weigh station. If they see four or more trucks in line, they will pass by the station and risk being caught and ticketed. What is the probability that a truck will pass by the station?

5.11. In Problem 5.8, the head of the Management Department at Tech is considering the addition of a second advisor in the college advising office to serve students waiting to have their schedules approved. This new advisor could serve the same number of students per hour as the present advisor. Determine L, L_q, W, and W_q for this altered advising system. As a student, would you recommend adding the advisor?

5.12. Annie Campbell is a nurse on the evening shift from 10:00 P.M. to 6:00 A.M. at Community Hospital. She is responsible for 15 patients in her area. She averages two calls from each of her patients every evening (Poisson distributed), and she must spend an average of 10 minutes (negative exponential distribution) with each patient who calls. Nurse Smith has indicated to her shift supervisor that although she has not kept records she believes her patients must wait about 10 minutes on average for her to respond and she has requested that her supervisor assign a second nurse to her area. The supervisor believes 10 minutes is too long to wait, but she does not want her nurses to be idle more than 40% of the time. Determine what the supervisor should do.

5.13. Wallace Publishers has a large number of employees who use the company's single fax machine. Employees arrive randomly to use the fax machine at an average rate of 20 per hour. This arrival process is approximated by a Poisson distribution. Employees spend an average of two minutes using the fax machine, either transmitting or receiving items. The time spent using the machine is distributed according to a negative exponential distribution. Employees line up in single file to use the machine, and they obtain access to it on a first-come, first-served basis. There is no defined limit to the number who can line up to use the machine.

Management has determined that by assigning an operator to the fax machine rather than allowing the employees to operate the machine themselves, it can reduce the average service time from the current 2 minutes to 1.5 minutes. However, the fax operator's salary is $8 per hour, which must be paid 8 hours per day even if there are no employees wishing to use the fax machine part of the time. Management has estimated the cost of employee time spent waiting in line and at the fax machine during service to be 17¢ per minute (based on an average salary of $10.20 per hour per employee). Should the firm assign an operator to the fax machine?

5.14. The Universal Manufacturing Company has a single assembly line that feeds two drill presses in parallel. As partially completed products come off the line, they are lined up to be worked on as drill presses become available. The units arrive at the workstation (containing both presses) at the rate of 90 per hour (Poisson distributed). Each press operator can process an average of 60 units per hour (Poisson distributed). Compute L, L_q, W, and W_q.

5.15. The Escargot is a small French restaurant with 6 waiters and waitresses. The average service time at the restaurant for a table (of any size) is 80 minutes (exponentially distributed). The restaurant does not take reservations and parties arrive for dinner (and stay and wait) every 16 minutes (Poisson distributed). The restaurant is concerned that a lengthy waiting time might hurt its business in the long run. What is the current waiting time and queue length for the restaurant? Discuss the quality implications of the current waiting time and any actions the restaurant might take.

5.16. Cakes baked by the Freshfood Bakery are transported from the ovens to be packaged by one of three wrappers. Each wrapper can wrap an average of 120 cakes per hour (Poisson distributed). The cakes are brought to the wrappers at the rate of 300 per hour (Poisson distributed). If a cake sits longer than 5 minutes before being wrapped, it will not be fresh enough to meet the bakery's quality control standards. Does the bakery need to hire another wrapper?

5.17. The Draper Clinic has two general practitioners who see patients daily. An average of 6.5 patients arrive at the clinic per hour (Poisson distributed). Each doctor spends an average of 15 minutes (exponentially distributed) with a patient. The patients wait in a waiting area until one of the two doctors is able to see them. However, since patients typically do not feel well when they come to the clinic, the doctors do not believe it is good practice to have a patient wait longer than an average of 20 minutes. Should this clinic add a third doctor, and, if so, will this alleviate the waiting problem?

5.18. The Wearever Shoe Company is going to open a new branch at a mall, and company managers are attempting to determine how many salespeople to hire. Based on an analysis of mall traffic, the company estimates that customers will arrive at the store at the rate of 9 per hour (Poisson distributed), and from past experience at its other branches, the company knows that salespeople can serve an average of 6 customers per hour (Poisson distributed). How many salespeople should the company hire in order to maintain a company policy that on average a customer should have to wait for service no more than 30% of the time?

5.19. When customers arrive at Gilley's Ice Cream Shop, they take a number and wait to be called to purchase ice cream from one of the counter servers. From experience in past summers, the store's staff knows that customers arrive at the rate of 35 per hour (Poisson distributed) on summer days between 3:00 P.M. and 10:00 P.M. and a server can serve 15 customers per hour on average (Poisson distributed). Gilley's wants to make sure that customers wait no longer than 5 minutes for service. Gilley's is contemplating keeping three servers behind the ice cream counter during the peak summer hours. Will this number be adequate to meet the waiting time policy?

5.20. Huang's television-repair service receives an average of four TV sets per 8-hour day to be repaired. The service manager would like to be able to tell customers that they can expect their TV back in 3 days. What average repair time per set will the repair shop have to achieve to provide 3-day service on the average? (Assume that the arrival rate is Poisson distributed and repair times are exponentially distributed.)

5.21. Partially completed products arrive at a workstation in a manufacturing operation at a mean rate of 40 per hour (Poisson distributed). The processing time at the workstation averages 1.2 minutes per unit (exponentially distributed). The manufacturing company estimates that each unit of in-process inventory at the workstation costs $31 per day (on the average). However, the company can add extra employees and reduce the processing time to 0.90 minute per unit at a cost of $52 per day. Determine whether the company should continue the present operation or add extra employees.

5.22. The Seaboard Shipping Company has a warehouse terminal in Spartanburg, South Carolina. The capacity of each terminal dock is three trucks. As trucks enter the terminal, the drivers receive numbers, and when one of the three dock spaces becomes available, the truck with the lowest number enters the vacant dock. Truck arrivals are Poisson distributed, and the unloading and loading times (service times) are exponentially distributed. The average arrival rate at the terminal is five trucks per hour, and the average service rate per dock is two trucks per hour (30 minutes per truck).

a. Compute L, L_q, W, and W_q.

b. The management of the shipping company is considering adding extra employees and equipment to improve the average service time per terminal dock to 25 minutes per truck. It would cost the company $18,000 per year to achieve this improved service. Management estimates that it will increase its profit by $750 per year for each minute it is able to reduce a truck's waiting time. Determine whether management should make the investment.

c. Now suppose that the managers of the shipping company have decided that truck waiting time is excessive and they want to reduce it. They have determined that there are two alternatives available for reducing the waiting time. They can add a fourth dock, or they can add extra employees and equipment at the existing docks, which will reduce the average service time per location from the original 30 minutes per truck to 23 minutes per truck. The costs of these alternatives are approximately equal. Management desires to implement the alternative that reduces waiting time by the greatest amount. Which alternative should be selected?

5.23. Drivers who come to get their licenses at the department of motor vehicles have their photograph taken by an automated machine that develops the photograph onto the license card and laminates the complete license. The machine requires a constant time of 4.5 minutes to develop a completed license. If drivers arrive at the machine at the mean rate of 11 per hour (Poisson distributed), determine the average length of the waiting line and the average waiting time.

5.24. A vending machine at Municipal Airport dispenses hot coffee, hot chocolate, or hot tea in a constant service time of 30 seconds. Customers arrive at the vending machine at a mean rate of 50 per hour, Poisson distributed. Determine the average length of the waiting line and the average time a customer must wait.

5.25. In Problem 5.20 suppose that Huang's television-repair service cannot accommodate more than 10 TV sets at a time (under repair and waiting for service). What is the probability that the number of TV sets on hand will exceed the shop capacity?

5.26. Norfolk, Virginia, a major seaport on the East Coast, has a ship coal-loading facility. Currently, coal trucks filled with coal arrive at the port facility at the mean rate of 149 per day (Poisson distributed). The facility operates 24 hours a day. The coal trucks are unloaded one at a time on a first-come, first-served basis by automated mechanical equipment that empties the trucks in a constant time of eight minutes per truck, regardless of truck size. The port authority is negotiating with a coal company for an additional 30 trucks per day. However, the coal company will not use this port facility unless the port authority can assure them that their coal trucks will not have to wait to be unloaded at the port facility for more than 12 hours per truck on the average. Can the port authority provide this assurance?

5.27. The Waterfall Buffet in the lower level of the National Art Gallery serves food cafeteria-style daily to visitors and employees. The buffet is self-service. From 7:00 A.M. to 9:00 A.M. customers arrive at the buffet at a rate of eight per minute; from 9:00 A.M. to noon, at four per minute; from noon to 2:00, at 14 per minute; and from 2:00 P.M. to closing at 5:00 P.M., at eight per minute (Poisson distributed). All the customers take about the same amount of time to serve themselves and proceed to the buffet. Once a customer goes through the buffet, it takes an average of 0.4 minute (exponentially distributed) to pay the cashier. The gallery does not want a customer to have to wait longer than four minutes to pay. How many cashiers should be working at each of the four times during the day?

5.28. The Hair Port is a hair-styling salon at Riverside Mall. Four stylists are always available to serve customers on a first-come, first-served basis. Customers arrive at an average rate of four per hour (Poisson distributed), and the stylists spend an average of 45 minutes (exponentially distributed) on each customer.

a. Determine the average number of customers in the salon, the average time a customer must wait, and the average number waiting to be served.

b. The salon manager is considering adding a fifth stylist. Would this have a significant impact on waiting time?

5.29. The Riverton Police Department has eight patrol cars that are on constant call 24 hours per day. A patrol car requires repairs every 30 days, on average, according to an exponential distribution. When a patrol car is in need of repair it is driven into the motor pool, which has a repairperson on duty at all times. The average time required to repair a patrol car is 12 hours (exponentially distributed). Determine the average time a patrol car is not available for use and the average number of patrol cars out of service at any one time, and indicate if the repair service seems adequate.

5.30. The Crosstown Cab Company has four cabs on duty during normal business hours. The cab company dispatcher receives requests for service every seven minutes, on average, according to an exponential distribution. The average time to complete a trip is 20 minutes (exponentially distributed). Determine the average number of customers waiting for service and the average time a customer must wait for a cab.

5.31. A retail catalog operation employs a bank of six telephone operators who process orders using computer terminals. When a terminal breaks down, it must be disconnected and taken to a nearby electronics repair shop, where it is repaired. The mean time between terminal breakdowns is six working days, and the mean time required to repair a terminal is two working days (both exponentially distributed). As a result of lost sales, it costs the mail-order operation an estimated $50 per day in lost profits each day a terminal is out for repair. The company pays the electronics repair shop $3000 per year on a service agreement to repair the terminals. The company is considering the possibility of signing a new service agreement with another electronics repair shop that will provide substitute terminals while the broken ones are at the repair shop. However, the new service agreement would cost the mail-order operation $15,000 per year. Assuming that there are 250 working days in a year, determine what the mail-order operation should do.

5.32. The Baytown Post Office has four stations for service. Customers line up in single file for service on an FIFO basis. The mean arrival rate is 40 per hour, Poisson distributed, and the mean service time per server is five minutes, exponentially distributed. Compute the operating characteristics for this operation. Does the operation appear to be satisfactory in terms of: (a) postal workers' (servers') idle time; (b) customer waiting time and/or the number waiting for service; and (c) the percentage of the time a customer can walk in and get served without waiting at all?

5.33. Andromeda Books is a small, independent publisher of fiction and nonfiction books. Each week the publisher receives an average of eight unsolicited manuscripts to review (Poisson distributed). The publisher has 12 freelance reviewers in the area who read and evaluate manuscripts. It takes a reviewer an average of 10 days (exponentially distributed) to read a manuscript and write a brief synopsis. (Reviewers work on their own, seven days a week.) Determine how long the publisher must wait on average to receive a reviewer's manuscript evaluation, how many manuscripts are waiting to be reviewed, and how busy the reviewers are.

5.34. Amanda Fall is starting up a new house painting business, Fall Colors. She has been advertising in the local newspaper for several months, and based on inquiries and informal surveys of the local housing market she anticipates that she will get painting jobs at the rate of four per week (Poisson distributed). Amanda has also determined that it will take a four-person team of painters an average of 0.7 week (exponentially distributed) for a typical painting job.

a. Determine the number of teams of painters Amanda needs to hire so that customers will have to wait no longer than two weeks to get their houses painted.

b. If the average price for a painting job is $1700 and Amanda pays a team of painters $500 per week, will she make any money?

5.35. The Associate Dean in the College of Business at Tech is attempting to determine which of two copiers he should lease for the college's administrative suite. A regular copier leases for $8 per hour and it takes an employee an average of six minutes (exponentially distributed) to complete a copying job. A deluxe, high-speed copier leases for $16 per hour, and it requires an average of three minutes to complete a copying job. Employees arrive at the copying machine at the rate of seven per hour (Poisson distributed) and an employee's time is valued at $10 per hour. Determine which copier the college should lease.

5.36. The Corner Cleaners 24-hour laundromat has 16 washing machines. A machine breaks down every 20 days (exponentially distributed). The repair service the laundromat contracts takes an average of one day to repair a machine (exponentially distributed). A washing machine averages $5 per hour in revenue. The laundromat is considering a new repair service that guarantees repairs in 0.50 day, but they charge $10 more per hour than the current repair service. Should the laundromat switch to the new repair service?

5.37. The Ritz Hotel has enough space for six taxicabs to load passengers, line up, and wait for guests at its entrance. Cabs arrive at the hotel every 10 minutes and if a taxi drives by the hotel and the line is full it must drive on. Hotel guests require taxis every five minutes on average and then it takes a cab driver an average of 3.5 minutes to load passengers and luggage and leave the hotel (exponentially distributed).

a. What is the average time a cab must wait for a fare?

b. What is the probability that the line will be full when a cab drives by and it must drive on?

5.38. The local Quick Burger fast food restaurant has a drive-through window. Customers in cars arrive at the window at the rate of 10 per hour (Poisson distributed). It requires an average of four minutes (exponentially distributed) to take and fill an order. The restaurant chain has a service goal of an average waiting time of three minutes.

a. Will the current system meet the restaurant's service goal?

b. If the restaurant is not meeting its service goal, it can add a second drive-in window that will reduce the service time per customer to 2.5 minutes. Will the additional window enable the restaurant to meet its service goal?

c. During the two-hour lunch period the arrival rate of drive-in customers increases to 20 per hour. Will the two-window system be able to achieve the restaurant's service goal during the rush period?

5.39. From 3:00 P.M. to 8:00 P.M. the local Big-W Supermarket has a steady arrival of customers. Customers finish shopping and arrive at the checkout area at the rate of 80 per hour (Poisson distributed). It is assumed that when customers arrive at the cash registers they will divide themselves relatively evenly so that all the checkout lines are even. The average checkout time at a register is seven minutes (exponentially distributed). The store manager's service goal is for customers to be out of the store within 12 minutes (on average) after they complete their shopping and arrive at the cash register. How many cash registers must the store have open in order to achieve the manager's service goal?

5.40. Customers arrive at the lobby of the exclusive and expensive Ritzy Hotel at the rate of 40 per hour (Poisson distributed) to check in. The hotel normally has three clerks available at the desk to check guests in. The average time for a clerk to check in a guest is four minutes (exponentially distributed). Clerks at the Ritzy are paid $12 per hour and the hotel assigns a goodwill cost of $2 per minute for the time a guest must wait in line. Determine if the present check-in system is cost effective; if it is not, recommend what hotel management should do.

5.41. The Delacroix Inn in Alexandria is a small exclusive hotel with 20 rooms. Guests can call housekeeping from 8:00 A.M. to midnight for any of their service needs. Housekeeping keeps one person on duty during this time to respond to guest calls. Each room averages 0.7 calls per day to housekeeping (Poisson distributed), and a guest request requires an average response time of 30 minutes (exponentially distributed) from the staff person. Determine the portion of time the staff person is busy and how long a guest must wait for his or her request to be addressed. Does the housekeeping system seem adequate?

5.42. Jim Carter builds custom furniture, primarily cabinets, bookcases, small tables, and chairs. He only works on one piece of furniture for a customer at a time. It takes him an average of five weeks (exponentially distributed) to build a piece of furniture. An average of 14 customers approach Jim to order pieces of furniture each year (Poisson distributed); however, Jim will only take a maximum of eight advance orders. Determine the average time a customer must wait to receive a furniture order once it is placed and how busy Jim is. What is the probability that a customer will be able to place an order with Jim?

5.43. Judith Lewis is a doctoral student at State University, and she also works full time as an academic tutor for 10 scholarship student athletes. She took the job hoping it would leave her free time between tutoring to devote to her own studies. An athlete visits her for tutoring an average of every 16 hours (exponentially distributed), and she spends an average 1.5 hours (exponentially distributed) with the athlete. She is able to tutor only one athlete at a time, and athletes study while they are waiting.

a. Determine how long a player must wait to see her and the percentage of time Judith is busy. Does the job seem to meet Judith's expectations, and does the system seem adequate to meet the athlete's needs?

b. If the results in part (a) indicate that the tutoring arrangement is ineffective, suggest an adjustment that could make it better for both the athletes and Judith.

5.44. Agents at the security gate at the Hurtsfield County Regional Airport are able to check passengers and process them through the security gate at the rate of 52 per hour (Poisson distributed). Passengers arrive at the gate throughout the day at the rate of 45 per hour (Poisson distributed).

a. Determine the average waiting time and length of the waiting line.

b. The passenger traffic arriving at the airport security gate varies significantly during the day and flight takeoffs tend to cluster, making the passenger traffic very heavy at specific times while at other times there is little or no passenger traffic through the security gate. At the times leading up to flight takeoffs passengers arrive at a rate of 125 per hour (Poisson distributed). Develop and solve a waiting line system that can accommodate this increased level of passenger traffic.

5.45. The inland port at Pittsburgh is a transportation hub that transfers shipping containers from trucks coming from eastern seaports to rail cars for shipment to inland destinations. Containers arrive at the inland ports at the rate of nine per hour. It takes 25 minutes (exponentially distributed) for a crane to unload a container from a truck, place it on a flatbed railcar, and secure it. Suggest a waiting line system that will effectively handle this level of container traffic at the inland port.

5.46. The Dominion Landing theme park has a new water ride, the Raging Rapids. The ride holds 36 people in boat-cars and it takes 4.1 minutes to complete the ride circuit. It also takes the ride attendants another 3.5 minutes (with virtually no variation) to load and unload passengers. Passengers arrive at the ride during peak park hours at the rate of 4.4 per minute (Poisson distributed). Determine the length of the waiting line for the ride.

5.47. The food court at Tech has a single checkout counter over the weekends staffed by one employee who takes an average of 2 minutes to checkout a customer. Students arrive to the food court at a rate of 25 per hour. The campus newspaper has recently published complaints from students about slow service in the food court on weekends. Use queuing theory to calculate the following:

a. The average number of students in the system
b. The average number of students in the waiting line
c. The average time a student spends in the line
d. The probability that the cashier would be busy and thus the student would have to wait
e. What assumptions about the distribution of arrival rates and service rates are you making in deriving the above values? Are the student complaints valid? Discuss.

5.48. After reviewing your report above, Tech has decided to improve the checkout process through training, clearer signage about prices, and bar code stickers on the most popular items purchased. With the improvements in place, it now takes an average of 1.5 minutes to check out a customer from the food court. As a result of the shorter checkout lines, more students are visiting the food court on weekends, arriving at an average rate of 30 customers per hour. Recalculate the measures above (a through d in Problem 5.47). Has customer service improved in the new system?

5.49. Aisha works at the local Yourizon store on Friday nights, usually with two other employees. This Friday, her boss has told her she will be the only sales associate present. Aisha wants to convince the manager that having only one worker on duty will result in dissatisfied customers and lost business. She pulls out her OM textbook and flips to the chapter on queuing.

a. If customers arrive at an average rate of 12 customers per hour and can be served at a rate of 15 customers per hour, will any customers have to wait? Why or why not?
b. Yourizon policy states that the average time a person waits in line for service should be no longer than 10 minutes. Does Aisha have a case?
c. The manager is averse to idle employees. What is the probability that Aisha will be idle on Friday night at the store?
d. Yourizon has learned that when there are more than three customers in the store at any time, new customers passing by will not enter. What is the probability that the average number of customers in the system is more than three?

5.50. Cannera Bread Bistro usually has two workers behind the counter after morning rush hour. One worker takes the orders and the other one fills the orders. On average, 10 customers arrive per hour, and the average service time is four minutes (i.e., two minutes to take the order and two minutes to fill the order). The manager is wondering if each worker should be an order taker *and* an order filler, thus opening up two lines. Performing both tasks of taking and filling an order would take an average of six minutes total. Assuming that customers will line up in equal numbers in front of each register, calculate the average waiting time in line and the average queue length for each configuration. Which configuration would you recommend?

Case Problems

Case Problem 5.1 Streamlining the Refinancing Process

With mortgage rates at an all-time low, National Bank has been swamped with refinancing requests this year. To handle the increased volume, it divided the process into five distinct stages and created departments for each stage.

The process begins with a customer completing a loan application for a *loan agent*. The loan agent discusses the refinancing options with the customer and uses its online pre-approval program and customer-reported data to see if the customer qualifies for loan approval. If the numbers work, the customer signs a few papers to allow a credit check and goes home to wait for notification of the loan's approval.

The customer's electronic file is then passed on to a *loan processor*, who requests a credit check, verification of loans or mortgages from other financial institutions, an appraisal of the property, and employment verification. If any problems are encountered, the loan processor goes to the loan agent for advice. If items appear on the credit report that are not on the application or if other agencies have requested the credit report, the customer is required to explain the discrepancies in writing. If the explanation is acceptable, the letter is placed in the customer's file and the file is sent electronically to the *loan* agent (and sometimes the bank's board) for final approval.

The customer receives notification of loan approval and is asked to call the *closing agent* to schedule a closing date and to lock in a loan rate if the customer has not already done so.

The closing agent requests the name of the customer's attorney to forward the loan packet. The attorney is responsible for arranging a termite inspection, a survey, a title search, and insurance and for preparing the closing papers. The attorney and the closing agent correspond back and forth to verify fees, payment schedules, and payoff amounts.

The *loan-servicing specialist* makes sure the previous loan is paid off and the new loan is set up properly. After the closing takes place, the bank's *loan-payment specialist* takes care of issuing payment books or setting up the automatic drafting of mortgage fees and calculating the exact monthly payments, including escrow amounts. The loan-payment specialist also monitors late payment of mortgages.

It is difficult to evaluate the success or failure of the process, since the volume of refinancing requests is so much greater than it has ever been before. However, customer comments solicited by the loan-servicing specialist have been disturbing to management.

Customer Comments:

- I refinanced with the same bank that held my original loan, thinking erroneously that I could save time and money. You took two months longer processing my loan than the other bank would have, and the money I saved on closing costs was more than eaten up by the extra month's higher mortgage payments.
- I just got a call from someone at your bank claiming my mortgage payment was overdue. How can it be overdue when you draft it automatically from my checking account?
- If I haven't made any additions to my house or property in the past year, you appraised it last year, and you have access to my tax assessment, why bother with another appraisal? You guys just like to pass around the business.
- I never know who to call for what. You have so many people working on my file. I know I've repeated the same thing to a dozen different people.
- It took so long to get my loan approved that my credit report, appraisal report, and termite inspection ran out. You should pay for the new reports, not me.
- I drove down to your office in person today to deliver the attorney's papers, and I hoped to return them with your signature and whatever else you add to the closing packet. The loan specialist said that the closing agent wouldn't get to my file until the morning of the scheduled closing and that if she hit a snag, the closing could be postponed! I'm taking off half a day from work to attend the closing and "rescheduling" is not convenient. I know you have lots of business, but I don't like being treated this way.
- I received a letter from one of your loan-payment specialists today, along with a stack of forms to complete specifying how I want to set up my mortgage payments. I signed all these at closing—don't you read your own work? I'm worried that if I fill them out again you'll withdraw the payment twice from my account!

1. Create a service blueprint of the refinancing process. Why do you think the bank organized its process this way? What problems have ensued?

2. Examine the process carefully. Look at customer/provider interactions. Which steps create value for the customer? Which steps can be eliminated? Construct a new blueprint showing how the overall process can be improved.

Case Problem 5.2 Herding the Patient

Bayside General Hospital is trying to streamline its operations. A problem-solving group consisting of a nurse, a technician, a doctor, an administrator, and a patient is examining outpatient procedures in an effort to speed up the process and make it more cost-effective. Listed here are the steps that a typical patient follows for diagnostic imaging:

- Patient enters main hospital entrance.
- Patient takes a number and waits to be called to registration desk.
- Patient registers.
- Patient is taken to diagnostic imaging department.
- Patient registers at diagnostic imaging reception.
- Patient sits in department waiting area until dressing area clears.
- Patient changes in dressing area.
- Patient waits in dressing area.
- Patient is taken to exam room.
- Exam is performed.
- Patient is taken to dressing area.
- Patient dresses.
- Patient leaves.

1. Create a service blueprint of the procedure and identify opportunities for improvement.

2. Describe what elements of a servicescape would make this service more palatable to the customer and efficient for the hospital staff.

Case Problem 5.3 The College of Business Copy Center

The copy center in the College of Business at State University has become an increasingly contentious item among the college administrators. The department heads have complained to the associate dean about the long lines and waiting times for their secretaries at the copy center. They claim that it is a waste of scarce resources for the secretaries to wait in line talking when they could be doing more productive work in the office. Hanford Burris, the associate dean, says the limited operating budget will not allow the college to purchase a new copier or copiers to relieve the problem. This standoff has been going on for several years.

To make her case for improved copying facilities, Lauren Moore, a teacher in Operations Management, assigned students in her class to gather some information about the copy center as a class project. The students were to record the arrivals at the center and the length of time it took to do a copy job once the secretary actually reached a copy machine. In addition, the students were to describe how the copy center system worked.

When the students completed the project, they turned in a report to Professor Moore. The report described the copy center as containing two machines. When secretaries arrive for a copy job, they join a queue, which looked more like milling around to the students, but they acknowledged that each secretary knew when it was his or her turn, and, in effect, the secretaries formed a single queue for the first available copy machine. Also, since copy jobs are assigned tasks, secretaries always stayed to do the job no matter how long the line was or how long they had to wait. They never left the queue.

From the data the students gathered, Professor Moore was able to determine that secretaries arrived every eight minutes for a copy job and that the arrival rate was Poisson distributed. Furthermore, she was able to determine that the average time it takes to complete a job was 12 minutes, and this is exponentially distributed.

Using her department's personnel records and data from the university personnel office, Dr. Moore determined that a secretary's average salary is $8.50 per hour. From her academic calendar she added up the actual days in the year when the college and departmental offices were open and found there were 247. However, as she added up working days, it occurred to her that during the summer months the workload is much less, and the copy center would probably get less traffic. The summer included about 70 days, during which she expected the copy center traffic would be about half of what it is during the normal year, but she speculated that the average time of a copying job would remain about the same.

Professor Moore next called a local office supply firm to check the prices on copiers. A new copier of the type in the copy center now would cost $36,000. It would also require $8000 per year for maintenance and would have a normal useful life of six years.

Do you think Dr. Moore will be able to convince the associate dean that a new copy machine will be cost effective?

Case Problem 5.4 Northwoods Backpackers

Bob and Carol Packer operate a successful outdoor wear store in Vermont called Northwoods Backpackers. They stock mostly cold-weather outdoor items such as hiking and backpacking clothes, gear, and accessories. They established an excellent reputation throughout New England for quality products and service. Eventually, Bob and Carol noticed that more and more of their sales were from customers who did not live in the immediate vicinity but were calling in orders on the telephone. As a result, the Packers decided to distribute a catalog and establish a phone-order service. The order department consisted of five operators working eight hours per day from 10:00 A.M. to 6:00 P.M., Monday through Friday. For a few years the mail-order service was only moderately successful; the Packers just about broke even on their investment. However, during the holiday season of the third year of the catalog order service, they were overwhelmed with phone orders. Although they made a substantial profit, they were concerned about the large number of lost sales they estimated they incurred. Based on information provided by the telephone company regarding call volume and complaints from customers, the Packers estimated they lost sales of approximately $100,000. Also they felt they had lost a substantial number of old and potentially new customers because of the poor service of the catalog order department.

Prior to the next holiday season, the Packers explored several alternatives for improving the catalog order service. The current system includes the five original operators with computer terminals who work eight-hour days, five days per week. The Packers have hired a consultant to study this system, and she reported that the time for an operator to take a customer order is exponentially distributed with a mean of 3.6 minutes. Calls are expected to arrive at the telephone center during the six-week holiday season according to a Poisson distribution with a mean rate of 175 calls per hour. When all operators are busy, callers are put on hold, listening to music until an operator can answer. Waiting calls are answered on a first-in, first-out basis. Based on her experience with other catalog telephone order operations and data from Northwoods Backpackers, the consultant has determined that if Northwoods Backpackers can reduce customer call waiting time to approximately one-half minute or less, the company will save $135,000 in lost sales during the coming holiday season.

Therefore, the Packers have adopted this level of call service as their goal. However, in addition to simply avoiding lost sales, the Packers believe it is important to reduce waiting time to maintain their reputation for good customer service. Thus, they would like about 70% of their callers to receive immediate service.

The Packers can maintain the same number of workstations/computer terminals they currently have and increase their service to 16 hours per day with two operator shifts running from 8:00 A.M. to midnight. The Packers believe when customers become aware of their extended hours the calls will spread out uniformly, resulting in a new call average arrival rate of 87.5 calls per hour (still Poisson distributed). This schedule change would cost Northwoods Backpackers approximately $11,500 for the six-week holiday season.

Another alternative for reducing customer waiting times is to offer weekend service. However, the Packers believe that if they do offer weekend service, it must coincide with whatever service they offer during the week. In other words, if they have phone order service eight hours per day during the week, they must have the same service during the weekend; the same is true with 16-hours-per-day service. They feel that if weekend hours differ from weekday hours it will confuse customers. If eight-hour service is offered seven days per week, the new call arrival rate will be reduced to 125 calls per hour at a cost of $3600. If Northwoods offers 16-hour service, the mean call arrival rate will be reduced to 62.5 calls per hour, at a cost of $7300.

Still another possibility is to add more operator stations. Each station includes a desk, an operator, a phone, and a computer terminal. An additional station that is in operation five days per week, eight hours per day, will cost $2900 for the holiday season. For a 16-hour day the cost per new station is $4700. For seven-day service, the cost of an additional station for eight-hour-per-day service is $3800; for 16-hour-per-day service the cost is $6300.

The facility Northwoods Backpackers uses to house its operators can accommodate a maximum of 10 stations. Additional operators in excess of 10 would require the Packers to lease, remodel, and wire a new facility, which is a capital expenditure they do not want to undertake this holiday season. Alternatively, the Packers do not want to reduce their current number of operator stations.

Determine what order service configuration the Packers should use to achieve their goals, and explain your recommendation.

References

Bitner, M. J., A. Ostrom, and F. Morgan, "Service Blueprinting: A Practical Technique for Service Innovation," California Management Review, Vol. 50, No. 3 (2008).

Cooper, R. B. *Introduction to Queuing Theory*, 2nd ed. New York: North Holland, 1981.

Davis, M., and J. Heineke. *Operations Management*. New York: McGraw-Hill/Irwin, 2004.

Fitzsimmons, J., and M. Fitzsimmons. *Service Management*. New York: McGraw-Hill/Irwin, 8e, 2013.

Gross, D., and C. Harris. *Fundamentals of Queuing Theory*, 2nd ed. New York: Wiley, 1985.

Hillier, F. S., and O. S. Yu. *Queuing Tables and Graphics*. New York: North Holland, 1981.

Jacobs, R., and R. Chase. *Operations and Supply Chain Management*. New York: McGraw-Hill/ Irwin, 2014.

Jargon, J. "At Starbucks, Baristas Told No More Than Two Drinks," *The Wall Street Journal* (October 13, 2010).

Kleinrock, L. *Queuing Systems*, vols. 1 and 2. New York: Wiley, 1975.

Lee, A. *Applied Queuing Theory*. New York: St. Martin's Press, 1966.

Lovelock, C. H. and J. Wirtz. *Services Marketing*. Englewood Cliffs, NJ. Prentice Hall, 2011.

Morse, P. M. *Queues, Inventories, and Maintenance*. New York: Wiley, 1958.

Prahalad, C. K., and Venkat Ramaswamy. *The Future of Competition: Co-creating Unique Value with Customers*. Boston: Harvard Business School Press, 2004.

Saaty, T. L. *Elements of Queuing Theory with Applications*. New York: Dover, 1983.

Sampson, S. E. Understanding Service Businesses. Salt Lake City, UT: Brigham Young University, 1999.

Shostack, G. L. "Designing Services That Deliver." *Harvard Business Review* (January–February 1984), pp. 133–139.

Solomon, S. L. *Simulation of Waiting Line Systems*. Upper Saddle River, NJ: Prentice Hall, 1983.

White, J. A., J. W. Schmidt, and G. K. Bennett. *Analysis of Queuing Systems*. New York: Academic Press, 1975.

Zeithaml, V. *Service Quality*. Cambridge, MA: Marketing Science Institute, 2004

CHAPTER 6

Processes and Technology

Bloomberg/Getty Images, Inc.

LEARNING OBJECTIVES

After reading this chapter, you will be able to:

- Evaluate strategic options in process planning, including whether or not to outsource.
- Differentiate among different types of production processes.
- Understand the effect of volume and standardization on process selection.
- Appreciate the difficulties in translating a design to a process.
- Use simple flowcharting tools to improve everyday processes.
- Investigate the use of technology in manufacturing and service processes.

From Sand to Silicon to Smartphone

The semiconductor industry makes the chips that are the brains of smartphones. The process of making a chip is long and involved, over 300 steps in all, and takes place in the highly automated clean room environment of a foundry or *fab* (i.e., fabricator), as shown in the photo above. It begins with silicone (e.g., sand), which is purified, melted, and cooled into a solid crystallized ingot, commonly with a diameter of 300 mm. The ingot is sliced into discs called wafers, each about one mm thick. The wafers are polished and packaged for shipment to the next process or to an outside manufacturer. Photolithography then imprints a specific pattern on the wafer, deposits a liquid called photo resist, and exposes it to ultraviolet light. Many more steps are performed and repeated depending on the complexity of the chip; material and ions are added, diffused, etched, cleaned, and doped in precise sequences layer after layer. Transistors control the electrical current in the chip and are added layer by layer as well. The wafers are tested and then sliced into individual pieces and packaged into what we know as a chip. Depending on the size of each chip, its quality, and its intended use, one wafer can produce tens of thousands of chips.

The entire process is complex in both design and execution, *and* it is microscopic. With today's technology, over 30 million transistors can fit across the width of a single human hair. Smaller sizes mean more powerful chips and a faster and more powerful processor for your smartphone.

In this chapter, we'll talk about different types of processes and technologies, from highly automated advanced manufacturing to low-tech manual assembly operations. We'll examine how to select the right process, how to plan it out, and how to improve it.

Source: ITA, "Semiconductors and Semiconductor Manufacturing Equipment Top Markets Report," Washington, DC: International Trade Administration, July 2015; S. Gibbs, "Moore's law wins: new chips have circuits 10,000 times thinner than hairs," *The Guardian*, (July 9, 2015); "How Intel Makes Chips: Transistors to Transformations," Intel, Corporate brochure, 2015.

A **process** is a group of related tasks with specific inputs and outputs. Processes exist to create value for the customer, the shareholder, or society. *Process design* defines what tasks need to be done and how they are to be coordinated among functions, people, and organizations. Planning, analyzing, and improving processes is the essence of operations management. Processes are planned, analyzed, and redesigned as required by changes in strategy and emerging technology.

Process A group of related tasks with specific inputs and outputs.

Process strategy is an organization's overall approach for physically producing goods and providing services. Process decisions should reflect how the firm has chosen to compete in the marketplace, reinforce product decisions, and facilitate the achievement of corporate goals. A firm's process strategy defines its:

Process strategy An organization's overall approach for physically producing goods and services.

- ***Vertical integration:*** The extent to which the firm will produce the inputs and control the outputs of each stage of the production process.
- ***Capital intensity:*** The mix of capital (i.e., equipment, automation) and labor resources used in the production process.
- ***Process flexibility:*** The ease with which resources can be adjusted in response to changes in demand, technology, products or services, and resource availability.
- ***Customer involvement:*** The role of the customer in the production process.

In this chapter we examine the planning, analysis, and innovation of processes, as well as technology decisions related to those processes.

Process Planning

Process planning determines *how* a product will be produced or a service provided. It decides which components will be made in-house and which will be purchased from a supplier, selects processes, and develops and documents the specifications for manufacture and delivery. In this section, we discuss outsourcing decisions, process selection, and process plans.

Process planning Converts designs into workable instructions for manufacture or delivery.

Outsourcing

A firm that sells the product, assembles the product, makes all the parts, and extracts the raw material is completely **vertically integrated**. But most companies cannot or will not make all of the parts that go into a product. A major strategic decision, then, is how much of the work should be done outside the firm. The decision involves questions of dependence, competency-building, and proprietary knowledge, as well as cost.

Vertical integration The degree to which a firm produces the parts that go into its products.

On what basis should particular items be made in-house? When should items be outsourced? How should suppliers be selected? What type of relationship should be maintained with suppliers—arm's length, controlling, partnership, alliance? What is expected from the suppliers? How many suppliers should be used? How can the quality and dependability of suppliers be ensured? How can suppliers be encouraged to collaborate?

For process planning, we need to decide which items will be purchased from an outside supplier and which items will be produced in our own factories. More advanced sourcing decisions and a discussion of the questions posed above are covered in Chapter 10.

The basic outsourcing decision rests on an evaluation of the following factors:

1. ***Cost.*** Would it be cheaper to make the item or buy it? To perform the service in-house or outsource it? The cost of *buying* the item from a supplier includes the purchase price, transportation costs, and various tariffs, taxes, and fees (referred to as landed cost in Chapter 10). The cost of coordinating production over long distances and increased inventory levels to cover demand during a lengthy lead time can also run high. The cost of *making* the item includes labor, material, and overhead. Existing overhead does not disappear when some products are outsourced. Spreading overhead over fewer products can actually increase unit costs.

   In some situations a company may decide to buy an item rather than make it (or vice versa) when, from a cost standpoint, it would be cheaper to do otherwise. The remaining factors in this list represent noneconomic factors that can influence or dominate the economic considerations.

2. ***Capacity.*** Companies that are operating at less than full capacity may elect to make components rather than buy them, especially if maintaining a level workforce or capability to produce is important. Sometimes the available capacity is not sufficient to make all the components, so choices have to be made. Typically, it is better to produce more customized or volatile products in-house, and to outsource steady products with high volume/high standardization.
3. ***Quality.*** The capability to provide quality parts consistently is an important consideration in the outsourcing decision. It is easier to control the quality of items produced in your own factory. However, standardization of parts, supplier certification, and supplier involvement in design can improve the quality of supplied parts. In the event that quality becomes a problem, increased monitoring of the supplier can significantly increase costs.
4. ***Speed.*** The savings from purchasing an item from a far-off vendor can be eaten up by the lengthy transit time of offshore shipments. At other times, a smaller supplier can be more flexible, and can adapt more quickly to design and technology changes. Of course, speed is useful only if it is reliable.

5. ***Reliability.*** Suppliers need to be reliable in both the quality and the timing of what they supply. Unexpected delays in shipments or partially filled orders because of quality rejects can wreak havoc with the manufacturing system. Many companies today are requiring that their suppliers meet certain quality and delivery standards to be certified as an approved supplier. As discussed in Chapter 2, the most common quality certification is ISO 9000. Other companies assess huge penalties for unreliable supply. Some automakers, for example, fine their suppliers $30,000 for each *hour* an order is late.
6. ***Expertise.*** Companies that are especially good at making or designing certain items may want to keep control over their production. Coca-Cola would not want to release its formula to a supplier, even if there were guarantees of secrecy. Although automakers might outsource many of their component parts, they need proprietary control over major components such as engines, transmissions, and electronic guidance systems. Japanese, Taiwanese, and Korean firms are currently learning U.S. expertise in aircraft design and manufacture by serving as suppliers of component parts. Chinese markets are often flooded with cheap knockoffs of goods manufactured by suppliers in that country. The protection of intellectual property is a major concern in extended supply chains.

The outsourcing decision can be made along a continuum from a single purchasing decision to a joint venture, as shown in Figure 6.1. Single contracts are used if the outsourcing decision is temporary, or the products are standardized (like commodities) and suppliers are chosen based on lowest cost. Strategic alliances signify that the supplier is an important long-term partner, and the cost or consequences of switching suppliers would be significant. Companies share more information with strategic suppliers and work with them to solve problems or improve processes. Joint ventures are used when entering a foreign country for the first time, or as a condition for operating in another country. Risks, resources, and rewards are shared among equity partners of a joint venture.

Process Selection

The next step in process planning is to select a production process for those items we will produce in-house. Production processes can be classified into projects, batch production, mass production, and continuous production.

FIGURE 6.1 **The Sourcing Continuum**

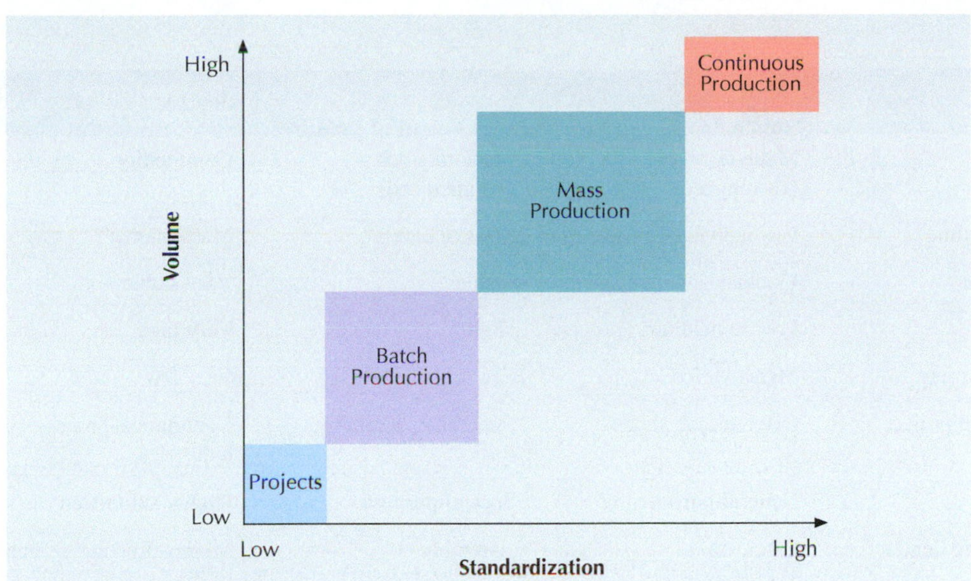

Source: Adapted from Robert Hayes and Steven Wheelwright, *Restoring the Competitive Edge: Competing Through Manufacturing* (New York, John Wiley & Sons, 1984), p. 209.

FIGURE 6.2 The Product-Process Matrix

Projects take a long time to complete, involve a large investment of funds and resources, and produce one item at a time to consumer order. Examples include construction projects, shipbuilding, new-product development, and aircraft manufacturing.

Projects One-at-a-time production of a product to customer order.

Batch production processes many different jobs through the production system at the same time in groups or batches. Products are typically made to customer order, volume (in terms of customer order size) is low, and demand fluctuates. Examples of batch production include printers, bakeries, machine shops, education, and furniture making.

Batch production Processing many different jobs at the same time in groups (or batches).

Mass production produces large volumes of a standard product for a mass market. Product demand is stable, and product volume is high. Goods that are mass produced include automobiles, televisions, personal computers, fast food, and most consumer goods.

Mass production Producing large volumes of a standard product for a mass market.

Continuous production is used for *very* high-volume commodity products that are *very* standardized. The system is *highly* automated and is typically in operation continuously 24 hours a day (as seen in the photo). Refined oil, treated water, paints, chemicals, steel and foodstuffs are produced by continuous production.

Continuous production Producing very high-volume commodity products.

The process chosen to create the product or service must be consistent with product and service characteristics. The most important product characteristics (in terms of process choice) are degree of *standardization* and *demand volume*. Figure 6.2 shows a product-process matrix that matches product characteristics with process choice.

The best process strategy is found on the diagonal of the matrix. Companies or products that are off the diagonal have either made poor process choices or have found a means to execute a competitive advantage. For example, technological advancements in flexible automation allow Motorola to mass produce customized pagers. Volvo and Rolls Royce occupy a special market niche by producing cars in a crafted, customized fashion. Examples of poor process choice include Texas Instruments' attempt to produce consumer products for mass markets by the same process that had been successful in the production of scientific products for specialized markets, and Corning's production of low-volume consumer items, such as range covers, with the same continuous process used for other items formed from glass.

Table 6.1 summarizes the characteristics of each type of process. Examples of each type of process are shown in the photos that follow. As we move from projects to continuous production, demand volume increases; products become more standardized; systems become more capital-intensive, more automated, and less flexible; and customers become less involved.

Process Selection With Breakeven Analysis

Several quantitative techniques are available for selecting a process. One that bases its decision on the cost tradeoffs associated with demand volume is **breakeven analysis**. The components of breakeven analysis are volume, cost, revenue, and profit.

Breakeven analysis Examines the cost trade-offs associated with demand volume.

TABLE 6.1 Types of Processes

	PROJECT	BATCH PRODUCTION	MASS PRODUCTION	CONTINUOUS PRODUCTION
Type of product	Unique	Made-to-order (customized)	Made-to-stock (standardized)	Commodity
Type of customer	One-at-a-time	Few individual customers	Mass market	Mass market
Product demand	Infrequent	Fluctuates	Stable	Very stable
Demand volume	Very low	Low to medium	High	Very high
No. of different products	Infinite variety	Many, varied	Few	Very few
Production system	Long-term project	Discrete, job shops	Repetitive, assembly lines	Continuous, process industries
Equipment	Varied	General-purpose	Special-purpose	Highly automated
Primary type of work	Specialized contracts	Fabrication	Assembly	Mixing, treating, refining
Worker skills	Experts, craftspersons	Wide range of skills	Limited range of skills	Equipment monitors
Advantages	Custom work, latest technology	Flexibility, quality	Efficiency, speed, low cost	Highly efficient, large capacity, ease of control
Disadvantages	Nonrepetitive, small customer base, expensive	Costly, slow, difficult to manage	Capital investment, lack of responsiveness	Difficult to change, far-reaching errors, limited variety
Examples	Construction, shipbuilding, spacecraft	Machine shops, print shops, bakeries, education	Automobiles, televisions, computers, fast food	Paint, chemicals, foodstuffs

Volume is the level of production, usually expressed as the number of units produced and sold. We assume that the number of units produced can be sold.

Cost is divided into two categories: fixed and variable. *Fixed costs* remain constant regardless of the number of units produced, such as plant and equipment and other elements of overhead. *Variable costs* vary with the volume of units produced, such as labor and material. The total cost of a process is the sum of its fixed cost and its total variable cost (defined as volume times per unit variable cost).

Revenue on a per-unit basis is simply the price at which an item is sold. *Total revenue* is price times volume sold. *Profit* is the difference between total revenue and total cost. These components can be expressed mathematically as follows:

$$\begin{aligned}
\text{Total cost} &= \text{fixed cost} + \text{total variable cost} \\
\text{TC} &= c_f + vc_v \\
\text{Total revenue} &= \text{volume} \times \text{price} \\
\text{TR} &= vp \\
\text{Profit} &= \text{total revenue} - \text{total cost} \\
Z &= \text{TR} - \text{TC} \\
&= vp - (c_f + vc_v)
\end{aligned}$$

where

c_f = fixed cost
v = volume (i.e., number of units produced and sold)
c_v = variable cost per unit
p = price per unit

Continuous Production. *A paper manufacturer produces a continuous sheet of paper from wood pulp surry, which is mixed, pressed, dried, and wound onto reels. Later winders will cut the paper into customer size rolls for wrapping and labeling. Production per day exceeds 1700 tons or the equivalent of 680,000 reams of paper.*

Philip Gould/Getty Images, Inc.

More Standardized,
Higher Volume

Bloomberg/Getty Images, Inc.

Mass Production. *At this Flextronics factory in Fort Worth, Texas, workers assemble more than 100,000 MotoZ cellphones per week. Work is arranged in a line with assembly tasks performed in sequence. Each task takes less than a minute to complete.*

Matt Rourke/AP Images

Batch Production. *At Martin Guitar, skilled craftsmen and women carefully construct and assemble the numerous parts of a guitar. Except for rough cutting and sanding, most of the 150 steps required to make an acoustic guitar are performed by hand. One of the most crucial steps for quality sound is fitting the neck to the body. While some manufacturers use computer-aided manufacturing (CAM) for this, at Martin, a master neck setter fits, shaves and refits the joint by hand for superior quality. Even with such careful attention to detail, the factory can produce approximately 200 guitars a day.*

JUNG YEON-JE/Getty Images, Inc.

Project. *The construction of an aircraft carrier is an enormous project. The USS Nimitz, shown here, took more than four years to build at a cost of $4.5 billion. The carrier accommodates a crew of more than 6000 people and a full-load displacement of 100,000 tons. The carrier also houses two nuclear reactors, enabling it to operate for 13 years without refueling. Modular construction, in which a ship is built in sections or modules, has cut the production time of carriers and other ships in half. This is accomplished by outfitting several modules at one time and then adding them to the hull. Extensive use of CAD/CAM, precise tolerances, and careful quality control ensure that the modules fit together perfectly.*

In selecting a process, it is useful to know at what volume of sales and production we can expect to earn a profit. We want to make sure that the cost of producing a product does not exceed the revenue we will receive from the sale of the product. By equating total revenue with total cost and solving for v, we can find the volume at which profit is zero. This is called the **breakeven point**. At any volume above the breakeven point, we will make a profit. A mathematical formula for the breakeven point can be determined as follows:

$$\begin{aligned} \text{TR} &= \text{TC} \\ vp &= c_f + vc_v \\ vp - vc_v &= c_f \\ v(p - c_v) &= c_f \\ v &= \frac{c_f}{p - c_v} \end{aligned}$$

The Image Bank/Getty Images, Inc.

Continuous processes are used for very-high-volume, commodity products whose output is measured rather than counted. The production system is capital-intensive and highly automated (with workers who monitor the equipment rather than perform the work) and is typically operated 24 hours a day. Here a worker monitors steel production from a control center at ThyssenKrupp AG in Germany.

EXAMPLE 6.1 | Breakeven Analysis

Travis and Jeff own Up Right Paddlers, a new startup company with the goal of designing, making, and marketing stand-up paddle boards for streams and rivers. A new fitness craze, stand-up paddle boards are similar to surfboards in appearance, but are used by individuals to navigate down rivers in an upright position with a single long pole (or paddle), instead of sitting in tubes or rafts and floating down. River boards are constructed from heavy-duty raft material that is inflatable, rather than fiberglass used in ocean boards. Unlike ocean boards that market for \$500 to \$1000 each, river boards are typically sold for between \$100 and \$400. Since Travis and Jeff are just starting out and the demand for paddle boards on the East Coast has not been firmly established, they anticipate selling their product for \$100 each. Travis estimates the fixed cost for equipment and space will be \$2000, and the material and labor costs will run \$50 per unit. What volume of demand will be necessary for Travis and Jeff to break even on their new venture?

Solution:

$$\text{Fixed cost} = c_f = \$2000$$
$$\text{Variable cost} = c_v = \$50 \text{ per board}$$
$$\text{Price} = p = \$100 \text{ per board}$$
$$v = \frac{c_f}{p - c_v} = \frac{2000}{100 - 50} = 40 \text{ units}$$

The solution is shown graphically in the following figure. The x-axis represents production or demand volume, and the y-axis represents dollars of revenue, cost, or profit. The total revenue line extends from the origin, with a slope equal to the unit price of a board. The total cost line intersects the y-axis at a level corresponding to the fixed cost of the process and has a slope equal to the per-unit variable cost. The intersection of these two lines is the breakeven point. If demand is less than the breakeven point, the company will operate at a loss. But if demand exceeds the breakeven point, the company will be profitable. The company needs to sell more than 40 paddle boards to make a profit.

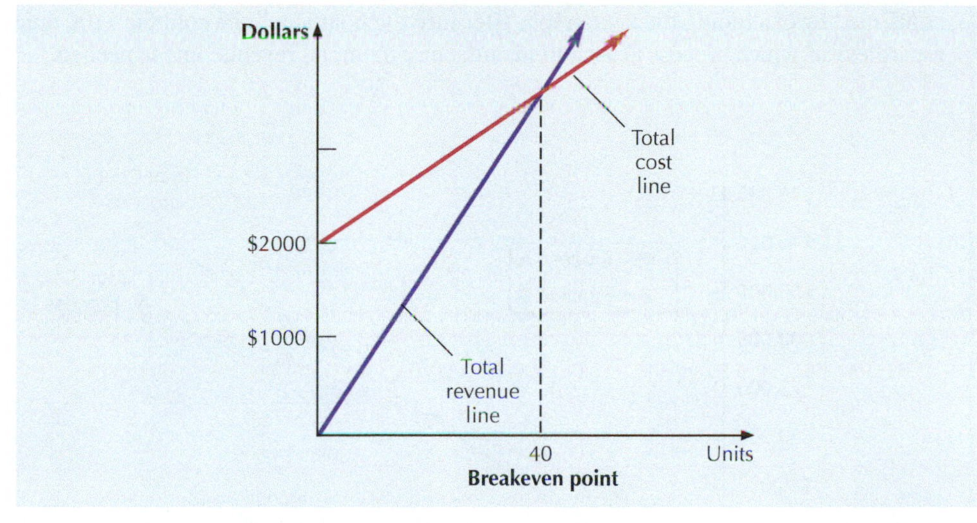

Breakeven analysis is especially useful when evaluating different degrees of automation. More automated processes have higher fixed costs but lower variable costs. The "best" process depends on the anticipated volume of demand for the product and the tradeoffs between fixed and variable costs. Example 6.2 shows how breakeven analysis can guide the selection of a process among two alternatives. The example uses this procedure:

1. Formulate a total cost equation for each process considered.
2. Calculate the ***point of indifference*** between two alternative processes (i.e., the volume at which the total cost of manufacturing is the same for the two processes) by setting their total cost equations equal to each other and solving for v, demand volume.
3. Above the point of indifference, choose the alternative with the lowest variable cost.
4. Below the point of indifference, choose the alternative with the lowest fixed cost.

For an example of choosing the best process among three alternatives, see the Solved Problem at the end of the chapter.

EXAMPLE 6.2 | Process Selection

Jeff, the more optimistic of the two owners of UpRight Paddlers, believes that demand for paddle boards will exceed the breakeven point of 40 units calculated in Example 6.1. He proposes spending $10,000 in fixed costs to buy more automated equipment that would reduce the materials and labor cost to $30 per board. The boards would sell for $100, regardless of which manufacturing process is chosen. Compare the two processes and determine for what level of demand each process would be preferred. Label Travis's proposal as Process A and Jeff's proposal as Process B.

Solution:

$$\begin{aligned} &\textit{Process A} \qquad\qquad \textit{Process B} \\ \$2{,}000 + \$50v &= \$10{,}000 + \$30v \\ \$20v &= \$8{,}000 \\ v &= 400 \text{ units} \end{aligned}$$

If demand is less than or equal to 400 boards, the alternative with the lowest fixed cost, *process A,* should be chosen. If demand is greater than or equal to 400 boards, the alternative with the lowest variable cost, *process B,* is preferred. Our decision can be confirmed by examining the next graph. (Because the boards will be sold for $100 apiece regardless of which process is used to manufacture them, no revenue line is needed.)

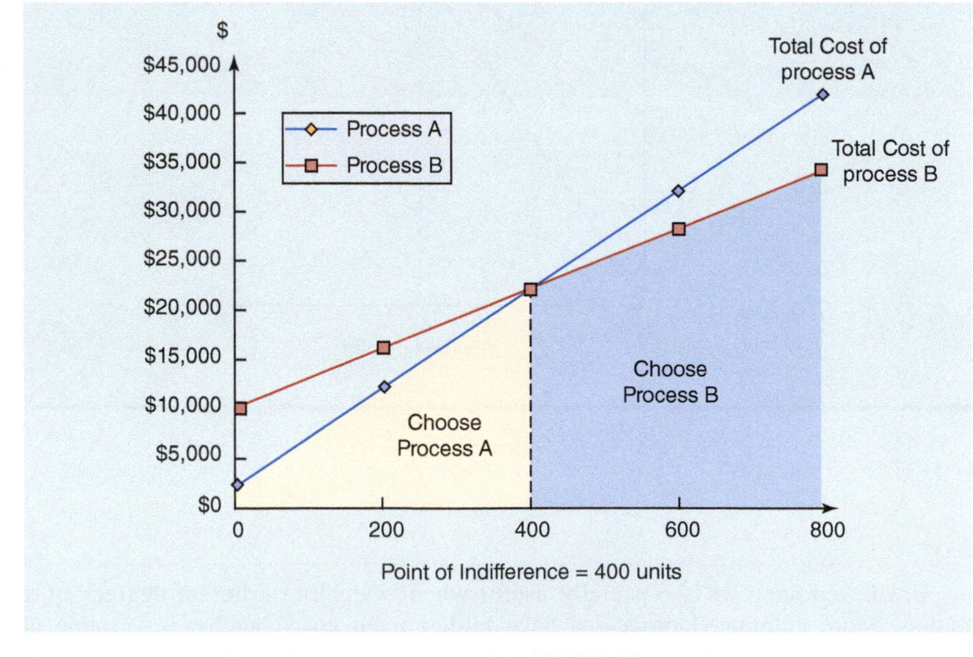

Process Plans

Process plans A set of documents that detail manufacturing and service delivery specifications.

Assembly charts A schematic diagram of a product that shows the relationship of component parts to parent assemblies.

Process plans are a set of documents that detail manufacturing and service delivery specifications. They begin with detailed drawings of product design (usually from a CAD system) and include **assembly charts** or bills of material (showing the parts and materials needed and how they are to be assembled together), *operations sheets* or routing sheets (listing the operations to be performed with details on equipment, tools, skills, etc.), and *quality-control checksheets* (specifying quality standards and quality data to be recorded).

Process plans are used in both manufacturing and service settings. A hospital, for example, has a set of process plans (often called protocols) for different types of medical

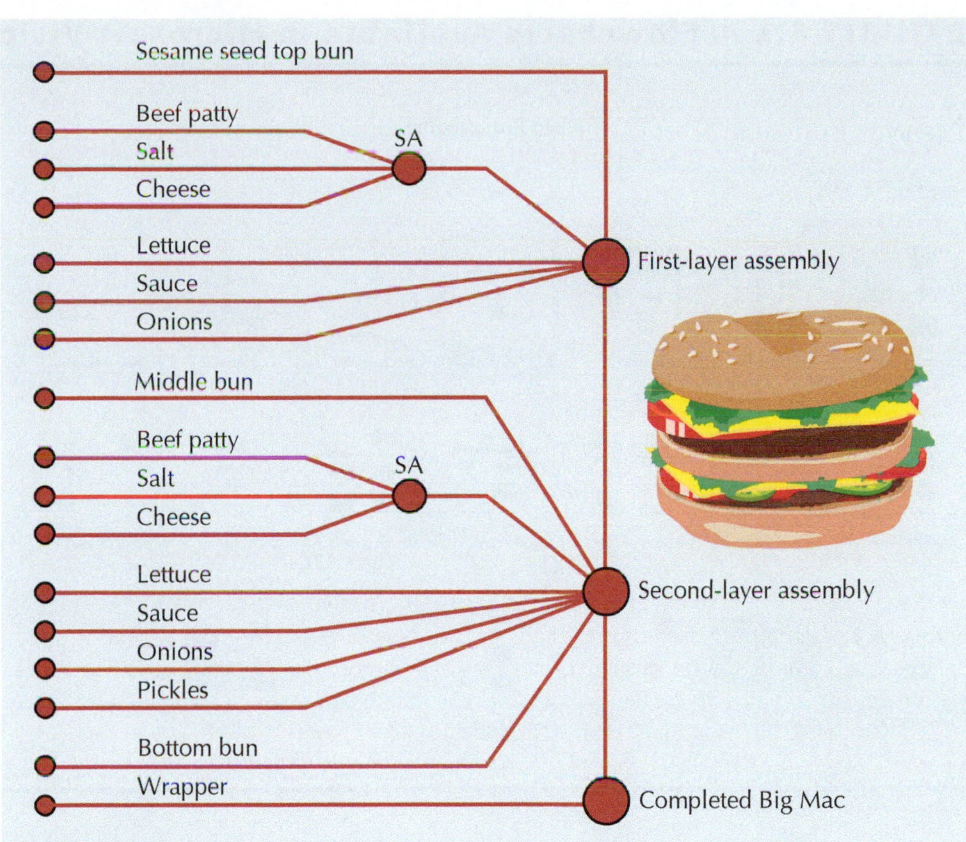

FIGURE 6.3 An Assembly Chart for a Big Mac

procedures and service plans for each particular patient. Similarly, in manufacturing, some process plans are standard, and others are created for each customer order. Figure 6.3 shows an assembly chart for a Big Mac. Figure 6.4 shows an operations sheet for a plastic molded vacuum cleaner attachment.

Process Analysis

Process analysis is the systematic examination of all aspects of a process to improve its operation—to make it faster, more efficient, less costly, or more responsive to the customer. The basic tools of process analysis are process flowcharts, diagrams, and maps.

FIGURE 6.4 An Operations Sheet for a Plastic Part

Part name: Crevice Tool
Part No.: 52074
Usage: Hand-Vac
Assembly No.: 520

Oper. No.	Description	Dept.	Machine/Tools	Time
10	Pour in plastic bits	041	Injection molding	1 min
20	Insert mold	041	#076	2 min
30	Check settings and start machine	041	113, 67, 650	20 min
40	Collect parts and lay flat	051	Plastics finishing	10 min
50	Remove and clean mold	042	Parts washer	15 min
60	Break off rough edges	051	Plastics finishing	10 min

EXHIBIT 6.1 | Flowcharts Available in Microsoft Visio

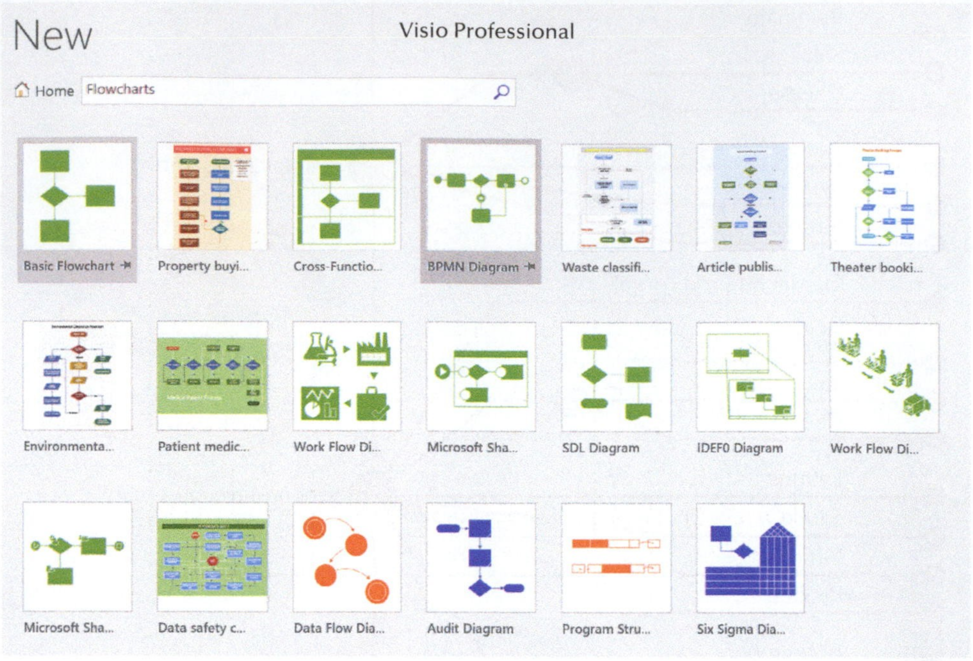

Exhibit 6.1 shows the various flowcharts available in Microsoft Visio to map out business processes.

These flowcharts come in many different sizes, shapes, and forms; several are depicted in this chapter. While the format and symbols used may vary, the "process" of building a flowchart follows these steps:

1. Determine objectives.
2. Define process boundaries.
3. Define units of flow (i.e., patients, products, data).
4. Choose type of chart.
5. Observe process and collect data.
6. Map out process.
7. Validate chart (with user, expert, or observation).

Process FlowCharts

Process flowchart A document that uses standardized symbols to chart the productive and nonproductive flow of activities involved in a process.

The classic **process flowchart** looks at the manufacture of a product or delivery of a service from a broad perspective. The chart uses five standard symbols, shown in Figure 6.5, to describe a process: ○ for operations, □ for inspections, ⇒ for transportation, D for delay, and ▽ for storage. The details of each process are not necessary for this chart; however, the time required to perform each process and the distance between processes are often included. By incorporating nonproductive activities (*inspection, transportation, delay, storage*), as well as productive activities (*operations*), process flowcharts may be used to analyze the efficiency of a series of processes and to suggest improvements. They also provide a standardized method for documenting the steps in a process and can be used as a training tool. Automated versions of these charts are available that will superimpose the charts on floor plans of facilities. In this fashion, bottlenecks can be identified and layouts can be adjusted. Process flowcharts are used in both manufacturing and service operations. They are a basic tool for process innovation, as well as for job design.

FIGURE 6.5 A Process Flowchart of Apple Processing

Date: 9-30-17						Location: Graves Mountain		
Analyst: TLR						Process: Applesauce		
Step	Operation	Transport	Inspect	Delay	Storage	Description of process	Time (min)	Distance (feet)
1	○	⇨	□	D	▽	Unload apples from truck	20	
2	○	⇨	□	D	▽	Move to inspection station		100 ft
3	○	⇨	□	D	▽	Weigh, inspect, sort	30	
4	○	⇨	□	D	▽	Move to storage		50 ft
5	○	⇨	□	D	▽	Wait until needed	360	
6	○	⇨	□	D	▽	Move to peeler		20 ft
7	○	⇨	□	D	▽	Peel and core apples	15	
8	○	⇨	□	D	▽	Soak in water until needed	20	
9	○	⇨	□	D	▽	Place on conveyor	5	
10	○	⇨	□	D	▽	Move to mixing area		20 ft
	Page 1 of 3					Total	450	190 ft

Process improvement teams are likely to make a first pass at diagramming a process, with adhesive notes plastered on large sheets of paper connected with hand-drawn arrows. As documentation of the process becomes more complete, departments or companies may prefer particular symbols to represent inputs, outputs, decisions, activities, and resources.

Flowcharts can take many forms, from freehand drawings to animated simulations. Flowcharting tools are available from Microsoft Visio, SmartDraw (www.smartdraw.com), iGrafx (www.igrafx.com), and others. You may be able to download free trial copies of the software for limited periods of time.

Figure 6.6 shows a *process map*, or swimlane chart, so called because it maps out the activities performed by various people in the process. Often process maps will include a time scale as well. **Figure 6.7** shows a simple value chain flowchart from supplier to customer.

Processes are analyzed to reduce cost, speed time-to-completion, increase customer satisfaction, and, for environmental reasons, to reduce energy consumption or increase sustainability. The "Along the Supply Chain" box that follows discusses New Belgium Brewery's series of process improvements to reduce the carbon footprint of Fat Tire Ale and to use renewable sources of energy.

Process Innovation

Processes are *planned* in response to new facilities, new products, new technologies, new markets, or new customer expectations. Processes should be *analyzed* for improvement on a continuous basis. When continual improvement efforts have been exhausted and performance expectations still cannot be reached with an existing process, it is time to completely redesign or innovate the process.

Process innovation[1] projects are typically chartered in response to a *breakthrough* goal for rapid, dramatic improvement in process performance. Performance improvement

Process innovation The total redesign of a process for breakthrough improvements.

[1]Process innovation is also known as business process reengineering (BPR), process redesign, restructuring, and many other company-specific terms.

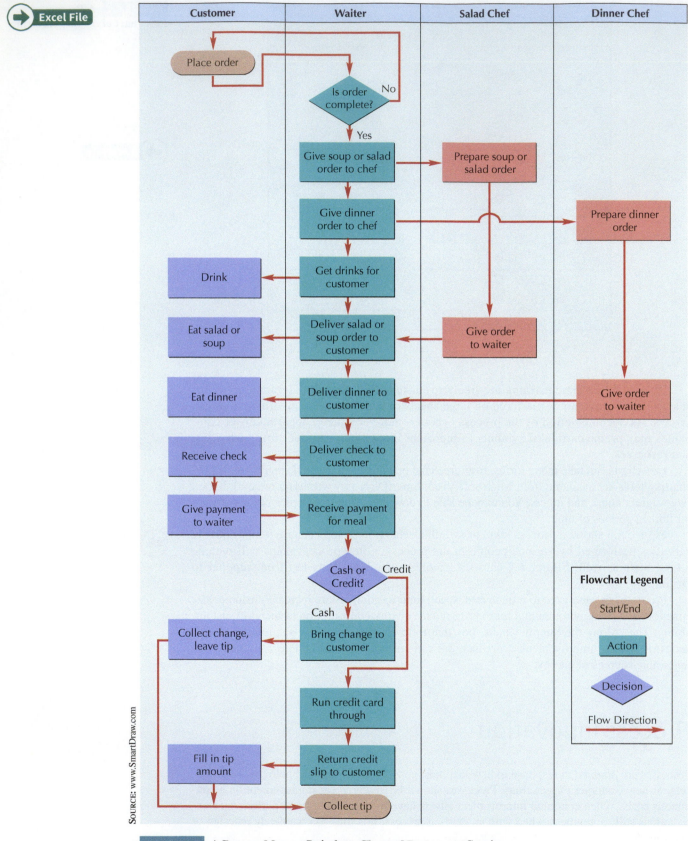

FIGURE 6.6 A Process Map or Swimlane Chart of Restaurant Service

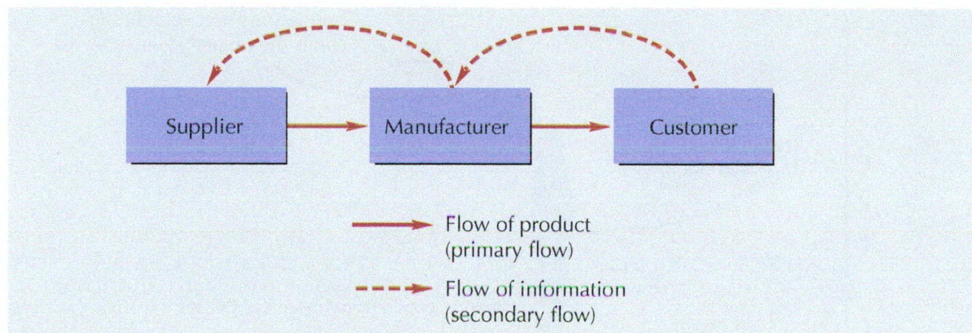

FIGURE 6.7 A Simple Value Chain Flowchart

Along the Supply Chain

Fat Tire Ale's Carbon Footprint

Fat Tire Ale is a product of the New Belgium Brewing Company, located in Fort Collins, Colorado. The company is a certified B Corp, meaning its purpose is to benefit society as well as to make a profit. For New Belgium, that benefit is expressed in employee ownership and concern for the environment.

Breweries use a lot of water; in fact, more than four glasses of water are used to create one glass of beer. New Belgium wants to reduce that amount to 3.5 glasses of water by 2017 and to continue to reduce it after that. Breweries use electricity to cool the beer for fermentation and maturation, and natural gas to boil water and malt to extract sugars and create wort for fermentation.

Reducing energy consumption is one of the first steps to sustainability. New Belgium does so through conservation, energy-efficient equipment, and heat exchangers. The company has also found a way to generate energy from wastewater treatment. As wastewater from the brewing process gets treated, it generates methane gas, which powers a generator that is used to fill 15% of the brewery's energy needs. Solar power now supplies electricity to the company's Packaging Hall, accounting for 3% of its energy use. A Smart Grid installed between the company and the city's utility allows excess energy to be transferred to the city's grid.

New Belgium is an employee-owned company. When an environmental audit showed that the largest contributor to the company's carbon footprint came from coal-powered electricity, the employees voted unanimously to use their bonus checks to subscribe to the City of Fort Collins' Wind Program, which bought wind power from Medicine Bow, Wyoming. Thus, New Belgium Brewing became the country's first brewery to generate 100% of its electricity through wind power.

New Belgium keeps track of its carbon footprint with greenhouse gas (GHG) accounting. The most recent report shows that almost 38% of its carbon footprint is accounted for by the glass bottle. The environmental impact of glass versus aluminum cans is an ongoing discussion at the brewery. In the meantime, the thickness of the glass in the container has been reduced to save GHG emissions. Barley has the second largest footprint at 18%, mainly due to fertilizers and irrigation. New Belgium is working with its barley farmers and maltsters to reduce their impact, and has considered organic farming as an alternative source of supply. Distribution (i.e., trucking the beer all over the country) accounted for 11% of the carbon footprint, a number consistent with other carbon footprint studies across industries. University of Michigan's Center for Sustainable Systems estimates the carbon footprint of a six-pack of Fat Tire Amber Ale at 7 pounds, compared to 7.2 pounds for a gallon of milk, 31 pounds for half a gallon of laundry detergent, 66 pounds for a jacket, 121 pounds for leather boots, and 97,000 pounds for an automobile.

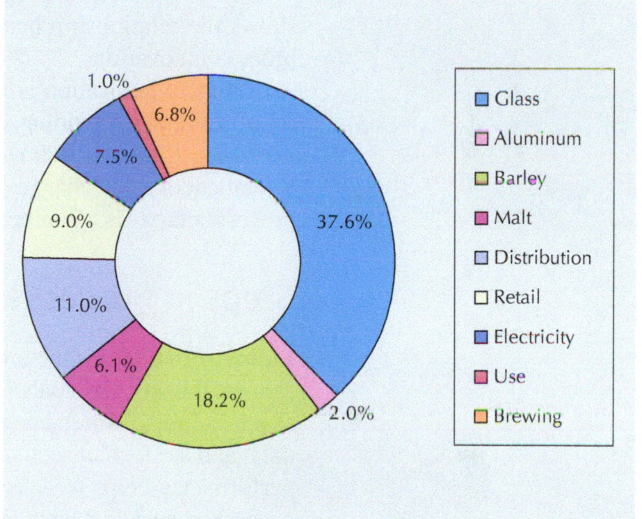

Finally, New Belgium reuses or recycles 99.8% of its waste. There are no dumpsters outside its plants, just a variety of recycling containers.

1. Explore the environmental impact of packaging beer in glass bottles versus aluminum cans. List pros and cons and make a recommendation to New Belgium.
2. Read about New Belgium's new brewery site in Asheville, NC. What factors impacted the location decision? What is a brownfield site?
3. As a consumer, does it matter to you whether a company values sustainability? Why or why not?

Sources: 2015 New Belgium Sustainabiity Report, www.newbelgium.com/sustainability, accessed February 10, 2016; Jeffrey Ball, "Six Products, Six Carbon Footprints," *The Wall Street Journal* (October 6, 2008).

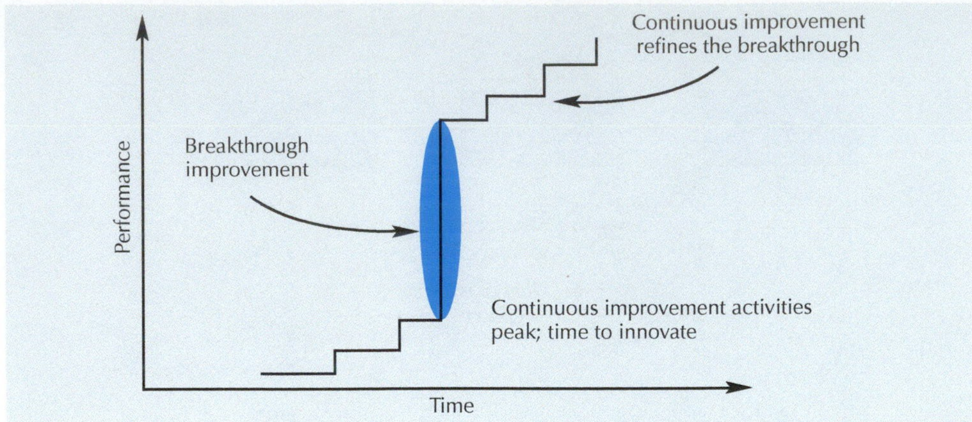

FIGURE 6.8 **Continuous Improvements and Breakthroughs**

of 50% to 100% within 12 months is common. In order to achieve such spectacular results, an innovation team is encouraged to start with a clean sheet of paper and rethink all aspects of a process, from its purpose to its outputs, structure, tasks, and technology. **Figure 6.8** shows the relationship between continuous improvement, breakthrough improvement, and process innovation.

Process innovation is most successful in organizations that can view their system as a set of processes providing value to the customer, instead of functional areas vying for limited resources. **Figure 6.9** shows this change from a functional to a process orientation. In an environment of rapid change, the ability to learn faster, reconfigure processes faster, and execute processes faster is a competitive advantage.

Steps in Process Innovation

Figure 6.10 outlines the innovation process. Let's review the process step by step. The initial step establishes the goals for process performance. Data from the existing process are used as a baseline to which benchmarking data on best industry practices, customer requirements data, and strategic directives are compared.[2] Analyzing the gap between current and desired performance helps to determine whether the process needs to be redesigned. If redesign is necessary, a project team is chartered and provided with the preliminary analysis and resulting goals and specifications for process performance. Although the goals for a process may be specific, the specifications are not (or else the creativity of the group is hampered). It is important that the project team be convinced that total redesign of the process is absolutely necessary to achieve the performance objectives.

A useful tool in beginning the redesign of a process is a *high-level process map*. Pared to its simplest form, a high-level map contains only the essential building blocks of a process. As shown in **Figure 6.11**, it is prepared by focusing on the performance goal—stated in customer terms—and working backward through the desired output, subprocesses, and

FIGURE 6.9 **From Function to Process**

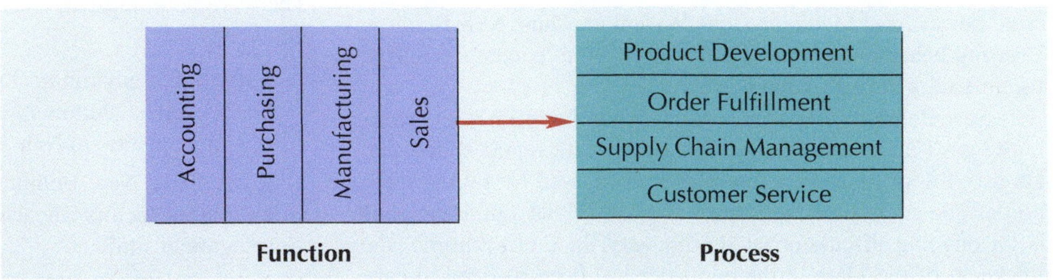

[2]Although process innovation means redesigning the process from scratch, it does not mean that the existing process should be ignored. The existing process should be studied long enough to understand "what" the process is and "why" it is performed. Exactly "how" it is performed is less relevant because the how will change dramatically during the course of the project.

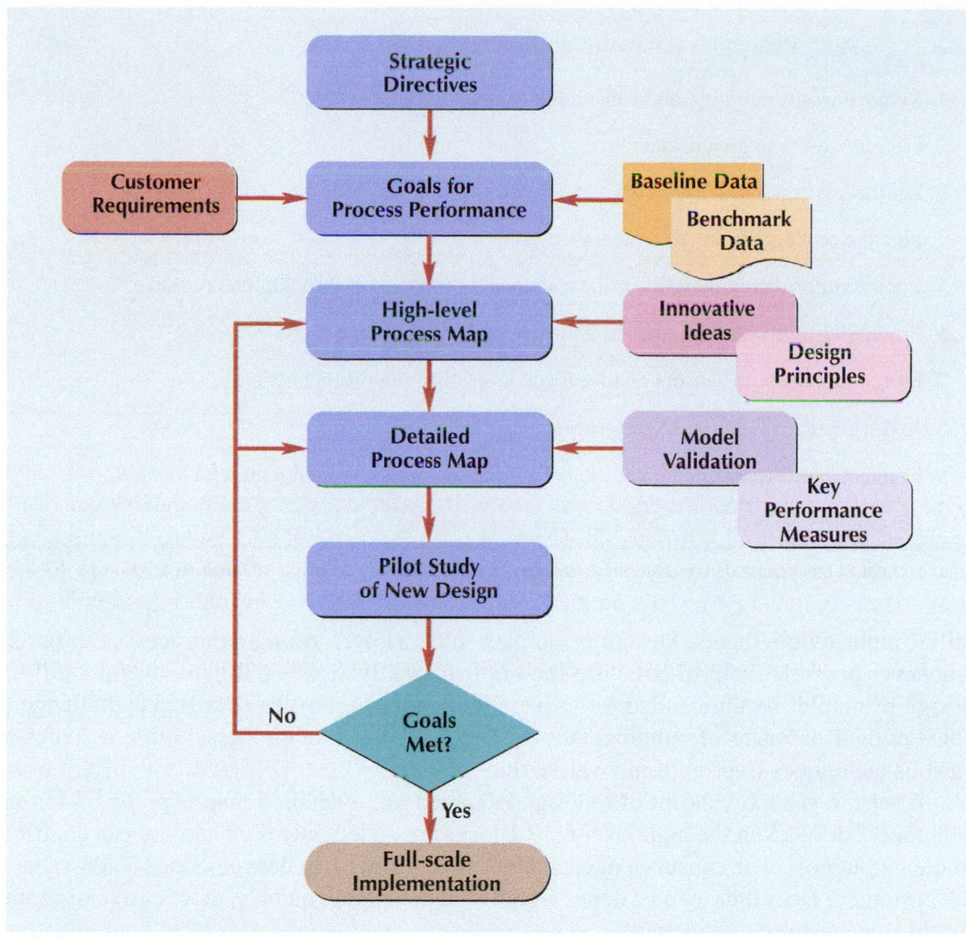

FIGURE 6.10 Process Innovation

(a) Generic

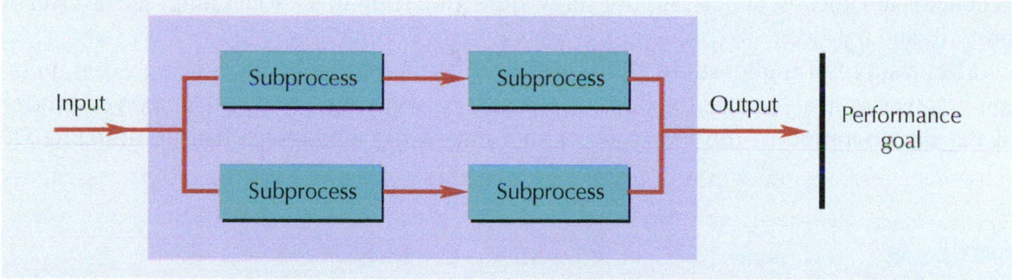

(b) Online Order Processing

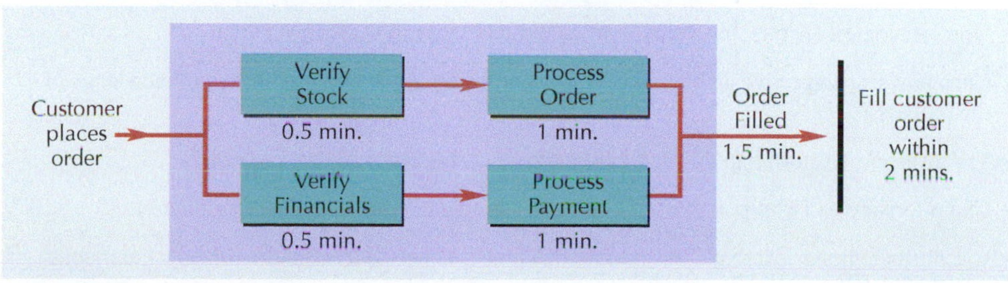

FIGURE 6.11 A High-Level Process Map

TABLE 6.2 Principles for Redesigning Processes

1. Remove waste, simplify, and consolidate similar activities.
2. Link processes to create value.
3. Let the swiftest and most capable enterprise execute the process.
4. Flex the process for any time, any place, any way.
5. Capture information digitally at the source and propagate it through the process.
6. Provide visibility through fresher and richer information about process status.
7. Fit the process with sensors and feedback loops that can prompt action.
8. Add analytic capabilities to the process.
9. Connect, collect, and create knowledge around the process through all who touch it.
10. Personalize the process with the preference and habits of participants.

Source: Omar El Sawy, *Redesigning Enterprise Processes for e-Business* (New York: McGraw-Hill, 2001), pp. 57–75.

initial input requirements. Design principles, such as performing subprocesses in parallel whenever possible, help to structure the map efficiently. Table 6.2 lists several additional design principles recommended for process innovation. Innovative ideas can challenge the conventional ordering of subprocesses, or the need for a subprocess. Table 6.3 presents various techniques to prompt innovative thinking.

After the general concept of redesign is agreed on, a detailed map is prepared for each subprocess or block in the high-level map. Blocks are added only if an activity can contribute to the output goal. The existence of each block or activity is challenged: Does it add value for the customer? Does it have to be done? Could it be done more quickly, more easily, or sooner? Could someone else do it better?

A detailed map guides decisions on allocation of resources and work methods. To guarantee that the detailed map will produce the desired results, key performance measures are determined and set in place. The model is also validated through simulation, interviewing, and partial testing. When the team is satisfied that the performance objective can be reached with the new design, a pilot study is conducted.

Process innovation is not like other projects, which can be carefully planned and flawlessly executed. Innovation is by definition something new and untested. Milestones, costs, and benefits are guesses at best. A pilot study allows the team to try something, see if it works, modify it, and try again.

After a successful pilot study, full-scale implementation can begin. Since process innovation involves radical change, the transition period between introducing the changed process and the incorporation of the new process into day-to-day operations can be difficult. The

TABLE 6.3 Techniques for Generating Innovative Ideas

• Vary the entry point to a problem. (In trying to untangle fishing lines, it's best to start from the fish, not the poles!)
• Draw analogies. (A previous solution to an old problem might work.)
• Change your perspective. (Think like a customer; bring in persons who have no knowledge of the process.)
• Try inverse brainstorming. (What would increase cost? displease the customer?)
• Chain forward as far as possible. (If I solve this problem, what is the next problem?)
• Use attribute brainstorming. (How would this process operate if . . . our workers were mobile and flexible? there were no monetary constraints? we had perfect knowledge?)

Source: Adapted from AT&T Quality Steering Committee, *Reengineering Handbook* (Indianapolis: AT&T Technical Publications Center, 1991).

Anastasia Thatcher

Senior Business Process Manager for a Public Sector Healthcare Company

Roberta Russell

I'm a process manager for the public sector division of one of the largest and best performing healthcare corporations in the United States. My region is the Northeast where the processes I oversee are responsible for the healthcare of over 400,000 lives.

I began my work auditing claims processing, and then became interested in how a claim works its way through the system. I noticed all sorts of inefficiencies. For example, high-dollar claims were manually handled with 10 different touch points. The Claims Processor would identify high-dollar claims and then forward it to the Special Matters Expert, who would work with the Claims Liaison, who would need approval from the Executive Director of the plan, who would consult the Claims Analyst, who would ask Contracting to get back to them so that they could inform the Executive Director, who would make a decision and send it to the Liaison, who would notify the Special Matters Expert, who would lastly pass along the decision to the Claims Processor, who would pay the claim. After redesign, the approval goes from Claims Processor to Special Matters Expert to Executive Director, period. The process flows more efficiently using fewer resources, and the providers are happier because they receive their payments more quickly, which ultimately ensures that members get access to the best care possible.

Like a lot of manufacturing firms, we have more data than we can process efficiently, and it seems that people are always looking for the same information. I remember one situation in particular with case management of high-risk pregnancies. There was a two-month backlog, which meant that by the time the case manager got around to contacting the patient, the pregnancy was too far along for treatment to make much of a difference. I analyzed the process and found that if we developed a shared database between the applicants, the case managers, and the nurses, we could eliminate the manual data entry of cases. That one change reduced the backlog to zero, saved the company millions, and most importantly reduced the number of detained babies (those that need to stay in the hospital after the mother had been released) by 50%. In this job, you can make a real difference. You can save lives.

I was amazed when I took the operations management class at NYU that there's a field of study for what I do. I live by flowcharts and Pareto analysis. We're always configuring and reconfiguring systems. If it doesn't work, we try something else. It's important to take a step back and look at the broader picture. Then you have to take risks and make decisions, and always look for ways of improving the process.

redesigned process may involve changing the way executives manage, the way employees think about their work, or how workers interact. The transition needs to be managed with a special concern for the "people" aspects of change. The innovation process is complete when the transition has been weathered and the new process consistently reaches its objective.

The concept of process innovation emerged in response to rapid changes in technology that rendered existing processes obsolete. In the next section, we discuss the impact of technology decisions and provide resources for a more in-depth study of technology.

Technology Decisions

Technology decisions involve large sums of money and can have a tremendous impact on the cost, speed, quality, and flexibility of operations. More importantly, they define the future capabilities of a firm and set the stage for competitive interactions. Thus, it is dangerous to delegate technology decisions to technical experts or financial analysts. A manager's ability to ask questions and understand the basic thrust of proposed technology is invaluable in making wise technology choices.

In this section we discuss the financial justification of new technology, followed by a brief technology primer. One technology that is changing the way we think about the economics of production is 3D printing, described in the Along the Suppy Chain box that follows.

Financial Justification of Technology

After it is decided that a part will be produced or service provided in-house, specific technology decisions can be made. Alternatives include using, replacing, or upgrading existing equipment, adding additional capacity, or purchasing new equipment. Any alternative that involves an outlay of funds is considered a *capital investment*. Capital investments involve the commitment of

Along the Supply Chain

3D Printing and Other Advances in Additive Manufacturing

Traditional manufacturing works by subtraction—that is, carving out a part or product from a solid block of metal or wood, often resulting in 90% of the material being cut away. Additive manufacturing builds up a part or product by spraying layers of material back and forth across a build platform as directed by a special CAD model. It converts a digital model into a 3D product, and since the process resembles how a dot-matrix printer operates, it's called 3D printing (see photo). Similar to those desktop printers, a 3D printer can be purchased and operated on your desktop to produce a vast variety of shapes, parts, and products. Right now, the time required to "print" those parts can be lengthy—two to three hours, or overnight—and precision is limited, but there are some interesting possibilities that make this technology revolutionary.

Monty Rakuse /Getty Images, Inc.

Additive manufacturing technology has actually been available for some time and has been used to prepare prototypes before building working products. It went by the name *rapid prototyping* and used patented processes such as *stereolithography* in which parts are formed by successively layering thin amounts of liquid resin. Advances in the technology now allow fully functional products to be built by this method out of a variety of materials beyond plastics. Metals are used in powder form and are either mixed with a binding agent or fused with a laser beam as they are deposited on the platform or build tray. After each layer is complete, the build tray is lowered by a fraction of a millimeter and the next layer is added. The layers are defined by software that takes a series of digital slices through a CAD design (see Chapter 4) and sends those descriptions to the 3D printer. Materials can also be mixed, such as lightweight composites, one layer at a time. 3D printing is especially useful for aerospace, as weight is critical in making aircraft. A reduction of 1 kg in the weight of an airliner, for example, will save around $3000 worth of fuel a year and significantly cut carbon-dioxide emissions.

From a business perspective, additive manufacturing lowers the cost of entry into an industry, shortens the time-to-market of new designs, allows mass customization, eliminates the need for costly inventory or the supply chain to provide it, saves resources (materials, energy, labor, tooling, etc.), and is better for the environment. Replacement parts, for example, can be printed instead of ordered; no need for stocking thousands of parts in inventory, or making them in advance of need. Think about how much weight could be jettisoned from aircraft carriers or spacecraft with no need for those extra parts; or how your local Advanced Auto store would house a printer or two, instead of shelves of inventory. Some stores or repair centers may cease to exist because individuals would have their own "printers."

3D printing can also create more intricate designs (and more rounded shapes) than is possible from conventional manufacturing, and it can make production profitable at lower volumes (nixing economies of scale). For example, since each item is created separately rather than from a mold, a build tray could hold 100 items that are different in design, and produce them at the same cost as 100 items of the same design. Invisalign currently uses 3D printing in this way to produce customized retainers for its large suite of patients who need new ones every two weeks as part of the orthodontic procedure. It's also used to produce custom orthotics, hearing aids, and dental crowns faster and at a much reduced cost than traditional means.

Silver inks are now available to print circuit boards (Xerox); stainless steel powders are used to print repair parts (Shapeways); gold "dust" prints customized jewelry (Concept Laser); concrete fixtures are printed for building structures (Loughborough University), and organic polymers build customized cartilage and joint replacements (BioRap). Bioprinters are now producing functional human tissue for medical research and regenerative therapies, such as lung tissue, blood vessels, heart valves, and kidney cells. The U.S. military is considering the use of in situ bioprinting to help treat wounds on the battlefield. One day in the future, we may even be able to design and print human organs for transplants from layering human tissue.

1. For what types of products and markets is 3D printing currently best suited? What future possibilities do you see for technology such as 3D printing?
2. How might additive manufacturing change the way companies provide products and customers purchase products? What are the social, commercial, and legal ramifications of this new approach to manufacture?

Sources: Based on Johnny Ryan, "Manufacturing 2.0," *Fortune* (May 23, 2011); "The Printed World," *The Economist* (February 10, 2011); "The Third Industrial Revolution," *The Economist* (April 21, 2012); "Solid Print," *The Economist* (April 21, 2012); "Additive Manufacturing: Pursuing the Promise," U.S. Department of Energy, Advanced Manufacturing Office, DOE/EE-0776 (August 2012); Robert Hotz, "Printing Evolves: An Inkjet for Living Tissue," *The Wall Street Journal* (September 18, 2012), D1.

funds in the present with an expectation of returns over some future time period. The expenditures are usually large and can have a significant effect on the future profitability of a firm. These decisions are analyzed carefully and typically require top management approval.

The most effective quantitative techniques for capital investment consider the time value of money as well as the risks associated with benefits that will not accrue until the future. These techniques, known collectively as *capital budgeting* techniques, include payback period, net present value, and internal rate of return. Detailed descriptions can be found in any basic finance text. Although capital budgeting techniques are beyond the scope of this text, we do need to comment on several factors that are often overlooked in the financial analysis of technology.

PURCHASE COST The initial investment in equipment consists of more than its basic purchase price. The cost of special tools and fixtures, installation, training, maintenance, and engineering or programming adjustments can represent a significant additional investment. Operating costs are often underestimated as well.

OPERATING COSTS To assess more accurately the requirements of the new technology, it is useful to consider, step by step, how the equipment will be operated, started, stopped, loaded, unloaded, changed over, upgraded, networked, maintained, repaired, cleaned up, speeded up, and slowed down.

ANNUAL SAVINGS Most new technology is justified based on direct labor savings. However, other savings can actually be more important. For example, a more efficient process may be able to use less material and require less machine time or fewer repairs, so that downtime is reduced. A process that produces a better-quality product can result in fewer inspections and less scrap and rework. New processes (especially those that are automated) may significantly reduce safety costs, in terms of compliance with required regulations, as well as fines or compensation for safety violations.

REVENUE ENHANCEMENT Increases in revenue due to technology upgrades or new-equipment purchases are often ignored in financial analysis because they are difficult to predict. Improvements in product quality, price reductions due to decreased costs, and more rapid or dependable delivery can increase market share and, thus, revenue. Flexibility of equipment can also be important in adapting to the changing needs of the customer.

REPLACEMENT ANALYSIS As existing equipment ages, it may become slower, less reliable, and obsolete. The decision to replace old equipment with state-of-the-art equipment depends in large measure on the competitive environment. If a major competitor upgrades to a newer technology that improves quality, cost, or flexibility and you do not, your ability to compete will be severely damaged. In some industries, technology changes so rapidly that a replacement decision also involves determining whether this generation of equipment should be purchased or if it would be better to wait for the next generation. Replacement analysis maps out different schedules for equipment purchases over a two- to five-year period and selects a replacement cycle that will minimize cost.

RISK AND UNCERTAINTY Investment in new technology can be risky. Estimates of equipment capabilities, length of life, and operating cost may be uncertain. Because of the risk involved, financial analysts tend to assign higher hurdle rates (i.e., required rates of return) to technology investments, making it difficult to gain approval for them.

PIECEMEAL ANALYSIS Investment in equipment and new technology is also expensive. Rarely can a company afford to automate an entire facility all at once. This has led to the proposal and evaluation of equipment purchases in a piecemeal fashion, resulting in pieces of technology that don't fit into the existing system and fail to deliver the expected returns.

A Technology Primer

Technology is important in both manufacturing and service operations. Cars now have hundreds of embedded systems performing thousands of computerized functions. Pacemakers, vending machines, copiers, and store shelves notify the manufacturer when repairs or restocking are needed. Wearable technology measures vital statistics and notifies a physician or recommends changes in medication regimes. Refrigerators can pre-order ingredients to match weekly menus or order milk when the supply is low. We discuss many of the information technology advances that support these systems in more detail in Chapters 10 and 15. In this section, we present a brief overview of technology advances in manufacturing systems.

Technology in manufacturing includes computer-aided design, robots, automated guided vehicles, computer numerically controlled machines, automated storage and retrieval systems, and flexible manufacturing systems. Automated manufacturing systems integrated through computer technology have aptly been called computer-integrated manufacturing (CIM). While that term is still used, a new era in automated manufacturing has emerged that is more digital, networked, and collaborative.

The digital revolution we spoke about in Chapter 1 has made its way to manufacturing. Digital or smart manufacturing technologies are changing how products are designed and made, how processes are controlled, how suppliers are monitored, and how value is delivered to the customer. More than automation, it is the connectivity and intelligence of these devices that is driving the new "digital" industrial revolution. Countries are preparing their industries to compete in this new era of manufacturing as evidenced by the U.S. National Network for Manufacturing Innovation, Germany's Industry 4.0 initiative, and China's Made in China 2025.

Digital manufacturing Also called smart manufacturing; using digital technologies to design, manufacture, and control production, even remotely.

Digital manufacturing uses advanced digital technologies to integrate product, process, manufacture, and information technology over the life of the product. Sensors embedded in a product can record status and conditions of use, determine when the product needs repair or replacement, and send updates or begin working on a replacement part before the customer places an order. Products can be made to exact customer specifications, and settings to improve operation can be modified in real-time. Machines, cells, and factories can be controlled remotely and adjusted on-demand to reflect changing needs, resources, or preferences. Operations managers can monitor production in supplier plants down to the settings on machines and break times for workers. Vision systems can perform 100% inspection and trigger rework when needed. Repair shops (or customers, for that matter) can make their own replacement parts through 3D printing technology. In order to facilitate this meshing of product, process, and technology, protocols for communication must be established and ICT infrastructure and security measures must be in place.

IIOT (Industrial Internet of Things) Sensors to collect information and control processes; enables digital manufacture.

Sensors used to control automated equipment and communicate information to remote locations are referred to collectively as the industrial internet of things or **IIoT.** Figure 6.12

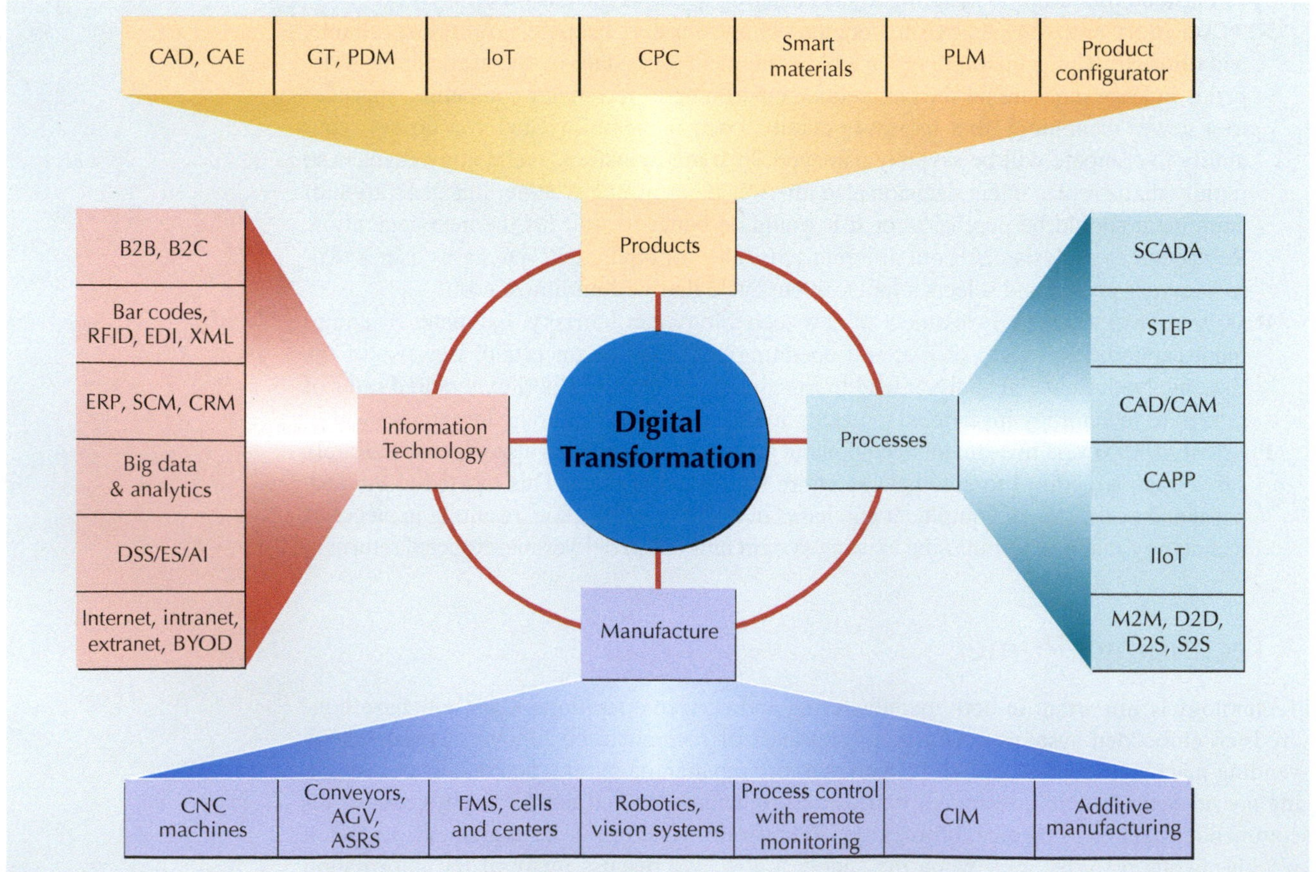

FIGURE 6.12 **Components of a Digital Transformation**

summarizes the technologies needed for a digital transformation in four essential areas: product, process, manufacture, and information. Table 6.4 serves as a technology primer, briefly defining the terms listed in the figure. Together, these resources provide a good starting point for investigating the advanced digital technologies that are becoming an integral part of lives.

TABLE 6.4 A Technology Primer

PRODUCT TECHNOLOGY		
CAD, CAE	Computer-aided design, computer-aided engineering	Creates, communicates, and tests product designs electronically
GT, PDM	Group technology; Product data management	Classifies designs into families for easy retrieval and modification; keeps track of design specs and revisions for the life of the product
CPC	Collaborative product commerce	Facilitates electronic communication and exchange of information among designers and suppliers
PLM	Product lifecycle management	Integrates the decisions of those involved in product development, manufacturing, sales, customer service, recycling, and disposal
Product configurator		Defines products "configured" by customers who have selected among various options, usually from a website
Smart materials	Materials with properties that react to changes in the environment	Examples: self-healing, shape-memory, conduction, etc.
IoT	Internet of Things	Embedded sensors that detect & relay information
PROCESS TECHNOLOGY		
STEP	Standard for exchange of product model data (ISO 10303)	Sets standards for communication among different CAD vendors; translates CAD data into requirements for automated inspection and manufacture
CAD/CAM	Computer-aided design and manufacture	The electronic link between automated design (CAD) and automated manufacture (CAM)
CAPP	Computer-aided process planning	Generates process plans based on a database of similar requirements
SCADA	Supervisory Control and Data Acquisition	An industrial automation control system for remote monitoring; used for critical infrastructure
M2M	Machine-to-machine communication	Sensors on one machine can direct other machines to turn on/off, adjust, etc.
D2D	Device-to-device communication	Integrates intelligent machines or devices; real-time applications
S2S	Server-to-server communication	For web services and business apps
D2S	Device-to-server communication	For data collection and remote monitoring
MANUFACTURING TECHNOLOGY		
CNC	Computer numerically controlled	Machines controlled by software code to perform a variety of operations with the help of automated tool changers; also collects processing information and quality data
FMS	Flexible manufacturing system	A collection of CNC machines connected by an automated material handling system to produce a wide variety of parts
Robots	Pick-and-place, articulated; Smart robots	Manipulators that can be programmed to perform repetitive tasks at varying levels of difficulty. Smart robots can detect, act, and learn.
Conveyors		Fixed-path material handling; moves items along a belt or overhead chain; "reads" packages via bar code or RFID tag and diverts them to different directions; can be very fast

(*continued*)

TABLE 6.4 A Technology Primer (*continued*)

MANUFACTURING TECHNOLOGY		
AGV	Automatic guided vechicle	A driverless truck that moves material along a specified path; directed by wire or tape embedded in the floor or by radio frequencies; very flexible
ASRS	Automated storage and retrieval system	An automated warehouse—some 26 stories high—in which items are placed in a carousel-type storage system and retrieved by fast-moving stacker cranes; controlled by computer
Process Control		Continuous monitoring of automated equipment; makes real-time decisions on ongoing operation, maintenance, and quality; can be employed remotely
CIM	Computer-integrated manufacturing	Automated manufacturing systems integrated through computer technology; a precursor to digital manufacturing
3D printing	Additive manufacturing	Building up a product layer by layer from digital instructions
INFORMATION TECHNOLOGY		
B2B, B2C	Business-to-business; Business-to-consumer	Electronic transactions between businesses, or between businesses and the consumer, usually over the Internet
Internet, Intranet, Extranet		A global information system of computer networks. Intranets are communication networks internal to an organization. Extranets give suppliers, customers, and trading partners access to select portions of a company's intranet through secure portals.
Bar codes		A series of vertical lines printed on most packages that identifies the item and other information when read by a scanner
RFID	Radio frequency identification tags	An integrated circuit embedded in a tag that can send and receive information; a 21st-century bar code with read/write capabilities
EDI	Electronic data interchange	A computer-to-computer exchange of business documents over a proprietary network; very expensive and inflexible
XML	Extensible markup language	A programming language that enables computer-to-computer communication over the Internet by tagging data before it is sent
ERP, SCM, CRM	Enterprise resource planning, Supply chain management, Customer relationship management	A suite of software products for managing the business processes of an enterprise (see Chapter 15); SCM software manages suppliers and supply chain networks; CRM manages customer and sales data.
Big data & analytics	Big data is characterized by its volume, variety (structured and unstructured data), and velocity	Anaytics uses techniques such as statistics, math programming, data mining, and text mining to find patterns in data and make inferences
DSS	Decision support systems	An information system that helps managers make decisions; includes a quantitative modeling component and an interactive component for what-if? analysis
ES	Expert systems	A computer system that uses an expert knowledge base to diagnose or solve a problem
AI	Artificial intelligence	A field of study that attempts to replicate elements of human thought in computer processes; includes expert systems, genetic algorithms, neural networks, and fuzzy logic (see Chapter 17)

Summary

Important issues in process design are types of processes, process planning, analysis and innovation, and technology decisions. The type of production process selected depends primarily on demand volume and degree of product standardization. *Projects* are produced one at a time to customer order. *Batch production* is used to process a variety of low-volume jobs. *Mass production* produces large volumes of a standard product for a mass market. *Continuous production* is used for very-high-volume commodity products.

Process planning consists of converting product designs into workable instructions for manufacture. They often take the form of assembly charts, process flowcharts, operations sheets, and manufacturing or delivery specifications. On a broader scale, process planning involves process selection, technology decisions, and decisions on outsourcing. Process analysis drives the continuous improvement of operations; process innovation drives breakthrough improvements. Digital manufacturing has been called the next industrial revolution due to the dramatic changes in production possibilities that it brings to factories, entities, and workers worldwide.

Key Terms

assembly chart A schematic diagram of a product that shows the relationship of component parts to parent assemblies, the groupings of parts that make up a subassembly, and the overall sequence of assembly.

batch production The low-volume production of customized products.

breakeven analysis A technique that determines the volume of demand needed to be profitable; it takes into account the trade-off between fixed and variable costs.

continuous production The production of a very-high-volume commodity product with highly automated equipment.

digital manufacturing Also called smart manufacturing; using digital technologies to design, manufacture, and control production, even remotely.

IIoT Industrial Internet of Things; sensors to collect information and control processes; enables digital manufacture

mass production The high-volume production of a standard product for a mass market.

process A group of related tasks with specific inputs and outputs.

process flowchart A document that uses standardized symbols to chart the productive and nonproductive flow of activities involved in a process; it may be used to document current processes or as a vehicle for process improvement.

process innovation The total redesign of a process.

process planning The conversion of designs into workable instructions for manufacture, along with associated decisions on component purchase or fabrication, and process and equipment selection.

process plans A set of documents that detail manufacturing or service delivery specifications.

process strategy An organization's overall approach for physically producing goods and services.

project The one-of-a-kind production of a product to customer order that requires a long time to complete and a large investment of funds and resources.

vertical integration The degree to which a firm produces the parts that go into its products

Key Formulas

Breakeven point

$$v = \frac{c_f}{p - c_v}$$

Point of indifference

$$\left| \frac{c_{f2} - c_{f1}}{c_{v1} - c_{v2}} \right|$$

Solved Problems

Texloy Manufacturing Company must select a process for its new product, TX2, from among three different alternatives. The following cost data have been gathered:

	PROCESS A	PROCESS B	PROCESS C
Fixed cost	$10,000	$40,000	$70,000
Variable cost	$5/unit	$2/unit	$1/unit

For what volume of demand would each process be desirable?

Solution

If v represents the number of TX2s demanded (and, we assume, produced), then

$$\text{Total cost for process A} = \$10{,}000 + \$5v$$
$$\text{Total cost for process B} = \$40{,}000 + \$2v$$
$$\text{Total cost for process C} = \$70{,}000 + \$1v$$

Next, we calculate the points of indifference between each pair of processes by equating their total costs and solving for demand volume, v. Always begin with the process that has the lowest fixed cost and compare it to the process with the next lowest fixed cost, and so on. For this example that means we'll compare process A to process B and process B to process C.

Comparison 1: Process A versus Process B

$$\begin{array}{cc} \textit{Process A} & \textit{Process B} \\ \$10{,}000 + \$5v = & \$40{,}000 + \$2v \\ & v = 10{,}000 \text{ units} \end{array}$$

If demand is less than or equal to 10,000, we should choose the alternative with the lowest fixed cost, process A. Conversely, if demand is greater than 10,000, we should choose the aternative with the lowest variable cost, process B. At 10,000 units we can actually choose either A or B.

Comparison 2: Process B versus Process C

$$\begin{array}{cc} \textit{Process B} & \textit{Process C} \\ \$40{,}000 + \$2v = & \$70{,}000 + \$1v \\ & v = 30{,}000 \text{ units} \end{array}$$

If demand is greater than 30,000 units, we should choose process C. If demand is less than 30,000 but greater than 10,000 (see comparison 1), we should choose process B. At 30,000, we can choose either B or C.

The Excel solution to this problem is shown in Exhibit 6.2.

To summarize, from the graph in Exhibit 6.2 and our decision rules, we can recommend the following process selection:

- Below 10,000 units, choose process A.
- Between 10,000 and 30,000 units, choose process B.
- Above 30,000 units, choose process C.

EXHIBIT 6.2 | Using Excel for the Point of Indifference

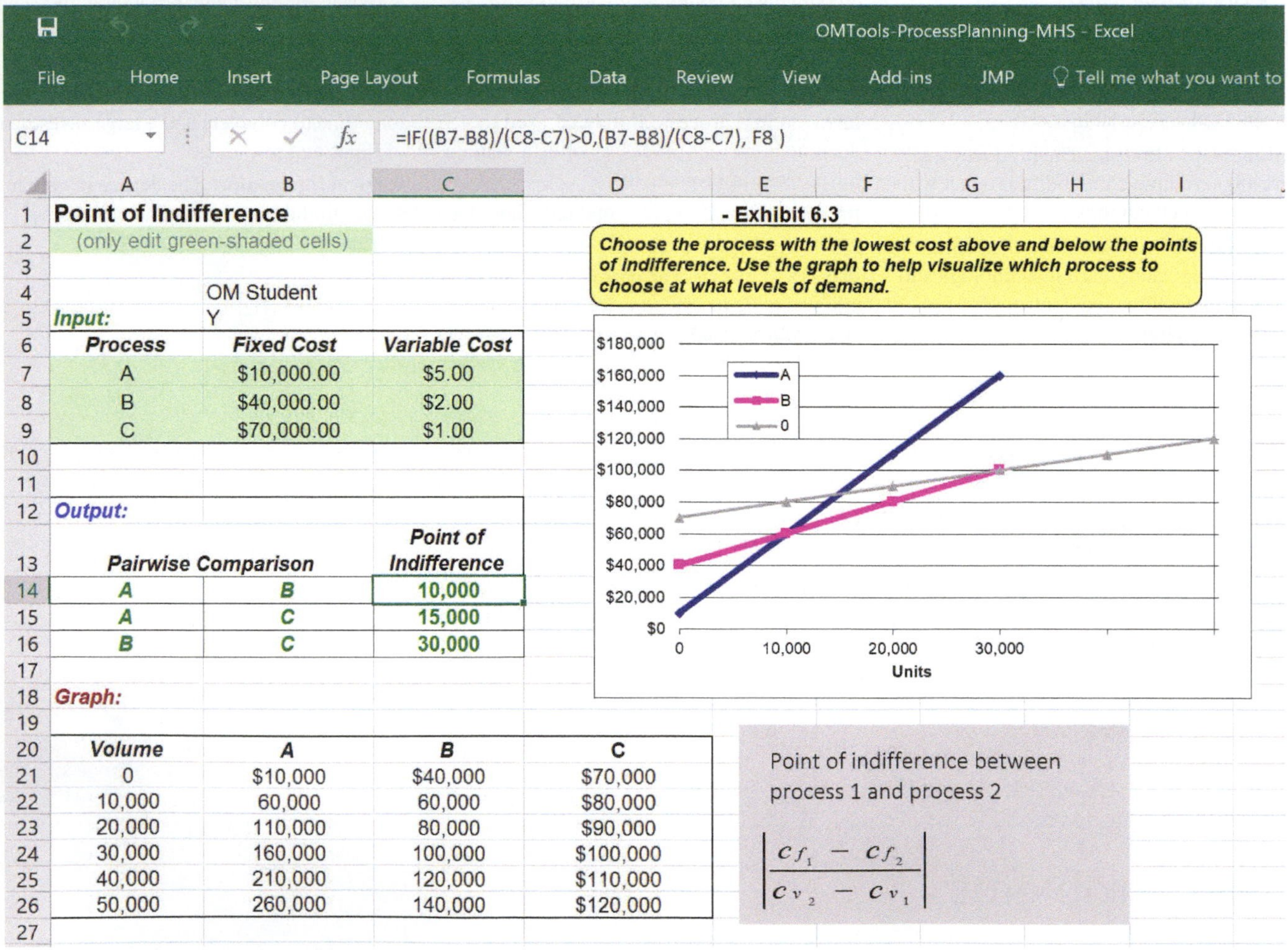

OMTools-ProcessPlanning-MHS - Excel

File Home Insert Page Layout Formulas Data Review View Add-ins JMP Tell me what you want to

C14 =IF((B7-B8)/(C8-C7)>0,(B7-B8)/(C8-C7), F8)

Point of Indifference - Exhibit 6.3

(only edit green-shaded cells)

OM Student

Y

Choose the process with the lowest cost above and below the points of indifference. Use the graph to help visualize which process to choose at what levels of demand.

Input:

Process	Fixed Cost	Variable Cost
A	$10,000.00	$5.00
B	$40,000.00	$2.00
C	$70,000.00	$1.00

Output:

Pairwise Comparison		Point of Indifference
A	B	10,000
A	C	15,000
B	C	30,000

Graph:

Volume	A	B	C
0	$10,000	$40,000	$70,000
10,000	60,000	60,000	$80,000
20,000	110,000	80,000	$90,000
30,000	160,000	100,000	$100,000
40,000	210,000	120,000	$110,000
50,000	260,000	140,000	$120,000

$180,000 $160,000 $140,000 $120,000 $100,000 $80,000 $60,000 $40,000 $20,000 $0

A B 0

0 10,000 20,000 30,000

Units

Point of indifference between process 1 and process 2

$$\left|\frac{cf_1 - cf_2}{cv_2 - cv_1}\right|$$

Questions

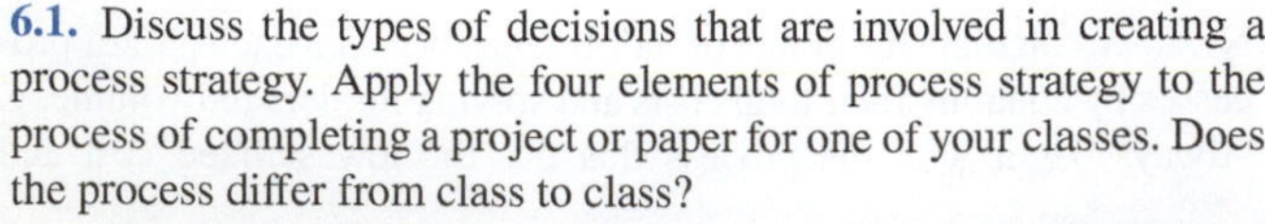

6.1. Discuss the types of decisions that are involved in creating a process strategy. Apply the four elements of process strategy to the process of completing a project or paper for one of your classes. Does the process differ from class to class?

6.2. List and explain six factors that affect the decision to outsource. Explain the sourcing continuum.

6.3. Describe the four basic types of production processes. What are the advantages and disadvantages of each? When should each be used?

6.4. What are the major cost factors considered in process selection? How is breakeven analysis used for process selection?

6.5. What kind of information do the following documents communicate?

a. Assembly chart

b. Operations sheet

c. Process flowchart

6.6. What does process planning entail? How would process planning differ for batch and continuous processes?

6.7. Explain the basic steps involved in process innovation.

6.8. Our thinking process, limited by the paradigms under which we operate, can become very rigid. Try these out-of-box thinking exercises:

a. Where does the letter Z belong in this pattern, above or below the line? Why?

BCD G J OPQRS U
A EF HI KLMN T VWXY

b. What letter comes next in the following pattern? Why?

OTTFF

c. Connect the nine dots below with four straight lines. Do not lift your pencil.

• • •
• • •
• • •

d. Circle the three errors in the following sentence: There is three mistakes in this sentence.

6.9. Describe the factors often overlooked in the financial justification of new technology.

6.10. Briefly discuss the components of digital or smart manufacturing. In what ways can companies collaborate in producing goods and services? Report on at least one web source on collaborative manufacturing, digital manufacturing, or additive manufacturing.

6.11. Read about issues in outsourcing from a search on the Web. Then, examine the website of a company with which you are familiar for its outsourcing strategy and supplier policies.

6.12. Create a flowchart for the process of building flowcharts described in the Process Analysis section of this chapter.

6.13. Explore the sustainability requirements of production outsourced to different parts of the world.

Problems

6.1. Construct a process flowchart of a process with which you are familiar. Identify bottlenecks, potential failure points, and opportunities for improvement.

6.2. Create an operations chart for making pancakes.

6.3. T.W. Smitty, an emerging rapper, has reserved a recording studio for $5000 to cut his first album, called "Smart Rap." The cost of recording the album is $5000 and copies are $5 apiece. If the vinyl albums are priced at $15 each, how many must be sold to break even? What is the breakeven point in dollars?

6.4. T.W. Smitty is confident that demand for his Smart Rap album will substantially exceed the break even point computed in Problem 6.3, so T.W. is contemplating having his album cut at a classier (and pricier) studio. The recording costs would rise to $9000. However, since this new studio works with very high volume, production costs would fall to $2 per vinyl album.

a. What is the breakeven point for this new process?

b. Compare this process to the process proposed in the previous problem. For what volume of demand should T.W. choose the classier studio?

6.5. Patricia Zell, a dollmaker from Olney, Maryland, is interested in the mass marketing and production of a ceramic doll of her own design called Tiny Trisha. The initial investment required for plant and equipment is estimated at $25,000. Labor and material costs are approximately $10 per doll. If the dolls can be sold for $50 each, what volume of demand is necessary for the Tiny Trisha doll to break even?

6.6. Although it will fulfill her lifelong dream, Patricia is not confident that demand for her Tiny Trisha doll will exceed the breakeven point computed in Problem 6-5. If she chooses a less appealing site and does more of the work by hand, her initial investment cost can be reduced to $5000, but her per-unit cost of manufacture will rise to $15 per doll.

a. What is the breakeven point for this new process?

b. Compare this process to the process proposed in the previous problem. For what volume of demand should Patricia choose this process?

6.7. David Austin recently purchased a chain of dry cleaners in northern Wisconsin. Although the business is making a modest profit now, David suspects that if he invests in a new press, he could recognize a substantial increase in profits. The new press costs $15,400 to purchase and install and can press 40 shirts an hour (or 320 per day). David estimates that with the new press, it will cost $0.25 to launder and press each shirt. Customers are charged $1.10 per shirt.

a. How many shirts will David have to press to break even?

b. So far, David's workload has varied from 50 to 200 shirts a day. How long would it take to break even on the new press at the low-demand estimate? at the high-demand estimate?

c. If David cuts his price to $0.99 a shirt, he expects to be able to stabilize his customer base at 250 shirts per day. How long would it take to break even at the reduced price of $0.99? Should David cut his price and buy the new press?

6.8. The school cafeteria can make pizza for approximately $0.30 a slice. The cost of kitchen use and cafeteria staff runs about $200 per day. The Pizza Den nearby will deliver whole pizzas for $9.00 each. The cafeteria staff cuts the pizza into eight slices and serves them in the usual cafeteria line. With no cooking duties, the staff can be reduced by half, for a fixed cost of $75 per day. Should the school cafeteria make or buy its pizzas?

6.9. Soft Key is trying to determine how best to produce its newest product, DVORK keyboards. The keyboards could be produced in-house using either process A or process B, or purchased from a supplier. Cost data are given below. For what levels of demand should each process be chosen?

	FIXED COST	VARIABLE COST
Process A	$ 8,000	$10
Process B	$20,000	$ 4
Supplier	$ 0	$20

6.10. NanoTech is ready to begin production of its exciting new technology. The company is evaluating three methods of production: (A) a small production facility with older equipment, (B) a larger production facility that is more automated, and (C) subcontracting to an electronics manufacturer in Singapore. The costs of each alternative are shown below. Determine for what level of demand each production process should be chosen.

PROCESS	FIXED COST	VARIABLE COST
A	$200,000	$40
B	$600,000	$20
C	$ 0	$60

6.11. Creative Designs makes intricate jewelry out of precious metal. The company is introducing a new line and needs to select a manufacturing process. Three options are available. The first involves using a mold to mass produce the design for pendants, earrings, and bracelets. The second option laser cuts the design from a block of metal using a pattern directed by the software. The third option builds the design out of metal powder (gold, silver, and bronze) via a 3D printer. The company is uncertain about demand for the new design.

OPTION	FIXED COST	VARIABLE COST
1	$10,000	$10
2	$ 5,000	$30
3	$ 3,000	$50

a. If Creative Designs expects to sell 200 pieces of the new design, which process should it use?

b. If Creative Designs expects to sell 1000 pieces of the new design, which process should it use?

c. Create a decision rule that specifies which process to select for different levels of demand.

6.12. Merrimac Manufacturing Company has always purchased a certain component part from a supplier on the East Coast for $50 per part. The supplier is reliable and has maintained the same price structure for years. Recently, improvements in operations and reduced product demand have cleared up some capacity in Merrimac's own plant for producing component parts. The particular part in question could be produced at $40 per part, with an annual fixed investment of $25,000. Currently, Merrimac needs 300 of these parts per year.

a. Should Merrimac make or buy the component part?

b. As another alternative, a new supplier located nearby is offering volume discounts for new customers of $50 per part for the first 100 parts ordered and $45 per part for each additional unit ordered. Should Merrimac make the component in-house, buy it from the new supplier, or stick with the old supplier?

c. Would your decision change if Merrimac's annual demand increased to 2000 parts? increased to 5000 parts?

d. Develop a set of rules that Merrimac can use to decide when to make this component, when to buy it from the old supplier, and when to buy it from the new supplier.

6.13. Prydain Pharmaceuticals is reviewing its employee healthcare program. Currently, the company pays a fixed fee of $300 per month for each employee, regardless of the number or dollar amount of medical claims filed. Another healthcare provider has offered to charge the company $100 per month per employee and $30 per claim filed. A third insurer charges $200 per month per employee and $10 per claim filed. Which healthcare program should Prydain join? How would the average number of claims filed per employee per month affect your decision?

6.14. Gemstone Quarry is trying to decide whether to invest in a new material-handling system. The current system (which is old and completely paid for) has an annual maintenance cost of $10,000 and costs approximately $25 to transport each load of material. The two new systems that are being considered vary both in sophistication and cost. System 1 has a fixed cost of $40,000 and a cost per load estimated at $10. System 2 has a fixed cost of $100,000 but a per-load cost of $5. At what volume of demand (i.e., number of loads) should Gemstone purchase System 1? System 2?

6.15. Tribal Systems, Inc., is opening a new plant and has yet to decide on the type of process to employ. A labor-intensive process would cost $10,000 for tools and equipment and $14 for labor and materials per item produced. A more automated process costs $50,000 in plant and equipment but has a labor/material cost of $8 per item produced. A fully automated process costs $300,000 for plant and equipment and $2 per item produced. If process selection were based solely on lowest cost, for what range of production would each process be chosen?

6.16. Lydia and Jon order their holiday gifts online. They have spent many evenings at home comparison-shopping on various websites and have found all the things they need from three online retailers, B.B. Lean, Spoogle's, and Sea's End. The purchase price for their selections from each retailer is given here. The shipping and handling charge per item is also given. If Lydia and Jon want to order all their gifts from the same source, which retailer should they choose? How does the number of items ordered affect your recommendation?

	B.B. LEAN	SPOOGLE'S	SEA'S END
Purchase price	$400	$500	$460
Shipping/handling per item	$ 6	$ 3	$ 4

6.17. Sandra Saunders and her design team are analyzing the production costs for three alternative monitor designs. Given the cost information below, and assuming form and function are similar for each design, which monitor design would you recommend?

MONITOR	FIXED COST	VARIABLE COST
A	$ 700,000	$250
B	$1,000,000	$125
C	$1,500,000	$100

6.18. Three Bags Full is a small grocery store chain in the Lehigh Valley. The company is trying to decide whether to include a bakery section in its stores. You have been asked to run the numbers using pies as an example. Baking the pies in-house would cost $80 per day and $1 per pie. Pies can be purchased for $4 each from a local bakery, or $3 each from a large regional bakery. The regional bakery requires a minimum purchase of 25 pies per day. Which alternative would you recommend? (Hint: Graph the problem.)

6.19. Keisha has been inundated with product-of-the-month offers from various marketing companies. She is considering joining a service that allows movies to be streamed from a members-only website, but can't decide which membership offers the best deal. Given the cost information below, which service would you recommend for Keisha?

SERVICE	MEMBERSHIP FEE	COST PER MOVIE
Almost Free Flicks	$ 40	$5
Best Movies	$ 65	$4
Choice Cinema	$100	$3

6.20. Pete Patel is the sports liaison for the student government association. During the fall semester, the group promotes school spirit with "orange effect" t-shirts. The shirts feature a special screen-printed logo that can be expensive to make. Pete's supplier, Classic Tees, has quoted three prices for the shirts with differing logo packages.

a. If the t-shirts are sold for $6 each, how many shirts would have to be sold to break even with Package 1?

b. Pete is considering selling the shirts for $8 each. What is the breakeven point for packages 1 and 2 with an $8 price?

c. Which logo package would you recommend if Pete expects to sell 75 shirts? 200 shirts?

d. Assuming the shirts would be sold at the same price regardless of the logo package, create a decision rule for Pete to use based on anticipated sales volume.

PACKAGE	COST OF LOGO	COST PER SHIRT
1	$300	$4
2	$100	$6
3	$ 0	$8

6.21. Sized Rite is trying to determine how best to produce its new line of shoes for "expanded" feet. Demand for its w-i-d-e products is uncertain. Given the alternative processes and costs below, determine at what level of demand you would choose each process.

	FIXED COST	VARIABLE COST
Process A	$20,000	$ 5
Process B	$10,000	$10
Supplier C	$ 0	$20

6.22. Matthew Richter has recently upgraded his smartphone and is now looking to upgrade his data plan. Flat rates are shown in the table below. Amounts over the maximum allowable gigabytes (GB) for each plan are charged $15 per GB, fractional amounts included. Matthew is uncertain how many GB he might use because of the new phone's additional features, but his best bet is 10 GB, which doesn't align directly with any plan.

PLAN	BASE PRICE	MAX # OF GB
A	$60	5
B	$85	7
C	$140	12
D	$150	15

a. If Matthew uses 10 GB of data, which plan should he choose?

b. At what level of usage should Matthew upgrade from Plan B to Plan C?

c. At what level of usage should Matthew upgrade from Plan C to Plan D?

d. Summarize the decision rules for when Matthew should choose each plan.

6.23. Devonte Price is a self-published author finishing up his seventh book. His books are sold regionally through book fairs, conferences, and special events. He does not sell through online booksellers, as royalties are typically only $1 a book and the availability online eats up in-person sales. Having an inventory of books at the various live venues is critical to making a sale, but with too much inventory Devonte is stuck with lots of doorstoppers. The table below provides sales data on Books 1 through 6. Devonte anticipates charging $28.50 for Book 7. The printing company that he uses charges $175 to set up for each run, $8 per book to print, and $60 per case (holds approximately 30 books) to ship.

BOOK	SALES	PRICE	TOTAL REVENUE
1	500	$17.95	$8,975.00
2	450	$17.95	$8,077.50
3	300	$12.95	$3,885.00
4	375	$14.95	$5,606.25
5	400	$17.95	$7,180.00
6	125	$14.95	$1,868.75
7	?	?	?

a. How many books should Devonte order of Book 7 to break even?

b. Devonte thinks Book 7 will sell at least as many as his top seller. If that is the case and he orders that many books from the printer, what would be the net return for the project?

c. How many books should Devonte order (and sell) if he hopes to net $20,000 on the project?

d. The printer has looked at Book 7 and thinks Devonte should opt for a deluxe package with glossy paper and true color photography. The increased setup fee is $500 and the per book printing cost is $10. Shipping costs remain the same. The printer recommends that Devonte increase the price of the book to $32.50 to cover the extra cost of printing. If Devonte opts for a deluxe printing of Book 7 and adjusts the price as suggested, how many copies should he order (and sell) to break even? How many copies would Devonte have to sell to net $20,000?

e. Devonte is worried about how the new book will sell. If he can only sell 150 books, which version should he order (basic or deluxe)?

f. If Devonte can only sell 500 books, which version should he order (basic or deluxe)?

g. At what level of anticipated sales should Devonte switch from the basic to the deluxe printing of Book 7?

Case Problems

Case Problem 6.1 A Manager's Woes

Kyle Peschken has been a manager for the discount store Zelmart for the past two years. It's time for his annual performance review, and Kyle would like to make a big impression on the corporate staff. Walking through the store, he makes a mental note of which departments need to be straightened, which ones need to be reorganized, and which employees he'd like to schedule during the week of his review. And then he sees it—blocking the aisles, creating commotion, and looking very unprofessional—the long line in the electronics department. It's time to confront Chris, the sales clerk.

"Chris, what's the holdup here?"

"I'm waiting for a manager to approve this $120 check. And then I have to show this lady a digital camera from the display cabinet. She's been waiting half an hour, and then. . . ."

"Alright Chris . . . I can help out for awhile . . ."

Two hours later, Kyle exited the electronics department disheartened. That's no way for a store manager to spend his afternoon. There's got to be a logical way to solve this, thought Kyle. He walked back to his office and wrote down the facts as he knew them.

1. Customer service managers (CSMs) must approve all checks over $100, and over 50% of purchases in electronics exceed $100.
2. It's more efficient to stage CSMs at the front of the store by the 12 checkout lines.
3. It takes an average of 10 minutes for the CSM to reach electronics after being paged.
4. Because of cost controls, the number of CSMs is limited to two per shift, and there is no room in the budget for additional hires of any type.
5. Electronics must be purchased in the electronics department (to prevent theft).
6. Store policy allows customers to check out other items at the electronics counter if they are making purchases in that department. (This makes sense especially if the customer wants to write a check for the entire purchase.)
7. Store clerks must monitor the locked cabinets and stay with a customer who wants to view an item from the cabinet.
8. Because of the size of the enclosed department, only two checkout counters will fit in electronics.
9. Moving the electronics department to the front of the store would not be wise because shoppers tend to pick up impulse items on their way to the center of the store where electronics are located.
10. The average time a customer spends in electronics during peak periods is an unacceptable 40 minutes.

Help Kyle come up with a solution to his inefficient department. Draw a flowchart of the current process from the customer's point of view and try to identify areas for improvement. If small improvements will not fix the problem, try a more innovative approach. Chart out your suggestions and bring them to class. (It may help to visit a similar store and watch their checkout process.)

Case Problem 6.2 Wrong Meds, Again!

"It was horrible," said the distraught client. "No matter how many times I provided the information, no one listened to me. And they obviously didn't listen to each other either, because they used the wrong meds . . . again."

"Okay, calm down. Now tell me what happened from the beginning," urged Melanie Torrent, the Quality Assurance Manager for Hope Memorial Hospital.

"I got a call at work saying my father was being taken to the hospital from the nursing home. The nursing home always sends a list of medications with the ambulance, but when I got to the emergency room, they were asking my dad what medications he was taking. Of course my dad told them he wasn't taking any medications and they believed him! He's sent to the emergency room from a nursing home and they decide it's reasonable for him not to be on any medications . . . so of course I corrected him and told them to find the medication list. I don't know whether the ambulance driver forgot to bring in the list, or gave it to the wrong person, or what, but they couldn't find it. My dad must be on 12 different medications so I wasn't sure I could remember them correctly. I called the nursing home and we went over the list with them, and then I gave the handwritten list to the nursing station.

In the meantime, my dad was admitted to the hospital and moved to a hospital room. Again, a nurse came in with a computer and asked me to tell them what meds he was talking. I tried to tell them that the emergency room had the list, but she said it would be the next morning before the list got updated online. Nevertheless, the nurse called down to the emergency room and was faxed up the list of medications. Only the fax was unreadable, so they came back to me. It was a few hours before his next meds were due, so I drove over to the nursing home, had them make several legible copies of the meds list and drove back to the hospital. I gave the nurse the list, kept one for myself and posted the other on the bulletin board in my dad's room. The nurse thanked me and said she'd take care of it at the end of her shift.

After a long night at the hospital, I woke up the next morning to see my dad hallucinating. I knew immediately what had happened—there's a certain drug that he has this reaction to. I ran down to the nurse's station and had her look up the medications he had been given. Sure enough, it was there, along with several other medications he should no longer be taking. Turns out, the list was from two years ago when he had last been admitted to the hospital! How could they have made that kind of mistake—using data from two years ago?"

"That is something we'll look into. More importantly, has your father been taken off the drug?"

"Yes."

"And has the medication list been corrected?"

"Yes."

"And how is he doing today?"

"Fine today, but it could have been more serious and I think you should look into changing your procedures so this doesn't happen again . . . "

"I appreciate you bringing this to my attention. I will speak to the persons involved and I assure you this will not happen again. Hope Memorial prides itself on being a caring and responsible healthcare provider. Now if you'll excuse me, I have another client to see . . . "

1. Trace the path of the medication list and denote possible failure points. Construct a process flowchart of the existing process and create a new chart of an improved process.
2. Was the medication error a failure of individuals or a failure of the process? Explain.
3. Think about the different settings: the ambulance, the emergency room, the hospital room, and the nurse's station. How is data handled in each setting? Can the process of recording information be changed so that every one is using the same data? How can the accuracy of the data be assured?
4. Given Melanie's reaction, do you think this error will happen again? Why or why not?

Case Problem 6.3 The DPA Protocol

Blake is an intern in the Department of Performing Arts (DPA) at State University. One of his duties is to schedule end-of-term recitals for the department's graduating seniors and to create and distribute programs for those recitals. The recitals for each student include several performance pieces and often feature classical pieces with foreign titles and composers. The students submit a request for recital online and are sent an email confirmation of their recital schedule (from Blake). With that confirmation is a reminder that the material for the program needs to be submitted by a certain time. Generally, these are emailed to Blake, who puts them in standard program format and prints, folds, and distributes them to the recital venue on the evening of the performance. The department has recently been embarrassed by mistakes in the programs, and after verifying that the source of the error is usually with the student, not Blake, the department has created a new protocol to improve the process.

Following are copies of emails about the new protocol. Create a flowchart of the old and new protocols and identify where problems or delays might occur. Do you think this new protocol will improve the quality of the programs? What would you do to improve the process?

Sent: March 1, 2017
To: DPA Faculty, Staff and Interns
From: Dr. Salvatore, Chair, DPA

To ensure that the Department is putting out the best-quality recital programs, a new protocol has been established.

New Protocol for Recital Programs

- Students submit programs to their program directors.
- Program directors edit and submit programs to Ingrid.
- Ingrid submits programs to interns.
- Interns format programs and submit to Naomi for final edits.
- Naomi submits programs to Dr. Salvatore for final approval.
- Interns print, fold, and distribute programs.

Please refer any questions to Ingrid or Naomi.

Sent: March 5, 2017
To: Ingrid and Naomi
From: Blake

I am a little confused about the sequence of the programs. Do the students send their programs to their program directors before they send it to Ingrid, or do we send it to their program directors after we format it?

Thanks,
Blake

Sent: March 6, 2017
To: Blake
From: Ingrid, Head Secretary, DPA

I know this is a bit confusing so let me clarify as best as I can. When the students send me their programs, I inform them that their programs should be edited and approved by their program directors before they send it to me. I then forward it to you for proper formatting, then you send it to Naomi for editing, and then she sends it back to you for printing.

Sent: March 7, 2017
To: Blake
From: Naomi, Administrative Assistant, DPA

They send it to Ingrid, she sends it to you for formatting, and then you send it to the program director. Ingrid or I will keep you posted if there are any changes to the protocol.

References

__________, "3D Printing: The printed world," *The Economist* (February 10, 2011), http://www.economist.com/node/18114221/print, accessed February 17, 2012.

__________, "Print Me a Stradivarius," *The Economist* (February 10, 2011), http://www.economist.com/node/18114327/print, accessed February 17, 2012.

Arup Foresight, "Rethinking the Factory," 2015, http://www.driversofchange.com (accessed February 15, 2016).

Bedworth, D., M. Henderson, and P. Wolfe. *Computer-Integrated Design and Manufacturing*. New York: McGraw-Hill, 1991.

Bylinsky, Gene. "Hot New Technologies for American Factories." *Fortune Now* (June 26, 2000).

El Sawy, Omar. *Redesigning Enterprise Processes for e-Business*. New York: McGraw-Hill, 2001.

Hagel, J., Brown, J., Kulasooriya, D., Giffi, C., and Chen, M., "The Future of Manufacturing: Making things in a changing world," Deloitte University Press, 2015.

Hammer, Michael, and James Champy. *Reengineering the Corporation*. New York: HarperCollins, 1993.

Hammer, Michael, and Steven Stanton. *The Reengineering Revolution*. New York: HarperCollins, 1995.

Hartmann, B., King, W., and Narayanan, S., "Digital manufacturing: The revolution will be virtualized," McKinsey & Company, August 2015.

Hayes, Robert, Gary Pisano, David Upton, and Steven Wheelwright. *Operations Strategy and Technology: Pursuing the Competitive Edge*. Hoboken, NJ: Wiley, 2005.

Hunt, V. Daniel. *Process Mapping*. New York: Wiley, 1996.

Keen, Peter. *The Process Edge*. Boston: Harvard Business School Press, 1997.

Nevens, J., D. Whitney, T. DeFazio, A. Edsall, R. Gustavson, R. Metzinger, and W. Dvorak. *Concurrent Design of Products and Process: A Strategy for the Next Generation in Manufacturing*. New York: McGraw-Hill, 1989.

Richards, Bill. "Superplant." *eCompany Now* (November 2000).

Schneider, S., "Understanding the Protocols behind the Internet of Things," Electronic Design, October 2013.

Schwab, K., "The Fourth Industrial Revolution: What it Means, How to Respond," Foreign Affairs, December 12, 2015.

Semle, Aaron, "IIoT Protocols to Watch," White Paper, Kepware Technologies, https://www.kepware.com (accessed February 16, 2016).

Skinner, W. *Manufacturing: The Formidable Competitive Weapon*. New York: Wiley, 1985.

Teresko, John. "The Dawn of e-Manufacturing." *Industry Week* (October 2, 2000).

Valery, N. "Factory of the Future." *The Economist* (May 30, 1987), pp. 3–18.

WEC, "Industrial Internet of Things: Unleashing the Potential of Connected Products and Services," *World Economic Forum*, January 2015.

CHAPTER 7

Capacity and Facilities Design

John Carl D'Annibale/AP Images

LEARNING OBJECTIVES

After reading this chapter, you will be able to:

- Evaluate different strategies for capacity expansion, and explain the concepts of economies of scale, best operating level, and capacity cushion.
- Describe the advantages and disadvantages of basic types of layouts in both manufacturing and service settings.
- Visualize work flow and utilize algorithmic problem solving to design product and process layouts.
- Create and evaluate hybrid layouts and hybrid solutions to problems.

Making Capacity Decisions

The semiconductor industry is a high tech, high volume, expensive fabrication environment. The major players, Intel, Global Foundries (see photo), Samsung, and TSMC, are centered in the United States, South Korea, and Taiwan. Less sophisticated, lower cost foundries and specialty fabs are more common in Japan and Europe. *Fabless* companies who design semiconductors and contract out their manufacturing (e.g., Qualcomm, Nvidia, IBM) are mainly U.S. companies. Technology advances in chip design can make products obsolete in six months to two years.

While there are many places to manufacture different kinds of chips, from low–cost, general-purpose foundries to specialty and captive fabs, there is a limit to how many wafers (and chips) the industry can produce each day. For advanced products, the cost of outfitting new, state-of-the-art fabs can be prohibitive: TSMC's new foundry in Taiwan cost \$9.3 billion and Samsung's new Austin foundry cost \$13 billion. For less advanced products, expanding existing facilities can be challenging because equipment (new or used) can be difficult to find. As a result, capacity tends to remain relatively stable.

Demand, however, does not. Large consumer electronics companies such as Apple or Qualcomm consume huge portions of available capacity at the leading foundries. A shift by either of those players from one foundry to another could seriously impact capacity elsewhere in the industry. In addition, any change in the new product introduction cycle design, say from 24 months to 18 months, could cause severe capacity shortages in multiple foundries.

Demand patterns in the electronics industry vary by type of product. For example, while demand for computer products is decreasing and demand for consumer electronics has stabilized, demand for sensors and other IoT (i.e., Internet of Things) devices is increasing rapidly. Sensors use simpler technology; smartphones and computers use the most advanced technology. So demand currently favors older fabs, but companies are hesitant to build new foundries based on older technology. To complicate the decision, the lead time for getting a new foundry online is two to three years.

China, the world's largest manufacturer and assembler of electronics products, imports 91% of its semiconductor needs. The Chinese government is investing $150 billion into developing its domestic semiconductor industry over the next ten years. We'll see what kind of capacity they build and how that affects the rest of the industry.

Making capacity decisions into an uncertain future is difficult. In this chapter, we discuss issues with capacity planning and facility-related decisions on size, location, and layout. These decisions can have a long-term effect on the profitability of a firm, especially in the electronics industry.

Sources: E. Sperling, "Manufacturing Constraint Fears Grow," *Semiconductor Engineering*, December 18, 2014; D. Lammers, "Fabs in the Internet of Things Era," *NanoChip*, Vol. 8, Issue 2, pp. 20–23; ITA, "Semiconductors and Semiconductor Manufacturing Equipment Top Markets Report," Washington, DC: International Trade Administration, July 2015.

Capacity Planning

Capacity is the maximum capability to produce. Capacity planning takes place at several levels of detail. We discuss long-term capacity planning in this chapter, intermediate-term capacity planning in Chapter 14, and short-term capacity planning in Chapters 15 and 16.

Capacity The maximum capability to produce.

Long-term **capacity planning** is a strategic decision that establishes a firm's overall level of resources. It extends over a time horizon long enough to obtain those resources—usually a year or more for building or expanding facilities or acquiring new businesses. Capacity decisions affect product lead times, customer responsiveness, operating costs, and a firm's ability to compete. Inadequate capacity can lose customers and limit growth. Excess capacity can drain a company's resources and prevent investments in more lucrative ventures. *When* to increase capacity and *how much* to increase it are critical decisions.

Capacity planning Establishes the overall level of productive resources for a firm.

Figure 7.1*a*, *b*, and *c* show three basic strategies for the timing of capacity expansion in relation to a steady growth in demand.

1. ***Capacity lead strategy***. Capacity is expanded in anticipation of demand growth. This aggressive strategy is used to lure customers from competitors who are capacity constrained or to gain a foothold in a rapidly expanding market. It also allows companies to respond to unexpected surges in demand and to provide superior levels of service during peak demand periods.
2. ***Average capacity strategy***. Capacity is expanded to coincide with average expected demand. This is a moderate strategy in which managers are certain they will be able to sell at least some portion of expanded output, and endure some periods of unmet demand. Approximately half of the time capacity leads demand, and half of the time capacity lags demand.
3. ***Capacity lag strategy***. Capacity is increased after an increase in demand has been documented. This conservative strategy produces a higher return on investment but may lose customers in the process. It is used in industries with standard products and cost-based or weak competition. The strategy assumes that lost customers will return from competitors after capacity has expanded.

Consider higher education's strategy in preparing for a tripling of the state's college-bound population in the next decade. An established university, guaranteed applicants even in lean years, may follow a capacity lag strategy. A young university might lead capacity expansion in hopes of capturing students not admitted to the more established universities. A community college may choose the average capacity strategy to fulfill its mission of educating the state's youth but with little risk.

How much to increase capacity depends on (1) the volume and certainty of anticipated *demand;* (2) *strategic objectives* in terms of growth, customer service, and competition; and (3) the *costs* of expansion and operation.

FIGURE 7.1 Capacity Expansion Strategies

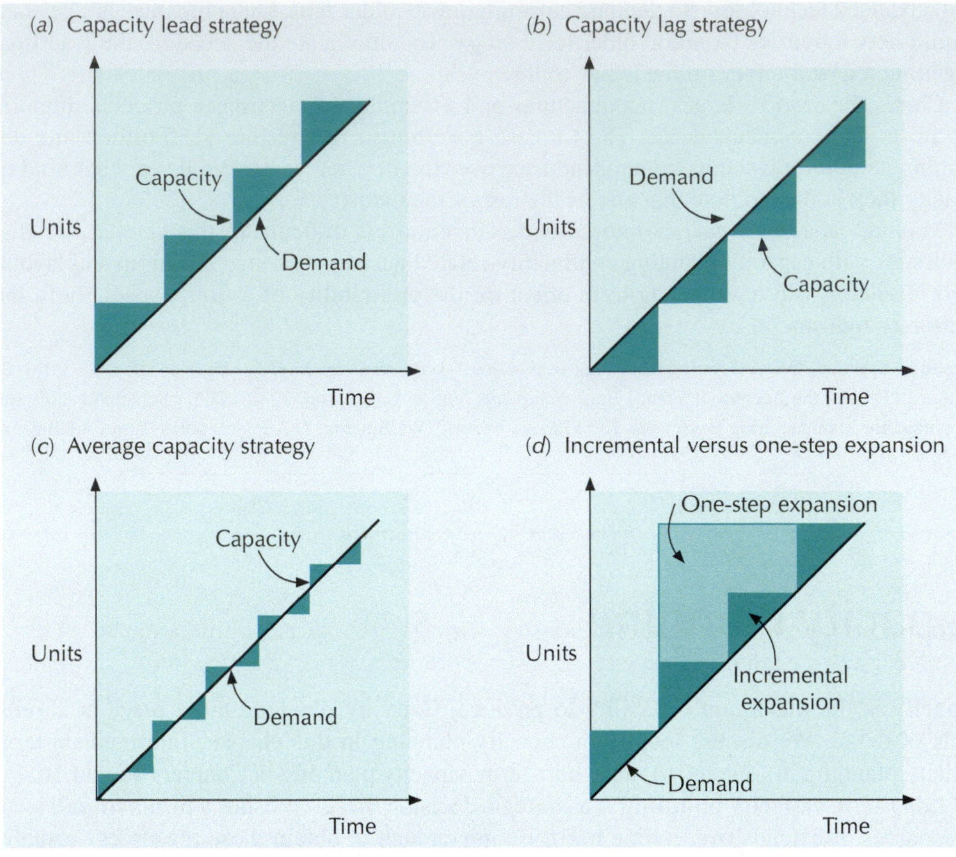

Capacity can be increased incrementally or in one large step, as shown in Figure 7.1*d*. Incremental expansion is less risky but more costly. An attractive alternative to expanding capacity is *outsourcing*, in which suppliers absorb the risk of demand uncertainty.

Best operating level The percent of capacity utilization that minimizes unit costs.

The **best operating level** for a facility is the percent of capacity utilization that minimizes average unit cost. Rarely is the best operating level at 100% of capacity—at higher levels of utilization, productivity slows and things start to go wrong. Average capacity

The 50-story Bahrain World Trade Center is powered by three huge wind turbines that connect twin sail-shaped towers. The shape of the towers funnels and accelerates the wind toward the turbines. Wind was chosen as a clean energy alternative, instead of solar, because of the intense heat in Manama, Bahrain. Green buildings of many different types are gaining popularity worldwide.

Orhan Cam/Shutterstock

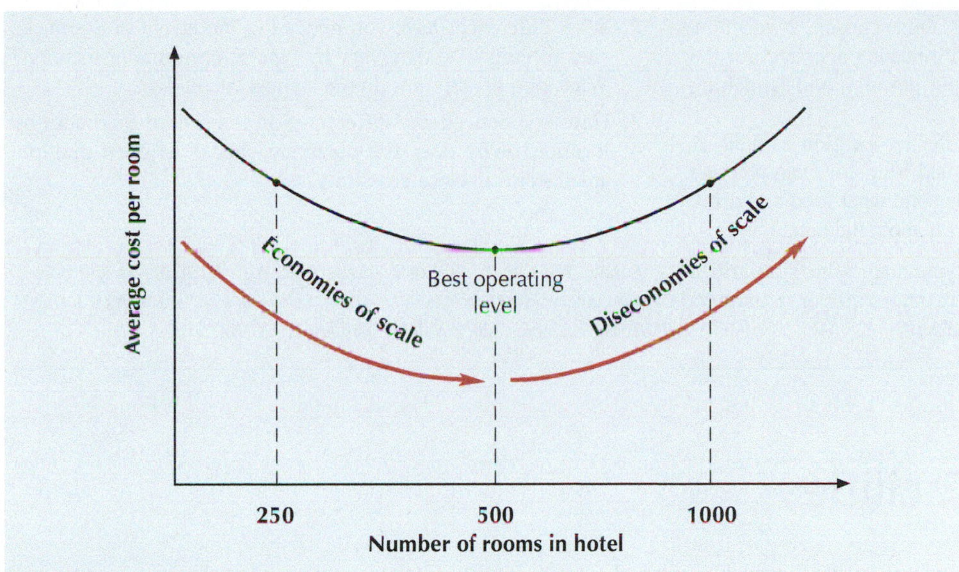

FIGURE 7.2 Best Operating Level for a Hotel

utilization differs by industry. An industry with an 80% average utilization would have a 20% **capacity cushion** for unexpected surges in demand or temporary work stoppages. Large-capacity cushions are common in industries in which demand is highly variable, resource flexibility is low, and customer service is important. Utilities, for example, maintain a 20% capacity cushion. Capital-intensive industries with less flexibility and higher costs maintain cushions under 10%. Airlines maintain a negative cushion by overbooking flights. Best operating level can also refer to the most economic size of a facility.

Capacity cushion The percent of capacity held in reserve for unexpected occurrences.

Figure 7.2 shows the best operating level—in this case, the number of rooms for a hotel—as the point at which the *economies of scale* have reached their peak and the **diseconomies of scale** have not yet begun.

Diseconomies of scale When higher levels of output cost more per unit to produce.

Economies of scale When it costs less per unit to produce high levels of output.

Economies of scale occur when it costs less per unit to produce or operate at high levels of output. This holds true when:

- Fixed costs can be spread over a larger number of units,
- Production or operating costs do not increase linearly with output levels,
- Quantity discounts are available for material purchases, and
- Operating efficiency increases as workers gain experience.

The electronics industry provides a good case example of economies of scale. The average cost per chip placement for printed circuit-board assembly is 32 cents in factories with a volume of 25 million placements, 15 cents in factories with 200 million placements, and only 10 cents in factories with 800 million placements.[1]

Capacity decisions provide a framework for further facility decisions, such as where to locate a new facility and how to arrange the flow of work in the facility. Facility location is discussed in the supplement to this chapter. The remainder of the chapter presents various alternatives for laying out a facility.

Along the Supply Chain

Is There Really a Starbucks at Every Corner?

Starbucks may seem to spring up overnight at seemingly random locations, but be assured, where to locate a new store (and what menu items to offer there) is the result of careful analysis. There's even an app for that.

Atlas is the market planning and store development application built by Starbucks. Basically a big data analytics tool layered onto a geographic information system (GIS), Atlas allows Starbucks to visualize a range of variables that lead to success in existing locations and then identify sites with similar data patterns for new store locations. For example, a city map showing current Starbucks locations can be layered with demographic information, daily traffic volume, availability of parking or public transportation, and locations (or soon-to-be locations) of other stores, offices, and eating establishments. These same factors can then

[1]"High Volumes Yield Profits for High-Tech Factories." *HE Solutions* (April 1996), p. 8.

be used to identify new potential sites. Once chosen, a workflow screen appears to guide the process of securing approval for the new site at corporate, filing the proper permits, and launching the store.

Menus, décor, and layout can differ by location as well. A map of purchasing patterns for wine and beer, for example, can determine the hours a Starbucks is open and what food and drink are offered. For Starbucks, location is all about the data.

1. Look at the Starbucks locations in your area. What similarities do those locations provide? Are there other stores or restaurants that seem to be paired with Starbucks?
2. What differences have you noticed in the layout of Starbucks sites recently? Do they vary by type of customer or location? What kind of activities do the layouts encourage?
3. Have you noticed any differences in the size of Starbucks by location? Why does the company choose to open multiple small stores in close proximity?

Source: Jeff Vance, "Big data secrets from Airbnb, Starbucks and Sonic," Computerworld (February 17, 2015); Paul Ausick, "Starbucks Closing 4 Teavanna Stores," 24/7 Wall St. (January 22, 2016).

Facilities

Facilities make a difference. They can provide a competitive edge by enabling and leveraging the latest process concepts. For example, Tesla, featured in the "Along the Supply Chain" box, is building an exemplary facility showcasing green design. Green buildings, such as the Bahrain World Trade Center shown previously, can save energy costs and increase worker productivity. Facility design has an impact on both quality and productivity. Facilities affect how efficiently workers can do their jobs, how much and how fast goods can be produced, how difficult it is to automate a system, and how responsive the system can be to changes in product or service design, product mix, or demand volume. Facilities must be planned, located, and laid out.

Facility layouts are more flexible than ever before. Factories that once positioned shipping and receiving departments at one end of the building now construct T-shaped buildings so that deliveries can be made directly to points of use within the factory. Stores sport portable kiosks for customer inquiry and checkout at various locations throughout the facility. Classrooms incorporate desks on wheels to be repositioned for different teaching styles and student interaction. Effective layouts can have many different objectives.

Objectives of Facility Layout

Facility layout The arrangement of areas within a facility.

Facility layout refers to the arrangement of activities, processes, departments, workstations, storage areas, aisles, and common areas within an existing or proposed facility. The basic objective of the layout decision is to ensure a smooth flow of work, material, people, and information through the system. Effective layouts also do the following:

- Minimize movement and material handling costs;
- Utilize space efficiently;
- Utilize labor efficiently;
- Eliminate bottlenecks;
- Facilitate communication and interaction between workers, between workers and their supervisors, and between workers and customers;
- Reduce manufacturing cycle time and customer service time;
- Eliminate wasted or redundant movement;
- Facilitate the entry, exit, and placement of material, products, and people;
- Incorporate safety and security measures;
- Promote product and service quality;
- Encourage proper maintenance activities;
- Provide a visual control of activities;
- Provide flexibility to adapt to changing conditions;
- Increase capacity.

Along the Supply Chain

Tesla's Gigafactory Produces Energy As Well As Batteries

Tesla's gigafactory is the biggest lithium-ion battery factory in the world. When completed, its 13 million sq ft footprint will rival the largest building in the world. At full production, the factory will produce half a million batteries per day, and require 100 megawatts of energy to operate. And yet, the factory, run by solar panels, a 85-turbine wind farm, and geothermal energy, will itself generate 20% more power than it can use. The excess power will provide electricity to nearby Reno, Nevada. The location of the factory, as shown in the photo, was carefully calculated to provide maximum sun exposure (5+ hours per day), abundant land, and access to geothermal and wind energy. Elon Musk built the factory to reduce the cost of batteries for its Tesla electric car, and to provide homes, businesses, and industry with their own "Powerpacks."

1. What are the advantages and disadvantages of building one enormous factory instead of multiple normal-sized factories in more diverse locations?
2. Panasonic makes batteries for the current line of Tesla cars and is expected to continue as a supplier. Why would Elon Musk build the new factory instead of Panasonic?

The Washington Post/Getty Images, Inc.

3. Less than 1% of LEED certified buildings are manufacturing and distribution centers, and yet these types of facilities are the biggest users of energy and materials. Why do you think this is the case?

Source: Katie Fehrenbacher, "Tesla is Already Making Grid Batteries at the Gigafactory," *Fortune*, (November 3, 2015); Max Chaffin, "Elon Musk Powers Up: Inside Tesla's $5 Billion Gigafactory," Fast Company (December/January 2016).

Basic Layouts

Layouts can take many different forms. In the next section, we discuss three basic layout types: process, product, and fixed-position. Later in the chapter, we discuss three hybrid layouts: cellular layouts, flexible manufacturing systems, and mixed-model assembly lines.

Process Layouts

Process layouts Group similar activities together according to the process or function they perform.

Process layouts, also known as *functional layouts*, group similar activities together in departments or work centers according to the process or function they perform. For example, in a machine shop, all drills would be located in one work center, lathes in another work center, and milling machines in still another work center. In a department store, women's clothes, men's clothes, children's clothes, cosmetics, and shoes are located in separate departments. A process layout is characteristic of service shops, job shops, or batch production, i.e., intermittent operations that serve different customers with different needs. The volume of each customer's order is low, and the sequence of operations required to complete a customer's order can vary considerably.

The equipment in a process layout is general purpose, and the workers are skilled at operating the equipment in their particular department. The advantage of this layout is flexibility. The disadvantage is inefficiency. Jobs or customers do not flow through the system in an orderly manner, backtracking is common, movement from department to department can take a considerable amount of time, and queues tend to develop. In addition, each new arrival may require that an operation be set up differently for its particular processing requirements. Although workers can operate a number of machines or perform a number of different tasks in a single department, their workload often fluctuates—from queues of jobs or customers waiting to be processed to idle time between jobs or customers. Figures 7.3 and 7.4 show schematic diagrams of process layouts in services and manufacturing.

Material storage and movement are directly affected by the type of layout. Storage space in a process layout is large to accommodate the large amount of in-process inventory.

FIGURE 7.3 A Process Layout in Services

Women's lingerie	Shoes	Housewares
Women's dresses	Cosmetics and jewelry	Children's department
Women's sportswear	Entry and display area	Men's department

The factory may look like a warehouse, with work centers strewn between storage aisles. In-process inventory is high because material moves from work center to work center in batches waiting to be processed. Finished goods inventory, on the other hand, is low because the goods are being made for a particular customer and are shipped out to that customer on completion.

Process layouts in manufacturing firms require flexible material handling equipment (such as forklifts, carts or AGVs) that can follow multiple paths, move in any direction, and carry large loads of in-process goods. A *forklift* moving pallets of material from work center to work center needs wide aisles to accommodate heavy loads and two-way movement. Scheduling of forklifts is typically controlled by radio dispatch and varies from day to day and hour to hour. Routes have to be determined and priorities given to different loads competing for pickup.

Process layouts in service firms require large aisles for customers to move back and forth and ample display space to accommodate different customer preferences.

The major layout concern for a process layout is where to locate the departments or machine centers in relation to each other. Although each job or customer potentially has a different route through the facility, some paths will be more common than others. Past information on customer orders and projections of customer orders can be used to develop patterns of flow through the shop.

Product Layouts

Product layouts Arrange activities in a line according to the sequence of operations for a particular product or service.

Product layouts, better known as *assembly lines*, arrange activities in a line according to the sequence of operations that need to be performed to assemble a particular product. Each product has its own "line" specifically designed to meet its requirements. The flow of work is orderly and efficient, moving from one workstation to another down the assembly line until a finished product comes off the end of the line, as shown in the photo below.

FIGURE 7.4 A Process Layout in Manufacturing

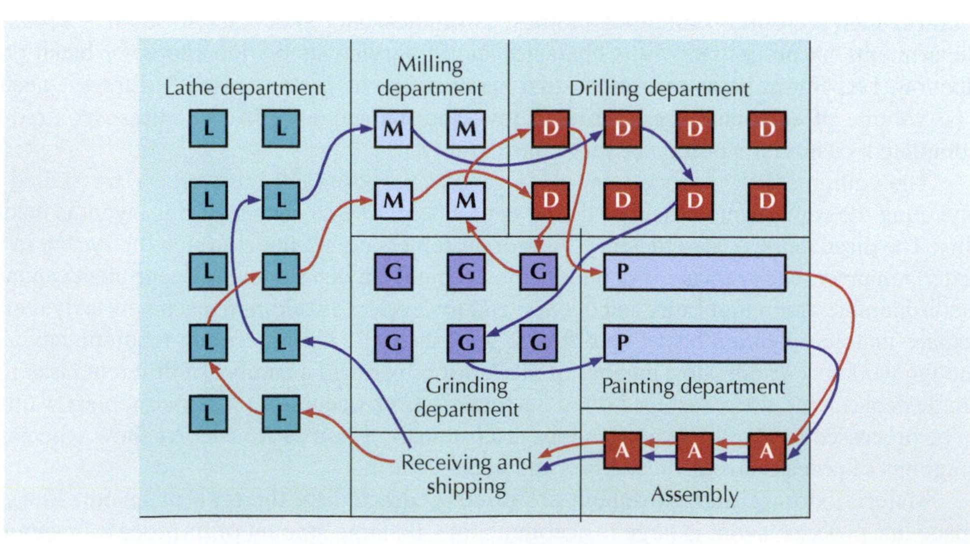

Bloomberg/Getty Images, Inc.

In this Porsche AG factory in Leipzig, Germany SUV chassis are moving down a paced assembly line with robots performing welding and other production tasks. The product layout is so named because the order of operations is standardized according to how a particular product is put together. Today's factories are increasingly automated, clean and orderly.

Since the line is set up for one type of product or service, special machines can be purchased to match a product's specific processing requirements. Product layouts are suitable for mass production or repetitive operations in which demand is stable and volume is high. The product or service is a standard one made for a general market, not for a particular customer. Because of the high level of demand, product layouts are more automated than process layouts, and the role of the worker is different. Workers perform narrowly defined assembly tasks that do not demand as high a wage rate as those of the more versatile workers in a process layout.

The advantage of the product layout is its efficiency and ease of use. The disadvantage is its inflexibility. Significant changes in product design may require that a new assembly line be built and new equipment be purchased. This is what happened to U.S. automakers when demand shifted to smaller cars. The factories that could efficiently produce six-cylinder engines could not be adapted to produce four-cylinder engines. A similar inflexibility occurs when demand volume slows. The fixed cost of a product layout (mostly for equipment) allocated over fewer units can send the price of a product soaring.

The major concern in a product layout is balancing the assembly line so that no one workstation becomes a bottleneck and holds up the flow of work through the line. Figure 7.5 shows the product flow in a product layout. Contrast this with the flow of products through the process layout shown in Figure 7.4.

A product layout needs material moved in one direction along the assembly line and always in the same pattern. Conveyors are the most common material handling equipment for product layouts. Conveyors can be *paced* (automatically set to control the speed of work) or *unpaced* (stopped and started by the workers according to their pace). Assembly work can be performed *online* (i.e., on the conveyor) or *offline* (at a workstation serviced by the conveyor).

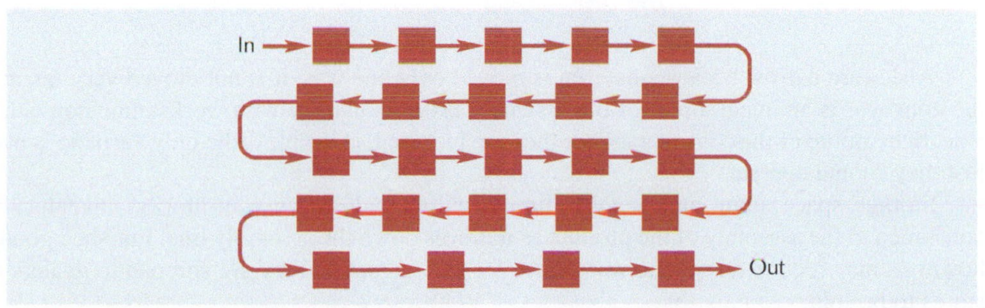

FIGURE 7.5 A Product Layout

Along the Supply Chain

Stihl's Manufacturing Complex

© Kevin Brine - Editorial / Alamy Stock Photo

Stihl, Inc., a venerable 100-year-old German engineering and manufacturing firm, has a 150-acre manufacturing complex in Virginia Beach, VA, consisting of six factories, 2 million square feet of production space, and several supporting buildings (e.g., offices, warehouses, and testing facilities). The complex employs over 1900 people and produces 275 different models of handheld outdoor power equipment, such as chain saws (see photo), trimmers, blowers, and shredders. Stihl also manufactures its own engines on site, as well as machined and plastic parts for its products. In addition, Stihl designs and builds much of its own production and testing equipment, including machine vision robots. This degree of vertical integration is unusual today.

The newest building on site is a 60,000-square-foot guide bar factory that sports fully automated stamping, welding, riveting, painting, and packaging processes. In another building, seven chain saw assembly lines (or cells) produce more than 35 different models, while 15 power tool assembly lines build more than 100 models. The two sections of assembly are separated by a kanban supermarket of key components that feed the lines (we discuss kanbans in Chapter 16). Workstations along the assembly line are ergonomically designed and electric fastening tools employ smart-arm technology.

The assembly lines are flexible and assembly line workers are cross-trained on a variety of lines, so that work can be quickly reconfigured to reflect seasonal demand for products. Demand is higher for trimmers during the spring and summer, and blowers in the fall; demand for chain saws peaks during hurricane season from summer through fall. Production takes place in the off season prior to demand peaks.

The variety of chain saws assembled range from a 9-pound tool for homeowners to a professional lumberjack's tool with a 25" guide bar that can fell and buck large-diameter trees. Product options for power-landscaping tools include engine displacements, driveshafts, filter systems, fuel tanks, mufflers, cutting heads, and attachments. One of the trimmer assembly lines, for instance, runs three shifts and handles over 500 product variations, including advanced engine technology (i.e., 2-cycle, 4-cycle, and hybrid engines) requiring different emissions testing. Stihl has 137 test cells where every product coming off the assembly line is run-in for quality checks. Finally, since 45% of manufacturing output is sent overseas, warning labels, instruction manuals, and packaging are added in more than a dozen languages.

The Stihl complex is heavily invested in lean production. In addition to the kanban supermarket, the plant uses 5S, kaizen, visual control, value-stream mapping, and andon boards that display production rates, takt time, safety records, and quality ratings for specific assembly lines. Continuous improvement methodologies are used by teams of workers and engineers to streamline both manual and automated processes. For example, in the plastics factory, one operator can run 27 different injection molding machines at a time. With over 150 robots across factories at the site, many of the improvement projects address machine vision or the collaborative work of humans and machines. Employees that make suggestions for process improvement can get paid up to 25 percent of the first-year's cost savings.

Consistent with German tradition, the Virginia Beach complex also includes an apprenticeship program that trains workers in robotics, tool and die making, polymer technology, CNC machining, quality assurance, and plant maintenance.

1. Explore the Stihl corporate website and other online resources. How does Stihl fare in various product markets? What is their positioning strategy, i.e., on what do they compete? (see Chapter 1)
2. Make a list of the ways in which Stihl controls the inputs to its manufacturing processes. Why do you think Stihl is so invested in vertical integration?
3. For what reasons might Stihl have built this large manufacturing complex in the United States? Comment on both the size and location. Where else in the world are Stihl products manufactured?
4. There are several different types of production processes exhibited in the Stihl manufacturing complex. What kinds of items are produced in batch production? When does mass production take place? How are hybrid layouts used?

Sources: Austin Weber, "STIHL Stays a Cut Above the Competition," *Assembly Magazine* (October 3, 2014); Bill Bregar, "Stihl cuts through the competition," *Plastics News* (February 10, 2015).

Aisles are narrow because material is moved only one way, it is not moved very far, and the conveyor is an integral part of the assembly process, usually with workstations on either side. Scheduling of the conveyors, once they are installed, is simple—the only variable is how fast they should operate.

Storage space along an assembly line is quite small because in-process inventory is consumed in the assembly of the product as it moves down the assembly line. Finished goods, however, may require a separate warehouse for storage before they are shipped to dealers or stores to be sold.

TABLE 7.1 A Comparison of Product and Process Layouts

	PRODUCT LAYOUT	PROCESS LAYOUT
1. Description	Sequential arrangement of activities	Functional grouping of activities
2. Type of process	Continuous, mass production, mainly assembly	Intermittent, job shop, batch production, mainly fabrication
3. Product	Standardized, made to stock	Varied, made to order
4. Demand	Stable	Fluctuating
5. Volume	High	Low
6. Equipment	Special purpose	General purpose
7. Workers	Limited skills	Varied skills
8. Inventory	Low in-process, high finished goods	High in-process, low finished goods
9. Storage space	Small	Large
10. Material handling	Fixed path (conveyor)	Variable path (forklift)
11. Aisles	Narrow	Wide
12. Scheduling	Part of balancing	Dynamic
13. Layout decision	Line balancing	Machine location
14. Goal	Equalize work at each station	Minimize material handling cost
15. Advantage	Efficiency	Flexibility

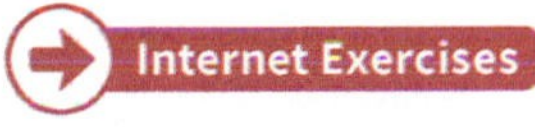

Product and process layouts look different, use different material handling methods, and have different layout concerns. Table 7.1 summarizes the differences between product and process layouts.

Fixed-Position Layouts

Fixed-position layouts are typical of projects in which the product produced is too fragile, bulky, or heavy to move. Ships, houses, and aircraft (see photo) are examples. In this layout, the product remains stationary for the entire manufacturing cycle. Equipment, workers, materials,

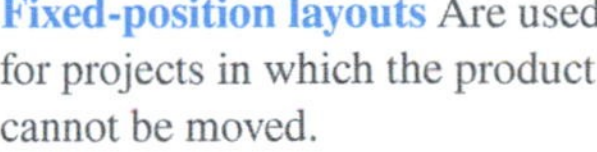

Fixed-position layouts Are used for projects in which the product cannot be moved.

Kevin P. Casey/Bloomberg/Getty Images, Inc.

Aircraft production generally takes place in a fixed-position layout due to the size and complexity of assembly. Shown here is a Boeing 787 Dreamliner being outfitted.

and other resources are brought to the production site. Equipment utilization is low because it is often less costly to leave equipment idle at a location where it will be needed again in a few days, than to move it back and forth. Frequently, the equipment is leased or subcontracted because it is used for limited periods of time. The workers called to the work site are highly skilled at performing the special tasks they are requested to do. For instance, pipefitters may be needed at one stage of production, and electricians or plumbers at another. The wage rate for these workers is much higher than minimum wage. Thus, if we were to look at the cost breakdown for fixed-position layouts, the fixed cost would be relatively low (equipment may not be owned by the company), whereas the variable costs would be high (due to high labor rates and the cost of leasing and moving equipment).

Fixed-position layouts are specialized to individual projects and thus are beyond the scope of this book. Projects are covered in more detail in the next chapter. In the sections that follow, we examine some quantitative approaches for designing product and process layouts.

Designing Process Layouts

In designing a process layout, we want to minimize movement or material handling cost, which is a function of the amount of material moved times the distance it is moved. This implies that departments that incur the most interdepartment movement should be located closest to each other, and those that do not interact should be located further away. Two techniques used to design process layouts, block diagramming and relationship diagramming, are based on logic and the visual representation of data.

Block Diagramming

Unit load The quantity in which material is normally moved.

We begin with data on historical or predicted movement of material between departments in the existing or proposed facility. This information is typically provided in the form of a from/to chart, or *load summary chart*. The chart gives the average number of **unit loads** transported between the departments over a given period of time. A unit load can be a single unit, a pallet of material, a bin of material, or a crate of material—however material is normally moved from location to location. In automobile manufacturing, a single car represents a unit load. For a ball-bearing producer, a unit load might consist of a bin of 100 or 1000 ball bearings, depending on their size.

The next step in designing the layout is to calculate the *composite movements* between departments and rank them from most movement to least movement. Composite movement, represented by a two-headed arrow, refers to the back-and-forth movement between each pair of departments.

Finally, trial layouts are placed on a grid that graphically represents the relative distances between departments in the form of uniform blocks. The objective is to assign each department to a block on the grid so that *nonadjacent loads* are minimized. The term *nonadjacent* is defined as a distance farther than the next block, either horizontally, vertically, or diagonally. The trial layouts are scored on the basis of the number of nonadjacent loads. Ideally, the optimal layout would have zero nonadjacent loads. In practice, this is rarely possible, and the process of trying different layout configurations to reduce the number of nonadjacent loads continues until an acceptable layout is found.

EXAMPLE 7.1 | Process Layout

Barko, Inc., makes *bark scalpers*, processing equipment that strips the bark off trees and turns it into nuggets or mulch for gardens. The facility that makes bark scalpers is a small-job shop that employs 50 workers and is arranged into five departments: (1) bar stock cutting, (2) sheet metal, (3) machining, (4) painting, and (5) assembly. The average number of loads transported between the five departments per month is given in the accompanying load summary chart. The current layout of the facility is shown schematically on the 2 × 3 grid. Notice that there is quite a bit of flexibility in the facility, as indicated by the six possible locations (i.e., intersections) available for five departments. In addition, the forklift used in the facility is very flexible, allowing horizontal, vertical, and diagonal movement of material.

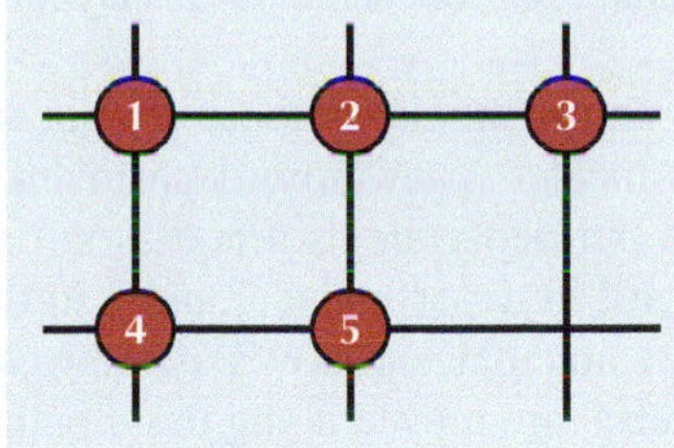

LOAD SUMMARY CHART					
	DEPARTMENT				
FROM/TO DEPARTMENT	1	2	3	4	5
1	—	100	50		
2		—	200	50	
3	60		—	40	50
4		100		—	60
5		50			—

Barko management anticipates that a new bark scalper plant will soon be necessary and would like to know if a similar layout should be used or if a better layout can be designed. You are asked to evaluate the current layout in terms of nonadjacent loads, and if needed, propose a new layout on a 2 × 3 grid that will minimize the number of nonadjacent loads.

Solution: In order to evaluate the current layout, we need to calculate the composite, or back-and-forth, movements between departments. For example, the composite movement between department 1 and department 3 is the sum of 50 loads moved from 1 to 3, plus 60 loads moved from 3 to 1, or 110 loads of material. If we continue to calculate composite movements and rank them from highest to lowest, the following list results:

COMPOSITE	MOVEMENTS	COMPOSITE	MOVEMENTS
2 ↔ 3	200 loads	3 ↔ 5	50 loads
2 ↔ 4	150 loads	2 ↔ 5	50 loads
1 ↔ 3	110 loads	3 ↔ 4	40 loads
1 ↔ 2	100 loads	1 ↔ 4	0 loads
4 ↔ 5	60 loads	1 ↔ 5	0 loads

Next, we evaluate the "goodness" of the layout by scoring it in terms of nonadjacent loads. The results are shown visually in Grid 1.

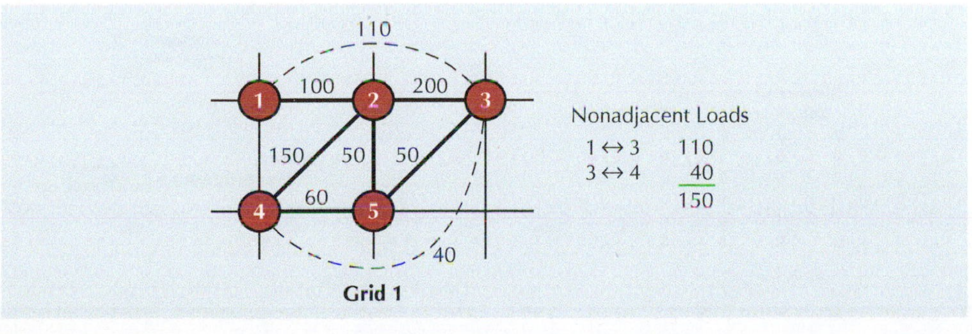

Grid 1

The adjacent moves are marked with a solid line and the nonadjacent moves are shown with a curved dashed line to highlight the fact that material is moved farther than we would like, that is, across more than one square. Following our composite movement list, $2 \leftrightarrow 3$ and $2 \leftrightarrow 4$ are adjacent moves, but $1 \leftrightarrow 3$ is not. Our nonadjacent score starts with 110 loads of material from $1 \leftrightarrow 3$. Continuing down our list, all moves are adjacent and are marked with solid lines until $3 \leftrightarrow 4$. Movement $3 \leftrightarrow 4$ is nonadjacent, so we designate it as such and add 40 loads to our nonadjacent score. The remaining movements have zero loads. Thus, our score for this layout is $110 + 40 = 150$ nonadjacent loads.

To improve the layout, we note that departments 3 and 4 should be located adjacent to department 2, and that departments 4 and 5 may be located away from department 1 without adding to the score of nonadjacent loads. Let's put departments 4 and 5 on one end of the grid and department 1 on the other and then fill in departments 2 and 3 in the middle. The revised solution is shown in Grid 2. The only nonadjacent moves are between departments 1 and 4, and 1 and 5. Since no loads of material are moved along those paths, the score for this layout is zero.

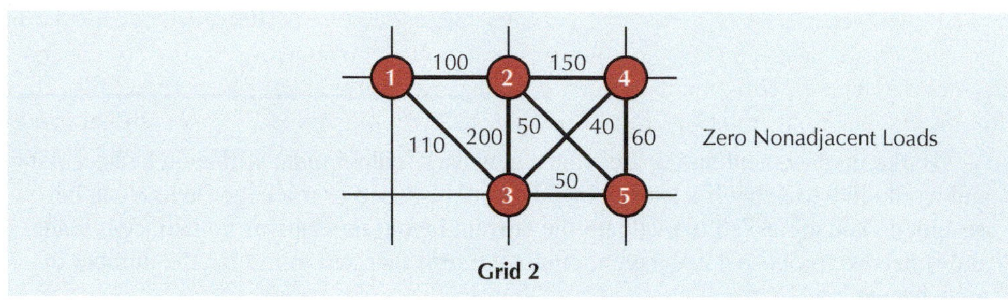

The Excel setup for this problem is shown in Exhibit 7.1.

EXHIBIT 7.1

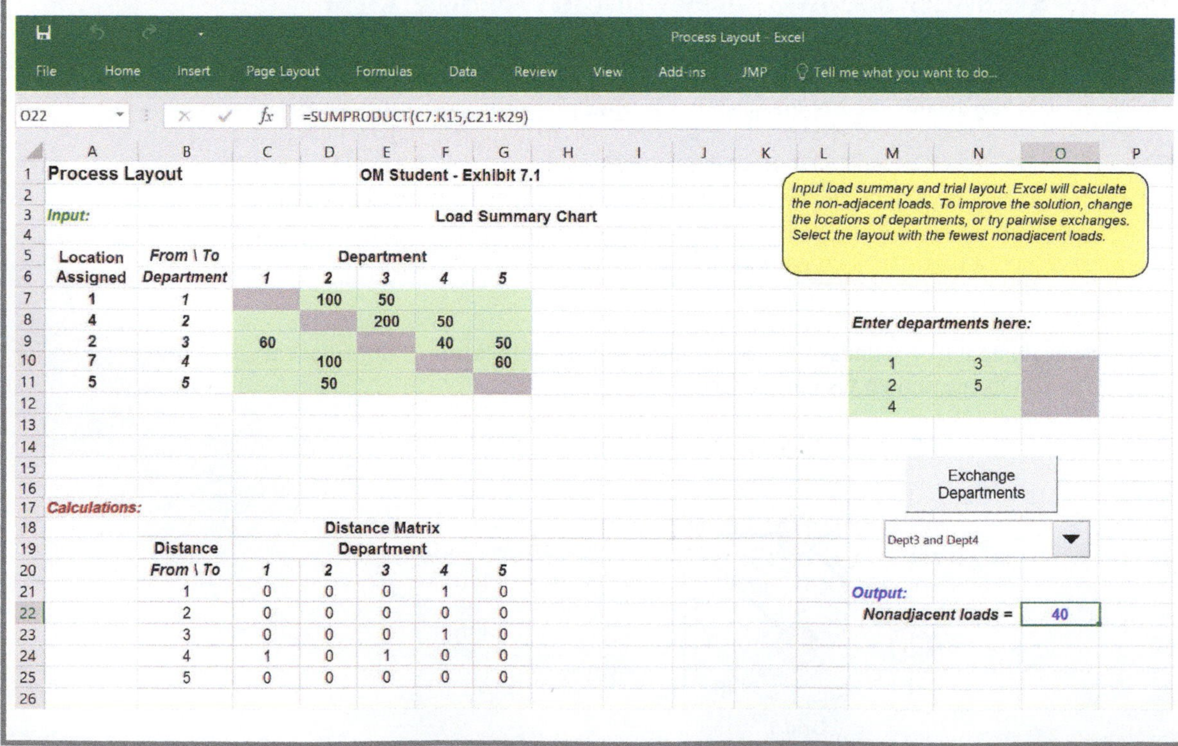

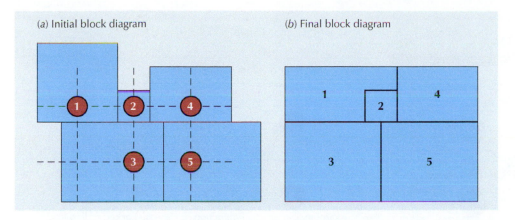

FIGURE 7.6 **Block Diagrams**

(*a*) Initial block diagram

(*b*) Final block diagram

The layout solution in Grid 2 represents the relative position of each department. The next step in the layout design is to add information about the space required for each department. Recommendations for workspace around machines can be requested from equipment vendors or found in safety regulations or operating manuals. In some cases, vendors provide templates of equipment layouts, with work areas included. Workspace allocations for workers can be specified as part of job design, recommended by professional groups, or agreed on through union negotiations. A **block diagram** can be created by "blocking in" the work areas around the departments on the grid. The *final block diagram* adjusts the block diagram for the desired or proposed shape of the building. Standard building shapes include rectangles, L shapes, T shapes, and U shapes.

Block diagram A type of schematic layout diagram that includes space requirements.

Figure 7.6*a* shows an initial block diagram for Example 7.1, and Figure 7.6*b* shows a final block diagram. Notice that the space requirements vary considerably from department to department, but the relative location of departments has been retained from the grid.

Relationship Diagramming

The preceding solution procedure is appropriate for designing process layouts when quantitative data are available. However, in situations for which quantitative data are difficult to obtain or do not adequately address the layout problem, the load summary chart can be replaced with subjective input from analysts or managers. Richard Muther developed a format for displaying manager preferences for departmental locations, known as **Muther's grid**.[2] The preference information is coded into six categories associated with the five vowels, *A, E, I, O*, and *U*, plus the letter *X*. As shown in Figure 7.7, the vowels match the first letter of the closeness rating for locating two departments next to each other. The diamond-shaped grid is read similarly to mileage charts on a road map. For example, reading down the highlighted row in Figure 7.7, it is *okay* if the offices are located next to production, *absolutely necessary* that the stockroom be located next to production, *important* that shipping and receiving be located next to production, *especially important* that the locker room be located next to production, and *absolutely necessary* that the toolroom be located next to production.

Muther's grid A format for displaying manager preferences for department locations.

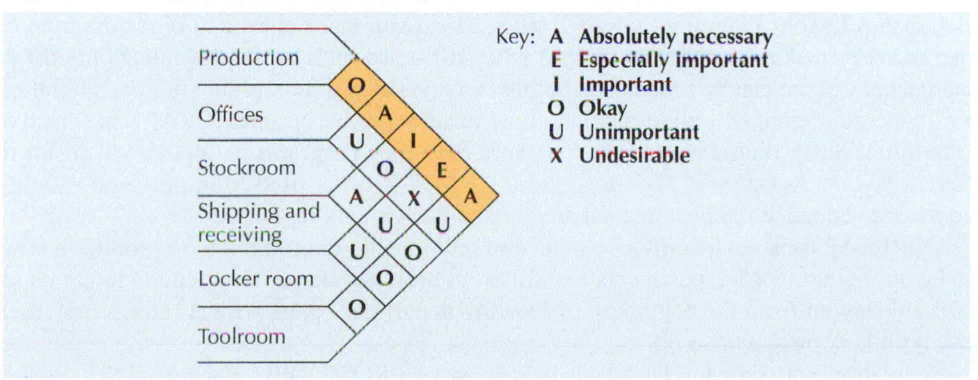

FIGURE 7.7 **Muther's Grid**

[2]R. Muther, *Systematic Layout Planning* (Boston: Industrial Education Institute, 1961).

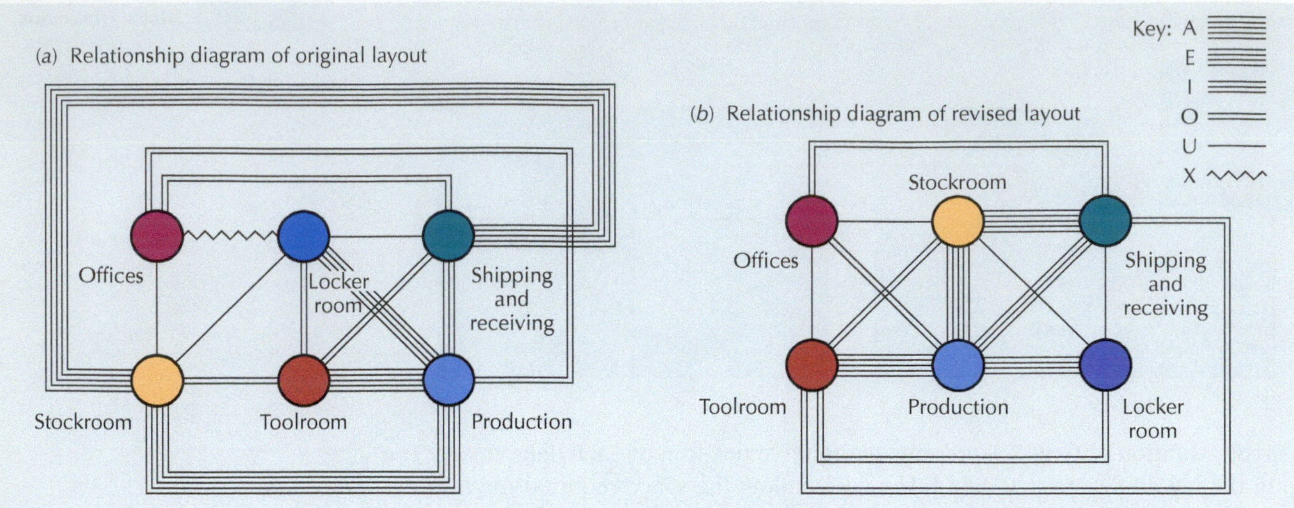

FIGURE 7.8 **Relationship Diagrams**

Relationship diagram A schematic diagram that uses weighted lines to denote location preference.

The information from Muther's grid can be used to construct a **relationship diagram** that evaluates existing or proposed layouts. Consider the relationship diagram shown in Figure 7.8*a*. A schematic diagram of the six departments from Figure 7.7 is given in a 2 × 3 grid. Lines of different thicknesses are drawn from department to department. The thickest lines (three, four, or five strands) identify the closeness ratings with the highest priority—that is, for which departments it is *important, especially important*, or *absolutely necessary* that they be located next to each other. The priority diminishes with line thickness. *Undesirable* closeness ratings are marked with a zigzagged line. Visually, the best solution would show short heavy lines and no zigzagged lines (undesirable locations are noted only if they are adjacent). Thin lines (one or two strands, representing *unimportant* or *okay*) can be of any length and for that reason are sometimes eliminated from the analysis. An alternative form of relationship diagramming uses colors instead of line thickness to visualize closeness ratings.

From Figure 7.8*a*, it is obvious that production and shipping and receiving are located too far from the stockroom and that the offices and locker room are located too close to one another. Figure 7.8*b* shows a revised layout and evaluates the layout with a relationship diagram. The revised layout appears to satisfy the preferences expressed in Muther's grid. The heavy lines are short and within the perimeter of the grid. The lengthy lines are thin, and there are no zigzagged lines (X's are shown only if the departments are adjacent).

Computerized Layout Solutions

The diagrams just discussed help formulate ideas for the arrangement of departments in a process layout, but they can be cumbersome for large problems. Fortunately, several computer packages are available for designing process layouts. The best known are CRAFT (Computerized Relative Allocation of Facilities Technique) and CORELAP (Computerized Relationship Layout Planning). CRAFT takes a load summary chart and block diagram as input and then makes pairwise exchanges of departments until no improvements in cost or nonadjacency score can be found. The output is a revised block diagram after each iteration for a rectangular-shaped building, which may or may not be optimal. CRAFT is sensitive to the initial block diagram used; that is, different block diagrams as inputs will result in different layouts as outputs. For this reason, CRAFT is often used to improve on existing layouts or to enhance the best manual attempts at designing a layout.

CORELAP uses nonquantitative input and relationship diagramming to produce a feasible layout for up to 45 departments and different building shapes. It attempts to create an acceptable layout from the beginning by locating department pairs with A ratings first, then those with E ratings, and so on.

Simulation software for layout analysis such as PROMODEL and EXTEND provide visual feedback and allow the user to quickly test a variety of scenarios. Three-D modeling and CAD-integrated layout analysis are available in VisFactory and similar software.

The Washington Post/Getty Images, Inc.

Trends in office layouts include flexibility, shared spaces, and ergonomic desks, like the one here at Motley Fool's headquarters, that can transition from sitting to standing and may even include a treadmill.

Designing Service Layouts

Most service organizations use process layouts. This makes sense because of the variability in customer requests for service. Service layouts are designed in much the same way as process layouts in manufacturing firms, but the objectives may differ. For example, instead of minimizing the flow of materials through the system, services may seek to minimize the flow of paperwork or to maximize customer exposure to as many goods as possible. Grocery stores take this approach when they locate milk on one end of the store and bread on the other, forcing the customer to travel through aisles of merchandise that might prompt additional purchases.

In addition to the location of departments, service layouts are concerned with the circulation of customer traffic through the facility. There are a variety of ways to prompt the flow of customers through various processes or departments. You may have experienced a free-flow layout in The Disney Store, a grid layout in your grocery store, a spine layout in Barnes and Noble, or a loop layout in Kohl's department store. These layouts are shown in Figure 7.9. *Freeflow layouts* encourage browsing, increase impulse purchasing, and are flexible and visually appealing. *Grid layouts* encourage customer familiarity, are low cost, easy to clean and secure, and good for repeat customers. *Loop layouts* and *spine layouts* fall between the extremes of free flow and grids. They

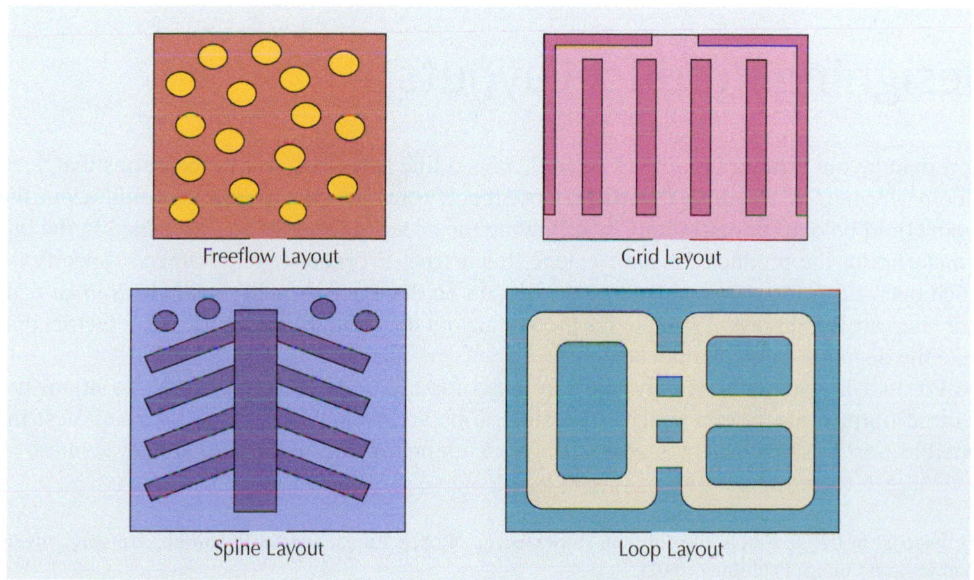

FIGURE 7.9 Types of Store Layouts

Along the Supply Chain

Inviting Retail Layouts

In contrast to manufacturing layouts, retail layouts need to be inviting to the customer. The invitation begins at the threshold, the first 5 to 15 feet of space at the entry to a facility. This is where customers get their first impression of the store and its merchandize, and where they "decompress" or transition to the retail environment. No need to put displays, signage, or product here; customers will walk right by them.

Research shows that 90% of customers turn right upon entering a store. Knowing that, retailers typically have a display wall or area to the right of store entry; subsequent displays lead customers along walking paths through the store usually in a circular pattern from front to back and then up to the front again. The path is not always as long or as obvious as the one IKEA leads its customers down, but a customer journey is indeed mapped out by the placement of aisles, displays, signage, and other visual cues.

The purpose of a retail layout is not efficiency, but rather maximum exposure to products. In fact, retail stores often create "speed bumps" to slow the customer's pace through the store and encourage impulse purchases. And saving space is not usually the top goal in retail layouts. Shopping anthropologist Paco Underhill found that narrow or crowded aisles discourage shoppers who fear the "butt-brush effect" of close proximity to other customers. Who knew?

1. Compare your grocery store layout to another type of retail store. What differences do you find in the "walking path"?
2. Think about how layouts can affect human behavior. Give an example from your own experience.

Source: Gus Lubin, "This Heat Map reveals the secret to IKEA's Store Design," *Business Insider* (January 21, 2014); Humayun Khan, "How to Create Retail Store Interiors That Get People to Purchase Your Products," https://www.shopify.com/blog/12927757, posted March 19, 2014 (accessed January 23, 2016).

both increase customer sightlines and exposure to products, while encouraging the customer to circulate through the entire store.[3]

Service layouts are also concerned with the allocation of space to departments, the location of special displays, the efficiency of checkout procedures, and protection from pilferage. Space allocation is determined by evaluating the sales per square foot of a product or product line versus the willingness of a vendor to pay for product placement. Queuing analysis, discussed in Chapter 5, is a quantitative technique for improving waiting lines that often form at checkouts.

Industry-specific recommendations are available for layout and display decisions. Computerized applications, such as SLIM (Store Labor and Inventory Management) and COSMOS (Computerized Optimization and Simulation Modeling for Operating Supermarkets), consider shelf space, demand rates, profitability, and stockout probabilities in layout design.

Finally, services may have both a *back office* (invisible to the customer) and a *front office* (in full view of the customer) component. Back offices may be organized for employee efficiency, functionality or well-being (see photo), while front office layouts must be aesthetically pleasing to the customer as well as functional. For that reason, service layouts are often considered part of the service design process.

Designing Product Layouts

A product layout arranges machines or workers in a line according to the operations that need to be performed to assemble a particular product. From this description, it would seem the layout could be determined simply by following the order of assembly as contained in the bill of material for the product. To some extent, this is true. Precedence requirements, specifying which operations must precede others, which can be done concurrently and which must wait until later, are an important input to the product layout decision. But there are other factors that make the decision more complicated.

Product layouts or assembly lines are used for high-volume production. To attain the required output rate as efficiently as possible, jobs are broken down into their smallest indivisible portions, called *work elements*. Work elements are so small that they cannot be

[3]The material in this section is adapted from Patrick Dunne, Robert Lusch, and David Griffith, *Retailing*, 4th ed. (Southwestern College Publishing, 2001).

performed by more than one worker or at more than one workstation. But it is common for one worker to perform several work elements as the product passes through his or her workstation. Part of the layout decision is concerned with grouping these work elements into workstations so products flow through the assembly line smoothly. A *workstation* is any area along the assembly line that requires at least one worker or one machine. If each workstation on the assembly line takes the same amount of time to perform the work elements that have been assigned, then products will move successively from workstation to workstation with no need for a product to wait or a worker to be idle. The process of equalizing the amount of work at each workstation is called **line balancing**.

Line balancing Tries to equalize the amount of work at each workstation.

Line Balancing

Assembly-line balancing operates under two constraints: precedence requirements and cycle time restrictions.

Precedence requirements are physical restrictions on the *order* in which operations are performed on the assembly line. For example, we would not ask a worker to package a product before all the components were attached, even if he or she had the time to do so before passing the product to the next worker on the line. To facilitate line balancing, precedence requirements are often expressed in the form of a precedence diagram. The *precedence diagram* is a network, with work elements represented by circles or nodes and precedence relationships represented by directed line segments connecting the nodes. We will construct a precedence diagram later in Example 7.2.

Precedence requirements Physical restrictions on the order in which operations are performed.

Cycle time, the other restriction on line balancing, refers to the maximum amount of time the product is allowed to spend at each workstation if the targeted production rate is to be reached. *Desired cycle time* is calculated by dividing the time available for production by the number of units scheduled to be produced:

Cycle time The maximum amount of time a product is allowed to spend at each workstation.

$$C_d = \frac{\text{production time available}}{\text{desired units of output}}$$

Suppose a company wanted to produce 120 units in an 8-hour day. The cycle time necessary to achieve the production quota is

$$C_d = \frac{(8 \text{ hours} \times 60 \text{ minutes/hour})}{(120 \text{ units})}$$

$$= \frac{480}{120} = 4 \text{ minutes}$$

Cycle time can also be viewed as the time between completed items rolling off the assembly line. Consider the three-station assembly line shown here.

Flow time = 4 + 4 + 4 = 12 minutes

Cycle time = max {4, 4, 4} = 4 minutes

It takes 12 minutes (i.e., 4 + 4 + 4) for each item to pass completely through all three stations of the assembly line. The time required to complete an item is referred to as its *flow time*. However, the assembly line does not work on only one item at a time. When fully operational, the line will be processing three items at a time, one at each workstation, in various stages of assembly. Every 4 minutes a new item enters the line at workstation 1, an item is passed from workstation 1 to workstation 2, another item is passed from workstation 2 to workstation 3, and a completed item leaves the assembly line. Thus, a completed item rolls off the assembly line every 4 minutes. This 4-minute interval is the actual cycle time of the line.

The *actual cycle time*, C_a, is the maximum workstation time on the line. It differs from the desired cycle time when the production quota does not match the maximum output attainable by the system. Sometimes the production quota cannot be achieved because the time required for one work element is too large. To correct the situation, the quota can be revised downward or parallel stations can be set up for the bottleneck element.

Line balancing is basically a trial-and-error process. We group elements into workstations recognizing time and precedence constraints. For simple problems, we can evaluate all feasible groupings of elements. For more complicated problems, we need to know when to stop trying different workstation configurations. The *efficiency* of the line can provide one type of guideline; the *theoretical minimum number of workstations* provides another. The formulas for efficiency, E, and minimum number of workstations, N, are

$$E = \frac{\sum_{i=1}^{j} t_i}{nC_a}; \qquad N = \frac{\sum_{i=1}^{j} t_i}{C_d}$$

where

t_i = completion time for element i

j = number of work elements

n = actual number of work stations

C_a = actual cycle time

C_d = desired cycle time

Balance delay The total idle time of the line.

The total idle time of the line, called **balance delay**, is calculated as (1 − efficiency). Efficiency and balance delay are usually expressed as percentages. In practice, it may be difficult to attain the theoretical number of workstations or 100% efficiency.

The line balancing process can be summarized as follows:

1. Draw and label a precedence diagram.
2. Calculate the desired cycle time required for the line.
3. Calculate the theoretical minimum number of workstations.
4. Group elements into workstations, recognizing cycle time and precedence constraints.
5. Calculate the efficiency of the line.
6. Determine if the theoretical minimum number of workstations or an acceptable efficiency level has been reached. If not, go back to step 4.

EXAMPLE 7.2 | Line Balancing

Real Fruit Snack Strips are made from a mixture of dried fruit, food coloring, preservatives, and glucose. The mixture is pressed out into a thin sheet, imprinted with various shapes, rolled, and packaged. The precedence and time requirements for each step in the assembly process are given below. To meet demand, Real Fruit needs to produce 6000 fruit strips every 40-hour week. Design an assembly line with the fewest number of workstations that will achieve the production quota without violating precedence constraints.

	WORK ELEMENT	PRECEDENCE	TIME (MIN)
A	Press out sheet of fruit	—	0.1
B	Cut into strips	A	0.2
C	Outline fun shapes	A	0.4
D	Roll up and package	B, C	0.3

Solution:

First, we draw the precedence diagram as follows.

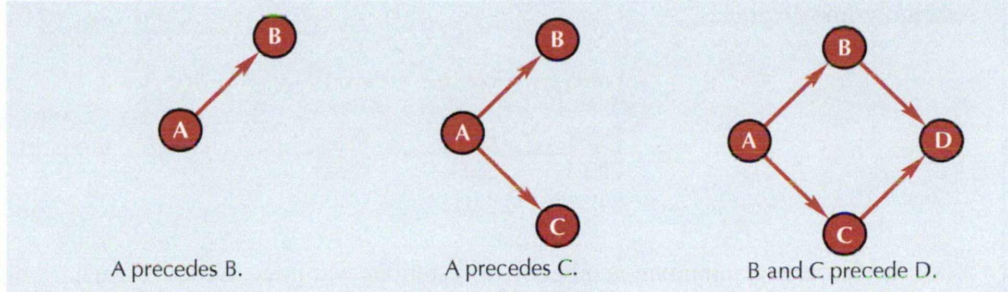

The precedence diagram is completed by adding the time requirements beside each node. Next, we calculate the desired cycle time and the theoretical minimum number of workstations:

$$C_d = \frac{40 \text{ hours} \times 60 \text{ minutes/hour}}{6000 \text{ units}} = \frac{2400}{6000} = 0.4 \text{ minutes}$$

$$N = \frac{0.1 + 0.2 + 0.3 + 0.4}{0.4} = \frac{1.0}{0.4} = 2.5 \approx 3 \text{ workstations (round up)}$$

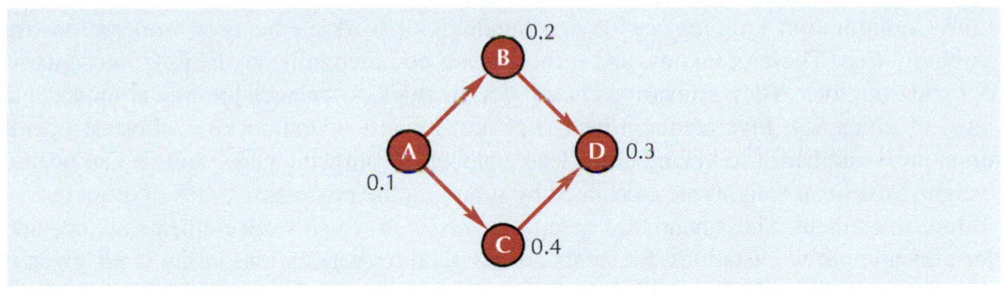

To balance the line, we must group elements into workstations so that the sum of the element times at each workstation is less than or equal to the desired cycle time of 0.4 minutes. Examining the precedence diagram, we begin with A since it is the only element that does not have a precedence. We assign A to workstation 1. B and C are now available for assignment. Cycle time is exceeded with A and C in the same workstation, so we assign B to workstation 1 and place C in a second workstation. No other element can be added to workstation 2, due to cycle time constraints. That leaves D for assignment to a third workstation. Elements grouped into workstations are circled on the precedence diagram and placed into workstations shown on the assembly line diagram.

WORKSTATION	ELEMENT	REMAINING TIME	REMAINING ELEMENTS
1	A	0.3	B, C
	B	0.1	C, D
2	C	0.0	D
3	D	0.1	none

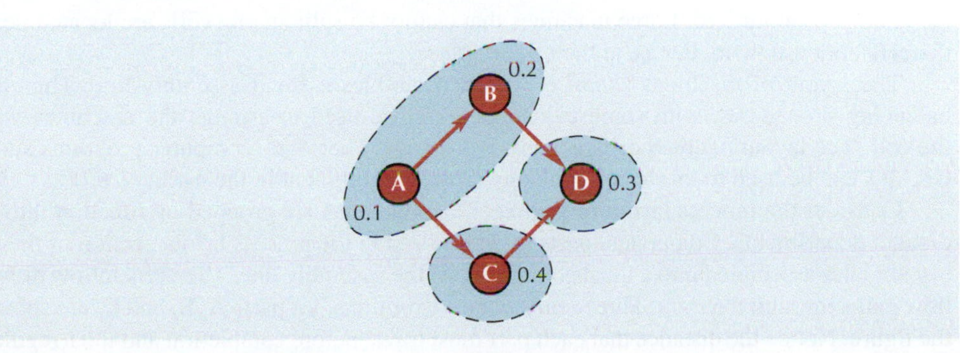

Assembly-line diagram:

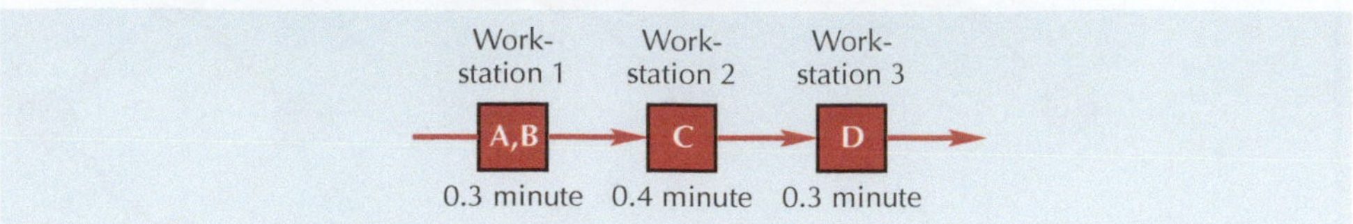

Since the theoretical minimum number of workstations was three, we know we have balanced the line as efficiently as possible. The assembly line has an efficiency of

$$E = \frac{0.1 + 0.2 + 0.3 + 0.4}{3(0.4)} = \frac{1.0}{1.2} = 0.833 = 83.3\%$$

Computerized Line Balancing

Line balancing by hand becomes unwieldy as the problems grow in size. Fortunately, there are software packages that will balance large lines quickly. IBM's COMSOAL (Computer Method for Sequencing Operations for Assembly Lines) and GE's ASYBL (Assembly Line Configuration Program) can assign hundreds of work elements to workstations on an assembly line. These programs, and most that are commercially available, do not guarantee optimal solutions. They use various *heuristics*, or rules, to balance the line at an acceptable level of efficiency. Five common heuristics are: longest operation time, shortest operation time, most number of following tasks, least number of following tasks, and ranked positional weight. Positional weights are calculated by summing the processing times of those tasks that follow an element. These heuristics specify the *order* in which work elements are considered for allocation to workstations. Elements are assigned to workstations in the order given until the cycle time is reached or until all tasks have been assigned. The most number of following tasks heuristic was used in Example 7.2.

Hybrid Layouts

Hybrid layouts modify and/or combine some aspects of product and process layouts. We discuss three hybrid layouts: cellular layouts, flexible manufacturing systems, and mixed-model assembly lines.

Cellular Layouts

Cellular layouts Group dissimilar machines into work centers (called cells) that process families of parts with similar shapes or processing requirements.

Cellular layouts attempt to combine the flexibility of a process layout with the efficiency of a product layout. Based on the concept of group technology (GT), dissimilar machines or activities are grouped into work centers, called *cells*, to process families of parts or customers with similar requirements. (Figure 7.10 shows a family of parts with similar shapes and a family of related grocery items.) The cells are arranged in relation to each other so that material movement is minimized. Large machines that cannot be split among cells are located near to the cells that use them, that is, at their *point of use*.

The layout of machines *within* each cell resembles a small assembly line. Thus, line-balancing procedures, with some adjustment, can be used to arrange the machines within the cell. The layout *between* cells is a process layout. Therefore, computer programs such as CRAFT can be used to locate cells and any leftover equipment in the facility.

Consider the process layout in Figure 7.11. Machines are grouped by function into four distinct departments. Component parts manufactured in the process layout section of the factory are later assembled into a finished product on the assembly line. The parts follow different flow paths through the shop. Three representative routings, for parts A, B, and C, are shown in the figure. Notice the distance that each part must travel before completion and the irregularity

FIGURE 7.10 Group Technology: (*a*) A family of similar parts; (*b*) A family of related grocery items.

Source: Adapted from Mikell P. Groover, *Automation, Production Systems, and Computer Integrated Manufacturing* © 1987. Adapted by permission of Pearson Education, Inc., Upper Saddle River, NJ.

of the part routings. A considerable amount of "paperwork" is needed to direct the flow of each individual part and to confirm that the right operation has been performed. Workers are skilled at operating the types of machines within a single department and typically can operate more than one machine at a time.

Figure 7.11 gives the complete part routing matrix for the eight parts processed through the facility. In its current form, there is no apparent pattern to the routings. **Production flow analysis (PFA)** is a group technology technique that reorders part routing matrices to identify families of parts with similar processing requirements. The reordering process can be as simple as using the "Data Sort" command in Excel for the most common machines, or as sophisticated as pattern-recognition algorithms from the field of artificial intelligence. Figure 7.12 shows the results of reordering. Now the part families and cell formations are clear. Cell 1, consisting of machines 1, 2, 4, 8, and 10, will process parts A, D, and F; Cell 2, consisting of machines 3, 6, and 9, will process products C and G; and Cell 3, consisting of machines 5, 7, 11, and 12, will process parts B, H, and E. A complete cellular layout showing the three cells feeding a final assembly line is also given in Figure 7.12. The representative part flows for parts A, B, and C are much more direct than those in the process layout. There is no backtracking or crisscrossing of routes, and the parts travel a shorter distance to be processed. Notice that parts G and E cannot be completely processed within cells 2 and 3, to which they have been assigned. However, the two cells are located in such a fashion that the transfer of parts between the cells does not involve much extra movement.

Production flow analysis Reorders part routing matrices to identify families of parts with similar processing requirements.

The U shape of cells 1 and 3 is a popular arrangement for manufacturing cells because it facilitates the rotation of workers among several machines. Workers in a cellular layout typically operate more than one machine, as was true in the process layout. However, workers who are assigned to each cell must now be multifunctional—that is, skilled at operating many different kinds of machines, not just one type, as in the process layout. In addition, workers are assigned a *path* to follow among the machines that they operate, which may or may not coincide with the path the product follows through the cell. Figure 7.13 shows a U-shaped manufacturing cell including worker paths.

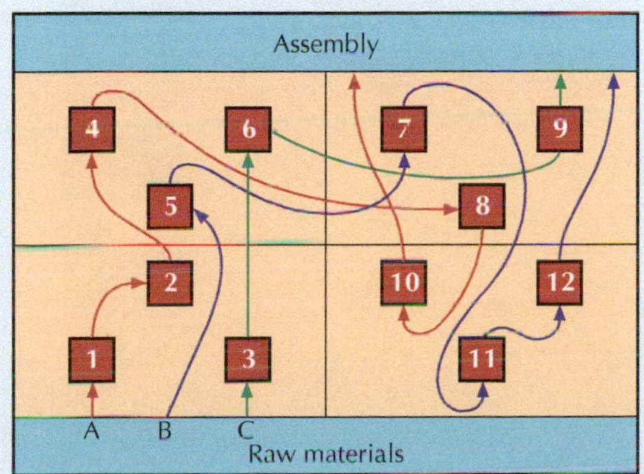

Parts	Machines 1	2	3	4	5	6	7	8	9	10	11	12
A	×	×		×				×		×		
B					×		×				×	×
C			×			×			×			
D	×	×		×				×		×		
E					×	×						×
F	×			×				×				
G			×			×			×			×
H							×				×	×

FIGURE 7.11 Original Process Layout with Routing Matrix

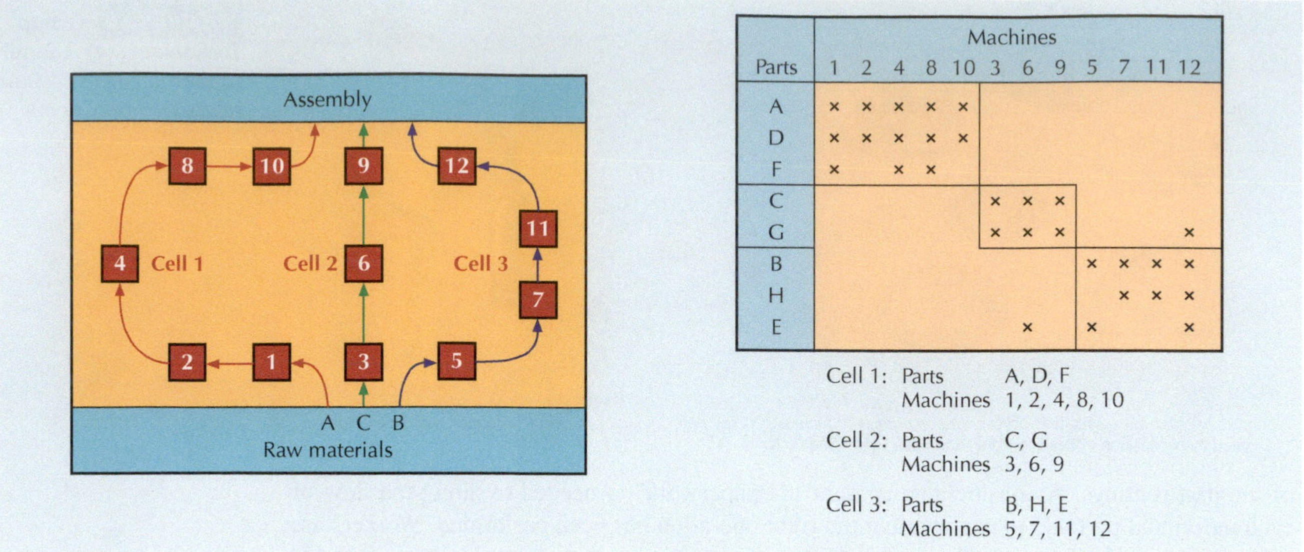

Parts	1	2	4	8	10	3	6	9	5	7	11	12
A	×	×	×	×	×							
D	×	×	×	×	×							
F	×		×	×								
C						×	×	×				
G						×	×	×				×
B									×	×	×	×
H										×	×	×
E							×		×			×

(Machines)

Cell 1: Parts A, D, F
Machines 1, 2, 4, 8, 10

Cell 2: Parts C, G
Machines 3, 6, 9

Cell 3: Parts B, H, E
Machines 5, 7, 11, 12

FIGURE 7.12 **Revised Cellular Layout with Reordered Routing Matrix**

Advantages of Cellular Layouts Cellular layouts have become popular in the past decade as the backbone of modern factories. Cells can differ considerably in size, in automation, and in the variety of parts processed. As small interconnected layout units, cells are common in services, as well as manufacturing.

The advantages of cellular layouts are as follows:

- ***Reduced material handling and transit time***. Material movement is more direct. Less distance is traveled between operations. Material does not accumulate or wait long periods of time to be moved. Within a cell, the worker is more likely to carry a partially finished item from machine to machine than wait for material-handling equipment, as is characteristic of process layouts where larger loads must be moved farther distances.

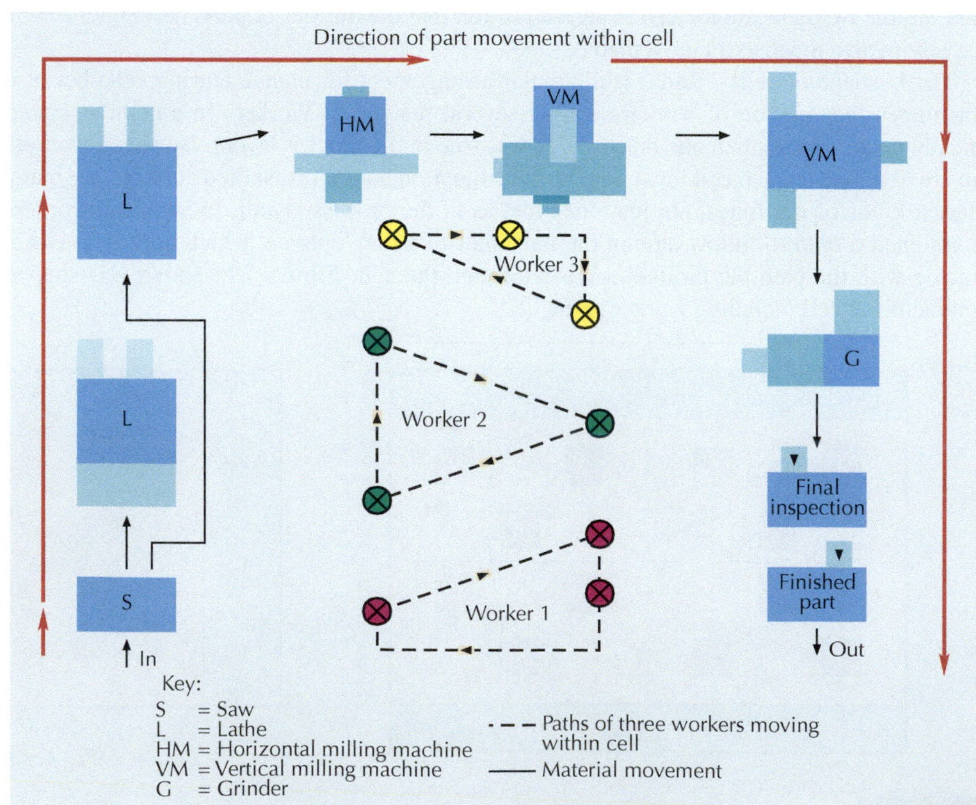

FIGURE 7.13 **A Manufacturing Cell with Worker Paths**

Source: J.T. Black, "Cellular Manufacturing Systems Reduce Setup Time, Make Small Lot Production Economical." *Industrial Engineering* (November 1983). Reprinted with the permission of the Institute of Industrial Engineers, 3577 Parkway Lane, Suite 200, Norcross, GA 30092, 770-449-0461. © 1983.

- ***Reduced setup time***. Since similar parts are processed together, the adjustments required to set up a machine should not be that different from item to item. If it does not take that long to change over from one item to another, then the changeover can occur more frequently, and items can be produced and transferred in very small batches or lot sizes.
- ***Reduced work-in-process inventory***. In a work cell, as with assembly lines, the flow of work is balanced so that no bottleneck or significant buildup of material occurs between stations or machines. Less space is required for storage of in-process inventory between machines, and machines can be moved closer together, thereby saving transit time and increasing communication.
- ***Better use of human resources***. Typically, a cell contains a small number of workers responsible for producing a completed part or product. The workers act as a self-managed team, in most cases more satisfied with the work that they do and more particular about the quality of their work. Labor in cellular manufacturing is a flexible resource. Workers in each cell are multifunctional and can be assigned to different routes within a cell or between cells as demand volume changes.
- ***Easier to control***. Items in the same part family are processed in a similar manner through the work cell. There is a significant reduction in the paperwork necessary to document material travel, such as where an item should be routed next, if the right operation has been performed, and the current status of a job. With fewer jobs processed through a cell, smaller batch sizes, and less distance to travel between operations, the progress of a job can be verified visually.
- ***Easier to automate***. Automation is expensive. Rarely can a company afford to automate an entire factory all at once. Cellular layouts can be automated one cell at a time. Figure 7.14 shows an automated cell with one robot in the center to load and unload material from several

FIGURE 7.14 An Automated Manufacturing Cell

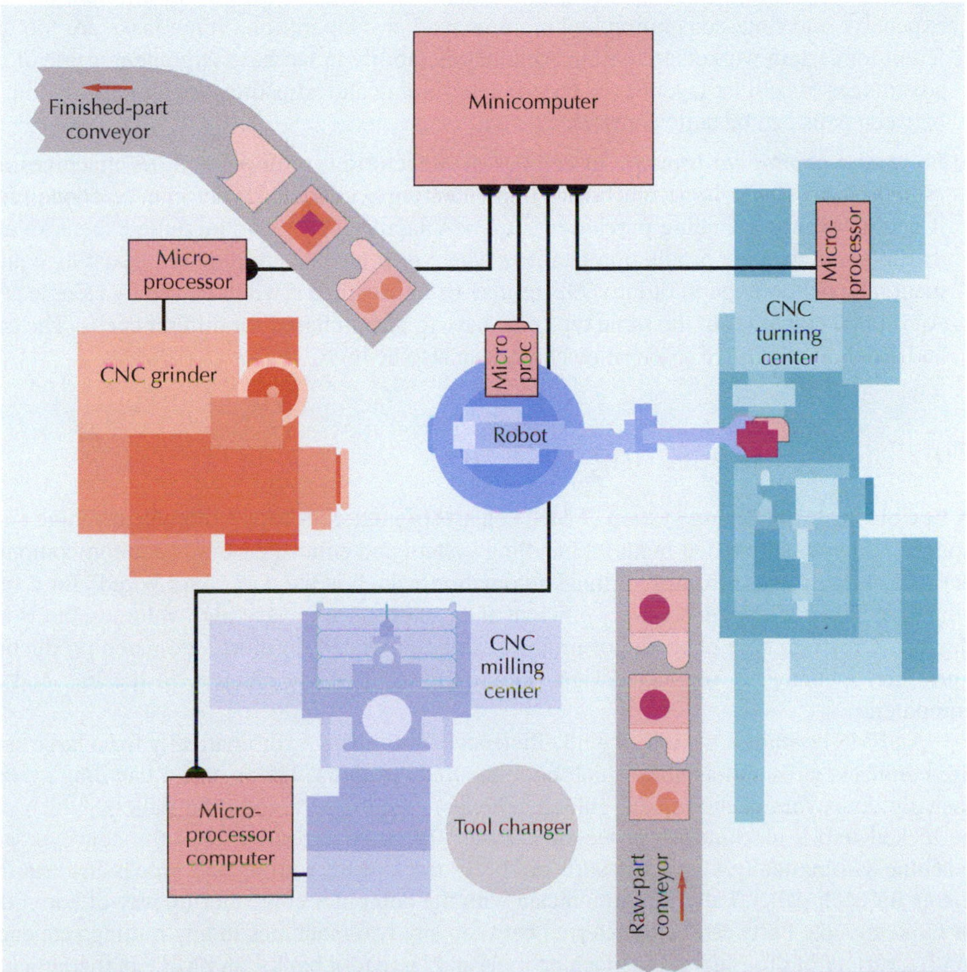

Source: J. T. Black, "Cellular Manufacturing Systems Reduce Setup Time, Make Small Lot Production Economical." *Industrial Engineering* (November 1983). Reprinted with the permission of the Institute of Industrial Engineers, 3577 Parkway Lane, Suite 200, Norcross, GA 30092, 770-449-0461, © 1983.

CNC machines and an incoming and outgoing conveyor. Automating a few workstations on an assembly line will make it difficult to balance the line and achieve the increases in productivity expected. Introducing automated equipment in a job shop has similar results, because the "islands of automation" speed up only certain processes and are not integrated into the complete processing of a part or product.

Disadvantages of Cellular Layouts In spite of their many advantages, cellular layouts are not appropriate for all types of businesses. The following disadvantages of cellular layouts must be considered:

- ***Inadequate part families***. There must be enough similarity in the types of items processed to form distinct part families. Cellular manufacturing is appropriate for medium levels of product variety and volume. The formation of part families and the allocation of machines to cells is not always an easy task. Part families identified for design purposes may not be appropriate for manufacturing purposes.
- ***Poorly balanced cells***. Balancing the flow of work through a cell is more difficult than assembly-line balancing because items may follow different sequences through the cell that require different machines or processing times. The sequence in which parts are processed can thus affect the length of time a worker spends at a certain stage of processing and thus delay his arrival to a subsequent stage in his worker path. Poorly balanced cells can be very inefficient. It is also important to balance the workload among cells in the system, so that one cell is not overloaded while others are idle. This may be taken care of in the initial cellular layout, only to become a problem as changes occur in product designs or product mix. Severe imbalances may require the reformation of cells around different part families, and the cost and disruption that implies.
- ***Expanded training and scheduling of workers***. Training workers to do different tasks is expensive and time-consuming and requires worker cooperation. Some tasks are too different for certain workers to master. Although flexibility in worker assignment is one of the advantages of cellular layouts, the task of determining and adjusting worker paths within or between cells can be quite complex.
- ***Increased capital investment***. In cellular manufacturing, multiple smaller machines are preferable to single large machines. Implementing a cellular layout can be economical if new machines are being purchased for a new facility, but it can be quite expensive and disruptive in existing production facilities where new layouts are required. Existing equipment may be too large to fit into cells or may be underutilized when placed in a single cell. Additional machines of the same type may have to be purchased for different cells. The cost and downtime required to move machines can also be high.

Flexible Manufacturing Systems

Flexible manufacturing system
Can produce an enormous variety of items.

A **flexible manufacturing system (FMS)** consists of numerous programmable machine tools connected by an automated material handling system and controlled by a common computer network. It is different from traditional automation, which is fixed or "hard wired" for a specific task. *Fixed automation* is very efficient and can produce in very high volumes, but is not flexible. Only one type or model of product can be produced on most automated production lines, and a change in product design would require extensive changes in the line and its equipment.

An FMS combines flexibility with efficiency. Tools change automatically from large storage carousels at each machine, which hold hundreds of tools. The material-handling system (usually conveyors or automated guided vehicles) carries workpieces on pallets, which can be locked into a machine for processing. Pallets are transferred between the conveyor and machine automatically. Computer software keeps track of the routing and processing requirements for each pallet. Pallets communicate with the computer controller by way of bar codes or radio signals. Parts can be transferred between any two machines in any routing sequence. With a variety of programmable machine tools and large tool banks, an FMS can theoretically produce thousands of different items as efficiently as a thousand of the same item.

The efficiency of an FMS is derived from reductions in setup and queue times. Setup activities take place *before* the part reaches the machine. A machine is presented only with

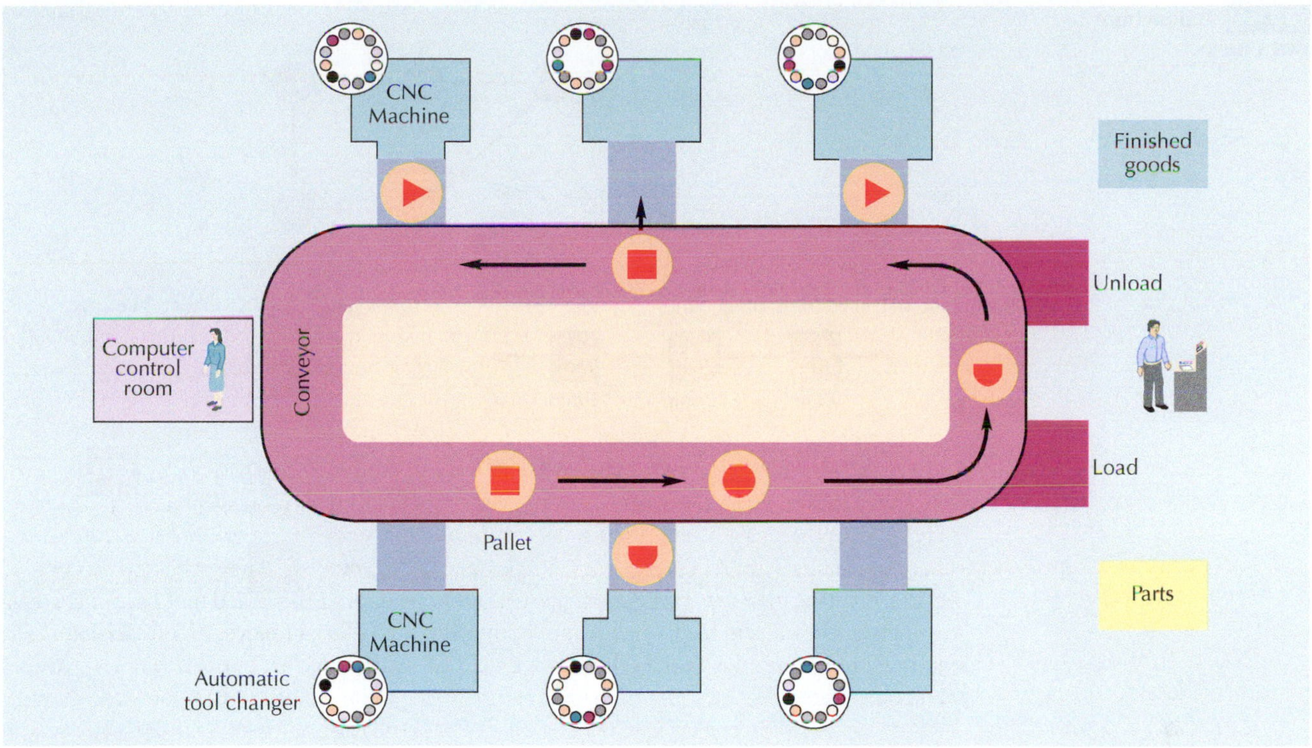

FIGURE 7.15 **A Flexible Manufacturing System**

parts and tools ready for immediate processing. Queuing areas at each machine hold pallets ready to move in the moment the machine finishes with the previous piece. The pallet also serves as a work platform, so no time is lost transferring the workpiece from pallet to machine or positioning and fixturing the part. The machines in an advanced FMS, such as five-axis CNC *machining centers*, simultaneously perform up to five operations on a workpiece that would normally require a series of operations on individual machines.

FMS layouts differ based on the variety of parts that the system can process, the size of the parts processed, and the average processing time required for part completion. Figure 7.15 shows a simple FMS where parts rotate on a conveyor until a machine is available for processing.

Mixed-Model Assembly Lines

Traditional assembly lines, designed to process a single model or type of product, can be used to process more than one type of product but not efficiently. Models of the same type are produced in long production runs, sometimes lasting for months, and then the line is shut down and changed over for the next model. The next model is also run for an extended time, producing perhaps half a year to a year's supply; then the line is shut down again and changed over for yet another model; and so on. The problem with this arrangement is the difficulty in responding to changes in customer demand. If a certain model is selling well and customers want more of it, they have to wait until the next batch of that model is scheduled to be produced. On the other hand, if demand is disappointing for models that have already been produced, the manufacturer is stuck with unwanted inventory.

Recognizing that this mismatch of production and demand is a problem, some manufacturers concentrated on devising more sophisticated forecasting techniques. Others changed the manner in which the assembly line was laid out and operated so that it really became a **mixed-model assembly line**. First, they reduced the time needed to change over the line to produce different models. Then they trained their workers to perform a variety of tasks and allowed them to work at more than one workstation on the line, as needed. Finally, they changed the way in which the line was arranged and scheduled. The following factors are important in the design and operation of mixed-model assembly lines.

Mixed-model assembly line Processes more than one product model.

- ***Line balancing***. In a mixed-model line, the time to complete a task can vary from model to model. Instead of using the completion times from one model to balance the line, a

FIGURE 7.16 Balancing U-Shaped Lines

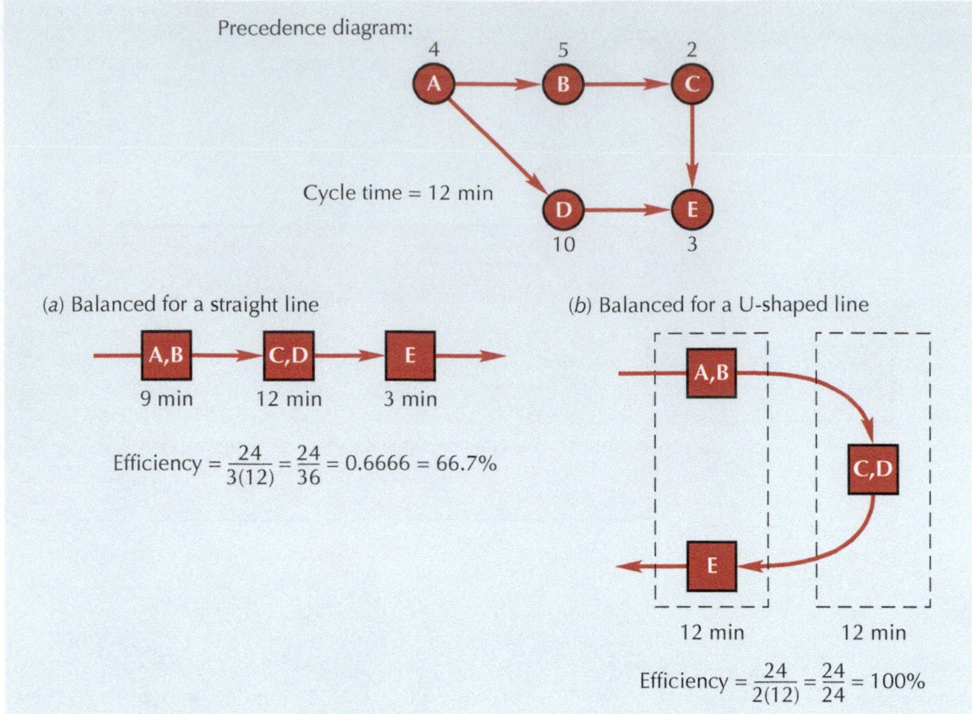

distribution of possible completion times from the array of models must be considered. In most cases, the expected value, or average, times are used in the balancing procedure. Otherwise, mixed-model lines are balanced in much the same way as single-model lines.

- ***U-shaped lines***. To compensate for the different work requirements of assembling different models, it is necessary to have a flexible workforce and to arrange the line so that workers can assist one another as needed. Figure 7.16 shows how the efficiency of an assembly line can be improved when a U-shaped line is used.
- ***Flexible workforce***. Although worker paths are predetermined to fit within a set cycle time, the use of average time values in mixed-model lines will produce variations in worker performance. Hence, the flexibility of workers helping other workers makes a tremendous difference in the ability of the line to adapt to the varied length of tasks inherent in a mixed-model line.
- ***Model sequencing***. Since different models are produced on the same line, mixed-model scheduling involves an additional decision—the order, or sequence, of models to be run through the line. From a logical standpoint, it would be unwise to sequence two models back to back that require extra long processing times. It would make more sense to mix the assembling of models so that a short model (requiring less than the average time) followed a long one (requiring more than the average time). With this pattern, workers could "catch up" from one model to the next.

Another objective in model sequencing is to spread out the production of different models as evenly as possible throughout the time period scheduled. This concept of *uniform production* will be discussed in Chapter 16, "Lean Production."

Summary

Capacity planning is the process of establishing the overall level of productive resources for a firm. It involves long-term strategic activities, such as the acquisition of new facilities, technologies, or businesses, that take a year or more to complete.

Capacity expansion can *lead* demand, *lag* behind demand, or meet *average* demand. The *best operating level* for a facility often includes a *capacity cushion* for unexpected occurrences. The tendency of high levels of output to cost less per unit is known as *economies of scale*. This normally holds true up to a certain level of output, at which point *diseconomies of scale* can take over.

Facility decisions are an important part of operations strategy. An effective layout reflects a firm's competitive priorities and enables the firm to reach its strategic objectives. Batch production, which emphasizes flexibility, is most often organized into a *process layout*, whereas mass production uses a *product layout* for maximum efficiency. Because of their size and scope, projects tend to use *fixed-position layouts. Service layouts* may try to process customers through the system as quickly as possible or maximize customer exposure to products and services.

In the current manufacturing environment of new product introductions, rapidly changing technologies, and intense competition, the ability of a manufacturing system to adapt is essential. Thus, several hybrid layouts have emerged that combine flexibility and efficiency. Reductions in setup times have made *mixed-model assembly lines* feasible. The newest *flexible manufacturing systems (FMSs)* can process any item that fits the dimensions of the pallet on which it is transported. *Manufacturing cells* that resemble small assembly lines are designed to process families of items. Some companies are placing wheels and casters on their machines so that the cells can be adjusted as needed. Others are experimenting with modular conveyor systems that allow assembly lines to be rearranged while workers are on their lunch break.

As important as flexibility is, the cost of moving material is still a primary consideration in layout design. Today, as in the past, layout decisions are concerned with minimizing material flow. However, with reduced inventory levels, the emphasis has shifted from minimizing the *number* of loads moved to minimizing the *distance* they are moved. Instead of accumulating larger loads of material and moving them less often, machines are located closer together to allow the frequent movement of smaller loads. Planners, who used to devote a considerable amount of time to designing the location of storage areas and the movement of material into and out of storage areas, are now concerned with the rapid movement of material to and from the facility itself. The logistics of material transportation is discussed in Chapter 11, "Global Supply Chain Procurement and Distribution."

Key Terms

balance delay The total idle time of an assembly line.

best operating level The percent of capacity utilization at which unit costs are lowest.

block diagram A schematic layout diagram that includes the size of each work area.

capacity The maximum capability to produce.

capacity cushion A percent of capacity held in reserve for unexpected occurrences.

capacity planning A long-term strategic decision that establishes the overall level of productive resources for a firm.

cellular layout A layout that creates individual cells to process parts or customers with similar requirements.

cycle time The maximum amount of time an item is allowed to spend at each workstation if the targeted production rate is to be achieved; also, the time between successive product completions.

diseconomies of scale When higher levels of output cost more per unit to produce.

economies of scale When it costs less per unit to produce higher levels of output.

facility layout The arrangement of machines, departments, workstations, and other areas within a facility.

fixed-position layout A layout in which the product remains at a stationary site for the entire manufacturing cycle.

flexible manufacturing system (FMS) Programmable equipment connected by an automated material-handling system and controlled by a central computer.

line balancing A layout technique that attempts to equalize the amount of work assigned to each workstation on an assembly line.

mixed-model assembly line An assembly line that processes more than one product model.

Muther's grid A format for displaying manager preferences for department locations.

precedence requirements Physical restrictions on the order in which operations are performed.

process layout A layout that groups similar activities together into work centers according to the process or function they perform.

product layout A layout that arranges activities in a line according to the sequence of operations that are needed to assemble a particular product.

production flow analysis (PFA) A group technology technique that reorders part routing matrices to identify families of parts with similar processing requirements.

relationship diagram A schematic diagram that denotes location preference with different line thicknesses.

unit load The quantity in which material is normally moved, such as a unit at a time, a pallet, or a bin of material.

Key Formulas

Desired Cycle Time

$$C_d = \frac{\text{production time available}}{\text{desired units of output}}$$

Actual Cycle Time

$$C_a = \text{maximum workstation time}$$

Theoretical Minimum Number of Workstations

$$N = \frac{\sum_{i=1}^{j} t_i}{C_d}$$

Efficiency

$$E = \frac{\sum_{i=1}^{j} t_i}{nC_a}$$

Balance Delay

$$1 - \text{efficiency}$$

Solved Problems

1. Process Layout

Mohawk Valley Furniture Warehouse has purchased a retail outlet with six departments. The anticipated number of customers that move between the departments each week is given in the load summary chart.

a. Calculate the nonadjacent loads for the layout shown below.

b. Revise Mohawk's layout such that nonadjacent loads are minimized.

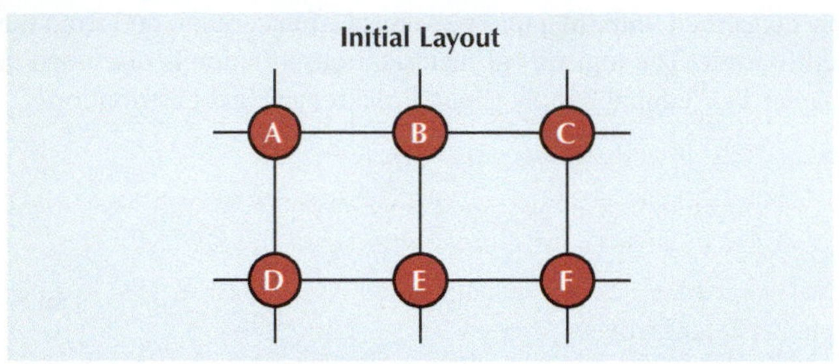

LOAD SUMMARY CHART						
DEPARTMENT	A	B	C	D	E	F
A	—	70				50
B		—			100	
C		70	—			
D			80	—		
E	40				—	30
F		60			100	—

Solution

a.

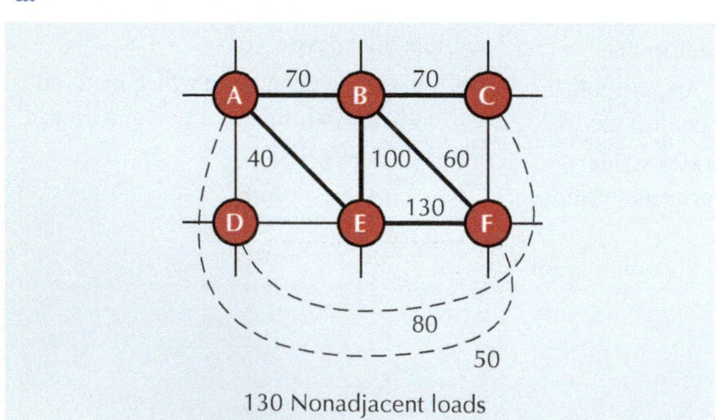

130 Nonadjacent loads

b.

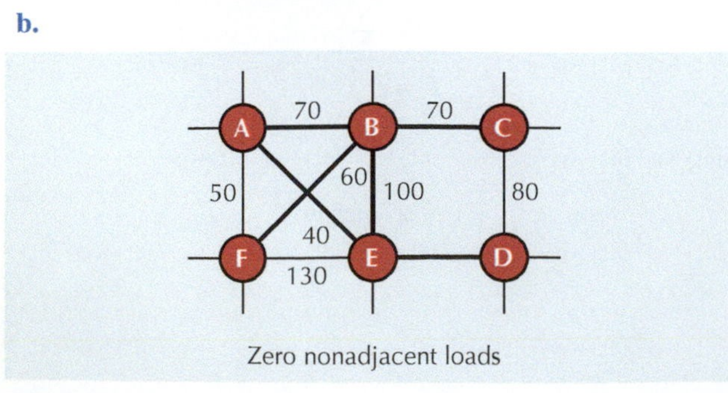

Zero nonadjacent loads

2. Product Layout

The Basic Block Company needs to produce 4000 boxes of blocks per 40-hour week to meet upcoming holiday demand. The process of making blocks can be broken down into six work elements. The precedence and time requirements for each element are as follows. Draw and label a precedence diagram for the production process. Set up a balanced assembly line and calculate the efficiency of the line.

WORK ELEMENT	PRECEDENCE	PERFORMANCE TIME (MIN)
A	—	0.10
B	A	0.40
C	A	0.50
D	—	0.20
E	C, D	0.60
F	B, E	0.40

Solution

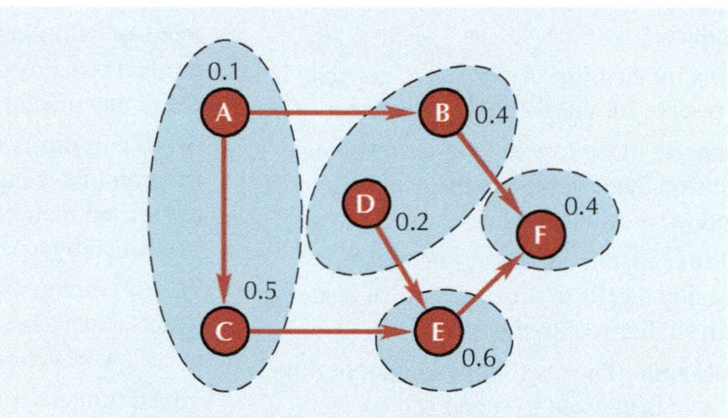

Start at the beginning of the network and group elements into workstations until cycle time has been reached. Do not violate precedence requirements.

$$C_d = \frac{\text{time}}{\text{units}} = \frac{40 \times 6}{4000} = \frac{2400}{4000} = 0.60$$

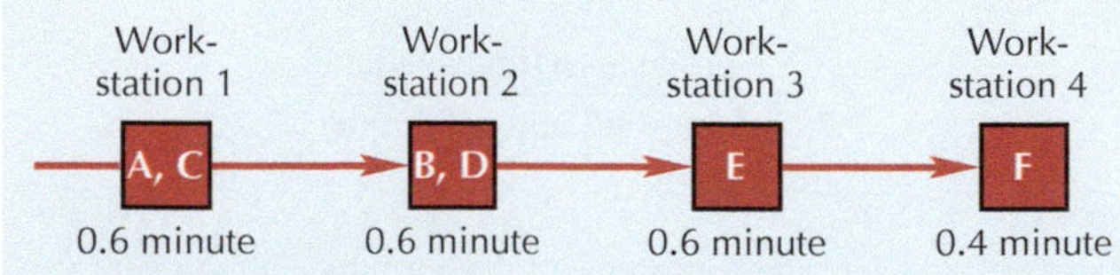

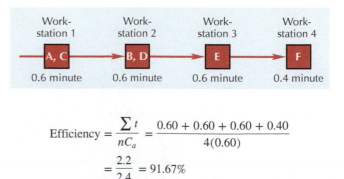

$$\text{Efficiency} = \frac{\sum t}{nC_a} = \frac{0.60 + 0.60 + 0.60 + 0.40}{4(0.60)}$$

$$= \frac{2.2}{2.4} = 91.67\%$$

Questions

7.1. Why is capacity planning strategically important?

7.2. Describe three strategies for expanding capacity. What are the advantages and disadvantages of incremental versus one-step expansion?

7.3. Explain economies and diseconomies of scale. Give an example of each.

7.4. Explore capacity planning at your university or place of business. How is capacity measured? What factors influence the acquisition and allocation of resources?

7.5. Look around your classroom. Which layout characteristics help the learning process, and which ones hinder it? How does layout affect the manner in which the class is taught?

7.6. Visit a local McDonald's, Burger King, and Taco Bell (or similar establishment). How do their layouts differ? Which appears to be most efficient? Why?

7.7. Does layout make a difference? Think of a time when the layout of a facility impeded a process with which you were involved. Think of a time when a layout made it easier for a process to be completed.

7.8. List five goals of facility layout. Give an example of a facility you know that emphasizes each goal.

7.9. Distinguish between a process and product layout. Give an example of each.

7.10. Give an example of a fixed-position layout for producing a product and providing a service.

7.11. What type of layout(s) would be appropriate for:

a. A grocery store?
b. Home construction?
c. Electronics assembly?
d. A university?

7.12. What are the fixed and variable cost tradeoffs among product, process, and fixed-position layouts? Draw a cost/volume graph to illustrate your answer.

7.13. What is the difference between block diagramming and relationship diagramming? When might each be used?

7.14. How do service layouts differ from manufacturing layouts? Give an example of a well-designed service layout and an example of a poorly designed service layout.

7.15. What are the objectives of line balancing? Describe several heuristic approaches to line balancing.

7.16. How are manufacturing cells formed? How does the role of the worker differ in cellular manufacturing?

7.17. Discuss the advantages and disadvantages of cellular layouts. How does a cellular layout combine a product and process layout?

7.18. Describe a flexible manufacturing system. How does it differ from a cellular layout?

7.19. How do mixed-model assembly lines differ from traditional assembly lines? What additional decisions are required?

7.20. Look for layout software packages on the Internet. What do systems like Proplanner do? Can you find any of the layout approaches discussed in the text?

7.21. Find a virtual plant tour on the Internet and describe the production system according to the criteria in Table 7.1.

7.22. Even better than virtual tours are actual tours. Take a tour of two production or distribution facilities in your area. Look for the basic and hybrid layouts discussed in this chapter. Also, look for bottlenecks and smooth flow. Write a paper comparing the two layouts.

Problems

7.1. Maureen Marcy is designing the layout for a new business in town, *The Collegiate Spa*. From visiting spas in neighboring towns, she has compiled the following data on movement between spa activities. Help Maureen determine where to locate each activity on a 2 × 3 grid so that nonadjacent moves are minimized.

FROM / TO	1	2	3	4	5	6
1 Relaxation Lounge		50	25		75	
2 Facial	10					75
3 Massage	30			50		50
4 Power Shower						25
5 Mineral Bath		50				50
6 Sauna						

7.2. Spiffy Dry Cleaners has recently changed management, and the new owners want to revise the current layout. The store performs six main services: (1) laundry, (2) dry cleaning, (3) pressing, (4) alterations, (5) delivery, and (6) tuxedo rental. Each is located in a separate department, as shown here. The load summary chart gives the current level of interaction between the departments. Calculate the number of nonadjacent loads for the current layout. Design an alternative layout to minimize the number of nonadjacent loads.

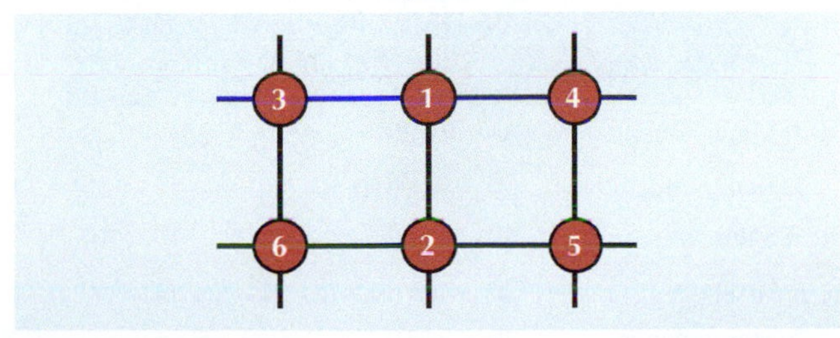

	LOAD SUMMARY CHART					
FROM / TO	1	2	3	4	5	6
1	—		125	40		
2		—	45	75		
3			—	20	235	200
4	60	30	10	—	85	50
5					—	10
6			40	30	150	—

7.3. Given the following load summary chart, design a layout on a 2 × 3 grid that will minimize nonadjacent loads.

	LOAD SUMMARY CHART				
FROM / TO	1	2	3	4	5
1	—		50		25
2		—	20	100	
3	30	10	—		75
4			40	—	
5		60			—

7.4. Pratt's Department Store is opening a new store in The Center's Mall. Customer movement tracked in its existing stores is shown below. Design a layout for Pratt's new store on a 2 × 3 grid that will minimize nonadjacent customer movement.

	NUMBER OF CUSTOMERS					
FROM / TO	WOMEN'S	MEN'S	BOYS'	GIRLS'	INFANTS	HOME
Women's	—	20	50	50	50	70
Men's		—	20	10		20
Boys'		20	—	20		
Girls'	30		50	—	30	
Infants	30				—	
Home	40					—

7.5. Rent-With-Us Management Inc. has purchased a large housing complex and must decide where to locate its offices and service facilities. The company has learned that locating each service in a different apartment building helps control the behavior of tenants, but it would also like to keep unnecessary transit time to a minimum. Data collected on movements between facilities during a six month period from a similar apartment complex are shown below. Construct a layout diagram on a 2 × 3 grid that minimizes nonadjacent movement.

	SITE TO SITE TRAVEL				
FROM / TO	1	2	3	4	5
1 Management	—	20	35	25	20
2 Rent collection	50	—			35
3 Sales	40		—		10
4 Grounds	20			—	40
5 Maintenance	20	10		50	—

7.6. Avalanche, Inc. is a manufacturer of premium snow skis. The work is a combination of precision machining and skilled craftsmanship. Before completion, skis are processed back and forth between six different departments: (1) molding, (2) cutting, (3) fiberglass weaving, (4) gluing, (5) finishing, and (6) waxing. Avalanche is opening a new production facility and wants to lay it out as efficiently as possible. The number of loads of material moved from department to department at existing operations in other plants is shown below. Arrange the department for Avalanche's new plant in a 2 × 3 grid so that nonadjacent loads are minimized.

	LOAD SUMMARY CHART					
FROM / TO	1	2	3	4	5	6
1	—	100	75		100	60
2	10	—		45	60	
3	30		—		85	
4	100	50		—	70	
5	25	70	30	40	—	65
6	65				35	—

7.7. Marillion Hospital is building a satellite clinic in the Cold Harbor area of Richmond. The design committee has collected data on patient movement from similar facilities in hopes of making the new facility more efficient and customer-friendly.

	PATIENT MOVEMENTS					
FROM / TO	1	2	3	4	5	6
1 Intake	—	50	10	25	10	100
2 Exam room		—	30	40	20	20
3 Radiology		40	—	20	60	40
4 Laboratory		10	10	—	10	40
5 Orthopedics		30	20	10	—	30
6 Waiting room	40	60	50	20	50	—

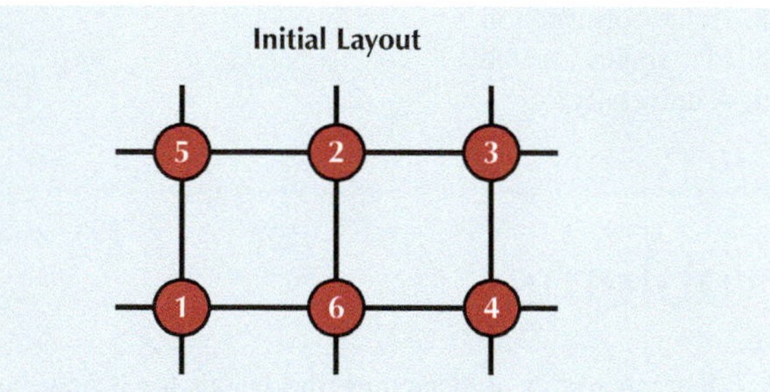

a. Calculate the nonadjacent loads for the initial layout.

b. Which pairwise exchange of departments would most improve the layout?

7.8. Social Services is moving into a new facility. Historical data on client visitation per month among its six departments is shown below. Design a layout for the new facility on a 2 × 3 grid that minimizes the distance clients must travel to receive services.

	CLIENT VISITATION					
FROM / TO	1	2	3	4	5	6
1	—	140				100
2		—			200	
3		100	—			
4			80	—		
5	70				—	60
6		60			100	—

7.9. Tech Express provides technical assistance to customers through six separate departments. While much of the communication is electronic, it is helpful for departments working together on a customer's request to be physically located near to each other. Given the following data on customer "flow" between departments, design a layout on a 2 × 3 grid that will facilitate the maximum collaboration among departments. How much customer flow is nonadjacent?

	CUSTOMER FLOW					
FROM / TO	1	2	3	4	5	6
1	—	50	100	25	60	
2	40	—	80		150	
3	10	70	—	55		
4	10		80	—		
5	40			80	—	30
6		60	50			—

7.10. Flying Flags is opening a new theme park in southern Indiana. The park will have six main attractions: (a) animal kingdom, (b) Broadway shows, (c) carousel and other kiddie rides, (d) daredevil roller coasters, (e) eating places, and (f) flying machines. Data on customer flow patterns from similar parks is shown here, along with the layout for a similar park in Virginia. Calculate the nonadjacent loads for the Virginia park; then improve the design for the new Indiana location.

	CUSTOMER FLOW					
FROM / TO	1	2	3	4	5	6
1	—	20	100	10	10	20
2		—	30		50	
3		20	—			
4	50			—	50	300
5	30	50	60	40	—	50
6	10			200	60	—

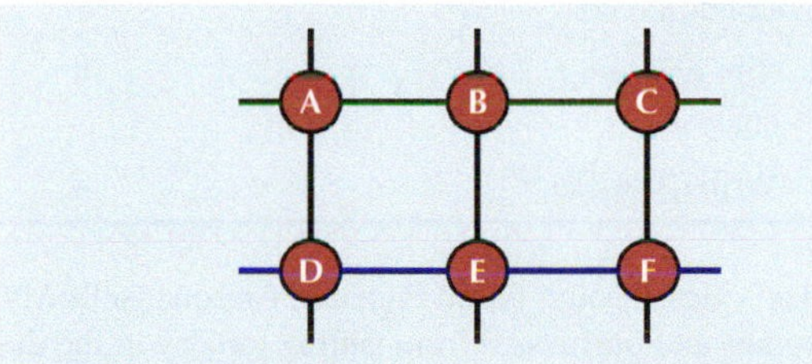

7.11. Design a layout on a 2 × 3 grid that satisfies the preferences listed here.

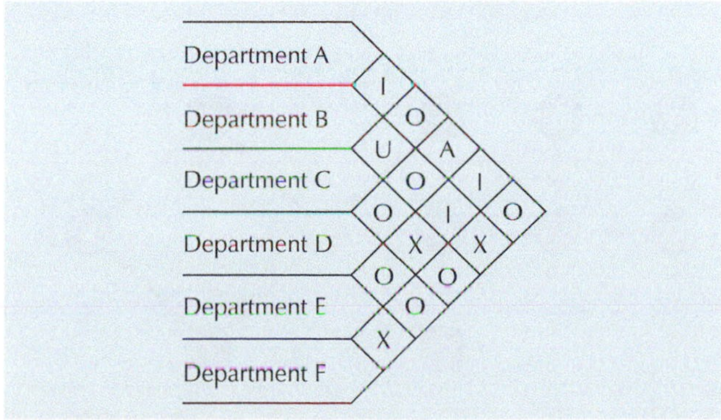

7.12. Design a layout on a 2 × 3 grid that satisfies these preferences.

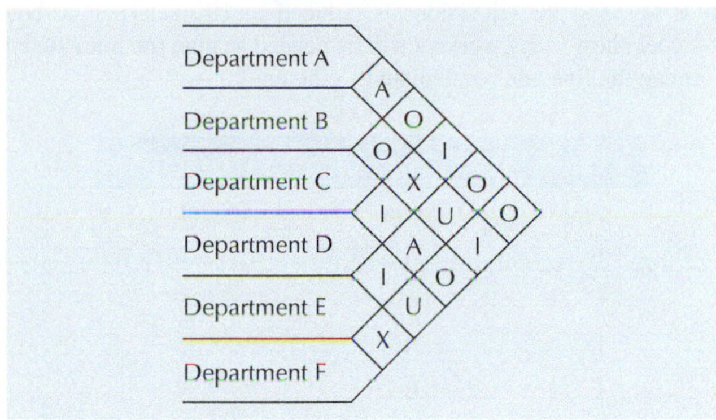

7.13. Amber Ale use a simple five-step process to prepare its products for shipment. Because of recent increases in demand, the company is setting up an assembly line to do the work. How should the line be constructed if Amber needs a new product off the line every 10 minutes? Draw a precedence diagram, group the tasks into workstations, determine the efficiency of the line, and calculate the expected output for an eight-hour day. (*There are multiple solutions to this problem.*)

TASK	PRECEDENCE	TIME (MINS)
A	None	5
B	A	2
C	A	4
D	A	7
E	B, C, D	5

7.14. The Henry Street Mission uses volunteers to assemble care packages for needy families during the holiday season. The mission would like to organize the work as efficiently as possible. A list of tasks, task times, and precedence requirements follows:

TASK	PRECEDENCE	TIME (MINS)
A	—	6
B	A	3
C	B	7
D	B	5
E	C, D	4
F	E	5

a. If the mission wants to complete a care package every 10 minutes, how many volunteers should be called in? Balance the line and calculate the efficiency. How many packages can be assembled in a four-hour period?

b. Suppose that volunteers are plentiful. Balance the line to maximize output. What is the efficiency of the line? How many care packages can be assembled in a four-hour period?

7.15. Best Vision is revamping its assembly lines to improve efficiency. As shown below, there are 10 steps to assembling a television set.

a. If Best needs to produce 120 televisions in a 40-hour work week, how should the line be balanced? Given that one worker is assigned to each workstation, how many workers are required to operate the line? What is the efficiency of the line?

b. If demand for televisions is reduced to 100 sets per 40-hour week, how many workers will be needed to man the line? Rebalance the line and recalculate its efficiency.

TASK	PRECEDENCE	TIME (MIN)
A	None	8
B	A	4
C	A	7
D	A	3
E	B	7
F	C, E	11
G	D	2
H	G	8
I	F, H	5
J	I	7

7.16. Professional Image Briefcases is an exclusive producer of handcrafted, stylish cases. The company assembles each case with care and attention to detail. This laborious process requires the completion of the six primary work elements listed here.

WORK ELEMENT		PRECEDENCE	TIME (MIN)
A	Tan leather	—	30
B	Dye leather	A	15
C	Shape case	B	10
D	Mold hinges and fixtures	—	5
E	Install hinges and fixtures	C, D	10
F	Assemble case	E	10

a. Construct a precedence diagram for the manufacturing of briefcases.

b. Compute the flow time required for assembling one briefcase and the cycle time necessary to assemble 50 cases in a 40-hour week.

c. Balance the line and compute its efficiency.

d. How would you change the line to produce 80 cases per week?

7.17. The TLB Yogurt Company must be able to make 600 party cakes in a 40-hour week. Use the following information to draw and label a precedence diagram, compute cycle time, compute the theoretical minimum number of workstations, balance the assembly line, and calculate its efficiency.

WORK ELEMENT	PRECEDENCE	PERFORMANCE TIME (MIN)
A	—	1
B	A	2
C	B	2
D	A, E	4
E	—	3
F	C, D	4

7.18. The Speedy Pizza Palace is revamping its order-processing and pizza-making procedures. In order to deliver fresh pizza fast, six elements must be completed.

WORK ELEMENT		PRECEDENCE	TIME (MIN)
A	Receive order	—	2
B	Shape dough	A	1
C	Prepare toppings	A	2
D	Assemble pizza	B, C	3
E	Bake pizza	D	3
F	Deliver pizza	E	3

a. Construct a precedence diagram and compute the lead time for the process.

b. If the demand for pizzas is 120 per night (5:00 P.M. to 1:00 A.M.), what is the cycle time?

c. Balance the line and calculate its efficiency.

d. How would the line change to produce 160 pizzas per night?

7.19. Professor Garcia has assigned 15 cases in his OM Seminar class to be completed in a 15-week semester. The students, of course, are moaning and groaning that the caseload cannot possibly be completed in the time allotted. Professor Garcia sympathetically suggests that the students work in groups and learn to organize their work efficiently. Knowing when a situation is hopeless, the students make a list of the tasks that have to be completed in preparing a case. These tasks are listed here, along with precedence requirements and estimated time in days. Assuming students will work five days a week on this assignment, how many students should be assigned to each group, and what is the most efficient allocation of tasks? Can 15 cases be completed in a semester? Explain your answer.

ELEMENT	DESCRIPTION	PRECEDENCE	TIME (DAYS)
a	Read case	—	1
b	Gather data	a	4
c	Search literature	a	3
d	Load in data	b	1
e	Run computer analysis	d	4
f	Write/type case	c, e	4

7.20. McCauley's Heating and Air in Phoenix, Arizona, sells Mystifiers to keep homes and businesses from getting too dry in the desert air. The precedence diagram and task times (in minutes) for assembling a Mystifier are shown here. Set up an assembly line to produce 125 mystifiers in a 40-hour week. Balance the line and calculate its efficiency.

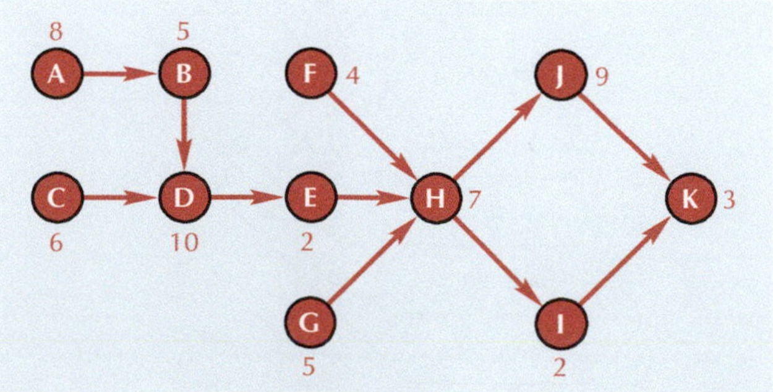

7.21. The precedence diagram and task times (in minutes) for assembling modular furniture are shown below. Set up an assembly line to assemble 1000 sets of modular furniture in a 40-hour week. Balance the line and calculate its efficiency.

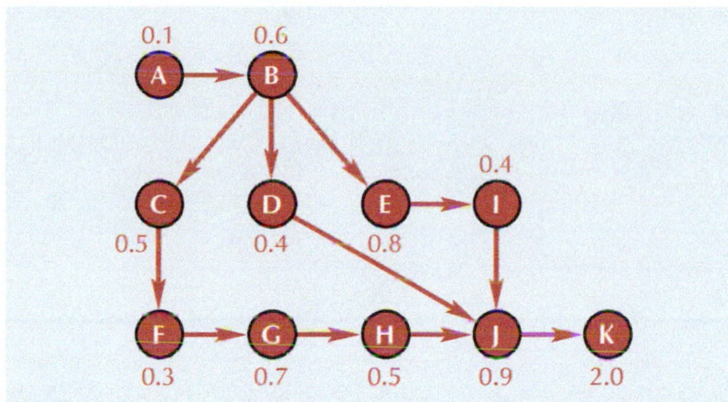

7.22. The Costplus Corporation has set a processing quota of 80 insurance claims per 8-hour day. The claims process consists of five elements, which are detailed in the following table. Costplus has decided to use an assembly-line arrangement to process the forms and would like to make sure they have set up the line in the most efficient fashion. Construct a precedence diagram for the claims process and calculate the cycle time required to meet the processing quota. Balance the assembly line and show your arrangement of workstations. Calculate the line's efficiency. How many claims can actually be processed on your line?

ELEMENT	PRECEDENCE	TIME (MIN)
A	—	4
B	A	5
C	B	2
D	A	1
E	C, D	3

7.23. Hanover Hospital beds can transform from a bed to a chair to a scale with the push of a button. As the design becomes more complicated, so does the assembly process. Given in the following table are tasks A–K necessary for final assembly of a hospital bed, the length of time needed to perform each task, and the operations that must be completed prior to subsequent operations. Construct a precedence diagram and balance the assembly line for a desired cycle time of 14 minutes. Draw a schematic diagram of the balanced line. How many beds can actually be assembled in an eight-hour period?

ELEMENT	PRECEDENCE	TIME (MIN)
A	None	4
B	None	5
C	None	8
D	A	4
E	A, B	3
F	B	3
G	D, E	5
H	F	7
I	G, H	1
J	I	7
K	C, J	4

7.24. Fine's Furniture is known for its fine cedar chests. Given in the following table are the tasks necessary for the assembly of cedar chests, the length of time needed to perform each task, and the operations that must be completed prior to subsequent operations.

ELEMENT	PRECEDENCE	TIME (MIN)
A	None	2
B	A	4
C	B	5
D	None	5
E	D	3
F	None	1
G	F	2
H	C, E, G	4

a. Calculate the cycle time necessary to complete 300 cedar chests in a 35-hour week.

b. What is the minimum number of workstations that can be used on the assembly line and still reach the production quota? Balance the line and calculate the line's efficiency.

c. Rebalance the line with a cycle time of 9 minutes. How do the number of workstations, output, and line efficiency change?

7.25. Quick Start Technologies (QST) helps companies design facility layouts. One of its clients is building five new assembly plants across the continental United States. QST will design the assembly-line layout and ship the layout instructions, along with the appropriate machinery to each new locale. Use the precedence and time requirements given below to design an assembly line that will produce a new product every 12 minutes. Construct a precedence diagram, group the tasks into workstations, determine the efficiency of the line, and calculate the expected output for an eight-hour day.

TASK	PRECEDENCE	TIME (MINS)
A	None	6
B	A	2
C	B	2
D	A	1
E	A	7
F	A	5
G	C	6
H	D, E, F	5
I	H	3
J	G	5
K	I, J	4

7-26. The Wet Wellies Corporation produces waterproof boots and assembles them with optional linings and other features on an assembly line. Due to global warming, the demand for wellies has increased and the company would like to be able to produce 1200 boots in an 8-hour day. The table below contains work elements involved in the production process, as well as time and precedence requirements.

DESCRIPTION	WORK ELEMENT	PRECEDENCE REQUIREMENT	TIME (MINS)
Cut vinyl R side	A	—	0.5
Cut sheepskin R side	B	—	0.6
Sew R sides together	C	A, B	1.0
Cut vinyl L side	D	—	0.5
Cut sheepskin L side	E	—	0.4
Sew L sides together	F	D, E	1.0
Prep back strip	G	—	0.4
Sew sides w/strip	H	C, F, G	1.5
Prep outer sole /heel	I	—	0.4
Assemble boot	J	H, I	0.6
Place insole inside	K	J	0.3

a. Calculate the desired cycle time for boot production.
b. Calculate the theoretical minimum number of workstations.
c. Draw a precedence diagram and balance the line.
d. Calculate the efficiency of the line.
e. Customer feedback and returns indicate there are problems with the outer sole of the boot. The QIT (quality improvement team) recommends either taking more time prepping the outer sole or taking more time assembling the outer sole to the boot. They estimate increasing the time of either work element I or J by 0.1 minutes would help fix the issue. Does it matter which work element time is increased? Why or why not?

7.27. Print-for-All is a family-owned print shop that has grown from a three-press two-color operation to a full-service facility capable of performing a range of jobs from simple copying to four-color printing, scanning, binding, and more. The company is moving into a new facility and would like some help arranging its 16 processes into an efficient, yet flexible, layout. A list of the most popular jobs and the processes associated with them is shown in the Print-for-All Process Manual below. Arrange the processes into cells to ensure an efficient *and* flexible operation.

	PRINT-FOR-ALL PROCESSES															
JOBS	1	2	3	4	5	6	7	8	9	10	11	12	13	14	15	16
A	X	X										X				
B						X		X								
C	X						X							X		
D	X	X					X							X		
E				X		X										
F						X		X			X					
G	X	X										X				
H					X					X					X	
I	X	X	X											X		
J						X					X					
K										X					X	X
L				X		X					X			X		
M		X							X			X				
N										X					X	X
O					X					X					X	X
P				X		X					X					
Q								X								

(continued)

7.28. Jetaway, a small manufacturer of replacement parts for the aircraft industry, had always maintained a simple layout—all like machines were located together. That way the firm could be as flexible as possible in producing small amounts of the variety of parts its customers required. No one questioned the production arrangement until Chris Munnelly started to work for the company. Chris was actually hired to upgrade Jetaway's computer system. In the process of creating a database of part routings, Chris began to see similarities in the parts produced. A part routing matrix for nine of the most popular parts is shown below, along with a schematic of the factory layout.

Chris, who was already tired of being a programmer, decided to reorder the matrix and see what he could find. If he could identify distinct part families, he could reorganize the placement of machines into the cells he had been reading about in his business magazines. Maybe then someone would notice his management potential.

Help Chris gain status in Jetaway by creating a cellular layout for the company. Show your results in a schematic diagram. Be sure to include the reordered routing matrix.

	Machines											
Parts	1	2	3	4	5	6	7	8	9	10	11	12
A	×			×	×							
B		×	×			×						
C								×			×	
D	×			×	×		×					
E		×	×			×			×			×
F								×		×	×	
G	×				×		×					
H		×	×			×			×			
I								×		×		

Jetaway Initial Layout

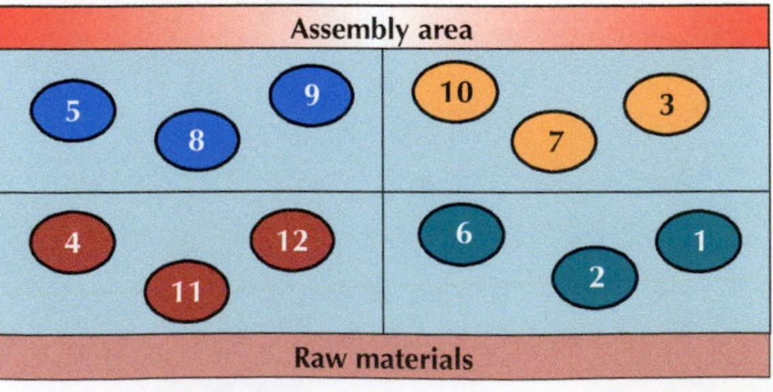

Case Problems

Case Problem 7.1 Workout Plus

Workout Plus is a health club that offers a full range of services to its clients. Recently, two other fitness clubs have opened up in town, threatening Workout's solvency. While Workout is tops among serious fitness buffs, it has not attracted a wide spectrum of members. Shannon Hiller, owner and manager, has decided it's time for a face lift. She started the process by sponsoring a week-long "ideathon" among club members. Nonmembers who frequented an adjacent grocery store were also canvassed for suggestions. Their comments are provided below, along with the current facility layout.

Current layout:

Free Weights	Circuit Training
Aerobics Room	Cardio Machines

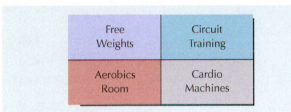

Member comments:

- The cardio machines fill up too fast on rainy days. Then everything else gets backed up.
- I don't feel like strutting through the gym from one end to the other just to finish my workout.
- How about a quick 30-minute workout routine for busy folks?
- I like working out with my friends, but aerobics is not for me. What other group activities are good for cardio?
- Separate the people who want to gab from the people who want to pump.
- It's so confusing with all those machines and weights. You need a novice section that's not so intimidating.
- It's hard to work yourself in when you come from across the gym. I'd like to see the machines I'll be using to gauge my time.
- Circuit training is for wimps. The next thing you know you'll be stopping and starting the music to tell us when to change machines.
- We all seem to arrive at the popular machines at once. Can you space us out?
- I'd like for my kids to get some exercise too while I'm working out. But I don't want them wandering all over the place trying to find me.
- This place is too crowded and disorganized. It's not fun anymore.
- You have classes only at busy times. During the day the gym is empty, but you don't provide many services. I think you're missing a great opportunity to connect with the not-so-fit at off-peak times.

1. How can Workout update its facility to attract new customers? What additional equipment or services would you suggest? How could something as simple as revising the layout help?
2. It is your job to design a new layout for Workout Plus. Visit a nearby gym to get ideas. Watch the customer flow, unused space, and bottlenecks. What aspects of a process layout do you see? a product layout? cells? Draw a simple diagram of your proposed layout. (You'll want to be more detailed than the original layout.) How does your layout respond to the comments collected by Shannon?

Case Problem 7.2 Photo Op—Please Line Up

Tech is modernizing its college ID system. Beginning this term, all faculty, staff, and students will be required to carry a "smart" identification card, called a student passport. What makes it smart is a magnetic strip with information on club memberships, library usage, class schedules (for taking exams), restrictions (such as no alcohol), medical insurance, emergency contacts, and medical conditions. If desired, it can also be set up as a debit card to pay fines or purchase items from the bookstore, vending machines, cash machines, copy machines, and several local retailers.

University administrators are excited about the revenue potential and increased control of the passport, but they are not looking forward to the process of issuing approximately 60,000 new cards. If applicants could be processed at the rate of 60 an hour, the entire university could be issued passports in a month's time (with a little overtime).

The steps in the process and approximate times follow. Steps 1 and 2 must be completed before step 3 can begin. Steps 3 and 4 must precede step 5, and step 5 must be completed before step 6.

Steps in Process	Time
1. Review application for correctness	10 seconds
2. Verify information and check for outstanding debt	60 seconds
3. Process and record payment	30 seconds
4. Take photo	20 seconds
5. Attach photo and laminate	10 seconds
6. Magnetize and issue passport	10 seconds

a. Is it possible to process one applicant every minute? Explain.

b. How would you assign tasks to workers in order to process 60 applicants an hour?

c. How many workers are required? How efficient is your line?

Case Problem 7.3 The Grab'n Go Café

The GNG Café, a new concept in on-campus dining, features homemade bakery items, upscale sandwiches and wraps, fresh salads, and signature soups. The modern café-style design allows customers the freedom to select their menu choices from individual stations throughout the café. While the restaurant has caught the imagination of the university community with its nifty interiors and quality food (which is a welcome change from "the bun"), space and layout restrictions have ensured that the customer when buying anything at GNG can neither "grab" nor "go."

It is undeniable that the quality of food offered at GNG is good, but GNG management should not forget that their target customers are students who possess a modest income. It is not unusual for students to reach the checkout and find themselves without sufficient funds to complete their transaction.

The first thing customers do when they enter the restaurant is stand and look for the various items they want to buy. While the food and drinks are displayed quite neatly and colorfully, customers still have a hard time figuring out where to go first and what price they should expect to pay for a particular product. Neither the product options nor their prices are prominently displayed. This is especially true of made-to-order sandwiches. Since customers don't have information about the sandwiches beforehand and the options are many, they can take quite some time deciding what kind of sandwich they

TABLE 7.3 Customer Flow Data

CUSTOMER	BAKERY ITEMS	FOUNTAIN DRINKS	SOUPS	BOTTLED DRINKS	FRESH FRUITS	SALADS	SANDWICHES (AND WRAPS)	COFFEE OR COOKIES	TOTAL TIME (MIN)
1	X		X					X	3.00
2	X		X				X		4.50
3	X	X	X						3.30
4		X	X				X		4.50
5	X		X	X					2.50
6	X	X							3.70
7	X	X							4.50
8	X						X		8.90
9		X	X				X		8.00
10	X	X				X			5.20
11		X					X	X	9.00
12		X					X		10.00
13			X	X					8.00
14	X				X				4.50
15								X	1.00
16			X	X			X		10.00
17	X	X							2.00
18						X		X	5.00
19	X			X					3.00
20	X	X	X		X				5.00
21						X			1.50
22	X	X							3.00
23	X			X					2.00
24		X							2.20
25			X				X		8.00

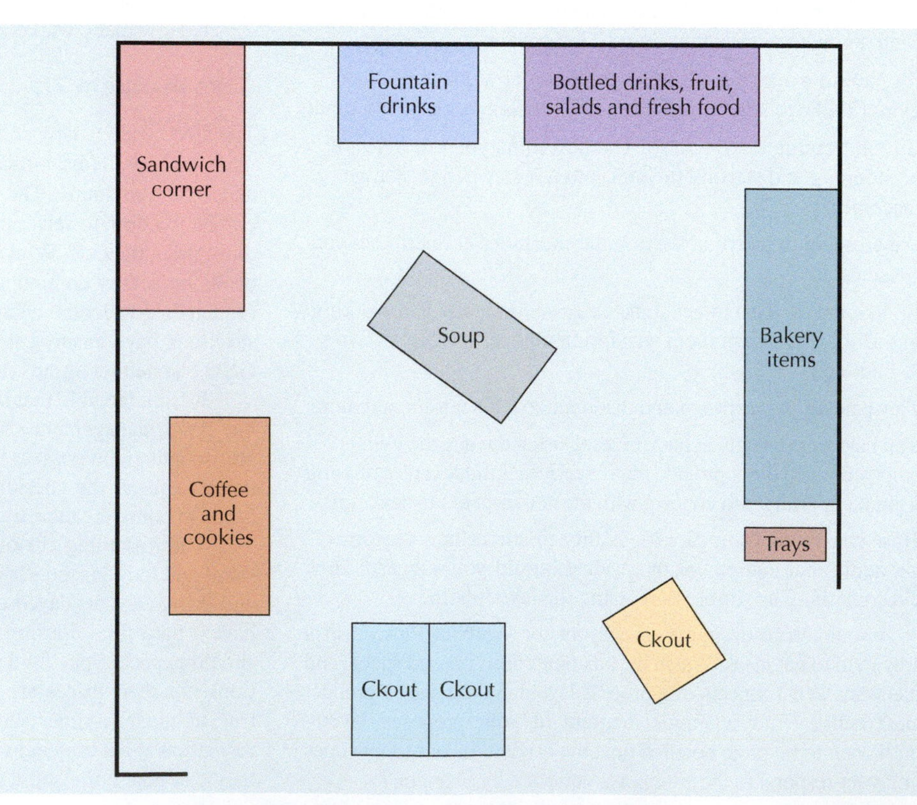

FIGURE 7.17 GNG Facility Layout

want to buy. This causes a traffic problem, especially at mealtimes, when a lot of people come in at the same time to order, and then must wait for their food in a small space. The overcrowding and open layout also present problems with pilfering of food, as students conveniently "forget" to pay upon exiting the facility.

GNG management has agreed to take on a student project to chart the flow of customers through the café and to make recommendations on facility changes. A schematic diagram of the existing layout follows, along with data on the flow of 25 customers. What changes in layout and operating procedures would you recommend for GNG?

References

Benjaafar, Saif, Sunderesh Heragu, and Shahrukh Irani. "Next Generation Factory Layouts: Research Challenges and Recent Progress." *Interfaces* (November/December 2002), pp. 58–78.

Black, J. T. *The Design of the Factory with a Future*. New York: McGraw-Hill, 1991.

Flanders, R. E. "Design, Manufacture and Production Control of a Standard Machine." *Transactions of ASME* 46 (1925).

Goetsch, D. *Advanced Manufacturing Technology*. Albany, NY: Delmar, 1990.

Hyer, Nancy, and Urban Wemmerlov. *Reorganizing the Factory: Competing Through Cellular Manufacturing*. Portland, OR: Productivity Press, 2002.

Jablonowski, J. "Reexamining FMSs." *American Machinist*, Special Report 774 (March 1985).

Luggen, W. *Flexible Manufacturing Cells and Systems*. Upper Saddle River, NJ: Prentice Hall, 1991.

Monden, Y. *Toyota Production System*, 3rd ed. Atlanta: IIE Press, 1993.

Muther, R. *Systematic Layout Planning*. Boston: Industrial Education Institute, 1961.

Russell, R. S., P. Y. Huang, and Y. Y. Leu. "A Study of Labor Allocation in Cellular Manufacturing." *Decision Sciences* 22 (3; 1991), pp. 594–611.

Sumichrast, R. T., R. S. Russell, and B. W. Taylor. "A Comparative Analysis of Sequencing Procedures for Mixed-Model Assembly Lines in a Just-In-Time Production System." *International Journal of Production Research* 30 (1; 1992), pp. 199–214.

Towards a New Era in Manufacturing Studies Board. Washington, DC: National Academy Press, 1986.

SUPPLEMENT TO CHAPTER 7

Operational Decision-Making Tools: Facility Location Models

- Types of Facilities
- Site Selection: Where to Locate
- Global Supply Chain Factors
- Location Analysis Techniques

The physical location of business facilities can have a significant impact on the success of a company. In this supplement we will briefly discuss some of the factors that are important in locating facilities. We will focus on several quantitative methods for facility location, including location factor ratings, the center-of-gravity technique, and the load-distance technique.

Types of Facilities

The type of facility is a major determinant of its location. The factors important in determining the location of a manufacturing plant are usually different from those important in locating a service facility or a warehouse. In this section we discuss the major categories of facilities and the different factors that are important in the location desired.

Heavy manufacturing facilities are plants that are large, require a lot of space, and are expensive to construct, such as automobile plants, steel mills, and oil refineries.

Factors in the location decision for plants include construction costs, land costs, modes of transportation for shipping heavy manufactured items and receiving bulk shipments of raw materials, proximity to raw materials, utilities, means of waste disposal, and labor availability. Sites for manufacturing plants are normally selected where construction and land costs can be kept at a minimum and raw material sources are nearby in order to reduce transportation costs. Access to railroads is frequently a factor in locating a plant. Environmental issues have increasingly become a factor in plant location decisions.

Light-industry facilities are perceived as cleaner plants that produce electronic equipment and components, computer products, or assembled products like TVs; breweries; or pharmaceutical firms.

Distribution centers for The Gap in Gallatin, Tennessee, Target in Augusta City, Virginia, and Home Depot in Savannah, Georgia, each encompass more than 1.4 million square feet of space—about 30 times bigger than the area of a football field! The UPS Worldwide Logistics warehouse in Louisville, Kentucky, includes 1.3 million square feet of floor space. Because of their role as intermediate points in the supply chain, transportation costs are often an important factor in the location decision for warehouses. The proximity to markets is also a consideration, depending on the delivery requirements, including frequency of delivery required by the customer.

Retail and service facilities are usually the smallest and least costly. Examples include retail facilities such as groceries and department stores, among many others, and such service facilities as restaurants, banks, hotels, cleaners, clinics, and law offices. However, there are always exceptions, and some service facilities, such as a hospital, a company headquarters, a resort hotel, or a university academic building, can be large and expensive. One of the most important factors for locating a service or retail facility is proximity to customers. It is often critical that a service facility be near the customers it serves, and a retail facility must be near the customers who buy from it. Construction costs tend to be less important, although land or leasing costs can be high. For retail operations, for which the saying "location is everything" is meaningful, site costs can be very high. Factors like zoning, utilities, transportation, environmental constraints, and labor tend to be less important for service operations, and closeness to suppliers is not usually as important as it is to manufacturing firms, which must be close to materials and parts suppliers.

Site Selection: Where to Locate

When we see in the news that a company has selected a site for a new plant, or a new store is opening, the announcement can appear trivial. Usually it is reported that a particular site was selected from among two or three alternatives, and a few reasons are provided, such as good community, heavy customer traffic, or available land. However, such media reports do not reveal the long, detailed process for selecting a site for a business facility. It is usually the culmination of a selection process that can take several years and the evaluation of dozens or hundreds of potential sites.

Decisions regarding where to locate a business facility or plant are not made frequently, but they tend to be crucial in terms of a firm's profitability and long-term survival. A mistake in location is not easily overcome. Business success often is being "in the right place at the right time." For a service operation such as a restaurant, hotel, or retail store, being in the right place usually means in a location that is convenient and easily accessible to customers.

Location decisions for services tend to be an important part of the overall market strategy for the delivery of their products or services to customers. However, a business cannot simply survey the demographic characteristics of a geographic area and build a facility at the location with the greatest potential for customer traffic; other factors, particularly financial considerations, must be part of the location decision. Obviously, a site on Fifth Avenue in New York City would be attractive for a McDonald's restaurant, but can enough hamburgers and french fries be sold to pay the rent? In this case, the answer is yes.

Location decisions are usually made more frequently for service operations than manufacturing facilities. Facilities for service-related businesses tend to be smaller and less costly, although a hospital or hotel can require a huge investment and be very large. Services depend on a certain degree of market saturation; the location is actually part of their product. Where to locate a manufacturing facility is also important, but for different reasons, not the least of which is the very high expense of building a plant or factory. Although the primary location criterion for a service-related business is usually access to customers, a different set of criteria is important for a manufacturing facility. These include the nature of the labor force and labor costs, proximity to suppliers and markets, distribution and transportation costs, energy availability and cost, the community infrastructure of roads, sewers, and utilities, quality of life in a community, and government regulations and taxes.

When the site selection process is initiated, the pool of potential locations for a manufacturing or service facility is, literally, global. In today's international marketplace, countries around the world become potential sites. The site selection process is one of gradually and methodically narrowing down the pool of alternatives until the final location is determined. In the following discussion, we identify some of the factors that companies consider when determining the country, region, community, and site at which to locate a facility.

Global Supply Chain Factors

U.S. companies frequently locate in foreign countries to be closer to newly emerging markets and to take advantage of lower labor costs. Trade agreements between countries have reduced trade barriers around the world and created new markets like the European Community (EC), Eastern Europe, and Asia.

Foreign firms have also begun to locate in the United States to be closer to their customers. For both U.S. and foreign companies, the motivation is the same—to reduce supply chain costs and better serve their customers. Relatively slow overseas transportation requires multinational companies to maintain large, costly inventories to serve their foreign customers in a timely manner. This drives up supply chain costs and makes it economical for companies to relocate closer to their markets.

While foreign markets offer great opportunities, the problems with locating in a foreign country can be substantial, making site location a very important part of supply chain design. For example, although China offers an extremely attractive market because of its huge population, growing economy, and cheap labor force, it has an inefficient transportation and distribution system, and numerous government regulations. Markets in Russia and the former Soviet states are attractive; however they can also be risky because of government regulations, theft, and logistics. Lack of familiarity with standard business practices and corruption can threaten success for foreign companies.

Some of the factors that multinational firms must consider when locating in a foreign country include the following:

- Government stability
- Government regulations
- Political and economic systems
- Economic stability and growth
- Exchange rates
- Culture
- Climate
- Export and import regulations, duties, and tariffs
- Raw material availability
- Number and proximity of suppliers
- Transportation and distribution systems
- Labor force cost and education
- Available technology
- Commercial travel
- Technical expertise
- Cross-border trade regulations
- Group trade agreements

Regional and Community Location Factors in the United States

Labor is one of the most important factors in a location decision, including the cost of labor, availability, work ethic, the presence of organized labor and labor conflict, and skill and educational level. Traditionally, labor costs have been lower and organized labor has been less visible across the South and Southwest. While labor conflict is anathema to many companies, in some cases labor unions have assisted in attracting new plants or in keeping existing plants from relocating by making attractive concessions.

The proximity of suppliers and markets are important location factors. Manufacturing companies need to be close to materials, and service companies like fast-food restaurants, retail stores, groceries, and service stations need to be close to customers and distribution centers. Transportation costs can be significant if frequent deliveries over long distances are required. The closeness of suppliers can determine the amount of inventory a company must keep on hand and how quickly it can serve its own customers. Uncertainty in delivery schedules from suppliers can require excessive inventories.

It is important for service-related businesses to be located near their customers. Many businesses simply look for a high volume of customer traffic as the main determinant of location, regardless of the competition. An interstate highway exit onto a major thoroughfare always has a number of competing service stations and fast-food restaurants. Shopping malls are an example of a location in which a critical mass of customer traffic is sought to support a variety of similar and dissimilar businesses.

Another important factor, **infrastructure**, is the collection of physical support systems of a location, including the roads, water and sewer, and utilities. If a community does not have a good infrastructure, it must make improvements if it hopes to attract new business facilities. From a company's perspective, an inadequate infrastructure will add to its supply chain costs and inhibit its customer service.

Infrastructure The roads, water and sewer, and utilities at a location.

Factors that are considered when selecting the part of the country and community for a facility are summarized as follows:

- Labor (availability, education, cost, and unions)
- Proximity of customers
- Number of customers
- Construction/leasing costs
- Land cost
- Modes and quality of transportation
- Transportation costs
- Community government
- Local business regulations
- Government services (e.g., Chamber of Commerce)
- Financial services
- Community inducements
- Business climate
- Community services
- Incentive packages
- Government regulations
- Environmental regulations
- Raw material availability
- Commercial travel
- Climate
- Infrastructure (e.g., roads, water, sewers)
- Quality of life
- Taxes
- Availability of sites
- Proximity of suppliers
- Education system

Location Incentives

Besides physical and societal characteristics, local incentives have increasingly become a major important factor in attracting companies to specific locations. Incentive packages typically include job tax credits, relaxed government regulations, job training, road and sewage infrastructure improvements, and sometimes just plain cash. These incentives plus the advantages of a superior location can significantly reduce a company's supply chain costs while helping it achieve its strategic goal for customer service.

States and communities cannot afford to overlook incentives if they hope to attract new companies and jobs. However, they must make sure that the amount of their investment in incentive packages and the costs they incur for infrastructure improvements are balanced against the number of new jobs developed and the expansion of the economy the new plant will provide. Incentives are a good public investment unless they bankrupt the locality. While some small communities are successful in attracting new businesses, they are left with little remaining tax base to pay for the infrastructure improvements needed to support the increased population drawn by job demand. Thus, states and communities, much like businesses, need a strategy for economic development that weighs the costs versus the benefits of attracting companies.

Geographic Information Systems

One tool that is used in the facility location and site selection process is a geographic information system or GIS. A GIS is a computerized system for storing, managing, creating, analyzing, integrating, and digitally displaying geographic (i.e., spatial) data. A GIS is both a database system and a set of operations for working with and analyzing this data. As a tool specifically used for site selection, it allows the user to interactively search and analyze the type of data and information (i.e., location factors) we discussed in the previous sections that might be related to the site selection process, such as population, labor, income, infrastructure, customer base, climate, taxes, and transportation. A GIS used for site selection will incorporate quantitative models (like the ones presented later in this chapter and text) and statistical analysis to help analyze the data.

FIGURE S7.1 A GIS Diagram

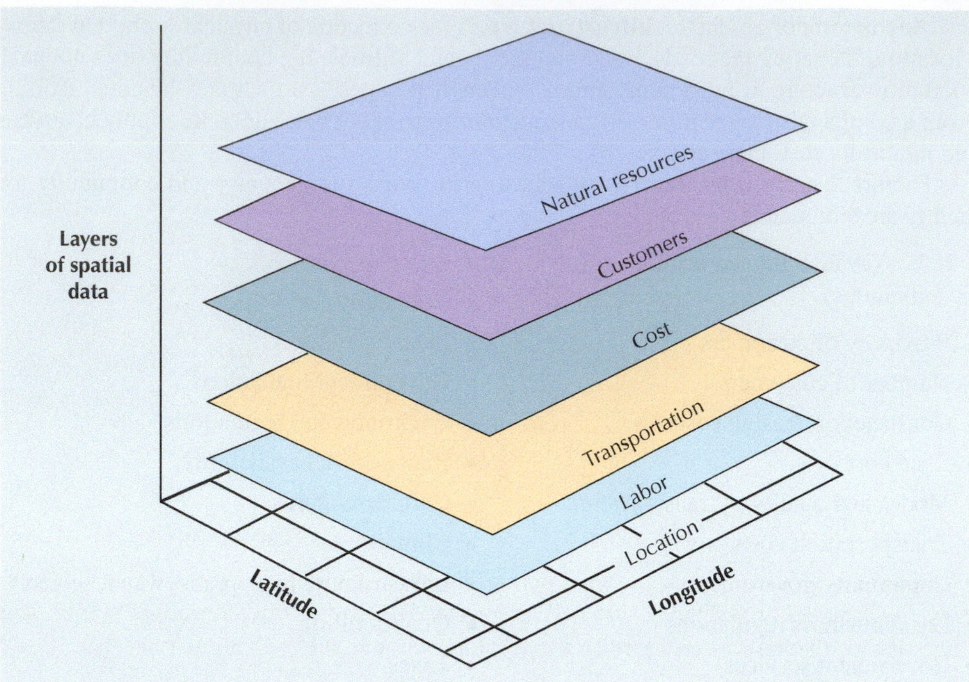

Figure S7.1 provides a simple schematic diagram of how a GIS for site selection might be constructed. Each layer (or spatial map) in this diagram contains information about one characteristic (or attribute) of the location being analyzed. Each layer that might relate to the site selection process is precisely overlaid on the other layers so that their corresponding geographic (spatial, locations) are exactly matched to each other. The bottom layer is a geographic grid that serves as a frame of reference (e.g., latitude and longitude), to which all the other layers are precisely matched.

Once these layers of data have been entered into the GIS, information about the layers can be compared and analyzed in combination. For example, transportation routes can be considered relative to the location of plants, distribution centers, and shippers, as well as labor markets and natural resources, such as water. Such comparative analyses are frequently in the form of digital computer displays as well as three-dimensional graphs and displays. The GIS may provide just statistical analyses for use in the decision-making process, or it may incorporate one or more quantitative models to provide a recommended decision about a site.

The advantage of a GIS is that it enables the user to integrate large quantities of information about potential facility sites and then analyze these data with a number of different, powerful analytical tools. The ability to consider hundreds of separate layers of spatial information and then combine it with other layers of information is the main reason GIS has become such a popular tool for location analysis and site selection.

GIS has come to be used extensively for utilities and infrastructure planning and management, including such things as energy use, cable and pipe networks, gas lines, electrical usage and networks, and transportation, as well as real estate analysis, demographic and marketing analysis, and various government applications such as emergency services and analyzing tax bases. GIS is also used in business applications. For example, GIS has been used to select distribution centers or hubs based on spatial data for shipping times, customer locations, and transportation routes. Bank of America upon entering the New York City market used a GIS to show the distribution of its own branch network relative to deposit potential in the New York market area; from this they determined where their market coverage was strong or weak. Levi Strauss used a GIS to create a geographic network of its existing retailers, potential retailers, and the customer base each served, so it could make sure that new stores that joined its retail network would not adversely affect sales in existing stores. Edens, Inc., one of the nation's leading retail real estate companies, has a GIS-based website that enables retailers to locate space in their inventory (at various shopping malls, etc.) that specifically matches their site selection criteria.

Today there are hundreds of commercial software systems that offer GIS capabilities for different applications, including site selection, and numerous consulting and software firms that specialize in the development of GIS for specific applications. The list of websites for this supplement includes links to several GIS software systems and some of the major companies that specialize in GIS development and applications.

Location Analysis Techniques

We will discuss three techniques to help make a location decision—the location rating factor, the center-of-gravity technique, and the load-distance technique. The location factor rating mathematically evaluates location factors, such as those identified in the previous section. The center-of-gravity and load-distance techniques are quantitative models that centrally locate a proposed facility among existing facilities.

Location Factor Rating

The decision where to locate is based on many different types of information and inputs. There is no single model or technique that will select the "best" site from a group. However, techniques are available that help to organize site information and that can be used as a starting point for comparing different locations.

In the **location factor rating** system, factors that are important in the location decision are identified. Each factor is weighted from 0 to 1.00 to prioritize the factor and reflect its importance. A subjective score is assigned (usually between 0 and 100) to each factor based on its attractiveness compared with other locations, and the weighted scores are summed. Decisions typically will not be made based solely on these ratings, but they provide a good way to organize and rank factors.

Location factor rating A method for identifying and weighting important location factors.

EXAMPLE S7.1 | Location Factor Rating

The Dynaco Manufacturing Company is going to build a new plant to manufacture ring bearings (used in automobiles and trucks). The site selection team is evaluating three sites, and they have scored the important factors for each as follows. They want to use these ratings to compare the locations.

		SCORES (0 TO 100)		
LOCATION FACTOR	WEIGHT	*SITE 1*	*SITE 2*	*SITE 3*
Labor pool and climate	.30	80	65	90
Proximity to suppliers	.20	100	91	75
Wage rates	.15	60	95	72
Community environment	.15	75	80	80
Proximity to customers	.10	65	90	95
Shipping modes	.05	85	92	65
Air service	.05	50	65	90

Solution: The weighted scores for each site are computed by multiplying the factor weights by the score for that factor. For example, the weighted score for "labor pool and climate" for site 1 is

$$(0.30)(80) = 24 \text{ points}$$

The weighted scores for each factor for each site and the total scores are summarized as follows:

	WEIGHTED SCORES		
LOCATION FACTOR	*SITE 1*	*SITE 2*	*SITE 3*
Labor pool and climate	24.00	19.50	27.00
Proximity to suppliers	20.00	18.20	15.00
Wage rates	9.00	14.25	10.80
Community environment	11.25	12.00	12.00
Proximity to customers	6.50	9.00	9.50
Shipping modes	4.25	4.60	3.25
Air service	2.50	3.24	4.50
Total score	77.50	80.80	82.05

Site 3 has the highest factor rating compared with the other locations; however, this evaluation would have to be used with other information, particularly a cost analysis, before making a decision.

Location Factor Rating with Excel and OM Tools

Exhibit S7.1 shows the Excel spreadsheet for Example S7.1. Notice that the location score for Site 1 is shown in cell E12 and the formula for the computation of the site 1 score (embedded in E12) is shown on the formula bar at the top of the spreadsheet.

Exhibit S7.2 shows the OM Tools spreadsheet for Example S7.1

Center-of-Gravity Technique

Center-of-gravity technique The center of movement in a geographic area based on transport weight and distance.

In general, transportation costs are a function of distance, weight, and time. The **center-of-gravity** or *weight center* technique is a quantitative method for locating a facility such as a

EXHIBIT S7.1

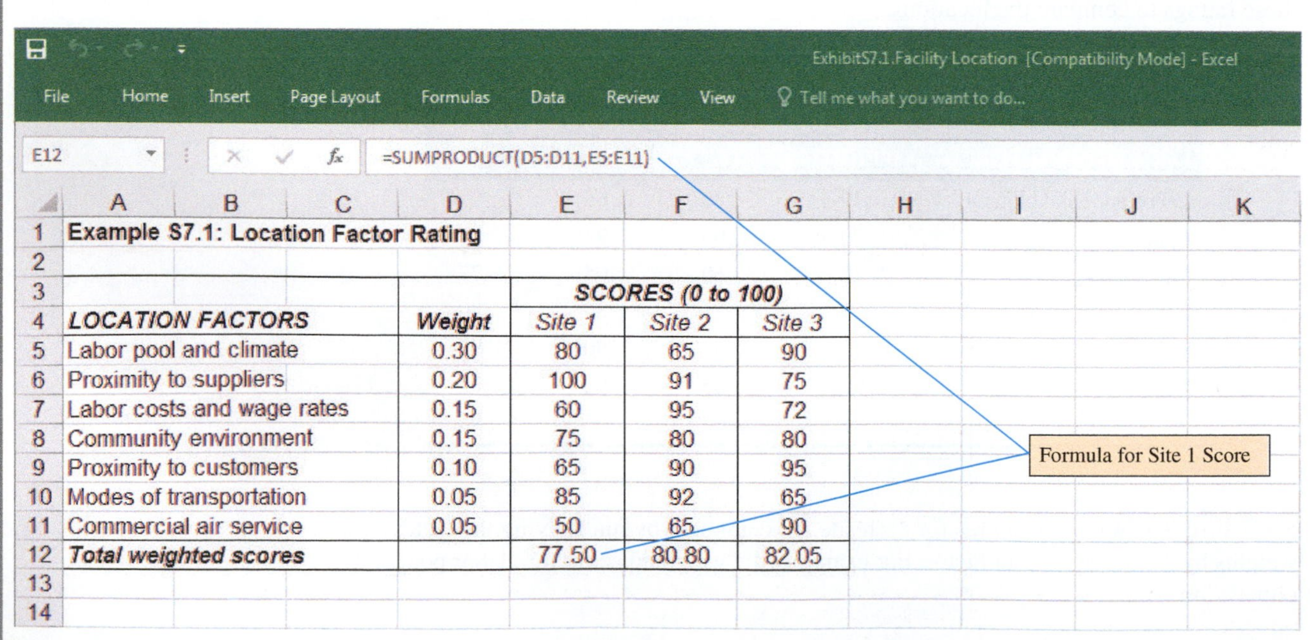

	A	B	C	D	E	F	G
1	Example S7.1: Location Factor Rating						
2							
3					SCORES (0 to 100)		
4	LOCATION FACTORS			Weight	Site 1	Site 2	Site 3
5	Labor pool and climate			0.30	80	65	90
6	Proximity to suppliers			0.20	100	91	75
7	Labor costs and wage rates			0.15	60	95	72
8	Community environment			0.15	75	80	80
9	Proximity to customers			0.10	65	90	95
10	Modes of transportation			0.05	85	92	65
11	Commercial air service			0.05	50	65	90
12	Total weighted scores				77.50	80.80	82.05
13							
14							

EXHIBIT S7.2

ExhibitS7.2.LocationFactorRating [Compatibility Mode] - Excel

File Home Insert Page Layout Formulas Data Review View Tell me what you want to do...

C17 =SUMPRODUCT($B$7:$B$13,C7:C13)

	A	B	C	D	E	F	G	H	I
1	**Location Factor Rating**			OM Student - Example S7.1					
2									
3		*Label the location factors, and input their weight and score for each site.*							
4	*Input:*								
5				*SCORES (0 to 100)*					
6	*LOCATION FACTORS*	*Weight*	*Site 1*	*Site 2*	*Site 3*				
7	Labor pool and climate	0.30	80	65	90				
8	Proximity to suppliers	0.20	100	91	75				
9	Wage rates	0.15	60	95	72				
10	Community environment	0.15	75	80	80				
11	Proximity to customers	0.10	65	90	95				
12	Shipping modes	0.05	85	92	65				
13	Air service	0.05	50	65	90				
14		1.00							
15									
16	*Output:*		*Site 1*	*Site 2*	*Site 3*				
17		*Total location score*	77.50	80.80	82.05				
18									

warehouse at the center of movement in a geographic area based on weight and distance. This method identifies a set of coordinates designating a central location on a map relative to all other locations.

The starting point for this method is a grid map set up on a Cartesian plane, as shown in Figure S7.2. There are three locations, 1, 2, and 3, each at a set of coordinates (x_i, y_i) identifying its location in the grid. The value W_i is the annual weight shipped from that location. The objective is to determine a central location for a new facility.

The coordinates for the location of the new facility are computed using the following formulas:

$$x = \frac{\sum_{i=1}^{n} x_i W_i}{\sum_{i=1}^{n} W_i}, \qquad y = \frac{\sum_{i=1}^{n} y_i W_i}{\sum_{i=1}^{n} W_i}$$

where

x, y = coordinates of the new facility at center of gravity
x_i, y_i = coordinates of existing facility i
W_i = annual weight shipped from facility i

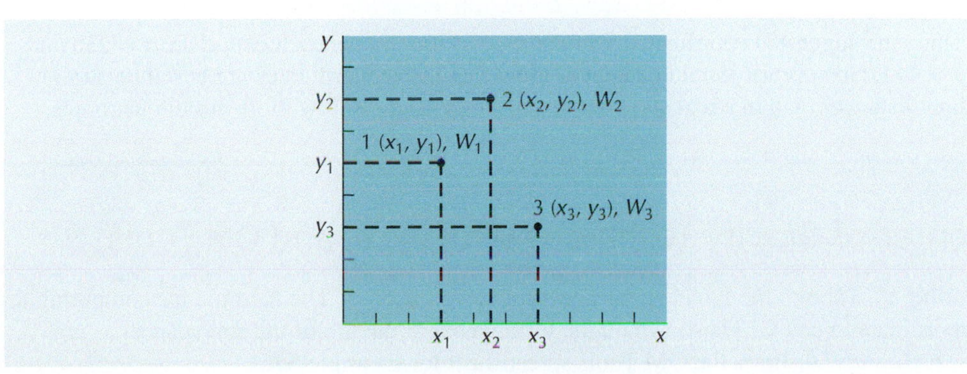

FIGURE S7.2 Grid Map Coordinates

EXAMPLE S7.2 | The Center-of-Gravity Technique

The Burger Doodle restaurant chain purchases ingredients from four different food suppliers. The company wants to construct a new central distribution center to process and package the ingredients before shipping them to its various restaurants. The suppliers transport ingredient items in 40-foot truck trailers, each with a capacity of 38,000 lbs. The locations of the four suppliers, A, B, C, and D, and the annual number of trailer loads that will be transported to the distribution center, are shown in the following figure:

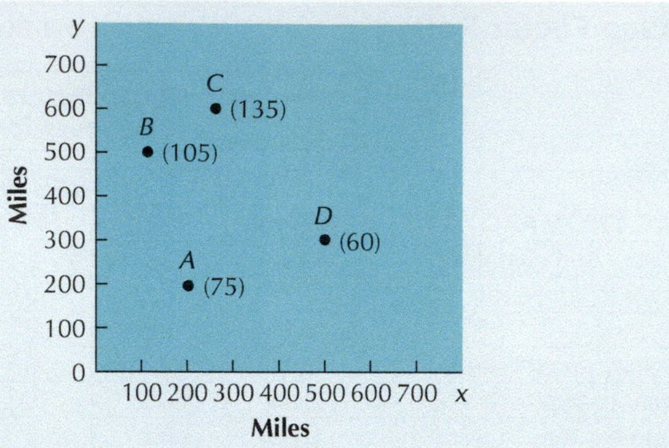

Using the center-of-gravity method, determine a possible location for the distribution center.

Solution:

A	B	C	D
$x_A = 200$	$x_B = 100$	$x_C = 250$	$x_D = 500$
$y_A = 200$	$y_B = 500$	$y_C = 600$	$y_D = 300$
$W_A = 75$	$W_B = 105$	$W_C = 135$	$W_D = 60$

$$x = \frac{\sum_{i=A}^{D} x_i W_i}{\sum_{i=A}^{D} W_i}$$

$$= \frac{(200)(75) + (100)(105) + (250)(135) + (500)(60)}{75 + 105 + 135 + 60}$$

$$= 238$$

$$y = \frac{\sum_{i=A}^{D} y_i W_i}{\sum_{i=A}^{D} W_i}$$

$$= \frac{(200)(75) + (500)(105) + (600)(135) + (300)(60)}{75 + 105 + 135 + 60}$$

$$= 444$$

Thus, the suggested coordinates for the new distribution center location are $x = 238$ and $y = 444$. However, it should be kept in mind that these coordinates are based on straight-line distances, and in a real situation actual roads might follow more circuitous routes.

Center-of-Gravity Technique With Excel and OM Tools

Exhibit S7.3 shows the Excel spreadsheet for Example S7.2. The formula for computing the x-coordinate in cell C13 is shown on the formula bar at the top of the spreadsheet.

Exhibit S7.4 shows the OM Tools spreadsheet for Example S7.2.

EXHIBIT S7.3

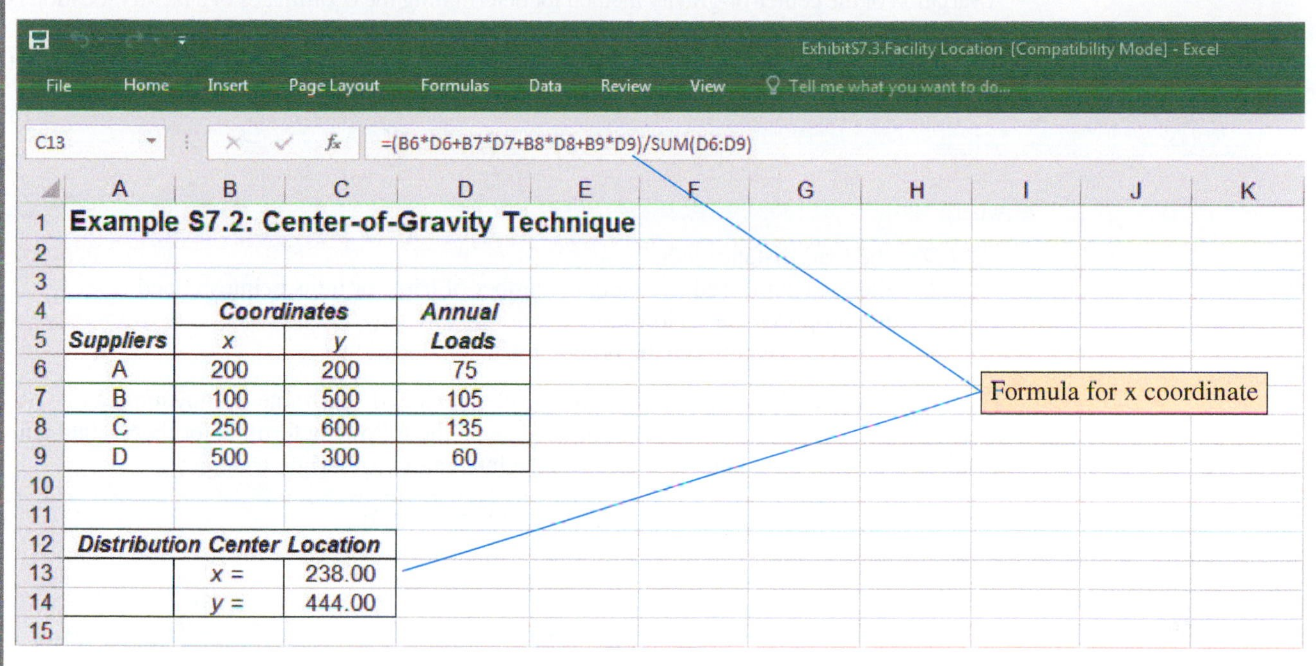

EXHIBIT S7.4

ExhibitS7.4.CenterofGravity [Compatibility Mode] - Excel

File Home Insert Page Layout Formulas Data Review View Tell me what you want to do...

C14 =(SUMPRODUCT(B7:B10,D7:D10))/SUM(D7:D10)

Center-of-Gravity Technique

OM Student - Example S7.2

Label the sites and input the load and x,y coordinates for each site.

Input:

	Coordinates		Loads
Sites	**x**	**y**	**W**
A	200	200	75
B	100	500	105
C	250	600	135
D	500	300	60

Output:

Center of Gravity	
x =	238.00
y =	444.00

Center of Gravity

700, 600, 500, 400, 300, 200, 100, 0

0, 100, 200, 300, 400, 500, 600

◆ Sites
■ Center of Gravity

Center-of-Gravity Coordinates

$$x = \frac{\sum_{i=1}^{n} x_i W_i}{\sum_{i=1}^{n} W_i}, \quad y = \frac{\sum_{i=1}^{n} y}{\sum_{i=1}^{n} 1}$$

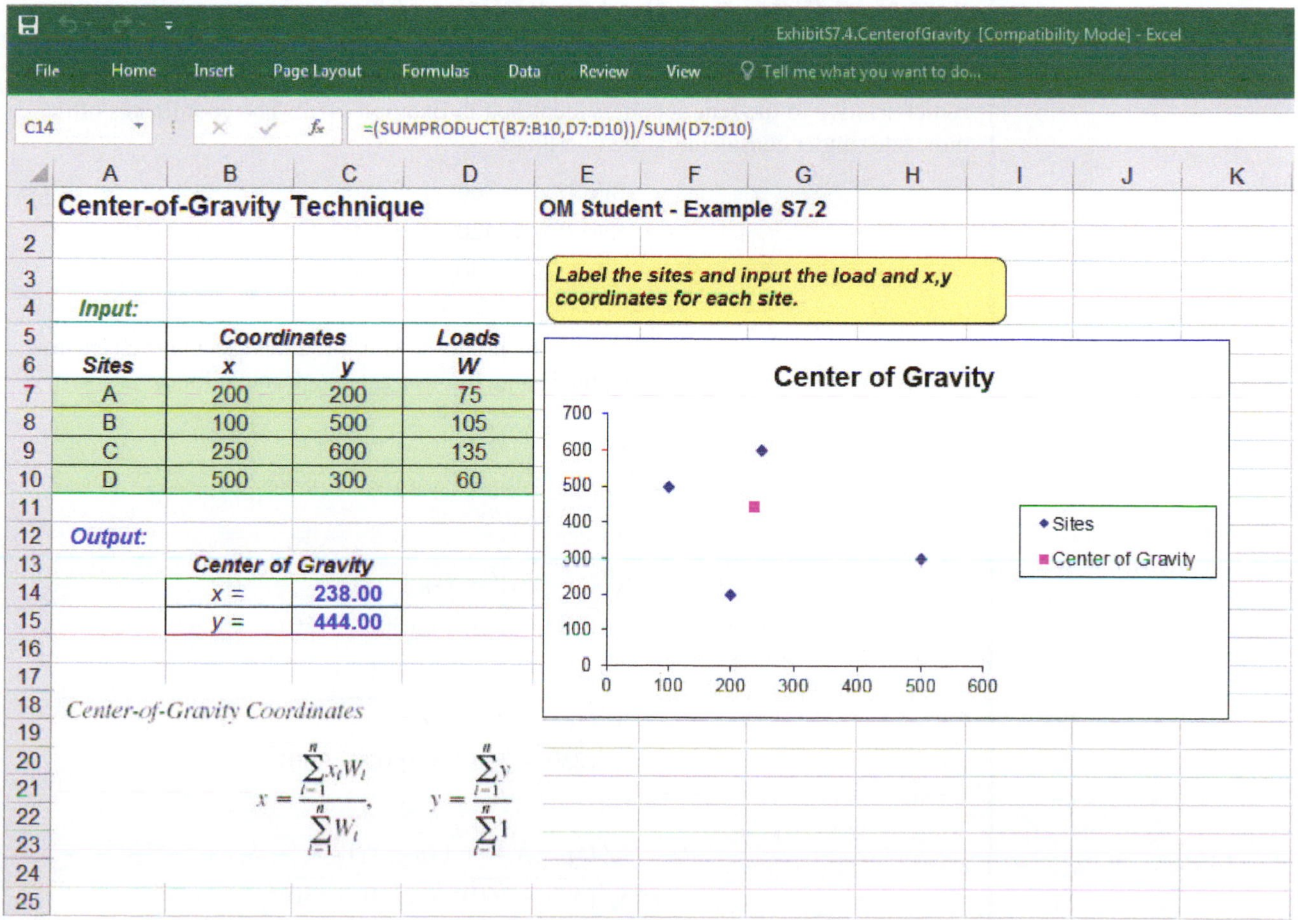

Load-Distance Technique

Load-distance technique A method of evaluating different locations based on the load being transported and the distance.

A variation of the center-of-gravity method for determining the coordinates of a facility location is the **load-distance technique**. In this method, a single set of location coordinates is not identified. Instead, various locations are evaluated using a load-distance value that is a measure of weight and distance. For a single potential location, a load-distance value is computed as follows:

$$LD = \sum_{i=1}^{n} l_i d_i$$

where

LD = the load-distance value
l_i = the load expressed as a weight, number of trips, or units being shipped from the proposed site to location i
d_i = the distance between the proposed site and location i

The distance d_i in this formula can be the travel distance, if that value is known or can be determined from a map. It can also be computed using the following formula for the straight-line distance between two points, which is also the hypotenuse of a right triangle:

$$d_i = \sqrt{(x_i - x)^2 + (y_i - y)^2}$$

where

(x, y) = coordinates of proposed site
(x_i, y_i) = coordinates of existing facility

The load-distance technique is applied by computing a load-distance value for each potential facility location. The implication is that the location with the lowest value would result in the minimum transportation cost and thus would be preferable.

EXAMPLE S7.3 | The Load-Distance Technique

Burger Doodle wants to evaluate three different sites it has identified for its new distribution center relative to the four suppliers identified in Example S7.2. The coordinates of the three sites under consideration are as follows:

$$\text{Site 1: } x_1 = 360,\ y_1 = 180$$
$$\text{Site 2: } x_2 = 420,\ y_2 = 450$$
$$\text{Site 3: } x_3 = 250,\ y_3 = 400$$

Solution: First, the distances between the proposed sites (1, 2, and 3) and each existing facility (A, B, C, and D), are computed using the straight-line formula for d_i:

$$\begin{aligned}
\text{Site 1: } d_A &= \sqrt{(x_A - x_1)^2 + (y_A - y_1)^2} \\
&= \sqrt{(200 - 360)^2 + (200 - 180)^2} \\
&= 161.2 \\
d_B &= \sqrt{(x_B - x_1)^2 + (y_B - y_1)^2} \\
&= \sqrt{(100 - 360)^2 + (500 - 180)^2} \\
&= 412.3 \\
d_C &= \sqrt{(x_C - x_1)^2 + (y_C - y_1)^2} \\
&= \sqrt{(250 - 360)^2 + (600 - 180)^2} \\
&= 434.2 \\
d_D &= \sqrt{(x_D - x_1)^2 + (y_D - y_1)^2} \\
&= \sqrt{(500 - 360)^2 + (300 - 180)^2} \\
&= 184.4
\end{aligned}$$

Site 2: $d_A = 333, d_B = 323.9, d_C = 226.7, d_D = 170$
Site 3: $d_A = 206.2, d_B = 180.3, d_C = 200, d_D = 269.3$

Next, the formula for load distance is computed for each proposed site:

$$\begin{aligned}
\text{LD (site 1)} &= \sum_{i=A}^{D} l_i d_i \\
&= (75)(161.2) + (105)(412.3) + (135)(434.2) + (60)(184.4) \\
&= 125{,}063 \\
\text{LD (site 2)} &= (75)(333) + (105)(323.9) + (135)(226.7) + (60)(170) \\
&= 99{,}789 \\
\text{LD (site 3)} &= (75)(206.2) + (105)(180.3) + (135)(200) + (60)(269.3) \\
&= 77{,}555
\end{aligned}$$

Since site 3 has the lowest load-distance value, it would be assumed that this location would also minimize transportation costs. Notice that site 3 is very close to the location determined using the center-of-gravity method in Example S7.2.

Load-Distance Technique with Excel and OM Tools

Exhibit S7.5 shows the Excel spreadsheet for Example S7.3. The formula for computing the distance from supplier location A to site 1 is embedded in C11 and is shown on the formula bar at the top of the spreadsheet. The formula for computing the location-distance formula for site 1 is shown in the callout box attached to cell C17.

Exhibit S7.6 shows the OM Tools spreadsheet for Example S7.3.

EXHIBIT S7.5

ExhibitS7.5.Facility Location [Compatibility Mode] - Excel

File Home Insert Page Layout Formulas Data Review View Tell me what you want to do...

C11 =SQRT((B5-H5)^2+(B6-H6)^2)

Example S7.3: Load-Distance Technique

	Supplier Locations						Distribution Center Sites		
	A	B	C	D			1	2	3
x	200	100	250	500		x	360	420	250
y	200	500	600	300		y	180	450	400
W	75	105	135	60					

Site 1 Distances		Site 2 Distances		Site 3 Distances	
A =	161.25	A =	333.02	A =	206.16
B =	412.31	B =	323.88	B =	180.28
C =	434.17	C =	226.72	C =	200.00
D =	184.39	D =	170.00	D =	269.26

LD (Site 1) =	125,061.8
LD (Site 2) =	99,790.5
LD (Site 3) =	77,546.3

EXHIBIT S7.6

ExhibitS7.6.LoadDistance [Compatibility Mode] - Excel

File | Home | Insert | Page Layout | Formulas | Data | Review | View | Tell me what you want to do...

C29 | =B9*B14+C9*B15+D9*B16+E9*B17

Load-Distance Technique — OM Student - Example S7.3

Input the x ,y coordinates for each destination and site. Enter the destination weights.

Input:

Map Coordinate	Destination			
	A	B	C	D
x	200	100	250	500
y	200	500	600	300
Weight	75	105	135	60

Map Coordinates	Sites		
	1	2	3
x	360	420	250
y	180	450	400

Calculations:

Site 1 Distances		Site 2 Distances		Site 3 Distances	
A	161.25	A	333.02	A	206.16
B	412.31	B	323.88	B	180.28
C	434.17	C	226.72	C	200.00
D	184.39	D	170.00	D	269.26

Load-Distance Formulas

$$LD = \sum_{i=1}^{n} l_i d_i$$

$$d_i = \sqrt{(x_i - x)^2 + (y_i - y)^2}$$

Output:

LD (Site 1) =	125,061.8
LD (Site 2) =	99,790.5
LD (Site 3) =	77,546.3

Map of Sites and Destinations

Destinations
Sites

0 100 200 300 400 500 600 700

0 100 200 300 400 500 600

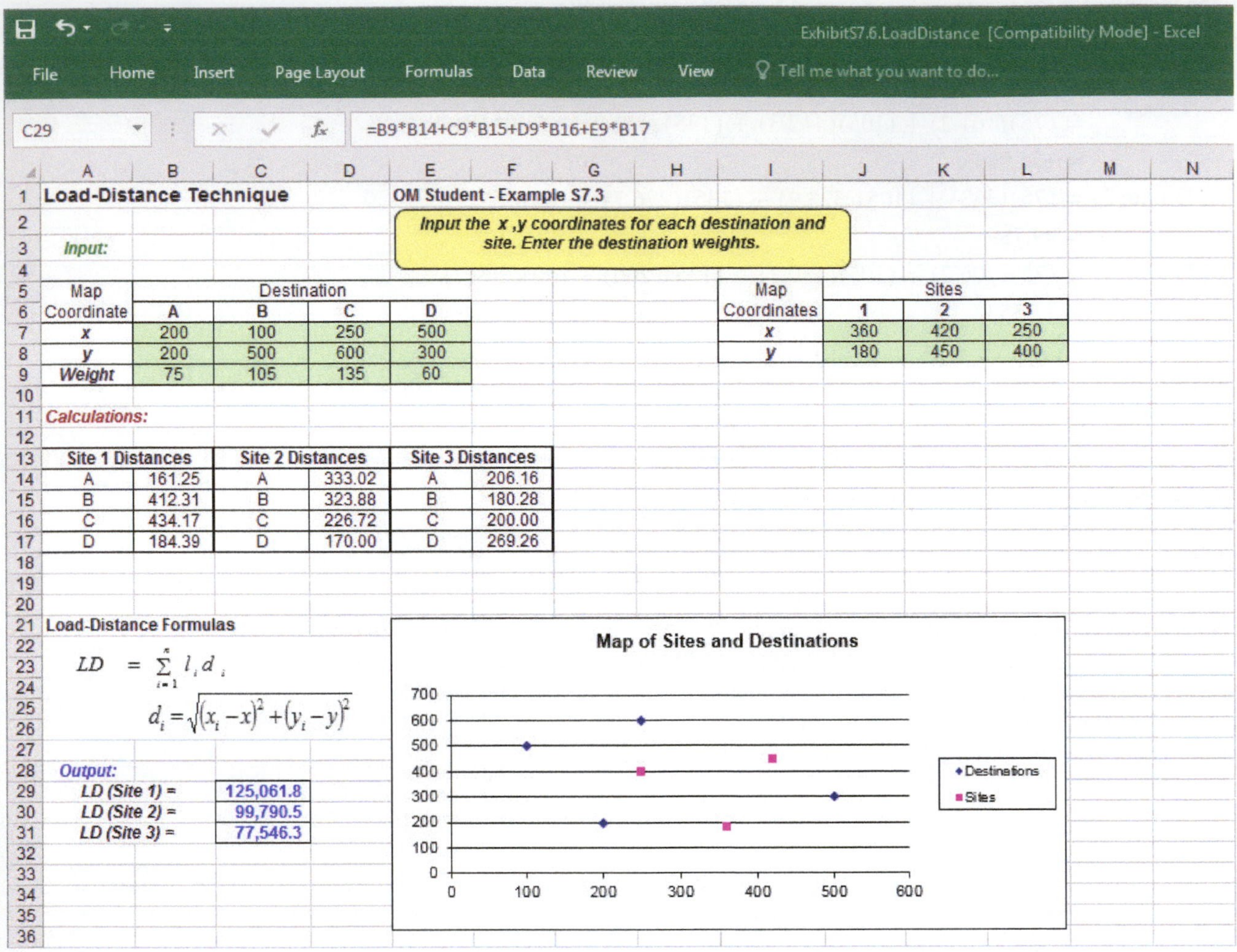

Summary

Facility location is an often overlooked but important aspect of a company's strategic plan. What kind of facility to build and where to locate it are expensive decisions. A location decision is not easily reversed if it is a bad one. For a service operation, the wrong location can result in too few customers to be profitable, whereas for a manufacturing operation, a wrong location can result in excessive costs, especially for transportation and distribution, and high inventories. The quantitative tools presented in this supplement are not usually sufficient for making an actual location decision, but they do provide means for helping in the location analysis and decision process.

Key Terms

center-of-gravity technique A quantitative method for locating a facility at the center of movement in a geographic area based on weight and distance.

infrastructure The physical support structures in a community, including roads, water and sewage systems, and utilities.

load-distance technique A quantitative method for evaluating various facility locations using a value that is a measure of weight and distance.

location factor rating A system for weighting the importance of different factors in the location decision, scoring the individual factors, and then developing an overall location score that enables a comparison of different location sites.

Key Formulas

Center-of-Gravity Coordinates

$$x = \frac{\sum_{i=1}^{n} x_i W_i}{\sum_{i=1}^{n} W_i}, \qquad y = \frac{\sum_{i=1}^{n} y_i W_i}{\sum_{i=1}^{n} W_i}$$

Load-Distance Technique

$$LD = \sum_{i=1}^{n} l_i d_i$$

$$d_i = \sqrt{(x_i - x)^2 + (y_i - y)^2}$$

Solved Problems

1. Center-of-Gravity Technique

A company is going to construct a new warehouse served by suppliers A, B, and C. The locations of the three suppliers and the annual number of truck carriers that will serve the warehouse are shown in the following figure:

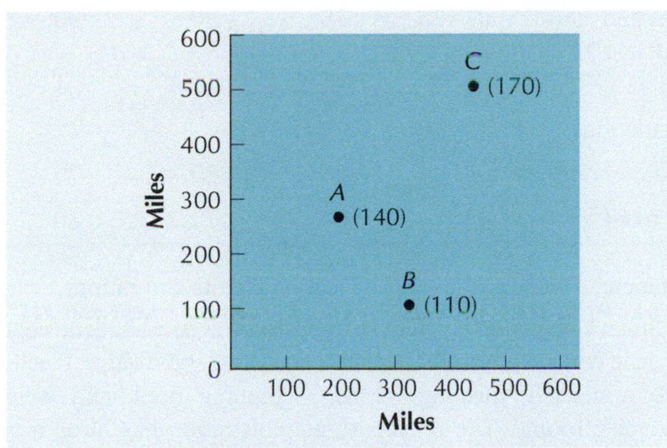

A	B	C
$x_A = 150$	$x_B = 300$	$x_C = 400$
$Y_A = 250$	$Y_B = 100$	$Y_C = 500$
$W_A = 140$	$W_B = 110$	$W_C = 170$

Determine the best site for the warehouse using the center of gravity technique.

Solution

$$x = \frac{\sum_{i=A}^{C} x_i W_i}{\sum_{i=A}^{C} W_i} = \frac{(150)(140) + (300)(110) + (400)(170)}{140 + 110 + 170}$$

$$= 290.5$$

$$y = \frac{\sum_{i=A}^{C} y_i W_i}{\sum_{i=A}^{C} W_i} = \frac{(250)(140) + (100)(110) + (500)(170)}{140 + 110 + 170}$$

$$= 311.9$$

The suggested coordinates for the new warehouse are $x = 290.5$ and $y = 311.9$.

Questions

S7.1. How are the location decisions for service operations and manufacturing operations similar, and how are they different?

S7.2. Indicate what you perceive to be general location trends for service operations and manufacturing operations.

S7.3. What factors make the southern region of the United States an attractive location for service and manufacturing businesses?

S7.4. Describe the positive and negative factors for a company contemplating locating in a foreign country.

S7.5. What would be the important location factors that McDonald's might consider before opening a new restaurant?

S7.6. The following businesses are considering locating in your community:

a. A pizza delivery service
b. A sporting goods store
c. A small brewery
d. A plant making aluminum cans

Describe the positive and negative location factors for each of these businesses.

S7.7. What location factors make small cities and towns in the Midwest attractive to companies?

S7.8. Select a major (light or heavy) manufacturing facility in your community or immediate geographic area (within a radius of 100 miles), and identify the factors that make it a good or poor site, in your opinion.

S7.9. Assume that you are going to open a Starbuck's in your community. Select three sites. Perform a location factor analysis for each and select the best site.

S7.10. Suppose your college or university was planning to develop a new student center and athletic complex with a bookstore, theaters, meeting areas, pool, gymnasium, and weight and exercise rooms. Identify three potential sites on your campus for this facility and rank them according to location factors you can identify.

S7.11. Select four fast-food restaurants (e.g., McDonald's, Burger King, Wendy's, Domino's, etc.) in your town, and develop a scoring model including decision criteria, weights, and grades to rank the restaurants from the best to worst.

Problems

WileyPLUS

S7.1. Sweats and Sweaters is a small chain of stores specializing in casual cotton clothing. The company currently has five stores in Georgia, South Carolina, and North Carolina, and it wants to open a new store in one of four new mall locations in the Southeast. A consulting firm has been hired to help the company decide where to locate its new store. The company has indicated five factors that are important to its decision, including proximity of a college, community median income, mall vehicle traffic flow and parking, quality and number of stores in the mall, and proximity of other malls or shopping areas. The consulting firm had the company weight the importance of each factor. The consultants visited each potential location and rated them according to each factor, as follows:

		SCORES (0 TO 100)			
LOCATION FACTOR	WEIGHT	MALL 1	MALL 2	MALL 3	MALL 4
College proximity	.30	40	60	90	50
Median income	.25	75	80	75	70
Vehicle traffic	.25	60	90	79	74
Mall quality and size	.10	90	100	80	90
Proximity of other shopping	.10	80	30	60	70

Given that all sites have basically the same leasing costs and labor and operating costs, recommend a location based on the rating factors.

S7.2. Exotech Computers manufactures computer components such as chips, circuit boards, motherboards, keyboards, LCD panels, and the like and sells them around the world. It wants to construct a new warehouse/distribution center in Asia to serve emerging Asian markets. It has identified sites in Shanghai, Hong Kong, and Singapore and has rated the important location factors for each site as follows:

		SCORES (0 TO 100)		
LOCATION FACTOR	WEIGHT	SHANGHAI	HONG KONG	SINGAPORE
Political stability	.25	50	80	90
Economic growth	.18	90	80	75
Port facilities	.15	60	95	90
Container support	.10	50	80	90
Land and construction cost	.08	90	50	30
Transportation/ distribution	.08	50	80	70
Duties and traffic	.07	70	90	90
Trade regulations	.05	70	95	95
Airline service	.02	60	80	70
Area roads	.02	60	70	80

Recommend a site based on these location factors and ratings.

S7.3. State University is going to construct a new student center and athletic complex that will include a bookstore, post office, theaters, market, mini-mall, meeting rooms, swimming pool, and weight and exercise rooms. The university administration has hired a site selection specialist to identify the best potential sites on campus for the new facility. The site specialist has identified four sites on campus and has rated the important location factors for each site as follows:

		SCORES (0 TO 100)			
LOCATION FACTOR	WEIGHT	SOUTH	WEST A	WEST B	EAST
Proximity to housing	.23	70	90	65	80
Student traffic	.22	75	80	60	85
Parking availability	.16	90	60	80	70
Plot size, terrain	.12	80	70	90	65
Infrastructure	0.10	50	60	40	60
Off-campus accessibility	0.06	90	70	70	70
Proximity to dining facilities	0.05	60	80	70	80
Visitor traffic	0.04	70	80	65	55
Landscape/ aesthetics	0.02	50	40	60	70

Recommend a site based on these location factors and ratings.

S7.4. Arsenal Electronics is going to construct a new $1.2 billion semiconductor plant and has selected four towns in the Midwest as potential sites. The important location factors and ratings for each town are as follows:

LOCATION FACTOR	WEIGHT	SCORES (0 TO 100)			
		ABBETON	BAYSIDE	CANE CREEK	DUNNVILLE
Work ethics	.18	80	90	70	75
Quality of life	.16	75	85	95	90
Labor laws/ unionization	.12	90	60	60	70
Infrastructure	.10	60	50	60	70
Education	.08	80	90	85	95
Labor skill and education	.07	75	65	70	80
Cost of living	.06	70	80	85	75
Taxes	.05	65	70	55	60
Incentive package	.05	90	95	70	80
Government regulations	.03	40	50	65	55
Environmental regulations	.03	65	60	70	80
Transportation	.03	90	80	95	80
Space for expansion	.02	90	95	90	90
Urban proximity	.02	60	90	70	80

Recommend a site based on these location factors and ratings.

S7.5. Herriott Hotels, Inc. wants to develop a new beachfront resort along the coast of South Carolina. A number of sites are available, and the hotel chain has narrowed the choice to five locations. They have graded their choices according to the weighted criteria shown as follows:

LOCATION FACTOR	WEIGHT	RESORT LOCATION SCORES (0 TO 100)				
		ALBER-MARLE	OCEAN-FRONT	CALYPSO	DAFUSKLE	EDENISLE
Annual tourist population	.40	80	70	70	90	60
Cost	.20	50	70	90	60	90
Road proximity to beach	.15	70	60	70	50	80
Quality of beach	.05	90	80	90	60	80
Infrastructure	.05	40	60	70	80	100
Shopping and restaurants	.05	70	90	90	80	90
Crowdedness of beach	.05	30	80	50	70	60
Other attractions	.05	100	70	90	80	90

Recommend a resort site based on these location factors and ratings.

S7.6. Robin Dillon has recently accepted a new job in the Washington, DC, area and has been hunting for a condominium to purchase. From friends and coworkers she has compiled a list of five possible condominium complexes that she might move into. The following table indicates the weighted criteria that Robin intends to use in her decision-making process and a grade indicating how well each complex satisfies each criterion.

LOCATION CRITERIA	WEIGHTS	CONDOMINIUM COMPLEXES				
		FAIRFAX FOREST	DUPONT GARDENS	TYSONS TERRACE	ALEXAN-DRIA COMMONS	MANASSAS FARMS
Purchase price	.30	92	85	75	62	79
Neighborhood location	.18	76	63	95	90	80
Proximity to Metro train	.12	78	75	76	85	60
Shopping	.10	65	80	98	92	75
Security	.10	75	78	90	95	83
Recreational facilities	.05	96	90	82	81	93
Distance to job	.05	85	67	95	75	65
Condo floor plan	.05	80	78	86	92	90
Complex size	.05	65	60	92	89	70

S7.7. Balston Healthcare operates three hospitals and a number of clinics in its citywide network. It is planning to open a new wellness center and clinic facility that focuses on geriatric clients in one of four suburbs. The following table shows the weighted criteria for each location.

LOCATION FACTORS	WEIGHT	SCORES (0 TO 100)			
		ASHCROFT	BRAINERD	CRABTREE	DOWLING
Elderly population	.55	75	80	65	75
Income level	.15	65	75	90	85
Land availability	.10	90	70	90	80
Average age	.10	80	70	80	75
Public trans-portation	.05	95	55	75	95
Crime rate	.05	95	70	85	90

Recommend a site for the new Balston Healthcare facility based on these weighted location factors and scores.

S7.8. The owners of the Midlands United professional soccer team currently located in a Midwestern city are concerned about declining attendance at their team's games, and they have decided to use a scoring model to help them decide which city in the south to relocate in—Atlanta, Birmingham, Charlotte, or Durham. They have graded the possible cities according to the following weighted criteria:

LOCATION FACTORS	WEIGHT	CITY SCORES (0 TO 100) ATLANTA	BIRMINGHAM	CHARLOTTE	DURHAM
Soccer interest	.25	70	40	75	90
Entertainment competition	.18	33	45	60	95
Playing facility	.12	50	65	70	85
Population (age 15 to 40)	.10	100	70	90	25
Media market	.07	100	65	95	40
Income level (age 15 to 40)	.05	80	70	80	60
Tax incentives	.05	20	40	75	60
Airline transportation	.05	100	70	95	65
Cultural diversity	.05	100	80	90	75
General sports interest	.03	75	95	85	65
Local government support	.03	30	60	75	90
Community support	.02	20	35	50	75

Develop a scoring model to help the owners decide on which city to select to relocate.

S7.9. As part of an aggressive expansion plan, StarTrack Coffee is planning to open three new retail stores in the city. The table shows the location factors it considers important indicators of future profitability, and how each location has been graded by management according to each one of these factors.

LOCATION	LOCATION FACTORS BUSINESS DENSITY	SHOPPING DENSITY	VEHICLE TRAFFIC	PEDESTRIAN TRAFFIC	LAND AND CONSTRUCTION COST
1	75	81	55	75	63
2	62	56	83	67	82
3	73	45	71	70	74
4	81	69	77	65	66
5	77	86	75	65	82
6	64	75	65	80	91
7	89	86	67	73	67
8	91	90	64	80	65
9	56	64	77	69	82
10	66	68	81	72	87
11	67	81	75	66	85
12	83	73	77	70	90

Use your own judgment to determine weights for each of the location factors and recommend the three new store sites. Are there other location factors that you think might be important?

S7.10. Federated Electronics, Ltd., manufactures display screens and monitors for computers and televisions, which it sells to companies around the world. It wants to construct a new warehouse and distribution center in Asia to serve emerging markets there. It has identified potential sites in the port cities of Shanghai, Singapore, Pusan, Kaohsiung, and Hong Kong. The following table shows the factors in the location decision and the grade of each location for each factor.

LOCATION FACTORS	PORT SCORES (0 TO 100) SHANGHAI	SINGAPORE	PUSAN	KAOHSIUNG	HONG KONG
Facility cost	65	75	80	90	55
Labor rates	75	70	85	95	60
Labor availability	70	65	85	80	70
Infrastructure	80	80	65	70	95
Transportation	75	65	75	75	90
Container availability	70	80	65	75	85
Expansion/ modernization	80	75	90	80	95
Political stability	65	70	85	80	90
Duties, tariffs, and fees	75	80	80	90	70
Trade regulations	65	75	80	80	75

The weights indicating the importance of each location factor are not included. Determine what you think these weights should be and recommend the best location for the new distribution center.

S7.11. The Western Jeans Company is going to select a new overseas supplier for denim jeans. The company has identified suppliers in Bangladesh, India, the Philippines, China, Pakistan, and Turkey. The following table shows the location factors that the company views as important in the selection process and management's grade for each of these factors.

LOCATION FACTORS	SCORES (0 TO 100) BANGLADESH	INDIA	PHILIPPINES	CHINA	PAKISTAN	TURKEY
Wage rate	90	75	90	85	80	70
Infrastructure	60	65	70	65	65	75
Suppliers	55	80	65	90	70	75
Labor sustainability	50	80	65	70	60	80
Environmental sustainability	60	75	70	55	60	75
Government stability	50	95	80	90	55	95
Quality program	75	90	80	70	80	90
Water supply	90	90	80	75	70	80
Language/ communication	80	95	80	60	75	65
Logistics	70	75	75	70	60	80
Port access	60	90	85	95	65	60
Export regulations	85	85	80	75	65	70
Risk	50	90	80	85	55	95

Use your own judgment to attach weights to each of the location factors and recommend the preferred supplier.

S7.12. The Federal Parcel Service wants to build a new distribution center in Charlotte, North Carolina. The center needs to be in the vicinity of uncongested Interstate-77 and Interstate-85 interchanges, and the Charlotte-Douglas International Airport. The coordinates of these three sites and the number of weekly packages that flow to each are as follows:

I-77	I-85	AIRPORT
$x = 14$	$x = 20$	$x = 30$
$y = 30$	$y = 8$	$y = 14$
$w = 17{,}000$	$w = 12{,}000$	$w = 9000$

Determine the best site location using the center-of-gravity technique.

S7.13. The Burger Doodle restaurant chain uses a distribution center to prepare the food ingredients it provides its individual restaurants. The company is attempting to determine the location for a new distribution center that will service five restaurants. The grid-map coordinates of the five restaurants and the annual number of 40-foot trailer trucks transported to each restaurant are as follows:

RESTAURANT	COORDINATES x	y	ANNUAL TRUCK SHIPMENTS
1	100	300	35
2	210	180	24
3	250	400	15
4	300	150	19
5	400	200	38

a. Determine the least-cost location using the center-of-gravity method.

b. Plot the five restaurants and the proposed new distribution center on a grid map.

S7.14. The Burger Doodle restaurant chain in Problem S7.13 is considering three potential sites, with the following grid-map coordinates, for its new distribution center: A(350, 300), B(150, 250), and C(250, 300). Determine the best location using the load-distance formula, and plot this location on a grid map with the five restaurants. How does this location compare with the location determined in Problem S7.13?

S7-15. The StarTrack Coffee Company has identified four possible high pedestrian traffic areas (resulting from nearby stores, hotels, and work places) in the city within a half-mile area it wants to open a new retail store in. The company has taken surveys to measure the volume of daily pedestrian traffic at each location area, which is shown in the table below together with the grid coordinates of each location within the area. The location coordinates shown (in yards) are not possible sites for the new store; what the company wants to determine are the best possible location coordinates according to distance and pedestrian traffic and then use this information to search for the nearest available property it can lease or buy for the store.

CITY LOCATION AREA	COORDINATES x	y	DAILY FOOT TRAFFIC
A	200	250	10,400
B	600	1,500	15,200
C	1,400	1,250	9,300
D	1,600	725	14,700

Determine the best possible site location for the company to search in using the center-of-gravity technique.

S7.16. A development company is attempting to determine the location for a new outlet mall. The region where the outlet mall will be constructed includes four towns, which together have a sizable population base. The grid-map coordinates of the four towns and the population of each are as follows:

TOWN	COORDINATES x	y	POPULATION (10,000s)
Four Corners	30	60	8.5
Whitesburg	50	40	6.1
Russellville	10	70	7.3
Whistle Stop	40	30	5.9

a. Determine the best location for the outlet mall using the center-of-gravity method.

b. Plot the four towns and the location of the new mall on a grid map.

S7.17. State University in Problem S7.3 is attempting to locate the best site for a new student center and athletic complex. The university administration would like to know what the best location is relative to the four main concentrations of student housing and classroom activity on campus. These coordinates of these housing and classroom areas (in yards) and daily student populations are shown on the previous page.

CAMPUS STUDENT CONCENTRATIONS: ANDERSON DORM COMPLEX	BALL HOUSING COMPLEX	CARTER CLASSROOM COMPLEX	DERRING CLASSROOM COMPLEX
$x_A = 1000$	$x_B = 1500$	$x_C = 2000$	$x_D = 32$
$y_A = 1250$	$y_B = 2700$	$y_C = 700$	$y_D = 25$
$w_A = 7000$	$w_B = 9000$	$w_C = 11{,}500$	$w_D = 4300$

Determine the best site using the center-of-gravity method.

S7.18. Mega-Mart, a discount store chain, wants to build a new superstore in an area in southwest Virginia near four small towns with populations between 8000 and 42,000. The coordinates (in miles) of these four towns and the market population in each are as follows:

WHITESBURG	ALTONVILLE	CAMBURG	MILLIGAN
$x = 12$	$x = 18$	$x = 30$	$x = 32$
$y = 20$	$y = 15$	$y = 7$	$y = 25$
$w = 26{,}000$	$w = 12{,}000$	$w = 18{,}300$	$w = 9700$

Determine the best site using the center-of-gravity technique.

S7.19. Home-Base, a home improvement/building supply chain, is going to build a new warehouse facility to serve its stores in six North Carolina cities—Charlotte, Winston-Salem, Greensboro, Durham, Raleigh, and Wilmington. The coordinates of these cities (in miles), using Columbia, South Carolina, as the origin (0,0) of a set of coordinates, and the annual truckloads that supply each city are shown as follows:

CHARLOTTE	WINSTON-SALEM	GREENSBORO
$x = 15$	$x = 42$	$x = 88$
$y = 85$	$y = 145$	$y = 145$
$w = 160$	$w = 90$	$w = 105$

DURHAM	RALEIGH	WILMINGTON
$x = 125$	$x = 135$	$x = 180$
$y = 140$	$y = 125$	$y = 18$
$w = 35$	$w = 60$	$w = 75$

a. Determine the best site using the center-of-gravity technique.

b. Look at a map of North Carolina, and identify the closest town to the grid coordinates developed in (a). Looking at the map, can you suggest a better location in the vicinity? Explain your answer.

S7.20. In Problem S7.19, Home-Base has two parcels of land in Fayetteville and Statesville, North Carolina. Use the load-distance technique (and a map of North Carolina) to determine which would be better.

S7.21. An army division in Iraq has five troop encampments in the desert, and the division leaders want to determine the best location for a supply depot to serve the camps. The (x, y) coordinates (in miles) of the camps, A, B, C, D, and E, and the daily amount of supplies (in tons) required at each camp are as follows:

	COORDINATES		
CAMP	x	y	DAILY TONNAGE (1000S)
A	110	120	85
B	70	300	110
C	520	350	75
D	300	450	60
E	400	600	100

Determine the best site for the supply depot using the center-of-gravity technique.

S7.22. In Problem S7.21, suppose the division commanders are limited to three possible sites for the supply depot because of airfield locations and enemy troop concentrations. The coordinates (in miles) of these three potential sites are site 1 (400, 250), site 2 (100, 200), and site 3 (200, 500). Using the load-distance technique, determine the best site for the supply depot.

S7.23. Somerset Furniture Company imports furniture components and pieces from several manufactures in China and then assembles the finished furniture pieces and adds hardware at a distribution center before shipping the finished pieces of furniture on to its customers' warehouses in several states. Furniture shipments arrive from China (in containers) at three U.S. ports in the United States—New Orleans, Savannah, and Norfolk. These containers are then transported to Somerset's distribution center for final furniture assembly before they are shipped in truckloads to five customer warehouses. The (x, y) coordinates of the ports and warehouses and the annual container truckload shipments are shown in the following table.

	COORDINATES		
PORT/ WAREHOUSE	x	y	ANNUAL TRUCKLOADS
New Orleans	1100	700	41
Savannah	2700	1400	27
Norfolk	2800	2200	34
1	200	1200	18
2	1400	1500	20
3	700	2300	32
4	1200	2700	24
5	2100	2600	18

Determine the best site for Somerset's distribution center using the center-of-gravity technique.

S7.24. In Problem S7.23, suppose Somerset furniture is considering three possible sites for its distribution center, which are the most economical in terms of land and building cost. The coordinates for the three potential sites are site A (1700, 800), site B (2400, 1700), and site C (1800, 2200). Using the load-distance technique, determine the best site for the distribution center.

S7.25. The Safora Company is a national chain of beauty products and cosmetic stores. It supplies all of its stores from a distribution center in Belcamp, Maryland; however, it has decided to construct a new distribution center for its stores west of the Mississippi River, and it will either continue to use its Belcamp facility to supply its stores in the east or open a new facility in the east. The following table shows Safora's monthly truck shipments to 12 major eastern and Midwest cities where the majority of Safora's stores are clustered.

CITY	MONTHLY TRUCKLOADS
Boston	24
New York	32
Philadelphia	17
Washington, DC	20
Miami	25
New Orleans	12
Atlanta	14
Charlotte	10
Nashville	8
Pittsburgh	11
Chicago	20
Detroit	15

Determine the best site if Safora decides to build a new eastern distribution center using the center-of-gravity technique.

S7.26. Using the load-distance technique, compare the best site for Safora's distribution center determined in problem S7.25 with the existing Belcamp, Maryland, site and explain which one you would select.

S7.27. The Safora Company in problem S7.25 also wants to build a new western distribution center. The following table shows Safora's monthly truck shipments to 12 major cities west of the Mississippi where the majority of Safora's stores are clustered.

CITY	MONTHLY TRUCKLOADS
San Diego	9
Los Angeles	25
San Francisco	15
Seattle	15
Phoenix	8
Houston	7
Las Vegas	11
Dallas	10
Denver	13
Kansas City	11
St. Louis	15

Determine the best location to build a new western distribution center using the center-of-gravity technique.

Case Problems

Case Problem S7.1 Selecting a European Distribution Center Site for American International Automotive Industries

American International Automotive Industries (AIAI) manufactures auto and truck engine, transmission, and chassis parts for manufacturers and repair companies in the United States, South America, Canada, Mexico, Asia, and Europe. The company transports to its foreign markets by container ships. To serve its customers in South America and Asia, AIAI has large warehouse/distribution centers. In Europe it ships into Hamburg and Gdansk, where it has contracted with independent distribution companies to deliver its products to customers throughout Europe. However, AIAI has been displeased with a recent history of late deliveries and rough handling of its products. For a time AIAI was not overly concerned since its European market wasn't too big and its European customers didn't complain. In addition, it had more pressing supply chain problems elsewhere. In the past five years, since trade barriers have fallen in Europe and Eastern European markets have opened up, its Europeans business has expanded, as has new competition, and its customers have become more demanding and quality conscious. As a result, AIAI has initiated the process to select a site for a new European warehouse/distribution center. Although it provides parts to a number of smaller truck and auto maintenance and service centers in Europe, it has seven major customers—auto and truck manufacturers—in Vienna, Leipzig, Budapest, Prague, Krakow, Munich, and Frankfurt. Its customers in Vienna and Budapest have adopted manufacturing processes requiring continuous replenishment of parts and materials.

AIAI's European headquarters is in Hamburg. The vice-president for construction and development in Dayton, Ohio, has asked the Hamburg office to do a preliminary site search based on location, geography, transportation, proximity to customers, and costs. The Hamburg office has identified five potential sites in Dresden, Lodz, Hamburg, Gdansk, and Frankfurt. The Hamburg office has forwarded information about each of these sites to corporate headquarters, including forecasts of the number of containers shipped annually to each customer as follows: Vienna, 160; Leipzig, 100; Budapest, 180; Prague, 210; Krakow, 90; Munich, 120; and Frankfurt, 50. When the vice-president of construction in Dayton received this information, he pulled out his map of Europe and began to study the sites.

Assist AIAI with its site selection process in Europe. Recommend a site form the five possibilities, and indicate what other location factors you might consider in the selection process.

References

Bowersox, D. J. *Logistics Management*, 2nd ed. New York: Macmillan, 1978.

Francis, R. L., and J. A. White. *Facilities Layout and Location: An Analytical Approach*. Upper Saddle River, NJ: Prentice Hall, 1987.

Fulton, M. "New Factors in Plant Location." *Harvard Business Review* (May–June 1971), pp. 4–17, 166–168.

Johnson, J. C., and D. F. Wood. *Contemporary Logistics*, 6th ed. Upper Saddle River, NJ: Prentice Hall, 1996.

Schmenner, R. W. *Making Business Location Decisions*. Upper Saddle River, NJ: Prentice Hall, 1982.

Human Resources

CHAPTER **8**

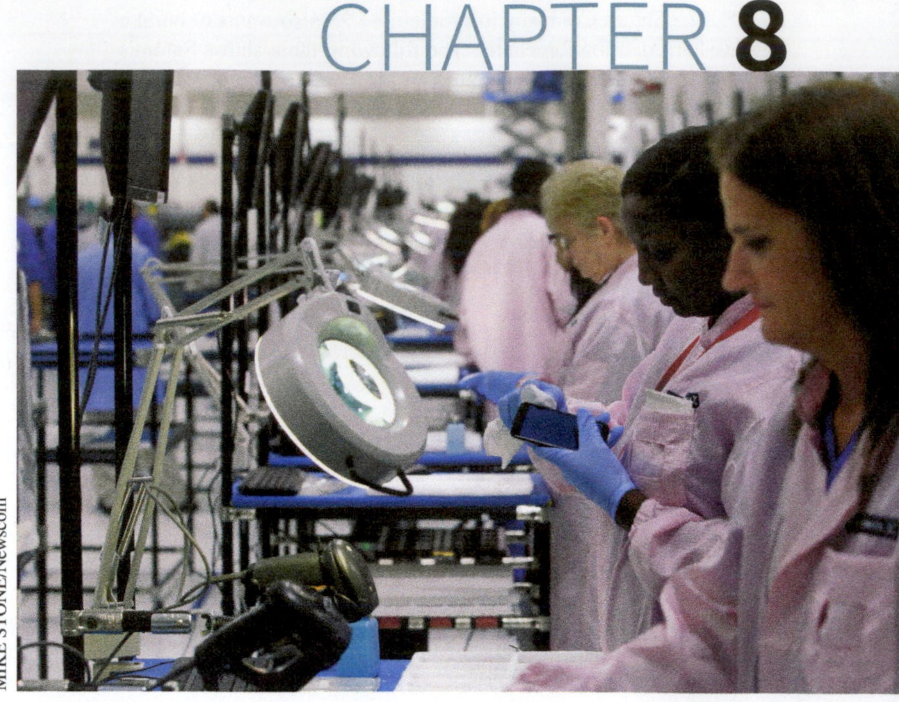
MIKE STONE/Newscom

LEARNING OBJECTIVES

After reading this chapter, you will be able to:

- Discuss the basic principles of human resource management in quality-focused companies.
- Discuss the changing nature of and contemporary trends in human resources management.
- Explain different methods of employee compensation.
- Describe the benefits of employee diversity and give examples of diversity initiatives.
- Describe the attributes and elements of a good job design.
- Use various tools to conduct a job analysis.
- Determine and explain the learning curve effect for work improvement.

A Commitment to Worker Sustainability at Apple

Apple has almost 100,000 full-time permanent employees who work directly for the company, and it has a reputation as a model employer. However, it also has over 1.5 million "quasi-employees" who work directly for Apple's global suppliers, the preponderance in East Asia and China. Increasingly Apple has been under intense pressure by global media to accept a degree of responsibility for these workers, which is linked to a growing sense of social responsibility around the world that multinational companies should develop and maintain a sustainable work force. Almost all of Apple's manufacturing is outsourced globally to over 750 supplier facilities, and enforcing work rules and policies in companies that are not your own and in countries that have very different government regulations than the United States or Europe can be a difficult process. However, in the past decade there were widely reported worker abuses, especially among Apple's Chinese suppliers, including worker suicides, workers forced to work excessive overtime (sometimes seven days a week), under-aged workers, students forced to work in factories for up to two years, factory explosions, and worker exposure to hazardous and toxic chemicals, crowded substandard living quarters, and instances where over half of workers' earnings were required by companies to pay for services such as rent and food.

To address these and other worker sustainability issues Apple established a "Supplier Code of Conduct" and "Supplier Responsibility Standards," that all of its suppliers are required to meet. Every Apple supplier factory must agree to follow this code and the standards and must agree to be audited. Factory audits are led by Apple auditors and supported by local third-party auditors who are experts in their fields and have been trained to use Apple's detailed auditing procedures. Suppliers are graded on various data points corresponding to categories in the code of conduct. The auditors review payroll documents, interview workers, assess the health and safety conditions in a facility, and inspect environmental conditions inside and outside of the factory. Suppliers are required to remediate all violations and submit a corrective action plan within two weeks of the audit. Severe violations can result in termination as an Apple supplier. A team of verification specialists checks in with suppliers every 30 days for three months to assess progress, and a separate third-party auditor is hired to visit the facility at 120 days to independently verify the corrective actions. Since 2007, when the program started, over 2000 audits have been conducted, which have resulted in 92 percent compliance with Apple's maximum 60-hour work week. In a recent year, audits resulted in almost $4 million repaid to foreign contact workers for excessive recruitment fees charged by labor brokers, almost $1 million paid to workers for unpaid overtime, and underage workers were sent back to school with full tuition and salary. In addition, Apple has undertaken worker empowerment and education programs that include millions of workers being trained on Apple's code of conduct and their rights. Since Apple's Supplier Employee Education and Development (SEED) program began in 2008, over 850,000 workers have taken coursers free of charge for personal development and some have received college degrees.

Sources: Apple, Inc. website at www.apple.com/supplier-responsibility; and C. Duhigg and D. Barboza, "In China, Human Costs are Built Into an iPad," *The NY Times* (January 25, 2012).

Employees—the people who work in an organization—are "resources," as important as other company resources, such as natural resources and technology. In fact, it is the one resource that all companies have available to them. A company in Taiwan, Japan, or Denmark may have different and few natural resources, certainly fewer than U.S. companies have, but they all have people. With the same or superior technologies as their competitors, and with good people, foreign companies can compete and thrive. Increasingly, *skilled* human resources are the difference between successfully competing or failing.

The traditional view of employees or labor was not so much as a valuable resource, but as a replaceable part of the productive process that must be closely directed and controlled. The trend toward quality management, more than anything else, changed this perspective. W. E. Deming, the international quality expert, emphasized that good employees who are always improving are the key to successful quality management and a company's ultimate survival. More than half of Deming's 14 points for quality improvement relate to employees. His point is that if a company is to attain its goals for quality improvement and customer service, its employees must be involved and committed. However, to get employees "with the program," the company must regard them and manage them as a valuable resource. Moreover, the company must have a commitment to its employees.

Another thing that has changed the way companies regard employees and work is the shift in the U.S. economy toward the service sector and away from manufacturing. Since services tend to be more people-intensive than capital-intensive, human resources are becoming a more important competitive factor for service companies. Advances in information technologies have also changed the working environment, especially in service companies. Because they rely heavily on information technology and communication, services need employees who are technically skilled and can communicate effectively with customers. They also need flexible employees who can apply these skills to a variety of tasks and who are continuously trained to keep up with rapid advances in information technology.

Increasing technological advances in equipment and machinery have also resulted in manufacturing work that is more technically sophisticated. Employees are required to be better educated, have greater skill levels and technical expertise, and are expected to take on greater responsibility. This work environment is a result of changing technologies and international market conditions, global competition that emphasizes diverse products, and an emphasis on product and service quality.

In this chapter we first discuss employees' role in achieving a company's goals for quality. Next we provide a perspective on how work has developed and changed in the United States and then look at some of the current trends in human resources. We will also discuss some of the traditional aspects of work and job design.

Human Resources and Quality Management

Most successful quality-oriented firms today recognize the importance of their employees when developing a competitive strategy. Quality management is an integral part of most companies' strategic design, and the role of employees is an important aspect of quality management. To change management's traditional control-oriented relationship with employees to one of cooperation, mutual trust, teamwork, and goal orientation necessary in a quality-focused company generally requires a long-term commitment as a key part of a company's strategic plan.

In the traditional management–employee relationship, employees are given precise directions to achieve narrowly defined individual objectives. They are rewarded with merit pay based on individual performance in competition with their coworkers. Often individual excellence is rewarded while other employees look on in envy. In a successful quality management program, employees are given broad latitude in their jobs, they are encouraged to improvise, and they have the power to use their own initiative to correct and prevent problems. Strategic goals are for quality and customer service instead of maximizing profit or minimizing cost, and rewards are based on group achievement. Instead of limited training for specific, narrowly defined jobs, employees are trained in a broad range of skills so they know more about the entire productive process, making them flexible in where they can work.

To manage human resources from this perspective, a company must focus on employees as a key, even central, component in their strategic design. All of the Malcolm Baldrige National Quality Award winners have a pervasive human resource focus. Companies that successfully integrate this kind of "employees first" philosophy into their strategic design share several common characteristics. Employee training and education are recognized as necessary long-term investments. Strategic planning for product and technological innovation is tied to the development of employees' skills, not only to help in the product development process but also to carry out innovations as they come to fruition. Motorola provides employees with 160 hours of training annually to keep up with technological changes and to learn how to understand and compete in newly emerging global markets.

To make sure their strategic design for human resources is working, companies regularly monitor employee satisfaction using surveys and make changes when problems are identified. All Baldrige Quality Award-winning companies conduct annual employee surveys to assess employee satisfaction and make improvements.

A safe, healthy working environment is a basic necessity to keep employees satisfied. Successful companies provide special services like recreational activities, day care, flexible work hours, cultural events, picnics, and fitness centers. Notice that these are services that treat employees like customers, an acknowledgment that there is a direct and powerful link between employee satisfaction and customer satisfaction.

Strategic goals for quality and customer satisfaction require teamwork and group participation. Quality-oriented companies want all employees to be team members to identify and solve quality-related problems. Team members and individuals are encouraged to make suggestions to improve processes. The motivation for employee suggestions is viewed as that of a concerned family member, not as a complainant or as "sticking one's nose in."

It is important that employees understand what the strategic goals of the company are and that they feel like they can participate in achieving these goals. Employees need to believe they make a difference in order to be committed to goals and have pride in their work. Employee commitment and participation in the strategic plan can be enhanced if employees are involved in the planning process, especially at the local level. As the strategic plan passes down through the organization to the employee level, employees can participate in the development of local plans to achieve overall corporate goals.

The Changing Nature of Human Resource Management

The principles of *scientific management* developed by F. W. Taylor in the 1880s and 1890s dominated operations management during the first part of the twentieth century. Taylor's approach was to break jobs down into their most elemental activities and to simplify job designs so that only limited skills were required to learn a job, thus minimizing the time required for learning. This approach divided the jobs requiring less skill from the work required to set up machinery and maintain it, which required greater skill. In Taylor's system, a **job** is the set of all the tasks performed by a worker and **tasks** are individual activities consisting of *elements*, which encompass several **job motions**, or basic physical movements.

Jobs Comprise a set of tasks, elements, and job motions (basic physical movements).

Tasks Individual, defined job activities that consist of one or more elements.

Scientific management broke down a job into its simplest elements and motions, eliminated unnecessary motions, and then divided the tasks among several workers so that each would require only minimal skill. This system enabled companies to hire large numbers of cheap, unskilled laborers, who were basically interchangeable and easily replaced. If a worker was fired or quit, another could easily be placed on the job with virtually no training expense. In this system, the timing of job elements (by stopwatch) enabled management to develop *standard times* for producing one unit of output. Workers were paid according to their total output in a *piece-rate system*. A worker was paid "extra" wages according to the amount he or she exceeded the "standard" daily output. Such a wage system is based on the premise that the single motivating factor for a worker to increase output is monetary reward.

F. W. Taylor's work was not immediately accepted or implemented. This system required high volumes of output to make the large number of workers needed for the expanded number of jobs cost effective. The principles of scientific management and mass production were brought together by Henry Ford and the assembly-line production of automobiles.

The Assembly Line

Between 1908 and 1929, Ford Motor Company created and maintained a mass market for the Model-T automobile, more than 15 million of which were eventually produced. During this period, Ford expanded production output by combining standardized parts and product design, continuous-flow production, and Taylor's scientific management. These elements were encompassed in the assembly-line production process.

On an assembly line, workers no longer moved from place to place to perform tasks, as they had in the factory/shop. Instead they remained at a single workplace, and the work was conveyed to them along the assembly line. Technology had advanced from the general-purpose machinery available at the turn of the century, which required the abilities of a skilled machinist, to highly specialized, semiautomatic machine tools, which required less skill to feed parts into or perform repetitive tasks. Fifteen thousand of these machines were installed at Ford's Highland Park plant. The pace of work was established mechanically by the line and not by the worker or management. The jobs along the line were broken down into highly repetitive, simple tasks.

The assembly line at Ford was enormously successful. The amount of labor time required to assemble a Model-T chassis was reduced from more than 12 hours in 1908 to a little less than 3 hours by 1913. By 1914 the average time for some tasks was as low as 1½ minutes. The basic assembly-line structure and many job designs that existed in 1914 remained virtually unchanged for the next 50 years.

Limitations of Scientific Management

Scientific management had obvious advantages. It resulted in increased output and lower labor costs. Workers could easily be replaced and trained at low cost, taking advantage of a large pool of cheap, unskilled labor shifting from farms to industry. Because of low-cost mass production, the U.S. standard of living was increased enormously and became the envy of the rest of the world. It also allowed unskilled, uneducated workers to gain employment based almost solely on their willingness to work hard physically at jobs that were mentally undemanding.

Scientific management also proved to have serious disadvantages. Workers frequently became bored and dissatisfied with the numbing repetition of simple job tasks that required little thought, ingenuity, or responsibility. The skill level required in repetitive, specialized tasks is so low that workers do not have the opportunity to prove their worth or abilities for advancement. Repetitive tasks requiring the same monotonous physical motions can result in unnatural physical and mental fatigue.

Employee Motivation

Motivation A willingness to work hard because that effort satisfies an employee need.

Modern psychologists and behaviorists in the 1950s and 1960s eschewed the principles of scientific management, and they developed theories that proposed that in order to get employees to work productively and efficiently they must be motivated (as summarized in Table 8.1). **Motivation** is a willingness by an employee to work hard to achieve the company's goals because that effort satisfies some employee's need or objective. Thus, employee motivation is a key factor in achieving company goals such as product quality and creating a quality workplace. However, different things motivate employees. Obviously, financial compensation is a major motivating factor, but it is not the only one and may not be the most important. Other factors that motivate employees include self-actualization (such as integrity, responsibility, and naturalness), achievement and accomplishment, recognition, relationships with coworkers and supervisors, the type and degree of work supervision, job interest, trust and responsibility, and the opportunity for growth and advancement.

In general, job performance is a function of motivation combined with ability. Ability depends on education, experience, and training, and its improvement can follow a slow but clearly defined process. On the other hand, motivation can be improved more quickly, but there is no clear-cut process for motivating people. However, certain basic elements in job design and management have been shown to improve motivation, including

- positive reinforcement and feedback
- effective organization and discipline
- fair treatment of people
- satisfaction of employee needs
- setting of work-related goals
- design of jobs to fit the employee
- work responsibility
- empowerment
- restructuring of jobs when necessary
- rewards based on company as well as individual performance
- achievement of company goals

TABLE 8.1 Evolution of Theories of Employee Motivation

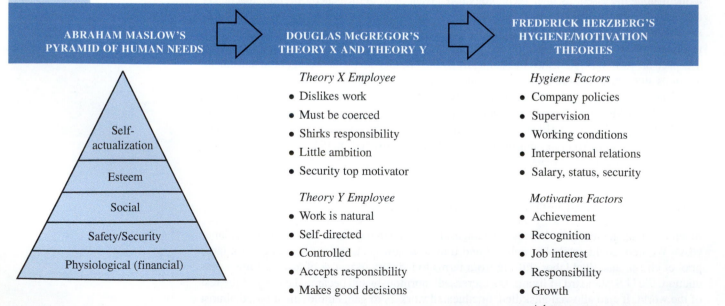

ABRAHAM MASLOW'S PYRAMID OF HUMAN NEEDS	DOUGLAS McGREGOR'S THEORY X AND THEORY Y	FREDERICK HERZBERG'S HYGIENE/MOTIVATION THEORIES
Self-actualization	*Theory X Employee*	*Hygiene Factors*
Esteem	• Dislikes work	• Company policies
Social	• Must be coerced	• Supervision
Safety/Security	• Shirks responsibility	• Working conditions
Physiological (financial)	• Little ambition	• Interpersonal relations
	• Security top motivator	• Salary, status, security
	Theory Y Employee	*Motivation Factors*
	• Work is natural	• Achievement
	• Self-directed	• Recognition
	• Controlled	• Job interest
	• Accepts responsibility	• Responsibility
	• Makes good decisions	• Growth
		• Advancement

Along the Supply Chain

Human Resources Management at Baldrige National Quality Award-Winning Companies

The Malcom Baldrige National Quality Award criteria include a set of basic principles for quality management; prominent among them is *employee satisfaction*. The "human resource focus" of a company is also an important award criteria. As a result, a common attribute among Baldrige Quality Award winners is their commitment to their employees and the resulting high level of employee satisfaction, which these companies monitor on a regular and continuing basis.

Baldrige Award winner Nestle Purina Petcare Company (NPPC), a St. Louis-based subsidiary of Nestle, S.A. with a workforce of approximately 7000, manufactures pet food and cat litter. The company has twice been named a "Number One Place to Work in St. Louis," based on employee surveys that includes categories such as trust, manager effectiveness, and job satisfaction. Its aggregate score was the benchmark for St. Louis businesses for three years running. NPPC has a commitment to hire and retain employees who love pets, are performance driven, and have a customer focus. NPPC assesses workforce engagement through external benchmark surveys, internal surveys, and focus groups. Absenteeism is consistently low, beating the national average by 65% to 75%.

The Pewaukee School District (outside Milwaukee), another Baldrige Award winner, was named one of Wisconsin's Top 100 Workplaces for two years running by the *Milwaukee Journal Sentinel*. The school district regularly surveys its staff and staff satisfaction is over 70% for salaries, 80% for benefits, 90% for engagement and involvement, and 98% for leadership—all metrics far exceeding national averages. Teachers are empowered to tailor classroom instruction to best serve the needs of each student.

The North Mississippi Health Service, a community-owned health service serving 24 rural counties in northeast Mississippi and northwest Alabama, has a workforce of 6400 employees and 490 physicians. Its employee retention rate has been at or above 90%, which exceeds the Bureau of Labor Statistics benchmark by 10%, and in surveys employees rate their job satisfaction as "best in class." Senior managers have created a culture that emphasizes "people first" as a critical success factor, which enables managers to build trust with employees, sustaining an empowered, accountable, and high performing workforce. Open communication is achieved through a "no secrets" culture and open door policy.

The City of Irving, Texas, located between Dallas and Fort Worth is the 13th most populous city in Texas with approximately 217,000 residents. Based on annual resident surveys Irving's overall rating for quality of service is 74%, approximately 25 points higher than ratings for the state, county, and U.S. governments. Employee surveys show that its employee ratings exceed the highest comparable scores achieved by a U.S. government agency. And 95% of Irving employees say the city is a good place to work.

K&N Management, an Austin, Texas, developer for Rudy's "Country Store" & Bar-B-Q and the creator of Mighty Fine Burgers, Fries and Shakes, two fast-casual restaurants, has been named "the best place to work in Austin" by the *Austin American-Statesman*. K&N's turnover rates among its workforce of 450 is less than 50% compared to the industry average of 85%, absenteeism is a little more than 1% compared to 5% for the best competitor. Over 95% of K&N team members indicate they are proud to work for the company.

These Baldrige Award–winning companies provide a benchmark for human resources management among companies committed to quality improvement and total quality management. They exhibit common human resource characteristics, including extensive job training, employee empowerment, incentive plans, rewards for good performance, teamwork, job flexibility, and close monitoring of employee satisfaction via annual surveys.

Go to the Baldrige Award Web site at www.quality.nist.gov and identify and discuss the different ways Baldrige Award winning companies assess employee satisfaction.

Source: Malcolm Baldrige National Quality Award website, http://www.nist.gov/baldrige/.

Contemporary Trends in Human Resource Management

During the last two decades of the twentieth century the competitive advantage gained by many Japanese companies in international markets, and especially in the automobile industry, caused U.S. firms to reevaluate their management practices vis-à-vis those of the Japanese. Human resource management is one area where there was a striking difference between Japanese and U.S. approaches and results. For example, in the 1980s one Japanese automobile company was able to assemble a car with half the blue-collar labor of a comparable U.S. auto company—about 14 hours in Japan, compared with 25 hours in the United States. Japan had not adopted the traditional Western approaches to work. Instead Japanese work allowed for more individual worker responsibility and less supervision, group work and interaction, higher worker skill levels, and training across a variety of tasks and jobs. There was initially a tendency among Americans to think that these characteristics were unique to the Japanese culture. However, the successes of U.S. companies such as Ford and Motorola in implementing quality-management programs, as well as successful Japanese companies operating in the United States, such as Nissan and Honda, showed that cultural factors were less important than management practices. As a result, certain contemporary trends in human resource management became the norm for successful companies in the United States and abroad.

Job Training

In companies with a commitment to quality, job training is extensive and varied. Expectations for performance and advancement from both the employee and management tend to be high. Typically, numerous courses are available for training in different jobs and functions. Job training is considered part of a structured career-development system that includes cross training and job rotation. This system of training and job rotation enhances the flexibility of the production process we mentioned earlier. It creates talent reserves that can be used as the need arises when products or processes change or the workforce is reduced.

Training is a major feature of all companies with quality management programs. Two of W. E. Deming's 14 points (See chapter 2, Table 2.2., page 61) refer to employee education and training. All Baldrige National Quality Award winners cite extensive job training programs as a key factor in their success.

Cross Training

Cross training An employee learns more than one job.

In **cross training** an employee learns more than one job in the company. Cross training has a number of attractive features that make it beneficial to the company and the employee. For the company it provides a safety measure with more job coverage in the event of employee resignations and absenteeism and sudden increases in a particular job activity. Employees are given more knowledge and variety so that they won't get as easily bored, they will find more value in what they do, and their interest level in the company will increase. Because of their increased knowledge, they will have the opportunity to move to other jobs within the company without leaving. Employees will respect each other because they will be more familiar with each other's jobs. However, cross training requires a significant investment in time and money, so the company should be committed to its implementation and sure of the benefits it hopes to realize from cross training.

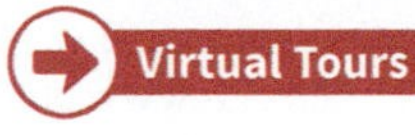

Job rotation The horizontal movement between two or more jobs according to a plan.

Job rotation is not exactly the same as cross training. Cross training gives an employee the ability to move between jobs if needed. Job rotation requires cross training, but it also includes the horizontal movement between two or more jobs according to a plan or schedule. This not only creates a flexible employee, but it also reduces boredom and increases employee interest.

Job Enrichment

The objective of job enrichment is to create more opportunities for individual achievement and recognition by adding variety, responsibility, and accountability to the job. This can also lead to greater worker autonomy, increased task identity, and greater direct contact with other workers. Frederick Herzberg (Table 8.1) developed the following set of principles for job enrichment:

Vertical job enlargement Allows employees control over their work.

Horizontal job enlargement An employee is assigned a complete unit of work with defined start and end.

- Allow employees control over their own work and some of the supervisory responsibilities for the job, while retaining accountability, also called **vertical job enlargement**.
- Assign each worker a complete unit of work that includes all the tasks necessary to complete a process or product with clearly defined start and end points so that the employee feels a sense of closure and achievement. This is also called **horizontal job enlargement**.
- Provide additional authority and freedom for employees.
- Make periodic reports available to workers instead of just supervisors.
- Introduce new and more difficult tasks into the job.
- Encourage development of expertise by assigning individuals to specialized tasks.

Empowerment

Empowerment Giving employees authority to make decisions.

Empowerment is giving employees responsibility and authority to make decisions. For quality management programs to work, it is generally conceded that employees must be empowered so that they are willing to innovate and act on their own in an atmosphere of trust and respect. Five of W. E. Deming's 14 points for quality improvement relate to employee empowerment. Empowerment requires employee education and training, and participation in goal setting. The advantages of empowerment include more attention to product quality and the ability to fix quality problems quickly, increased respect and trust among employees, lower absenteeism and higher productivity, more satisfying work, less conflict with management, and fewer middle managers. However, empowerment can also have some negative aspects. Employees may abuse the power given to them; empowerment may provide too much responsibility for some employees; it may create conflicts with middle management; it will require additional training for employees and managers that can be costly; group work, which often is an integral part of empowerment, can be time-consuming; and some employees may not make good decisions.

A Motorola sales representative is empowered to replace a customer's defective product up to six years after its purchase. GM plant employees can call in suppliers to help them solve problems. FedEx employees are empowered to do whatever it takes to ensure 100% customer satisfaction. The authority of employees to halt an entire production operation or line on their own initiative if they discover a quality problem is well documented at companies like AT&T. A Ritz-Carlton "lady or gentleman" can spend up to $2000 without approval to immediately solve a guest's problem.

Teams

Empowerment and employee involvement are often realized through work groups or teams. Quality circles, discussed in Chapter 2 ("Quality Management"), in which a group of 8 to 10 employees plus their supervisor work on problems in their immediate work area, is a well-known example of a team approach. Teams can differ according to their purpose, level of responsibility, and longevity. Some teams are established to work on a specific problem and then disband; others are more long-term, formed to monitor a work area or process for continual improvement. Most teams are not totally democratic and have some supervisory oversight, although some have more authority than others. Quality circles typically have a supervisor in charge. In general, for teams to be effective, they must know what their purpose and roles are relative to the company's goals, as well as the extent of their empowerment, have the skills and training necessary to achieve their goals, and possess the ability to work together as a team.

Self-directed teams, though not totally independent, are usually empowered to make decisions and changes relative to the processes in their own work area. This degree of responsibility is based on trust and management's belief that the people who are closest to a work process know how to make it work best. Team members tend to feel more responsibility to make their solutions work, and companies typically reward teams for performance improvement.

Self-directed teams generally require more training to work together as a team; however, benefits include less managerial control (and fewer managers), quicker identification and solution of problems, more job satisfaction, positive peer pressure, and a feeling of "not wanting to let the team down" common to sports teams and military groups. On the other hand, such teams can have some negative aspects. Supervisors and managers may have difficulty adjusting to their changed role in which they monitor and oversee rather than direct work. Also, conflict among team members can hinder a team's effectiveness.

Flexible Work Schedules

Flextime Part of a daily work schedule in which employees can choose time of arrival and departure.

Flexible work schedules or **flextime** are becoming an increasingly important workplace format. It refers to a variety of arrangements in which fixed times of arrival and departure are replaced by a combination of "core" or fixed time and flexible time. Core time is the designated period during which all employees are present, say 9:00 A.M. to 2:30 P.M. Flexible time is part of the

Along the Supply Chain

Creating Sustainable Workplaces

Sustainability, the ability for a company to make a profit without sacrificing the resources of its people, the community, and the planet, is a movement that is gaining momentum throughout the workplace. Moreover, it is increasingly seen as having a positive impact on a business's bottom line, and as a factor in achieving its strategic goals. Widely adopted "green" practices include recycling of office products; energy-efficient equipment such as lighting systems that use occupancy sensors; laptops instead of desktops; automatic shutoffs for equipment; developing green "habits" of turning off lights when leaving a room, and not adjusting thermostats too high or too low; using recycled or refurbished supplies such as toner cartridges and printers; promoting alternative transportation like walking and biking, and public transportation; partnering with environmentally friendly suppliers; minimizing pollution during production processes; and participating in community "green" projects and events. Besides promoting sustainability, most of these activities also result in cost savings.

Telecommuting has become an effective "green" activity since it reduces employee travel, thereby reducing gasoline consumption and reducing carbon emissions. Studies show that the over 3 million U.S. employees who telecommute save almost 400 million gallons of gas and prevent the release of 3.6 million tons of greenhouse gases each year. If all 60 million U.S. employees who hold telework-compatible jobs and who want to work at home were allowed to, it would save $900 billion annually and reduce our Persian Gulf imports by over 45%. The energy saved annually would exceed the output of all renewable energy sources combined. Replacing employee travel with videoconferencing reduces airplane fuel consumption and carbon emissions, as well as saving airline travel costs. Over 60% of U.S. companies offer some degree of telecommuting to employees, and about 10% of U.S. workers—over 13 million—work from home at least some of the time. More than 25% of IBM's almost 400,000 global employees participate in some form of telecommuting; 11% of Xerox's U.S. employees work remotely 100% of the time and many thousands more have telecommuting options available; 43% of Aetna's 48,000 employees telecommute in some form; 20% of Dell's 100,000 employees telecommute. Over 3% of federal government employees work from home, which is more workers than in any other job sector.

Building energy-efficient buildings using solar paneling, radiant heat, and lots of windows saves energy while reducing costs. Going green is also an effective employee recruitment and retention tool for companies. According to various surveys, U.S. employees, especially younger workers, overwhelmingly (i.e., 80% to 90%) prefer to work in a "green" workplace with a company that is environmentally friendly. Companies have discovered that promoting "green" in the workplace creates a sense of achievement and pride among employees that translates to their jobs and operations. Extending quality improvement initiatives beyond just a company's functional processes to the workplace and environment is both good citizenship and good business.

Discuss some reasons a company might not want to participate in sustainable or green activities in the workplace.

Source: Based on A. Fox, "Get in the Business of Being Green," *HR Magazine* 53 (6; June 2008), pp. 45–50; K. Lister and T. Harnish, "The State of Telework in the U.S.," *Telework Research Network* (June 2011), www.workshifting.com.

daily work schedule where employees can choose their time of arrival and departure. In some cases, an employee may bank or credit hours—that is, work more hours one day and bank those hours in order to take a shorter work day in the future. In other cases, an employee may vary work days during the week, for example, work four 10-hour days followed by a three-day weekend. While flextime helps the company attract and retain employees and promotes job satisfaction, it can make it difficult to compensate for sudden changes in the workload or problems that can arise that require quick reactions.

Alternative Workplaces and Telecommuting

Alternative workplace A nontraditional work location.

An **alternative workplace** is a combination of nontraditional work locations, settings, and practices that supplements or replaces the traditional office. An alternative workplace can be a home office, a satellite office, a shared office, a shared desk or an open workspace where many employees work side by side. Another form of alternative workplace is telecommuting, performing work electronically wherever the worker chooses.

The motivation for companies to create alternative workplaces is primarily financial. Eliminating physical office space—that is, real estate—and reducing related overhead costs can result in significant cost reductions. In one five-year period, IBM realized $1 billion in real estate savings alone by equipping and training 17% of its worldwide workforce to work in alternative workplaces. Alternative workplaces can increase productivity by relieving employees of typical time-consuming office routines, allowing them more time to devote to customers. They can also help companies recruit and retain talented, motivated employees who

© Mark Baigent Lifestyle/Alamy

Telecommuting, where employees work from home or some other alternative location, is becoming increasingly popular. It has been shown to increase productivity and job satisfaction and reduce facility costs.

find the flexibility of telecommuting or a home office very attractive. Eliminating commuting time to a remote office can save employees substantial work time. Customer satisfaction can also increase as customers find it easier to contact employees and receive more personalized attention.

In general, companies that use alternative workplaces employ a mix of different formats and tailor the workplace to fit specific company needs. There are also costs associated with establishing alternative workplace formats, including training, hardware and software, networks, phone charges, technical support, and equipment, although these costs are usually less than real estate costs, which are ever-increasing. Of course, alternative workplaces are not feasible for some companies, such as manufacturing companies, which require employees to be located at specific workstations, facilities, or stationary equipment or which require direct management supervision. Employees who work on an assembly line or in a hotel are not candidates for an alternative workplace. Alternative workplaces are more appropriate for companies that are informational—that is, they operate through voice and data communication between their employees and their customers.

Telecommuting Employees work electronically from a location they choose.

One of the more increasingly common new alternative workplace formats is **telecommuting**, also referred to as "telework," and a "virtual workplace," in which employees work electronically from whatever location they choose, either exclusively or some of the time, as shown in photo. It is estimated that about 40% of U.S. companies offer some form of telecommuting to employees. Companies that use telecommuting sites experience such benefits as lower real estate costs, reduced turnover, decreased absenteeism and leave usage, increased productivity, and increased ability to comply with federal workplace laws such as the Americans with Disabilities Act. IBM, one of the first and most visible companies to promote telecommuting, estimates that in one year in the United States alone, its telecommuting program conserves approximately 6 million gallons of fuel and avoids over 50,000 metric tons of CO_2 emissions. Sun Microsystems estimates its telecommuting program saves it $2.5 million in electricity bills annually, and its employees who telecommute average annual commuting savings of over $2300.

It has been estimated that through telecommuting, absenteeism can be reduced by as much as 25%. For employees, telecommuting eliminates commuting time and travel costs, allows for a more flexible work schedule, and allows them to blend work with family and personal responsibilities. Some companies that offer telecommuting indicate productivity increases 10% to 20% and job satisfaction also increases, which can result in a higher employee retention rate.

Telecommuting also has negative aspects. It may negatively affect the relationship between employees and their immediate supervisors. Supervisors and middle managers may feel uncomfortable not having employees under direct visual surveillance. Furthermore, they may feel that they do not have control and authority over their employees if they are not physically present. In fact, some employees may not be well suited for telecommuting; they may not be self-motivated and may require more direct supervision and external motivation. The technology that allows employees to work anywhere, anytime, can also lead to employees who cannot "disconnect" from their jobs. Studies show that the biggest barrier to telecommuting is management fear and mistrust. Some companies that previously allowed telecommunicating, most prominently Yahoo, have recently backed away from it.

Temporary and Part-Time Employees

A trend among service companies in particular is the use of temporary, or *contingent*, employees. Part-time employees have accounted for over 40% of job growth in the retail industry during the last two decades. Fast-food and restaurant chains, retail companies, package delivery services, and financial firms tend to use a large number of temporary employees. Companies that have seasonal demand make extensive use of temporary employees. L.L. Bean needs a lot more telephone service operators and UPS needs many more package sorters in the weeks before Christmas. Sometimes a company will undertake a project requiring technical expertise its permanent employees do not have. Instead of reassigning or retraining its employees, the company will bring in temporary employees having the necessary expertise. Some firms *lease* people for jobs, especially for computer services. As companies downsize to cut costs, they turn to temporary employees to fill temporary needs without adding to their long-term cost base. People with computer skills able to work from home have also increased the pool of available temporary workers.

Unfortunately, temporary employees do not always have the commitment to goals for quality and service that a company might want. Companies dependent on temporary employees may not only suffer the inconsistent levels of their work ethic and skills, they may also sacrifice productivity for lower costs. To offset this possible inconsistency and to protect product and service quality, firms sometimes try to hire temporary employees only into isolated work areas away from their core businesses that most directly affect quality.

Part-time employment is a key aspect at some companies like UPS, which hires more than 95,000 part-time, seasonal employees; however part-time employment does not always have positive results. As part of a retooling plan at Home Depot, an attempt was made to change the sales floor staff mix from 30% part-time to 50% in order to cut costs and gain flexibility to cover busy times of the day. The plan was abandoned after customers complained about bad service and full-time employees complained about the part-timers' lack of commitment. It also violated the perception among employees that Home Depot was a place where someone could build a career.

Employee Compensation

Good human resource management practices or motivation factors cannot compensate for insufficient monetary rewards. If the reward is perceived as good, other things will motivate employees to give their best performance. Self-motivation can go only so far—it must be reinforced by financial rewards. Merit must be measured and rewarded regularly; otherwise performance levels will not be sustained.

The two traditional forms of employee payment are the hourly wage and the individual incentive, or piece-rate, wage, both of which are tied to time. The hourly wage is self-explanatory; the longer someone works, the more he or she is paid. In a piece-rate system, employees are paid for the number of units they produce during the workday. The faster the employee performs, the more output generated and the greater the pay. These two forms of payment are also frequently combined with a guaranteed base hourly wage and additional incentive piece-rate payments based on the number of units produced above a standard hourly rate of output. Other basic forms of compensation include straight salary, the most common form of payment for management, and commissions, a payment system usually applied to sales and salespeople.

An individual piece-rate system provides incentive to increase output, but it does not ensure high quality. It can do just the opposite! In an effort to produce as much as possible, the worker will become sloppy, take shortcuts, and pay less attention to detail. As a result, some quality-focused companies have tried to move away from individual wage incentive systems based on output and time. There has been a trend toward other measures of performance, such as quality, productivity, cost reduction, and the achievement of organizational goals. These systems usually combine an hourly base payment or even a salary with some form of incentive payment. However, incentives are not always individual but are tied to group, team, or company performance.

Gainsharing is an incentive plan that includes employees in a common effort to achieve a company's objectives in which they share in the gains. Although gainsharing systems vary broadly, they all generally include some type of financial measurement and frequent feedback system to monitor company performance and distribute gains periodically in the form of bonuses. **Profit sharing** sets aside some portion of company profits and distributes it among employees, usually at the end of the fiscal year. The objective behind both incentive programs is to create a sense among employees that it is in their self-interest for the company to do well: the company wants employees to buy into the company's financial goals.

Gainsharing An incentive plan joins employees in a common effort to achieve company goals, who share in gain.

Profit sharing Sets aside a portion of profits for employees at year's end.

Both programs have been shown to result in an increase in employee productivity; however, gainsharing is different from profit sharing in several ways. Gainsharing programs provide frequent payouts or bonuses, sometimes weekly or monthly, while profit-sharing bonuses are awarded once a year. Thus, gainsharing provides a more frequent reinforcement of good performance for the average employee. It is also generally easier for average employees to see results of gainsharing than profit sharing. Gainsharing focuses more on performance measures that are directly linked to the performance of employees or groups of employees than does profit sharing. Gainsharing spells out clearly what employees need to do to achieve a short-term goal and what will happen when they do achieve it. Profit sharing does not have the same emphasis on specifically what needs to happen to achieve short-term (weekly or monthly) goals. For these reasons, profit sharing is typically an incentive program that is more applicable to higher level employees and executives.

Managing Diversity in the Workplace

Diversity in U.S. companies has been a critical management issue for several decades. However, as more and more companies move into the global marketplace, diversity has become an even more pervasive factor in human resource management around the world. The spread of global business combined with the geographic mobility of employees has resulted in companies with a more diverse workforce than ever before. U.S. companies outsource business activities and operate facilities and businesses overseas with a mix of foreign and U.S. management teams and employees, and foreign companies operate plants and businesses in the United States with similar mixes. Almost 40% of the U.S. workforce is considered diverse (i.e., people who differ from the majority of the workforce by race, gender, age, ethnicity, etc.). Today, 16% of the workforce is Hispanic and by 2050 that figure is expected to be over 30%. Women make up almost half of the U.S. workforce and by 2020 the number of women in the workforce is expected to exceed the number of men. Over 6% of the workforce is considered gay or transgender.

In order to be successful with a diverse workforce, companies must provide a climate in which all employees feel comfortable, can do their job, feel like they are valued by the organization, and perceive that they are treated fairly. However, inequalities too often exist for employees because of race, gender, religion, cultural origin, age, and physical or mental limitations. The elimination of racism, sexism, cultural indifference, and religious intolerance cannot be mandated by higher management or managed by financial incentives. Companies as a whole, starting with top management, must develop a strategic approach to managing diversity in order to meet the challenges posed by a diverse workforce.

Affirmative Action and Equal Opportunity

In the United States affirmative action and equal opportunity are sometimes confused with managing diversity, but they are not the same thing. Affirmative action is an outgrowth

Along the Supply Chain

English in the Workplace

In the United States, foreign-born workers make up over 16% of the workforce, and this percentage is predicted to increase as U.S.-born workers decrease and immigration increases. Hispanics currently constitute about 15% of the population, and by 2050 this percentage is expected to double. As a result, there has been a growing diversity of languages in the workplace, and increasingly employers must rely on the non-English-speaking labor force to fill jobs. However, while foreign-born workers can get a job, they typically need English proficiency to advance, and low-wage companies like construction, hotels, and restaurants have discovered that non-English employees can hurt business. As a result, many companies have instituted their own in-house English language training programs as a competitive necessity.

English language programs can have many profitable benefits for employees and employers, including improving compliance with safety policies, boosting worker productivity (by improving comprehension), ensuring employees understand pay and benefits, improving customer service, preventing errors and waste, enhancing communication between workers and managers, and improving recruitment and retention While some companies invest in their own English training programs, others work out arrangements with teaching institutions. For example, Marriott International has invested $500 million in portable, computerized recording devices to help Spanish-speaking workers learn English at home. McDonald's "English Under the Arches" is an English-language learning program specifically designed for McDonald's managers and management trainees to help them advance in their careers at McDonald's. Individual franchise owners select managers and trainees to participate, pay their tuition, and provide paid work time for employees to attend classes, mostly in a virtual classroom setting. Over 90% of participants complete the 50 weeks of course work, and over 70% of participants were still working for McDonald's four years after completing the program. However, despite the growing recognition of the need for English language training in the workplace, employer-provided training is still the exception, resulting in a number of legal issues for companies that seek to resolve the problem by only hiring workers who speak English. This would seem to be an untenable solution for the long run given the growing non-English-speaking workforce.

Source: Based on R. Zeidner, "One Workforce—Many Languages," *HR Magazine* 54 (1: January 2009), p. 37.

of laws and regulations and is government initiated and mandated. It contains goals and timetables designed to increase the level of participation by women and minorities to attain parity levels in a company's workforce. Affirmative action is not directly concerned with increasing company success or increasing profits. On the other hand, managing diversity is the process of creating a work environment in which all employees can contribute to their full potential in order to achieve a company's goals. It is voluntary in nature, not mandated. It seeks to improve internal communications and interpersonal relationships, resolve conflict, and in doing so increase product quality, productivity, and efficiency. Managing diversity is creating an environment where everyone works in concert to do the best job possible. Whereas affirmative action has a short-term result, managing diversity is a long-term process. The objective of managing diversity is to find a way to let everyone do their best so that the company can gain a competitive edge.

Although affirmative action and diversity management are not the same thing, they are not independent of each other. A company that successfully manages diversity and implements successful programs that eliminate diversity issues and discrimination will also eliminate costly affirmative action liability and government mandates.

Diversity Management Programs

Managing diversity Includes education, awareness, communication, fairness, and commitment.

Although there is no magic formula for successfully **managing diversity**, education, awareness, communication, fairness, and commitment are critical elements in the process. We have explained on several occasions that employee training is an essential element in achieving product quality; the same holds true for creating a quality work environment for a diverse workforce. Prejudice feeds on ignorance. Employees must be educated about racial, gender, religious, and ethnic differences; they must be made aware of what it is like to be someone who is different from themselves. This also requires that lines of communication be open between different groups, and between employees and management. Most importantly, successful diversity management requires a commitment from top management. Although top management cannot mandate that the workplace be diversity friendly, strong leadership can successfully influence it.

A company's diversity initiatives can help them to maintain a competitive advantage by improving corporate culture, improving employee morale, decreasing interpersonal conflict

Along the Supply Chain

A Commitment to a Sustainable Workplace at Hershey's

Hershey's is committed to a diverse and all-inclusive workforce. Hershey has a Corporate Social Responsibility (CSR) Department, which is directed by the Vice President of Corporate Communications and CSR, who reports directly to the company's Board of Directors. The company provides a variety of opportunities for its employees to learn and grow in the work environment and the community. Hershey's sponsors Business Resource Groups (BRGs) for women (who make up half of Hershey's North American workforce), Latinos, veterans, Asians and African Americans. Other BRGs include "Abilities First" for educating and informing about people with disabilities as valued members of the workplace and community; and "Prism," a resource for gay, lesbian, bisexual, and transgender employees, that seeks to improve the quality of the work environment for all of Hershey's employees.

Hershey's also holds an annual companywide Inclusion Day celebrating the diversity of local communities. "Lunch and Learn" speakers discuss such topics as new immigrant experiences and personal empowerment for women and minorities. An in-depth company website provides employees with information about an array of diversity subjects. Diversity email newsletters educate employees on specific aspects of diversity and educate them about why these differences are important to Hershey.

Hershey's Supplier Code of Conduct outlines policies that express zero tolerance for abusive child labor practices including keeping children from school to work on farms, carrying heavy loads, exposure to chemicals, and trafficking of children or forcing children to work. All of these efforts at Hershey's are aimed at helping the company realize its vision of "Great People Building Great Brands."

Investigate and discuss how your college or university achieves and supports diversity among its employees, including faculty and staff, and whether or not you think it is effective and successful.

Source: The Hershey Company website at www.thehersheycompany.com.

among employees, and increasing creativity and productivity, as well as improving employee recruitment and customer relations.

Many companies have discovered that a diverse workforce is no longer just a legally or culturally mandated requirement, but a beneficial aspect of their corporate culture that can have a bottom-line impact. At Frito-Lay, the snack food division of PepsiCo, the Latino Employee Network (called Adelante) played a major role in the development of Doritos Guacamole Flavored Tortilla Chips. Members of the network provided feedback on taste and packaging that ensured that the new product would be regarded as authentic. This helped make the new Doritos one of the most successful product launches in the company's history, with more than $100 million in sales in its first year. Aetna has discovered that it is critical for their employees to literally speak the language of their customers, making multilingual employees invaluable. Aetna often targets its recruiting efforts to identify individuals who can speak more than one language for specific functional segments in the company. Aetna, like many companies, has also found that diversity can impact community involvement and thus their marketplace. By supporting diversity-related community programs, Aetna enhances its presence and brand reputation in key markets, resulting in more business opportunities.

The most common diversity initiatives and programs are recruiting efforts designed to increase diversity; diversity training; education and awareness programs; and community outreach. However, these initiatives can be time consuming, costly, and sometimes generate false hopes.

One approach being used by a number of companies is to create groups or networks that enable employees with diverse backgrounds to interact with one another. Kodak has a number of diversity groups, including a Women's Forum and a gay-employees network, which collaborate on different workplace issues. Many employees belong to multiple groups and learn about each others' issues and concerns, which helps develop sensitivity and mutual respect. Unisys and AT&T have resource groups for disabled employees that allow them to provide suggestions for designing products to make them more accessible to people with disabilities. Other diversity initiatives that have shown success within companies include internships, mentoring programs, career management programs, and skill enhancement programs.

Global Workforce Diversity and Sustainability Issues

Trends toward the globalization of companies, the use of global teams within and across companies, and global outsourcing have resulted in unique diversity issues. Cultural and language

These Chinese workers are sewing jeans in a garment factory in Shenzhen, one of mainland China's "Special Economic Zones," which provide more flexible government economic policies including tax incentives for foreign investments, emphasis on joint sino-foreign ventures, greater independence for international trade activities, and export-oriented products.

differences and geography are significant barriers to managing a globally diverse workforce. Emails, faxes, the Internet, phones, and air travel make managing a global workforce possible but not necessarily effective.

In the case of culturally diverse groups, differences may be more subtle, and defined diversity programs may be less effective in dealing with them. Some nationalities and cultures have a more relaxed view of time than, say, Americans or Europeans; deadlines are less important. In some cultures, religious and national holidays have more significance than in others. Americans will frequently work at home in the evening, stay late at work, or work over the weekend or on vacations, and on the average take less vacation time than employees in most European countries; in many foreign countries such behavior is unheard of. Some cultures seem to have their own rules of communication. An employee in a foreign country, for example, may politely nod yes in response to a question from a U.S. manager as a polite face-saving gesture, when in fact it's not an indication of agreement at all.

Such cultural differences require unique forms of diversity management. Managers cannot interpret their employees' behavior through their own cultural background. It is important to identify critical cultural elements such as important holidays and a culturally acceptable work schedule, and to learn the informal rules of communication that may exist in a foreign culture among a diverse group of employees. It is often helpful to use a third party who is better able to bridge the cultural gap as a go-between. A manager who is culturally aware, and most importantly, speaks the language, is less likely to incorrectly interpret the behavior of diverse employees. Similarly, it is beneficial to teach employees the cultural norms for the organization so that they understand all the rules.

As a result of increased media attention, social networking, and Internet websites related to sustainability and social issues, there is an increased awareness of the plight of workers around the world, whose working conditions and treatment are generally perceived to be below acceptable norms. This has led to demands for major global companies (especially U.S. companies) to take responsibility for the condition of workers of the companies that they do business with in their extended supply chains (see photo). A number of high profile, socially conscious companies such as Walmart and Target have developed detailed employee standards with formal documentation, manuals, and audits that their suppliers are required to agree to, or not do business with these companies. These standards address working conditions related to areas such as compliance with local laws and regulations, voluntary labor, working hours, hiring practices, fair compensation, union organization and collective bargaining, health and safety, sanitation, living conditions, environmental laws, and corruption.

Job Design

In the preceding sections we have discussed how to motivate employees to perform well in their jobs. A key element in employee motivation and job performance is to make sure the

Along the Supply Chain

Target's Workplace Sustainability Standards for Its Global Suppliers' Employees

Target, a *Fortune 500* company headquartered in Minneapolis, Minnesota, is one of the largest and most well-known retail chains in the United States with over 1900 stores in 49 states and over 365,000 employees. For its hard good (nonfabric) products, such as toys, furniture, electronics, sporting goods, and kitchen goods, Target works with over 3200 factories around the world. When a factory joins the Target supply chain it is required to sign a "standards of supplier engagement" agreement that clearly spells out Target's requirements for employee treatment, which are nonnegotiable, and are the most important part of Target's partnering relationship with its suppliers. These requirements protect the Target brand by ensuring that its products are produced ethically and in accordance with its Standards of Vendor Engagement (SOVE), its Vendor Conduct Guide, and local laws. SOVE explicitly indicates that Target will not work with any company that does not comply with its ethical standards. Target's global business partners must provide safe and healthy workplaces that comply with local laws. If they provide residential facilities for their workers, they must be safe, healthy, and in compliance with local standards. There can be no forced or compulsory labor, no physical or mental punishment against employees, and no child (below age 14) labor.

While Target respects cultural differences, it believes workers should be employed based on their abilities, and suppliers are encouraged to eliminate workplace discrimination based on race, gender, personal characteristics, or beliefs. Suppliers should offer reasonable working hours and overtime, and workweeks should not exceed local laws or business customs. Target encourages its partners not to require more than a 60-hour workweek on a regularly scheduled basis (except for overtime compensated in compliance with local laws). Fair wages and benefits must be provided in compliance with local laws; in addition, partners are encouraged to improve wages and benefits to address the basic needs of workers and their families. Target requires its vendors to warrant that all goods are made in compliance with all applicable laws—both U.S. laws and the laws of the country in which the goods are produced, including the Fair Labor Standards Act of 1938, which governs how employers pay and treat their employees. Target has similar basic minimum requirements in countries where labor laws are not yet well developed. Target's vendor contracts authorize it to conduct unannounced social compliance audits at any time, which factories and suppliers must pass to continue as part of Target's supply chain. Each year Target's auditors conduct random, unannounced, mandatory social compliance audits at supplier factories and noncompliant factories are terminated.

Target has been a leader in creating a "sustainable" work environment for workers within its global supply chain. Identify other companies that have also been proactive in dealing with worker sustainability among their global suppliers.

Sources: Based on William H. Murphy, "Bull's Eye: An Inside Look at How Target Ensures Quality in a Complex Supply Chain," *Quality Progress* (June 2010), pp. 22–29; and the Target website at www.target.com.

employee is well suited for a job and vice versa. If a job is not designed properly and it is not a good fit for the employee, then it will not be performed well. Frederick Herzberg identified several attributes of good job design, as follows:

- An appropriate degree of repetitiveness
- An appropriate degree of attention and mental absorption
- Some employee responsibility for decisions and discretion
- Employee control over their own job
- Goals and achievement feedback
- A perceived contribution to a useful product or service
- Opportunities for personal relationships and friendships
- Some influence over the way work is carried out in groups
- Use of skills

In this section we will focus on the factors that must be considered in job design—the things that must be considered to create jobs with the attributes listed above.

The Elements of Job Design

The elements of job design fall into three categories: an analysis of the tasks included in the job, employee requirements, and the environment in which the job takes place. These categories address the questions of how the job is performed, who does it, and where it is done. Table 8.2 summarizes a selection of individual elements that would generally be considered in the job design process.

TABLE 8.2 Elements of Job Design

TASK ANALYSIS	WORKER ANALYSIS	ENVIRONMENTAL ANALYSIS
• Description of tasks to be performed	• Capability requirements	• Workplace location
• Task sequence	• Performance requirements	• Process location
• Function of tasks	• Evaluation	• Temperature and humidity
• Frequency of tasks	• Skill level	• Lighting
• Criticality of tasks	• Job training	• Ventilation
• Relationship with other jobs/tasks	• Physical requirements	• Safety
• Performance requirements	• Mental stress	• Logistics
• Information requirements	• Boredom	• Space requirements
• Control requirements	• Motivation	• Noise
• Error possibilities	• Number of workers	• Vibration
• Task duration(s)	• Level of responsibility	
• Equipment requirements	• Monitoring level	
	• Quality responsibility	
	• Empowerment level	

Task Analysis

Task analysis determines how to do each task and how all the tasks fit together to form a job. It includes defining the individual tasks and determining their most efficient sequence, their duration, their relationship with other tasks, and their frequency. Task analysis should be sufficiently detailed so that it results in a step-by-step procedure for the job. The sequence of tasks in some jobs is a logical ordering; for example, the wedges of material used in making a baseball cap must be cut before they can be sewn together, and they must all be sewn together before the cap bill can be attached. The *performance requirements of a task* can be the time required to complete the task, the accuracy in performing the task to specifications, the output level or productivity yield, or quality performance. The performance of some tasks requires information such as a measurement (cutting furniture pieces), temperature (food processing), weight (filling bags of fertilizer), or a litmus test (for a chemical process).

Worker Analysis

Worker analysis determines the characteristics the worker must possess to meet the job requirements, the responsibilities the worker will have in the job, and how the worker will be rewarded. Some jobs require manual labor and physical strength, whereas others require none. Physical requirements are assessed not only to make sure the right worker is placed in a job but also to determine if the physical requirements are excessive, necessitating redesign. The same type of design questions must be addressed for mental stress.

Environmental Analysis

Environmental analysis refers to the physical location of the job in the production or service facility and the environmental conditions that must exist. These conditions include things such as proper temperature, lighting, ventilation, and noise. The production of microchips requires an extremely clean, climatically controlled, enclosed environment. Detail work, such as engraving or sewing, requires proper lighting; some jobs that create dust levels, such as lint in textile operations, require proper ventilation. Some jobs require a large amount of space around the immediate job area.

Ergonomics

Put simply, **ergonomics** as it is applied to work is fitting the task to the person. It deals with the interaction of work, technology, and humans. Ergonomics applies human sciences like anatomy, physiology, and psychology to the design of the work environment and jobs, and objects and equipment used in work. The objective of ergonomics is to make the best use of employees' capabilities while maintaining the employees' health and well-being. The job should never limit the employee or compromise an employee's capabilities or physical and mental health because of poor job design. Good ergonomics shortens learning times; makes the job easier with less fatigue; improves equipment maintenance; reduces absenteeism, labor turnover, and job stress and injury; and meets legislative requirements for health and safety. In order to achieve these objectives, the job activity must be carefully analyzed, and the demands placed on the employee must be understood.

Ergonomics Fitting the task to the person in a work environment.

The contribution of anatomy in ergonomics is the improvement of the physical aspect of the job: achieving a good physical fit between the employee and the things the employee uses on the job, whether it's a hand tool, a computer, a video camera, a forklift, or a lathe. Physiology is concerned with how the body functions. It addresses the energy required from the employee to do the job as well as the acceptable workload and work rate and the physical working conditions—heat, cold, light, noise, vibration, and space. Psychology is concerned with the human mind. Its objective is to create a good psychological fit between the employee and the job.

Technology and Automation

The worker-machine interface is possibly the most crucial aspect of job design, both in manufacturing industries and in service companies where workers interface with computers. New

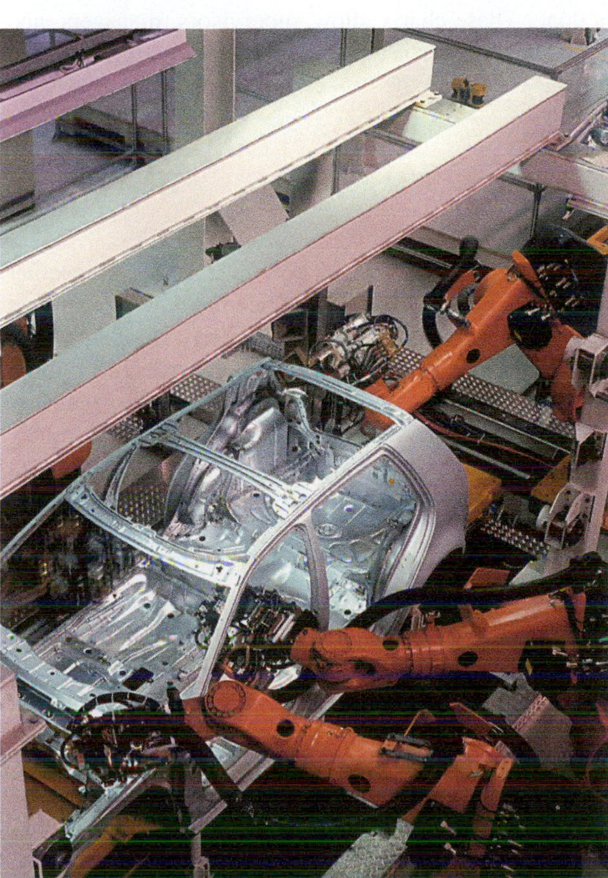

RicAguiar/iStockphoto

Robots do not necessarily perform a job faster than humans, but they can tolerate hostile environments, work longer hours, and do a job more consistently. Robots are used for a wide range of manufacturing jobs, including material handling, machining, assembly, and inspection.

technologies have increased the educational requirements and need for employee training. The development of computer technology and systems has heightened the need for workers with better skills and more job training.

There has been a substantial investment in new plants and equipment in the United States to compete globally. Companies have developed and installed a new generation of automated equipment and robotics that enhanced their abilities to achieve higher output and lower costs, for example, see the photo of the robots. This new equipment also reduced the manual labor necessary to perform jobs and improved safety. Computer systems provided workers with an expanded array of information that increased their ability to identify and locate problems in the production process and monitor product quality. New job designs and redesigns of existing jobs were required that reflected these new technologies.

Job Analysis

Part of job design is to study the *methods* used in the work included in the job to see how it should be done. This has traditionally been referred to as *methods analysis*, or simply *work methods*.

Methods analysis is used to redesign or improve existing jobs. An analyst will study an existing job to determine if the work is being done in the most efficient manner possible; if all the present tasks are necessary; or if new tasks should be added. The analyst might also want to see how the job fits in with other jobs—that is, how well a job is integrated into the overall production process or a sequence of jobs. The development and installation of new machinery or equipment, new products or product changes, and changes in quality standards can all require that a job be analyzed for redesign.

Methods analysis is also used to develop new jobs. In this case, the analyst must work with a description or outline of a proposed job and attempt to develop a mental picture of how the job will be performed.

The primary tools of methods analysis are a variety of charts that illustrate in different ways how a job or a work process is done. These charts allow supervisors, managers, and workers to see how a job is accomplished and to get their input and feedback on the design or redesign process. Two of the more popular charts are the *process flowchart* and the *worker-machine chart*.

Process Flowchart

Process flowchart A graph of the steps of a job.

A **process flowchart** is used to analyze how the steps of a job or how a set of jobs fit together into the overall flow of the production process. Examples might include the flow of a product through a manufacturing assembly process, the making of a pizza, the activities of a surgical team in an operating room, or the processing of a catalog mail or telephone order.

A process flowchart uses some basic symbols shown in Figure 8.1 to describe the tasks or steps in a job or a series of jobs. The symbols are connected by lines on the chart to show the flow of the process.

FIGURE 8.1 Symbols for a Process Flowchart

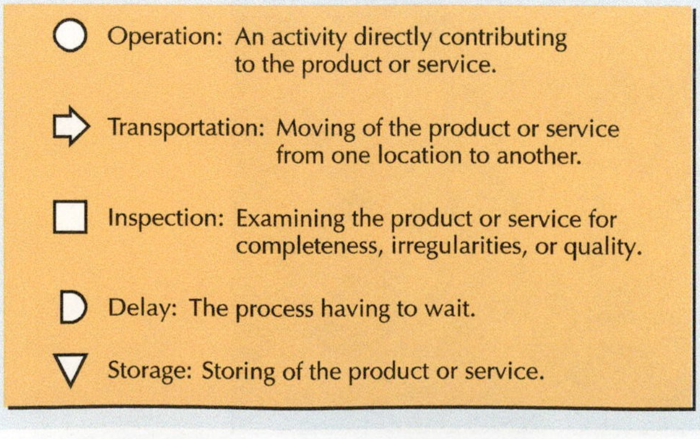

○ Operation: An activity directly contributing to the product or service.

⇨ Transportation: Moving of the product or service from one location to another.

□ Inspection: Examining the product or service for completeness, irregularities, or quality.

D Delay: The process having to wait.

▽ Storage: Storing of the product or service.

EXAMPLE 8.1 | Developing a Job Process Flowchart

The QuikCopy Store does copying jobs for walk-in customers. When a customer comes in with a copy job, a desk operator fills out a work order (name, number of copies, quality of paper, and so on) and places it in a box. An operator subsequently picks up the job, makes the copies, and returns the completed job to the cashier, where the job transaction is completed. The store would like a job process flowchart that describes this sequence of tasks.

Solution: The process flowchart for the steps in this copying job are shown in Figure 8.2. Although the process encompasses several operators and jobs, it focuses primarily on the tasks of the copy machine operator, who actually makes the copies.

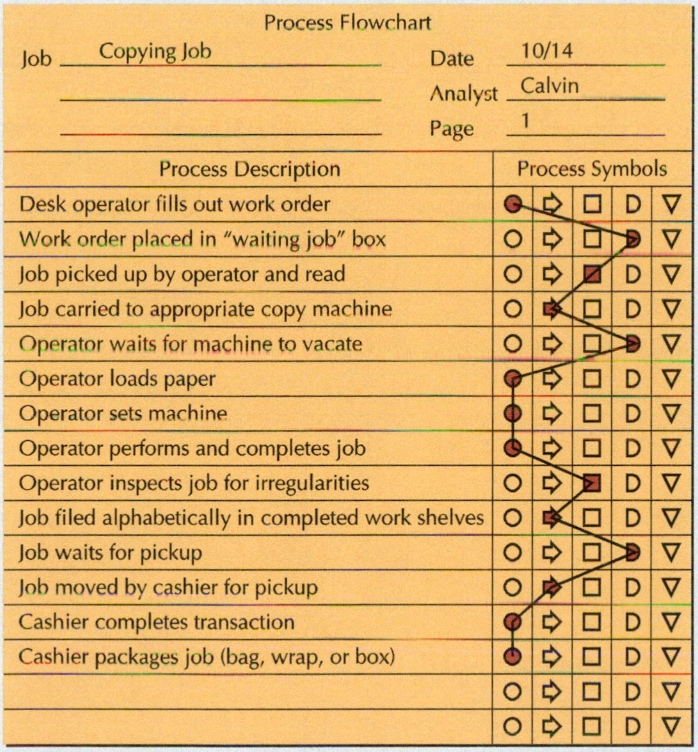

Process Flowchart

Job: Copying Job | Date: 10/14 | Analyst: Calvin | Page: 1

Process Description	Process Symbols				
Desk operator fills out work order	●	⇨	□	D	▽
Work order placed in "waiting job" box	O	⇨	□	**D** (filled)	▽
Job picked up by operator and read	O	⇨	■	D	▽
Job carried to appropriate copy machine	O	➡	□	D	▽
Operator waits for machine to vacate	O	⇨	□	**D** (filled)	▽
Operator loads paper	●	⇨	□	D	▽
Operator sets machine	●	⇨	□	D	▽
Operator performs and completes job	●	⇨	□	D	▽
Operator inspects job for irregularities	O	⇨	■	D	▽
Job filed alphabetically in completed work shelves	O	➡	□	D	▽
Job waits for pickup	O	⇨	□	**D** (filled)	▽
Job moved by cashier for pickup	O	➡	□	D	▽
Cashier completes transaction	●	⇨	□	D	▽
Cashier packages job (bag, wrap, or box)	●	⇨	□	D	▽
	O	⇨	□	D	▽
	O	⇨	□	D	▽

FIGURE 8.2 **Process Flowchart of Copying Job**

Often a process flowchart is used in combination with other types of methods analysis charts and a written job description to form a comprehensive and detailed picture of a job. Essentially, the methods analyst is a "job detective," who wants to get as much evidence as possible about a job from as many perspectives as possible in order to improve the job.

Worker-Machine Chart

A **worker-machine chart** illustrates the amount of time a worker and a machine are working or idle in a job. This type of chart is occasionally used in conjunction with a process flowchart when the job process includes equipment or machinery. The worker-machine chart shows if the worker's time and the machine time are being used efficiently—that is, if the worker or machine is idle an excessive amount of time.

Worker-machine chart
Determines if worker and machine time are used efficiently.

Another type of worker-machine chart is the *gang process chart*, which illustrates a job in which a team of workers are interacting with a piece of equipment or a machine. Examples include workers at a coal furnace in a steel mill or a military gunnery team on a battleship.

EXAMPLE 8.2 | Developing a Worker-Machine Chart

The QuikCopy Store described in Example 8.1 also makes photo ID cards. An operator types in data about the customer on a card, submits this to the photo machine, positions the customer for the photo, and takes the photograph. The machine processes the photo ID card. The store would like to develop a worker-machine chart for this job.

Solution: Figure 8.3 shows the worker-machine chart for the job of making photo ID cards.

The time scale along the left side of the chart provides a visual perspective of the amount of work and idle time in the job process. For this job, the summary at the bottom of Figure 8.3 indicates that the operator and machine were both working and idle approximately the same amount of time.

Worker–Machine Chart

Job: Photo-ID Cards | Date: 10/14

Time (min)	Operator	Time (min)	Photo Machine
1–2	*Key in customer data on card*	2.6	*Idle*
3	*Feed data card in*	0.4	*Accept card*
	Position customer for photo	1.0	*Idle*
4	*Take picture*	0.6	*Begin photo process*
5–7	*Idle*	3.4	*Photo/card processed*
8–9	*Inspect card and trim edges*	1.2	*Idle*
10			

Summary

	Operator Time	%	Photo Machine Time	%
Work	5.8	63	4.8	52
Idle	3.4	37	4.4	48
Total	9.2 min	100%	9.2 min	100%

FIGURE 8.3 **Worker-Machine Chart**

A gang chart is constructed the same way as the chart in Figure 8.3, except there are columns for each of the different operators. The purpose of a gang process chart is to determine if the interaction between the workers is efficient and coordinated.

Motion Study

Motion study Used to ensure efficiency of motion in a job.

The most detailed form of job analysis is **motion study**, the study of the individual human motions used in a task. The purpose of motion study is to make sure that a job task does not include any unnecessary motion by the worker and to select the sequence of motions that ensure that the task is being performed in the most efficient way.

Motion study originated with Frank Gilbreth, a colleague of F. W. Taylor's at the beginning of the twentieth century. F.W. Taylor's approach to the study of work methods was to select the best worker among a group of workers and use that worker's methods as the standard by which other workers were trained. Alternatively, Gilbreth studied many workers and from among them picked the best way to perform each activity. Then he combined these elements to form the "one best way" to perform a task.

Gilbreth and his wife Lillian used movies to study individual work motions in slow motion and frame by frame, called *micromotion analysis*. Using motion pictures, the Gilbreths carefully categorized the basic physical elements of motion used in work.

The Gilbreths' research eventually evolved into a set of widely adopted *principles of motion study*, which companies have used as guidelines for the efficient design of work. These principles are categorized according to the efficient use of the *human body*, the efficient arrangement of the *workplace*, and the efficient use of *equipment and machinery*. The principles of motion study include about 25 rules for conserving motion. These rules can be grouped in the three categories shown in **Table 8.3**.

Motion study and scientific management complemented each other. Motion study was effective for designing the repetitive, simplified, assembly-line-type jobs characteristic of manufacturing operations. Frank Gilbreth's first subject was a bricklayer; through his study of this worker's motions, he was able to improve the bricklayer's productivity threefold. However, in Gilbreth's day, bricklayers were paid on the basis of how many bricks they could lay in an hour in a piece-rate wage system. Who would be able to find a bricklayer today paid according to such a system!

There has been a movement away from task specialization and simple, repetitive jobs in lieu of greater job responsibility and a broader range of tasks, which has reduced the use of motion study. Nevertheless, motion study is still employed for repetitive jobs, especially in service industries, such as postal workers in mailrooms, who process and route thousands of pieces of mail.

The Gilbreths, together with F. W. Taylor and Henry Gantt, are considered pioneers in operations management. The Gilbreths' use of motion pictures is still popular today. Computer-generated images are used to analyze an athlete's movements to enhance performance, and video cameras are widely used to study everything from surgical procedures in the operating room to telephone operators.

TABLE 8.3 Summary of General Guidelines for Motion Study

EFFICIENT USE OF THE HUMAN BODY
• Work should be simplified, rhythmic, and symmetric.
• Hand/arm motions should be coordinated and simultaneous.
• The full extent of physical capabilities should be employed; all parts of the body should perform; the hand should never be idle.
• Energy should be conserved by letting machines perform tasks when possible, minimizing the distance of movements, and physical momentum should be in favor of the worker.
• Tasks should be simple, requiring minimal eye contact and minimal muscular effort, with no unnecessary motions, delays, or idleness.
EFFICIENT ARRANGEMENT OF THE WORKPLACE
• All tools, materials, and equipment should have a designated, easily accessible location that minimizes the motions required to get them.
• Seating and the general work environment should be comfortable and healthy.
EFFICIENT USE OF EQUIPMENT
• Equipment and mechanized tools enhance worker abilities.
• The use of foot-operated mechanized equipment that relieves the hand/arms of work should be maximized.
• Equipment should be constructed and arranged to fit worker use.

Learning Curves

Learning curve Illustrates the improvement rate of workers as a job is repeated.

A **learning curve**, or *improvement curve*, is a graph that reflects the fact that as workers repeat their tasks, they will improve performance. The learning curve effect was introduced in 1936 in an article in the *Journal of Aeronautical Sciences* by T. P. Wright, who described how the direct labor cost for producing airplanes decreased as the number of planes produced increased (see photo). This observation and the rate of improvement were found to be strikingly consistent across a number of airplane manufacturers. The premise of the learning curve is that improvement occurs because workers learn how to do a job better as they produce more and more units. However, it is generally recognized that other production-related factors also improve performance over time, such as methods analysis and improvement, job redesign, retooling, and worker motivation.

Figure 8.4 illustrates the general relationship defined by the learning curve; as the number of cumulative units produced increases, the labor time per unit decreases. Specifically, the learning curve reflects the fact that each time the number of units produced doubles, the processing time per unit decreases by a constant percentage.

The decrease in processing time per unit as production doubles will normally range from 10 to 20%. The convention is to describe a learning curve in terms of 1, or 100%, minus the percentage rate of improvement. For example, an 80% learning curve describes an improvement rate of 20% each time production doubles, a 90% learning curve indicates a 10% improvement rate, and so forth. As such, the lower the learning curve number, the steeper the slope and the faster the drop in costs. Standardized products and processes tend to have costs that decline more steeply than others.

The learning curve in Figure 8.4 is similar to an exponential distribution. The corresponding learning curve formula for computing the time required for the nth unit produced is

$$t_n = t_1 n^b$$

where

t_n = the time required for the nth unit produced
t_1 = time required for the first unit produced
n = the cumulative number of units produced
$b = \ln r / \ln 2$, where r is the learning curve percentage (decimal coefficient)

Learning curves are useful for measuring work improvement for nonrepetitive, complex jobs requiring a long time to complete, such as building airplanes or medical surgical procedures. For short, repetitive, and routine jobs, there may be little relative improvement, and it may occur in a brief time span during the first (of many) job repetitions. For that reason, learning curves can have limited use for mass production and assembly-line-type jobs. A learning

FIGURE 8.4 Learning Curve

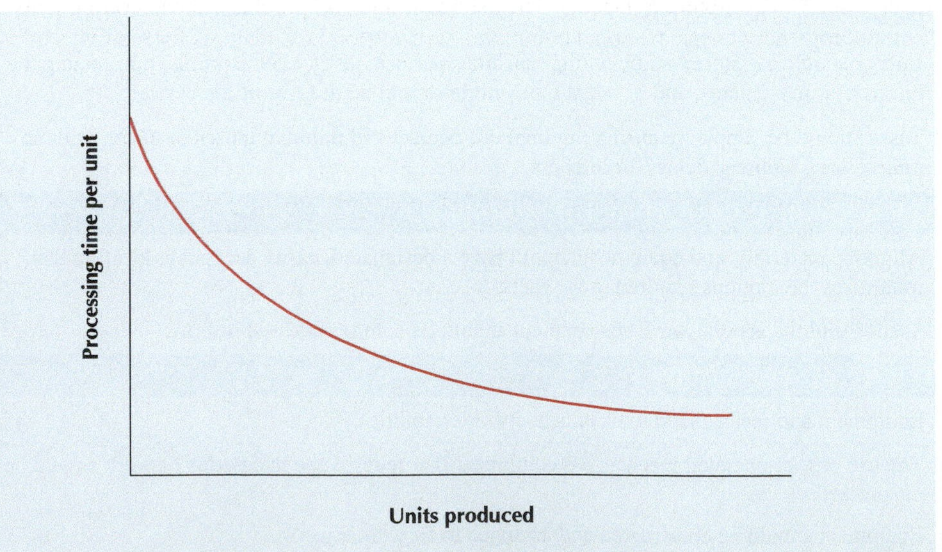

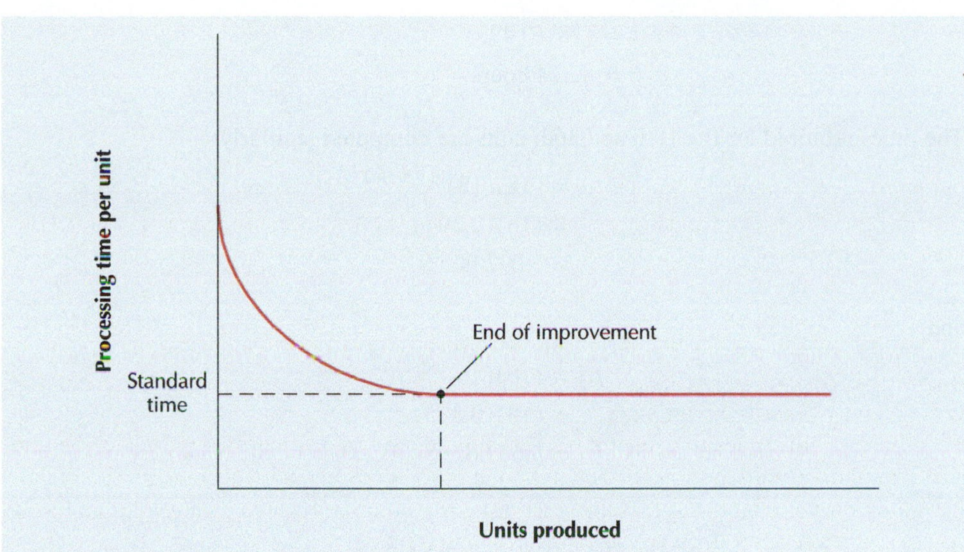

FIGURE 8.5 Learning Curve for Mass Production Job

curve for this type of operation sometimes achieves any improvement early in the process and then flattens out and shows virtually no improvement, as reflected in Figure 8.5.

Learning curves help managers project labor and budgeting requirements in order to develop production scheduling plans. Knowing how many production labor hours will be required over time can enable managers to determine the number of workers to hire. Also, knowing how many labor hours will eventually be required for a product can help managers make overall product cost estimates to use in bidding for jobs and later for determining the product selling price. However, product or other changes during the production process can negate the learning curve effect.

Although learning curves can be applied to many different businesses, its impact is most pronounced in businesses and industries that include complex, repetitive operations where the work pace is determined mostly by people, not machines. Examples of industries where the learning curve is used extensively include aerospace, electronics, shipbuilding, construction, and defense. The learning curve in the aerospace and shipbuilding industries is estimated to be 85%, while it is estimated to be 90% to 95% in the electronics industry. NASA, for example, uses the learning curve to estimate costs of space shuttle production and the times to complete tasks in space.

EXAMPLE 8.3 | Determining the Learning Curve Effect

Paulette Taylor and Maureen Becker, two undergraduates at State University, produce customized personal computer systems at night in their apartment (hence the name of their enterprise, PM Computer Services). They shop around and purchase cheap components and then put together generic personal computers with customized features for faculty, students, and local businesses. Each time they get an order, it takes them a while to assemble the first unit, but they learn as they go, and they reduce the assembly time as they produce more units. They have recently received their biggest order to date from the statistics department at State for 36 customized personal computers. It is near the end of the university's fiscal year, and the computers are needed quickly to charge them on this year's budget. Paulette and Maureen assembled the first unit as a trial and found that it took them 18 hours of direct labor. To determine if they can fill the order in the time allotted, they want to apply the learning curve effect to determine how much time the 9th, 18th, and 36th units will require to assemble. Based on past experience, they believe their learning curve is 80%.

Solution: The time required for the 9th unit is computed using the learning curve formula:

$$t_n = t_1 n^b$$
$$t_9 = (18)(9)^{\ln(0.8)/\ln 2}$$
$$= (18)(9)^{-0.322} = 18/(9)^{0.322}$$

$$= (18)(0.493)$$
$$= 8.874 \text{ hours}$$

The times required for the 18th and 36th units are computed similarly:

$$t_{18} = (18)(18)^{\ln(0.8)/\ln 2}$$
$$= (18)(0.394)$$
$$= 7.092 \text{ hours}$$

and

$$t_{36} = (18)(36)^{\ln(0.8)/\ln 2}$$
$$= (18)(0.315)$$
$$= 5.67 \text{ hours}$$

Learning Curves With Excel and OM Tools

The Excel spreadsheet for Example 8.3 is shown in **Exhibit 8.1**. Notice that cell C10 is highlighted and the learning curve formula for computing the time required for the 36th unit is shown on the toolbar at the top of the screen. This formula includes the learning curve coefficient in cell D4, the time required for the first unit produced in cell D3, and the target unit in B10.

Exhibit 8.2 shows the OM Tools spreadsheet for the learning curve in Example 8.3. Note that to determine the time required for a specific unit the unit number must first be input in cells B11 to B13.

Kevin P. Casey/Bloomberg/Getty Images, Inc.

Aircraft manufacturers have long relied on learning curves for production planning. Learning curves were first recognized in the aircraft industry in 1936 by T. P. Wright. Aircraft production at that time required a large amount of direct labor for assembly work; thus any marked increases in productivity were clearly recognizable. Based on empirical analysis, Wright discovered that on average when output doubled in the aircraft industry, labor requirements decreased by approximately 20%; that is, an 80% learning curve. During World War II when aircraft manufacturing proliferated, the learning curve became a tool for planning and an integral part of military aircraft contracts. Studies during these years demonstrated the existence of the learning curve in other industries as well. For example, studies of historical production figures at Ford Motor Company from 1909 to 1926 showed productivity improved for the Model T according to an 86% learning curve. The learning curve effect was subsequently shown to exist not only in labor-intensive manufacturing but also in capital-intensive manufacturing industries such as petroleum refining, steel, paper, construction, electronics and apparel, as well as in clerical operations.

EXHIBIT 8.1

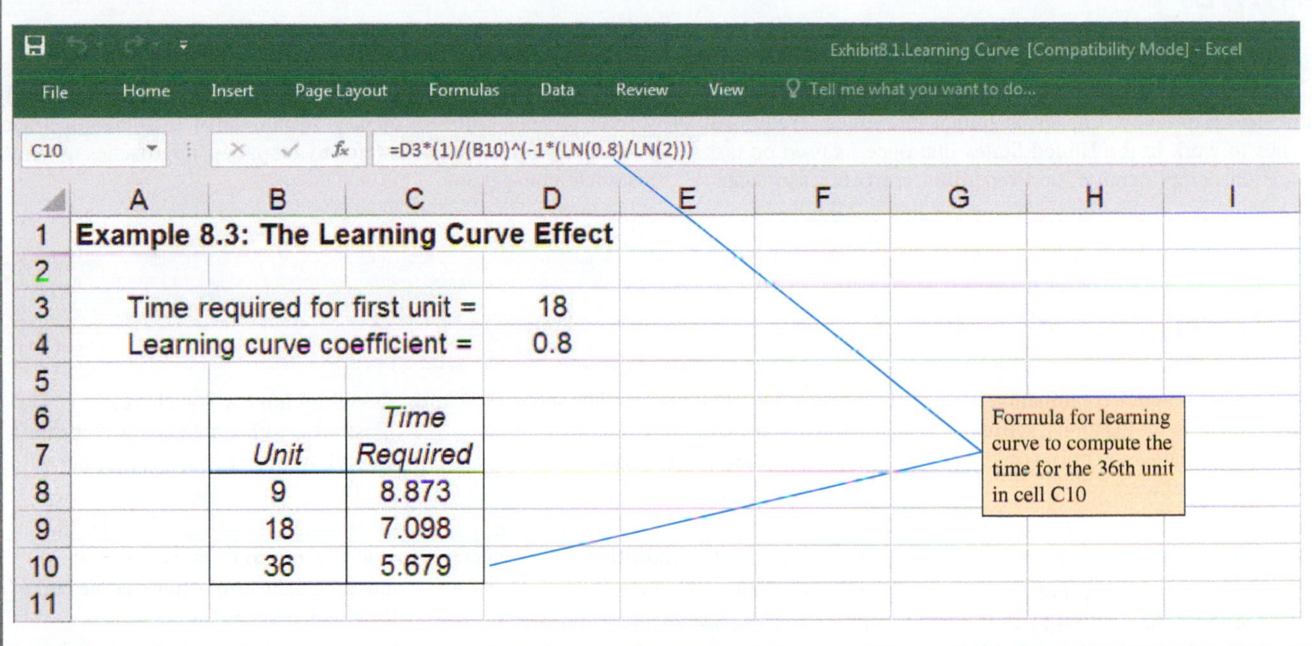

EXHIBIT 8.2

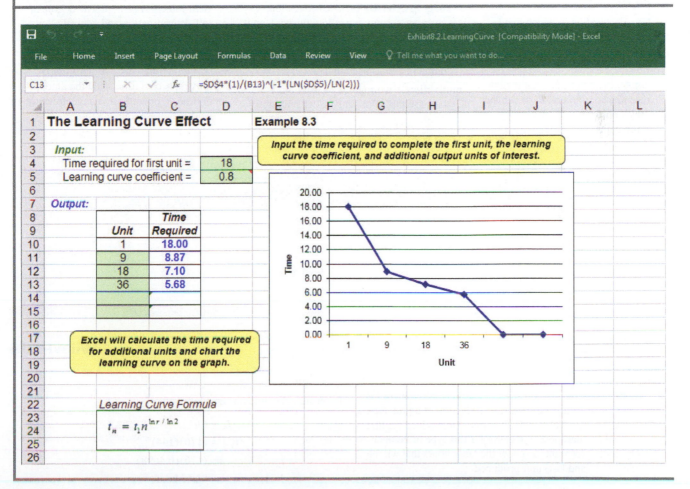

Exhibit8.2.LearningCurve [Compatibility Mode] - Excel

File Home Insert Page Layout Formulas Data Review View Tell me what you want to do...

C13 =$D$4*(1)/(B13)^(-1*(LN($D$5)/LN(2)))

The Learning Curve Effect **Example 8.3**

Input:

Time required for first unit =	18
Learning curve coefficient =	0.8

Input the time required to complete the first unit, the learning curve coefficient, and additional output units of interest.

Output:

Unit	Time Required
1	18.00
9	8.87
18	7.10
36	5.68

Excel will calculate the time required for additional units and chart the learning curve on the graph.

Time: 20.00, 18.00, 16.00, 14.00, 12.00, 10.00, 8.00, 6.00, 4.00, 2.00, 0.00

Unit: 1, 9, 18, 36

Learning Curve Formula

$$t_n = t_1 n^{\ln r / \ln 2}$$

Summary

As with many other areas in production and operations management, the quality movement and increased international competition have had a dramatic impact on human resources. Traditional approaches to work in the United States that once focused on task specialization, simplification, and repetition are being supplanted by approaches that promote higher job skill levels, broader task responsibility, more worker involvement, and, most importantly, worker responsibility for quality. A number of U.S. manufacturing and service firms have attempted to adopt new approaches to human resource management.

Key Terms

alternative workplace A combination of nontraditional work locations, settings, and practices that supplements or replaces the traditional office.

cross training An employee learns more than one job in the organization.

empowerment The authority and responsibility of the workers to alert management about job-related problems.

ergonomics The application of human sciences like anatomy, physiology, and psychology to the design of the work environment and jobs, and objects and equipment used in work; fitting the task to the person.

flextime A work schedule in which fixed times of arrival and departure are replaced by a combination of fixed and variable times.

gainsharing An incentive plan that includes employees in a common effort to achieve a company's objectives in which they share in the gains.

horizontal job enlargement The scope of a job that includes all tasks necessary to complete a product or process.

job A defined set of tasks that compose the work performed by employees that contributes to the production of a product or delivery of a service.

job rotation The horizontal movement between two or more jobs according to a plan or schedule.

learning curve A graph that reflects the improvement rate of workers as a job is repeated and more units are produced.

managing diversity Includes education, awareness, communication, fairness, and commitment.

motion study The study of the individual human motions used in a task.

motivation A willingness to work hard because that effort satisfies an employee need.

process flowchart A flowchart that illustrates, with symbols, the steps for a job or how several jobs fit together within the flow of the production process.

profit sharing The company sets aside a portion of profits and distributes it among employees, usually at the end of the fiscal year.

tasks Individual, defined job activities that consist of one or more elements.

telecommuting Employees work electronically from whatever location they choose, either exclusively or some of the time.

vertical job enlargement The degree of self-determination and control allowed workers over their own work; also referred to as job enrichment.

worker-machine chart A chart that illustrates on a time scale the amount of time an operator and a machine are working or are idle in a job.

Key Formulas

Learning Curve Formula

$$t_n = t_1 n^{\ln r/\ln 2}$$

Solved Problems

WileyPLUS

1. Learning Curve

A military contractor is manufacturing an electronic component for a weapons system. It is estimated from the production of a prototype unit that 176 hours of direct labor will be required to produce the first unit. The industrial standard learning curve for this type of component is 90%. The contractor wants to know the labor hours that will be required for the 144th (and last) unit produced.

Solution

Determine the time for the 144th unit.

$$\begin{aligned} t_n &= t_1 n^b \\ t_{144} &= (176)(144)^{\ln(0.9)/\ln 2} \\ &= (176)(0.4698) \\ &= 82.69 \text{ hours} \end{aligned}$$

Questions

8.1. Discuss how human resources is an integral part of a company's strategic planning process.

8.2. Why has human resources become a greater focus of companies in recent years?

8.3. Describe the characteristics of job design according to the scientific management approach.

8.4. Describe the contributions of F. W. Taylor and the Gilbreths to job design and analysis, and work measurement.

8.5. Explain the difference between horizontal and vertical job enlargement and how these concepts might work at a business like McDonald's or Starbucks.

8.6. What is the difference between tasks, elements, and motions in a basic job structure?

8.7. How did the development of the assembly-line production process at Ford Motor Company popularize the scientific management approach to job design?

8.8. What are some of the ways companies achieve sustainability in the workplace?

8.9. Using the Internet, identify a specific company that has adopted telecommuting and discuss how and to what extent the company is using telecommuting and its impact.

8.10. Companies with global supply chains often encounter workplace sustainability issues and problems with its overseas suppliers. Identify and discuss some of these possible issues and describe what companies do to resolve them.

8.11. Identify a specific company that has an extensive global supply chain, and using the Internet and the company's website discuss how the company is achieving workplace sustainability with its overseas suppliers.

8.12. Discuss the specific problems that U.S. companies with suppliers in China have with workplace sustainability issues in China, and their efforts to overcome these problems.

8.13. One of the seven major categories of criteria for an applicant for the Malcolm Baldrige National Quality Award is "human resource focus." A company or organization that applies for the Baldrige Award must show measurable results of efforts to improve the workplace and working environment for employees. Identify and discuss some of these efforts and measures cited by Baldrige Award winners.

8.14. Research the Baldrige Award website and describe some of the award-winning companies initiatives and efforts related to employee training and education.

8.15. Workplace diversity has become an important corporate objective for many companies, partly because of the media scrutiny this issue receives. Research three company websites and discuss their specific efforts in achieving and sustaining diversity.

8.16. What kind of diversity issues does a company with a global supply chain encounter with its overseas suppliers?

8.17. What role do you think social media and the Internet have had in raising the public's consciousness about workplace issues both in the United States and abroad?

8.18. The principles of scientific management were not adopted in Japan during the first half of the twentieth century as they were in the United States and other Western nations. Speculate as to why this occurred.

8.19. Contrast the traditional U.S. approaches to job design with current trends.

8.20. What are the advantages of the scientific management approach to job design (specifically, task specialization, simplicity, and repetition) to both management and the worker?

8.21. Describe the primary characteristics of the behavioral approach to job design.

8.22. How has the increased emphasis on quality improvement affected human resources management in the United States?

8.23. How successful have companies in the United States been in adapting trends in job design that mostly originated in Japan?

8.24. Describe the three major categories of the elements of job design.

8.25. Describe the differences between a process flowchart and a worker-machine chart and what they are designed to achieve.

8.26. Pick an activity you are familiar with in your daily life such as washing a car, cutting grass, or taking a shower, and develop a process flowchart for it.

8.27. Describe some of the advantages and disadvantages of telecommuting from both the employee and manager's perspective.

8.28. Why is empowerment a critical element in total quality management? What are the disadvantages of empowerment?

8.29. Select an article (or articles) from *HR Magazine* and write a report on a human resource management application in a company similar to the "Along the Supply Chain" boxes in this chapter.

8.30. Go to the Malcolm Baldrige website at http://www.nist.gov/baldrige/ and write a brief report on the role of human resource management at a Baldrige award-winning company or organization.

8.31. Select a workplace at your university such as an academic department office, the athletic department, the bookstore, or the cafeteria, and describe the compensation program for rank-and-file employees and any additional programs used to create job satisfaction and motivate employees. Also indicate the amount and type of job training and the involvement of employees in quality management. Identify any problems you see in the workplace environment and how it might be approved.

8.32. Describe a job you have had in the past or a job you are very familiar with and indicate the negative aspects of the job and how it could be improved with current human resource management techniques.

8.33. For what type of jobs are learning curves most useful?

8.34. What does a learning curve specifically measure?

8.35. Discuss some of the uses and limitations of learning curves.

Problems

WileyPLUS

8.1. The United Mutual and Accident Insurance Company has a large pool of clerical employees who process insurance application forms on networked computers. When the company hires a new clerical employee, it takes that person about 48 minutes to process a form. The learning curve for this job is 88%, but no additional learning will take place after about the 100th form is processed. United Mutual has recently acquired a smaller competitor that will add 800 new forms per week to its clerical pool. If an employee works six hours per day (excluding breaks, meals, and so on) per five-day week, how many employees would be hired to absorb the extra workload?

8.2. Professor Cook teaches operations management at State University. She is scheduled to give her class of 35 students a final exam on the last day of exam week, and she is leaving town the same day. She is concerned about her ability to finish grading her exams. She estimates that with everything else she has to do she has only five hours to grade the exams. From past experience she knows the first exam will take her about 12 minutes to grade. She estimates her learning curve to be about 90%, and it will be fully realized after about 10 exams. Will she get the exams graded on time?

8.3. Nite-Site, Inc., manufactures image intensification devices used in products such as night-vision goggles and aviator's night-vision imaging systems. The primary customer for these products is the U.S. military. The military requires that learning curves be employed in the bid process for awarding military contracts. The company is planning to make a bid for 120 image intensifiers to be used in a military vehicle. The company estimates the first unit will require 80 hours of direct labor to produce. The industry learning curve for this particular type of product is 92%. Determine how many hours will be required to produce the 60th and 120th units.

8.4. Global Distribution Systems installs warehouse management software systems for it clients and trains client employees in its use. As the company expands and contracts with new clients it hires and trains new project teams to install the software at its clients' warehouse facilities. At first it takes a new team about three weeks to install the system and train employees in its use. If a new team has an 88% learning curve, how many installations will be required before the team can complete the installation process in two weeks?

8.5. Jericho Vehicles manufactures special-purpose all-terrain vehicles primarily for the military and government agencies in the United States and for foreign governments. The company is planning to bid on a new all-terrain vehicle specially equipped for desert military action. The company has experienced an 87% learning curve in the past for producing similar vehicles. Based on a prototype model, it estimates the first vehicle produced will require 1600 hours of direct labor. The order is for 60 all-terrain vehicles. Determine the time that will be required for the 30th and 60th units.

8.6. Zippos.com is an online shoe retail store. While most customers shop online at the company's Internet site, many others call the company directly for specialized assistance with questions. After phone operators are first hired and trained they spend an average of 24 minutes talking to a customer, much of which is taken up with the new phone operators looking up answers to questions they don't know off-hand on the company's website. If phone operators have an 85% learning curve while learning typical responses to customer questions, how many calls will they have to experience until they can reduce their call time to 10 minutes?

8.7. Jericho Vehicles is considering making a bid for a mobile rocket-launching system for the U.S. military. However, the company has almost no experience in producing this type of vehicle. In an effort to develop a learning curve for the production of this new mobile weapon system, management has called contacts from several former competitors who went bankrupt. Although management could not obtain direct learning curve rates, they did learn from one contact that for a system with similar features, the first unit required 2400 hours of direct labor to produce and the 30th and final unit required 1450 hours to produce. Determine the learning curve rate for this vehicle.

8.8. PM Computer Services (described in Example 8.3) has received an order for 120 custom configured personal computers for a local business. Paulette and Maureen have so many orders that they can no longer perform the work themselves, and they must hire extra labor to assemble the units for this new order. They have hired eight students from the university to work part-time, 20 hours per week, to assemble the computers. Paulette and Maureen assembled a prototype unit and it required 26 hours of direct labor; from experience they know their computer assembly operation has an 84% learning curve. Approximately when will PM Computer Services be able to deliver the completed order?

8.9. Hanna's Super Service Burgers and Fries fast-food restaurant trains its new employees (all of whom are part-time) for three days to assemble its different burgers. The most time-consuming item to assemble is the Super Mega-Burger because it includes a lot of ingredients. After three days of training, an employee can assemble his or her first Mega-Burger as a regular employee in an average of 126 seconds. The learning curve for this assembly operation is estimated to be 85%, and no additional learning will take place after assembly of the eightieth Mega-Burger. Determine how many seconds will be required for an employee to assemble his or her eightieth Mega-Burger.

8.10. The housekeeping staff at the five-star Ritz Hotel has a specific, detailed list of activities for cleaning an occupied room. Each activity is completed whether or not it looks like it is necessary. When the hotel hires a new housekeeper, it takes that employee about 55 minutes to clean a room the first time. The learning curve for this job is 92%, and the average minimum time for an experienced housekeeper to clean a room is 32 minutes. How many rooms will a newly hired housekeeper have to clean before it can be done in 32 minutes? If a housekeeper has an eight-hour work day with 1.5 hours off for lunch and breaks, how many work days will be required before the housekeeper is fully proficient and able to clean a room in the minimum average time?

8.11. Prior to the invention of the printing press in the mid-1400s, the process of producing fine books, called illuminated manuscripts, was strictly manual and performed by skilled craftsmen. A scribe would copy the manuscript in ornate handwriting (or calligraphy) from an original text called an exemplar, and artists decorated (or illuminated) the books with pictures. It is estimated that an apprentice scribe could initially copy approximately 50 lines per day. This roughly translates to about 15 minutes per line for a scribe just starting out. A scribe was generally thought to have completed his apprenticeship and was considered a craftsman after completing eight books where each book consisted of about 17,000 lines. (After eight books a scribe would show little additional improvement in accurate copying speed.) Assuming a learning curve of 91%, how long would it take for an experienced scribe to copy a line, and how many lines could he copy in a day?

8.12. Dale Computer Company accepts orders from customers for computers online through its website and configures and builds them to order at one of its distribution centers from components it orders from its various suppliers in the United States and overseas. It is continually retaining new suppliers as its computer models change and as new computing technologies are developed. It promises its customers that when an order is placed the customer will receive it quickly, typically within a week, which in turn requires that Dale's suppliers provide component parts as quickly as they are demanded. Normally Dale sets a target of three days for a supplier to deliver parts once they are ordered, and Dale uses SPC charts (see Chapter 3) to monitor a supplier's delivery performance once this target value has been achieved. Dale has learned from past experiences working with many suppliers that it takes some time for new suppliers to improve their production and delivery processes to consistently meet Dale's target delivery time. It normally takes a supplier about 15 days to deliver Dale's first order. Determine approximately how many orders it will take a new supplier that has a 70% learning curve to be able to meet Dale's orders within the specified target time.

Case Problems

Case Problem 8.1 Maury Mills

The Maury Mills Company is a producer and distributor of food products and handmade crafts located in southwest Virginia. Anne Maury and Dana Mills were roommates in college when they started selling homemade cookies, candy, apple butter, and breads at craft fairs in the region. As they attended craft fairs, they made acquaintances with a number of craftspeople, artisans, and vendors who also had booths. After Anne and Dana graduated from college with degrees in English and Theater Arts, respectively, they decided to start their own business selling crafts they would buy from the artisans they knew from craft fairs and food items they would make themselves or contract with locals to make. They leased a building previously occupied by an auto parts store to use as an office, warehouse, and distribution center. Their plan was to sell their products to grocery stores, specialty food stores, and gift shops in the region.

Initially, Anne and Dana ran the business themselves. Anne did all the buying and bookkeeping while Dana handled sales. Both of them did a lot of telephoning and traveled around the region visiting their suppliers and potential customers, picking up purchased goods and making deliveries. In the evening and on weekends they made their own brand of cookies, candy, apple butter, breads, and cakes and packaged them. Their products sold well, primarily because of their high quality and uniqueness, and both suppliers and customers liked the two hard-working ladies. They were able to purchase the crafts they sold at modest prices from local artisans, and because they had relatively low overhead and expenses and no employees, their profit margin was high. However, their business soon exceeded their capacity, and they began to hire additional employees. Initially, they hired high school students part time to help with strictly physical work like packaging, picking up purchased items, and making deliveries. However, they soon realized they needed more skilled, reliable, full-time employees, including people to handle phone orders and customer service. They moved their business out of the old building they were using into a new office and warehouse facility that included an on-site bakery and food processing plant.

Anne and Dana moved more into a managerial role and spent less direct hands-on time with operations, which was a new experience for them and one for which they did not feel totally prepared. Managing employees was a particularly daunting task, and they were forced to learn as they went along. They used basic common sense and a commitment to treating their employees fairly and nicely, which proved to be successful. They could not help feeling responsible for their employees' well-being, and they soon considered themselves a large family of friends who were all working together for a common goal.

Maury Mills's sales continued to grow at a rapid pace, profits were high, and the employee base expanded. With the help of an e-business consultant, Maury Mills developed a website and a print catalog and began selling to individuals, stores, and shops around the country through its catalog and online. The two friends turned over more of the daily operation of the company to managers and stepped back to relax and take some time for their own lives. They enrolled in an executive MBA program in the Northeast. They also began to travel for business and pleasure, exploring new markets and suppliers overseas, and sometimes attending business seminars and workshops in Europe, Hong Kong, and the Caribbean to fill in some of the gaps in their business expertise.

Within a few years, the crafts and specialty products business became more competitive, and online websites and catalogues for craft items and food products began to proliferate. At Maury Mills this caused the cost of purchasing their products to increase, and profit margins began to decline. At the same time the economy went into recession, and sales decreased. Anne and Dana became concerned that the financial health of the business they worked so hard to establish and that had been so successful was in peril. They quickly reimmersed themselves in the daily operations of Maury Mills, but the problems seemed overwhelming. They felt that their employees had become complacent and spoiled and weren't as committed to the business as they had been when they were smaller and more of a family. Walking around their facilities, they felt they hardly knew anyone who worked for them. Despite the seminars and business courses they had attended, they decided to hire a management consulting firm to come in and advise them how to turn things around.

The consulting firm spent a month at Maury Mills analyzing the company's financial data and operations, and looking closely at its markets and customer base. Their report offered several sweeping recommendations. The consultants found that the market for craft and specialty products had become saturated while the market for their food products, especially in the region, was still strong. They therefore recommended Maury Mills cut back on its craft products business while expanding its food products business. Thus, the first recommendation was that the company workforce be cut by 20% in all areas except food products processing. Anne and Dana had earlier expressed their concern about employee malaise to the consulting team, and this group picked up on that. The consultants felt that the food products business could be increased without capital expansion by increasing productivity through adopting various incentive measures and compensation programs to motivate employees. They also suggested that employees in packaging and distribution be paid according to an incentive plan based on the number of packages they processed daily. Another recommendation was that all orders arriving in the distribution center by 3:00 P.M. should be processed and shipped that same day. These changes would not only increase productivity but also speed order fulfillment, which would appeal to customers. They recommended a group bonus plan tied to the percentage of incoming orders shipped the same day. The consultants also thought that phone operators currently spent too much time talking with customers and suppliers and that their calls should be cut from an average of seven minutes to less than four minutes. It was recommended that employees in the food products area should also increase their productivity. A group incentive plan was suggested for the food products area that would provide monthly bonuses for increased productivity and for process improvements that would save food processing time and result in higher production levels. The report recommended that the sales force be placed on a partial commission plan based on dollar sales and that salespeople be empowered to offer discounts to customers to gain orders especially at food stores. It was also recommended that buyers be empowered to shop for lower-cost goods and be paid a percentage of cost savings as bonuses. Anne and Dana adopted the consultants' recommendations across the board and instructed their managers to implement the changes.

Within a few months, productivity increased throughout the company; the volume of phone orders increased by over 50%; and despite cutbacks, the distribution center increased the number of packages it was processing on a daily basis by 40%, and the number of orders shipped the same day as received rose to 95%. The food products area showed an increase in its production rate of 30%. Sales were up and purchasing costs had decreased.

Anne and Dana felt a great sense of relief, but this feeling was short-lived. Six months later over the course of a few days, several events stunned them. First, Anne was grocery shopping at the local Kroger when she eavesdropped on the following conversation between two shoppers:

"I hear things aren't going so well over at M 'n' Ms."

"No, everybody seems to be at each other's throat and the whole place seems to be falling apart."

"What happened? It seemed to be such a great place to work when my sister was there back when they first started."

"Well, I don't know what it was like back then, but things aren't so nice now. We have a lot of irate customers and they're returning stuff right and left, and our supervisors are leaning on everyone to do more. Most of us are exhausted and fed up."

Anne couldn't believe what she had heard; she immediately told Dana, and they decided to investigate. Sure enough, they discovered that returns had increased substantially and were clogging the warehouse. When they asked the manager in charge why customers were returning items, he told them there were complaints of poor quality. The next day they received another jolt. Dana's secretary told her that a group of black and Hispanic employees from the warehouse and distribution center had asked for an appointment to see Anne and Dana. Upon asking what the purpose of the meeting was, Dana was told that there was a lot of built-up resentment over earlier cutbacks in the distribution center, which was made up mostly of minority employees, while at the same time there weren't any cutbacks in the food products area, which was made up mostly of Caucasian employees. Dana's secretary also said that she had heard some complaining about inequities in the incentive plan that had been set up. Later that same day Anne received a phone call from Jim Barnett, the regional manager for the Market Place grocery chain. He told Anne that as a courtesy he wanted to personally let her know that he was not going to continue to carry Maury Mills food products in the specialty foods sections at his stores. He said he regretted it, especially since they had enjoyed a long-standing positive relationship, and Maury Mills had been providing such low prices in recent months, but Market Place had received a lot of customer complaints about poor-quality items. It had also received a lot of incomplete, late, and messed-up orders; when managers would call to try and resolve problems, the people they talked to were abrupt and seemed to be in a hurry to get off the phone. Immediately after this conversation ended, Anne went down to the sales office and discovered that there were a number of other old, established customers who were no longer placing orders. She also tracked several recent shipments and found that while orders were being processed on time, they often sat at the loading dock or were a long time in transit.

Anne and Dana were dazed. They were in worse shape than they had been before the changes!

Why do you think Maury Mills got in the shape it is? What are some of the mistakes you think they may have made in managing their human resources? What would you recommend that Dana and Anne do to resolve their problems? Are their problems solvable?

References

Barnes, R. M. *Motion and Time Study: Design and Measurement of Work*, 8th ed. New York: Wiley, 1980.

Belkaoui, A. *The Learning Curve*. Westport, CT: Quorum Books, 1986.

Emerson, H. P., and D. C. E. Maehring. *Origins of Industrial Engineering*. Atlanta: Institute of Industrial Engineers, 1988.

Evans, J. R., and W. M. Lindsay. *The Management and Control of Quality*, 3rd ed. St. Paul, MN: West, 1996.

Gilbreth, F. *Motion Study*. New York: Van Nostrand, 1911.

Herzberg, F. "One More Time: How Do You Motivate Employees?" *Harvard Business Review* 81 (1; January 2003), pp. 87–96.

Knights, D., H. Willmott, and D. Collinson, eds. *Job Redesign: Critical Perspectives on the Labor Process*. Hants, England: Gower, 1985.

Taylor, F. W. *The Principles of Scientific Management*. New York: Harper, 1911.

Wood, S., ed. *The Transformation of Work*. London: Unwin Hyman, 1989.

SUPPLEMENT TO CHAPTER 8

Operational Decision-Making Tools: Work Measurement

- Time Studies
- Work Sampling

Work measurement is determining how long it takes to do a job. Managing human resources requires managers to know how much work employees can do during a specific period. Otherwise they cannot plan production schedules or output. Without a good idea of how long it takes to do a job, a company will not know if it can meet customer expectations for delivery or service time. Despite the unpopularity of wage-incentive systems among some quality proponents, they are still widely used in the United States, and work measurement is required to set the output standards on which incentive rates are based. These wage rates determine the cost of a product or service.

Work measurement has also seen a revival within the ever-growing service sector. Services tend to be labor-intensive, and service jobs, especially clerical ones, are often repetitive. For example, sorting mail in a postal service, processing income tax returns in the IRS, making hamburgers at McDonald's, and inputting data from insurance forms in a computer at Prudential are all repetitive service jobs that can be measured, and standards can be set for output and wages. As a result, work measurement is still an important aspect of operations management for many companies.

Time Studies

The traditional means for determining an estimate of the time to do a job has been the time study, in which a stopwatch is used to time the individual elements of a job. These elemental times are summed to get a time estimate for a job and then adjusted by a performance rating of the worker and an allowance factor for unavoidable delays, resulting in a **standard time**. The standard time is the time required by an "average" worker to perform a job once under normal circumstances and conditions.

Standard time The time required by an average worker to perform a job once.

Work measurement and time study were introduced by Frederick W. Taylor in the late 1880s and 1890s. One of his objectives was to determine a "fair" method of job performance evaluation and payment, which at that time was frequently a matter of contention between management and labor. The basic form of wage payment was an incentive piece-rate system, in which workers were paid a wage rate per unit of output instead of an hourly wage rate; the more workers produced, the more they earned. The problem with this system at the time was that there was no way to determine a "normal," or "fair," rate of output. Management wanted the normal rate high, labor wanted it low. Since management made pay decisions, the piece rate was usually "tight," making it hard for the worker to make the expected, or fair, output rate. Thus, workers earned less. This was the scenario in which Taylor introduced his time study approach to develop an equitable piece-rate wage system based on fair standard job times.

The stopwatch time study approach for work measurement was popular and widespread into the 1970s. Many union contracts in the automotive, textile, and other manufacturing industries for virtually every production job in a company were based almost entirely on standard times developed from time studies. However, the basic principle underlying an incentive wage system is that pay is the sole motivation for work. We pointed out in Chapter 8 that this principle has been disproved. In fact, in recent years incentive wage systems have been shown to inhibit quality improvement.

However, performance evaluation represents only one use for time study and work measurement. It is still widely used for planning purposes in order to predict the level of output a company might achieve in the future.

Stopwatch Time Study

The result of a time study is a *standard time* for performing a repetitious job once. Time study is a statistical technique that is accurate for jobs that are highly repetitive.

The basic steps in a time study are:

1. ***Establish the standard job method.*** The job should be analyzed using methods analysis to make sure the best method is being used.

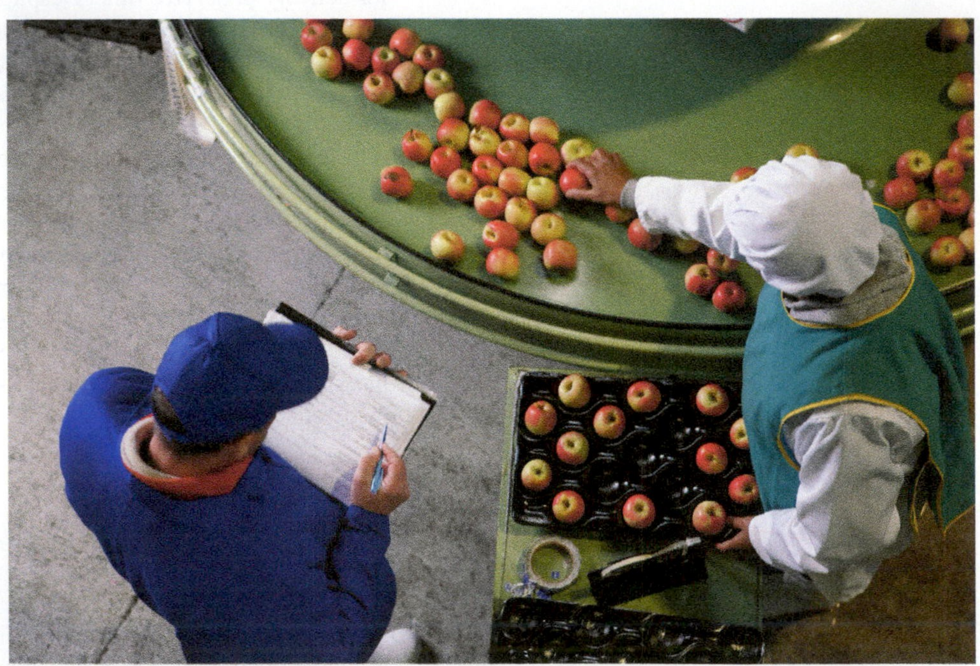

Alistair Berg//Getty Images, Inc.

This person is performing a time study of an employee doing a manual task. Although time studies are no longer as popular for establishing performance-based wage rates as they once were, they are still an effective means for studying jobs in order to improve them. Many jobs in manufacturing and especially in service businesses include simple, repetitive tasks, such as making a hamburger and wrapping it at McDonald's, checking in a rental car at Avis, or making a bed at a Ritz-Carlton. Reducing the time required to perform these tasks, while still making sure that they are done conscientiously and correctly by the employee, can result in quicker and more efficient customer service and improved quality. However, speed and quickness only translate to good quality if they result in customer satisfaction.

2. ***Break down the job into elements***. The job is broken down into short, elemental tasks with obvious "break points" between them. The more detailed the elements, the easier it is to eliminate elemental times that are not normally included in each job cycle and might abnormally affect the standard time.

3. ***Study the job***. Times studies have traditionally been conducted using a stopwatch attached to a clipboard, although handheld electronic time-study machines (similar to an electronic calculator) are now available that store elemental times in a memory that can be transferred to a computer for processing. To conduct a time study with a stopwatch, the industrial engineer or technician takes a position near the worker and records each elemental time on an observation sheet. In recent years, video cameras have been used to videotape jobs, with the time study conducted outside the workplace at a later time.

4. ***Rate the worker's performance***. As the time study is being conducted, the worker's performance is also rated by the person doing the study. The objective of the study is to determine a "normal," or average, time for the job, so the engineer/technician must adjust the elemental times up or down with a rating factor. A performance rating factor of 100% reflects normal work performance, below 100% represents a below-average performance, and above 100% indicates performance better than normal. Rating factors usually range between 80% and 120%.

   The observer conducting the study must, in effect, "judge" the difficulty of the job and mentally assess what normal performance is, primarily in terms of *speed*. Effort, or physical exertion, can also be a characteristic of performance; however, it must be viewed with caution, since a poor worker might exhibit a lot of exertion, whereas a good worker might exhibit little exertion in doing the same job.

   The performance rating factor is a crucial component of the time study, but it is also subjective. The person conducting the study must be very familiar with the job in order to rate the worker's performance accurately. Films and videos are available that show different levels of performance, effort, and speed for a variety of motions, tasks, and jobs. Even then it is often difficult to evaluate performance during an actual study.

   Workers are not always cooperative, and they sometimes resent time studies, especially if they know they are being used to set wages. They will purposely slow or speed up their normal work rate, make frequent mistakes, or alter the normal work methods, all designed to disrupt the work study.

   It is easy to understand why quality consultants and teachers perceive incentive wage systems and work measurement to be detrimental to quality improvement.

5. ***Compute the average time***. Once a sufficient number of job cycles have been observed, an average time for each work element is calculated. We talk more about the appropriate number of cycles to include in the study a little later.

6. ***Compute the normal time***. The **normal time** is calculated by multiplying the elemental average time by the performance rating factor:

Normal time The elemental average time multiplied by a performance rating.

$$\text{Normal time} = (\text{elemental average time})(\text{rating factor})$$

or

$$\mathrm{N}t = (\bar{t})(RF)$$

The normal cycle time (NT) is computed by summing the elemental normal times,

$$\mathrm{NT} = \Sigma \mathrm{N}t$$

7. ***Compute the standard time***. The standard time is computed by adjusting the normal cycle time by an allowance factor for unavoidable work delays (such as a machine breakdown), personal delays (such as using the rest room), and normal mental or physical fatigue. The allowance factor is a percentage increase in the normal cycle time. The standard time is calculated as follows:

$$\text{Standard time} = (\text{normal cycle time})(1 + \text{allowance factor})$$

or

$$\mathrm{ST} = (\mathrm{NT})(1 + \mathrm{AF})$$

EXAMPLE S8.1 | Performing a Time Study and Developing a Standard Time

The Metro Food Services Company delivers fresh sandwiches each morning to vending machines throughout the city. Workers work through the night to prepare the sandwiches for morning delivery. A worker normally makes several kinds of sandwiches. A time study for a worker making ham and cheese sandwiches is shown in **Figure S8.1** below. Notice that each element has two readings. Row t includes the individual elemental times, whereas the R row contains a cumulative (running) clock reading recorded going down the column. In this case the individual elemental times are determined by subtracting the cumulative times between sequential readings.

Solution: In Figure S8.1 the average element times are first computed as

$$\bar{t} = \frac{\Sigma t}{10}$$

For element 1 the average time is

$$\bar{t} = \frac{0.53}{10} = 0.053$$

Time Study Observation Sheet

Identification of operation: *Sandwich Assembly* — Date: *5/17*

Operator: *Smith* — Approval: *Jones* — Observer: *Russell*

			Cycles										Summary			
			1	2	3	4	5	6	7	8	9	10	Σt	$\bar{t}$	RF	Nt
1	*Grasp and lay out bread slices*	t	0.04	0.05	0.05	0.04	0.06	0.05	0.06	0.06	0.07	0.05	0.53	0.053	1.05	0.056
		R	0.04	0.38	0.72	1.05	1.40	1.76	2.13	2.50	2.89	3.29				
2	*Spread mayonnaise on both slices*	t	0.07	0.06	0.07	0.08	0.07	0.07	0.08	0.10	0.09	0.08	0.77	0.077	1.00	0.077
		R	0.11	0.44	0.79	1.13	1.47	1.83	2.21	2.60	2.98	3.37				
3	*Place ham, cheese, and lettuce on bread*	t	0.12	0.11	0.14	0.12	0.13	0.13	0.13	0.12	0.14	0.14	1.28	0.128	1.10	0.141
		R	0.23	0.55	0.93	1.25	1.60	1.96	2.34	2.72	3.12	3.51				
4	*Place top on sandwich, slice, and stack*	t	0.10	0.12	0.08	0.09	0.11	0.11	0.10	0.10	0.12	0.10	1.03	0.103	1.10	0.113
		R	0.33	0.67	1.01	1.34	1.71	2.07	2.44	2.82	3.24	3.61				
5		t														
		R														
6		t														
		R														
7		t														
		R														
8		t														
		R														
9		t														
		R														
10		t														
		R														

Normal cycle time *0.387* + Allowance *15%* = Std. time *0.445 min.*

FIGURE S8.1 Time Study Observation Sheet

The normal elemental times are computed by adjusting the average time, $\bar{t}$, by the performance rating factor, *RF*. For element 1 the normal time is

$$\begin{aligned} \mathrm{N}t &= (\bar{t})(RF) \\ &= (0.053)(1.05) \\ &= 0.056 \end{aligned}$$

The normal cycle time, NT, is computed by summing the normal times for all elements, which for this example is 0.387. The standard time is computed by adjusting the normal cycle time by an allowance factor,

$$\begin{aligned} \mathrm{ST} &= (\mathrm{NT})(1 + \mathrm{AF}) \\ &= (0.387)(1 + 0.15) \\ &= 0.445 \text{ min} \end{aligned}$$

If, for example, the company wants to know how many ham and cheese sandwiches can be produced in a two-hour period, they could simply divide the standard time into 120 minutes:

$$\frac{120 \text{ min}}{0.445 \text{ min/sandwich}} = 269.7 \text{ or } 270 \text{ sandwiches}$$

EXAMPLE S8.2 | An Incentive Piece-Rate System

If the Metro Food Services Company pays workers a piece-rate of $0.04 per sandwich, what would an average worker be paid per hour, and what would the subject of the time study in Example S8.1 expect to be paid?

Solution: The average worker would produce the following number of sandwiches in an hour:

$$\frac{60 \text{ min}}{0.445 \text{ min/sandwich}} = 134.8 \text{ or } 135 \text{ sandwiches}$$

The hourly wage rate would thus average

$$(135)(0.04) = \$5.40$$

Alternatively, the worker from Example S8.1 would produce at the average cycle time not adjusted by the rating factor, or 0.361 minute ($\Sigma\bar{t}$). Adjusting this time by the allowance time results in a time of

$$(0.361)(1 + 0.15) = 0.415 \text{ min}$$

This worker could be expected to produce the following number of sandwiches per hour:

$$\frac{60 \text{ min}}{0.415 \text{ min/sandwich}} = 144.6 \text{ or } 145 \text{ sandwiches}$$

The average hourly wage rate for this worker would be

$$(145)(0.04) = \$5.80$$

or $0.40 more per hour.

An Excel spreadsheet of the time study observation sheet shown in Figure S8.1 is shown in **Exhibit S8.1**.

EXHIBIT S8.1

Example S8.2. Performing a Time Study

Time Study Observation Sheet

Identification of Operation: *Sandwich Assembly* — Date: *5/17*

Operator: *Smith* **Approval:** *Jones* **Observer:** *Russell*

		Cycles										Summary			
		1	2	3	4	5	6	7	8	9	10	*Sum t*	$\bar{t}$	*RF*	*Nt*
1. Grasp and lay out	*t*	0.04	0.05	0.05	0.04	0.06	0.05	0.06	0.06	0.07	0.05	0.53	0.053	1.05	0.056
bread slices	*R*	0.04	0.38	0.72	1.05	1.40	1.76	2.13	2.50	2.89	3.29				
2. Spread mayonnaise	*t*	0.07	0.06	0.07	0.08	0.07	0.07	0.08	0.10	0.09	0.08	0.77	0.077	1.00	0.077
on both slices	*R*	0.11	0.44	0.79	1.13	1.47	1.83	2.21	2.60	2.98	3.37				
3. Place ham, cheese	*t*	0.12	0.11	0.14	0.12	0.13	0.13	0.13	0.12	0.14	0.14	1.28	0.128	1.10	0.141
and lettuce on bread	*R*	0.23	0.55	0.93	1.25	1.60	1.96	2.34	2.72	3.12	3.51				
4. Place top, slice	*t*	0.10	0.12	0.08	0.09	0.11	0.11	0.1	0.1	0.12	0.1	1.03	0.103	1.10	0.113
and stack	*R*	0.33	0.67	1.01	1.34	1.71	2.07	2.44	2.82	3.24	3.61				

Normal cycle time = *0.387* + Allowance *15%* Standard Time = *0.445* min.

Number of Cycles

In Example S8.1 the time study was conducted for 10 cycles. However, was this sufficient for us to have confidence that the standard time was accurate? The time study is actually a statistical sample distribution, where the number of cycles is the sample size.

Assuming that this distribution of sample times is normally distributed (a traditional assumption for time study), we can use the following formula to determine the sample size, n, for a time study:

$$n = \left(\frac{zs}{e\overline{T}}\right)^2$$

where

z = the number of standard deviations from the mean in a normal distribution reflecting a level of statistical confidence

$s = \sqrt{\dfrac{\Sigma(x_i - \bar{x})^2}{n - 1}}$ = sample standard deviation from the sample time study

$\overline{T}$ = the average job cycle time from the sample time study

e = the degree of error from the true mean of the distribution

EXAMPLE S8.3 | Determining the Number of Cycles for a Time Study

In Example S8.1 the Metro Food Services Company conducted a time study for 10 cycles of a job assembling ham and cheese sandwiches, which we will consider to be a sample. The average cycle time, $\overline{T}$, for the job was 0.361 minute, computed by dividing the total time for 10 cycles of the job, 3.61, by the number of cycles, 10. The standard deviation of the sample was 0.03 minute. The company wants to determine the number of cycles for a time study such that it can be 95% confident that the average time computed from the time study is within 5% of the true average cycle time.

Solution: The sample size is computed using $z = 1.96$ for a probability of .95, as follows:

$$
\begin{aligned}
n &= \left(\frac{zs}{eT}\right)^2 \\
&= \left[\frac{(1.96)(0.03)}{(0.05)(0.361)}\right]^2 \\
&= 10.61, \text{ or } 11
\end{aligned}
$$

The time study should include 11 cycles to be 95% confident that the time-study average job cycle time is within 5% of the true average job cycle time. The 10 cycles that were used in our time study were just about right. An OM Tools spreadsheet for Example S8.3 (as well as Example S8.1) is shown in **Exhibit S8.2.**

Elemental Time Files

Workers often do not like to be the subject of a time study and will not cooperate, and rating workers can be a difficult, subjective task. Time studies can also be time-consuming and costly. As an alternative, many companies have accumulated large files of time-study data over time for elements common to many jobs throughout their organization. Instead of conducting an actual time study, these **elemental standard time files** can be accessed to derive the standard time, or the elemental times in the files can be used in conjunction with current time-study data, reducing the time and cost required for the study.

Elemental standard time files Predetermined job element times.

It can be difficult, however, to put together a standard time without the benefit of a time study. The engineer/technician is left wondering if anything was left out or if the environment or job conditions have changed enough since the data were collected to alter the original elemental times. Also, the individuals who develop the current standard time must have a great deal of confidence in their predecessor's abilities and competence.

EXHIBIT S8.2

ExhibitS8.2 Time Study [Compatibility Mode] - Excel

B27 | f_x =(B26*B25/(F4*M21))^2

Stopwatch Time Study — **Examples S8.1and S8.3**

Input:

No. of work elements	4
No. of cycles	10
Allowance factor	0.15

Precision	0.05
Confidence level	0.95
Standard deviation	0.03

Input work elements, element times, rating factors, an allowance factor, and other model parameters. Excel will calculate normal time, standard time, and sample size.

Calculations:

	Element Cycle Times													
Work Element	**1**	**2**	**3**	**4**	**5**	**6**	**7**	**8**	**9**	**10**	**Rating Factor**	**Average element time**	**Normal element time**	**Standard element time**
Grasp and lay out bread slices	0.04	0.05	0.05	0.04	0.06	0.05	0.06	0.06	0.07	0.05	1.05	0.053	0.056	0.064
Spread mayonnaise	0.07	0.06	0.07	0.08	0.07	0.07	0.08	0.10	0.09	0.08	1.00	0.077	0.077	0.089
Place ham, cheese and lettuce	0.12	0.11	0.14	0.12	0.13	0.13	0.13	0.12	0.14	0.14	1.10	0.128	0.141	0.162
Place top, slice and stack	0.10	0.12	0.08	0.09	0.11	0.11	0.10	0.10	0.12	0.10	1.10	0.103	0.113	0.130
												0.000	0.000	0.000
												0.000	0.000	0.000
												0.000	0.000	0.000
												0.000	0.000	0.000
												0.000	0.000	0.000
												0.000	0.000	0.000
												0.361	0.387	0.445

Output:

Normal cycle time	0.387
Standard job time	0.445
Standard deviation	0.030
Z-value	1.960
Sample size	10.612

Normal Elemental Time	$Nt = (\bar{t})(RF)$
Normal Cycle Time	$NT = \sum Nt$
Standard Job Time	$ST = (NT)(1 + AF)$
Time Study Sample Size	$n = \left(\frac{zs}{eT}\right)^2$

Predetermined Motion Times

Predetermined motion times Predetermined times for basic micromotions.

The use of elemental standard times from company files is one way to construct a standard time without a time study, or before a task or job is even in effect yet. Another approach for developing time standards without a time study is to use a system of **predetermined motion times**. A predetermined motion time system provides normal times for basic, generic micromotions, such as reach, grasp, move, position, and release, that are common to many jobs. These basic motion times have been developed in a laboratory-type environment from studies of workers across a variety of industries and, in some cases, from motion pictures of workers.

To develop a standard time using predetermined motion times, a job must be broken down into its basic micromotions. Then the appropriate motion time is selected from a set of tables (or a computerized database), taking into account job conditions such as the weight of an object moved and the distance it might be moved. The standard time is determined by summing all the motion times. As might be suspected, even a very short job can have many motions; a job of only one minute can have more than 100 basic motions.

Several systems of predetermined motion times exist, the two most well known being methods time measurement (MTM) and basic motion time study (BMT). Table S8.1 provides an example of an MTM table for the motion *move*. The motion times are measured in *time*

TABLE S8.1 MTM Table For *Move*

DISTANCE MOVED (INCHES)	A	B	C	HAND IN MOTION B	WEIGHT (b) UP TO:	DYNAMIC FACTOR	STATIC CONSTANT TMU	CASE AND DESCRIPTION
¾ or less	2.0	2.0	2.0	1.7				
1	2.5	2.9	3.4	2.3	2.5	1.00	0	
2	3.6	4.6	5.2	2.9				A. Move object to other hand or against stop.
3	4.9	5.7	6.7	3.6	7.5	1.06	2.2	
4	6.1	6.9	8.0	4.3				
5	7.3	8.0	9.2	5.0	12.5	1.11	3.9	
6	8.1	8.9	10.3	5.7				
7	8.9	9.7	11.1	6.5	17.5	1.17	5.6	
8	9.7	10.6	11.8	7.2				
9	10.5	11.5	12.7	7.9	22.5	1.22	7.4	B. Move object to approximate or indefinite location.
10	11.3	12.2	13.5	8.6				
12	12.9	13.4	15.2	10.0	27.5	1.28	9.1	
14	14.4	14.6	16.9	11.4				
16	16.0	15.8	18.7	12.8	32.5	1.33	10.8	
18	17.6	17.0	20.4	14.2				
20	19.2	18.2	22.1	15.6	37.5	1.39	12.5	
22	20.8	19.4	23.8	17.0				
24	22.4	20.6	25.5	18.4	42.5	1.44	14.3	C. Move object to exact location.
26	24.0	21.8	27.3	19.8				
28	25.5	23.1	29.0	21.2	47.5	1.50	16.0	
30	27.1	24.3	30.7	22.7				
Additional	0.8	0.6	0.85			TMU per inch over 30 in.		

Source: MTM Association for Standards and Research.

measurement units, or *TMUs*, where one TMU equals 0.0006 minute and 100,000 TMUs equal one hour.

There are several advantages of using a predetermined motion time system. It enables a standard time to be developed for a new job before the job is even part of the production process. Worker cooperation and compliance are not required, and the workplace is not disrupted. Performance ratings are included in the motion times, eliminating this subjective part of developing standard times.

There are also disadvantages to a predetermined motion time system. It ignores the job context within which a single motion takes place—that is, where each motion is considered independently of all others. What the hand comes from doing when it reaches for an object may affect the motion time as well as the overall sequence of motion. Also, although predetermined motion times are generally determined from a broad sample of workers across several industries, they may not reflect the skill level, training, or abilities of workers in a specific company.

Work Sampling

Work sampling Determines the proportion of time a worker spends on activities.

Work sampling is a technique for determining the proportion of time a worker or machine spends on various activities. The procedure for work sampling is to make brief, random observations of a worker or machine over a period of time and record the activity in which they are involved. An estimate of the proportion of time that is being spent on an activity is determined by dividing the number of observations recorded for that activity by the total number of observations. A work sample can indicate the proportion of time a worker is busy or idle or performing a task or how frequently a machine is idle or in use. A secretary's work can be sampled to determine what portion of the day is spent word processing, answering the telephone, filing, and so on. It also can be used to determine the allowance factor that was used to calculate the standard time for a time study. (Recall that the allowance factor was a percentage of time reflecting worker delays and idle time for machine breakdowns, personal needs, and so on.)

The primary uses of work sampling are to determine *ratio delay*, which is the percentage of time a worker or machine is delayed or idle, and to analyze jobs that have *nonrepetitive tasks*—for example, a secretary, a nurse, or a police officer. The information from a work sample in the form of the percentage of time spent on each job activity or task can be useful in designing or redesigning jobs, developing job descriptions, and determining the level of work output that can be expected from a worker for use in planning.

The steps in work sampling are summarized as follows:

1. ***Define the job activities.*** The activities that are to be observed must be exhaustive so that any time an observation is made, an activity is clearly indicated. For example, if the activities of interest are "worker idle" and "worker not idle," this clearly defines all possible activities for the work sample.
2. ***Determine the number of observations in the work sample.*** The purpose of the work sample is to calculate a proportion of time that a worker is performing a specific job activity. The degree of accuracy of the work sample depends on the number of observations, or sample size. The larger the sample size, the more accurate the proportion estimate will be. The accuracy of the proportion, p, is usually expressed in terms of an allowable degree of error, e (for example, 3% or 4%), with a degree of confidence of, for example, 95% to 98%. Using these parameters and assuming the sample is approximately normally distributed, we can determine the sample size using the following formula:

$$n = \left(\frac{z}{e}\right)^2 p(1 - p)$$

where

n = the sample size (number of sample observations)
z = the number of standard deviations from the mean for the desired level of confidence

e = the degree of allowable error in the sample estimate
p = the proportion of time spent on a work activity estimated prior to calculating the work sample

3. ***Determine the length of the sampling period.*** The length of the work sampling study must be sufficient to record the number of observations for the work activity determined in step 2. The schedule of observations must be random. (If workers knew an observation would be taken every half hour, they might alter their normal work activity.) The most direct way to achieve randomness is to tie the observation schedule to a table or computer program of random numbers. For example, if a table of three-digit random numbers is used, the first one or two random numbers in the digit could specify the time in minutes between observations.
4. ***Conduct the work sampling study and record the observations.*** In this step the observations are tallied, and the proportion, p, is computed by dividing the number of activity observations by the total number of observations.
5. ***Periodically recompute the number of observations.*** Recall from step 2 that p is an estimate of the proportion of time spent on a work activity made prior to the sample. As the work sample is conducted, it may be discovered that the actual proportion is different from what was originally estimated. Therefore, it is beneficial periodically to recompute the sample size, n, based on preliminary values of p to see if more or fewer observations are needed than first determined.

EXAMPLE S8.4 | Conducting a Work Sampling Study

The Northern Lights Company is a retail catalog operation specializing in outdoor clothing. The company has a pool of 28 telephone operators to take catalog orders during the business hours of 9 A.M. to 5:00 P.M. (The company uses a smaller pool of operators for the remaining 16 off-peak hours.) The company has recently been experiencing a larger number of lost calls because operators are busy and suspects it is because the operators are spending around 30% of their time describing products to customers. The company believes that if operators knew more about the products instead of having to pull up a description screen on the computer each time a customer asked a question about a product, they could save a lot of operator time, so it is thinking about instituting a product awareness training program. However, first the company wants to perform a work sampling study to determine the proportion of time operators are answering product-related questions. The company wants the proportion of this activity to be accurate within ±2%, with a 95% degree of confidence.

Solution: First determine the number of observations to take, as follows:

$$n = \left(\frac{z}{e}\right)^2 p(1-p)$$

$$= \left(\frac{1.96}{0.02}\right)^2 (0.3)(0.7)$$

$$= 2016.84, \text{ or } 2017$$

This is a large number of observations; however, since there are 28 operators, only 2017/28, or 72, visits to observe the operators need to be made. Actually, the observations could be made by picking up a one-way phone line to listen in on the operator–customer conversation. The "conversation" schedule was set up using a two-digit random number table (similar to Table S13.3). The random numbers are the minutes between each observation, and since the random numbers ranged from 00 to 99, the average time between observations is about 50 minutes. The study was expected to take about eight days (with slightly more than nine observations per day).

EXHIBIT S8.3

ExhibitS8.3.Work Sampling [Compatibility Mode] - Excel

File Home Insert Page Layout Formulas Data Review View Tell me what you want to do...

C11 =((C10/C5)^2)*C9*(1-C9)

	A	B	C	D	E	F	G
1	**Work Sampling**				**Example S8.4**		
2							
3	*Input:*	No. of resources	28		***Observation***	***No. Idle***	***% Idle***
4		No. of observations	2		1		0.00
5		Precision	0.02		2		0.00
6		Confidence level	0.95				
7							
8							
9	*Output:*	**p-bar**	**0.3800**				
10		**Z-value**	**1.96**				
11		**Sample size**	**2263**				
15		*Work Sampling Sample Size*					

$$n = \left(\frac{z}{e}\right)^2 \bar{p}(1-\bar{p})$$

Input no. of resources, no. of times a resource was observed idle , and the precision and confidence level required.

Excel will calculate the average percent busy and the sample size.

In fact, after 10 observation trips and a total of 280 observations, the portion of time the operators spent answering the customers' product-related questions was 38%, so the random sample size was recomputed:

$$n = \left(\frac{1.96}{0.02}\right)^2 (0.38)(0.62)$$
$$= 2263$$

This number of observations is 246 more than originally computed, or almost nine additional observation trips, resulting in a total of 81. (As noted previously, it is beneficial periodically to recompute the sample size based on preliminary results in order to ensure that the final result will reflect the degree of accuracy and confidence originally specified.)

An OM Tools spreadsheet for Example S8.4 is shown in **Exhibit S8.3**. (Note that this example does not include individual "observations," so when entering the input data to start the "work sampling" module we arbitrarily entered a value of "2" for the number of observations in order to access the module.)

Work sampling is an easier, cheaper, and quicker approach to work measurement than time study. It tends to be less disruptive of the workplace and less annoying to workers, because it requires much less time to sample than time study. Also, the "symbolic" stopwatch is absent. A disadvantage is the large number of observations needed to obtain an accurate sample estimate, sometimes requiring the study to span several days or weeks.

Summary

As the nature of work changes, the techniques and approaches to methods analysis and work measurement also change. Time study has historically been used to establish piece-rate incentive wage systems; however, as such systems are increasingly being perceived as counter to quality-improvement efforts, work measurement and time study are being used less and less for that purpose. However, work-measurement techniques are still useful and widely used, especially in service companies, for production planning, scheduling, and cost control.

Key Terms

elemental standard time files Company files containing historical data of elemental time studies that can be used to develop a standard time.

normal time In a time study, the elemental average time multiplied by a performance rating.

predetermined motion times Normal times for basic, generic micromotions developed by an outside organization in a laboratory-type environment.

standard time The time required by an "average" worker to perform a job once under normal circumstances and conditions.

work sampling A technique for determining the proportion of time a worker or machine spends on job activities.

Key Formulas

Normal Elemental Time

$$Nt = (\bar{t})(RF)$$

Normal Cycle Time

$$NT = \Sigma Nt$$

Standard Job Time

$$ST = (NT)(1 + AF)$$

Time-Study Sample Size

$$n = \left(\frac{zs}{e\bar{T}}\right)^2$$

Work Sampling Sample Size

$$n = \left(\frac{z}{e}\right)^2 p(1 - p)$$

Solved Problems

WileyPLUS

1. Standard Job Time

A manufacturing company has conducted a time study for 10 cycles of a job. The job has five elements, and the total elemental times (minutes) for each element and performance rating factors are as follows:

ELEMENT	Σt(MIN)	*RF*
1	3.61	1.05
2	4.84	0.90
3	2.93	1.00
4	4.91	1.10
5	1.78	0.95

Compute the standard time using an allowance factor of 18%.

Solution

Step 1. Determine the normal elemental times by multiplying the average elemental times by the rating factors.

ELEMENT	Σt	$\bar{t}$	*RF*	*Nt*
1	3.61	0.361	1.05	0.379
2	4.84	0.484	0.90	0.436
3	2.93	0.293	1.00	0.293
4	4.91	0.491	1.10	0.542
5	1.78	0.178	0.95	0.169

Step 2. Compute the normal cycle time.

$$NT = \Sigma Nt$$
$$= 1.819 \text{ min}$$

Step 3. Compute the standard time.

$$ST = NT(1 + AF)$$
$$= 1.819(1 + 0.18)$$
$$= 2.146 \text{ min}$$

2. Time-Study Sample Size

For the previous problem, determine the sample size, n, for a time study so there is 98% confidence that the average time computed from the time study is within 4% of the actual average cycle time. The sample standard deviation is 0.23.

Solution

Step 1. Determine the value of z for a probability of .98 from the normal table in Appendix A and $\bar{t}$.

$$\bar{T} = \Sigma\bar{t} = 1.807 \text{ min}$$
$$z = 2.33$$

Step 2. Compute the sample size.

$$n = \left(\frac{zs}{e\bar{T}}\right)^2$$

$$= \left[\frac{(2.33)(0.23)}{(0.04)(1.807)}\right]^2$$

$$= 54.97, \text{ or } 55 \text{ cycles}$$

3. Work Sampling

A technician is conducting a work sampling study of a machine maintenance worker to determine the portion of the time the worker spends in one particular department. Management has indicated that they believe that repairs in this department consume 50% of the maintenance worker's time, and they want the estimate to be within ±5% of the true proportion, with 95% confidence.

Solution

Determine the number of observations in the sample.

$$n = \left(\frac{z}{e}\right)^2 p(1-p)$$

$$= \left(\frac{1.96}{0.05}\right)^2 (0.5)(0.5)$$

$$= 384.16, \text{ or } 385 \text{ observations}$$

Questions

S8.1. Compare the use of predetermined motion times for developing time standards instead of using time-study methods, and discuss the advantages and disadvantages.

S8.2. Describe the steps involved in conducting a time study, and discuss any difficulties you might envision at various steps.

S8.3. What are some of the criticisms of work measurement, in general, and time study, specifically, that have caused their popularity to wane in recent years?

S8.4. A traditional performance rating benchmark (or guideline) for "normal" effort, or speed, is dealing 52 cards into four piles, forming a square with each pile one foot apart, in 0.50 minute. Conduct an experiment with one or more fellow students in which one deals the cards and the others rate the dealer's performance, and then compare these subjective ratings with the actual time of the dealer.

S8.5. When conducting a work sampling study, how can the number of observations required by the study be reduced?

S8.6. When is work sampling a more appropriate work-measurement technique than time study?

S8.7. Describe the steps involved in conducting a work sample.

S8.8. Select a job that you are conveniently able to observe, such as a secretary, store clerk, or custodian, and design a work sampling study for a specific job activity. Indicate how the initial estimate of the proportion of time for the activity would be determined and how the observation schedule would be developed. (However, do not conduct the actual study.)

Problems

WileyPLUS

S8.1. A time-study technician at the Southern Textile Company has conducted a time study of an operator of a spinning machine that spins rough cotton yarn into a finer yarn on bobbins for use in a weaving operation. The time study was requested as the result of a union grievance. The average cycle time for the operator to replace all the full bobbins on the machine with empty bobbins was 3.62 minutes. The technician assigned an overall performance rating for the job of 100%, and the allowance factor specified by the union contract is 15%. Compute the standard time for this job.

S8.2. A sewing operator at the Gameday Sportswear Company assembles baseball-style caps with a team logo from precut wedges of material that form the crown, a precut bill, and additional precut pieces of material for the headband and reinforcing. The job encompasses seven basic elements. A time technician for the company has conducted a time study of the job for 20 cycles and accumulated for the following elemental times and assigned performance ratings:

ELEMENT	Σt	RF
1	3.15	1.10
2	8.67	1.05
3	14.25	1.10
4	11.53	1.00
5	6.91	0.95
6	5.72	1.05
7	5.38	1.05

Determine the standard time for this job using an allowance factor of 12%.

S8.3. The Braykup China Company makes an assortment of gift and commemorative items with team and college logos, such as plates, bowls, and mugs. One popular item is a commemorative stein. The steins are all

Time-Study Observation Sheet

Identification of operation	Stein assembly		Date 7/15
	Operator Smith	Approval Jones	Observer Russell

			Cycles										Summary			
			1	2	3	4	5	6	7	8	9	10	Σt	$\bar{t}$	RF	Nt
1	Place mug in vise/ holder upside down	t														
		R	0.12	2.05	4.04	5.92	7.86	9.80	11.73	13.65	15.64	17.59			1.05	
2	Press both bracket sides around handle	t														
		R	0.19	2.12	4.09	6.01	7.94	9.88	11.81	13.72	15.7	17.66			1.00	
3	Solder bracket seam on inside of handle	t														
		R	1.05	3.01	4.91	6.87	8.81	10.71	12.66	14.56	16.52	18.50			1.10	
4	Turn stein right side up	t														
		R	1.13	3.08	4.98	6.93	8.90	10.79	12.74	14.66	16.63	18.59			1.10	
5	Solder lid top to bracket	t														
		R	1.75	3.76	5.65	7.60	9.56	11.45	13.36	15.34	17.31	19.28			1.05	
6	Remove stein from holder and place in box	t														
		R	1.91	3.90	5.79	7.75	9.70	11.61	13.53	15.49	17.46	19.44			1.00	
		t														

physically identical, with the only style change being the team colors, name, and logo. The stein parts include a porcelain mug, a hinged pewter top that is opened up when someone drinks from the mug, and a bracket that attaches the top to the mug handle. The bracket is soldered together from two matching parts; on one end, the bracket encircles the handle and the other end attaches to the lid mechanism. The stein is assembled from these parts in one job. A time-study chart for this job with the elements of the job and the time observations obtained from a stopwatch time study are shown on at this bottom of this page.

a. Using an allowance factor of 15%, determine the standard time for this job.

b. If the company pays workers a piece rate of \$0.18 per stein, what wage would an average worker make per hour and what would the subject of this time study make per hour?

S8.4. Puff 'n' Stuff Services is a small company that assembles mailings for clients in the Atlanta area. Different-size envelopes are stuffed with various items such as coupons, advertisements, political messages, and so on, by a staff of workers who are paid on a piece-rate basis. A time study of a job has been conducted by an engineering consulting firm using a subject stuffing manila envelopes. The observations from the time study for 10 cycles of the five-element job and the performance rating for each element are as follows.

	ELEMENTAL TIMES (MIN)										
ELEMENT	1	2	3	4	5	6	7	8	9	10	RF
1	0.09	0.10	0.12	0.09	0.08	0.07	0.09	0.06	0.10	0.09	1.10
2	0.08	0.09	0.08	0.07	0.10	0.10	0.08	0.06	0.11	0.09	0.95
3	0.15	0.13	0.14	0.16	0.12	0.15	0.16	0.15	0.15	0.14	0.90
4	0.10	0.09	0.09	0.08	0.11	0.08	0.09	0.10	0.10	0.09	1.00
5	0.06	0.05	0.09	0.06	0.07	0.05	0.08	0.05	0.09	0.07	0.95

a. Using an allowance factor of 10%, compute the standard time for this job.

b. If the firm pays workers a piece rate of \$0.03 per envelope for this job, what would the average worker make per hour, and what would the subject of the study make per hour?

S8.5. The Konishi Electronics Company manufactures computer microchips. A particular job that has been under analysis as part of a quality-improvement program was the subject of a time study. The time study encompassed 20 job cycles, and the results include the following cumulative times and performance rating factors for each element:

ELEMENT	ΣT (MIN)	RF
1	10.52	1.15
2	18.61	1.10
3	26.20	1.10
4	16.46	1.05

a. Compute the standard time for this job using an allowance factor of 15%.

b. Using a sample standard deviation of 0.51 minutes, determine the number of cycles for this time study such that the company would be 95% confident that the average time from the time study is within 5% of the true average cycle time.

S8.6. Data Products, Inc., packages and distributes a variety of personal computer-related products. A time study has been conducted for a job packaging 3.5-inch personal computer diskettes for shipment to customers. The job requires a packager to place 20 diskettes in a rectangular plastic bag, close the bag with a twist tie, and place the filled bag into a bin, which is replaced by another worker when it is filled. The job can be broken into four basic elements. The elemental times (in minutes) were obtained from the time study for 10 job cycles shown in the following table.

	ELEMENTAL TIMES										
ELEMENT	1	2	3	4	5	6	7	8	9	10	*RF*
1	0.36	0.31	0.42	0.35	0.38	0.30	0.41	0.42	0.35	0.35	1.05
2	0.81	0.95	0.76	0.85	1.01	1.02	0.95	0.90	0.87	0.88	0.90
3	0.56	0.38	0.42	0.45	0.51	0.48	0.50	0.52	0.39	0.46	1.00
4	0.19	0.12	0.16	0.21	0.15	0.16	0.18	0.19	0.19	0.15	1.05

a. Using an allowance factor of 16%, determine the standard time for this job.

b. Determine the number of cycles for this time study such that the company would be 95% confident that the average time from the time study is within ±4% of the true average cycle time.

S8.7. In Problem S8.2, a time study was conducted for the job of sewing baseball-style caps. Using a sample standard deviation of 0.25, determine the number of cycles for the time study such that the company would be 98% confident that the average cycle time for the job is within 6% of the actual average cycle time.

S8.8. Determine the sample size for the time study of the stein assembly operation described in Problem S8.3. The Braykup China Company wants to be 95% confident that the average cycle time from the study is within 2% of the true average.

S8.9. Sonichi Electronics manufactures small electronic consumer items such as portable clocks, calculators, and radios. The company is concerned about the high cost of its product-inspection operation. As a result, it had its industrial engineering department conduct a time study of an inspector who inspects portable radios. The operation consists of seven elements, as follows: (1) The package is opened and the radio is removed; (2) the battery casing cover is removed; (3) two AA batteries are inserted; (4) the radio is turned on, and the inspector tunes to a station and listens briefly to at least two stations; (5) the radio is turned off and the batteries are removed; (6) the battery cover is replaced; and (7) the radio is repackaged. The time-study observations (in minutes) for 10 cycles are shown in the following table.

	ELEMENTAL TIMES										
ELEMENT	1	2	3	4	5	6	7	8	9	10	*RF*
1	0.23	0.20	0.19	0.20	0.18	0.18	0.24	0.25	0.17	0.20	1.05
2	0.12	0.10	0.08	0.09	0.10	0.10	0.13	0.14	0.10	0.11	1.00
3	0.16	0.18	0.17	0.17	0.17	0.20	0.16	0.15	0.18	0.18	1.05
4	0.26	0.28	0.32	0.19	0.35	0.33	0.22	0.28	0.28	0.27	0.95
5	0.10	0.08	0.09	0.10	0.11	0.11	0.09	0.12	0.12	0.12	1.00
6	0.06	0.08	0.08	0.08	0.07	0.06	0.10	0.08	0.09	0.11	1.00
7	0.20	0.28	0.25	0.36	0.17	0.22	0.33	0.19	0.20	0.16	1.05

a. The allowance factor for this job is 15%. Determine the standard time.

b. If management wants the estimate of the average cycle time to be within ±0.03 minute with a 95% level of confidence, how many job cycles should be observed?

c. Management is considering putting inspectors on a piece-rate wage system in order to provide them with greater incentive to inspect more items. What effect might this have on the quality-inspection function?

S8.10. Baker Street Stereo is a catalog ordering operation. The company maintains an ordering staff of 30 telephone operators, who take orders from customers. Management wants to determine the proportion of time that operators are idle. A work sampling study was conducted at random over a four-day period, and the following random observations were recorded:

OBSERVATION		OPERATOR IDLE
10/15:	1	6
	2	5
	3	4
	4	7
	5	5
	6	2
10/16:	7	4
	8	3
	9	5
	10	6
	11	4
10/17:	12	7
	13	3
	14	3
	15	6
	16	5
	17	7
	18	4
10/19:	19	5
	20	6

If management wants the proportion of time from the work sampling study to be ±2% accurate with a confidence level of 98%, how many additional sample observations should be taken?

S8.11. The associate dean of the college of business at Tech has succumbed to faculty pressure to purchase a new fax machine, although she has always contended that the machine would have minimal use. She has estimated that the machine will be used only 20% of the time. Now that the machine has been installed, she has asked the students in the introductory OM course to conduct a work sampling study to see what proportion of time the new fax machine is used. She wants the estimate to be within 3% of the actual proportion, with a confidence level of 95%. Determine the sample size for the work sample.

S8.12. The Rowntown Cab Company has 26 cabs. The local manager wants to conduct a work sampling study to determine what proportion of the time a cab driver is sitting idle, which he estimates is about 30%. The cabs were observed at random during a five-day period by the dispatcher, who simply called each cab and checked on its status. The manager wants the estimate to be within ±3% of the proportion, with a 95% level of confidence.

a. Determine the sample size for this work sampling study.

b. The results of the first 20 observations of the work sampling study are shown as follows.

OBSERVATION	IDLE CABS	OBSERVATION	IDLE CABS
1	4	11	6
2	3	12	4
3	5	13	3
4	8	14	5
5	7	15	2
6	5	16	0
7	3	17	3
8	6	18	4
9	4	19	5
10	3	20	4

What is the revised estimate of the sample size based on these initial results?

S8.13. The head of the department of management at State University has noticed that the four secretaries in the departmental office seem to spend a lot of time answering questions from students that could better be answered by the college advising office, by faculty advisors, or simply from the available literature; that is, course schedules, catalogs, the student handbook, and so on. As a result, the department head is considering remodeling the office with cubicles so students do not have easy access to the secretaries. However, before investing in this project the head has decided to conduct a work sampling study to determine the proportion of time the secretaries spend assisting students. The head arranged for a graduate assistant to make observations for the work sample, but the graduate student's schedule enabled her to make only 300 random observations in the time allotted for the study. The results of the work sampling study showed that the secretaries assisted students 12% of the time, somewhat less than the head anticipated.

a. Given the number of observations that were included in the work sampling study, how confident can the department head be that the sample result is within 3% of the actual proportion?

b. How many fewer or additional observations would be required for the department head to be 95% confident in the work sampling results?

S8.14. In Problem S8.11, the OM students have completed 100 observations of the work sampling study and have a preliminary result showing the fax machine is in use 31% of the time. How many additional observations are required based on this result?

S8.15. Northwoods Backpackers is a mail-order operation specializing in outdoor camping and hiking equipment and clothing. In addition to its normal pool of telephone operators to take customer orders, the company has a group of customer service operators to respond to customer complaints and product-related inquiries. The time required for customer service operators to handle customer calls differs, based on an operator's ability to think fast and quickly recall from memory product information (without using product description screens on the computer). The company wants to determine the standard time required for a customer service operator to complete a call without having to resort to a time study. Instead, management had a work sampling study of an operator conducted during an eight-hour workday that included 160 observations. The study showed the operator was talking to customers only 78% of the time, and call records indicated that the operator handled 120 customer calls during the day. The customer service manager has indicated that the particular operator that was studied performs at about 110% compared with a normal operator. Company policy allows 15% personal time on the job for lunch, breaks, and so on. Determine the standard time per customer call.

S8.16. In Problem S8.15, how confident can Northwoods Backpackers be in the standard time it computed if it assumed that the proportion of time that an operator is busy determined from the work sampling study is accurate within ±4%? How many additional observations might be needed for Northwoods to be 95% confident in the standard time per customer call?

S8.17. The manager of the order-distribution center for Northwoods Backpackers has a company directive to downsize his operation. He has decided to conduct work sampling studies of employees in the order-processing department, the warehouse area, and the packaging area. In the warehouse area he has 17 employees who locate items, pull them, and put them on conveyors to the packaging area. A work sampling study was conducted over a five-day period to determine the proportion of time warehouse employees were idle, and out of the 50 random observations, employees were idle 400 times.

a. How many observations should be taken if the manager wants to be 90% confident the estimate is within ±5% of the actual proportion of time a warehouse employee is idle?

b. The manager also conducted a work sampling study of the packaging area and discovered that the 28 employees were idle approximately 37% of the time. How might the manager redesign his operation to downsize and be more efficient?

S8.18. The manager of the Burger Doodle restaurant believes the time to fill orders at the drive-through window is too long. She suspects that the window cashier spends too much time making change, and she is considering using even pricing for most menu items to reduce the window time. She has decided to conduct a work sampling study to determine the proportion of time the cashier is making change. During a three-day period the manager checked the cashier 150 times and recorded 84 observations in which the cashier was making change.

a. How many more observations should be taken if the manager wants to be 99% confident that her estimate is within ±1% of the actual proportion of time the cashier is making change?

b. Based on the time required to take the first 150 observations, how many days will be required to conduct this study?

c. How could the manager reduce the number of days required to conduct in part (b)?

S8.19. The National Bank of Hamilton has opened up two new drive-through teller windows outside its main office building in downtown Hamilton. The bank is not sure that it needs both windows open all day so it has decided to conduct a work sampling study to determine the proportion of time the two tellers are idle between the hours of 10:00 A.M. to 11:30 A.M. and 1:00 P.M. to 3:00 P.M. The work sampling study was conducted at random over a five-day period, and the following observations were recorded:

OBSERVATION	TELLERS IDLE	OBSERVATION	TELLERS IDLE
1	1	11	1
2	1	12	1
3	0	13	2
4	0	14	2
5	0	15	0
6	2	16	1
7	1	17	2
8	2	18	2
9	2	19	0
10	1	20	1

21	2	26	1
22	2	27	0
23	2	28	2
24	0	29	0
25	1	30	2

a. Bank management wants the study to be ±5% accurate with a 95% confidence level. How many additional sample observations should be taken?

b. If the bank does not want to conduct a study of more than 100 observations, what level of confidence could it expect?

Case Problem

Case Problem S8.1 Measuring Faculty Work Activity at State University

At several recent meetings of the faculty senate at State University there has been discussion of media reports that college faculty are more concerned about their research than about teaching and, specifically, that faculty don't spend enough time working with students, which should be their main task. These media reports imply that faculty work only during the time they are in class, which for most faculty is between 6 and 12 hours per week. The faculty believes this information is misleading and dangerous to higher education in general. The faculty representatives on the senate claim that the time they spend in class is only a small portion of their actual workload, and although they spend some time on their research, they also dedicate a large portion of their time outside of class to class preparation and meeting with students. Unfortunately, few people outside of the faculty appear to believe this, including the students, parents, certain legislators, and, recently, several highly placed university administrators.

In an attempt to educate the students more about what faculty actually do with their time, the senate invited several student leaders to one of its meetings, where they discussed the issue. Among the students invited to this meeting was Mary Shipley, editor of *The Daily State*, the student newspaper. Subsequently, Mary wrote an editorial in the paper about how faculty members spent their time.

Mary was a student in the college of business at State; coincidentally, the topic currently under discussion in her operations management class was "Job Design and Work Measurement." The day after her editorial appeared, she was asked the following question in her class by a fellow student, Art Cohen:

"Mary, it looks like to me that all you did in your editorial was repeat what you had been told by the faculty at the faculty senate meeting. I don't really believe you have any idea about what faculty do, any more than the rest of us!"

Before Mary could respond, another student, Angela Watts, broke in, "Well, it shouldn't be too hard to check out. That's what we're studying in class right now—how to measure work. Why don't we check out how much time the faculty work at different tasks?"

At this point their teacher, Dr. Larry Moore, broke in. "That's a good idea, Angela, it sounds to me as if you just resolved our problem of a class project for this term. I'm going to break you all into teams and let each team monitor a specific faculty member, using work sampling to determine the amount of time the faculty member spends with students outside the classroom."

"That's not really going to provide any relevant information," interrupted Bobby Jenkins. "That will just provide us with a percentage of time faculty work with students. If professors spend 90% of their time working with students, that sounds great, but if they are only in their offices two hours a day, 90% of two hours is not very much."

"I see what you mean," Dr. Moore replied. "That's a good point. Somehow we need to determine how many hours a day a faculty member devotes to his or her job to have a frame of reference."

"The way it looks to me, a professor works only about three or four hours a day," said Rodney Jefferson. This drew laughter from the class and Dr. Moore.

"I don't think that's really true," responded Mary Shipley. "One of the things the faculty pointed out to me and I indicated in my editorial was that even though faculty members may not be in their offices all the time, they may still be working, either at home or in the library. And a lot of times they have committee work at various locations around campus." A lot of the class seemed to be in general agreement with this. "Anyway," Mary continued, "I don't think the issue is how much a professor works. I believe we all agree they put in a full seven- or eight-hour day like almost anyone else. The point as I see it is, what do they do with that time? Do they spend it all on their own research and writing or are they working with students?"

"Okay then," said Dr. Moore. "If we can all agree that the number of hours of work is a moot point, then let's set up our work sampling experiment. We'll break down the activities outside of classroom teaching as 'working with students,' or 'not working with students,' which could include anything else the faculty member is working on, such as research, making out tests, preparing for class, and so on. That should be all-inclusive. What proportion of time do you think a faculty member spends with students outside the classroom, to use a starting point? 10%? 20%?"

The class seemed to mull this over for a few minutes and someone shouted, "20%." Someone else said 30%, and after a few seconds people were simply talking back and forth.

"Okay, okay," said Dr. Moore, "everyone calm down. Let's say 20%. That sounds like a reasonable number to me, and you can always adjust it in the course of your experiment. Let's allow for an error of 3% and use a confidence level of 95%. Does this sound okay to everybody?" He waited a few moments for any negative reaction, but there seemed to be general agreement. "Good, I'll post teams on my office door by tomorrow, and I'll let each team select the faculty member they want to study. Let me know by the end of the week and I'll alert the faculty members so they will know what to expect. Also, it's possible someone might not want to participate, and I'll let you know that too so you can select someone else. Please be as unobtrusive as possible and try not to bother anybody. Okay, if there are no other questions, that's it. Get busy."

Describe how you would set up this work sampling experiment at your school, and, if your teacher is agreeable, carry out this project. Also, describe how you might alter the work sample to analyze other faculty work activities.

References

Barnes, R. M. *Motion and Time Study: Design and Measurement of Work*, 8th ed. New York: Wiley, 1980.

Emerson, H. P., and D. C. E. Maehring. *Origins of Industrial Engineering*. Atlanta: Institute of Industrial Engineers, 1988.

Gilbreth, F. *Motion Study*. New York: Van Nostrand, 1911.

Mundel, M. E. *Motion and Time Study: Improving Productivity*, 6th ed. Upper Saddle River, NJ: Prentice Hall, 1985.

Smith, G. L., Jr. *Work Measurement: A Systems Approach*. Columbus, OH: Grid Publishing, 1978.

Taylor, F. W. *The Principles of Scientific Management*. New York: Harper, 1911.

Wood, S., ed. *The Transformation of Work* (London: Unwin Hyman, 1989).

CHAPTER 9

Project Management

Connie Zhou/Google/Zuma Press

LEARNING OBJECTIVES

After reading this chapter, you will be able to:

- Discuss the project planning process, including planning tools, evaluation methods, and key elements.
- Discuss the benefits of and strategies for dealing with diverse project groups.
- Explain the basics of project scheduling and the use of Gantt charts.
- Define enterprise project management and discuss the key elements in project control.
- Develop and analyze both deterministic and probabilistic project networks.
- Use Microsoft Project for network analysis.
- Determine and explain project crashing and time-cost tradeoffs.

Sustainable "Cloud" Data Center Projects at Apple

In recent years Apple has undertaken major expansion projects to build new state-of-the-art data centers to support its current and future Internet services and iCloud activities. Apple's iCloud is the largest supplier of online media services for U.S. consumers, equaling the usage of Google and Dropbox combined. The company's data centers handle huge terabytes of data (where 1 terabyte equals 1 trillion bytes) for iMessages (over 2 billion per day) from its 250 million iCloud users, FaceTime calls, iCloud documents and photos, emails, calendars, contacts, iPhone location connections, iBooks, maps, Siri, iOS software updates, iTunes transactions, and app store titles.

Data centers are basically massive warehouses that cover several hundred thousand square feet packed with stacks of servers and thousands of miles of cable and wiring. They are major construction projects requiring years of planning, the involvement of large project teams, and precise scheduling to meet customers' rapidly expanding computing needs. They also require massive amounts of electricity to power their processors—one data center can consume as much electricity as a small town—and they generate a tremendous amount of heat that must be evacuated, requiring even more energy. It is estimated that data centers, in general, consume approximately 1.5 percent of the world's electricity, so their construction and operation is a significant issue for governments and green watchdog organizations. Apple has made a substantial commitment to minimize the impact of its products and company on the environment. As part of this commitment Apple powers its data centers entirely by clean and renewable sources such as solar, wind, biogas fuel cells, micro-hydro power, and geothermal energy from onsite and locally obtained resources, which means no matter how much data they handle, there is a zero greenhouse gas impact on the environment from their energy use.

One of Apple's recently constructed data centers in Maiden, North Carolina, cost $1 billion and encompasses a half million square-feet, placing it among the top ten largest data centers in the United States, and is estimated to hold over 100,000 web servers. On any given day, between 60 and 100 percent of the energy it uses is generated onsite through biogas fuel cells (using methane from nearby landfills), and two 20-megawatt solar arrays—the nation's largest privately owned renewable energy installation. It generates 167 million kilowatt-hours of renewable energy per year, enough to power the equivalent of 12,700 North Carolina homes; and the recent addition of another 17-megawatt solar array is capable of producing 39 million kWh per year.

Apple's data center in Prineville, Oregon, which will ultimately encompass almost 700,000 square-feet, has a micro-hydro system that harnesses the power of water that flows through local, 60-year-old irrigation canals. These micro-hydro projects generate 12 million kWh of clean, renewable energy a year. To supplement this micro-hydro generation, Apple has access to enough local wind energy to power the entire data center. At its Reno, Nevada, 400,000 square-foot data center, Apple, in conjunction with a local utility, constructed a 20-megawatt solar array using a new kind of photovoltaic solar panel with curved mirrors that concentrates sunlight, which is well-suited to the region's bright, sunny skies. The solar array has an annual production capacity of over 43 million kWh of clean, renewable energy, and additional solar arrays are planned as the data center expands.

These very successful and sustainable projects, and many more like them, enable Apple to both serve its millions of customers while fulfilling its commitment to the environment.

In this chapter we will learn how companies plan, manage, and schedule projects, including how they use project management tools like CPM/PERT.

Source: The Apple website at www.Apple.com.

Activity Individual job or work effort requiring labor, resources, and time, and subject to management control.

Project A unique, one-time operational activity or effort.

In other chapters we discuss the scheduling of repetitive operations and **activities**, such as work scheduling and job scheduling, as an important aspect of managing an operation. Operational schedules are established to keep the flow of products or services through the supply chain on time. However, not all operational activities are repetitive; some are unique, occurring only once within a specified time frame. Such unique, one-time activities are referred to as **projects**.

Project management is the management of the work to develop and implement an innovation or change in an existing operation. It encompasses planning the project and controlling the project activities, subject to resource and budget constraints, to keep the project on schedule. Examples of projects include constructing facilities and buildings, such as houses, factories, a shopping mall, an athletic stadium, or an arena; developing a military weapons system, new aircraft, or new ship; launching a satellite system; constructing an oil pipeline, developing and implementing a new computer system; planning a rock concert, football bowl game, or basketball tournament; and introducing new products into the market.

Projects have become increasingly pervasive in companies in recent years. The nature of the global business environment is such that new machinery and equipment, as well as new production processes and computer support systems, are constantly evolving. This provides the capability of developing new products and services, which generates consumer demand for even greater product diversity. As a result, a larger proportion of total organizational effort now goes toward project-oriented activities than in the past. Thus, the planning and management of projects has taken on a more crucial role in operations management.

In this chapter we focus on project management using CPM and PERT network scheduling techniques that are popular because they provide a graph or visual representation of the interrelationship and sequence of individual project activities. However, before presenting the CPM/PERT technique, we will discuss the primary elements of the project management process—planning, scheduling, and control.

Project Planning

The general management process is concerned with the planning, organization, and control of an ongoing process or activity such as the production of a product or delivery of a service. Project management is different in that it requires a commitment of resources and people to an important undertaking that is not repetitive and involves a relatively short period of time, after which the management effort is dissolved. A project has a unique purpose, it is temporary, and it draws resources from various areas in the organization; as a result, it is subject to more uncertainty than the normal management process. Thus, the features and characteristics of the project management process tend to be unique.

Figure 9.1 provides an overview of the project management process, which encompasses three other major processes—planning, scheduling, and control. It also includes a number of the more prominent elements of these processes. In the remainder of this section, we will discuss some features of the project planning process, and in the following few sections we will discuss the scheduling and control processes.

Elements of a Project Plan

Project plans generally include the following basic elements.

- *Objectives*—a detailed statement of what the project is to accomplish and how it will achieve the company's goals and meet the strategic plan; and an estimate of when it needs to be completed, the cost and the return.
- *Project scope*—a discussion of how to approach the project, the technological and resource feasibility, the major tasks involved, and a preliminary schedule; includes a justification of the project and what constitutes project success.
- *Contract requirements*—a general structure of managerial, reporting, and performance responsibilities, including a detailed list of staff, suppliers, subcontractors, managerial requirements and agreements, reporting requirements, and a projected organizational structure.
- *Schedules*—a list of all major events, tasks, and subschedules, from which a master schedule is developed.
- *Resources*—the overall project budget for all resource requirements and procedures for budgetry control.
- *Personnel*—identification and recruitment of personnel required for the project team, including special skills and training.
- *Control*—procedures for monitoring and evaluating progress and performance, including schedules and cost.
- *Risk and problem analysis*—anticipating and assessing uncertainties, problems, and potential difficulties that might increase the risk of project delays and/or failure and threaten project success.

Project Return

In order for a project to be selected to be undertaken it typically has to have some kind of positive gain or benefit for the organization that is considering it. In a business, one of the most popular measures of benefit is return on investment (ROI). ROI is a performance measure that is often used to evaluate the expected outcome of a project or to compare a number of different projects. To calculate ROI, the benefit (return) of a project is divided by the cost of the project; the result is expressed as a percentage or a ratio:

$$\text{ROI} = \frac{(\text{Gain from project} - \text{cost of project})}{\text{Cost of project}}$$

If a project does not have a positive ROI, or if there are other projects with a higher ROI, then the project might not be undertaken. ROI is a very popular metric for project planning because of its versatility and simplicity.

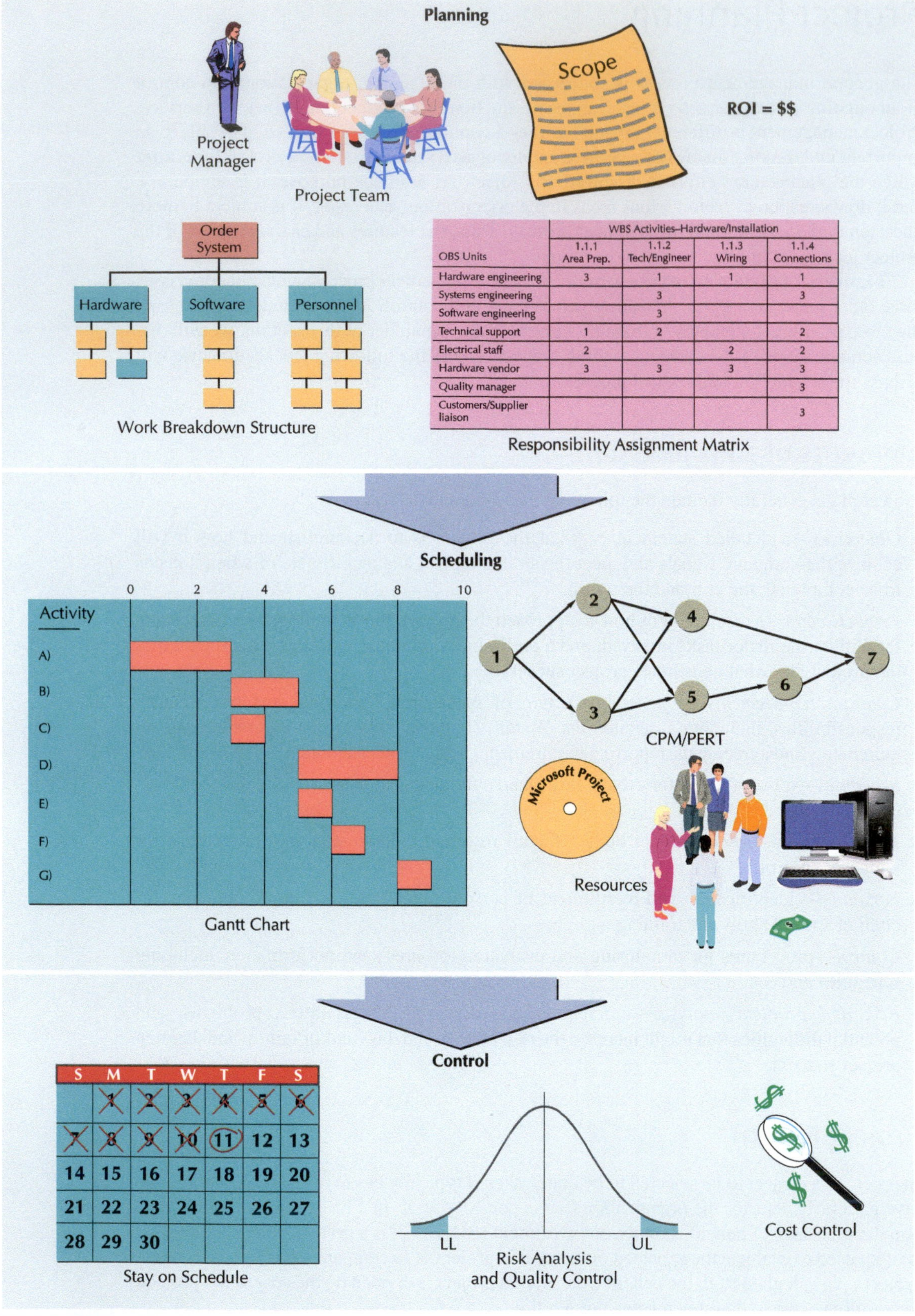

OBS Units	WBS Activities–Hardware/Installation 1.1.1 Area Prep.	1.1.2 Tech/Engineer	1.1.3 Wiring	1.1.4 Connections
Hardware engineering	3	1	1	1
Systems engineering		3		3
Software engineering		3		
Technical support	1	2		2
Electrical staff	2		2	2
Hardware vendor	3	3	3	3
Quality manager				3
Customers/Supplier liaison				3

FIGURE 9.1 The Project Management Process

However, projects sometimes have benefits that cannot be measured in a tangible way with something like an ROI, what's referred to as a "soft" return. For example, a project that has raising employee satisfaction as its goal can result in real benefits—increased productivity, improved quality, and lower costs—that are difficult to measure monetarily in the short run. A project by an Internet online retailer to install backup power generators to keep orders coming in and customers happy during a power outage is like insurance for something that may never happen, making an ROI difficult to determine. A "green" project may not have a tangible dollar ROI, but it can protect a company against regulatory infractions and improve its public image. In general, it may be more appropriate to measure a project's benefit not just in terms of financial return, but also in terms of the positive impact it may have on a company's employees and customers, that is, quality improvement.

Projects undertaken by government agencies or "not-for-profits" typically do not have an ROI-type benefit; they are undertaken to benefit the "public good," for example, the transportation construction projects in the "Along the Supply Chain" box. Cost containment is certainly an important consideration in such projects, but the actual benefit is not easy to measure in terms of dollars.

The Project Team

The project team is typically cross-functional, consisting of a group of individuals selected from other areas in the organization or from outside the organization because of their special skills, expertise, and experience related to the project activities. Members of the engineering staff are often assigned to project work because of their technical skills, especially if the project is related to production processes or equipment. The project team may also include managers and staff personnel from specific areas related to the project. Workers can also be involved on the project team if their job is a function of the project activity. For example, a project team for the construction of a new loading dock facility might include truck drivers, forklift operators, dock workers, and staff personnel and managers from purchasing, shipping, receiving, and packaging, as well as engineers to assess vehicle flow, routes, and space considerations.

The term **matrix organization** refers to a team approach to special projects. The team is developed from members of different functional areas or departments in the company. For example, team members might come from engineering, production, marketing, or human resources, depending on the specialized skills required by the project. The team members are, in effect, on loan from their home departments to work on a project. The term *matrix* is derived from the two-dimensional characteristics of this type of organizational structure. On one dimension, the vertical, is the company's normal organizational structure for performing jobs, whereas the horizontal dimension is the special functional structure (i.e., the functional team members) required by the project.

Matrix organization A team structure with members from different functional areas, depending on the skills required.

Assignment to a project team is usually temporary, which can have both positive and negative repercussions. The temporary loss of workers and staff from their permanent jobs can be disruptive for both the employee and the work area. The employee must sometimes "serve two masters," reporting to both the project manager and a regular supervisor. Since projects are usually exciting, they provide an opportunity to do work that is new and innovative, making the employee reluctant to report back to a more mundane, regular job after the project is completed.

The Project Manager

The most important member of the project team is the *project manager*. Managing a project is subject to lots of uncertainty and the distinct possibility of failure. Since a project is unique and usually has not been attempted previously, the outcome is not as certain as the outcome of an ongoing process would be. A degree of security is attained in the supervision of a continuing process that is not present in project management. The project team members are often from diverse areas of the organization and possess different skills, which must be coordinated into a single, focused effort to complete the project successfully. The project is subject to time and budgetary constraints that are not the same as normal work schedules and resource consumption in an ongoing process. There is usually more perceived and real pressure associated with project management than in a normal management position. However, there are potential opportunities, including demonstrating management abilities in a difficult situation, the challenge of working on a unique project, and the excitement of doing something new.

Along the Supply Chain

The Panama Canal Expansion Project

The Panama Canal, completed in 1914, stretches 48 miles across the Isthmus of Panama, connecting the Atlantic and Pacific Oceans, and is a key global shipping conduit, with approximately 12,000 ships passing through the canal each year. The canal consists of a set of locks at each end that lift ships up to Gatun Lake, 85 feet above sea level. The American Society of Civil Engineers lists the canal as one of the seven wonders of the modern world.

In 2007 an expansion project began to construct two new sets of locks at each end of the canal, excavate new channels to the locks, and widen and deepen existing channels. The project doubled the capacity of the canal and allowed larger ships to pass through at a projected cost of over $5 billion. The Canal could only accommodate ships with 4000 to 5000 TEUs (20 foot equivalent shipping containers) and the expansion allowed for ships with cargoes up to 24,000 TEUs. The project completion date was scheduled for August 2014, to coincide with the 100th anniversary of the canal, however the completion date was repeatedly pushed back and the expansion was opened on June 26, 2016. The project proved to be very complex and difficult, with contractors from around the world collaborating with each other and with the project team. In order to coordinate the many pieces of the project a small, close-knit project management office employing a program management information system was created. The project team effectively addressed a number of issues, including opposition from environmentalists and labor advocates (for the Panamanian people), and prevented some potential delays. The delays that did occur were not considered detrimental to the project's eventual success because of the expected increase in income, jobs, and economic growth resulting from the expanded canal.

Using the Internet, research and identify other construction mega-projects around the world.

Source: Based on Matt Alderton, "Moving Ahead," *PM Network* 28 (3): (March 2014), pp. 24–35.

Scope Statement

Scope statement A document that provides an understanding, justification, and expected result of a project.

The **scope statement** is a document that provides a common understanding of a project. It includes a justification for the project that describes which factors created a need within the company for the project. It also includes an indication of what the expected results of the project will be and what will constitute project success. The scope statement might also include a list of the types of planning reports and documents that are part of the project management process.

Statement of work A written description of the objectives of a project.

A similar planning document is the **statement of work**. In a large project, the statement of work is often prepared for individual team members, groups, departments, subcontractors, and suppliers. This statement describes the work in sufficient detail so that the team members responsible for it know what is required and whether they have sufficient resources to accomplish the work successfully and on time. For suppliers and subcontractors it is often the basis for determining whether they can perform the work and for bidding on it. Some companies require that a statement of work be part of an official contract with a supplier or subcontractor.

Work Breakdown Structure

Work breakdown structure (WBS) Breaks down a project into components, subcomponents, activities, and tasks.

The **work breakdown structure (WBS)** is a tool used for project planning. The WBS organizes the work to be done on a project. In a WBS, a project is broken down into its major components, referred to as modules. These components are then subdivided into detailed subcomponents, which are further broken down into activities and, finally, individual tasks. The end result is a project hierarchical organizational structure made up of different levels, with the overall project at the top of the structure and the individual tasks for each activity at the bottom level. The WBS format is a good way to identify activities and to determine the individual task, module, and project workloads and resources required. It also helps to identify relationships between modules and activities as well as unnecessary duplication of activities. Finally, it provides the basis for developing and managing the project schedule, resources, and modifications.

There is no specific model to follow for the development of a WBS. It can be in the form of a chart or a table. It can be organized around project groups, project phases, or project tasks and events. However, experience has shown that there are two good ways for a project team to develop a WBS. One way is to start at the top and work one's way down, asking, "What components constitute this level?" until the WBS is developed in sufficient detail. The other way is simply to brainstorm the entire project, writing down each item on a sticky note and then organizing them together into the branches of a WBS. The upper levels of the WBS hierarchy tend to

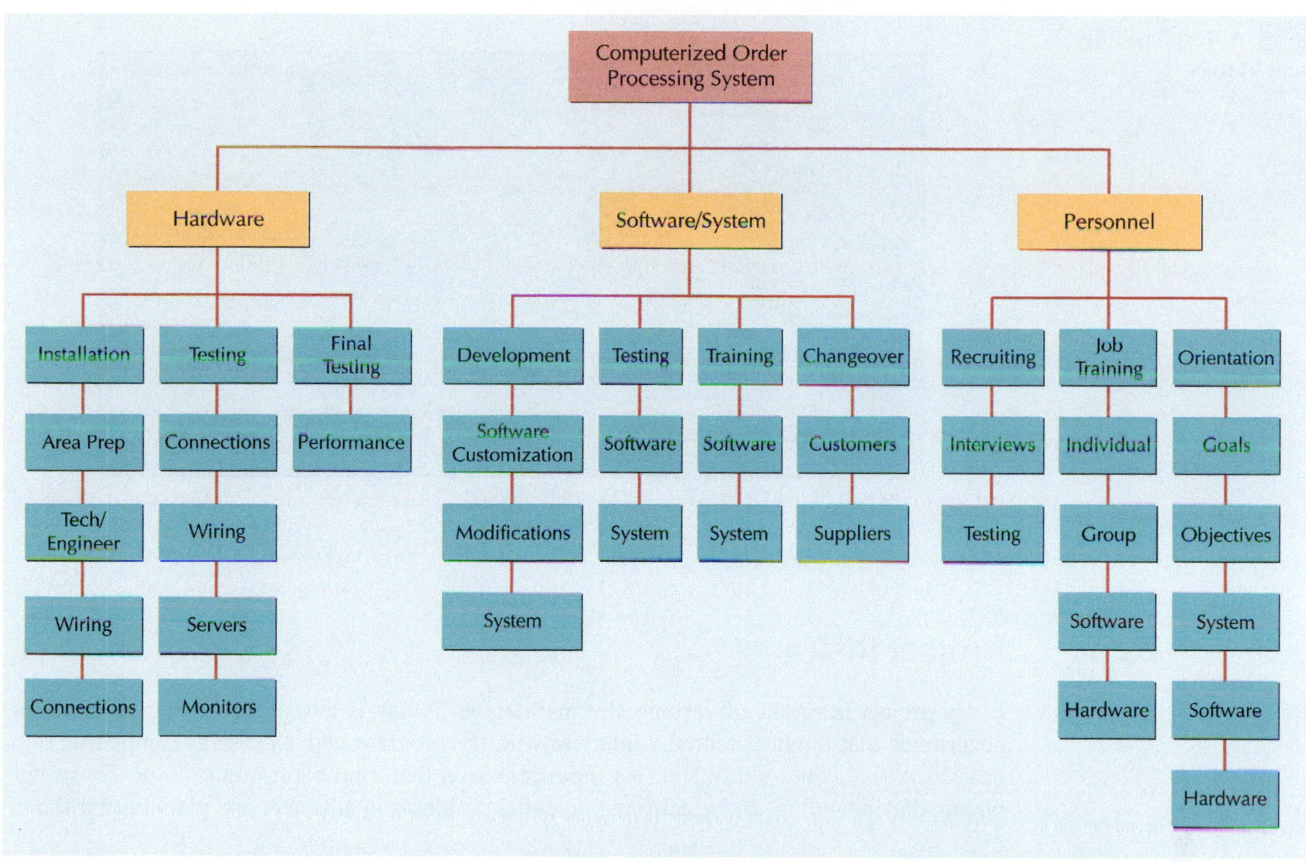

FIGURE 9.2 **Work Breakdown Structure for a Computer Order Processing System Project**

indicate the summary activities, major components, or functional areas involved in the project. They are typically described by nouns that indicate "what" is to be done. The lower levels of the WBS tend to describe the detailed work activities of the project required under the major components or areas. They are typically described by verbs that indicate "how" things are done.

Figure 9.2 shows a WBS for a project for installing a new computerized order processing system for a textile manufacturer that links customers, the manufacturer, and suppliers (see Example 9.1). The WBS is organized according to the three major project categories for development of the system—hardware, software/system, and personnel. Within each of these categories the major tasks and activities under those tasks are detailed. For example, under hardware, a major task is "installation," and activities required in installation include area preparation, technical/engineering layouts and configurations, and wiring and electrical connections.

Responsibility Assignment Matrix

After the work breakdown structure is developed, which organizes the project work into smaller, manageable elements, the project manager assigns the work elements to organizational units—departments, groups, individuals, or subcontractors—using an **organizational breakdown structure (OBS)**. The OBS is an organizational chart that shows which organizational units are responsible for work items. After the OBS is developed, the project manager can then develop a **responsibility assignment matrix (RAM)**. The RAM shows who in the organization is responsible for doing the work in the project. Figure 9.3 shows a RAM for the "Hardware/Installation" category from the work breakdown structure for the computerized order processing project shown in Figure 9.2. Notice that there are three levels of work assignment in the matrix, reflecting who is responsible for the work, who actually performs the work, and those who perform support activities. As with the WBS, both the OBS and RAM can take many different forms depending on the needs and preferences of the company, project team, and project manager.

Organizational breakdown structure (OBS) A chart that shows which organizational units are responsible for work items.

Responsibility assignment matrix (RAM) Shows who is responsible for the work in a project.

FIGURE 9.3 A Responsibility Assignment Matrix

OBS Units	WBS Activities–Hardware/Installation 1.1.1 Area Prep	1.1.2 Tech/Engineer	1.1.3 Wiring	1.1.4 Connections
Hardware engineering	3	1	1	1
Systems engineering		3		3
Software engineering		3		
Technical support	1	2		2
Electrical staff	2		2	2
Hardware vendor	3	3	3	3
Quality manager				3
Customer/supplier liaison				3

Level of responsibility: 1 = overall responsibility
2 = performance responsibility
3 = support

Project Risk

Every project has risks of varying size and degree. A risk is any uncertain factor, event, or occurrence that might potentially interfere with the progress and successful completion of a project. A risk is not a problem; it's the recognition that a problem might occur. By recognizing, understanding, and identifying potential problems in advance, and planning for them,

Along the Supply Chain

A Sustainable Wind Farm Project in Denmark

The Danish government has pledged to stop using fossil fuels and to rely solely on renewable energy sources by 2050, and by 2020 it is planned that half of the country's electricity will be from wind power. A major piece of this commitment was the completion of the Anholt offshore wind farm between the Danish mainland and the island of Anholt in the sea between Denmark and Sweden. It is the largest wind farm in Denmark and the third largest in the world, covering 34 square miles with 111 turbines and a capacity to generate 400 megawatts of electricity, enough for 400,000 Danish homes, corresponding to 4 percent of the country's energy consumption. The wind farm was constructed by the Danish company DONG Energy in 18 months and cost 1.35 billion euros. The contract included deadlines for the delivery of the first kWh by the end of 2012, and the total 400 MW by the end of 2013. Failure to meet the first deadline would result in a €80.5 million penalty for the company, and failure to meet the second deadline would result in a €53.6 million penalty. As a result, the project had to stay on schedule. With a tight schedule, risk management became an essential part of the project management process. Even before DONG was awarded the contract, project managers began working to minimize risks from unforeseen problems, primarily in the supply chain. The project team put down costly deposits for critical construction vessels, to make sure they would be ready when construction started. They arranged conditional contracts with Siemens for the turbines and hardware for the site. The project managers set up a rigorous but flexible schedule so that if one activity was delayed the next activity could be started without major delays or problems. They also built in buffers for the riskiest critical parts of the project: installing the underwater

Soren Kjeldgaard

turbine foundation and laying the underwater transmission cables. As construction began some initial problems arose, including the seabed being too soft in some spots where the placement of the turbines was planned, requiring the team to change the farm's layout, and there were also some supply chain bottlenecks. However, because of the project team's focus on planning, scheduling, and risk management, negative risk outcomes were kept at a minimum and no major delays occurred, allowing the company to meet the final operational deadline six months ahead of schedule.

Identify and discuss some potential sustainable projects at your school.

Source: Based on Clay Dillow, "Run Like the Wind," *PM Network* 27(8); (August 2013), pp. 46–51.

the project team and manager can attempt to prevent them. It's the job of the project team and manager to manage and minimize the risk in their projects.

Managing project risks is best addressed in the planning stage. A risk management plan documents how risks will be managed throughout the project. In addition to identifying potential risks, it specifies which team members are responsible for managing various areas of risk, how risks will be monitored throughout the project life cycle, how contingency plans for risks that materialize will be developed and implemented, and how project resources will be allocated to handle risk.

The approach to managing project risk is proactive. The first step is to identify all of the possible risks that can be anticipated in the project. This might include such things as resource changes, wrong assumptions, a change in company objectives and needs, technology changes, changes in the company's competitive environment, and anything new in the project, like technology. After as many risks as possible are identified, they should each be evaluated in terms of their impact and possible eventuality (i.e., probability), and possibly quantified. Although any kind of risk evaluation and measurement is obviously an estimate, the objective is to have a process to compare the risks to one another in order to prioritize them in terms of which ones will most threaten project success. The most important risks that are controllable can be mitigated, and strategies should be developed to mitigate those that can't be controlled.

Successfully managing project risk can have a very positive impact; it can keep projects within budget and save money, maintain project schedules, and result in the project success and quality results hoped for.

Global Cultural and Diversity Issues in Project Management

In the existing global business environment, project teams form a mosaic of different genders, cultures, ethnicities, nationalities, religions, and races. Only by acknowledging and embracing this diversity will companies be able to attract the best people and achieve project success. Diversity offers a significant business advantage by providing a more well rounded perspective on a project from team members with different views, experiences, and values. The project leader must focus on creating common goals and objectives for the project by using good communication techniques and developing a cooperative environment that identifies common values and fosters mutual respect for differences. However, while a globally diverse project team can have advantages, project success typically requires respect for cultural differences and a management style that acknowledges these differences.

Global projects that involve companies and team members from different countries have expanded dramatically in recent years as a result of increased information and communication technology. Teamwork is a critical element in achieving project success, and in global projects diversity among international team members can add an extra dimension to project planning. For projects to be successful, cultural differences, idiosyncrasies, and issues must be considered as important parts of the planning process. The basics of project management tend to be universal, but cultural differences in priorities, nuances, and terminology can result in communication failures. Since English is used widely around the world, language is not necessarily an overriding problem. However, often it is not what people say that matters but what they mean.

An example of one cultural difference that can play havoc with developing project schedules is the difference in work days and holidays in different countries. Southern Europeans take a lot of holidays, which can mess up a project schedule if they are not planned for. While the U.S. has 10 national holidays, China has 36 and India has 77, and France has 9 weeks of vacation. In the United States you can ask people to move their vacations or work while on vacation (via phone or Internet), but in countries like France or Italy, don't ask. In India, the work ethic is closer to the European than the U.S. model: when the day ends it's over, and weekends are inviolate. In some cultures, certain days are auspicious for starting a new venture or ending a task.

Some cultures tend to be less aggressive than others, and team members will avoid confrontation so that when problems on a project occur (such as cost overruns or missed due

Along the Supply Chain

Cross-Cultural Project Teams in China

In today's global economy cross-cultural project teams have become relatively common, but they still present unique situational problems that require an awareness of cultural differences on the part of U.S. team members and especially the project manager. In projects in China, Chinese team members will sometimes show more deference and politeness than Americans are used to, avoiding useful criticisms that are expected by U.S. team members. A project manager who asks for input from team members is often seen as weak, not inclusive. While U.S. companies value individualism, Chinese companies, reflecting 2,000 years of traditional Confucianism values, do not. Chinese project managers typically use a more collaborative leadership style than the more direct style of U.S. project managers. The Chinese word *guanxi* (gwan-shee) refers to the strong reliance of business on social connections. A Chinese business partner with strong, well-placed relationships can enhance project success; however, such relationships are developed slowly. The Chinese focus on the "long-term" rather than the "short-term" view prevalent in many Western companies; patience is a respected virtue in China. "Face" or *mianzi* (me-ahn-zee) is very important in China. Every conversation, meeting, meal, or social or business engagement is an opportunity for an individual to gain or lose stature. Rank is important in China; people of high rank are given an extraordinary degree of deference. As such, instructions from leaders are respected and followed, and advice from junior team members is not generally expected or valued. Planning for risks in a project runs counter to the culture since it implies things might go wrong. The U.S. way of doing business is not better than the Chinese way; it's just different.

U.S. project team members should research the culture of their Chinese team members to identify stereotypes and make sure they do not influence behavior. It is good practice to develop and show an interest in cultural differences and learn about traditions; communicate effectively and don't always assume you are being understood; and listen carefully and emphatically. Project managers should develop a skill known as "emotional intelligence"—the ability to read facial, verbal, and physical cues that reveal how a person from another culture is feeling. Team members and project managers need to develop a cultural sensitivity and understanding to see how cultural differences may impact the project environment in order to work together effectively to achieve project success, on time and within the budget.

Assume you and a classmate or fellow student from a different country or culture are project team members. Discuss cultural differences between yourselves that you think might have an effect on project success.

Source: Based on Bud Baker, "When in China…," PM Network 20 (6); (June 2006), pp. 24–25; and Jake Malooey, "Crossing Borders," *PM Network* 28 (4); (April 2014), pp. 28–35.

dates) they will not be as aggressively addressed as they might be in the United States or in Germany, for example. Some team members in underdeveloped countries may bow to the perceived superiority of those from developed countries and not press their points aggressively even though they may be correct. Some people may simply have trouble working with others with cultural differences. Team members may think they do not understand team members from a foreign country, when it's actually their culture they don't understand.

In Asian countries businesses typically employ a more methodical management style that values patience and building relationships. Project managers and team members in Japan consider establishing plans and providing direction to be more important managerial competencies than they are considered in the United States. What's considered to be micromanaging in the United States is the more common way of doing things in China. In Latin America a formal management style with specific managerial direction is a cultural trait. Business relationships are built slowly over time and they are based on trust and a sense of personal integrity. In Latin countries personal connections (that might include inquires into team members' personal lives) are often expected before business is transacted. In Malaysia a "boss" has almost absolute power over subordinates, whereas in Austria the perception is almost completely the opposite. The United States, Scandinavia, and many European countries fall somewhere in between. In countries like the United Kingdom, Sweden, and Denmark, people tend to cope with uncertainty and unexpected events much better than people in Italy and Portugal.

As a result, the project manager must address the issue of cultural diversity up front in the planning process. Project managers have to approach diversity differently from country to country. The project manager should never assume that something that works at home will work abroad or that what will work in country A will work in country B. This makes cultural research and communication important elements in the planning process. The manager must determine what cultural faux pas must be avoided—the things you don't do. It's important to discover at the start what holidays and cultural celebrations exist and the work ethic of team members.

The project manager must often find team members who are particularly adept at bridging cultural differences. It may be helpful to identify a team associate who can keep the project manager and other team members informed of important cultural differences. Although long-distance communication via phone or email is very easy, the face-to-face meeting is often better with someone with cultural differences, even with the added expense of travel.

Project Scheduling and Control

The project schedule evolves from the planning documents we discussed in the previous section. It is typically the most critical element in the project management process, especially during the implementation phase (i.e., the actual project work), and it is the source of most conflict and problems. One reason is that frequently the single most important criterion for the success of a project is that it be finished on time. If a stadium is supposed to be finished in time for the first game of the season and it's not, there will be a lot of angry ticket holders; if a school building is not completed by the time the school year starts, there will be a lot of angry parents; if a shopping mall is not completed on time, there will be a lot of angry tenants; if a new product is not completed by the scheduled launch date, millions of dollars can be lost; and if a new military weapon is not completed on time, it could affect national security. Time is also a measure of progress that is very visible. It is an absolute with little flexibility; you can spend less money or use fewer people, but you cannot slow down or stop the passage of time.

Developing a schedule encompasses the following basic steps. First, *define the activities* that must be performed to complete the project; second, *sequence the activities* in the order in which they must be completed; next, *estimate the time* required to complete each activity; and finally, *develop the schedule* based on this sequencing and time estimates of the activities.

Because scheduling involves a quantifiable measure, time, several quantitative techniques, including the Gantt chart and CPM/PERT networks, are available that can be used to develop a project schedule. There are also various computer software packages that can be used to schedule projects, including the popular Microsoft Project. Later in this chapter we are going to discuss CPM/PERT and Microsoft Project in greater detail. For now, we are going to describe one of the oldest and most widely used scheduling techniques, the Gantt chart.

The Gantt Chart

A **Gantt chart** (also called a *bar chart*) was developed by Henry Gantt, a pioneer in the field of industrial engineering, at the artillery ammunition shops of the Frankford Arsenal in 1914. The Gantt chart has been a popular project scheduling tool since its inception and is still widely used today. It is the direct precursor of the CPM/PERT technique, which we will discuss later.

Gantt chart A graph or bar chart with a bar for each project activity that shows the passage of time.

The Gantt chart is a graph with a bar representing time for each activity in the project being analyzed. Figure 9.4 illustrates a Gantt chart of a simplified project description for building a house. The project contains only seven primary activities, such as designing the house, laying the foundation, ordering materials, and so forth. The first activity is "design house and obtain financing," and it requires three months to complete, shown by the bar from left to right across the chart. After the first activity is finished, the next two activities, "lay foundation" and "order and receive materials," can start simultaneously. This set of activities demonstrates how a **precedence relationship** works: the design of the house and the financing must precede the next two activities.

Precedence relationship The sequential relationship of project activities to each other.

The activity "lay foundation" requires two months to complete, so it will be finished, at the earliest, at the end of month 5. "Order and receive materials" requires one month to complete, and it could be finished after month 4. However, observe that it is possible to delay the start of this activity one month until month 4. This delay would still enable the activity to be completed by the end of month 5, when the next activity, "build house," is scheduled to start. This extra time for the activity "order materials" is called slack. **Slack** is the amount by which an activity can be delayed without delaying any of the activities that follow it or the project as a whole. The remainder of the Gantt chart is constructed in a similar manner, and the project is scheduled to be completed at the end of month 9.

Slack The amount of time an activity can be delayed without delaying the project.

The Gantt chart provides a visual display of the project schedule, indicating when activities are scheduled to start, when they will be finished, and where extra time is available

FIGURE 9.4 **A Gantt Chart**

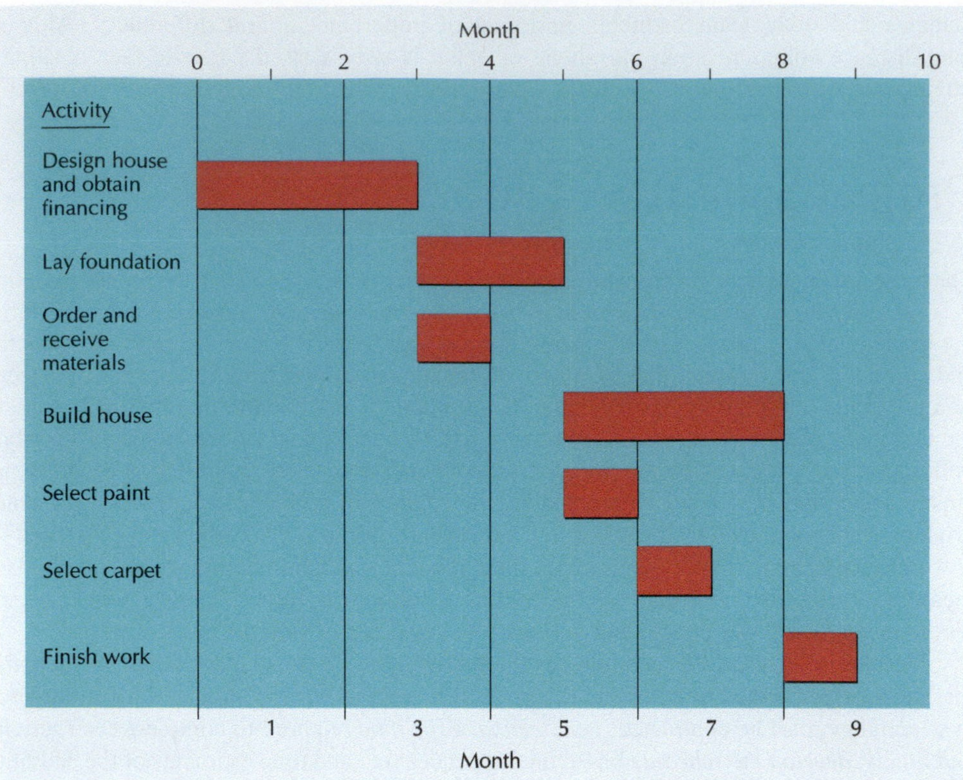

and activities can be delayed. The project manager can use the chart to monitor the progress of the activities and see which ones are ahead of schedule and which ones are behind schedule. The Gantt chart also indicates the precedence relationships between activities; however, these relationships are not always easily discernible. This problem is one of the disadvantages of the Gantt chart method, and it sometimes limits the chart's use to smaller projects with relatively few activities. The CPM/PERT network technique does not suffer this disadvantage.

Project Control

Project control is the process of making sure the project progresses toward a successful completion. It requires that the project be monitored and progress be measured so that any deviations from the project plan, and particularly the project schedule, are minimized. If the project is found to be deviating from the plan—that is, it is not on schedule, cost overruns are occurring, activity results are not as expected, and so on—then corrective action must be taken. In the rest of this section we will describe several key elements of project control, including time management, quality control, performance monitoring, and communication.

Time Management

Time management is the process of making sure the project schedule does not slip and is on time. This requires the monitoring of individual activity schedules and frequent updates. If the schedule is being delayed to an extent that jeopardizes the project success, then the project manager may have to shift resources to accelerate critical activities. Some activities may have slack time, and resources can be shifted from them to activities that are not on schedule. This is referred to as *time–cost tradeoff*. However, this can also push the project cost above budget. In some cases, the work may need to be corrected or made more efficient. In other cases, original activity time estimates upon implementation may prove to be unrealistic, with the result that the schedule must be changed and the repercussions of such changes on project success evaluated.

Cost Management

Cost management is often closely tied to time management because of the time–cost tradeoff occurrences that we mentioned previously. If the schedule is delayed, costs tend to increase in order to get the project back on schedule. Also, as the project progresses, some cost estimates may prove to be unrealistic or erroneous. Thus, it will be necessary to revise cost estimates and develop budget updates. If cost overruns are excessive, then corrective actions must be taken.

Quality Management

Quality management and control are an integral part of the project management process. The process requires that project work be monitored for quality and that improvements be made as the project progresses, just as in a normal production or manufacturing operation. Tasks and activities must be monitored to make sure that work is done correctly and that activities are completed correctly according to plan. If the work on an activity or task is flawed, subsequent activities may be affected, requiring rework, delaying the project, and threatening project success. Poor-quality work increases the risk of project failure, just as a defective part can result in a defective final product if not corrected. Thus, the principles of quality management and many of the same techniques for statistical analysis and statistical process control discussed in earlier chapters for traditional production processes can also be applied to the project management process.

Performance Management

Performance management is the process of monitoring a project and developing timed (i.e., daily, weekly, monthly) status reports to make sure that goals are being met and the plan is being followed. It compares planned target dates for events, milestones, and work completion with dates actually achieved to determine whether the project is on schedule or behind schedule. Key measures of performance include deviation from the schedule, resource usage, and cost overruns. These reports are developed by the project manager and by individuals and organizational units with performance responsibility.

Earned value analysis (EVA) is a specific system for performance management. Activities "earn value" as they are completed. EVA is a recognized standard procedure for numerically measuring a project's progress, forecasting its completion date and final cost, and providing measures of schedule and budget variation as activities are completed. For example, an EVA metric such as "schedule variance" compares the work performed during a time period with the work that was scheduled to be performed. A negative variance means the project is behind schedule. "Cost variance" is the budgeted cost of work performed minus the actual cost of the work. A negative variance means the project is over budget. EVA works best when it is used in conjunction with a work breakdown structure (WBS) that compartmentalizes project work into small packages that are easy to measure. The drawbacks of EVA are that it's sometimes difficult to measure work progress and the time required for data measurement can be considerable.

Earned value analysis (EVA) A standard procedure for numerically measuring a project's progress, forecasting its completion date and cost, and measuring schedule and budget variation.

Communication

Communication needs for project and program management control in today's global business environment tend to be substantial and complex. The distribution of design documents, budget and cost documents, plans, status reports, schedules, and schedule changes in a timely manner is often critical to project success. As a result, more and more companies are using the Internet to communicate project information, and are using company intranet project websites to provide a single location for team members to access project information. Internet communication and software combined with faxing, videoconferencing systems, phones, handheld computers, and jet travel are enabling transnational companies to engage in global project management.

Along the Supply Chain

Reconstructing the Pentagon after 9/11

On September 11, 2001, at 9:37 A.M. American Airlines Flight 77, which had been hijacked by terrorists, was flown into the west face of the Pentagon in Arlington, Virginia. More than 400,000 square feet of office space were destroyed, and an additional 1.6 million square feet were damaged. Almost immediately the "Phoenix Project" to restore the Pentagon was initiated. A deadline of one year was established for the project completion, which required the demolition and removal of the destroyed portion of the building followed by the building restoration including the limestone facade (see photo). The Pentagon consists of five rings of offices (housing 25,000 employees) that emanate from the center of the building; ring "A" is the innermost ring, while ring "E" is the outermost. Ten corridors radiate out from the building's hub bisecting the rings and forming the Pentagon's five distinctive wedges. At the time of the attack, the Pentagon was undergoing a 20-year, $1.2 billion renovation program and the renovation of Wedge 1 that was demolished in the attack was nearing completion. As a result, the Phoenix Project leaders were able to use the Wedge 1 renovation project structure and plans as a basis for its own reconstruction plan and schedule, saving much time in the process. Project leaders were in place and able to assign resources on the very day of the attack. The project included over 30,000 activities and a 3000-member project team and required 3 million man-hours of work during the project duration. Over 56,000 tons of contaminated debris were removed from the site, 2.5 million pounds of limestone were used to reconstruct the facade (using the original drawings from 1941), 21,000 cubic yards of concrete were poured, and 3800 tons of reinforcing steel were placed. The Phoenix Project was completed almost a month ahead of schedule and nearly $194 million under the original budget estimate of $700 million.

The project planning process for the reconstruction of the Pentagon began virtually on the day of the September 11 attack. The project was completed a month ahead of schedule and $194 million under budget.

Building construction is one of the main applications of project management; discuss some of the unique factors associated with the Pentagon project that made it different from other, more typical, construction projects.

Source: N. Bauer, "Rising from the Ashes," *PM Network*, 18 (5); (May 2004): 24–32.

Enterprise Project Management

In many companies, project control takes place within the larger context of a multiple project environment. *Enterprise project management* refers to the management and control of a companywide portfolio of projects. In the enterprise approach to managing projects, a company's goals are achieved through the coordination of simultaneous projects. The company grows, changes, and adds value by systematically implementing projects of all types across the enterprise. The aggregate result of an organization's portfolio of projects becomes the company's bottom line. As such, program management is a managerial approach that sits above project management. Whereas project management concentrates on delivering a clearly defined, tangible outcome with its own scope and goals within a specified time frame, in a program management environment the company's goals and changes are achieved through a carefully planned and coordinated set of projects. Programs tend to cut across and affect all business areas and thus require a higher degree of cross-business functional coordination than individual projects.

Agile Project Management

Agile project management Approach that focuses on adaptability to rapid and unexpected change.

Agile project management, a relatively recent addition to the project management lexicon, evolved out of the unique problems and challenges encountered in managing IT and software development projects. The agile approach to project management is very different from the formal, planned approach we have described so far. It focuses more on adaptability to rapid and unexpected change (i.e., uncertainty) in the project environment, which is especially prevalent in the IT and software development business.

Agile is a way to deal with change in project management by using an iterative and incremental approach. Unlike the traditional, straightforward and linear project management process with a predetermined and planned set of steps (i.e., a scope statement, project network, etc.), as, for example, would exist in a construction project, the agile method breaks down tasks into small increments with minimal planning. It promotes adaptive planning, evolutionary development, and an iterative approach, and encourages rapid and flexible response to changes. Its primary benefit is that it's adaptable to constant adjustments to change through a collaborative process. This type of iterative process is more conducive to software projects, for example, that are subject to very rapid and unforeseen changes, which may be, in part, the result of customers not knowing entirely at the outset what they want the product to look like. Iterations are for short time frames (called time-boxes) that might last several weeks, at the end of which a working product (i.e., the software) is delivered and demonstrated to the customer. This reduces the overall risk and allows the project to adapt to changes quickly. For a software or IT development project, an iteration might not result in a market-ready product, with multiple iterations required for release of the full (software) product or new features.

Team composition in an agile project is usually cross-functional and typically includes a customer representative. Face-to-face communication among team members is emphasized, and is frequent, usually daily (in short meetings called *scrums*), which helps to reveal problems as they arise. Team size is typically small (5–9 people) to simplify team communication and collaboration. When a team works in different locations, they maintain daily contact through videoconferencing, voice, email, and so on. At the end of each iteration, stakeholders and the customer representative review progress and re-evaluate priorities with a view to optimizing the ROI and ensuring the project is aligned with customer needs and goals.

The agile approach differs from traditional project management by responding to change rather than following a plan; by relying on individuals who interact instead of formal processes and tools; and by frequently communicating and collaborating with the customer. As global business environments have become subject to more and more rapid and constant change, the agile approach to project management is spreading beyond IT and software development into other sectors, particularly business environments that are dynamic and turbulent, such as technology-based companies, financial services, insurance, telecommunications, pharmaceuticals, utilities, and manufacturing. While the agile approach has benefited some companies, it also has limitations and is not universally applicable to project management, even if the projects involve significant change. It requires small groups of experienced, talented, cross-functional team members that work well together, and some companies cannot (nor need to) adapt to the absence of a formal planning process.

CPM/PERT

In 1956, a research team at E. I. du Pont de Nemours & Company, Inc., led by a du Pont engineer, Morgan R. Walker, and a Remington-Rand computer specialist, James E. Kelley Jr., initiated a project to develop a computerized system to improve the planning, scheduling, and reporting of the company's engineering programs (including plant maintenance and construction projects). The resulting network approach is known as the *critical path method (CPM)*. At the same time, the U.S. Navy established a research team composed of members of the Navy Special Projects Office, Lockheed, and the consulting firm of Booz, Allen, and Hamilton, led by D. G. Malcolm. They developed a similar network approach for the design of a management control system for the development of the Polaris Missile Project (a ballistic missile-firing nuclear submarine). This network scheduling technique was named the *program evaluation and review technique*, or *PERT*. The Polaris project (see photo) eventually included 23 PERT networks encompassing 3000 activities.

Both CPM and PERT are derivatives of the Gantt chart and, as a result, are very similar. There were originally two primary differences between CPM and PERT. With CPM a single estimate for activity time was used that did not allow for any variation in activity times—activity times were treated as if they were known for certain, or "deterministic." With PERT, multiple time estimates were used for each activity that allowed for variation in activity times—activity times were treated as "probabilistic." The other difference was related to the mechanics of drawing the project network. In PERT, activities were represented as arcs, or arrowed lines, between two nodes, or circles, whereas in CPM activities were represented as

The nuclear powered missile submarine shown here launching a Tomahawk cruise missile, is a direct descendant of the USS George Washington, the first nuclear submarine of this type. In the late 1950s the Polaris Fleet Ballistic Missile Project included more than 250 prime contractors and 9000 subcontractors. The Navy Department credited PERT with bringing the Polaris missile submarine to combat readiness approximately two years ahead of the originally scheduled completion date.

the nodes or circles. However, over time CPM and PERT have been effectively merged into a single technique conventionally referred to as CPM/PERT.

The advantage of CPM/PERT over the Gantt chart is in the use of a network to depict the precedence relationships between activities. The Gantt chart does not clearly show precedence relationships, a disadvantage that limited its use to small projects. The CPM/PERT network is a more efficient and direct means of displaying precedence relationships. In other words, in a network it is visually easier to see the precedence relationships, which makes CPM/PERT popular with managers and other users, especially for large projects with many activities.

The Project Network

A CPM/PERT network consists of *branches* and *nodes*, as shown in Figure 9.5. When CPM and PERT were first developed, they employed different conventions for constructing a network. With CPM the nodes, or circles in Figure 9.5, represented the project activities. The arrows in between the nodes indicated the precedence relationships between activities. For the network in Figure 9.5, activity 1, represented by node 1, precedes activity 2, and 2 precedes 3. This approach to network construction is called **activity-on-node (AON)**. With PERT the opposite convention was taken. The branches represented the activities, and the nodes in between them reflected **events**, or points in time such as the end of one activity and the beginning of another. In this approach, referred to as **activity-on-arrow (AOA)**, the activities are normally identified by the node numbers at the start and end of an activity. For example, activity 1–2 precedes activity 2–3 in Figure 9.5. In this book, we will focus on the AON convention, but we will also provide an overview of AOA networks.

Activity-on-node (AON) Nodes represent activities and arrows show precedence relationships.

Events Completion or beginning of an activity.

Activity-on-arrow (AOA) Arrows represent activities and nodes are events for points in time.

AOA Network

To demonstrate how these components are used to construct the two types of network, we will use our example project of building a house used in the Gantt chart in Figure 9.4. The

FIGURE 9.5 **Network Components**

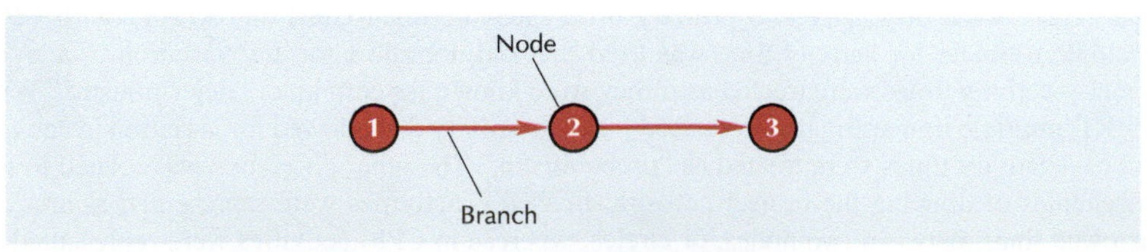

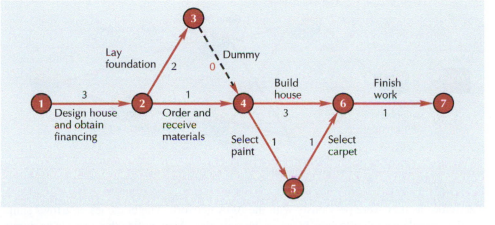

FIGURE 9.6 **The AOA Project Network for Building a House**

comparable AOA CPM/PERT network for this project is shown in Figure 9.6. The precedence relationships are reflected in this network by the arrangement of the arrowed (or directed) branches in Figure 9.6. The first activity (1–2) in the project is to design the house and obtain financing. This activity must be completed before any subsequent activities can begin. Thus, activities 2–3, laying the foundation, and 2–4, ordering and receiving materials, can start only when node 2 is *realized*, indicating the event that activity 1–2 is finished. (Notice in Figure 9.6 that a time estimate of three months has been assigned for the completion of this activity.) Activity 2–3 and activity 2–4 can occur concurrently; neither depends on the other, and both depend only on the completion of activity 1–2.

When the activities of laying the foundation (2–3) and ordering and receiving materials (2–4) are completed, then activities 4–5 and 4–6 can begin simultaneously. However, before discussing these activities further, notice activity 3–4, referred to in the network as a dummy.

A **dummy** activity is inserted into the network to show a precedence relationship, but it does not represent any actual passage of time. Activities 2–3 and 2–4 have the precedence relationship shown in Figure 9.7a. However, in an AOA network, two or more activities are not allowed to share the same starting and ending nodes. Instead, activity 3–4 is inserted to give two activities separate end nodes and, thus, two separate identities as shown in Figure 9.7b. Notice, however, that a time of zero months has been assigned to activity 3–4. The dummy activity shows that activity 2–3 must be completed prior to any activities beginning at node 4, but it does not represent the passage of time.

Dummy Two or more activities cannot share the same start and end nodes.

Returning to the network in Figure 9.6, we see that two activities start at node 4. Activity 4–6 is the actual building of the house, and activity 4–5 is the search for and selection of the paint for the exterior and interior of the house. Activity 4–6 and activity 4–5 can begin simultaneously and take place concurrently. Following the selection of the paint (activity 4–5) and the realization of node 5, the carpet can be selected (since the carpet color depends on the paint color). This activity can also occur concurrently with the building of the house (activity 4–6). When the building is completed and the paint and carpet are selected, the house can be finished (activity 6–7).

AON Network

Figure 9.8 shows the comparable AON network to the AOA network in Figure 9.6 for our house building project. Notice that the activities and activity times are on the nodes and not on

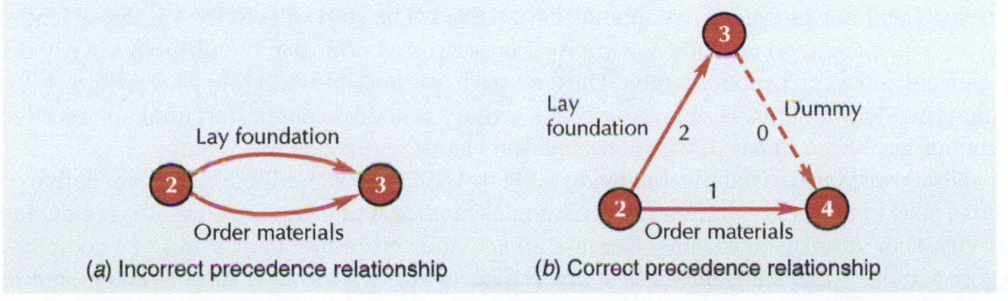

FIGURE 9.7 **Concurrent Activities**

FIGURE 9.8 **AON Network for House Building Project**

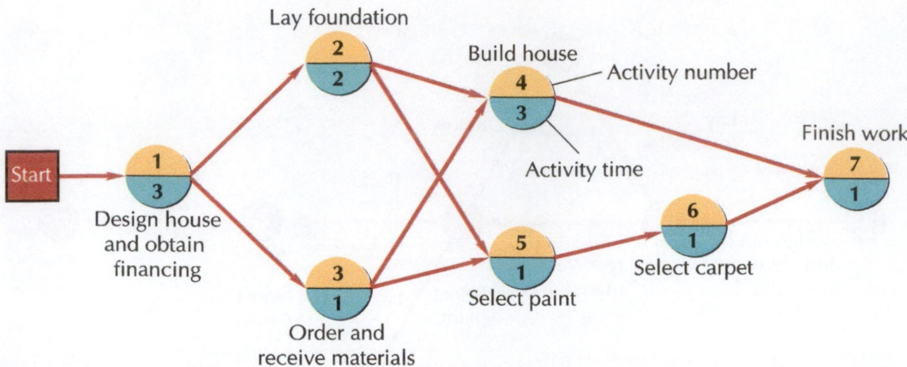

the activities as they were previously with the AOA network. The branches or arrows simply show the precedence relationships between the activities. Also, notice that there is no dummy activity; dummy activities are not required in an AON network since two activities will never be confused because they have the same start and end nodes. In general, both of the two methods accomplish the same thing, and the one that is used is usually a matter of individual preference. However, for our purposes the AON network has one distinct advantage—it is the convention used in the popular *Microsoft Project* software package, and because we want to demonstrate how to use this software, we will use the AON convention in this chapter.

The Critical Path

A network path is a sequence of connected activities that runs from the start to the end of the network. The network in Figure 9.8 has several paths through it. In fact, close observations of this network show four paths, identified as A, B, C, and D:

A: $1-2-4-7$
B: $1-2-5-6-7$
C: $1-3-4-7$
D: $1-3-5-6-7$

The project cannot be completed (i.e., the house cannot be built) sooner than the time required by the longest path in the network, in terms of time. The path with the longest duration of time is referred to as the **critical path**.

Critical path The longest path through a network; it is the minimum project completion time.

By summing the activity times (shown in Figure 9.8) along each of the four paths, we can compute the length of each path, as follows:

Path A: $1-2-4-7$
$3+2+3+1=9$ months
Path B: $1-2-5-6-7$
$3+2+1+1+1=8$ months
Path C: $1-3-4-7$
$3+1+3+1=8$ months
Path D: $1-3-5-6-7$
$3+1+1+1+1=7$ months

Because path A is the longest, it is the critical path; thus, the minimum completion time for the project is nine months. Now let us analyze the critical path more closely. From Figure 9.9 we can see that activity 3 cannot start until three months have passed. It is also easy to see that activity 4 will not start until five months have passed. The start of activity 4 is dependent on two activities leading into node 4. Activity 2 is completed after five months, but activity 3 is completed at the end of four months. Thus, we have two possible start times for activity 4, five months and four months. However, since the activity at node 4 cannot start until all preceding activities have been finished, the soonest node 4 can be realized is five months.

Now consider the activity following node 4. Using the same logic as before, activity 7 cannot start until after eight months (five months at node 4 plus the three months required by activity 4) or after seven months. Because all activities preceding node 7 must be completed before activity 7 can start, the earliest this can occur is eight months. Adding one month for

Start at 5 months
Finish at 9 months
Start at 6 months
Start at 3 months

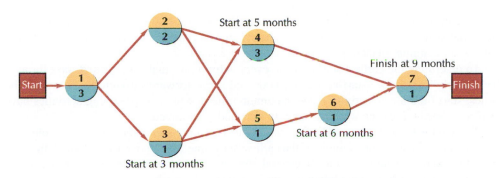

FIGURE 9.9 **Activity Start Times**

activity 7 to the start time at node 7 gives a project duration of nine months. This is the time of the longest path in the network—the critical path.

This brief analysis demonstrates the concept of a critical path and the determination of the minimum completion time of a project. However, this was a cumbersome method for determining a critical path. Next, we discuss a mathematical approach to scheduling the project activities and determining the critical path.

Activity Scheduling

In our analysis of the critical path, we determined the earliest time that each activity could be finished. For example, we found that the earliest time activity 4 could start was five months. This time is referred to as the **earliest start time**, and it is expressed symbolically as **ES**. In order to show the earliest start time on the network as well as some other activity times, we

Earliest start time (ES) The earliest time an activity can start.

Along the Supply Chain

The Costa Concordia Cruise Ship Salvage Project

On January 13, 2012, the Costa Concordia, a 300-meter, 114,000 ton cruise ship with 4000 passengers and crew members, ran aground near the island of Giglio off the coast of Tuscany, Italy. Thirty-two people were killed and the ship was left partially submerged and rolled onto her starboard side, sitting precariously on a rocky underwater ledge. The Costa Concordia was twice the size of the Titanic, and the largest capsized ship ever, resulting in the largest naval salvage project in history.

In the planning stage the project team identified three priorities—protect the water environment near Giglio, maintain a safe working environment, and complete the project as quickly as possible. The first step in the project was to carefully remove the ship's 2380 tons of fuel and sewage, which was completed two months after the wreck. Next, over a 16-month period, the 500-person project team cleaned and prepared the ship for a "parbuckling" procedure that would rotate the ship 65 degrees to an upright position, and then the ship would be floated away for salvage operations. The preparation stage included anchoring the ship to the sea bottom with steel cables to prevent it from slipping off the ledge it sat on, and then building a horizontal underwater platform below the ship for it to rest on after it was rotated upright. Throughout the project, the project team conducted risk management using computer simulations to test responses to potential risks including bad weather events. Airtight tanks called "sponsons" were attached to the port side of the hull, which was above the water. The parbuckling process began by using jacks to dislodge the ship from the sea bottom, a process that took three hours. Then the sponsons were filled with sea water using remote controlled valves. This exerted a downward force on the ship's port side hull until the ship sat upright on the underwater platform.

VINCENZO PINTO/Getty Images, Inc.

The rotation process took 19 hours and the entire parbuckling operation was conducted remotely by engineers from a barge near the ship, using sonar managing to detect problems. Additional sponsons were attached to the now above-water starboard side of the ship and the ship was refloated. Approximately two-and-a-half years after it ran aground, after a four-day journey (at a speed of 2 knots and with a 14-ship escort), the Costa Concordia arrived at the port in Genoa for scrapping operations, which required over a year. The total cost of the salvage operation, including repairing damage to Giglio Island, was expected to be approximately €1.5 billion.

Using the Internet, identify and research some other projects that have resulted because of accidents or disasters.

Source: Based on Ambreen Ali, "In Shipshape," *PM Network* 28(3); (March 2014), pp. 54–59.

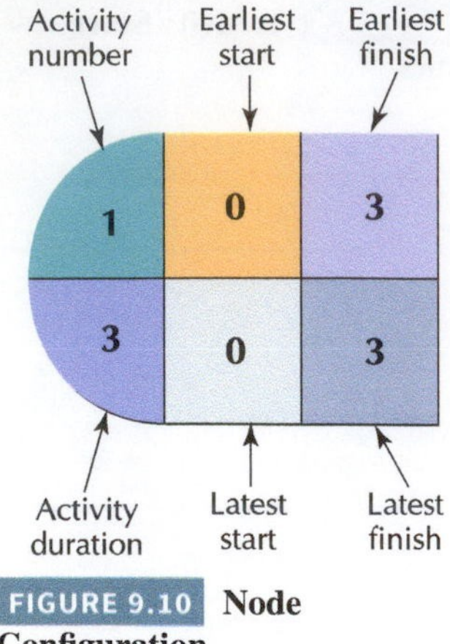

FIGURE 9.10 **Node Configuration**

Forward pass Starts at the beginning of a CPM/PERT network to determine the earliest activity times.

Earliest finish time (EF) Is the earliest start time plus the activity time.

will develop in the scheduling process, we will alter our node structure a little. Figure 9.10 shows the structure for node 1, the first activity in our example network for designing the house and obtaining financing.

To determine the earliest start time for every activity, we make a **forward pass** through the network. That is, we start at the first node and move forward through the network. The earliest start time for an activity is the maximum time in which all preceding activities have been completed—the time when the activity start node is realized.

The **earliest finish time (EF)** for an activity is simply the earliest start time plus the activity time estimate. For example, if the earliest start time for activity 1 is at time 0, then the earliest finish time is three months. In general, the earliest start and finish times for an activity are computed according to the following mathematical relationship.

$$\text{ES} = \text{maximum (EF) of immediate predecessors}$$
$$\text{EF} = \text{ES} + t$$

The earliest start and earliest finish times for all the activities in our project network are shown in Figure 9.11.

The earliest start time for the first activity in the network (for which there are no predecessor activities) is always 0, or, ES = 0. This enables us to compute the earliest finish time for activity 1 as

$$\begin{aligned}\text{EF} &= \text{ES} + t\\ &= 0 + 3\\ &= 3 \text{ months}\end{aligned}$$

The earliest start for activity 2 is

$$\begin{aligned}\text{ES} &= \max\text{ (EF immediate predecessors)}\\ &= 3 \text{ months}\end{aligned}$$

and the corresponding earliest finish time is

$$\begin{aligned}\text{EF} &= \text{ES} + t\\ &= 3 + 2\\ &= 5 \text{ months}\end{aligned}$$

For activity 3 the earliest start time (ES) is three months, and the earliest finish time (EF) is four months.

Now consider activity 4, which has two predecessor activities. The earliest start time is

$$\begin{aligned}\text{ES} &= \max\text{ (EF immediate predecessors)}\\ &= \max\ (5, 4)\\ &= 5 \text{ months}\end{aligned}$$

FIGURE 9.11 **Earliest Activity Start and Finish Times**

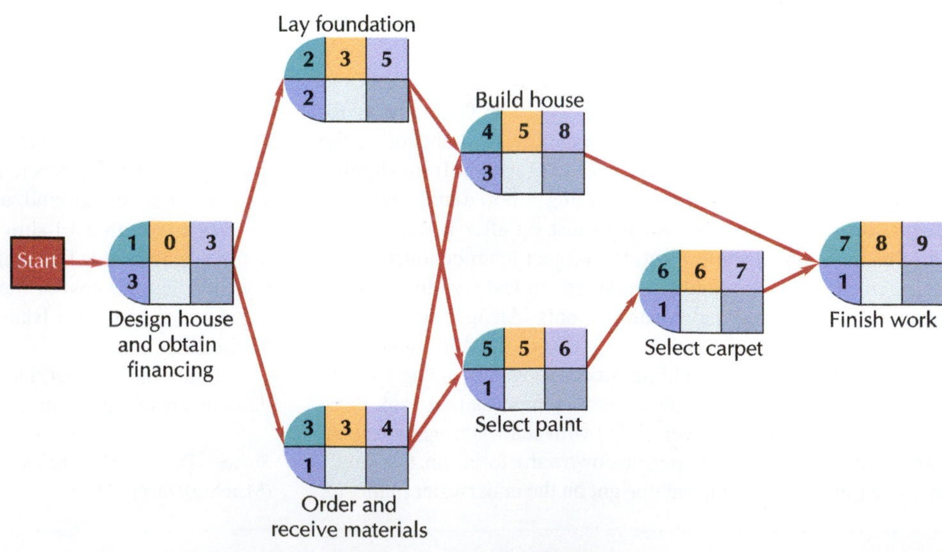

and the earliest finish time is

$$\begin{aligned} EF &= ES + t \\ &= 5 + 3 \\ &= 8 \text{ months} \end{aligned}$$

All the remaining earliest start and finish times are computed similarly. Notice in Figure 9.11 that the earliest finish time for activity 7, the last activity in the network, is nine months, which is the total project duration, or critical path time.

Companions to the earliest start and finish are the **latest start** and **latest finish times**, **LS** and **LF**. The latest start time is the latest time an activity can start without delaying the completion of the project beyond the project critical path time. For our example, the project completion time (and earliest finish time) at node 7 is nine months. Thus, the objective of determining latest times is to see how long each activity can be delayed without the project exceeding nine months.

Latest start time (LS) The latest time an activity can start without delaying critical path time.

Latest finish time (LF) The latest time an activity can be completed and still maintain the project critical path time.

In general, the latest start and finish times for an activity are computed according to the following formulas:

$$\begin{aligned} LS &= LF - t \\ LF &= \min \text{ (LS immediate following activities)} \end{aligned}$$

Whereas a forward pass through the network is made to determine the earliest times, the latest times are computed using a **backward pass**. We start at the end of the network at node 7 and work backward, computing the latest times for each activity. Since we want to determine how long each activity in the network can be delayed without extending the project time, the latest finish time at node 7 cannot exceed the earliest finish time. Therefore, the latest finish time at node 7 is nine months. This and all other latest times are shown in Figure 9.12.

Backward pass Determines latest activity times by starting at the end of a CPM/PERT network and working forward.

Starting at the end of the network, the critical path time, which is also equal to the earliest finish time of activity 7, is nine months. This automatically becomes the latest finish time for activity 7, or

$$LF = 9 \text{ months}$$

Using this value, the latest start time for activity 7 is

$$\begin{aligned} LS &= LF - t \\ &= 9 - 1 \\ &= 8 \text{ months} \end{aligned}$$

The latest finish time for activity 6 is the minimum of the latest start times for the activities following node 6. Since activity 7 follows node 6, the latest finish time is

$$\begin{aligned} LF_6 &= \min \text{ (LS following activities)} \\ &= 8 \text{ months} \end{aligned}$$

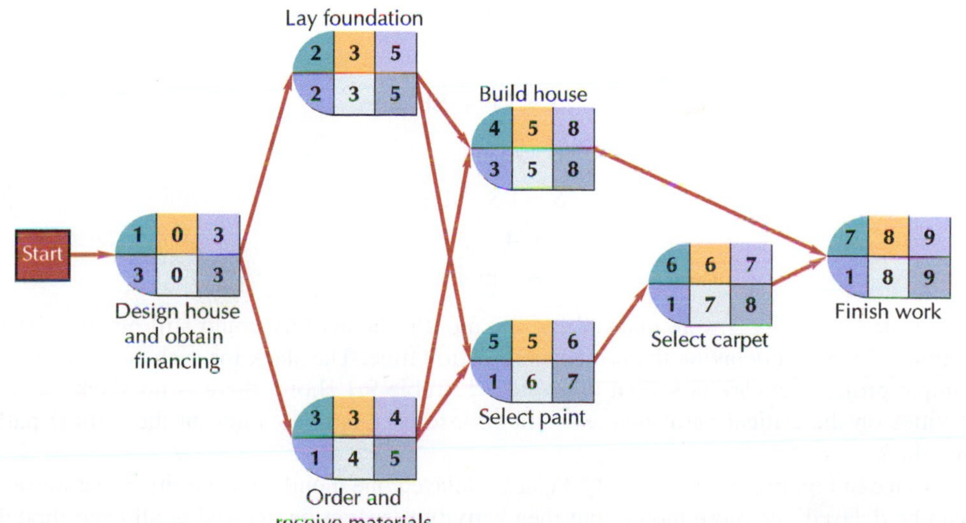

FIGURE 9.12 Latest Activity Start and Finish Times

The latest start time for activity 6 is

$$\begin{aligned} LS &= LF - t \\ &= 8 - 1 \\ &= 7 \text{ months} \end{aligned}$$

For activity 4, the latest finish time (LF) is eight months, and the latest start time (LS) is five months; for activity 5, the latest finish time (LF) is seven months, and the latest start time (LS) is six months.

Now consider activity 3, which has two activities, 4 and 5, following it. The latest finish time is computed as

$$\begin{aligned} LF &= \min (\text{LS following activities}) \\ &= \min (5, 6) \\ &= 5 \text{ months} \end{aligned}$$

The latest start time is

$$\begin{aligned} LS &= LF - t \\ &= 5 - 1 \\ &= 4 \text{ months} \end{aligned}$$

All the remaining latest start and latest finish times are computed similarly. Figure 9.12 includes the earliest and latest start times and earliest and latest finish times for all activities.

Activity Slack

The project network in Figure 9.12, with all activity start and finish times, highlights the critical path (1–2–4–7) we determined earlier by inspection. Notice that for the activities on the critical path, the earliest start times and latest start times are equal. This means that these activities on the critical path must start exactly on time and cannot be delayed at all. If the start of any activity on the critical path is delayed, then the overall project time will be increased. We now have an alternative way to determine the critical path besides simply inspecting the network. The activities on the critical path can be determined by seeing for which activities ES = LS or EF = LF. In Figure 9.12 the activities 1, 2, 4, and 7 all have earliest start times and latest start times that are equal (and EF = LF); thus, they are on the critical path.

For activities not on the critical path for which the earliest and latest start times (or earliest and latest finish times) are not equal, *slack* time exists. We introduced slack with our discussion of the Gantt chart in Figure 9.4. Slack is the amount of time an activity can be delayed without affecting the overall project duration. In effect, it is extra time available for completing an activity.

Slack, S, is computed using either of the following formulas:

$$S = LS - ES$$

or

$$S = LF - EF$$

For example, the slack for activity 3 is

$$\begin{aligned} S &= LS - ES \\ &= 4 - 3 \\ &= 1 \text{ month} \end{aligned}$$

If the start of activity 3 were delayed for one month, the activity could still be completed by month 5 without delaying the project completion time. The slack for each activity in our example project network is shown in **Table 9.1**. Table 9.1 shows there is no slack for the activities on the critical path (marked with an asterisk); activities not on the critical path have slack.

Notice in Figure 9.12 that activity 3 can be delayed one month and activity 5 that follows it can be delayed one more month, but then activity 6 cannot be delayed at all even though

TABLE 9.1 Activity Slack

ACTIVITY	LS	ES	LF	EF	SLACK S
*1	0	0	3	3	0
*2	3	3	5	5	0
3	4	3	5	4	1
*4	5	5	8	8	0
5	6	5	7	6	1
6	7	6	8	7	1
*7	8	8	9	9	0

*Critical path.

it has one month of slack. If activity 3 starts late at month 4 instead of month 3, then it will be completed at month 5, which will not allow activity 5 to start until month 5. If the start of activity 5 is delayed one month, then it will be completed at month 7, and activity 6 cannot be delayed at all without exceeding the critical path time. The slack on these three activities is called *shared slack*. This means that the sequence of activities 3–5–6 can be delayed two months jointly without delaying the project, but not three months.

Slack is beneficial to the project manager because it enables resources to be temporarily diverted from activities with slack and used for other activities that might be delayed for various reasons or for which the time estimate has proved to be inaccurate.

The times for the network activities are simply estimates, for which there is usually not a lot of historical basis (since projects tend to be unique undertakings). As such, activity time estimates are subject to quite a bit of uncertainty. However, the uncertainty inherent in activity time estimates can be reflected to a certain extent by using probabilistic time estimates instead of the single, deterministic estimates we have used so far.

Probabilistic Activity Times

In the project network for building a house in the previous section, all activity time estimates were single values. By using only a single activity time estimate, we are, in effect, assuming that activity times are known with certainty (i.e., they are deterministic). For example, in Figure 9.8, the time estimate for activity 2 (laying the foundation) is two months. Since only this one value is given, we must assume that the activity time does not vary (or varies very little) from two months. It is rare that activity time estimates can be made with certainty. Project activities are likely to be unique with little historical evidence that can be used as a basis to predict activity times. Recall that one of the primary differences between CPM and PERT is that PERT uses probabilistic activity times.

Probabilistic Time Estimates

In the PERT-type approach to estimating activity times, three time estimates for each activity are determined, which enables us to estimate the mean and variance of a **beta distribution** of the activity times.

Beta distribution A probability distribution traditionally used in CPM/PERT.

We assume that the activity times can be described by a beta distribution for several reasons. The beta distribution mean and variance can be approximated with three time estimates. Also, the beta distribution is continuous, but it has no predetermined shape (such as the bell shape of the normal curve). It will take on the shape indicated—that is, be skewed—by the time estimates given. This is beneficial, since typically we have no prior knowledge of the shapes of the distributions of activity times in a unique project network. Although other types of distributions have been shown to be no more or less accurate than the beta, it has become traditional to use the beta distribution to estimate probabilistic activity times.

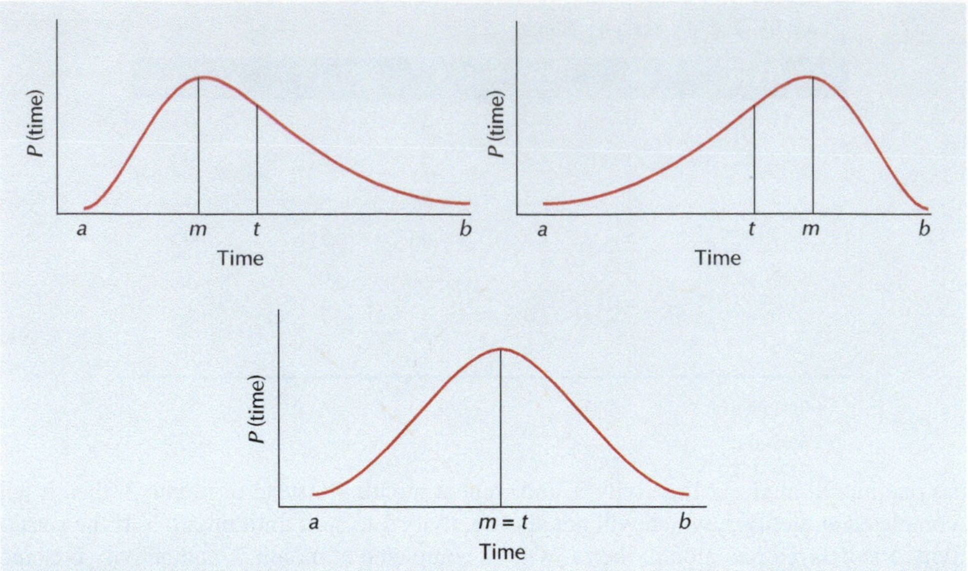

FIGURE 9.13 Examples of the Beta Distribution

Optimistic (a), most likely (m), and pessimistic (b) Time estimates for an activity.

The three time estimates for each activity are the **most likely time (m)**, the **optimistic time (a)**, and the **pessimistic time (b)**. The most likely time is a subjective estimate of the activity time that would most frequently occur if the activity were repeated many times. The optimistic time is the shortest possible time to complete the activity if everything went right. The pessimistic time is the longest possible time to complete the activity assuming everything went wrong. The person most familiar with an activity or the project manager makes these "subjective" estimates to the best of his or her knowledge and ability.

These three time estimates are used to estimate the mean and variance of a beta distribution, as follows:

$$\text{Mean (expected time): } t = \frac{a + 4m + b}{6}$$

$$\text{Variance: } \sigma^2 = \left(\frac{b - a}{6}\right)^2$$

where

a = optimistic time estimate
m = most likely time estimate
b = pessimistic time estimate

These formulas provide a reasonable estimate of the mean and variance of the beta distribution, a distribution that is continuous and can take on various shapes, or exhibit skewness.

Figure 9.13 illustrates the general form of beta distributions for different relative values of a, m, and b.

EXAMPLE 9.1 | A Project Network with Probabilistic Time Estimates

The Southern Textile Company has decided to install a new computerized order processing system that will link the company with customers and suppliers. In the past, orders were processed manually, which contributed to delays in delivery orders and resulted in lost sales. The new system will improve the quality of the service the company provides. The company wants to develop a project network for the installation of the new system. The network for the installation of the new order processing system is shown in the following figure.

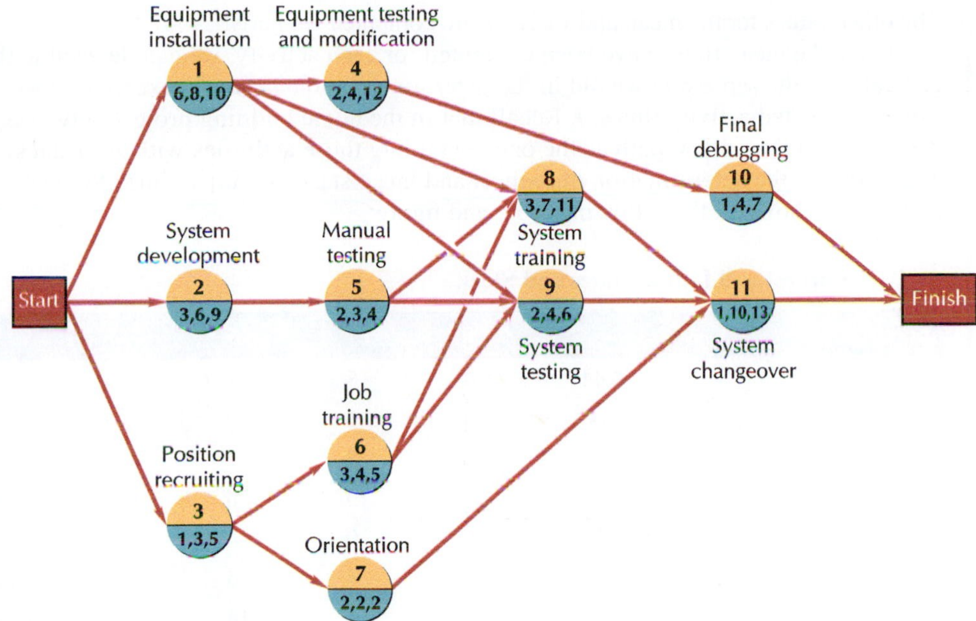

The network begins with three concurrent activities: The new computer equipment is installed (activity 1); the computerized order processing system is developed (activity 2); and people are recruited to operate the system (activity 3). Once people are hired, they are trained for the job (activity 6), and other personnel in the company, such as marketing, accounting, and production personnel, are introduced to the new system (activity 7). Once the system is developed (activity 2) it is tested manually to make sure that it is logical (activity 5). Following activity 1, the new equipment is tested, any necessary modifications are made (activity 4), and the newly trained personnel begin training on the computerized system (activity 8). Also, node 9 begins the testing of the system on the computer to check for errors (activity 9). The final activities include a trial run and changeover to the system (activity 11), and final debugging of the computer system (activity 10).

The three time estimates, the mean, and the variance for all the activities in the network as shown in the figure are provided in the following table.

Activity Time Estimates

	TIME ESTIMATES (WEEKS)			MEAN TIME	VARIANCE
ACTIVITY	a	m	b	t	σ^2
1	6	8	10	8	0.44
2	3	6	9	6	1.00
3	1	3	5	3	0.44
4	2	4	12	5	2.78
5	2	3	4	3	0.11
6	3	4	5	4	0.11
7	2	2	2	2	0.00
8	3	7	11	7	1.78
9	2	4	6	4	0.44
10	1	4	7	4	1.00
11	1	10	13	9	4.00

Solution: As an example of the computation of the individual activity mean times and variance, consider activity 1. The three time estimates ($a = 6$, $m = 8$, $b = 10$) are substituted in the formulas as follows:

$$t = \frac{a + 4m + b}{6} = \frac{6 + 4(8) + 10}{6} = 8 \text{ weeks}$$

$$\sigma^2 = \left(\frac{b - a}{6}\right)^2 = \left(\frac{10 - 6}{6}\right)^2 = \frac{4}{9} \text{ week}$$

The other values for the mean and variance are computed similarly.

Once the mean times have been computed for each activity, we can determine the critical path the same way we did in the deterministic time network, except that we use the expected activity times, *t*. Recall that in the home building project network, we identified the critical path as the one containing those activities with zero slack. This requires the determination of earliest and latest start and finish times for each activity, as shown in the following table and figure:

Activity Earliest and Latest Times and Slack

ACTIVITY	t	σ^2	ES	EF	LS	LF	S
1	8	0.44	0	8	1	9	1
2	6	1.00	0	6	0	6	0
3	3	0.44	0	3	2	5	2
4	5	2.78	8	13	16	21	8
5	3	0.11	6	9	6	9	0
6	4	0.11	3	7	5	9	2
7	2	0.00	3	5	14	16	11
8	7	1.78	9	16	9	16	0
9	4	0.44	9	13	12	16	3
10	4	1.00	13	17	21	25	8
11	9	4.00	16	25	16	25	0

From the table, we can see that the critical path encompasses activities 2–5–8–11, since these activities have no available slack. We can also see that the expected project completion time (t_p) is the same as the earliest or latest finish for activity 11, or $t_p =$ 25 weeks. To determine the project variance, we *sum the variances for the activities on the critical path.* Using the variances shown in the table for the critical path activities, we can compute the total project variance as follows:

$$\begin{aligned}\sigma^2 &= \sigma_2^2 + \sigma_5^2 + \sigma_8^2 + \sigma_{11}^2 \\ &= 1.00 + 0.11 + 1.78 + 4.00 \\ &= 6.89 \text{ weeks}\end{aligned}$$

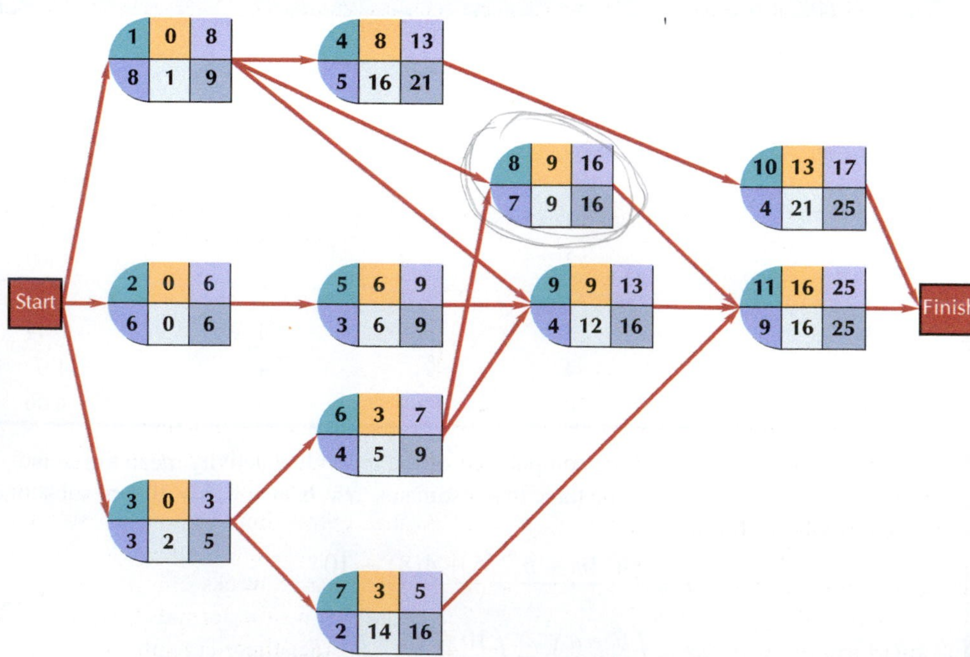

Along the Supply Chain

U.S. Transportation Construction Mega-Projects

One of the most frequent applications of project management is for transportation construction projects, some of which can reach massive proportions. One example is the California High-Speed Rail project currently under construction. The first phase, scheduled to be completed in 2029, will cover 520 miles, connecting Los Angeles with San Francisco with train speeds up to 220 miles per hour, with an estimated cost of $68 billion, making it the most expensive public works project in U.S. history. Phase 2, which has no schedule yet, will connect Sacramento and San Diego to Los Angeles. The project has experienced a number of legal issues over financing, property rights, and routing that have caused delays. To manage the project the California High-Speed Rail Authority divided it into nine matrixed project sections in order to ensure rapid decision-making. A risk management program has also been implemented to address problem issues and delays that will certainly arrive from a project of this size and complexity.

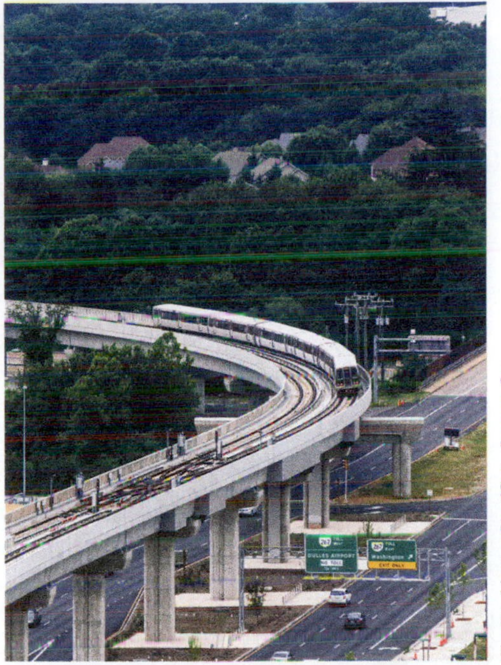

The Washington Post/Getty Images, Inc.

Another major construction project is the BeltLine project in Atlanta, a multi-use trail being built in stages within a former abandoned railway corridor. It is designed to include light rail transit, 1,300 acres of parks, 5,600 units of affordable housing, and 33 miles of multi-use trails. The total length of the BeltLine will be 22 miles, running about 3 miles on both sides of Atlanta's central business district. The entire project, scheduled to be completed by 2030 at a cost of $3 billion, will encompass approximately 120 individual projects across 45 communities, which must be managed simultaneously as they progress through different stages. Communication with all stakeholders is critical to the project's eventual success since public monies are involved, which some constituents believe should be used for things other than parks and trails.

A third major transportation project currently underway is the Dulles Corridor Metrorail Project in Northern Virginia that will extend the Washington, DC, Metrorail 23 miles to Dulles Airport, scheduled to be completed around 2020 at a projected cost of almost $7 billion (see photo). The project is being constructed in two phases; phase 1 has been completed and extended the rail system 12 miles to the Reston East station in Fairfax County, Virginia. Phase 2, which is scheduled to be completed about 2020, will extend the rail line to Dulles Airport. The project will also include 11 new rail stations and several parking lots and garages.

Using the Internet, research these and several other public transportation construction projects and describe some of the problems these mega-projects have in common.

Source: Matt Alderton, "Moving Ahead," *PM Network* 28 (3); (March 2014); pp. 24–35; and Dulles Metrorail Project at www.dullesmetro.com/.

CPM/PERT Analysis with OM Tools

The "Project Management" module in OM Tools has the capability to develop both single-time estimate and three-time estimate networks. Exhibit 9.1 shows the OM Tools spreadsheet for the "Order Processing System" project in Example 9.1.

Probabilistic Network Analysis

The CPM/PERT method assumes that the activity times are statistically independent, which allows us to sum the individual expected activity times and variances to get an expected project time and variance. It is further assumed that the network mean and variance are normally distributed. This assumption is based on the central limit theorem of probability, which for CPM/PERT analysis and our purposes states that if the number of activities is large enough and the activities are statistically independent, then the sum of the means of the activities along the critical path will approach the mean of a normal distribution. For the small examples in this chapter, it is questionable whether there are sufficient activities to guarantee that the mean project completion time and variance are normally distributed.

EXHIBIT 9.1

OM Tools

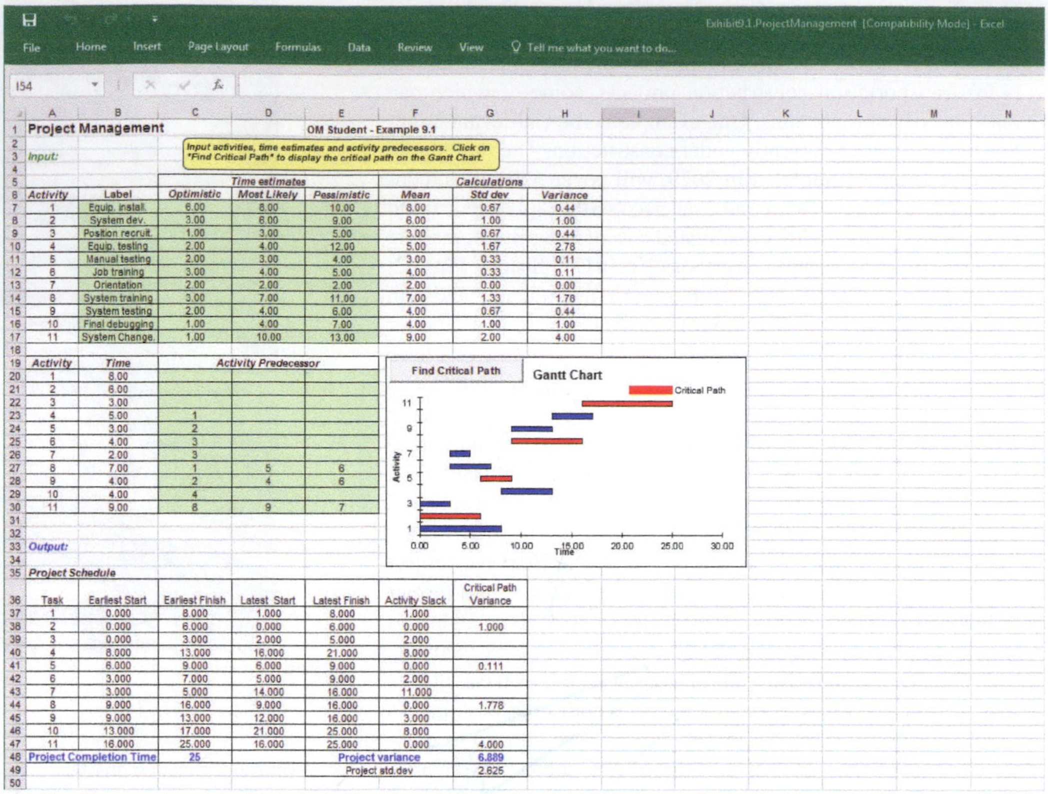

Project Management — OM Student - Example 9.1

Input:

Input activities, time estimates and activity predecessors. Click on "Find Critical Path" to display the critical path on the Gantt Chart.

		Time estimates			Calculations		
Activity	Label	Optimistic	Most Likely	Pessimistic	Mean	Std dev	Variance
1	Equip. install.	6.00	8.00	10.00	8.00	0.67	0.44
2	System dev.	3.00	6.00	9.00	6.00	1.00	1.00
3	Position recruit.	1.00	3.00	5.00	3.00	0.67	0.44
4	Equip. testing	2.00	4.00	12.00	5.00	1.67	2.78
5	Manual testing	2.00	3.00	4.00	3.00	0.33	0.11
6	Job training	3.00	4.00	5.00	4.00	0.33	0.11
7	Orientation	2.00	2.00	2.00	2.00	0.00	0.00
8	System training	3.00	7.00	11.00	7.00	1.33	1.78
9	System testing	2.00	4.00	6.00	4.00	0.67	0.44
10	Final debugging	1.00	4.00	7.00	4.00	1.00	1.00
11	System Change.	1.00	10.00	13.00	9.00	2.00	4.00

Activity	Time	Activity Predecessor		
1	8.00			
2	6.00			
3	3.00			
4	5.00	1		
5	3.00	2		
6	4.00	3		
7	2.00	3		
8	7.00	1	5	6
9	4.00	2	4	6
10	4.00	4		
11	9.00	8	9	7

Find Critical Path

Gantt Chart

Critical Path

Activity: 1, 3, 5, 7, 9, 11

Time: 0.00, 5.00, 10.00, 15.00, 20.00, 25.00, 30.00

Output:

Project Schedule

Task	Earliest Start	Earliest Finish	Latest Start	Latest Finish	Activity Slack	Critical Path Variance
1	0.000	8.000	1.000	8.000	1.000	
2	0.000	6.000	0.000	6.000	0.000	1.000
3	0.000	3.000	2.000	5.000	2.000	
4	8.000	13.000	16.000	21.000	8.000	
5	6.000	9.000	6.000	9.000	0.000	0.111
6	3.000	7.000	5.000	9.000	2.000	
7	3.000	5.000	14.000	16.000	11.000	
8	9.000	16.000	9.000	16.000	0.000	1.778
9	9.000	13.000	12.000	16.000	3.000	
10	13.000	17.000	21.000	25.000	8.000	
11	16.000	25.000	16.000	25.000	0.000	4.000
Project Completion Time		25		Project variance		6.889
				Project std.dev		2.625

Although it has become conventional in CPM/PERT analysis to employ probability analysis using the normal distribution regardless of the network size, the prudent user should bear this limitation in mind.

Probabilistic analysis of a CPM/PERT network is the determination of the probability that the project will be completed within a certain time period given the mean and variance of a normally distributed project completion time. This is illustrated in **Figure 9.14**. The value Z is computed using the following formula:

$$Z = \frac{x - \mu}{\sigma}$$

FIGURE 9.14 **Normal Distribution of Project Time**

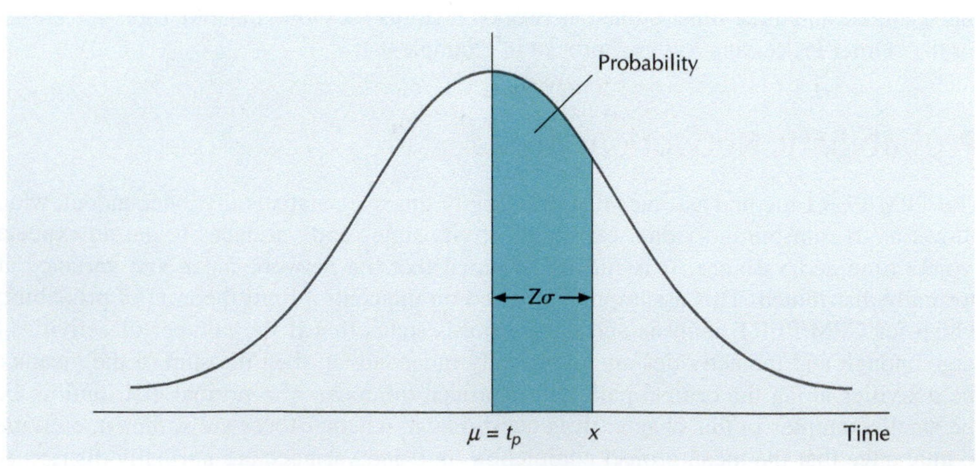

where

$$\mu = t_p = \text{project mean time}$$
$$x = \text{the proposed project time}$$
$$Z = \text{number of standard deviations } x \text{ is from the mean}$$

This value of Z is then used to find the corresponding probability in Table A.1 (Appendix A).

EXAMPLE 9.2 | Probabilistic Analysis of the Project Network

The Southern Textile Company in Example 9.1 has told its customers that the new order processing system will be operational in 30 weeks. What is the probability that the system will be ready by that time?

Solution: The probability that the project will be completed within 30 weeks is shown as the shaded area in the accompanying figure. To compute the Z value for a time of 30 weeks, we must first compute the standard deviation (σ) from the variance (σ^2).

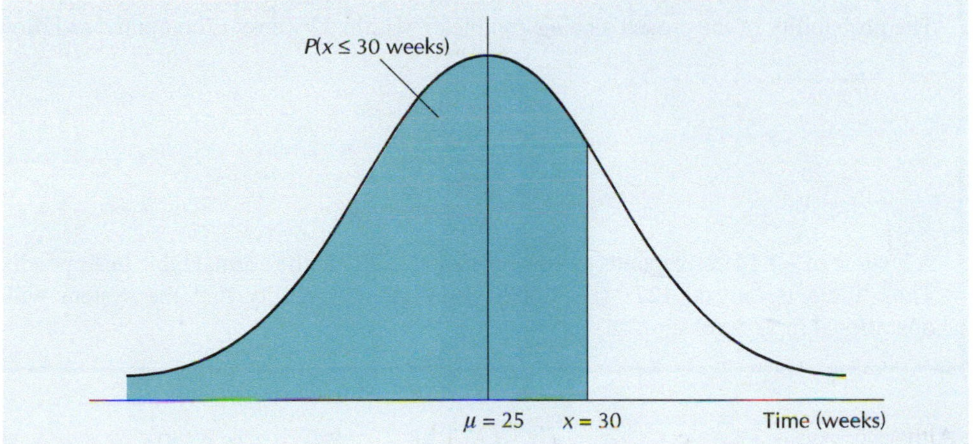

$$\sigma^2 = 6.89 \text{ weeks}$$
$$\sigma = \sqrt{6.89}$$
$$= 2.62 \text{ weeks}$$

Next we substitute this value for the standard deviation along with the value for the mean, 25 weeks, and our proposed project completion time, 30 weeks, into the following formula:

$$Z = \frac{x - \mu}{\sigma}$$
$$= \frac{30 - 25}{2.62}$$
$$= 1.91$$

A Z value of 1.91 corresponds to a probability of .4719 in Table A.1 in Appendix A. This means that there is a .9719 probability of completing the project in 30 weeks or less (adding the probability of the area to the left of $\mu = 25$, or .5000, to .4719).

EXAMPLE 9.3 | Probabilistic Analysis of the Project Network

A customer of the Southern Textile Company has become frustrated with delayed orders and told the company that if the new ordering system is not working within 22 weeks, it will not do any more business with the textile company. What is the probability the order processing system will be operational within 22 weeks?

Solution: The probability that the project will be completed within 22 weeks is shown as the shaded area in the accompanying figure.

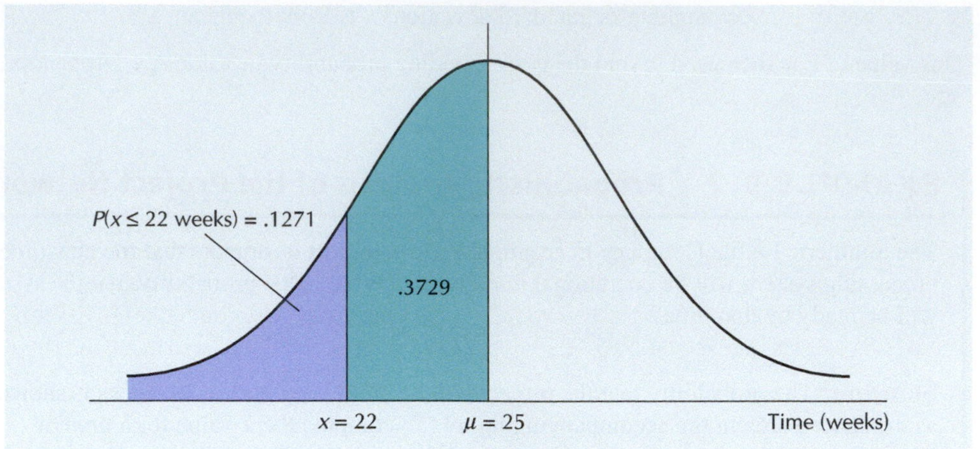

The probability of the project's being completed within 22 weeks is computed as follows:

$$\begin{aligned} Z &= \frac{22 - 25}{2.62} \\ &= \frac{-3}{2.62} \\ &= -1.14 \end{aligned}$$

A Z value of -1.14 corresponds to a probability of .3729 in the normal table in Appendix A. Thus, there is only a .1271 (i.e., .5000 − .3729) probability that the system will be operational in 22 weeks.

Microsoft Project

Microsoft Project is a popular and widely used software package for project management and CPM/PERT analysis. It is also relatively easy to use. We will demonstrate how to use Microsoft Project using the project network for building a house shown in Figure 9.8.

When you open *Microsoft Project,* a screen comes up for a new project, as shown in **Exhibit 9.2**. Notice that the "Gantt Chart Tools" tab on the toolbar ribbon at the top of the screen is highlighted. The initial step is to set the project up in this window. First type in the activity name, "Design and finance" under the "Task Name" column, and then type in the activity duration in the "Duration" column, which is three months for this activity. This only requires that you type "3 mo" and it will be recognized as three months. Next, type in a "Start" date, which we have selected to be "March 14, 2016." The start date can also be selected from the drop-down calendar. (Note that a start date must be designated for all starting activities that don't have predecessors, which for this example is only the first activity.) This first activity has no predecessor, so leave the "Predecessor" cell for this activity blank, and drop down to the next line to enter the next activity, "Lay foundation." Repeat the process followed for the first activity by typing in the duration, "2 mos," but do not type in the start and finish dates; the program will do this automatically once you start identifying activity predecessors. Toggle over to the "Predecessor" cell for this activity and type in "1" (indicating that activity 1 is the predecessor activity for this activity, 2. Next, drop down to the next line and type in the information for activity 3, "Order materials," the duration of "1 mo," and that its "Predecessor" is activity 1. Exhibit 9.2 shows our progress so far.

Before proceeding to finishing inputting the project data, we'll make a few comments. First, note the emerging Gantt chart forming on the calendar part of your window (on the

EXHIBIT 9.2

Microsoft Project

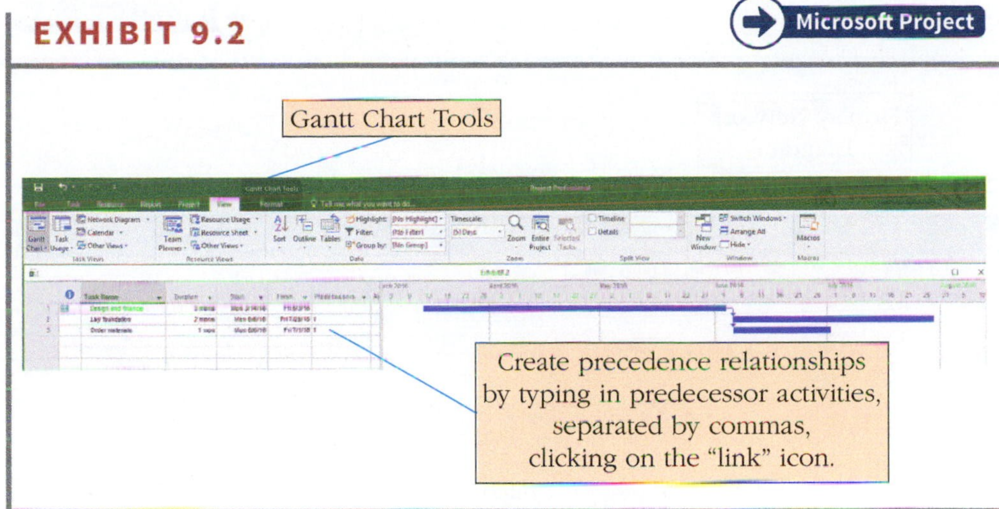
Gantt Chart Tools
Create precedence relationships by typing in predecessor activities, separated by commas, clicking on the "link" icon.

right-hand part of the screen) for the activities we've entered. This chart might not be on your screen when you start because the timescale on the calendar does not conform to your start date. If the Gantt chart is not there, you can make it appear by moving the tab at the bottom of the calendar part of the screen ahead (i.e., to the right) until your start date appears, and this view should contain the beginning of your Gantt chart. Also, notice at the top of the window that we have switched to the "View" tab. On this toolbar ribbon, if you click on "Timescale," you can insert the time units of the project, which in this case is months, or you can accomplish the same thing by "right-clicking" on the timcline just above the Gantt chart and then clicking on "Timescale" from the drop-down menu. You can also condense the size of your Gantt chart to fit on the calendar part of your screen by clicking on the button on the "Entire Project" icon on the toolbar.

Microsoft Project uses a "standard" calendar for scheduling project activities; for example, it automatically removes weekend days as working days. Holidays and vacation days can also be designated by first clicking on the "Project" tab, then clicking on the "Change Working Time" icon. This will bring up a window with a calendar and menu for changing work times.

Next, we will finish typing in the rest of the information for our project as shown in Exhibit 9.3. On this screen if we can switch back to the "Format" tab under "Gantt Chart Tools," we can select the "Critical Tasks" button to highlight the critical path on the Gantt chart in red. The "pin" icons in the cells next to each activity in the "Task Mode" column on our data window indicate that we have manually scheduled the activities (or tasks); the other "Task Mode" option is to allow *Microsoft Project* to automatically schedule the activities. For our purposes, manual scheduling is sufficient.

EXHIBIT 9.3

Microsoft Project

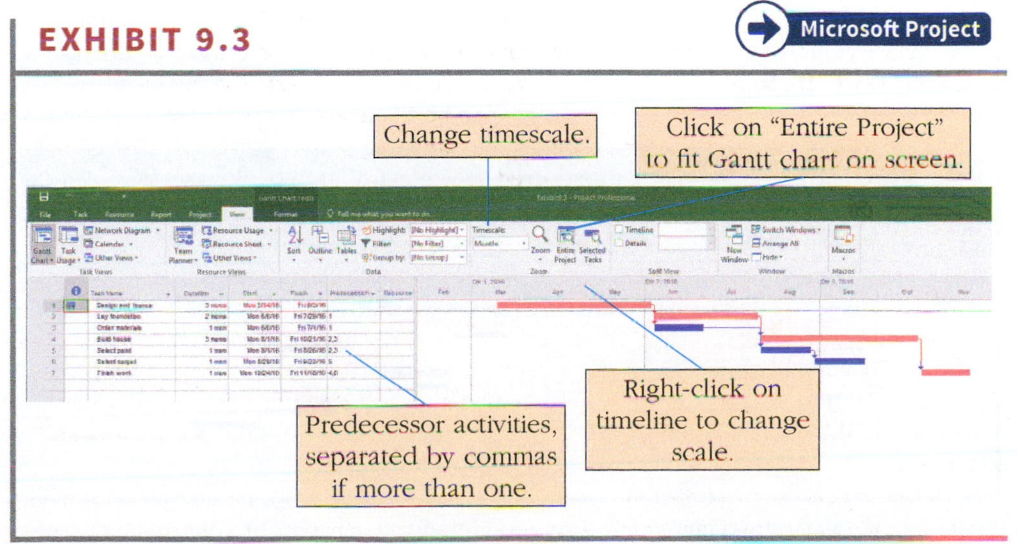
Change timescale.
Click on "Entire Project" to fit Gantt chart on screen.
Predecessor activities, separated by commas if more than one.
Right-click on timeline to change scale.

EXHIBIT 9.4

Microsoft Project

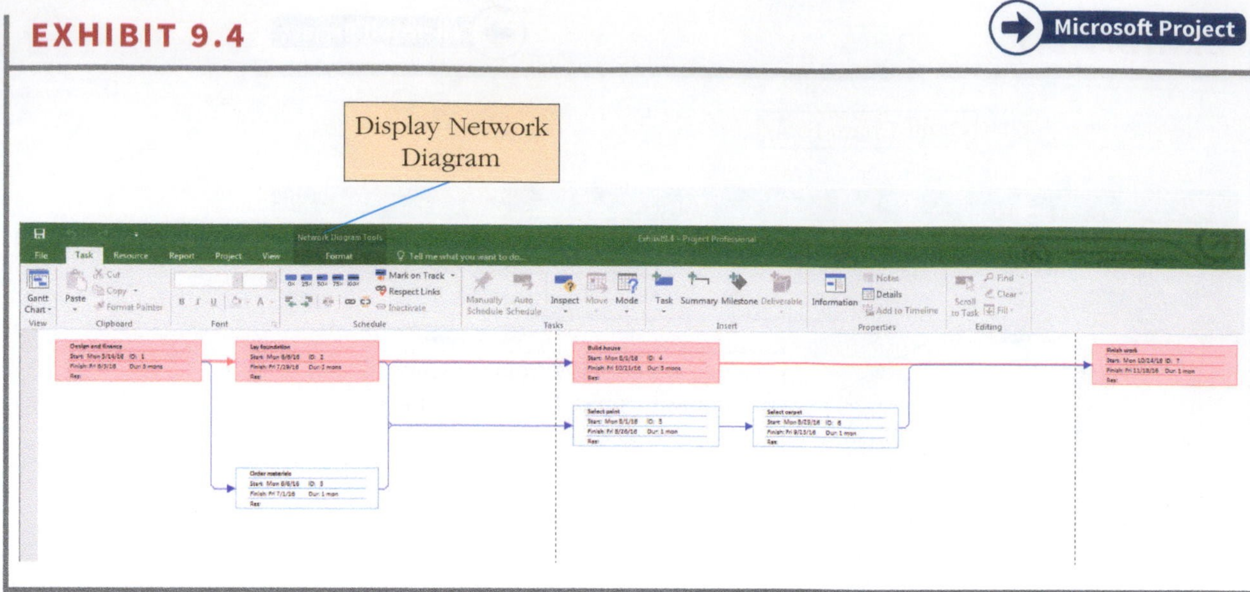

In order to show the network diagram of our project, click on "View" on the toolbar and then on "Network Diagram," which results in the screen shown in Exhibit 9.4. (We also used the "Zoom" icon to make the network larger.) Notice that the critical path is highlighted in red, which, as we noted, can be achieved from the "Format" tab.

Microsoft Project does not have PERT (three time estimates) capabilities (although software add-in apps are available to do this). Thus, to use *Microsoft Project* when you have three time estimates you must first manually (or using Excel) compute the mean activity times and use these as single time estimates in *Microsoft Project*. Exhibit 9.5 shows the Gantt chart window for our "Order Processing System" project example where the mean activity time estimates are used. Exhibit 9.6 shows the network diagram. Notice that we gave this project a start date of April 4, 2016, which had to be designated as the start date for all three of our starting activities (that do not have predecessors): 1, 2, and 3.

Microsoft Project also has many additional tools and features, including project updating and activity completion, resource management, work stoppages, and changing work times, including shortened days, holidays, and vacation time. To learn about these features, access the various "Help" screens from the different *Microsoft Project* windows or press the F1 key.

EXHIBIT 9.5

Microsoft Project

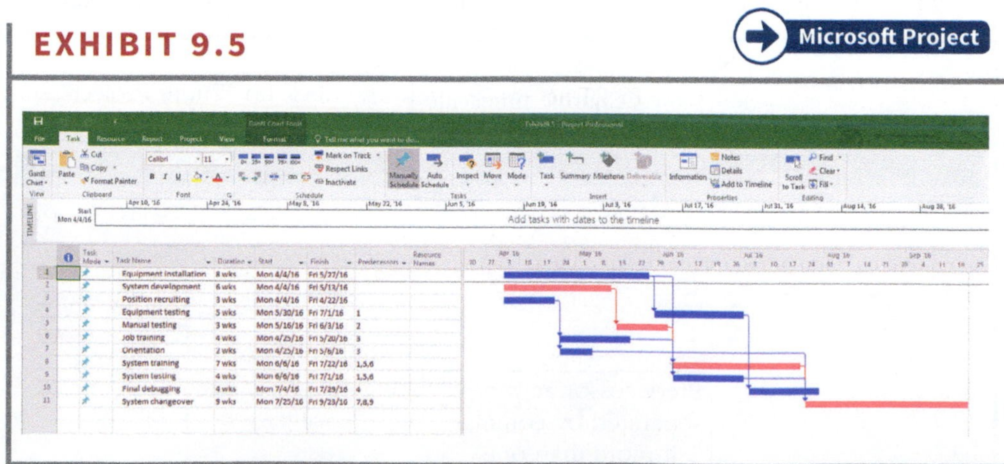

	Task Name	Duration	Start	Finish	Predecessors
1	Equipment installation	8 wks	Mon 4/4/16	Fri 5/27/16	
2	System development	6 wks	Mon 4/4/16	Fri 5/13/16	
3	Position recruiting	3 wks	Mon 4/4/16	Fri 4/22/16	
4	Equipment testing	5 wks	Mon 5/30/16	Fri 7/1/16	1
5	Manual testing	3 wks	Mon 5/16/16	Fri 6/3/16	2
6	Job training	4 wks	Mon 4/25/16	Fri 5/20/16	3
7	Orientation	2 wks	Mon 4/25/16	Fri 5/6/16	3
8	System training	7 wks	Mon 6/6/16	Fri 7/22/16	1,5,6
9	System testing	4 wks	Mon 6/6/16	Fri 7/1/16	1,5,6
10	Final debugging	4 wks	Mon 7/4/16	Fri 7/29/16	4
11	System changeover	9 wks	Mon 7/25/16	Fri 9/23/16	7,8,9

EXHIBIT 9.6 Microsoft Project

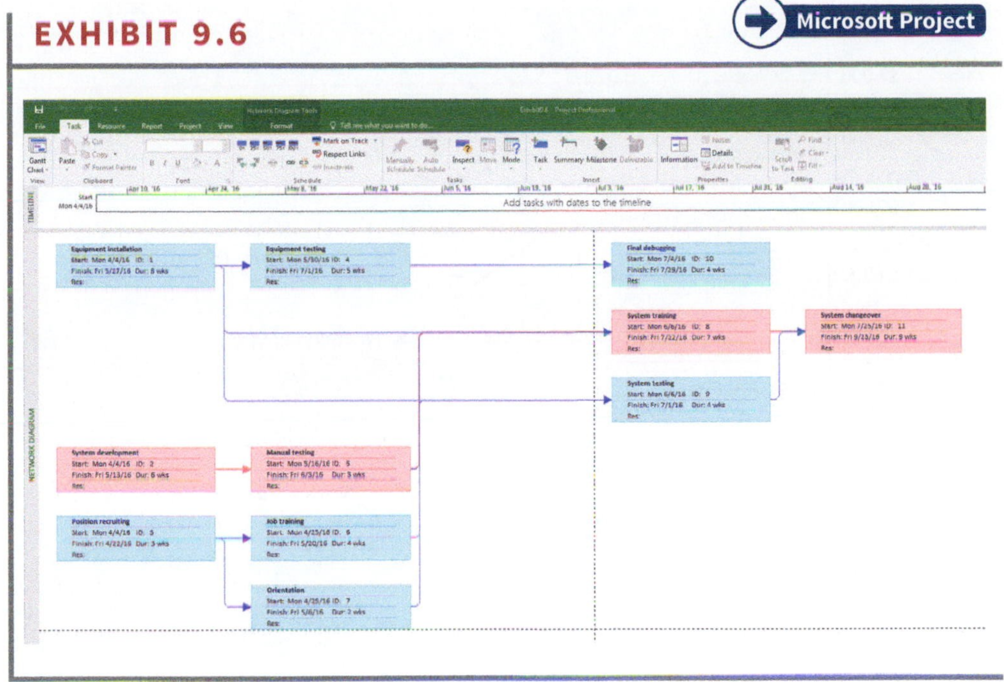

Project Crashing and Time-Cost Tradeoff

The project manager is frequently confronted with having to reduce the scheduled completion time of a project to meet a deadline. In other words, the manager must finish the project sooner than indicated by the CPM/PERT network analysis. Project duration can often be reduced by assigning more labor to project activities, in the form of overtime, and by assigning more resources (material, equipment, and so on). However, additional labor and resources increase the project cost. Thus, the decision to reduce the project duration must be based on an analysis of the tradeoff between time and cost. *Project crashing* is a method for shortening the project duration by reducing the time of one (or more) of the critical project activities to less than its normal activity time. This reduction in the normal activity time is referred to as **crashing**. Crashing is achieved by devoting more resources, usually measured in terms of dollars, to the activities to be crashed.

Crashing Reducing project time by expending additional resources.

Project Crashing

To demonstrate how project crashing works, we will employ the CPM/PERT network for constructing a house in Figure 9.8. This network is repeated in Figure 9.15, except that the activity times previously shown as months have been converted to weeks. Although this sample network encompasses only single-activity time estimates, the project crashing procedure can be applied in the same manner to PERT networks with probabilistic activity time estimates.

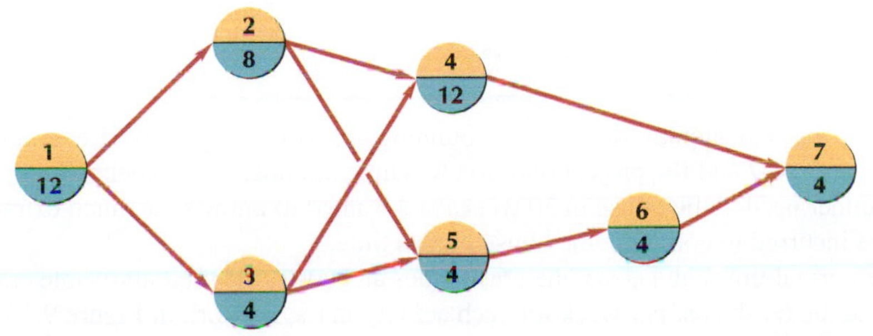

FIGURE 9.15 The Project Network for Building a House

FIGURE 9.16 **The Relationship Between Normal Time and Cost, and Crash Time and Cost**

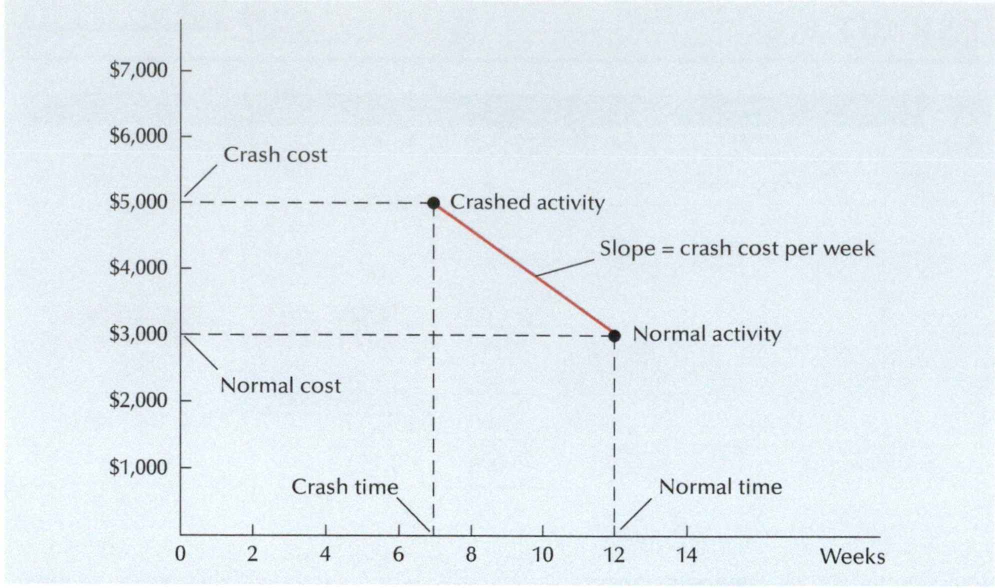

We will assume that the times (in weeks) shown on the network activities are the normal activity times. For example, 12 weeks are normally required to complete activity 1. Furthermore, we will assume that the cost required to complete this activity in the time indicated is \$3000. This cost is referred to as the *normal activity cost*. Next, we will assume that the building contractor has estimated that activity 1 can be completed in seven weeks, but it will cost \$5000 instead of \$3000 to complete the activity. This new estimated activity time is known as the **crash time**, and the cost to achieve the crash time is referred to as the **crash cost**.

Crash time An amount of time by which an activity is reduced.

Crash cost The cost of reducing activity time.

Activity 1 can be crashed a total of five weeks (normal time − crash time = 12 − 7 = 5 weeks) at a total crash cost of \$2000 (crash cost − normal cost = \$5000 − 3000 = \$2000). Dividing the total crash cost by the total allowable crash time yields the crash cost per week:

$$\frac{\text{Total crash cost}}{\text{Total crash time}} = \frac{\$2000}{5} = \$400 \text{ per week}$$

If we assume that the relationship between crash cost and crash time is linear, then activity 1 can be crashed by any amount of time (not exceeding the maximum allowable crash time) at a rate of \$400 per week. For example, if the contractor decided to crash activity 1–2 by only two weeks (reducing activity time to 10 weeks), the crash cost would be \$800 (\$400 per week × 2 weeks). The linear relationships between crash cost and crash time and between normal cost and normal time are illustrated in Figure 9.16.

The objective of project crashing is to reduce project duration while minimizing the cost of crashing. Since the project completion time can be shortened only by crashing activities on the critical path, it may turn out that not all activities have to be crashed. However, as activities are crashed, the critical path may change, requiring crashing of previously noncritical activities to reduce the project completion time even further.

EXAMPLE 9.4 | Project Crashing

Recall that the critical path for the house building network in Figure 9.15 encompassed activities 1–2–4–7 and the project duration was nine months, or 36 weeks. Suppose the home builder needed the house in 30 weeks and wanted to know how much extra cost would be incurred to complete the house by this time.

The normal times and costs, the crash times and costs, the total allowable crash times, and the crash cost per week for each activity in the network in Figure 9.15 are summarized in the following table:

Normal Activity and Crash Data

ACTIVITY	NORMAL TIME (WEEKS)	CRASH TIME (WEEKS)	NORMAL COST	CRASH COST	TOTAL ALLOWABLE CRASH TIME (WEEKS)	CRASH COST PER WEEK
1	12	7	$3,000	$5,000	5	$400
2	8	5	2,000	3,500	3	500
3	4	3	4,000	7,000	1	3,000
4	12	9	50,000	71,000	3	7,000
5	4	1	500	1,100	3	200
6	4	1	500	1,100	3	200
7	4	3	15,000	22,000	1	7,000
			$75,000	$110,700		

Solution: We start by looking at the critical path and seeing which activity has the minimum crash cost per week. Observing the preceding table and the figure below, we see activity 1 has the minimum crash cost of $400. Activity 1 will be reduced as much as possible. The table shows that the maximum allowable reduction for activity 1 is five weeks, but we can reduce activity 1 only to the point at which another path becomes critical. When two paths simultaneously become critical, activities on both must be reduced by the same amount. If we reduce the activity time beyond the point at which another path becomes critical, we may be incurring an unnecessary cost. This last stipulation means that we must keep up with all the network paths as we reduce individual activities, a condition that makes manual crashing very cumbersome. For that reason the computer is generally required for project crashing; however, we will solve this example manually in order to demonstrate the logic of project crashing.

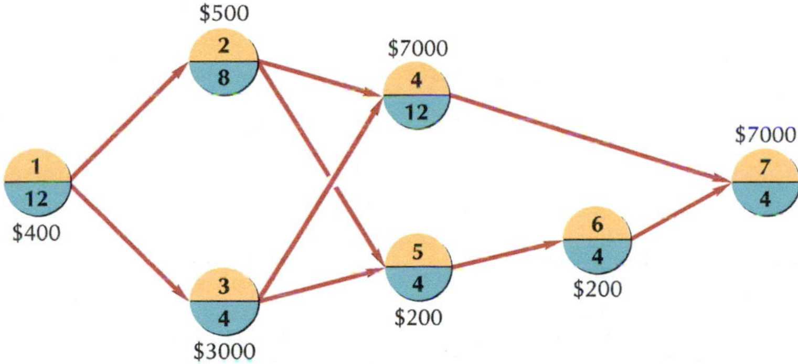

It turns out that activity 1 can be crashed by the total amount of five weeks without another path becoming critical, since activity 1 is included in all four paths in the network. Crashing this activity results in a revised project duration of 31 weeks at a crashing cost of $2000. The revised network is shown in the following figure.

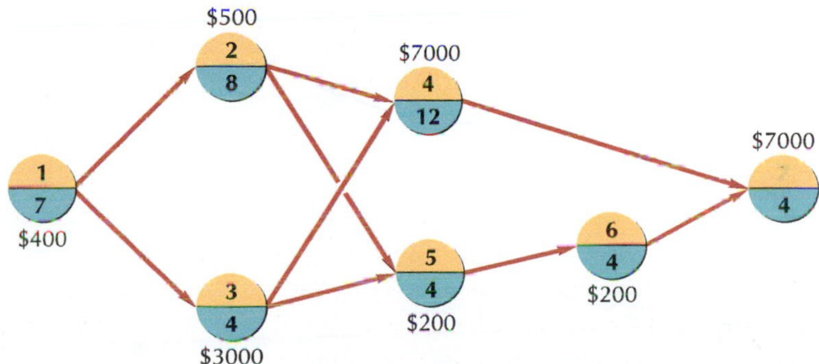

Since we have not reached our crashing goal of 30 weeks, we must continue, and the process is repeated. The critical path in the preceding figure remains the same, and the minimum activity crash cost on the critical path is $500 for activity 2. Activity 2 can be crashed a total of three weeks, but since the contractor desires to crash the network only to 30 weeks, we need to crash activity 2 by only one week. Crashing activity 2 by one week does not result in any other path becoming critical, so we can safely make this reduction. Crashing activity 2 to seven weeks (i.e., a one-week reduction) costs $500 and reduces the project duration to 30 weeks.

The total cost of crashing the project to 30 weeks is $2500. The contractor could inform the customer that an additional cost of only $2500 would be incurred to finish the house in 30 weeks.

Suppose we wanted to continue to crash this network, reducing the project duration down to the minimum time possible—that is, crashing the network the maximum amount possible. We can determine how much the network can be crashed by crashing each activity the maximum amount possible and then determining the critical path of this completely crashed network. For example, activity 1 is seven weeks, activity 2 is five weeks, 3 is three weeks, and so on. The critical path of this totally crashed network is 1–2–4–7, with a project duration of 24 weeks. This is the smallest amount of time in which the project can be completed. If we crashed all the activities by their maximum amount, the total crashing cost would be $35,700, computed by subtracting the total normal cost of $75,000 from the total crash cost of $110,700 in the preceding table. However, if we followed the crashing procedure outlined in this example, the network could be crashed to 24 weeks at a cost of $31,500, a savings of $4000.

The General Relationship of Time and Cost

In our discussion of project crashing, we demonstrated how the project critical path time could be reduced by increasing expenditures for labor and other direct resources. The objective of crashing was to reduce the scheduled completion time to reap the results of the project sooner. However, there may be other reasons for reducing project time. As projects continue over time, they consume *indirect costs*, including the cost of facilities, equipment, and machinery, interest on investment, utilities, labor, personnel costs, and the loss of skills and labor from members of the project team who are not working at their regular jobs. There also may be direct financial penalties for not completing a project on time. For example, many construction contracts and government contracts have penalty clauses for exceeding the project completion date.

In general, project crashing costs and indirect costs have an inverse relationship: crashing costs are highest when the project is shortened, whereas indirect costs increase as the project duration increases. This time–cost relationship is illustrated in Figure 9.17. The best, or optimal, project time is at the minimum point on the total cost curve.

FIGURE 9.17 **The Time–Cost Tradeoff**

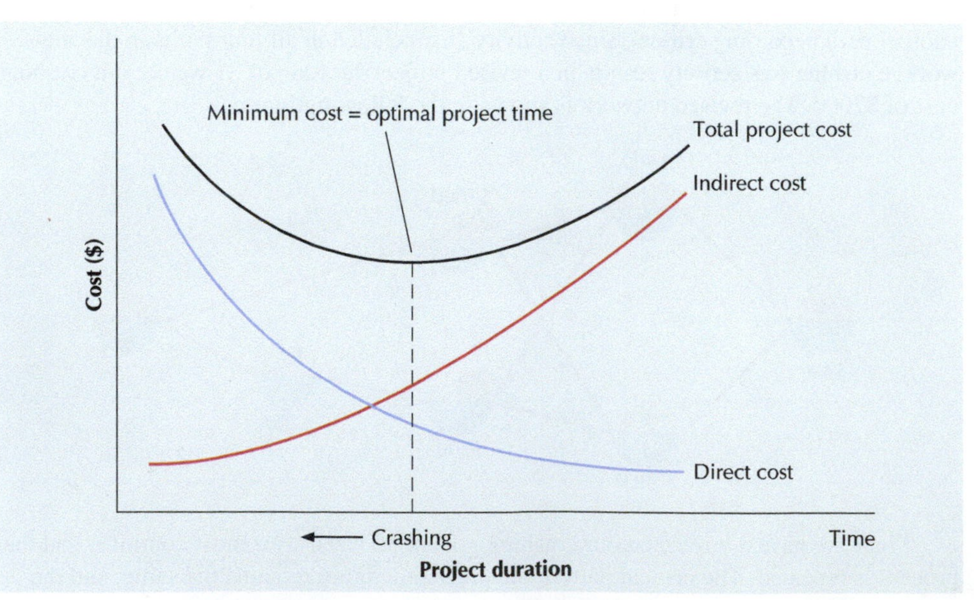

Summary

Since the development of CPM/PERT in the 1950s, it has been applied in a variety of government agencies concerned with project control, including military agencies, NASA, the Federal Aviation Agency (FAA), and the General Services Administration (GSA). These agencies are frequently involved in large-scale projects involving millions of dollars and many subcontractors. CPM/PERT has also been widely applied in the private sector. Two of the areas of application of CPM/PERT in the private sector have been research and development (R&D) and construction.

One reason for this popularity is that a network analysis provides a visual display of the project that is easy for managers and staff to understand and interpret. It is a powerful tool for identifying and organizing the activities in a project and controlling the project schedule. However, beyond that it provides an effective focal point for organizing the efforts of management and the project team. Currently, hundreds of project management software packages are commercially available for personal computers, ranging in cost from several hundred dollars to thousands of dollars.

CPM/PERT also has certain limitations. The project manager tends to rely so heavily on the project network that errors in the precedence relationship or missing activities can be overlooked, until a point in time where these omissions become a problem. Attention to critical path activities can become excessive to the extent that other project activities may be neglected, or they may be delayed to the point that other paths become critical. Obtaining accurate single-time estimates and even three probabilistic time estimates is difficult and subject to a great deal of uncertainty. Since persons directly associated with the project activity within the organization are typically the primary source for time estimates, they may be overly pessimistic if they have a vested interest in the scheduling process or overly optimistic if they do not. Personal interests aside, it is frequently difficult to define, within the context of an activity, what an optimistic or pessimistic time means. Nevertheless, such reservations have not diminished the popularity of CPM/PERT because most people feel its usefulness far outweighs any speculative or theoretical drawbacks.

Key Terms

activity Performance of an individual job or work effort that requires labor, resources, and time and is subject to management control.

activity-on-arrow (AOA) A convention for constructing a CPM/PERT network in which the branches between nodes represent project activities.

activity-on-node (AON) A convention for constructing a CPM/PERT network in which the nodes represent project activities.

agile project management An approach to project management that focuses on adaptability to rapid and unexpected change.

backward pass Starting at the end of a CPM/PERT network, a procedure for determining latest activity times.

beta distribution A probability distribution traditionally used in CPM/PERT for estimating the mean and variance of project activity times.

crash cost The cost of reducing the normal activity time.

crash time The amount of time an activity is reduced.

crashing A method for shortening the project duration by reducing the time of one or more critical activities at a cost.

critical path The longest path through a CPM/PERT network, indicating the minimum time in which a project can be completed.

dummy An activity in a network that shows a precedence relationship but represents no passage of time.

earliest finish time (EF) The earliest time an activity can be completed.

earliest start time (ES) The earliest time an activity can begin subject to preceding activities.

earned value analysis (EVA) A standard procedure for measuring a project's progress, forecasting its completion time and cost, and measuring schedule and budget variation.

event The completion or beginning of an activity in a project.

forward pass Starting at the beginning of a CPM/PERT network, a procedure for determining earliest activity times.

Gantt chart A graphical display using bars (or time lines) to show the duration of project activities and precedence relationships.

latest finish time (LF) The latest time an activity can be completed and still maintain the project critical path time.

latest start time (LS) The latest time an activity can begin and not delay subsequent activities.

matrix organization An organizational structure of project teams that includes members from various functional areas in the company.

most likely time (m) The subjective estimate of the time that would occur most frequently if the activity were repeated many times.

optimistic time (a) The shortest possible time to complete the activity if everything went right.

organizational breakdown structure (OBS) A chart that shows which organizational units are responsible for work items.

pessimistic time (b) The longest possible time to complete the activity given that everything went wrong.

precedence relationship The sequential relationship of project activities to each other.

project A unique, one-time operation or effort.

responsibility assignment matrix (RAM) Shows who in the organization is responsible for doing the work in the project.

scope statement A document that provides an understanding, justification, and expected result for the project.

slack The amount by which an activity can be delayed without delaying any of the activities that follow it or the project as a whole.

statement of work A written description of the objectives of a project.

work breakdown structure (WBS) A method for subdividing a project into different hierarchical levels of components.

Key Formulas

Earliest Start and Finish Times

$$ES = \max\ (\text{EF of immediately preceding activities})$$
$$EF = ES + t$$

Latest Start and Finish Times

$$LS = LF - t$$
$$LF = \min\ (\text{LS of immediately following activities})$$

Activity Slack

$$S = LS - ES = LF - EF$$

Mean Activity Time and Variance

$$t = \frac{a + 4m + b}{6}$$
$$\sigma^2 = \left(\frac{b - a}{6}\right)^2$$

Solved Problem

WileyPLUS

CPM/PERT Network Analysis

Given the following network and activity time estimates, determine earliest and latest activity times, slack, the expected project completion time and variance, and the probability that the project will be completed in 28 days or less.

	TIME ESTIMATES (DAYS)		
ACTIVITY	*a*	*m*	*b*
1	5	8	17
2	7	10	13
3	3	5	7
4	1	3	5
5	4	6	8
6	3	3	3
7	3	4	5

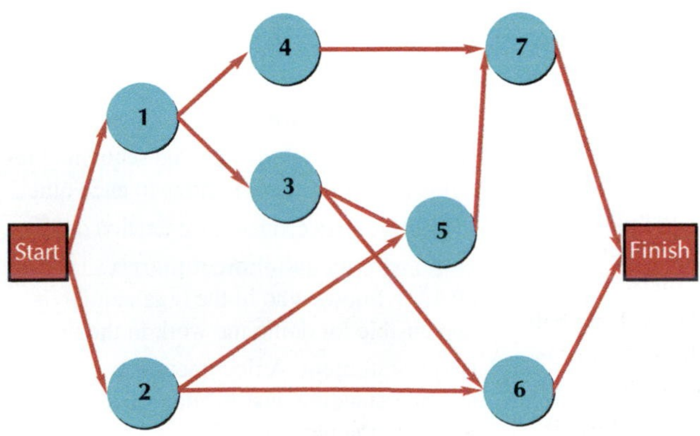

Solution

Step 1. Compute the expected activity times and variances:

$$t = \frac{a + 4m + b}{6}$$
$$\sigma^2 = \left(\frac{b - a}{6}\right)^2$$

For example, the expected time and variance for activity 1 are

$$t = \frac{5 + 4(8) + 17}{6} = 9 \text{ days}$$
$$\sigma^2 = \left(\frac{17 - 5}{6}\right)^2 = 4 \text{ days}$$

These values and the remaining expected times and variances for each activity are shown in the following table:

ACTIVITY	t	σ^2
1	9	4
2	10	1
3	5	4/9
4	3	4/9
5	6	4/9
6	3	0
7	4	1/9

Step 2. Determine the earliest and latest activity times and activity slack:

ACTIVITY	t	ES	EF	LS	LF	S
1	9	0	9	0	9	0
2	10	0	10	4	14	4
3	5	9	14	9	14	0
4	3	9	12	17	20	8
5	6	14	20	14	20	0
6	3	14	17	21	24	7
7	4	20	24	20	24	0

As an example, the earliest start and finish times for activity 1 are

$$\begin{aligned} ES &= \max\ (\text{EF immediate predecessors}) \\ &= 0 \\ EF &= ES + t \\ &= 0 + 9 \\ &= 9 \end{aligned}$$

The latest start and finish times for activity 7 are

$$\begin{aligned} LF &= \min \text{ (LS following activities)} \\ &= 24 \\ LS &= LF - t \\ &= 24 - 4 \\ &= 20 \end{aligned}$$

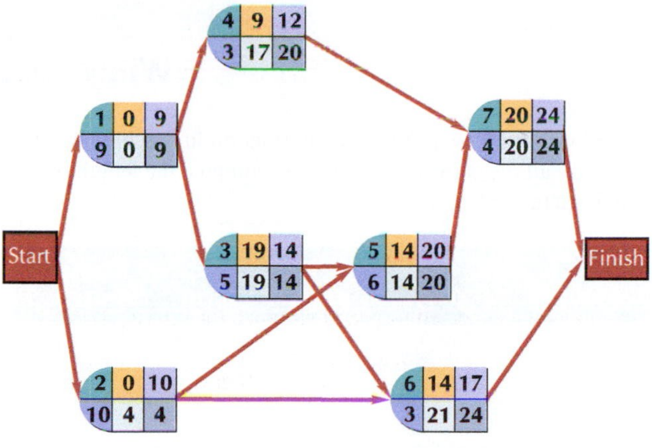

Step 3. Identify the critical path and compute expected project completion time and variance. Observing the preceding table and those activities with no slack (i.e., $s = 0$), we can identify the critical path as 1–3–5–7. The expected project completion time (t_p) is 24 days. The variance is computed by summing the variances for the activities in the critical path:

$$\begin{aligned} \sigma^2 &= 4 + \frac{4}{9} + \frac{4}{9} + \frac{1}{9} \\ &= 5 \text{ days} \end{aligned}$$

Step 4. Determine the probability that the project will be completed in 28 days or less. The following normal probability distribution describes the probability analysis.

Compute Z using the following formula:

$$\begin{aligned} Z &= \frac{x - \mu}{\sigma} \\ &= \frac{28 - 24}{\sqrt{5}} \\ &= 1.79 \end{aligned}$$

The corresponding probability from the normal table in Appendix A is .4633; thus,

$$P(x \leq 28) = .9633$$

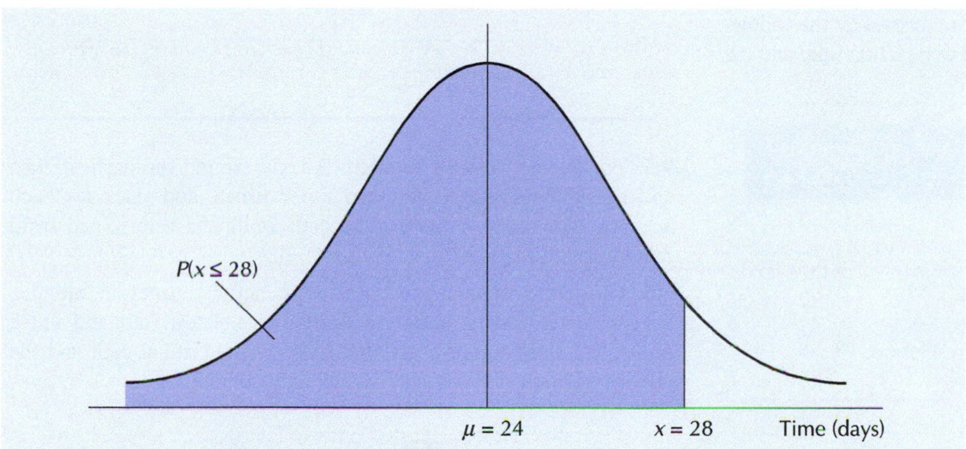

Questions

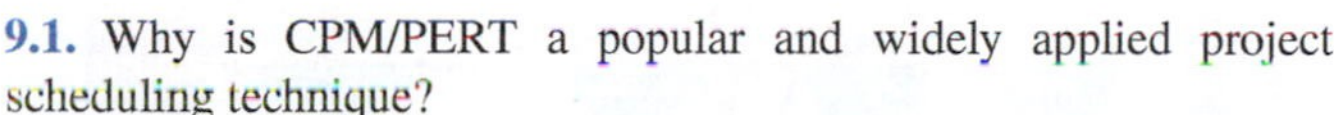

9.1. Why is CPM/PERT a popular and widely applied project scheduling technique?

9.2. What is the purpose of a CPM/PERT network?

9.3. Why are dummy activities used in a CPM/PERT network?

9.4. What is the critical path, and what is its importance in project planning?

9.5. What is slack, and how is it computed?

9.6. How are the mean activity times and activity variances computed in probabilistic CPM/PERT analysis?

9.7. How is total project variance determined in CPM/PERT analysis?

9.8. What is the purpose of project crashing analysis?

9.9. Describe the process of manually crashing a project network.

9.10. Which method for determining activity time estimates, deterministic or probabilistic, do you perceive to be preferable? Explain.

9.11. Explain how a Gantt chart differs from a CPM/PERT network, and indicate the advantage of the latter.

9.12. Discuss the relationship of direct and indirect costs in project management.

9.13. Describe the limitations and disadvantages of CPM/PERT.

9.14. Describe the difference between activity-on-node and activity-on-arrow project networks.

9.15. Identify and briefly describe the major elements of project management.

9.16. Select an everyday "project" you are familiar with such as a class project, preparing a meal, making a pizza, or repairing your car. Develop a list of the activities, a CPM/PERT network (with time estimates), and a work breakdown schedule for the project.

9.17. Prepare a WBS for a spaghetti with meatballs dinner that includes a Caesar salad, a loaf of Italian bread, and wine. (Include the different components of the dinner at the upper level and the various detailed work activities required by each component at the lower level.)

9.18. Write a paper summarizing an actual project reported on in the magazine *PM Network*.

9.19. Describe and discuss the cultural differences between the United States and a country of your choice that might affect the management of a project in this foreign country.

Problems

WileyPLUS

9.1. Construct a Gantt chart for the project described by the following set of activities, and indicate the project completion time:

ACTIVITY	ACTIVITY PREDECESSOR	TIME (WEEKS)
1	—	5
2	—	4
3	1	3
4	2	6

9.2. Construct a Gantt chart for the project described by the following set of activities, and indicate the project completion time and the available slack for each activity:

ACTIVITY	ACTIVITY PREDECESSOR	TIME (WEEKS)
1	—	3
2	—	7
3	1	2
4	2	5
5	2	6
6	4	1
7	5	4

9.3. Use the project activities that follow to determine the following:

a. Construct a Gantt chart; indicate the project completion time and slack for each activity.

b. Construct the CPM/PERT network, compute the length of each path in the network, and indicate the critical path.

ACTIVITY	ACTIVITY PREDECESSOR	TIME (WEEKS)
1	—	4
2	—	7
3	1	8
4	1	3
5	2	9
6	3	5
7	3	2
8	4, 5, 6	6
9	2	5

9.4. Construct a network from the information in the following table and identify all the paths in the network, compute the length of each, and indicate the critical path.

ACTIVITY	ACTIVITY PREDECESSOR	TIME (WEEKS)
1	—	7
2	—	10
3	1	6
4	2	5
5	2	4
6	3, 4	3
7	5, 6	2

9.5. For the network in Problem 9.4, determine the earliest start and finish times, latest start and finish times, and slack for each activity. Indicate how the critical path would be determined from this information.

9.6. Given the following network with activity times in months, determine the earliest start and finish times, latest start and finish times, and slack for each activity. Indicate the critical path and the project duration.

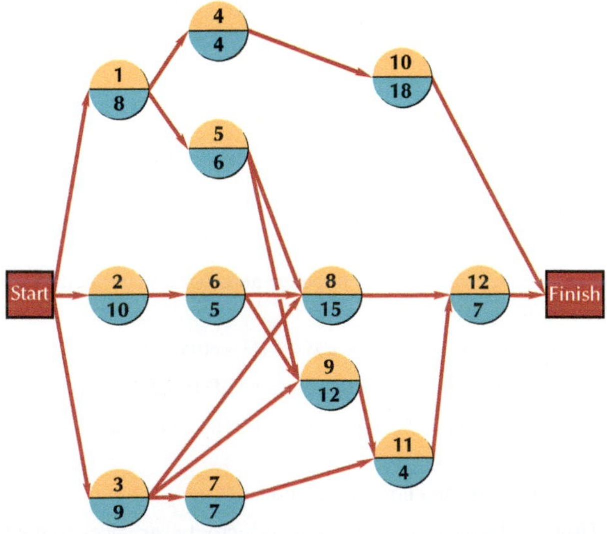

9.7. Given the following network with activity times in weeks, determine the earliest start and finish times, latest start and finish times, and slack for each activity. Indicate the critical path and the project duration.

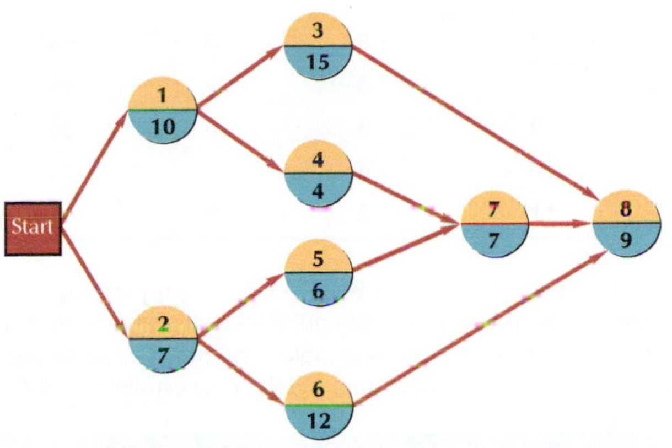

a. Determine all paths through the network from node a to node f and the duration of each, and indicate the critical path.
b. Determine the earliest and latest activity start and finish times.
c. Determine the slack for each activity.

9.9. In one of the little-known battles of the Civil War, General Tecumseh Beauregard lost the Third Battle of Bull Run because his preparations were not complete when the enemy attacked. If the critical path method had been available, the general could have planned better. Suppose that the project network below with activity times in days had been available. Determine the earliest start and finish times, latest start and finish times, and activity slack for the network. Indicate the critical path and the time between the general's receipt of battle orders and the onset of battle.

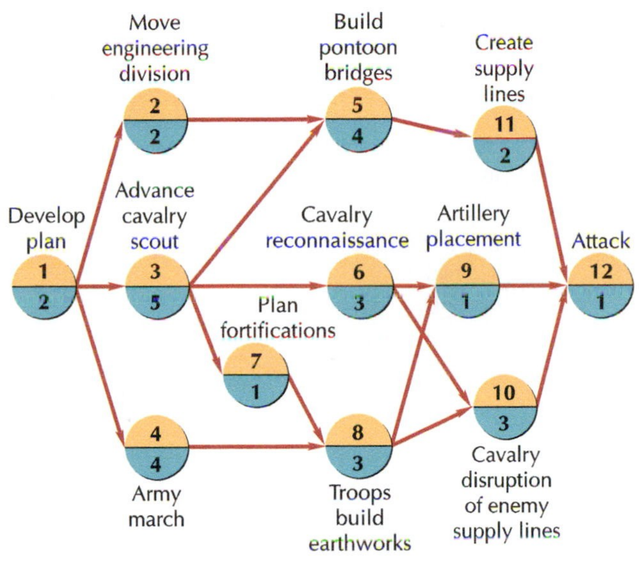

9.8. A marketing firm is planning to conduct a survey of a segment of the potential product audience for one of its customers. The planning process for preparing to conduct the survey consists of six activities with procedure relationships and activity time estimates as follows:

ACTIVITY	DESCRIPTION	ACTIVITY PREDECESSOR	TIME ESTIMATES (DAYS)
a	Determine survey objectives	—	3
b	Select and hire personnel	a	3
c	Design questionnaire	a	5
d	Train personnel	b, c	4
e	Select target audience	c	3
f	Make personnel assignments	d, e	2

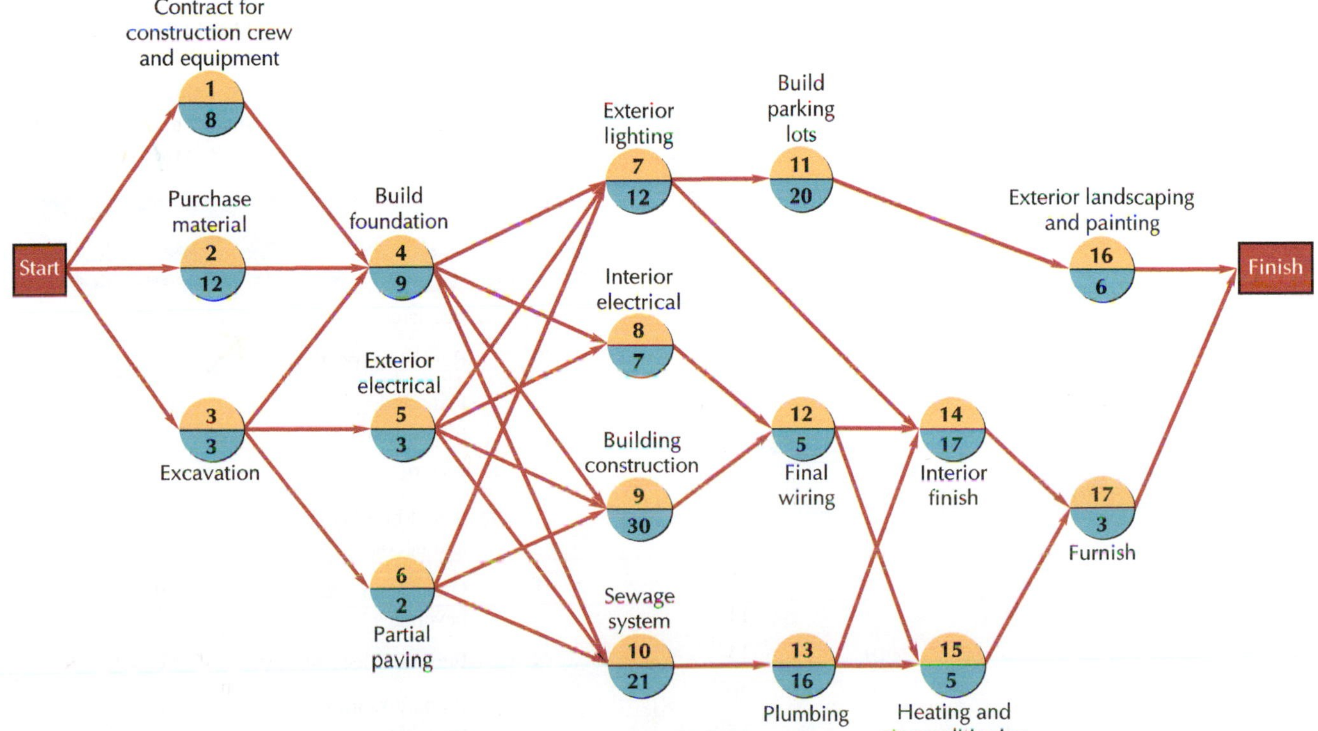

9.10. A group of developers is building a new shopping center. A consultant for the developers has constructed the CPM/PERT network above and assigned activity times in weeks. Determine the earliest start and finish times, latest start and finish times, activity slack, critical path, and duration for the project.

9.11. The management of a factory is going to erect a maintenance building with a connecting electrical generator and water tank. The activities, activity descriptions, and estimated durations are given in the following table:

ACTIVITY	DESCRIPTION	ACTIVITY PREDECESSOR	ACTIVITY DURATION (WEEKS)
a	Excavate	—	2
b	Erect building	a	6
c	Install generator	a	4
d	Install tank	a	2
e	Install maintenance equipment	b	4
f	Connect generator and tank to building	b, c, d	5
g	Paint on a finish	b	3
h	Check out facility	e, f	2

Construct the network for this project, identify the critical path, and determine the project duration time.

9.12. Given the following network and probabilistic activity time estimates, determine the expected time and variance for each activity and indicate the critical path:

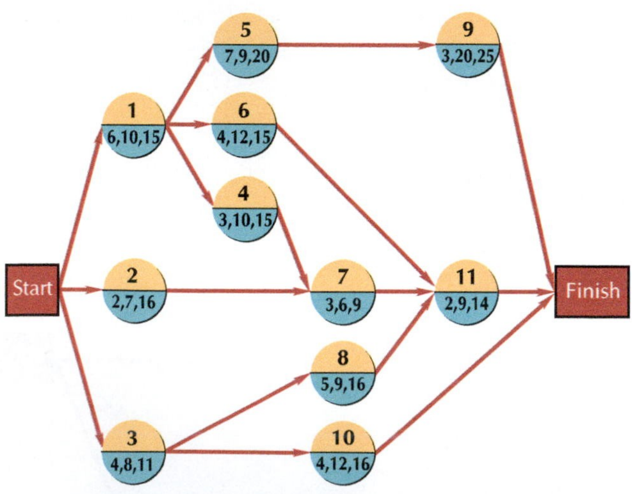

ACTIVITY	TIME ESTIMATES (WEEKS) a	m	b
1	6	10	15
2	2	7	16
3	4	8	11
4	3	10	15
5	7	9	20
6	4	12	15
7	3	6	9
8	5	9	16
9	3	20	35
10	4	12	16
11	2	9	14

9.13. The Farmer's American Bank of Leesburg is planning to install a new computerized accounts system. Bank management has determined the activities required to complete the project, the precedence relationships of the activities, and activity time estimates as follows:

ACTIVITY	DESCRIPTION	ACTIVITY PREDECESSOR	TIME ESTIMATES (WEEKS) a	m	b
a	Position recruiting	—	5	8	17
b	System development	—	3	12	15
c	System training	a	4	7	10
d	Equipment training	a	5	8	23
e	Manual system test	b, c	1	1	1
f	Preliminary system changeover	b, c	1	4	13
g	Computer-personnel interface	d, e	3	6	9
h	Equipment modification	d, e	1	2.5	7
i	Equipment testing	h	1	1	1
j	System debugging and installation	f, g	2	2	2
k	Equipment changeover	g, i	5	8	11

Determine the earliest and latest activity times, the expected completion time and standard deviation, and the probability that the project will be completed in 40 weeks or less.

9.14. Samantha and Levi Taylor are planning an anniversary party for their parents in December and they want it to have a holiday theme. They have identified the following planning activities and time estimates:

ACTIVITY	DESCRIPTION	ACTIVITY PREDECESSOR	TIME ESTIMATE (DAYS)
a	Set date	—	3
b	Reserve a location	—	5
c	Print and send invitations	a, b	4
d	RSVPs	c	10
e	Select holiday theme and decor	—	2
f	Order food and beverages	d	3
g	Purchase decorations	e	2
h	Prepare seating chart for tables	d	2

i	Pick up food and beverages and prepare	f	1
j	Decorate	g	1

Construct the network for this project, identify the critical path and determine the project duration time.

9.15. Lindsey Brinton is moving into a rental house near campus at the beginning of the new fall semester at Tech with three friends. Each of the four friends will have a bedroom that they can redecorate as they wish. Lindsey wants to wallpaper her room and put down new carpet and she has identified the following activities and the times they will take that she will need to accomplish in order to complete the project before school starts.

ACTIVITY	DESCRIPTION	ACTIVITY PREDECESSOR	TIME ESTIMATE (HOURS)
a	Clean walls	—	6
b	Wash and clean woodwork	a	4
c	Select and buy paint	—	6
d	Paint woodwork (first coat)	b, c	5
e	Fill holes	a	3
f	Select and buy wallpaper	b, c	4
g	Paper walls	d, e, f	10
h	Paint woodwork (second coat)	d	4
i	Lay new carpet	g, h	8

Construct the network for this project, identify the critical path, and determine the project duration time.

9.16. The following probabilistic activity time estimates are for the network in Problem 9.6:

	TIME ESTIMATES (MONTHS)		
ACTIVITY	a	m	b
1	4	8	12
2	6	10	15
3	2	10	14
4	1	4	13
5	3	6	9
6	3	6	18
7	2	8	12
8	9	15	22
9	5	12	21
10	7	20	25
11	5	6	12
12	3	8	20

Determine the following:

a. Expected activity times
b. Earliest start and finish times
c. Latest start and finish times
d. Activity slack
e. Critical path
f. Expected project duration and standard deviation

9.17. The following probabilistic activity time estimates are for the CPM/PERT network in Problem 9.9:

	TIME ESTIMATES (DAYS)				TIME ESTIMATES (DAYS)		
ACTIVITY	a	m	b	ACTIVITY	a	m	b
1	1	2	6	7	1	1.5	2
2	1	3	5	8	1	3	5
3	3	5	10	9	1	1	5
4	3	6	14	10	2	4	9
5	2	4	9	11	1	2	3
6	2	3	7	12	1	1	1

Determine the following:

a. Expected activity times
b. Earliest start and finish times
c. Latest start and finish times
d. Activity slack
e. Critical path
f. Expected project duration and standard deviation

9.18. For the CPM/PERT network in Problem 9.16, determine the probability that the network duration will exceed 50 months.

9.19. The Stone River Textile Mill was inspected by OSHA and found to be in violation of a number of safety regulations. The OSHA inspectors ordered the mill to alter some existing machinery to make it safer (e.g., add safety guards); purchase some new machinery to replace older, dangerous machinery; and relocate some machinery to make safer passages and unobstructed entrances and exits. OSHA gave the mill only 35 weeks to make the changes; if the changes were not made by then, the mill would be fined $300,000. The mill determined the activities in a PERT network that would have to be completed and then estimated the indicated activity times, as shown in the table below. Construct the PERT network for this project and determine the following:

			TIME ESTIMATES (WEEKS)		
ACTIVITY	DESCRIPTION	ACTIVITY PREDECESSOR	a	m	b
a	Order new machinery	—	1	2	3
b	Plan new physical layout	—	2	5	8
c	Determine safety changes in existing machinery	—	1	3	5
d	Receive equipment	a	4	10	25
e	Hire new employees	a	3	7	12
f	Make plant alterations	b	10	15	25
g	Make changes in existing machinery	c	5	9	14
h	Train new employees	d, e	2	3	7
i	Install new machinery	d, e, f	1	4	6
j	Relocate old machinery	d, e, f, g	2	5	10
k	Conduct employee safety orientation	h, i, j	2	2	2

a. Expected activity times
b. Earliest and latest activity times and activity slack
c. Critical path
d. Expected project duration and variance
e. The probability that the mill will be fined $300,000

9.20. In the Third Battle of Bull Run, for which a CPM/PERT network was developed in Problem 9.17, General Beauregard would have won if his preparations had been completed in 15 days. What would the probability of General Beauregard's winning the battle have been?

9.21. On May 21, 1927, Charles Lindbergh landed at Le Bourget Field in Paris, completing his famous transatlantic solo flight. The preparation period prior to his flight was quite hectic and time was critical, since several other famous pilots of the day were also planning transatlantic flights. Once Ryan Aircraft was contracted to build the *Spirit of St. Louis*, it took only a little over 2½ months to construct the plane and fly it to New York for the takeoff. If CPM/PERT had been available to Charles Lindbergh, it no doubt would have been useful in helping him plan this project. Use your imagination and assume that a CPM/PERT network, as shown in the figure below, with the following estimated activity times, was developed for the flight.

ACTIVITY	TIME ESTIMATES (DAYS) a	m	b
1	1	3	5
2	4	6	10
3	20	35	50
4	4	7	12
5	2	3	5
6	8	12	25
7	10	16	21
8	5	9	15
9	1	2	2
10	6	8	14
11	5	8	12
12	5	10	15
13	4	7	10
14	5	7	12
15	5	9	20
16	1	3	7

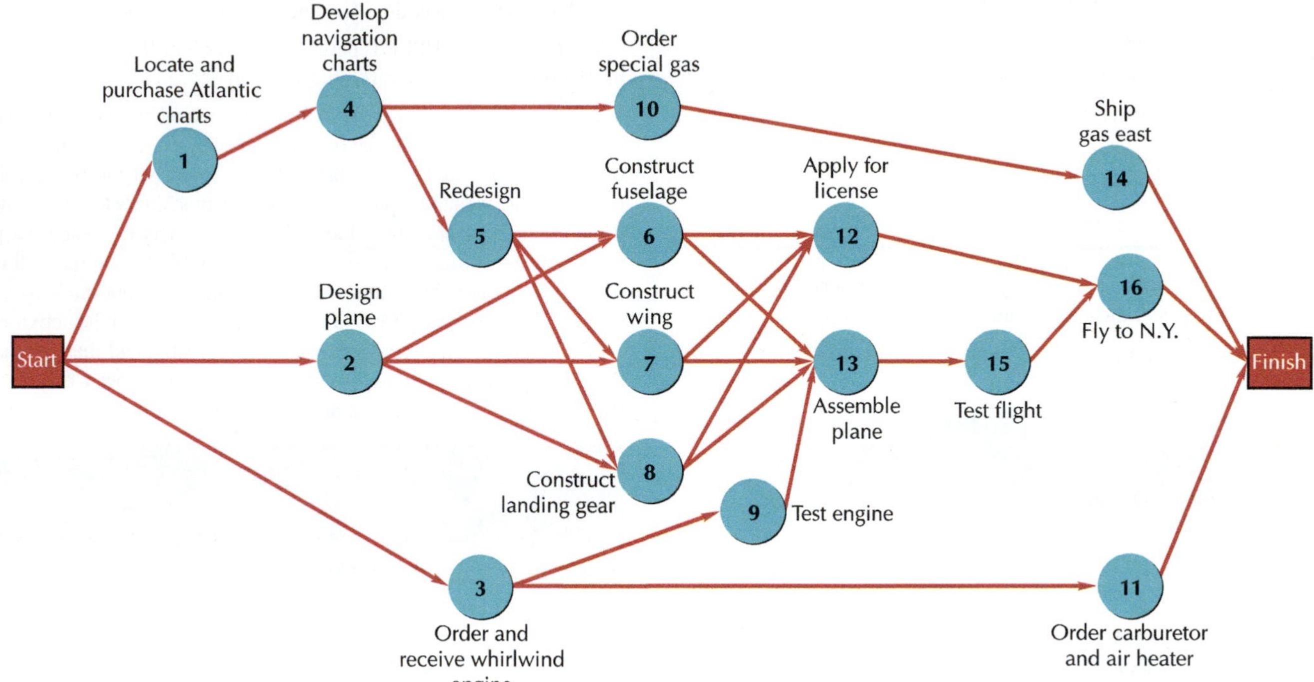

Determine the expected project duration and variance and the probability of completing the project in 67 days.

9.22. RusTech Tooling, Inc., is a large job shop operation that builds machine tools and dies to manufacture parts for specialized items. The company bids primarily on contracts for government-related activities to produce parts for things such as military aircraft, weapons systems, and the space program. The company is bidding on a contract to produce a component part for the fuselage assembly in a new space shuttle. A major criterion for selecting the winning bid besides low cost is the time required to produce the part. However, if the company is awarded the contract it will be held strictly to the completion date specified in the bid, and any delays will result in severe financial penalties. In order to determine the project completion time to put in its bid, the company has identified the project activities, precedence relationships, and activity times shown in the following table:

ACTIVITY	ACTIVITY PREDECESSOR	TIME ESTIMATES (WEEKS) a	m	b
a	—	3	5	9
b	a	2	5	8
c	a	1	4	6
d	a	4	6	10
e	b	2	8	11
f	b	5	9	16
g	c	4	12	20
h	c	6	9	13
i	d	3	7	14

j	d	8	14	22
k	f, g	9	12	20
l	h, i	6	11	15
m	e	4	7	12
n	j	3	8	16
o	n	5	8	10

If RusTech, Inc., wants to be 90% certain that it can deliver the part without incurring a penalty, what time frame should it specify in the bid?

9.23. PM Computers is an international manufacturer of computer equipment and software. It is going to introduce a number of new products in the coming year, and it wants to develop marketing programs to accompany the product introductions. The marketing program includes the preparation of printed materials distributed directly by the company and used by the company's marketing personnel, vendors, and representatives; print advertising in regular magazines, trade journals, and newspapers; and television commercials. The program also includes extensive training programs for marketing personnel, vendors, and representatives about the new products. A project management team with members from the marketing department and manufacturing areas has developed the following list of activities for the development of the marketing program:

ACTIVITY	DESCRIPTION	ACTIVITY PREDECESSOR	TIME ESTIMATES (DAYS)		
			a	m	b
a	Preliminary budget and plan approval	—	10	15	20
b	Select marketing personnel for training	—	5	9	12
c	Develop overall media plan	a	15	25	30
d	Prepare separate media plans	c	12	20	25
e	Develop training plan	c	5	8	12
f	Design training course	e	6	14	20
g	Train marketing personnel	b, f	16	20	25
h	Plan TV commercial with agency	d	15	25	35
i	Draft in-house print materials	d	8	15	20
j	Develop print advertising layouts with agency	d	16	23	30
k	Review print advertising layouts	j	4	9	12
l	Review TV commercial	h	3	7	12
m	Review and print in-house materials	i	3	5	7
n	Release advertising to print media	g, i, k,	2	4	8
o	Release TV commercials to networks	l	4	7	10
p	Final marketing personnel review	g, i, k	4	5	9
q	Run media advertising, mailings	m, n, o	15	20	30

Construct the network for this project and determine the activity schedule. Identify the critical path and determine the expected project duration time and variance. What is the probability the program can be completed within four months?

9.24. The following table provides the information necessary to construct a project network and project crash data:

ACTIVITY	ACTIVITY PREDECESSOR	ACTIVITY TIME (WEEKS)		ACTIVITY COST ($)	
		NORMAL	CRASH	NORMAL	CRASH
1	—	20	8	1000	1480
2	—	24	20	1200	1400
3	—	14	7	700	1190
4	1	10	6	500	820
5	3	11	5	550	730

a. Construct the project network.
b. Determine the maximum possible crash time for the network, and crash the network the maximum amount possible.
c. Compute the normal project cost and the cost of the crashed project.

9.25. The following table provides the information necessary to construct a project network and project crash data:

ACTIVITY	ACTIVITY PREDECESSOR	ACTIVITY TIME (WEEKS)		ACTIVITY COST ($)	
		NORMAL	CRASH	NORMAL	CRASH
b	—	14	9	1000	1800
c	a	8	6	500	700
d	a	5	4	600	1300
e	b	4	2	1500	3000
f	b	6	4	800	1600
g	c	10	7	3000	4500
h	d, e	15	10	5000	8000

Construct the project network, and crash the network the maximum amount possible.

9.26. For the Solved Problem above, assume that the most likely times (m) are the normal activity times and the optimistic times (a)

are the activity crash times. Further assume that the activities have the following normal and crash costs:

ACTIVITY	COSTS (NORMAL COST, CRASH COST)
1	($100, 400)
2	($250, 400)
3	($400, 800)
4	($200, 400)
5	($150, 300)
6	($100, 100)
7	($300, 500)

Crash the network the maximum amount possible and indicate the total crash cost.

9.27. The following table provides the crash data for the project network in Problem 9.13. The normal activity times are considered to be deterministic and not probabilistic.

	ACTIVITY TIME (WEEKS)		ACTIVITY COST ($)	
ACTIVITY	NORMAL	CRASH	NORMAL	CRASH
a	9	7	4,800	6,300
b	11	9	9,100	15,500
c	7	5	3,000	4,000
d	10	8	3,600	5,000
e	1	1	0	0
f	5	3	1,500	2,000
g	6	5	1,800	2.000
h	3	3	0	0
i	1	1	0	0
j	2	2	0	0
k	8	6	5,000	7,000

Crash the network the maximum amount, indicate how much it would cost the bank, and identify the new critical path(s).

9.28. The Center for Information Technology at State University has outgrown its office in Bates (B) Hall and is moving to Allen (A) Hall, which has more space. The move will take place during the three-week break between the end of summer semester and the beginning of fall semester. Movers will be hired from the university's physical plant to move the furniture, boxes of books, and files that the faculty will pack. The center has hired a local retail computer firm to move its office computers so they will not be damaged. Following is a list of activities, their precedence relationships, and probabilistic time estimates for this project:

			TIME ESTIMATES (DAYS)		
ACTIVITY	DESCRIPTION	PREDECESSOR	a	m	b
a	Pack "A" offices	—	1	3	5
b	Network "A" offices	—	2	3	5
c	Pack "B" offices	—	2	4	7
d	Movers move "A" offices	a	1	3	4
e	Paint and clean "A" offices	d	2	5	8
f	Move computers	b, e	1	2	2
g	Movers move "B" offices	b, c, e	3	6	8
h	Computer installation	f	2	4	5
i	Faculty move and unpack	g	3	4	6
j	Faculty set up computers and offices	h, i	1	2	4

Determine the earliest and latest start and finish times, the critical path, and the expected project duration. What is the probability the center will complete its move before the start of the fall semester?

9.29. The Eastern Shore Hospital has encountered a problem in bed turnaround time (i.e., the time taken to discharge a patient from a bed and admit a new patient). This, in turn, has caused delays in the hospital operating room, resulting in physician and patient dissatisfaction. The hospital initiated a Six Sigma project to resolve the problem, initially focusing on one surgical nursing unit, which had almost 3000 patients in one year. The Six Sigma DMAIC process employed by the project team included the following project activities, activity times, and precedence relationships.

			TIME ESTIMATES (DAYS)		
ACTIVITY	DESCRIPTION	ACTIVITY PREDECESSOR	a	m	b
a	Develop process map	—	4	7	10
b	VoC survey of RNs	a	6	12	15
c	Establish turnaround target time	b	2	5	8
d	Measure process, define defects	a, c	5	7	11
e	Cause & effect diagram (identify variables that are effected by turnaround time)	b	3	9	14
f	Statistical analysis of variables	e	4	6	10
g	Analyze possible solutions	c, d, f	5	9	14
h	Identify solution approach	g	3	7	9

i	Improve process	h	10	14	20
j	Monitor and control process with SPC	i	15	23	30
k	Apply improved process across hospital	j	12	18	25

Construct the network for this project. Determine the earliest and latest activity times and the critical path.

9.30. The Valley United Soccer Club is planning a soccer tournament for the weekend of April 29–30. The club's officers know that by March 30 they must send out acceptances to teams that have applied to enter and by April 15 they must send out the tournament game schedule to teams that have been selected to play. Their tentative plan is to begin the initial activities for tournament preparation including sending out the application forms to prospective teams, on January 20. Following is a list of tournament activities, their precedence relationships, and estimates of their duration in days. Develop a project network for the club's tournament preparation process and determine the likelihood that they will meet their schedule milestones and complete the process according to the scheduled tournament start date of April 29.

ACTIVITY	ACTIVITY DESCRIPTION	ACTIVITY PREDECESSOR	TIME ESTIMATES (DAYS)		
			a	m	b
a	Send application forms	—	5	7	10
b	Get volunteer workers	—	10	18	26
c	Line up referees	—	7	10	14
d	Reserve fields	—	14	21	35
e	Receive and process forms	a	30	30	30
f	Determine age divisions	b, c, d, e	4	9	12
g	Assign fields to divisions	f	4	7	10
h	Sell program ads	b	14	21	30
i	Acquire donated items for team gift bags	b	15	20	26
j	Schedule games	g	6	14	18
k	Design ads	h	5	8	10
l	Fill gift bags	i	9	12	17
m	Process team t-shirt orders	e	7	10	14
n	Send acceptance letters	f	4	7	12
o	Design and print programs	j, k, l, n	14	18	24
p	Put together registration boxes (programs, gifts, etc.)	o	5	7	10
q	Send out game schedules	j, k, l, n	5	8	12
r	Assign referees to games	j, k, l, n	4	7	10
s	Get trophies	f	20	28	35
t	Silk-screen t-shirts	m	12	17	25
u	Package team t-shirt orders	t	5	8	12

9.31. The Horizon Aircraft Company is preparing a contract proposal to submit to the Global Airlines Company for a new commercial aircraft, the JK60. Part of the proposal is a development and productions schedule for completion of the first aircraft. The project consists of three primary categories: (1) engine design and development; (2) development and production of the airframe (e.g., the aircraft body); and (3) the design and development of the aircraft avionics (e.g., the electronic systems, equipment, and other devices used to operate and control the aircraft). Following is a table listing the project activities with time estimates (in months).

ACTIVITY	DESCRIPTION	ACTIVITY PREDECESSOR	TIME ESTIMATES (DAYS)		
			a	m	b
1	General design	—	6	10	24
2	Design engines	—	20	35	60
3	Airframe design	1	5	17	33
4	Avionics design	1	2	8	21
5	Develop test engine	2	6	9	15
6	Develop test airframe	3	7	12	17
7	Develop interim avionics	4	6	16	27
8	Engine development	2	18	25	42
9	Assemble test aircraft	5, 6, 7	5	8	11
10	Test avionics	4	4	11	16
11	Engine/airframe flight trials	9	5	10	13
12	Avionics flight trials	10	5	9	26
13	Engine production	8	10	15	18
14	Airframe production	11	11	14	21
15	Avionics production	11, 12	12	16	26
16	Final assembly/ Finish	13, 14, 15	3	5	6

Develop the project network, and determine the critical path, the expected project duration, and variance. What is the probability the project will be completed within 8 years?

9.32. The Virginia Department of Transportation is undertaking a construction project to widen a large section of interstate highway near Washington, DC, which includes the construction of a number of new bridges, interchanges, and overpasses. The first step in the project is the appointment of a project manger and the development of a project team, some of which will be departmental employees and others will be private consultants and operatives. The team for a project this size also requires a large support staff with varying technical skills. Once the team is selected and the staff is in place the first task is to select a primary contractor to manage and oversee the actual construction. The following activities are standard for the planning and scheduling of this process:

ACTIVITY	DESCRIPTION	ACTIVITY PREDECESSOR	TIME ESTIMATES (WEEKS)		
			a	m	b
a	Select project manager	—	1	2	2
b	Develop team recruitment plan	a	1	2	3
c	Implement team recruitment process	b	3	6	8
d	Staff needs assessment	b	1	2	3
e	Staff recruitment advertising	d	1	1	1
f	Staff selection evaluation procedures	b	1	2	4
g	Select project team members	c	2	4	6
h	Develop contractor bid requirements	a	1	4	6
i	Develop contractor bid evaluation procedure	g, h	2	3	4
j	Staff applicant evaluation and selection	e, f, g	2	4	5
k	Solicit contractor bids	i, j	4	6	10
l	Contractor bid evaluation	k	3	6	8
m	Select contractor and complete negotiations	l	2	3	5

Construct the CPM/PERT network for this project and determine the project schedule. Identify the critical path and determine the expected project duration time and variance. Determine the probability that the team and contractor will be in place and the project started within six months; within one year.

9.33. The Carriage Auto Parts Company near Nashville, Tennessee, is a direct supplier for the nearby Sigma auto manufacturing plant. In order to gain a competitive advantage and meet quality requirements by its customer, Carriage has undertaken a project to achieve ISO/TS 16949 registration. TS 16949 provides the requirements for the application of ISO 9001:2015 standards for automotive production and relevant service parts organizations. The goal of ISO/TS 16949 is the development of a quality management system that provides for continual improvement emphasizing defect prevention and the reduction of process variation and waste. (See Chapter 2 for a discussion of ISO certification.) The project management team has developed the following list of required activities necessary to achieve ISO certification:

ACTIVITY	DESCRIPTION	ACTIVITY PREDECESSOR	TIME ESTIMATES (WEEKS)		
			a	m	b
a	Appointment of company taskforce	—	1	2	3
b	Development of feasibility plan	a	2	3	4
c	Selection of third party registrar and auditor	b	1	2	3
d	Development of quality manual, procedure, and instruction documents	b	10	14	20
e	Quality system training for all employees	b	4	7	10
f	Outside training for company quality managers and internal plant auditors	b	4	7	10
g	Plant preparation and organization to meet ISO 9001:2015 standards including use of SPC charts to identify non-conforming processes	e	18	24	32
h	Preparation of ISO application documents with outside auditor; set schedule for submissions to registrar	c	4	6	10

i	Internal audit of plant	d, f, h, g	10	12	16
j	Corrective action plans for necessary process improvements	i	8	12	20
k	Outside auditor visit and audit	j	1	2	3
l	Corrective action plans developed based on auditor report and implemented	k	2	4	5
m	Follow-up visit and re-audit by auditor	l	1	2	4
n	Auditor recommendation to registrar for ISO certification	m	1	2	2

Construct the network for this project and determine the project schedule. Identify the critical path and determine the expected project duration time and variance. Determine the probability that the certification project can be completed with one year; within 18 months.

9.34. During a violent thunderstorm with very high wind gusts in the third week of March, the broadcast tower for the public radio station, WVPR, atop Poor Mountain in Roanoke, Virginia, collapsed. This greatly reduced the strength of the station's signal in the area. The station management immediately began plans to construct a new tower. Following is a list of the required activities for building the new tower with most likely (*m*), optimistic (*a*), and pessimistic (*b*) time estimates (in days). However, the sequence of the activities has not been designated.

		TIME ESTIMATES (DAYS)		
	ACTIVITY	a	m	b
a	Removal of debris	5	8	12
b	Survey new tower site	3	6	8
c	Procure structural steel	15	21	30
d	Procure electrical/broadcasting equipment	18	32	40
e	Grade tower site	4	7	10
f	Pour concrete footings and anchors	10	18	22
g	Deliver and unload steel	3	5	9
h	Deliver and unload electrical/ broadcast equipment	1	2	4
i	Erect tower	25	35	50
j	Connect electrical cables between tower and building	4	6	10
k	Construct storm drains and tiles	10	15	21
l	Backfill and grade tower site	4	7	9
m	Clean up	3	6	10
n	Obtain inspection approval	1	4	7

Using your best judgment, develop a CPM/PERT network for this project and determine the expected project completion time. Also determine the probability that the station signal will be back at full strength within three months.

9.35. The following table contains the activities for planning a wedding and the activity time estimates. However, the precedence relationships between activities are not included.

		TIME (DAYS)		
	ACTIVITY	a	m	b
a	Determine date	1	10	15
b	Obtain marriage license	1	5	8
c	Select bridal attendants	3	5	7
d	Order dresses	10	14	21
e	Fit dresses	5	10	12
f	Select groomsmen	1	2	4
g	Order tuxedos	3	5	7
h	Find and rent church	6	14	20
i	Hire florist	3	6	10
J	Develop/print programs	15	22	30
k	Hire photographer	3	10	15
l	Develop guest list	14	25	40
m	Order invitations	7	12	20
n	Address and mail invitations	10	15	25
o	Compile RSVP list	30	45	60
p	Reserve reception hall	3	7	10
q	Hire caterer	2	5	8
r	Determine reception menu	10	12	16
s	Make final order	2	4	7
t	Hire band	10	18	21
u	Decorate reception hall	1	2	3
v	Wedding ceremony	.5	.5	.5
w	Wedding reception	.5	.5	.5

Using your best judgment, determine the project network, critical path, and expected project duration. If it is the first of January and a couple is planning a June 1 wedding, what is the probability that it can be done on time?

Case Problems

Case Problem 9.1 The Bloodless Coup Concert

John Aaron had just called the meeting of the Programs and Arts Committee of the Student Government Association to order.

"Okay, okay, everybody, quiet down. I have an important announcement to make," he shouted above the noise. The room got quiet and John started again. "Well, you guys, we can have the Coup."

His audience looked puzzled and Randy Jones asked, "What coup have we scored this time, John?"

"The Coup, the Coup! You know, the rock group, the Bloodless Coup!"

Everyone in the room cheered and started talking excitedly. John stood up, waved his arms, and shouted, "Hey, calm down, everybody, and listen up." The room quieted again and everyone focused on John. "The good news is that they can come." He paused a moment. "The bad news is that they will be here in 18 days."

The students groaned and seemed to share Jim Hasting's feelings, "No way, man. It can't be done. Why can't we put it off for a couple of weeks?"

John answered, "They're just starting their new tour and are looking for some warm-up concerts. They will be traveling near here for their first concert date in D.C. and saw they had a letter from us, so they said they could come now—but that's it, now or never." He looked around the room at the solemn faces. "Look you guys, we can handle this. Let's think of what we have to do. Come on, perk up. Let's make a list of everything we have to do to get ready and figure out how long it will take. So somebody tell me what we have to do first!"

Anna Mendoza shouted from the back of the room, "We have to find a place; you know, get an auditorium somewhere. I've done that before, and it should take anywhere from 2 days up to 7 days, most likely about 4 days."

"Okay, that's great," John said as he wrote down the activity "secure auditorium" on the blackboard with the times out to the side. "What's next?"

"We need to print tickets and quick," Tracey Shea blurted. "It could only take a day if the printer isn't busy, but it could take up to 4 days if it is. It should probably take about 2 days."

"But we can't print tickets until we know where the concert will be because of the security arrangement," Andy Taylor noted.

"Right," said John. "Get the auditorium first, then print the tickets. What else?"

"We need to make hotel and transportation arrangements for the Coup and their entourage while they are here," Jim Hastings said. "But we better not do that until we get the auditorium. If we can't find a place for the concert, everything falls through."

"How long do you think it will take to make the arrangements?" John asked.

"Oh, between 3 and 10 days, probably about 5, most likely," Jim answered.

"We also have to negotiate with the local union for concert employees, stagehands, and whomever else we need to hire," said Reggie Wilkes. "That could take a day or up to 8 days, but 3 days would be my best guess."

"We should probably also hold off on talking to the union until we get the auditorium," John added. "That will probably be a factor in the negotiations."

"After we work things out with the union we can hire some stagehands," Reggie continued. "That could take as few as 2 days but as long as 7. I imagine it'll take about 4 days. We should also be able to get some student ushers at the same time once we get union approval. That could take only a day, but it has taken 5 days in the past; 3 days is probably the most likely."

"We need to arrange a press conference," said Art Cohen, leaning against a wall. "This is a heavy group, big-time."

"But doesn't a press conference usually take place at the hotel?" John asked.

"Yeah, that's right," said Art. "We can't make arrangements for the press conference until we work things out with the hotel. When we do that it should take about 3 days to set up a press conference, 2 days if we're lucky and 4 at the most."

The room got quiet as everyone thought.

"What else?" John said.

"Hey, I know," said Annie Roark. "Once we hire the stagehands they have to set up the stage. I think that could be done in a couple of days, but it could take up to 6 days, with 3 most likely." She paused for a moment before adding, "And we can assign the ushers to their jobs once we hire them. That shouldn't take long, maybe only a day, 3 days worst. Probably 2 days would be a good time to put down."

"We also have to do some advertising and promotion if we want anyone to show for this thing," said Art nonchalantly. "I guess we need to wait until we print the tickets first so we'll have something to sell. That depends on the media, the paper, and radio stations. I've worked with this before. It could get done really quick, like 2 days, if we can make the right contacts, but it could take a lot longer, like 12 days, if we hit any snags. We probably ought to count on 6 days as our best estimate."

"Hey, if we're going to promote this, shouldn't we also have a preliminary act, some other group?" said Annie.

"Wow, I forgot all about that," said John. "Hiring another act will take me between 4 and 8 days; I can probably do it in 5. I can start on that right away at the same time you guys are arranging for an auditorium." He thought for a moment. "But we really can't begin to work on the promotion until I get the lead-in group. So what's left?"

"Sell the tickets," shouted several people at once.

"Right," said John, "we have to wait until they are printed; but I don't think we have to wait for the advertising and promotion to start do we?"

"No," said Jim, "but we should hire the preliminary act first so people will know what they're buying a ticket for."

"Agreed," said John. "The tickets could go quick; I suppose in the first day."

"Or," interrupted Mike Eggleston, "it could take longer. I remember two years ago it took 12 days to sell out for the Cosmic Modem."

"Okay, so it's between 1 and 12 days to sell the tickets," said John, "but I think about 5 days is more likely. Everybody agree?"

The group nodded in unison and they all turned at once to the list of activities and times John had written on the blackboard.

Use PERT analysis to determine the probability the concert preparations will be completed in time.

Case Problem 9.2 Moore Housing Contractors

Moore Housing Contractors is negotiating a deal with Countryside Realtors to build six houses in a new development. Countryside wants Moore Contractors to start in late winter or early spring when the weather begins to moderate and build through the summer into the fall. The summer months are a busy time for the realty company, and it believes it can sell the houses almost as soon as they are ready—sometimes before. The houses all have similar floor plans and are of approximately equal size; only the exteriors are noticeably different. The completion time is so critical for Countryside Realtors that it is insisting a project management network accompany the contractor's bid for the job with an estimate of the completion time for a house.

ACTIVITY	DESCRIPTION	PREDECESSOR	TIME (DAYS) a	m	b
a	Excavation, pour footers	—	3	4	6
b	Lay foundation	a	2	3	5
c	Frame and roof	b	2	4	5
d	Lay drain tiles	b	1	2	4
e	Sewer (floor) drains	b	1	2	3
f	Install insulation	c	2	4	5
g	Pour basement floor	e	2	3	5
h	Rough plumbing, pipes	e	2	4	7
i	Install windows	f	1	3	4
j	Rough electrical wiring	f	1	2	4
k	Install furnace, air conditioner	c, g	3	5	8
l	Exterior brickwork	i	5	6	10
m	Install plasterboard, mud, plaster	j, h, k	6	8	12
n	Roof shingles, flashing	l	2	3	6
o	Attach gutter, downspouts	n	1	2	5
p	Grading	d, o	2	3	7
q	Lay subflooring	m	3	4	6
r	Lay driveway, walks, landscape	p	4	6	10
s	Finish carpentry	q	3	5	12
t	Kitchen cabinetry, sink, and appliances	q	2	4	8
u	Bathroom cabinetry, fixtures	q	2	3	6
v	Painting (interior and exterior)	t, u	4	6	10
w	Finish wood floors, lay carpet	v, s	2	5	8
x	Final electrical, light fixtures	v	1	3	4

The realtor also needs to be able to plan its offerings and marketing for the summer. The realtor wants each house to be completed within 45 days after it is started. If a house is not completed within this time frame, the realtor wants to be able to charge the contractor a penalty. Mary and Sandy Moore, the president and vice president of Moore Housing Contractors, are concerned about the prospect of a penalty. They want to be confident they can meet the deadline for a house before entering into any agreement with a penalty involved. (If there is a reasonable likelihood they cannot finish a house within 45 days, they want to increase their bid to cover potential penalty charges.)

The Moores are experienced home builders, so it was not difficult for them to list the activities involved in building a house or to estimate activity times. However, they made their estimates conservatively and tended to increase their pessimistic estimates to compensate for the possibility of bad weather and variations in their workforce. Following is a list of the activities for building a house and the activity time estimates:

1. Develop a CPM/PERT network for Moore House Contractors and determine the probability that the contractors can complete a house within 45 days. Does it appear that the Moores might need to increase their bid to compensate for potential penalties?
2. Indicate which project activities Moore Contractors should be particularly diligent to keep on schedule by making sure workers and materials are always available. Also indicate which activities the company might shift workers from as the need arises.

References

Burman, P. J. *Precedence Networks for Project Planning and Control*. New York: McGraw-Hill, 1972.

Cleland, D. I., and W. R. King. *Project Management Handbook*. New York: Van Nostrand Reinhold, 1983.

Levy, F., G. Thompson, and J. Wiest. "The ABC's of the Critical Path Method." *Harvard Business Review* 41(5; October 1963).

Moder, J., C. R. Phillips, and E. W. Davis. *Project Management with CPM and PERT and Precedence Diagramming*, 3rd ed. New York: Van Nostrand Reinhold, 1983.

O'Brian, J. *CPM in Construction Management*. New York: McGraw-Hill, 1965.

Wiest, J. D., and F. K. Levy. *A Management Guide to PERT/CPM*, 2nd ed. Upper Saddle River, NJ: Prentice Hall, 1977.

CHAPTER 10

Supply Chain Management Strategy and Design

Bloomberg/Contributor/Getty Images, Inc.

LEARNING OBJECTIVES

After reading this chapter, you will be able to:

- Describe the key characteristics and management strategies of the modern supply chain.
- Discuss sustainable supply chain practices and the impact of the environment on supply chain decisions.
- Describe the role of information technology in supply chains, and the need for supply chain integration.
- Present the SCOR model and calculate key performance indicators for monitoring supply chain performance.

Smartphone Supply Chain Strategies at Samsung and Apple

Together Samsung and Apple account for about half of all smartphones sold around the world. A key ingredient in their success is each company's management of an efficient supply chain. In Gartner's annual ranking of the top 25 supply chains, Apple is one of two companies (with Proctor and Gamble) in a special "Masters" category achieved because they have been ranked in the top five for at least 7 out of 10 years; and Samsung consistently ranks in the top 10. Their supply chains consist of a vast network of suppliers that manufacture and ship the ever-increasing and complicated number of components in smartphones. Every day billions of smartphone components are being shipped around the world. With annual global smartphone sales of over 1.2 billion, the number of components being manufactured and shipped each year is enormous, almost a trillion. This number will continue to increase as smartphones and other mobile devices become even more complex and sophisticated, as will the importance of a well-managed supply chain. However, managing a global supply chain is filled with the risk of delays and there are numerous and frequent examples of delayed product launches that resulted in lost sales and reduced market share. At Google, supply chain issues affected the availability of a version of its flagship Nexus smartphone, causing critical shortages at its launch, and HTC experienced significant device shortages because its phone camera component suppliers had inaccurate product and component forecasts.

It is apparent that Apple and Samsung gain an advantage over their competitors from their superior supply chains and their efficient management of billions of components, although each company does it quite differently. Most of Samsung's supply chain is in-house, from product development to final assembly, and it only uses suppliers (that are easily replaceable) for low-cost components. Also, Samsung is the largest manufacturer in its region, which gives it bargaining power and flexibility with its suppliers to increase or decrease the size of its orders, which in turn reduces inventory costs. Alternatively, Apple outsources almost all of its manufacturing. It has almost 750 suppliers, over 600 in Asia, which Apple closely monitors. Apple does not offer as many smartphone variations as Samsung, which allows them to focus on the supply of fewer components. Apple also has the highest loyalty rate in the smartphone industry, giving it significant bargaining power with its manufacturing suppliers.

A new smartphone model will include unique and perhaps exclusive components that create risk and uncertainty in the supply chain, requiring suppliers who have the needed capacity and are willing and able to steadily supply these components before, during, and after the product launch. A Samsung Galaxy smartphone has over a thousand component parts and major components often have many subcomponents, which can also be made up of subcomponents. And while the number of components and capabilities of devices have increased, the relative size of these devices has decreased, making the manufacturing process more complex than ever. The supply of these many hundreds of individual parts takes significant time, resources, and technical expertise. It's not surprising that timing is crucial to any smartphone's success in the market. Delays in any part of the supply chain, from raw materials to manufacturing, can significantly affect commercial success. Samsung and Apple, with two different strategies, have built reliable and consistently excellent supply chains that are the industry's best, which enable them to manage a steady stream of billions of components, meet customer demand, and thwart competitors from eating into their combined market share.

In this chapter we will learn about supply chains and the key role supply chain management plays in successfully integrating all the operations and processes involved in producing a product like smartphones.

Supply Chains

Globalization and the evolution of information technology have provided the catalysts for supply chain management to become the strategic means for companies to manage quality, satisfy customers, and remain competitive. A **supply chain** encompasses all activities associated with the flow and transformation of goods and services from the raw materials stage to the end user (customer), as well as the associated information flows. In essence, it is all the assets, information, and processes that provide "supply." It is made up of many interrelated members, starting with raw material suppliers, and including parts and components suppliers, subassembly suppliers, the product or service producer, and distributors, and ending with the end-use customer.

Supply chain The facilities, functions, and activities involved in producing and delivering a product or service from suppliers (and their suppliers) to customers (and their customers).

Figure 10.1 illustrates the stages, facilities, and physical movement of products and services in a supply chain. The supply chain begins with suppliers, which can be as basic as raw material providers. These suppliers are referred to as *upstream* supply chain members, while the distributors, warehouses, and eventual end-use customers are referred to as *downstream* supply chain members. The stream at the bottom of the figure denotes the flow of goods and services (i.e., demand) as the supply chain moves downstream. Notice that the stream is very rough at the upstream end and gets smoother as it moves downstream, a characteristic we will discuss in greater detail later. Also note that "information" is at the center of Figure 10.1; it is the "heart and brains" of the supply chain, another characteristic we will talk more about later.

The supply chain in Figure 10.1 can represent a single producer directly linked to one level of suppliers and one set of end-use customers. A grocery store that gets food products like milk, eggs, or vegetables directly from a farmer (and not through a distributor) and sells them directly to the customer who consumes them reflects this basic level of supply chain. However, supply chains are more typically a series of linked suppliers and customers; every customer is in turn a supplier to the next, up to the final end user of the product or service. For example, **Figure 10.2** shows the supply chain for denim jeans, a straightforward manufacturing process with a distinct set of suppliers. Notice that the jeans manufacturer has suppliers that produce denim who in turn have suppliers who produce cotton and dye.

As Figures 10.1 and 10.2 show, the delivery of a product or service to a customer is a complex process, encompassing many different interrelated processes and activities. First, demand for a product or service is forecast, and plans and schedules are made to meet demand within a time frame. The product or service can require multiple suppliers (who have their

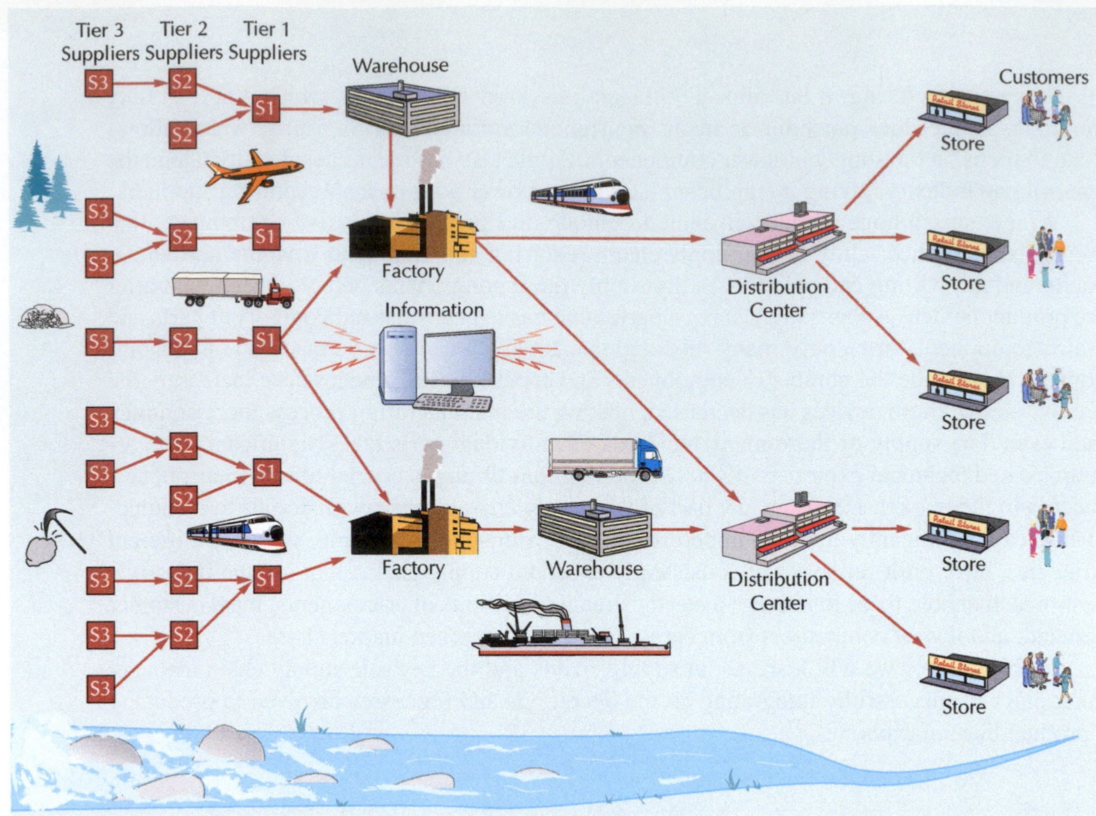

FIGURE 10.1 The Supply Chain

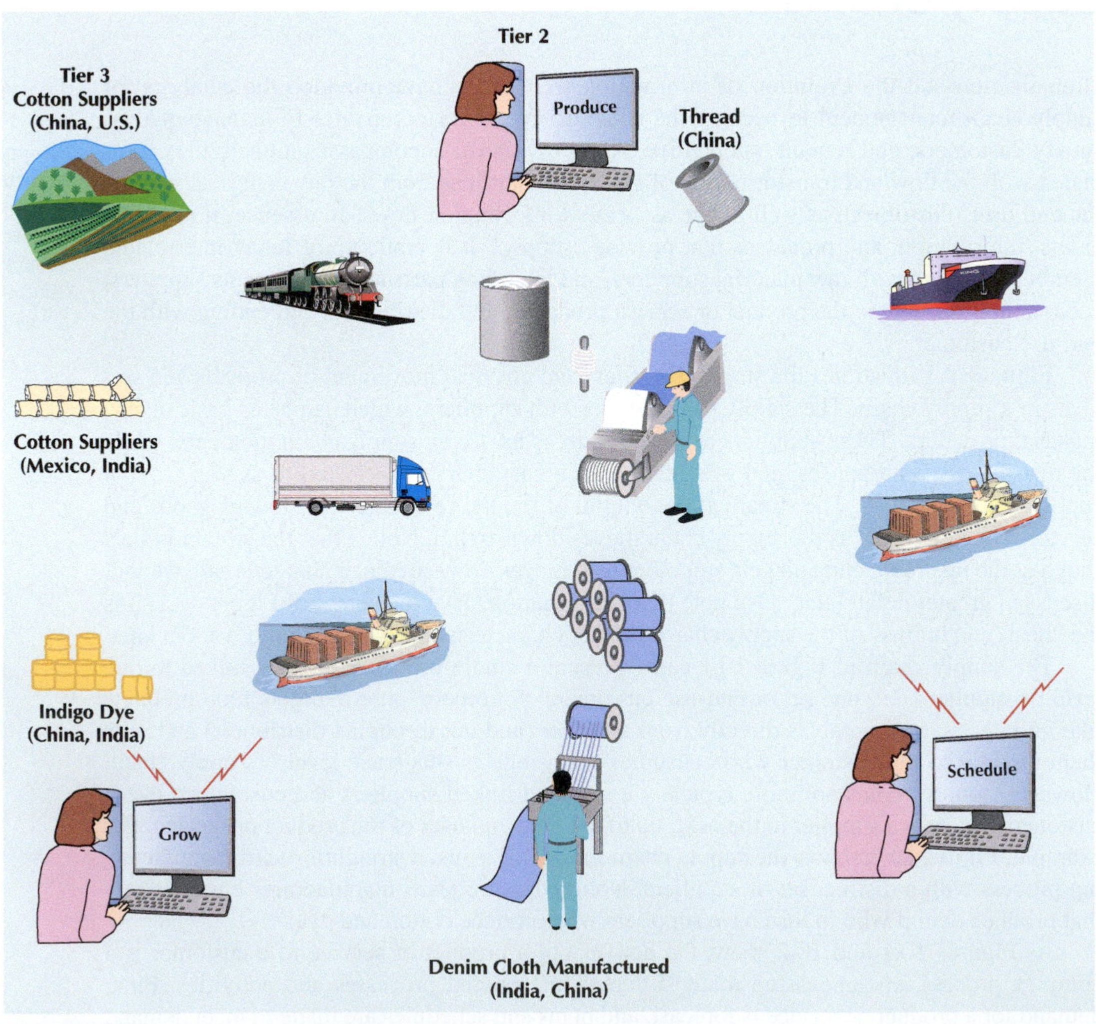

FIGURE 10.2 The Supply Chain for Denim Jeans

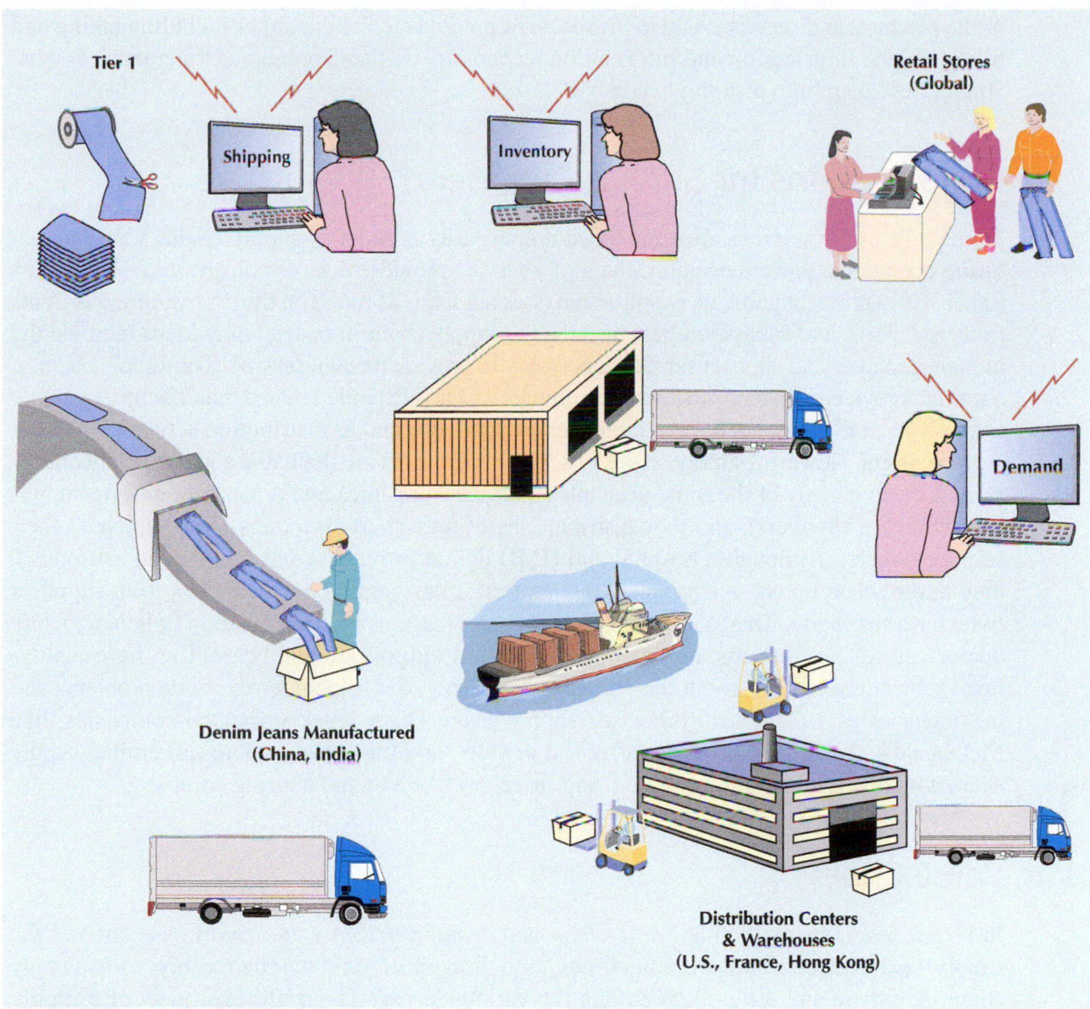

FIGURE 10.2 **(continued)**

own suppliers) who prepare and then ship parts and materials to manufacturing or service sites. A large manufacturer like Procter & Gamble has over 80,000 suppliers including first-tier suppliers that supply it directly, second-tier suppliers that supply those suppliers, third-tier suppliers that supply second-tier suppliers, and so on. Parts and materials are transformed into final products or services. These products may then be stored at a distribution center or warehouse. Finally, these products are transported by carriers to external or internal customers. However, this may not be the final step at all, as these customers may transform the product or service further and ship it on to their customers. All of this is part of the supply chain—that is, the flow of goods and services from the materials stage to the end user.

The supply chain is also an integrated group of business processes and activities with the same goal—providing customer satisfaction. As shown in Figure 10.3, these processes include the **procurement** of services, materials, and components from suppliers; *production*

procurement Purchasing goods and services from suppliers.

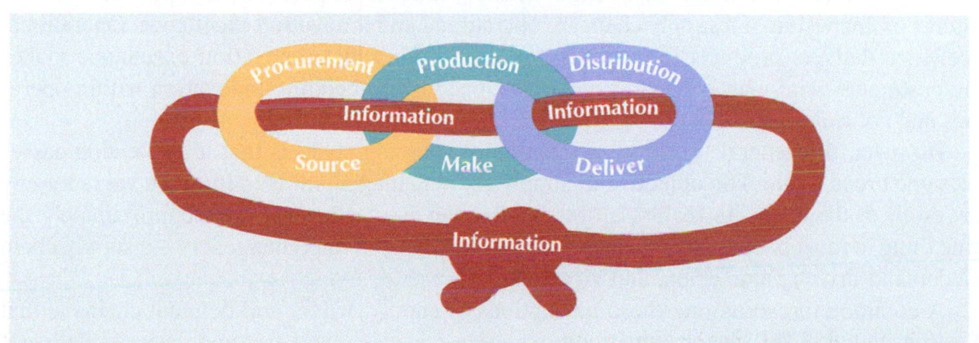

FIGURE 10.3 **Supply Chain Processes**

of the products and services; and *distribution* of products to the customer including taking and filling orders. Information and information technology tie these processes together; it is what "integrates" them into a supply chain.

Supply Chains for Service Providers

Supply chains for services are sometimes not as easily defined as supply chains for manufacturing operations. Since the supply chain of a service provider does not always provide the customer with a physical good, its supply chain does not focus as much on the flow of physical items (material, parts, and subassemblies) through the supply chain. It instead may focus more on the human resources and support services necessary to provide its own service. The supply chain of a service provider also tends to be more compact and less extended than a manufacturing supply chain. It generally does not have as many tiers of suppliers, and its distribution network is smaller or nonexistent. However, supply chains of service companies are definable and can be effectively managed using many of the same principles. Service companies and organizations have suppliers (who have suppliers), and they distribute their products to customers (who may have their own customers). Although a hospital and HMO do not provide actual goods to its customers, they nevertheless purchase equipment, computers, drugs, and medical supplies from suppliers (who have suppliers). They also contract for services (such as food preparation or laundry); hire doctors, nurses, accountants, administrators, and staff; and provide healthcare. They have quality-management issues throughout their supply chain. They also encounter the same problems and inefficiencies as a manufacturing-based supply chain. Other service-oriented companies, like McDonald's, do, in fact, provide a physical product, and thus have a more discernible supply chain with distribution, transportation, and inventory like a manufacturing company.

Value Chains

In recent years, terms such as *value chain* and *demand-driven value chain* have entered the supply chain lexicon and are sometimes used instead of, or interchangeably with, supply chain. Are there any differences among the various terms? The traditional view of a supply chain was that it focused somewhat narrowly on the activities and processes associated with material management and logistics that convert raw materials and subassemblies into a manufactured product—plan, source, make, and deliver. However, a **value chain** is thought to have a broader focus with a more important and visible corporate presence that might also include such functions as customer management, new product innovation and launch, post-sales support, and change management. In this context, the ultimate goal of a value chain is the delivery of maximum value to the end user.

Value chain A more contemporary name for a supply chain.

A demand-driven value chain is considered to be a global supply chain that is organized according to three overlapping areas of responsibility:

- Supply management—manufacturing, logistics, supply planning, and sourcing
- Demand management—marketing, sales, demand planning, and service
- Product management—R&D, innovation, engineering, and product development

When these processes work together, are visible to each other, and communicate, then a company can respond quickly and efficiently to opportunities that arise from customer or market demand (i.e., it is demand-driven, and thus creates value for all parts of the supply chain). Key features of this vision of a supply chain are operational and innovation excellence. Operational excellence delivers products to customers as promised; while innovation excellence makes sure customers want what's being made and shipped by embedding innovation within operations and not isolating it in a lab.

However, the general "current" perception of a supply chain is that it also encompasses this same broad focus. The objective of supply chain management is to increase value for any part or all of the chain. In reality, all of these names have come to mean approximately the same thing to most people, and the terms are frequently used interchangeably—a supply chain is a demand-driven value chain, and vice versa.

Value The creation of value for the customer is an important aspect of supply chain management.

A common thread among these perceptions of supply, value, and demand chains is that of **value**. Value to the customer is good quality, a fair price, and fast and accurate delivery.

Along the Supply Chain

The Denim Jeans Supply Chain

The United States is the world's largest market for denim jeans. Out of the 2 billion pairs of jeans sold each year worldwide about 40% are sold in the United States. The favorite jeans of consumers are U.S. brands such as Levi's, Lee, Wrangler, Gap, Old Navy, and American Eagle. However, almost all denim jeans sold in U.S. stores (approximately 98%), are imported from suppliers in countries around the world, even though the United States is the world's third largest cotton producer and the largest cotton exporter. This means that the denim jeans industry encompasses a supply chain that is geographically and financially one of the largest in the world, with the United States as a major (cotton) supplier on one end of the supply chain, the predominant jeans consumer on the other end, but with virtually none of the production process in between. China, India, the United States, and Pakistan produce almost 80% of the world's cotton. Much of the cotton grown in China, India, and Pakistan supply manufacturing facilities within these countries that produce denim cloth and then jeans, while cotton from the United States (as well as other major exporters like India, Brazil, and Australia) is exported to these countries as well as other major denim fabric and jeans producing countries like Mexico and Bangladesh. China, Mexico, and Bangladesh are the top jeans suppliers to the United States, accounting for almost 70% percent of U.S. imports. Mexico is the largest U.S. supplier of men's and boy's jeans (approximately 40%) while China is the primary supplier for women's and girl's jeans (about 44% percent). The jeans manufacturing process can occur at facilities entirely within a country or between countries. For example, cotton grown in the United States, can be shipped to China where it is stored in warehouses, then transported by truck or rail to a Chinese facility where it is spun into yarn, which is then shipped to another city in China where denim cloth is produced, which is then shipped to Bangladesh where jeans are sewn, and buttons, rivets, and zippers are added from other plants before the finished denim jeans are shipped back to the United States to complete the supply chain.

Discuss how the supply chain for a product like denim, which is somewhat straightforward and simple, differs from a supply chain for a more complex product like smartphones.

Sources: Based on "Denim Jeans: State of the U.S. Market", www.lifestylemonitor.cottoninc.com, 2011; and, Summer R. Oakes, "Textile Talk: DenimNation-Series 1.1" www.source4style.com, 2011.

To achieve value for the customer, the members of the supply chain must act as partners to systematically create value at every stage of the supply chain. Thus, companies not only look for ways to create value internally in their own production processes, but they also look to their supply chain partners to create value by improving product design and quality, enhancing supply chain performance and speed, and lowering costs. To accomplish these value enhancers, supply chain members must collaborate with each other and integrate their processes, topics that we will continually return to in this chapter.

The Management of Supply Chains

Supply chain management (SCM) focuses on integrating and managing the flow of goods and services and information through the supply chain in order to make it responsive to customer needs while lowering total costs. Traditionally, each segment of the supply chain was managed as a separate (stand-alone) entity focused on its own goals. However, to compete in today's global marketplace a company has to count on the combined and coordinated effort of all members of the supply chain.

Supply chain management (SCM) Requires managing the flow of information through the supply chain in order to attain the level of synchronization that will make it more responsive to customer needs while lowering costs.

Supply chains require close collaboration, cooperation, and communication among members to be effective. Suppliers and their customers must share information. It is the rapid flow of information among customers, suppliers, distributors, and producers that characterizes today's supply chain management. Suppliers and customers must also have the same goals. They need to be able to trust each other. Customers need to be able to count on the quality and timeliness of the products and services of their suppliers. Furthermore, suppliers and customers must participate together in the design of the supply chain to achieve their shared goals and to facilitate communication and the flow of information.

Supply Chain Uncertainty and Inventory

One of a company's main objectives in managing its supply chain is to synchronize the upstream flow of incoming materials, parts, subassemblies, and services with production and distribution downstream so that it can respond to uncertainty in customer demand without creating costly excess inventory. Examples of factors that contribute to uncertainty, and hence variability, in the supply chain are inaccurate demand forecasting, long variable lead times for orders, late deliveries, incomplete shipments, product changes, batch ordering, price fluctuations and discounts, and inflated orders. The primary negative effects of supply chain uncertainty and variability are lateness and incomplete orders. If deliveries from suppliers are late or incomplete, they slow down the flow of goods and services through the supply chain, ultimately resulting in poor-quality customer service. Companies cope with this uncertainty and try to avoid delays with their own form of "insurance," **inventory**.

Inventory Insurance against supply chain uncertainty.

Supply chain members carry buffer (or extra) inventory at various stages of the supply chain to minimize the negative effects of uncertainty and to keep goods and services flowing smoothly from suppliers to customers. For example, if a parts order arrives late (or does not arrive at all) from a supplier, the producer is able to continue production and maintain its delivery schedule to its customers by using parts it has stored in inventory for just such an occurrence.

Companies also accumulate inventory because they may order in large batches in order to keep down order and transportation costs or to receive a discount or special price from a supplier. However, inventory is very costly. Products sitting on a shelf or in a warehouse are just like money sitting there not being used when it could be used for something else. It is estimated that the cost of carrying a retail product in inventory for one year is between 18% and 35% of what the item cost. Inventory-carrying costs are almost $500 billion per year in the United States. As such, suppliers and customers would like to minimize or eliminate it.

The Bullwhip Effect

Distorted information or the lack of information, such as inaccurate demand data or forecasts from the customer end can ripple back upstream through the supply chain and magnify demand variability at each stage. This can result in high buffer inventories, poor customer service, missed production schedules, wrong capacity plans, inefficient shipping, and high costs. This phenomenon, which has been observed across different industries, is known as the **bullwhip effect**. It occurs when slight to moderate demand variability becomes magnified as demand information is transmitted back upstream in the supply chain. In Figure 10.1 the stream at the bottom of the figure reflects this occurrence; the flow is greater (and the waters more turbulent) further upstream. Figure 10.4 presents a detailed perspective of the bullwhip effect.

Bullwhip effect Occurs when slight demand variability is magnified as information moves back upstream.

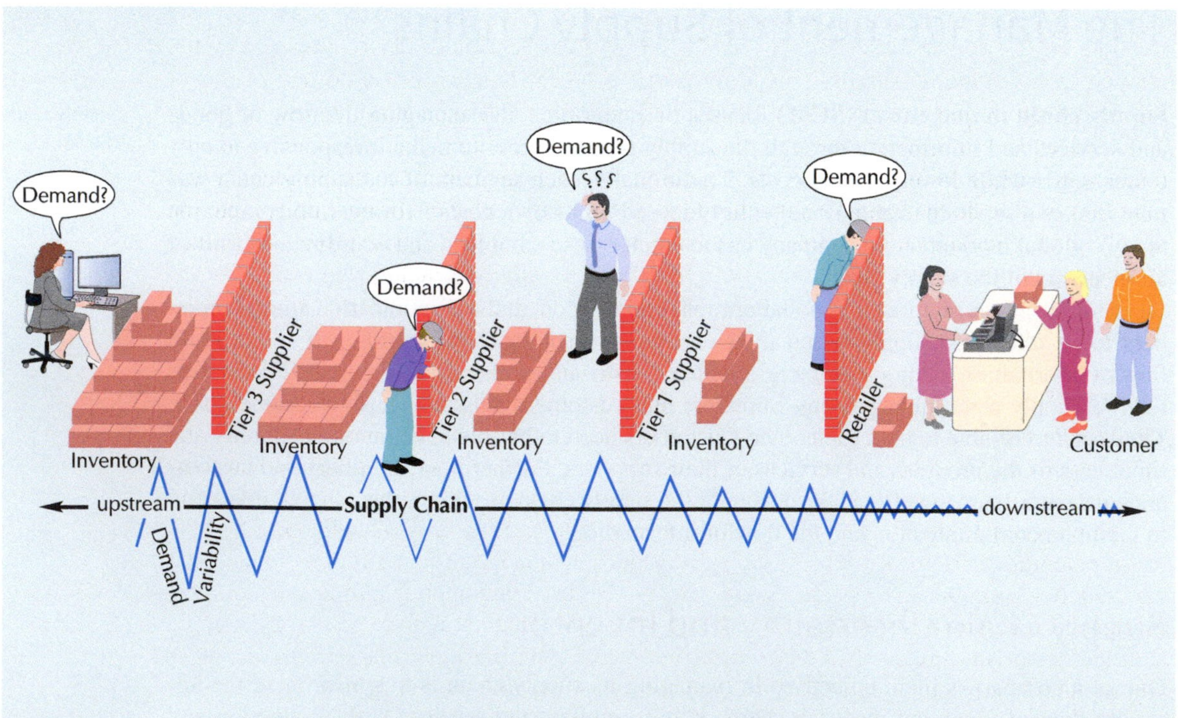

FIGURE 10.4 **The Bullwhip Effect**

The bullwhip effect is created when supply chain members make ordering decisions with an eye to their own self-interest and/or they do not have accurate demand information from the adjacent supply chain members. If each supply chain member is uncertain and not confident about what the actual demand is for the succeeding member it supplies and is making its own demand forecast, then it will stockpile extra inventory to compensate for the uncertainty. In other words, they create a security blanket of inventory. As shown in Figure 10.4, demand for the end user is relatively stable and the inventory is small. However, if slight changes in demand occur, and the distributor does not know why this change occurred, then the distributor will tend to overreact and increase its own demand, or conversely reduce its own demand too much if demand from its customer unexpectedly drops. This creates an even greater overreaction by the manufacturer who supplies the distributor and the suppliers who supply the manufacturer. One way to cope with the bullwhip effect is for supply chain members to share information, especially demand forecasts. If the supply chain exhibits *transparency*, then members can have access to each other's information, which reduces or eliminates uncertainty.

Managing Supply Chain Risk

When supply chains stretch over long distances and multiple locations around the world, uncertainty, and therefore risk, increase. In "lean" supply chains there is little redundancy and slack (i.e., inventory), so when disruptions occur—natural or otherwise—the effects can cascade through the supply chain, slowing or stopping normal operations and eventual customer order fulfillment. As suggested previously, one way to offset uncertainty is by carrying extra inventory at various points along the supply chain, however, as we have also noted, this is an expensive solution for handling uncertainty and risk. Instead, a number of innovative companies with top supply chains have begun to engage in formal "risk management" to cope with supply chain uncertainty.

For the first time, risk is being incorporated into the latest version of ISO 9001:2015, which establishes the requirements of a quality management system (see the section on standards in Chapter 2). The ISO defines risk as "the effect of uncertainty on an expected result." As part of the ISO 9001:2015 standard, organizations are required to determine the processes needed for a quality management system, which includes the identification of risks and the opportunities and actions needed to address them. Management is required to demonstrate leadership and commitment to customers by taking a risk-based approach, to make sure risks that affect products, services, and the ability to enhance customer satisfaction are identified and addressed.

Risk management requires due diligence to evaluate and anticipate the likelihood and possible impact of unexpected supply chain disruptions, which can be operational, economic, marketplace, or natural, and plan ahead for them. In recent years as a result of a global economic downturn and several natural disasters, including an earthquake in Japan, floods in Thailand, and a volcanic eruption in Iceland, companies have altered their approach to supply chain management to incorporate formal ongoing risk management processes to identify and plan for possible disruptions. This is referred to as building *resiliency* (or continuity) into the supply chain. (See the "Along the Supply Chain" for Cisco Systems.) These processes include identifying circumstances in advance that could cause disruptions, monitoring events worldwide to anticipate disruptions, and developing contingency plans for the occurrence of disruptions, including a pool of alternative suppliers, logistics providers, and energy sources to fall back on when disruptions occur. After the Japanese earthquake in 2011, one international automaker that sourced a microcontroller exclusively from a company in Japan had lined up an alternate supplier as part of its proactive risk management contingency plan, which allowed the company to avoid being forced to cut production by half following the earthquake, and enabled it to return to normal operations within a few months.

However, risks do not just evolve from natural disasters. Risks are also inherent in a variety of potential operational issues including transportation and logistics disruptions; customer and supplier communication failures; product, processes, and supply chain design failures; changes in regulatory/customs documentation and environmental requirements; security issues and terrorism threats; data thefts and computer system breaches; marketplace changes; and supplier insolvency to name just a few of the many possible sources of risk.

Risk pooling is an approach to managing risks in which an attempt is made to aggregate risks to reduce the impact of individual risks. One way to pool risks is to combine inventories

Risk pooling: An approach to risk management that aggregates risk to reduce its impact.

The devastation in Northeast Japan following a major earthquake and tsunami that hit the island in March 2011. For months this natural disaster disrupted the global supply chains of many companies with Japanese suppliers.

The Asahi Shimbun/Getty Images, Inc.

from multiple at-risk locations into a few, or one, location, like a warehouse or distribution center, in a more risk-free environment. It is well known that it is more economical to hold inventory at a single location than to disperse it across a number of customer locations. Doing so reduces the overall inventory investment needed to achieve a target service level across all the customers supplied by a distribution center, which, in effect, reduces demand variability. Adding a distribution center between a supplier and a customer can also shorten lead times, which is another way to pool risks (i.e., it's more costly to meet variations in demand from several locations than from one).

Another way to manage risks is to build risk tradeoffs into product and service designs to include fewer parts and product variability. Reducing the number of product components

Along the Supply Chain

Supply Chain Resiliency at Cisco Systems

Cisco Systems, the San Jose-based designer and manufacturer of networking equipment with annual revenues over $47 billion, outsources all of the manufacturing of its products. It has a global supply chain of more than 600 direct suppliers and numerous manufacturing partners that supply around 80,000 parts for its products. Its supply chain was ranked sixth best in *Gartner's* 2015 annual Top 25 ranking of company's supply chains. Following Hurricane Katrina in 2005, Cisco found that it was not capable of responding quickly and effectively enough to meet demand from its customers for $1 billion in telecommunication replacement parts in the Gulf Coast region. As a result, Cisco created a centralized risk management team within its supply chain operations organization that works with other organizational functions (like engineering and customer operations) to ensure supply chain resiliency in the face of possible disruptions. Cisco achieves resiliency through four processes. Product resiliency identifies strategic priorities for product categories and determines risk trade-offs early in the development and sourcing of products. Supply chain resiliency identifies supply chain vulnerabilities and mitigates circumstances that could limit recovery from a major disruption within a certain time frame. Business continuity planning compiles resiliency data points for critical suppliers including such things as emergency contacts, alternate power providers, and estimated recovery time as part of the supply chain design process. The supply chain incident management process monitors events worldwide on a 24/7 basis for any potential disruption that could impact suppliers, transportation, or manufacturing. In 2011, six years after the lessons learned from Hurricane Katrina these processes helped Cisco weather the Japanese earthquake that impacted over 7000 parts and involved 300 suppliers. Cisco was able to execute 900 new supply sources three times faster than the average time and incurred only minimal customer order fulfillment disruption and virtually no loss of revenue. Cisco was also able to react to similar natural disruptions, including floods in Thailand and an Iceland volcano eruption, due to its supply chain resiliency processes.

Do you think Cisco's centralized approach to risk management would be appropriate and useful for retail companies like P&G and Walmart?

Sources: Based on Mary Siegfried, "Building a Resilient Supply Chain," *Inside Supply Chain Management*, (www.ism.ws), vol. 23, no. 3, April 2012, p. 24; and, Maria Jesus Saenz and Elena Revilla, "Creating More Resilient Supply Chains," *MIT Sloan Management Review*, (www.sloanreview.mit.edu), Summer 2014.

allows a company to meet demand with fewer products and fewer suppliers. Having common product components that can be used in a lot of different products enables a company to pool its forecasts for component demand, resulting in fewer demand forecasts. (The more forecasts, the more chances for errors.) Reducing product offerings can have the same effect—it's easier to forecast demand for a smaller number of product configurations than a larger number.

Supply Chain Sustainability

Achieving **sustainability**, also referred to as "going green," has become one of the most visible recent trends in operations and supply chain management. Sustainability, according to the United Nations, is "meeting present needs without compromising the ability of future generations to meet their needs." Implicit in this definition is not depleting or abusing our natural resources like air, water, land, and energy in a way that's going to harm current or future generations. For businesses it also means sustaining human and social resources. However, to many companies, sustainability means becoming environmentally friendly and socially conscious (i.e., "green") at *the expense of competitiveness and higher costs.* A common perception among many U.S. and European corporations is that requiring suppliers, especially in developing countries, to use green practices is not feasible because they do not face the same governmental, cultural, and social pressures; that green manufacturing will require costly new equipment and processes; and that the customer market for products designed with green attributes is "soft." As a result, companies often view social and environmental responsibility separately from business objectives.

sustainability Meeting present needs without compromising the ability of future generations to meet their needs.

Along the Supply Chain

Walmart's Commitment to Sustainability

Walmart is the world's largest company by revenue (over $480 billion annually) and also the largest retailer, with over 11,500 retail locations in 28 countries. Walmart has more than 2.2 million employees around the world and has a global supply chain with over 100,000 suppliers. The company has made a major commitment to have an environmentally sustainable supply chain to make a difference for the environment and communities around the world. It has established corporate sustainability goals "to be supplied 100 percent by renewable energy, create zero waste, and sell products that sustain people and the environment." To achieve these goals Walmart closely monitors and scrutinizes the environmental performance of its extended supply chain, suggests improvements to its suppliers, and helps its suppliers implement sustainable solutions. Walmart employs a sustainability index that measures supplier performance related to energy and climate, material efficiency, natural resources, and ethical production. The index helps Walmart direct its suppliers on what they need to be doing to meet the company's sustainability goals. Over 1,300 U.S. suppliers, representing 65% of the goods sold in Walmart stores, use the sustainability index to drive sustainable production.

Walmart has developed a number of sustainability initiatives, including a goal to eliminate 20 million metric tons of greenhouse gas (GHG) emissions (the amount of its direct emissions in 2010) from its global supply chain by 2016. By 2014 Walmart had over 335 renewable energy projects around the world that provided its facilities with over 2.2 billion kilowatt hours of electricity. The U.S. Environmental Protection Agency (EPA) ranks Walmart as the sixteenth-largest onsite green power generator in the United States. Combined with other renewable energy sources, in 2015 Walmart generated over 26% of its global electricity needs with renewable energy. The company procured over 3 billion kWh globally achieving about 43% of its goal of procuring 7 billion kWh by 2020. Another energy initiative is to double Walmart's distribution fleet efficiency from a 2005 baseline by working with suppliers to use fuel-saving technologies and better driving techniques, and to load trucks more efficiently, improve routing, and use alternatively fueled trucks. It has committed to sending zero waste to U.S. landfills by 2025. In 2015 the company kept almost 82% of all waste from its U.S. operations and 68% internationally out of landfills, which had the potential to reduce CO_2 emissions by over 12 million tons annually.

In 2009 Walmart joined with several other companies that provided seed money to start The Sustainability Consortium (TSC), jointly run by the University of Arkansas and Arizona State University, that now includes over 100 of the world's largest retailers and consumer products companies including Coca-Cola, Pepsico, P&G, and Kellogg's. The consortium determines what makes certain products more sustainable than others and has developed guidelines for sustainability for over 100 product categories. In an effort to make its customers more sustainability conscious, Walmart's ecommerce (virtual) site now labels over 3000 products made by more than 100 of its suppliers with a badge reading "Made by a Sustainability Leader."

Identify the top five companies that are on the EPAs list of the top onsite green power generators and discuss their sustainability initiatives.

Sources: Based on the Walmart website at http://corporate.walmart.com/global-responsibility/; and Erica Plambeck and Lyn Denend, "The Greening of Walmart's Supply Chain . . . Revisted," *Supply Chain Management Review*, 5; (September/October 2011), pp. 16–23.

However, there is a growing realization among many companies that the social and environmental benefits of developing sustainable products do not have to come at the expense of reduced profits and competiveness. In an IBM survey of 320 global companies in 31 countries, almost 37% indicated that they were utilizing sustainability as part of their company's innovation and growth strategy. As these companies have learned, sustainability can, in fact, be cost-effective and profitable and provide the impetus for product and process innovations. Green initiatives can lower costs because fewer resources are used, and additional revenues can result from better products or new businesses. Although Toyota realized huge costs in developing its hybrid Prius, it created a whole new successful and potentially profitable product and market just as gasoline prices were rising. Further, by designing products that can be recycled or reused, companies can reduce waste, thereby lowering costs. Thus, while a commitment to green practices can create a better image for companies among consumers (and the government), they can also reduce costs and increase revenues.

The impetus for, and commitment to, sustainability generally comes from downstream in the supply chain and moves back upstream to include suppliers. Companies have found that suppliers can account for as much as 80% of the resources consumed in a product's supply chain. Companies must work with and guide suppliers to reduce the inefficient use of resources, reduce the use of raw materials, reduce waste, and recycle. Suppliers can be coerced into using green practices by threats, demands, or incentives, or a combination.

Sustainability and Quality Management

Many companies already have quality improvement programs in place that require suppliers to adhere to continuous improvement goals of eliminating returned products, thus reducing waste; poor quality translates to wasted resources. The same quality management focus on reducing waste can work to achieve sustainability goals. As we discussed in Chapter 2, the cost of poor quality can have a significant impact on a company's profitability and competitiveness, and quality costs may often come from suppliers along the supply chain, including the cost of materials, labor, and resources for reworking defective products; the cost of shipping delays and customer service errors; and the cost of product replacement and waste.

Improving fuel efficiency in a distribution fleet, having employees telecommute, using eco-friendly packaging materials, building energy efficient facilities, reducing the use of wooden pallets, and even turning the thermostat up in summer and down in winter are initiatives that improve processes and reduce costs, and also achieve sustainability goals. As part of the U.S. General Services Administration's smart building strategy, IBM is installing smart building technology in 50 of the federal government's highest-energy-consuming buildings, saving taxpayers $15 million annually. By consolidating distribution centers, COSCO, China's largest shipping and logistics services supplier, reduced its overall fuel costs by 25%. Dow Chemical estimates that its sustainability initiatives have saved more than $8 billion in fuel costs.

Along the Supply Chain

Reducing Costs with Sustainability at UPS and FedEx

UPS is the world's largest package delivery company delivering more than 16 million packages per day to more than 6 million customers in over 200 companies around the world. FedEx is the world's largest express transportation company with 4 million package deliveries daily to over 220 countries and territories with a fleet of 675 aircraft and 48,000 vehicles. Both companies are major providers of supply chain logistics, distribution, and transportation services, and are key partners in many companies' supply chains. Both have also been leaders in achieving sustainability that also cut their costs.

FedEx Express has a holistic three-tiered vehicle sustainability strategy to improve the fuel efficiency of its fleet—"reduce, replace, and revolutionize." In 2008 FedEx set a goal to improve fuel efficiency in its fleet of global vehicles by 20% by 2020, and when it surpassed this goal in 2012 it revised it to 30%. A "Fuel Sense" program based on the concept that "every drop counts" was developed and executed by a FedEx Express fleet team by making incremental changes to make fuel consumption in their aircraft fleet more efficient. Specific examples include pilots consciously waiting to start their last engine during taxi out, or shutting the first one down while taxiing in rather than at the gate; ramp agents loading more efficiently with an aft center of gravity (CG), which can reduce drag by 1.5%, representing an annual fuel savings potential of over $7 million; technicians connecting ground power to aircraft quickly to reduce the usage of auxiliary aircraft power at ten times the cost; dispatchers reducing the amount of optional fuel planned on every flight, which saved $1 million for every minute reduced across the fleet for a year; and ramp agents keeping the parking gates clear to allow taxiing aircraft to arrive and get into position quickly and efficiently, saving very expensive aircraft wait-time. Since 2007, when the program started, it has saved over 350 million gallons of jet fuel, enough energy to power 270,000 homes for a year, with a cost savings equal to four jet Boeing freighters, and it eliminates almost a half million metric tons of carbon emissions every year. FedEx is also putting old airplanes out of service, and replacing them with new more energy-efficient Boeing 767s, each one saving the company $10 million per year in costs. The company is also adding new fuel-efficient ground vehicles to its fleet. The company works with a variety of manufacturers to advance vehicle technologies and make the best use of the conventional vehicles operated by the company. Simply matching the right vehicle to each route has made the biggest single impact on the fleet's overall fuel efficiency.

Since 2001 UPS's sustainability initiatives have saved almost 400 million miles of travel. It uses a number of technologies, analytics, and "big data" to achieve fuel efficiency across its ground fleet of 80,000 vehicles. Fuel efficiency starts even before the engines are turned on; UPS uses package-flow technologies that load vans effectively, minimizing the time it takes a driver to find the right package, thus quickening delivery. This translates into fewer miles traveled, which conserves fuel and reduces emissions. For years UPS route planners have designed routes to avoid left turns, reducing the amount of time spent idling waiting to turn left, which conserves fuel and reduces emissions, and is also a lot safer. In North America in the past decade UPS's no-left-turns policy has saved 10 million gallons of gas and reduced CO_2 emissions by 100,000 metric tons. In general, the company maintains a strict anti-idle policy, which has cut the time trucks idle by 24 minutes per driver per day, resulting in a fuel savings of $188 per driver per year. Routes are also designed to have the minimum number of stops and starts and still be on time. UPS tries to match the vehicle (i.e., powertrain) to the needs of the routes to get the best mileage, and it's constantly looking for ways to make its vehicles more fuel efficient regardless of the powertrain. It worked with Isuzu and Utilimaster to develop lighter-weight composite-body diesel vans that achieved a 40% increase in fuel economy over traditional aluminum vans in testing. UPS also expects to save 40% in fuel costs by switching its long-haul semi-tractor trailer fleet to natural gas with prices 30% to 40% lower than diesel.

It employs a computer system called Orion (On Road Integrated Optimization and Navigation). The system employs telematics technology, which is geospatial mapping information combined with real-time communications with drivers to give them precise, optimized driving directions each morning and then update them during the day as customers request specific drop-off times, new drop-off destinations, and new pickups. Sensors capture over 200 data points for more than 80,000 vehicles every day to help determine what packages are loaded on each truck; plan and track routes; provide insight into engine performance and condition; capture driver behavior and safety habits; report on emissions and fuel consumption; and monitor deliveries and customer service. By optimizing deliveries UPS estimates that in one year it saved over 206 million minutes of idling time, which saved more than 1.5 million gallons of fuel; it also reduced miles per delivery by over 12 million miles, avoiding 13,000 metric tons of CO_2 emissions and saving 39 million gallons of gas.

Information Technology: A Supply Chain Enabler

Information is the essential link between all supply chain processes and members. Computer and information technology allows real-time, online communications throughout the supply chain. Technologies that enable the efficient flow of products and services through the supply chain are referred to as "enablers," and information technology has become the most important enabler of effective supply chain management.

Supply chain managers like to use the phrase "in modern supply chain management, information replaces inventory." Although this statement is not literally true—companies need inventory at some point, not just information—information does change the way supply chains are managed, and these changes can lead to lower inventories. Without information technology, supply chain management would not be possible at the level it is currently being accomplished on a global basis. Some of the more important IT supply chain enablers are shown in Figure 10.5.

Electronic Business

E-business replaces physical processes with electronic ones. In e-business, supply chain transactions are conducted via a variety of electronic media, including electronic data interchange

E-business The replacement of physical business processes with electronic ones.

FIGURE 10.5 **Supply Chain Enablers**

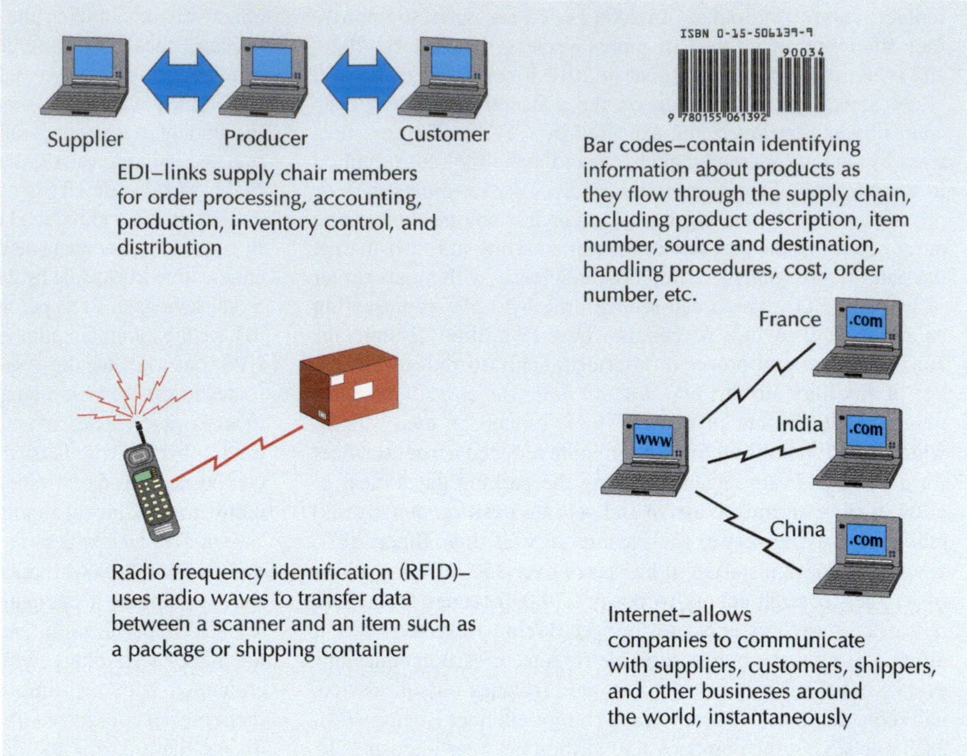

(EDI), email, electronic funds transfer (EFT), electronic publishing, image processing, electronic bulletin boards, shared databases, bar coding, fax, automated voice mail, CD-ROM catalogs, the Internet, websites, and so on. Companies are able to automate the process of moving information electronically between suppliers and customers. This saves both labor costs and time.

Some of the features that e-business brings to supply chain management include:

- Cost savings and price reductions derived from lower transaction costs (including labor and document savings)
- Reduction or elimination of the role of intermediaries and even retailers and service providers, thus reducing costs
- Shortening supply chain response and transaction times for ordering and delivery
- Gaining a wider presence and increased visibility for companies
- Greater choices and more information for customers
- Improved service as a result of instant accessibility to services
- Collection and analysis of voluminous amounts of customer data and preferences
- The creation of virtual companies like Amazon.com that distribute only through the Web, which can afford to sell at lower prices because they do not need to maintain retail space
- Leveling the playing field for small companies, which lack resources to invest in infrastructure (plant and facilities) and marketing
- Gaining global access to markets, suppliers, and distribution channels

Electronic Data Interchange

Electronic data interchange (EDI) A computer-to-computer exchange of business documents.

Electronic data interchange (EDI) is a computer-to-computer exchange of business documents in a standard format, which has been established by the American National Standards Institute (ANSI) and the International Standards Organization (ISO). It creates a data exchange that allows trading partners to use Internet transactions instead of paper when performing purchasing, shipping, and other business. EDI links supply chain members together for order processing, accounting, production, and distribution. It provides quick access to information, allows better customer service, reduces paperwork, allows better communication, increases productivity, improves tracking and expediting, and improves billing and cost efficiency.

EDI can be effective in reducing or eliminating the bullwhip effect discussed earlier in this chapter. With EDI, supply chain members are able to share demand information in real time, and thus are able to develop more accurate demand forecasts and reduce the uncertainty that tends to be magnified at each upstream stage of the supply chain.

Bar Codes

A bar code is what is referred to as an "automated data collection" system, or "auto-ID." In bar coding, computer-readable codes are attached to items flowing through the supply chain, including products, containers, packages, and even vehicles. The bar code contains identifying information about the item. It might include such things as a product description, item number, its source and destination, special handling procedures, cost, and order number. A food product can be identified down to the farmer who grew it and the field it was grown in. When the bar code information is scanned into a company's computer by an electronic scanner, it provides supply chain members with critical information about the item's location in the supply chain.

Bar code technology has had a huge influence on supply chain management, and it is used by thousands of companies in different situations. Package delivery companies like FedEx and UPS use bar codes to provide themselves and customers with instantaneous detailed tracking information. Supermarkets use scanners at cash registers to read prices, products, and manufacturers from Universal Product Codes (UPCs).

When bar codes are scanned at checkout counters, it also creates **point-of-sale data**—an instantaneous computer record of the sale of a product. This piece of information can be instantly transmitted throughout the supply chain to update inventory records. Point-of-sale data enable supply chain members—suppliers, producers, and distributors—to quickly identify trends, order parts and materials, schedule orders and production, and plan for deliveries.

Point-of-sale data Creates an instantaneous computer record of a sale.

Radio Frequency Identification

While a barcode is the most commonly used auto-ID system, a more technologically advanced system is **radio frequency identification (RFID)**. RFID technology uses radio waves to transfer data between a reader (that is, a scanner) and an item such as a shipping container or a carton. RFID consists of a tiny microchip and computer, often a small, thin ribbon, which can be put in almost any form—for example between layers of cardboard in a box, or on a piece of tape or a label. An RFID "tag" stores a unique identification number, as shown in photos. RFID scanners transmit a radio signal via an antenna to "access" the tag, which then responds

Radio frequency identification (RFID) Can send product data from an item to a reader via radio waves.

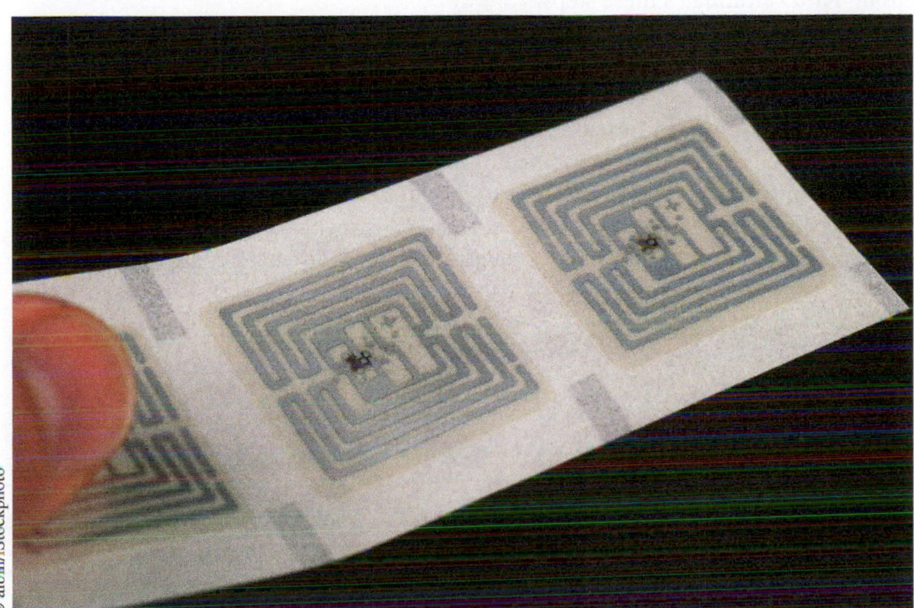

© albln/iStockphoto

Marc F. Henning/Alamy Stock Photo

With RFID technology, small individual electronic "tags" like these are attached to cartons, packages, or containers, which allows companies and organizations to track their every move around the world.

Along the Supply Chain

Managing Ford's Supply Chain Risks and Helping the Automaker's Recovery

In 2006, Ford mortgaged virtually the entire company against private bank loans of almost $27 billion (while rivals GM and Chrysler accepted $25 billion of government bailout money). A condition of the loans was that its debt would have to be rated investment grade by two major rating agencies before Ford could get back its brand, buildings, and factories. By mid-2012, following three years of solid revenue growth, Ford received investment grade ratings from Fitch Ratings and Moody's Investor Services. In 2010, it surpassed Toyota as the second-largest auto seller in the United States.

A significant factor in Ford's recovery has been attributed to tight management of its large and complex supply chain. Ford builds around 6 million cars a year with a supply chain that includes 70 plants around the world drawing 34 billion parts from 1400 tier 1 suppliers at 4400 manufacturing sites, with as many as 10 tiers of suppliers between the automaker and its raw material sources. A key to Ford's supply chain management strategy was simplification, by building cars on a smaller number of base vehicles. This is one of the primary trends of the top company supply chains identified by *Gartner's* in its annual report (see the "Along the Supply Chain" box).

Ford also mirrored top supply chain performers by introducing *resiliency* in its supply chain through good risk planning. Ford was able to weather several major disruptions during its recovery, including a fire at the trim factory of a Michigan supplier and severe floods in Thailand that affected a tooling plant. The company worked to proactively identify the areas of greatest risk, especially among its tier 1 suppliers where disruptions could halt production, by keeping approved, qualified alternative suppliers available to minimize risk and prevent supply disruptions.

Using the Internet, identify some of the major natural, economic, or political global disruptions in the past five years that would have posed a risk situation to U.S. companies with a global supply chain.

Source: Based on Robert J. Bowman, "How Ford's Supply Chain Put the Company Back in the Driver's Seat," *SupplyChainBrain,* (June 18, 2012), www.supplychainbrain.com.

with its number. The tag could be an Electronic Product Code (EPC), which could be linked to databases with detailed information about a product item.

RFID has several advantages over barcodes. RFID tags do not need a direct "line of sight" to read, and many tags can be read simultaneously over a long distance. When products arrive at a location, such as a retail store, shipping dock, or warehouse, each barcode has to be scanned individually, whereas RFID readers placed at an entry site (like a door) can scan a whole pallet of different products automatically and instantaneously. As such, RFID provides complete visibility of product location, is faster, reduces labor usage, and is more accurate than barcodes. With barcodes it is difficult to know how much product is in a store; however, RFID readers inside a store (or warehouse) can continuously monitor what is available, and when the inventory reaches a certain level it can be reordered. When items are stored in a warehouse, the barcode on the item to be stored has to be scanned as well as the barcode fixed to the location; RFID eliminates these steps.

In a global supply chain RFID tags make it possible for suppliers or retailers to know automatically what goods they have and where they are around the world. For example, a retailer could distinguish between three cartons of the same product and know that one was in the warehouse in Asia, one was in the store, and one was in ocean transit, which would speed up product location, delivery, and replenishment. **Figure 10.6** shows some of the advantages RFID could provide. RFID technology also has obvious security benefits by being able to identify all items being shipped into the United States on an airplane or a ship.

Walmart, an early proponent of RFID, estimated that the following benefits would result from RFID:

- Labor to scan barcodes on cases and pallets will be eliminated.
- On-shelf monitoring will decrease stock-outs in stores.
- Product shrinkage, vendor fraud, and theft will be prevented.
- Tracking over 1 billion pallets annually will reduce distribution center costs.
- RFID will provide inventory visibility, enabling a 20% reduction in inventory levels.
- Savings of over $8 billion per year are projected.

However, RFID technology does have disadvantages. RFID technology is not yet standardized, which makes it difficult to track items that move from one system to another. Using RFID is more costly than using barcodes: individual RFID tags are expensive relative to barcodes, and the readers are costly. Radio waves don't go through metal and are diffused by water.

DC
RFID directs packages through a conveyor system in distribution center
RFID reads item in inventory at a store or DC plus items in transit so company knows up-to-date inventory status and can synchronize supply chain
Employee finds items in bins or puts items in bins with RFID
RFID checks arriving truckloads for security and updates inventory
RFID keeps track of items on ships and planes leaving global ports or coming into U.S. for security
Customer finds pair of jeans with his size (with chip sewn into label) on store shelf with radio wand provided by store; pays with cell phone RFID technology

FIGURE 10.6 RFID Capabilities

Walmart originally mandated that its top suppliers put RFID tags carrying EPC codes on their pallets and cases. However, a number of its suppliers balked due to technical problems and costs. Many consumer products such as toilet paper and detergent have very thin profit margins, so requiring tags on every pallet and case could turn profit into loss very quickly. Walmart also thought other retailers would follow their lead and also implement RFID on a wide scale, and when this didn't happen, suppliers were left with the cost of maintaining two inventory systems—one for Walmart and one for everyone else. As a result, Walmart scaled back its expectations for implementing RFID throughout its supply chain to a smaller number of top suppliers. Where RFID has found a niche is inside retail stores. Walmart, Zara, Macy's, Bloomingdale's, and Lord and Taylor are examples of retailers that are using RFID to track shelf inventory and maintain the right mix of sizes and styles for customers. It's much less costly and time-consuming to scan a store shelf with RFID tags than to use hand sorting or barcode scanning.

The Internet

No technology has a bigger impact on supply chain management, and business in general, than the Internet. Through the Internet a business can communicate with customers and other businesses within its supply chain anywhere in the world in real time.

The Internet has eliminated geographic barriers, enabling companies to access markets and suppliers around the world that were previously inaccessible. By doing so, the Internet has shifted the advantage in the transaction process from the seller to the buyer, because the Internet makes it easier for companies to deal with many more suppliers around the world in order to get lower prices and better service.

The Internet adds speed and accessibility to the supply chain. Companies are able to reduce or eliminate traditional time-consuming activities associated with ordering and purchasing transactions by using the Internet to link directly to suppliers, factories, distributors, and customers. It enables companies to speed up ordering and delivery, track orders and delivery in real time, instantaneously update inventory information, and get instantaneous feedback from customers. This combination of accurate information and speed allows companies to reduce uncertainty and inventory. Internet commerce is expected to exceed $6 trillion in this decade.

Build-To-Order (BTO)

Dell was the first computer company to move to a direct-sell-to-customers model over the Internet. Its popular build-to-order (BTO) models were initially based on telephone orders by customers. Dell created an efficient supply chain using a huge number of weekly purchase orders faxed to suppliers. However, Dell now sends out orders to suppliers over the Internet every few hours or less. Dell's suppliers are able to access the company's inventories and production plans, and they receive constant feedback on how well they are meeting shipping schedules.

Dell's website allows the customer to configure a PC with the desired features; to order and track the order status, allowing the customer to follow their purchase in real time from order to delivery; and to be notified by email as soon as the order is shipped. Also, Dell created secure private sites for corporate and public sector customers to provide access to service and support information customized to the customer's products. In addition, Dell provides online access to technical reference materials and self-diagnostic tools that include symptom-specific troubleshooting modules that walk customers interactively through common systems problems.

Supply Chain Integration

One of the keys to having a successful, efficient supply chain is to get the various supply chain members to collaborate and work together, that is, to get "in sync." This level of coordination is referred to as *supply chain integration*. Information technology is the key element in achieving supply chain integration through four areas—information sharing, collaborative planning, workflow coordination, and the adoption of new models and technologies. **Table 10.1** describes the positive effect each of these elements can have on supply chain performance.

Information sharing includes any data that are useful to other members of the supply chain such as demand data, inventory stocks, and production and shipping schedules—anything that can help the supply chain members improve performance. Information needs to be transparent (i.e., not hidden) and easily accessible online. Collaborative planning defines *what* is done with the information that is shared. Workflow coordination defines *how* supply chain partners work together to coordinate their activities. Finally, adopting new business models and technologies is how supply chain members redesign and improve their supply chain performance.

Collaborative planning, forecasting, and replenishment (CPFR) A process for two or more companies in a supply chain to synchronize their demand forecasts into a single plan to meet customer demand.

Collaborative planning, forecasting, and replenishment (CPFR) is a process for two or more companies in a supply chain to synchronize their individual demand forecasts in order to develop a single plan for meeting customer demand. With CPFR, parties electronically exchange a series of written comments and supporting data, which includes past sales trends, point-of-sale data, on-hand inventory, scheduled promotions, and forecasts. This allows participants to coordinate joint forecasts by concentrating on differences in forecast numbers. They

TABLE 10.1 Supply Chain Integration

Information sharing among supply chain members
- Reduced bullwhip effect
- Early problem detection
- Faster response
- Builds trust and confidence

Collaborative planning, forecasting, replenishment, and design
- Reduced bullwhip effect
- Lower costs (material, logistics, operating, etc.)
- Higher capacity utilization
- Improved customer service levels

Coordinated workflow, production and operations, procurement
- Production efficiencies
- Fast response
- Improved service
- Quicker to market

Adopt new business models and technologies
- Penetration of new markets
- Creation of new products
- Improved efficiency
- Mass customization

review the data together, compare calculations, and collaborate on what is causing discrepancies. If there are no exceptions they can develop a purchase order and ship. CPFR does not require EDI; data can be sent via spreadsheets or over the Internet. CPFR is actual collaboration because both parties do the work and both parties share in fixing the problems. Sharing forecasts in this type of collaborative system can result in a significant decrease in inventory levels for both the manufacturer and distributor since it tends to reduce the "bullwhip effect" and thus lower costs. Many companies, including General Mills, Procter & Gamble, Hershey's, and Cisco Systems participate in some form of CPFR with their suppliers.

Supply Chain Management (SCM) Software

Enterprise resource planning (ERP) is software that helps integrate the components of a company, including most of the supply chain processes, by sharing and organizing information and data among supply chain members. It transforms transactional data like sales into useful information that supports business decisions in other parts of the company. For example, when data such as a sale becomes available in one part of the business, it is transmitted through ERP software, which automatically determines the effects of the transaction on other areas, such as manufacturing, inventory, procurement, invoicing, distribution, and accounting, and on suppliers. Through these information flows ERP organizes and manages a company's supply chain. Most ERP vendors systems handle external, Web-based interactions, and have software specifically for supply chain management called "SCM."

Enterprise resource planning (ERP) Software that integrates the components of a company by sharing and organizing information and data.

SAP was the first ERP software provider and is the largest, which has made it almost synonymous with ERP applications software. mySAP.com is the umbrella brand name for the SAP software. mySAP.com is a suite of Web-enabled SAP modules that allow a company to collaborate with its customers and business partners along its supply chain. When a customer submits an order, that transaction ripples throughout the company's supply chain, adjusting inventory, part supplies, accounting entries, production schedules and shipping schedules, and balance sheets. Different nations' laws, currencies, and business practices are embedded in the software, which enables it to translate sales transactions smoothly between business partners in different countries—for example, a company in Taiwan and its customer in Brazil.

ERP is discussed in greater detail in Chapter 15, "Resource Planning."

Measuring Supply Chain Performance

As we indicated in previous sections, inventory is a key element in supply chain management. On one hand, it enables a company to cope with uncertainty by serving as a buffer between stages in the supply chain. Inventory allows items to flow smoothly through the system to meet customer demand when stages are not in sync. On the other hand, inventory can be very costly. Thus, it is important for a company to maintain an efficient supply chain by lowering inventory levels (and costs) as much as possible. In order to accomplish this objective, several numerical measures, also called **key performance indicators (KPIs)** or metrics, are often used to measure supply chain performance. Three of the more widely used key performance indicators are *inventory turnover*, *inventory days of supply*, and *fill rate*.

Key performance indicators (KPIs) Metrics used to measure supply chain performance.

Key Performance Indicators

Inventory turns A supply chain performance metric computed by dividing the cost of goods sold by the average aggregate value of inventory.

Inventory turnover (or turns) is computed by dividing the cost of goods sold (i.e., the cost of annual sales) by the average aggregate inventory value:

$$\text{Inventory turns} = \frac{\text{Cost of goods sold}}{\text{Average aggregate value of inventory}}$$

The average aggregate value of inventory is the total value (at cost) of all items being held in inventory, including such things as raw materials, work-in-process (WIP), and finished goods. It is computed by summing, for all individual inventory items, the product of the average number of units on hand in inventory at any one time multiplied by the unit value:

$$\text{Average aggregate value of inventory} = \sum (\text{average inventory for item } i) \times (\text{unit value item } i)$$

The cost of goods sold is only for finished goods, valued at cost, not the final sale price (which might include discounts or markups).

Every time product items are sold that are equal to the average amount of money that was invested in those items, then the inventory has been turned. An item whose inventory is sold (i.e., turns over) once a year has higher holding costs (for rent, utilities, insurance, theft, etc.) than one that turns over twice, three times, or more in that same time period. For example, if a firm that sells products that cost \$10,000 in a year has a total revenue from the sale of these products of \$15,000, the gross profit is \$5000. However, suppose instead the company only purchased \$5000 worth of product at the first of the year, and then just before running out of stock, it bought an additional \$5000 of product with part of the revenues from selling the first batch. The company still invested \$10,000 in products and made revenues of \$15,000, but only on an investment of \$5000. Which strategy is better—making \$5000 gross profit on an investment of \$10,000 or \$5000? It is better to invest the smaller amount; with a \$5000 investment the company has freed up \$5000 for part of the year to invest in other things it could make a profit on, and it has reduced its holding costs. However, the trick is to invest the minimum amount possible in products and reorder at just the right time to avoid stockouts. This is why a company with good supply chain management has more inventory turns than a company that does not.

A poor, or comparatively low, inventory turnover indicates that a large amount of inventory is required to satisfy demand. In general, a good (or poor) number of inventory turns is relative to what is being achieved at various stages across a company and what the industry norm is. Only comparisons of inventory turns for companies within the same industry are meaningful. Comparing a supermarket to a car dealer is not meaningful; a supermarket sells fast-moving products so its inventory turns will be higher than a car dealer that sells slow-moving items. In the 1980s, inventory turns for many manufacturing companies were less than five; however, the advent of lean production (see Chapter 16) and the increased focus on quality management and supply chain management have increased inventory turns in much of the manufacturing sector to about six turns per year for a typical company. Although this seems like a small change, it still represents a significant decrease in costs and increase in profits. On the other hand, a typical computer company or grocery store will have 12 turns or more per year.

Toyota had inventory turns in the 60s in the 1980s when its supply chain was mostly in Japan, but this has fallen to between 10 and 12 in recent years as it has expanded globally

Along the Supply Chain

Amazon Leader Among Top-Ten Supply Chains

Bloomberg/Getty Images, Inc.

In Gartner Inc.'s annual "Supply Chain Top 25" report in 2015, Amazon was ranked first followed in the top ten by retail and manufacturing giants McDonald's, Unilever, Intel, Inditex, Cisco Systems, H&M, Samsung, Colgate-Palmolive, and Nike. Perennial first place supply chain company, Apple, and top-five company, Proctor & Gamble, were placed in a new category, "Supply Chain Masters," recognizing companies that have consistently been among the top five supply chains for at least seven out of the past ten years. The report identifies the manufacturers and retailers that exhibit superior supply chain capabilities and performance based on a score derived from supply chain financial metrics—three-year weighted return on assets, three-year weighted revenue growth, and inventory turns—plus a survey of supply chain professionals, and Gartner's analysts' opinions. Among the top 25 companies, Amazon's overall score was only about 2% higher than second-ranked McDonald's. For the three metrics Gartner uses to develop its scores, Amazon had zero weighted average return on assets due to large investments in future products and services; the eighth highest inventory turns (8.7 compared to second-ranked McDonald's 157.3); and the highest revenue growth (21.7% compared to Qualcomm, ranked nineteenth at 17.8%), which is the highest weighted score metric. Amazon's 8.7 inventory compared to McDonald's 157.3 is impressive given that McDonald's sells a huge number of food items on a daily basis, while Amazon sells a massive variety of consumer products.

In its ranking report Gartner cited three recent trends among the top-ranked companies—bimodal supply chain strategies, increased customer intimacy, and emerging digital business models. It defines a bimodal strategy as one where companies will devote as much time to growing and innovating as they will streamlining and promotion efficiency, which promotes flexibility and growth. It sees companies focusing on the customer experience within the supply chain as a top priority, as well as companies leveraging digital capabilities to support new business models. In addition, most of the top-25 companies are product and supply chain innovators who have successfully introduced new products and features and that have successfully been able to improve the resiliency of their global supply chains to mitigate the risk of supply and demand disruptions, such as natural disasters and catastrophes. Supply chain leaders also streamline their supply chains by simplifying their products lines and eliminating less profitable products. These leaders also eliminate infrequently used product features, service offerings, distribution network capacity, and supply chain layers that do not add sufficient value to customers. All of the top supply chain companies have forward-thinking, cost-saving programs for environmental, social, and labor sustainability throughout their global supply chains.

Identify some of the other companies on Gartner Inc.'s Top 25 list and describe their similarities with other companies on the list.

Sources: Based on Stan Aronow, Michael Burkett, Kimberly Nilles, and Jim Romano, "The Gartner Supply Chain Top 25 for 2015," www.gartner.com, (May 13, 2015).

and the complexities of its supply chain have increased accordingly. High-tech companies typically have around six turns per year, but Dell has achieved inventory turns greater than 50, attesting to its supply chain success. On the other hand, pharmaceutical giant Pfizer has had recent inventory turns as low as 1.5. However, this does not mean that Pfizer is doing poorly financially—it has been very profitable. It does mean that perhaps it could manage its supply chain more efficiently.

Another commonly used KPI is days (or weeks) of supply. This is a measure of how many days (or weeks) of inventory is available at any point in time. It is computed by dividing the aggregate average value of inventory by the daily (or weekly) cost of goods sold,

$$\text{Days of supply} = \frac{\text{Average aggregate value of inventory}}{(\text{Cost of goods sold})/(365 \text{ days})}$$

Automotive companies typically carry about 60 days of finished goods supply.

Another frequently used KPI is **fill rate**. Fill rates are the fraction of orders placed by a customer with a supplier distribution center or warehouse that are filled within a specific period of time, typically one day. High fill rates indicate that inventory is moving from the supplier to the customer at a faster rate, which thereby reduces inventory at the distribution center. For example, Nabisco's fill rate for its Planter's peanuts at Wegman's grocery store chain is 97%, meaning that when the store places an order with the Nabisco distribution center, 97% of the time it is filled within one day.

Fill rate The fraction of orders filled by a distribution center within a specific time period.

EXAMPLE 10.1 | Computing Key Performance Indicators

The Tomahawk Motorcycle Company manufactures motorcycles. Last year the cost of goods sold was $425 million. The company had the following average value of production materials and parts, work-in-process, and finished goods inventory:

Production materials and parts	$ 4,629,000
Work-in-process	17,465,000
Finished goods	12,322,000
Total average aggregate value of inventory	$34,416,000

The company wants to know the number of inventory turns and days of supply being held in inventory.

Solution:

$$\text{Inventory turns} = \frac{\text{Cost of goods sold}}{\text{Average aggregate value of inventory}}$$

$$= \frac{\$425{,}000{,}000}{34{,}416{,}000}$$

$$\text{Inventory turns} = 12.3$$

$$\text{Days of supply} = \frac{\text{Average aggregate value of inventory}}{(\text{Cost of goods sold})/(365 \text{ days})}$$

$$= \frac{\$34{,}416{,}000}{(425{,}000{,}000)/(365)}$$

$$\text{Days of supply} = 29.6$$

Process Control

In Chapter 2, "Quality Management," we talked about various techniques that could be employed to monitor product and service quality. One of the more powerful techniques we presented was statistical process control, the subject of Chapter 3. Although we tend to think that process control is used to monitor and control quality for manufacturing operations, it can also be used to monitor and control any of the processes in the supply chain. If products are defective, then the effects are obvious. However, other problems along the supply chain that create uncertainty and variability are most often caused by errors. If deliveries are missed or are late, if orders are lost, if errors are made in filling out forms, if items with high obsolescence rates (like PCs) or perishable items are allowed to stay too long in inventory, if demand forecast errors are made, if plant and equipment are not properly maintained, then the supply chain can be disrupted, thereby reducing supply chain performance. Thus, at any stage in the process, statistical process control charts can be used to monitor process performance.

SCOR

Supply chain operations reference (SCOR) A cross-industry supply chain diagnostic tool maintained by the Supply Chain Council.

The **supply chain operations reference (SCOR)** model is a supply chain diagnostic tool that provides a cross-industry standard for supply chain management. It was developed by the Supply Chain Council, a global not-for-profit trade association organized in 1996 with membership open to companies interested in improving supply chain efficiency primarily through the use of SCOR. The Supply Chain Council (SCC) has almost 1,000 corporate members around the world, including many Fortune 500 companies. In 2014 the SCC merged with the

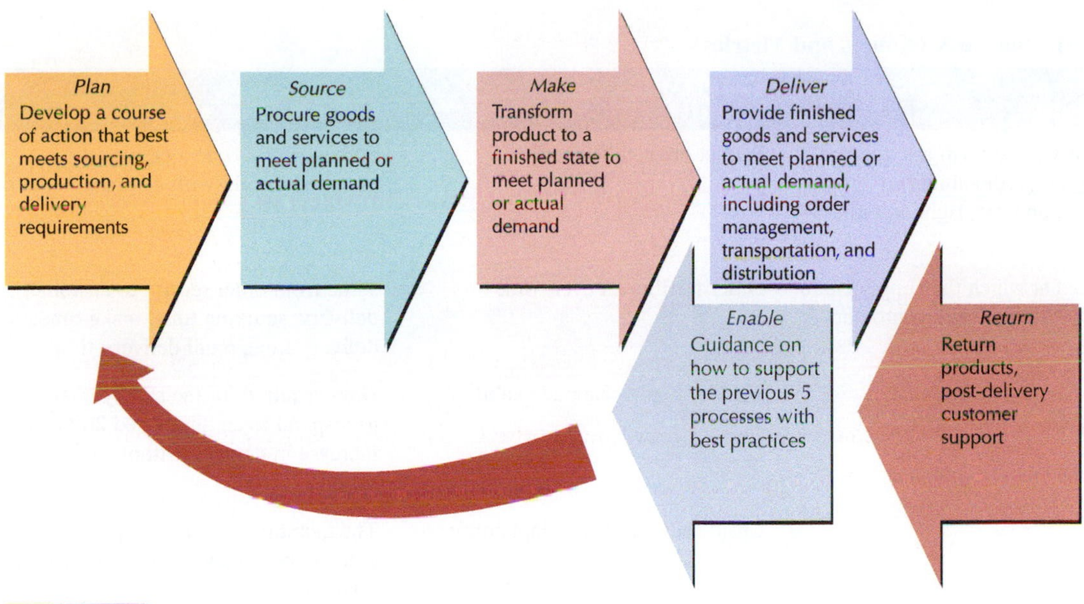

FIGURE 10.7 **SCOR Level Processes**

American Production and Inventory Control Society (APICS), with 43,000 members, which maintains the SCOR model.

The purpose of the SCOR model is to define a company's current supply chain processes, quantify the performance of similar companies to establish targets to achieve "best-in-class" performance, and identify the practices and software solutions that will yield "best in class" performance. It is organized around a set of six primary management processes—plan, source, make, deliver, return, and enable as shown in Figure 10.7. These processes provide a common set of definitions, or building blocks, that SCOR uses to describe any supply chain, from simple to complex. This allows supply chains for different companies to be linked and compared. The closed loop nature of these processes is similar to the Deming Wheel (PDCA cycle) and the Six Sigma DMAIC steps (chapter 2).

A primary feature of the SCOR model is a set of five performance attributes of a supply chain—reliability, responsiveness, agility, costs, and asset management—that enable it to be analyzed and evaluated against other competing supply chains. Reliability, responsiveness, and agility are more customer-focused attributes while cost and asset management are more internally focused. Associated with each performance attribute are various quantitative metrics that an organization can calculate to determine how well its supply chain is performing within its industry. There are over 250 SCOR metrics organized within a three tiered hierarchy according to level 1 (strategic), level 2 (processes), and level 3 (diagnostic). Table 10.2 summarizes and defines the SCOR performance attributes and shows the level 1 metrics for each attribute with their description.

These metrics can be used to develop a "SCOR mark" that benchmarks a company's current supply chain performance for different processes against its industry competitors' metrics. The company then projects the level of metrics it needs to be on a par with its competitors, to have an advantage over its competitors, or to be superior. The value associated with these measured improvements in performance is then projected for the different performance attributes. For example, a company may know that the industry "median fill rate (the percentage of orders shipped from stock within 24 hours of order receipt)" is 90% and the industry best-in-class performance is 99%. The company has determined that its current fill rate is 65%, and that a fill rate of 90% will give it parity with its competitors, a 95% fill rate will give it an advantage, and a 99% fill rate will make it superior to most of its competitors. The company may then project that the improvement in its fill rate plus improvements in the other supply chain reliability attributes (i.e., delivery performance and perfect order fulfillment) will increase supply chain value by $10 million in revenue. SCOR provides a framework not only for measuring performance but for diagnosing problems and identifying practices and solutions that will enable a company to achieve its competitive performance objectives.

TABLE 10.2 SCOR Performance Attributes and Metrics

PERFORMANCE ATTRIBUTE	DEFINITION	STRATEGIC METRICS	DEFINITION
Reliability	The ability to perform as expected, focusing on predictability of processes; on time, right amount, quality	Perfect order fulfillment	Percentage of orders delivered on time and in full, with no errors
Responsiveness	The speed at which the supply chain provides products to the cutomer	Order fulfillment cycle time	Time from order receipt to customer delivery, sourcing time, make time, delivery time, retail delivery time
Agility	Responsiveness to external influences and marketplace changes	Upside supply chain adaptability	Days required for the supply chain to respond to an unplanned 20% increase in demand without a cost penalty
		Upside supply chain adaptability	The quantity of increased production that can be achieved and sustained in 30 days
		Downside supply chain adaptability	The reduction in quantities ordered 30 days pror to delievry with no cost penalties
		Overall value at risk (VAR)	measures the impact of supply chain disruptions; the sum of the probablity of risk events multiplied by the financial impact of the events for all supply chain processes
Cost	The cost of operating the supply chain including labor, material, transportation, and management	Total cost to serve	The direct and indirect costs to plan source, make and deliver product and services, including material and labor
Asset management efficiency	Efficiently utilizing assets including inventory reduction and in-sourcing vs. outsourcing	Cash-to-cash cycle time	Inventory days of supply (WIP)
		Return on fixed assets	Fixed supply chain asset value, supply chain revenue
		Return on working capital	Accounts payable, receivable, and inventory

SCOR also has a special application called GreenSCOR designed to address environmental sustainability efforts. The SCOR framework provides a structure for measuring environmental performance and where it can be improved using the following strategic metrics: carbon emissions, air pollutant emissions, liquid waste, solid waste, and percent recycled waste.

Summary

Supply chain management is one of the most important strategic aspects of operations management because it encompasses so many related functions. Who to buy materials from, how to transport goods and services, and how to distribute them in the most cost-effective, timely manner constitutes much of an organization's strategic planning. Contracting with the wrong supplier can result in poor-quality materials and late deliveries. Selecting the wrong mode of transportation or carrier can mean late deliveries to customers that will require high, costly inventories to offset. All of these critical functional supply chain decisions are complicated by the fact that they often occur in a global environment within cultures and markets at a distance and much different from those in the United States.

Key Terms

bullwhip effect Occurs when demand variability is magnified at various upstream points in the supply chain.

collaborative planning, forecasting, and replenishment (CPFR) A process for two or more companies in a supply chain to synchronize their demand forecasts into a single plan to meet customer demand.

e-business The replacement of physical business processes with electronic ones.

electronic data interchange (EDI) A computer-to-computer exchange of business documents.

enterprise resource planning (ERP) Software that connects the components of a company by sharing and organizing information and data.

fill rate The fraction of orders placed by a customer with a supplier distribution center or warehouse that are filled within 24 hours.

inventory Insurance against supply chain uncertainty held between supply chain stages.

inventory turns A supply chain performance metric computed by dividing the cost of goods sold by the average aggregate value of inventory.

key performance indicator (KPI) A metric used to measure supply chain performance.

point-of-sale data Computer records of sales at retail sites.

procurement Purchasing goods and services from suppliers.

radio frequency identification (RFID) Radio waves used to transfer data, like an electronic product code, between an item with an embedded microchip and a reader.

risk pooling An approach to risk management that aggregates risk to reduce its impact.

SCOR The supply chain operations reference model; a diagnostic tool that provides a cross-industry standard for supply chain management.

supply chain The facilities, functions, and activities involved in producing and delivering a product or service from suppliers (and their suppliers) to customers (and their customers).

supply chain management (SCM) Managing the flow of information through the supply chain in order to attain the level of synchronization that will make it more responsive to customer needs while lowering costs.

sustainability Meeting present needs without compromising the ability of future generations to meet their needs.

value The creation of value for the customer is an important aspect of supply chain management.

value chain A more contemporary name for a supply chain.

Key Formulas

$$\text{Inventory turns} = \frac{\text{Cost of goods sold}}{\text{Average aggregate value of inventory}}$$

$$\text{Days of supply} = \frac{\text{Average aggregate value of inventory}}{(\text{Cost of goods sold})/(365\text{ days})}$$

Solved Problem

WileyPLUS

Inventory Turns and Days of Supply

A manufacturing company had the following average raw materials, work-in-process, and finished goods inventory on hand at any one time during the past year.

RAW MATERIALS	AVERAGE INVENTORY	UNIT COST
1	135	$26.50
2	67	18.20
3	210	9.75
4	97	31.25
WORK-IN-PROCESS		
5	40	$165.00
6	65	230.00

FINISHED GOODS	AVERAGE INVENTORY	UNIT COST
7	25	$ 670.00
8	18	1050.00
9	35	520.00

The company's cost of goods sold last year was $2.73 million, and it operates 365 days per year.

Determine the company's inventory turns and days of supply.

Solution

Step 1. Compute the average aggregate value of inventory.

Raw materials: (135)($26.50) = $3,577.50
(67)(18.20) = 1,219.40
(210)(9.75) = 2,047.50

$$(97)(31.25) = 3{,}031.25$$
$$\text{Work-in-process: } (40)(165) = 6{,}600.00$$
$$(65)(230) = 14{,}950.00$$
$$\text{Finished goods: } (25)(670) = 16{,}750.00$$
$$(18)(1050) = 18{,}900.00$$
$$(35)(520) = 18{,}200.00$$
$$\text{Total } \$85{,}275.65$$

Step 2. Compute inventory turns.

$$\text{Inventory turns} = \frac{\text{Cost of good sold}}{\text{Average aggregate value of inventory}} = \frac{2{,}730{,}000}{85{,}275.65} = 32$$

Step 3. Compute days of supply.

$$\text{Days of supply} = \frac{\text{Average aggregate value of inventory}}{(\text{cost of goods sold})/(365)} = \frac{85{,}275.65}{(2{,}730{,}000)/(365)} = 11.4 \text{ days}$$

Questions

10.1. Compare the supply chains, in general terms, for McDonald's and for Toyota.

10.2. Define the strategic goals of supply chain management, and indicate how each element of a supply chain (purchasing, production, inventory, and transportation and distribution) affects these goals.

10.3. Identify three service businesses in your community and describe their supply chains.

10.4. Discuss, in general, the differences in the supply chains of service providers and manufacturing companies.

10.5. Describe how a business you are familiar with uses IT enablers in its supply chain management.

10.6. Select a company and determine the type of suppliers it has, then indicate the criteria that you think the company might use to evaluate and select suppliers.

10.7. Locate an e-marketplace site on the Internet and describe it and the type of producers and suppliers it connects.

10.8. Explore the website of an ERP provider and describe the services that it indicates it provides.

10.9. *Supply Chain Management Review* is a trade magazine with articles that include many examples of supply chain management at various companies. Research an article from *Supply Chain Management Review* and write a brief paper on a company reporting on its supply chain activities similar to the "Along the Supply Chain" boxes in this chapter.

10.10. Many websites and trade magazines focusing on supply chain management include numerous articles reporting on specific companies' experiences with different aspects of supply chain management. Using the Internet, find a magazine or website article dealing with transportation and distribution, and write a brief paper similar to the "Along the Supply Chain" boxes in this chapter.

10.11. Several automobile manufacturers have programs for "build-to-order" cars. Identify an auto company that has a BTO program and describe what it entails. Contrast the BTO program of this manufacturer with a company experienced in BTO production like Dell Computers. Discuss the differences in the supply chains between these companies that might make BTO production more difficult for an auto manufacturer.

10.12. Explain why radio frequency identification (RFID) offers enhanced opportunities for security in global transportation and distribution, and how this, in turn, could improve supply chain efficiency.

10.13. Walmart is one of the leaders in promoting the development and use of RFID and electronic product codes. Explain how Walmart uses RFID, why Walmart wants its suppliers to adopt RFID, and what obstacles have been shown to exist for this new technology.

10.14. It has been suggested that SCOR might serve as an international supply chain certification tool much like ISO certification for quality. Explain how you think SCOR might be used as a certification tool.

10.15. Describe the supply chain for your university or college. Who are the suppliers, producers, and distributors in this supply chain? Are there different supplier tiers? How would you evaluate this supply chain? Does inventory even exist, and if it does, what form does it take?

10.16. What is the bullwhip effect and what are its causes?

10.17. Identify and discuss the types of risk a company with a global supply chain might encounter with its overseas suppliers.

10.18. What are some of the ways companies manage risks in a global supply chain?

10.19. Identify the quality problems that a company might encounter with the following global supply chain components:

- **a.** Oversesas suppliers
- **b.** Container ships
- **c.** Transportation
- **d.** Packaging
- **e.** Distribution
- **f.** Warehousing

10.20. Identify a business that employs EDI in its supply chain management and describe how it is used.

10.21. Surf the Internet and identify a company with a strong commitment to sustainability and discuss its green initiatives.

10.22. What green initiatives have recently been taken at your school? What additional green initiatives do you think your school should undertake? Discuss whether you think the initiatives that have been taken have been for cosmetic purposes for public consumption or have resulted in real quality improvement. Discuss whether you think they have been cost-effective.

10.23. Discuss how sustainability might fit in with a company's quality management program.

10.24. What are some of the unique sustainability challenges that a company might face in a global supply chain?

10.25. What type of sustainability issues might a U.S. company face with a supplier in China? Mexico?

10.26. How are companies able to save money through their sustainability efforts?

10.27. Using the Internet, identify three U.S. companies with a strong reputation for sustainability. Describe the common characteristics of their sustainability efforts.

10.28. How do sustainability initiatives differ between a service provider and a manufacturing firm?

10.29. Identify some applications of barcode technology at your school. Would switching to RFID technology for any of these applications be cost-effective?

10.30. Select a local business and discuss how it is applying any auto-ID technologies.

10.31. Describe the differences between a traditional supply chain for a physical product and a *digital supply chain*. Identify a company that employs a digital supply chain and describe the processes involved.

10.32. Identify some of the common characteristics among the companies in *Gartner's* annual "Supply Chain Top 25."

10.33. How does *Gartner's* compute the scores that it uses to rank companies in its annual "Supply Chain Top 25"?

10.34. What companies that have typically been in *Gartner's* annual "Supply Chain Top 25" in the past have recently dropped out, and why?

10.35. Select a service provider and a manufacturer from *Gartner's* annual "Supply Chain Top 25" and write a brief profile comparing the supply chain attributes of each company.

Problems

WileyPLUS

10.1. The Fizer Drug Company manufactures over-the-counter and prescription drugs. Last year the company's cost of goods sold was $470 million. It carried average raw material inventory of $17.5 million, average work-in-process of $9.3 million, and average finished goods inventory of $6.4 million. The company operates 365 days per year. Compute the company's inventory turns and days of supply for last year.

10.2. Tigongzhe Company is a Chinese supplier of smartphone camera parts to manufacturing companies in China that assemble smartphones. Last year it had cost of goods sold of $63.7 million and the following average value of production materials and parts, work-in-process, and finished goods inventory:

Production materials and parts	$1,216,000
Work-in-process	6,490,000
Finished goods	4,336,000

Determine the company's inventory turns and days of supply being held in inventory.

10.3. The Ashton Furniture Company manufactures coffee tables and chests of drawers. Last year the company's cost of goods sold was $3,700,000, and it carried inventory of oak, pine, stains, joiners, and brass fixtures, work-in-process of furniture frames, drawers and wood panels, and finished chests and coffee tables. Its average inventory levels for a 52-week business year were as follows.

RAW MATERIALS	AVERAGE INVENTORY	UNIT COST
Oak	8000	$6.00
Pine	4500	4.00
Brass fixtures	1200	8.00
Stains	3000	2.00
Joiners	900	1.00
WORK-IN-PROCESS		
Frames	200	$30
Drawers	400	10
Panels	600	50
Chests	120	110
Tables	90	90
FINISHED GOODS		
Chests	300	$500
Coffee tables	200	350

Determine the number of inventory turns and the days of supply for the furniture company.

10.4. Barington Mills manufactures denim cloth from two primary raw materials, cotton and dye. Work-in-process includes lapped cotton, spun yarn, and undyed cloth, while finished goods includes three grades of dyed cloth. The average inventory amounts on hand at any one time last year and the unit costs are as follows.

RAW MATERIALS	AVERAGE INVENTORY	UNIT COST
Cotton	70,000 lb.	$2.75
Dye	125,000 gal.	5.00
WORK-IN-PROCESS		
Lapped cotton	2000 rolls	$10.50
Spun yarn	5000 spools	6.75
Undyed cloth	500 rolls	26.10
FINISHED GOODS		
Grade 1 cloth	250 rolls	$65.00
Grade 2 cloth	190 rolls	80.00
Grade 3 cloth	310 rolls	105.00

The company operates 50 weeks per year, and its cost of goods sold for the past year was $17.5 million.

Determine the company's inventory turns and weeks of supply.

10.5. House Max Builders constructs modular homes, and last year their cost of goods sold was $18,500,000. It operates 50 weeks per year. The company has the following inventory of raw materials, work-in-process, and finished goods.

RAW MATERIALS	AVERAGE INVENTORY	UNIT COST
1	7200	$8.50
2	4500	7.20
3	3200	15.40
4	4800	13.70
5	6900	10.50
WORK-IN-PROCESS	**AVERAGE INVENTORY**	**UNIT COST**
A	100	$16,200
B	70	13,500
C	60	6,100
D	35	14,400
FINISHED GOODS		
Model X	20	$78,700
Model Y	10	65,300
Model Z	10	86,000

Determine the number of inventory turns and the days of supply for House Max.

10.6. The PM Computer Company makes build-to-order (BTO) computers at its distribution center year round. The following table shows the average value (in $ millions) of component parts, work-in-process, and finished computers at the DC for the past four years.

	YEAR			
	1	2	3	4
Component parts	$20.5	27.8	30.8	37.3
Work-in-process	4.2	6.7	7.1	9.5
Finished computers	3.6	7.2	8.6	10.1
Cost of goods sold	226.0	345.0	517.0	680.0

a. Determine the number of inventory turns and the days of supply for each year.

b. As the company has grown, does it appear that the company's supply chain performance has improved? Explain your answer.

c. If the company wants to improve its supply chain performance, what items should it focus on? Why?

10.7. Delph Manufacturing Company is going to purchase an auto parts component from one of two competing suppliers. Delph is going to base its decision, in part, on the supply chain performance of the two suppliers. The company has obtained the following data for average raw materials, work-in-process, and finished goods inventory value, as well as cost of goods sold for the suppliers.

	SUPPLIER 1	SUPPLIER 2
Cost of goods sold	$8,360,000	$14,800,000
Raw materials	275,000	870,000
Work-in-process	62,000	550,000
Finished goods	33,000	180,000

Each company operates 52 weeks per year.

Determine which supplier has the best supply chain performance according to inventory turns and weeks of supply. What other factors would the company likely take into account in selecting a supplier?

10.8. Solve Problem 3.8 in Chapter 3 to construct a *c*-chart for monitoring invoice errors at Telecom Manufacturing Company.

10.9. Solve Problem 3.9 in Chapter 3 to construct a *c*-chart to monitor late order deliveries at the National Bread Company.

10.10. Solve Problem 3.10 in Chapter 3 to construct a *p*-chart to monitor order problems at BooksCDs.com

10.11. Solve Problem 3.11 in Chapter 3 to construct an *x*-chart in conjunction with an *R*-chart for order fulfillment lead time at Valtec Electronics.

10.12. Solve Problem 3.36 in Chapter 3 to construct an *x*-bar chart in conjunction with an *R*-chart for delivery time at the Great Outdoors Clothing Company.

Case Problem

Case Problem 10.1 Somerset Furniture Company's Global Supply Chain

The Somerset Furniture Company was founded in 1957 in Randolph County, Virginia. It traditionally has manufactured large, medium-priced, ornate residential wood furniture such as bedroom cabinets and chests of drawers, and dining and living room cabinets, tables, and chairs, at its primary manufacturing facility in Randolph County. It employed a marketing strategy of rapidly introducing new product lines every few years. Over time it developed a reputation for high-quality, affordable furniture for a growing U.S. market of homeowners during the last half of the twentieth century. The company was generally considered to be an innovator in furniture manufacturing processes and in applying QM principles to furniture manufacturing. However, in the mid-1990s, faced with increasing foreign competition, high labor rates, and diminishing profits, the Somerset Company contracted to outsource several of its furniture product lines to manufacturers in China, simultaneously reducing the size of its own domestic manufacturing facility and labor force. This initially proved to be very successful in reducing costs and increasing profits, and by 2000 Somerset had decided to close its entire manufacturing facility in the United States and outsource all of its manufacturing to suppliers in China. The company set up a global supply chain in which it arranges for shipments of wood from the United States and South America to manufacturing plants in China where the furniture products are produced by hand by Chinese laborers. The Chinese manufacturers are very good at copying the Somerset ornate furniture designs by hand without expensive machinery. The average labor rate for furniture manufacturing in the United States is between $9 and $20 per hour, whereas the average labor rate for furniture manufacturers in China is $2 per day. Finished furniture products are shipped by container ship from Hong Kong or Shanghai to Norfolk, Virginia, where the containers are then transported by truck to Somerset warehouses in Randolph County. Somerset supplies retail furniture stores from this location. All hardware is installed on the furniture at the retail stores in order to reduce the possibility of damage during transport.

The order processing and fulfillment system for Somerset includes a great deal of variability, as do all aspects of the company's global supply chain. The company processes orders weekly and biweekly. In the United States it takes between 12 and 25 days for the company to develop a purchase order and release it to its Chinese suppliers. This process includes developing a demand forecast, which may take from one to two weeks; converting the forecast to an order fulfillment schedule; and then developing a purchase order. Once the purchase order is processed overseas by the Chinese manufacturer, which may take 10 to 20 days depending on the number of changes made, the manufacturing process requires approximately 60 days. The foreign logistics process requires finished furniture items to be transported from the manufacturing plants to the Chinese ports, which can take up to several weeks depending on trucking availability and schedules. An additional 5 to 10 days are required to arrange for shipping containers and prepare the paperwork for shipping. However, shipments can then wait from one day to a week for enough available containers. There are often too few containers at the ports because large U.S. importers, like "Big W" discount stores in the United States, reserve all the available containers for their continual stream of overseas shipments. Once enough containers are secured, it requires three to six days to optimally load the containers. The furniture pieces often have odd dimensions that result in partially filled containers. Since 9/11, random security checks of containers can delay shipment another one to three weeks, and smaller companies like Somerset are more likely to be extensively checked than larger shippers like Big W, whom the port authorities don't want upset with delays. The trip overseas to Norfolk requires 28 days. Once in port, one to two weeks are required for a shipment to clear customs and to be loaded onto trucks for transport to Somerset's warehouse in Randolph County, which takes from one to three days. When a shipment arrives, it can take from one day up to a month to unload a trailer, depending on the urgency to fill store orders from the shipment.

Because of supply chain variability, shipments can be off schedule (i.e., delayed) by as much as 40%. The company prides itself on customer service and fears that late deliveries to its customers would harm its credibility and result in cancelled orders and lost customers. At the same time, keeping excess inventories on hand in its warehouses is very costly, and since Somerset redesigns its product lines so frequently a real problem of product obsolescence arises if products remain in inventory very long. Somerset has also been experiencing quality problems. The Chinese suppliers employ quality auditors who rotate among plants every few weeks to perform quality control tests and monitor the manufacturing process for several days before visiting another plant. However, store and individual customer complaints have forced Somerset to inspect virtually every piece of furniture it receives from overseas before forwarding it to stores. In some instances, customers have complained that tables and chairs creak noisily during use. Somerset subsequently discovered that the creaking was caused by humidity differences between the locations of the Chinese plants and the geographic areas in the United States where their furniture is sold. Replacement parts (like cabinet doors or table legs) are difficult to secure because the Chinese suppliers will only agree to provide replacement parts for the product lines currently in production. However, Somerset provides a one-year warranty on its furniture, which means that they often need parts for a product no longer being produced. Even when replacement parts were available, it took too long to get them from the supplier in order to provide timely customer service.

Although Somerset was initially successful at outsourcing its manufacturing process on a limited basis, it has since discovered, as many companies do, that outsourcing can result in a host of supply chain problems, as indicated. Discuss Somerset's global supply chain and possible remedies for its supply chain problems, including strategic and tactical changes that might improve the company's supply chain performance, reduce system variability, and improve quality and customer service.

References

Chopra, S. and P. Meindl. *Supply Chain Management*, 2nd ed. Upper Saddle River, N.J.: Prentice Hall, 2004.

Christopher, M. *Logistics and Supply Chain Management*, 2nd ed. Upper Saddle River, N.J.: Prentice Hall, 1998.

Dornier, P., R. Ernst, M. Fender and P. Kouvelis. *Global Operations and Logistics*. New York: John Wiley & Sons, 1998.

Schecter, D. and Gordon S. *Delivering the Goods: The Art of Managing Your Supply Chain*. New York: John Wiley & Sons, 2002.

CHAPTER 11

Global Supply Chain Procurement and Distribution

REUTERS/Bobby Yip/ReutersPictures

LEARNING OBJECTIVES

After reading this chapter, you will be able to:

- Discuss outsourcing as a strategic decision.
- Explain the basic elements of procurement, e-procurement, and spend analysis.
- Describe distribution strategies, systems, and processes.
- Assess the advantages and disadvantages of different modes of transportation.
- Discuss issues and trends in the global supply chain.

China and Apple's Global Supply Chain

Apple's overall company success is in large part attributable to outsourcing its manufacturing processes to Asia, and particularly China. Over 330 of Apple's almost 750 global suppliers, and 14 out of 18 Apple's final assembly facilities, are in China. These assembly plants include seven Foxconn plants, a Taiwanese electronics manufacturing company with over a million employees that is the principal manufacturer of Apple products and components. A major reason for Apple's reliance on Chinese-based suppliers is low wage rates; the average wage rate for Apple workers in these Chinese plants ranges from $1.50 to $2.50 per hour, low by U.S. and European standards but high for Chinese workers. This low wage enables Apple to capture almost 60% of the value of an iPhone, despite the fact that its manufacture is entirely outsourced. The labor costs in China account for the smallest share, around 2%, or, for example, $12 for an iPhone that sells for $600. Although both Apple and Foxconn rely on an army of Chinese workers working 60-hour weeks to meet demand, the cost of Chinese labor in manufacturing is relatively insignificant in Apple's overall profitability.

Another critical part of Apple's supply chain is logistics and distribution, moving components to assembly factories in China and then finished iPhones from these factories in China to its customers, all of which must be done quickly, on schedule, and seamlessly while achieving the lowest cost possible. The distribution process of a new iPhone model begins months before it is formally launched; Apple first pre-books and coordinates flights and trucks to move components from suppliers to assembly plants in China. Apple company representatives from sales, marketing, operations, and finance collaborate to forecast how many devices the company expects to sell. The accuracy of this forecast is critical to knowing how many component parts to order and ship, and how much transport to book. Once a forecast is made, millions of iPhones are manufactured and remain in China while Apple's software team at its headquarters in Cupertino, California, finishes work on the iOS software that runs on the device, and when the software is finished, it is loaded on the smartphones. Before a new iPhone model is formally introduced, it is shipped to distribution centers and retail stores around the world so the new model is in stores everywhere at exactly the same time.

Apple primarily ships its iPhones to the United States using FedEx Boeing 777s, which can make the non-stop flight from China to the main U.S. hub in Memphis, Tennessee, in about 15 hours. The planes can each carry about 450,000 iPhones and cost about $250,000 to charter. The iPhone's high price and light weight, and the ability to pack many devices into air shipments, enable Apple to maximize profit margins despite the relative high cost of air freight, instead of using sea cargo as was historically the case with consumer electronics. Once the iPhone goes on sale the procedure changes, and Apple manages online orders from customers for specific colors and memory. Online orders are received directly at the supplier factories in China, where workers customize the smartphones and put them on pallets with others destined for customers in a similar part of the world. Shipping online orders directly from the factory to the customer, and thus avoiding the phones sitting in warehouses, eliminates inventory costs. Apple continuously monitors sales from its retail stores, website, and third-party sellers (like Best Buy), and reallocates phones to where demand is strongest. For example, smartphones coming off the assembly line in China originally destined for retail stores in Europe could be used to fill a jump in online orders in the United States. Once the initial iPhone launch is over, Apple's supply chain team at the Apple headquarters in California analyzes what went wrong and plans how to improve the process for its next launch.

In this chapter we will learn how companies like Apple and many others manage their global supply chains, including procurement, outsourcing, logistics, and distribution, and doing so in a sustainable manner.

In Chapter 10 we introduced the topic of supply chain management and focused on the strategy and design of supply chains. We discussed the various aspects, components, and implications of supply chain management in a broad context, giving more of a *macro*-view of supply chains. Early in Chapter 10, in Figure 10.3 we identified the primary processes related to supply chain management—the procurement of supply, production, and the distribution of products and services. In this chapter we are going to focus more closely on two of these processes—procurement and distribution, which also includes transportation; this entails a more *micro*-view of supply chains. We will begin with a discussion of procurement, which is the process of obtaining *supply*: the goods and services that are used in the production process (whether it be goods or services).

Supply chains begin with supply at the farthest upstream point in the supply chain, inevitably from raw materials, as was shown in Figure 10.1. Purchased materials have historically accounted for about half of U.S. manufacturing costs, and many manufacturers purchase over half of their parts. Companies want the materials, parts, and services necessary to produce their products to be delivered on time, to be of high quality, and to be low cost, which are the responsibility of their suppliers. If deliveries are late from suppliers, a company will be forced to keep large, costly inventories to keep their own products from being late to their customers. Thus, purchasing goods and services from suppliers, or **procurement**, plays a crucial role in supply chain management.

Procurement The purchase of goods and services from suppliers.

Procurement

A key element in the development of a successful partnership between a company and a supplier is the establishment of linkages. The most important linkage is information flow; companies and suppliers must communicate—about product demand, about costs, about quality, and so on—in order to coordinate their activities. To facilitate communication and the sharing of information, many companies use teams. *Cross-enterprise teams* coordinate processes between a company and its supplier. For example, suppliers may join a company in its product-design process. Instead of a company designing a product and then asking a supplier if it can provide the required part or a company trying to design a product around an existing part, the supplier works with the company in the design process to ensure the most effective design possible. This form of cooperation makes use of the expertise and talents of both parties. It also ensures that quality features will be designed into the product.

On-demand (direct-response) delivery Requires the supplier to deliver goods when demanded by the customer.

Continuous replenishment Supplying orders in a short period of time according to a predetermined schedule.

In an attempt to minimize inventory levels, companies frequently require that their suppliers provide **on-demand**, also referred to as **direct-response**, delivery to support a just-in-time (JIT) or comparable inventory system. In **continuous replenishment**, a company shares real-time demand and inventory data with its suppliers, and goods and services are provided as they are needed. For the supplier, these forms of delivery often mean making more frequent, partial deliveries, instead of the large-batch orders suppliers have traditionally been used to filling. While large-batch orders are easier for the supplier to manage, and less costly, they increase the customer's inventory. They also reduce the customer's flexibility to deal with sudden market changes because of their large investment in inventory. Every part used at Honda's Marysville, Ohio, plant is delivered on a daily basis. Sometimes parts deliveries are required several times a day. This often requires that suppliers move their location to be close to their customer. For example, most of the U.S. suppliers for Honda are within a 150-mile radius of their Marysville, Ohio, assembly plant.

In addition to meeting their customers' demands for quality, lower inventory, and prompt delivery, suppliers are also expected to help their customers lower product cost by lowering the price of its goods and services. These customer demands on its suppliers—high quality, prompt delivery, and lower prices—are potentially very costly to suppliers. Prompt delivery of products and services as they are demanded from its customers may require the supplier to maintain excessive inventories itself. These demands require the supplier to improve its own processes and make its own supply chain more efficient. Suppliers require of their own suppliers what has been required of them—high quality, lower prices, process improvement, and better delivery performance.

Along the Supply Chain

Boeing's Supplier Rating System

Boeing is one of the world's largest aerospace companies, manufacturing commercial jetliners and defense systems, with over 13,000 suppliers in 47 countries with procurement expenditures over $62 billion. Supplier-provided components and assemblies make up more than 60% of the cost of Boeing products. Monitoring and measuring supplier quality are critical to Boeing's competitive success and to meeting customer expectations. To achieve supply chain quality, Boeing uses a supplier evaluation and rating system that tracks performance for products and services monthly with a final rating based on a 12-month rolling average. Their rating system includes five color-coded threshold standards—gold (the best), silver, bronze, yellow, and red (the worst). Within each color-coded standard a supplier is graded in three areas—on-time delivery; a general performance assessment (GPA), which provides a comprehensive assessment of a supplier's management performance; and quality and value. Each of these areas is graded: 5 (gold), 4 (silver), 3 (bronze), 1 (yellow), and 0 (red). For example, if a supplier's quality is bronze, they receive a 3, if their delivery also rates a bronze they receive a 3, and if their GPA is yellow, they receive a 1. The average of these scores is a GPA summary rating of 2.33, and within the rating system, GPA summary scores above 1 and less than 2.8 fall in the yellow category. An overall yellow rating indicates that improvement in supplier performance is needed to meet Boeing's expectations. Alternatively, a gold rating denotes exceptional supplier performance that clearly exceeds expectations, which includes 100% on-time delivery and 100% quality, while a red rating denotes unsatisfactory supplier performance that clearly fails to meet expectations with deliveries less than 90% and quality below 98%. Boeing's rating system helps it make sourcing decisions, monitor supplier performance, and recognize supplier excellence, and it also provides suppliers with valuable feedback that enables them to improve performance. The Aerospace Industries Association has recognized Boeing's rating system as the industry's best supplier rating system.

Discuss how Boeing's supplier rating system might be applied to a service organization, like a hospital or restaurant.

Source: Based on Kirsten Parks and Timothy Connor, "The Way to Engage, An Inside Look at How Boeing's Supplier Rating System Keeps the Aviation Giant Focused on Continuous Improvement," Quality Progress 44 (4) (April 2011), pp. 21–27.

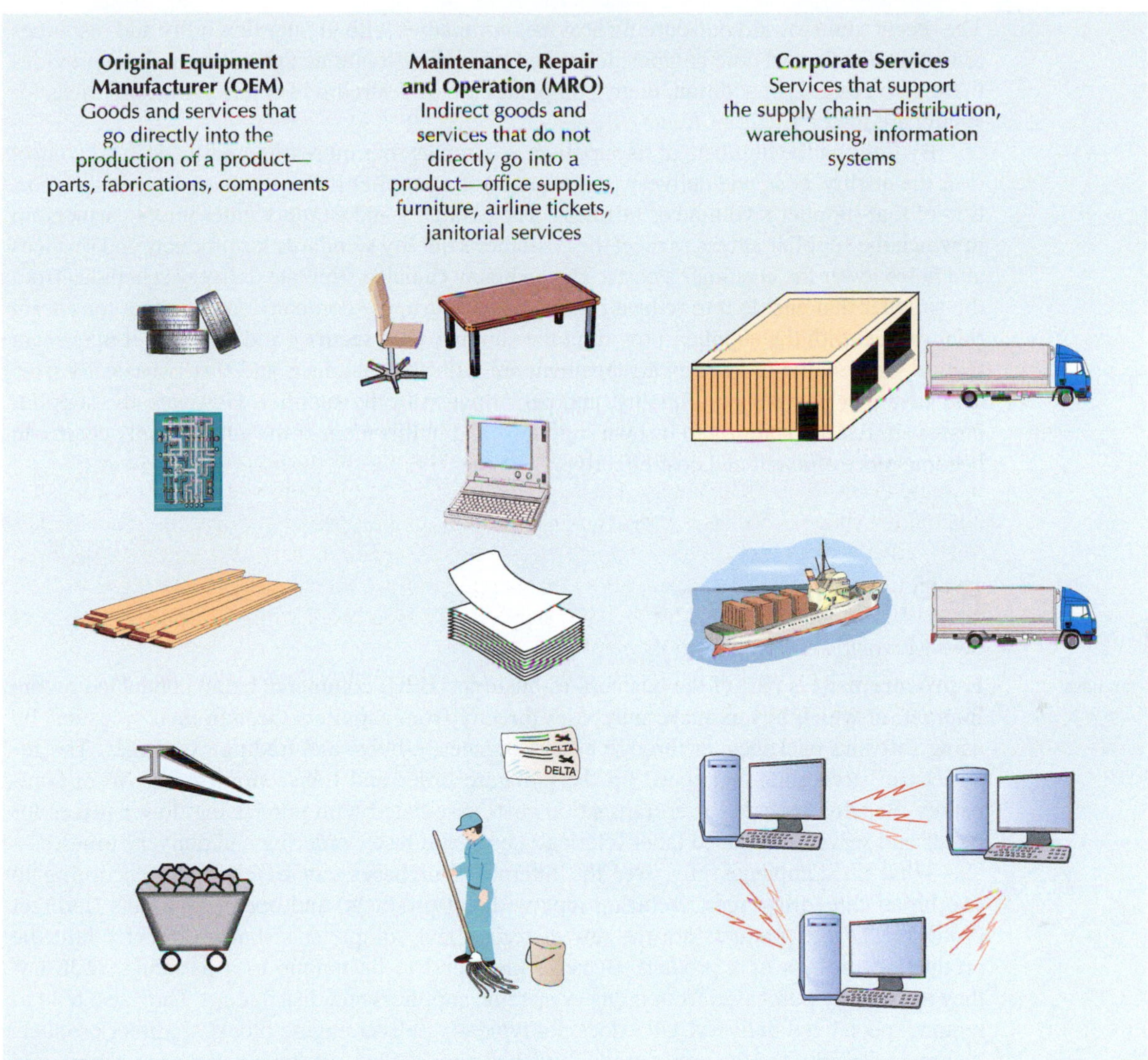

Original Equipment Manufacturer (OEM)
Goods and services that go directly into the production of a product—parts, fabrications, components
Maintenance, Repair and Operation (MRO)
Indirect goods and services that do not directly go into a product—office supplies, furniture, airline tickets, janitorial services
Corporate Services
Services that support the supply chain—distribution, warehousing, information systems
DELTA
DELTA

FIGURE 11.1 Categories of Goods and Services that Companies Outsource

Outsourcing

The selection of suppliers is called **sourcing**: suppliers are literally the "source" of supply. **Outsourcing** is the act of purchasing goods and services that were originally produced in-house from an outside supplier. Outsourcing is nothing new; for decades companies have outsourced as a short-term solution to problems such as an unexpected increase in demand, breakdowns in plants and equipment, testing products, or a temporary lack of plant capacity. However, outsourcing has become a long-term strategic decision instead of simply a short-term tactical one. Companies, especially large multinational companies, are moving more production, service, and inventory functions into the hands of suppliers. Figure 11.1 shows the three major categories of goods and services that companies tend to outsource.

Sourcing The selection of suppliers.

Outsourcing The purchase of goods and services from an outside supplier.

Many companies are outsourcing as a strategic move so that they can focus more on their **core competencies**, that is, what they do best. They let a supplier do what the company is not very good at or doesn't have much experience with, what the supplier is most competent to do. Traditionally, many companies, especially large ones, attempted to own and operate all of their sources of supply and distribution along the supply chain so that they would have direct managerial control and reduce their dependence on potentially unreliable suppliers. They also thought it was more cost effective. However, this stretched these companies' resources thin, and they discovered they did not have the expertise to do everything well. In addition, management of unwieldy, complex supply chains was often difficult. Large inventories were kept throughout the supply chain to buffer against uncertainties and poor management practices.

Core competencies What a company does best.

The recent trend toward outsourcing provides companies with greater flexibility and resources to focus on their own core competencies, and partnering relationships with suppliers provides them with control. In addition, many companies are outsourcing in countries where prices for supply are lower, such as China.

By limiting the numbers of its suppliers, a company has more direct influence and control over the quality, cost, and delivery performance of a supplier if the company has a major portion of that supplier's volume of business. The company and supplier enter into a partnership in which the supplier agrees to meet the customer's quality standards for products and services and helps lower the customer's costs. The company can also stipulate delivery schedules from the supplier that enable it to reduce inventory. In return, the company enters into a long-term relationship with the supplier, providing the supplier with security and stability. It may seem that all the benefits of such an arrangement are with the customer, and that is basically true. The customer dictates cost, quality, and performance to the supplier. However, the supplier passes similar demands on to its own suppliers, and in this manner the entire supply chain can become more efficient and cost-effective.

E-Procurement

E-procurement Direct purchase from suppliers over the Internet.

E-procurement is part of the business-to-business (B2B) commerce being conducted on the Internet, in which buyers make purchases directly from suppliers through their websites, by using software packages, or through e-marketplaces, e-hubs, and trading exchanges. The Internet can streamline and speed up the purchase order and transaction process from companies. Benefits include lower transaction costs associated with purchasing, lower prices for goods and services, reduced labor (clerical) costs, and faster ordering and delivery times.

What do companies buy over the Internet? Purchases can be classified according to two broad categories: manufacturing inputs (direct products) and operating inputs (indirect products). Direct products are the raw materials and components that go directly into the production process of a product. Because they tend to be unique to a particular industry, they are usually purchased from industry-specific suppliers and distributors. They also tend to require specialized delivery; UPS does not typically deliver engine blocks. Indirect products do not go directly into the production of finished goods. They are the maintenance, repair, and operation (MRO) goods and services we mentioned previously (Figure 11.1). They tend not to be industry specific; they include things like office supplies, computers, furniture, janitorial services, and airline tickets. As a result, they can often be purchased from vendors like Staples, and they can be delivered by services like UPS.

More companies tend to purchase indirect goods and services over the Internet than direct goods. One reason is that a company does not have to be as careful about indirect goods since they typically cost less than direct products and they do not directly affect the quality of the company's own final product. Companies that purchase direct goods over the Internet tend to do so through suppliers with whom they already have an established relationship.

Spend Analysis

Spend analysis A formal process usually incorporating software for analyzing spend data to lower procurement costs.

Spend analysis is a relatively recent addition to the supply chain management lexicon that has evolved out of the challenges encountered in managing procurement activities, especially in far-reaching, complex global business environments. It is a formal process of collecting, cleansing, classifying, and analyzing spending data in order to reduce procurement costs and improve the efficiency of the procurement process. Spend analysis attempts to assess the who, what, when, where, why, and how of a company's expenditure process and thereby answer the questions: How much is being spent? With which suppliers? Is the promised value being realized?

Spend data can come from many different sources including supplier data and contracts, purchasing transactions, financial data, and risk data. Figure 11.1 shows three basic categories of spend data—original equipment manufacturer (OEM); maintenance, repair, and operation (MRO); and corporate services. Within all of these categories, spend data can come from different suppliers, where there are too many suppliers for the same commodity. For example, in the OEM category a company could purchase office supplies and furniture from several different office supply companies and could work with a number of printing services, copier companies, and couriers; employees could use different travel agents, etc. Within the OEM and corporate services categories, spend data can come from an ERP system and accounts payable. Many companies attempt to consolidate this data on spreadsheets; however, even if all the data from multiple sources is accurately collected, in order to effectively manage spending and realize maximum cost savings, a formal process must be in place to analyze and manage spending, which is the basic premise of spend analysis. A formal spend analysis system can be automated with spend analysis software products, of which there are many, or by outsourcing spend analysis with an outside vendor.

Whatever automated system is used, companies that have a spend analysis process in place tend to have significantly lower procurement costs, have fewer suppliers, have a more efficient supply chain in terms of speed and quality, and tend to use more advanced e-procurement systems, such as vendor-managed inventory. Spend analysis helps companies find opportunities to save money. This can be as simple as determining who is buying what within a company so that purchases can be consolidated and volume discounts can be achieved. This might also include the use of Pareto analysis to see which few items make up the largest spending categories. It can identify suppliers in different business units or in different geographic locations that are providing better buying terms than suppliers in other parts of the business; or it can indicate if contract prices are not being adhered to. One important potential benefit is the analysis of total supply chain cost for a product that integrates spend data not only for supply purchase cost but also for transportation, tariffs and duties, inventory carrying cost, insurance, and so on.

E-Marketplaces

E-marketplaces or e-hubs consolidate suppliers' goods and services at one Internet site like a catalog. For example, e-hubs for MROs include consolidated catalogs from a wide array of suppliers that enable buyers to purchase low-value goods and services with relatively high transaction costs more cheaply and efficiently over the Internet. E-hubs for direct goods and services are similar in that they bring together groups of suppliers at a few easy-to-use websites.

E-marketplaces Websites where companies and suppliers conduct business-to-business activities.

E-marketplaces like Ariba provide a neutral ground on the Internet where companies can streamline supply chains and find new business partners. An e-marketplace also offers services such as online auctions where suppliers bid on order contracts, online product catalogs with multiple supplier listings that generate online purchase orders, and request-for-quote (RFQ) services, through which buyers can submit an RFQ for their needs and users can respond.

Along the Supply Chain

Spend Analysis at Mount Sinai Medical Center

Mount Sinai Medical Center in Miami, Florida, with over 3000 employees and 700 physicians, is the largest private, not-for-profit, teaching hospital in South Florida. It has been designated as one of "America's Top Hospitals" by *U.S. News & World Report*. In 2001, Mount Sinai had a projected operating loss of over $60 million, and as a result it initiated an aggressive spend analysis program to manage expenses. The hospital perceived that because supplier contracts were becoming so complex and there was so many of them, it needed to collect the correct purchasing data and automate its spend management. As a result, the hospital enhanced its in-house purchasing system with spend analysis software, which gave it the ability to look at its overall spend picture and benchmark it against other successful hospitals. For example, if the hospital was evaluating pacemaker purchases, it would use the spend analysis software program to collect data and determine how many devices were being used. Next, using other contract software the hospital would confirm that it was purchasing the pacemakers from the correct supplier at the lowest price. Next, using benchmark software it would compare its purchase process for the devices with other hospitals. This information taken together would then allow the hospital to negotiate a better price from suppliers.

By the end of the decade, using its automated spend analysis program, Mount Sinai was generating a positive annual net income, and had accumulated a positive surplus of over $14 million.

What kind of goods and services would another service provider, like a restaurant, have in a spend analysis program?

Source: Based on Karen Minich-Pourshadi, "Hospital Business Analytics: Elevating the Spend Analysis," www.HealthLeadersMedia.com, January 13, 2011.

E-Auctions

E-auction A company posts orders on the Internet for suppliers to bid on.

A process used by e-marketplaces for buyers to purchase items is the **e-auction**, also known as a reverse auction. In a reverse auction, a company posts contracts for items it wants to purchase that suppliers can bid on. The auction is usually open for a specified time frame, and vendors can bid as often as they want in order to provide the lowest purchase price. When the auction is closed, the company can compare bids on the basis of purchase price, delivery time, and supplier reputation for quality. Some e-marketplaces restrict participation to vendors who have been previously screened or certified for reliability and product quality. e-auctions are not only used to purchase manufacturing items but are also being used to purchase services. For example, transportation exchanges hold reverse auctions for carriers to bid on shipping contracts and for air travel. Google has over 60,000 suppliers and negotiates about 20% of its total supply spending with e-auctions, saving an estimated 18% on prices and saving time, taking only 50 minutes to complete a live auction.

Sometimes companies use reverse auctions to create price competition among the suppliers it does business with; other times companies simply go through a reverse auction only to determine the lowest price without any intention of awarding a contract. It only wants to determine a baseline price to use in negotiations with its regular supplier. Companies that award contracts to low bidders in auctions can later discover their purchases are delivered late or not at all, and are of poor quality. Suppliers are often able to see online their rank in the bidding process relative to other bidders (who are anonymous), which provides pricing information to them for the future.

Distribution

Distribution encompasses all of the channels, processes, and functions, including warehousing and transportation, that a product passes through on its way to the final customer (end user). It is the actual movement of products and materials between locations. Distribution management involves managing the handling of materials and products at receiving docks, storing products and materials, packaging, and the shipment of orders. The focus of distribution, what it accomplishes, is referred to as **order fulfillment**. It is the process of ensuring on-time delivery of the customer's order.

Order fulfillment The process of ensuring on-time delivery of an order.

Logistics The transportation and distribution of goods and services.

Distribution and transportation are also often referred to as **logistics**. Logistics management in its broadest interpretation is similar to supply chain management. However, it is frequently more narrowly defined as being concerned with just transportation and distribution, in which case logistics is a subset of supply chain management. In this decade total annual U.S. business logistics is over $1.4 trillion.

Speed and Quality

Distribution is not simply a matter of moving products from point A to point B. The driving force behind distribution and transportation in today's highly competitive business environment is *speed*. One of the primary quality attributes on which companies compete is speed of service. Customers have gotten used to instant access to information, rapid Internet-based order transactions, and quick delivery of goods and services. As a result, walking next door to check on what's in the warehouse is not nearly fast enough when customers want to buy a product now and a company has to let them know if it's in stock. That demands real-time inventory information. Calling a trucking firm and asking it when it will have a truck in the vicinity to pick up a delivery is not nearly fast enough when a customer has come to expect delivery in a few days or overnight. That also requires real-time information about carrier location, schedules, and capacity. Thus, the key to distribution speed is information, as it has been in our discussion of other parts of the supply chain.

Internet Companies: Amazon.com

Distribution is a particularly important supply chain component for Internet companies like Amazon.com, whose supply chains consist almost entirely of supply and distribution. These

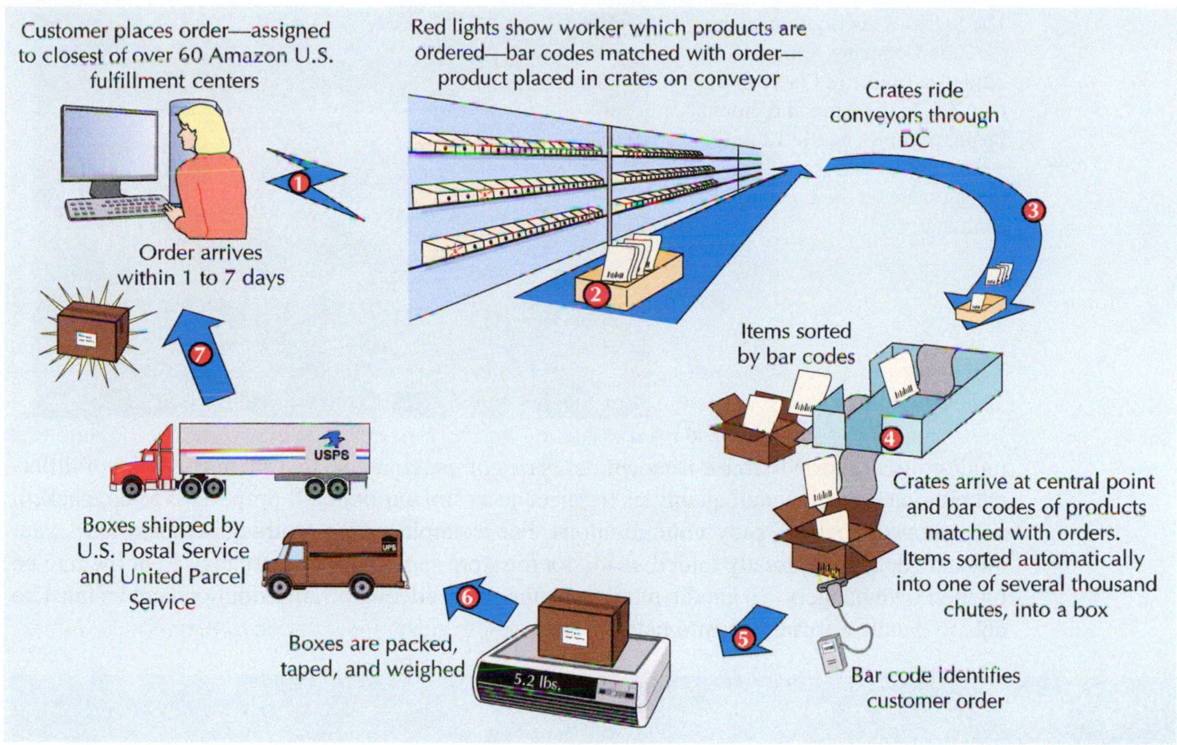
Customer places order—assigned to closest of over 60 Amazon U.S. fulfillment centers
Red lights show worker which products are ordered—bar codes matched with order—product placed in crates on conveyor
Crates ride conveyors through DC
Order arrives within 1 to 7 days
Items sorted by bar codes
USPS
Crates arrive at central point and bar codes of products matched with orders. Items sorted automatically into one of several thousand chutes, into a box
Boxes shipped by U.S. Postal Service and United Parcel Service
Boxes are packed, taped, and weighed
5.2 lbs.
Bar code identifies customer order

FIGURE 11.2 **Order Fulfillment at Amazon.com**

companies have no production process; they simply sell and distribute products that they acquire from suppliers. They are not driven from the front end of the supply chain—the website—but by distribution at the back end. Their success ultimately depends on the capability to ship each order when the customer needs or wants it.

Figure 11.2 illustrates the order fulfillment process at Amazon.com when one of its millions of customers places an order via the Internet (or by phone). The order is transmitted to the closest distribution center (DC) where items are stored in a warehouse in shelved bins. Computers send workers to retrieve items from the shelves, and they place each item in a crate with other orders. When the crate is full it moves by conveyor through the plant to a central point. At this central sorting area bar codes are matched with order numbers to determine which items go with which order, and the items that fulfill an order are sorted into chutes. The items that make up an order are placed in a box as they come off the chute with a new bar code that identifies the order. The boxes are then packed, taped, weighed, and shipped by a carrier, for example, the U.S. Postal Service or UPS.

Distribution Centers and Warehousing

Distribution centers, which typically incorporate warehousing and storage, are buildings that are used to receive, handle, store, package, and then ship products (see photo). Some of the largest business facilities in the United States are distribution centers. The Target Import DC in Lacey, Washington, has 2 million square feet of floor space—over 37 times bigger than the area of a football field and almost the same floor space as the Empire State Building; one of the largest Amazon fulfillment centers in Phoenix, Arizona, is over 1.6 million square feet. The annual cost of warehousing in the U.S. is over $470 billion.

As in other areas of supply chain management, information technology has a significant impact on distribution management. The Internet has altered how companies distribute goods by adding more frequent orders in smaller amounts and higher customer service expectations to the already difficult task of rapid response fulfillment. To fill Internet orders successfully, warehouses and distribution centers must be set up as "flow-through" facilities, using automated material-handling equipment to speed up the processing and delivery of orders.

Retailers have shifted from buying goods in bulk and storing them to pushing inventory and storage and final configuration back up the supply chain (upstream). They expect suppliers

The logistics distribution center of the Zara Company, known as the Zaragoza Logistics Platform or PLAZA, in the Aragon region of Spain, occupies nearly 13 million square meters and is the largest logistics site on the European continent.

Xurxo Lobato/Cover/Getty Images

(and/or distributors) to make frequent deliveries of merchandise that includes a mix of different product items in small quantities (referred to as "mixed-pallet"), properly labeled, packed, and shipped in store-ready configurations. For example, some clothing retailers may want sweaters delivered already folded, ready for the store shelf, while others may want them to be on their own hangers. To handle retailer requirements adequately, distribution centers must be able to handle a variety of automated tasks.

Along the Supply Chain

Adding a New Distribution Center to the Sephora Supply Chain

Cheng Xuliang/ZUMA Press/Newcom

Sephora, the beauty products brand and chain of cosmetics stores (shown in photo), was founded in Paris and is owned by French conglomerate LVMH (Louis Vuitton Moet Hennessy). The Sephora supply chain includes more than 900 stores in 29 countries, carrying over 250 brands, along with its own private label. Sephora has over 360 stores in the United States and Canada, which until 2008 were served by a single 316,000 square-foot distribution center in Belcamp, Maryland. Precipitated by its rapid growth and becoming the exclusive provider of beauty products for over 300 J.C. Penney stores across the United States in 2006, Sephora began investigating alternatives for its distribution network, including replacing the Belcamp facility with a larger, more optimally located distribution center, opening a second distribution center, or simply keeping the Belcamp facility. The company engaged an outside supply chain consulting firm to undertake a project to investigate these alternatives.

The project team, consisting primarily of Sephora's internal logistics team and members from the consulting firm, first developed a model of the existing Sephora distribution network to better understand how store replenishment worked and what level of service they needed. The network model included transactional data for its stores and Internet site, plus logistics data for freight costs, warehouse operating costs, shipment volumes, and store locations. Next, the objectives for the future distribution network were established, which required an understanding of future store growth patterns including possible locations.

After growth projections were included in the model, the team addressed two possible scenarios—what was the best East Coast site if Belcamp was closed, and if Belcamp stayed open, what was the best site for a second facility. For each scenario the model was evaluated with data for different possible locations, including the average cost per square foot and freight rates, and based on these model results the sites were rated and then ranked according to service cost. The model results showed first that the absolute optimal site was near Philadelphia, only 80 miles from Belcamp, such that the minimal savings in transportation costs would not offset the relocation costs, and thus Belcamp was fixed as one site. Next, the model was reevaluated for second-site candidates that would optimize transportation costs, lead times and expenses. Salt Lake City was selected as the site for the second distribution center not only because of optimal transportation costs, but also because of the support of local and state governments. The Salt Lake City distribution center opened in 2008 and relieved the capacity at Belcamp, increased Sephora's customer service capabilities, and reduced its shipping costs. In 2013, Sephora began considering a third North American distribution center as it expanded into Brazil and Mexico. In 2014 Sephora replaced the Belcamp facility with a new distribution center a few miles away in Perryman, Maryland, that's almost double the size of the Belcamp warehouse.

Do you think the process Sephora used to determine the site of its new distribution center could be universally applied to other retail companies?

Source: Based on Maida Napolitano, "Sephora's Gorgeous Network Reorganization," *Supply Chain Management Review* 15 (11); (November 2011), pp. S40–S50.

Postponement

Postponement moves some final manufacturing steps like assembly or individual product customization into the warehouse or distribution center. Generic products or component parts (like computer components) are stored at the warehouse, and then final products are built-to-order (BTO), or personalized, to meet individual customer demand. It is a response to the adage that whoever can get the desired product to the customer first gets the sale. Postponement actually pulls distribution into the manufacturing process, allowing lead times to be reduced so that demand can be met more quickly. However, postponement also usually means that a distributor must stock a large number of inventory items at the warehouse to meet the final assembly or customization requirements; this can create higher inventory-carrying costs. The manufacturing and distribution supply chain members must therefore work together to synchronize their demand forecasts and carefully manage inventory.

Postponement Moves some manufacturing steps into the distribution center.

Warehouse Management Systems

In order to handle the new trends and demands of distribution management, companies employ sophisticated, highly automated **warehouse management systems (WMS)** to run day-to-day operations of a distribution center and keep track of inventories. The WMS places an item in storage at a specific location (a *putaway*), locates and takes an item out of storage (a *pick*), packs the item, and ships it via a *carrier*. The WMS acknowledges that a product is available to ship, and, if it is not available, the system will determine from suppliers in real time when it will be available.

Warehouse management system (WMS) An automated system that runs the day-to-day operations of a distribution center.

Figure 11.3 illustrates the features of a WMS. Orders flow into a WMS through an *order management system* (OMS). The OMS enables the distribution center to add, modify, or cancel orders in real time. When the OMS receives customer order information online, it provides a snapshot of product availability from the WMS and from suppliers via EDI. If an item is not

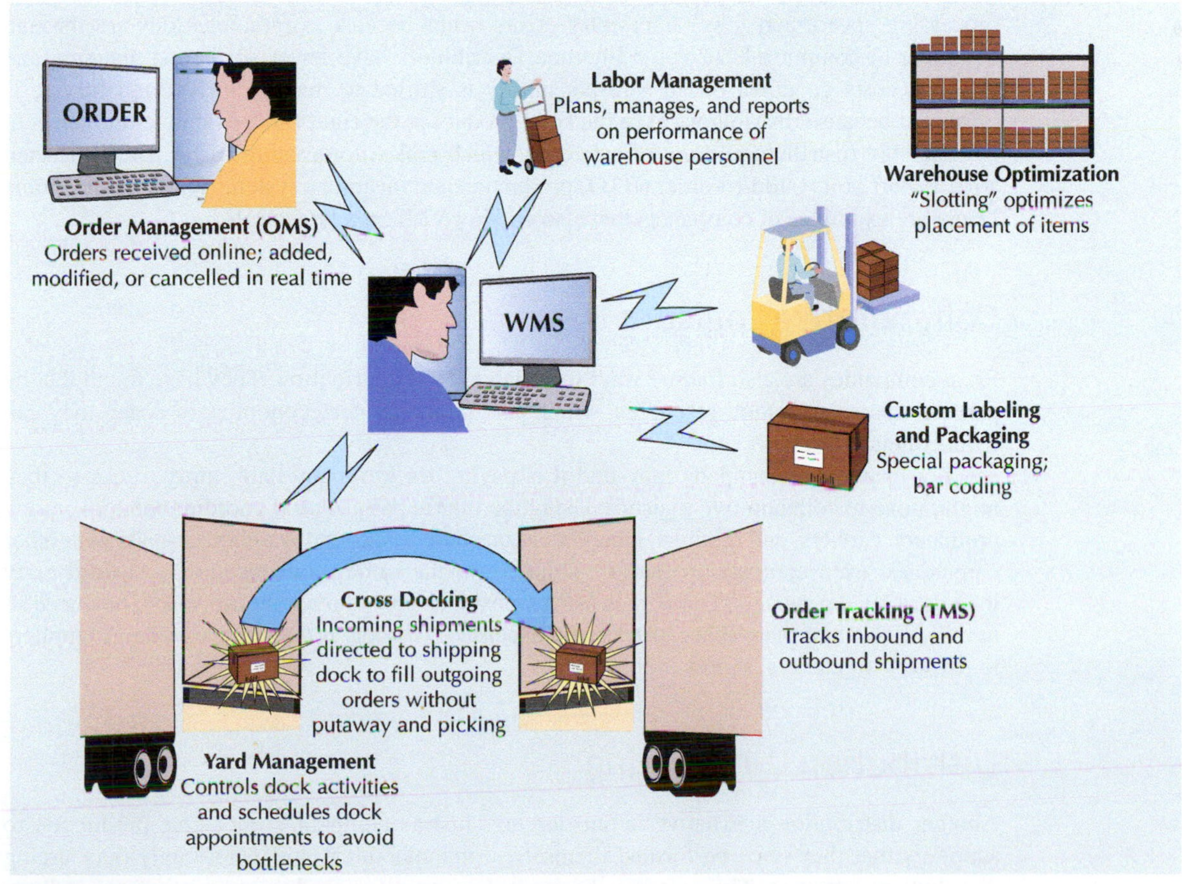

FIGURE 11.3 A Warehouse Management System (WMS)

in stock, the OMS looks into the supplier's production schedule to see when it will be available. The OMS then allocates inventory from the warehouse site to fill an order, establishes a delivery date, and passes these orders onto the transportation management system for delivery.

The *transportation management system (TMS)* allows the DC to track inbound and outbound shipments, to consolidate and build economical loads, and to select the best carrier based on cost and service. *Yard management* controls activities at the facility's dock and schedules dock appointments to reduce bottlenecks. *Labor management* plans, manages, and reports the performance level of warehouse personnel. *Warehouse optimization* optimizes the warehouse placement of items, called "slotting," based on demand, product groupings, and the physical characteristics of the item. A WMS also creates custom labeling and packaging. A WMS facilitates **cross-docking**, a system that Walmart originated that allows a DC to direct incoming shipments straight to a shipping dock to fill outgoing orders, eliminating costly put-away and picking operations. In a cross-docking system, products are delivered to a warehouse on a continual basis, where they are stored, repackaged, and distributed to stores without sitting in inventory. Goods "cross" from one loading dock to another, usually in 48 hours or less.

Cross-docking Goods "cross" from one loading dock to another in 48 hours or less.

Vendor-Managed Inventory

Vendor-managed inventory (VMI) Manufacturers rather than vendors generate orders.

With **vendor-managed inventory (VMI)** (also called supplier managed inventory or SMI), manufacturers, instead of distributors or retailers, generate orders. Under VMI, manufacturers receive data electronically via EDI or the Internet about distributors' sales and stock levels. Manufacturers can see which items distributors carry, as well as several years of point-of-sale data, expected growth, promotions, new and lost business, and inventory goals, and use this information to create and maintain a forecast and an inventory plan. VMI is a form of "role reversal"—usually the buyer completes the administrative tasks of ordering; with VMI the responsibility for planning shifts to the manufacturer.

VMI is usually an integral part of supply chain collaboration. The vendor has more control over the supply chain and the buyer is relieved of administrative tasks, thereby increasing supply chain efficiency. Both manufacturers and distributors benefit from increased processing speed, and fewer data entry errors occur because communications are through computer-to-computer EDI or the Internet. Distributors have fewer stockouts; planning and ordering costs go down because responsibility is shifted to manufacturers; and service is improved because distributors have the right product at the right time. Manufacturers benefit by receiving distributors' point-of-sale data, which makes forecasting easier. Dell perfected VMI as part of its build-to-order (BTO) production and inventory system; Walmart and Home Depot are examples of companies that also employ VMI on a large scale.

Collaborative Logistics

Rival companies are also finding ways to collaborate in distribution. They have found that by pooling their distribution resources, which can create greater economies of scale, they can reduce their costs.

For example, a company may find it is paying for too many half-empty trucks so they might move to collaborative logistics. Using the Internet as a central coordination tool among producers, carriers, and retailers, companies can share trucks and warehouse space with other companies, even competitors that are shipping to the same retail locations. At third-party logistics (3PL) providers, companies use a website to post the warehouse space they need or have available and share space, trucks, and expenses. The goal is that everyone, from suppliers to truckers to retailers, shares in the savings.

Distribution Outsourcing

Another distribution alternative is outsourcing. Just as companies outsource production to suppliers that they once performed themselves, manufacturers are increasingly outsourcing distribution activities. The reason is basically the same for producers as it is for suppliers: outsourcing allows the company to focus on its core competencies. It also takes advantage of the expertise that distribution companies have developed. Outsourcing distribution activities to third-party logistics (3PL) providers tends to lower inventory levels and reduce costs for the outsourcing company, plus it allows companies to focus on its core competencies.

Transportation

In a supply chain, *transportation* is the movement of a product from one location to another as it makes its way to the end-use customer. Although supply chain experts agree that transportation sometimes falls through the supply chain management cracks, receiving less attention than it should, it can be a significant supply chain cost. For some manufacturing companies, transportation costs can be as much as 20% of total production costs and run as high as 6% of revenue. Over $860 billion is spent on supply chain transportation costs in the United States each year. For some retail companies primarily involved in the distribution of goods, such as L.L. Bean and Amazon.com, transportation is not only a major cost of doing business, it is also a major determinant of quick delivery service. L.L. Bean ships over 15 million packages in a year—over one million in its busiest week—mostly by UPS.

The principal modes of transportation within the United States are railroads, air, truck, intermodal, water, package carriers, and pipeline. In the United States, the greatest amount of freight is shipped by trucking, followed by railroad, pipeline, and inland waterways. The different transport modes and some of their advantages and disadvantages are shown in Figure 11.4.

Railroads, with more than 160,000 miles of track in the United States, are cost-effective for transporting products such as raw materials, coal, minerals, ores, and especially containers over long distances. However, railroads operate on less flexible and slower schedules than trucks, and they usually cannot go directly from one business location to another as trucks can. Railroad freight service also has the worst record of quality performance of all modes of freight transport, with a higher incidence of product damage and almost 10 times more late deliveries than trucking.

Trucking is the main mode of freight transportation in the United States, annually carrying over 60% of U.S. freight tonnage, and generating almost 80% of the nation's total freight cost each year. Trucks provide flexible point-to-point service, delivering small loads over short and long distances over widely dispersed geographic areas.

Air freight is the most expensive and fastest mode of freight transportation. For companies that use air freight, service is more important than price. For some companies, production stoppages because of missing parts or components can be much more expensive than the

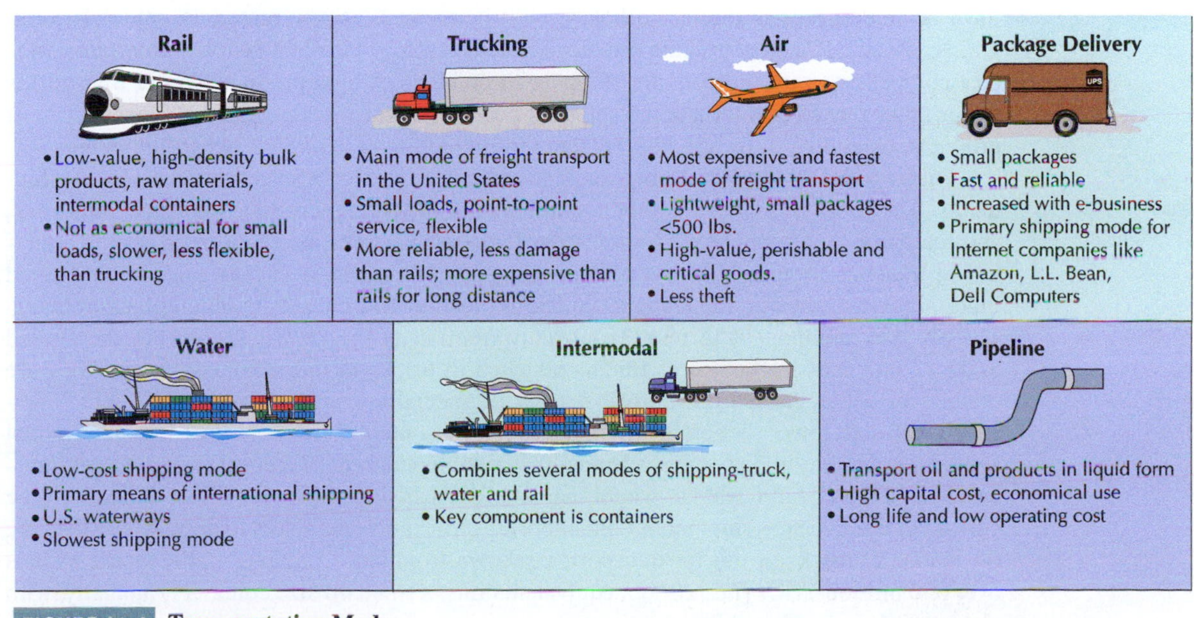

FIGURE 11.4 Transportation Modes

Federal Express superhubs consolidate and distribute shipments from a central location. FedEx is the industry leader in overnight package delivery service.

Bloomberg via Getty Images

increased cost of air freight. For high-value goods such as pharmaceuticals, high technology, and consumer electronics, speed to market is important. In addition, shorter shipping times reduce the chances for theft and other losses. The general rule for international air freight is that anything that is physically or economically perishable has to move by air instead of by ship. The major product groups that are shipped by international air freight, from largest to smallest, are perishables, construction and engineering equipment, textiles and wearing apparel, documents and small package shipments, and computers, peripherals, and spare parts.

Air freight is growing particularly fast in Asia and specifically China. The lack of adequate ground infrastructure makes rail and trucking transport difficult between countries in Asia and regions in China. Companies with manufacturing plants in one place in Asia and suppliers in another often use air freight to connect the two.

Package carriers such as UPS, FedEx, and the U.S. Postal Service transport small packages, up to about 150 pounds. The growth of e-business has significantly increased the use of package carriers. Package carriers combine various modes of transportation, mostly air and truck, to ship small packages rapidly. They are not economical for large-volume shipments; however, they are fast and reliable, and they provide unique services that some companies must have. Package carriers have been innovative in the use of bar codes and the Internet to arrange and track shipments. The FedEx website attracts more than 50 million package tracking requests daily, and it receives 70% of its customer orders electronically. FedEx, as shown in photo, delivers around 9 million packages daily in over 220 countries.

Waterways in the United States include 26,000 navigable miles over inland waterways, canals, the Great Lakes, and along coastlines. Water transport is a slow but very low-cost form of shipping. It is limited to heavy, bulk items such as raw materials, minerals, ores, grains, chemicals, and petroleum products. If delivery speed is not a factor, water transport is cost competitive with railroads for shipping these kinds of bulk products. Water transport is the primary means of international shipping between countries separated by oceans for most products. Over 80% of freight imports into the United States arrive via ocean shipping.

Intermodal transportation Combines several modes of transportation to move shipments.

Intermodal transportation combines several modes of transportation to move shipments. The most common intermodal combination in the United States is truck–rail–truck, and the truck–water–rail/truck combination is the primary means of global transport. Intermodal transportation carries over 35% of all freight shipments over 500 miles in the United States. Intermodal truck–rail shipping can be as much as 40% cheaper than long-haul trucking.

The key component in intermodal transportation is the *container*. Within the United States, containers are hauled as trailers attached to trucks to rail terminals, where they are double- or triple-stacked on railroad flatcars or specially designed "well cars," which feature a well-like lower section in which the trailer or container rides (70% of U.S. intermodal shipping over a million containers annually) is double-stacked. The containers are then transported to another rail terminal, where they are reattached to trucks for direct delivery to the customer. For overseas shipments, container ships transport containers to ports where they are off-loaded to trucks or rail for transport, as shown in photo. Container traffic world wide is over 650 million TEUs (i.e., 20-foot equivalent units, a standard size container) annually, with almost 10% in the United States.

Along the Supply Chain

Supply Chain Operations at Food Distributor Sysco Corporation

Houston-based Sysco Corporation, with annual revenues over $44 billon, is the global leader in the food services industry. Each year Sysco ships over 21 million tons of produce, meats, prepared meals, and other food-related products to over 425,000 customers, supplying one in three restaurants, cafeterias, and sports stadiums in the United States. Sysco's supply chain, which stretches from the farm to the dinner table, is especially complex because a jar of caviar must be handled differently from a box of frozen onion rings or a tub of flour. As a result of its unique inventory and distribution systems, Sysco is constantly seeking to cut costs and speed delivery times. In one of its sorting and distribution centers, such as its 450,000-square-foot facility in Jersey City, New Jersey, restaurant supplies are sorted and loaded before being sent to their final destination. Forklift drivers, called selectors, wear a wireless scanner plus a printer on their hip that provides exact instructions on what to load; they point their scanners at a bar code above an item, grab it, and put it on a pallet. Software determines how each pallet should be arranged based on the weight of its items, its location, and its destination. The sorting facility is arranged so that work is all done in one direction, drivers never double back, and the aisles are organized according to weight and temperature. Heavier items are put on one side of the warehouse, while lighter items, like potato chips, are put on the other side, in order to maximize efficiency. This sorting facility turns over 11,000 inventory items every 17 days. To achieve this kind of turnover rate each product has an expiration date; if an item passes its expiration, inventory management software alerts workers to pull it, or if supplies are too low the software tells the center to replenish. Sysco uses redistribution centers where truck deliveries from suppliers are consolidated and packed into trucks for delivery to sorting centers. Sysco realizes savings through cross-docking, taking full truckloads from a supplier, bringing them to a cross-dock, mixing the freight and shipping full truckloads to a customer. In some cases pallets are packed and ready for delivery to customers at the redistribution centers so that only a few additional pallets must be assembled at the sorting center before the truck is sent out for delivery, resulting in fewer and fuller trucks. Sysco also uses Roadnet routing software developed by UPS to determine the most efficient routes for its trucks, which in addition to lowering costs, also has the sustainable result of reducing diesel fuel usage.

In a number of ways the warehouse and distribution system used by Sysco is similar to other large retailers like Walmart, Target, L.L. Bean, and Amazon. Discuss the similarities and differences in supply chain operations between Sysco and these other retailers.

Source: Jia Lynn Yang, 'Veggie Tales', *Fortune*, 159 (12); (June 2009), p. 25.

There are over 2 million miles of *pipelines* in the United States, 75% of which are used primarily for transporting oil and petroleum products. Pipelines called slurry lines carry other products such as coal and kaolin that have been pulverized and transformed into liquid form. Once the product arrives at its destination, the water is removed, leaving the solid material. Although pipelines require a high initial capital investment to construct, they are economical because they can carry materials over terrain that would be difficult for trucks or trains to travel across, for example, the Trans-Alaska pipeline. Once in place, pipelines have a long life and are low cost in terms of operation, maintenance, and labor.

Sheila Fitzgerald/Shutterstock

One of the most popular forms of intermodal transportation uses containers that are transported via rail or truck to ports where they are loaded onto container ships for shipment overseas, and then loaded back onto trucks or rail at destination ports for delivery to end-use customers.

Internet Transportation Exchanges

Internet transportation exchanges bring together shippers who post loads and carriers who post their available capacity in order to arrange shipments. In some exchanges once the parties have matched up at a website, all the negotiation is done offline. In others the online service manages the load matches automatically; the services match up shipments and carriers based on shipment characteristics, trailer availability, and the like. For example, shippers tender load characteristics, and the online service returns with recommendations on carrier price and service levels. Some services also provide an online international exchange structured as a reverse auction. The shippers will tender their loads, and carriers will bid on the shipment. Shipments remain up for bid until a shipper-specified auction closing time (like auctions on eBay). However, the lowest price, or lowest bid, is not always conducive to quality service. At some sites the low bid does not necessarily win; the service takes into account quality issues such as transit time, the carrier, and availability in addition to price.

One of the more well-known Internet exchange services is www.freightquote.com. At this site (and others like it) shippers and carriers identify their available shipment or capacity needs and their business requirements. The exchanges automatically match compatible shippers with carriers based on price and service. Automated processes make the trade within a few hours with no phone calls, invoices, and so on.

The Global Supply Chain

A number of factors have combined to create a global marketplace. International trade barriers have fallen, and new trade agreements between countries and nations have been established. The dissolution of communism opened up new markets in Russia and Middle and Eastern Europe, and the creation of the European Union resulted in the world's largest economic market—500 million people. Europe, with a total population of 730 million, is the largest, best-educated economic group in the world. Emerging markets in China, growing Asian export-driven economies, burgeoning global trading centers in Hong Kong and Singapore, and an increasingly robust economy in India have linked with the rest of the world to form a vigorous global economic community. Global trade now exceeds $27 trillion per year.

Along the Supply Chain

Global Supply Chain Management at Li & Fung

Li & Fung Limited, headquartered in Hong Kong, is the world's leading consumer goods sourcing company supplying high volume, time-sensitive apparel products to over 8000 customers worldwide. It is the recognized world leader in supply chain management, providing a spectrum of services that covers the entire supply chain. It has over 300 offices and distribution centers with 26,000 employees in over 40 countries. Garments, including denim jeans, make up about two-thirds of Li & Fung's business; it is involved in the production of between 40% to 50% of the clothes you'll find in any U.S. shopping mall.

Li & Fung's extensive global network of over 15,000 suppliers includes product design and development, raw material and factory sourcing, production planning and management, quality assurance, shipping and distribution, warehousing, customs brokerage, and export documentation. It manages the supply chain of large retailers such as Walmart, Kohl's, Sears, JC Penney, Target, Abercrombie & Fitch, Marks and Spencer, and Talbots, helping them (and all their customers) optimize the flow of inventory and information to reduce cost and improve service level. For apparel products like denim jeans, Li & Fung finds raw materials and factories and takes on manufacturing responsibilities to make sure factories meet labor standards and deliver jeans at set prices and quickly (although Li & Fung generally owns few factories itself).

Several years ago Li & Fung took over Liz Claiborne Inc.'s sourcing operations, which encompasses all aspects of its production, from acquiring materials to manufacturing and delivery. Liz Claiborne, which includes Juicy Couture, Kate Spade, and Lucky Brand, retained its design and marketing functions—for example, it gives jeans designs to Li & Fung, and Li & Fung then bids them out worldwide to the manufacturer with the best combination of quality, speed-to-market, and price. Liz Claiborne recognized that Li & Fung, with its vast sourcing network and supply chain expertise, could manage its supply chain better than it could itself.

Sources: Based on Li & Fung's website at www.lifunggroup.com; "Bruce Einhorn, "Li & Fung: A Factory Sourcer Shines," www.businessweek.com/magazine (May 14, 2009); and Sandeep Agarwal, "Li & Fung – Operations, Emerging Supply Chain Changes & More…," www.denim-andjeans.com (October 8, 2011).

Globalization is no longer restricted to giant companies. Technology advances have made it possible for middle-tier companies to establish a global presence. Companies previously regional in scope are using the Internet to become global overnight. Information technology is the "enabler" that lets companies gain global visibility and link disparate locations, suppliers, and customers. However, many companies are learning that it takes more than a glitzy website to be a global player. As with the domestic U.S. market, it takes a well-planned and coordinated supply chain to be competitive and successful.

Obstacles to Global Supply Chain Management

Moving products across international borders is like negotiating an intricate maze, riddled with potential pitfalls. For U.S. companies eager to enter new and growing markets, trading in foreign countries is not "business as usual." Global supply chain management, though global in nature, must still take into account national and regional differences. Customs, business practices, and regulations can vary widely from country to country and even within a country. Foreign markets are not homogeneous and often require customized service in terms of packaging and labeling. Quality can be a major challenge when dealing with emerging markets in countries with different languages and customers.

Some of the other major differences between domestic and global supply chain transactions include:

- Increased documentation for invoices, cargo insurance, letters of credit, ocean bills of lading or air waybills, and inspections
- Ever-changing regulations that vary from country to country and govern the import and export of goods
- Trade groups, tariffs, duties, and landing costs
- Limited shipping modes and infrastructure
- Differences in communication technology and availability
- Different business practices as well as language barriers
- Government codes and reporting requirements that vary from country to country
- Numerous players, including forwarding agents, custom house brokers, financial institutions, insurance providers, multiple transportation carriers, and government agencies
- Numerous security regulations and requirements

Duties, Tariffs, and Global Trading Groups

The proliferation of trade agreements has changed global markets and has accelerated global trade activity. Nations have joined together to form trading groups, also called **nation groups**, and customs unions, and within these groups products move freely with no import tax, called **tariffs** or **duties**, charged on member products. The members of a group charge uniform import duties to nations outside their group, thus removing tariff trade barriers within the group and raising barriers for outsiders. The group adopts rules and regulations for freely transporting goods across borders that, combined with reduced tariffs, give member nations a competitive advantage over nonmembers. These trade advantages among member nations lower supply chain costs and reduce cycle time—that is, the time required for products to move through the supply chain.

Nation groups Nations joined together into trading groups.

Tariffs (duties) Taxes on imported goods.

Two of the most prominent international groups that trade with the United States are NAFTA, the North American Free Trade Agreement, and EU, the European Union trade group.

The World Trade Organization (WTO) is an international organization dealing with the global rules of trade. It ensures that trade flows as smoothly and freely as possible among its 161 members. The trade agreements and rules are negotiated and signed by governments, and their purpose is to help exporters and importers conduct business. Most-favored-nation trade (MFN) status is an arrangement in which WTO member countries must extend to other members the most favorable treatment given to any trading partner. For example, MFN status for China translates into lower duties on goods entering the United States, and fewer trade regulations for companies.

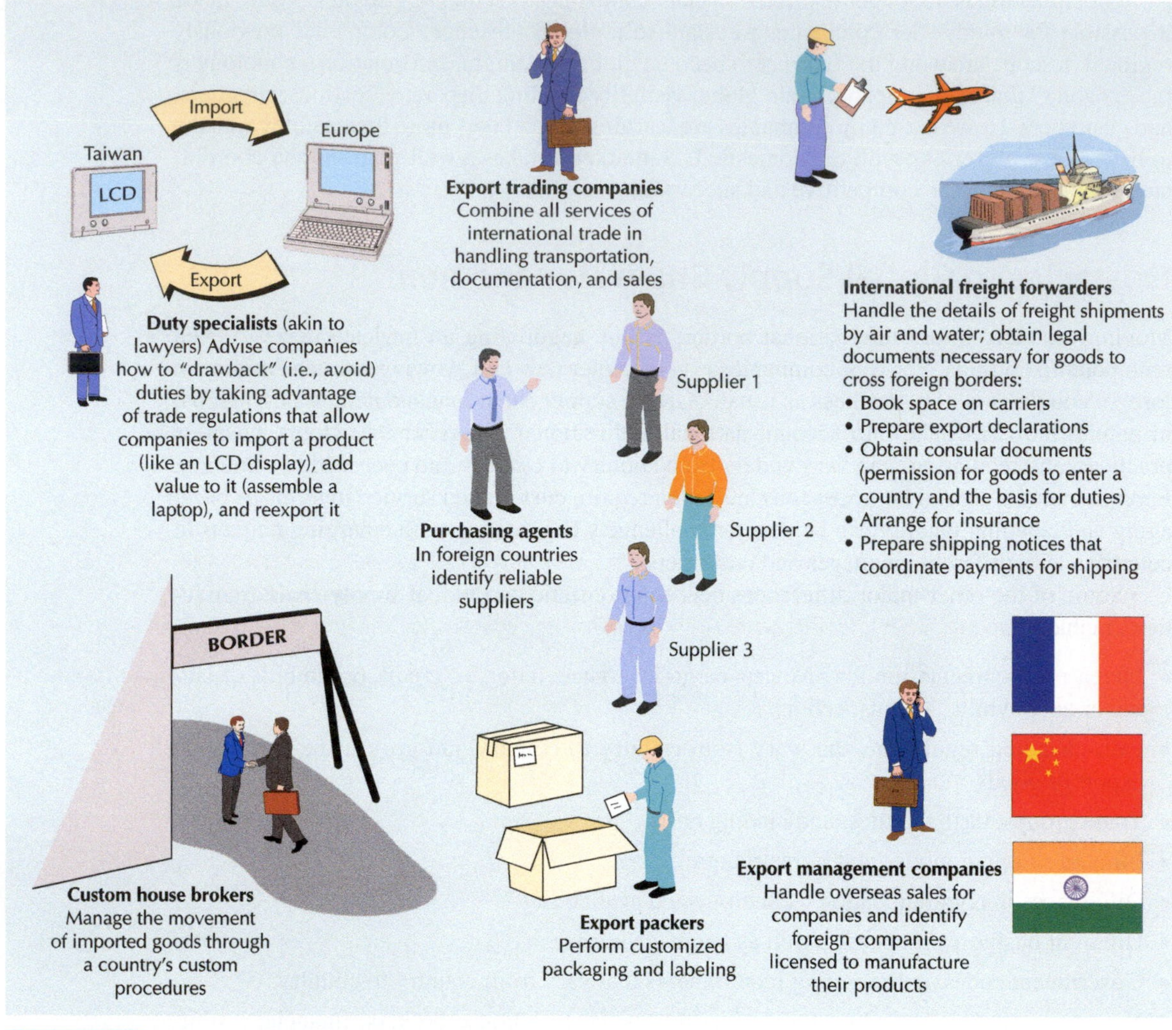

FIGURE 11.5 **International Trade Specialists**

Trade specialists Include freight forwarders, customs house brokers, export packers, and export management and trading companies.

To overcome the obstacles and problems of global supply chain management, many companies hire one or more international **trade specialists**. Figure 11.5 summarizes the activities of different types of trade specialists.

Landed Cost

Landed cost The total cost of producing, storing, and transporting a product to its destination or port.

Value-added tax (VAT) An indirect tax assessed on the increase in value of a good at any stage of the production process from raw material to final product.

In global trade **landed cost** is the total cost of producing, storing, and transporting a product to the site of consumption or another port. It can include such costs as brokerage and logistics fees, port fees, custom duties, tariffs, taxes, insurance, currency conversion, and handling fees; as many as 80 components can be included in landed cost. However, 85% of these components fall into two broad categories: (1) transportation cost and duty, and (2) governmental charges such as **value added tax (VAT)** and excise tax. Landed costs are important because the duty assessed by different governments incorporates varying portions of landed costs. For example, for U.S. imports, duty is charged free on board (FOB) the factory. This means that transportation costs from the point of entry into the United States to the factory destination are not calculated as part of the import duty charge. However, in other countries the duty assessed can include the cost of transportation from beginning to end.

By knowing the landed cost of a product before it is purchased, a company can make more informed decisions, while poorly projected landed costs can balloon the price of a product move. Accurately estimating true landed costs helps avoid "clicker shock." Clicker shock occurs when an overseas customer places an order with a company that does not have the capability of calculating landed cost. Then the order gets shipped, and along the way tariffs get added on top—in some cases this can double the original purchase price.

Web-Based International Trade Logistics Systems

As we have indicated, global supply chain management involves a stunningly complex matrix of language barriers, currency conversions, international trade agreements, taxes, tariffs, embargoes, duties, quotas, document requirements, local rules, and new trading partners. These factors require an automated information technology solution for any company with any real volume of international shipments. International trade logistics (ITL) companies use web-based software products that link directly to customers' websites to eliminate or reduce the obstacles to global trade. They convert language and currency from the U.S. system into those used by many of the United States's trading partners, giving potential buyers in other nations easy access to product and price information. ITL systems also provide information on tariffs, duties, and customs processes and some link with financial institutions to facilitate letters of credit and payment. Through the use of extensive databases these systems can attach the appropriate weights, measurements, and unit prices to individual products ordered over the Web. These systems can also incorporate transportation costs and conversion rates so that purchasers can electronically see the landed cost of ordering a product and having it delivered. Some ITL systems use a landed cost search engine that calculates shipping costs online while a company enters an order so it will know exactly what the costs will be in U.S. funds. They also track global shipments.

Through their websites and software products, ITL companies do many of the things international trade specialists do (Figure 11.5). They let their customers know which international companies they can do business with and which companies can do business with them. They identify export and import restrictions between buyers and vendors. They provide the documents required to export and import products, and they determine the duties, taxes, and landed costs and other government charges associated with importing a product.

Livingston International (www.livingstonintl.com) is an example of a global trade management company that enables customers through its web-based software products to calculate landed costs, screen for restricted parties, generate shipment documentation, and manage duties, and it also handles repairs and returns. It has an online library of trade regulations for different countries.

Fan Jun/Xinhua / Zuma Press

The Port of Singapore handles over 10 million TEUs (20-foot container equivalent units) annually at three container terminals. The Brani terminal has 9 berths, 31 quay cranes, and a capacity of 5.5 million TEUs. The Port of Singapore has been the world's busiest port in terms of shipping tonnage since 1986.

Along the Supply Chain

Hewlett-Packard Sustainability Initiatives in China

Hewlett-Packard is a company recognized for its commitment to helping its global supply chain partners, specifically in China, make continual improvement in their sustainable processes. Up until 2010, HP manufacturing and assembly factories had been mainly in coastal regions of China. This was common practice among electronics and tech companies; Chinese manufacturing incubated in Shanghai and Hong Kong—cities ideally located for exports. However, a constant challenge was a shortage of locally based labor, which caused huge migratory labor flows, resulting in workers traveling long distances from inland China to jobs in coastal cities. By 2010 two-thirds of HP's labor supply was not from coastal provinces, which meant that workers were migrating seasonally and forced to work far away from their homes and families. The situation was stressful for workers who did not receive the same rights as workers in the local provinces, and who were not accustomed to local dialects and cuisine outside of their home provinces. HP also began to notice inflationary pressures on workers' living expenses because of rising food and energy prices, all of which contributed to high staff turnover and absenteeism. In response, HP decided to encourage its suppliers to build new facilities in Chongqing, over 1000 miles west of Shanghai, with an urban population approaching 13 million, and an additional 15 million workers in nearby rural areas. HPs "Go West" strategy incorporates all three elements of human, economic, and environmental sustainability, and it also builds resiliency into the supply chain by not locating all of its factories in one area of coastal China, which was a risk. By relocating its suppliers to Chongqing, HP was able to reduce its costs, increase staff retention, and improve the working conditions of the tens of thousands of workers in its suppliers' factories who no longer needed to move from their homes to coastal cities to find work. Approximately 80% of its Chongqing workers are local or from the surrounding province; its suppliers employ 80,000 workers in Chongqing, making over 20 million laptops and 15 million printers a year.

However, moving manufacturing to Chongqing in inland China brought with it some logistical challenges since it was so far away from coastal ports. HP worked with the Chinese government (who provided incentives) to develop a new freight railway line rail route to ship products from Chongqing to markets in Europe. The rail line mirrors the fabled Silk Road, the ancient web of routes used to transport spices, gems, and silk fabric by camel from China to markets in Europe between about 115 BC to AD 1450. The modern-day version spans almost 7000 miles, covers two continents, and crosses six countries. It takes about three weeks for HP's express trains to complete a one-way journey to HP's European distribution center, in Oostrum, the Netherlands, traveling at speeds of up to 50 miles per hour and safeguarded by armed security guards. The rail cost is about one-third the price of air transport. It also saves time—shipping products by rail takes approximately three weeks—less time than the 35 days required to transport products by sea from Shanghai. Rail transportation also reduces HP's carbon footprint from transport by up to 95%, reduces oil consumption for sea transport, and results in one-thirtieth of the carbon footprint associated with air freight.

Another HP sustainability initiative in China is their "Student and Dispatch Worker Standard for Supplier Facilities in the People's Republic of China," to address the significant increase in the use of student and temporary workers in China. Many factories in China have long relied on high school students, vocational school students, and temporary workers to cope with periodic surges in orders as factory labor becomes increasingly scarce. Students complained of being ordered by school administrators to put in very long hours on short notice at jobs with no relevance to their studies; local governments sometimes ordered schools to provide labor, and the factories management paid school administrators a bonus. Enforcing workplace rules in China is difficult, as Chinese laws on labor practices are often ignored by some manufacturers as they struggle to keep up with production demand amid labor shortages, and the nation's labor force has begun to slowly shrink because of the rigorous one-child policy through the 1980s and 1990s. HP's policy requires that all student work be voluntary, local regulations on student workers are met, only limited numbers of student workers can be used for HP production (below 20% of the total workforce), and students are employed in roles that further their education. Further, students and temporary workers must be able to leave work at any time upon reasonable notice without negative repercussions, and they must have access to reliable and reprisal-free grievance mechanisms. HP monitors progress through key performance indicators that track student and young workers, which Chinese suppliers report to HP monthly.

Using the Internet research the recent sustainability initiatives in China of several other large global companies.

Source: The Hewlett-Packard website at http://www.hp.com.

Trends in Globalization for U.S. Companies

Two significant changes that prompted many U.S. companies to expand globally were the passage of NAFTA, which opened up business opportunities with Mexico, and the admission of China into the World Trade Organization. Approximately 700 of the *Fortune* 1000 companies have a portion of their operations, production components, or affiliates in Mexico. Besides cheap labor, Mexico is also close to the United States, and thus Mexican companies can meet the just-in-time requirements of many U.S. companies. However, Mexico's economic gains also lead to more jobs and increased worker skills, and as a result, higher wages, which, in turn, has led U.S. and foreign companies away from Mexico to China with its even lower wage rates. The hourly manufacturing wage rate in China is around \$2 to \$3, compared to approximately \$7 in Mexico, \$9 in Singapore, \$9 in Taiwan, \$36 in Japan, and \$25 in the United States. As companies have moved their manufacturing into China because of lower labor costs, new low-cost Chinese suppliers have also emerged, and United States, Japanese, Taiwanese, and Korean suppliers (among others) have set up operations in China as well. This is basically the same pattern followed previously in Japan in the 1960s and 1970s and later in Korea, Taiwan, and Singapore (see photo) before Mexico became a global hot spot.

Both Mexico and China have positive and negative aspects in terms of supply chain development for U.S. companies. You can ship from Mexico to the United States in about eight hours; however, it takes 21 to 23 days to ship from China. Many people speak English in Mexico, and many Americans speak Spanish; the same situation does not exist in China (although English is becoming more prevalent). Government regulations, especially in terms of business ownership, are sometimes restrictive in China, but in China a company can work 24 hours a day, 7 days a week, compared to an average workweek in Mexico of approximately 44 hours. Trade regulations and tariffs are increasingly being lowered in Mexico and China. Quality is a problem in both Mexico and China, where it can vary dramatically between companies. Chinese and Mexican suppliers generally lack quality-management systems, and do not often use statistical process control or have ISO certification, unless they are imposed by their global customers.

China's Role in the Global Supply Chain

It has become commonplace for companies in the United States and abroad to develop a global supply chain by sourcing in low-cost countries, and no country has received more attention as a supplier than China. China has become one of the world's premier sources of supply. Walmart, for example, has more than 50,000 suppliers in China. Not only are companies looking to China as a low-cost supplier of goods and services, but some companies are relocating their procurement operations to China. IBM moved its global purchasing headquarters from Westchester County, New York, to Shenzhen, China—the first time IBM located the headquarters of one of its global corporate functions outside the United States. It relocated, in part, to help the company develop stronger relationships with its suppliers in China, and to have more control over quality and logistics.

Companies are looking to China (as well as other emerging low-cost sources of supply such as Central/Eastern Europe, India, Bangladesh, the Philippines, and Pacific Rim countries) for several reasons. First there is an abundance of low-wage labor; China has a labor market of 750 million people, and the country's average hourly wage, although increasing, is still lower than in most other emerging markets. The average worker earns about $2 to $3 an hour, and migrant workers (who account for one-fifth of the labor market) typically earn less than $200 per month. Almost half of China's population has a middle-school or greater education. Most companies that are global sourcing also want to position their source countries as future markets, and China is one of the world's fastest-growing markets, and the world's second largest economy. China's exports increased by 500% and were almost $9 trillion in the first decade of this century. China's retail spending has been increasing by as much 12% to 16% annually in recent years. China has introduced a number of regulatory changes that has liberalized its market.

Traditionally, China exported consumer goods, clothing, and textiles; however, it is now increasingly exporting products with a higher technology content as its manufacturing sector matures. This is what most low-cost emerging countries do: ramp up with labor-intensive manufacturing and then migrate slowly toward more skilled, higher-value products and services. In particular, high-tech industries are looking to China as a low-cost supplier. Because high-tech companies operate on razor-thin margins, with intense competition and very fast product lifecycles, they have no choice but to look to countries like China as a source of low-cost supply. The Microsoft Xbox game system was first built in Mexico and Hungary, but production was shifted to China. Laptop computer manufacturing in Taiwan is moving to China.

United States companies generally follow one of several models in doing business in China. One option is to employ local third-party trading agents such as Chinese import and export companies (like Li & Fung) to help identify local suppliers, negotiate prices, and arrange logistics. Companies can develop their own international procurement offices that have specialized teams performing different sourcing functions like logistics. This has proven to be the most successful, especially for large manufacturing firms.

Sourcing from China is not without challenges. Dramatic differences in organization, cultural relationships, and technology can result in significant problems to overcome. Many U.S.

companies have spent years and resources building a network of reliable, high-quality suppliers, and disrupting that system in order to global outsource (often to remain competitive) can be a daunting task. Simply getting reliable information about Chinese suppliers in order to compare companies is much more difficult than in the United States. Information technology is less advanced and sophisticated in China than in the United States. Cultural relationships are more difficult to establish in China than in the United States. *Guanxi* (or personal relation ships) will frequently trump commercial considerations in the negotiation process and in doing business. Worker turnover rates among low-skilled workers are extremely high, averaging 30%–40% annually, and the turnover rate among new university graduates is also extremely high compared to industrialized nations. The piracy of U.S. intellectual properties is increasingly problematic.

Although China has become a burgeoning global supplier market, the country's underdeveloped transportation infrastructure, fragmented distribution systems, lack of sophisticated technology, limited logistics skills, regulatory restrictions, and local protectionism hinder efficient logistics and make supply chain management a challenge. Companies entering the Chinese market often find they cannot manage transportation and distribution as they might in their home country. The government-controlled rail service is China's cheapest distribution mode; however, capacity shortages often occur, although there has been significant investment in the railway infrastructure with over $350 billion spent between 2009 and 2012, and over $2 trillion on infrastructure projects between 2014 and 2016. Roads are the preferred mode of distribution for packaged finished goods; however, demand exceeds capacities, and China's road transport industry is fragmented although improving. Airfreight is subject to high prices, inadequate capacity, fragmented routes, and limited information exchange between airlines and freight forwarders. Ocean and inland water transport is the most developed distribution mode in China, and China's shipping companies rank among the world's largest. However, inland water distribution is sometimes underutilized because ports often cannot process and manage cargo efficiently, bureaucratic delays and theft are common, and some ports cannot accommodate larger vessels. Distribution is also hampered by poor warehousing, which is predominantly government controlled. Warehouse designs are inefficient with low ceilings and poor lighting, and goods are usually handled manually without warehouse automation.

Logistics oversight in China is shared by different government entities such as various planning and trade commissions, and this shared responsibility creates problems with things like customs clearance including excessive paperwork, inefficient procedures, and short business hours. Complicated and excessive regulatory controls are also common. Foreign trade companies must sell goods through distributors and cannot sell directly to stores, and they are forbidden to own distribution channels. A foreign company can sell goods manufactured in China, but it cannot sell or distribute goods imported into the country, including those produced by a company's plants outside of China. Thus, foreign companies must rely on small local distribution companies to move goods. Regulations also have created a shortage of third-party logistics providers.

However, despite these problems China's distribution and logistics sector is growing and improving rapidly. Trillions of dollars are being spent annually on new highways, airport construction and expansion, inland water transportation, and the construction of distribution and logistics centers. China's emergence as an economic power has forced the country to progressively remove regulations and restrictions that prevent foreign companies from participating in transportation and distribution functions, which has made it possible for foreign companies to establish subsidiaries and offices that manage a variety of supply chain functions. The demand for third-party logistics service providers has also expanded the outsourcing of logistics and transportation.

Reverse Globalization and Nearshoring

U.S. and European companies expanded their supply chains and shifting operations into Asia, and specifically China, because of cheaper labor and raw materials. However, the trend toward partnering with Asian and Far Eastern suppliers shows signs of reversing itself as the gloss of global sourcing has begun to tarnish for some companies. With an improved infrastructure and a higher standard of living, China is rapidly approaching a level of parity with other developed nations, mirroring a transition experienced in the past by other foreign countries like Japan, Taiwan, and India. Wage rates in Asia are steadily rising, thus negating one of the primary

Along the Supply Chain

U.S. Nearshoring in Central and South America

U.S. companies that are increasingly concerned about problems with extended Asian supply chains, and Chinese suppliers in particular, are looking more closely at reverse globalization and near shore suppliers. Chinese wages are growing at a rate of 15% to 20% per year. In 2004 India had 70% of the world's outsourcing market, but by 2015 it was 44%; North American nearshore outsourcing is growing at an annual rate of 10.5% while offshore outsourcing is growing at a 4% rate. There are a number of reasons for the growing attractiveness of nearshoring in Central and South America for U.S. companies. Latin American countries fall in the same time zone as the United States, which allows for real time communication, work, and travel. There is a large, highly skilled pool of college-educated talent in Latin America. Brazil has the most JAVA programmers in the world, and a large number of Latin American professionals attended universities in the United States. Spanish is the second language in the United States, spoken by an estimated 45 million people. Many Latin American countries have signed trade agreements with the United States that guarantee intellectual property (IP) rights while China and India pose a real threat for IP piracy.

Brazil, for example, offers a number of advantages to U.S. companies as a nearshore supplier and as a consumer market. Since 2000, Brazilian exports have grown at an annual rate of 17%, positioning it as one of the world's foremost emerging economies and global trading partners. With annual exports over $161 billion it is the twenty-fourth leading exporter in the world, and enjoys a trade balance of over $35 billion. Brazil has become a potential supply chain source for U.S. companies because of several factors. The country's electrical system is based mainly on hydroelectric power, which is inexpensive and sustainable. It has a favorable climate for agro-commodities, which has increased productivity compared to other northern hemisphere countries for almost all crops. It has a wealth of natural resource reserves including petroleum, making it relatively independent of resource shortages that have plagued other countries. Brazil has an established sustainable ethanol production and distribution network that provides more than 80% of the energy for passenger vehicles produced and sold in the country, and making it probably the first country that will be independent of fossil fuels for its light vehicle fleet. It has a well-established local supply base of small industrial companies that support a variety of industry sectors. It has substantially lower labor costs compared to developed countries. Although China is a major sourcing and consumer market for many U.S. and European companies, Brazil's closeness to the United States in geography, distance, and time zone results in comparatively less risky, less expensive, more sustainable supply chains (see photo). Shipping routes do not pass through global hot spots in the Mideast; freight rates are 30% lower than rates from Asia; and there are lower carbon emissions. In addition, the western culture of Brazilian businessmen is more closely related to that of North Americans and Western Europeans. Brazil, as well as the rest of Latin America, does have some drawbacks: the manufacturing wage rates are still significantly higher than China and Asia; the industrial capacity in some sectors is not sufficient to supply some U.S. manufacturing industries; advanced technology skills are insufficient in some hi-tech industry sectors; and the country's infrastructure is lacking and any exporter will likely be required to make a significant investment in shipping capacity and reliability. Still, Brazil and Latin America offer enough positive benefits for many U.S. companies to start looking south for a new supply chain member.

Investigate and discuss some of the other countries that might be possible near shore supply sources for the United States in the future.

Sources: Based on Ricardo Ruiz-Huidobro and Markus Stricker, "Brazil, A Country of Regeneration," *Inside Supply Management*, vol. 20, (9: September 2009), pp. 26–28; and, Jake Ryan, "Why Nearshoring is a Better Option for North American Companies," *Material Handling & Logistics* (at http://mhlnews.com), (November 19, 2014).

reasons for global sourcing. While Far Eastern and Asian countries are instituting new laws and port and trade regulations, countries in Latin America, South America, and Canada are investing more in education and infrastructure and developing larger and more modern port facilities, making it more appealing to source in this hemisphere. Volatile oil prices have made it more costly to ship items long distances and more difficult to predict costs; oil prices now account for nearly half of total freight costs. Shipping products over long distances while companies are demanding faster delivery times in a JIT-type competitive environment have contributed to an increase in containerization and faster ship speeds, which have increased fuel consumption. Increases in global transport costs have now effectively offset many of the trade liberalization agreements of the last 30 years.

Combined with these factors are the continuing unreliability of delivery times in longer global supply chains and quality failures, in China in particular. Surveys show that companies are increasingly concerned about the risk of poor product and supply chain quality (for example, the problem of lead paint in toys produced in China), and the infringement on intellectual property and security breaches in China. Long lead times resulting from distance and uncertainties in the shipping processes for global sourcing mean ordering far in advance, which can backfire if the product market changes or the economy sours. It is often difficult for U.S. companies to gain visibility into the financial health of foreign suppliers; during the recent global recession many overseas suppliers went bankrupt, creating supply chain delays for U.S. buyers. All of these factors—increasing oil prices, higher foreign wage rates, increasing

luoman/iStockphoto

Brazil has 36 deep water ports, making it an attractive "near shore supplier" for the United States. Rio de Janeiro is the third busiest port in Brazil in terms of cargo volume and container movement; the port of Santos is the largest.

raw material costs, poor quality, and long delivery times—have made what's referred to as *near-shore* sourcing, and redesigning supply chains with multilocal operations, in this hemisphere more attractive.

Gartner's annual survey of Top 25 supply chains, which includes companies like Apple, Dell, Amazon, Cisco, Walmart, and Procter & Gamble, indicates that an emerging trend among companies with top-ranked supply chains was a reassessment of the tradeoff between global economies of scale and the demand for local responsiveness, and as a result, they are exploring redesigning their supply chains to support a more regionalized approach. Although these companies' supply chains may be designed to address a global marketplace, manufacturing and supply capabilities are often being situated at numerous regional localities, rather than in a central location like China. This change is being driven by several factors including local government incentives, organized labor concessions, high annual wage increases and rising logistics expenses in China, combined with the demand to be more responsive to local markets and to reduce supply chain risks.

Although wage rates are higher, many U.S. companies are moving operations and facilities back to the United States, are partnering with U.S. suppliers or suppliers in this hemisphere, including South America, Mexico and the Caribbean, and some are insourcing. Near-shoring allows companies to reduce or avoid many of the risks associated with global sourcing, and shorter supply chains enable companies to gain more control and flexibility. Some companies, embracing customer concerns about service quality, are moving customer service and ordering processes from India back to the United States; even though it's more costly, maintaining customers and customer satisfaction is being recognized as the more important consideration.

Security within Global Supply Chains

The events of 9/11 affected global supply chains as they did much else in our lives. The two primary modes of transport in global supply chains are airfreight and ocean carriers, both of which enter the United States through portals from the outside world and thus are obvious security risks. The U.S. government in concert with countries around the world has adopted security measures that, besides increasing security, have added time to supply chain schedules and increased supply chain costs. Air and ocean carriers must file an advance manifest with the U.S. government 24 hours before loading the containers on a U.S.-bound ship or airplane so the government can conduct "risk screening." This 24-hour rule requires extensive documentation at the airport or seaport of origin, which can extend supply chain time by three to four days. Even if shipments reach the U.S. port on time, stricter customs inspections can leave the shipment tied up for hours or days. For example, food imports can be diverted for inspections for possible bioterrorism alterations. For airfreight, a delay of three or four days would negate the benefit of shipping by air at all. As a result of new security measures after 9/11, inventory levels increased almost 5%, requiring more than $75 billion in extra working capital, as companies coped with delays with buffer inventory. The cost of insuring U.S. imports increased from $36 billion in 2001 to over $40 billion to 2002. The Brookings Institute has estimated that the cost of slowing the delivery of imported goods by one day because of additional security checks is approximately $7 billion per year. These costs do not even include the costs of new people, technologies, equipment, surveillance, communication, security systems, and training necessary for screening at airports and seaports around the world.

In 2003 the U.S. Customs and Border Protection (CPB) agency was established as part of the Department of Homeland Security to ensure that all imports and exports are legal and comply with U.S. laws and regulations. The CPB has implemented a comprehensive cargo security system designed to protect national security that includes the 24-hour manifest rule, a container security initiative, a customs-trade partnership against terrorism (C-PAT), nonintrusion inspection techniques, automated targeting systems, the national targeting center, and recently the secure freight initiative. The secure freight initiative, announced in 2008, went into effect in January 2010. Also known as the "10 + 2" initiative, it is intended to reduce the rise of terrorism by using the latest tracking and tracing, and communication and reporting, technologies. It provides for a detailed security account of goods and materials shipped into the United States, called the Importer Security Filing (ISF), that distinguishes between potentially risky cargo and lower risk cargo, and more efficiently allocates agency resources to focus on true security threats. ISF 10 + 2 is mandatory for all importers; it includes 10 specific data elements related to container manufacturer, seller, buyer, content, importer, schedule, origin, and destination, that must be electronically filed 24 hours before loading any container on a ship bound for the United States. The "+2" are data files which the carrier must file within 48 hours of the departure time, and includes the location of all containers on the ship and information on the movement of containers and any status changes as they move through the supply chain. 10 + 2 was expected to increase annual supply chain shipping costs from $400 million to $700 million as a result of government filing fees and the additional reporting information required.

Key Terms

continuous replenishment Supplying orders in a short period of time according to a predetermined schedule.

core competencies The activities that a company does best.

cross-docking Crossing of goods from one loading dock to another without being placed in storage.

e-auction A company posts items it wants to purchase on an Internet e-marketplace for suppliers to bid on.

e-marketplaces Websites where companies and suppliers conduct business-to-business activities.

e-procurement Business-to-business commerce in which purchases are made directly through a supplier's website.

intermodal transportation Combines several modes of transportation.

landed cost Total cost of producing, storing, and transporting a product to the site of consumption.

logistics The transportation and distribution of goods and services.

nation groups Nations joined together into trading groups.

on-demand (direct-response) delivery Requires the supplier to deliver goods when demanded by the customer.

order fulfillment The process of ensuring on-time delivery of a customer's order.

outsourcing Purchasing goods and services that were originally produced in-house from an outside supplier.

postponement Moving some final manufacturing steps like final assembly or product customization into the warehouse or distribution center.

procurement Purchasing goods and services from suppliers.

sourcing The selection of suppliers.

spend analysis A formal process for analyzing procurement data to lower costs.

tariffs (duties) Taxes on imported goods.

trade specialists Specialists who help manage transportation and distribution operations in foreign countries.

value added tax (VAT) An indirect tax on the increase in value of a good at any stage in the supply chain from raw material to final product.

vendor-managed inventory (VMI) A system in which manufacturers instead of distributors generate orders.

warehouse management system (WMS) An automated system that runs the day-to-day operations of a warehouse or distribution center and keeps track of inventory.

Questions

11.1. Describe in general terms how you think the distribution system for McDonald's works.

11.2. Discuss why single-sourcing is attractive to some companies.

11.3. Define the strategic goals of supply chain management, and indicate how procurement and transportation and distribution have an impact on these goals.

11.4. Identify five businesses in your community and determine what modes of transportation are used to supply them.

11.5. Pick a business you are familiar with and describe its primary transportation model and its transport routes.

11.6. Select a company and determine the type of suppliers it has, then indicate the criteria that you think the company might use to evaluate and select suppliers.

11.7. Select a company that has a global supply chain and describe it, including purchasing, production, distribution, and transportation.

11.8. Locate an e-marketplace on the Internet and describe it and the type of suppliers, and producers it connects.

11.9. Locate a transportation exchange on the Internet, describe the services it provides to its users, and indicate some of the customers that use it.

11.10. Explore the website of an enterprise resource planning provider and describe the transportation and distribution services it indicates it provides.

11.11. Locate an international logistics provider on the Internet; describe the services it provides and identify some of its customers.

11.12. *Supply Chain Management Review* (at www.scmr.com) and *Inside Supply Management* are trade magazines that focus on all aspects of supply chain management. Its articles include examples of supply chain management at various companies. Research an article (or articles) and write a brief paper on a company (or companies) related to procurement similar to the "Along the Supply Chain" boxes in this chapter.

11.13. The two magazines in question 11.12 also include articles on logistics, transportation, and distribution. Select an article (or articles) and write a brief paper about these processes similar to the "Along the Supply Chain" boxes in this chapter.

11.14. Describe the global supply and distribution channels of the retail company L.L. Bean.

11.15. Walmart is one of the leaders in promoting the development and use of radio frequency identification (RFID) and electronic product codes. Explain how Walmart uses RFID in its procurement and distribution and why Walmart wants its suppliers to adopt RFID.

11.16. Describe the differences and/or similarities between VMI and postponement, and explain how the two might complement each other.

11.17. Explain how Walmart has used cross-docking to improve its supply chain efficiency.

11.18. Describe the supply chain for your university or college. Who are the suppliers and distributors in this supply chain?

11.19. Identify three countries (other than Canada) that you think would be possible near-shore suppliers for U.S. companies and discuss their advantages and disadvantages.

11.20. Discuss how sustainability can be achieved in transportation and distribution functions.

11.21. Using the Internet, find an article and write a report about how an actual company is achieving sustainability though improved processes in its transportation and distribution functions.

11.22. Discuss some of the disadvantages of U.S. companies using Chinese suppliers that might drive them to near-shore their supply chains.

11.23. Discuss why you think reverse globalization may, or may not, be a long-term trend.

11.24. Describe what spend analysis is and how it can improve procurement activities for a company with a global supply chain.

11.25. Compare the positive and negative aspects of a U.S. company outsourcing in China, Mexico, and Brazil.

11.26. Apple, Amazon, and Procter & Gamble are recognized year after year as companies with top-rated global supply chains. Describe the supply chains of each company and discuss their similarities and differences.

11.27. Walmart employs numerous suppliers in China; describe some of the difficulties that it experiences in its sustainability efforts.

11.28. For each of the principal modes of product transportation—rail, air, truck, intermodal, water, package carriers, and pipeline—identify a company that employs the mode of transportation, and for which of its products.

11.29. Using the Internet, identify a third-party logistics (3PL) provider and describe the type of services it offers and the advantages it might provide the outsourcing company.

11.30. Describe some of the problems a company faces with global supply chain management.

11.31. Study the website of the World Trade Organization (WTO) and describe the type of services it provides its members—that is, what it is and what it does.

11.32. Describe the "10 benefits of the WTO trading system" outlined on the World Trade organization website.

11.33. Describe the differences among tariffs, duties, landed costs, and value-added taxes.

11.34. The World Trade Organization (WTO) maintains large databases about the trade statistics of its member countries on its website. Access a "trade profile" for a country of your choosing and the United States for the most recent available year, and write a summary report describing and comparing the trade profiles of the two countries.

11.35. Describe the European Union—what it is, its history, and how it promotes and advances international trade.

11.36. Using the Internet, identify an "international trade specialist" and describe the services it provides companies with a global supply chain.

11.37. Using the Internet, research and write a report on intermodal shipping, including its different forms, its technical aspects, its use around the world, some examples of companies that use it, and the type of products that are transported using intermodal.

11.38. Referring to *Gartner's* list of "Top 25 Supply Chains," describe any trends you can identify among the companies on the list for managing their global supply chains.

11.39. Using the Internet, identify the five busiest global ports according to whatever measure of port traffic or volume you choose.

11.40. Write a report describing the North American Free Trade Agreement (NAFTA), including its history, what it is, what it does, and its effectiveness in promoting trade between its member companies.

Case Problem

Case Problem 11.1 Somerset Furniture Company's Global Supply Chain—Continued

For the Somerset Furniture Company described in Case Problem 10.1 in Chapter 10, determine the product lead time by developing a time line from the initiation of a purchase order to product delivery. Discuss the company's possible transportation modes and channels in China and to and within the United States, and the likelihood of potential problems. Identify and discuss how international trade specialist(s), trade logistics companies, and/or Internet exchanges might help Somerset reduce its product lead time and variability.

SUPPLEMENT TO CHAPTER 11

Operational Decision-Making Tools: Transportation and Transshipment Models

IN THIS SUPPLEMENT, YOU WILL LEARN ABOUT . . .

- The Transportation Model
- The Transshipment Model

An important factor in supply chain management is determining the lowest-cost transportation provider from among several alternatives. In most cases, items are transported from a plant or warehouse to a producer, a retail outlet, or distributor via truck, rail, or air. Sometimes the modes of transportation may be the same, but the company must decide among different transportation carriers—for example, different trucking firms. Two quantitative techniques that are used for determining the least cost means of transporting goods or services are the *transportation method* and the *transshipment method*.

The Transportation Model

Transportation model Involves transporting items from sources with fixed supply to destinations with fixed demand at the lowest cost.

A **transportation model** is formulated for a class of problems with the following characteristics: (1) a product is *transported* from a number of sources to a number of destinations at the minimum possible cost, and (2) each source is able to supply a fixed number of units of the product and each destination has a fixed demand for the product. The following example demonstrates the formulation of the transportation model.

EXAMPLE S11.1 | A Transportation Problem

Potatoes are grown and harvested on farms in the Midwest and then shipped to distribution centers in Kansas City, Omaha, and Des Moines, where they are cleaned and sorted. These distribution centers supply three manufacturing plants operated by the Frodo-Lane Foods Company, located in Chicago, St. Louis, and Cincinnati, where they make potato chips. Potatoes are shipped to the manufacturing plants by railroad or truck. Each distribution center is able to supply the following tons of potatoes to the plants on a monthly basis:

DISTRIBUTION CENTER	SUPPLY
1. Kansas City	150
2. Omaha	175
3. Des Moines	275
	600 tons

Each plant demands the following tons of potatoes per month:

PLANT	DEMAND
A. Chicago	200
B. St. Louis	100
C. Cincinnati	300
	600 tons

The cost of transporting 1 ton of potatoes from each distribution center (source) to each plant (destination) differs according to the distance and method of transport. These costs are shown next. For example, the cost of shipping 1 ton of potatoes from the distribution center at Omaha to the plant at Chicago is $7.

DISTRIBUTION CENTER	PLANT		
	CHICAGO	*ST. LOUIS*	*CINCINNATI*
Kansas City	$6	$8	$10
Omaha	7	11	11
Des Moines	4	5	12

The problem is to determine how many tons of potatoes to transport from each distribution center to each plant on a monthly basis to minimize the total cost of transportation. A diagram of the different transportation routes with supply, demand, and cost figures is given in **Figure S11.1**.

Transportation models are solved within the context of a transportation table, which for our example is shown as follows. Each cell in the table represents the amount transported from one source to one destination. The smaller box within each cell contains the unit transportation cost for that route. For example, in the cell in the upper-left-hand corner, the value $6 is the cost of transporting 1 ton of potatoes from Kansas City to Chicago. Along the outer rim of the table are the supply and demand constraint quantity values, referred to as *rim requirements*.

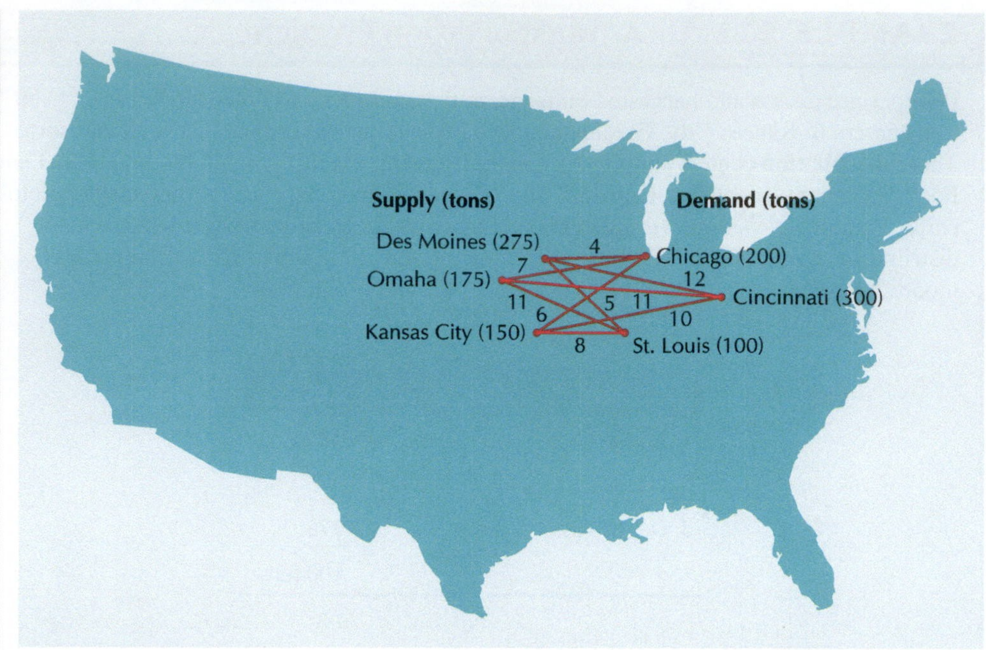

FIGURE S11.1 **Network of Transportation Routes**

The Transportation Table

FROM \ TO	*CHICAGO*	*ST. LOUIS*	*CINCINNATI*	*SUPPLY*
Kansas City	6	8	10	150
Omaha	7	11	11	175
Des Moines	4	5	12	275
Demand	200	100	300	600

There are several quantitative methods for solving transportation models manually, including the *stepping-stone method* and the *modified distribution method*. These methods require a number of computational steps and are very time consuming if done by hand. We will not present the detailed solution procedure for these methods here. We will focus on the computer solution of the transportation model using Excel.

Solution of the Transportation Model with Excel

Transportation models can be solved using spreadsheets like Microsoft Excel. **Exhibit S11.1** shows the initial Excel screen for Example S11.1 (which can be downloaded from the text website).

The "target" cell containing total cost is C10, and it is set equal to "min" since our objective is to minimize cost. The "variables" in our problem representing individual shipments from each distributor to each plant are cells C5 to E7 inclusive. This is designated as "C5:E7." (Excel adds the $s.) The constraints mathematically specify that the amount shipped equals the amount available or demanded. For example, C9:E9 = C8:E8 means the amount shipped from all three distribution centers will equal demand at all three plants. First, the "variables non-negative" box must be checked, and "Simplex LP" must be selected as the "solving method," as shown in **Exhibit S11.2**. Once all the model parameters have been entered into the solver, click on "Solve." The solution is shown on the Excel screen in **Exhibit S11.3**.

Interpreting this solution, we find that 125 tons are shipped from Kansas City to Cincinnati, 175 tons are shipped from Omaha to the plant at Cincinnati, and so on. The total shipping cost is $4525. The company could use these results to make decisions about how to ship potatoes and to negotiate new rate agreements with railway and trucking shippers.

EXHIBIT S11.1

Excel File

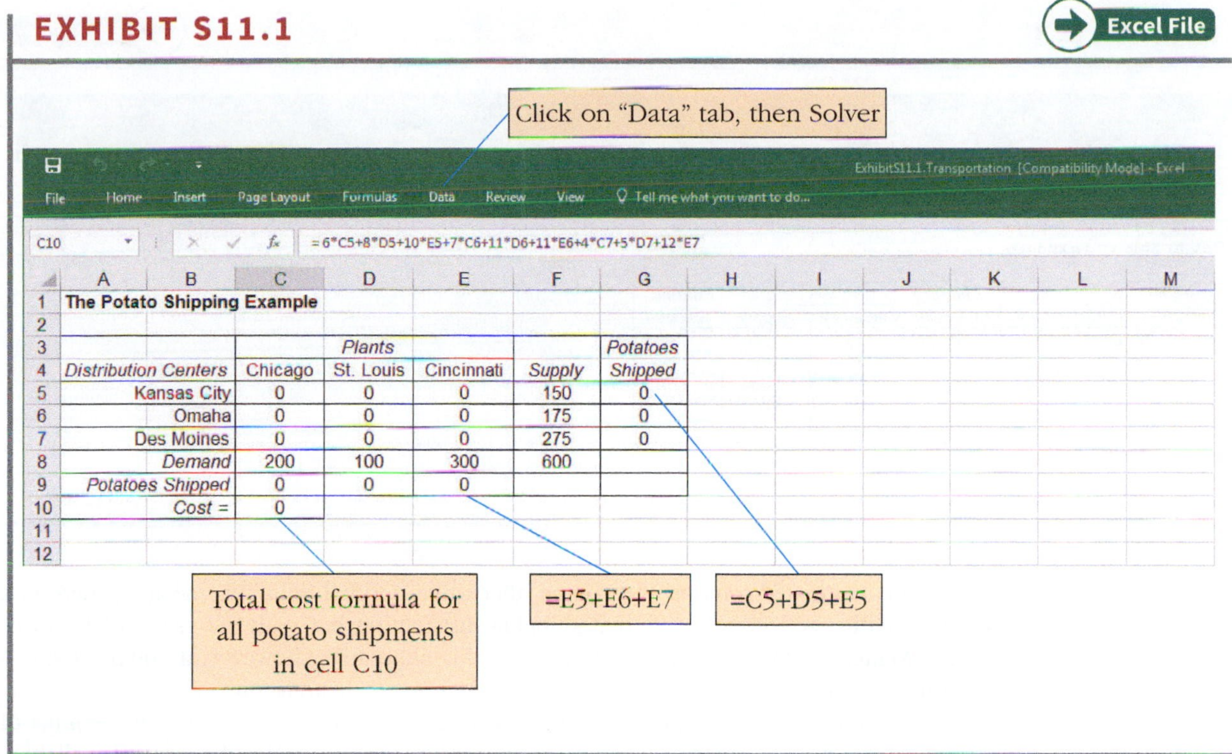
Click on "Data" tab, then Solver
C10
=6*C5+8*D5+10*E5+7*C6+11*D6+11*E6+4*C7+5*D7+12*E7
The Potato Shipping Example
Plants
Potatoes Shipped
Distribution Centers
Chicago
St. Louis
Cincinnati
Supply
Kansas City
Omaha
Des Moines
Demand
Potatoes Shipped
Cost =
Total cost formula for all potato shipments in cell C10
=E5+E6+E7
=C5+D5+E5

EXHIBIT S11.2

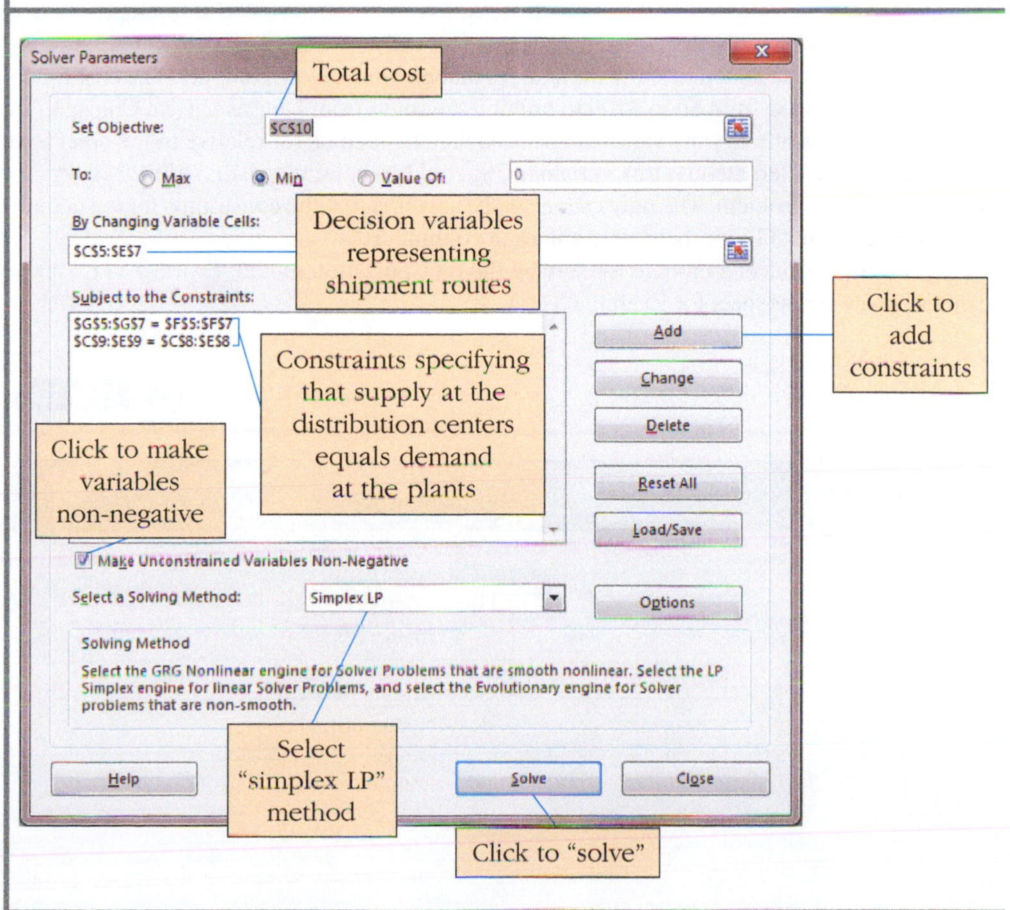
Solver Parameters
Total cost
Set Objective:
$C$10
To:
Max
Min
Value Of:
By Changing Variable Cells:
$C$5:$E$7
Decision variables representing shipment routes
Subject to the Constraints:
$G$5:$G$7 = $F$5:$F$7
$C$9:$E$9 = $C$8:$E$8
Constraints specifying that supply at the distribution centers equals demand at the plants
Add
Change
Delete
Reset All
Load/Save
Click to add constraints
Click to make variables non-negative
Make Unconstrained Variables Non-Negative
Select a Solving Method:
Simplex LP
Options
Solving Method
Select the GRG Nonlinear engine for Solver Problems that are smooth nonlinear. Select the LP Simplex engine for linear Solver Problems, and select the Evolutionary engine for Solver problems that are non-smooth.
Help
Select "simplex LP" method
Solve
Close
Click to "solve"

EXHIBIT S11.3

Excel File

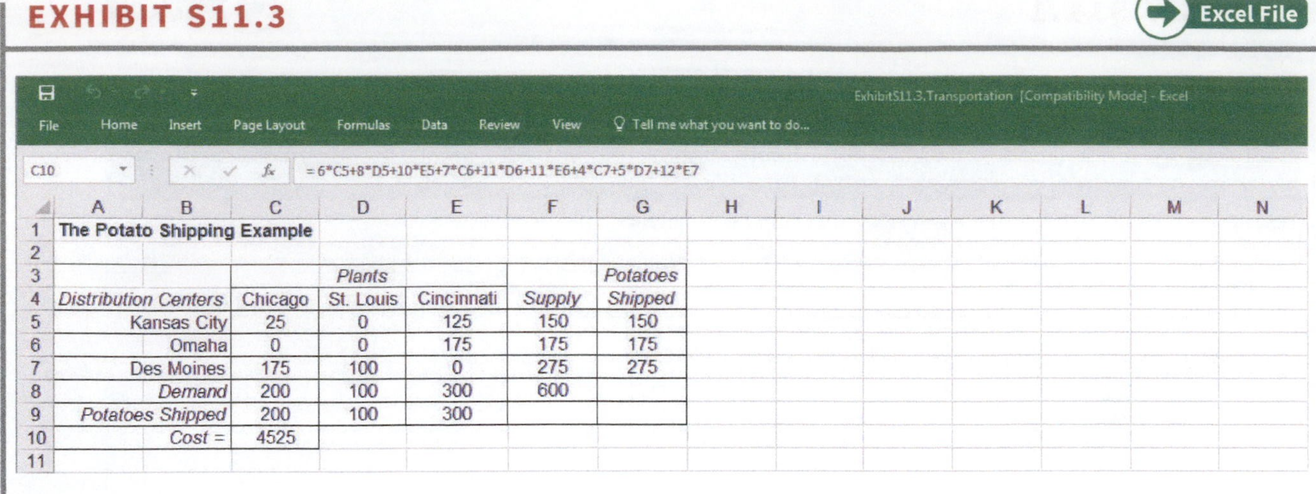
ExhibitS11.3.Transportation [Compatibility Mode] - Excel

C10 = 6*C5+8*D5+10*E5+7*C6+11*D6+11*E6+4*C7+5*D7+12*E7

The Potato Shipping Example

	Plants				Potatoes
Distribution Centers	Chicago	St. Louis	Cincinnati	*Supply*	*Shipped*
Kansas City	25	0	125	150	150
Omaha	0	0	175	175	175
Des Moines	175	100	0	275	275
Demand	200	100	300	600	
Potatoes Shipped	200	100	300		
Cost =	4525				

In this computer solution there is an alternative optimal solution, meaning there is a second solution reflecting a different shipping distribution but with the same total cost of $4525. Manual solution is required to identify this alternative; however, it could provide a different shipping pattern that the company might view as advantageous.

Prohibited route Transportation route over which goods cannot be transported.

In Example S11.1 the unique condition occurred in which there were the same number of sources as destinations, three, and the supply at all three sources equaled the demand at all three destinations, 600 tons. This is the simplest form of transportation model; however, solution is not restricted to these conditions. Sources and destinations can be unequal, and total supply does not have to equal total demand, which is called an *unbalanced* problem. In addition, there can be **prohibited routes**. If a route is prohibited, units cannot be transported from a particular source to a particular destination.

Exhibit S11.4 shows the solution for a modified version of our potato shipment example in which supply at Des Moines has been increased to 375 tons and the shipping route from Kansas City to Chicago is prohibited because of a railway track being repaired. An extra column (H) has been added to show the sources that now have excess supply. The cost for cell C5 has been changed from $6 to $100 to prohibit the route from Kansas City to Chicago. The value of $100 is arbitrary; any value can be used that is much larger relative to the other route shipping costs. (Alternatively, this variable, CS, could be eliminated.) Exhibit S11.5 shows the solver for this problem. The only change in the solver is that the constraints for the potatoes shipped in column "G" are the supply values in column "F."

OM Tools also has a module for solving the transportation model. Exhibit S11.6 shows the OM Tools spreadsheet for Example S11.1.

EXHIBIT S11.4

Excel File

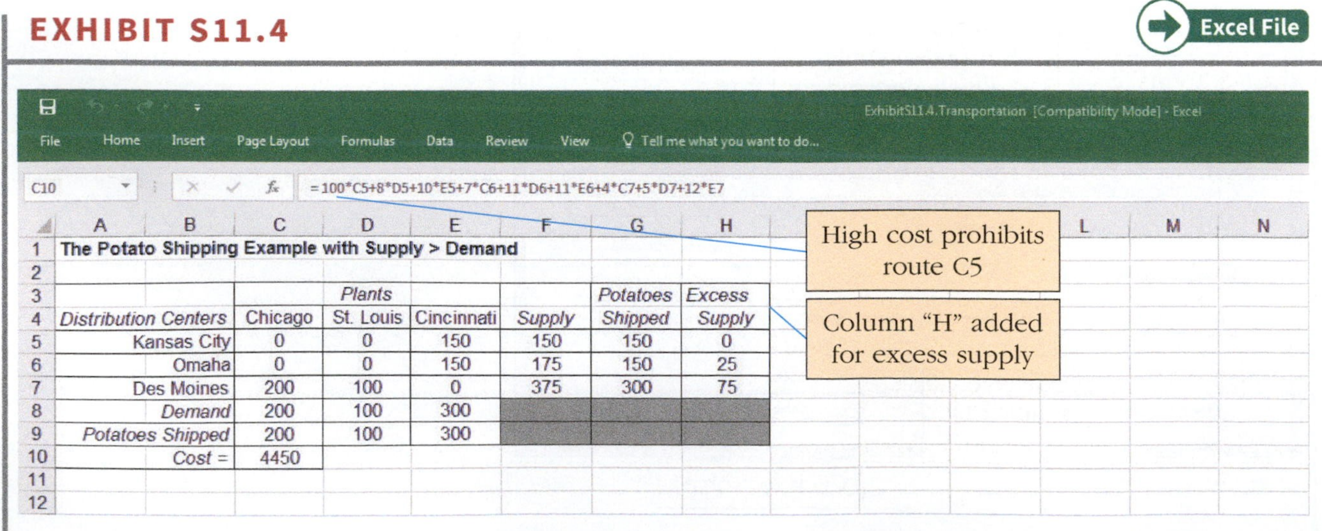
High cost prohibits route C5
Column "H" added for excess supply
ExhibitS11.4.Transportation [Compatibility Mode] - Excel

C10 = 100*C5+8*D5+10*E5+7*C6+11*D6+11*E6+4*C7+5*D7+12*E7

The Potato Shipping Example with Supply > Demand

	Plants				Potatoes	Excess
Distribution Centers	Chicago	St. Louis	Cincinnati	*Supply*	*Shipped*	*Supply*
Kansas City	0	0	150	150	150	0
Omaha	0	0	150	175	150	25
Des Moines	200	100	0	375	300	75
Demand	200	100	300			
Potatoes Shipped	200	100	300			
Cost =	4450					

EXHIBIT S11.5

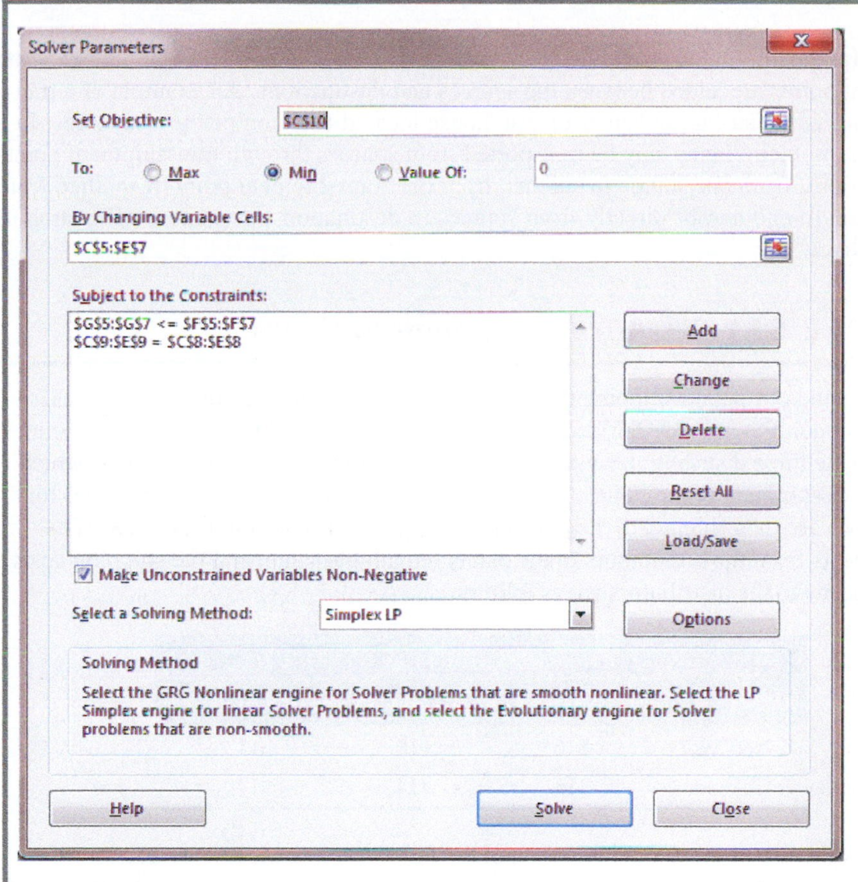

EXHIBIT S11.6

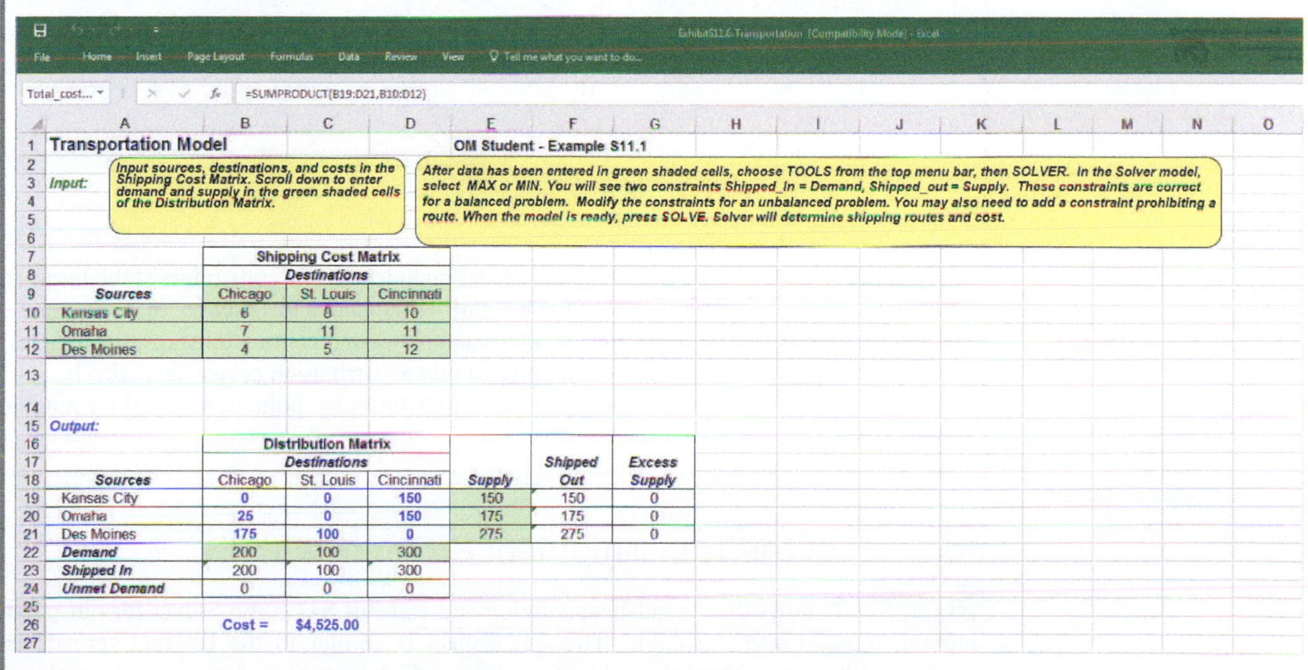

Total_cost... =SUMPRODUCT(B19:D21,B10:D12)

Transportation Model — OM Student - Example S11.1

Input: Input sources, destinations, and costs in the Shipping Cost Matrix. Scroll down to enter demand and supply in the green shaded cells of the Distribution Matrix.

After data has been entered in green shaded cells, choose TOOLS from the top menu bar, then SOLVER. In the Solver model, select MAX or MIN. You will see two constraints Shipped_In = Demand, Shipped_out = Supply. These constraints are correct for a balanced problem. Modify the constraints for an unbalanced problem. You may also need to add a constraint prohibiting a route. When the model is ready, press SOLVE. Solver will determine shipping routes and cost.

	Shipping Cost Matrix		
	Destinations		
Sources	Chicago	St. Louis	Cincinnati
Kansas City	6	8	10
Omaha	7	11	11
Des Moines	4	5	12

Output:

	Distribution Matrix					
	Destinations				Shipped	Excess
Sources	Chicago	St. Louis	Cincinnati	Supply	Out	Supply
Kansas City	0	0	150	150	150	0
Omaha	25	0	150	175	175	0
Des Moines	175	100	0	275	275	0
Demand	200	100	300			
Shipped In	200	100	300			
Unmet Demand	0	0	0			

Cost = $4,525.00

The Transshipment Model

Transshipment model A variation of the transportation model with intermediate points between sources and destinations.

The **transshipment model** is an extension of the transportation model in which intermediate transshipment points are added between the sources and destinations. An example of a transshipment point is a distribution center or warehouse located between plants and stores. In a transshipment problem, items may be transported from sources through transshipment points on to destinations, from one source to another, from one transshipment point to another, from one destination to another, or directly from sources to destinations, or some combination of these alternatives.

EXAMPLE S11.2 | A Transshipment Problem

We will expand our potato shipping example to demonstrate the formulation of a transshipment model. Potatoes are harvested at farms in Nebraska and Colorado before being shipped to the three distribution centers in Kansas City, Omaha, and Des Moines, which are now transshipment points. The amount of potatoes harvested at each farm is 300 tons. The potatoes are then shipped to the plants in Chicago, St. Louis, and Cincinnati. The shipping costs from the distributors to the plants remain the same, and the shipping costs from the farms to the distributors are as follows.

	DISTRIBUTION CENTER		
FARM	3. KANSAS CITY	4. OMAHA	5. DES MOINES
1. Nebraska	$16	10	12
2. Colorado	15	14	17

The basic structure of this model is shown in the following graphical network.

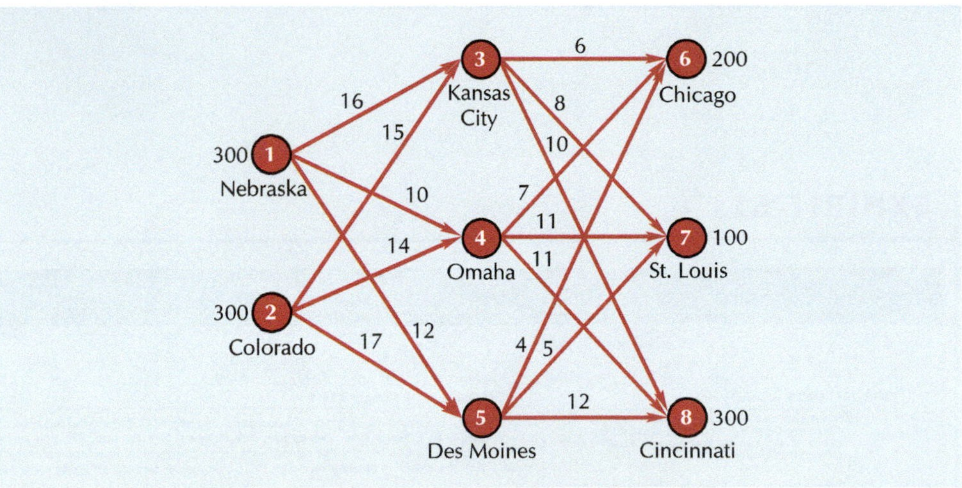

As with the transportation problem, this model includes supply constraints at the farms in Nebraska and Colorado, and demand constraints at the plants in Chicago, St. Louis, and Cincinnati. However, there are several additional mathematical relationships that express the condition that whatever amount is shipped into a distribution center must also be shipped out; that is, the amount shipped into a transshipment point must equal the amount shipped out.

Solution of the Transshipment Problem with Excel

Exhibit S11.7 shows the spreadsheet solution and Exhibit S11.8 the Solver for our potato shipping transshipment example. The spreadsheet is similar to the original spreadsheet for the regular transportation problem in Exhibit S11.1, except there are two tables of

EXHIBIT S11.7

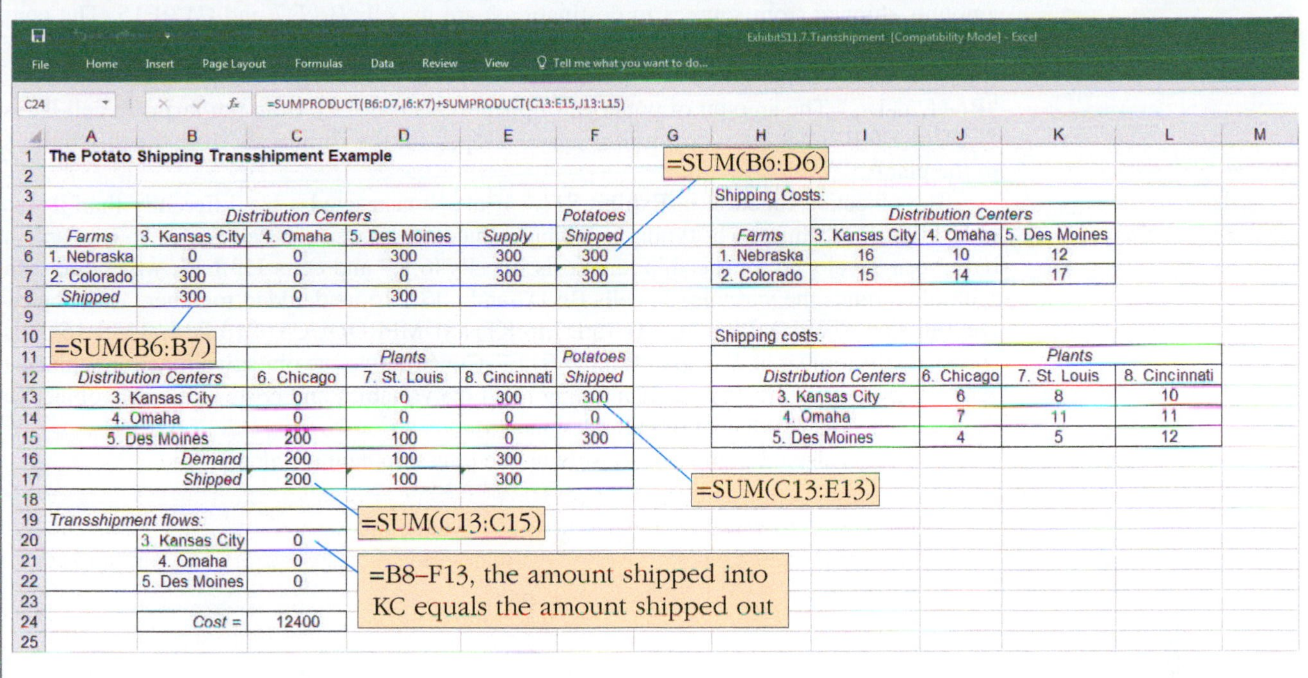

The Potato Shipping Transshipment Example

Farms	3. Kansas City	4. Omaha	5. Des Moines	Supply	Potatoes Shipped
1. Nebraska	0	0	300	300	300
2. Colorado	300	0	0	300	300
Shipped	300	0	300		

Distribution Centers	6. Chicago	7. St. Louis	8. Cincinnati	Potatoes Shipped
3. Kansas City	0	0	300	300
4. Omaha	0	0	0	0
5. Des Moines	200	100	0	300
Demand	200	100	300	
Shipped	200	100	300	

Transshipment flows:	
3. Kansas City	0
4. Omaha	0
5. Des Moines	0
Cost =	12400

Shipping Costs:

Farms	3. Kansas City	4. Omaha	5. Des Moines
1. Nebraska	16	10	12
2. Colorado	15	14	17

Shipping costs:

Distribution Centers	6. Chicago	7. St. Louis	8. Cincinnati
3. Kansas City	6	8	10
4. Omaha	7	11	11
5. Des Moines	4	5	12

EXHIBIT S11.8

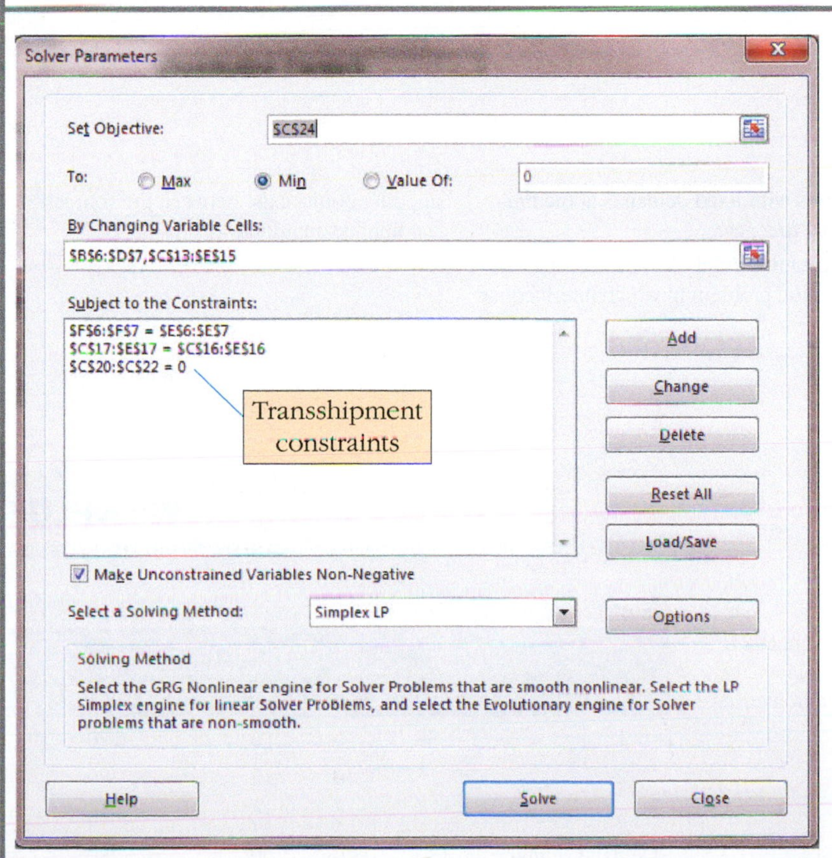

variables—one for shipping from the farms to the distribution centers and one for shipping potatoes from the distribution centers to the plants. Thus, the decision variables (i.e., the amounts shipped from sources to destinations) are in cells B6:D7 and C13:E15. The constraint for the amount of potatoes shipped from the farm in Nebraska to the three distributors (i.e., the supply constraint for Nebraska) in cell F6 is "=SUM(B6:D6)," which sums cells "B6+C6+D6." The amount of potatoes shipped to Kansas City from the farms in cell B8 is "=SUM(B6:B7)." Similar constraints are developed for the shipments from the distributors to the plants.

The objective function in Exhibit S11.7 is also constructed a bit differently than it was in Exhibit S11.1. Instead of typing in a single objective function in cell C24, two cost arrays have been developed for the shipping costs in cells I6:K7 and cells J13:L15, which are then multiplied times the variables in cells B6:D7 and C13:E15, and added together. This objective function, "=SUMPRODUCT(B6:D7,I6:K7)+SUMPRODUCT(C13:E15, J13:L15)," is shown on the toolbar at the top of Exhibit S11.7. Constructing the objective function with cost arrays like this is a little easier than typing in all the variables and costs in a single objective function when there are a lot of variables and costs.

OM Tools also has a module for solving the transshipment problem.

Summary

Transportation and transshipment models are quantitative techniques that are used to analyze logistical supply chain problems, specifically the distribution of items from sources to destinations. The objective is frequently to minimize transportation costs. Both models can be solved using Excel spreadsheets that were demonstrated in this chapter.

Key Terms

prohibited route A transportation route over which items cannot be transported.

transportation model Transporting items from sources with fixed supplies to destinations with fixed demands at the minimum cost, time, etc.

transshipment model A special case of the transportation problem in which intermediate shipping points exist between the sources and final destinations.

Solved Problems

WileyPLUS
ANIMATED DEMO PROBLEM

Transportation Model

A manufacturing firm ships its finished products from three plants to three distribution warehouses. The supply capacities of the plants, the demand requirements at the warehouses, and the transportation costs per ton are shown as follows:

	WAREHOUSES			
PLANT	*A*	*B*	*C*	SUPPLY (UNITS)
1	$8	5	6	120
2	15	10	12	80
3	3	9	10	80
Demand (units)	150	70	60	280

Solve this problem using Excel.

Solution

EXHIBIT S11.9

ExhibitS11 - Solved Problem [Compatibility Mode] - Excel

File Home Insert Page Layout Formulas Data Review View Tell me what you want to do...

C10 f_x =8*C5+5*D5+6*E5+15*C6+10*D6+12*E6+3*C7+9*D7+10*E7

	A	B	C	D	E	F	G
1	Solved Problem						
2							
3				Warehouses			Units
4	Plant		A	B	C	Supply	Shipped
5		1	70	0	50	120	120
6		2	0	70	10	80	80
7		3	80	0	0	80	80
8		Demand	150	70	60	280	
9		Units shipped	150	70	60		
10		Cost =	1920				
11							

Problems

WileyPLUS

S11.1. Steel mills in three cities produce the following amounts of steel:

LOCATION	WEEKLY PRODUCTION (TONS)
A. Bethlehem	180
B. Birmingham	260
C. Gary	310
	740

These mills supply steel to four cities, where manufacturing plants have the following demand:

LOCATION	WEEKLY DEMAND (TONS)
1. Detroit	160
2. St. Louis	120
3. Chicago	170
4. Norfolk	220
	670

Shipping costs per ton of steel are as follows:

	TO			
FROM	*1*	*2*	*3*	*4*
A.	$130	$ 90	$140	$170
B.	120	110	70	100
C.	180	130	100	210

Because of a truckers' strike, shipments are prohibited from Birmingham to Chicago. Solve this problem.

S11.2. In Problem S11.1, what would be the effect of a reduction in production capacity at the Gary location from 310 tons to 260 tons per week?

S11.3. Oranges are grown, picked, and then processed and packaged at distribution centers in Tampa, Miami, and Fresno. These centers supply oranges to markets in New York, Philadelphia, Chicago, and Boston. The following table shows the shipping costs per truckload ($100s), supply, and demand:

	TO				
FROM	NEW YORK	PHILADELPHIA	CHICAGO	BOSTON	SUPPLY
Tampa	$ 9	$ 14	$ 12	$ 17	300
Miami	11	10	6	10	200
Fresno	12	8	15	7	250
Demand	160	210	130	180	

Because of an agreement between distributors, shipments are prohibited from Miami to Chicago. Solve this problem.

S11.4. In Exhibit S11.4, shipments are prohibited from Kansas City to Chicago because of railroad construction. Once the rail construction is completed, what will be the effect on the optimal shipping routes?

S11.5. A manufacturing firm produces diesel engines in four cities—Phoenix, Seattle, St. Louis, and Detroit. The company is able to produce the following numbers of engines per month:

PLANT	PRODUCTION
1. Phoenix	10
2. Seattle	20
3. St. Louis	15
4. Detroit	25

Three trucking firms purchase the following numbers of engines for their plants in three cities:

FIRM	DEMAND
A. Greensboro	10
B. Charlotte	20
C. Louisville	15

The transportation costs per engine ($100s) from sources to destinations are as shown:

	TO		
FROM	*A*	*B*	*C*
1.	$ 7	$ 8	$ 5
2.	6	10	6
3.	10	4	5
4.	3	9	11

However, the Charlotte firm will not accept engines made in Seattle, and the Louisville firm will not accept engines from Detroit; therefore, these routes are prohibited. Solve this problem.

S11.6. The US-Haul Truck Rental firm has accumulated extra trucks at three of its truck leasing outlets, as shown:

LEASING OUTLET	EXTRA TRUCKS
1. Atlanta	70
2. St. Louis	115
3. Charlotte	60
	245

The firm also has four outlets with shortages of rental trucks, as follows:

LEASING OUTLET	TRUCK SHORTAGE
A. New Orleans	80
B. Buffalo	50
C. Dallas	90
D. Pittsburgh	25
	245

The firm wants to transfer trucks from the outlets with extras to those with shortages at the minimum total cost. The following costs of transporting these trucks from city to city have been determined:

	TO			
FROM	*A*	*B*	*C*	*D*
1.	$ 70	$100	$ 90	$60
2.	120	80	50	40
3.	110	140	120	70

Solve this problem.

S11.7. In Problem S11.6, what would be the effect on the optimal solution if there were no shortage of rental trucks at the New Orleans outlet?

S11.8. The John Adams Brewing Company has breweries in three cities; the breweries can supply the following numbers of barrels of draft beer to the company's distributors each month:

BREWERY	MONTHLY SUPPLY (BARRELS)
A. Tampa	4,000
B. St. Louis	5,000
C. Chicago	3,500
	12,500

The distributors, spread throughout six states, have the following total monthly demand:

DISTRIBUTOR	MONTHLY DEMAND (BARRELS)
1. Tennessee	1800
2. Georgia	2100
3. North Carolina	1700
4. South Carolina	1050
5. Kentucky	2350
6. Virginia	1400
	10.400

The company must pay the following shipping costs per barrel:

	TO					
FROM	*1*	*2*	*3*	*4*	*5*	*6*
A.	$0.50	$0.35	$0.60	$0.45	$0.80	$0.75
B.	0.25	0.65	0.40	0.55	0.20	0.65
C.	0.40	0.70	0.55	0.50	0.35	0.50

Determine the minimum cost shipping routes for the company.

S11.9. In Problem S11.8, the Adams Brewing Company management has negotiated a new shipping contract with a trucking firm between its Tampa brewery and its distributor in Kentucky that reduces the shipping cost per barrel from $0.80 per barrel to $0.55 per barrel. How will this cost change affect the optimal solution?

S11.10. Systems Unlimited sells personal computers to universities and colleges on the East Coast and ships them from three distribution warehouses. The firm is able to supply the following numbers of computers to the universities by the beginning of the academic year:

DISTRIBUTION WAREHOUSE	SUPPLY (COMPUTERS)
1. Richmond	420
2. Atlanta	610
3. Washington, DC	340
	1370

Four universities have ordered computers that must be delivered and installed by the beginning of the academic year:

UNIVERSITY	DEMAND (COMPUTERS)
A. Tech	560
B. A & M	280
C. State	410
D. Central	340
	1590

The shipping and installation costs per computer from each distributor to each university are as follows:

	TO			
FROM	*A*	*B*	*C*	*D*
1.	$22	17	30	18
2.	15	35	20	25
3.	28	21	16	14

Determine the shipments that will minimize total costs.

S11.11. In Problem S11.10, Systems Unlimited wants to meet demand more effectively at the four universities it supplies. It is considering two alternatives: (1) expand its warehouse at Richmond to a capacity of 600 at a cost equivalent to an additional $6 in handling and shipping per unit; or (2) purchase a new warehouse in Charlotte that can supply 300 units with shipping costs of $19 to Tech, $26 to A&M, $22 to State, and $16 to Central. Which alternative should management select based solely on transportation costs (i.e., no capital costs)?

S11.12. A manufacturing company is closing three of its existing plants and intends to transfer some of its more skilled employees to three plants that will remain open. The number of employees available for transfer from each closing plant is as follows:

CLOSING PLANT	TRANSFERABLE EMPLOYEES
1.	60
2.	105
3.	70
	235

The following number of employees can be accommodated at the three plants remaining open:

OPEN PLANTS	EMPLOYEES DEMANDED
A.	55
B.	80
C.	40
	175

Each transferred employee will increase product output (units) per day at each plant as follows:

	TO		
FROM	*A*	*B*	*C*
1.	5	8	6
2.	10	9	12
3.	7	6	8

Determine the best way to transfer employees in order to ensure the maximum increase in product output.

S11.13. The Sunshine Rental Car Agency has six lots in Orlando, and it wants to have a certain number of cars available at each lot at the beginning of each day for local rental. The agency would like a model it could quickly solve at the end of each day that would tell how to redistribute the cars among the six lots at the minimum total mileage. The distances between the six lots are as follows:

	TO (MILES)					
FROM	*1*	*2*	*3*	*4*	*5*	*6*
1.	—	12	17	18	10	20
2.	14	—	10	19	16	15
3.	14	10	—	12	8	9
4.	8	16	14	—	12	15
5.	11	21	16	18	—	10
6.	24	12	9	17	15	—

The agency would like the following number of cars at each lot at the end of the day. Also shown is the number of available cars at each lot at the end of a particular day. Determine the optimal reallocation of rental cars that will minimize the total mileage.

LOT	1	2	3	4	5	6
Available	42	21	18	23	35	27
Desire	27	26	22	44	31	16

S11.14. The Roadnet Shipping Company has expanded its shipping capacity by purchasing 90 trailer trucks from a competitor that went bankrupt. The company subsequently located 30 of the purchased trucks at each of its shipping warehouses in Charlotte, Memphis, and Louisville. The company makes shipments from each of these warehouses to terminals in St. Louis, Atlanta, and New York. Each truck is capable of making one shipment per week. The terminal managers have each indicated their capacity for extra shipments. The manager at St. Louis can accommodate 30 additional trucks per week, the manager at Atlanta can accommodate 50 additional trucks, and the manager at New York can accommodate 40 additional trucks. The company makes the following profit per truckload shipment from each warehouse to each terminal. The profits differ as a result of differences in products shipped, shipping costs, and transport rates.

	TERMINAL		
WAREHOUSE	ST. LOUIS	ATLANTA	NEW YORK
Charlotte	$1800	$2100	$1600
Memphis	1000	700	900
Louisville	1400	800	2200

Determine how many trucks to assign to each route (i.e., warehouse to terminal) to maximize profit.

S11.15. The Beacon Publishing Company hires eight college students as salespeople to sell children's books during the summer. The company desires to distribute them to three sales territories. Territory 1 requires three salespeople, and territories 2 and 3 require two salespeople each. It is estimated that each salesperson will be able to generate the following amounts of dollar sales per day in each of the three territories:

	TERRITORY		
SALESPERSON	*1*	*2*	*3*
A	$110	$150	$130
B	90	120	80
C	205	160	175
D	125	100	115
E	140	105	150
F	100	140	120
G	180	210	160
H	110	120	70

Determine which salespeople to allocate to the three territories so that sales will be maximized.

S11.16. The Big Ten Athletic Conference has nine basketball officials who must be assigned to three conference games, three to each game. The conference office wants to assign the officials so that the time they travel the total distances will be minimized. The hours each official would have to travel to each game is given in the following table:

	GAME		
OFFICIAL	COLUMBUS	MADISON	BLOOMINGTON
1	2.3	4.5	1.6
2	4.1	8.7	7.2
3	6.5	7.0	2.9
4	3.4	6.3	4.5
5	8.1	1.9	5.2
6	6.4	2.6	3.5
7	3.9	4.8	7.4
8	5.2	4.2	6.5
9	4.6	5.6	3.9

Determine the optimal game assignments that will minimize the total time traveled by the officials.

S11.17. Maryville has built a new elementary school so that the town now has a total of four schools—Addison, Beeks, Canfield, and Daley. Each has a capacity of 400 students. The city wants to assign children to schools so that their travel time by bus is as short as possible. It has partitioned the town into five districts conforming to population density—north, south, east, west, and central. The average bus travel time from each district to each school is shown as follows:

	TRAVEL TIME (MIN)				
DISTRICT	ADDISON	BEEKS	CANFIELD	DALEY	STUDENT POPULATION
North	12	23	35	17	270
South	26	15	21	27	310
East	18	20	22	31	320
West	29	24	35	10	220
Central	15	10	23	16	280

Determine the number of children that should be assigned from each district to each school in order to minimize total student travel time.

S11.18. In Problem S11.17, the school board has determined that it does not want any of the schools to be overly crowded compared with the other schools. It would like to assign students from each district to each school so that enrollments are evenly balanced between the four schools. However, the school board is concerned that this might significantly increase travel time. Determine the number of students to be assigned from each district to each school such that school enrollments are evenly balanced. Does this new solution appear to significantly increase travel time per student?

S11.19. The Atlantic Grocery chain operates in major metropolitan areas on the eastern seaboard. The stores have a "no-frills" approach, with low overhead and high volume. They generally buy their stock in volume at low prices. However, in some cases they actually buy stock at stores in other areas and ship it in. They can do this because of high prices in the cities they operate in compared with costs in other locations. One example is baby food. Atlantic purchases baby food at stores in Albany, Binghamton, Claremont, Dover, and Edison, and then trucks it to six stores in and around New York City. The stores in the outlying areas know what Atlantic is up to, so they limit the number of cases of baby food Atlantic can purchase. The following table shows the profit Altantic makes per case of baby food based on where the chain purchases it and which store it is sold at, plus the available baby food per week at purchase locations and the shelf space available at each Atlantic store per week:

	ATLANTIC STORE						
PURCHASE LOCATION	*1*	*2*	*3*	*4*	*5*	*6*	SUPPLY
Albany	9	8	11	12	7	8	26
Binghamton	10	10	8	6	9	7	40
Claremont	8	6	6	5	7	4	20
Dover	4	6	9	5	8	10	40
Edison	12	10	8	9	6	7	45
Demand	25	15	30	18	27	35	

Determine where Atlantic should purchase baby food and how the food should be distributed in order to maximize profit.

S11.20. Suppose that in Problem S11.19 Atlantic could purchase all the baby food it needs from a New York City distributor at a price that would result in a profit of $9 per case at stores 1, 3, and 4, $8 per case at stores 2 and 6, and $7 per case at store 5. Should Atlantic purchase all, none, or some of its baby food from the distributor rather than purchasing it at other stores and trucking it in?

S11.21. During the war in Iraq large amounts of military material and supplies had to be shipped daily from supply depots in the United Sates to bases in the Middle East. The critical factor in the movement of these supplies was speed. The following table shows the number of planeloads of supplies available each day from each of six supply depots and the number of daily loads demanded at each of five bases. (Each planeload is approximately equal in tonnage.) Also included in the table are the transport hours per plane (where transport hours include loading and fueling time, actual flight time, and unloading and refueling times).

	MILITARY BASE					
SUPPLY DEPOT	*A*	*B*	*C*	*D*	*E*	SUPPLY
1	36	40	32	43	29	8
2	28	27	29	40	38	12
3	34	35	41	29	31	7
4	41	42	35	27	36	10
5	25	28	40	34	38	9
6	31	30	43	38	40	6
Demand	9	6	12	8	10	

Determine the optimal daily flight schedule that will minimize total transport time.

S11.22. A severe winter ice storm has swept across North Carolina and Virginia followed by more than a foot of snow and frigid, single-digit temperatures. These weather conditions have resulted in numerous downed power lines and power outages in the region, causing dangerous conditions for much of the population. Local utility companies have been overwhelmed and have requested assistance from unaffected utility companies across the Southeast. The following table shows the number of utility trucks with crews available from five different companies in Georgia, South Carolina, and Florida; the demand for crews in seven different areas that local companies cannot get to; and the weekly cost ($1000s) of a crew going to a specific area (based on the visiting company's normal charges, the distance the crew has to come, and living expenses in an area). Determine the number of crews that should be sent from each utility to each affected area that will minimize total costs.

CREW	AREA (COST = $1000s)							CREWS AVAILABLE
	NC-E	NC-SW	NC-P	NC-W	VA-SW	VA-C	VA-T	
GA-1	15.2	14.3	13.9	13.5	14.7	16.5	18.7	14
GA-2	12.8	11.3	10.6	12.0	12.7	13.2	15.6	12
SC-1	12.4	10.8	9.4	11.3	13.1	12.8	14.5	15
FL-1	18.2	19.4	18.2	17.9	20.5	20.7	22.7	16
FL-2	19.3	20.2	19.5	20.2	21.2	21.3	23.5	11
Crews Needed	9	7	5	8	10	9	7	

S11.23. TransAm Foods Company has five plants where it processes and packages fruits and vegetables. It has suppliers in six cities in California, Texas, Alabama, and Florida. The company has owned and operated its own trucking system in the past for transporting fruits and vegetables from its suppliers to its plants. However, it is now considering transferring all of its shipping to outside trucking firms and getting rid of its own trucks. It currently spends $245,000 per month to operate its own trucking system. It has determined monthly shipping costs (in $1000s per ton) using outside shippers from each of its suppliers to each of its plants, as shown in the following table.

SUPPLIERS	PROCESSING PLANTS ($1000s PER TON)					SUPPLY (TONS)
	DENVER	ST. PAUL	LOUISVILLE	AKRON	TOPEKA	
Sacramento	3.7	4.6	4.9	5.5	4.3	19
Bakersfield	3.4	5.1	4.4	5.9	5.2	14
San Antonio	3.3	4.1	3.7	2.9	2.6	12
Montgomery	1.9	4.2	2.7	5.4	3.9	10
Jacksonville	6.1	5.1	3.8	2.5	4.1	22
Ocala	6.6	4.8	3.5	3.6	4.5	17
Demand (tons)	20	15	15	15	20	

Should National Foods continue to operate its own shipping network or sell its trucks and outsource its shipping to independent trucking firms?

S11.24. In Problem S11.23, TransAm Foods would like to know what the effect would be on the optimal solution and the company's decision regarding its shipping if it negotiates with its suppliers in Sacramento, Jacksonville, and Ocala to increase their capacity to 25 tons per month. What would be the effect of negotiating instead with its suppliers at San Antonio and Montgomery to increase their capacity to 25 tons each?

S11.25. Orient Transport Express (OTE) is a global distribution company that transports its clients' products to customers in Hong Kong, Singapore, and Taipei. All of the products OTE ships are stored at three distribution centers—one in Los Angeles, one in Savannah, and one in Galveston. For the coming month the company has 450 containers of computer components available at the Los Angeles center, 600 containers available at Savannah, and 350 containers available in Galveston. The company has orders for 600 containers from Hong Kong, 500 containers from Singapore, and 500 containers from Taipei. The shipping costs per container from each U.S. port to each of the overseas ports are shown in the following table:

U.S. DISTRIBUTION CENTER	OVERSEAS PORT		
	HONG KONG	SINGAPORE	TAIPEI
Los Angeles	$300	210	340
Savannah	490	520	610
Galveston	360	320	500

OTE, as the overseas broker for its U.S. customers, is responsible for unfulfilled orders, and it incurs stiff penalty costs from overseas customers if it does not meet an order. The Hong Kong customers charge a penalty cost of $800 per container for unfulfilled demand, Singapore customers charge a penalty cost of $920 per container, and Taipei customers charge $1100 per container. Formulate and solve a transportation model to determine the shipments from each U.S. distribution center to each overseas port that will minimize shipping costs. Indicate what portion of the total cost is a result of penalties.

S11.26. The Southern Atlantic Railroad's rail network covers most of the U.S. Middle Atlantic and Southeast region. On a daily basis it sends empty freight cars from various locations in its rail network to its customers at other rail hubs for their use to meet demand. The transportation costs for shipping empty freight cars, shown at the bottom of the page, are directly related to distance travelled and the number of rail centers that must handle the car movement.

Determine the number of empty freight cars that should be sent from each rail network location to customers to meet demand at the minimum total cost on a given day when supply and demand are as shown.

FREIGHT CAR LOCATION	CUSTOMER LOCATION									SUPPLY
	A. ATLANTA	B. JACKSONVILLE	C. NASHVILLE	D. LOUISVILLE	E. RICHMOND	F. ROANOKE	G. NORFOLK	H. MEMPHIS	I. WILMINGTON	
1. New Orleans	29	34	25	31	34	29	40	18	33	85
2. Jackson	26	35	25	28	27	31	47	14	26	110
3. Savannah	10	18	23	24	22	27	38	48	35	73
4. Mobile	20	24	21	24	29	24	32	21	47	45
5. Birmingham	9	18	19	22	23	22	44	30	28	29
6. Houston	47	44	48	49	37	35	45	24	48	112
8. Charleston	15	14	15	18	23	25	19	30	9	88
9. Shreveport	24	31	26	31	26	27	38	15	44	143
Demand	63	102	72	116	41	96	8	65	122	

S11.27. The MidLands Trucking Company based in Louisville has eight trucks located throughout the Mideast that have delivered their loads and are available for shipments. Through their Internet logistics site MidLands has received shipping requests from 12 customers. The following table shows the mileage for a truck to travel to a customer location, pick up the load, and deliver it.

	CUSTOMERS											
TRUCK	A	B	C	D	E	F	G	H	I	J	K	L
1	500	730	620	410	550	600	390	480	670	710	440	590
2	900	570	820	770	910	660	650	780	840	950	590	670
3	630	660	750	540	680	750	810	560	710	1200	490	650
4	870	1200	810	670	710	820	1200	630	700	900	540	620
5	950	910	740	810	630	590	930	650	840	930	460	560
6	1100	860	800	590	570	550	780	610	1300	840	550	790
7	610	710	910	550	810	730	910	720	850	760	580	630
8	560	690	660	640	720	670	830	690	880	1000	710	680

Determine the optimal assignment of trucks to customers that will minimize the total mileage.

S11.28. In Problem S11.27, assume that the customers have the following truck capacity loads:

	CUSTOMERS											
	A	B	C	D	E	F	G	H	I	J	K	L
Capacity	87	76	92	81	93	84	85	77	70	93	76	84

Determine the optimal assignment of trucks to customers that will minimize total mileage while also achieving at least an average truck load capacity of 87%. Does this load capacity requirement significantly increase the total mileage?

S11.29. The Heartland Produce Company owns farms in the Midwest, where it grows and harvests potatoes. It then ships these potatoes to three processing plants in St. Louis, New Orleans, and Chicago, where different varieties of potato products, including potato chips, are produced. The company is experiencing increased demand, so it wants to buy one or more new farms to produce more potato products. The company is considering six new farms with the following annual fixed costs and projected harvest:

FARM	FIXED ANNUAL COSTS ($1,000s)	PROJECTED ANNUAL HARVEST (THOUSANDS OF TONS)
1	$405	11.2
2	390	10.5
3	450	12.8
4	368	9.3
5	520	10.8
6	465	9.6

The company currently has the following additional available production capacity (tons) at its three plants, which it wants to utilize:

PLANT	AVAILABLE CAPACITY (THOUSANDS OF TONS)
St. Louis	12
Dallas	10
Chicago	14

The shipping costs ($) per ton from the farms being considered for purchase to the plants are as follows:

	PLANT (SHIPPING COSTS, $/TON)		
FARM	ST. LOUIS	DALLAS	CHICAGO
1	18	15	12
2	13	10	17
3	16	14	18
4	19	15	16
5	17	19	12
6	14	16	12

Which of the six farms should the company purchase to meet available production capacity at the minimum total cost (including annual fixed costs and shipping costs)?

S11.30. Arkind, based in India, is a global supplier of denim jeans for apparel companies around the world. They purchase raw cotton from producers in Louisiana, Mississippi and Texas, where it is picked, ginned and baled and then transported by flat-bed trucks to ports in Houston, New Orleans, Savannah and Charleston, where it is loaded into 80-foot containers and shipped to factories overseas. For the coming year Arkind has contracted with its U.S. broker for 71,000 (550 lb.) bales of cotton and the transportation and handling costs from each cotton processing facility to each port, and the available containers at each port are, as follows.

	PORTS				
COTTON FARMS	HOUSTON	SAVANNAH	NEW ORLEANS	CHARLESTON	SUPPLY (BALES)
Louisiana	$18	$23	$15	$23	31,000
Mississippi	26	19	14	27	45,000
Texas	14	29	21	32	27,000
Demand (bales)	26,000	19,000	14,000	12,000	

Determine the optimal shipments from each processing facility to each port that will result in the minimum shipping cost.

S11.31. Arkind in problem S11.30 ships the cotton it has purchased from the U.S. ports to overseas ports in Singapore, Karachi and Mumbai, where its denim fabric factories are also located. The shipping and handling costs per bale of cotton from each U.S. port to each of Arkind's overseas factories and the demand at these factories, is as follows.

	PORTS/DENIM FABRIC PLANTS		
PORTS	SINGAPORE	KARACHI	MUMBAI
Houston	$23	$28	$30
Savannah	28	24	32
New Orleans	26	26	27
Charleston	29	23	34
Demand (bales)	34,000	22,000	15,000

Determine the optimal shipments that will result in the minimum total shipping cost.

S11.32. Arkind in problem S11.31 manufactures denim fabric at its factories in Singapore, Karachi and Mumbai and ships it to its denim jeans manufacturing facilities in China, India, Japan, Turkey and Italy. A bale of cotton will produce approximately 325 yards of denim fabric. Following is the fabric demand at each denim jeans plant and the shipping and handling costs per yard from the fabric manufacturing facilities to the jeans plants.

DENIM FABRIC PLANTS	DENIM JEANS FACTORIES				
	CHINA	INDIA	JAPAN	TURKEY	ITALY
Singapore	$0.027	$0.043	$0.036	$0.055	$0.075
Karachi	0.034	0.025	0.046	0.049	0.058
Mumbai	0.049	0.037	0.037	0.067	0.063
Demand (1000 yds)	5,425	6,350	3,450	4,750	3,100

Determine the optimal shipments from each of the fabric plants to the denim jeans manufacturing facilities and the minimum total shipping cost.

S11.33. Arkind in problem S11.32 supplies its finished denim jeans to its customers' distribution centers in the U.S. in Philadelphia and New Orleans, and in Europe in London and Rotterdam. Denim jeans require 1.5 yards of denim fabric. Following are the contracted deliveries of jeans for each of Arkind's customer's distribution centers, and the shipping and handling costs per jeans from the jeans factories to the distribution centers.

DENIM JEANS FACTORIES	PORT/DISTRIBUTION CENTERS			
	PHILADELPHIA	LONDON	ROTTERDAM	NEW ORLEANS
China	$0.45	$0.51	$0.56	$0.41
India	0.40	0.47	0.48	0.46
Japan	0.53	0.55	0.61	0.47
Turkey	0.39	0.42	0.45	0.51
Italy	0.47	0.48	0.52	0.48
Jeans Demand (1000s)	7,127	2,435	3,422	2,400

Determine the optimal shipments from each jeans factory to each distribution center and the optimal total shipping cost.

S11.34. Mill Mountain Coffee Company produces various blends of Free Trade, organic specialty coffees that it sells to wholesale customers. The company imports 28 million pounds of coffee beans annually from coffee plantations in Brazil, Indonesia, Kenya, Colombia, Cote D'lvoire, and Guatemala. The beans are shipped from these countries to U.S. ports in Galveston, New Orleans, Savannah, and Jacksonville, where they are loaded onto container trucks and shipped to the company's plant in upstate New York. The shipping costs ($/million lbs) from the countries to the U.S. ports, the amount of beans (in millions of lbs) contracted from the growers in each country, and the port capacities are shown in the following table.

GROWER COUNTRY	U.S. PORT				
	7. Mobile	8. New Orleans	9. Savannah	10. Jacksonville	Supply
1. Brazil	$30,000	$36,000	$29,000	$41,000	5.9
2. Colombia	19,000	23,000	28,000	35,000	4.3
3. Indonesia	53,000	47,000	45,000	39,000	3.8
4. Kenya	45,000	54,000	48,000	41,000	6.7
5. Cote d'Ivoire	35,000	33,000	27,000	29,000	2.5
6. Guatemala	14,000	17,000	24,000	28,000	4.8

The shipping costs from each port to the plant in New York are shown in the following table.

U.S. PORT	11. NEW YORK
7. Mobile	$61,000
8. New Orleans	55,000
9. Savannah	38,000
10. Jacksonville	43,000

Determine the optimal shipments from the grower countries to the plant in New York that will minimize shipping costs.

S11.35. Globalnet Foods, Inc., imports food products such as meats, cheeses, and pastries to the United States from warehouses at ports in Hamburg, Marseille, and Liverpool. Ships from these ports deliver the products to Norfolk, New York, and Savannah, where they are stored in company warehouses before being shipped to distribution centers in Dallas, St. Louis, and Chicago. The products are then distributed to specialty food stores and sold through catalogs. The shipping costs ($/1000 lb) from the European ports to the U.S. cities and the available supply (1000 lb) at the European ports are provided in the following table.

EUROPEAN PORT	U.S. CITIES			
	4. NORFOLK	5. NEW YORK	6. SAVANNAH	SUPPLY
1. Hamburg	$420	$390	$610	55
2. Marseilles	510	590	470	78
3. Liverpool	450	360	480	37

The transportation costs ($/1000 lb) from each U.S. warehouse to the three distribution centers and the demand (1000 lb) at the distribution centers are as follows.

WAREHOUSE	DISTRIBUTION CENTER		
	7. DALLAS	8. ST. LOUIS	9. CHICAGO
4. Norfolk	$75	$63	$81
5. New York	125	110	95
6. Savannah	68	82	95
	60	45	50

Determine the optimal shipments between the European ports and the warehouses and the distribution centers that will minimize total transportation costs.

S11.36. A sports apparel company has received an order for a college basketball team's national championship T-shirt. The company can purchase the T-shirts from textile factories in Mexico, Puerto Rico, and Haiti. The shirts are shipped from the factories to companies in the United States that silk-screen the shirts before they are shipped to distribution centers. Following are the production and transportation costs ($/shirt) from the T-shirt factories to the silk-screen companies to the distribution centers, plus the supply of T-shirts at the factories and demand for the shirts at the distribution centers.

T-SHIRT FACTORY	SILK-SCREEN COMPANIES			
	4. MIAMI	5. ATLANTA	6. HOUSTON	SUPPLY (1000s)
1. Mexico	$4	$6	$3	18
2. Puerto Rico	3	5	5	15
3. Haiti	2	4	4	23

SILK-SCREEN COMPANY	DISTRIBUTION CENTERS 7. NEW YORK	8. ST. LOUIS	9. LOS ANGELES
4. Miami	$5	$7	$9
5. Atlanta	7	6	10
6. Houston	8	6	8
Demand (1000s)	20	12	20

Determine the optimal shipments that will minimize total production and transportation costs for the apparel company.

S11.37. Walsh's Fruit Company contracts with growers in Ohio, Pennsylvania, and New York to purchase grapes. The grapes are processed into juice at the farms and stored in refrigerated vats. Then the juice is shipped to two plants, where it is processed into bottled grape juice and frozen concentrate. The juice and concentrate are then transported to four food warehouses/distribution centers. The transportation costs per ton from the farms to the plants and from the plants to the distributors, and the supply at the farms and demand at the distribution centers are summarized in the following tables.

FARM	PLANT 4. INDIANA	5. GEORGIA	SUPPLY (1000 TONS)
1. Ohio	$16	$21	72
2. Pennsylvania	18	16	105
3. New York	22	25	83

PLANT	DISTRIBUTION CENTERS 6. VIRGINIA	7. KENTUCKY	8. LOUISIANA
4. Indiana	$23	$15	$29
5. Georgia	20	17	24
Demand (1000 tons)	90	80	120

a. Determine the optimal shipments from farms to plants to distribution centers that will minimize total transportation costs.

b. What would be the effect on the solution if the capacity at each plant was 140,000 tons?

S11.38. A national catalog and Internet retailer has three warehouses and three major distribution centers located around the country. Normally, items are shipped directly from the warehouses to the distribution centers; however, each of the distribution centers can also be used as an intermediate transshipment point. The transportation costs ($/unit) between warehouses and distribution centers, the supply at the warehouses (100 units), and the demand at the distribution centers (100 units) for a specific week are shown in the following table.

WAREHOUSE	DISTRIBUTION CENTER *A*	*B*	*C*	SUPPLY
1	$12	$ 11	$ 7	70
2	8	6	14	80
3	9	10	12	50
Demand	60	100	40	

The transportation costs ($/unit) between the distribution centers are

DISTRIBUTION CENTER	DISTRIBUTION CENTER *A*	*B*	*C*
A	—	8	3
B	1	—	2
C	7	2	—

Determine the optimal shipments between warehouses and distribution centers that will minimize total transportation costs.

S11.39. Horizon Computers manufactures laptops in Germany, Belgium, and Italy. Because of high tariffs between international trade groups, it is sometimes cheaper to ship partially completed laptops to factories in Puerto Rico, Mexico, and Panama and have them completed before final shipment to U.S. distributors in Texas, Virginia, and Ohio. The cost ($/unit) of the completed laptops plus tariffs and shipment costs from the European plants directly to the United States and supply and demand are shown as follows.

EUROPEAN PLANTS	U.S. DISTRIBUTORS 7. TEXAS	8.VIRGINIA	9. OHIO	SUPPLY (1000s)
1. Germany	$2600	$1900	$2300	5.2
2. Belgium	2200	2100	2600	6.3
3. Italy	1800	2200	2500	4.5
Demand (1000s)	2.1	3.7	7.8	

Alternatively, the unit costs of shipping partially completed laptops to plants for finishing before sending them to the United States are as follows.

EUROPEAN PLANTS	FACTORIES 4. PUERTO RICO	5. MEXICO	6. PANAMA
1. Germany	$1400	$1200	$1100
2. Belgium	1600	1100	900
3. Italy	1500	1400	1200

FACTORIES	U.S. DISTRIBUTORS 7. TEXAS	8. VIRGINIA	9. OHIO
4. Puerto Rico	$800	$700	$900
5. Mexico	600	800	1100
6. Panama	900	700	1200

Determine the optimal shipments of laptops that will meet demand at the U.S. distributors at the minimum total cost.

S11.40. The MidAm Produce Company contracts with potato farmers in Idaho, Nebraska, South Dakota, and Michigan for monthly potato shipments. MidAm picks up the potatoes at the farms and ships mostly by truck (and sometimes by rail) to its sorting and distribution centers in Indiana, Kansas, and Arkansas. At these centers the potatoes are cleaned, rejects are discarded, and they are sorted according to size and quality. They are then shipped to combination plants and distribution centers in Maryland, Ohio, South Carolina, and Alabama where the company produces a variety of potato products and distributes bags of potatoes to stores. An exception is the Indiana distribution center, which will only accept potatoes from farms in Nebraska, South Dakota, and Michigan, and the Alabama plant, which won't accept shipments from Indiana because of disagreements over delivery schedules and quality issues. Following are summaries of the shipping costs from the farms to the distribution centers and the processing and shipping costs from the distribution centers to the plants, as well as the available monthly supply at each farm, the processing capacity at the distribution centers, and the final demand at the plants (in bushels).

	DISTRIBUTION CENTERS ($/BUSHEL)			
FARM	5. INDIANA	6. KANSAS	7. ARKANSAS	SUPPLY (BUSHELS)
1. Idaho	—	1.09	1.26	1,600
2. Nebraska	0.89	1.32	1.17	1,100
3. South Dakota	0.78	1.22	1.36	1,400
4. Michigan	1.19	1.25	1.42	1,900
Processing Capacity (bushels)	1,800	2,200	1,600	

	PLANTS ($/BUSHEL)			
DISTRIBUTION CENTER	8. MARYLAND	9. OHIO	10. SOUTH CAROLINA	11. ALABAMA
5. Indiana	4.56	3.98	4.94	—
6. Kansas	3.43	5.74	4.65	5.01
7. Arkansas	5.39	6.35	5.70	4.87
Demand (bushels)	1,200	900	1,100	1,500

Determine the optimal monthly shipments from the farms to the distribution centers and from the distribution centers to the plants that will minimize total shipping and processing costs.

S11.41. Phillups Corporation is a global distributor of electrical parts and components. Its customers are electronics companies in the United States, including computer manufacturers and audio/visual product manufacturers. The company contracts to purchase components and parts from manufacturers in Europe and has them delivered to warehouses in three ports: Antwerp, Barcelona, and Cherbourg. The various components and parts are loaded into containers based on demand from their U.S. customers. Each port has a limited fixed number of containers available each month. The containers are then shipped overseas by container ships to the ports of Boston, Savannah, Mobile, and Houston. From these seaports the containers are typically coupled with trucks and hauled to inland ports in Ohio, Texas, and North Carolina. There are fixed numbers of freight haulers available at each port each month. These inland ports are sometimes called "freight villages" or intermodal junctions where the containers are collected and transferred from one transport mode to another—from truck to rail or vice-versa. From the inland ports the containers are transported to the Phillups distribution centers in Phoenix, Columbus, Kansas City, Louisville, and Memphis. Following are the handling and shipping costs ($/container) between each of the embarkation and destination points along this overseas supply chain and the available containers at each port.

	U.S. PORTS				
EUROPEAN PORTS	4. BOSTON	5. SAVANNAH	6. MOBILE	7. HOUSTON	AVAILABLE CONTAINERS
1. Antwerp	1725	1800	2345	2700	125
2. Barcelona	1825	1750	1945	2320	210
3. Cherbourg	2060	2175	2050	2475	160

	INLAND PORTS			
U.S. PORTS	8. OHIO	9. TEXAS	10. NORTH CAROLINA	INTERMODAL CAPACITY (CONTAINERS)
4. Boston	825	545	320	85
5. Savannah	750	675	450	110
6. Mobile	325	605	690	100
7. Houston	270	510	1050	130
Intermodal Capacity (containers)	170	240	140	

	DISTRIBUTION CENTERS				
INLAND PORT	11. PHOENIX	12. COLUMBUS	13. KANSAS CITY	14. LOUISVILLE	15. MEMPHIS
8. Ohio	450	830	565	420	960
9. Texas	880	520	450	380	660
10. North Carolina	1,350	390	1,200	450	310
Demand	85	60	105	50	120

Determine the optimal shipments from each point of embarkation to each destination along this supply chain that will result in the minimum total shipping cost.

S11.42. In Problem S11.41 Phillups Corporation is just as concerned that its U.S. distributors receive shipments in the minimum amount of time as they are about minimizing their shipping costs. Suppose each U.S. distributor receives one major container shipment each month. Following are summaries of the shipping times (in days) between each of the embarkation and destination points along the Phillups global supply chain. These times not only encompass travel time but also processing, loading, and unloading times at each port.

	U.S. PORTS			
EUROPEAN PORT	4. BOSTON	5. SAVANNAH	6. MOBILE	7. HOUSTON
1. Antwerp	22	24	27	30
2. Barcelona	17	20	23	26
3. Cherbourg	25	21	24	26

	INLAND PORTS		
U.S. PORTS	8. OHIO	9. TEXAS	10. NORTH CAROLINA
4. Boston	10	8	6
5. Savannah	12	9	8
6. Mobile	8	7	10
7. Houston	12	6	8

	DISTRIBUTION CENTERS				
INLAND PORT	11. PHOENIX	12. COLUMBUS	13. KANSAS CITY	14. LOUISVILLE	15. CLEVELAND
8. Ohio	5	6	5	7	8
9. Texas	6	4	4	5	7
10. North Carolina	10	5	7	4	6

a. Determine the optimal shipping route for each distribution center along this supply chain that will result in the minimum total shipping time. Determine the shipping route and time for each U.S. distributor.

b. Suppose the European ports can only accommodate three shipments each. How will this affect the solution in part (a)?

S11.43. The Pandora Company, a U.S.-based manufacturer of furniture and appliances that offshores all of its manufacturing operations to Asia, has distribution centers at various locations on the East Coast near ports where their items are imported on container ships. In many cases, their appliances and furniture arrive partially assembled, and they complete the assembly at their distribution centers before sending the finished products to retailers. For example, appliance motors, electric controls, housings, and furniture pieces might arrive from different Asian manufacturers in separate containers. Recently, the company began exporting its products to various locations in Europe, and demand steadily increased. As a result, the company determined that shipping items to the United States, assembling the products, and then turning around and shipping them to Europe was inefficient and not cost-effective. The company now plans to open three new distribution centers near ports in Europe, so that it will ship the items from Asian ports to its distribution centers at the European ports, offload some of the items for final product assembly, and then ship the partially filled containers on to its U.S. distribution centers. The table above shows the seven possible distribution center locations near container ports in Europe and their container capacities; the container shipments from each of its Asian ports; and the container shipping cost from each of its Asian ports to each possible distribution center location.

	PROPOSED DISTRIBUTION CENTERS							
ASIAN PORT CENTER COST	F. ROTTERDAM $16,725,000	G. HAMBURG 19,351,000	H. ANTWERP 13,766,000	I. BREMEN 15,463,000	J. VALENCIA 12,542,000	K. LISBON 13,811,000	L. LE HAVRE 22,365,000	CONTAINER SHIPMENTS
A. Hong Kong	$3466	$3560	3125	3345	3060	3120	3658	235
B. Shanghai	3190	3020	3278	3269	2987	2864	3725	170
C. Busan	2815	2700	2890	3005	2465	2321	3145	165
D. Mumbai	2412	2560	2515	2875	2325	2133	2758	325
E. Kaoshiung	2600	2800	2735	2755	2473	2410	2925	405
Capacity	565	485	520	490	310	410	605	

The following table shows the demand from each of the U.S. ports and the cost for container shipments from each of the possible distribution center locations to each of the U.S. ports.

	U.S. PORT			
PROPOSED DISTRIBUTION CENTERS	M. NEW YORK	N. SAVANNAH	O. MIAMI	P. NEW ORLEANS
F. Rotterdam	2045	1875	1675	2320
G. Hamburg	2875	2130	1856	2415
H. Antwerp	2415	2056	1956	2228
I. Bremen	2225	1875	2075	2652
J. Valencia	1865	1725	1548	1815
K. Lisbon	1750	1555	1420	1475
L. Le Havre	3056	2280	2065	2425
Demand	440	305	190	365

Determine the three distribution center locations in Europe that Pandora should select, and the shipments from each of the Asian ports to these selected distribution centers, and from the European distribution centers to the U.S. ports.

S11.44. In Problem S11.43, select the three new distribution center locations in Europe within a budget of $45 million, while minimizing Pandora's shipping costs. What is the difference in this solution, if any?

S11.45. Formulate and solve a transshipment model for the shipments of cottons from the cotton processing facilities to the U.S. ports and to the overseas ports and Arkind's fabric factories as described in problems S11.30 and S11.31.

Case Problems

Case Problem S11.1 Stateline Shipping and Transport Company

Rachel Sundusky is the manager of the South-Atlantic office of the Stateline Shipping and Transport Company. She is in the process of negotiating a new shipping contract with Polychem, a company that manufactures chemicals for industrial use. Polychem wants Stateline to pick up and transport waste products from its six plants to four waste disposal sites. Rachel is very concerned about this proposed arrangement. The chemical wastes that will be hauled can be hazardous to humans and the environment if they leak. In addition, a number of towns and communities in the region where the plants are located prohibit hazardous materials from being shipped through their municipal limits. Thus, not only will the shipments have to be handled carefully and transported at reduced speeds, they will also have to traverse circuitous routes in many cases.

Rachel has estimated the cost of shipping a barrel of waste from each of the six plants to each of the three waste disposal sites as shown in the following table:

	WASTE DISPOSAL SITES		
PLANTS	WHITEWATER	LOS CANOS	DURAS
Kingsport	$12	$15	$17
Danville	14	9	10
Macon	13	20	11
Selma	17	16	19
Columbus	7	14	12
Allentown	22	16	18

Each week the plants generate amounts of waste as shown in the following table:

PLANT	WASTE PER WEEK (BBL)
Kingsport	35
Danville	26
Macon	42
Selma	53
Columbus	29
Allentown	38

The three waste disposal sites at Whitewater, Los Canos, and Duras can accommodate a maximum of 65, 80, and 105 barrels per week, respectively.

The estimated shipping cost per barrel between each of the three waste disposal sites is shown in the following table:

WASTE DISPOSAL SITE	WHITEWATER	LOS CANOS	DURAS
Whitewater	—	$12	$10
Los Canos	12	—	15
Duras	10	15	—

In addition to shipping directly from each of the six plants to one of the three waste disposal sites, Rachel is also considering using each of the plants and waste disposal sites as intermediate shipping points. Trucks would be able to drop a load at a plant or disposal site to be picked up and carried on to the final destination by another truck, and vice versa. Stateline would not incur any handling costs since Polychem has agreed to take care of all local handling of the waste materials at the plants and the waste disposal sites. In other words, the only cost Stateline incurs is the actual transportation cost. So Rachel wants to be able to consider the possibility that it may be cheaper to drop and pick up loads at intermediate points rather than shipping them directly.

The following table shows how much Rachel estimates the shipping costs per barrel between each of the six plants to be.

PLANTS	KINGSPORT	DANVILLE	MACON	SELMA	COLUMBUS	ALLENTOWN
Kingsport	—	$6	$1	$9	$7	$8
Danville	6	—	11	10	12	7
Macon	5	11	—	3	7	15
Selma	9	10	3	—	3	16
Columbus	7	12	7	3	—	14
Allentown	8	7	15	16	14	—

Rachel wants to determine the shipping routes that will minimize Stateline's total cost in order to develop a contract proposal to submit to Polychem for waste disposal. She particularly wants to know if it is cheaper to ship directly from the plants to the waste sites or if she should drop and pick up some loads at the various plants and waste sites. Develop a model to assist Rachel and solve the model to determine the optimal routes.

Case Problem S11.2 Global Supply Chain Management at Cantrex Apparel International

Cantrex Apparel International manufactures clothing items around the world. It has currently contracted with a U.S. retail clothing wholesale distributor for men's goatskin and lambskin leather jackets for the next Christmas season. The distributor has distribution centers in Ohio, Tennessee, and New York. The distributor supplies the leather jackets to a discount retail chain, a chain of mall boutique stores, and a department store chain. The jackets arrive at the distribution centers unfinished, and at the centers the distributor adds a unique lining and label specific to each of its customers. The distributor has contracted with Cantrex to deliver the following number of leather jackets to its distribution centers in late fall:

DISTRIBUTION CENTER	GOATSKIN JACKETS	LAMBSKIN JACKETS
Ohio	1000	780
Tennessee	1400	950
New York	1600	1150

Cantrex has tanning factories and clothing manufacturing plants to produce leather jackets in Spain, France, Italy, Venezuela, and Brazil. Its tanning facilities are in Mende in France, Foggia in Italy, Saragosa in Spain, Feira in Brazil, and El Tigre in Venezuela. Its manufacturing plants are in Limoges, Naples, and Madrid in Europe, and São Paulo and Caracas in South America. Following are the supplies of available leather from each tanning facility and the processing capacity at each plant (in lb) for this particular order of leather jackets.

TANNING FACTORY	GOATSKIN SUPPLY (lb)	LAMBSKIN SUPPLY (lb)
Mende	4000	4400
Foggia	3700	5300
Saragosa	6500	4650
Feira	5100	6850
El Tigre	3600	5700

PLANT	PRODUCTION CAPACITY (lb)
Madrid	7800
Naples	5700
Limoges	8200
São Paulo	7600
Caracas	6800

In the production of jackets at the plants 37.5% of the goatskin leather and 50% of the lambskin leather are waste (i.e., it is discarded during the production process and sold for other byproducts). After production, a goatskin jacket weighs approximately 3 lb and a lambskin jacket weighs approximately 2.5 lb (neither with linings, which are added in the United States).

Following are the costs/lb (in U.S.$) for tanning the uncut leather, shipping it, and producing the leather jackets at each plant.

TANNING FACTORY	PLANTS ($/lb)				
	MADRID	NAPLES	LIMOGES	SÃO PAULO	CARACAS
Mende	24	22	16	21	23
Foggia	31	17	22	19	22
Saragosa	18	25	28	23	25
Feira	XX	XX	XX	16	18
El Tigre	XX	XX	XX	14	15

Note that the cost of jacket production is the same for goatskin and lambskin. Also, leather can be tanned in France, Spain, and Italy and shipped directly to the South American plants for jacket production, but the opposite is not possible (due to high tariff restrictions); that is, tanned leather is not shipped to Europe for production.

Once the leather jackets are produced at the plants in Europe and South America, Cantrex uses load match sites and international trade logistics (ITL) systems on the Internet to contract for available rail, truck, and ship transport from the plants to ports in Lisbon, Marseilles, and Caracas, and for shipping from these ports to U.S. ports in New Orleans, Jacksonville, and Savannah. Cantrex has arrangements with trade specialists in these port cities to handle the legal import and export regulations and documentations. The available shipping capacity at each port and transportation costs from the plants to the ports are as follows:

PLANTS	PORTS ($/lb)		
	LISBON	MARSEILLES	CARACAS
Madrid	0.75	1.05	XX
Naples	3.45	1.35	XX
Limoges	2.25	0.60	XX
São Paulo	XX	XX	1.15
Caracas	XX	XX	0.20
Capacity (lb)	8000	5500	9000

The shipping costs ($/lb) from each port in Europe and South America to the U.S. ports, and the available truck and rail capacity for transport at the U.S. ports are as follows.

PORTS	U.S. PORTS ($/lb)		
	NEW ORLEANS	JACKSONVILLE	SAVANNAH
Lisbon	2.35	1.90	1.80
Marseille	3.10	2.40	2.00
Caracas	1.95	2.15	2.40
Capacity (lb)	8000	5200	7500

Once in the United States, Cantrex outsources transportation to third-party logistics companies it has used previously, and it makes use of load match sites on the Internet. The transportation costs ($/lb) from the U.S. ports to the three distribution centers are as follows.

U.S. PORTS	DISTRIBUTION CENTERS ($/lb)		
	OHIO	TENNESSEE	NEW YORK
New Orleans	0.65	0.52	0.87
Jacksonville	0.43	0.41	0.65
Savannah	0.38	0.34	0.50

Cantrex wants to determine the least costly flow of materials and goods along this supply chain that will meet the demand at the U.S. distribution centers. Develop a transshipment supply chain model for Cantrex that will result in a minimum cost solution.

References

Hitchcock, F. L. "The Distribution of a Product from Several Sources to Numerous Localities." *Journal of Mathematics and Physics* 20 (1941), pp. 224, 230.

Taylor, B. W. *Introduction to Management Science*, 9th ed. Upper Saddle River, NJ: Prentice Hall, 2004.

CHAPTER 12

Forecasting

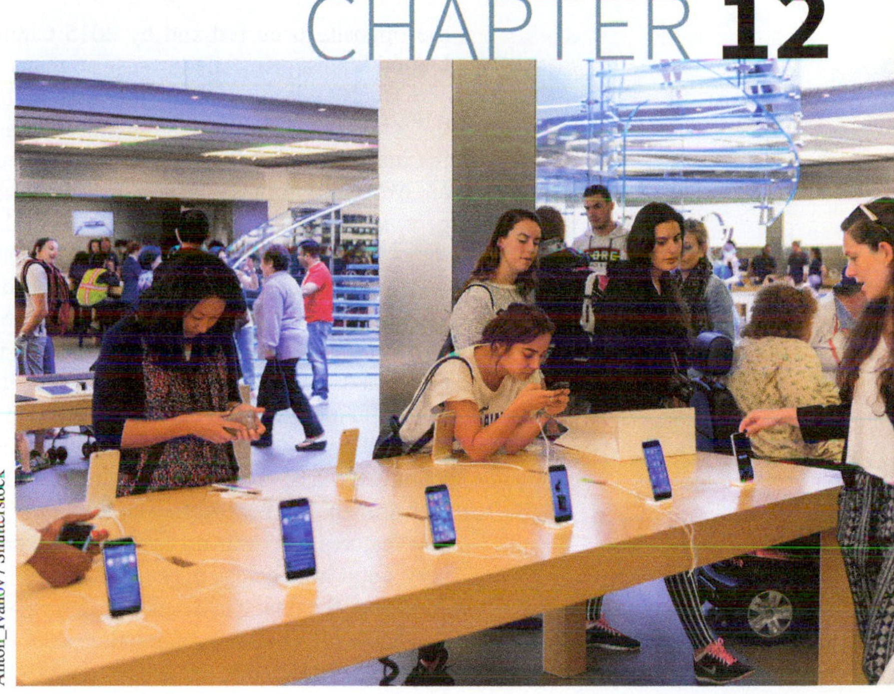

Anton_Ivanov / Shutterstock

LEARNING OBJECTIVES

After reading this chapter, you will be able to:

- Discuss the strategic role of forecasting in supply chain management.
- Describe the forecasting process and identify the components of forecasting demand.
- Forecast demand using various time series models, including exponential smoothing, and trend and seasonal adjustments.
- Discuss and calculate various methods for evaluating forecast accuracy.
- Use Excel to create various forecast models.
- Develop forecasting models with linear and multiple regression analysis.

Forecasting the Global Smartphone Market

Since the introduction of both the first iPhone by Apple and the Android platform in 2007, the global smartphone market has experienced extraordinary growth with steadily increasing sales. In 2008, 140 million smartphones were sold worldwide, and by 2015 sales with a market value over $300 billion had increased to over 1.4 billion units, a 900% increase, and the forecast is for this trend to continue with sales of smartphones estimated to approach 2 billion by 2019. As smartphone sales have increased, the sale of mobile non-smartphones have correspondingly decreased from over a billion in 2008 to 620 million in 2015. Further, various forecasts estimate that by 2018 mobile devices (e.g., smartphones and tablets) will constitute almost 90% of the market for devices that connect to the Internet compared to a little over 10% for PCs and laptops, and this trend will also likely continue into the future.

In the immediate (five-year) future, smartphone sales are forecast to continue to grow, but likely at a much slower rate. In the first part of this decade emerging markets in China and India dominated new user sales as the smartphone market in Europe, Japan, Australia, and North America increasingly became more dependent on the replacement phone market as the number of new users dwindled. In 2015, a little over 420 million smartphones were sold in China, an increase of almost 450% from the 77 million sold in 2011. However, there is evidence that the market for new (first-time) users in China has slowed, and with a 90% market penetration, China has now become a replacement market as well, and will continue to be so in the future. As the Chinese smartphone market emerged many forecasters predicted Apple would not be able to take advantage of the world's largest smartphone market with over 520 million possible users because of its high-end pricing strategy. However, almost the opposite occurred and by 2015 China became Apple's largest market, superseding the United States, primarily because so many consumers in China joined the middle class.

By 2019 it is estimated that new mobile phone users will account for only around 7% of the total global market. As the global smartphone market growth slows and new players enter the market, especially in China, the selling price of a smartphone is expected to decline from an average of about $300 in 2014 to about $240 by 2019, reducing revenues. Forecasters expect Apple and Samsung to continue to dominate the smartphone market, but perhaps not to the extent as in the past as competition increases among traditional and new competitors, especially in China, that are expected to introduce smartphones priced below $150 for consumers who currently own less-sophisticated mobile phones and will switch to low-priced devices.

Although Apple's global market share is expected to decline, its product and pricing strategy aimed at users at the high end of the market should enable it to continue to retain the largest portion of market revenues and profits, while Android-platform smartphones (e.g., Samsung) are likely to continue to make deep penetrations into the market. In the future in China and other mature markets, convincing existing users to upgrade to new smartphones will be the key to further growth. For competitive smartphone companies this will likely depend heavily on creating new features that users do not currently know they want or need (something that Apple has been very good at), increasingly large expenditures on marketing and advertising (something that Apple has the financial assets to do), trying to expand sales through companies' own-brand retail shops and direct-to-customer online sales (something Apple already does well), and introducing smartphones aimed at the high-end user to compete directly with Apple.

In this chapter we will learn about the important role forecasting plays in supply chain management, and some of the quantitative models, techniques, and technologies that companies in the supply chain use to forecast product demand.

A forecast is a prediction of what will occur in the future. Meteorologists forecast the weather, sportscasters and gamblers predict the winners of football games, and companies attempt to predict how much of their product will be sold in the future. A forecast of product demand is the basis for most important planning decisions. Planning decisions regarding scheduling, inventory, production, facility layout and design, workforce, distribution, purchasing, and so on, are functions of customer demand. Long-range strategic plans by top management are based on forecasts of the type of products consumers will demand in the future and the size and location of product markets.

Forecasting is an uncertain process. It is not possible to predict consistently what the future will be, even with the help of a crystal ball or a deck of tarot cards. Management generally hopes to forecast demand with as much accuracy as possible, which is becoming increasingly difficult to do. In the current international business environment, consumers have more product choices and more information on which to base choices. They also demand and receive greater product diversity, made possible by rapid technological advances. This makes forecasting products and product demand more difficult. Consumers and markets have never been stationary targets, but they are moving more rapidly now than they ever have before.

Qualitative forecast methods Subjective methods.

Quantitative forecast methods Are based on mathematical formulas.

Companies sometimes use **qualitative forecast methods** based on judgment, opinion, past experience, or best guesses, to make forecasts. A number of **quantitative forecasting methods** are also available to aid management in making planning decisions. In this chapter, we discuss two of the traditional types of mathematical forecasting methods, time series analysis and regression, as well as several nonmathematical, qualitative approaches to forecasting. Although no technique will result in a totally accurate forecast, these methods can provide reliable guidelines in making decisions.

The Strategic Role of Forecasting in Supply Chain Management

In today's global business environment, strategic planning and design tend to focus on supply chain management and quality management.

Supply Chain Management

A company's supply chain encompasses all of the facilities, functions, and activities involved in producing a product or service from suppliers (and their suppliers) to customers (and their customers). Supply chain functions include purchasing, inventory, production, scheduling, facility location, transportation, and distribution. All these functions are affected in the short run by product demand and in the long run by new products and processes, technology advances, and changing markets.

Forecasts of product demand determine how much inventory is needed, how much product to make, and how much material to purchase from suppliers to meet forecasted customer needs. This in turn determines the kind of transportation that will be needed and where plants, warehouses, and distribution centers should be located so that products and services can be delivered on time. Without accurate forecasts, large stocks of costly inventory must be kept at each stage of the supply chain to compensate for the uncertainties of customer demand. If there are insufficient inventories, customer service suffers because of late deliveries and stockouts. This is especially hurtful in today's competitive global business environment, where customer service and on-time delivery are critical factors. Figure 12.1 illustrates the effects of bad forecasting on the supply chain.

While accurate forecasts are necessary, completely accurate forecasts are never possible. Hopefully, the forecast will reduce uncertainty about the future as much as possible, but it will never eliminate uncertainty. Thus, all of the supply chain processes need to be flexible to respond to some degree of uncertainty.

In Chapter 10 on supply chain management, we talked about the "bullwhip effect" and its negative impact on the supply chain. The bullwhip effect is the distortion of information about product demand (including forecasts) as it is transmitted back through the supply chain toward

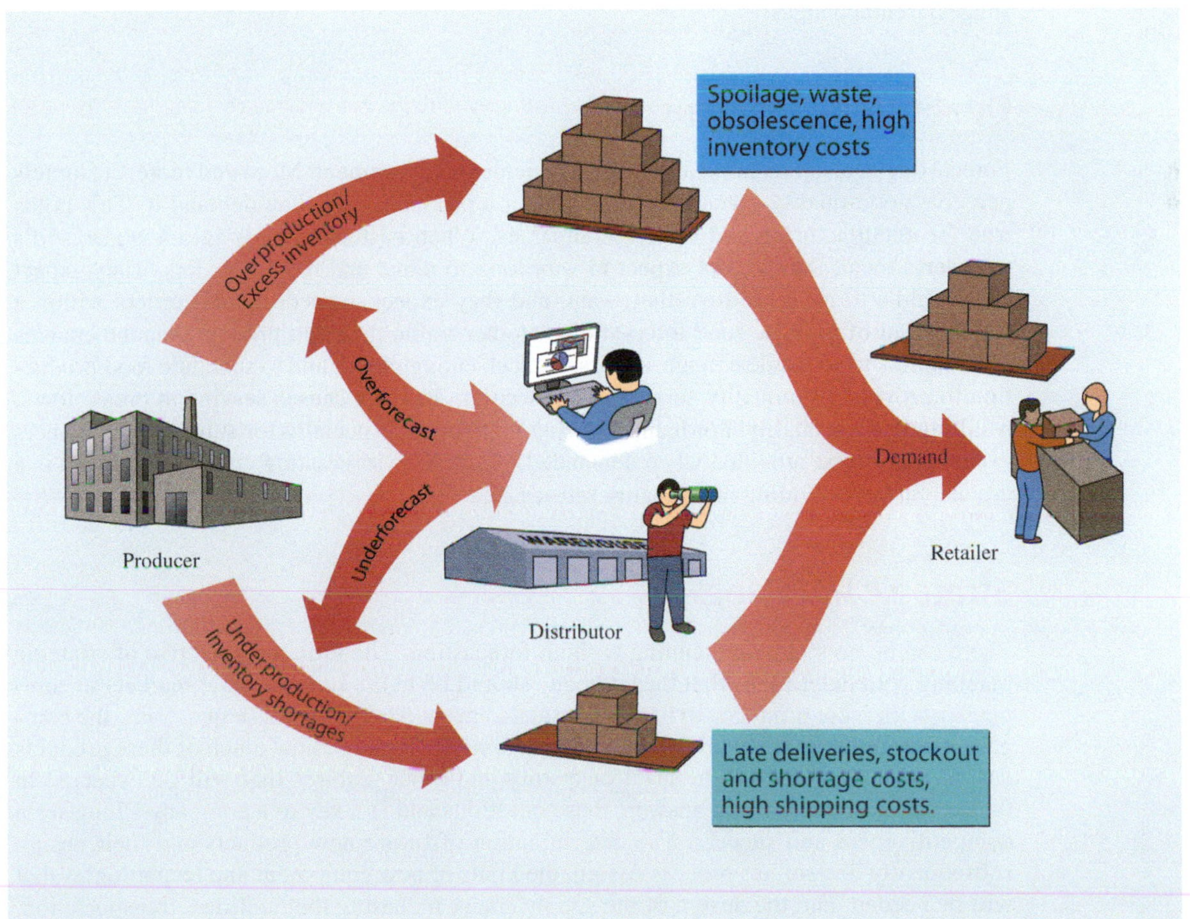

FIGURE 12.1 The Effect of Inaccurate Forecasting on the Supply Chain

suppliers. As demand moves further away from the ultimate end-use consumer, the variation in demand becomes greater and demand forecasts become less reliable. This increased variation can result in excessive, costly safety stock inventories at each stage in the supply chain and poorer customer service.

The bullwhip effect is caused when slight demand variability is magnified as information moves back upstream in the supply chain (see Figure 10.4). It is created when supply chain members make ordering decisions with an eye to their own self-interest and/or they do not have accurate demand forecasts from adjacent supply chain members. If each supply chain member is uncertain and not confident about what the actual demand is for the succeeding member it supplies, and it's making its own demand forecast, then it will stockpile extra inventory to compensate for the uncertainty; that is, the member creates a security blanket of inventory. One way to cope with the bullwhip effect is to develop demand forecasts that will reduce uncertainty and for supply chain members to share these forecasts with one another. Ideally, a single forecast of demand for the final customer in the supply chain would drive the development of subsequent forecasts for each supply chain member back up through the supply chain.

One trend in supply chain design is *continuous replenishment,* wherein continuous updating of data is shared between suppliers and customers. In this system, customers are continuously being replenished, daily or even more often, by their suppliers based on actual sales. Continuous replenishment, typically managed by the supplier, reduces inventory for the company and speeds customer delivery. Variations of continuous replenishment include quick response, just-in-time (JIT), VMI (vendor-managed inventory), SMI (supplier managed inventory), and stockless inventory. Such systems rely heavily on accurate short-term forecasts, usually on a weekly basis, of end-use sales to the ultimate customer. The supplier at one end of a company's supply chain must forecast the company's customer demand at the other end of the supply chain in order to maintain continuous replenishment. The forecast also has to be able to respond to sudden, quick changes in demand. Longer forecasts based on historical sales data for 6 to 12 months into the future are also generally required to help make weekly forecasts and suggest trend changes.

Quality Management

Forecasting is also crucial in a quality management environment. More and more, customers perceive good-quality service to mean having a product when they demand it. This holds true for manufacturing and service companies. When customers walk into a McDonald's to order a meal, they do not expect to wait long to place and receive orders. They expect McDonald's to have the item they want, and they expect to receive their orders within a short period of time. A good forecast of customer traffic flow and product demand enables McDonald's to schedule enough servers, to stock enough food, and to schedule food production to provide high-quality service. An inaccurate forecast causes service to break down, resulting in poor quality. For manufacturing operations, especially for suppliers, customers expect parts to be provided when demanded. Accurately forecasting customer demand is a crucial part of providing high-quality service.

Strategic Planning

There can be no strategic planning without forecasting. The ultimate objective of strategic planning is to determine what the company should be in the future—what markets to compete in, with what products, to be successful and grow. To answer these questions, the company needs to know what new products its customers will want, how much of these products customers will want, and the level of quality and other features that will be expected in these products. Forecasting answers these questions and is a key to a company's long-term competitiveness and success. The determination of future new products and their design subsequently determines process design, the kinds of new equipment and technologies that will be needed, and the design of the supply chain, including the facilities, transportation, and distribution systems that will be required. These elements are ultimately based on the company's forecast of the long-run future.

Along the Supply Chain

Forecasting Denim Jeans Trends

Denim jeans consumers may think that new apparel trends just happen out of the "blue," however, that's rarely the case. In most cases, jeans looks, styles, and colors can be traced back months and often years, and are the result of vast amounts of data and information, sophisticated forecasting methodologies, and expert professional analysis. In the denim jeans industry trends evolve over time, as distinct from fads, which are short term and are driven by extraneous factors like instant celebrity or a music video. Most large-volume denim jeans brands like Levi's, Gap, Lee, and Wrangler, and more fashionable brands like H&M, Calvin Klein, Tommy Hilfiger, and Zara, follow a similar methodology for trend forecasting. They first identify basic fundamental facts about past trends and forecasts such as the colors and styles that have had the greatest demand, then they determine what factors caused changes in the past and compare differences between past forecasts and what actually occurred. Next they determine what factors are most likely to affect future trends, which can be economic and technological changes as well as fashion changes. Factors that go into denim jeans trend forecasting could include new cotton fiber innovations, the price and availability of cotton, advances in manufacturing processes and machinery, shifts in global manufacturing locations, shipping changes, shifting global markets (for example into less economically developed countries), and sustainability issues, in addition to fashion factors like design, style, color, media, blogs, celebrity, and apparel trade shows. The resulting information and data are used in forecasting tools and techniques to develop trend forecasts, with particular attention paid to accuracy and reliability. Once the trend forecast is developed it is closely monitored to determine reasons for significant deviations from what is actually happening, and the forecast is revised as needed. Ultimately it is this trend forecast combined with shorter term and seasonal forecasts that drives a jeans company's global supply chain; and it is sudden changes in fashion trends and customer tastes that alter the forecast and make the denim jeans supply chain so complex and difficult to manage.

Discuss how forecasting trends for an apparel item like denim jeans is different from forecasting trends for an electronic device like a smartphone or tablet.

Source: Based on Randi Gollin, "Trend Forecasters Talk Fall/Winter 2012/2013," *Apparel Insiders*, www.apparelinsiders.com.

Components of Forecasting Demand

The type of forecasting method to use depends on several factors, including the **time frame** of the forecast (i.e., how far in the future is being forecasted), the *behavior* of demand, and the possible existence of patterns (trends, seasonality, and so on), and the *causes* of demand behavior.

Time frame Indicates how far into the future is forecast.

Time Frame

Forecasts are either short- to mid-range, or long-range. **Short-range (to mid-range) forecasts** are typically for daily, weekly, or monthly sales demand for up to approximately two years into the future, depending on the company and the type of industry. They are primarily used to determine production and delivery schedules and to establish inventory levels. At Hewlett-Packard monthly forecasts for printers are constructed from 12 to 18 months into the future, while at Levi Strauss weekly forecasts for jeans are prepared for five years into the future.

Short- to mid-range forecast Typically encompasses the immediate future—daily up to two years.

A **long-range forecast** is usually for a period longer than two years into the future. A long-range forecast is normally used for strategic planning—to establish long-term goals, plan new products for changing markets, enter new markets, develop new facilities, develop technology, design the supply chain, and implement strategic programs. At Unisys, long-range strategic forecasts project three years into the future; Hewlett-Packard's long-term forecasts are developed for years 2 through 6; and at Fiat, the Italian automaker, strategic plans for new and continuing products go 10 years into the future.

Long-range forecast Usually encompasses a period of time longer than two years.

These classifications are generalizations. The line between short- and long-range forecasts is not always distinct. For some companies a short-range forecast can be several years, and for other firms a long-range forecast can be in terms of months. The length of a forecast depends a lot on how rapidly the product market changes and how susceptible the market is to technological changes.

Demand Behavior

Demand sometimes behaves in a random, irregular way. At other times it exhibits predictable behavior, with trends or repetitive patterns, which the forecast may reflect. The three types of demand behavior are *trends*, *cycles*, and *seasonal patterns*.

Trend A gradual, long-term up or down movement of demand.

Random variations Movements in demand that do not follow a pattern.

Cycle An up-and-down repetitive movement in demand.

Seasonal pattern An up-and-down repetitive movement in demand occurring periodically.

A **trend** is a gradual, long-term up or down movement of demand. For example, the demand for houses has followed an upward trend during the past few decades, without any sustained downward movement in the market. Trends are often the starting points for developing forecasts. Figure 12.2(*a*) illustrates a demand trend in which there is a general upward movement, or increase. Notice that Figure 12.2(*a*) also includes several random movements up and down. **Random variations** are movements that are not predictable and follow no pattern (and thus are virtually unpredictable). They are routine variations that have no "assignable" cause.

A **cycle** is an up-and-down movement in demand that repeats itself over a lengthy time span (i.e., more than a year). For example, new housing starts and, thus, construction-related products tend to follow cycles in the economy. Automobile sales also tend to follow cycles. The demand for winter sports equipment increases every four years before and after the Winter Olympics. Figure 12.2(*b*) shows the behavior of a demand cycle.

A **seasonal pattern** is an oscillating movement in demand that occurs periodically (in the short run) and is repetitive. Seasonality is often weather-related. For example, every winter the demand for snowblowers and skis increases, and retail sales in general increase during the holiday season. However, a seasonal pattern can occur on a daily or weekly basis. For example, some restaurants are busier at lunch than at dinner, and shopping mall stores and theaters tend to have higher demand on weekends. At FedEx seasonalities include the month of the year, day of the week, and day of the month, as well as various holidays. Figure 12.2(*c*) illustrates a seasonal pattern in which the same demand behavior is repeated each year at the same time.

Demand behavior frequently displays several of these characteristics simultaneously. Although housing starts display cyclical behavior, there has been an upward trend in new house construction over the years. Demand for skis is seasonal; however, there has been an upward trend in the demand for winter sports equipment during the past two decades. Figure 12.2(*d*) displays the combination of two demand patterns, a trend with a seasonal pattern.

Instances when demand behavior exhibits no pattern are referred to as *irregular movements,* or variations. For example, a local flood might cause a momentary increase in carpet demand, or a competitor's promotional campaign might cause a company's product demand

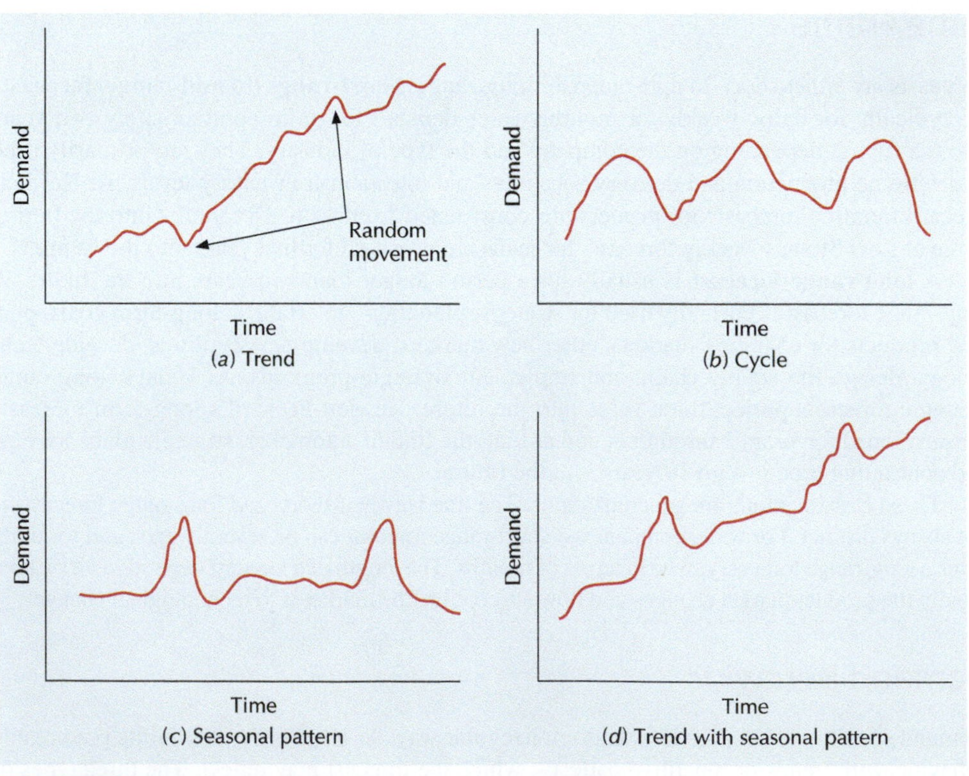

FIGURE 12.2 **Forms of Forecast Movement**

to drop for a time. Although this behavior has a cause and, thus, is not totally random, it still does not follow a pattern that can be reflected in a forecast.

Forecasting Methods

The factors discussed previously in this section determine to a certain extent the type of forecasting method that can or should be used. In this chapter we are going to discuss three basic types of forecasting: *time series methods, regression methods,* and *qualitative methods.*

Time series methods are statistical techniques that use historical demand data to predict future demand. **Regression** (or causal) **forecasting methods** attempt to develop a mathematical relationship (in the form of a regression model) between demand and factors that cause it to behave the way it does. Most of the remainder of this chapter will be about time series and regression forecasting methods. In this section we will focus our discussion on qualitative forecasting.

Regression forecasting methods Relate demand to other factors that cause demand behavior.

Qualitative (or judgmental) methods use management judgment, expertise, and opinion to make forecasts. Often called "the jury of executive opinion," they are the most common type of forecasting method for the long-term strategic planning process. There are normally individuals or groups within an organization whose judgments and opinions regarding the future are as valid or more valid than those of outside experts or other structured approaches. Top managers are the key group involved in the development of forecasts for strategic plans. They are generally most familiar with their firms' own capabilities and resources and the markets for their products. The sales force of a company represents a direct point of contact with the consumer. This contact provides an awareness of consumer expectations in the future that others may not possess. Engineering personnel have an innate understanding of the technological aspects of the type of products that might be feasible and likely in the future.

Consumer (or market) *research* is an organized approach using surveys and other research techniques to determine what products and services customers want and will purchase, and to identify new markets and sources of customers. Consumer and market research is normally conducted by the marketing department within an organization, by industry organizations and groups, and by private marketing or consulting firms. Although market research can provide accurate and useful forecasts of product demand, it must be skillfully and correctly conducted, and it can be expensive.

The **Delphi method** is a procedure for acquiring informed judgments and opinions from knowledgeable individuals using a series of questionnaires to develop a consensus forecast about what will occur in the future. It was developed at the Rand Corporation shortly after World War II to forecast the impact of a hypothetical nuclear attack on the United States. Although the Delphi method has been used for a variety of applications, forecasting has been one of its primary uses. It has been especially useful for forecasting technological change and advances.

Delphi method Involves soliciting forecasts about technological advances from experts.

Technological forecasting has become increasingly crucial to compete in the modern international business environment. New enhanced computer technology, new production methods, and advanced machinery and equipment are constantly being made available to companies. These advances enable them to introduce more new products into the marketplace faster than ever before. The companies that succeed manage to get a "technological" jump on their competitors by accurately predicting what technology will be available in the future and how it can be exploited. What new products and services will be technologically feasible, when they can be introduced, and what their demand will be are questions about the future for which answers cannot be predicted from historical data. Instead, the informed opinion and judgment of experts are necessary to make these types of single, long-term forecasts.

Data mining is a recent addition to the library of methods and techniques companies have available for forecasting, brought about by the evolution in information technology. It is a process and set of tools for analyzing large amounts of data in order to identify patterns, trends, and relationships among and between groups of customers, markets, and products. Data mining is made possible by the vast amounts of data that companies now have available to them from various electronic transactions throughout their supply chains, and the ability to store this amount of data inexpensively.

Data mining Process and set of tools for analyzing large amounts of data.

Forecasting Process

Forecasting is not simply identifying and using a method to compute a numerical estimate of what demand will be in the future. It is a continuing process that requires constant monitoring and adjustment illustrated by the steps in Figure 12.3.

In the next few sections we present several different forecasting methods applicable for different patterns of demand behavior. Thus, one of the first steps in the forecasting process is to plot the available historical demand data and, by looking at them, to attempt to determine the forecasting method that best seems to fit the patterns the data exhibit. Historical demand is usually past sales or orders data. There are several measures for comparing historical demand with the forecast to see how accurate the forecast is. Following our discussion of the forecasting methods, we present several measures of forecast accuracy. If the forecast does not seem to be accurate, another method can be tried until an accurate

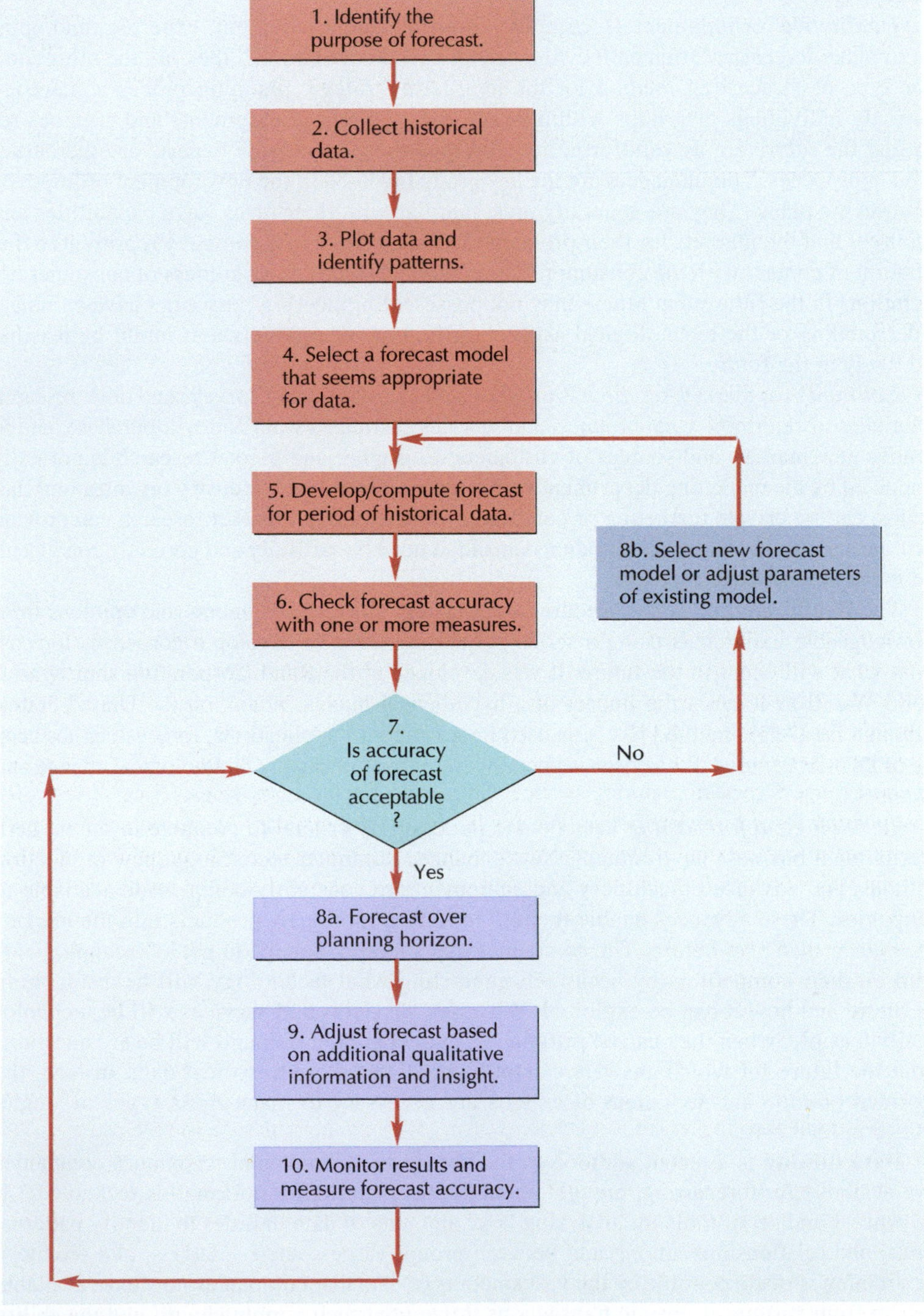

FIGURE 12.3 **Steps of the Forecasting Process**

Along the Supply Chain

Global Supply Chain Forecasting at Hershey's

Global companies such as Hershey's have numerous opportunities to use forecasting along various points in its supply chain. Downstream in its supply chain Hershey's attempts to forecast product demand, which is subject to uncertainties resulting from new and current products from competitors, competitors' promotional events and price changes, and changing consumer tastes for its own current and new products. Issues related to product quality and safety, ingredients, or packaging could adversely affect demand. Negative publicity related to product recalls due to contamination or product tampering, whether valid or not, might also negatively impact product demand. All of these factors affect the forecasting process. Upstream in its supply chain, Hershey's sources many different commodities including cocoa products, sugar, dairy products, peanuts, almonds, corn sweeteners, natural gas, and fuel oil. Commodities are subject to price volatility and changes in supply caused by numerous factors, including commodity market fluctuations and speculative influences; currency exchange rates; the effect of weather on crop yield and distribution channels; trade agreements among producing and consuming nations; political unrest in producing countries; and changes in governmental agricultural programs and energy policies. Other factors that can create uncertainties in its global supply chain and operations that make forecasting difficult include global economic and environmental changes that can result in interruptions in supply and decreased demand for its products overseas; changes in tariff and trade agreements; political instability; nationalization of Hershey's properties; and disruptions in shipping or reduced availability of freight transportation.

Given the various uncertainties inherent in the forecasting process at Hershey's, what kind of forecasting models might you suggest for the company?

Source: Hershey's website at www.thehersheycompany.com

forecast method is identified. After the forecast is made over the desired planning horizon, it may be possible to use judgment, experience, knowledge of the market, or even intuition to adjust the forecast to enhance its accuracy. Finally, as demand actually occurs over the planning period, it must be monitored and compared with the forecast in order to assess the performance of the forecast method. If the forecast is accurate, then it is appropriate to continue using the forecast method. If it is not accurate, a new model or adjusting the existing one should be considered.

Moving Average

Time series methods are statistical techniques that make use of historical data accumulated over a period of time. Time series methods assume that what has occurred in the past will continue to occur in the future. As the name *time series* suggests, these methods relate the forecast to only one factor—time. These methods assume that identifiable historical patterns or trends for demand over time will repeat themselves. They include the moving average, exponential smoothing, and linear trend line, and they are among the most popular methods for short-range forecasting among service and manufacturing companies. Time series is the most popular forecasting method by far. It's likely that the majority of businesses have used time series to some extent. One of the reasons time series models are so popular is that they are relatively easy to understand and use. The survey also showed that the most popular time series models are moving averages and exponential smoothing.

Time series methods Use historical demand data over a period of time to predict future demand.

A time series forecast can be as simple as using demand in the current period to predict demand in the next period. This is sometimes called a *naive* or *intuitive* forecast. For example, if demand is 100 units this week, the forecast for next week's demand is 100 units; if demand turns out to be 90 units instead, then the following week's demand is 90 units, and so on. This type of forecasting method does not take into account historical demand *behavior*; it relies only on demand in the current period. It reacts directly to the normal, random movements in demand.

The simple **moving average** method uses several demand values during the recent past to develop a forecast. This tends to *dampen*, or *smooth out*, the random increases and decreases of a forecast that uses only one period. The simple moving average is useful for forecasting demand that is stable and does not display any pronounced demand behavior, such as a trend or seasonal pattern.

Moving average Method uses average demand for a fixed sequence of periods.

Moving averages are computed for specific periods, such as three months or five months, depending on how much the forecaster desires to "smooth" the demand data. The longer the moving average period, the smoother it will be. (Alternatively, a shorter moving average is more susceptible to simple random variation.) The formula for computing the simple moving average is

$$MA_n = \frac{\sum_{i=1}^{n} D_i}{n}$$

where

n = number of periods in the moving average
D_i = demand in period i

The disadvantage of the moving average method is that it does not react to variations that occur for a reason, such as cycles and seasonal effects. Factors that cause changes are generally ignored. It is basically a "mechanical" method that reflects historical data in a consistent way. However, the moving average method does have the advantage of being easy to use, quick, and relatively inexpensive. In general, this method can provide a good forecast for the short run, but it should not be pushed too far into the future.

EXAMPLE 12.1 | Computing a Simple Moving Average

The Heartland Produce Company sells and delivers food produce to restaurants and catering services within a 100-mile radius of its warehouse. The food supply business is competitive, and the ability to deliver orders promptly is a factor in getting new customers and keeping old ones. The manager of the company wants to be certain enough drivers and vehicles are available to deliver orders promptly and they have adequate inventory in stock. Therefore, the manager wants to be able to forecast the number of orders that will occur during the next month (i.e., to forecast the demand for deliveries).

From records of delivery orders, management has accumulated the following data for the past 10 months, from which it wants to compute three- and five-month moving averages.

MONTH	ORDERS	MONTH	ORDERS
January	120	June	50
February	90	July	75
March	100	August	130
April	75	September	110
May	110	October	90

Solution: Let us assume that it is the end of October. The forecast resulting from either the three- or five-month moving average is typically for the next month in the sequence, which in this case is November. The moving average is computed from the demand for orders for the prior three months in the sequence according to the following formula:

$$MA_3 = \frac{\sum_{i=1}^{3} D_i}{3} = \frac{90 + 110 + 130}{3} = 110 \text{ orders for November}$$

The five-month moving average is computed from the prior five months of demand data as follows:

$$MA_5 = \frac{\sum_{i=1}^{5} D_i}{5} = \frac{90 + 110 + 130 + 75 + 50}{5} = 91 \text{ orders for November}$$

The three- and five-month moving average forecasts for all the months of demand data are shown in the following table. Actually, the manager would use only the forecast for November based on the most recent monthly demand. However, the earlier forecasts for prior months allow us to compare the forecast with actual demand to see how accurate the forecasting method is—that is, how well it does.

Three- and Five-Month Averages

MONTH	ORDERS PER MONTH	THREE-MONTH MOVING AVERAGE	FIVE-MONTH MOVING AVERAGE
January	120	—	—
February	90	—	—
March	100	—	—
April	75	103.3	—
May	110	88.3	—
June	50	95.0	99.0
July	75	78.3	85.0
August	130	78.3	82.0
September	110	85.0	88.0
October	90	105.0	95.0
November	—	110.0	91.0

Both moving average forecasts in the preceding table tend to smooth out the variability occurring in the actual data. This smoothing effect can be observed in the following figure in which the three-month and five-month averages have been superimposed on a graph of the original data:

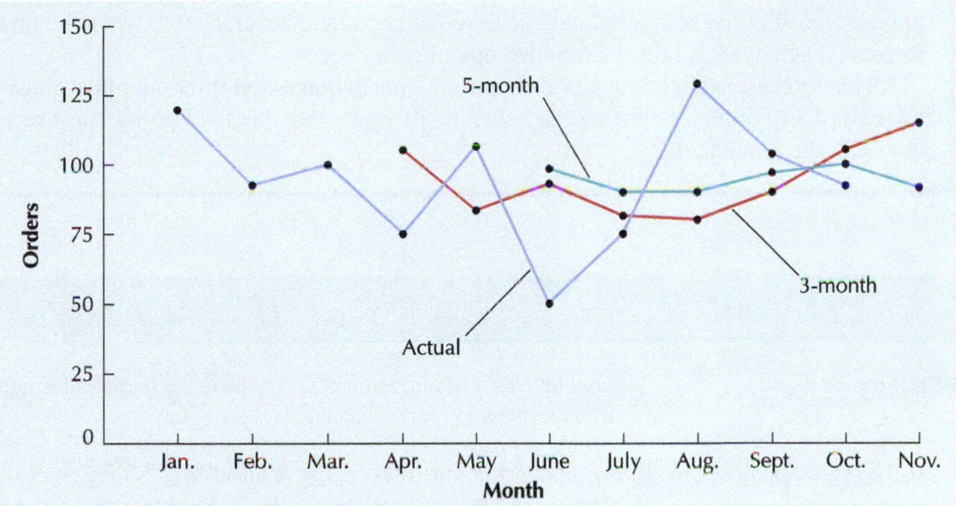

The five-month moving average in the previous figure smooths out fluctuations to a greater extent than the three-month moving average. However, the three-month average more closely reflects the most recent data available to the produce company manager. In general, forecasts using the longer-period moving average are slower to react to recent changes in demand than those made using shorter-period moving averages. The extra periods of data dampen the speed with which the forecast responds. Establishing the appropriate number of periods to use in a moving average forecast often requires some amount of trial-and-error experimentation.

Weighted Moving Average

The moving average method can be adjusted to more closely reflect fluctuations in the data. In the **weighted moving average** method, weights are assigned to the most recent data according to the following formula:

Weighted moving average Weights are assigned to the most recent data.

$$WMA_n = \sum_{i=1}^{n} W_i D_i$$

where

W_i = the weight for period i, between 0 and 100 percent
$\Sigma w_i = 1.00$

Determining the precise weights to use for each period of data usually requires some trial-and-error experimentation, as does determining the number of periods to include in the moving average. If the most recent periods are weighted too heavily, the forecast might overreact to a random fluctuation in demand. If they are weighted too lightly, the forecast might underreact to actual changes in demand behavior.

EXAMPLE 12.2 | Computing a Weighted Moving Average

The Heartland Produce Company in Example 12.1 wants to compute a three-month weighted moving average with a weight of 50% for the October data, a weight of 33% for the September data, and a weight of 17% for the August data. These weights reflect the company's desire to have the most recent data influence the forecast most strongly.

Solution: The weighted moving average is computed as

$$\begin{aligned} WMA_3 &= \sum_{i=1}^{3} W_i D_i \\ &= (0.50)(90) + (0.33)(110) + (0.17)(130) \\ &= 103.4 \text{ orders} \end{aligned}$$

Notice that the forecast includes a fractional part, 0.4. In general, the fractional parts need to be included in the computation to achieve mathematical accuracy, but when the final forecast is achieved, it must be rounded up or down.

This forecast is slightly lower than our previously computed three-month average forecast of 110 orders, reflecting the lower number of orders in October (the most recent month in the sequence).

Along the Supply Chain

Demand Forecasts for Solar Energy Development at GE

General Electric (GE) Energy is a global leader in energy technology involved in all areas of the energy industry, including conventional energy sources, coal, oil, natural gas, nuclear energy, and renewable sources such as water, wind, solar, biogas, and other alternative fuels. GE has received support from the U.S. Department of Energy to produce electricity generated from solar (photoelectric) cells that convert sunlight into electricity, as shown in photo, and make its generation and distribution cost competitive with conventional sources of electricity. GE Energy expects its emerging solar business to grow to over $1 billion in revenues by mid-decade and for it to continue to grow rapidly in the future. However, the solar industry is in an embryonic stage and thus requires GE to not only engage in R&D to develop solar cell technology, but to also establish partnerships with companies to develop a manufacturing and distribution infrastructure to install solar energy systems for commercial and utility consumers. This requires a significant capital investment for manufacturing solar power equipment for high-volume consumer usage, which requires estimating costs and forecasting solar energy demand in order to make good investment decisions in the face of uncertainties in technology, costs, demand, and energy policy.

A key aspect of this development process for GE is being able to forecast solar energy demand by year, region of the country, and market type over a 10- to 15-year period, as well as research and development costs. GE's forecasting model for solar energy demand first forecasts the potential in megawatts that can physically be installed on rooftops by region of the country, using existing data for available floor space. GE then estimates potential revenues generated by an average rooftop installation, which when compared with installation costs enables GE to determine the payback period for its investment. These forecasts are then used in combination with previously developed solar energy market penetration functions to determine market penetration in megawatts as a function of payback years.

Solar energy is an emerging technology; discuss how GE might use "subjective" expert opinions as a forecasting tool.

Source: Based on Bex G. Thomas and Srinivas Bollapragada, "General Electric Uses an Integrated Framework for Product Costing, Demand Forecasting, and Capacity Planning of New Photovoltaic Technology Products," *Interfaces*, 40 (5) (September–October 2010), pp. 353–367.

gmalandra/iStockphoto

Solar parks are becoming increasingly popular, especially in Europe. Although, solar power accounts for less than 1 percent of all electricity generation worldwide, it is growing at an annual rate above 50 percent, which makes forecasting solar demand for energy companies critically important.

Exponential Smoothing

Exponential smoothing is also an averaging method that weights the most recent data more strongly. As such, the forecast will react more to recent changes in demand. This is useful if the recent changes in the data are significant and unpredictable instead of just random fluctuations (for which a simple moving average forecast would suffice).

Exponential smoothing An averaging method that reacts more strongly to recent changes in demand.

Exponential smoothing is one of the more popular and frequently used forecasting techniques, for a variety of reasons. Exponential smoothing requires minimal data. Only the forecast for the current period, the actual demand for the current period, and a weighting factor called a smoothing constant are necessary. The mathematics of the technique are easy for management to understand. Virtually all forecasting computer software packages include modules for exponential smoothing. Most importantly, exponential smoothing has a good track record of success. It has been employed over the years by many companies that have found it to be an accurate method of forecasting.

The exponential smoothing forecast is computed using the formula

$$F_{t+1} = \alpha D_t + (1 - \alpha)F_t$$

where

F_{t+1} = the forecast for the next period
D_t = actual demand in the present period
F_t = the previously determined forecast for the present period
α = a weighting factor referred to as the **smoothing constant**

Smoothing constant The weighting factor given to the most recent data in exponential smoothing forecasts.

The smoothing constant, α, is between 0.0 and 1.0. It reflects the weight given to the most recent demand data. For example, if $\alpha = .20$,

$$F_{t+1} = 0.20D_t + 0.80F_t$$

which means that our forecast for the next period is based on 20% of recent demand (D_t) and 80% of past demand (in the form of forecast F_t, since F_t is derived from previous demands and forecasts). If we go to one extreme and let $\alpha = 0.0$, then

$$\begin{aligned} F_{t+1} &= 0D_t + 1F_t \\ &= F_t \end{aligned}$$

and the forecast for the next period is the same as the forecast for this period. In other words, *the forecast does not reflect the most recent demand at all.*

On the other hand, if $\alpha = 1.0$, then

$$\begin{aligned} F_{t+1} &= 1D_t + 0F_t \\ &= 1D_t \end{aligned}$$

and we have considered only the most recent data (demand in the present period) and nothing else. Thus, the higher α is, the more sensitive the forecast will be to changes in recent demand, and the smoothing will be less. The closer α is to zero, the greater will be the dampening, or smoothing, effect. As α approaches zero, the forecast will react and adjust more slowly to differences between the actual demand and the forecasted demand. The most commonly used values of α are in the range of .01 to .50. However, the determination of α is usually judgmental and subjective and is often based on trial-and-error experimentation. An inaccurate estimate of α can limit the usefulness of this forecasting technique. (As α approaches 1.0, the forecast is the same as the naive result.)

EXAMPLE 12.3 | Computing an Exponentially Smoothed Forecast

HiTek Computer Services repairs and services personal computers at its store, and it makes local service calls. It primarily uses part-time State University students as technicians. The company has had steady growth since it started. It purchases generic computer parts in volume at a discount from a variety of sources whenever it sees a good deal. Thus, they need a good forecast of demand for repairs so that they will know how many computer component parts to purchase and stock, and how many technicians to hire.

The company has accumulated the demand data shown in the accompanying table for repair and service calls for the past 12 months, from which it wants to consider exponential smoothing forecasts using smoothing constants (α) equal to .30 and .50.

Demand for Repair and Service Calls

PERIOD	MONTH	DEMAND	PERIOD	MONTH	DEMAND
1	January	37	7	July	43
2	February	40	8	August	47
3	March	41	9	September	56
4	April	37	10	October	52
5	May	45	11	November	55
6	June	50	12	December	54

Solution: To develop the series of forecasts for the data in this table, we will start with period 1 (January) and compute the forecast for period 2 (February) using $\alpha = .30$. The formula for exponential smoothing also requires a forecast for period 1, which we do not have, so we will use the demand for period 1 as both *demand* and *forecast* for period 1. (Other ways to determine a starting forecast include averaging the first three or four periods or making a subjective estimate.) Thus, the forecast for February is

$$\begin{aligned} F_2 &= \alpha D_1 + (1 - \alpha)F_1 \\ &= (0.30)(37) + (0.70)(37) \\ &= 37 \text{ service calls} \end{aligned}$$

The forecast for period 3 is computed similarly:

$$\begin{aligned} F_3 &= \alpha D_2 + (1 - \alpha)F_2 \\ &= (0.30)(40) + (0.70)(37) \\ &= 37.9 \text{ service calls} \end{aligned}$$

The remainder of the monthly forecasts are shown in the following table. The final forecast is for period 13, January, and is the forecast of interest to HiTek:

$$
\begin{aligned}
F_{13} &= \alpha D_{12} + (1 - \alpha)F_{12} \\
&= (0.30)(54) + (0.70)(50.84) \\
&= 51.79 \text{ service calls}
\end{aligned}
$$

Exponential Smoothing Forecasts, $\alpha = .30$ and $\alpha = .50$

			FORECAST, F_{t+1}	
PERIOD	MONTH	DEMAND	$\alpha = .30$	$\alpha = .50$
1	January	37	—	—
2	February	40	37.00	37.00
3	March	41	37.90	38.50
4	April	37	38.83	39.75
5	May	45	38.28	38.37
6	June	50	40.29	41.68
7	July	43	43.20	45.84
8	August	47	43.14	44.42
9	September	56	44.30	45.71
10	October	52	47.81	50.85
11	November	55	49.06	51.42
12	December	54	50.84	53.21
13	January	—	51.79	53.61

This table also includes the forecast values using $\alpha = .50$. Both exponential smoothing forecasts are shown in the following figure together with the actual data.

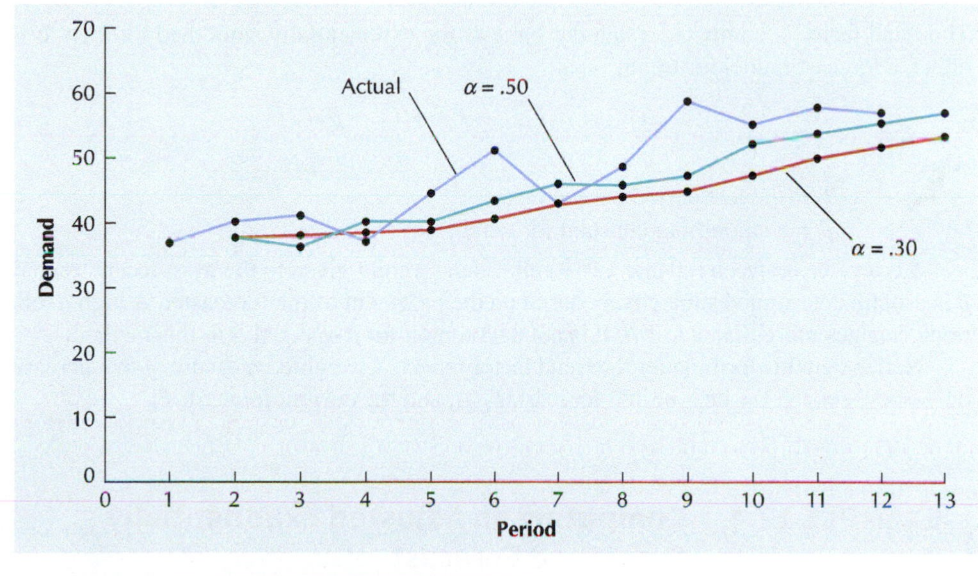

In Example 12.3, the forecast using the higher smoothing constant, $\alpha = .50$, seems to react more strongly to changes in demand than does the forecast with $\alpha = .30$, although both smooth out the random fluctuations in the forecast. Notice that both forecasts lag behind the actual demand. For example, a pronounced downward change in demand in July is not reflected in the forecast until August. If these changes mark a change in trend (i.e., a long-term upward or downward movement) rather than just a random fluctuation, then the forecast will always lag behind this trend. We can see a general upward trend in service calls throughout the year. Both forecasts tend to be consistently lower than the actual demand; that is, the forecasts lag the trend.

Based on simple observation of the two forecasts in Example 12.3, $\alpha = .50$ seems to be the more accurate of the two in the sense that it seems to follow the actual data more closely. (Later in this chapter we discuss several quantitative methods for determining forecast accuracy.) When demand is relatively stable without any trend, a small value for α is more appropriate to simply smooth out the forecast. When actual demand displays an increasing (or decreasing) trend, as is the case in the figure, a larger value of α is better. It will react more quickly to more recent upward or downward movements in the actual data. In some approaches to exponential smoothing, the accuracy of the forecast is monitored in terms of the difference between the actual values and the forecasted values. If these differences become larger, then α is changed (higher or lower) in an attempt to adapt the forecast to the actual data. However, the exponential smoothing forecast can also be adjusted for the effects of a trend.

In Example 12.3, the final forecast computed was for one month, January. A forecast for two or three months could have been computed by grouping the demand data into the required number of periods and then using these values in the exponential smoothing computations. For example, if a three-month forecast were needed, demand for January, February, and March could be summed and used to compute the average forecast for the next three-month period, and so on, until a final three-month forecast results. Alternatively, if a trend is present, the final period forecast can be used for an extended forecast by adjusting it by a trend factor.

Adjusted Exponential Smoothing

Adjusted exponential smoothing forecast An exponential smoothing forecast with an adjustment for a trend added to it.

The **adjusted exponential smoothing forecast** consists of the exponential smoothing forecast with a trend adjustment factor added to it:

$$AF_{t+1} = F_{t+1} + T_{t+1}$$

where

T = an exponentially smoothed trend factor

The trend factor is computed much the same as the exponentially smoothed forecast. It is, in effect, a forecast model for trend:

$$T_{t+1} = \beta(F_{t+1} - F_t) + (1 - \beta)T_t$$

where

T_t = the last period's trend factor
β = a smoothing constant for trend

β is a value between 0.0 and 1.0. It reflects the weight given to the most recent trend data. β is usually determined subjectively based on the judgment of the forecaster. A high β reflects trend changes more than a low β. It is not uncommon for β to equal α in this method.

Notice that this formula for the trend factor reflects a weighted measure of the increase (or decrease) between the next period forecast, F_{t+1}, and the current forecast, F_t.

EXAMPLE 12.4 | Computing an Adjusted Exponentially Smoothed Forecast

HiTek Computer Services now wants to develop an adjusted exponentially smoothed forecast using the same 12 months of demand shown in the table for Example 12.3. It will use the exponentially smoothed forecast with $\alpha = .5$ computed in Example 12.3 with a smoothing constant for trend, β, of .30.

Solution: The formula for the adjusted exponential smoothing forecast requires an initial value for T_t to start the computational process. This initial trend factor is often an estimate determined subjectively or based on past data by the forecaster. In this case, since we have a long sequence of demand data (i.e., 12 months), we will start with the trend T_t equal to zero. By the time the forecast value of interest F_{13} is computed, we should have a relatively good value for the trend factor.

The adjusted forecast for February, AF_2, is the same as the exponentially smoothed forecast, since the trend computing factor will be zero (i.e., F_1 and F_2 are the same and $T_2 = 0$). Thus, we compute the adjusted forecast for March, AF_3, as follows, starting with the determination of the trend factor, T_3:

$$\begin{aligned} T_3 &= \beta(F_3 - F_2) + (1 - \beta)T_2 \\ &= (0.30)(38.5 - 37.0) + (0.70)(0) \\ &= 0.45 \end{aligned}$$

and

$$\begin{aligned} AF_3 &= F_3 + T_3 \\ &= 38.5 + 0.45 \\ &= 38.95 \text{ service cells} \end{aligned}$$

This adjusted forecast value for period 3 is shown in the accompanying table, with all other adjusted forecast values for the 12-month period plus the forecast for period 13, computed as follows:

$$\begin{aligned} T_{13} &= \beta(F_{13} - F_{12}) + (1 - \beta)T_{12} \\ &= (0.30)(53.61 - 53.21) + (0.70)(1.77) \\ &= 1.36 \end{aligned}$$

and

$$\begin{aligned} AF_{13} &= F_{13} + T_{13} \\ &= 53.61 + 1.36 \\ &= 54.97 \text{ service calls} \end{aligned}$$

Adjusted Exponential Smoothing Forecast Values

PERIOD	MONTH	DEMAND	FORECAST F_{t+1}	TREND T_{t+1}	ADJUSTED FORECAST AF_{t+1}
1	January	37	37.00	—	—
2	February	40	37.00	0.00	37.00
3	March	41	38.50	0.45	38.95
4	April	37	39.75	0.69	40.44
5	May	45	38.37	0.07	38.44
6	June	50	41.68	1.04	42.73
7	July	43	45.84	1.97	47.82
8	August	47	44.42	0.95	45.37
9	September	56	45.71	1.05	46.76
10	October	52	50.85	2.28	53.13
11	November	55	51.42	1.76	53.19
12	December	54	53.21	1.77	54.98
13	January	—	53.61	1.36	54.97

The adjusted exponentially smoothed forecast values shown in the above table are compared with the exponentially smoothed forecast values and the actual data in the figure. Notice that the adjusted forecast is consistently higher than the exponentially smoothed forecast and is thus more reflective of the generally increasing trend of the actual data. However, in general, the pattern, or degree of smoothing, is very similar for both forecasts.

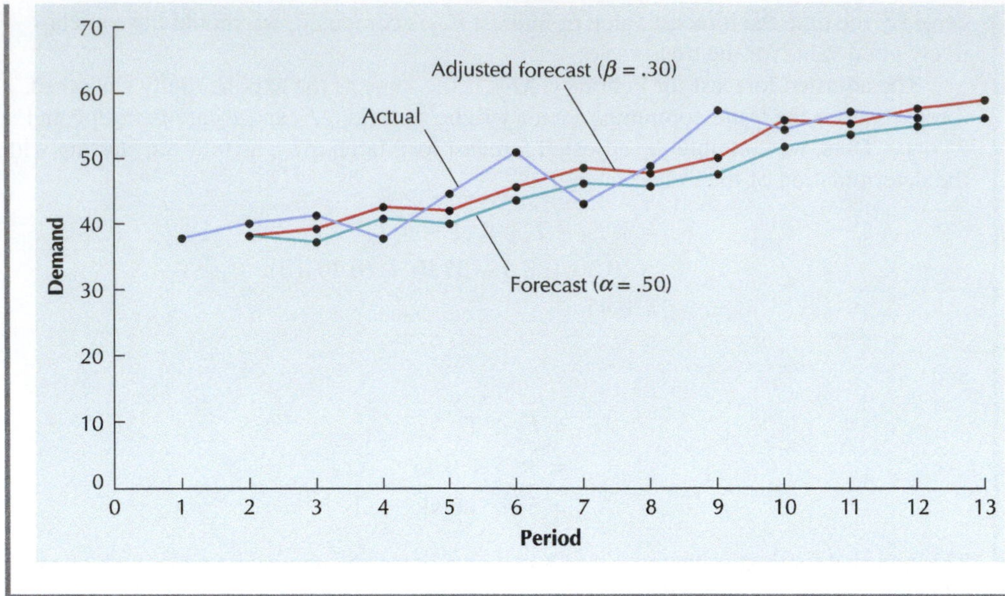

Linear Trend Line

Linear trend line A linear regression model relating demand to time.

Linear regression is a method of forecasting in which a mathematical relationship is developed between demand and some other factor that causes demand behavior. However, when demand displays an obvious trend over time, a least squares regression line, or **linear trend line**, that relates demand to time can be used to forecast demand.

A linear trend line relates a dependent variable, which for our purposes is demand, to one independent variable, time, in the form of a linear equation:

$$y = a + bx$$

where

$$\begin{aligned} a &= \text{intercept (at period 0)} \\ b &= \text{slope of the line} \\ x &= \text{the time period} \\ y &= \text{forecast for demand for period } x \end{aligned}$$

These parameters of the linear trend line can be calculated using the least squares formulas for linear regression:

$$b = \frac{\sum xy - n\overline{x}\overline{y}}{\sum x^2 - n\overline{x}^2}$$

$$a = \overline{y} - b\overline{x}$$

where

$$\begin{aligned} n &= \text{number of periods} \\ \overline{x} &= \frac{\sum x}{n} = \text{the mean of the } x \text{ values} \\ \overline{y} &= \frac{\sum y}{n} = \text{the mean of the } y \text{ values} \end{aligned}$$

EXAMPLE 12.5 | Computing a Linear Trend Line

The data for HiTek Computer Services (shown in the table for Example 12.3) appears to follow an increasing linear trend. The company wants to compute a linear trend line to see if it is more accurate than the exponential smoothing and adjusted exponential smoothing forecasts developed in Examples 12.3 and 12.4.

Solution: The values required for the least squares calculations are as follows:

Least Squares Calculations

x (PERIOD)	y (DEMAND)	xy	x^2
1	37	37	1
2	40	80	4
3	41	123	9
4	37	148	16
5	45	225	25
6	50	300	36
7	43	301	49
8	47	376	64
9	56	504	81
10	52	520	100
11	55	605	121
12	54	648	144
78	557	3867	650

Using these values, we can compute the parameters for the linear trend line as follows:

$$\bar{x} = \frac{78}{12} = 6.5$$

$$\bar{y} = \frac{557}{12} = 46.42$$

$$\begin{aligned} b &= \frac{\Sigma xy - n\bar{x}\bar{y}}{\Sigma x^2 - n\bar{x}^2} \\ &= \frac{3867 - (12)(6.5)(46.42)}{650 - 12(6.5)^2} \\ &= 1.72 \end{aligned}$$

$$\begin{aligned} a &= \bar{y} - b\bar{x} \\ &= 46.42 - (1.72)(6.5) \\ &= 35.2 \end{aligned}$$

Therefore, the linear trend line equation is

$$y = 35.2 + 1.72x$$

To calculate a forecast for period 13, let $x = 13$ in the linear trend line:

$$\begin{aligned} y &= 35.2 + 1.72(13) \\ &= 57.56 \text{ service calls} \end{aligned}$$

The graph shows the linear trend line compared with the actual data. The trend line appears to reflect closely the actual data—that is, to be a good fit—and would thus be a good forecast model for this problem. However, a disadvantage of the linear trend line is that it will not adjust to a change in the trend, as the exponential smoothing forecast methods will; that is, it is assumed that all future forecasts will follow a straight line. This limits the use of this method to a shorter time frame in which you can be relatively certain that the trend will not change.

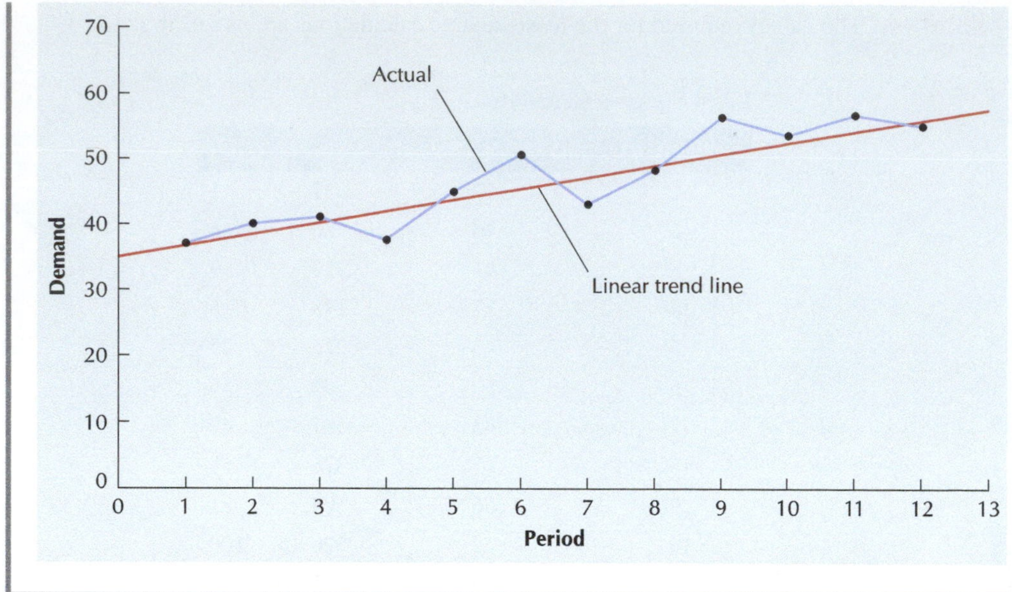

Seasonal Adjustments

A seasonal pattern is a repetitive increase and decrease in demand. Many demand items exhibit seasonal behavior. Clothing sales follow annual seasonal patterns, with demand for warm clothes increasing in the fall and winter and declining in the spring and summer

Snow skiing is an industry that exhibits several different patterns of demand behavior. It is primarily a seasonal (i.e., winter) industry and over a long period of time has exhibited a generally increasing growth trend. Random factors can cause variations, or abrupt peaks and valleys, in demand. For example, demand for skiing products always shows a pronounced increase after the Winter Olympics.

as the demand for cooler clothing increases. Another example is the snow skiing industry as shown in photo. Demand for many retail items, including toys, sports equipment, clothing, electronic appliances, hams, turkeys, wine, and fruit, increases during the holiday season. Greeting card demand increases in conjunction with special days such as Valentine's Day and Mother's Day. Seasonal patterns can also occur on a monthly, weekly, or even daily basis. Some restaurants have higher demand in the evening than at lunch or on weekends as opposed to weekdays. Traffic—hence sales—at shopping malls picks up on Friday and Saturday.

There are several methods for reflecting seasonal patterns in a time series forecast. We will describe one of the simpler methods using a *seasonal factor*. A **seasonal factor** is a numerical value that is multiplied by the normal forecast to get a seasonally adjusted forecast.

Seasonal factor Adjust for seasonality by multiplying the normal forecast by a seasonal factor.

One method for developing a demand for seasonal factors is to divide the demand for each seasonal period by total annual demand, according to the following formula:

$$S_i = \frac{D_i}{\Sigma D}$$

The resulting seasonal factors between 0 and 1.0 are, in effect, the portion of total annual demand assigned to each season. These seasonal factors are multiplied by the annual forecasted demand to yield adjusted forecasts for each season.

EXAMPLE 12.6 | Computing a Forecast with Seasonal Adjustments

Wishbone Farms grows turkeys to sell to a meat-processing company throughout the year, as seen in photo. However, its peak season is obviously during the fourth quarter of the year, from October to December. Wishbone Farms has experienced the demand for turkeys for the past three years shown in the following table:

Demand for Turkeys at Wishbone Farms

	DEMAND (1000s) PER QUARTER				
YEAR	1	2	3	4	TOTAL
2014	12.6	8.6	6.3	17.5	45.0
2015	14.1	10.3	7.5	18.2	50.1
2016	15.3	10.6	8.1	19.6	53.6
Total	42.0	29.5	21.9	55.3	148.7

Solution: Because we have three years of demand data, we can compute the seasonal factors by dividing total quarterly demand for the three years by total demand across all three years:

$$S_1 = \frac{D_1}{\Sigma D} = \frac{42.0}{148.7} = 0.28$$

$$S_2 = \frac{D_2}{\Sigma D} = \frac{29.5}{148.7} = 0.20$$

$$S_3 = \frac{D_3}{\Sigma D} = \frac{21.9}{148.7} = 0.15$$

$$S_4 = \frac{D_4}{\Sigma D} = \frac{55.3}{148.7} = 0.37$$

Next, we want to multiply the forecasted demand for the next year, 2014, by each of the seasonal factors to get the forecasted demand for each quarter. To accomplish this, we need a demand forecast for 2017. In this case, since the demand data in the table seem to exhibit a generally increasing trend, we compute a linear trend line for the three years of data in the table to get a rough forecast estimate:

$$\begin{aligned} y &= 40.97 + 4.30x \\ &= 40.97 + 4.30(4) \\ &= 58.17 \end{aligned}$$

Thus, the forecast for 2017 is 58.17, or 58,170 turkeys.

Using this annual forecast of demand, we find that the seasonally adjusted forecasts, SF_i, for 2017 are

$$\begin{aligned} SF_1 &= (S_1)(F_5) = (0.28)(58.17) = 16.28 \\ SF_2 &= (S_2)(F_5) = (0.20)(58.17) = 11.63 \\ SF_3 &= (S_3)(F_5) = (0.15)(58.17) = 8.73 \\ SF_4 &= (S_4)(F_5) = (0.37)(58.17) = 21.53 \end{aligned}$$

Comparing these quarterly forecasts with the actual demand values in the table, we see that they would seem to be relatively good forecast estimates, reflecting both the seasonal variations in the data and the general upward trend.

Along the Supply Chain

Demand Forecasting for Global Distribution at Zara

Zara is a subsidiary of the Inditex Group, one of the world's largest clothing retailers, that includes over 100 companies involved in textile design, manufacturing, and distribution. Zara is one of the world's most recognized and successful apparel retailers with more than 2000 stores in 88 countries and annual revenues over 11.5 billion euros. Its supply chain model involves frequent and rapid store changes with trendy fashion items provided at competitive prices. Within Zara's supply chain a continual flow of information from stores to designers conveys customer's changing tastes and instigates rapid orders for new designs from manufacturing suppliers.

Zara's supply chain includes four primary logistics platforms (warehouses and distribution centers) in Spain that receive finished clothing shipments from suppliers around the world and then ship items directly to stores around the world twice a week. The time between when orders are received at distribution centers to store delivery averages 24 hours in Europe and is less than 48 hours to U.S. and Asian stores. Individual store managers differentiate between major (S, M, and L) sizes and minor sizes (XXS, XXL, etc.), and when a store runs out of a major size for a clothing article it pulls all the item's inventory from the shelves and replaces it with a new article, so that customers won't be frustrated by wanting to buy an item that's not available in their size. The removed article may be returned to the store shelves if missing sizes can be shipped from warehouses, or the removed inventory may be transferred to another store where it is consolidated.

The challenge for Zara is to determine the exact number of units of each of eight sizes, of each of up to 3,000 items, to include in a shipment to each of its 1,500 stores. These order decisions, which across Zara's supply chain can reach several million each week, must be determined in a few hours after the store manager receives the relevant information including store inventory and the previous day's sales history. Any further delays can delay store replenishment by a day because of warehouse processing times and transportation schedules. Zara uses previous store shipment orders and past sales data to develop demand forecasts, which are combined with the current store and warehouse inventory to determine optimal shipment quantities that will maximize global sales. The demand forecasting model uses standard regression analysis to predict the upcoming weekly demand for each size of each article in each of Zara's stores.

As an apparel retailer, what are some of the unique supply chain forecasting factors that might affect Zara?

Sources: Based on Felipe Caro, Jeremie Gallien, Miguel Diaz, Javier Garcia, Jose Corredoira, Marcos Montes, Jose A. Ramos, and Juan Correa, "Zara Uses Operations Research to Reengineer Its Global Distribution Process," *Interfaces* 40 (1) (January–February 2010), pp. 71–84; and Zara website at www.zara.com.

Alamy Images

Turkeys are an example of a product with a long-term trend for increasing demand with a seasonal pattern. Turkey sales show a distinct seasonal pattern by increasing markedly during the Thanksgiving holiday season. For example, turkey sales are lowest from January to May, they begin to rise in June and July and peak in August when distributors begin to build up their inventory of frozen turkeys for increased sales in November. Sales remain high for September, October, and November and then begin to decline in December and January.

Forecast Accuracy

A forecast is never completely accurate; forecasts will always deviate from the actual demand. This difference between the forecast and the actual is the **forecast error**. Although forecast error is inevitable, the objective of forecasting is that it be as slight as possible. A large degree of error may indicate that either the forecasting technique is the wrong one or it needs to be adjusted by changing its parameters (for example, α in the exponential smoothing forecast).

Forecast error The difference between the forecast and actual demand.

There are different measures of forecast error. We will discuss several of the more popular ones: mean absolute deviation (MAD), mean absolute percent deviation (MAPD), cumulative error, and average error or bias ($\overline{E}$).

Mean Absolute Deviation

The **mean absolute deviation**, or **MAD**, is one of the most popular and simplest to use measures of forecast error. MAD is an average of the difference between the forecast and actual demand, as computed by the following formula:

Mean absolute deviation (MAD) The average absolute difference between the forecast and demand.

$$\text{MAD} = \frac{\Sigma|D_t - F_t|}{n}$$

where

t = the period number
D_t = demand in period t
F_t = the forecast for period t
n = the total number of periods
$||$ = absolute value

EXAMPLE 12.7 | Measuring Forecasting Accuracy with MAD

In Examples 12.3, 12.4, and 12.5, forecasts were developed using exponential smoothing ($\alpha = .30$ and $\alpha = .50$), adjusted exponential smoothing ($\alpha = .50$, $\beta = .30$), and a linear trend line, respectively, for the demand data for HiTek Computer Services. The company wants to compare the accuracy of these different forecasts using MAD.

Solution: We will compute MAD for all four forecasts; however, we will present the computational detail for the exponential smoothing forecast with $\alpha = .30$ only. The following table shows the values necessary to compute M for the exponential smoothing forecast:

Computational Values for MAD

PERIOD	DEMAND, D_t	FORECAST F_t ($\alpha_i = .30$)	ERROR (e_t) ($D_t - F_i$)	$\lvert D_t - F_t \rvert$
1	37	37.00	—	—
2	40	37.00	3.00	3.00
3	41	37.90	3.10	3.10
4	37	38.83	−1.83	1.83
5	45	38.28	6.72	6.72
6	50	40.29	9.69	9.69
7	43	43.20	−0.20	0.20
8	47	43.14	3.86	3.86
9	56	44.30	11.70	11.70
10	52	47.81	4.19	4.19
11	55	49.06	5.94	5.94
12	54	50.84	3.15	3.15
	557		49.32	53.38

[a]The computation of MAD will be based on 11 periods, periods 2 through 12, excluding the initial demand and forecast values for period 1 since they both equal 37.

Using the data in the table, MAD is computed as

$$\text{MAD} = \frac{\Sigma|D_t - F_t|}{n}$$

$$= \frac{53.39}{11}$$

$$= 4.85$$

The smaller the value of MAD, the more accurate the forecast, although viewed alone, MAD is difficult to assess. In this example, the data values were relatively small, and the MAD value of 4.85 should be judged accordingly. Overall, it would seem to be a "low" value; that is, the forecast appears to be relatively accurate. However, if the magnitude of the data values were in the thousands or millions, then a MAD value of a similar magnitude might not be bad, either. The point is, you cannot compare a MAD value of 4.85 with a MAD value of 485 and say the former is good and the latter is bad; they depend to a certain extent on the relative magnitude of the data.

One benefit of MAD is to compare the accuracy of several different forecasting techniques, as we are doing in this example. The MAD values for the remaining forecasts are as follows:

$$\text{Exponential smoothing}(\alpha = .50)\text{: MAD} = 4.04$$

$$\text{Adjusted exponential smoothing}(\alpha = .50, \beta = .30)\text{: MAD} = 3.81$$

$$\text{Linear trend line: MAD} = 2.29$$

Since the linear trend line has the lowest MAD value of 2.29, it would seem to be the most accurate, although it does not appear to be significantly better than the adjusted exponential smoothing forecast. Furthermore, we can deduce from these MAD values that increasing α from .30 to .50 enhanced the accuracy of the exponentially smoothed forecast. The adjusted forecast is even more accurate.

mean absolute percent deviation (MAPD) The absolute error as a percentage of demand.

The **mean absolute percent deviation (MAPD)** measures the absolute error as a percentage of demand rather than per period. As a result, it eliminates the problem of interpreting the measure of accuracy relative to the magnitude of the demand and forecast values, as MAD does. The mean absolute percent deviation is computed according to the following formula:

$$\text{MAPD} = \frac{\Sigma|D_t - F_t|}{\Sigma D_t}$$

Using the data from the table in Example 12.7 for the exponential smoothing forecast ($\alpha = .30$) for HiTek Computer Services, we find

$$\begin{aligned}\text{MAPD} &= \frac{53.39}{557} \\ &= 0.096 \text{ or } 9.6\%\end{aligned}$$

A lower percent deviation implies a more accurate forecast. The MAPD values for our other three forecasts are

$$\begin{aligned}\text{Exponential smoothing}(\alpha = .50)\text{: MAPD} &= 7.9\% \\ \text{Adjusted exponential smoothing}(\alpha = .50, \beta = .30)\text{: MAPD} &= 7.5\% \\ \text{Linear trend line: MAPD} &= 4.9\%\end{aligned}$$

Cumulative Error

Cumulative error is computed simply by summing the forecast errors, as shown in the following formula.

Cumulative error The sum of the forecast errors.

$$E = \Sigma e_t$$

A large positive value indicates that the forecast is probably consistently lower than the actual demand, or is biased low. A large negative value implies that the forecast is consistently higher than actual demand, or is biased high. Also, when the errors for each period are scrutinized, a preponderance of positive values shows the forecast is consistently less than the actual value and vice versa.

The cumulative error for the exponential smoothing forecast ($\alpha = .30$) for HiTek Computer Services can be read directly from the table in Example 12.7; it is simply the sum of the values in the "Error" column:

$$\begin{aligned}E &= \Sigma e_t \\ &= 49.31\end{aligned}$$

This large positive error for cumulative error, plus the fact that the individual errors for all but two of the periods in the table are positive, indicates that this forecast is consistently below the actual demand. A quick glance back at the plot of the exponential smoothing ($\alpha = .30$) forecast in Example 12.3 visually verifies this result.

The cumulative error for the other forecasts are

$$\begin{aligned}\text{Exponential smoothing } (\alpha = .50)\text{: } E &= 33.21 \\ \text{Adjusted exponential smoothing } (\alpha = .50, \beta = .30)\text{: } E &= 21.14\end{aligned}$$

We did not show the cumulative error for the linear trend line. E will always be near zero for the linear trend line.

A measure closely related to cumulative error is the **average error**, or *bias*. It is computed by averaging the cumulative error over the number of time periods:

Average error The per-period average of cumulative error.

$$\bar{E} = \frac{\Sigma e_t}{n}$$

For example, the average error for the exponential smoothing forecast ($\alpha = .30$) is computed as follows. (Notice a value of 11 was used for n, since we used actual demand for the first-period forecast, resulting in no error, that is, $D_1 = F_1 = 37$.)

$$\bar{E} = \frac{49.32}{11} = 4.48$$

TABLE 12.1 Comparison of Forecasts for HiTek Computer Services

FORECAST	MAD	MAPD	E	$\bar{E}$
Exponential smoothing ($\alpha = .30$)	4.85	9.6%	49.31	4.48
Exponential smoothing ($\alpha = .50$)	4.04	8.5%	33.21	3.02
Adjusted exponential smoothing ($\alpha = .50, \beta = .30$)	3.81	7.5%	21.14	1.92
Linear trend line	2.29	4.9%	—	—

The average error is interpreted similarly to the cumulative error. A positive value indicates low bias, and a negative value indicates high bias. A value close to zero implies a lack of bias.

Table 12.1 summarizes the measures of forecast accuracy we have discussed in this section for the four example forecasts we developed in Examples 12.3, 12.4, and 12.5 for HiTek Computer Services. The results are consistent for all four forecasts, indicating that for the HiTek Computer Services example data, a larger value of α is preferable for the exponential smoothing forecast. The adjusted forecast is more accurate than the exponential smoothing forecasts, and the linear trend is more accurate than all the others. Although these results are for specific examples, they indicate how the different forecast measures for accuracy can be used to adjust a forecasting method or select the best method.

Forecast Control

There are several ways to monitor forecast error over time to make sure that the forecast is performing correctly—that is, the forecast is in control. Forecasts can go "out of control" and start providing inaccurate forecasts for several reasons, including a change in trend, the unanticipated appearance of a cycle, or an irregular variation such as unseasonable weather, a promotional campaign, new competition, or a political event that distracts consumers.

Tracking signal Monitors the forecast to see if it is biased high or low.

A **tracking signal** indicates if the forecast is consistently biased high or low. It is computed by dividing the cumulative error by MAD, according to the formula

$$\text{Tracking signal} = \frac{\Sigma(D_t - F_t)}{\text{MAD}} = \frac{E}{\text{MAD}}$$

The tracking signal is recomputed each period, with updated, "running" values of cumulative error and MAD. The movement of the tracking signal is compared to *control limits*: as long as the tracking signal is within these limits, the forecast is in control.

Typically, forecast errors are normally distributed, which results in the following relationship between MAD and the standard deviation of the distribution of error, σ:

$$1 \text{ MAD} \cong 0.8\sigma$$

EXAMPLE 12.8 | Developing a Tracking Signal

In Example 12.7, the mean absolute deviation was computed for the exponential smoothing forecast ($\alpha = .30$) for HiTek Computer Services. Using a tracking signal, monitor the forecast accuracy using control limits of ± 3 MADs.

Solution: To use the tracking signal, we must recompute MAD each period as the cumulative error is computed.

Using MAD = 3.00, we find that the tracking signal for period 2 is

$$TS_2 = \frac{E}{\text{MAD}} = \frac{3.00}{3.00} = 1.00$$

The tracking signal for period 3 is

$$TS_3 = \frac{6.10}{3.05} = 2.00$$

The remaining tracking signal values are shown in the following table:

Tracking Signal Values

PERIOD	DEMAND, D_t	FORECAST, F_t	ERROR, $D_t - F_t$	$E = \sum(D_t - F_t)$	MAD	TRACKING SIGNAL
1	37	37.00	—	—	—	—
2	40	37.00	3.00	3.00	3.00	1.00
3	41	37.90	3.10	6.10	3.05	2.00
4	37	38.83	−1.83	4.27	2.64	1.62
5	45	38.28	6.72	10.99	3.66	3.00
6	50	40.29	9.69	20.68	4.87	4.25
7	43	43.20	−0.20	20.48	4.09	5.01
8	47	43.14	3.86	24.34	4.06	6.00
9	56	44.30	11.70	36.04	5.01	7.19
10	52	47.81	4.19	40.23	4.92	8.18
11	55	49.06	5.94	46.17	5.02	9.20
12	54	50.84	3.15	49.32	4.85	10.17

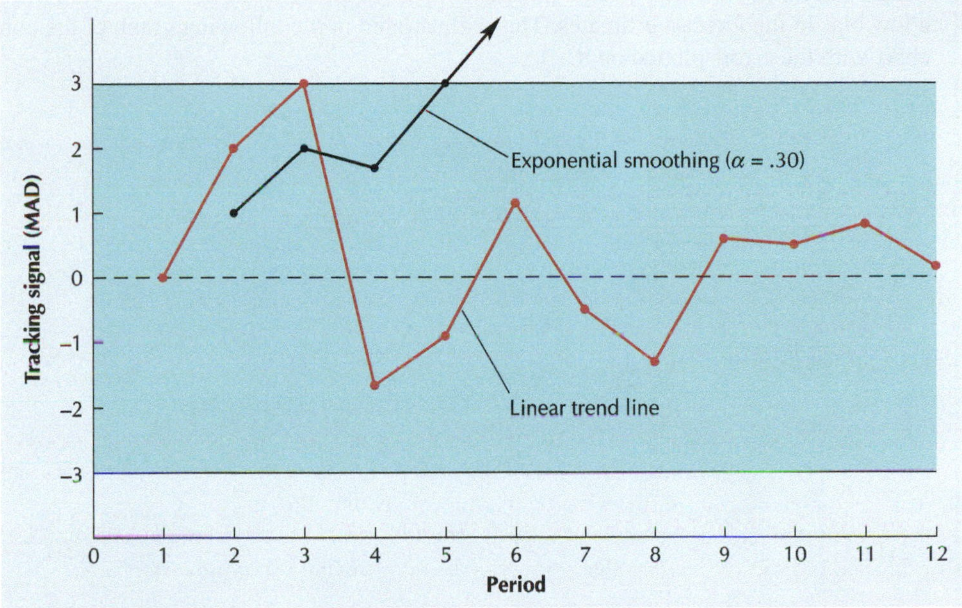

The tracking signal values in the table above move outside ±3 MAD control limits (i.e., ±3.00) in period 5 *and* continue increasing. This suggests that the forecast is not performing accurately or, more precisely, is consistently biased low (i.e., actual demand consistently exceeds the forecast). This is illustrated in the graph. Notice that the tracking signal moves beyond the upper limit of 3 following period 5 and continues to rise. For the sake of comparison, the tracking signal for the linear trend line forecast computed in Example 12.5 is also plotted on this graph. Notice that it remains within the limits (touching the upper limit in period 3), indicating a lack of consistent bias.

This enables us to establish statistical control limits for the tracking signal that correspond to the more familiar normal distribution. For example, statistical control limits of ±3 standard deviations, corresponding to 99.7% of the errors, would translate to ±3.75 MADs; that is, $3\sigma \div 0.8 = 3.75$ MADs. Control limits of ±2 to ±5 MADs are used most frequently.

Another method for monitoring forecast error is statistical control charts. For example, $\pm 3\sigma$ control limits would reflect 99.7% of the forecast errors (assuming they are normally distributed). The sample standard deviation, σ, is computed as

$$\sigma = \sqrt{\frac{\Sigma(D_t - F_t)^2}{n - 1}}$$

Mean squared error (MSE) The average of the squared forecast errors.

This formula without the square root is known as the **mean squared error (MSE)**, and it is sometimes used as a measure of forecast error. It reacts to forecast error much as MAD does. (For our Example 12.8, MSE = 37.57.)

EXAMPLE 12.9 | Forecast Error with Statistical Control Charts

Using the same example for the exponential smoothing forecast ($\alpha = .30$) for HiTek Computer Services as in Example 12.8, we compute the standard deviation as

$$\sigma = \sqrt{\frac{375.61}{10}} = 6.13$$

Using this value of σ we can compute statistical control limits for forecast errors for our exponential smoothing forecast ($\alpha = .30$) example for HiTek Computer Services. Plus or minus 3σ control limits, reflecting 99.7% of the forecast errors, gives $\pm 3(6.13)$, or ± 18.39. Although it can be observed from the table in Example 12.8 that all the error values are within the control limits, we can still detect that most of the errors are positive, indicating a low bias in the forecast estimates. This is illustrated in the following graph of the control chart with the errors plotted on it.

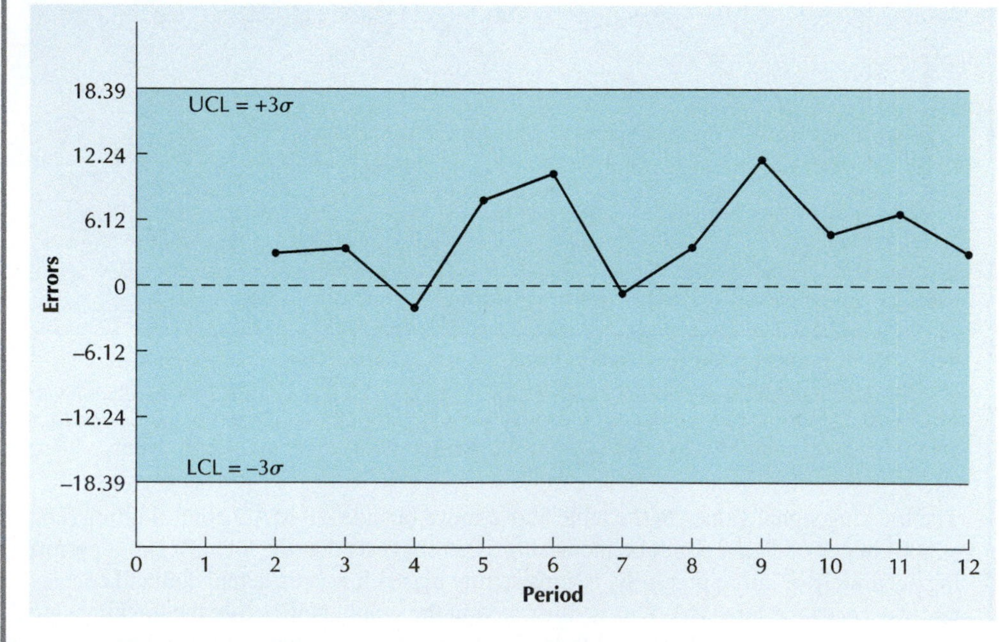

Time Series Forecasting Using Excel

Excel can be used to develop forecasts using the moving average, exponential smoothing, adjusted exponential smoothing, and linear trend line techniques. Various surveys of companies across different industries that use forecasting, show that over half use Excel spreadsheets for forecasting, and most use a variety of different forecasting software packages.

First we will demonstrate how to determine exponentially smoothed and adjusted exponentially smoothed forecasts using Excel, as shown in Exhibit 12.1. We will demonstrate Excel using Examples 12.3 and 12.4 for forecasting demand at HiTek Computer Services, including the Excel spreadsheets showing the exponentially smoothed forecast with $\alpha = .5$ and the adjusted exponentially smoothed forecast with $\beta = .3$. We have also computed the values for MAD, MAPD, and E.

EXHIBIT 12.1

Excel File

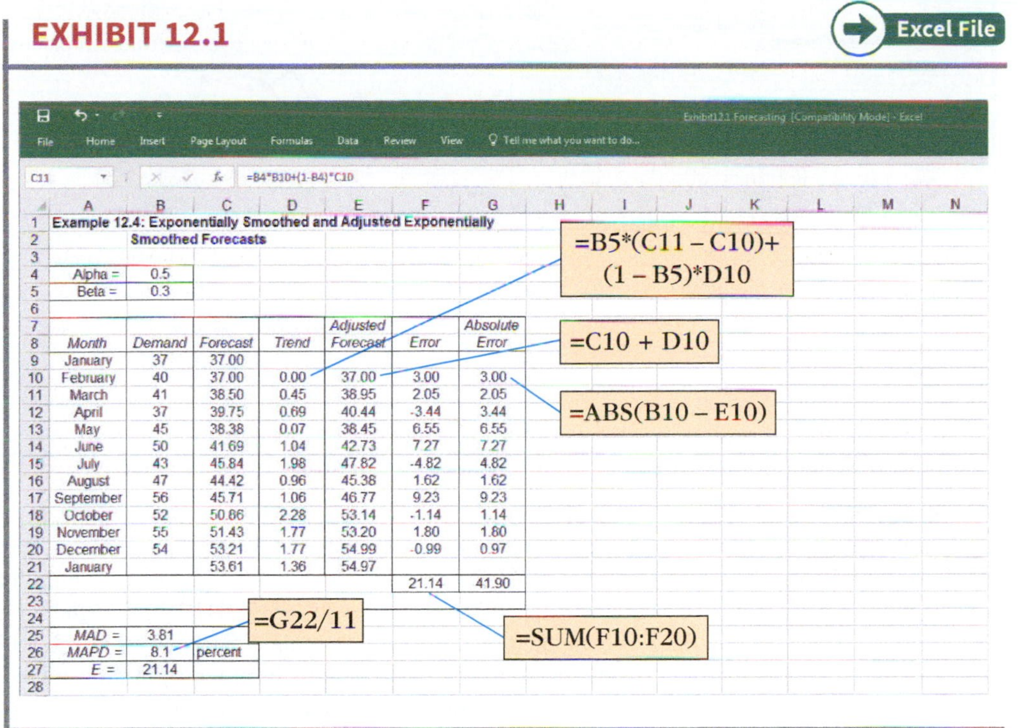

Example 12.4: Exponentially Smoothed and Adjusted Exponentially Smoothed Forecasts

Alpha =	0.5
Beta =	0.3

Month	Demand	Forecast	Trend	Adjusted Forecast	Error	Absolute Error
January	37	37.00				
February	40	37.00	0.00	37.00	3.00	3.00
March	41	38.50	0.45	38.95	2.05	2.05
April	37	39.75	0.69	40.44	-3.44	3.44
May	45	38.38	0.07	38.45	6.55	6.55
June	50	41.69	1.04	42.73	7.27	7.27
July	43	45.84	1.98	47.82	-4.82	4.82
August	47	44.42	0.96	45.38	1.62	1.62
September	56	45.71	1.06	46.77	9.23	9.23
October	52	50.86	2.28	53.14	-1.14	1.14
November	55	51.43	1.77	53.20	1.80	1.80
December	54	53.21	1.77	54.99	-0.99	0.97
January		53.61	1.36	54.97		
					21.14	41.90

MAD =	3.81	
MAPD =	8.1	percent
E =	21.14	

Along the Supply Chain

Forecasting Empty Shipping Containers

Compana Sud Americana de Vapores (CSAV), headquartered in Chile, is one of the world's largest shipping companies. It ships cargo using containers transported by over 180 ships operated by CSAV or other companies. Its fleet consists of about 70,000 containers of different sizes and types, about 5% of which CSAV owns with the rest leased on long-term contracts. Each week the company makes hundreds of thousands of container logistics decisions over its vast shipping network, involving different nationalities, culture, and time zones, which makes the decision-making process very difficult. Typically an empty container is first loaded on a truck at a container depot and transported to a shipper by truck, filled and then shipped by truck to a port where it is loaded on a vessel after meeting customs requirements. At its destination port the container is unloaded from the vessel, and transported by truck, train, or feeder vessel to the customer, who unloads the container and returns it to the shipping company. Managing this fleet of empty containers is a complex process partly as a result of the imbalance in demand among regions; some regions are net exporters whereas some regions are net importers of containers. Another challenge is forecasting demand for empty containers of different types and sizes at each location for specific dates, given the uncertainty in the demand for empty containers, which depends on factors like market conditions, travel times, delays in returning empty containers, and the availability of vessel capacity to transport empty containers. To forecast demand CSAV uses a combination of several forecasting approaches. It forecasts returned containers using a moving average of the past n days, and a trended seasonal moving average using past demand from the same season with a yearly trend computed from previous years. These time series forecasts are complemented by a sales forecast based on the demand expectations of their sales agents around the world. Over a million and a half demand forecasts are generated based on updated information and revised settings. Logistics planners at various locations then use the forecast model that best fits their own experience and forecast accuracy at their location. These forecasts are subsequently used in a network flow optimization model to plan the movement of empty containers in CSAV's system. This solution approach resulted in savings of $81 million in the first year it was implemented.

Using the Internet, identify and discuss forecasting demand of another part or process (other than containers) related to distribution and transportation in the supply chain.

Sources: Based on R. Epstein, A. Neely, A. Weintraub, F. Valenzuela, S. Hurtado, G. Gonzalez, A. Beiza, M. Naveas, F. Infante, F. Alarcon, G. Angulo, C. Berner, J. Catalan, C. Gonzalez and D. Yung, "A Strategic Empty Container Logistics Optimization in A Major Shipping Company," *Interfaces* 42, no. 1 (January–February 2012): 5–16.

EXHIBIT 12.2

Excel File

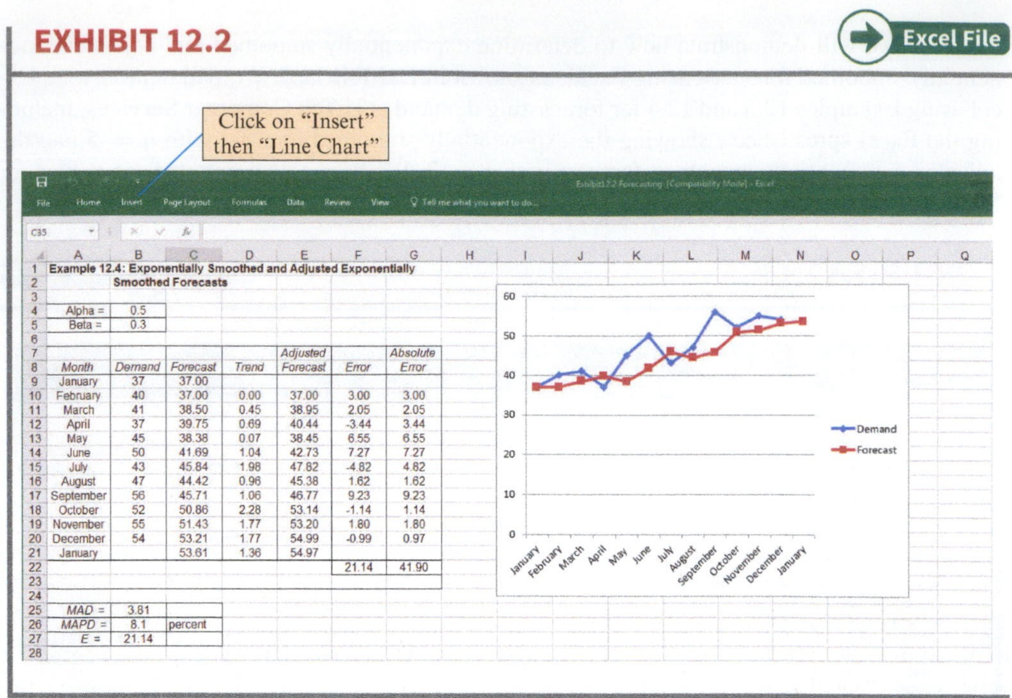

Example 12.4: Exponentially Smoothed and Adjusted Exponentially Smoothed Forecasts

Alpha = 0.5
Beta = 0.3

Month	Demand	Forecast	Trend	Adjusted Forecast	Error	Absolute Error
January	37	37.00				
February	40	37.00	0.00	37.00	3.00	3.00
March	41	38.50	0.45	38.95	2.05	2.05
April	37	39.75	0.69	40.44	-3.44	3.44
May	45	38.38	0.07	38.45	6.55	6.55
June	50	41.69	1.04	42.73	7.27	7.27
July	43	45.84	1.98	47.82	-4.82	4.82
August	47	44.42	0.96	45.38	1.62	1.62
September	56	45.71	1.06	46.77	9.23	9.23
October	52	50.86	2.28	53.14	-1.14	1.14
November	55	51.43	1.77	53.20	1.80	1.80
December	54	53.21	1.77	54.99	-0.99	0.97
January		53.61	1.36	54.97		
					21.14	41.90

MAD = 3.81
MAPD = 8.1 percent
E = 21.14

Notice that the formula in Exhibit 12.1 for computing the exponentially smoothed forecast for March is embedded in cell C11 and shown on the formula bar at the top of the screen. The same formula is used to compute all the other forecast values in column C. The formula for computing the trend value for March is = B5*(C11 − C10) + (1 − B5)*D10. The formula for the adjusted forecast in column *E* is computed by typing the formula = C10 + D10 in cell E10 and copying it to cells E11:E21 (using the copy and paste options from the right mouse key). The error is computed for the adjusted forecast, and the formula for computing the error for March is = B11 − E11, while the formula for absolute error for March is = ABS (F11).

A graph of the forecast can also be developed with Excel. To plot the exponentially smoothed forecast in column C and demand in column B, cover all cells from A8 to C21 with the mouse and click on "Insert" on the toolbar at the top of the worksheet. Next click on "Line" on the "Chart" toolbar. The resulting graph for demand and the exponentially smoothed forecast for our example are shown in **Exhibit 12.2**.

The exponential smoothing forecast can also be developed directly from Excel without "customizing" a spreadsheet and entering formulas as we did in Exhibit 12.1. From the Tools menu at the top of the spreadsheet select the "Data" option and then "Data Analysis" option. **Exhibit 12.3** shows the "Data Analysis" window and the "Exponential Smoothing" menu item, which should be selected by clicking on "OK." The resulting "Exponential Smoothing" window is shown in **Exhibit 12.4**. The "input range" includes the demand values in column B in Exhibit 12.1, the damping factor is α, which in this case is .5, and the output should be placed in column C in Exhibit 12.1. Clicking on "OK" will result in the same forecast values

EXHIBIT 12.3

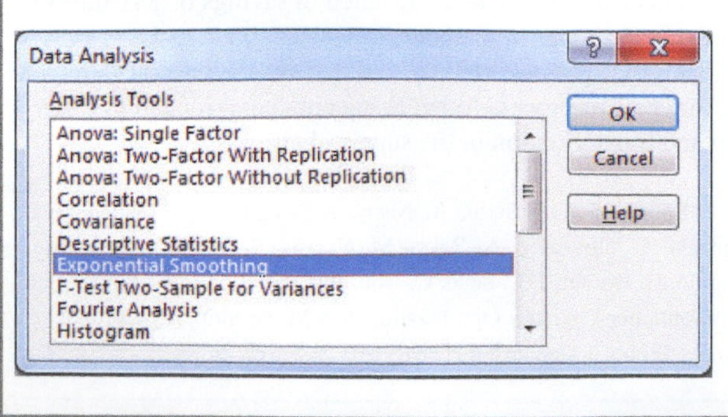

EXHIBIT 12.4

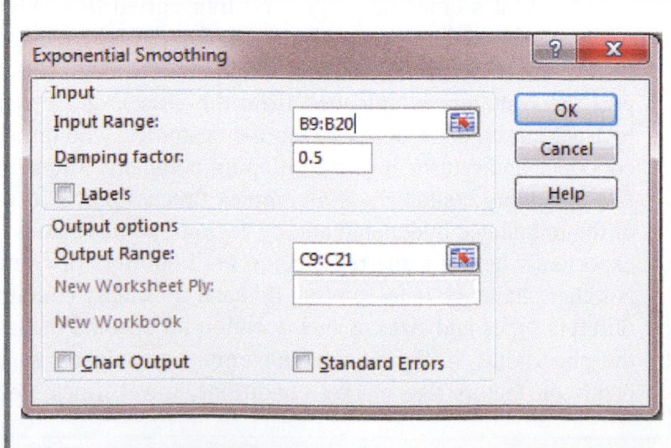

EXHIBIT 12.5

Excel File

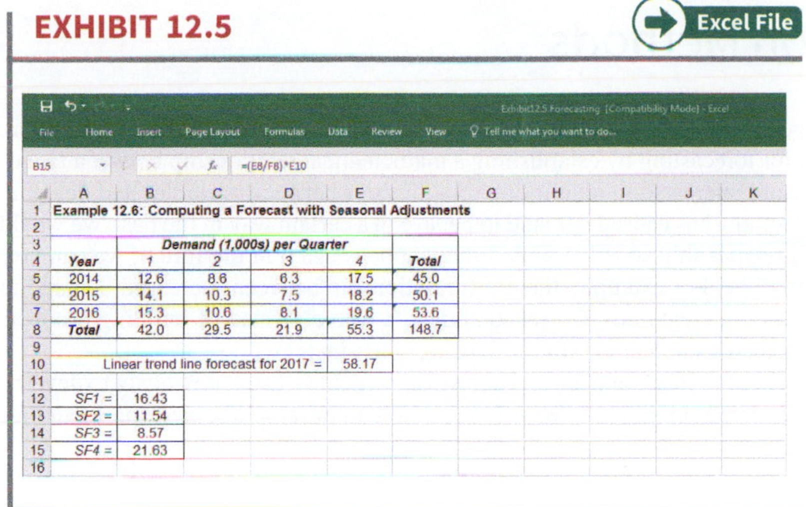

B15 | f_x =(E8/F8)*E10

Example 12.6: Computing a Forecast with Seasonal Adjustments

	Demand (1,000s) per Quarter				
Year	*1*	*2*	*3*	*4*	*Total*
2014	12.6	8.6	6.3	17.5	45.0
2015	14.1	10.3	7.5	18.2	50.1
2016	15.3	10.6	8.1	19.6	53.6
Total	42.0	29.5	21.9	55.3	148.7

Linear trend line forecast for 2017 =	58.17

SF1 =	16.43
SF2 =	11.54
SF3 =	8.57
SF4 =	21.63

in column C of Exhibit 12.1 as we computed using our own exponential smoothing formula. Note that the Data Analysis group of analysis tools does not have an adjusted exponential smoothing selection; that is one reason we developed our own customized spreadsheet in Exhibit 12.1. The "Data Analysis" tools also have a moving average menu item that you can use to compute a moving average forecast.

Excel can also be used to develop more customized forecast models, like seasonal forecasts. **Exhibit 12.5** shows an Excel screen for the seasonal forecast model developed in Example 12.6. Notice that the computation of the seasonal forecast for the first quarter (SF1) in cell B12 uses the formula shown on the formula bar at the top of the screen. The forecast value for SF1 is slightly different from the value in Example 12.6 because of rounding.

Forecasting with OM Tools

OM Tools has modules for all of the forecasting methods presented in this chapter. As an example, **Exhibit 12.6** shows the OM Tools spreadsheet for the exponential smoothing model ($\alpha = .30$) in Example 12.3.

EXHIBIT 12.6

OM Tools

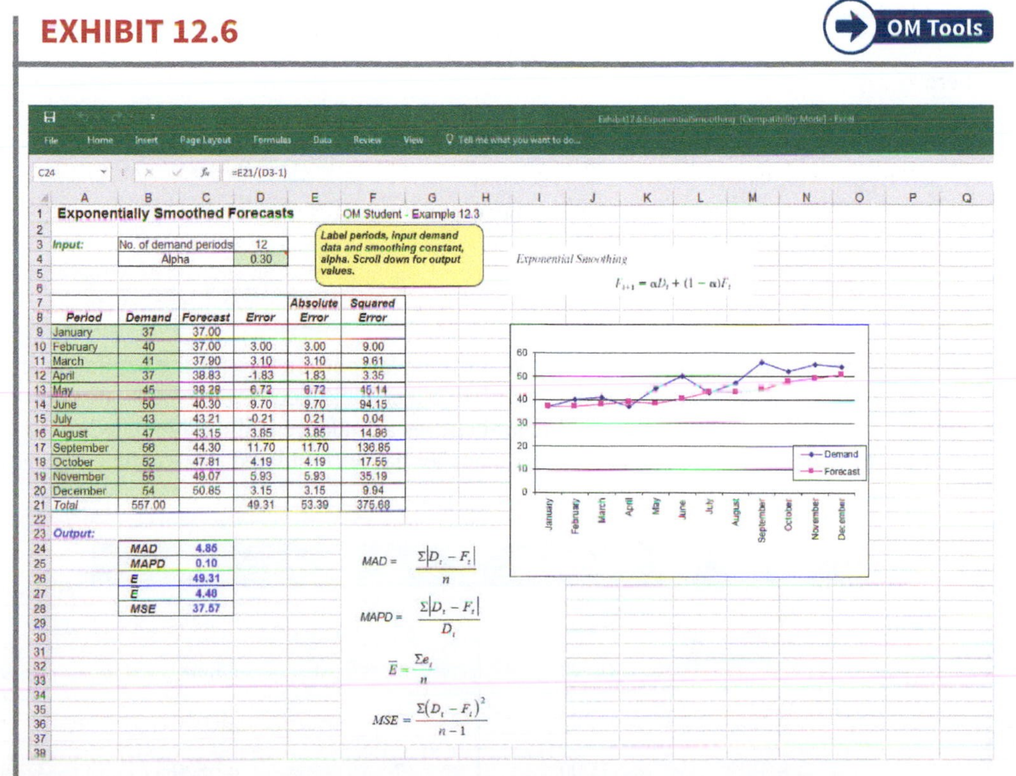

C24 | f_x =E21/(D3-1)

Exponentially Smoothed Forecasts — OM Student - Example 12.3

Input:

No. of demand periods	12
Alpha	0.30

Label periods, input demand data and smoothing constant, alpha. Scroll down for output values.

Period	*Demand*	*Forecast*	*Error*	*Absolute Error*	*Squared Error*
January	37	37.00			
February	40	37.00	3.00	3.00	9.00
March	41	37.90	3.10	3.10	9.61
April	37	38.83	-1.83	1.83	3.35
May	45	38.28	6.72	6.72	45.14
June	50	40.30	9.70	9.70	94.15
July	43	43.21	-0.21	0.21	0.04
August	47	43.15	3.85	3.85	14.86
September	56	44.30	11.70	11.70	136.85
October	52	47.81	4.19	4.19	17.55
November	55	49.07	5.93	5.93	35.19
December	54	50.85	3.15	3.15	9.94
Total	557.00		49.31	53.39	375.68

Output:

MAD	4.86
MAPD	0.10
E	49.31
$\bar{E}$	4.40
MSE	37.57

$$MAD = \frac{\Sigma|D_t - F_t|}{n}$$

$$MAPD = \frac{\Sigma|D_t - F_t|}{D_t}$$

$$\bar{E} = \frac{\Sigma e_t}{n}$$

$$MSE = \frac{\Sigma(D_t - F_t)^2}{n-1}$$

Regression Methods

The second most popular forecasting technique among various industrial firms is regression. Regression is used for forecasting by establishing a mathematical relationship between two or more variables. We are interested in identifying relationships between variables and demand. If we know that something has caused demand to behave in a certain way in the past, we would like to identify that relationship so if the same thing happens again in the future, we can predict what demand will be. For example, there is a relationship between increased demand in new housing and lower interest rates. Correspondingly, a whole myriad of building products and services display increased demand if new housing starts increase.

The simplest form of regression is linear regression, which we used previously to develop a linear trend line for forecasting. Now we will show how to develop a regression model for variables related to demand other than time.

Linear Regression

Linear regression A mathematical technique that relates a dependent variable to an independent variable in the form of a linear equation.

Linear regression is a mathematical technique that relates one variable, called an *independent variable*, to another, the *dependent variable*, in the form of an equation for a straight line. A linear equation has the following general form:

$$y = a + bx$$

where

y = the dependent variable
a = the intercept
b = the slope of the line
x = the independent variable

Because we want to use linear regression as a forecasting model for demand, the dependent variable, y, represents demand, and x is an independent variable that causes demand to behave in a linear manner.

To develop the linear equation, the slope, b, and the intercept, a, must first be computed using the following least squares formulas:

$$a = \overline{y} - b\overline{x}$$

$$b = \frac{\Sigma xy - n\,\overline{x}\overline{y}}{\Sigma x^2 - n\,\overline{x}^2}$$

where

$$\overline{x} = \frac{\Sigma x}{n} = \text{mean of the } x \text{ data}$$

$$\overline{y} = \frac{\Sigma y}{n} = \text{mean of the } y \text{ data}$$

EXAMPLE 12.10 | Developing a Linear Regression Forecast

The State University athletic department wants to develop its budget for the coming year using a forecast for football attendance. Football attendance accounts for the largest portion of its revenues, and the athletic director believes attendance is directly related to the number of wins by the team. The business manager has accumulated total annual average attendance figures for the past eight years.

WINS	ATTENDANCE	WINS	ATTENDANCE
4	36,300	6	44,000
6	40,100	7	45,600
6	41,200	5	39,000
8	53,000	7	47,500

Given the number of returning starters and the strength of the schedule, the athletic director believes the team will win at least seven games next year. Develop a simple regression equation for this data to forecast attendance for this level of success.

Solution: The computations necessary to compute a and b using the least squares formulas are summarized in the accompanying table. (Note that y is given in 1000s to make manual computation easier.)

Least Squares Computations

x (WINS)	y (ATTENDANCE, 1000s)	xy	x^2
4	36.3	145.2	16
6	40.1	240.6	36
6	41.2	247.2	36
8	53.0	424.0	64
6	44.0	264.0	36
7	45.6	319.2	49
5	39.0	195.0	25
7	47.5	332.5	49
49	346.9	2167.7	311

$$\bar{x} = \frac{49}{8} = 6.125$$

$$\bar{y} = \frac{346.9}{8} = 43.36$$

$$\begin{aligned} b &= \frac{\Sigma xy - n\bar{x}\bar{y}}{\Sigma x^2 - n\bar{x}^2} \\ &= \frac{(2167.7) - (8)(6.125)(43.36)}{(311) - (8)(6.125)^2} \\ &= 4.06 \end{aligned}$$

$$\begin{aligned} a &= \bar{y} - b\bar{x} \\ &= 43.36 - (4.06)(6.125) \\ &= 18.46 \end{aligned}$$

Substituting these values for a and b into the linear equation line, we have

$$y = 18.46 + 4.06x$$

Thus, for $x = 7$ (wins), the forecast for attendance is

$$\begin{aligned} y &= 18.46 + 4.06(7) \\ &= 46.88, \text{ or } 46{,}880 \end{aligned}$$

The data points with the regression line are shown in the following figure. Observing the regression line relative to the data points, it would appear that the data follow a distinct upward linear trend, which would indicate that the forecast should be relatively accurate. In fact, the MAD value for this forecasting model is 1.41, which suggests an accurate forecast.

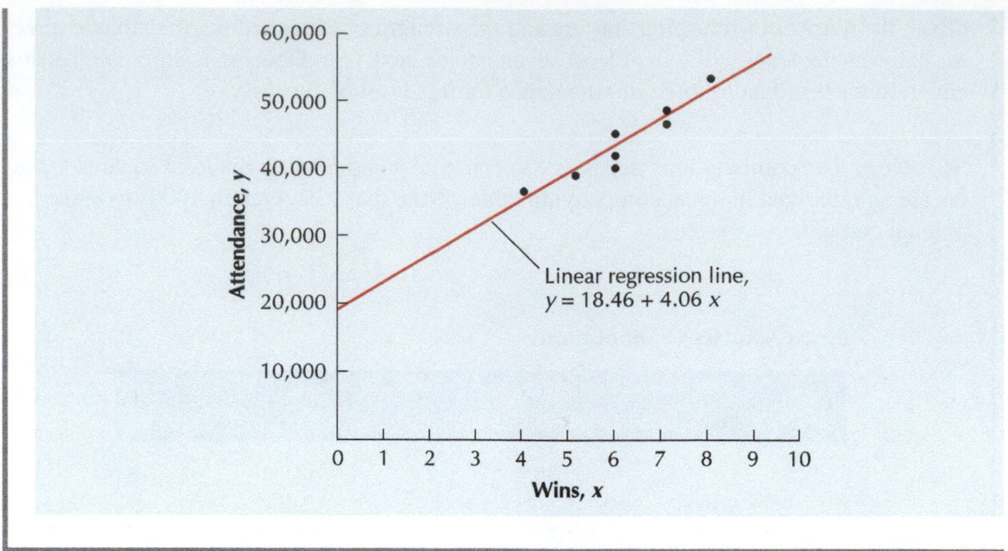

Correlation

Correlation A measure of the strength of the relationship between independent and dependent variables.

Correlation in a linear regression equation is a measure of the strength of the relationship between the independent and dependent variables. The formula for the correlation coefficient is

$$r = \frac{n\Sigma xy - \Sigma x \Sigma y}{\sqrt{[n\Sigma x^2 - (\Sigma x)^2][n\Sigma y^2 - (\Sigma y)^2]}}$$

The value of r varies between -1.00 and -1.00, with a value of $+1.00$ indicating a strong linear relationship between the variables. If $r = 1.00$, then an increase in the independent variable will result in a corresponding linear increase in the dependent variable. If $r = -1.00$, an increase in the dependent variable will result in a linear decrease in the dependent variable. A value of r near zero implies that there is little or no linear relationship between variables.

We can determine the correlation coefficient for the linear regression equation determined in Example 12.10 by substituting most of the terms calculated for the least squares formula (except for Σy^2) into the formula for r:

$$r = \frac{(8)(2167.7) - (49)(346.9)}{\sqrt{[(8)(311) - (49)^2][(8)(15{,}224.7) - (346.9)^2]}}$$
$$= 0.947$$

This value for the correlation coefficient is very close to 1.00, indicating a strong linear relationship between the number of wins and home attendance.

Coefficient of determination The percentage of the variation in the dependent variable that results from the independent variable.

Another measure of the strength of the relationship between the variables in a linear regression equation is the **coefficient of determination.** It is computed by squaring the value of r. It indicates the percentage of the variation in the dependent variable that is a result of the behavior of the independent variable. For our example, $r = 0.947$; thus, the coefficient of determination is

$$r^2 = (0.947)^2$$
$$= 0.897$$

This value for the coefficient of determination means that 89.7% of the amount of variation in attendance can be attributed to the number of wins by the team (with the remaining 10.3% due to other unexplained factors, such as weather, a good or poor start, or publicity). A value of 1.00 (or 100%) would indicate that attendance depends totally on wins. However, since 10.3% of the variation is a result of other factors, some amount of forecast error can be expected.

Regression Analysis with Excel

The development of the simple linear regression equation and the correlation coefficient for our example was not too difficult because the amount of data was relatively small. However, manual computation of the components of simple linear regression equations can become very time-consuming and cumbersome as the amount of data increases. Excel has the capability of performing linear regression.

Exhibit 12.7 shows a spreadsheet set up to develop the linear regression forecast for Example 12.10 for the State University Athletic Department. Notice that Excel computes the slope directly with the formula "=SLOPE(B5:B12,A5:A12)" entered in cell E7 and shown on the formula bar at the top of the spreadsheet. The formula for the intercept in cell E6 is "=INTERCEPT(B5:B12,A5:A12)." The values for the slope and intercept are subsequently entered into cells E9 and G9 to form the linear regression equation. The correlation coefficient in cell E13 is computed using the formula "=CORREL(B5:B12, A5:A12)." Although it is not shown on the spreadsheet, the coefficient of determination (r^2) could be computed using the formula "=RSQ(B5:B12,A5:A12)."

A linear regression forecast can also be developed directly with Excel using the "Data Analysis" option from the Tools menu we accessed previously to develop an exponentially smoothed forecast. Exhibit 12.8 shows the selection of "Regression" from the Data Analysis menu, and Exhibit 12.9 shows the Regression window. We first enter the cells from

EXHIBIT 12.7

Excel File

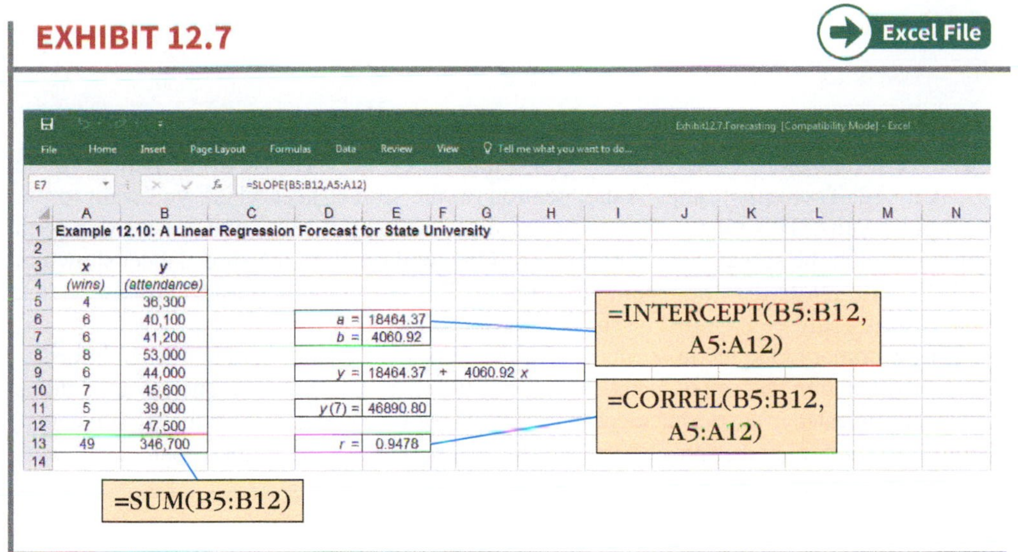

EXHIBIT 12.8

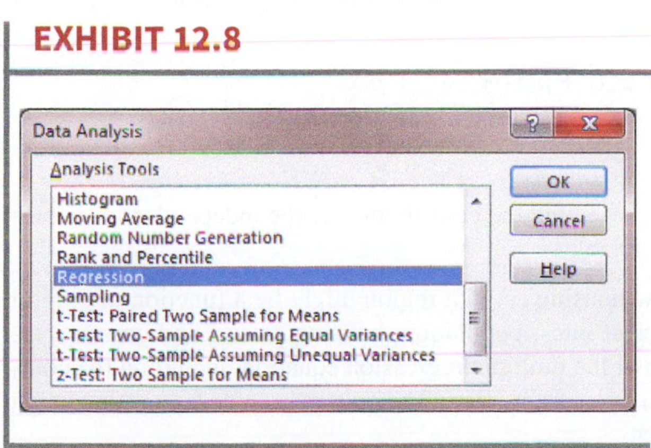

EXHIBIT 12.9

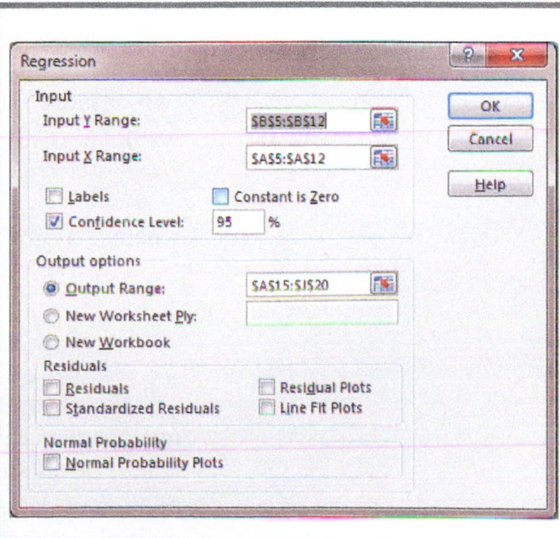

EXHIBIT 12.10

Example 12.10: State University Athletic Department

x (wins)	y (attendance)
4	36,300
6	40,100
6	41,200
8	53,000
6	44,000
7	45,600
5	39,000
7	47,500
49	346,700

SUMMARY OUTPUT

Regression Statistics	
Multiple R	0.948
R Square	0.898
Adjusted R Square	0.881
Standard Error	1839.311
Observations	8

ANOVA

	df	*SS*	*MS*	*F*	*Significance F*
Regression	1	179340359.2	179340359.2	53.01120495	0.00034182
Residual	6	20298390.8	3383065.134		
Total	7	199638750			

	Coefficients	*Standard Error*	*t Stat*	*P-value*	*Lower 95%*	*Upper 95%*	*Lower 95.0%*	*Upper 95.0%*
Intercept	18464.37	3477.57	5.31	0.00	9955.06	26973.68	9955.06	26973.68
X Variable 1	4060.92	557.75	7.28	0.00	2696.15	5425.69	2696.15	5425.69

Exhibit 12.7 that include the y values (for attendance), B5:B12. Next enter the x value cells, A5:A12. The output range is the location on the spreadsheet where you want to put the output results. This range needs to be large (18 cells by 9 cells) and not overlap with anything else on the spreadsheet. Clicking on "OK" will result in the spreadsheet shown in Exhibit 12.10. (Note that the "Summary Output" has been slightly moved around so that all the results could be included on the screen in Exhibit 12.9.)

The "Summary Output" in Exhibit 12.10 provides a large amount of statistical information, the explanation and use of which are beyond the scope of this book. The essential items that we are interested in are the intercept and slope (labeled "X Variable 1") in the "Coefficients" column at the bottom of the spreadsheet, and the "Multiple R" (or correlation coefficient) value shown under "Regression Statistics."

Multiple Regression with Excel

Multiple regression A relationship of demand to two or more independent variables.

Another causal method of forecasting is **multiple regression**, a more powerful extension of linear regression. Linear regression relates demand to one other independent variable, whereas multiple regression reflects the relationship between a dependent variable and two or more independent variables. A multiple regression model has the following general form:

$$y = \beta_0 + \beta_1 x_1 + \beta_2 x_2 + \cdots + \beta_k x_k$$

where

β_0 = the intercept
$\beta_1, \ldots, \beta_k$ = parameters representing the contribution of the independent variables
$x_1, \ldots, x_k$ = independent variables

For example, the demand for new housing (y) in a region might be a function of several independent variables, including interest rates, population, housing prices, and personal income. Development and computation of the multiple regression equation, including the compilation of data, is more complex than linear regression. The only means for forecasting using multiple regression is with a computer.

EXAMPLE 12.11 | Developing a Multiple Regression Forecast with Excel

To demonstrate the capability to solve multiple regression problems with Excel spreadsheets, we will expand our State University athletic department Example 12.10 for forecasting attendance at football games that we used to demonstrate linear regression. Instead of attempting to predict attendance based on only one variable, wins, we will include a second variable for advertising and promotional expenditures as follows:

WINS	PROMOTION ($)	ATTENDANCE
4	29,500	36,300
6	55,700	40,100
6	71,300	41,200
8	87,000	53,000
6	75,000	44,000
7	72,000	45,600
5	55,300	39,000
7	81,600	47,500

We will use the "Data Analysis" option (add-in) from the Tools menu at the top of the spreadsheet that we used in the previous section to develop our linear regression equation, and then the "Regression" option from the "Data Analysis" menu. The resulting spreadsheet with the multiple regression statistics is shown in Exhibit 12.11.

Solution: Note that the data must be set up on the spreadsheet so that the two x variables are in adjacent columns (in this case A and B). Then we enter the "Input X Range" as **A4:B12** as shown in Exhibit 12.12.

The regression coefficients for our x variables, wins and promotion, are shown in cells B27 and B28. Thus, the multiple regression equation is formulated as

$$y = 19{,}094.42 + 3560.99x_1 + 0.0368x_2$$

This equation can now be used to forecast attendance based on both projected football wins and promotional expenditure. For example, if the athletic department expects the team to win seven games and plans to spend \$60,000 on promotion and advertising, the forecasted attendance is

$$\begin{aligned} y &= 19{,}094.42 + 3560.99(7) + 0.0368(60{,}000) \\ &= 46{,}229.35 \end{aligned}$$

If the promotional expenditure is held constant, every win will increase attendance by 3560.99, whereas if the wins are held constant, every \$1000 of advertising spent will increase attendance by 36.8 fans. This would seem to suggest that the number of wins has a more significant impact on attendance than promotional expenditures.

r^2, the coefficient of determination shown in cell B19, is 0.900, which suggests that 90% of the amount of variation in attendance can be attributed to the number of wins and the promotional expenditures. However, as we have already noted, the number of wins would probably appear to account for a larger part of the variation in attendance.

A problem often encountered in multiple regression is *multicollinearity*, or the amount of "overlapping" information about the dependent variable that is provided by several independent variables. This problem usually occurs when the independent variables are highly correlated, as in this example, in which wins and promotional expenditures are both positively

EXHIBIT 12.11

Excel File

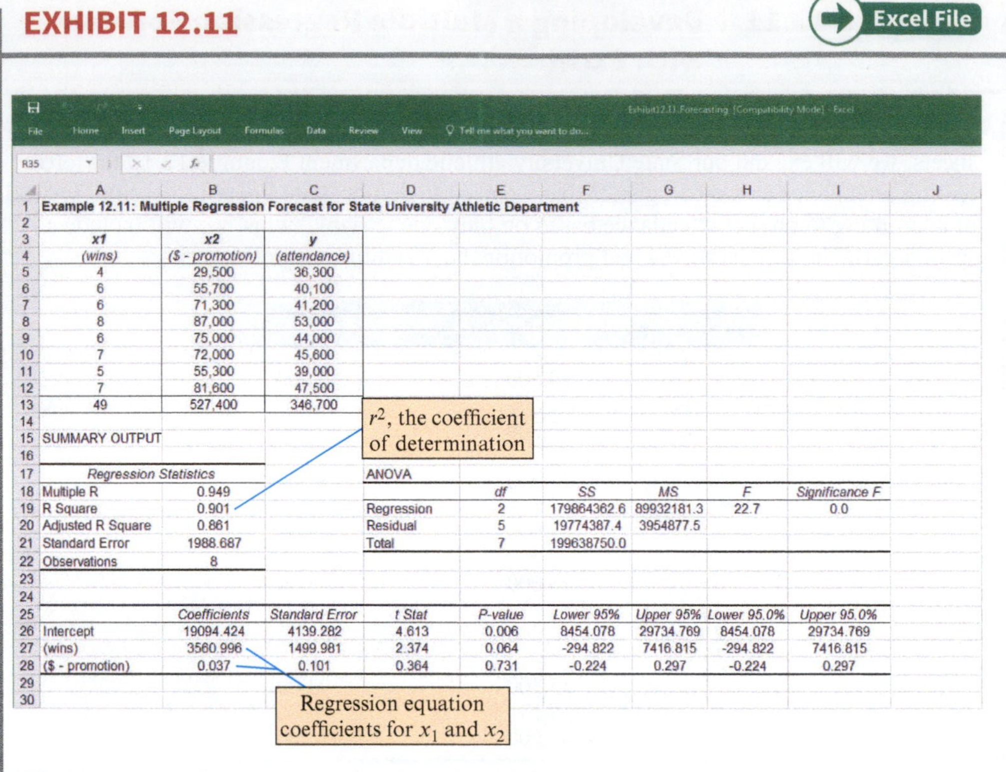

Example 12.11: Multiple Regression Forecast for State University Athletic Department

x1 (wins)	x2 ($ - promotion)	y (attendance)
4	29,500	36,300
6	55,700	40,100
6	71,300	41,200
8	87,000	53,000
6	75,000	44,000
7	72,000	45,600
5	55,300	39,000
7	81,600	47,500
49	527,400	346,700

SUMMARY OUTPUT

Regression Statistics	
Multiple R	0.949
R Square	0.901
Adjusted R Square	0.861
Standard Error	1988.687
Observations	8

ANOVA

	df	SS	MS	F	Significance F
Regression	2	179864362.6	89932181.3	22.7	0.0
Residual	5	19774387.4	3954877.5		
Total	7	199638750.0			

	Coefficients	Standard Error	t Stat	P-value	Lower 95%	Upper 95%	Lower 95.0%	Upper 95.0%
Intercept	19094.424	4139.282	4.613	0.006	8454.078	29734.769	8454.078	29734.769
(wins)	3560.996	1499.981	2.374	0.064	-294.822	7416.815	-294.822	7416.815
($ - promotion)	0.037	0.101	0.364	0.731	-0.224	0.297	-0.224	0.297

EXHIBIT 12.12

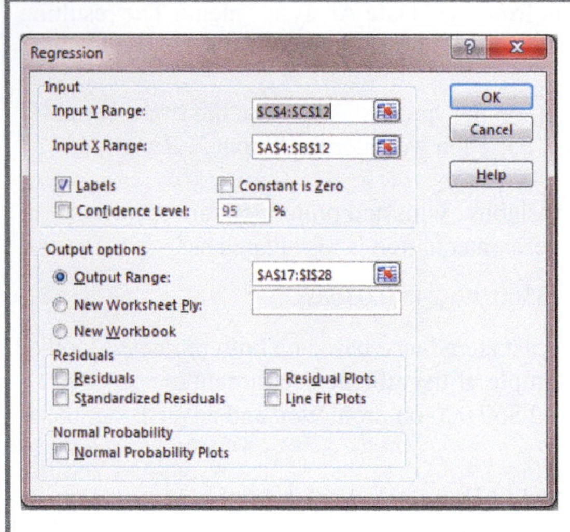

correlated (i.e., more wins coincide with higher promotional expenditures and vice versa). (Possibly the athletic department increased promotional expenditures when it thought it would have a better team that would achieve more wins.) The topic of multicollinearity and how to cope with it is beyond the scope of this book and this brief section on multiple regression; however, most statistics textbooks discuss this topic in detail.

Data Mining

At one time, business forecasters typically did not have enough data to develop accurate forecasts; however, that's no longer a problem. In fact, the situation is just the opposite—businesses are overwhelmed with data. Data are collected wherever and whenever a customer swipes a credit card or accesses a website, or a company employee scans a box or a pallet in a warehouse or goods on a store shelf. It is estimated that all the data in databases in the world double in less than every two years. In addition, large, inexpensive storage devises make it possible for companies to store this explosion of data. Thus, the problem for forecasters is no longer having enough data, it's how to use the huge amount of data they now have for forecasting purposes. Data mining helps forecasters use this wealth of data to develop useful forecasts.

Uses for Data Mining

Data mining is a process of exploring, categorizing, and modeling large amounts of data in order to identify meaningful, logical patterns and relationships among key variables. It is used to discover trends, predict future events, and assess possible courses of action. For example, police can use data mining to predict when and where crimes might occur; weather analysts use data mining to discover weather patterns and make forecasts; utility companies use data mining to forecast energy consumption under different weather conditions in different geographic regions; hotels can use data mining to determine returning customers' preferences. Data mining allows companies to search for useful information such as patterns or trends that might be useful for forecasting—for example, to determine if certain products are sold together, if events trigger the sale of certain products, or, if more of a product is sold in a certain geographic region. Data mining can help companies like Amazon or Barnes & Noble determine what types of books or music various groups of customers categorized by such things as age, gender, income, or location might prefer; or help denim jeans companies identify fashion trends.

Data mining for business forecasting purposes is different from time series and regression methods. In these traditional forecasting methods forecasters first attempt to determine if there is a pattern in the demand data such as a trend or seasonality, and then find the forecasting model (i.e., exponential smoothing, weighted average, regression, etc.) that best fits the data pattern. When they find a model that reflects the data they use it to forecast future demand. The opposite happens with data mining; forecasters don't attempt to know what patterns may fit the data; many times, forecasters don't even know what kind of pattern they're looking for and or that may be found. Instead, data mining is a way of letting the data identify patterns and then using that information for forecasting.

Tools of Data Mining

Data mining uses and analyzes data that are stored in *databases*, *data warehouses*, and *data marts*. A database is a collection of related data organized to help a company analyze some relevant activity—for example, historical sales data for a specific product. A data warehouse is typically a company's repository for its own current and historical data, including information from its own operations (i.e., marketing, sales, ERP systems, supply chain, and external data) for such things as markets, demographics, customers, materials, competitors, suppliers, and financial data. Data warehouses can be subdivided into data marts, which store subsets of data that hold special information, and data that is grouped to help the company make decisions. Data mining employs several tools or tasks that are used to extract patterns and relationships from databases, data warehouses, and data marts. All of these categories of tools employ various software packages, such as SAS, SPSS, and Excel products, to mine data—to import, process, and analyze data, and help identify patterns and relationships.

Association rule learning is a data mining tool that searches for relationships between variables, such as a retail store determining which apparel products are frequently purchased together by certain categories of customers, such as a shirt with denim jeans; or common features across a variety of product variations that a group of customers prefer. *Clustering analysis* is a tool that uses software packages to identify groups in the data that naturally fall together, such as suppliers who use a type of packaging or method of transportation, or an age or income group that purchases a type of jeans. *Classification* tools attempt to distinguish different classes of objects or actions. For example, an email may be classified as "legitimate" or "spam," or a company or product (like jeans) may be considered "green" or not. *Prediction* tools are adopted from traditional forecasting methods, such as regression, for predicting a variable's value, like monthly demand. *Summarization* provides a compact representation of the data, including a report.

Summary

Forecasts of product demand are a necessity for almost all aspects of operational planning. Short-range demand forecasts determine the daily resource requirements needed for production, including labor and material, as well as for developing work schedules and shipping dates and controlling inventory levels. Long-range forecasts are needed to plan new products for development and changes in existing products and to acquire the plant, equipment, personnel, resources, and supply chain necessary for future operations.

We have presented several methods of forecasting useful for different time frames. These quantitative forecasting techniques are easy to understand, simple to use, and not especially costly unless the data requirements are substantial. They also have exhibited a good track record of performance for many companies that have used them. For these reasons, regression methods, and especially times series, are popular.

When managers and students are first introduced to forecasting methods, they are sometimes surprised and disappointed at the lack of exactness of the forecasts. However, they soon learn that forecasting is not easy, and exactness is not possible. Nonetheless, companies that have the skill and experience to obtain more accurate forecasts than their competitors' will gain a competitive edge.

Key Terms

adjusted exponential smoothing An exponential smoothing forecast adjusted for trend.

average error The cumulative error averaged over the number of time periods.

coefficient of determination The correlation coefficient squared; it measures the portion of the variation in the dependent variable that can be attributed to the independent variable.

correlation A measure of the strength of the causal relationship between the independent and dependent variables in a linear regression equation.

cumulative error A sum of the forecast errors; also known as bias.

cycle An up-and-down movement in demand over time.

data mining Is a process for analyzing large amounts of data to identify patterns, trends, and relationships in groups.

Delphi method A procedure for acquiring informed judgments and opinions from knowledgeable individuals to use as a subjective forecast.

exponential smoothing An averaging method that weights the most recent data more strongly than more distant data.

forecast error The difference between actual and forecasted demand.

linear regression A mathematical technique that relates a dependent variable to an independent variable in the form of a linear equation.

linear trend line A forecast using the linear regression equation to relate demand to time.

long-range forecast A forecast encompassing a period longer than two years into the future.

mean absolute deviation (MAD) The per-period average of the absolute difference between actual and forecasted demand.

mean absolute percent deviation (MAPD) The absolute forecast error measured as a percentage of demand.

mean squared error (MSE) The average of the squared forecast errors.

moving average Average demand for a fixed sequence of periods including the most recent period.

multiple regression A mathematical relationship that relates a dependent variable to two or more independent variables.

qualitative forecast methods Nonquantitative, subjective forecasts based on judgment, opinion, experience, and expert opinion.

quantitative forecast methods Forecasts derived from a mathematical formula.

random variations Movements in demand that are not predictable and follow no pattern.

regression forecasting methods A class of mathematical techniques that relate demand to factors that cause demand behavior.

seasonal factor A numerical value that is multiplied by the normal forecast to get a seasonally adjusted forecast.

seasonal pattern An oscillating movement in demand that occurs periodically in the short run and is repetitive.

short- to mid-range forecast A forecast encompassing the immediate future, usually days or weeks, but up to two years.

smoothing constant The weighting factor given to the most recent data in exponential smoothing forecasts.

time frame How far into the future something is forecasted.

time series methods A class of statistical methods that uses historical demand data over a period of time to predict future demand.

tracking signal A measure computed by dividing the cumulative error by MAD; used for monitoring bias in a forecast.

trend A gradual, long-term up or down movement of demand.

weighted moving average A moving average with more recent demand values adjusted with weights.

Key Formulas

Moving Average

$$MA_n = \frac{\sum_{i=1}^{n} D_i}{n}$$

Weighted Moving Average

$$WMA_n = \sum_{i=1}^{n} W_i D_i$$

Exponential Smoothing

$$F_{t+1} = \alpha D_t + (1 - \alpha) F_t$$

Adjusted Exponential Smoothing

$$AF_{t+1} = F_{t+1} + T_{t+1}$$

Trend Factor

$$T_{t+1} = \beta(F_{t+1} - F_t) + (1 - \beta)T_t$$

Linear Trend Line

$$y = a + bx$$

Least Squares

$$b = \frac{\Sigma xy - n\bar{x}\bar{y}}{\Sigma x^2 - n\bar{x}^2}$$

$$a = \bar{y} - b\bar{x}$$

Seasonal Factor

$$S_i = \frac{D_i}{\Sigma D}$$

Seasonally Adjusted Forecast

$$SF_i = (S_i)(F_t)$$

Mean Absolute Deviation

$$MAD = \frac{\Sigma |D_t - F_t|}{n}$$

Mean Absolute Percent Deviation

$$MAPD = \frac{\Sigma |D_t - F_t|}{\Sigma D_t}$$

Cumulative Error

$$E = \Sigma e_t$$

Average Error (Bias)

$$\bar{E} = \frac{\Sigma e_t}{n}$$

Tracking Signal

$$TS = \frac{\Sigma (D_t - F_t)}{MAD} = \frac{E}{MAD}$$

Mean Squared Error

$$MSE = \frac{\Sigma (D_t - F_t)^2}{n - 1}$$

Linear Regression Equation

$$y = a + bx$$

Correlation Coefficient

$$r = \frac{n\Sigma xy - \Sigma x \Sigma y}{\sqrt{[n\Sigma x^2 - (\Sigma x)^2][n\Sigma y^2 - (\Sigma y)^2]}}$$

Coefficient of Determination

$$\text{Coefficient of determination} = r^2$$

Solved Problems

WileyPLUS

1. Moving Average

A manufacturing company has monthly demand for one of its products as follows:

MONTH	DEMAND
February	520
March	490
April	550
May	580
June	600
July	420
August	510
September	610

Develop a three-period moving average forecast and a three-period weighted moving average forecast with weights of .50, .30, and .20 for the most recent demand values, in that order. Calculate MAD for each forecast, and indicate which would seem to be most accurate.

Solution

Step 1. Compute the three-month moving average using the formula

$$MA_3 = \sum_{i=1}^{3} \frac{D_i}{3}$$

For May, the moving average forecast is

$$MA_3 = \frac{520 + 490 + 550}{3} = 520$$

Step 2. Compute the three-month weighted moving average using the formula

$$WMA_3 = \Sigma W_i D_i$$

For May, the weighted average forecast is

$$\begin{aligned} WMA_3 &= (0.50)(550) + (0.30)(490) + (0.20)(520) \\ &= 526.00 \end{aligned}$$

The values for both moving average forecasts are shown in the following table:

MONTH	DEMAND	MA_3	WMA_3
February	520	—	—
March	490	—	—
April	550	—	—
May	580	520.00	526.00
June	600	540.00	553.00
July	420	576.67	584.00
August	510	533.33	506.00
September	610	510.00	501.00
October	—	513.33	542.00

Step 3. Compute the MAD value for both forecasts:

$$\text{MAD} = \frac{\Sigma|D_t - F_t|}{n}$$

The MAD value for the three-month moving average is 80.0, and the MAD value for the three-month weighted moving average is 75.6, indicating there is not much difference in accuracy between the two forecasts, although the weighted moving average is slightly better.

2. Exponential Smoothing

A computer software firm has experienced the following demand for its "Personal Finance" software package:

PERIOD	UNITS
1	56
2	61
3	55
4	70
5	66
6	65
7	72
8	75

Develop an exponential smoothing forecast using $\alpha = .40$ and an adjusted exponential smoothing forecast using $\alpha = .40$ and $\beta = .20$. Compare the accuracy of the two forecasts using MAD and cumulative error.

Solution

Step 1. Compute the exponential smoothing forecast with $\alpha = .40$ using the following formula:

$$F_{t+1} = \alpha D_t + (1 - \alpha)F_t$$

For period 2, the forecast (assuming $F_1 = 56$) is

$$\begin{aligned} F_2 &= \alpha D_t + (1 - \alpha)F_1 \\ &= (0.40)(56) + (0.60)(56) \\ &= 56 \end{aligned}$$

For period 3, the forecast is

$$\begin{aligned} F_3 &= (0.40)(61) + (0.60)(56) \\ &= 58 \end{aligned}$$

The remaining forecasts are computed similarly and are shown in the accompanying table.

Step 2. Compute the adjusted exponential smoothing forecast with $\alpha = .40$ and $\beta = .20$ using the formula

$$\begin{aligned} \text{AF}_{t+1} &= F_{t+1} + T_{t+1} \\ T_{t+1} &= \beta(F_{t+1} - F_t) + (1 - \beta)T_t \end{aligned}$$

Starting with the forecast for period 3 (since $F_1 = F_2$, and we will assume $T_2 = 0$),

$$\begin{aligned} T_3 &= \beta(F_3 - F_2) + (1 - \beta)T_2 \\ &= (0.20)(58 - 56) + (0.80)(0) \\ &= 0.40 \\ \text{AF}_3 &= F_3 + T_3 \\ &= 58 + 0.40 \\ &= 58.40 \end{aligned}$$

The remaining adjusted forecasts are computed similarly and are shown in the following table:

PERIOD	D_t	F_t	AF_t	$D_t - F_t$	$D_t - AF_t$
1	56	—	—	—	—
2	61	56.00	56.00	5.00	5.00
3	55	58.00	58.40	−3.00	−3.40
4	70	56.80	56.88	13.20	13.12
5	66	62.08	63.20	3.92	2.80
6	65	63.65	64.86	1.35	0.14
7	72	64.18	65.26	7.81	6.73
8	75	67.31	68.80	7.68	6.20
9	—	70.39	72.19	—	—
				35.97	30.60

Step 3. Compute the MAD value for each forecast:

$$\begin{aligned} \text{MAD}(F_t) &= \frac{\Sigma|D_t - F_t|}{n} \\ &= \frac{41.97}{7} \\ &= 5.99 \\ \text{MAD}(\text{AF}_t) &= \frac{37.39}{7} \\ &= 5.34 \end{aligned}$$

Step 4. Compute the cumulative error for each forecast:

$$\begin{aligned} E(F_t) &= 35.97 \\ E(\text{AF}_t) &= 30.60 \end{aligned}$$

Because both MAD and the cumulative error are less for the adjusted forecast, it would appear to be the most accurate.

3. Linear Regression

A local building products store has accumulated sales data for 2 × 4 lumber (in board feet) and the number of building permits in its area for the past 10 quarters:

QUARTER	BUILDING PERMITS x	LUMBER SALES (1000s OF BOARD FEET)$_y$
1	8	12.6
2	12	16.3
3	7	9.3

4	9	11.5
5	15	18.1
6	6	7.6
7	5	6.2
8	8	14.2
9	101	15.0
10	12	17.8

Develop a linear regression model for these data and determine the strength of the linear relationship using correlation. If the model appears to be relatively strong, determine the forecast for lumber given ten building permits in the next quarter.

Solution

Step 1. Compute the components of the linear regression equation, $y = a + bx$, using the least squares formulas

$$\bar{x} = \frac{92}{10} = 9.2$$

$$\bar{y} = \frac{128.6}{10} = 12.86$$

$$b = \frac{\Sigma xy - n\bar{x}\bar{y}}{\Sigma x^2 - n\bar{x}^2}$$

$$= \frac{(1290.3) - (10)(9.2)(12.86)}{(932) - (10)(9.2)^2}$$

$$b = 1.25$$

$$a = \bar{y} - b\bar{x}$$

$$= 12.86 - (1.25)(9.2)$$

$$a = 1.36$$

Step 2. Develop the linear regression equations:

$$y = a + bx$$

$$y = 1.36 + 1.25x$$

Step 3. Compute the correlation coefficient:

$$r = \frac{n\Sigma xy - \Sigma x\Sigma y}{\sqrt{[n\Sigma x^2 - (\Sigma x)^2][(n\Sigma y^2 - (\Sigma y)^2]}}$$

$$= \frac{(10)(1290.3) - (92)(128.6)}{\sqrt{[(10)(932) - (92)^2][(10)(1810.48) - (128.6)^2]}}$$

$$= 0.925$$

Thus, there appears to be a strong linear relationship.

Step 4. Calculate the forecast for $x = 10$ permits.

$$y = a + bx$$

$$= 1.36 + 1.25(10)$$

$$= 13.86 \text{ or } 13{,}860 \text{ board feet}$$

Questions

12.1. List some of the operations and functions in a company that are dependent on a forecast for product demand.

12.2. What is the difference between quantitative forecast methods and qualitative forecast methods?

12.3. Describe the difference between short- and long-range forecasts.

12.4. Discuss the role of forecasting in supply chain management.

12.5. Why is accurate forecasting so important to companies that use a continuous replenishment inventory system?

12.6. Discuss the relationship between forecasting and quality management.

12.7. What kinds of forecasting methods are used for long-range strategic planning?

12.8. Describe the Delphi method for forecasting.

12.9. What is the difference between a trend and a cycle and a seasonal pattern?

12.10. How is the moving average method similar to exponential smoothing?

12.11. In the chapter examples for time series methods, the starting forecast was always assumed to be the same as actual demand in the first period. Suggest other ways that the starting forecast might be derived in actual use.

12.12. What effect on the exponential smoothing model will increasing the smoothing constant have?

12.13. How does adjusted exponential smoothing differ from exponential smoothing?

12.14. What determines the choice of the smoothing constant for trend in an adjusted exponential smoothing model?

12.15. How does the linear trend line forecasting model differ from a linear regression model for forecasting?

12.16. Of the time series models presented in this chapter, including the moving average and weighted moving average, exponential smoothing and adjusted exponential smoothing, and linear trend line, which one do you consider the best? Why?

12.17. What advantages does adjusted exponential smoothing have over a linear trend line for forecasted demand that exhibits a trend?

12.18. Describe how a forecast is monitored to detect bias.

12.19. Explain the relationship between the use of a tracking signal and statistical control limits for forecast control.

12.20. Selecting from MAD, MAPD, MSE, E, and $\bar{E}$, which measure of forecast accuracy do you consider superior? Why?

12.21. What is the difference between linear and multiple regression?

12.22. Define the different components (y, x, a, and b) of a linear regression equation.

12.23. A company that produces video equipment, including video cameras and televisions, is attempting to forecast what new products and product innovations might be technologically feasible and customers might demand 10 years into the future. Speculate on what type of qualitative methods it might use to develop this type of forecast.

Problems

12.1. The Hartley-Davis motorcycle dealer in the Minneapolis–St. Paul area wants to be able to forecast accurately the demand for the Roadhog Super motorcycle during the next month. From sales records, the dealer has accumulated the data in the following table for the past year.

MONTH	MOTORCYCLE SALES
January	9
February	7
March	10
April	8
May	7
June	12
July	10
August	11
September	12
October	10
November	14
December	16

a. Compute a three-month moving average forecast of demand for April through January (of the next year).

b. Compute a five-month moving average forecast for June through January.

c. Compare the two forecasts computed in parts (a) and (b) using MAD. Which one should the dealer use for January of the next year?

12.2. The manager of the I-85 Carpet Outlet needs to be able to forecast accurately the demand for Soft Shag carpet (its biggest seller). If the manager does not order enough carpet from the carpet mill, customers will buy their carpets from one of the outlet's many competitors. The manager has collected the following demand data for the past eight months.

MONTH	DEMAND FOR SOFT SHAG CARPET (1000 yd)
1	5
2	10
3	6
4	8
5	14
6	10
7	9
8	12

a. Compute a three-month moving average forecast for months 4 through 9.

b. Compute a weighted three-month moving average forecast for months 4 through 9. Assign weights of .55, .33, and .12 to the months in sequence, starting with the most recent month.

c. Compare the two forecasts using MAD. Which forecast appears to be more accurate?

12.3. The LawnPlus Fertilizer Company distributes fertilizer to various lawn and garden shops. The company must base its quarterly production schedule on a forecast of how many tons of fertilizer will be demanded from it. The company has gathered the following data for the past three years from its sales records.

YEAR	QUARTER	DEMAND FOR FERTILIZER (TON)
1	1	105
	2	150
	3	93
	4	121
2	5	140
	6	170
	7	105
	8	150
3	9	150
	10	170
	11	110
	12	130

a. Compute a three-quarter moving average forecast for quarters 4 through 13 and compute the forecast error for each quarter.

b. Compute a five-quarter moving average forecast for quarters 6 through 13 and compute the forecast error for each quarter.

c. Compute a weighted three-quarter moving average forecast using weights of .50, .33, and .17 for the most recent, next recent, and most distant data, respectively, and compute the forecast error for each quarter.

d. Compare the forecasts developed in parts (a), (b), and (c) using cumulative error. Which forecast appears to be most accurate? Do any exhibit any bias?

12.4. Graph the demand data in Problem 12.3. Can you identify any trends, cycles, and/or seasonal patterns?

12.5. The chairperson of the department of management at Tech wants to forecast the number of students who will enroll in operations management next semester in order to determine how many sections to schedule. The chair has accumulated the following enrollment data for the past eight semesters:

SEMESTER	STUDENTS ENROLLED IN OM
1	270
2	310
3	250
4	290
5	370
6	410
7	400
8	450

a. Compute a three-semester moving average forecast for semesters 4 through 9.
b. Compute the exponentially smoothed forecast ($\alpha = .20$) for the enrollment data.
c. Compare the two forecasts using MAD and indicate the most accurate.

12.6. The manager of the Excom Service Station wants to forecast the demand for unleaded gasoline next month so that the proper number of gallons can be ordered from the distributor. The owner has accumulated the following data on demand for unleaded gasoline from sales during the past 10 months:

MONTH	GASOLINE DEMANDED (GAL)
October	800
November	725
December	630
January	500
February	645
March	690
April	730
May	810
June	1200
July	980

a. Compute an exponentially smoothed forecast using an α value of .30.
b. Compute an adjusted exponentially smoothed forecast ($\alpha = .30$ and $\beta = .20$).
c. Compare the two forecasts using MAPD and indicate which seems to be the most accurate.

12.7. The Intrepid mutual fund of growth stocks has had the following average monthly price for the past 10 months.

MONTH	FUND PRICE
1	62.7
2	63.9
3	68.0
4	66.4
5	67.2
6	65.8
7	68.2
8	69.3
9	67.2
10	70.1

Compute the exponentially smoothed forecast with $\alpha = .40$, the adjusted exponentially smoothed forecast with $\alpha = .40$ and $\beta = .30$, and the linear trend line forecast. Compare the accuracy of the three forecasts using cumulative error and MAD, and indicate which forecast appears to be most accurate.

12.8. The Oceanside Hotel is adjacent to City Coliseum, a 24,000-seat arena that is home to the city's professional basketball and ice hockey teams and that hosts a variety of concerts, trade shows, and conventions throughout the year. The hotel has experienced the following occupancy rates for the nine years since the coliseum opened:

YEAR	OCCUPANCY RATE
1	75%
2	70
3	72
4	77
5	83
6	81
7	86
8	91
9	87

Compute an exponential smoothing forecast with $\alpha = .20$, an adjusted exponential smoothing forecast with $\alpha = .20$ and $\beta = .20$, and a linear trend line forecast. Compare the three forecasts using MAD and average error ($\bar{E}$), and indicate which forecast seems to be most accurate.

12.9. Mary Hernandez has invested in a stock mutual fund and she is considering liquidating and investing in a bond fund. She would like to forecast the price of the stock fund for the next month before making a decision. She has collected the following data on the average price of the fund during the past 20 months.

MONTH	FUND PRICE	MONTH	FUND PRICE
1	63 1/4	11	68 1/8
2	60 1/8	12	63 1/4
3	61 3/4	13	64 3/8
4	64 1/4	14	68 5/8
5	59 3/8	15	70 1/8
6	57 7/8	16	72 3/4
7	62 1/4	17	74 1/8
8	65 1/8	18	71 3/4
9	68 1/4	19	75 1/2
10	65 1/2	20	76 3/4

a. Using a three-month moving average, forecast the fund price for month 21.
b. Using a three-month weighted average with the most recent month weighted .60, the next most recent month weighted .30, and the third month weighted .10, forecast the fund price for month 21.
c. Compute an exponentially smoothed forecast using $\alpha = .40$ and forecast the fund price for month 21.
d. Compare the forecasts in (a), (b), and (c) using MAD and indicate the most accurate.

12.10. Globetron manufactures components for use in small electronic products such as computers, CD players, and radios at plants in Belgium, Germany, and France. The parts are transported by truck to Hamburg, where they are shipped overseas to customers in Mexico, South America, the United States, and the Pacific Rim. The company has to reserve space on ships months and sometimes years in advance, and thus needs an accurate forecasting model. Following are the number of cubic feet of container space the company has used in each of the past 18 months.

MONTH	SPACE (1000s ft^3)	MONTH	SPACE (1000s ft^3)
1	10.6	10	19.2
2	12.7	11	16.3
3	9.8	12	14.7
4	11.3	13	18.2
5	13.6	14	19.6
6	14.4	15	21.4
7	12.2	16	22.8
8	16.7	17	20.6
9	18.1	18	18.7

Develop a forecasting model that you believe would provide the company with relatively accurate forecasts for the next year and indicate the forecasted shipping space required for the next three months.

12.11. The Bee Line Café is well known for its popular homemade ice cream, which it makes in a small plant in back of the cafe. People drive long distances to buy the ice cream. The two ladies who own the café want to develop a forecasting model so they can plan their ice cream production operation and determine the number of employees they need to sell ice cream in the café. They have accumulated the following sales records for their ice cream for the past 12 quarters:

YEAR/QUARTER	ICE CREAM SALES (gal)
1:1	350
2	510
3	750
4	420
2:5	370
6	480
7	860
8	500
3:9	450
10	550
11	820
12	570

Develop an adjusted exponential smoothing model with $\alpha = .50$ and $\beta = .50$ to forecast demand, and assess its accuracy using cumulative error (E) and average error ($\bar{E}$). Does there appear to be any bias in the forecast?

12.12. For the demand data in Problem 12.11, develop a seasonally adjusted forecast for year 4. (Use a linear trend line model to develop a forecast estimate for year 4.) Which forecast model do you perceive to be the most accurate, the adjusted exponential smoothing model from Problem 12.11 or the seasonally adjusted forecast?

12.13. Develop a seasonally adjusted forecast for the demand data for fertilizer in Problem 12.3. Use a linear trend line model to compute a forecast estimate for demand in year 4.

12.14. Backstreet's Pizza delivery service has randomly selected eight weekdays during the past month and recorded orders for pizza at four different time periods per day, as follows:

	DAYS							
TIME PERIOD	1	2	3	4	5	6	7	8
10:00 A.M.–3:00 P.M.	62	49	53	35	43	48	56	43
3:00 P.M.–7:00 P.M.	73	55	81	77	60	66	85	70
7:00 P.M.–11:00 P.M.	42	38	45	50	29	37	35	44
11:00 P.M.–2:00 P.M.	35	40	36	39	26	25	36	31

Develop a seasonally adjusted forecasting model for daily pizza demand and forecast demand for each of the time periods for a single upcoming day.

12.15. The Willow River Mining Company mines and ships coal. It has experienced the following demand for coal during the past eight years:

YEAR	COAT SALES (TONS)
1	4260
2	4510
3	4050
4	3720
5	3900
6	3470
7	2890
8	3100

Develop an adjusted exponential smoothing model ($\alpha = .30$, $\beta = .20$) and a linear trend line model, and compare the forecast accuracy of the two using MAD. Indicate which forecast seems to be most accurate.

12.16. The Great Northwest Outdoor Company is a catalog sales operation that specializes in outdoor recreational clothing. Demand for its items is very seasonal, peaking during the holiday season and during the spring. It has accumulated the following data for order per "season" (quarter) during the past five years:

	ORDERS (1000s)				
QUARTER/YEAR	1	2	3	4	5
January–March	18.6	18.1	22.4	23.2	24.5
April–June	23.5	24.7	28.8	27.6	31.0
July–September	20.4	19.5	21.0	24.4	23.7
October–December	41.9	46.3	45.5	47.1	52.8

a. Develop a seasonally adjusted forecast model for these order data. Forecast demand for each quarter for year 6 (using a linear trend line forecast estimate for orders in year 6).

b. Develop a separate linear trend line forecast for each of the four seasons and forecast each season for year 6.

c. Which of the two approaches used in parts (a) and (b) appear to be the most accurate? Use MAD to verify your selection.

12.17. Townside Food Vending operates vending machines in office buildings, the airport, bus stations, colleges, and other businesses and agencies around town and operates vending trucks for building and construction sites. The company believes its sandwich sales follow a seasonal pattern. It has accumulated the following data for sandwich sales per season during the past four years.

SEASON/YEAR	SANDWICH SALES (1000s) 1	2	3	4
Fall	42.7	44.3	45.7	40.6
Winter	36.9	42.7	34.8	41.5
Spring	51.3	55.6	49.3	47.3
Summer	62.9	64.8	71.2	74.5

Develop a seasonally adjusted forecast model for these sandwich sales data. Forecast demand for each season for year 5 using a linear trend line estimate for sales in year 5. Do the data appear to have a seasonal pattern?

12.18. The town aquatic center has an indoor pool that has lanes for lap swimming and an open area for recreational swimming and water exercises. When local schools are in session from mid-August to late May, during weekdays the pool operates from 7:00 A.M. to 9:00 P.M. The center requires a lifeguard to pool user ratio of 30:1. The center director has to submit a new yearly budget to the town and wants to develop a forecast of hourly pool attendance in order to determine the number of lifeguards she'll have to hire in the coming year. The director believes pool attendance follows a seasonal pattern during the day and she has accumulated the following data for average daily attendance for each hour of the day that the pool is open to the public for the past six years.

TIME	YEAR 1	2	3	4	5	6
7:00 A.M.	56	64	66	60	72	65
8:00	31	41	37	44	52	46
9:00	15	22	24	30	19	26
10:00	34	35	38	31	28	33
11:00	45	52	55	49	57	50
Noon	63	71	57	65	75	70
1:00 P.M.	35	30	41	42	33	45
2:00	24	28	32	30	35	33
3:00	27	19	24	23	25	27
6:00	31	47	36	45	40	46
7:00	25	35	41	43	39	45
8:00	14	20	18	17	23	27
9:00	10	8	16	14	15	18

Develop a seasonally adjusted forecast for these data for hourly pool attendance. Forecast average pool attendance for each hour for year 7 by using a linear trend line estimate for pool attendance in year 7. Do the data appear to have a seasonal pattern?

12.19. Develop an adjusted exponential smoothing forecast ($\alpha = .30$, $\beta = .20$) for the annual pool attendance data in Problem 12.18. Does this forecast appear to be more or less accurate than the forecast based on the linear trend line model to forecast hourly pool attendance in Problem 12.18?

12.20. During the past five months the emergency room at the new County Hospital has observed the number of patients during two parts of every other week—the weekend (Friday through Sunday) and weekdays (Monday through Thursday). They typically experience greater patient traffic on weekends than during the week:

WEEK	NUMBER OF PATIENTS WEEKEND	WEEKDAYS
1	105	73
2	119	85
3	122	89
4	128	83
5	117	96
6	136	78
7	141	91
8	126	100
9	143	83
10	140	101

Develop a seasonally adjusted forecasting model for number of patients during each part of the week for week 11.

12.21. At its craft store and through its website, the Highlands Craft Store makes and sells bowls and mugs that are hand-made by local artisans. Since making these items requires a special type of clay and a large amount of individual man-hours, for planning purposes the company would like to forecast future demand, specifically through their website, which has increasingly become the primary source of their sales. Following is the company's website demand (in items sold) for the past 36 months.

MONTH	SALES	MONTH	SALES	MONTH	SALES
1	345	13	415	25	344
2	411	14	395	26	286
3	266	15	298	27	455
4	347	16	377	28	634
5	506	17	418	29	502
6	278	18	522	30	388
7	411	19	421	31	427
8	510	20	384	32	561
9	198	21	455	33	447
10	387	22	506	34	395
11	344	23	478	35	414
12	412	24	613	36	522

Develop a linear trend forecast model, an exponentially smoothed model ($\alpha = .20$) and a 5-month moving average forecast model and indicate which one seems best to forecast website demand.

12.22. A group of business students at Tech organized a student club called Prism to develop and disseminate content about business majors through a website they created. They would like the college and various academic departments to use their club website to provide information about, and promote, their majors, and to post possible job opportunities from potential employers. In order to convince the college administration and department heads to use their site, they want to develop a forecast of future website visits. Following is the number of weekly visits the club's website has received for the past 24 weeks while it has been in existence.

WEEK	WEBSITE VISITS	WEEK	WEBSITE VISITS
1	537	13	822
2	375	14	677
3	419	15	1,031
4	276	16	657
5	445	17	983
6	512	18	774
7	670	19	1,210
8	561	20	811
9	705	21	1,137
10	619	22	763
11	768	23	1,225
12	645	24	941

Develop a linear trend line forecast, an exponential smoothing forecast ($\alpha = .60$) and a three-month weighted moving average (with the most recent month weighted by .50, the next closest month by .30 and the final month by .20). Indicate which one seems to be the most accurate forecast model and the forecast for week 25.

12.23. Temco Industries has developed a forecasting model that was used to forecast during a ten-month period. The forecasts and actual demand are shown as follows:

MONTH	ACTUAL DEMAND	FORECAST DEMAND
1	160	170
2	150	165
3	175	157
4	200	166
5	190	183
6	220	186
7	205	203
8	210	204
9	200	207
10	220	203

Measure the accuracy of the forecast using MAD, MAPD, and cumulative error. Does the forecast method appear to be accurate?

12.24. Monitor the forecast in Problem 12.23 for bias using a tracking signal and a control chart with ±3 MAD. Does there appear to be any bias in the forecast?

12.25. Develop a statistical control chart for the forecast error in Problem 12.11 using 3σ control limits, and indicate if the forecast seems to be biased.

12.26. Monitor the adjusted exponential smoothing forecast in Problem 12.15 for bias using a tracking signal and a control chart with ±3 MAD.

12.27. RAP Computers assembles computers from generic parts it purchases at discount and sells the units via phone orders it receives from customers responding to their ads in trade journals. The business has developed an exponential smoothing forecast model to forecast future computer demand. Actual demand for their computers for the past eight months is as follows:

MONTH	DEMAND	FORECAST
March	120	—
April	110	120.0
May	150	116.0
June	130	129.6
July	160	129.7
August	165	141.8
September	140	151.1
October	155	146.7
November	—	150.0

a. Using the measure of forecast accuracy of your choice, ascertain if the forecast appears to be accurate.

b. Determine if a three-month moving average would provide a better forecast.

c. Use a tracking signal to monitor the forecast in part (a) for bias.

12.28. Develop an exponential smoothing forecast with $\alpha = .20$ for the demand data in Problem 12.1. Compare this forecast with the three-month moving average computed in 12.1(a) using MAD and indicate which forecast seems to be most accurate.

12.29. The Fieldale Dairy produces cheese, which it sells to supermarkets and food processing companies. Because of concerns about cholesterol and fat in cheese, the company has seen demand for its products decline during the past decade. It is now considering introducing some alternative low-fat dairy products and wants to determine how much available plant capacity it will have next year. The company has developed an exponential smoothing forecast with $\alpha = .40$ to forecast cheese. The actual demand and the forecasts from its model are shown as follows:

YEAR	DEMAND (1000s lb)	FORECAST
1	16.8	—
2	14.1	16.8
3	15.3	15.7
4	12.7	15.5
5	11.9	14.4
6	12.3	13.4
7	11.5	12.9
8	10.8	12.4

Assess the accuracy of the forecast model using MAD and cumulative error, and determine if the forecast error reflects bias using a tracking signal and ±3 MAD control limits. If the exponential smoothing forecast model is biased, determine if a linear trend model would provide a more accurate forecast.

12.30. Global smartphone sales experienced extraordinary growth starting in 2007 with the introduction of both the iPhone and Android-platform based devices (see the Chapter Introduction). Following are the yearly global sales (in million units) for smartphones beginning in 2008 through 2015:

YEAR	SALES
2008	140
2009	173
2010	305
2011	495
2012	730
2013	1030
2014	1300
2015	1430

Develop a linear trend line model to forecast smartphone sales for 2016, 2017, and 2018, and compare these forecasts with those reported on the Internet.

12.31. Arkind, an Indian company, is a global manufacturer and supplier of denim jeans to apparel retailers around the world. It purchases baled cotton around the world, ships it to its denim fabric factories, then to its denim jeans manufacturing facilities. Its cotton purchases and manufacturing and shipping plans depend on an accurate forecast of denim jeans demand. Arkind believes there might be a strong relationship between cotton production and denim jeans demand that will enable them to include cotton production as part of its forecasting process. Following are global cotton production and denim jeans sales for the past six years.

YEAR	COTTON PRODUCTION (MILLION BALES)	DENIM JEANS SALES (MILLIONS OF PAIRS)
1	123	1830
2	109	2010
3	118	1903
4	114	1875
5	103	2110
6	109	2005

Develop a linear regression model for these data, forecast denim jeans demand for cotton production of 115 million bales, and explain why you think the model should or should not be used to forecast denim jeans demand.

12.32. The manager of the Commander Hotel near City Stadium believes that how well the local Blue Sox professional baseball team is playing has an impact on the occupancy rate at the hotel during the summer months. Following are the number of victories for the Blue Sox (in a 162-game schedule) for the past eight years and the hotel occupancy rates:

YEAR	NUMBER OF BLUE SOX WINS	OCCUPANCY RATE
1	70	81%
2	65	74
3	81	83
4	88	84
5	80	85
6	92	91
7	83	88
8	64	80

Develop a linear regression model for these data, and forecast the occupancy rate for next year if the Blue Sox win 85 games. Does there appear to be a strong relationship between wins and occupancy rate?

12.33. The I-85 Carpet Outlet wants to develop a means to forecast its carpet sales. The store manager believes that the store's sales are directly related to the number of new housing starts in town. The manager has gathered data from county records of monthly house construction permits and from store records on monthly sales. These data are as follows:

MONTHLY CARPET SALES (1000s yd)	MONTHLY CONSTRUCTION PERMITS
5	17
12	30
6	12
5	14
8	18
4	10
14	38
9	20
9	16
16	31

a. Develop a linear regression model for this data and forecast carpet sales if 25 construction permits for new homes are filed.

b. Determine the strength of the causal relationship between monthly sales and new home construction using correlation.

12.34. The manager of Sarah's Ice Cream store needs an accurate forecast of the demand for ice cream. The store orders ice cream from a distributor a week ahead, and if too little is ordered the store loses business. If it orders too much, it must be thrown away. The manager believes that a major determinant of ice cream sales is temperature; that is, the hotter it is, the more ice cream people buy. Using an almanac, the manager has determined the average daytime temperature for 10 weeks selected at random and then, from store records, has determined the ice cream consumption for the same 10 weeks. The data are summarized as follows:

WEEK	TEMPERATURE	(GALLONS SOLD)
1	75	95
2	67	90
3	83	125
4	89	150
5	77	85
6	80	115
7	84	110
8	92	145
9	89	130
10	65	100

a. Develop a linear regression model for this data and forecast the ice cream consumption if the average weekly daytime temperature is expected to be 80.

b. Determine the strength of the linear relationship between temperature and ice cream consumption using correlation.

12.35. Compute the coefficient of determination for the data in Problem 12.34 and explain its meaning.

12.36. The registrar at State University believes that decreases in the number of freshman applications that have been experienced are directly related to tuition increases. They have collected the following enrollment and tuition data for the past decade:

YEAR	FRESHMAN APPLICATIONS	ANNUAL TUITION ($)
1	6010	3600
2	5560	3600
3	6100	4000
4	5330	4400
5	4980	4500
6	5870	5700
7	5120	6000
8	4750	6000
9	4615	7500
10	4100	8000

a. Develop a linear regression model for these data and forecast the number of applications for State University if tuition increases to $10,000 per year and if tuition is lowered to $7000 per year.

b. Determine the strength of the linear relationship between freshman applications and tuition using correlation.

c. Describe the various planning decisions for State University that would be affected by the forecast for freshman applications.

12.37. Employees at Hubbell Engine Parts Company produce parts using precision machine tools according to exact design specifications. The employees are paid partially according to a piece rate system wherein if they work faster and produce more parts, they are eligible for monthly bonuses. Management suspects that this method of pay may contribute to a high number of defective parts. A specific part requires a normal, standard time of 23 minutes to produce. The quality control manager has checked the actual average times to produce this part for 10 different employees during 20 days selected at random during the past month, and determined the corresponding percentage of defective parts, as follows.

AVERAGE TIME (MIN)	% DEFECTIVE	AVERAGE TIME (MIN)	% DEFECTIVE
21.6	4.1	20.8	3.1
22.5	4.6	18.9	6.1
23.1	1.2	21.4	3.8
24.6	1.5	23.7	1.9
22.8	2.6	23.8	1.7
23.7	1.9	24.9	0.8
20.9	3.7	19.8	4.3
19.7	5.3	19.7	5.1
24.5	1.8	21.2	3.9
26.7	2.3	20.8	1.7

Develop a linear regression model relating average production time to percentage defects to determine if a relationship exists, and the percentage of defective items that would be expected with the normal production time of 23 minutes.

12.38. Apperson and Fitz is a chain of clothing stores that caters to high school and college students. It publishes a quarterly catalog and operates a website that features provocatively attired males and females. The website is very expensive to maintain, and company executives are not sure if the number of hits at the site relate to sales; that is, people may be looking at the site for the pictures rather than as potential customers. The webmaster has accumulated the following data for hits per month and orders placed at the website for the past 20 months.

HITS (1000s)	ORDERS (1000s)	HITS (1000s)	ORDERS (1000s)
34.2	8.2	52.3	10.4
28.5	5.7	35.2	7.5
36.7	9.1	27.9	6.2
42.3	7.5	31.4	4.8
25.8	6.3	29.4	5.3
46.7	9.1	28.9	4.4
43.5	7.2	26.4	5.2
52.6	10.7	39.4	6.8
61.8	9.3	44.7	8.4
37.3	3.1	46.3	7.9

Develop a linear regression model for these data and indicate if there appears to be a strong relationship between website hits and orders. What would be the forecast for orders with 60,000 hits per month?

12.39. Develop a linear trend line model for the freshman applications data at State University in Problem 12.36.

a. Does this forecast appear to be more or less accurate than the linear regression forecast developed in Problem 12.36? Justify your answer.

b. Compute the correlation coefficient for the linear trend line forecast and explain its meaning.

12.40. Explain what the numerical value of the slope of the linear regression equation in Problem 12.34 means.

12.41. ITown is a large computer discount store that sells computers and ancillary equipment and software in the town where State University is located. It has collected historical data on computer sales and printer sales for the past 10 years as follows:

YEAR	PERSONAL COMPUTER SALES	PRINTERS SOLD
1	1045	381
2	1610	579
3	860	312
4	1211	501
5	975	296
6	1117	415
7	1066	535
8	1310	592
9	1517	607
10	1246	473

a. Develop a linear trend line forecast to forecast printer demand in year 11.

b. Develop a linear regression model relating printer sales to computer sales to forecast printer demand in year 11 if 1500 computers are sold.

c. Compare the forecasts developed in parts (a) and (b) and indicate which one appears to be the best.

12.42. Develop an exponential smoothing model with $\alpha = .30$ for the data in Problem 12.41 to forecast printer demand in year 11, and compare its accuracy to the linear regression forecast developed in Problem 12.41(a).

12.43. Arrow Air is a regional East Coast airline. It has collected data for the percentage of available seats occupied on its flights for four quarters—(1) January–March, (2) April–June, (3) July–September, and (4) October–December—for the past five years. The company also has collected data for the average percentage fare discount for each of these quarters as follows:

YEAR	QUARTER	% SEAT OCCUPANCY	% AVERAGE FARE DISCOUNT
1	1	63	21
	2	75	34
	3	76	18
	4	58	26
2	1	59	18
	2	62	40
	3	81	25
	4	76	30
3	1	65	23
	2	70	28
	3	78	30
	4	69	35
4	1	59	20
	2	61	35
	3	83	26
	4	71	30
5	1	60	25
	2	66	37
	3	86	25
	4	74	30

a. Develop a seasonally adjusted forecast model for seat occupancy. Forecast seat occupancy for year 6 (using a linear trend line forecast estimate for seat occupancy in year 6).

b. Develop linear regression models relating seat occupancy to discount fares to forecast seat occupancy for each quarter in year 6. Assume a fare discount of 20% for quarter 1, 36% for quarter 2, 25% for quarter 3, and 30% for quarter 4.

c. Compare the forecasts developed in parts (a) and (b) and indicate which one appears to be the best.

12.44. Develop an adjusted exponential smoothing forecast model ($\alpha = .40$ and $\beta = .40$) for the data in Problem 12.43 to forecast seat occupancy, and compare its accuracy with the seasonally adjusted model developed in Problem 12.43(a).

12.45. The consumer loan department at National Bank wants to develop a forecasting model to help determine its potential loan application volume for the coming year. Since adjustable-rate home mortgages are based on government long-term Treasury note rates, the bank has collected the following data for three- to five-year Treasury note interest rates for the past 24 years:

YEAR	RATE	YEAR	RATE	YEAR	RATE
1	5.77	3	6.92	5	7.49
2	5.85	4	7.82	6	6.67
7	6.69	13	10.45	19	8.55
8	8.29	14	11.89	20	8.26
9	9.71	15	9.64	21	6.80
10	11.55	16	7.06	22	6.12
11	14.44	17	7.68	23	5.48
12	12.92	18	8.26	24	6.09

Develop an appropriate forecast model for the bank to use to forecast Treasury note rates in the future, and indicate how accurate it appears to be compared to historical data.

12.46. The Vantage Fund is a balanced mutual fund that includes a mix of stocks and bonds. Following are the year-end share prices of the fund and Dow Jones Industrial Average for a 20-year period.

YEAR	SHARE PRICE	DJIA	YEAR	SHARE PRICE	DJIA
1	14.75	1,046	11	19.08	3,301
2	15.06	1,258	12	20.40	3,754
3	14.98	1,211	13	19.39	3,834
4	15.73	1,546	14	24.43	5,117
5	16.11	1,895	15	26.46	6,448
6	16.07	1,938	16	29.45	7,908
7	16.78	2,168	17	29.35	9,181
8	17.69	2,753	18	27.96	11,497
9	16.90	2,633	19	28.21	10,786
10	17.81	3,168	20	27.26	10,150

Develop a linear regression model for these data and forecast the fund share price for a DJIA of 12,000. Does there appear to be a strong relationship between the fund's share price and the DJIA?

12.47. Delaplane Computers gets most of its component parts from suppliers in Pacific Rim countries, who ship to the company's main distribution center near Long Beach, California, where computers are built to order for customers. This type of assembly operation at the company's distribution center allows it to carry little of its own inventory by pushing inventory down to its suppliers, who provide components as demanded. However, the suppliers also want to minimize their own inventory, and one way to do that is to develop an accurate demand forecast. Following is the demand data (units) from Delaplane for the past 24 months for one specific supplier who provides the screens for laptops.

MONTH	YEAR 1 DEMAND	YEAR 2 DEMAND
January	2447	2561
February	1826	1733
March	1755	1693
April	1456	1484
May	1529	1501
June	1633	1655
July	2346	2412
August	3784	4017

MONTH	YEAR 1 DEMAND	YEAR 2 DEMAND
September	4106	3886
October	3006	2844
November	2257	2107
December	3212	3415

Closely observe the demand data and develop a forecast model for year 3 that would be the most accurate for the supplier.

12.48. The CableCast Cable TV Company is a national chain that services the small college town where Tech, with a student population of almost 30,000, is located. The company has generally been able to handle service calls and installations in the past, but a growth trend in the town and occasional significant jumps in service requests, especially for new Internet installations, have made it more difficult for the company to determine the number of technicians and trucks it needs to maintain good service for its customers. Following is the demand for service calls during the past 36 months.

	YEAR 1	YEAR 2	YEAR 3
MONTH	SERVICE CALLS	SERVICE CALLS	SERVICE CALLS
January	1048	1155	1135
February	326	319	365
March	303	324	341
April	351	344	370
May	673	712	694
June	274	306	310
July	219	245	266
August	1347	1455	1505
September	973	1056	981
October	536	545	555
November	312	298	317
December	577	481	562

Develop a monthly forecast for the upcoming year for CableCast. What are possible reasons for the occasional increases and decreases in the monthly demand for service calls?

12.49. Chlorex, a household products company, has developed a natural, cold-water detergent called "Nature Clean." The company's marketing department thinks that sales jump when there are several major environmental (i.e., sustainability) episodes in the national media, such as an oil spill or the government issuing a major pollution report. Thus, the marketing department wants to develop a linear regression forecasting model that relates the number of "green" episodes reported monthly in the national media to monthly sales of the detergent. The marketing department had several staff members go through various media sources for the last two years and count the number of major national green episodes reported on, which, with monthly sales, is shown in the following table.

MONTH	SALES	GREEN EPISODES	MONTH	SALES	GREEN EPISODES
1	34,175	3	4	27,666	1
2	28,366	2	5	31,299	1
3	41,819	4	6	37,456	4
7	52,444	5	16	40,005	2
8	46,712	3	17	38,912	2
9	37,222	2	18	31,777	1
10	44,981	2	19	30,367	0
11	40,006	2	20	34,566	1
12	47,321	4	21	29,078	1
13	55,732	7	22	45,876	3
14	26,004	4	23	48,556	4
15	49,188	5	24	51,022	6

Develop a linear regression model and determine the sales forecast if three green episodes are reported in the media. Discuss the value and usefulness of this type of relational forecast for Chlorex's detergent sales.

12.50. Chlorex in Problem 12.49 is planning to introduce another "sustainable product," an all-purpose cleaner. The company is attempting to forecast what demand might be like five years into the future. However, it has no historical demand data to use to develop a forecast model. The marketing department has made its own estimate of first-year sales and acquired estimates for the new cleaner from four other sources—top management, the sales force, a household products trade association, and an independent marketing firm. Top management estimates first-year sales to be 34,000 units; the marketing department's estimate is 47,000 units; the sales force suggests 41,000 units; the trade association estimates first-year sales will be 28,000 units; and the independent marketing firm estimates sales will be 51,000 units. Using these estimates and the demand data and forecast model for the detergent in Problem 12.49, develop a forecast for planning purposes for year five for the new cleaner.

12.51. The admission data for freshmen at Tech during the past 10 years are as follows:

YEAR	APPLICANTS	OFFERS	% OFFERS	ACCEPTANCES	% ACCEPTANCES
1	13,876	11,200	80.7	4112	36.7
2	14,993	11,622	77.8	4354	37.3
3	14,842	11,579	78.0	4755	41.1
4	16,285	13,207	81.1	5068	38.0
5	16,922	11,382	73.2	4532	39.8
6	16,109	11,937	74.1	4655	39.0
7	15,883	11,616	73.1	4659	40.1
8	18,407	11,539	62.7	4620	40.0
9	18,838	13,138	69.7	5054	38.5
10	17,756	11,952	67.3	4822	40.3

Tech's admission objective is a class of 5000 entering freshmen, and it wants to forecast the percentage of offers it will likely have to make in order to achieve this objective.

a. Develop a linear trend line to forecast next year's applicants and percentage acceptances and use these results to estimate the percentage offers that Tech should expect to make.

b. Develop a linear trend line to forecast the percentage offers that Tech should expect to make and compare this result with the result in part (a). Which forecast do you think is more accurate?

c. Assume Tech receives 18,300 applicants in year 11. How many offers do you think it should make to get 5000 acceptances?

12.52. The Port of Charleston is considering an expansion of their container terminal. The port has experienced the following container throughput during the past 12 years, expressed as TEUs (i.e., 20 feet equivalent units, a standard unit of measure for containers).

YEAR	TEUs (1,000s)
1	526.1
2	549.4
3	606.0
4	627.0
5	695.7
6	734.9
7	761.1
8	845.4
9	1,021.1
10	1,137.1
11	1,173.6
12	1,233.4

a. Develop a linear trend line forecast for these data and forecast the number of TEUs for the next year.

b. How strong is the linear relationship for these data?

12.53. The County Arsenal Travel Soccer Club has boys and girls travel soccer teams at all age levels up to 18 years old. The club has been successful and grown in popularity over the years; however, an obstacle to its continued growth is a shortage of practice and game soccer fields in the area. The club has tried to make a case to the County Board of Supervisors for more soccer fields to accommodate the increasing number of kids who want to play on a club travel team. The number of kids who have played soccer on a club team, and the county's population for the last 10 years are as follows.

YEAR	CLUB SOCCER PLAYERS	TOWN POPULATION
1	246	38,060
2	235	38,021
3	259	38,110
4	261	38,125
5	276	38,240
6	290	38,231
7	327	38,306
8	318	38,477
9	335	38,506
10	331	38,583
11	339	38,609
12	351	38,745
13	366	39,003
14	401	39,062
15	427	39,114

The soccer club wants to develop a forecasting model to demonstrate to the board of supervisors its expected growth in the future.

a Develop a linear trend line forecast to predict the number of soccer players the club can expect next year.

b. The county planning department has told the soccer club that the county expects to grow to a population of 39,300 by next year and to 40,000 in five years. Develop a linear regression model using the county's population as a predictor of the number of club soccer players and compare this forecasting model to the one developed in part (a). Which forecasting model should the club use to support its request for new fields?

12.54. The Dean of the College of Business at State University has initiated a fund-raising campaign. One of the selling points she plans to use with potential donors is that increasing the college's private endowment will improve its ranking among business schools as published in various news magazines. She would like to demonstrate that there is a relationship between funding and the rankings. She has collected the following data showing the private endowments ($ millions), and annual budgets ($ millions) from state and private sources, for eight of State's peer institutions plus State, and the ranking of each school.

PRIVATE ENDOWMENT	ANNUAL BUDGET	RANKING
2.5	8.1	87
52.0	26.0	20
12.7	7.5	122
63.0	33.0	32
46.0	12.0	54
27.1	16.1	76
23.3	17.0	103
46.4	14.9	40
48.9	21.8	98

a. Use Excel to develop a linear regression model for the amount of the private endowment and the ranking, and forecast a ranking for a private endowment of $70 million. Does there appear to be a strong relationship between the endowment and ranking?

b. Using Excel, develop a multiple regression equation for all of these data including private endowment and annual budget, and forecast a ranking for a private endowment of $70 million and an annual budget of $40 million. How does this forecast compare to the forecast in part (a)?

12.55. Some members of management of the Fairface Cosmetics Firm believe that demand for its products is related to the promotional activities of local department stores where its cosmetics are sold. However, others in management believe that other factors, such as local demographics, are stronger determinants of demand behavior. The following data for local annual promotional expenditures for all Fairface products and local annual unit sales for Fairface lip gloss have been collected from 20 stores selected at random from different localities:

STORE	ANNUAL UNIT SALES ($1000s)	ANNUAL PROMOTIONAL EXPENDITURES ($1000s)
1	5.3	12.6
2	4.2	15.5
3	3.1	10.8
4	2.7	8.7
5	5.9	20.3
6	5.6	21.9

STORE	ANNUAL UNIT SALES ($1000s)	ANNUAL PROMOTIONAL EXPENDITURES ($1000s)
7	10.3	25.6
8	4.1	14.3
9	9.9	15.1
10	5.7	18.7
11	3.5	9.6
12	3.2	12.7
13	8.1	16.3
14	3.6	8.1
15	5.3	7.5
16	5.8	12.4
17	8.1	17.3
18	6.1	11.2
19	3.1	18.5
20	9.5	16.7

Based on these data, does it appear that the strength of the relationship between lip gloss sales and promotional expenditures is sufficient to warrant using a linear regression forecasting model? Explain your response.

12.56. The Pro Apparel company manufactures baseball-style caps with various team logos. The caps come in an assortment of designs and colors. The company has had monthly sales for the past 24 months as follows:

MONTH	DEMAND (1000s)	MONTH	DEMAND (1000s)
1	8.2	13	10.3
2	7.5	14	10.5
3	8.1	15	11.7
4	9.3	16	9.8
5	9.1	17	10.8
6	9.5	18	11.3
7	10.4	19	12.6
8	9.7	20	11.5
9	10.2	21	10.8
10	10.6	22	11.7
11	8.2	23	12.5
12	9.9	24	12.8

Develop a forecast model using the method you believe best, and justify your selection using a measure (or measures) of forecast accuracy.

12.57. State University administrators believe their freshman applications are influenced by two variables: tuition and the size of the applicant pool of eligible high school seniors in the state. The following data for an eight-year period show the tuition rates (per semester) and the sizes of the applicant pool for each year:

TUITION ($)	APPLICANT POOL	APPLICANTS
900	76,200	11,060
1250	78,050	10,900
1375	67,420	8,670
1400	70,390	9,050
1550	62,550	7,400
1625	59,230	7,100
1750	57,900	6,300
1930	60,080	6,100

a. Using Excel, develop the multiple regression equation for these data.

b. What is the coefficient of determination for this regression equation?

c. Determine the forecast for freshman applicants for a tuition rate of $1500 per semester with a pool of applicants of 60,000.

12.58. In Problem 12.41, ITown believes its printer sales are also related to the average price of its printers. It has collected historical data on average printer prices for the past 10 years as follows:

YEAR	AVERAGE PRINTER PRICES ($)
1	475
2	490
3	520
4	420
5	410
6	370
7	350
8	300
9	280
10	250

a. Using Excel, develop the multiple regression equation for these data.

b. What is the coefficient of determination for this regression equation?

c. Determine a forecast for printer sales based on personal computer sales of 1500 units and an average printer price of $300.

12.59. The manager of the Salem police department motor pool wants to develop a forecast model for annual maintenance on police cars based on mileage in the past year and age of the cars. The following data have been collected for eight different cars:

MILES DRIVEN	CAR AGE (YEARS)	MAINTENANCE COST ($)
14,320	6	$1120
15,100	7	1610
17,415	8	1545
9,370	3	900
7,230	3	650
12,045	5	1500
8,100	2	550
6,300	3	730

a. Using Excel, develop a multiple regression equation for these data.

b. What is the coefficient of determination for this regression equation?

c. Forecast the annual maintenance cost for a police car that is four years old and will be driven 10,000 miles in one year.

12.60. The busiest time of the day at the Taco Town fast-food restaurant is between 11:00 A.M. and 2:00 P.M. Taco Town's service is very labor-dependent, and a critical factor for providing quick service is the number of employees on hand during this three-hour period. In order to determine the number of employees it needs during each hour of the three-hour lunch period Taco Town requires an accurate forecasting model. Following are the number of customers served at Taco Town during each hour of the lunch period for the past 20 weekdays.

	HOUR				HOUR		
DAY	11–12	12–1	1–2	DAY	11–12	12–1	1–2
1	90	125	87	11	57	114	106
2	76	131	93	12	68	125	95
3	87	112	99	13	75	206	102
4	83	149	78	14	94	117	118
5	71	156	83	15	103	145	122
6	94	178	89	16	67	121	93
7	56	101	124	17	94	113	76
8	63	91	66	18	83	166	94
9	73	146	119	19	79	124	87
10	101	104	96	20	81	118	115

Develop a forecast model that you believe will best forecast Taco Town's customer demand for the next day and explain why you selected this model.

12.61. The State of Virginia has instituted a series of Standards of Learning (SOL) tests in math, history, English, and science that all high school students must pass with a grade of 70 before they are allowed to graduate and receive their diploma. The school superintendent of Montgomery County believes the tests are unfair because they are closely related to teacher salaries and teacher school tenure (i.e., the years a teacher has been at a school). The superintendent has sampled 12 other county school systems in the state and accumulated the following data for average teacher salaries and average teacher tenure.

SCHOOL	AVERAGE SOL SCORE	AVERAGE TEACHER SALARIES ($)	AVERAGE TEACHER TENURE (yr)
1	81	$34,300	9.3
2	78	28,700	10.1
3	76	26,500	7.6
4	77	36,200	8.2
5	84	35,900	8.8
6	86	32,500	12.7
7	79	31,800	8.4
8	91	38,200	11.5
9	68	27,100	8.3
10	73	31,500	7.3
11	90	37,600	12.3
12	85	40,400	14.2

a. Using Excel, develop the multiple regression equation for these data.

b. What is the coefficient of determination for this regression equation? Do you think the superintendent is correct in his beliefs?

c. Montgomery County has an average SOL score of 74 with an average teacher's salary of $27,500 and an average teacher tenure of 7.8 years. The superintendent has proposed to the school board a salary increase that would raise the average salary to $30,000 and a benefits program with a goal of increasing the average tenure to nine years. He has suggested that if the board passes his proposals the average SOL score will increase to 80. Is he correct according to the forecasting model?

Case Problems

Case Problem 12.1 Forecasting at State University

During the past few years the legislature has severely reduced funding for State University. In reaction, the administration at State has significantly raised tuition each year for the past five years. A bargain five years ago, State is now considered an expensive state-supported university. Some parents and students now question the value of a State education, and applications for admission have declined. Since a portion of state educational funding is based on a formula tied to enrollments, State has maintained its enrollment levels by going deeper into its applicant pool and accepting less qualified students.

On top of these problems, an increase in the college-age population is expected in this decade. Key members of the state legislature have told the university administration that State will be expected to absorb additional students during this decade. However, because of the economic outlook and the budget situation, State should not expect any funding increases for additional facilities, classrooms, dormitory rooms, or faculty. The university already has a classroom deficit in excess of 25%, and class sizes are above the average of their peer institutions.

The president of the university, Tanisha Lindsey, established several task forces consisting of faculty and administrators to address these problems. These groups made a number of recommendations, including the implementation of total quality management (TQM) practices and more in-depth, focused planning.

Discuss in general terms how forecasting might be used for planning to address these specific problems and the role of forecasting in initiating a TQM approach. Include in your discussion the types of forecasting methods that might be used.

Case Problem 12.2 The University Bookstore Student Computer Purchase Program

The University Bookstore is owned and operated by State University through an independent corporation with its own board of directors. The bookstore has three locations on or near the State University campus. It stocks a range of items, including textbooks, trade books, logo apparel, drawing and educational supplies, and computers and related products such as printers, modems, and software. The bookstore has a program to sell personal computers to incoming freshmen and other students at a substantial educational discount partly passed on from computer manufacturers. This means that the bookstore just covers computer costs with a very small profit margin remaining.

Each summer all incoming freshmen and their parents come to the State campus for a three-day orientation program. The students come in groups of 100 throughout the summer. During their visit the students and their parents are given details about the bookstore's computer purchase program. Some students place their computer orders for the fall semester at this time, while others wait until later in the summer. The bookstore also receives orders from returning students throughout the summer. This program presents a challenging supply chain management problem for the bookstore.

Orders come in throughout the summer, many only a few weeks before school starts in the fall, and the computer suppliers require at least six weeks for delivery. Thus, the bookstore must forecast computer demand to build up inventory to meet student demand in the fall. The student computer program and the forecast of computer demand have repercussions all along the bookstore supply chain. The bookstore has a warehouse near campus where it must store all computers since it has no storage space at its retail locations. Ordering too many computers not only ties up the bookstore's cash reserves but also takes up limited storage space and limits inventories for other bookstore products during the bookstore's busiest sales period. Since the bookstore has such a low profit margin on computers, its bottom line depends on these other products. As competition for good students has increased, the university has become very quality-conscious and insists that all university facilities provide exemplary student service, which for the bookstore means meeting all student demands for computers when the fall semester starts. The number of computers ordered also affects the number of temporary warehouse and bookstore workers that must be hired for handling and assisting with PC installations. The number of truck trips from the warehouse to the bookstore each day of fall registration is also affected by computer sales.

The bookstore student computer purchase program has been in place for 14 years. Although the student population has remained stable during this period, computer sales have been somewhat volatile. Following is the historical sales data for computers during the first month of fall registration:

YEAR	COMPUTERS SOLD	YEAR	COMPUTERS SOLD
1	518	8	792
2	651	9	877
3	708	10	693
4	921	11	841
5	775	12	1009
6	810	13	902
7	856	14	1103

Develop an appropriate forecast model for bookstore management to use to forecast computer demand for the next fall semester and indicate how accurate it appears to be. What other forecasts might be useful to the bookstore in managing its supply chain?

Case Problem 12.3 Cascades Swim Club

The Cascades Swim Club has 300 stockholders, each holding one share of stock in the club. A share of club stock allows the shareholder's family to use the club's heated outdoor pool during the summer upon payment of annual membership dues of $175. The club has not issued any stock in years, and only a few of the existing shares come up for sale each year. The board of directors administers the sale of all stock. When a shareholder wants to sell, he or she turns the stock into the board, which sells it to the person at the top of the waiting list. For the past few years, the length of the waiting list has remained relatively steady at approximately 20 names.

However, during the past winter two events occurred that have suddenly increased the demand for shares in the club. The winter was especially severe, and subzero weather and heavy ice storms caused both the town and the county pools to buckle and crack. The problems were not discovered until maintenance crews began to prepare the pools for the summer, and repairs cannot be completed until the fall. Also during the winter, the manager of the local country club had an argument with her board of directors and one night burned down the clubhouse. Although the pool itself was not damaged, the dressing room facilities, showers, and snack bar were destroyed. As a result of these two events, the Cascades Swim Club was inundated with applications to purchase shares. The waiting list suddenly grew to 250 people as the summer approached.

The board of directors of the swim club had refrained from issuing new shares in the past because there never was a very great demand, and the demand that did exist was usually absorbed within a year by stock turnover. In addition, the board has a real concern about overcrowding. It seemed that the present membership was about right, and there were very few complaints about overcrowding, except on holidays such as Memorial Day and the Fourth of July. However, at a recent board meeting a number of new applicants had attended and asked the board to issue new shares. In addition, a number of current shareholders suggested that this might be an opportunity for the club to raise some capital for needed repairs and to improve some of the existing facilities. This was tempting to the board. Although it had set the share price at $500 in the past, the board could set it at a much higher level now. In addition, an increase in attendance could create a need for more lifeguards.

Before the board of directors could make a decision on whether to sell more shares and, if so, how many, the board members felt they needed more information. Specifically, they would like a forecast of the average number of people (family members, guests, etc.) who might attend the pool each day during the summer with the current number of shares.

The board of directors has the following daily attendance records for June through August from the previous summer; it thinks the figures would provide accurate estimates for the upcoming summer.

M-139	W-380	F-193	Su-399	T-177	Th-238
T-273	Th-367	Sa-378	M-197	W-161	F-224
W-172	F-359	Su-461	T-273	Th-308	Sa-368
Th-275	Sa-463	M-242	W-213	F-256	Su-541
F-337	Su-578	T-177	Th-303	Sa-391	M-235
Sa-402	M-287	W-245	F-262	Su-400	T-218
Su-487	T-247	Th-390	Sa-447	M-224	W-271
M-198	W-356	F-284	Su-399	T-239	Th-259
T-310	Th-322	Sa-417	M-275	W-274	F-232
W-347	F-419	Su-474	T-241	Th-205	Sa-317

Th-393	Sa-516	M-194	W-190	F-361	Su-369
F-421	Su-478	T-207	Th-243	Sa-411	M-361
Sa-595	M-303	W-215	F-277	Su-419	
Su-497	T-223	Th-304	Sa-241	M-258	
M-341	W-315	F-331	Su-384	T-130	
T-291	Th-258	Sa-407	M-246	W-195	

Develop a forecasting model to forecast daily demand during the summer.

Case Problem 12.4 Forecasting Passenger Arrivals at the Gotham International Airport

Since the terrorist attacks of 9/11 and the ensuing measures by the federal Transportation Security Administration (TSA) to increase airline security, airports have faced the problem of long waiting lines and waiting times at security gates. One of the key components of any effort by the TSA to operationally improve airport security procedures while reducing passenger waiting times and inconvenience is forecasting passenger arrivals at security checkpoints in order to determine how many security checkpoints and staff are needed. At the Gotham International Airport, TSA operations analysts would like to forecast passenger arrivals for next July, the airport's busiest travel month of the year, for the purpose of determining how many security checkpoints they should staff during the month in order that waiting lines and times will not be excessively long. Demand for airline travel has generally been increasing during the past three years. There are two main concourses at Gotham International, East and West, each serving different airlines. The following table shows passenger arrivals at the West concourse for 10 days (selected randomly) in two-hour segments from 4:00 A.M. to 10:00 P.M. for the month of July for the past three years.

	DAY	4–6 A.M.	6–8 A.M.	8–10 A.M.	10–NOON	NOON–2 P.M.	2–4 P.M.	4–6 P.M.	6–8 P.M.	8–10 P.M.
	1	2400	2700	3200	1400	1700	1800	1600	800	200
	2	1900	2500	3100	1600	1800	2000	1800	900	300
	3	2300	3100	2500	1500	1500	1800	1900	1100	200
	4	2200	3200	3100	2200	1900	2400	2100	1200	400
Year 1	5	2400	3300	3400	1700	2200	2100	2000	1000	600
	6	2600	2800	3500	1500	1700	1900	1500	1100	300
	7	1900	2800	3100	1200	1500	2000	1400	900	400
	8	2000	2700	2500	1500	2000	2300	1900	1000	200
	9	2400	3200	3600	1600	2100	2500	1800	1400	200
	10	2600	3300	3100	200	2500	2600	2400	1100	400
	11	3100	3900	4100	2200	2600	2300	2500	1100	300
	12	2800	3400	3900	1900	2100	2500	2000	1200	300
	13	2700	3800	4300	2100	2400	2400	2400	1200	400
	14	2400	3500	4100	2400	3000	3200	2600	1200	700
Year 2	15	3300	3700	4000	2600	2600	2700	2900	1000	300
	16	3500	4000	3800	2300	2700	3100	3000	900	200
	17	2900	4100	3900	2400	3000	3200	2500	1100	500
	18	3400	3800	4200	2000	2500	3000	2200	1000	300
	19	3600	3600	4000	2300	2600	2800	2600	1200	200
	20	3700	3700	4000	2200	2600	2700	2400	1200	200
	21	4400	4400	4500	2600	3300	3400	3000	1200	400
	22	4200	4500	4300	2500	3400	3600	3100	1400	300
	23	4500	4500	4700	2700	3400	3500	2900	1200	300
	24	4600	4600	4600	2500	3200	3500	2800	1300	300
Year 3	25	4500	4300	4400	2900	3300	3300	3300	1500	400
	26	4200	4300	4500	3000	4000	3400	3000	1500	600
	27	4500	4500	5100	3300	4000	3700	3100	1200	300
	28	4300	4200	4300	2800	3500	4000	3300	1100	400
	29	4900	4100	4200	3100	3600	3900	3400	1400	500
	30	4700	4500	4100	3000	4000	3700	3400	1200	500

Develop a forecast for daily passenger arrivals at the West concourse at Gotham for each time period for July of year 4. Discuss the various forecast model variations that might be used to develop this forecast.

References

Box, G. E. P., and G. M. Jenkins. *Time Series Analysis: Forecasting and Control*, 2nd ed. Oakland, CA: Holden-Day, 1976.

Brown, R. G. *Statistical Forecasting for Inventory Control*. New York: McGraw-Hill, 1959.

Chambers, J. C., K. M. Satinder, and D. D. Smith. "How to Choose the Right Forecasting Technique." *Harvard Business Review* (July–August 1971), pp. 45–74.

Gardner, E. S. "Exponential Smoothing: The State of the Art." *Journal of Forecasting* 4(1; 1985).

Gardner, E. S., and D. G. Dannenbring. "Forecasting with Exponential Smoothing: Some Guidelines for Model Selection." *Decision Sciences* 11(2; 1980), pp. 370–383.

Makridakis, S., S. C. Wheelwright, and V. E. McGee. *Forecasting: Methods and Applications,* 2nd ed. New York: John Wiley, 1983.

Tersine, R. J., and W. Riggs. "The Delphi Technique: A Long-Range Planning Tool." *Business Horizons* 19(2; 1976).

CHAPTER 13

Inventory Management

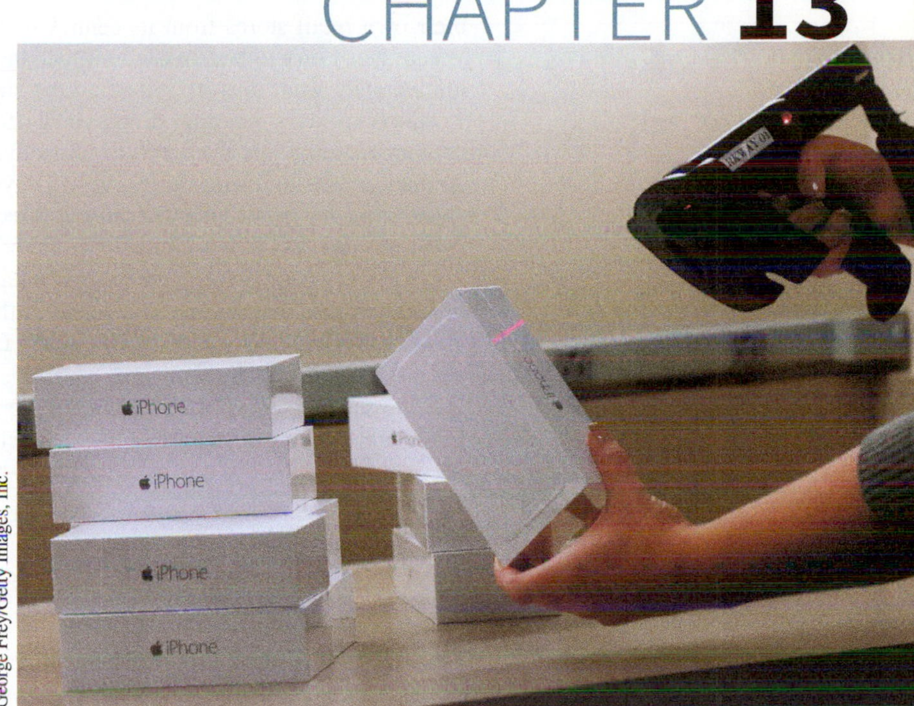

George Frey/Getty Images, Inc.

LEARNING OBJECTIVES

After reading this chapter, you will be able to:

- Explain why companies keep inventory and how advances in IT have impacted inventory decisions.
- Discuss the key elements and costs of inventory, and the relationship between inventory costs and customer service.
- Contrast continuous and periodic inventory systems, and classify inventory according to the ABC system.
- Utilize basic inventory models to calculate order quantity and related measures, as well as the annual cost of inventory.
- Determine the appropriate reorder point in a continuous inventory system based on a target service level.
- Calculate the order quantity for a periodic inventory system.

World-class Inventory Management at Apple

From 2008 to 2014 Apple ranked first every year in the Gartner Supply Chain Top 25 ranking, and in 2015 it was placed (with Proctor & Gamble) in a new "Supply Chain Masters" category that recognizes a company's sustained supply chain leadership. A primary reason for Apple's supply chain success and this ultimate special categorization is how it manages its inventory. Accurate demand forecasting and eliminating excess inventory is absolutely critical in the computer-related industry. Keeping little inventory on hand is important because of inventory (warehouse) costs and new products from competitors. A sudden new product announcement or a new innovation can immediately reduce the value of products in inventory. New products cannibalize old ones very quickly and the inventory for technology like smartphones, tablets, and laptops depreciates very rapidly, losing an estimated 1% to 2% of value each week. Apple CEO, Tim Cook, has stated that "inventory is fundamentally evil. You kind of want to manage it like you're in the dairy business. If it gets past its freshness date, you have a problem."

Apple manages its inventory much better than competitors like Samsung, Dell, and Motorola, with a higher number of inventory turns (i.e., how many times a company's inventory can be sold and replaced over a specific period of time). In general, a fundamental part of Apple's inventory management planning process is to sell everything it makes, with no waste from unsold inventory. Apple operates its supply chain by purchasing components and materials from various suppliers, has them shipped to assembly plants primarily in China, and then ships the finished products directly to their customers (via UPS and FedEx) who purchase them online. Apple ships products to other distributors and their own retail stores from its central warehouse and call center in Elk Grove, California. When Tim Cook joined Apple in 1998 (the same year Steve Jobs rejoined the company) he immediately went to work remaking the supply chain by slashing inventory from a month's worth to six days, shutting down 10 of 19 warehouses to limit overstocking, and reducing component suppliers from 100 to 24 to make them compete for Apple's business. By 2012 Apple was turning its inventory every 5 days compared to Samsung's 21 days. Apple is better able to manage its inventory because it forecasts demand better than its competitors by having fewer product SKUs to keep track of, and because its products tend to have a longer life cycle. The company has also been remarkably adept at predicting (and sometimes initiating) the kind of technologies that will be in demand in the future, which limits imitations, and which also allows them to place orders with suppliers farther in advance, thus reducing costs and closing out competitors' orders.

In this chapter we will learn about some of the different inventory models, techniques, and technologies companies use to determine the lowest-cost amount of inventory to order and keep on hand, which is one of the primary objectives of supply chain management.

Source: Based on Clara Lu, "Apple Had the Best Supply Chain in the World for the Last Four years – Here is What You Can Learn from It," http://www.tradegecko.com (April 3, 2014).

The objective of inventory management has been to keep enough inventory to meet customer demand and also be cost effective. However, inventory has not always been perceived as an area to control cost. Traditionally, companies maintained "generous" inventory levels to meet long-term customer demand because there were fewer competitors and products in a generally sheltered market environment. In the current global business environment, with more competitors and highly diverse markets in which new products and new product features are rapidly and continually introduced, the cost of inventory has increased due in part to quicker product obsolescence. At the same time, companies are continuously seeking to lower costs so they can provide a better product at a "lower" price.

Inventory is an obvious candidate for cost reduction. It is estimated that U.S. companies carry over a half trillion dollars in inventory spread out along their supply chains. It is also estimated that the average holding cost of inventory in the United States is between 18% and 35% of the total value of the inventory. That means if a company has \$10 million worth of products in inventory, and the cost of holding the inventory (including insurance, obsolescence, depreciation, interest, opportunity costs, storage costs, and so on) is approximately 30% or \$3 million; if inventory could be reduced by half, to \$5 million, then \$1.5 million would be saved, a significant cost reduction.

The high cost of inventory has motivated companies to focus on efficient supply chain management and quality management. They believe that inventory can be significantly reduced by reducing uncertainty at various points along the supply chain. In many cases, uncertainty is created by poor quality on the part of the company or its suppliers or both. This can be in the form of variations in delivery times, uncertain production schedules caused by late deliveries, or large numbers of defects that require higher levels of production or service than what should be necessary, large fluctuations in customer demand, or poor forecasts of customer demand.

With efficient supply chain management, products or services are moved from one stage in the supply chain to the next according to a system of constant communication between customers and suppliers. Items are replaced as they are diminished without maintaining larger buffer stocks of inventory at each stage to compensate for late deliveries, inefficient service, poor quality, or uncertain demand. An efficient, well-coordinated supply chain reduces or eliminates these types of uncertainty so that this type of system will work.

Some companies maintain in-process, buffer inventories between production stages to offset irregularities and problems and keep the supply chain flowing smoothly. Quality-oriented companies consider large buffer inventories to be a costly crutch that masks problems and inefficiency primarily caused by poor quality. Adherents of quality management believe that inventory should be minimized. However, this works primarily for a production or manufacturing process. For the retailer who sells finished goods directly to the consumer or the supplier who sells parts or materials to the manufacturer, inventory is a necessity. Few shoe stores, discount stores, or department stores can stay in business with only one or two items on their shelves or racks. For these supply chains, the traditional inventory decisions of how much to order and when to order continue to be important. In addition, the traditional approaches to inventory management are still widely used by most companies.

In this chapter we review the basic elements of traditional inventory management and discuss several of the more popular models and techniques for making cost-effective inventory decisions. These decisions are basically *how much to order* and *when to order* to replenish inventory to an optimal level.

The Role of Inventory in Supply Chain Management

A company employs an inventory strategy for many reasons. The main reason is holding inventories of finished goods to meet customer demand for a product, especially in a retail operation. However, customer demand can also be a secretary going to a storage closet to get a printer cartridge or paper, or a carpenter getting a board or nails from a storage shed.

Since demand is usually not known with certainty, it is not possible to produce exactly the amount demanded. An additional amount of inventory, called safety, or buffer, stocks, is kept on hand to meet variations in product demand. In the *bullwhip effect* (which we have discussed previously in our chapters on supply chain and forecasting), demand information is distorted as it moves away from the end-use customer. This uncertainty about demand back upstream in the supply chain causes distributors, manufacturers, and suppliers to stock increasingly higher safety stock inventories to compensate.

Additional stocks of inventories are sometimes built up to meet demand that is seasonal or cyclical. Companies will continue to produce items when demand is low to meet high seasonal demand for which their production capacity is insufficient. For example, toy manufacturers produce large inventories during the summer and fall to meet anticipated demand during the holiday season. Doing so enables them to maintain a relatively smooth supply chain flow throughout the year. They would not normally have the production capacity or logistical support to produce enough to meet all of the holiday demand during that season. In the same way retailers might find it necessary to keep large stocks of inventory on their shelves to meet peak seasonal demand, or for display purposes to attract buyers.

At the other end of the supply chain from finished goods inventory, a company might keep large stocks of parts and material inventory to meet variations in supplier deliveries. Inventory provides independence from vendors that a company does not have direct control over. Inventories of raw materials and purchased parts are kept on hand so that the production process will not be delayed as a result of missed or late deliveries or shortages from a supplier.

A company will purchase large amounts of inventory to take advantage of price discounts, as a hedge against anticipated price increases in the future, or because it can get a lower price by purchasing in volume. Walmart stores have been known to purchase a manufacturer's entire stock of soap powder or other retail item because they can get a very low price, which they subsequently pass on to their customers. Companies purchase large stocks of low-priced items when a supplier liquidates. In some cases, large orders will be made simply because the cost of ordering may be very high, and it is more cost-effective to have higher inventories than to order frequently.

Many companies find it necessary to maintain buffer inventories at different stages of their production process to provide independence between stages and to avoid work stoppages or delays. Inventories are kept between stages in the manufacturing process so that production can continue smoothly if there are temporary machine breakdowns or other work stoppages. Similarly, a stock of finished parts or products allows customer demand to be met in the event of a work stoppage or problem with transportation or distribution.

Information Technology and Inventory Management

As we pointed out in previous chapters, information technology (IT) has become an enabler for effective supply chain management. Traditionally inventory was owned by the buyer (as opposed to the supplier), it was kept at the buyer's location, and the buyer controlled how and when its inventory was replenished. However, in recent years these traditional aspects of inventory management have changed, due in large part to advances in IT. Because of technology and software—including such IT tools as enterprises resource planning (ERP) systems (including forecasting software), barcodes, radio frequency identification (RFID), EDI, and point-of-sales data—companies can track and locate inventory throughout their supply chain, which enables them to locate inventory somewhere other than their own facility, and control it remotely or have someone else control it. These technologies have enabled modern supply chain management practices such as vendor managed inventory (VMI), continuous replenishment programs (CRP), supplier hubs, and outsourcing operations to third-party service providers (3PL). In these practices inventory can be located at the supplier's facility, at the buyer's, or somewhere in between. Unlike traditional practices, the supplier owns inventory until the buyer needs it and it is delivered, thus relieving the buyer of inventory costs; order sizes are reduced, deliveries (which the supplier pays for) are increased, and the buyer avoids maintaining storage facilities. However, for this to be effective the supplier must be able to minimize its own inventory costs and optimize its own supply chain, which can be achieved if the buyer shares end-use demand and sales data with its suppliers through IT. This enables suppliers to make replenishment decisions and provide inventory to the buyer, as it's needed. A recent supply chain management practice is for inventory to be located at "supplier hubs" that are usually at, or in very close proximity to, the buyer, and are often owned and operated by a 3PL provider, which shifts all responsibility and liability for inventory to the suppliers that share the hub. For a supplier hub to work, the supply chain members—buyers, suppliers, and 3PL providers—must share information through information technology. The 3PL provider uses information provided by the buyer and suppliers (including forecasts and sales data) to consolidate shipping among suppliers, plan and execute all logistics, connect and coordinate all supply chain members through an IT system, and operate the hub facility. Supplier hubs are being used successfully by such companies as Dell, Apple, Fiat, Hewlett-Packard, Nokia, Cisco, Sam's Club, Samsung, and Volkswagen.

Inventory and Quality Management in the Supply Chain

A company maintains inventory to meet its own demand and its customers' demand for items in the supply chain. The ability to meet effectively internal organizational demand or external customer demand in a timely, efficient manner is referred to as the *level of customer service*. A primary objective of supply chain management is to provide as high a level of customer service in terms of on-time delivery as possible. This is especially important in today's highly competitive business environment, where quality is such an important product characteristic. Customers for finished goods usually perceive quality service as availability of goods they want when they want them. (This is equally true of internal customers, such as company departments or employees.) To provide this level of quality customer service, the tendency is to maintain large stocks of all types of items. However, there is a cost associated with carrying items in inventory, which creates a cost tradeoff between the quality level of customer service and the cost of that service.

As the level of inventory increases to provide better customer service, inventory costs increase, whereas quality-related customer service costs, such as lost sales and loss of customers, decrease. The conventional approach to inventory management is to maintain a level of inventory that reflects a compromise between inventory costs and customer service. However, according to the contemporary "zero defects" philosophy of quality management, the long-term benefits of quality in terms of larger market share outweigh lower short-term production-related costs, such as inventory costs. Attempting to apply this philosophy to inventory management is not simple because one way of competing in today's diverse business environment is to reduce prices through reduced inventory costs.

The Elements of Inventory Management

Inventory A stock of items kept to meet demand.

Inventory is a stock of items kept by an organization to meet internal or external customer demand. Virtually every type of organization maintains some form of inventory. Department stores and grocery stores carry inventories of all the retail products they sell; a nursery has inventories of different plants, trees, and flowers; a rental-car agency has inventories of cars; and a major league baseball team maintains an inventory of players on its minor league teams. Even a family household maintains inventories of items such as food, clothing, medical supplies, and personal hygiene products.

Most people think of inventory as a final product waiting to be sold to a retail customer—a new car or a can of tomatoes. This is certainly one of its most important uses. However, especially in a manufacturing firm, inventory can take on forms besides finished goods, including:

- Raw materials
- Purchased parts and supplies
- Partially complete work in process (WIP)
- Items being transported
- Tools and equipment

The purpose of *inventory management* is to determine the amount of inventory to keep in stock—how much to order and when to replenish, or order. In this chapter we describe several different inventory systems and techniques for making these determinations.

Demand

The starting point for the management of inventory is customer demand. Inventory exists to meet customer demand. Customers can be inside the organization, such as a machine operator waiting for a part or partially completed product to work on. Customers can also be outside the organization—for example, an individual purchasing groceries or a new DVD player. In either case, an essential determinant of effective inventory management is an accurate forecast of demand. For this reason the topics of forecasting (Chapter 12) and inventory management are directly interrelated.

In general, the demand for items in inventory is either dependent or independent. **Dependent demand** items are typically component parts or materials used in the process of producing a final product. If an automobile company plans to produce 1000 new cars, then it will need 5000 wheels and tires (including spares). The demand for wheels is dependent on the production of cars—the demand for one item depends on demand for another item (see photo).

Dependent demand Items are used internally to produce a final product.

Cars, retail items, grocery products, and office supplies are examples of independent demand items. **Independent demand** items are final or finished products that are not a function of, or dependent on, internal production activity. Independent demand is usually determined by external market conditions and, thus, is beyond the direct control of the organization. In this chapter we focus on the management of inventory for independent demand items.

Independent demand Items are final products demanded by external customers.

Bloomberg/Getty Images, Inc.

These offloaded cars at a port are an example of independent demand, as are appliances, computers, and houses. The tires on these cars are an example of a dependent demand item.

Inventory Costs

Three basic costs are associated with inventory: carrying, or holding, costs; ordering costs; and shortage costs.

Carrying costs The costs of holding an item in inventory.

Carrying (or holding) costs are the costs of holding items in inventory. Annual inventory carrying costs in the United States are estimated to be over $400 billion. These costs vary with the level of inventory in stock and occasionally with the length of time an item is held. That is, the greater the level of inventory over a period of time, the higher the carrying costs. In general, any cost that grows linearly with the number of units in stock is a carrying cost. Carrying costs can include the following items:

- Facility storage (rent, depreciation, power, heat, cooling, lighting, security, refrigeration, taxes, insurance, etc.)
- Material handling (equipment)
- Labor
- Record keeping
- Borrowing to purchase inventory (interest on loans, taxes, insurance)
- Product deterioration, spoilage, breakage, obsolescence, pilferage

Carrying costs are normally specified in one of two ways. The usual way is to assign total carrying costs, determined by summing all the individual costs just mentioned, on a per-unit basis per time period, such as a month or year. In this form, carrying costs are commonly expressed as a per-unit dollar amount on an annual basis; for example, $10 per unit per year. Alternatively, carrying costs are sometimes expressed as a percentage of the value of an item or as a percentage of average inventory value. It is generally estimated that carrying costs range from 10% to 40% of the value of a manufactured item.

Ordering costs The costs of replenishing inventory.

Ordering costs are the costs associated with replenishing the stock of inventory being held. These are normally expressed as a dollar amount per order and are independent of the order size. Annual ordering costs vary with the number of orders made—as the number of orders increases, the ordering cost increases. In general, any cost that increases linearly with the number of orders is an ordering cost. Costs incurred each time an order is made can include requisition and purchase orders, transportation and shipping, receiving, inspection, handling, and accounting and auditing costs.

Ordering costs react inversely to carrying costs. As the size of orders increases, fewer orders are required, reducing ordering costs. However, ordering larger amounts results in higher inventory levels and higher carrying costs. In general, as the order size increases, ordering costs decrease and carrying costs increase.

Shortage costs Temporary or permanent loss of sales when demand cannot be met.

Shortage costs, also referred to as *stockout costs*, occur when customer demand cannot be met because of insufficient inventory. If these shortages result in a permanent loss of sales, shortage costs include the loss of profits. Shortages can also cause customer dissatisfaction and a loss of goodwill that can result in a permanent loss of customers and future sales. Some studies have shown that approximately 8% of shoppers will not find the product they want to purchase in stock, which will ultimately result in total lost sales of about 3%.

In some instances, the inability to meet customer demand or lateness in meeting demand results in penalties in the form of price discounts or rebates. When demand is internal, a shortage can cause work stoppages in the production process and create delays, resulting in downtime costs and the cost of lost production (including indirect and direct production costs).

Costs resulting from lost sales because demand cannot be met are more difficult to determine than carrying or ordering costs. Therefore, shortage costs are frequently subjective estimates and sometimes an educated guess.

Shortages occur because carrying inventory is costly. As a result, shortage costs have an inverse relationship to carrying costs—as the amount of inventory on hand increases, the carrying cost increases, whereas shortage costs decrease.

The objective of inventory management is to employ an inventory control system that will indicate how much should be ordered and when orders should take place so that the sum of the three inventory costs just described will be minimized.

Inventory Control Systems

An inventory system controls the level of inventory by determining how much to order (the level of replenishment) and when to order. There are two basic types of inventory systems: a *continuous* (or *fixed-order-quantity*) *system* and a *periodic* (or *fixed-time-period*) *system.* In a continuous system, an order is placed for the same constant amount whenever the inventory on hand decreases to a certain level, whereas in a periodic system, an order is placed for a variable amount after specific regular intervals.

Continuous Inventory Systems

Continuous inventory system A constant amount is ordered when inventory declines to a predetermined level.

In a **continuous inventory system** (also referred to as a *perpetual system* and a *fixed-order-quantity system*), a continual record of the inventory level for every item is maintained. Whenever the inventory on hand decreases to a predetermined level, referred to as the *reorder point*, a new order is placed to replenish the stock of inventory. The order that is placed is for a fixed amount that minimizes the total inventory costs. This amount, called the *economic order quantity*, is discussed in greater detail later.

A positive feature of a continuous system is that the inventory level is continuously monitored, so management always knows the inventory status. This is advantageous for critical items such as replacement parts or raw materials and supplies. However, maintaining a continual record of the amount of inventory on hand can also be costly.

A simple example of a continuous inventory system is a ledger-style checkbook that many of us use on a daily basis. Our checkbook comes with 300 checks; after the 200th check has been used (and there are 100 left), there is an order form for a new batch of checks. This form, when turned in at the bank, initiates an order for a new batch of 300 checks. Many office inventory systems use *reorder cards* that are placed within stacks of stationery or at the bottom of a case of pens or paper clips to signal when a new order should be placed. If you look behind the items on a hanging rack in a Kmart store, there will be a card indicating it is time to place an order for the item for an amount indicated on the card.

Continuous inventory systems often incorporate information technology tools to improve the speed and accuracy of data entry. A familiar example is the computerized checkout system with a laser scanner used by many supermarkets and retail stores. The laser scanner reads the universal product code (UPC), or bar code, from the product package; the transaction is instantly recorded and the inventory level updated. Such a system is not only quick and accurate, it also provides management with continuously updated information on the status of inventory levels. Many manufacturing companies' suppliers and distributors also use bar code systems and handheld laser scanners to inventory materials, supplies, equipment, in-process parts, and finished goods, as shown in the photo.

Periodic Inventory Systems

Periodic inventory system An order is placed for a variable amount after a fixed passage of time.

In a **periodic inventory system** (also referred to as a *fixed-time-period system* or a *periodic review system*), the inventory on hand is counted at specific time intervals—for example, every week or at the end of each month. After the inventory in stock is determined, an order is placed for an amount that will bring inventory back up to a desired level. In this system, the inventory level is not monitored at all during the time interval between orders, so it has the advantage of little or no required record keeping. The disadvantage is less direct control. This typically results in larger inventory levels for a periodic inventory system than in a continuous system to guard against unexpected stockouts early in the fixed period. Such a system also requires that a new order quantity be determined each time a periodic order is made.

An example of a periodic inventory system is a college or university bookstore. Textbooks are normally ordered according to a periodic system, wherein a count of textbooks in stock (for every course) is made after the first few weeks of a semester or quarter. An order for new textbooks for the next semester is then made according to estimated course enrollments for the next term (i.e., demand) and the amount remaining in stock. Smaller retail stores, drugstores, grocery stores, and offices sometimes use periodic systems—the stock level is checked every week or month, often by a vendor, to see how much should be ordered.

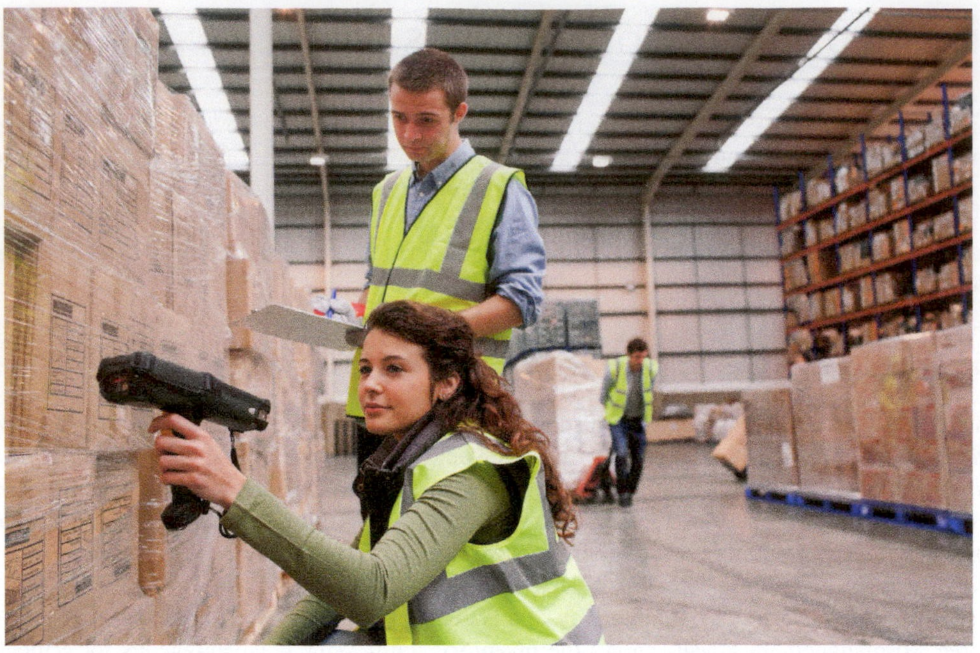

To consumers the most familiar type of bar code scanner is used with cash registers at retail stores, where the bar code is a single line with 11 digits, the first 6 identifying a manufacturer and the last 5 assigned to a specific product by the manufacturer. This employee is using a portable hand-held bar code scanner to scan a bar code for inventory control. In addition to identifying the product, it can indicate where a product came from, where it is supposed to go, and how the product should be handled in transit.

Clerkenwell_Images/iStockphoto

The ABC Classification System

ABC system An inventory classification system in which a small percentage of (A) items account for most of the inventory value.

The **ABC system** is a method for classifying inventory according to several criteria, including its dollar value to the firm. Typically, thousands of independent demand items are held in inventory by a company, especially in manufacturing, but a small percentage is of such a high dollar value to warrant close inventory control. In general, about 5% to 15% of all inventory items account for 70% to 80% of the total dollar value of inventory. These are classified as *A*, or *Class A*, items. *B* items represent approximately 30% of total inventory units but only about 15% of total inventory dollar value. *C* items generally account for 50% to 60% of all inventory units but represent only 5% to 10% of total dollar value. For example, a discount store such as Walmart normally stocks a relatively small number of televisions, a somewhat larger number of bicycles or sets of sheets, and hundreds of boxes of soap powder, bottles of shampoo, and AA batteries. Figure 13.1 shows the approximate ABC classes.

In ABC analysis each class of inventory requires different levels of inventory monitoring and control—the higher the value of the inventory, the tighter the control. Class A items should experience tight inventory control; B and C require more relaxed (perhaps minimal)

FIGURE 13.1 ABC Classifications

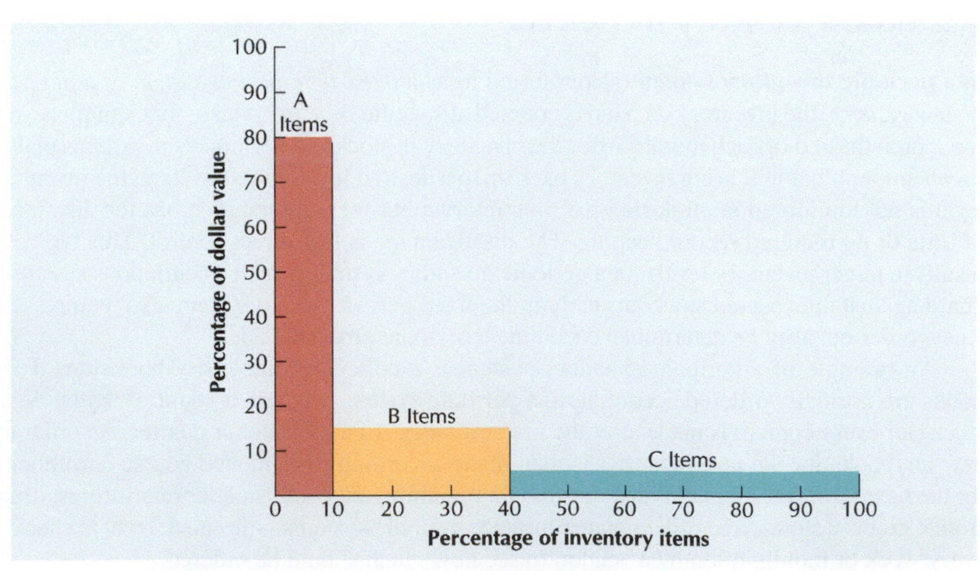

attention. However, the original rationale for ABC analysis was that continuous inventory monitoring was expensive and not justified for many items. The wide use of bar code scanners may have eroded that reasoning. At least for larger companies, bar codes have made continuous monitoring cheap enough to use for all item classes.

The first step in ABC analysis is to classify all inventory items as A, B, or C. Each item is assigned a dollar value, which is computed by multiplying the dollar cost of one unit by the annual demand for that item. All items are then ranked according to their annual dollar value, with, for example, the top 10% classified as A items, the next 30% as B items, and the last 60% as C items. These classifications will not be exact, but they have been found to be close to the actual occurrence in firms with remarkable frequency.

The next step is to determine the level of inventory control for each classification. Class A items require tight inventory control because they represent such a large percentage of the total dollar value of inventory. These inventory levels should be as low as possible, and safety stocks minimized. This requires accurate demand forecasts and detailed record keeping. The appropriate inventory control system and inventory modeling procedure to determine order quantity should be applied. In addition, close attention should be given to purchasing policies and procedures if the inventory items are acquired from outside the firm. B and C items require less stringent inventory control. Since carrying costs are usually lower for C items, higher inventory levels can sometimes be maintained with larger safety stocks. It may not be necessary to control C items beyond simple observation. In general, A items frequently require a continuous control system, where the inventory level is continuously monitored; a periodic review system with less monitoring will suffice for C items.

Although cost is the predominant reason for inventory classification, other factors such as scarcity of parts or difficulty of supply may also be reasons for giving items a higher priority. For example, long lead times for some parts might be a problem for a company in Australia ordering from Europe, thus requiring a higher-priority classification for those parts.

EXAMPLE 13.1 | ABC System Classification

The maintenance department for a small manufacturing firm has responsibility for maintaining an inventory of spare parts for the machinery it services. The parts inventory, unit cost, and annual usage are as follows:

PART	UNIT COST	ANNUAL USAGE
1	$60	90
2	350	40
3	30	130
4	80	60
5	30	100
6	20	180
7	10	170
8	320	50
9	510	60
10	20	120

The department manager wants to classify the inventory parts according to the ABC system to determine which stocks of parts should most closely be monitored.

Solution: First rank the items according to their total value and also compute each item's percentage of total value and quantity.

PART	TOTAL VALUE	% OF TOTAL VALUE	% OF TOTAL QUANTITY	% CUMULATIVE
9	$30,600	35.9	6.0	6.0
8	16,000	18.7	5.0	11.0
2	14,000	16.4	4.0	15.0
1	5,400	6.3	9.0	24.0
4	4,800	5.6	6.0	30.0
3	3,900	4.6	13.0	43.0
6	3,600	4.2	18.0	61.0
5	3,000	3.5	10.0	71.0
10	2,400	2.8	12.0	83.0
7	1,700	2.0	17.0	100.0
	$85,400			

Based on simple observation, it appears that the first three items form a group with the highest value, the next three items form a second group, and the last four items constitute a group. Thus, the ABC classification for these items is as follows:

CLASS	ITEMS	% OF TOTAL VALUE	% OF TOTAL QUANTITY
A	9, 8, 2	71.0	15.0
B	1, 4, 3	16.5	28.0
C	6, 5, 10, 7	12.5	57.0

Along the Supply Chain

Inventory Management at Zara

Zara, a subsidiary of the Inditex Group, is one of the world's most successful apparel retailers with more than 2000 stores in 88 countries. It was ranked fifth in Gartner, Inc.'s 2015 Global Supply Chain Top 25, and one prominent reason is its unique approach to inventory management. Zara controls more of its supply chain than most retailers with most of its production in-house. It is renowned for its ability to deliver new clothes to stores quickly and in small batches. The company produces over 450 million items a year for its stores. Twice a week, at precise times, store managers order clothes, and twice a week, on schedule, new garments arrive. This results in frequent shipments and higher numbers of customer visits to the stores, creating a perception of shortages and uniqueness. This sense of scarcity and exclusiveness allows Zara to sell more items at full price. Zara gets 85 percent of the full price on its clothes, while the industry average is 60 to 70 percent. Unsold items account for less than 10 percent of its inventory stock, compared with an industry average of 17 to 20 percent.

Inventory optimization models help the company determine the quantity that should be delivered to every one of its retail stores in twice weekly shipments. The stock that is delivered is strictly limited, ensuring that each store only receives just what they need. This follows Zara's strategy of being exclusive while avoiding inventories of unpopular stock. If the design Zara hastily creates in an attempt to chase the latest fashion trend does not sell well, since the shipment is small, there's not a lot of unsold inventory to get rid of. Zara's inventory management models enable the store managers to communicate customer feedback to designers on what they are looking for, what they like, and what they dislike. Constant small design changes allows Zara to sell more items at full price; and fewer mark-downs means less inventory throughout the supply chain from raw materials to finished products.

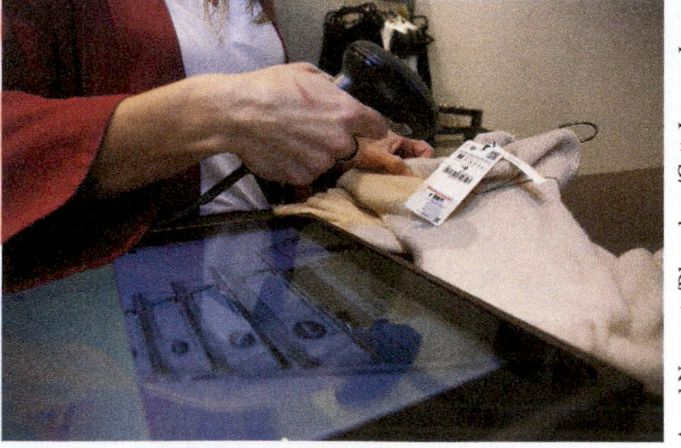
Angel Navarrete/Bloomberg/Getty Images, Inc.

Zara also makes extensive use of RFID technology for inventory management. RFID chips are inserted inside the slightly larger plastic security tags Zara attaches to each item, which protects the chips, allowing for their reuse after they are removed at checkout. The RFID chips and scanning devices require fewer Zara store employees to take inventory and about half the time, compared to scanning individual barcodes one at a time. Because of the time saved, store inventories can be conducted about every six weeks instead of every six months, which provides a more accurate picture of what styles are selling well and ones that are not. Also, each time an item is sold, data from its chip triggers an instant order to the stockroom (as with JIT) for an identical item.

Using the Internet identify several other retail companies that are using RFID technology for inventory management.

Sources: Based on Christopher Bjork, "Zara Builds its Business Around RFID," *The Wall Street Journal*, http://wsj.com (September 16, 2014); Clara Lu, "Zara's Secret to Retail Success — Its Supply Chain," *tradegecko*, https://www.tradegecko.com (December 4, 2014).

Economic Order Quantity Models

In a continuous, or fixed-order-quantity, system when inventory reaches a specific level, referred to as the *reorder point*, a fixed amount is ordered. The most widely used and traditional means for determining how much to order in a continuous system is the **economic order quantity (EOQ)** model, also referred to as the economic lot-size model. The earliest published derivation of the basic EOQ model formula in 1915 is credited to Ford Harris, an employee at Westinghouse.

Economic order quantity (EOQ) The optimal order quantity that will minimize total inventory costs.

The function of the EOQ model is to determine the optimal order size that minimizes total inventory costs. There are several variations of the EOQ model, depending on the assumptions made about the inventory system. We will describe two model versions: the basic EOQ model and the production quantity model.

The Basic EOQ Model

The *basic EOQ model* is a formula for determining the optimal order size that minimizes the sum of carrying costs and ordering costs. The model formula is derived under a set of simplifying and restrictive assumptions, as follows:

- Demand is known with certainty and is constant over time.
- No shortages are allowed.
- Lead time for the receipt of orders is constant.
- The order quantity is received all at once.

These basic model assumptions are reflected in **Figure 13.2**, which describes the continuous-inventory **order cycle** system inherent in the EOQ model. An order quantity, Q, is received and is used up over time at a constant rate. When the inventory level decreases to the reorder point, R, a new order is placed; a period of time, referred to as the *lead time*, is required for delivery. The order is received all at once just at the moment when demand depletes the entire stock of inventory—the inventory level reaches 0—so there will be no shortages. This cycle is repeated continuously for the same order quantity, reorder point, and lead time.

Order cycle The time between receipt of orders in an inventory cycle.

As we mentioned, the economic order quantity is the order size that minimizes the sum of carrying costs and ordering costs. These two costs react inversely to each other. As the order size increases, fewer orders are required, causing the ordering cost to decline, whereas the average amount of inventory on hand will increase, resulting in an increase in carrying costs. Thus, in effect, the optimal order quantity represents a compromise between these two inversely related costs.

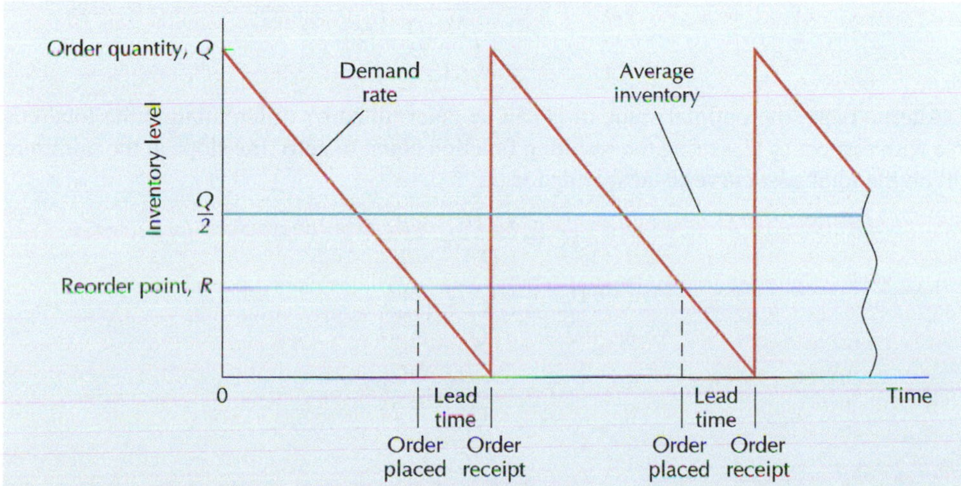

FIGURE 13.2 The Inventory Order Cycle

FIGURE 13.3 **The EOQ Cost Model**

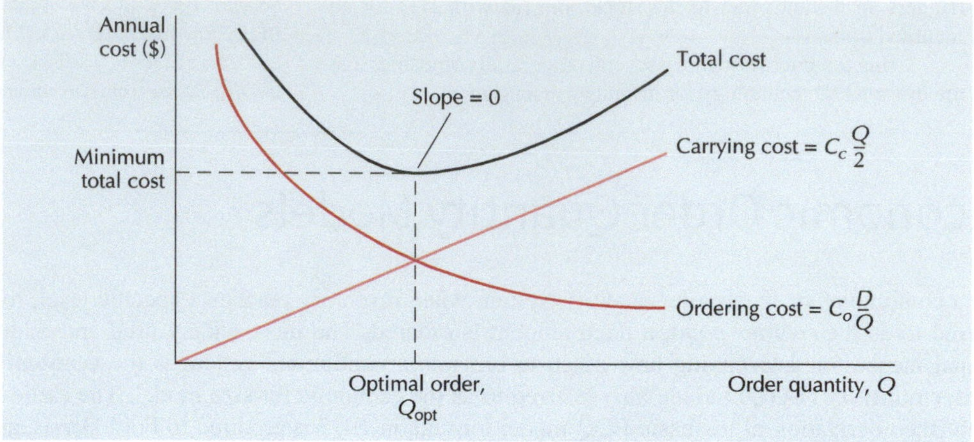

The total annual ordering cost is computed by multiplying the cost per order, designated as C_o, times the number of orders per year. Since annual demand, D, is assumed to be known and to be constant, the number of orders will be D/Q, where Q is the order size and

$$\text{Annual ordering cost} = \frac{C_o D}{Q}$$

The only variable in this equation is Q; both C_o and D are constant parameters. Thus, the relative magnitude of the ordering cost is dependent on the order size.

Total annual carrying cost is computed by multiplying the annual per-unit carrying cost, designated as C_c, by the average inventory level. The average inventory level is one-half of Q or $Q/2$, as shown in Figure 13.2.

$$\text{Annual carrying cost} = \frac{C_c Q}{2}$$

The total annual inventory cost is the sum of the ordering and carrying costs:

$$\text{TC} = \frac{C_o D}{Q} + \frac{C_c Q}{2}$$

The graph in **Figure 13.3** shows the inverse relationship between ordering cost and carrying cost, resulting in a convex total cost curve.

The optimal order quantity occurs at the point in Figure 13.3 where the total cost curve is at a minimum, which coincides exactly with the point where the carrying cost curve intersects the ordering cost curve. This enables us to determine the optimal value of Q by equating the two cost functions and solving for Q:

$$\frac{C_o D}{Q} = \frac{C_c Q}{2}$$

$$Q^2 = \frac{2C_o D}{C_c}$$

$$Q_{\text{opt}} = \sqrt{\frac{2C_o D}{C_c}}$$

Alternatively, the optimal value of Q can be determined by differentiating the total cost curve with respect to Q, setting the resulting function equal to zero (the slope at the minimum point on the total cost curve), and solving for Q:

$$\text{TC} = \frac{C_o D}{Q} + \frac{C_c Q}{2}$$

$$\frac{\partial \text{TC}}{\partial Q} = -\frac{C_o D}{Q^2} + \frac{C_c}{2}$$

$$0 = -\frac{C_o D}{Q^2} + \frac{C_c}{2}$$

$$Q_{\text{opt}} = \sqrt{\frac{2C_o D}{C_c}}$$

The total minimum cost is determined by substituting the value for the optimal order size, Q_{opt}, into the total cost equation:

$$TC_{min} = \frac{C_o D}{Q_{opt}} + \frac{C_c Q_{opt}}{2}$$

EXAMPLE 13.2 | The Economic Order Quantity

The ePaint Store stocks paint in its warehouse and sells it online on its website. The store stocks several brands of paint; however, its biggest seller is Sharman-Wilson Ironcoat paint. The company wants to determine the optimal order size and total inventory cost for Ironcoat paint given an estimated annual demand of 10,000 gallons of paint, an annual carrying cost of \$0.75 per gallon, and an ordering cost of \$150 per order. It would also like to know the number of orders that will be made annually and the time between orders (i.e., the order cycle).

Solution:

$$C_c = \$0.75 \text{ per gallon}$$
$$C_o = \$150$$
$$D = 10{,}000 \text{ gallons}$$

The optimal order size is

$$Q_{opt} = \sqrt{\frac{2C_o D}{C_c}} = \sqrt{\frac{2(150)(10{,}000)}{(0.75)}} = 2000 \text{ gallons}$$

The total annual inventory cost is determined by substituting Q_{opt} into the total cost formula:

$$TC_{min} = \frac{C_o D}{Q_{opt}} + \frac{C_c Q_{opt}}{2} = \frac{(150)(10{,}000)}{2000} + \frac{(0.75)(2000)}{2} = \$750 + 750 = \$1500$$

The number of orders per year is computed as follows:

$$\text{Number of orders per year} = \frac{D}{Q_{opt}} = \frac{10{,}000}{2000} = 5 \text{ orders per year}$$

Given that the company processes orders 311 days annually (365 days minus 52 Sundays, Thanksgiving, and Christmas), the order cycle is

$$\text{Order cycle time} = \frac{311 \text{ days}}{D/Q_{opt}} = \frac{311}{5} = 62.2 \text{ days}$$

The optimal order quantity, determined in this example and in general, is an approximate value, since it is based on estimates of carrying and ordering costs as well as uncertain demand (although all of these parameters are treated as known, certain values in the EOQ model). In practice it is desirable to round the Q values off to some nearby pragmatic value. The precision of a decimal place is generally not necessary. In addition, because the optimal order quantity is computed from a square root, errors or variations in the cost parameters and demand tend to be dampened. For instance, in Example 13.2, if the order cost had actually been 30% higher, or \$200, the resulting optimal order size would have varied only by a little under 10% (i.e., 2190 gallons instead of 2000 gallons). Variations in both inventory costs will tend to offset each other, since they have an inverse relationship. As a result, the EOQ model is relatively resilient to errors in the cost estimates and demand, or is *robust*, which has tended to enhance its popularity.

The Production Quantity Model

Production quantity model An inventory system in which an order is received gradually, as inventory is simultaneously being depleted.

A variation of the basic EOQ model is the **production quantity model**, also referred to as the *gradual usage* and *non-instantaneous receipt* model. In this EOQ model the assumption that orders are received all at once is relaxed. The order quantity is received gradually over time, and the inventory level is depleted at the same time it is being replenished. This situation is commonly found when the inventory user is also the producer, as in a manufacturing operation where a part is produced to use in a larger assembly. This situation also can occur when orders are delivered continuously over time or when a retailer is also the producer.

The noninstantaneous receipt model is shown graphically in Figure 13.4. The inventory level is gradually replenished as an order is received. In the basic EOQ model, average inventory was half the maximum inventory level, or $Q/2$, but in this model variation, the maximum inventory level is not simply Q; it is an amount somewhat lower than Q, adjusted for the fact the order quantity is depleted during the order receipt period.

In order to determine the average inventory level, we define the following parameters unique to this model:

p = daily rate at which the order is received over time, also known as the *production rate*
d = daily rate at which inventory is demanded

The demand rate cannot exceed the production rate, since we are still assuming that no shortages are possible, and, if $d = p$, there is no order size, since items are used as fast as they are produced. For this model the production rate must exceed the demand rate, or $p \geq d$.

Observing Figure 13.4, we see that the time required to finish receiving an order is the order quantity divided by the rate at which the order is received, or Q/p. For example, if the order size is 100 units and the production rate, p, is 20 units per day, the order will be received over five days. The amount of inventory that will be depleted or used up during this time period is determined by multiplying by the demand rate: $(Q/p)d$. For example, if it takes five days to receive the order and during this time inventory is depleted at the rate of two units per day, then 10 units are used. As a result, the maximum amount of

FIGURE 13.4 The Production Quantity Model

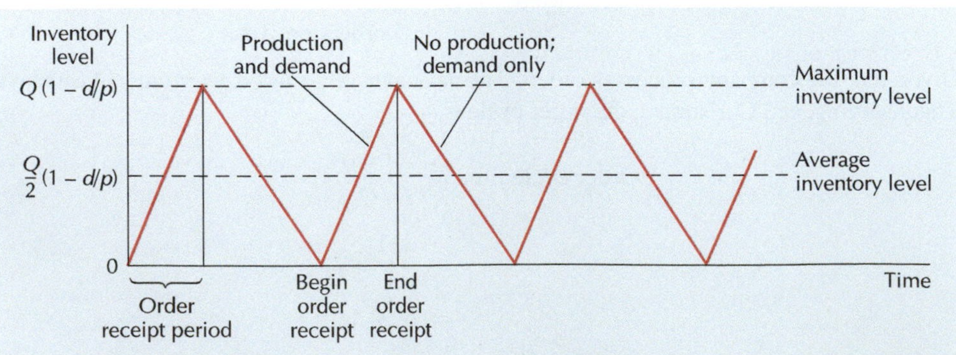

inventory on hand is the order size minus the amount depleted during the receipt period, computed as

$$\text{Maximum inventory level} = Q - \frac{Q}{p}d$$
$$= Q\left(1 - \frac{d}{p}\right)$$

Since this is the maximum inventory level, the average inventory level is determined by dividing this amount by 2:

$$\text{Average inventory level} = \frac{1}{2}\left[Q\left(1 - \frac{d}{p}\right)\right]$$
$$= \frac{Q}{2}\left(1 - \frac{d}{p}\right)$$

The total carrying cost using this function for average inventory is

$$\text{Total carrying cost} = \frac{C_c Q}{2}\left(1 - \frac{d}{p}\right)$$

In this case the ordering cost, C_o, is often the setup cost for production.

Thus, the total annual inventory cost is determined according to the following formula:

$$\text{TC} = \frac{C_o D}{Q} + \frac{C_c Q}{2}\left(1 - \frac{d}{p}\right)$$

Solving this function for the optimal value Q,

$$Q_{\text{opt}} = \sqrt{\frac{2C_o D}{C_c\left(1 - \frac{d}{p}\right)}}$$

EXAMPLE 13.3 | The Production Quantity Model

Assume that the ePaint Store has its own manufacturing facility in which it produces Ironcoat paint. The ordering cost, C_o, is the cost of setting up the production process to make paint. $C_o = \$150$. Recall that $C_c = \$0.75$ per gallon and $D = 10{,}000$ gallons per year. The manufacturing facility operates the same days the store is open (i.e., 311 days) and produces 150 gallons of paint per day. Determine the optimal order size, total inventory cost, the length of time to receive an order, the number of orders per year, and the maximum inventory level.

Solution:

$$C_o = \$150$$
$$C_c = \$0.75 \text{ per gallons}$$
$$D = 10{,}000 \text{ gallons}$$
$$d = \frac{10{,}000}{311} = 32.2 \text{ gallons per day}$$
$$p = 150 \text{ gallons per day}$$

The optimal order size is determined as follows:

$$Q_{\text{opt}} = \sqrt{\frac{2C_o D}{C_c\left(1 - \frac{d}{p}\right)}}$$
$$= \sqrt{\frac{2(150)(10{,}000)}{0.75\left(1 - \frac{32.2}{150}\right)}}$$
$$= 2256.8 \text{ gallons}$$

Although an order of 2256.8 gallons should be rounded to 2257, we will use the 2256.8 to compute total cost.

This value is substituted into the following formula to determine total minimum annual inventory cost:

$$TC_{\min} = \frac{C_o D}{Q} + \frac{C_c Q}{2}\left(1 - \frac{d}{p}\right)$$
$$= \frac{(150)(10{,}000)}{2256.8} + \frac{(0.75)(2256.8)}{2}\left(1 - \frac{32.2}{150}\right)$$
$$= \$1329$$

The length of time to receive an order for this type of manufacturing operation is commonly called the length of the *production run*.

$$\text{Production run} = \frac{Q}{p}$$
$$= \frac{2256.8}{150}$$
$$= 15.05 \text{ days per order}$$

The number of orders per year is actually the number of production runs that will be made:

$$\text{Number of production runs (from orders)} = \frac{D}{Q}$$
$$= \frac{10{,}000}{2256.8}$$
$$= 4.43 \text{ runs per year}$$

Finally, the maximum inventory level is

$$\text{Maximum inventory level} = Q\left(1 - \frac{d}{p}\right)$$
$$= 2256.8\left(1 - \frac{32.2}{150}\right)$$
$$= 1772 \text{ gallons}$$

Thus, ePaint will need to set aside storage space sufficient to accommodate these 1772 gallons of paint.

Solution Of EOQ Models with Excel

EOQ analysis can be done with Excel. The Excel solution screen for Example 13.2 is shown in **Exhibit 13.1**. The Excel screen for the production quantity model in Example 13.3 is shown in **Exhibit 13.2**.

EXHIBIT 13.1

Excel File

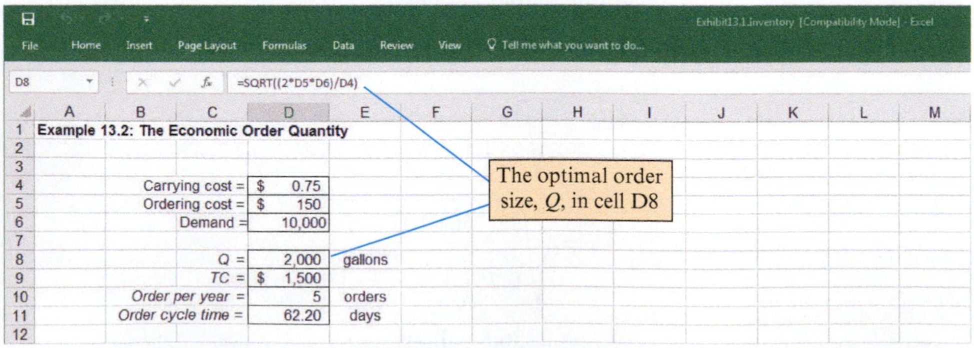

Exhibit13.1.Inventory [Compatibility Mode] - Excel

File Home Insert Page Layout Formulas Data Review View Tell me what you want to do...

D8 =SQRT((2*D5*D6)/D4)

	A	B	C	D	E
1	Example 13.2: The Economic Order Quantity				
2					
3					
4			Carrying cost =	$ 0.75	
5			Ordering cost =	$ 150	
6			Demand =	10,000	
7					
8			Q =	2,000	gallons
9			TC =	$ 1,500	
10			Order per year =	5	orders
11			Order cycle time =	62.20	days
12					

The optimal order size, Q, in cell D8

EXHIBIT 13.2

Excel File

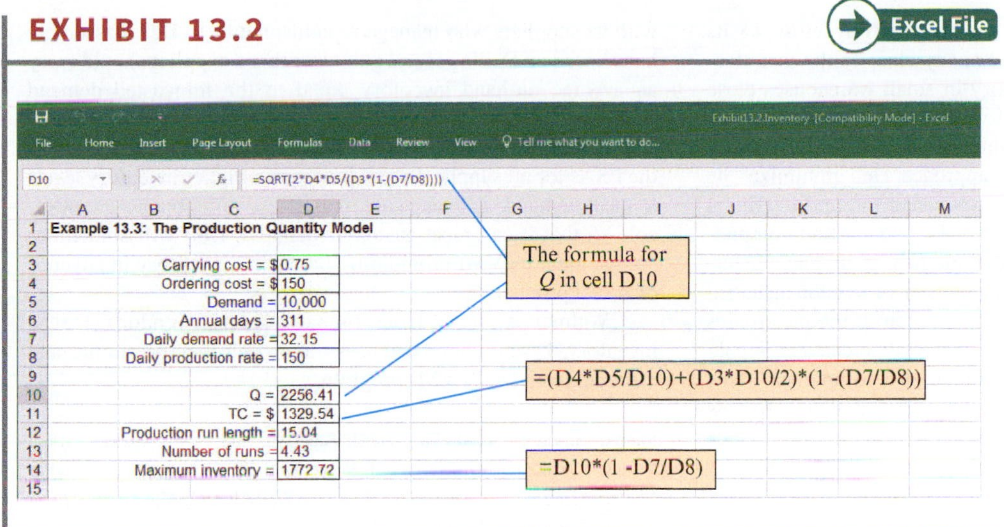

Solution Of EOQ Models with OM Tools

OM tools has modules to solve all the various inventory models illustrated in this chapter, including the ABC model for Example 13.1, the EOQ and production quality models for Examples 13.2 and 13.3, the quantity discount model (Example 13.4), the recorder point model (Examples 13.5 and 13.6), and the fixed-period model (Example 13.7). As an example, **Exhibit 13.3** shows the OM Tools spreadsheet for the EOQ Model in Example 13.2.

EXHIBIT 13.3

Excel File

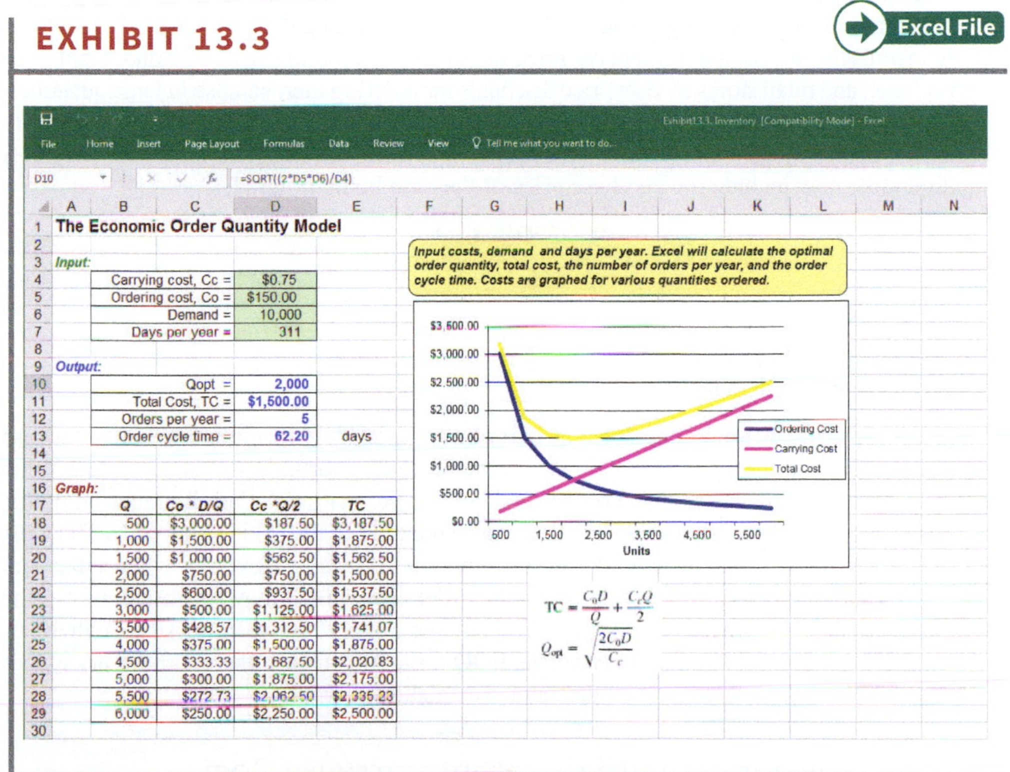

Q	Co * D/Q	Cc *Q/2	TC
500	$3,000.00	$187.50	$3,187.50
1,000	$1,500.00	$375.00	$1,875.00
1,500	$1,000.00	$562.50	$1,562.50
2,000	$750.00	$750.00	$1,500.00
2,500	$600.00	$937.50	$1,537.50
3,000	$500.00	$1,125.00	$1,625.00
3,500	$428.57	$1,312.50	$1,741.07
4,000	$375.00	$1,500.00	$1,875.00
4,500	$333.33	$1,687.50	$2,020.83
5,000	$300.00	$1,875.00	$2,175.00
5,500	$272.73	$2,062.50	$2,335.23
6,000	$250.00	$2,250.00	$2,500.00

Along the Supply Chain

Vendor-Managed Inventory (VMI) at Dell

With annual revenues over $60 billion, Dell is the third largest personal computer vendor in the world behind Lenovo and HP, and is the number one supplier of PC monitors. From its start Dell has been an innovator in supply chain management, pioneering the "direct-to-customer" manufacturing model that delivers PCs to customers according to their individual specifications. To minimize the time between a PC order and its delivery Dell also employs a just-in-time (JIT) approach to manufacturing, which requires that product manufacturing be relatively close to its customers, and that suppliers be relatively close to the manufacturer. Dell's suppliers keep inventory in small warehouses close to Dell's assembly plants and Dell withdraws inventory from its suppliers as needed (e.g., JIT), which reduces Dell's inventory at its assembly plants. Using this approach Dell minimizes its own inventory costs, which Dell is renowned for, and is critical in the computer-related industry where PC models and components depreciate very quickly. To complement their manufacturing approach Dell also was an early pioneer of vendor-managed inventory (VMI), which has become common in the electronics industry. VMI programs typically include a "percentage supply allocation (PSA)," which is a percentage of a component part's overall demand (multi-sourced from many suppliers) that is pre-negotiated with an individual supplier to provide. Dell's goals for its VMI program are to meet customer demand, minimize its own inventory, and meet the PSAs for all of its suppliers of a part. Using collaborative forecasting, Dell shares its demand forecasts with its suppliers who manage replenishments to Dell's assembly hubs based on Dell's general guideline that a supplier should carry an average on-hand inventory equal to the forecasted demand (provided by Dell) for the next ten days, i.e., ten days of inventory supply. Because of demand variability Dell might not always meet the PSAs for all suppliers or might require higher inventory levels to meet demand. To make sure that critical components are available so that it can meet customer demand, Dell will sometimes complement its VMI program by procuring inventory in advance of actual production.

Walmart is another large company that uses vendor-managed inventory. Discuss how Walmart's approach may be similar and different from Dell's VMI program.

Source: Based on Abhilasha Prakash Katariya, Sila Cetinkaya, and Eylem Tekin, "Cyclic Consumption and Replenishment Decisions for Vendor-Managed Inventory of Multisourced Parts in Dell's Supply Chain," *Interfaces* 44 (3) (May–June 2014), pp. 300–16.

Quantity Discounts

Quantity discount Given for specific higher order quantities.

A **quantity discount** is a price discount on an item if predetermined numbers of units are ordered. In the back of a magazine you might see an advertisement for a firm stating that it will produce a coffee mug (or hat) with a company or organizational logo on it, and the price will be \$5 per mug if you purchase 100, \$4 per mug if you purchase 200, or \$3 per mug if you purchase 500 or more. Many manufacturing companies receive price discounts for ordering materials and supplies in high volume, and retail stores receive price discounts for ordering merchandise in large quantities.

The basic EOQ model can be used to determine the optimal order size with quantity discounts; however, the application of the model is slightly altered. The total inventory cost function must now include the purchase price of the item being ordered:

$$\text{TC} = \frac{C_oD}{Q} + \frac{C_cQ}{2} + PD$$

where

P = per-unit price of the item
D = annual demand

Purchase price was not considered as part of our basic EOQ formulation earlier because it had no impact on the optimal order size. In the preceding formula PD is a constant value that would not alter the basic shape of the total cost curve; that is, the minimum point on the cost curve would still be at the same location, corresponding to the same value of Q. Thus, the optimal order size is the same no matter what the purchase price is. However, when a discount price is available, it is associated with a specific order size, which may be different from the optimal order size, and the customer must evaluate the tradeoff between possibly higher carrying costs with the discount quantity versus EOQ cost. As a result, the purchase price does affect the order-size decision when a discount is available.

Quantity Discounts with Constant Carrying Cost

The EOQ cost model with constant carrying costs for a pricing schedule with two discounts, d_1 and d_2, is illustrated in Figure 13.5 for the following discounts:

ORDER SIZE	PRICE
0–99	\$10
100–99	$8(d_1)$
200+	$6(d_2)$

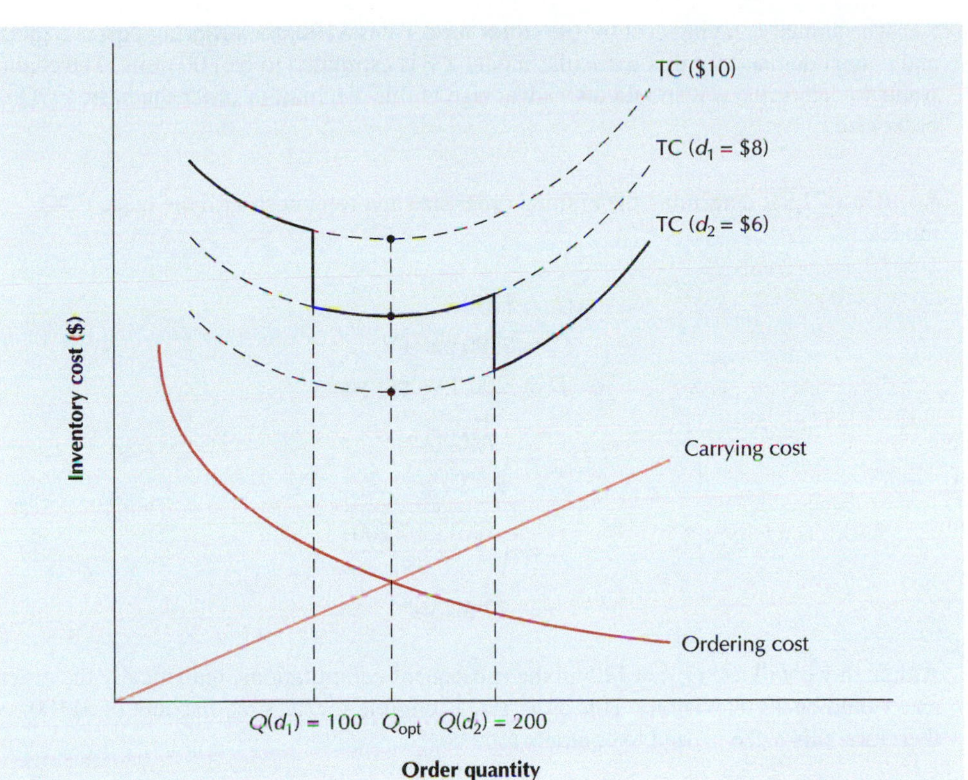

FIGURE 13.5 Quantity Discounts with Constant Carrying Cost

Notice in Figure 13.5 that the optimal order size, Q_{opt}, is the same regardless of the discount price. Although the total cost curve decreases with each discount in price (i.e., d_1 and d_2), since ordering and carrying cost are constant, the optimal order size, Q_{opt}, does not change.

The graph in Figure 13.5 reflects the composition of the total cost curve resulting from the discounts kicking in at two successively higher order quantities. The first segment of the total cost curve (with no discount) is valid only up to 99 units ordered. Beyond that quantity, the total cost curve (represented by the topmost dashed line) is meaningless because above 100 units there is a discount (d_1). Between 100 and 199 units the total cost drops down to the middle curve. This middle-level cost curve is valid only up to 199 units because at 200 units there is another, lower discount (d_2). So the total cost curve has two discrete steps, starting with the original total cost curve, dropping down to the next level cost curve for the first discount, and finally dropping to the third-level cost curve for the final discount.

Notice that the optimal order size, Q_{opt}, is feasible only for the middle level of the total cost curve, TC(d_1)—it does not coincide with the top level of the cost curve, TC, or the lowest level, TC(d_2). If the optimal EOQ order size had coincided with the lowest level of the total cost curve, TC(d_2), it would have been optimal order size for the entire discount price schedule. Since it does not coincide with the lowest level of the total cost curve, the total cost with Q_{opt} must be compared to the lower-level total cost using $Q(d_2)$ to see which results in the minimum total cost. In this case the optimal order size is 200.

EXAMPLE 13.4 | A Quantity Discount with Constant Carrying Cost

Avtek, a distributor of audio and video equipment, wants to reduce a large stock of televisions. It has offered a local chain of stores a quantity discount pricing schedule, as follows:

QUANTITY	PRICE
1–49	$1400
50–89	1100
90+	900

The annual carrying cost for the stores for a TV is \$190, the ordering cost is \$2500, and annual demand for this particular model TV is estimated to be 200 units. The chain wants to determine if it should take advantage of this discount or order the basic EOQ order size.

Solution: First determine the optimal order size and total cost with the basic EOQ model.

$$C_o = \$2500$$
$$C_c = \$190 \text{ per TV}$$
$$D = 200 \text{ TVs per year}$$

$$Q_{\text{opt}} = \sqrt{\frac{2C_cD}{C_c}}$$
$$= \sqrt{\frac{2(2500)(200)}{190}}$$
$$= 72.5 \text{ TVs}$$

Although we will use $Q_{\text{opt}} = 72.5$ in the subsequent computations, realistically the order size would be 73 televisions. This order size is eligible for the first discount of \$1100; therefore, this price is used to compute total cost:

$$\text{TC}_{\text{min}} = \frac{C_0D}{Q_{\text{opt}}} + \frac{C_cQ_{\text{opt}}}{2} + PD$$
$$= \frac{(2500)(200)}{72.5} + \frac{(190)(72.5)}{2} + (1100)(200)$$
$$\text{TC}_{\text{min}} = \$233{,}784$$

Since there is a discount for a larger order size than 50 units (i.e., there is a lower cost curve), this total cost of \$233,784 must be compared with total cost with an order size of 90 and a discounted price of \$900:

$$\text{TC} = \frac{C_oD}{Q} + \frac{C_cQ}{2} + PD$$
$$= \frac{(2500)(200)}{90} + \frac{(190)(90)}{2} + (900)(200)$$
$$= \$194{,}105$$

Since this total cost is lower (\$194,105 < \$233,784), the maximum discount price should be taken, and 90 units should be ordered. We know that there is no order size larger than 90 that would result in a lower cost, since the minimum point on this total cost curve has already been determined to be 73.

Quantity Discount Model Solution with Excel

It is also possible to use Excel to solve the quantity-discount model with constant carrying cost. **Exhibit 13.4** shows the Excel solution screen for Example 13.4. Notice that the selection of the appropriate order size, Q, that results in the minimum total cost for each discount range is determined by the formulas embedded in cells E8, E9, and E10. For example, the formula for the first quantity-discount range, "1–49," is embedded in cell E8 and shown on the formula bar at the top of the screen, "=IF(D8≥B8,D8,B8)." This means that if the discount order size in cell D8 (i.e., $Q = 72.55$) is greater than or equal to the quantity in cell B8 (i.e., 1), then

EXHIBIT 13.4

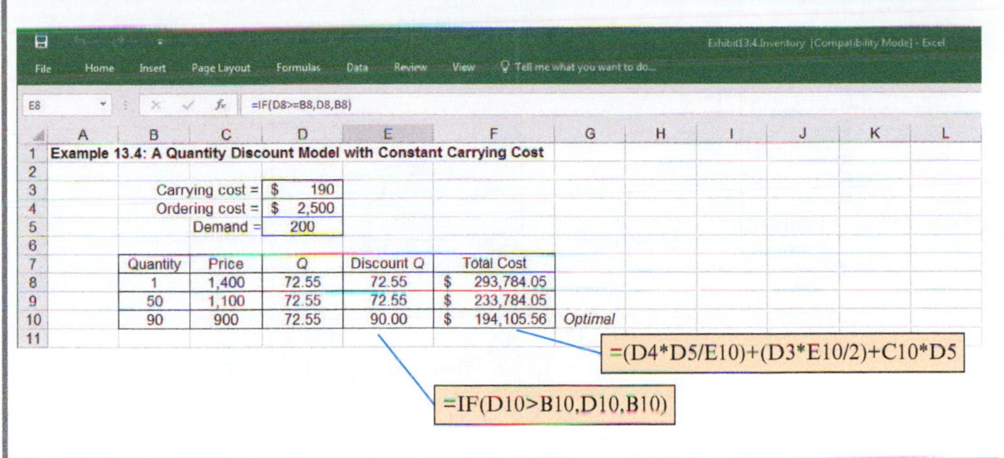

Example 13.4: A Quantity Discount Model with Constant Carrying Cost

Carrying cost =	$ 190
Ordering cost =	$ 2,500
Demand =	200

Quantity	Price	Q	Discount Q	Total Cost	
1	1,400	72.55	72.55	$ 293,784.05	
50	1,100	72.55	72.55	$ 233,784.05	
90	900	72.55	90.00	$ 194,105.56	Optimal

the quantity in cell D8 (72.55) is selected; otherwise the amount in cell B8 is selected. The formulas in cells E9 and E10 are constructed similarly. The result is that the order quantity for the final discount range, $Q = 90$, is selected.

Reorder Point

In our description of the EOQ models in the previous sections, we addressed how much should be ordered. Now we will discuss the other aspect of inventory management, when to order. The determinant of when to order in a continuous inventory system is the **reorder point**, the inventory level at which a new order is placed.

Reorder point The level of inventory at which a new order should be placed.

The reorder point for our basic EOQ model with constant demand and a constant lead time to receive an order is equal to the amount demanded during the lead time,

$$R = dL$$

where

d = demand rate per period (e.g., daily)
L = lead time

EXAMPLE 13.5 | Reorder Point for the Basic EOQ Model

The ePaint Internet Store in Example 13.2 is open 311 days per year. If annual demand is 10,000 gallons of Ironcoat paint and the lead time to receive an order is 10 days, determine the reorder point for paint.

Solution:

$$\begin{aligned} R &= dL \\ &= \left(\frac{10{,}000}{311}\right)(10) \\ &= 321.54 \text{ gallons} \end{aligned}$$

When the inventory level falls to approximately 321 gallons of paint, a new order is placed. Notice that the reorder point is not related to the optimal order quantity or any of the inventory costs.

FIGURE 13.6 Variable Demand with a Reorder Point

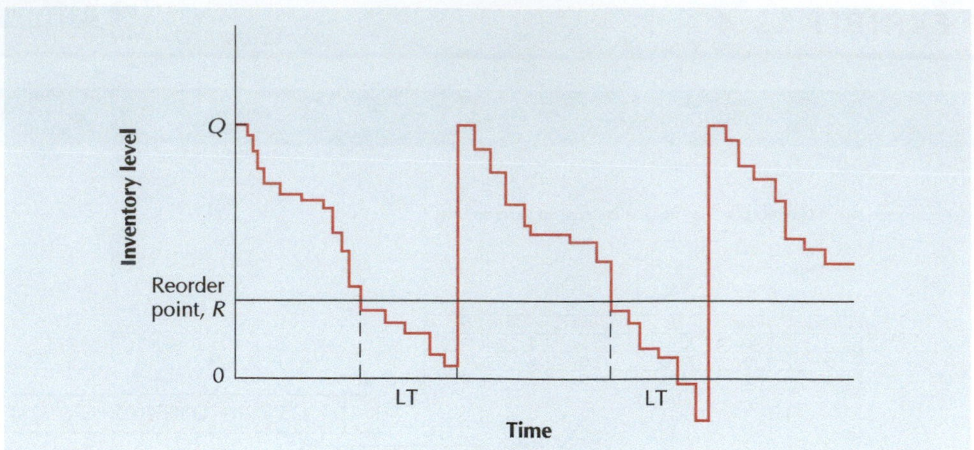

Safety Stocks

In Example 13.5, an order is made when the inventory level reaches the reorder point. During the lead time, the remaining inventory in stock will be depleted at a constant demand rate, such that the new order quantity will arrive at exactly the same moment as the inventory level reaches zero. Realistically, demand—and, to a lesser extent lead time—are uncertain. The inventory level might be depleted at a faster rate during lead time. This is depicted in Figure 13.6 for uncertain demand and a constant lead time.

Stockout An inventory shortage.

Safety stock A buffer added to the inventory on hand during lead time.

Notice in the second order cycle that a **stockout** occurs when demand exceeds the available inventory in stock. As a hedge against stockouts when demand is uncertain, a **safety stock** of inventory is frequently added to the expected demand during lead time. The addition of a safety stock to the stockout occurrence shown in Figure 13.6 is displayed in Figure 13.7.

Service Level

Service level The probability that the inventory available during lead time will meet demand.

There are several ways to determine the amount of the safety stock. One popular method is to establish a safety stock that will meet a specified **service level**. The service level is the probability that the amount of inventory on hand during the lead time is sufficient to meet expected demand—that is, the probability that a stockout will not occur. The term *service* is used, since the higher the probability that inventory will be on hand, the more likely that customer demand will be met—that is, that the customer can be served. A service level of 90% means that there is a .90 probability that demand will be met during the lead time, and the probability that a stockout will occur is 10%. The service level is typically a policy decision based on a number of factors, including carrying costs for the extra safety stock and lost sales if customer demand cannot be met.

FIGURE 13.7 Reorder Point with a Safety Stock

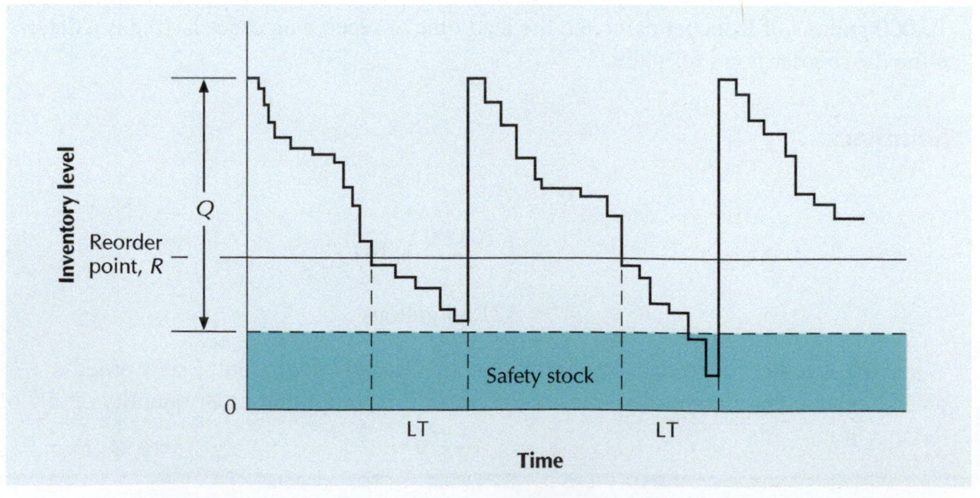

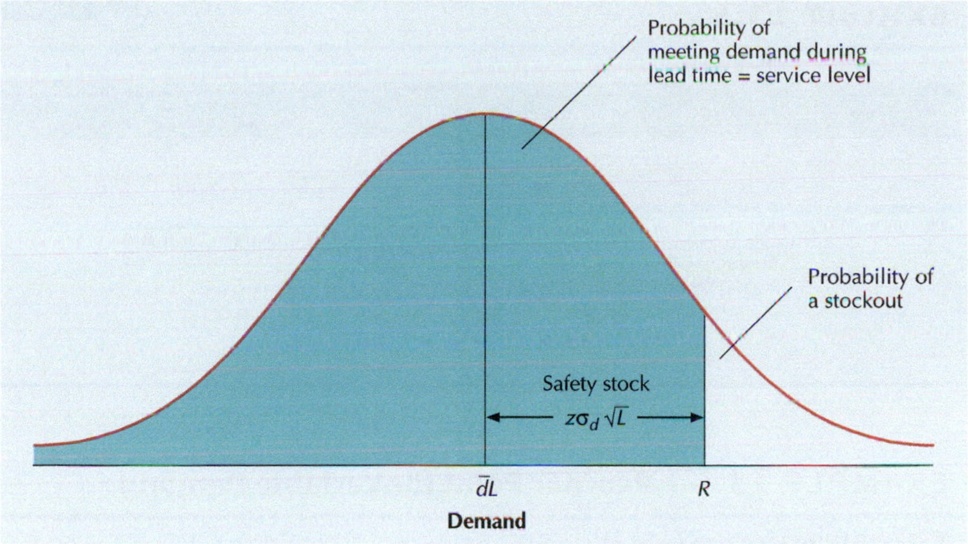

FIGURE 13.8 Reorder Point for a Service Level

Reorder Point with Variable Demand

To compute the reorder point with a safety stock that will meet a specific service level, we will assume the demand during each day of lead time is uncertain, independent, and can be described by a normal distribution. The average demand for the lead time is the sum of the average daily demand for the days of the lead time, which is also the product of the average daily demands multiplied by the lead time. Similarly, the variance of the distribution is the sum of the daily variances for the number of days in the lead time. Using these parameters, we can compute the reorder point to meet a specific service level as

$$R = \bar{d}L + z\sigma_d\sqrt{L}$$

where

$\bar{d}$ = average daily demand

L = lead time

σ_d = the standard deviation of daily demand

z = number of standard deviations corresponding to the service level probability

$z\sigma_d\sqrt{L}$ = safety stock

The term $\sigma_d\sqrt{L}$ in this formula for the reorder point is the square root of the sum of the daily variances during lead time:

$$\text{Variance} = (\text{daily variance}) \times (\text{number of days of lead time})$$

$$= \sigma_d^2 L$$

$$\text{Standard deviation} = \sqrt{\sigma_d^2 L}$$

$$= \sigma_d\sqrt{L}$$

The reorder point relative to the service level is shown in Figure 13.8. The service level is the shaded area, or probability, to the left of the reorder point, *R*.

Determining the Reorder Point with Excel

Excel can be used to determine the reorder point for variable demand. Exhibit 13.5 shows the Excel screen for Example 13.6. Notice that the reorder point is computed using the formula in cell E7, which is shown on the formula bar at the top of the screen.

EXHIBIT 13.5

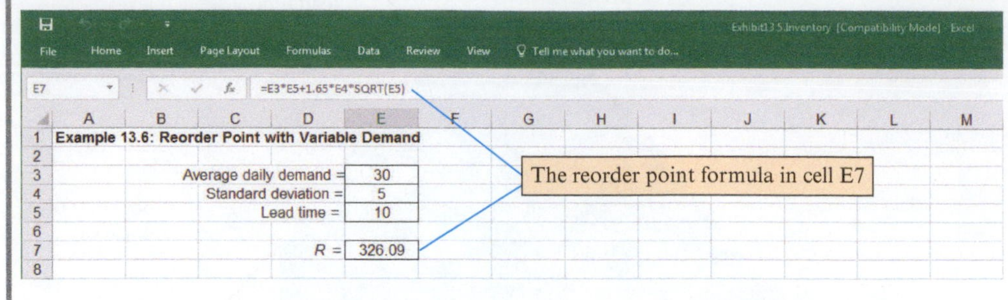

EXAMPLE 13.6 | Reorder Point for Variable Demand

For the ePaint Internet Store in Example 13.2, we will assume that daily demand for Ironcoat paint is normally distributed with an average daily demand of 30 gallons and a standard deviation of 5 gallons of paint per day. The lead time for receiving a new order of paint is 10 days. Determine the reorder point and safety stock if the store wants a service level of 95%—that is, the probability of a stockout is 5%.

Solution:

$$\bar{d} = 30 \text{ gallons per day}$$
$$L = 10 \text{ days}$$
$$\sigma_d = 5 \text{ gallons per day}$$

For a 95% service level, the value of z (from the Normal table in Appendix A) is 1.65. The safety stock is:

$$\begin{aligned}\text{Safety stock} &= z\sigma_d\sqrt{L}\\ &= (1.65)(5)(\sqrt{10})\\ &= 26.1 \text{ gallons}\end{aligned}$$

The reorder point is computed as follows:

$$\begin{aligned}R &= \bar{d}L + z\sigma_d\sqrt{L}\\ &= 30(10) + (1.65)(5)(\sqrt{10})\\ &= 300 + 26.1\\ &= 326.1 \text{ gallons}\end{aligned}$$

Along the Supply Chain

Multi-Echelon Inventory Optimization at Procter & Gamble

The various EOQ models presented in this chapter are known as single-stage models; they only attempt to optimize inventory of a single item at a single location. The items are considered in isolation, and not how this single item's inventory level might affect the entire supply chain. This is a somewhat simplistic but necessary view of inventory optimization for many companies, because of the complexity involved in considering the relationship among many different inventory items at many locations for an end-to-end supply chain. However, many *Fortune 500* and other companies across a wide range of industries are now approaching inventory optimization from a total supply chain perspective. This relatively new approach, called *multi-echelon* inventory optimization, uses various software packages designed for the purpose to scientifically determine the minimum inventory levels for multiple materials, parts, subassemblies, and finished goods across the entire supply chain. One company that has had great success with the multi-echelon inventory optimization approach is Procter & Gamble.

Procter & Gamble, headquartered in Cincinnati, Ohio, is one of the world's leading and best-known consumer products companies with sales over $80 billion in 180 countries for such products as Crest, Tide, Pantene, Pampers, Charmin, Cascade, Duracell, Cover Girl, and Gillette, among many others. Each of its three global business units—beauty and grooming, household care, and health and well-being—individually is large enough to be on the *Fortune 200* list. P&G's supply chain network consists of 500 supply chains that include 145 P&G-owned manufacturing facilities and 300 contract manufacturers. Inventory management across a supply chain network of this size and magnitude is a complex process. P&G's logistics management workforce that plans material supply, capacity, inventory, and logistics across its supply chain network has over 5000 individuals. P&G's inventory management process is implemented in a two-step approach. First, spreadsheet–based inventory models (employing assorted mathematical inventory optimization tools) are applied locally to optimize each stage in the supply chain. These models are used in about 70% of P&G's business units. Next, multi-echelon inventory optimization software is implemented in about 30% of P&G's business units across more complex supply chains.

The North American supply chain for cosmetics liquid makeup in P&G's beauty products division includes 500 stages with 8 raw materials, 10 uncolored work-in-process materials, 24 colored work-in-process materials, 150 packaging materials, 18 intermediate partially assembled products, and 75 finished goods that move from packaging to U.S. and Canadian distribution centers and then to retail customers. Material lead times ranged from 7 days to 8 weeks, production times from 1 to 2 days, review periods from 7 to 28 days, transportation times from 1 to 7 days, and quality assurance from 1 to 5 days. Demand forecasts were based on the immediate past 13 weeks of shipments and a forecast for the future 13 weeks. Among a number of improvements, P&G's application of a multi-echelon inventory approach changed the location of safety stocks within the supply chain and reduced safety stock investment for the supply chain by 17% and total inventory by 5%, while maintaining its 99.5% service level. The multi-echelon approach at Procter & Gamble reduced inventory in its beauty division by $100 million, and in one year alone saved the company $1.5 billion in inventory costs across all of its supply chains.

Discuss some of the problems a company such as Procter & Gamble might face in managing inventory across such a large, complex global supply chain.

Source: Based on I. Farsyn, S. Humair, J.L. Kahn, J.J. Neale, O. Rosen, J. Ruark, W. Tarlton, W. Van de Velde, G. Wegryn, and S. Willems, "Inventory Optimization at Procter & Gamble: Achieving Real Benefits Through User Adoption of Inventory Tools," *Interfaces* 41 (1) (January–February 2011), pp. 66–78; and Sean R. Williams,"How Inventory Optimization Opens Pathways to Profitability," *Supply Chain Management Review,* 5 (March/April 2011), pp. 30–36.

Order Quantity for a Periodic Inventory System

We defined a continuous, or fixed-order-quantity, inventory system as one in which the order quantity was constant and the time between orders varied. So far this type of inventory system has been the focus of our discussion. The less common *periodic*, or *fixed-time-period, inventory system* is one in which the time between orders is constant and the order size varies. Small retailers often use this sytem. Drugstores are one example of a business that sometimes uses a fixed-period inventory system. Drugstores stock a number of personal hygiene- and health-related products such as shampoo, toothpaste, soap, bandages, cough medicine, and aspirin.

Normally, the vendors who provide these items to the store will make periodic visits—every few weeks or every month—and count the stock of inventory on hand for their product. If the inventory is exhausted or at some predetermined reorder point, a new order will be placed for an amount that will bring the inventory level back up to the desired level. The drugstore managers will generally not monitor the inventory level between vendor visits but instead will rely on the vendor to take inventory.

Under this system, the vendor would bundle many small, low-cost items into a single order and delivery, thereby saving costs. Since the items are generally of low value, larger safety stocks will not pose a significant cost. Also, if the items are noncritical, even if there is a stockout, it is not a big deal. However, inventory might be exhausted early in the time period between visits, resulting in a stockout that will not be remedied until the next scheduled order. As a result, a larger safety stock for more critical items is sometimes required for the fixed-interval system.

Order Quantity with Variable Demand

If the demand rate and lead time are constant, then the fixed-period model will have a fixed-order quantity that will be made at specified time intervals, which is the same as the fixed-quantity (EOQ) model under similar conditions. However, as we have already explained, the fixed-period model reacts differently from the fixed-order model when demand is a variable.

The order size for a fixed-period model given variable daily demand that is normally distributed is determined by

$$Q = \left[\bar{d}(t_b + L) + z\sigma_d\sqrt{t_b + L}\right] - I$$

where

$$\begin{aligned} \bar{d} &= \text{average demand rate} \\ t_b &= \text{the fixed time between orders} \\ L &= \text{lead time} \\ \sigma_d &= \text{standard deviation of demand} \\ z\sigma_d\sqrt{t_b + L} &= \text{safety stock} \\ I &= \text{inventory in stock} \end{aligned}$$

The first term in this formula, $\bar{d}(t_b + L)$, is the average demand during the order cycle time plus the lead time. It reflects the amount of inventory that will be needed to protect against the entire time from this order to the next and the lead time until the order is received. The second term, $z\sigma_d\sqrt{t_b + L}$, is the safety stock for a specific service level, determined in much the same way as previously described for a reorder point. These first two terms combined are a "target" level of inventory to maintain. The final term, I, is the amount of inventory on hand when the inventory level is checked and an order is made.

Figure 13.9 shows a periodic inventory system in which variable order sizes (Q) are placed at fixed time intervals (t_b), and Example 13.7 illustrates this system.

Determining the Order Quantity for the Fixed-Period Model with Excel

The order quantity for the fixed-period model with variable demand can be determined using Excel. The Excel screen for Example 13.7 is shown in **Exhibit 13.6**. Notice that the order quantity in cell D10 is computed with the formula shown on the formula bar at the top of the screen.

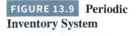

FIGURE 13.9 **Periodic Inventory System**

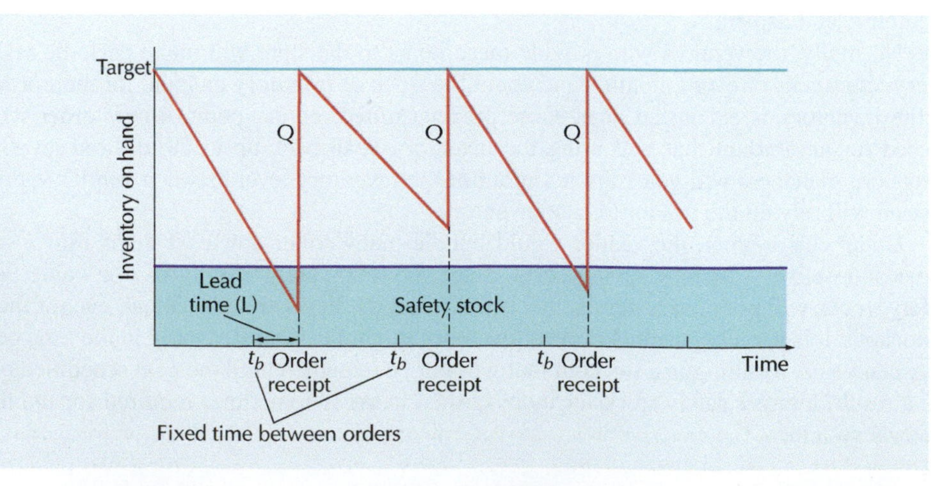

EXHIBIT 13.6

D10 | f_x =D3*(D4+5)+D7-D8

	A	B	C	D	E	F
1	**Example 13.7: Fixed Period Model with Variable Demand**					
2						
3			Average demand rate =	6	packages per day	
4			Time between orders =	60	days	
5			Lead time =	5	days	
6			Standard deviation of demand =	1.2	packages	
7			Safety stock =	15.96	packages	
8			Inventroy in stock =	8	packages	
9						
10			Q =	397.96	packages	
11						

Formula for order size, Q, in cell D10

EXAMPLE 13.7 | Order Size for Fixed-Period Model with Variable Demand

The KVS Pharmacy stocks a popular brand of over-the-counter flu and cold medicine. The average demand for the medicine is six packages per day, with a standard deviation of 1.2 packages. A vendor for the pharmaceutical company checks KVS's stock every 60 days. During one visit the store had eight packages in stock. The lead time to receive an order is five days. Determine the order size for this order period that will enable KVS to maintain a 95% service level.

Solution:

$$\bar{d} = 6 \text{ packages per day}$$
$$\sigma_d = 1.2 \text{ packages}$$
$$t_b = 60 \text{ days}$$
$$L = 5 \text{ days}$$
$$I = 8 \text{ packages}$$
$$z = 1.65 \text{ (for a 95 service level)}$$
$$Q = \bar{d}(t_b + L) + z\sigma_d\sqrt{t_b + L} - I$$
$$= (6)(60 + 5) + (1.65)(1.2)\sqrt{60 + 5} - 8$$
$$= 397.96 \text{ packages}$$

This will be rounded to 398 packages, or perhaps 400 if it is shipped in boxes of 100 packages.

Summary

The two types of systems for managing inventory are continuous and periodic, and we presented several models for determining how much to order and when to order for each system. However, we focused our attention primarily on the more commonly used continuous, fixed-order-quantity systems with EOQ models for determining order size and reorder points for determining when to order.

The objective of these order quantity models is to determine the optimal tradeoff between inventory carrying costs and ordering costs that would minimize total inventory cost. However, a drawback of approaching inventory management in this manner is that it can delude management into thinking that if it determines the minimum cost order quantity, it has achieved all it can in reducing inventory costs, which is not the case. Management should continually strive both to accurately assess and to reduce individual inventory costs. If management has accurately determined carrying and order costs, then it can seek ways to lower them that will reduce overall inventory costs regardless of the order size and reorder point.

Key Terms

ABC system A method for classifying inventory items according to their dollar value to the firm based on the principle that only a few items account for the greatest dollar value of total inventory.

carrying costs The cost of holding an item in inventory, including lost opportunity costs, storage, rent, cooling, lighting, interest on loans, and so on.

continuous inventory system A system in which the inventory level is continually monitored; when it decreases to a certain level, the reorder point, a fixed amount is ordered.

dependent demand Typically, component parts or materials used in the process to produce a final product.

economic order quantity (EOQ) A fixed-order quantity that minimizes total inventory costs.

independent demand Final or finished products whose demand is not a function of, or dependent on, internal production activity.

inventory A stock of items kept by an organization to meet internal or external customer demand.

order cycle The time between the receipt of orders in an inventory system.

ordering costs The cost of replenishing the stock of inventory including requisition cost, transportation and shipping, receiving, inspection, handling, and so forth.

periodic inventory system A system in which the inventory level is checked after a specific time period and a variable amount is ordered, depending on the inventory in stock.

production quantity model Also known as the production lot-size model; an inventory system in which an order is received gradually and the inventory level is depleted at the same time it is being replenished.

quantity discount A pricing schedule in which lower prices are provided for specific (higher) order quantities.

reorder point A level of inventory in stock at which a new order is placed.

safety stock An amount added to the expected amount demanded during the lead time (the reorder point level) as a hedge against a stockout.

service level The probability that the amount of inventory on hand during the lead time is sufficient to meet expected demand.

shortage costs Temporary or permanent loss of sales that will result when customer demand cannot be met.

stockout An inventory shortage occurring when demand exceeds the inventory in stock.

Key Formulas

Basic EOQ Model

$$\text{TC} = \frac{C_oD}{Q} + \frac{C_cQ}{2}$$

$$Q_{\text{opt}} = \sqrt{\frac{2C_oD}{C_c}}$$

EOQ Model with Noninstantaneous Receipt

$$\text{TC} = \frac{C_oD}{Q} + \frac{C_cQ}{2}\left(1 - \frac{d}{p}\right)$$

$$Q_{opt} = \sqrt{\frac{2C_oD}{C_o\left(1 - \frac{d}{p}\right)}}$$

Inventory Cost for Quantity Discounts

$$\text{TC} = \frac{C_oD}{Q} + \frac{C_cQ}{2} + PD$$

Reorder Point with Constant Demand and Lead Time

$$R = dL$$

Reorder Point with Variable Demand

$$R = \bar{d}L + z\sigma_d\sqrt{L}$$

Fixed-Time-Period Order Quantity with Variable Demand

$$Q = \bar{d}(t_b + L) + z\sigma_d\sqrt{t_b + L} - I$$

Solved Problems

1. Basic EOQ Model

Electronic Village stocks and sells a particular brand of personal computer. It costs the store $450 each time it places an order with the manufacturer for the personal computers. The annual cost of carrying the PCs in inventory is $170. The store manager estimates that annual demand for the PCs will be 1200 units. Determine the optimal order quantity and the total minimum inventory cost.

Solution

$$D = 1200 \text{ personal computers}$$
$$C_c = \$170$$
$$C_o = \$450$$
$$Q_{\text{opt}} = \sqrt{\frac{2C_oD}{C_c}}$$
$$= \sqrt{\frac{2(450)(1200)}{170}}$$
$$= 79.7 \text{ personal computers}$$
$$\text{TC} = \frac{C_oD}{Q_{\text{opt}}} + \frac{C_cQ_{\text{opt}}}{2}$$
$$= 450\left(\frac{1200}{79.7}\right) + 170\left(\frac{79.7}{2}\right)$$
$$= \$13{,}549.91$$

2. Production Quantity Model

I-75 Discount Carpets manufactures Cascade carpet, which it sells in its adjoining showroom store near the interstate. Estimated annual demand is 20,000 yards of carpet with an annual carrying cost of \$2.75 per yard. The manufacturing facility operates the same 360 days the store is open and produces 400 yards of carpet per day. The cost of setting up the manufacturing process for a production run is \$720. Determine the optimal order size, total inventory cost, length of time to receive an order, and maximum inventory level.

Solution

$$C_o = \$720$$
$$C_c = \$2.75 \text{ per yard}$$
$$D = 20{,}000 \text{ yards}$$
$$d = \frac{20{,}000}{360} = 55.56 \text{ yards per day}$$
$$p = 400 \text{ yards per day}$$
$$Q_{\text{opt}} = \sqrt{\frac{2C_oD}{C_c\left(1 - \frac{d}{p}\right)}}$$
$$= \sqrt{\frac{2(720)(20{,}000)}{2.75\left(1 - \frac{55.56}{400}\right)}}$$
$$= 3487.4 \text{ yards}$$
$$\text{TC}_{\text{min}} = \frac{C_oD}{Q} + \frac{C_cQ}{2}\left(1 - \frac{d}{p}\right)$$
$$= \frac{(720)(20{,}000)}{3487.4} + \frac{(2.75)(3487.4)}{2}\left(1 - \frac{55.6}{400}\right)$$
$$= \$8258.33$$
$$\text{Production run} = \frac{Q}{p}$$
$$= \frac{3487.4}{400}$$
$$= 8.72 \text{ days per order}$$

$$\text{Maximum inventory level} = Q\left(1 - \frac{d}{p}\right)$$
$$= 3487.4\left(1 - \frac{55.6}{400}\right)$$
$$= 3003 \text{ yards}$$

3. Quantity Discount

A manufacturing firm has been offered a particular component part it uses according to the following discount pricing schedule provided by the supplier.

1–199	\$65
200–599	59
600+	56

The manufacturing company uses 700 of the components annually, the annual carrying cost is \$14 per unit, and the ordering cost is \$275. Determine the amount the firm should order.

Solution

First, determine the optimal order size and total cost with the basic EOQ model.

$$C_o = \$275$$
$$C_c = \$14$$
$$D = 700$$
$$Q_{\text{opt}} = \sqrt{\frac{2C_oD}{C_c}}$$
$$= \sqrt{\frac{2(275)(700)}{14}}$$
$$Q_{\text{opt}} = 165.83$$
$$\text{TC} = \frac{C_oD}{Q_{\text{opt}}} + \frac{C_cQ_{\text{opt}}}{2} + PD$$
$$= \frac{(275)(700)}{165.83} + \frac{(14)(165.83)}{2} + (\$65)(700)$$
$$= \$47{,}821$$

Next, compare the order size with the second-level quantity discount with an order size of 200 and a discount price of \$59.

$$\text{TC} = \frac{(275)(700)}{200} + \frac{(14)(200)}{2} + (59)(700)$$
$$= \$43{,}662.50$$

This discount results in a lower cost.

Finally, compare the current discounted order size with the fixed-price discount for $Q = 600$.

$$\text{TC} = \frac{(275)(700)}{600} + \frac{(14)(600)}{2} + (56)(700)$$
$$= \$43{,}720.83$$

Since this total cost is higher, the optimal order size is 200 with a total cost of \$43,662.50.

4. Reorder Point with Variable Demand

A computer products store stocks color graphics monitors, and the daily demand is normally distributed with a mean of 1.6 monitors and a standard deviation of 0.4 monitor. The lead time to receive an order from the manufacturer is 15 days. Determine the reorder point that will achieve a 98% service level.

Solution

$$\bar{d} = 1.6 \text{ monitors per day}$$
$$L = 15 \text{ days}$$
$$\sigma_d = 0.4 \text{ monitor per day}$$
$$z = 2.05 (\text{for a } 98\% \text{ service level})$$
$$\begin{aligned} R &= \bar{d}L + z\sigma_d\sqrt{L} \\ &= (1.6)(15) + (2.05)(0.4)\sqrt{15} \\ &= 24 + 3.18 \\ &= 27.18 = 28 \text{ monitors} \end{aligned}$$

Questions

13.1. Describe the difference between independent and dependent demand and give an example of each for a pizza restaurant such as Domino's or Pizza Hut.

13.2. Distinguish between a fixed-order-quantity system and fixed-time-period system and give an example of each.

13.3. Discuss customer service level for an inventory system within the context of quality management.

13.4. Explain the ABC inventory classification system and indicate its advantages.

13.5. Identify the two basic decisions addressed by inventory management and discuss why the responses to these decisions differ for continuous and periodic inventory systems.

13.6. Describe the major cost categories used in inventory analysis and their functional relationship to each other.

13.7. Explain how the order quantity is determined using the basic EOQ model.

13.8. What are the assumptions of the basic EOQ model, and to what extent do they limit the usefulness of the model?

13.9. How are the reorder point and lead time related in inventory analysis?

13.10. Describe how the production quantity model differs from the basic EOQ model.

13.11. How must the application of the basic EOQ model be altered in order to reflect quantity discounts?

13.12. Why do the basic EOQ model variations not include the price of an item?

13.13. In the production quantity EOQ model, what would be the effect of the production rate becoming increasingly large as the demand rate became increasingly small, until the ratio d/p was negligible?

13.14. Explain in general terms how a safety stock level is determined using customer service level.

13.15. Explain the difference between a single-stage approach to inventory management and a multi-echelon approach.

Problems

WileyPLUS
GO TUTORIAL

13.1. AV City stocks and sells a particular brand of laptop. It costs the firm $625 each time it places an order with the manufacturer for the laptops. The cost of carrying one laptop in inventory for a year is $130. The store manager estimates that total annual demand for the laptops will be 1500 units, with a constant demand rate throughout the year. Orders are received within minutes after placement from a local warehouse maintained by the manufacturer. The store policy is never to have stockouts of the laptops. The store is open for business every day of the year except Christmas Day. Determine the following:

- **a.** Optimal order quantity per order
- **b.** Minimum total annual inventory costs
- **c.** The number of orders per year
- **d.** The time between orders (in working days)

13.2. AV City (Problem 13.1) assumed with certainty that the ordering cost is $625/order and the inventory carrying cost is $130/unit/year. However, the inventory model parameters are frequently only estimates that are subject to some degree of uncertainty. Consider four cases of variation in the model parameters as follows: (a) Both ordering cost and carrying cost are 10% less than originally estimated; (b) both ordering cost and carrying cost are 10% higher than originally estimated; (c) ordering cost is 10% higher and carrying cost is 10% lower than originally estimated; and (d) ordering cost is 10% lower and carrying cost is 10% higher than originally estimated. Determine the optimal order quantity and total inventory cost for each of the four cases. Prepare a table with values from all four cases and compare the sensitivity of the model solution to changes in parameter values.

13.3. A firm is faced with the attractive situation in which it can obtain immediate delivery of an item it stocks for retail sale. The firm has therefore not bothered to order the item in any systematic way. However, recently profits have been squeezed due to increasing competitive pressures, and the firm has retained a management consultant to study its inventory management. The consultant has determined that the various costs associated with making an order for the item stocked are approximately $70 per order. She has also determined that the costs of carrying the item in inventory amount to approximately $27 per unit per year (primarily direct storage costs and forgone profit on investment in inventory). Demand for the item is reasonably constant over time, and the forecast is for 16,500 units per year. When an order is placed for the item, the entire order is immediately delivered to the firm by the supplier. The firm operates 6 days a week plus a few Sundays, or approximately 320 days per year. Determine the following:

a. Optimal order quantity per order
b. Total annual inventory costs
c. Optimal number of orders to place per year
d. Number of operating days between orders, based on the optimal ordering

13.4. The Sofaworld Company purchases upholstery material from Barrett Textiles. The company uses 45,000 yards of material per year to make sofas. The cost of ordering material from the textile company is $1500 per order. It costs Sofaworld $0.70 annually to hold a yard of material in inventory. Determine the optimal number of yards of material Sofaworld should order, the minimum total inventory cost, the optimal number of orders per year, and the optimal time between orders.

13.5. The Wallace Stationery Company purchases paper from the Seaboard Paper Company. Wallace produces stationary that require 1,415,000 sq. yards of stationery per year. The cost per order for the company is $2200; the cost of holding 1 yard of paper in inventory is $0.08 per year. Determine the following:

a. Economic order quantity
b. Minimum total annual cost
c. Optimal number of orders per year
d. Optimal time between orders

13.6. The Ambrosia Bakery makes cakes for freezing and subsequent sale. The bakery, which operates five days a week, 52 weeks a year, can produce cakes at the rate of 116 cakes per day. The bakery sets up the cake-production operation and produces until a predetermined number (Q) has been produced. When not producing cakes, the bakery uses its personnel and facilities for producing other bakery items. The setup cost for a production run of cakes is $700. The cost of holding frozen cakes in storage is $9 per cake per year. The annual demand for frozen cakes, which is constant over time, is 6000 cakes. Determine the following:

a. Optimal production run quantity (Q)
b. Total annual inventory costs
c. Optimal number of production runs per year
d. Optimal cycle time (time between run starts)
e. Run length in working days

13.7. The EastCoasters Bicycle Shop operates 364 days a year, closing only on Christmas Day. The shop pays $300 for a particular bicycle purchased from the manufacturer. The annual holding cost per bicycle is estimated to be 25% of the dollar value of inventory. The shop sells an average of 18 bikes per week. The ordering cost for each order is $250. Determine the optimal order quantity and the total minimum cost.

13.8. The Chemco Company uses a highly toxic chemical in one of its manufacturing processes. It must have the product delivered by special cargo trucks designed for safe shipment of chemicals. As such, ordering (and delivery) costs are relatively high, at $3600 per order. The chemical product is packaged in 1-gallon plastic containers. The cost of holding the chemical in storage is $50 per gallon per year. The annual demand for the chemical, which is constant over time, is 7000 gallons per year. The lead time from time of order placement until receipt is 10 days. The company operates 310 working days per year. Compute the optimal order quantity, total minimum inventory cost, and the reorder point.

13.9. The Food Place Supermarket stocks Munchkin Cookies. Demand for Munchkins is 5000 boxes per year (365 days). It costs the store $80 per order of Munchkins, and it costs $0.50 per box per year to keep the cookies in stock. Once an order for Munchkins is placed, it takes four days to receive the order from a food distributor. Determine the following:

a. Optimal order size
b. Minimum total annual inventory cost
c. Reorder point

13.10. Kroft Foods makes cheese to supply to stores in its area. The dairy can make 350 pounds of cheese per day, and the demand at area stores is 205 pounds per day. Each time the dairy makes cheese, it costs $175 to set up the production process. The annual cost of carrying a pound of cheese in a refrigerated storage area is $12. Determine the optimal order size and the minimum total annual inventory cost.

13.11. The Shotz Brewery produces an ale that it stores in barrels in its warehouse and supplies to its distributors on demand. The demand for ale is 1800 barrels per day. The brewery can produce 3000 barrels per day. It costs $7500 to set up a production run for ale. Once it is brewed, the ale is stored in a refrigerated warehouse at an annual cost of $60 per barrel. Determine the economic order quantity and the minimum total annual inventory cost.

13.12. The purchasing manager for the Pacific Steel Company must determine a policy for ordering coal to operate 12 converters. Each converter requires exactly 5 tons of coal per day to operate, and the firm operates 360 days per year. The purchasing manager has determined that the ordering cost is $80 per order, and the cost of holding coal is 20% of the average dollar value of inventory held. The purchasing manager has negotiated a contract to obtain the coal for $12 per ton for the coming year.

a. Determine the optimal quantity of coal to receive in each order.
b. Determine the total inventory-related costs associated with the optimal ordering policy (do not include the cost of the coal).
c. If five days' lead time is required to receive an order of coal, how much coal should be on hand when an order is placed?

13.13. The TransCanada Lumber Company and Mill processes 10,000 logs annually, operating 250 days per year. Immediately upon receiving an order, the logging company's supplier begins delivery to the lumber mill at the rate of 60 logs per day. The lumber mill has determined that the ordering cost is $1600 per order, and the cost of carrying logs in inventory before they are processed is $15 per log on an annual basis. Determine the following:

a. The optimal order size
b. The total inventory cost associated with the optimal order quantity
c. The number of operating days between orders
d. The number of operating days required to receive an order

13.14. The Goodstone Tire Company produces a brand of tire called the Rainpath. The annual demand at its distribution center is 12,400 tires per year. The transport and handling costs are $2600 each time a shipment of tires is ordered at the distribution center. The annual carrying cost is $3.75 per tire.

a. Determine the optimal order quantity and the minimum total annual cost.
b. The company is thinking about relocating its distribution center, which would reduce transport and handling costs to $1900 per order but increase carrying costs to $4.50 per tire per year. Should the company relocate based on inventory costs?

13.15. The Deer Valley Farm produces a natural organic fertilizer, which it sells mostly to gardeners and homeowners. The annual demand for fertilizer is 220,000 pounds. The farm is able to produce 305,000 pounds annually. The cost to transport the fertilizer from the plant to the farm is $620 per load. The annual carrying cost is $0.12 per pound.

a. Compute the optimal order size, the maximum inventory level, and the total minimum cost.
b. If the farm can increase production capacity to 360,000 pounds per year, will it reduce total inventory cost?

13.16. Tradewinds Imports is an importer of ceramics from overseas. It has arranged to purchase a particular type of ceramic pottery from a Korean artisan. The artisan makes the pottery in 120-unit batches and will ship only that exact amount. The transportation and handling cost of a shipment is $7600 (not including the unit cost). The importer estimates its annual demand to be 1400 units. What storage and handling cost per unit does it need to achieve in order to minimize its inventory cost?

13.17. The KVS Pharmacy is open from 10:00 A.M. to 8:00 P.M., and it receives 200 calls per day for delivery orders. It costs the pharmacy \$25 to send out its cars to make deliveries. The pharmacy estimates that each minute a customer spends waiting for their order costs the pharmacy \$0.20 in lost sales.

a. How frequently should KVS send out its delivery cars each day? Indicate the total daily cost of deliveries.

b. If a car could only carry six orders how often would deliveries be made and what would be the cost?

13.18. The Olde Town Microbrewery makes Townside beer, which it bottles and sells in its adjoining restaurant and by the case. It costs \$1700 to set up, brew, and bottle a batch of the beer. The annual cost to store the beer in inventory is \$1.25 per bottle. The annual demand for the beer is 21,000 bottles and the brewery has the capacity to produce 30,000 bottles annually.

a. Determine the optimal order quantity, total annual inventory cost, the number of production runs per year, and the maximum inventory level.

b. If the microbrewery has only enough storage space to hold a maximum of 2500 bottles of beer in inventory, how will that affect total inventory costs?

13.19. JAL Trading is a Hong Kong manufacturer of electronic components. During the course of a year it requires container cargo space on ships leaving Hong Kong bound for the United States, Mexico, South America, and Canada. The company needs 280,000 cubic feet of cargo space annually. The cost of reserving cargo space is \$7000 and the cost of holding cargo space is \$0.80/ft^3. Determine how much storage space the company should optimally order, the total cost, and how many times per year it should place an order to reserve space.

13.20. Southwood Furniture Company is a U.S.-based furniture manufacturer that offshored all of its actual manufacturing operations to China about a decade ago. It set up a distribution center in Hong Kong from which the company ships its items to the United States on container ships. The company learned early on that it could not rely on local Chinese freight forwarders to arrange for sufficient containers for the company's shipments, so it contracted to purchase containers from a Taiwanese manufacturer and then sell them to shipping companies at the U.S. ports the containers are shipped to. Southwood needs 715 containers each year. It costs \$1200 to hold a container at its distribution center, and it costs \$6000 to receive an order for the containers. Determine the optimal order size, minimum total annual inventory cost, number of annual orders, and time between orders.

13.21. In Problem 12.1 in Chapter 12, the Hartley-Davis motorcycle dealership in the Minneapolis–St. Paul orders the Roadhog Super motorcycle it sells from the manufacturer in Japan. Using the three-month moving average forecast of demand for January as the monthly forecast for the next year, an annual carrying cost of \$375, an order cost of \$3200, and a lead time to receive an order of one month, determine the optimal order size, the minimum total annual inventory cost, the optimal time between orders, the number of orders, and the reorder point.

13.22. In Problem 12-2 in Chapter 12, Carpet City orders Soft Shag carpet from its own mill. Using the three-month moving average forecast of demand for month 9 as the monthly forecasts for all of next year, a production rate at the mill of 1200 yards per day (and the mill operates 260 days per year), an annual carrying cost of \$0.63, the cost of setting up a production run and delivering the carpet to the store is \$425, and a lead time to receive an order of 7 days, determine the optimal order size, the minimum total annual inventory cost, and the reorder point (given that Carpet City is open 360 days per year).

13.23. In Problem 12.47 in Chapter 12, Delaplane Computers supplier receives shipments of laptop screens from its manufacturing facility in the Philippines, which has maximum production rate of 200 units per day. Using the forecast of demand developed in 12-47, an annual carrying cost of \$115.75 (which includes an average obsolescence cost), a shipping cost from Asia of \$6500 per shipment, and a lead time to receive an order of 25 days, determine the optimal order size, the minimum total annual inventory cost, the maximum inventory level, and the reorder point (given that the Delaplane assembly operation operates 365 days per year).

13.24. The State University power plant burns coal to generate steam and electricity for campus buildings. It takes three days to transport coal by railroad from the coalfields, and the cost of shipping and handling coal by rail is \$19.50 per ton. The coal demand for the coming year is forecasted to be 48,000 tons, and the annual handling and storage cost at the Tech power plant is \$112 per ton. Determine the power plant's ordering policy and total annual inventory cost.

13.25. Arkind is a global manufacturer and supplier of denim jeans to apparel retailers around the world. It purchases baled cotton from cotton producers in Louisiana, Texas, Georgia, and South Carolina and ships it to its warehouse at the port of Savannah, where it then ships it overseas to its distribution center in India that supplies its nearby denim fabric and denim jeans factories. The demand from these overseas manufacturing facilities averages about 1,245,000 bales per year. The monthly handling and storage cost for a bale of cotton at Arkind's distribution center in India is \$15.75. Each time Arkind needs cotton it ships from Savannah on its own container ship at a cost of \$2.3 million. Determine the optimal order quantity, minimum total annual inventory cost, number of shipments per year, and the time between shipments.

13.26. County Hospital orders syringes from a hospital supply firm. The hospital expects to use 40,000 per year. The cost to order and have the syringes delivered is \$800. The annual carrying cost is \$1.90 per syringe because of security and theft. The hospital supply firm offers the following quantity discount pricing schedule.

QUANTITY	PRICE
0–9,999	\$3.40
10,000–19,999	3.20
20,000–29,999	3.00
30,000–39,999	2.80
40,000–49,999	2.60
50,000+	2.40

Determine the order size for the hospital.

13.27. The Interstate Carpet Discount Store has annual demand of 10,000 yards of Super Shag carpet. The annual carrying cost for a yard of this carpet is \$1.25, and the ordering cost is \$300. The carpet manufacturer normally charges the store \$8 per yard for the carpet. However, the manufacturer has offered a discount price of \$6.50 per yard if the store will order 5000 yards. How much should the store order, and what will be the total annual inventory cost for that order quantity?

13.28. Kelly's Tavern buys Shamrock draft beer by the keg from a local distributor. The bar has an annual demand of 900 kegs, which it purchases at a price of \$60 per keg. The annual carrying cost is \$7.20, and the cost per order is \$160. The distributor has offered the bar a reduced price of \$52 per barrel if it will order a minimum of 300 barrels. Should the bar take the discount?

13.29. The bookstore at Tech purchases jackets emblazoned with the school name and logo from a vendor. The vendor sells the jackets to the store for $38 apiece. The cost to the bookstore for placing an order is $120, and the annual carrying cost is 25% of the cost of a jacket. The bookstore manager estimates that 1700 jackets will be sold during the year. The vendor has offered the bookstore the following volume discount schedule:

ORDER SIZE	DISCOUNT
1–299	0%
300–499	2%
500–799	4%
800+	5%

What is the bookstore's optimal order quantity, given this quantity discount information?

13.30. Determine the optimal order quantity of jackets and total annual cost in Problem 13.29 if the carrying cost is a constant $8 per jacket per year.

13.31. The office manager for the Metro Life Insurance Company orders letterhead stationery from an office products firm in boxes of 500 sheets. The company uses 6500 boxes per year. Annual carrying costs are $3 per box, and ordering costs are $28. The following discount price schedule is provided by the office supply company:

ORDER QUANTITY (BOXES)	PRICE PER BOX
200–999	$16
1000–2999	14
3000–5999	13
6000+	12

Determine the optimal order quantity and the total annual inventory cost.

13.32. Determine the optimal order quantity and total annual inventory cost for boxes of stationery in Problem 13.31 if the carrying cost is 20% of the price of a box of stationery.

13.33. The 21,000-seat Air East Arena houses the local professional ice hockey, basketball, indoor soccer, and arena football teams as well as various trade shows, wrestling and boxing matches, tractor pulls, and circuses. Arena vending annually sells large quantities of soft drinks and beer in plastic cups with the name of the arena and the various team logos on them. The local container cup manufacturer that supplies the cups in boxes of 100 has offered arena management the following discount price schedule for cups:

ORDER QUANTITY (BOXES)	PRICE PER BOX
2,000–6,999	$47
7,000–11,999	43
12,000–19,999	41
20,000+	38

The annual demand for cups is 2.3 million, the annual carrying cost per box of cups is $1.90, and ordering cost is $320. Determine the optimal order quantity and total annual inventory cost.

13.34. Determine the optimal order quantity and total annual inventory cost for cups in Problem 13.33 if the carrying cost is 5% of the price of a box of cups.

13.35. The amount of denim used daily by the Southwest Apparel Company in its manufacturing process to make jeans is normally distributed with an average of 4000 yards of denim and a standard deviation of 600 yards. The lead time required to receive an order of denim from the textile mill is a constant 7 days. Determine the safety stock and reorder point if the company wants to limit the probability of a stockout and work stoppage to 5%.

13.36. In Problem 13.35, what level of service would a safety stock of 2000 yards provide?

13.37. The Paramount Paper company produces paper from wood pulp ordered from a lumber products firm. The paper company's daily demand for wood pulp is normally distributed, with a mean of 9000 pounds and a standard deviation of 1900 pounds. Lead time is eight days. Determine the reorder point if the paper company wants to limit the probability of a stockout and work stoppage to 2%.

13.38. Kelly's Tavern serves Shamrock draft beer to its customers. The daily demand for beer is normally distributed, with an average of 20 gallons and a standard deviation of 4 gallons. The lead time required to receive an order of beer from the local distributor is 12 days. Determine the safety stock and reorder point if the restaurant wants to maintain a 90% service level. What would be the increase in the safety stock if a 95% service level were desired?

13.39. The daily demand for Ironcoat paint at the Top Value Hardware Store in North Bay is normally distributed, with a mean of 30 gallons and a standard deviation of 10 gallons. The lead time for receiving an order of paint from the paint distributor is eight days. Since this is the only paint store in North Bay, the manager is interested in maintaining only a 75% service level. What reorder point should be used to meet this service level? The manager subsequently learned that a new paint store would open soon in North Bay, which has prompted her to increase the service level to 95%. What reorder point will maintain this service level?

13.40. IM Systems assembles microcomputers from generic components. It purchases its color monitors from a manufacturer in Taiwan; thus, there is a long lead time of 25 days. Daily demand is normally distributed with a mean of 3.5 monitors and a standard deviation of 1.2 monitors. Determine the safety stock and reorder point corresponding to a 90% service level.

13.41. IM Systems (Problem 13.40) is considering purchasing monitors from a U.S. manufacturer that would guarantee a lead time of eight days, instead of from the Taiwanese company. Determine the new reorder point given this lead time and identify the factors that would enter into the decision to change manufacturers.

13.42. KVS Pharmacy fills prescriptions for a popular children's antibiotic, Amoxycilin. The daily demand for Amoxycilin is normally distributed with a mean of 200 ounces and a standard deviation of 80 ounces. The vendor for the pharmaceutical firm that supplies the drug calls the drugstore's pharmacist every 30 days and checks the inventory of Amoxycilin. During a call the druggist indicated the store had 60 ounces of the antibiotic in stock. The lead time to receive an order is four days. Determine the order size that will enable the drugstore to maintain a 99% service level.

13.43. Food Place Market stocks frozen pizzas in a refrigerated display case. The average daily demand for the pizzas is normally distributed, with a mean of 8 pizzas and a standard deviation of 2.5 pizzas. A vendor for a packaged food distributor checks the market's inventory of frozen foods every 10 days; during a particular visit there were no pizzas in stock. The lead time to receive an order is three days. Determine the order size for this order period that will result in a 98% service level. During the vendor's following visit there were 5 frozen pizzas in stock. What is the order size for the next order period?

13.44. The Mediterranean Restaurant stocks a red Chilean table wine it purchases from a wine merchant in a nearby city. The daily demand for the wine at the restaurant is normally distributed, with a mean of 18 bottles and a standard deviation of 4 bottles. The wine merchant sends a representative to check the restaurant's wine cellar every 30 days, and during a recent visit there were 25 bottles in stock. The lead time to receive an order is two days. The restaurant manager has requested an order size that will enable him to limit the probability of a stockout to 5%.

13.45. The Aztec Company stocks a variety of parts and materials it uses in its manufacturing processes. Recently, as demand for its finished goods has increased, management has had difficulty managing parts inventory; they frequently run out of some crucial parts and seem to have an endless supply of others. In an effort to control inventory more effectively, they would like to classify their inventory of parts according to the ABC approach. Following is a list of selected parts and the annual usage and unit value for each:

ITEM NUMBER	ANNUAL USAGE	UNIT COST	ITEM NUMBER	ANNUAL USAGE	UNIT COST
1	36	$350	16	60	$610
2	510	30	17	120	20
3	50	23	18	270	15
4	300	45	19	45	50
5	18	1900	20	19	3200
6	500	8	21	910	3
7	710	4	22	12	4750
8	80	26	23	30	2710
9	344	28	24	24	1800
10	67	440	25	870	105
11	510	2	26	244	30
12	682	35	27	750	15
13	95	50	28	45	110
14	10	3	29	46	160
15	820	1	30	165	25

Classify the inventory items according to the ABC approach using dollar value of annual demand.

13.46. The EastCoasters Bicycle Shop stocks bikes; helmets; clothing; a variety of bike parts including chains, gears, tires, wheels; and biking accessories. The shop is in a storefront location on a busy street and it has very limited storage space for inventory. It often runs out of items and is unable to serve customers. To help manage its inventory the shop would like to classify the stock using the ABC system. Following is a list of items the shop stocks and the annual demand and unit value for each:

ITEM NUMBER	ANNUAL DEMAND	UNIT COST	ITEM NUMBER	ANNUAL DEMAND	UNIT COST
1	10	$8	17	110	$23
2	18	16	18	74	18
3	36	30	19	8	610
4	9	1230	20	10	935
5	4	760	21	7	270
6	3	810	22	5	1400
7	19	420	23	5	900
8	56	35	24	46	67
9	105	17	25	32	160
10	27	350	26	101	45
11	19	36	27	83	12
12	12	115	28	54	16
13	7	2300	29	14	42
14	10	245	30	9	705
15	6	665	31	7	37
16	18	28	32	16	26

Classify the inventory items according to the ABC approach using dollar value of annual demand.

13.47. Tara McCoy is the office administrator for the Department of Management at State University. The faculty uses a lot of printer paper and Tara is constantly reordering and frequently runs out. She orders the paper from the university central stores and several faculty have determined that the lead time to receive an order is normally distributed, with a mean of 2 days and a standard deviation of 0.5 day. The faculty have also determined that daily demand for the paper is normally distributed, with a mean of 2.6 packages and a standard deviation of 0.8 packages. What reorder point should Tara use in order not to run out 99% of the time?

13.48. The concession stand at the Shelby High School stadium sells slices of pizza during boys' and girls' soccer games. Concession stand sales are a primary source of revenue for the high school athletic programs, so the athletic director wants to sell as much food as possible; however, any pizza not sold is given away free to the players, coaches, and referees or it is thrown away. Thus, the athletic director wants to determine a reorder point that will meet the demand for pizza. Pizza sales are normally distributed with a mean of 6 pizzas per hour and a standard deviation of 2.5 pizzas. The pizzas are ordered from Pizza Beth's restaurant, and the mean delivery time is 30 minutes, with a standard deviation of 8 minutes.

a. Currently the concession stand places an order when there is 1 pizza left. What level of service does this result in?

b. What should the reorder point be to have a 98% service level?

Case Problems

Case Problem 13.1 The Instant Paper Clip Office Supply Company

Christie Levine is the manager of the Instant Paper Clip Office Supply Company in Louisville. The company attempts to gain an advantage over its competitors by providing quality customer service, which includes prompt delivery of orders by truck or van and always being able to meet customer demand from its stock. In order to achieve this degree of customer service, it must stock a large volume of items on a daily basis at a central warehouse and at three retail stores in the city and suburbs.

Christie maintains these inventory levels by borrowing cash on a daily basis from the First American Bank. She estimates that for the coming fiscal year the company's demand for cash to pay for inventory will be $17,000 per day for 305 working days. Any money she borrows during the year must be repaid with interest by the end of the year. The annual interest rate currently charged by the bank is 9%. Any time Christie takes out a loan to purchase inventory, the bank charges the company a loan origination fee of $1200 plus 2¼ points (2.25% of the amount borrowed).

Christie often uses EOQ analysis to determine optimal amounts of inventory to order for different office supplies. Now she is wondering if she can use the same type of analysis to determine an optimal borrowing policy. Determine the amount of the loan Christie should borrow from the bank, the total annual cost of the company's borrowing policy, and the number of loans the company should obtain during the year. Also determine the level of cash on hand at which the company should apply for a new loan given that it takes 15 days for a loan to be processed by the bank.

Suppose the bank offers Christie a discount as follows. On any loan amount equal to or greater than $500,000, the bank will lower the number of points charged on the loan origination fee from 2.25% to 2.00%. What would be the company's optimal amount borrowed?

Case Problem 13.2 The Texas Gladiators Apparel Store

The Texas Gladiators won the Super Bowl last year. As a result, sportswear such as hats, sweatshirts, sweatpants, and jackets with the Gladiators' logo are popular. The Gladiators operate an apparel store outside the football stadium. It is near a busy highway, so the store has heavy customer traffic throughout the year, not just on game days. In addition, the stadium has high school or college football and soccer games almost every week in the fall, and baseball games in the spring and summer. The most popular single item the stadium store sells is a red and silver baseball-style cap with the Gladiators' logo on it. The cap has an elastic headband inside it, which conforms to different head sizes. However, the store has had a difficult time keeping the cap in stock, especially during the time between the placement and receipt of an order. Often customers come to the store just for the hat; when it is not in stock, customers are upset, and the store management believes they tend to go to other competing stores to purchase their Gladiators' clothing. To rectify this problem, the store manager, Jessica James, would like to develop an inventory control policy that would ensure that customers would be able to purchase the cap 99% of the time they asked for it. Jessica has accumulated the following demand data for the cap for a 30-week period. (Demand includes actual sales plus a record of the times a cap has been requested but not available and an estimate of the number of times a customer wanted a cap when it was not available but did not ask for it.)

The store purchases the hats from a small manufacturing company in Jamaica. The shipments from Jamaica are erratic, with a lead time of 20 days.

In the past, Ms. James has placed an order whenever the stock got down to 150 caps. What level of service does this reorder point correspond to? What would the reorder point and safety stock need to be to achieve the desired service level? Discuss how Jessica James might determine the order size of caps and what additional, if any, information would be needed to determine the order size.

WEEK	DEMAND	WEEK	DEMAND	WEEK	DEMAND
1	38	4	60	7	29
2	51	5	35	8	46
3	25	6	42	9	55
10	19	17	62	24	46
11	28	18	53	25	47
12	41	19	46	26	41
13	37	20	41	27	39
14	44	21	52	28	50
15	45	22	48	29	28
16	56	23	49	30	34

Case Problem 13.3 Pharr Foods Company

Pharr Foods Company produces a variety of food products including a line of candies. One of its most popular candy items is "Far Stars," a bag of a dozen individually wrapped star-shaped candies made primarily from a blend of dark and milk chocolates, macadamia nuts, and a blend of heavy cream fillings. The item is relatively expensive, so Pharr Foods only produces it for its eastern market encompassing urban areas such as New York, Atlanta, Philadelphia, and Boston. The item is not sold in grocery or discount stores but mainly in specialty shops and specialty groceries, candy stores, and department stores. Pharr Foods supplies the candy to a single food distributor, which has several warehouses on the East Coast. The candy is shipped in cases with 60 bags of the candy per case. Far Stars sell well despite the fact that they are expensive at $9.85 per bag (wholesale). Pharr uses high-quality, fresh ingredients and does not store large stocks of the candy in inventory for very long periods of time.

Pharr's distributor believes that demand for the candy follows a seasonal pattern. It has collected demand data (i.e., cases sold) for Far Stars from its warehouses and the stores it supplies for the past three years, as follows.

	DEMAND (CASES)		
MONTH	YEAR 1	YEAR 2	YEAR 3
January	192	212	228
February	210	223	231
March	205	216	226
April	260	252	293
May	228	235	246
June	172	220	229
July	160	209	217
August	147	231	226
September	256	263	302
October	342	370	410
November	261	260	279
December	273	277	293

The distributor must hold the candy inventory in climate-controlled warehouses and be careful in handling it. The annual carrying cost is $116 per case. The item must be shipped a long distance from the manufacturer to the distributor. In order to keep the candy as fresh as possible, trucks must be air-conditioned and shipments must be direct, and are often less-than-truckload. As a result, ordering cost is $4700.

Pharr Foods makes Far Stars from three primary ingredients it orders from different suppliers: dark and milk chocolate, macadamia nuts, and, a special heavy cream filling. Except for its unique star shape, a Far Star is almost like a chocolate truffle. Each Far Star weighs 1.2 ounces and requires 0.70 ounce of blended chocolates, 0.50 ounce of macadamia nuts, and 0.40 ounce of filling to produce (including spillage and waste). Pharr Foods orders chocolate, nuts, and filling from its suppliers by the pound. The annual ordering cost is $5700 for chocolate, and the carrying cost is $0.45 per pound. The ordering cost for macadamia nuts is $6300, and the annual carrying cost is $0.63 per pound. The ordering cost for filling is $4500, and the annual average carrying cost is $0.55 per pound.

Each of the suppliers offers the candy manufacturer a quantity-discount price schedule for the ingredients as follows:

CHOCOLATE		MACADAMIA NUTS		FILLING	
PRICE	QUANTITY (lb)	PRICE	QUANTITY (lb)	PRICE	QUANTITY (lb)
$3.05	0–50,000	$6.50	0–30,000	$1.50	0–40,000
2.90	50,001–100,000	6.25	30,001–70,000	1.35	40,001–80,000
2.75	100,001–150,000	5.95	70,001+	1.25	80,001+
2.60	150,001+				

Determine the inventory order quantity for Pharr's distributor. Compare the optimal order quantity with a seasonally adjusted forecast for demand. Does the order quantity seem adequate to meet the seasonal demand pattern for Far Stars? That is, is it likely that shortages or excessive inventories will occur? Can you identify the causes of the seasonal demand pattern for Far Stars? Determine the inventory order quantity for each of the three primary ingredients that Pharr Foods orders from its suppliers. Discuss the possible impact of the order policies of the food distributor and Pharr Foods on quality management and supply chain management.

References

Brown, R. G. *Decision Rules for Inventory Management.* New York: Holt, Rinehart and Winston, 1967.

Buchan, J., and E. Koenigsberg. *Scientific Inventory Management.* Upper Saddle River, N.J.: Prentice Hall, 1963.

Buffa, E. S., and Jefferey Miller. *Production-Inventory Systems: Planning and Control*, rev. ed. Homewood, IL: Irwin, 1979.

Churchman, C. W., R. L. Ackoff, and E. L. Arnoff. *Introduction to Operations Research.* New York: Wiley, 1957.

Fetter, R. B., and W. C. Dalleck. *Decision Models for Inventory Management.* Homewood, IL: Irwin, 1961.

Greene, J. H. *Production and Inventory Control.* Homewood, IL: Irwin, 1974.

Hadley, G., and T. M. Whitin. *Analysis of Inventory Systems.* Upper Saddle River, N.J.: Prentice Hall, 1963.

McGee, J. F., and D. M. Boodman. *Production Planning and Inventory Control*, 2nd ed. New York: McGraw-Hill, 1967.

Starr, M. K., and D. W. Miller. *Inventory Control: Theory and Practice.* Upper Saddle River, N.J.: Prentice Hall, 1962.

Wagner, H. M. *Statistical Management of Inventory Systems.* New York: Wiley, 1962.

Whitin, T. M. *The Theory of Inventory Management.* Princeton, N.J.: Princeton University Press, 1957.

SUPPLEMENT TO CHAPTER 13

Operational Decision-Making Tools: Simulation

IN THIS SUPPLEMENT, YOU WILL LEARN ABOUT . . .

- Monte Carlo Simulation
- Computer Simulation with Excel
- Areas of Simulation Application

Simulation A mathematical and computer modeling technique for replicating real-world problem situations.

Simulation is popular because it can be applied to virtually any type of problem. It can frequently be used when there is no other applicable quantitative method; sometimes it is the technique of last resort for a problem. It is a modeling approach primarily used to analyze probabilistic problems. It does not normally provide a solution; instead, it provides information that is used to make a decision.

Much of the experimentation in space flight was conducted using physical **simulation** that recreated the conditions of space. Conditions of weightlessness were simulated using rooms filled with water. Other examples include wind tunnels that simulate the conditions of flight and treadmills that simulate automobile tire wear in a laboratory instead of on the road.

This supplement is concerned with another type of simulation, *computerized mathematical simulation*. In this form of simulation, systems are replicated with mathematical models, which are analyzed with a computer. This type of simulation is very popular and has been applied to a wide variety of operational problems.

Monte Carlo Simulation

Monte Carlo technique A method for selecting numbers randomly from a probability distribution for use in a simulation.

Some problems are difficult to solve analytically because they consist of random variables represented by probability distributions. Thus, a large proportion of the applications of simulations are for probabilistic models.

The term *Monte Carlo* has become synonymous with probabilistic simulation in recent years. However, the **Monte Carlo technique** can be more narrowly defined as a technique for selecting numbers *randomly* from a probability distribution (i.e., sampling) for use in a *trial* (computer) run of a simulation. As such, the Monte Carlo technique is not a type of simulation model but rather a mathematical process used within a simulation.

The name *Monte Carlo* is appropriate, since the basic principle behind the process is the same as in the operation of a gambling casino in Monaco. In Monaco devices like roulette wheels, dice, and playing cards produce numbered results at random from well-defined populations. For

TABLE S13.1 Probability Distribution of Demand

LAPTOPS DEMANDED PER WEEK, X	FREQUENCY OF DEMAND	PROBABILITY OF DEMAND $P(X)$
0	20	.20
1	40	.40
2	20	.20
3	10	.10
4	10	.10
	100	1.00

example, a 7 resulting from thrown dice is a random value from a population of 11 possible numbers (i.e., 2 through 12). This same process is employed, in principle, in the Monte Carlo process used in simulation models.

The Monte Carlo process of selecting random numbers according to a probability distribution will be demonstrated using the following example. The manager of ComputerWorld, a store that sells computers and related equipment, is attempting to determine how many laptops the store should order each week. A primary consideration in this decision is the average number of laptops that the store will sell each week and the average weekly revenue generated from the sale of laptops. A laptop sells for \$4300. The number of laptops demanded each week is a random variable (which we will define as x) that ranges from 0 to 4. From past sales records, the manager has determined the frequency of demand for laptops for the past 100 weeks. From this frequency distribution, a probability distribution of demand can be developed, as shown in Table S13.1.

The purpose of the Monte Carlo process is to generate the random variable, demand, by "sampling" from the probability distribution, $P(x)$. The demand per week could be randomly generated according to the probability distribution by spinning a roulette wheel that is partitioned into segments corresponding to the probabilities, as shown in Figure S13.1.

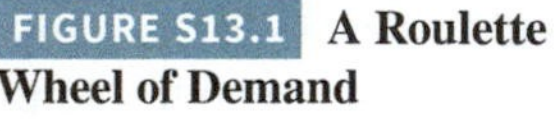
FIGURE S13.1 A Roulette Wheel of Demand

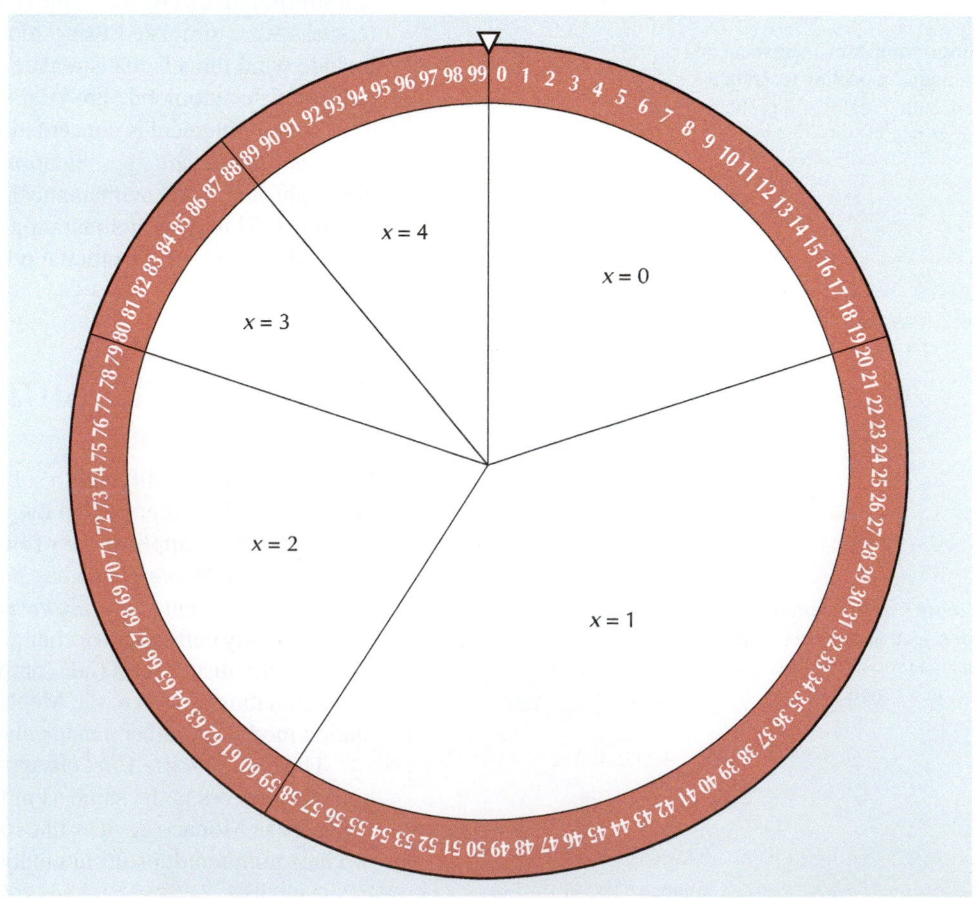

TABLE S13.2 Generating Demand from Random Numbers

DEMAND, x	RANGES OF RANDOM NUMBERS, r	
0	0–19	
1 ◄———	20–59 ◄———	$r = 39$
2	60–79	
3	80–89	
4	90–99	

There are 100 numbers from 0 to 99 on the outer rim of the wheel, and they have been partitioned according to the probability of each demand value. For example, 20 numbers from 0 to 19 (i.e., 20% of the total 100 numbers) correspond to a demand of zero laptops. Now we can determine the value of demand by the number the wheel stops at and the segment of the wheel.

When the manager spins this wheel, the demand for laptops will be determined by a number. For example, if the number 71 comes up on a spin, the demand is 2 laptops per week; the number 30 indicates a demand of 1. Since the manager does not know which number will come up prior to the spin and there is an equal chance of any of the 100 numbers occurring, the numbers occur at random. That is, they are **random numbers**.

Random numbers Numbers that have an equal likelihood of being selected at random.

It is not generally practical to predict weekly demand for laptops by spinning a wheel. Alternatively, the process of spinning a wheel can be replicated using random numbers alone.

First, we will transfer the ranges of random numbers for each demand value from the roulette wheel to a table, as in **Table S13.2**. Next, instead of spinning the wheel to get a random number, we will select a random number from **Table S13.3**, which is referred to as a *random number table*. (These random numbers have been generated by computer so that they are *equally likely to occur*, just as if we had spun a wheel.) As an example, let us select the number 39 in Table S13.3. Looking again at Table S13.2, we can see that the random number 39 falls in the range 20–59, which corresponds to a weekly demand of 1 laptop.

By repeating this process of selecting random numbers from Table S13.3 (starting anywhere in the table and moving in any direction but not repeating the same sequence) and then determining weekly demand from the random number, we can simulate demand for a period of time. For example, **Table S13.4** shows demand simulated for a period of 15 consecutive weeks.

These data can now be used to compute the estimated average weekly demand.

$$\text{Estimated average demand} = \frac{31}{15}$$
$$= 2.07 \text{ laptops per week}$$

The manager can then use this information to determine the number of laptops to order each week.

Although this example is convenient for illustrating how simulation works, the average demand could have been more appropriately calculated *analytically* using the formula for expected value. The *expected value*, or average, for weekly demand can be computed analytically from the probability distribution, $P(x)$, as follows:

$$E(x) = (0.20)(0) + (0.40)(1) + (0.20)(2) + (0.10)(3) + (0.10)(4)$$
$$= 1.5 \text{ laptops per week}$$

The analytical result of 1.5 laptops is not very close to the simulated result of 2.07 laptops. The difference (0.57 laptops) between the simulated value and the analytical value is a result of the

TABLE S13.3 Random Number Table

39 65 76 45 45	19 90 69 64 61	20 26 36 31 62	58 24 97 14 97	95 06 70 99 00
73 71 23 70 90	65 97 60 12 11	31 56 34 19 19	47 83 75 51 33	30 62 38 20 46
72 18 47 33 84	51 67 47 97 19	98 40 07 17 66	23 05 09 51 80	59 78 11 52 49
75 12 25 69 17	17 95 21 78 58	24 33 45 77 48	69 81 84 09 29	93 22 70 45 80
37 17 79 88 74	63 52 06 34 30	01 31 60 10 27	35 07 79 71 53	28 99 52 01 41
02 48 08 16 94	85 53 83 29 95	56 27 09 24 43	21 78 55 09 82	72 61 88 73 61
87 89 15 70 07	37 79 49 12 38	48 13 93 55 96	41 92 45 71 51	09 18 25 58 94
98 18 71 70 15	89 09 39 59 24	00 06 41 41 20	14 36 59 25 47	54 45 17 24 89
10 83 58 07 04	76 62 16 48 68	58 76 17 14 86	59 53 11 52 21	66 04 18 72 87
47 08 56 37 31	71 82 13 50 41	27 55 10 24 92	28 04 67 53 44	95 23 00 84 47
93 90 31 03 07	34 18 04 52 35	74 13 39 35 22	68 95 23 92 35	36 63 70 35 33
21 05 11 47 99	11 20 99 45 18	76 51 94 84 86	13 79 93 37 55	98 16 04 41 67
95 89 94 06 97	27 37 83 28 71	79 57 95 13 91	09 61 87 25 21	56 20 11 32 44
97 18 31 55 73	10 65 81 92 59	77 31 61 95 46	20 44 90 32 64	26 99 76 75 63
69 08 88 86 13	59 71 74 17 32	48 38 75 93 29	73 37 32 04 05	60 82 29 20 25
41 26 10 25 03	87 63 93 95 17	81 83 83 04 49	77 45 85 50 51	79 88 01 97 30
91 47 14 63 62	08 61 74 51 69	92 79 43 89 79	29 18 94 51 23	14 85 11 47 23
80 94 54 18 47	08 52 85 08 40	48 40 35 94 22	72 65 71 08 86	50 03 42 99 36
67 06 77 63 99	89 85 84 46 06	64 71 06 21 66	89 37 20 70 01	61 65 70 22 12
59 72 24 13 75	42 29 72 23 19	06 94 76 10 08	81 30 15 39 14	81 33 17 16 33
63 62 06 34 41	79 53 36 02 95	94 61 09 43 62	20 21 14 68 86	84 95 48 46 45
78 47 23 53 90	79 93 96 38 63	34 85 52 05 09	85 43 01 72 73	14 93 87 81 40
87 68 62 15 43	97 48 72 66 48	53 16 71 13 81	59 97 50 99 52	24 62 20 42 31
47 60 92 10 77	26 97 05 73 51	88 46 38 03 58	72 68 49 29 31	75 70 16 08 24
56 88 87 59 41	06 87 37 78 48	65 88 69 58 39	88 02 84 27 83	85 81 56 39 38
22 17 68 65 84	87 02 22 57 51	68 69 80 95 44	11 29 01 95 80	49 34 35 36 47
19 36 27 59 46	39 77 32 77 09	79 57 92 36 59	89 74 39 82 15	08 58 94 34 74
16 77 23 02 77	28 06 24 25 93	22 45 44 84 11	87 80 61 65 31	09 71 91 74 25
78 43 76 71 61	97 67 63 99 61	30 45 67 93 82	59 73 19 85 23	53 33 65 97 21
03 28 28 26 08	69 30 16 09 05	53 58 47 70 93	66 56 45 65 79	45 56 20 19 47
04 31 17 21 56	33 73 99 19 87	26 72 39 27 67	53 77 57 68 93	60 61 97 22 61
61 06 98 03 91	87 14 77 43 96	43 00 65 98 50	45 60 33 01 07	98 99 46 50 47
23 68 35 26 00	99 53 93 61 28	52 70 05 48 34	56 65 05 61 86	90 92 10 70 80
15 39 25 70 99	93 86 52 77 65	15 33 59 05 28	22 87 26 07 47	86 96 98 29 06
58 71 96 30 24	18 46 23 34 27	85 13 99 24 44	49 18 09 79 49	74 16 32 23 02
93 22 53 64 39	07 10 63 76 35	87 03 04 79 88	08 13 13 85 51	55 34 57 72 69
78 76 58 54 74	92 38 70 96 92	52 06 79 79 45	82 63 18 27 44	69 66 92 19 09
61 81 31 96 82	00 57 25 60 59	46 72 60 18 77	55 66 12 62 11	08 99 55 64 57
42 88 07 10 05	24 98 65 63 21	47 21 61 88 32	27 80 30 21 60	10 92 35 36 12
77 94 30 05 39	28 10 99 00 27	12 73 73 99 12	49 99 57 94 82	96 88 57 17 91

TABLE S13.4 The Simulation Experiment

WEEK	*r*	DEMAND (*X*)	REVENUE ($)
1	39	1	4,300
2	73	2	8,600
3	72	2	8,600
4	75	2	8,600
5	37	1	4,300
6	02	0	0
7	87	3	12,900
8	98	4	17,200
9	10	0	0
10	47	1	4,300
11	93	4	17,200
12	21	1	4,300
13	95	4	17,200
14	97	4	17,200
15	69	2	8,600
		$\Sigma = 31$	$133,300

number of periods over which the simulation was conducted. The results of any simulation study are subject to the number of times the simulation occurred (i.e., the number of *trials*). Thus, the more periods for which the simulation is conducted, the more accurate the result. For example, if demand were simulated for 1000 weeks, in all likelihood an average value exactly equal to the analytical value (1.5 laptops per week) would result.

Once a simulation has been repeated enough times, it reaches an average result that remains constant, called a **steady-state result**. For this example, 1.5 laptops is the long-run average or steady-state result, but we have seen that the simulation would have to be repeated more than 15 times (i.e., weeks) before this result is reached.

Steady-state result An average result that remains constant after enough trials.

Computer Simulation with Excel

The simulation we performed manually for this example was not too difficult. However, if we had performed the simulation for 1000 weeks, it would have taken several hours. On the other hand, this simulation could be done on the computer in several seconds. Also, our simulation example was not very complex. As simulation models get progressively more complex, it becomes virtually impossible to perform them manually, making the computer a necessity.

Although we will not develop a simulation model in computer language, we will demonstrate how a computerized simulation model is developed using Excel spreadsheets. We will do so by simulating our inventory example for ComputerWorld.

The first step in developing a simulation model is to generate random numbers. Random numbers between 0 and 1 can be generated in Excel by entering the formula, =RAND(), in a cell. Exhibit S13.1 is an Excel spreadsheet with 100 random numbers generated by entering the formula, =RAND(), in cell A3 and copying to the cells in the range A3:J12. We can copy things into a range of cells in two ways. You can first cover cells A3:J12 with the cursor; then type the formula "=RAND()" into cell A3; and finally hit the "Ctrl" and "Enter" keys simultaneously. Alternatively, you can type "=RAND()" into cell A3, "copy" this cell (using the right mouse button), then cover cells A4:J12 with the cursor, and (again with the right mouse button) paste this formula into these cells.

EXHIBIT S13.1

Excel File

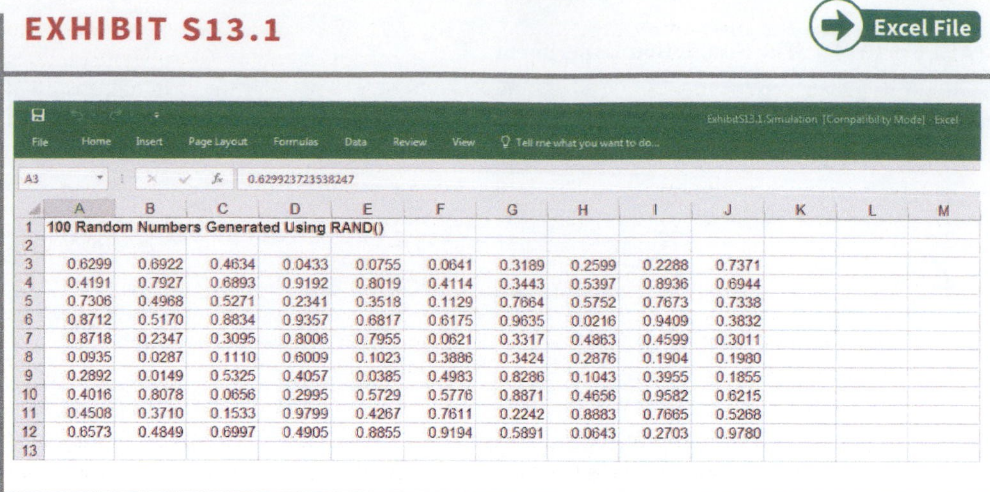

A3 = 0.629923723538247

100 Random Numbers Generated Using RAND()

	A	B	C	D	E	F	G	H	I	J
3	0.6299	0.6922	0.4634	0.0433	0.0755	0.0641	0.3189	0.2599	0.2288	0.7371
4	0.4191	0.7927	0.6893	0.9192	0.8019	0.4114	0.3443	0.5397	0.8936	0.6944
5	0.7306	0.4968	0.5271	0.2341	0.3518	0.1129	0.7664	0.5752	0.7673	0.7338
6	0.8712	0.5170	0.8834	0.9357	0.6817	0.6175	0.9635	0.0216	0.9409	0.3832
7	0.8718	0.2347	0.3095	0.8006	0.7955	0.0621	0.3317	0.4863	0.4599	0.3011
8	0.0935	0.0287	0.1110	0.6009	0.1023	0.3886	0.3424	0.2876	0.1904	0.1980
9	0.2892	0.0149	0.5325	0.4057	0.0385	0.4983	0.8286	0.1043	0.3955	0.1855
10	0.4016	0.8078	0.0656	0.2995	0.5729	0.5776	0.8871	0.4656	0.9582	0.6215
11	0.4508	0.3710	0.1533	0.9799	0.4267	0.7611	0.2242	0.8883	0.7665	0.5268
12	0.6573	0.4849	0.6997	0.4905	0.8855	0.9194	0.5891	0.0643	0.2703	0.9780

If you attempt to replicate this spreadsheet you will generate random numbers different from those shown in Exhibit S13.1. Every time you generate random numbers they will be different. In fact, any time you recalculate anything on your spreadsheet the random numbers will change. You can see this by hitting the F9 key and observing that all the random numbers change. However, sometimes it is useful in a simulation model to be able to use the same set (or stream) of random numbers over and over. You can freeze the random numbers you are using on your spreadsheet by first covering the cells with random numbers in them with the cursor, for example cells A3:J12 in Exhibit S13.1. Next copy these cells (using the right mouse button); then click on the "Edit" menu at the top of your spreadsheet and select "Paste Special" from this menu. Next select the "Values" option and click on "OK." This procedure pastes a copy of the numbers in these cells over the same cells with (=RAND()) formulas in them, thus freezing the numbers in place.

Notice one more thing from Exhibit S13.1: the random numbers are all between 0 and 1, whereas the random numbers in Table S13.3 are whole numbers between 0 and 100. We used whole random numbers previously for illustrative purposes; however, computer programs like Excel generally provide random numbers between 0 and 1.

Now we are ready to duplicate our example simulation model for the ComputerWorld store using Excel. The spreadsheet in **Exhibit S13.2** includes the simulation model originally developed in Table S13.4.

EXHIBIT S13.2

Excel File

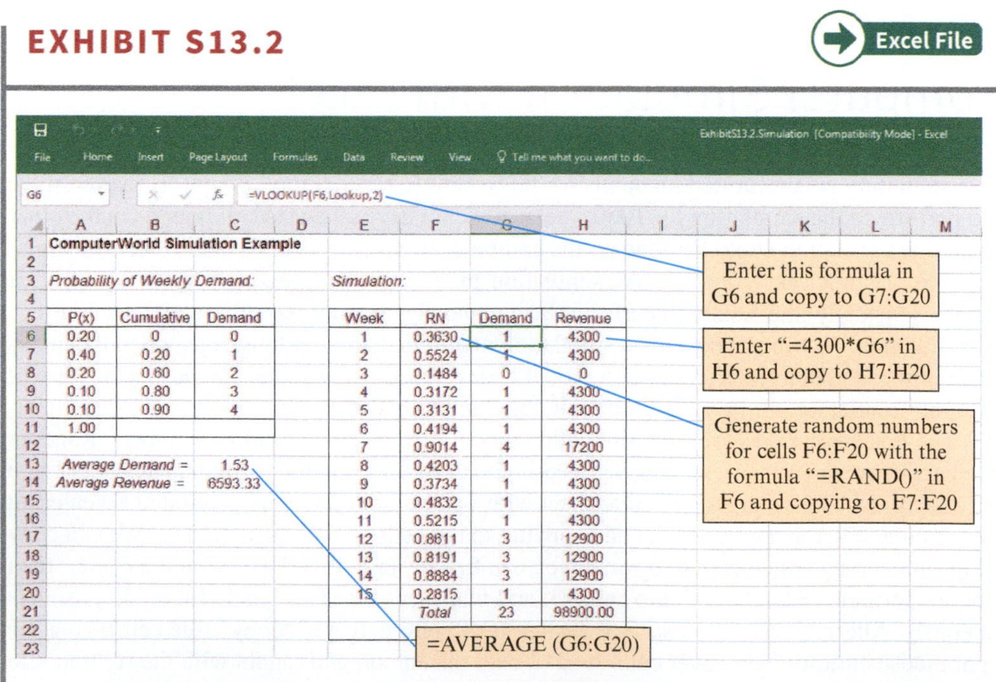

G6 = =VLOOKUP(F6,Lookup,2)

ComputerWorld Simulation Example

Probability of Weekly Demand:

P(x)	Cumulative	Demand
0.20	0	0
0.40	0.20	1
0.20	0.60	2
0.10	0.80	3
0.10	0.90	4
1.00		

Average Demand = 1.53

Average Revenue = 6593.33

Simulation:

Week	RN	Demand	Revenue
1	0.3630	1	4300
2	0.5524	1	4300
3	0.1484	0	0
4	0.3172	1	4300
5	0.3131	1	4300
6	0.4194	1	4300
7	0.9014	4	17200
8	0.4203	1	4300
9	0.3734	1	4300
10	0.4832	1	4300
11	0.5215	1	4300
12	0.8611	3	12900
13	0.8191	3	12900
14	0.8884	3	12900
15	0.2815	1	4300
Total		23	98900.00

First note that the probability distribution for the weekly demand for laptops has been entered in cells A5:C11. Also notice that we have entered a set of cumulative probability values in column B. We generated these cumulative probabilities by first entering 0 in cell B6, then entering the formula "=A6+B6" in cell B7, and copying this formula to cells B8:B10. This cumulative probability creates a range of random numbers for each demand value. For example, any random number less than 0.20 will result in a demand value of 0, whereas any random number greater than 0.20 but less than 0.60 will result in a demand value of 1, and so on.

Random numbers are generated in cells F6:F20 by entering the formula "=RAND()" in cell F6 and copying it to the range of cells in F7:F20.

Now we need to be able to generate demand values for each of these random numbers in column F. We accomplish this by first covering the cumulative probabilities and the demand values in cells B6:C10 with the cursor. Then we give this range of cells the name "Lookup." This can be done by typing "Lookup" directly on the formula bar in place of B6 or by clicking on the "Insert" button at the top of the spreadsheet and selecting "Name" and "Define" and then entering the name "Lookup." This has the effect of creating a table called "Lookup" with the ranges of random numbers and associated demand values in it. Next we enter the formula "=VLOOKUP(F6,Lookup,2)" in cell G6 and copy it to the cells in the range G7:G20. This formula will compare the random numbers in column F with the cumulative probabilities in B6:B10 and generate the correct demand value from cells C6:C10.

Once the demand values have been generated in column G we can determine the weekly revenue values by entering the formula "=4300*G6" in H6 and copying it to cells H7:H20.

Average weekly demand is computed in cell C13 by using the formula "=AVERAGE(G6:G20)," and the average weekly revenue is computed by entering a similar formula in cell C14.

Notice that the average weekly demand value of 1.53 in Exhibit S13.2 is different from the simulation result (2.07) we obtained from Table S13.4. This is because we used a different stream of random numbers. As we mentioned previously, to acquire an average closer to the true steady state value the simulation needs to include more repetitions than 15 weeks. As an example, Exhibit S13.3 simulates demand for 100 weeks. The window has been "frozen" at row 16 and scrolled up to show the first 10 weeks and the last 6 on the screen in Exhibit S13.3.

Decision Making with Simulation

In our previous example, the manager of the ComputerWorld store acquired some useful information about the weekly demand and revenue for laptops that would be helpful in making a decision about how many laptops would be needed each week to meet demand. However,

EXHIBIT S13.3

Excel File

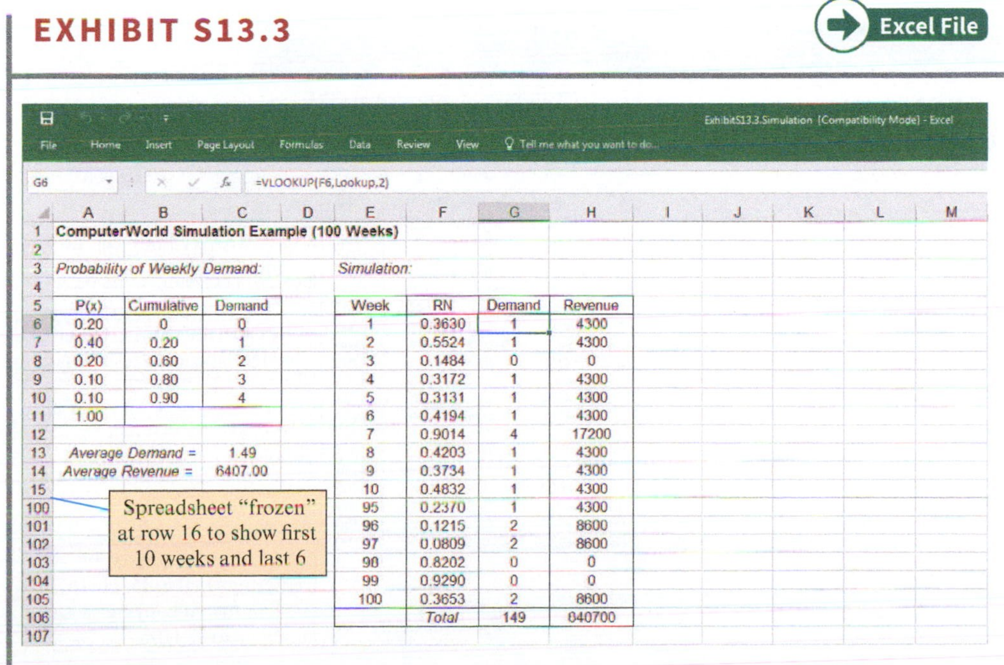
G6 =VLOOKUP(F6,Lookup,2)

ComputerWorld Simulation Example (100 Weeks)

Probability of Weekly Demand:

P(x)	Cumulative	Demand
0.20	0	0
0.40	0.20	1
0.20	0.60	2
0.10	0.80	3
0.10	0.90	4
1.00		

Average Demand = 1.49

Average Revenue = 6407.00

Simulation:

Week	RN	Demand	Revenue
1	0.3630	1	4300
2	0.5524	1	4300
3	0.1484	0	0
4	0.3172	1	4300
5	0.3131	1	4300
6	0.4194	1	4300
7	0.9014	4	17200
8	0.4203	1	4300
9	0.3734	1	4300
10	0.4832	1	4300
95	0.2370	1	4300
96	0.1215	2	8600
97	0.0809	2	8600
98	0.8202	0	0
99	0.9290	0	0
100	0.3653	2	8600
	Total	149	640700

this example did not lead directly to a decision. Next we will expand our ComputerWorld store example so that a possible decision will result.

From the simulation in Exhibit S13.3 the manager of the store knows that the average weekly demand for laptop PCs will be approximately 1.49; however, the manager cannot order 1.49 laptops each week. Since fractional laptops are not possible, either 1 or 2 must be ordered. Thus, the manager wants to repeat the earlier simulation with two possible order sizes, 1 and 2. The manager also wants to include some additional information in the model that will affect the decision.

If too few laptops are on hand to meet demand during the week, not only will there be a loss of revenue, but there will also be a shortage, or customer goodwill, cost of $500 per unit incurred because the customer will be unhappy. However, each laptop still in stock at the end of each week that has not been sold will incur an inventory or storage cost of $50. Thus, it costs the store money either to have too few or too many laptops on hand each week. Given this scenario, the manager wants to order either one or two laptops, depending on which order size will result in the greatest average weekly revenue.

Exhibit S13.4 shows the Excel spreadsheet for this revised example. The simulation is for 100 weeks. The columns labeled "1," "2," and "4" for "Week," "RN," and "Demand" were constructed similarly to the model in Exhibit S13.3. The array of cells B6:C10 were given the name "Lookup," and the formula "=VLOOKUP(F6,Lookup,2)" was entered in cell H6 and copied to cells H7:H105.

The simulation in Exhibit S13.4 is for an order size of one laptop each week. The "Inventory" column (3) keeps track of the amount of inventory available each week—the one laptop that comes in on order plus any laptops carried over from the previous week. The cumulative inventory is computed each week by entering the formula "=1+MAX(G6-H6,0)" in cell G7 and copying it to cells G8:G105. This formula adds the one laptop on order to either the amount left over from the previous week (G6–H6) or 0 if there were not enough laptops on hand to meet demand. It does not allow for negative inventory levels, called backorders. In other words, if a sale cannot be made due to a shortage, it is gone. The inventory values in column 3 are eventually multiplied by the inventory cost of $50 per unit in column 8 using the formula "=G6*50."

If there is a shortage it is recorded in column 5 labeled "Shortage." The shortage is computed by entering the formula "=MIN(G6-H6,0)" in cell I6 and copying it to cells I7:I105. Shortage costs are computed in column 7 by multiplying the shortage values in

EXHIBIT S13.4

Excel File

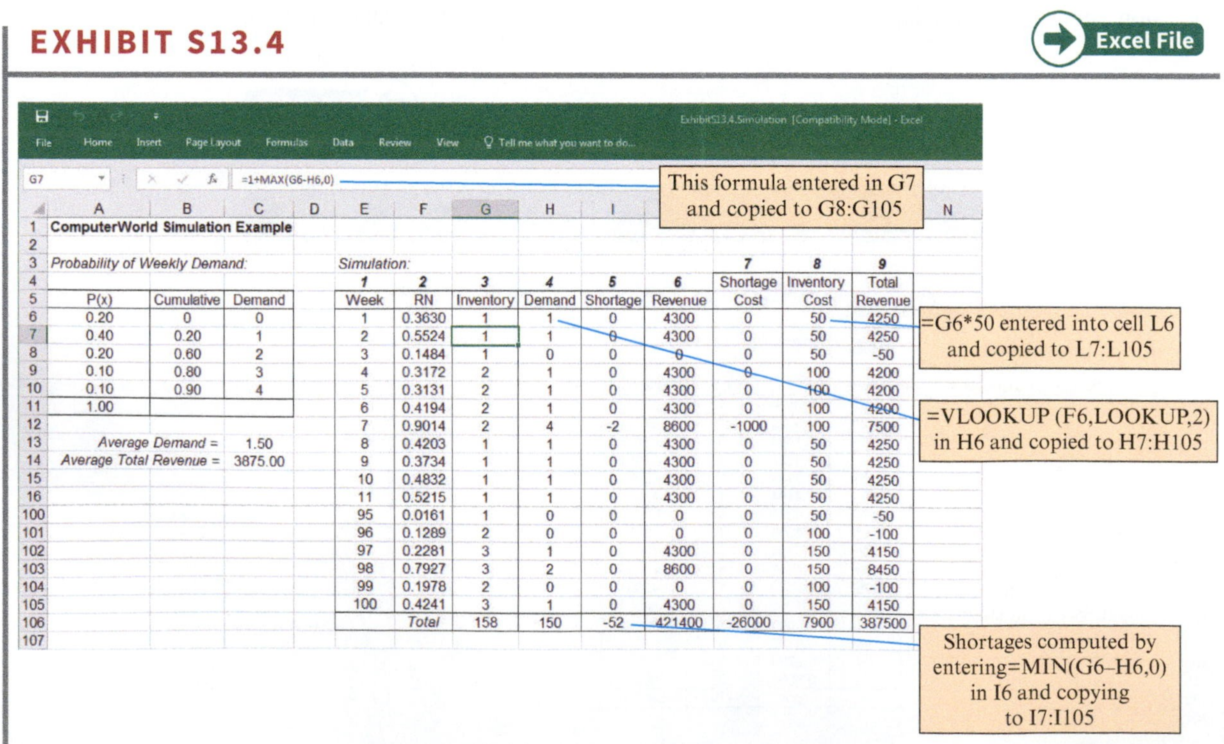

G7
=1+MAX(G6-H6,0)
This formula entered in G7 and copied to G8:G105
=G6*50 entered into cell L6 and copied to L7:L105
=VLOOKUP (F6,LOOKUP,2) in H6 and copied to H7:H105
Shortages computed by entering=MIN(G6–H6,0) in I6 and copying to I7:I105

ComputerWorld Simulation Example

Probability of Weekly Demand:

P(x)	Cumulative	Demand
0.20	0	0
0.40	0.20	1
0.20	0.60	2
0.10	0.80	3
0.10	0.90	4
1.00		

Average Demand = 1.50
Average Total Revenue = 3875.00

Simulation:

1	2	3	4	5	6	7	8	9
Week	RN	Inventory	Demand	Shortage	Revenue	Shortage Cost	Inventory Cost	Total Revenue
1	0.3630	1	1	0	4300	0	50	4250
2	0.5524	1	1	0	4300	0	50	4250
3	0.1484	1	0	0	0	0	50	-50
4	0.3172	2	1	0	4300	0	100	4200
5	0.3131	2	1	0	4300	0	100	4200
6	0.4194	2	1	0	4300	0	100	4200
7	0.9014	2	4	-2	8600	-1000	100	7500
8	0.4203	1	1	0	4300	0	50	4250
9	0.3734	1	1	0	4300	0	50	4250
10	0.4832	1	1	0	4300	0	50	4250
11	0.5215	1	1	0	4300	0	50	4250
95	0.0161	1	0	0	0	0	50	-50
96	0.1289	2	0	0	0	0	100	-100
97	0.2281	3	1	0	4300	0	150	4150
98	0.7927	3	2	0	8600	0	150	8450
99	0.1978	2	0	0	0	0	100	-100
100	0.4241	3	1	0	4300	0	150	4150
	Total	158	150	-52	421400	-26000	7900	387500

column 5 by $500, entering the formula "=I6*500" in cell K6, and copying it to cells K7:K105.

Weekly revenues are computed in column 6 by entering the formula "=4300*MIN(H6,G6)" in cell J6 and copying it to cells J7:J105. In other words, the revenue is determined by either the inventory level in column 3 or the demand in column 4, whichever is smaller.

Total weekly revenue is computed by summing revenue, shortage costs, and inventory costs in column 9 by entering the formula "=J6 + K6 – L6" in cell M6 and copying it to cells M7:M105.

The average weekly demand, 1.50, is shown in cell C13. The average weekly revenue, $3875, is computed in cell C14.

Next we must repeat this same simulation for an order size of two laptops each week. The spreadsheet for an order size of 2 is shown in **Exhibit S13.5**. Notice that the only actual difference is the use of a new formula to compute the weekly inventory level in column 3. This formula in cell G7 reflecting two laptops ordered each week is shown on the formula bar at the top of the spreadsheet.

This second simulation in Exhibit S13.5 results in average weekly demand of 1.52 laptops and average weekly total revenue of $5,107.50. This is higher than the total weekly revenue of $3875 achieved in the first simulation run in Exhibit S13.4, even though the store would incur significantly higher inventory costs. Thus, the correct decision—based on weekly revenue—would be to order two laptops per week. However, there are probably additional aspects of this problem the manager would want to consider in the decision-making process, such as the increasingly high inventory levels as the simulation progresses. For example, there may not be enough storage space to accommodate this much inventory. Such questions as this and others can also be analyzed with simulation. In fact, that is one of the main attributes of simulation—its usefulness as a model to experiment on, called "what if?" analysis.

This example briefly demonstrates how simulation can be used to make a decision (i.e., to "optimize"). In this example we experimented with two order sizes and determined the one that resulted in the greatest revenue. The same basic modeling principles can be used to solve larger problems with hundreds of possible order sizes and a probability distribution for demand with many more values plus variable lead times (i.e., the time it takes to receive an order), the ability to backorder and other complicating factors. These factors make the simulation model larger and more complex, but such models are frequently developed and used in business.

EXHIBIT S13.5

Excel File

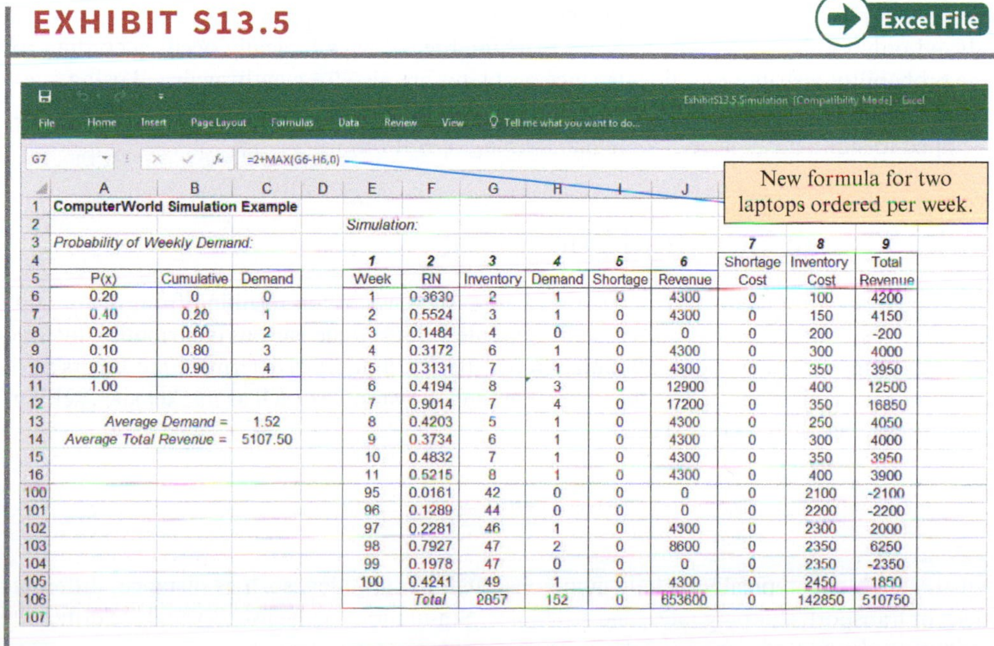

ComputerWorld Simulation Example

Probability of Weekly Demand:

P(x)	Cumulative	Demand
0.20	0	0
0.40	0.20	1
0.20	0.60	2
0.10	0.80	3
0.10	0.90	4
1.00		

Average Demand = 1.52

Average Total Revenue = 5107.50

Simulation:

1 Week	2 RN	3 Inventory	4 Demand	5 Shortage	6 Revenue	7 Shortage Cost	8 Inventory Cost	9 Total Revenue
1	0.3630	2	1	0	4300	0	100	4200
2	0.5524	3	1	0	4300	0	150	4150
3	0.1484	4	0	0	0	0	200	-200
4	0.3172	6	1	0	4300	0	300	4000
5	0.3131	7	1	0	4300	0	350	3950
6	0.4194	8	3	0	12900	0	400	12500
7	0.9014	7	4	0	17200	0	350	16850
8	0.4203	5	1	0	4300	0	250	4050
9	0.3734	6	1	0	4300	0	300	4000
10	0.4832	7	1	0	4300	0	350	3950
11	0.5215	8	1	0	4300	0	400	3900
95	0.0161	42	0	0	0	0	2100	-2100
96	0.1289	44	0	0	0	0	2200	-2200
97	0.2281	46	1	0	4300	0	2300	2000
98	0.7927	47	2	0	8600	0	2350	6250
99	0.1978	47	0	0	0	0	2350	-2350
100	0.4241	49	1	0	4300	0	2450	1850
	Total	2057	152	0	653600	0	142850	510750

Areas of Simulation Application

Simulation is one of the most popular of all quantitative techniques because it can be applied to operational problems that are too difficult to model and solve analytically. Some analysts feel that complex systems should be studied via simulation whether or not they can be analyzed analytically, because it provides an easy vehicle for experimenting on the system. Surveys indicate that a large majority of major corporations use simulation in such functional areas as production, planning, engineering, financial analysis, research and development, information systems, and personnel. Following are descriptions of some of the more common applications of simulation.

Waiting Lines/Service

A major application of simulation has been in the analysis of waiting line, or queuing, systems. For complex queuing systems, it is not possible to develop analytical formulas, and simulation is often the only means of analysis. For example, for a busy supermarket with multiple waiting lines, some for express service and some for regular service, simulation may be the only form of analysis to determine how many registers and servers are needed to meet customer demand.

Inventory Management

Product demand is an essential component in determining the amount of inventory a commercial enterprise should keep. Many of the traditional mathematical formulas used to analyze inventory systems make the assumption that this demand is certain (i.e., not a random variable). In practice, however, demand is rarely known with certainty. Simulation is one of the best means for analyzing inventory systems in which demand is a random variable. Simulation has been used to experiment with innovative inventory systems such as just-in-time (JIT). Companies use simulation to see how effective and costly a JIT system would be in their own manufacturing environment without having to implement the system physically.

Production and Manufacturing Systems

Simulation is often applied to production problems, such as production scheduling, production sequencing, assembly line balancing (of in-process inventory), plant layout, and plant location analysis. Many production processes can be viewed as queuing systems that can be analyzed only by using simulation. Since machine breakdowns typically occur according to some probability distributions, maintenance problems are also frequently analyzed using simulation. In the past few years, several software packages for the personal computer have been developed to simulate all aspects of manufacturing operations.

Capital Investment and Budgeting

Capital budgeting problems require estimates of cash flows, often resulting from many random variables. Simulation has been used to generate values of the various contributing factors to derive estimates of cash flows. Simulation has also been used to determine the inputs into rate-of-return calculations, where the inputs are random variables such as market size, selling price, growth rate, and market share.

Logistics

Logistics problems typically include numerous random variables, such as distance, different modes of transport, shipping rates, and schedules. Simulation can be used to analyze different distribution channels to determine the most efficient logistics system.

Service Operations

The operations of police departments, fire departments, post offices, hospitals, court systems, airports, and other public service systems have been analyzed using simulation. Typically, such operations are so complex and contain so many random variables that no technique except simulation can be employed for analysis.

Environmental and Resource Analysis

Some of the more recent innovative applications of simulation have been directed at problems in the environment. Simulation models have been developed to ascertain the impact of projects such as manufacturing plants, waste-disposal facilities, and nuclear power plants. In many cases, these models include measures to analyze the financial feasibility of such projects. Other models have been developed to simulate waste and population conditions. In the area of resource analysis, numerous simulation models have been developed in recent years to simulate energy systems and the feasibility of alternative energy sources.

Summary

Simulation has become an increasingly important quantitative technique for solving problems in operations. Surveys have shown simulation to be one of the techniques most widely applied to real-world problems. Evidence of this popularity is the number of specialized simulation languages that have been developed by the computer industry and academia to deal with complex problem areas.

The popularity of simulation is due in large part to the flexibility it allows in analyzing systems, compared with more confining analytical techniques. In other words, the problem does not have to fit the model (or technique); the simulation model can be constructed to fit the problem. Simulation is popular also because it is an excellent experimental technique, enabling systems and problems to be tested within a laboratory setting.

In spite of its versatility, simulation has limitations and must be used with caution. One limitation is that simulation models are typically unstructured and must be developed for a system or problem that is also unstructured. Unlike some of the structured techniques presented in this book, the models cannot simply be applied to a specific type of problem. As a result, developing simulation models often requires a certain amount of imagination and intuitiveness that is not required by some of the more straightforward solution techniques we have presented. In addition, the validation of simulation models is an area of serious concern. It is often impossible to validate simulation results realistically or to know if they accurately reflect the system under analysis. This problem has become an area of such concern that *output analysis* of simulation results is a field of study in its own right. Another limiting factor in simulation is the cost in terms of money and time of model building. Because simulation models are developed for unstructured systems, they often take large amounts of staff, computer time, and money to develop and run. For many business companies, these costs can be prohibitive.

The computer programming aspects of simulation can also be quite difficult. Fortunately, generalized simulation languages have been developed to perform many of the functions of a simulation study. Each of these languages requires at least some knowledge of a scientific or business-oriented programming language.

Key Terms

Monte Carlo technique A technique for selecting numbers randomly from a probability distribution for use in a simulation model.

random numbers Numbers in a table or generated by a computer, each of which has an equal likelihood of being selected at random.

simulation An approach to operational problem solving in which a real-world problem situation is replicated within a mathematical model.

steady-state result An average model result that approaches constancy after a sufficient passage of time or enough repetitions or trials.

Solved Problems

WileyPLUS

Simulation

Members of the Willow Creek Emergency Rescue Squad know from past experience that they will receive between zero and six emergency calls each night, according to the following discrete probability distribution:

CALLS	PROBABILITY
0	.05
1	.12
2	.15
3	.25
4	.22
5	.15
6	.06
	1.00

The rescue squad classifies each emergency call into one of three categories: minor, regular, or major emergency. The probability that a particular call will be each type of emergency is as follows:

EMERGENCY TYPE	PROBABILITY
Minor	.30
Regular	.56
Major	.14
	1.00

The type of emergency call determines the size of the crew sent in response. A minor emergency requires a two-person crew, a regular call requires a three-person crew, and a major emergency requires a five-person crew.

Simulate the emergency calls received by the rescue squad for 10 nights, compute the average number of each type of emergency call each night, and determine the maximum number of crew members that might be needed on any given night.

Solution

Step 1. Develop random number ranges for the probability distributions.

CALLS	PROBABILITY	CUMULATIVE PROBABILITY	RANDOM NUMBER RANGE, r_1
0	.05	.05	1–5
1	.12	.17	6–17
2	.15	.32	18–32
3	.25	.57	33–57
4	.22	.79	58–79
5	.15	.94	80–94
6	.06	1.00	95–99.00
	1.00		

EMERGENCY TYPES	PROBABILITY	CUMULATIVE PROBABILITY	RANDOM NUMBER RANGE, r_2
Minor	.30	.30	1–30
Regular	.56	.86	31–86
Major	.14	1.00	87–99.00
	1.00		

Step 2. Set up a tabular simulation. Use the second column of random numbers in Table S13.3.

NIGHT	r_1	NUMBER OF CALLS	r_2	EMERGENCY TYPE	CREW SIZE	TOTAL PER NIGHT
1	65	4	71	Regular	3	
			18	Minor	2	
			12	Minor	2	
			17	Minor	2	9
2	48	3	89	Major	5	
			18	Minor	2	
			83	Regular	3	10
3	08	1	90	Regular	3	3
4	05	0	—	—	—	—
5	89	5	18	Minor	2	
			08	Minor	2	
			26	Minor	2	
			47	Regular	3	
			94	Major	5	14
6	06	1	72	Regular	3	3
7	62	4	47	Regular	3	
			68	Regular	3	
			60	Regular	3	
			88	Major	5	14
8	17	1	36	Regular	3	3
9	77	4	43	Regular	3	
			28	Minor	2	
			31	Regular	3	
			06	Minor	2	10
10	68	4	39	Regular	3	
			71	Regular	3	
			22	Minor	2	
			76	Regular	3	11

Step 3. Compute the results.

$$\text{Average number of minor emergency calls per night} = \frac{10}{10} = 1.0$$

Average number of regular emergency calls per night $= \frac{14}{10} = 1.4$

Average number of major emergency calls per night $= \frac{3}{10} = 0.30$

If all the calls came in at the same time, the maximum number of squad members required during any one night would be 14.

Questions

S13.1. Explain what the Monte Carlo technique is and how random numbers are used in a Monte Carlo process.

S13.2. How are steady-state results achieved in a simulation?

S13.3. What type of information for decision making does simulation typically provide?

Problems

WileyPLUS

S13.1. The Hoylake Rescue Squad receives an emergency call every 1, 2, 3, 4, 5, or 6 hours, according to the following probability distribution:

TIME BETWEEN EMERGENCY CALLS (HOURS)	PROBABILITY
1	.05
2	.10
3	.30
4	.30
5	.20
6	.05
	1.00

The squad is on duty 24 hours per day, 7 days per week.

a. Simulate the emergency calls for three days (note that this will require a "running," or cumulative, hourly clock) using the random number table.

b. Compute the average time between calls and compare this value with the expected value of the time between calls from the probabilistic distribution. Why are the results different?

c. How many calls were made during the three-day period? Can you logically assume that this is an average number of calls per three-day period? If not, how could you simulate to determine such an average?

S13.2. The Dynaco Manufacturing Company produces a product in a process consisting of operations of five machines. The probability distribution of the number of machines that will break down in a week is as follows:

MACHINE BREAKDOWNS PER WEEK	PROBABILITY
0	.10
1	.10
2	.20
3	.25
4	.30
5	.05
	1.00

Every time a machine breaks down at the Dynaco Manufacturing Company, either one, two, or three hours are required to fix it, according to the following probability distribution:

REPAIR TIME (HOURS)	PROBABILITY
1	.30
2	.50
3	.20
	1.00

a. Simulate the repair time for 20 weeks and compute the average weekly repair time.

b. If the random numbers that are used to simulate breakdowns per week are also used to simulate repair time per breakdown, will the results be affected in any way? Explain.

c. If it costs $50 per hour to repair a machine when it breaks down (including lost productivity), determine the average weekly breakdown cost.

d. The Dynaco Company is considering a preventive maintenance program that would alter probabilities of machine breakdowns per week as follows:

MACHINE BREAKDOWNS PER WEEK	PROBABILITY
0	.20
1	.30
2	.20
3	.15
4	.10
5	.05
	1.00

The weekly cost of the preventive maintenance program is $150. Using simulation, determine whether the company should institute the preventive maintenance program.

S13.3. The Stereo Warehouse in Georgetown sells stereo sets, which it orders from Fuji Electronics in Japan. Because of shipping and handling costs, each order must be for five stereos. Because of the time it takes to receive an order, the warehouse outlet places an order every time the present stock drops to five stereos. It costs $100 to place an order. It costs the warehouse $400 in lost sales when a customer asks for a stereo and the warehouse is out of stock. It costs $40 to keep each stereo stored in the warehouse. If a customer cannot purchase a stereo when it is requested, the customer will not wait until one comes in but will go to a competitor. The following probability distribution for demand for stereos has been determined:

DEMAND PER WEEK	PROBABILITY
0	.04
1	.08
2	.28
3	.40
4	.16
5	.02
6	.02
	1.00

The time required to receive an order once it is placed has the following probability distribution:

TIME TO RECEIVE AN ORDER (WEEKS)	PROBABILITY
1	.60
2	.30
3	.10
	1.00

The warehouse presently has five stereos in stock. Orders are always received at the beginning of the week. Simulate the Stereo Warehouse's ordering and sales policy for 20 weeks, using the first column of random numbers in Table S13.3. Compute the average weekly cost.

S13.4. A baseball game consists of plays that can be described as follows:

PLAY	DESCRIPTION
No advance	An out where no runners advance. This includes strikeouts, pop ups, short flies, and the like.
Groundout	All runners can advance one base.
Possible double play	Double play if there is a runner on first base and fewer than two outs. The lead runner can be forced out; runners not out advance one base. If there is no runner on first or there are two outs this play is treated as a "no advance."
Long fly	A runner on third base can score.
Very long fly	Runners on second and third base advance one base.
Walk	Includes a hit batter.
Infield single	All runners advance one base.
Outfield single	A runner on first base advances one base, but a runner on second or third base scores.
Long single	All runners can advance a maximum of two bases.
Double	Runners can advance a maximum of two bases.
Long double	All runners score.
Triple	
Home run	

Note: Singles also include a factor for errors, allowing the batter to reach first base.

Distributions for these plays for two teams, the White Sox (visitors) and the Yankees (home), are as follows:

Team: White Sox

PLAY	PROBABILITY
No advance	.03
Groundout	.39
Possible double play	.06
Long fly	.09
Very long fly	.08
Walk	.06
Infield single	.02
Outfield single	.10
Long single	.03
Double	.04
Long double	.05
Triple	.02
Home run	.03
	1.00

Team: Yankees

PLAY	PROBABILITY
No advance	.04
Groundout	.38
Possible double play	.04
Long fly	.10
Very long fly	.06
Walk	.07
Infield single	.04
Outfield single	.10
Long single	.04
Double	.05
Long double	.03
Triple	.01
Home run	.04
	1.00

Simulate a nine-inning baseball game using this information.[1]

[1]This problem was adapted from R. E. Trueman, "A Computer Simulation Model of Baseball: with Particular Application to Strategy Analysis," in R. E. Machol, S. P. Ladany, and D. G. Morrison, eds., *Management Science in Sports* (New York: North Holland Publishing, Co., 1976), pp. 1–14.

S13.5. The Saki automobile dealer in the Minneapolis–St. Paul area orders the Saki sport compact, which gets 50 miles per gallon of gasoline, from the manufacturer in Japan. However, the dealer never knows for sure how many months it will take to receive an order once it is placed. It can take one, two, or three months with the following probabilities:

MONTHS TO RECEIVE AN ORDER	PROBABILITY
1	.30
2	.30
3	.20
	1.00

The demand per month is given by the following distribution:

DEMAND PER MONTH (CARS)	PROBABILITY
1	.10
2	.30
3	.40
4	.20
	1.00

The dealer orders when the number of cars on the lot gets down to a certain level. In order to determine the appropriate level of cars to use as an indicator of when to order, the dealer needs to know how many cars will be demanded during the time required to receive an order. Simulate the demand for 30 orders, and compute the average number of cars demanded during the time required to receive an order. At what level of cars in stock should the dealer place an order?

S13.6. The Paymor Rental Car Agency rents cars in a small town. It wants to determine how many rental cars it should maintain. Based on market projections and historical data, the manager has determined probability distributions for the number of rentals per day and rental duration (in days only) as shown in the following tables:

NUMBER OF CUSTOMERS/DAY	PROBABILITY
0	.20
1	.20
2	.50
3	.10

RENTAL DURATION (DAYS)	PROBABILITY
1	.10
2	.30
3	.40
4	.10
5	.10

Design a simulation experiment for the car agency and simulate, using a fleet of four rental cars, for 10 days. Compute the probability that the agency will not have a car available on demand. Should the agency expand its fleet? Explain how a simulation experiment could be designed to determine the optimal fleet size for the Paymor Agency.

S13.7. The emergency room of the community hospital in Farmburg has a receptionist, one doctor, and one nurse. The emergency room opens at time zero, and patients begin to arrive sometime later. Patients arrive at the emergency room according to the following probability distribution:

TIME BETWEEN ARRIVALS (MIN)	PROBABILITY
5	.06
10	.10
15	.23
20	.29
25	.18
30	.14

The attention needed by a patient who comes to the emergency room is defined by the following probability distribution:

PATIENT NEEDS TO SEE	PROBABILITY
Doctor alone	.50
Nurse alone	.20
Both	.30

If a patient needs to see both the doctor and the nurse, he or she cannot see one before the other; that is, the patient must wait to see both together. The length of the patient's visit (in minutes) is defined by the following probability distributions:

DOCTOR	PROBABILITY	NURSE	PROBABILITY	BOTH	PROBABILITY
10	.22	5	.08	15	.07
15	.31	10	.24	20	.16
20	.25	15	.51	25	.21
25	.12	20	.17	30	.28
30	.10			35	.17
				40	.11

Simulate the arrival of 20 patients to the emergency room and compute the probability that a patient must wait and the average waiting time. Based on this one simulation, does it appear this system provides adequate patient care?

S13.8. A robbery has just been committed at the Corner Market in the downtown area of the city. The market owner was able to activate the alarm, and the robber fled on foot. Police officers arrived a few minutes later and asked the owner, "How long ago did the robber leave?" "He left only a few minutes ago," the store owner responded. "He's probably 10 blocks away by now," one of the officers said to the other. "Not likely," said the store owner. "He was so stoned on drugs that I bet even if he has run 10 blocks, he's still only within a few blocks of here! He's probably just running in circles!"

Perform a simulation experiment that will test the store owner's hypothesis. Assume that at each corner of a city block there is an equal chance that the robber will go in any one of the four possible directions, north, south, east, or west. Simulate for five trials and then indicate in how many of the trials the robber is within two blocks of the store.

S13.9. Compcomm Inc. is an international communications and information technology company that has seen the value of its common stock appreciate substantially in recent years. A stock analyst would like to predict the stock prices of Compcomm for an extended period with simulation. Based on historical data, the analyst has developed the following probability distribution for the movement of Compcomm stock prices per day:

STOCK PRICE MOVEMENT	PROBABILITY
Increase	.45
Same	.30
Decrease	.25

The analyst has also developed the following probability distributions for the amount of the increases or decreases in the stock price per day:

	PROBABILITY	
STOCK PRICE CHANGE	INCREASE	DECREASE
1/8	.40	.12
1/4	.17	.15
3/8	.12	.18
1/2	.10	.21
5/8	.08	.14
3/4	.07	.10
7/8	.04	.05
1	.02	.05

The price of the stock is currently 62.

Develop a Monte Carlo simulation model to track the stock price of Compcomm stock and simulate for 30 days. Indicate the new stock price at the end of the 30 days. How would this model be expanded to conduct a complete simulation of one year's stock price movement?

S13.10. The Western Outfitter Store specializes in denim jeans. The variable cost of the jeans varies according to several factors, including the cost of the jeans from the distributor, labor costs, handling, packaging, and so on. Price also is a random variable that varies according to competitors' prices. Sales volume also varies each month. The probability distributions for price, volume, and variable costs each month are as follows:

SALES VOLUME	PROBABILITY
300	.12
400	.18
500	.20
600	.23
700	.17
800	.10
	1.00

PRICE	PROBABILITY
$22	.07
23	.16
24	.24
25	.25
26	.18
27	.10
	1.00

VARIABLE COST	PROBABILITY
$8	.17
9	.32
10	.29
11	.14
12	.08
	1.00

Fixed costs are $9000 per month for the store.

Simulate 20 months of store sales and compute the probability the store will at least break even.

S13.11. Randolph College and Salem College are within 20 miles of each other, and the students at each college frequently date. The students at Randolph College are debating how good their dates are at Salem College. The Randolph students have sampled several hundred of their fellow students and asked them to rate their dates from 1 to 5 (where 1 is excellent and 5 is poor) according to physical attractiveness, intelligence, and personality. Following are the resulting probability distributions for these three traits:

PHYSICAL ATTRACTIVENESS	PROBABILITY
1	.27
2	.35
3	.14
4	.09
5	.15
	1.00

INTELLIGENCE	PROBABILITY
1	.10
2	.16
3	.45
4	.17
5	.12
	1.00

PERSONALITY	PROBABILITY
1	.15
2	.30
3	.33
4	.07
5	.15
	1.00

Simulate 20 dates and compute an average overall rating of the Salem students.

S13.12. In Problem S13.11 discuss how you might assess the accuracy of the average rating for Salem College students based on only 20 simulated dates.

References

Banks, J., and J. S. Carson. *Discrete-Event System Simulation*. Upper Saddle River, NJ: Prentice Hall, 1984.

Christy, D., and H. Watson. "The Applications of Simulation: A Survey of Industry Practice." *Interfaces* 13 (5; October 1983), pp. 47–52.

Hammersly, J. M., and D. C. Handscomb. *Monte Carlo Methods*. New York: Wiley, 1984.

Law, A. M., and W. D. Kelton. *Simulation Modeling and Analysis*. New York: McGraw-Hill, 1982.

Meier, R. C., W. T. Newell, and H. L. Pazer. *Simulation in Business and Economics*. Upper Saddle River, NJ: Prentice Hall, 1969.

Naylor, T. H., J. L. Balintfy, D. S. Burdinck, and K. Chu. *Computer Simulation Techniques*. New York: Wiley, 1966.

Payne, J. A. *Introduction to Simulation*. New York: McGraw-Hill, 1982.

Pritsker, A. A. B., C. E. Sigal, and R. D. Hammesfahr. *SLAM II: Network Models for Decision Support*. Upper Saddle River, NJ: Prentice Hall, 1989.

Taha, H. A. *Simulation Modeling and Simen*. New York: McGraw-Hill, 1988.

Taylor, B. W. *Introduction to Management Science*, 5th ed. Upper Saddle River, NJ: Prentice Hall, 1996.

CHAPTER **14**

Sales and Operations Planning

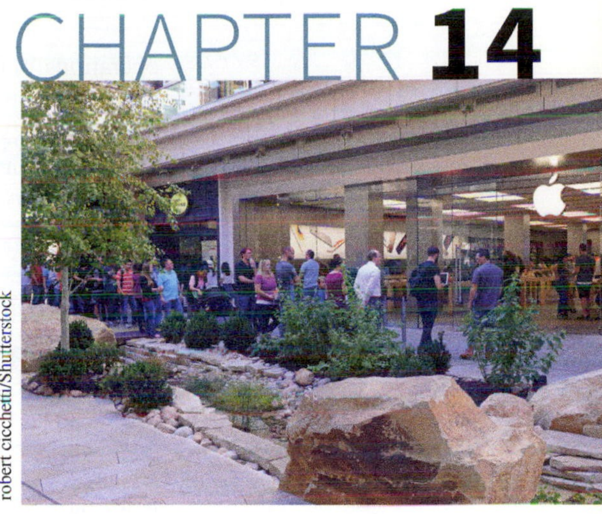
robert cicchetti/Shutterstock

LEARNING OBJECTIVES

After reading this chapter, you will be able to:

- Appreciate the interface of marketing, finance, and operations in S&OP planning.
- Describe the monthly S&OP process and the importance of reconciling differences.
- Utilize various tools and techniques to adjust capacity and manage demand.
- Evaluate a demand scenario and select an appropriate S&OP strategy.
- Describe hierarchical planning and the process of determining available-to-promise.
- Determine overbooking, single orders, and fare class strategies for revenue management in services.

Ramping Up and Down for iPhone Demand

For an Apple supplier, life has its ups and downs, particularly for iPhone production. To protect secrecy before product launch, few new models are produced initially, only to ramp up dramatically in the months that follow. The ramp up was especially steep for the iPhone 5, launched in September of 2012. By October and into the next year, factories in Asia were churning out 3.7 million phones *per week*. Hiring enough workers to staff the assembly lines and supplier factories became problematic, as Apple's own supplier audits later showed. To hire 60,000 new workers in Malaysia alone, employment brokers turned to a network of underground subagents who engaged in questionable recruiting and retention practices. Charges of kickbacks, illegal payments, maltreatment of foreign workers, and human rights violations damaged Apple's reputation, while Apple lost billions in market value by failing to meet demand.

For the iPhone 6, again introduced in September, 10 million phones were sold the first weekend and 80 million units were shipped by year end (see photo). The supply chain staggered under the weight of 2014 sales but held production steady for 2015. The problem then became too *much* inventory, as later sales did not materialize as predicted; so much so that suppliers in Japan, South Korea, and Europe (e.g., Pegatron, Dialog, Jabal, Alps Electronics, Sharp, Kyocera, LG Display, Japan Display) reduced their workforce by 30% or more. As for the iPhone 7, pre-orders are four times bigger than for the iPhone 6 and manufacturers are scrambling to keep pace.

Forecasting demand is tricky, and with cellular carriers moving away from the two year requirement for upgrading to a new phone, customer upgrade behavior will be even more difficult to predict. How do companies cope with this kind of uncertainty?

Matching supply and demand is important in all industries, but especially critical for high tech industries where inventories of unused products can quickly become obsolete, and where being slow to incorporate the latest technology in new products can mean lost opportunities and damaged reputations. In this chapter, we introduce sales and operations planning (S&OP), a process that seeks to synchronize demand forecasts with supply planning and take corrective action when misalignments occur.

Source: Cam Simpson, "An iPhone Tester Caught in Apple's Supply Chain," *Bloomberg Businessweek* (November 7, 2013); "Apple's iPhone 6s Supply Chain: Can They Handle the Global Demand?" *Supply Chain 24/7* (September 28, 2015); "Suppliers Prepare for iPhone Supply Chain Cut," *Supply Chain 24/7* (January 7, 2016).

The Sales and Operations Planning Process

Sales & operations planning (S&OP) A process for coordinating supply and demand.

Sales and operations planning (S&OP) is an aggregate planning process that determines the resource capacity a firm will need to meet its demand over an intermediate time horizon—6 to 12 months in the future. While the planning horizon varies by industry (as shown in the photo below), within this time frame, it is usually not feasible to increase capacity by building new facilities or purchasing new equipment; however, it *is* feasible to hire or lay off workers, increase or reduce the workweek, add an extra shift, subcontract out work, use overtime, or build up and deplete inventory levels.

We use the term *aggregate* because the plans are developed for product lines or product families, rather than individual products. An aggregate operations plan might specify how many bicycles are to be produced but would not identify them by color, size, tires, or type of brakes. Resource capacity is also expressed in aggregate terms, typically as labor or machine hours. Labor hours would not be specified by type of labor, nor machine hours by type of machine. And they may be given only for critical processes.

For services, capacity is often limited by *space*—number of airline seats, number of hotel rooms, number of hospital beds. *Time* can also affect capacity. The number of customers who can be served lunch in a restaurant is limited by the number of seats, as well as the number of hours lunch is served. In some overcrowded schools, lunch begins at 10:00 A.M. so that all students can be served by 2:00 P.M.!

There are two objectives to sales and operations planning:

1. To establish a companywide game plan for allocating resources, and
2. To develop an economic strategy for meeting demand.

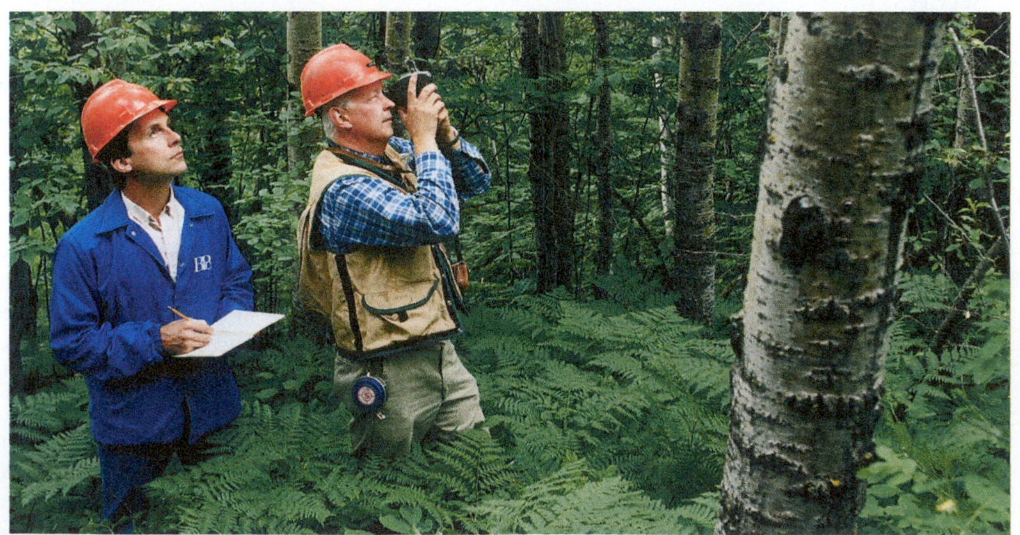

Photo Courtesy of Blandin Paper Company, Carlson & Kirwan, and Jeffrey Frey & Associates.

Producers of pulp, paper, lumber, and other wood products have an interesting aggregate planning problem—they must plan for the renewable resource of trees. Aggregate planning starts with a mathematical simulation model of tree growth that determines the maximum sustainable flow of wood fiber from each acreage. Decisions are made as to which trees to harvest now; which ones to leave until later; where to plant new trees; and the type, amount, and location of new timberland that should be purchased. The planning horizon is the biological lead time to grow trees—more than 80 years!

The first objective refers to the long-standing battle between the sales and operations functions within a firm. Personnel who are evaluated solely on sales volume have the tendency to make unrealistic sales commitments (either in terms of quantity or timing) that operations is expected to meet, sometimes at an exorbitant price. Operations personnel who are evaluated on keeping manufacturing costs down may refuse to accept orders that require additional financial resources (such as overtime wage rates) or hard-to-meet completion dates. The job of operations planning is to match forecasted demand with available capacity. If capacity is inadequate, it can usually be expanded, but at a cost. The company needs to determine if the extra cost is worth the increased revenue from the sale, and if the sale is consistent with the strategy of the firm. Thus, the aggregate plan should not be determined by manufacturing personnel alone; rather, it should be agreed on by top management from all the functional areas of the firm—operations, marketing, and finance. Because this is such an important decision, companies engage in a structured, collaborative decision-making process called *sales and operations planning (S&OP)*. **Figure 14.1** outlines the S&OP process.

As shown in Figure 14.1, the sales and operations plan should reflect company policy (such as avoiding layoffs, limiting inventory levels, and maintaining a specified customer service level) and strategic objectives (such as capturing a certain share of the market or achieving targeted levels of quality or profit). Other inputs include financial constraints, demand forecasts (from sales), and capacity constraints (from operations).

Given these inputs, the sales function develops a monthly sales plan. A forecasting model is run to create preliminary demand figures, then adjusted based on input from key customers and sales personnel in the field. The forecast is further adjusted for planned promotions, product introductions, and special offers. Finally, a customer service level is set that specifies the percent of customer demand that should be satisfied.

The sales plan is then shared with the operations function that must convert sales to production requirements as economically as possible. Operations develops a schedule of production per month by product family that includes the number of workers and other resources needed, and whether the production plan requires overtime or subcontracting. The production plan also shows anticipated inventory levels, backlog (work not yet completed), backorders (work performed later for customers willing to wait for their order), and lost sales (customers whose orders could not be completed or were not accepted).

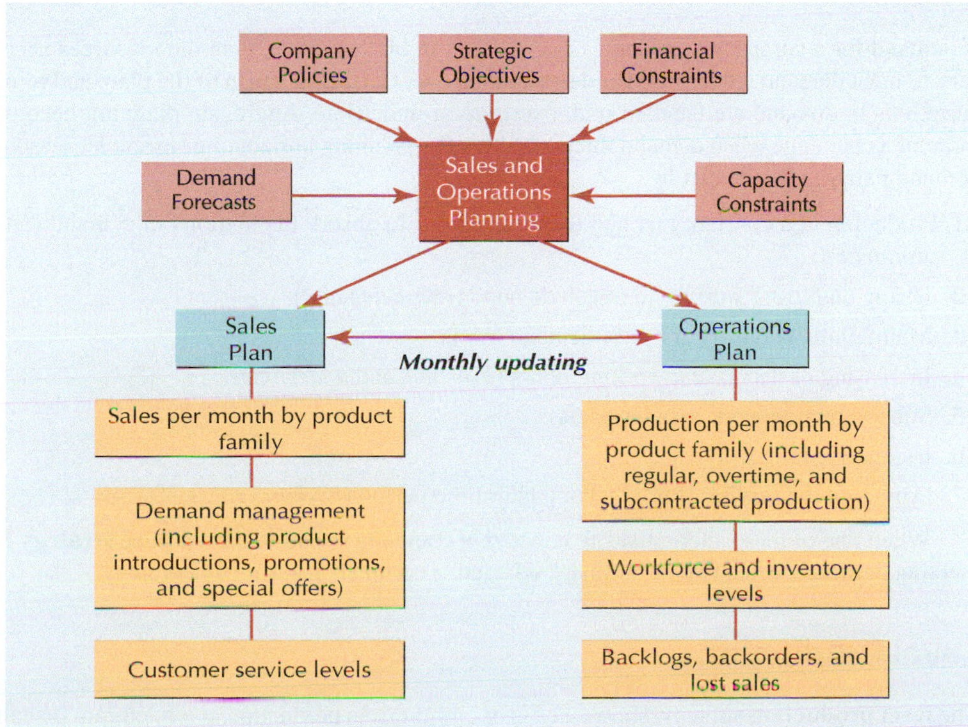

FIGURE 14.1 **Sales and Operations Planning**

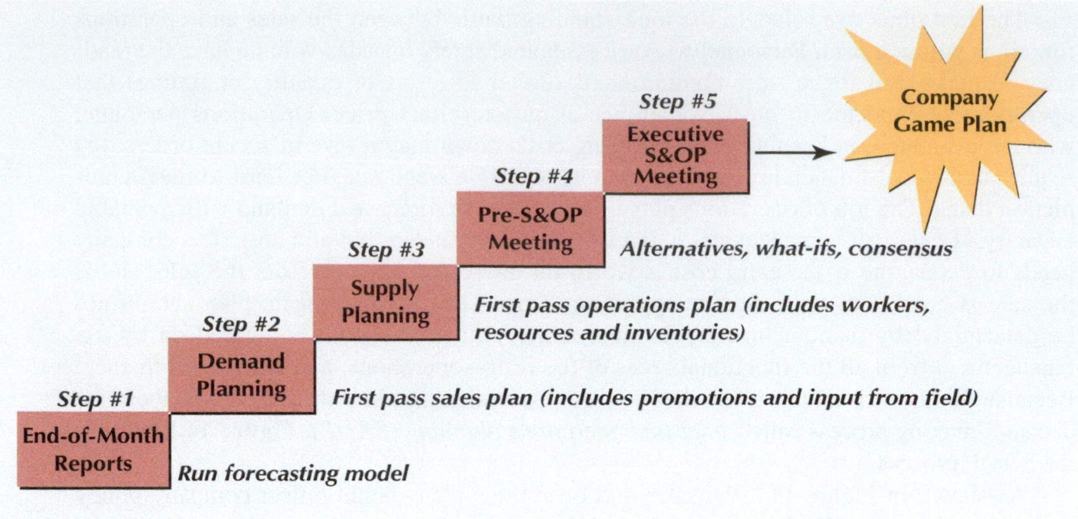

FIGURE 14.2 **The Monthly S&OP Planning Process**

The sales and operations planning process does not stop here. The two plans must be reconciled. Typically this involves creating an annual plan and updating it with monthly meetings that culminate in executive approval of the final plan. The process is diagrammed in Figure 14.2.

Because of the various factors and viewpoints considered, the sales and operations plan is often referred to as the company's *game plan* for the coming year, and deviations from the plan are carefully monitored. Monthly S&OP meeting reconcile differences in supply, demand, and new product plans.

An economic strategy for meeting demand can be attained by either *adjusting capacity* or *managing demand*. We discuss both approaches in the following sections. Please note that the terms *operations plan, production plan,* and *aggregate plan* are used interchangeably in this textbook.

Strategies for Adjusting Capacity

If demand for a company's products or services is stable over time, then the resources necessary to meet demand are acquired and maintained over the time horizon of the plan, and minor variations in demand are handled with overtime or undertime. Aggregate planning becomes more of a challenge when demand fluctuates over the planning horizon. For example, seasonal demand patterns can be met by:

1. Producing at a constant rate and using inventory to absorb fluctuations in demand (*level production*)
2. Hiring and firing workers to match demand (*chase demand*)
3. Maintaining resources for high-demand levels
4. Increasing or decreasing working hours (*overtime* and *undertime*)
5. Subcontracting work to other firms
6. Using part-time workers
7. Providing the service or product at a later time period (*backordering*)

Pure strategy Adjusting only one capacity factor to meet demand.

When one of these alternatives is selected, a company is said to have a **pure strategy** for meeting demand. When two or more are selected, a company has a mixed strategy.

Level Production

Level production Producing at a constant rate and using inventory as needed to meet demand.

The **level production** strategy, shown in Figure 14.3*a*, sets production at a fixed rate (usually to meet average demand) and uses inventory to absorb variations in demand. During periods

Along the Supply Chain

Chevron's Best Mix

PICHITBO/Shutterstock

Chevron, one of the world's largest oil companies, is involved in every stage of the oil, natural gas, and petrochemical supply chain, from exploration, production, and refining, to marketing, logistics, and sales. An oil and gas platform in the Gulf of Thailand is shown in the accompanying photo. Crude oil can be refined into a variety of fuels, including gasoline, jet fuel, diesel, and fuel oil. The refinery process (and which refinery to use) depends on the type of fuel being produced, the destination of the final product, and the source of the crude. Although one barrel of crude can be used to make many different products, crude sourced from the United States, United Kingdom, Saudi Arabia, and Nigeria tends to be processed into gasoline, whereas crude from Mexico, Russia, and Canada is more suited to lubricants, fuel oil, and petrochemicals. These are just a few of the variables considered in the production planning software created by Chevron, called Petro.

Petro is a massive linear programming model that is used at all levels of S&OP: strategic planning (5 years), aggregate planning (1 year), and operational planning (monthly). The model considers supply (crude sources), demand (product mix), production (refinery capabilities), transportation, and the fluctuating prices characteristic of the industry. A large multi-time period single refinery problem can involve 100,000 constraints and one million variables; even so, it takes less than a minute to solve. This is important since Petro may be processing 200 different models at a time from different users across the company.

Petro has been licensed to other users in the industry, but what sets Petro apart at Chevron is the manner in which the company uses the software. Analysts sit next to traders in each of Chevron's commodity trading locations and, through real-time connections with refineries, weather services, and stock market and other data, run Petro to advise traders on whether to bid crude and how much to bid. Once the bid is secured, Petro helps analysts decide how every bit of a barrel of oil will be used, which refinery will handle the processing, and how the final products will be transported to market. Petro data is constantly being updated with lab analysis of crude from different locales, changes in refinery process capabilities, changes in government or industry specifications, economic ups and downs, seasonal demand patterns, and price structures in the industry. All in all, it's an impressive, dynamic system that saves Chevron about $1 billion each year.

1. Besides cost, what outside factors might affect how Chevron allocates its production?
2. What kind of capacity limitations do oil companies face? How is inventory accounted for and used?
3. Think about the time factor of sourcing, production, and distribution, as well as price increases and declines. How do long term and short term decisions interact?
4. Why is Petro so valuable to Chevron?

Source: Robert Creek, "Optimizing Chevron's Refineries," Franz Edelman Award Presentation, INFORMS National Conference, San Antonio (April 8, 2013); Chevron corporate website, http://www.chevron.com/next/enhancingdownstreamefficiency/ (accessed February 3, 2016).

of low demand, overproduction is stored as inventory, to be depleted in periods of high demand. The cost of this strategy is the cost of holding inventory, including the cost of obsolete or perishable items that may have to be discarded.

Chase Demand

The **chase demand** strategy, shown in Figure 14.3*b*, matches the production plan to the demand pattern and absorbs variations in demand by hiring and firing workers. During periods of

Chase demand Changing workforce levels so that production matches demand.

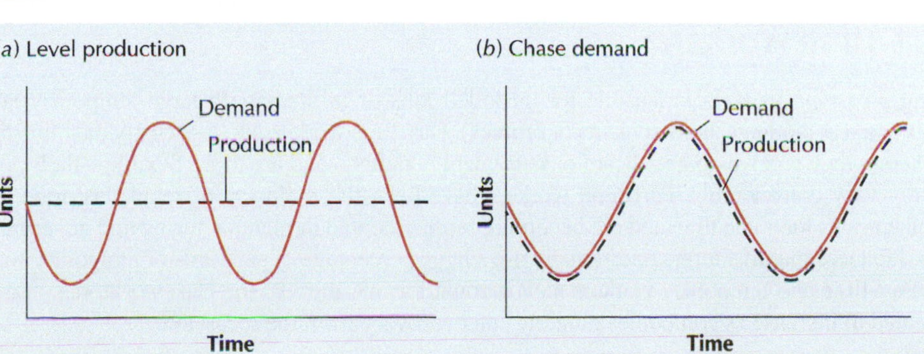

FIGURE 14.3 **Pure Strategies for Meeting Demand**

low demand, production is cut back and workers are laid off. During periods of high demand, production is increased and additional workers are hired. The cost of this strategy is the cost of hiring and firing workers. This approach would not work for industries in which worker skills are scarce or competition for labor is intense, but it can be quite cost-effective during periods of high unemployment or for industries with low-skilled workers.

A variation of chase demand is *chase supply*. For some industries, the production planning task revolves around the supply of raw materials, not the demand pattern. Consider Motts, the applesauce manufacturer, whose raw material is available only 40 days during a year. The workforce size at its peak is 1500 workers, but it normally consists of around 350 workers. Almost 10% of the company's payroll is made up of unemployment benefits—the price of doing business in that particular industry.

Peak Demand

Peak demand Staffing for high levels of customer service.

Maintaining resources for **peak demand** levels ensures high levels of customer service but can be very costly in terms of the investment in extra workers and machines that remain idle during low-demand periods. This strategy is used when superior customer service is important (as for Nordstrom's department store) or when customers are willing to pay extra for the availability of critical staff or equipment. Professional services trying to generate more demand may keep staff levels high, defense contractors may be paid to keep extra capacity "available," child-care facilities may elect to maintain staff levels for continuity when attendance is low, and full-service hospitals may invest in specialized equipment that is rarely used but is critical for the care of a small number of patients.

Overtime and Undertime

Overtime and *undertime* are common strategies when demand fluctuations are not extreme. A competent staff is maintained, hiring and firing costs are avoided, and demand is met temporarily without investing in permanent resources. Disadvantages include the premium paid for overtime work, a tired and potentially less efficient workforce, and the possibility that overtime alone may be insufficient to meet peak demand periods.

Undertime can be achieved by working fewer hours during the day or fewer days per week. In addition, vacation time can be scheduled during months of slow demand. For example, furniture manufacturers typically shut down the entire month of July, while shipbuilding goes dormant in December. During the recent recession, 35% of U.S. employers surveyed used unpaid furloughs in lieu of more layoffs to adjust to decreased demand. Europe routinely uses shorter workweeks and mandatory vacations in economic downturns.

Subcontracting

Subcontracting or outsourcing is a feasible alternative if a supplier can reliably meet quality and time requirements. This is a common solution for component parts when demand exceeds expectations for the final product. The outsourcing decision requires maintaining strong ties with possible subcontractors and first-hand knowledge of their work. Disadvantages include reduced profits, loss of control over production, long lead times, and the potential that the subcontractor may become a future competitor.

Part-Time Workers

Using *part-time workers* is feasible for unskilled jobs or in areas with large temporary labor pools (such as students, homemakers, or retirees). Part-time workers are less costly than full-time workers—they receive no healthcare or retirement benefits—and are more flexible—their hours usually vary considerably. Part-time workers have been the mainstay of retail, fast-food, and other services for some time and are becoming more accepted in manufacturing and government jobs. Japanese manufacturers traditionally use a large percentage of part-time or temporary workers. Part-time and temporary workers now account for one-third of the U.S. workforce, and are expected to increase as companies gingerly enter recovery from the recession.

Along the Supply Chain

Supply and Demand in the Spirits Industry

A beverage retailer in the spirits industry often sells products from around the world, each with its own unique supply chain. Beverages for mass consumption (beers and most wines) have a limited shelf life; fine wines and spirits have an extended life but, at a $100 to $3000 per bottle, can tie up needed cash in inventory. Stocking the latest trendy or seasonal beverage can be difficult because of lengthy lead times and the sheer number of SKUs (stock keeping units) available (see photo). A shipment of wine from Argentina, for example, takes an average of 60 days to arrive stateside. Craft beers may be produced in limited quantities and are marketed for specific seasons, so a single order placed a year in advance may be the only opportunity to guarantee supply.

Weight is another problem in the spirits supply chain. A typical 20-foot shipping container packed with bottled product will hit weight restrictions long before reaching FTL (full truck load) by volume. And different countries have different weight restrictions. Several solutions have been proposed. One is transporting mixed loads by partnering with a company whose product follows a similar geographic path but is lightweight. Another is transporting the product in bulk for the longest portion of the trip and bottling it nearer to major markets. Flexible plastic containers (called KN blue tanks) designed to fill a twenty-foot shipping container are more commonly used by producers in Australia and South America. Multiple bottling facilities, however, can add cost, and errors in estimating demand can mean a product needs to be transported further than anticipated to find a receptive market. Finally, the finished product itself can be sold in bags, boxes, or pouches instead of bottles. Astro pouches with colorful designs have become quite popular for some types of alcoholic beverages.

Climate controlled transport is expensive, too, especially for ocean routes; so much so that shippers of wine and beer to northern markets may travel to less accessible warm weather ports and then use heated trucks for transport to final destinations in colder climes. Some companies only ship product during the more temperate months of the year, further restricting supply.

Fine wines present their own special problems. Most wines travel from vineyard to producer to distributor to retailer within a year. However, fine wines may not be ready to drink for 10 years and may have a shelf life of 50 years. Ownership can change many times from production to consumption, and inventory must be carefully stored. Transporting these wines often or over long distances can damage them and expose the owner to fraud and theft. A pallet of Chateau Lafite-Rothschild Bordeaux, for example, may be valued at half a million dollars. So a new industry has emerged that keeps fine wines in climate controlled storage and transfers ownership (in a database), instead of product, when sales are made.

Faiz Zaki/Shutterstock

1. Sometimes what seems like a cool marketing idea is actually a cost-savings idea that is reframed to appeal to customers, like the Astro pouches. Can you think of other examples?
2. What kind of strategy might you have for stocking inventory in a retail store that serves the alcoholic beverage market?
3. How would you handle demand forecasting and product ordering when the lead time to obtain a product is lengthy?
4. We often don't think of transportation as being a major cost of production. Is it appropriate to include the cost of logistics in the retail price of an item? How would you do that? Give an example.
5. How might sales and operations planning be used to handle logistical problems and changing demand patterns in the spirits industry?

Source: Merrill Douglas, "Cheers! Managing the Spirited Supply Chain," *Inbound Logistics* (January 2012).

Backlogs, Backordering, and Lost Sales

Companies that offer customized products and services accept customer orders and fill them at a later date. The accumulation of these orders creates a **backlog** that grows during periods of high demand and is depleted during periods of low demand. The planned backlog is an important part of the aggregate plan. For make-to-stock companies, customers who request an item that is temporarily out of stock may have the option of **backordering** the item. If the customer is unwilling to wait for the backordered item, the sale will be lost. Although in general both backorders and **lost sales** should be avoided, the aggregate plan may include an estimate of both. Backorders are added to the next period's requirements; lost sales are not.

Backlog Accumulated customer orders to be completed at a later date.

Backordering Ordering an item that is temporarily out of stock.

Lost sales Forfeited sales for out-of-stock items.

Strategies for Managing Demand

Aggregate planning can also involve proactive demand management. Strategies for managing demand include:

- Shifting demand into other time periods with incentives, sales promotions, and advertising campaigns;
- Offering products or services with countercyclical demand patterns; and
- Partnering with suppliers to reduce information distortion along the supply chain.

Winter coat specials in July, bathing-suit sales in January, early-bird discounts on dinner, lower health club rates mid-mornings, and getaway weekends at hotels during the off-season are all attempts to shift demand into different time periods. Electric utilities are especially skilled at off-peak pricing. Promotions can also be used to extend high demand into low-demand seasons. Holiday gift buying is encouraged earlier each year, and beach resorts plan festivals in September and October to extend the season. Successful demand management depends on accurate forecasts of demand and accurate forecasts of the changes in demand brought about by sales, promotions, and special offers.

For industries with extreme variations in demand, offering products or services with countercyclical demand patterns helps smooth out resource requirements. This approach involves examining the idleness of resources and creating a demand for those resources. McDonald's offers breakfast to keep its kitchens busy during the prelunch hours, pancake restaurants serve lunch and dinner, heating firms also sell air conditioners, and lawn services also remove snow (see photos).

Amadas Industries, a small U.S. manufacturer of peanut harvesting equipment, does an especially good job of finding countercyclical products to smooth the load on its manufacturing facilities. The company operates a job shop production system with general-purpose equipment, 50 highly skilled workers, and a talented engineering staff. With these flexible resources, the company can make virtually anything its engineers can design. Inventories of finished goods are limited because of the significant investment in funds and the size of the finished product. Demand for the product is highly seasonal. Peanut-harvesting equipment is generally purchased on an as-needed basis from August to October, so during the spring and early summer, the company makes bark-scalping equipment for processing mulch and pine nuggets used by landscaping services. Demand for peanut-harvesting equipment is also affected by the weather each growing season, so during years of extensive drought, the company produces and sells irrigation equipment. The company also decided to market its products internationally with a special eye toward countries whose growing seasons are opposite to that of the United States. Thus, many of its sales are made in China and India during the very months when demand in the United States is low.

Another approach to managing demand recognizes the information distortion caused by ordering goods in batches along a supply chain. Even though a customer may require

Vincenzo Lombardo/Photographer's Choice RF/Getty Images

vm/E+/Getty Images

A carefully planned mix of services can smooth out resource requirements. At this resort, the pristine golf course during the summer months becomes a cross-country skiing path during the winter. The same company that maintains the fairways grooms the snow for the skiers.

Along the Supply Chain

Disney's Magic Numbers

Sales and operations planning at Disney World is all about people—how many people visit the parks and what they do while there. The Disney property in Florida includes 4 parks, 20 hotels, 27,500 rooms, 160 miles of roads, and 56,000 employees. Forecasting attendance and guest behavior helps plan for more than 1 billion customer interactions per year, and the purchase of 9 million hamburgers, 50 million Cokes, and tons of "tangible memories."

Planning begins with a five-year forecast of attendance based on a combination of econometric models, experience-based models, extensive research, and a magic mirror. The econometric model examines the international economies of seven key countries, their GDP growth, foreign exchange rate, and consumer confidence. The experience-based model looks at demographics, planned product introductions, capacity expansions, and marketing strategies. Extensive research is conducted by 35 analysts and 70 field personnel year round. Over 1 million surveys are administered to key household segments, current guests, cast members, and travel industry personnel. The magic mirror is the patented part of the forecasting procedure that, in part, accounts for the mere 5% error in the five-year attendance forecast and the 0% error in annual forecasts.

Disney's five-year plan is converted to an annual operating plan (AOP) for each park. Demand is highly seasonal and varies by month and day of the week. Economic conditions affect annual plans, as do history and holidays, school calendars, societal behavior, and sales promotions. The AOP is updated monthly with information from airline specials, hotel bookings, recent forecast accuracies, website monitoring, and competitive influences. A daily forecast of attendance is made by tweaking the AOP and adjusting for monthly variations, weather forecasts, and the previous day's crowds. Attendance drives all other decisions.

Disney is a master at adjusting its capacity and managing its demand. Capacity can be increased by lengthening park hours, opening more rides or shows, adding roving food and beverage carts, and deploying more "cast members." To maintain flexibility, cast members are scheduled in 15-minute intervals at various jobs throughout the park. Demand is managed by limiting access to the park, shifting crowds to street activities, taking reservations for attractions, and notifying patrons when room becomes available. Operating standards strictly regulate when these actions are taken. Obsessive collection of data ensures the response is timely.

© Helen Sessions/Alamy Stock Photo

The collection of data is easier and more timely with a new vacation management system implemented by Disney, called My Magic+. The system transforms how visitors navigate the park, and hopefully provides them with a better customer experience. It also provides Disney with more consumer behavior information on which to make decisions. Each guest is issued a rubber bracelet (the MagicBand) equipped with RFID tags (see photo). The MagicBands contain ticket information, credit card information, contact information, and other personal information, as allowed, as well as fast passes and updated information on the guest's interactions during their day at the park. Turnstiles throughout the park are replaced by bracelet readers, stores will soon no longer take cash, and, if activated, a child's name, birthday, and other information can be relayed to park staff so that interaction with costumed characters can really be magical. Lines are virtually eliminated with visitors "pinged" when it's their time for a particular ride or attraction, or when they pass by an attraction on their preferred list that has empty seats.

1. Comment on the extensiveness of Disney's planning process and its ability to react to updated data during the course of a day. What other types of industries could benefit from this flexible type of planning?
2. Think about the future of RFID tags in our daily lives. What are the pros and cons of the MagicBands? Of other types of RFID?

Source: Based on Joni Newkirk and Mark Haskell, "Forecasting in the Service Sector," presented at the Twelfth Annual Meeting of the Production Operations Management Society, Orlando, FL, April 1, 2001; Brooks Barnes, "At Disney Parks, a Bracelet Meant to Build Loyalty (and Sales)," *The New York Times* (January 7, 2013).

daily usage of an item, he or she probably does not purchase that item daily. Neither do retail stores restock their shelves continuously. By the time a replenishment order reaches distributors, wholesalers, manufacturers, and their suppliers, the demand pattern for a product can appear extremely erratic. This *bullwhip effect* was discussed in Chapter 10. To control the situation, manufacturers, their suppliers, and customers form partnerships in which demand information is shared and orders are placed in a more continuous fashion.

Quantitative Techniques for Aggregate Planning

Aggregate planning The process of determining the quantity and timing of production over an intermediate time frame.

One **aggregate planning** strategy is not always preferable to another. The most effective strategy depends on the demand distribution, competitive position, and cost structure of a firm or product line. Several quantitative techniques are available to help with the aggregate planning decision. In the sections that follow, we discuss pure and mixed strategies, linear programming, the *transportation method*, and other quantitative techniques.

Pure Strategies

Solving aggregate planning problems involves formulating strategies for meeting demand, constructing production plans from those strategies, determining the cost and feasibility of each plan, and selecting the lowest cost plan from among the feasible alternatives. The effectiveness of the aggregate planning process is directly related to management's understanding of the cost variables involved and the reasonableness of the scenarios tested. Example 14.1 compares the cost of two pure strategies: *level production* and *chase demand*.

EXAMPLE 14.1 | Aggregate Planning Using Pure Strategies

The Good and Rich Candy Company makes a variety of candies in three factories worldwide. Its line of chocolate candies exhibits a highly seasonal demand pattern, with peaks during the winter months (for the holiday season and Valentine's Day) and valleys during the summer months (when chocolate tends to melt and customers are watching their weight). Given the following costs and quarterly sales forecasts, determine whether (a) level production or (b) chase demand would more economically meet the demand for chocolate candies:

QUARTER	SALES FORECAST (lbs)
Spring	80,000
Summer	50,000
Fall	120,000
Winter	150,000

Hiring cost = \$100 per worker
Firing cost = \$500 per worker
Inventory carrying cost = \$0.50 per pound per quarter
Regular production cost per pound = \$2.00
Production per employee = 1000 pounds per quarter
Beginning workforce = 100 workers

Solution:

a. For the level production strategy, we first need to calculate average quarterly demand.

$$\frac{(80{,}000 + 50{,}000 + 120{,}000 + 150{,}000)}{4} = \frac{400{,}000}{4} = 100{,}000 \text{ pounds}$$

This becomes our planned production for each quarter. Since each worker can produce 1000 pounds a quarter, 100 workers will be needed each quarter to meet the production requirements of 100,000 pounds. Production in excess of demand is stored in inventory, where it remains until it is used to meet demand in a later period. Demand in excess of production is met by using inventory from the previous quarter. The production plan and resulting inventory costs are as follows:

QUARTER	DEMAND	REGULAR PRODUCTION	INVENTORY
Spring	80,000	100,000	(100,000 − 80,000) = 20,000
Summer	50,000	100,000	(20,000 + 100,000 − 50,000) = 70,000
Fall	120,000	100,000	(70,000 + 100,000 − 120,000) = 50,000
Winter	150,000	100,000	(50,000 + 100,000 − 150,000) = 0
Total	*400,000*	*400,000*	*140,000*

Cost of Level Production Strategy $= (400{,}000 \times \$2.00) + (140{,}000 \times \$.50) = \$870{,}000$

b. For the chase demand strategy, production each quarter matches demand. To accomplish this, workers are hired at a cost of $100 each and fired at a cost of $500 each. Since each worker can produce 1000 pounds per quarter, we divide the quarterly sales forecast by 1000 to determine the required workforce size each quarter. We begin with 100 workers and hire and fire as needed. The production plan and resulting hiring and firing costs are given here.

QUARTER	DEMAND	REGULAR PRODUCTION	WORKERS NEEDED	WORKERS HIRED	WORKERS FIRED
Spring	80,000	80,000	80,000/1000 = 80		(100 − 80) = 20
Summer	50,000	50,000	50,000/1000 = 50		(80 − 50) = 30
Fall	120,000	120,000	120,000/1000 = 120	(120 − 50) = 70	
Winter	150,000	150,000	150,000/1000 = 150	(150 − 120) = 30	
Total	*400,000*	*400,000*		*100*	*50*

Cost of Chase Demand Strategy $= (400{,}000 \times \$2.00) + (100 \times \$100) + (50 \times \$500) = \$835{,}000$

Comparing the cost of level production with chase demand, we find that chase demand is the best strategy for the Good and Rich line of candies.

The problem can also be solved using Excel. Exhibit 14.1 shows two worksheets from the Excel file, Exhibit 14.1.xls, available on the text website.

Although chase demand is the better strategy for Good and Rich from an economic point of view, it may seem unduly harsh on the company's workforce. An example of a good "fit" between a company's chase demand strategy and the needs of the workforce is Hershey's, located in rural Pennsylvania, with a demand and cost structure much like that of Good and Rich. The location of the manufacturing facility is essential to the effectiveness of the company's production plan. During the winter, when demand for chocolate is high, the company hires farmers from surrounding areas, who are idle at that time of year. The farmers are let go during the spring and summer, when they are anxious to return to their fields and the demand for chocolate falls. The plan is cost-effective, and the extra help is content with the sporadic hiring and firing practices of the company.

EXHIBIT 14.1a | Level Production for Good and Rich

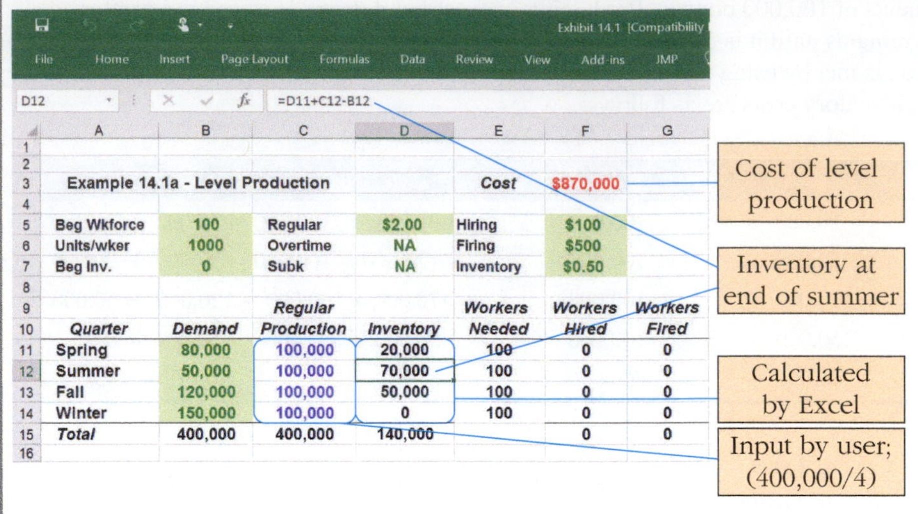

	A	B	C	D	E	F	G
3	Example 14.1a - Level Production				Cost	$870,000	
5	Beg Wkforce	100	Regular	$2.00	Hiring	$100	
6	Units/wker	1000	Overtime	NA	Firing	$500	
7	Beg Inv.	0	Subk	NA	Inventory	$0.50	
9			Regular		Workers	Workers	Workers
10	Quarter	Demand	Production	Inventory	Needed	Hired	Fired
11	Spring	80,000	100,000	20,000	100	0	0
12	Summer	50,000	100,000	70,000	100	0	0
13	Fall	120,000	100,000	50,000	100	0	0
14	Winter	150,000	100,000	0	100	0	0
15	Total	400,000	400,000	140,000		0	0

EXHIBIT 14.1b | Chase Demand for Good and Rich

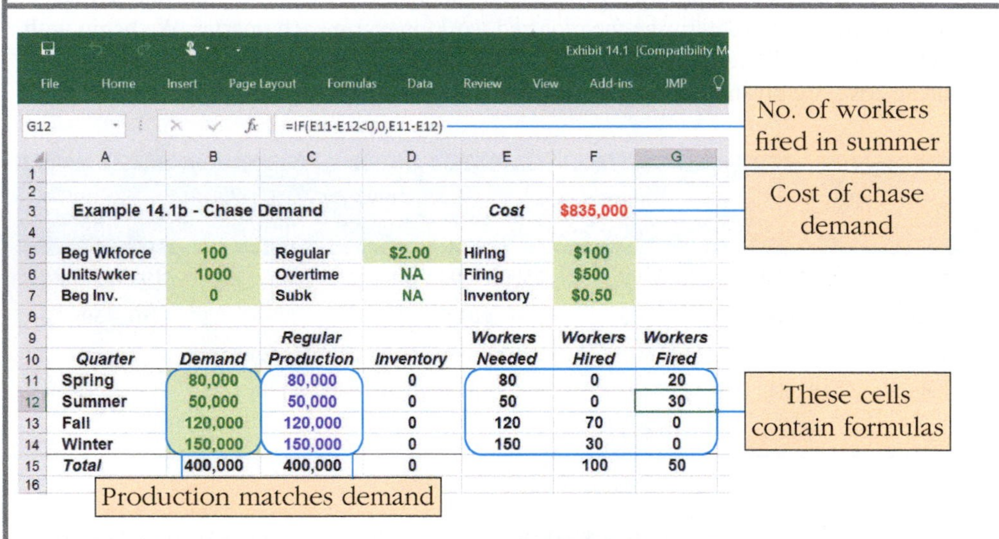

	A	B	C	D	E	F	G
3	Example 14.1b - Chase Demand				Cost	$835,000	
5	Beg Wkforce	100	Regular	$2.00	Hiring	$100	
6	Units/wker	1000	Overtime	NA	Firing	$500	
7	Beg Inv.	0	Subk	NA	Inventory	$0.50	
9			Regular		Workers	Workers	Workers
10	Quarter	Demand	Production	Inventory	Needed	Hired	Fired
11	Spring	80,000	80,000	0	80	0	20
12	Summer	50,000	50,000	0	50	0	30
13	Fall	120,000	120,000	0	120	70	0
14	Winter	150,000	150,000	0	150	30	0
15	Total	400,000	400,000	0		100	50

General Linear Programming Model

Strategies for production planning may be easy to evaluate, but they do not necessarily provide an optimal solution. Consider the Good and Rich Company of Example 14.1. The *optimal* production plan is probably some combination of inventory and workforce adjustment. We could simply try different combinations and compare the costs (i.e., the trial-and-error approach), or we could find the optimal solution by using *linear programming*. If you are unfamiliar with linear programming, please review the supplement to this chapter. Example 14.2 develops an optimal production plan for Good and Rich chocolate candies using linear programming.

EXAMPLE 14.2 | Production Planning Using Linear Programming

Formulate a linear programming model for Example 14.1 that will satisfy demand for Good and Rich chocolate candies at minimum cost. Solve the model with Excel Solver.

Solution:

Model Formulation:

$$\text{Minimize } Z = \$100\,(H_1 + H_2 + H_3 + H_4) + \$500\,(F_1 + F_2 + F_3 + F_4)$$

$$+ \$0.50\ (I_1 + I_2 + I_3 + I_4)$$
$$+ \$2\ (P_1 + P_2 + P_3 + P_4)$$

subject to

Demand constraints

$$P_1 - I_1 = 80{,}000 \quad (1)$$
$$I_1 + P_2 - I_2 = 50{,}000 \quad (2)$$
$$I_2 + P_3 - I_3 = 120{,}000 \quad (3)$$
$$I_3 + P_4 - I_4 = 150{,}000 \quad (4)$$

Production constraints

$$1000W_1 = P_1 \quad (5)$$
$$1000W_2 = P_2 \quad (6)$$
$$1000W_3 = P_3 \quad (7)$$
$$1000W_4 = P_4 \quad (8)$$

Workforce constraints

$$100 + H_1 - F_1 = W_1 \quad (9)$$
$$W_1 + H_2 - F_2 = W_2 \quad (10)$$
$$W_2 + H_3 - F_3 = W_3 \quad (11)$$
$$W_3 + H_4 - F_4 = W_4 \quad (12)$$

where

H_t = number of workers hired for period t
F_t = number of workers fired for period t
I_t = units in inventory at the end of period t
P_t = units produced in period t
W_t = workforce size for period t

- ***Objective function***: The objective function seeks to minimize the cost of hiring workers, firing workers, holding inventory, and production. Cost values are provided in the problem statement for Example 14.1. The number of workers hired and fired each quarter and the amount of inventory held are variables whose values are determined by solving the linear programming (LP) problem.
- ***Demand constraints***: The first set of constraints ensures that demand is met each quarter. Demand can be met from production in the current period and inventory from the previous period. Units produced in excess of demand remain in inventory at the end of the period. In general form, the demand equations are constructed as

  $$I_{t-1} + P_t = D_t + I_t$$

  where D_t is the demand in period t, as specified in the problem. Leaving demand on the right-hand side, we have

  $$I_{t-1} + P_t - I_t = D_t$$

  There are four demand constraints, one for each quarter. Since there is no beginning inventory, $I_0 = 0$, and it can be dropped from the first demand constraint.
- ***Production constraints***: The four production constraints convert the workforce size to the number of units that can be produced. Each worker can produce 1000 units a quarter, so the production each quarter is 1000 times the number of workers employed, or

  $$1000W_t = P_t$$
- ***Workforce constraints***: The workforce constraints limit the workforce size in each period to the previous period's workforce plus the number of workers hired in the current period minus the number of workers fired.

  $$W_{t-1} + H_t - F_t = W_t$$

  Notice the first workforce constraint shows a beginning workforce size of 100.
- ***Additional variables and constraints***: Additional variables, such as overtime and subcontracting, can be added to the LP formulation as needed. The cost of those variables is then added to the objective function. Additional constraints such as limiting the amount of overtime or subcontracting can also be added in the Solver model.

The LP model is formulated in Excel in Exhibit 14.2a and solved using Excel Solver in Exhibit 14.2b. The Excel file, Exhibit 14.2.xls, is available on the text website. The cost of the optimum solution is \$832,000, an improvement of \$3000 over the chase demand strategy and \$38,000 over the level production strategy.

EXHIBIT 14.2a | Setting up the Spreadsheet

Exhibit 14.1 [Compatibility Mode] - Excel

File | Home | Insert | Page Layout | Formulas | Data | Review | View | Add-ins | JMP | Tell me what you want to do...

H11 | =D10+C11-D11

	A	B	C	D	E	F	G	H	I	J
1										
2	Exhibit 14.2b - LP Solution				Cost	$0				
3										
4	Beg Wkforce	100	Regular	$2.00	Hiring	$100				
5	Units/wker	1000	Overtime	NA	Firing	$500				
6	Beg Inv.	0	Subk	NA	Inventory	$0.50				
7										
8–9	Quarter	Demand	Regular Production	Inventory	Workers Needed	Workers Hired	Workers Fired	Demand Constraint	Production Constraint	Workforce Constraint
10	Spring	80,000						0	0	100
11	Summer	50,000						0	0	0
12	Fall	120,000						0	0	0
13	Winter	150,000						0	0	0
14	Total	400,000	0	0		0	0			
15										

Solver Parameters

Set Objective: $F$2

To: Max ◉ Min Value Of: 0

By Changing Variable Cells: $C$10:$G$13

Subject to the Constraints:
DemandConstraint = Demand
ProductionConstraint = RegularProduction
workforceConstraint = WorkersNeeded

Add | Change | Delete | Reset All | Load/Save

☑ Make Unconstrained Variables Non-Negative

Select a Solving Method: Simplex LP | Options

Solving Method
Select the GRG Nonlinear engine for Solver Problems that are smooth nonlinear. Select the LP Simplex engine for linear Solver Problems, and select the Evolutionary engine for Solver problems that are non-smooth.

Help | Solve | Close

Cost of solution goes here

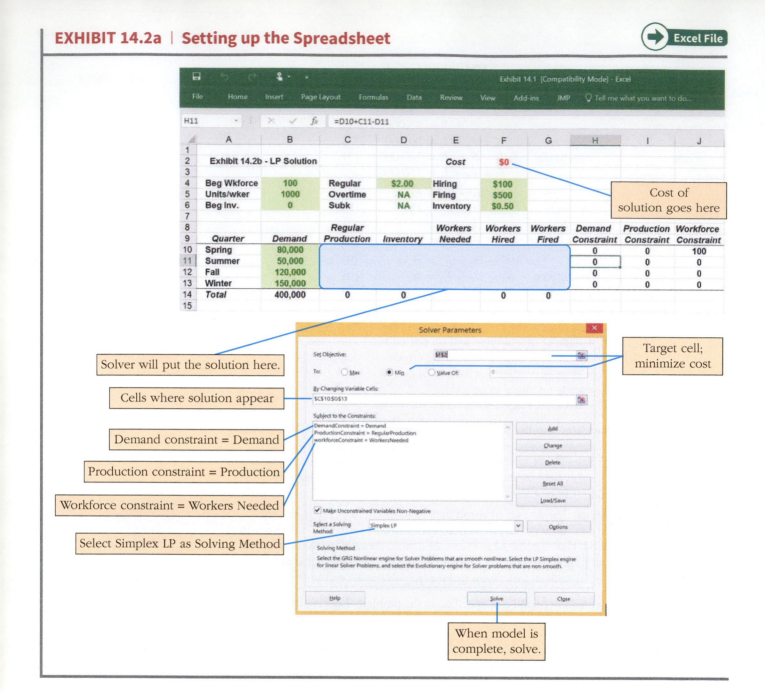

Solver will put the solution here.

Target cell; minimize cost

Cells where solution appear

Demand constraint = Demand

Production constraint = Production

Workforce constraint = Workers Needed

Select Simplex LP as Solving Method

When model is complete, solve.

EXHIBIT 14.2b | Solver Solution

Excel File

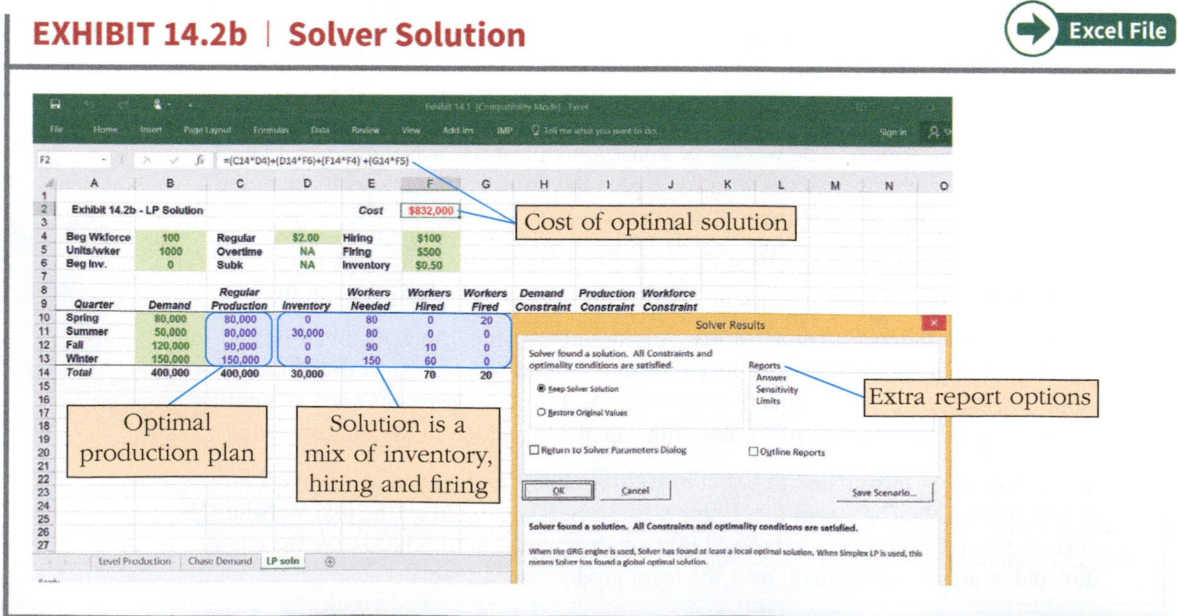

Mixed Strategies

Most companies use **mixed strategies** for production planning. Mixed strategies can incorporate management policies, such as "no more than x% of the workforce can be laid off in one quarter" or "inventory levels cannot exceed x dollars." They can also be adapted to the quirks of a company or industry. For example, many industries that experience a slowdown during part of the year may simply shut down manufacturing during the low-demand season and schedule employee vacations during that time.

Mixed strategy Varying two or more capacity factors to determine a feasible production plan.

Example 14.3 compares pure and mixed strategies in a more extensive aggregate planning problem. Excel spreadsheets are used to make the calculations. The user inputs demand and cost data, as well as values for regular, overtime, and subcontracted production. The spreadsheet calculates resulting inventory levels, workforce levels, hiring/firing and total cost. The Excel file for this example, Exhibit 14.3.xls, is available on the textbook website. Although this problem can be solved by hand, you may wish to use the spreadsheet as a template for solving other aggregate planning problems.

EXAMPLE 14.3 | Aggregate Planning Using Pure and Mixed Strategies

Demand for Quantum Corporation's action toy series follows a seasonal pattern—growing through the fall months and culminating in December, with smaller peaks in January (for after-season markdowns, exchanges, and accessory purchases) and July (for Christmas-in-July specials).

MONTH	DEMAND (CASES)	MONTH	DEMAND (CASES)
January	1000	July	500
February	400	August	500
March	400	September	1000
April	400	October	1500
May	400	November	2500
June	400	December	3000

Each worker can produce on average 100 cases of action toys each month. Overtime is limited to 300 cases, and subcontracting is unlimited. No action toys are currently in inventory. The wage rate is $10 per case for regular production, $15 for overtime production, and $25 for subcontracting. No stockouts are allowed. Holding cost is $1 per case per month. Increasing the workforce costs approximately $1000 per worker; decreasing the workforce costs $500 per worker.

Management wishes to test the following scenarios for planning production:

a. Level production over the 12 months.
b. Produce to meet demand each month.
c. Solve the problem with linear programming (LP) using Excel Solver.

Solution: Excel was used to evaluate the three planning scenarios. The solution printouts are shown in Exhibit 14.3. LP produced a mixed strategy of chase demand through August, then level production September through December.

EXHIBIT 14.3a | Level Production for Quantum

Excel File

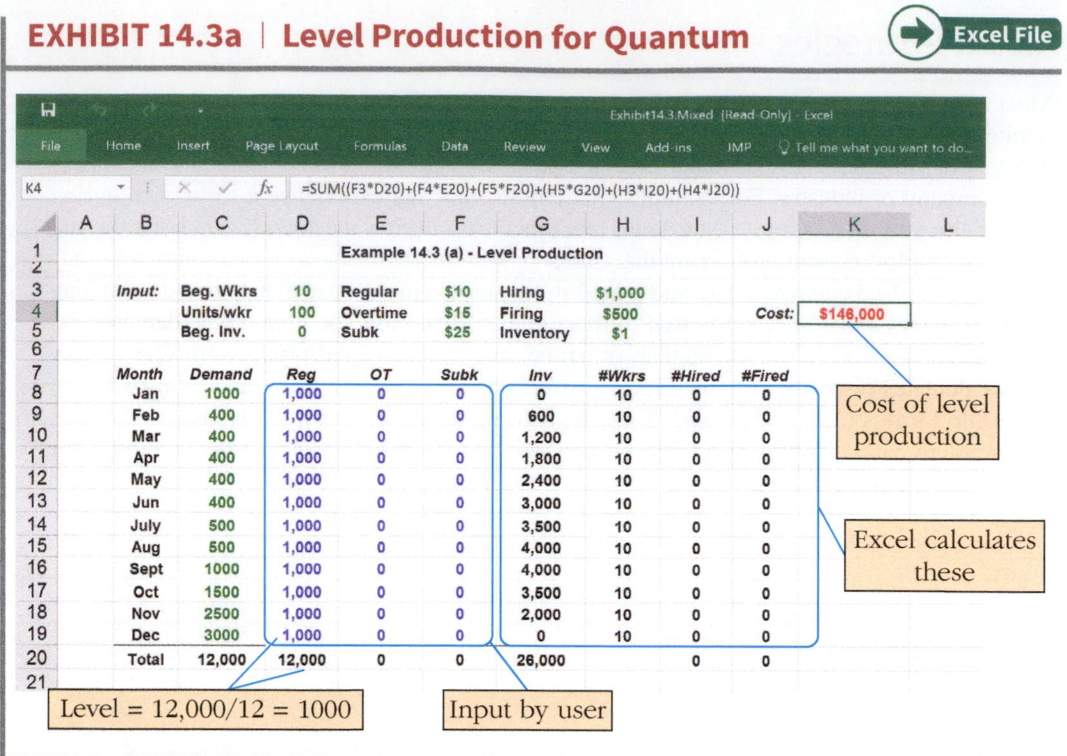

K4: =SUM((F3*D20)+(F4*E20)+(F5*F20)+(H5*G20)+(H3*I20)+(H4*J20))

Example 14.3 (a) - Level Production

Input:	Beg. Wkrs	10	Regular	$10	Hiring	$1,000		*Cost:*	$146,000
	Units/wkr	100	Overtime	$15	Firing	$500			
	Beg. Inv.	0	Subk	$25	Inventory	$1			

Month	*Demand*	*Reg*	*OT*	*Subk*	*Inv*	*#Wkrs*	*#Hired*	*#Fired*
Jan	1000	1,000	0	0	0	10	0	0
Feb	400	1,000	0	0	600	10	0	0
Mar	400	1,000	0	0	1,200	10	0	0
Apr	400	1,000	0	0	1,800	10	0	0
May	400	1,000	0	0	2,400	10	0	0
Jun	400	1,000	0	0	3,000	10	0	0
July	500	1,000	0	0	3,500	10	0	0
Aug	500	1,000	0	0	4,000	10	0	0
Sept	1000	1,000	0	0	4,000	10	0	0
Oct	1500	1,000	0	0	3,500	10	0	0
Nov	2500	1,000	0	0	2,000	10	0	0
Dec	3000	1,000	0	0	0	10	0	0
Total	12,000	12,000	0	0	26,000		0	0

EXHIBIT 14.3b | Chase Demand for Quantum

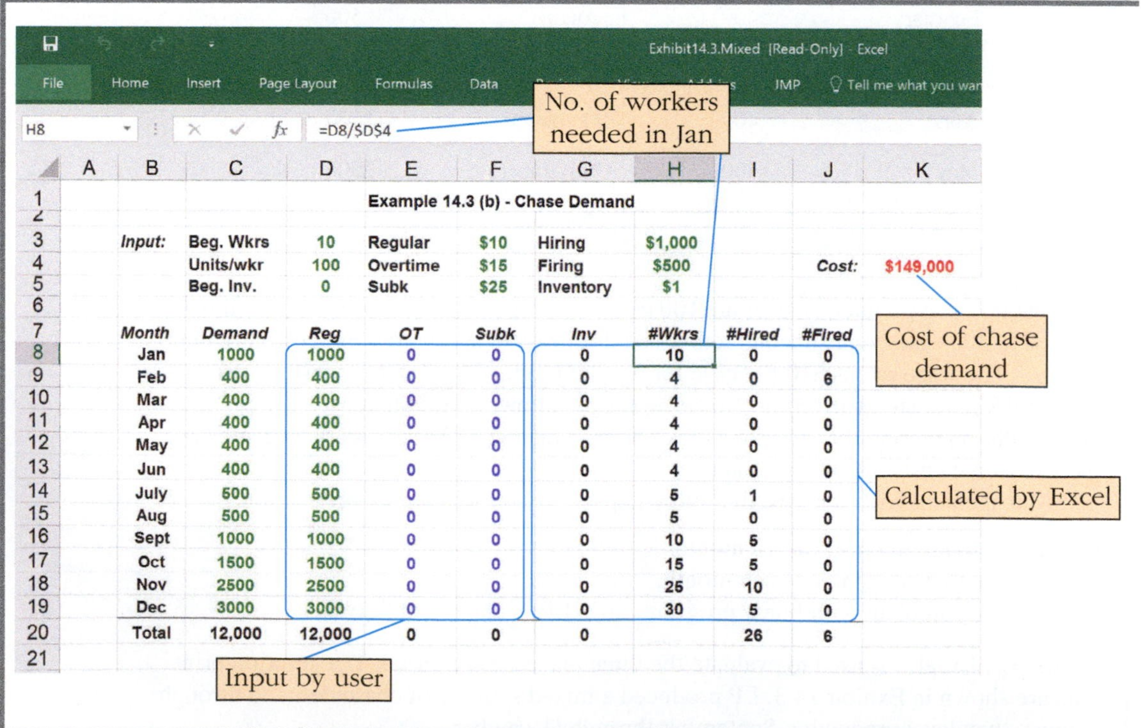

H8: =D8/$D$4

Example 14.3 (b) - Chase Demand

Input:	Beg. Wkrs	10	Regular	$10	Hiring	$1,000		*Cost:*	$149,000
	Units/wkr	100	Overtime	$15	Firing	$500			
	Beg. Inv.	0	Subk	$25	Inventory	$1			

Month	*Demand*	*Reg*	*OT*	*Subk*	*Inv*	*#Wkrs*	*#Hired*	*#Fired*
Jan	1000	1000	0	0	0	10	0	0
Feb	400	400	0	0	0	4	0	6
Mar	400	400	0	0	0	4	0	0
Apr	400	400	0	0	0	4	0	0
May	400	400	0	0	0	4	0	0
Jun	400	400	0	0	0	4	0	0
July	500	500	0	0	0	5	1	0
Aug	500	500	0	0	0	5	0	0
Sept	1000	1000	0	0	0	10	5	0
Oct	1500	1500	0	0	0	15	5	0
Nov	2500	2500	0	0	0	25	10	0
Dec	3000	3000	0	0	0	30	5	0
Total	12,000	12,000	0	0	0		26	6

EXHIBIT 14.3c | Linear Programming Solution for Quantum

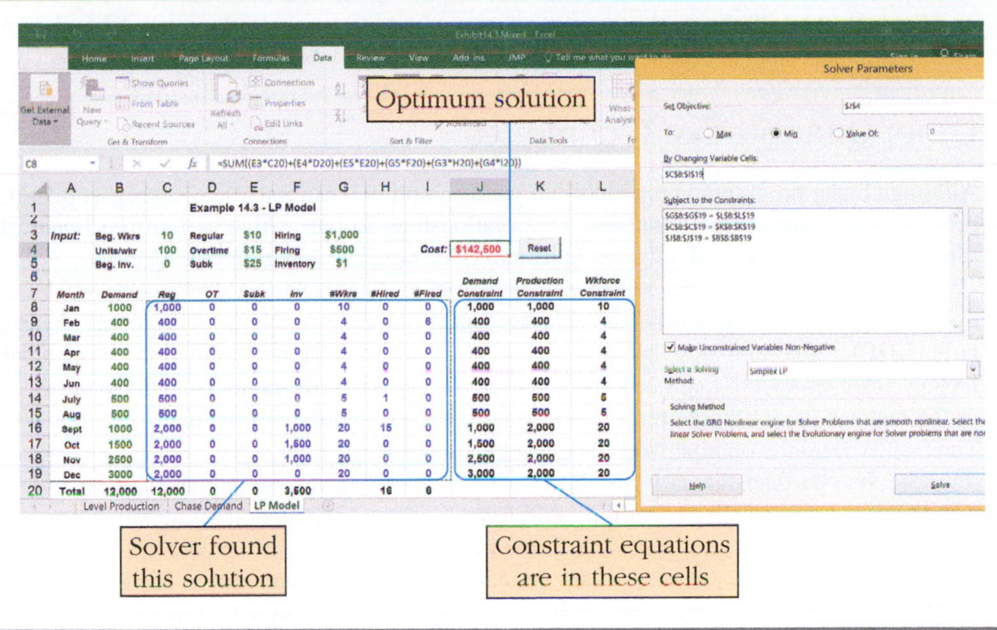

The Transportation Method

For cases in which the decision to change the size of the workforce has already been made or is prohibited, the transportation method of linear programming can be used to develop an aggregate production plan. (See Supplement 11 for an introduction to the transportation method.) The transportation method gathers all the cost information into one matrix and plans production based on the lowest-cost alternatives. Table 14.1 shows a blank transportation tableau with *i* for inventory, *h* for holding cost, *r* for regular production cost, *o* for overtime, *s* for subcontracting, and *b* for backordering. The capital letters indicate individual capacities or demand. The

TABLE 14.1 Transportation Tableau

PERIOD OF PRODUCTION		PERIOD OF USE 1	2	3	4	UNUSED CAPACITY	CAPACITY
	Beginning Inventory	0	h	$2h$	$3h$		I
1	Regular	r	$r+h$	$r+2h$	$r+3h$		R_1
	Overtime	o	$o+h$	$o+2h$	$o+3h$		O_1
	Subcontract	s	$s+h$	$s+2h$	$s+3h$		S_1
2	Regular	$r+b$	r	$r+h$	$r+2h$		R_2
	Overtime	$o+b$	o	$o+h$	$o+2h$		O_2
	Subcontract	$s+b$	s	$s+h$	$s+2h$		S_2
3	Regular	$r+2b$	$r+b$	r	$r+h$		R_3
	Overtime	$o+2b$	$o+b$	o	$o+h$		O_3
	Subcontract	$s+2b$	$s+b$	s	$s+h$		S_3
4	Regular	$r+3b$	$r+2b$	$r+b$	r		R_4
	Overtime	$o+3b$	$o+2b$	$o+b$	o		O_4
	Subcontract	$s+3b$	$s+2b$	$s+b$	s		S_4
	Demand	D_1	D_2	D_3	D_4		

h = holding cost per unit
r = regular production cost per unit
o = overtime cost per unit
s = subcontracting cost per unit
b = backordering cost per unit
D = demand
I = beginning inventory
R = regular capacity
O = overtime capacity
S = subcontracting capacity

periods of production, along with the production options, appear in the first column. The periods of use (regardless of when the items are produced) appear across the top row. Cost entries in the period-of-use columns differ by the cost of holding the item in inventory before its use.

Example 14.4 illustrates the transportation method of aggregate planning. A blank transportation tableau and an Excel file of Example 14.4 are available online.

Other Quantitative Techniques

Although linear programming models will yield an optimal solution to the aggregate planning problem, there are some limitations. The relationships among variables must be linear, the model is deterministic, and only one objective is allowed (usually minimizing cost).

Linear decision rule (LDR) A mathematical technique for aggregate planning.

Search decision rule (SDR) A pattern search technique for aggregate planning.

Management coefficients model A regression technique for aggregate planning

The linear decision rule, search decision rule, and management coefficients model use different types of cost functions to solve aggregate planning problems. The **linear decision rule (LDR)** is an optimizing technique originally developed for aggregate planning in a paint factory. It solves a set of four quadratic equations that describe the major capacity-related costs in the factory: payroll costs, hiring and firing, overtime and undertime, and inventory costs. The results yield the optimal workforce level and production rate.

The **search decision rule (SDR)** is a pattern search algorithm that tries to find the minimum cost combination of various workforce levels and production rates. Any type of cost function can be used. The search is performed by computer and may involve the evaluation of thousands of possible solutions, but an optimal solution is not guaranteed. The **management coefficients model** uses regression analysis to improve the consistency of planning decisions. Techniques like SDR and management coefficients are often embedded in commercial decision support systems or expert systems for aggregate planning.

EXAMPLE 14.4 | The Transportation Method of Aggregate Planning

Burruss Manufacturing Company uses overtime, inventory, and subcontracting to absorb fluctuations in demand. An aggregate production plan is devised annually and updated quarterly. Cost data, expected demand, and available capacities in units for the next four quarters are given here. Demand must be satisfied in the period it occurs; that is, no back-ordering is allowed. Design a production plan that will satisfy demand at minimum cost.

QUARTER	EXPECTED DEMAND	REGULAR CAPACITY	OVERTIME CAPACITY	SUBCONTRACT CAPACITY
1	900	1000	100	500
2	1500	1200	150	500
3	1600	1300	200	500
4	3000	1300	200	500

Regular production cost per unit	$20
Overtime production cost per unit	$25
Subcontracting cost per unit	$28
Inventory holding cost per unit per period	$ 3
Beginning inventory	300 units

Solution: The problem is solved using the transportation tableau shown in Table 14.2. The tableau is a worksheet that is completed as follows:

- **Rim requirements:** To set up the tableau, demand requirements for each quarter are listed on the bottom row, and capacity constraints for each type of production (i.e., regular, overtime, or subcontracting) are placed in the far right column, around the rim of the table.
- **Beginning inventory:** Next, cost figures are entered into the small square at the corner of each cell. Starting with the beginning inventory row, inventory on hand in

TABLE 14.2

PERIOD OF PRODUCTION		PERIOD OF USE 1		2		3		4		UNUSED CAPACITY	CAPACITY
	Beginning Inventory	300	0	—	3	—	6	—	9		300
1	Regular	600	20	300	23	100	26	—	29		1000
	Overtime		25		28		31	100	34		100
	Subcontract		28		31		34		37	500	500
2	Regular			1200	20	—	23	—	26		1200
	Overtime				25		28	150	31		150
	Subcontract				28		31	250	34	250	500
3	Regular					1300	20	—	23		1300
	Overtime					200	25	—	28		200
	Subcontract						28	500	31		500
4	Regular							1300	20		1300
	Overtime							200	25		200
	Subcontract							500	28		500
	Demand	900		1500		1600		3000		250	

period 1 that is used in period 1 incurs zero cost. Inventory on hand in period 1 that is not used until period 2 incurs a $3 holding cost. Inventory held until period 3, costs $3 more, or $6. Similarly, inventory held until period 4 costs an additional $3, or $9.

- **Cost figures:** For regular production, a unit produced in period 1 and used in period 1 costs $20. A unit produced under regular production in period 1 but not used until period 2 incurs a production cost of $20 plus an inventory cost of $3, or $23. If the unit is held until period 3, it costs $3 more, or $26. If held until period 4, it costs $29. The cost calculations continue for overtime and subcontracting, beginning with production costs of $25 and $28, respectively.
- **No backorders:** The costs for production in periods 2, 3, and 4 are determined in a similar fashion, with one exception. Half of the remaining transportation tableau is blocked out as infeasible. This occurs because no backordering is allowed for this problem, and production cannot take place in one period to satisfy demand for a period that has already passed.
- **Period 1:** Now that the tableau is set up, we can begin to allocate units to the cells and develop our production plan. The procedure is to assign units to the lowest-cost cells in a column so that demand requirements for the column are met, yet capacity constraints of each row are not exceeded. Beginning with the first demand column for period 1, we have 300 units of beginning inventory available to us at no cost. If we use all 300 units in period 1, there is no inventory left for use in later periods. We indicate this fact by putting a dash in the remaining cells of the beginning inventory row. We can satisfy the remaining 600 units of demand for period 1 with regular production at a cost of $20 per unit.
- **Period 2:** In period 2, the lowest-cost alternative is regular production in period 2. We assign 1200 units to that cell and, in the process, use up all the capacity for that row. Dashes are placed in the remaining cells of the row to indicate that they are no longer feasible choices. The remaining units needed to meet demand in period 2 are taken from regular production in period 1 that is inventoried until period 2, at a cost of $23 per unit. We assign 300 units to that cell.
- **Period 3:** Continuing to the third period's demand of 1600 units, we fully utilize the 1300 units available from regular production in the same period and 200 units of

TABLE 14.3 The Production Plan

		PRODUCTION PLAN			
PERIOD	DEMAND	REGULAR PRODUCTION	OVERTIME	SUBCONTRACT	ENDING INVENTORY
1	900	1000	100	0	500
2	1500	1200	150	250	600
3	1600	1300	200	500	1000
4	3000	1300	200	500	0
Total	7000	4800	650	1250	2100

overtime production. The remaining 100 units are produced with regular production in period 1 and held until period 3, at a cost of $26 per unit. As noted by the dashed line, period 1's regular production has reached its capacity and is no longer an alternative source of production.

- **Period 4:** Of the fourth period's demand of 3000 units, 1300 units come from regular production, 200 from overtime, and 500 from subcontracting in the same period. One hundred fifty more units can be provided at a cost of $31 per unit from overtime production in period 2 and 500 from subcontracting in period 3. The next-lowest alternative is $34 from overtime in period 1 or subcontracting in period 2. At this point, we can make a judgment call as to whether our workers want overtime or whether it would be easier to subcontract out the entire amount. As shown in Table 14.2, we decide to use overtime to its full capacity of 100 units and fill the remaining demand of 250 from subcontracting.
- **Unused capacity:** The unused capacity column is filled in last. In period 2, 250 units of subcontracting capacity are available but unused. This information is valuable because it tells us the flexibility the company has to accept additional orders.

The optimal production plan, derived from the transportation tableau, is given in Table 14.3.[1] The values in the production plan are taken from the transportation tableau one row at a time.

For example, the 1000 units of a regular production for period 1 is the sum of 600 + 300 + 100 from the second row of the transportation tableau. Ending inventory is calculated by summing beginning inventory and all forms of production for that period, and then subtracting demand. For example, the ending inventory for period 1 is

$$\begin{aligned}&(\text{Beginning inventory} + \text{Regular production}\\&\quad + \text{Overtime production} + \text{Subcontracting}) - \text{Demand}\\&\quad = (300 + 1000 + 100 + 0) - 900 = 500\end{aligned}$$

The cost of the production plan can be determined directly from the transportation tableau by multiplying the units in each cell times the cost in the corner of the cell and summing them. Alternatively, the cost can be determined from the production plan by multiplying the total units produced in each production category, or held in inventory, by their respective costs and summing them, as follows:

$$(4800 \times \$20) + (650 \times \$25) + (1250 \times \$28) + (2100 \times \$3) = \$153{,}550$$

An Excel solution to this problem is shown in Exhibit 14.4.

[1]For this example, our initial solution to the production problem happens to be optimal. In other cases, it may be necessary to iterate to additional transportation tableaux before an optimal solution is reached. Students unfamiliar with the transportation method should review the topic in the Supplement to Chapter 11.

EXHIBIT 14.4 | Using Excel for the Transportation Method of Aggregate Planning

Exhibit14.4.Transportation [Read-Only] [C

File Home Insert Page Layout Formulas Data Review View Add-ins JMP

F32 f_x =(E30*D7)+(G30*D8)+(I30*D9)+(K30*F6)

Exhibit 14.4 - The Transportation Method of Aggregate Planning

Period of Production		Period of Use 1	2	3	4	Units Produced	Capacity	Unused Capacity
	Beg. Inventory	300 (0)	0 (3)	0 (6)	(9)	300	300	0
1	Regular	600 (20)	300 (23)	100 (26)	(29)	1,000	1,000	0
	Overtime	(25)	0 (28)	0 (31)	100 (34)	100	100	0
	Subk	0 (28)	0 (31)	0 (34)	0 (37)	0	500	500
2	Regular	0	1,200 (20)	(23)	0 (26)	1,200	1,200	0
	Overtime	0	(26)	0 (28)	150 (31)	150	150	0
	Subk	0	(28)	0 (31)	250 (34)	250	500	250
3	Regular	0	0	1,300 (20)	0 (23)	1,300	1,300	0
	Overtime	0	0	200 (25)	0 (28)	200	200	0
	Subk	0	0	0 (28)	500 (31)	500	500	0
4	Regular	0	0	0	1,300 (20)	1,300	1,300	0
	Overtime	0	0	0	200 (25)	200	200	0
	Subk	0	0	0	500 (28)	500	500	0
	Units Produced	900	1,500	1,600	3,000	7,000	7,000	750
	Demand	900	1,500	1,600	3,000	7,000		
	Unmet Demand	0	0	0	0		Total Cost =	$153,550

Production Plan

Period	Demand	Reg. Prod.	Overtime	Subk	Ending Inventory
1	900	1,000	100	0	500
2	1,500	1,200	150	250	600
3	1,600	1,300	200	500	1,000
4	3,000	1,300	200	500	0
Total	7,000	4,800	650	1,250	2,100

Total Cost = $153,550

Regular production for period 1

Cost of solution

The Hierarchical Nature of Planning

Planning involves a hierarchy of decisions. By determining a strategy for meeting and managing demand, aggregate planning provides a framework within which shorter term production and capacity decisions can be made. The levels of production and capacity planning are shown in Figure 14.4. In production planning, the next level of detail is a *master production schedule*, in which weekly (not monthly or quarterly) production plans are specified by individual final product (not product line). At another level of detail, *material requirements planning* plans the production of the components that go into the final products. *Shop floor scheduling* schedules the manufacturing operations required to make each component.

In capacity planning, we might develop a *resource requirements plan*, to verify that a sales and operations plan is doable, and a *rough-cut capacity plan* as a quick check to see if the master production schedule is feasible. One level down, we would develop a much more detailed *capacity requirements plan* that matches the factory's machine and labor resources to the material requirements plan. Finally, we would use *input/output control* to monitor the production that takes place at individual machines or work centers.

At each level, decisions are made within the parameters set by the higher-level decisions. The process of moving from the aggregate plan to the next level down is called **disaggregation**. We examine this process more thoroughly in Chapter 15. In the next section, we discuss two important tools for planning in an e-business environment: collaborative planning and available-to-promise.

Disaggregation The process of breaking an aggregate plan into more detailed plans.

Collaborative Planning

Collaborative planning is part of the supply chain process of collaborative planning, forecasting, and replenishment (CPFR) presented in Chapter 10. In terms of production, CPFR

Collaborative planning Sharing information and synchronizing production across the supply chain.

FIGURE 14.4 **Hierarchical Planning**

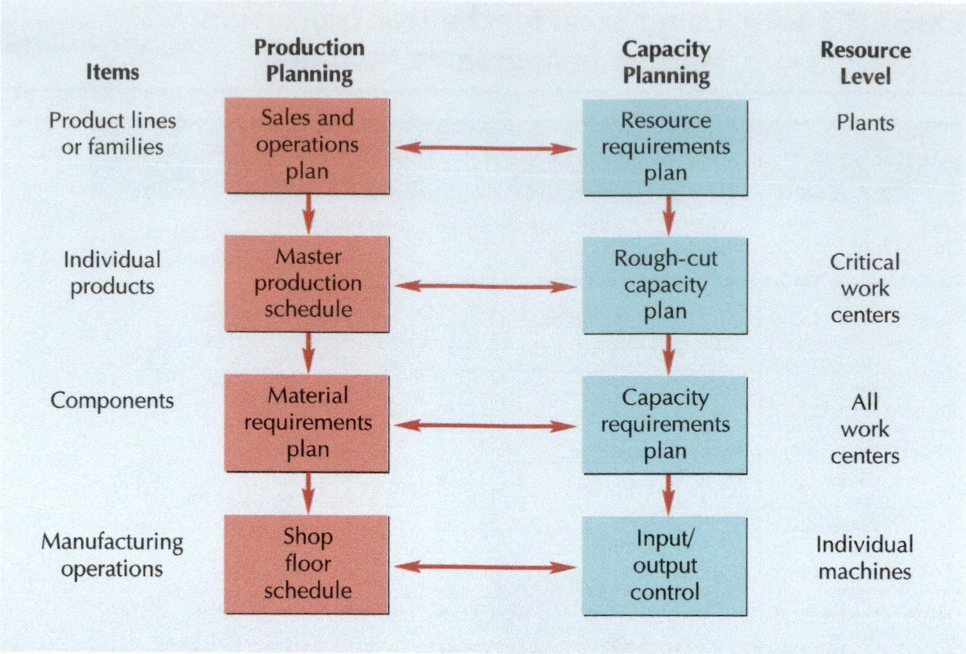

involves selecting the products to be jointly managed, creating a single forecast of customer demand, and synchronizing production across the supply chain. Consensus among partners is reached first on the sales forecast, then on the production plan. Although the process differs by software vendor, basically each partner has access to an Internet-enabled planning book in which forecasts, customer orders, and production plans are visible for specific items. Partners agree on the level of aggregation to be used. Events trigger responses by partners. Alerts warn partners of conditions that require special action or changes to the plan.

One example of an event that requires collaboration among trading partners is quoting available-to-promise dates for customers.

Available-to-Promise

Available-to-promise [ATP] The quantity of items that can be promised to the customer; the difference between planned production and customer orders already received.

In the current business environment of outsourcing and build-to-order products, companies must be able to provide the customer with accurate promise dates. Recall that S&OP is the company's *game plan* for matching supply and demand. As the time horizon grows shorter and more information becomes available, we develop and execute more detailed plans of action. For example, we convert the sales and operations plan for product families into a master schedule for individual products based on best estimates of future demand. As customer orders come in *consuming the forecast*, the remaining quantities are **available-to-promise** to future customers. Example 14.5 illustrates the process.

Available-to-promise is the difference between customer orders (CO) and planned production. In the first period of the planning horizon, available-to-promise is calculated by summing the on-hand quantity and planned production, then subtracting customer orders up until the next period of planned production. In subsequent periods, the ATP is simply planned production minus customer orders. No on-hand quantities are used. However, if customer orders exceed production, units can be taken from the ATP of previous periods.

ATP in period 1 = (On-hand quantity + MPS in period 1) − (CO until the next period of planned production)

ATP in period n = (MPS in period n) − (CO until the next period of planned production)

As companies venture beyond their boundaries to complete customer orders, so available-to-promise inquiries extend beyond a particular plant or distribution center to

EXAMPLE 14.5 | Available-to-Promise

East Coast Bicycle Company has recently begun to accept customer orders over the Internet. The company uses both an aggregate production plan for families and a master production schedule for individual products. Now East Coast wants to add available-to-promise functionality to the planning process. Using the information given below, determine how many girls' 26″ bikes are available-to-promise in April, May, and June.

Sales and Operations Plan

PRODUCT FAMILY	QUARTER 1	2	3	4
Juvenile Bikes	800	1000	1500	4000
Master Production Schedule for Qtr 2				
	April	May	June	Total
Boys' 26″ Bike	150	100	150	400
Girls' 26″ Bike	100	100	100	300
Boys' 20″ Bike	30	20	50	100
Girls' 20″ Bike	40	20	140	200
Total	320	240	440	1000
Available-to Promise for Girls' 26″ Bike				
On Hand = 10	April	May	June	Total
Forecast	50	100	150	300
Customer Orders	70	110	50	230
Master Production Schedule	100	100	100	300
Available-to-Promise				

Solution: The available-to-promise (ATP) row is calculated by summing the on-hand quantity with the scheduled production units and subtracting the customer orders up until the next period of planned production. The negative ATP in May is offset by using 10 units of ATP from April.

ON HAND = 10	APRIL	MAY	JUNE
Forecast	50	100	150
Customer Orders	70	110	150
Master Production Schedule	100	100	100
Available-to-Promise	30	0	50

ATP in April = (10 + 100) − 70 = ~~40~~ 30

ATP in May = 100 − 110 = ~~−10~~ 0 Take excess units from April

ATP in June = 100 − 50 = 50

a network of plants and supplier's plants worldwide. ATP may also involve drilling down beyond the end item level to check the availability of critical components. Supply chain and enterprise planning software vendors such as SAP and i2 have available-to-promise modules that execute a series of rules when assessing product availability, and alert the planner when customer orders exceed or fall short of forecasts. The rules prescribe product substitutions, alternative sources, and allocation procedures as shown in Figure 14.5. When the product is not available, the system proposes a **capable-to-promise** date that is subject to customer approval.

Capable-to-promise The quantity of items that can be produced and made available at a later date.

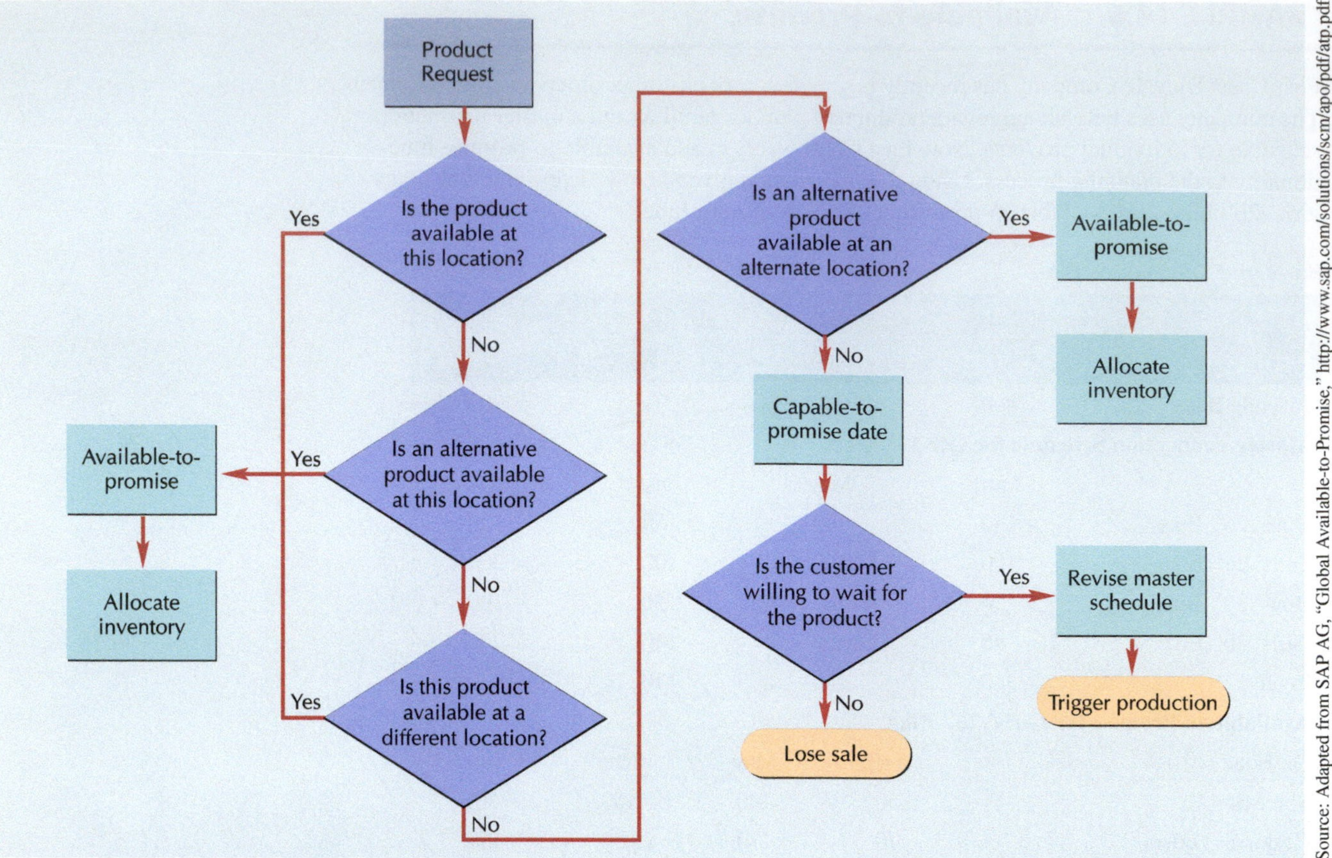

FIGURE 14.5 **Rules-Based ATP**

Aggregate Planning for Services

The aggregate planning process is different for services in the following ways:

1. ***Most services cannot be inventoried***. It is impossible to store an airline seat, hotel room, or hair appointment for use later when demand may be higher. When the goods that accompany a service can be inventoried, they typically have a very short life. Newspapers are good for only a day; flowers, at most a week; and cooked hamburgers, only 10 minutes.
2. ***Demand for services is difficult to predict***. Demand variations occur frequently and are often severe. The exponential distribution is commonly used to simulate the erratic demand for services—high-demand peaks over short periods of time with long periods of low demand in between. *Customer service levels* established by management express the percentage of demand that must be met and, sometimes, how quickly demand must be met. This is an important input to aggregate planning for services.
3. ***Capacity is also difficult to predict***. The variety of services offered and the individualized nature of services make capacity difficult to predict. The "capacity" of a bank teller depends on the number and type of transactions requested by the customer. Units of capacity can also vary. Should a hospital define capacity in terms of number of beds, number of patients, size of the nursing or medical staff, or number of patient hours?
4. ***Service capacity must be provided at the appropriate place and time***. Many services have branches or outlets widely dispersed over a geographic region. Determining the range of services and staff levels at each location is part of aggregate planning.
5. ***Labor is usually the most constraining resource for services***. This is an advantage in aggregate planning because labor is very flexible. Variations in demand can be handled by

hiring temporary workers, using part-time workers, or using overtime. Summer recreation programs and theme parks hire teenagers out of school for the summer. FedEx staffs its peak hours of midnight to 2 A.M. with area college students. McDonald's, Walmart, and other retail establishments woo senior citizens as reliable part-time workers. Workers can also be cross-trained to perform a variety of jobs and can be called upon as needed. A common example is the sales clerk who also stocks inventory. Less common are police officers who are cross-trained as firefighters and paramedics.

There are several services that have unique aggregate planning problems. Doctors, lawyers, and other professionals have emergency or priority calls for their service that must be meshed with regular appointments. Hotels and airlines routinely *overbook* their capacity in anticipation of customers who do not show up. Airlines design complex pricing structures for different routes and classes of customers. Planners incorporate these decisions in a process called revenue management.

Revenue Management

Revenue management (also called *yield management*) seeks to maximize profit or yield from time-sensitive products and services. It is used in industries with inflexible and expensive capacity, perishable products or services, segmented markets, advanced sales, and uncertain demand. The types of problems addressed by revenue management include overbooking, partitioning demand into fare classes, and single order quantities.

Revenue management Maximizes the yield of time-sensitive products and services.

Overbooking Services with reservation systems can lose money when customers fail to show up, or cancel reservations at the last minute. It is not unusual for no-shows to account for 10% to 30% of an aircraft's available seats. Thus, hotels, airlines, and restaurants routinely overbook their capacity. Managers who underestimate the number of no-shows must then compensate a customer who has been "bumped" by providing the service free of charge at another time or place.

Fare Classes Hotels, airlines, stadiums, and theaters typically offer different ticket prices for certain classes of seats or customers. Planners must determine the number of seats or rooms to allocate to these different fare classes. Too many high-priced seats can lose customers, while too few high-priced seats can lower profits. Sabre estimates that airlines make more profits from the 3% of customers who are "business travelers" than the rest of customers who have discounted fares.

With the volume of data now available from digital "footprints," companies can now offer one-to-one marketing deals to online customers, changing prices for each customer based on previous buying habits, or to close a sale for an item left in the shopping cart unpurchased. *Congestion prices* vary on the newest toll road for the D.C. metro region, where drivers may choose to pay a toll for access to less congested roadways. The price of the toll changes as traffic on the main road increases. Smart vending machines can change prices, too, depending on inventory levels or outside temperature.

Single Order Quantities The useful life for products such as newspapers, flowers, baked goods, and seasonal items is so short that in many instances only one order for production can take place. Determining the size of that single order can be difficult.

Table 14.4 shows the various types of revenue management problems with cost descriptions. In each of these problems, the cost of overestimating demand (times the probability that it will occur) must be balanced with the cost of underestimating demand and its probability of occurrence.

The optimum probability is where the cost of underestimating demand is equal to or just greater than the cost of overestimating demand. The derivation of the formula is shown below, followed by an example.

TABLE 14.4 Types of Revenue Management Problems

TYPE OF PROBLEM	TYPE OF BUSINESS	PROBABILITY OF OVERESTIMATING DEMAND OR NO-SHOWS, $P(N < X)$	OPTIMAL PROBABILITY OF DEMAND OR NO-SHOW $\frac{C_u}{(C_u + C_o)}$	COST DESCRIPTION
Overbooking	Hotel, airlines, restaurants	N = number of no-shows X = number of overbooked rooms or seats	C_o = cost of overbooking C_u = cost of underbooking	Replacement cost Lost profit
Fare Classes	Airlines, cruise ships, passenger trains, extended stay hotel	N = number of full-fare tickets that can be sold X = seats reserved for full-fare passengers	C_o = cost of overestimating full-fare passengers C_u = cost of underestimating full-fare passengers	Lost full-fare (Full-fare–discounted fare)
Premium Seats	Stadiums, theaters	N = number of premium tickets that can be sold X = seats reserved for premium ticket holders	C_o = cost of overestimating premium ticket sales C_u = cost of underestimating premium ticket sales	Lost regular revenue (Premium ticket–regular ticket revenue)
Single Order Quantities	Newspapers, magazines, florists, nurseries, bakeries, sale items	N = number of items that can be sold X = number of items ordered	C_o = cost of overestimating demand C_u = cost of underestimating demand	(Cost–salvage value) Lost profit

$$\text{Cost of underestimating demand} \geq \text{Cost of overestimating demand}$$
$$P(N \geq X)C_u \geq P(N < X)C_o$$
$$[1 - P(N < X)]C_u \geq P(N < X)C_o$$
$$P(N < X) \leq \frac{C_u}{C_u + C_o}$$

where

C_o = cost of overestimating demand or no-shows
C_u = cost of underestimating demand or no-shows
$P(N < X)$ = probability of overestimating demand or no-shows
$P(N \geq X)$ = probability of underestimating demand or no-shows
N = number of units demanded or no-shows
X = units ordered or overbooked

Given cost information and a distribution of demand or no-shows from past data, we can now match our planning policy with the optimum probability of overestimating demand. Example 14.6 illustrates the procedure for overbooking. A single order quantity problem is included in the solved problems at the end of this chapter.

EXAMPLE 14.6 | Types of Revenue Management Problems

Lauren Lacy, manager of the Lucky Traveler Inn in Las Vegas, is tired of customers who make reservations and then don't show up. Rooms rent for $100 a night and cost $25 to maintain per day. Overflow customers can be sent to the Motel 7 for $70 a night. Lauren's records of no-shows over the past six months are given below. Should the Lucky Traveler start overbooking? If so, how many rooms should be overbooked?

NO-SHOWS	PROBABILITY
0	0.15
1	0.25
2	0.30
3	0.30

Solution:

$$C_o = \$70$$
$$C_u = \$100 - \$25 = \$75$$
$$P(N < X) \leq \frac{C_u}{C_u + C_o} = \frac{75}{75 + 70} = 0.517$$

Adding a cumulative probability column of no-shows being less than expected gives us:

NO-SHOWS	PROBABILITY	$P(N < X)$
0	0.15	0.00
1	0.25	0.15
2	0.30	0.40 ←0.517
3	0.30	0.70

The optimal probability of no-shows falls between 0.40 and 0.70. Since we are concerned with no-shows *less than or equal to* 0.517 we choose the next lowest value, or 0.40. Following across the table, the Lucky Traveler should overbook by two rooms.

Summary

Sales and Operations Planning (S&OP) is a structured collaborative process for matching supply and demand. The sales plan and operations plan are expressed in aggregate terms, hence the name *aggregate planning*.

Aggregate planning is critical for companies with seasonal demand patterns and for services. Variations in demand can be met by *adjusting capacity* or *managing demand*. There are several mathematical techniques for aggregate planning, including linear programming, linear decision rule, search decision rule, and management coefficient model.

Production and capacity plans are developed at several levels of detail. The process of deriving more detailed production and capacity plans from the aggregate plan is called *disaggregation*. Collaborative planning sets production plans in concert with suppliers and trading partners. *Available-to-promise* often involves collaboration along a supply chain.

Aggregate planning for services is somewhat different from that for manufacturing because the variation in demand is usually more severe and occurs over shorter time frames. Fortunately, the constraining resource in most services is labor, which is quite flexible. Services use part-time workers, overtime, and undertime. *Revenue management* is a special aggregate planning tool for industries with time-sensitive products and segmented customer classes.

Key Terms

aggregate planning The process of determining the quantity and timing of production over an intermediate time frame.

available-to-promise The quantity of items that can be promised to the customer; the difference between planned production and customer orders already received.

backlog Accumulated customer orders to be completed at a later date.

backordering Ordering an item that is temporarily out of stock.

capable-to-promise The quantity of items that can be produced and made available at a later date.

chase demand An aggregate planning strategy that schedules production to match demand and absorbs variations in demand by adjusting the size of the workforce.

collaborative planning Sharing information and synchronizing production plans across the supply chain.

disaggregation The process of breaking down the aggregate plan into more detailed plans.

level production An aggregate planning strategy that produces units at a constant rate and uses inventory to absorb variations in demand.

linear decision rule (LDR) A mathematical technique for aggregate planning.

lost sales Forfeited sales for out-of-stock items

management coefficients model A regression technique for aggregate planning.

mixed strategy Varying two or more capacity factors to determine a feasible production plan.

peak demand Staffing for high levels of customer service.

pure strategy Varying only one capacity factor in aggregate planning.

sales & operations planning (S&OP) A process for coordinating supply and demand.

search decision rule (SDR) A pattern search technique for aggregate planning.

revenue management The process of determining the percentage of seats or rooms to be allocated to different fare classes.

Solved Problems

WileyPLUS

1. Fabulous Fit Fibers produces a line of sweatclothes that exhibits a varying demand pattern. Given the following demand forecasts, production costs, and constraints, design a production plan for Fabulous Fit using the transportation method of LP. Also, calculate the cost of the production plan.

PERIOD	DEMAND
September	100
October	130
November	200
December	300

Maximum regular production	100 units/month
Maximum overtime production	50 units/month
Maximum subcontracting	50 units/month
Regular production costs	$10/unit
Overtime production costs	$25/unit
Subcontracting costs	$35/unit
Inventory holding costs	$5/unit/month
Beginning inventory	0

Solution

PERIOD OF PRODUCTION		PERIOD OF USE 1	2	3	4	UNITS PRODUCED	CAPACITY	UNUSED CAPACITY
	Beg. Inventory	[0]	[5]	[10]	[15]	0	0	0
1	Regular	50 [10]	0 [15]	0 [20]	50 [25]	100	100	0
	Overtime	50 [25]	0 [30]	0 [35]	0 [40]	50	50	0
	Subk	0 [35]	0 [40]	0 [45]	0 [50]	0	50	50
2	Regular	0	50 [10]	50 [15]	0 [20]	100	100	0
	Overtime	0	50 [25]	0 [30]	0 [35]	50	50	0
	Subk	0	30 [35]	0 [40]	0 [45]	30	50	20
3	Regular	0	0	100 [10]	0 [15]	100	100	0
	Overtime	0	0	50 [25]	0 [30]	50	50	0
	Subk	0	0	0 [35]	50 [40]	50	50	0
4	Regular	0	0	0	100 [10]	100	100	0
	Overtime	0	0	0	50 [25]	50	50	0
	Subk	0	0	0	50 [35]	50	50	0
	Units Produced	100	130	200	300	730	730	70
	Demand	100	130	200	300	730		
	Unmet Demand	0	0	0	0		Total Cost = $14,800	

		PRODUCTION PLAN			
PERIOD	DEMAND	*REGULAR PRODUCTION*	*OVER-TIME*	*SUBCONTRACT*	ENDING INVENTORY
Sept	100	100	50	0	50
Oct	130	100	50	30	100
Nov	200	100	50	50	100
Dec	300	100	50	50	0
Total	730	400	200	130	250

$$\begin{aligned}\text{Cost} &= (400 \times \$10) + (200 \times \$25) + (130 \times \$35) + (250 \times \$5)\\ &= 4000 + 5000 + 4550 + 1250\\ &= \$14{,}800\end{aligned}$$

2. Calculate the available-to-promise for periods 1, 3, and 5.

ON HAND = 50	PERIOD 1	2	3	4	5	6
Forecast	100	100	100	100	100	100
Customer orders	90	120	130	70	20	10
Master production schedule	200			200	200	
Available-to-promise						

Solution

ON HAND = 50	PERIOD 1	2	3	4	5	6
Forecast	100	100	100	100	100	100
Customer orders	90	120	130	70	20	10
Master production schedule	200		200		200	
Available-to-promise	40		0		170	

ATP in period 1 = (50 + 200) − (90 + 120) = 40
ATP in period 3 = 200 − (130 + 70) = 0
ATP in period 5 = 200 − (20 + 10) = 170

3. Doughman Bakery bakes a variety of pastries, but none is more popular than its jumbo doughnuts. Doughnuts are made fresh every morning at 4:00 A.M. and sold throughout the day. Leftover doughnuts are put in a grab bag and sold at 75% discount the next day. Fresh doughnuts are sold for $1.20 each. The cost to make each doughnut is $0.45. The bakery has recorded first-day sales data for the last 200 days. Determine how many doughnuts Doughman Bakery should bake in the morning.

DOZENS OF DOUGHNUTS	FREQUENCY
2	14
3	18
4	26
5	32
6	30
7	26
8	20
9	18
10	12
11	2
12	2

Solution

DOZENS OF DOUGHNUTS	FREQUENCY	PROBABILITY	$P(N < X)$
2	14	0.07	0.00
3	18	0.09	0.07
4	26	0.13	0.16
5	32	0.16	0.29
6	30	0.15	0.45
7	26	0.13	0.60
8	20	0.10	0.73
9	18	0.09	0.83 ← 0.83
10	12	0.06	0.92
11	2	0.01	0.98
12	2	0.01	0.99
Total	200	1.00	

$$C_u = \$1.20 - \$0.45 = \$0.75$$

$$C_o = \$0.45 - \$0.30 = \$0.15$$

$$P(N < X) \leq \frac{C_u}{C_u + C_o} = \frac{0.75}{0.75 + 0.15} = 0.83$$

Doughman should make 9 dozen doughnuts.

Questions

14.1. What is the purpose of sales and operations planning? Describe the S&OP process.

14.2. List several alternatives for adjusting capacity. List several alternatives for managing demand.

14.3. Describe the output of aggregate planning. When is aggregate planning most useful?

14.4. How do linear programming, the linear decision rule, the search decision rule, and the management coefficients model differ in terms of cost functions and output?

14.5. Identify several industries that have highly variable demand patterns. Explore how they adjust capacity.

14.6. What options are available for altering the capacity of (a) an elementary school, (b) a prison, and (c) an airline?

14.7. Discuss the advantages and disadvantages of using part-time workers, subcontracting work, and building up inventory as strategies for meeting demand.

14.8. Describe the levels of production and capacity planning in the hierarchical planning process.

14.9. Explain the process of collaborative planning. How is available-to-promise involved?

14.10. Access a major vendor of business software, such as SAP or Oracle. Read about their demand management, available-to-promise, and production planning products. What kinds of capabilities do these systems have?

14.11. How is the aggregate planning process different when used for services rather than for manufacturing?

14.12. What does revenue management entail? What types of businesses, besides hotels and airlines, would benefit from revenue management? As a consumer, how do you view the practice?

Problems

14.1. Care Alliance (CA), a manufacturer of emergency care kits for disaster relief, has received the annual disaster readiness plans from its major constituents and now must develop an operations plan to set production, labor, and inventory levels of its basic emergency products for the next four quarters. Demand for the kits, given below, varies with seasonal weather, political climate, and economic conditions. The average worker at CA can produce 10,000 kits a quarter at a cost of $9 per kit. The cost of holding inventory is $2 per kit per quarter. Due to the medical nature of many of its products and concern for quality, hiring and firing costs are $700 per worker. CA currently employs 20 workers. Given the demand forecast below, develop a quarterly operations production plan for CA using (a) chase demand and (b) level production.

QUARTER	DEMAND
1	150,000
2	250,000
3	350,000
4	250,000

14.2. Bioway, Inc., a manufacturer of medical supplies, uses aggregate planning to set labor and inventory levels for the year. While a variety of items are produced, a standard kit composed of basic supplies is used for planning purposes. Demand varies with seasonal illnesses and the quarterly ordering policies of hospitals. The average worker at Bioway can produce 1000 kits a month at a cost of $9 per kit during regular production hours and $10 a kit during overtime production. Completed kits can also be purchased from outside suppliers at $12 each. Inventory carrying costs are $2 per kit per month. Overtime is limited to regular production, but subcontracting is unlimited. Due to high quality standards and extensive training, hiring and firing costs are $1500 per worker. Bioway currently employs 25 workers. Given the demand forecast below, develop a six-month aggregate production plan for Bioway using (a) chase demand and (b) a mixed strategy where the current workforce is kept for April through August, and supplemented with overtime and subcontracting as needed.

MONTH	DEMAND
April	60,000
May	22,000
June	15,000
July	46,000
August	80,000
September	15,000

14.3. Demand for Quiggly Pops follows an up-and-down pattern over the four quarters of a year, with peaks in the spring and winter months when special promotions are held. Production is handled by a highly skilled local workforce during a regular 40-hour week (i.e., overtime and subcontracting are not used). The company likes to zero out its inventory at the end of a year so that it can start fresh each January. QP currently uses a level production strategy but would like to evaluate other options. Create a production plan and calculate the cost of the plan for each strategy listed below. Which plan would you recommend to QP?

a. Level production
b. Chase demand
c. Produce 70,000 in period 1, and 100,000 in periods 2 through 4.
d. Produce 90,000 in periods 1 through 3, and 100,000 in period 4.

QUARTER	DEMAND FORECAST
1	70,000
2	100,000
3	50,000
4	150,000

Beginning workforce = 40 workers
Production per employee = 1,250 units per quarter
Hiring cost = $500 per worker
Firing cost = $500 per worker
Inventory carrying cost = $1 per unit per quarter
Regular production cost = $10 per unit

14.4. Rowley Apparel, manufacturer of the famous "Race-A-Rama" swimwear line, needs help planning production for next year. Demand for swimwear follows a seasonal pattern, as shown here. Given the following costs and demand forecasts, test these four strategies for meeting demand: (a) level production with overtime and subcontracting, as needed, (b) level production with backorders as needed, (c) chase demand, and (d) 3000 units regular production from April through September and as much regular, overtime, and subcontracting production in the other months as needed to meet annual demand. Determine the cost of each strategy. Which strategy would you recommend?

MONTH	DEMAND FORECAST
January	1000
February	500
March	500
April	2000
May	3000
June	4000
July	5000
August	3000
September	1000
October	500
November	500
December	3000

Beginning workforce	8 workers
Subcontracting capacity	unlimited
Overtime capacity	2000 units/month
Production rate per worker	250 units/month
Regular wage rate	$15 per unit
Overtime wage rate	$25 per unit
Subcontracting cost	$30 per unit
Hiring cost	$100 per worker

Firing cost	$200 per worker
Holding cost	$0.50 per unit/month
Backordering cost	$10 per unit/month

14.5. Mama's Stuffin' is a popular food item during the fall and winter months, but it is marginal in the spring and summer. Use the following demand forecasts and costs to determine which of the following production planning strategies is best for Mama's Stuffin':

a. Level production over the 12 months.

b. Produce to meet demand each month. Absorb variations in demand by changing the size of the workforce.

c. Keep the workforce at its current level. Supplement with overtime and subcontracting as necessary.

MONTH	DEMAND FORECAST
March	2000
April	1000
May	1000
June	1000
July	1000
August	1500
September	2500
October	3000
November	9000
December	7000
January	4000
February	3000

Overtime capacity per month	Regular production
Subcontracting capacity per month	Unlimited
Regular production cost	$30 per pallet
Overtime production cost	$40 per pallet
Subcontracting cost	$50 per pallet
Holding cost	$2 per pallet
Beginning workforce	10 workers
Production rate	200 pallets per worker per month
Hiring cost	$5000 per worker
Firing cost	$8000 per worker

14.6. FansForYou is a small, privately owned company that manufactures fans. Large variations in demand due to seasonality have contributed to high costs for the company. FansForYou currently uses a level production strategy because it prefers not to hire and fire employees. However, if there is enough cost justification, the company will consider alternative production plans.

a. What is the cost of the current production plan?

b. How much would FansForYou save by using a chase demand strategy?

c. How much would FansForYou save by keeping a steady workforce of 20 workers and supplementing with overtime and subcontracting as needed?

MONTH	DEMAND
September	1500
October	1000
November	600
December	600
January	600
February	800
March	1000
April	1000
May	4000
June	6500
July	6000
August	4000

Beginning inventory	0
Beginning workforce	25 workers
Production rate	100 fans per worker per month
Regular production cost	$40 per fan
Overtime production cost	$60 per fan
Subcontracting cost	$70 per fan
Overtime capacity	Not to exceed regular production
Subcontracting capacity	Unlimited
Holding cost	$8 per fan
Hiring cost	$2000
Firing cost	$3000

14.7. Slopes & Sleds (S&S) makes skis, snowboards, and high-end sledding equipment. As shown below, the demand for its products is highly seasonal. The company employs 10 workers who can each produce 200 units of various equipment per month. The cost of regular production is $8 per unit, overtime $12, and subcontracting $16. Overtime is limited to regular production each period. Subcontracting is unlimited. Hiring and firing costs are $500 per worker. Inventory holding costs are $2 per unit per month. Given the estimates of demand below, create an aggregate production plan for Slopes & Sleds and calculate the cost of the plan using:

a. the current workforce level (supplemented with overtime and subcontracting as needed),

b. chase demand.

c. linear programming with Solver.

d. subcontracting. The global sourcing department of Slopes & Sleds has located a company in China that can make S&S products for $9 a unit. Revise the production plan using Solver. How much money can be saved by outsourcing to China?

MONTH	DEMAND
January	6400
February	7000
March	1500
April	500
May	600
June	1400
July	1600
August	2000
September	1400
October	1500
November	5200
December	6900

14.8. Sawyer Furniture is one of the few remaining domestic manufacturers of wood furniture. In the current competitive environment, cost containment is the key to its continued survival. Demand for furniture follows a seasonal demand pattern with increased sales in the summer and fall months, culminating with peak demand in November.

a. The cost of production is $16 per unit for regular production, $24 for overtime, and $33 for subcontracting. Hiring and firing costs are $500 per worker. Inventory holding costs are $20 per unit per month. There is no beginning inventory. Ten workers are currently employed. Each worker can produce 50 pieces of furniture per month. Overtime cannot exceed regular production. Given the following demand data, use Excel Solver to design an aggregate production plan for Sawyer Furniture that will meet demand at the lowest possible cost.

b. In an attempt to stem the flow of jobs overseas, the local labor union has negotiated a penalty clause for layoffs. The new contract increases the firing cost per worker to $2500. Create a revised aggregate plan with these new cost figures. Assuming any subcontracting is, in fact, foreign production, does the penalty work? Why or why not?

MONTH	DEMAND
January	500
February	500
March	1000
April	1200
May	2000
June	400
July	400
August	1000
September	1000
October	1500
November	7000
December	500

14.9. Midlife Shoes, Inc. is a manufacturer of sensible shoes for aging baby-boomers. The company is having great success, and although demand is seasonal, it is expected to increase steadily over the next few years. The company is purchasing a new facility to accommodate the increase in demand, but the facility will not open until 13 months from now. The current facility can only accommodate 15 workers. Hiring and firing costs are negligible. Using the information below, help Midlife manage this transition year by deriving a production plan that will meet demand at the lowest cost. With the limited workforce size, neither chase demand nor level production is viable.

MONTH	DEMAND
January	1000
February	1200
March	1200
April	3000
May	3000
June	3000
July	2200
August	2200
September	4000
October	4000
November	2200
December	3000

Beginning inventory	0 units
Beginning workforce	8 workers
Production rate	100 units per worker per month
Regular capacity	Maximum of 15 workers
Overtime capacity	Half of regular production
Subcontracting capacity	1000 units
Regular production cost	$36 per unit
Overtime production cost	$54 per unit
Subcontracting cost	$70 per unit
Inventory holding cost	$10 per unit

14.10. Design a production plan for Rowley Apparel in Problem 14.4 using linear programming and Excel Solver.

14.11. Design a production plan for Mama's Stuffin' in Problem 14.5 using linear programming and Excel Solver.

14.12. Design a production plan for FansForYou in Problem 14.6 using linear programming and Excel Solver.

14.13. Froggatt Enterprises, a premier educational products company, experiences ups and downs in demand each year corresponding to major school holidays. The company maintains a steady workforce and uses overtime, inventory, and subcontracting to absorb fluctuations in demand. Expected demand, available capacities, and costs for the next four quarters are given below. There is no beginning inventory. Design a production plan that will satisfy demand at minimum cost.

PERIOD	DEMAND	REGULAR CAPACITY	OVERTIME CAPACITY	SUBCONTRACTING CAPACITY
1	600	1000	500	500
2	2100	1000	500	500
3	800	1000	500	500
4	1800	1000	500	500

Regular production cost per unit	$ 8
Overtime production cost per unit	$10
Subcontracting cost per unit	$12
Inventory holding cost per unit per period	$ 1

14.14. The Wetski Water Ski Company is the world's largest producer of water skis. As you might suspect, water skis exhibit a highly seasonal demand pattern, with peaks during the summer months and valleys during the winter months. Given the following costs and quarterly sales forecasts, use the transportation method to design a production plan that will economically meet demand. What is the cost of the plan?

QUARTER	SALES FORECAST
1	50,000
2	150,000
3	200,000
4	52,000

Inventory carrying cost	$3.00 per pair of skis per quarter
Production per employee	1000 pairs of skis per quarter
Regular workforce	50 workers
Regular capacity	50,000 pairs of skis
Overtime capacity	50,000 pairs of skis
Subcontracting capacity	40,000 pairs of skis
Cost of regular production	$50 per pair of skis
Cost of overtime production	$75 per pair of skis
Cost of subcontracting	$85 per pair of skis

14.15. College Press publishes textbooks for the college market. The demand for college textbooks is high during the beginning of each semester and then tapers off during the semester. The unavailability of books can cause a professor to switch adoptions, but the cost of storing books and their rapid obsolescence must also be considered. Given the demand and cost factors shown here, use the transportation method to design an aggregate production plan for College Press that will economically meet demand. What is the cost of the production plan?

MONTHS	DEMAND FORECAST
February–April	5,000
May–July	10,000
August–October	30,000
November–January	25,000

Regular capacity per quarter	10,000 books
Overtime capacity per quarter	5,000 books
Subcontracting capacity per qtr	10,000 books
Regular production rate	$20 per book
Overtime wage rate	$30 per book
Subcontracting cost	$35 per book
Holding cost	$2.00 per book

14.16. Bits and Pieces uses overtime, inventory, and subcontracting to absorb fluctuations in demand. An annual production plan is devised and updated quarterly. Expected demand over the next four quarters is 600, 800, 1600, and 1900 units, respectively. The capacity for regular production is 1000 units per quarter with an overtime capacity of 100 units a quarter. Subcontracting is limited to 500 units a quarter. Regular production costs $20 per unit, overtime $25 per unit, and subcontracting $30 per unit. Inventory holding costs are assessed at $3 per unit per period. There is no beginning inventory. Design a production plan that will satisfy demand at minimum cost.

14.17. GF Incorporated, a manufacturer of power systems, uses overtime, inventory, and subcontracting to absorb fluctuations in demand. An annual production plan is devised and updated quarterly. The expected demand and available capacities for the next four quarters are as follows:

PERIOD	DEMAND	REGULAR CAPACITY	OVERTIME CAPACITY	SUBCONTRACTING CAPACITY
1	2000	1000	1000	5000
2	4500	1000	1000	5000
3	7500	1000	1000	5000
4	3000	1000	1000	5000

Relevant cost data are as follows:

Regular production cost per unit	$20
Overtime production cost per unit	$25
Subcontracting cost per unit	$30
Inventory holding cost per unit per period	$ 3
Beginning inventory	0

Design a production plan that will satisfy demand at minimum cost.

14.18. Caltex uses overtime, inventory, and subcontracting to absorb fluctuations in demand. An annual production plan is devised and updated quarterly. Expected demand, available capacities, and costs for the next four quarters are given below. Design a production plan that will satisfy demand at minimum cost.

PERIOD	DEMAND	REGULAR CAPACITY	OVERTIME CAPACITY	SUBCONTRACTING CAPACITY
1	1500	1000	200	500
2	1900	1000	200	500
3	500	1000	200	500
4	2000	1000	200	500

Regular production cost per unit	$10
Overtime production cost per unit	$15
Subcontracting cost per unit	$20
Inventory holding cost per unit per period	$ 2

14.19. MTI, a global telecommunications company, manufactures cable boxes and DVRs for its customers. Demand varies considerably from quarter to quarter. Using the demand, capacities, and cost figures given below, devise an aggregate production plan for MTI that minimizes costs.

PERIOD	DEMAND	REGULAR CAPACITY	OVERTIME CAPACITY	SUBCONTRACTING CAPACITY
1	500	1000	200	500
2	1200	1000	200	500
3	2500	1000	200	500
4	1900	1000	200	500

Regular production cost per unit	$20
Overtime production cost per unit	$25
Subcontracting cost per unit	$30
Inventory holding cost per unit per period	$ 3

14.20. Minions-for-the-Masses uses overtime, inventory, and subcontracting to absorb fluctuations in demand for its fantasy action figures. Production is planned on an annual basis in cases per quarter. New product launches, regional tournaments, and user conventions cause demand to fluctuate considerably from quarter to quarter. Figures become outdated quickly so the cost of obsolete inventory is high. Quarterly demand data, costs of production, and production capacities are given as follows. Develop a production plan that will meet demand at the least possible cost.

QUARTER	DEMAND	REGULAR CAPACITY	OVERTIME CAPACITY	SUBCONTRACTING CAPACITY
1	500	1000	200	500
2	2200	1000	200	500
3	700	1000	200	500
4	1900	1000	200	500

Regular production cost per case	$100
Overtime production cost per case	$150
Subcontracting cost per case	$200
Inventory holding cost per case per period	$ 20

14.21. Panettones are fluffy dome-shaped Italian cakes popular during the holiday season. For Baluci's Bakery in Milan, sales of panettones in December account for 50% of its income for the year. The bakery has worked out a way to extend the shelf life of the popular pastry so it can begin production in September for the December market. Output is limited by the capacity of its ovens on site, but work can be outsourced to other bakeries nearby after normal hours of operation. Workers at Baluci can also work an extra shift if necessary at an overtime rate of time-and-a-half. Panettones are produced in batch sizes of 100. Given the data below (in batches), determine a production plan for Baluci that meets demand at the lowest possible cost.

MONTH	DEMAND	REGULAR CAPACITY	OVERTIME CAPACITY	SUBCONTRACTING CAPACITY
Sept	1600	1600	1600	1000
Oct	2000	1600	1600	1000
Nov	3600	1600	1600	1000
Dec	8000	1600	1600	1000

Regular production cost	$30 per batch
Overtime production cost	$45 per batch
Subcontracting cost	$50 per batch
Inventory holding cost	$10 per batch per period

14.22. Robotic Pet Products uses overtime, inventory, and subcontracting to absorb fluctuations in demand. As expected, demand in the fourth quarter during the holiday season is particularly high, followed by first quarter demand for customers purchasing accessories for their R-pets. Given the demand and available capacities shown below, design a production plan that will satisfy demand at minimum cost.

QUARTER	DEMAND	REGULAR CAPACITY	OVERTIME CAPACITY	SUBCONTRACTING CAPACITY
1	1000	1000	100	500
2	800	1000	100	500
3	600	1000	100	500
4	2600	1000	100	500

Regular production cost per unit	$10
Overtime production cost per unit	$15
Subcontracting cost per unit	$20
Inventory holding cost per unit per period	$ 3
Beginning inventory	100

14.23. How many units are available-to-promise in period 1? period 4?

	PERIOD					
ON HAND = 60	1	2	3	4	5	6
Forecast	50	100	100	100	100	50
Customer Orders	85	125	95	85	45	15
Master Production Schedule	250			250		
Available-to-Promise						

14.24. Complete the available-to-promise table below.

	PERIOD					
ON HAND = 10	1	2	3	4	5	6
Forecast	50	50	50	50	50	50
Customer Orders	56	17	75	50	16	14
Master Production Schedule	100		100		100	
Available-to-Promise						

14.25. Complete the available-to-promise table below.

	PERIOD					
ON HAND = 30	1	2	3	4	5	6
Forecast	100	50	100	50	100	50
Customer Orders	75	50	116	73	45	23
Master Production Schedule	100	50	100	50	100	50
Available-to-Promise						

14.26. Calculate the available-to-promise row in the following matrix.

	PERIOD					
ON HAND = 100	1	2	3	4	5	6
Forecast	50	100	50	100	50	100
Customer Orders	50	125	75	175	45	15
Master Production Schedule	200			200		
Available-to-Promise						

14.27. Complete the following table. How many Bs are available-to-promise in week 2? How soon could you fill an order for 250 Bs?

	PERIOD					
Bs ON HAND = 10	1	2	3	4	5	6
Forecast	100	100	100	100	100	100
Customer Orders	25	50	137	72	23	5
Master Production Schedule	100	100	100	100	100	100
Available-to-Promise						

14.28. Managers at the Dew Drop Inn are concerned about the increasing number of guests who make reservations but fail to show up. They have decided to institute a policy of overbooking like larger hotel chains. The profit from a paying guest averages $50 per room per night. The cost of putting up a guest at another hotel is $100 per room per night. Records show the following number of no-shows over the past three months:

NO-SHOWS	FREQUENCY
0	18
1	36
2	27
3	9

How many rooms should Dew Drop overbook?

14.29. Atlanta Airlines routinely overbooks its flight from Atlanta to Boston. Overbooking discounted seats can be expensive because providing a bumped passenger with a last-minute flight on a competing carrier can cost $450. A 120-passenger jet costs about $6000 to operate from Atlanta to Boston. The average ticket price is $300.

a. Given the frequency of no-shows in the following table, how many seats should be overbooked?

b. Atlanta Air offers special rates on its Atlanta/Boston route for the holidays. How would a $200 ticket price affect the number of seats overbooked?

NO-SHOWS	FREQUENCY
1	15
2	10
3	10
4	5
5	3
6	5

14.30. The Blue Roof Inn overbooks two rooms a night. Room rates run $100 a night but cost only $30 to maintain. Bumped customers are sent to a nearby hotel for $80 a night. What is the cost of overbooking? What is the cost of underbooking? Given the following distribution of no-shows, should Blue Roof continue its current policy?

NO-SHOWS	PROBABILITY
0	0.30
1	0.20
2	0.10
3	0.30
4	0.10

14.31. FlyUs Airlines is unhappy with the number of empty seats on its New York to Philadelphia flight. To remedy the problem, the airline is offering a special discounted rate of $89 instead of the normal $169, but only for 7-day advance purchases and for a limited number of seats per flight. The aircraft flown from NY to Philly holds 100 passengers. Last month's distribution of full-fare passengers is shown below. How many seats should FlyUs reserve for full-fare passengers?

FULL-FARE	FREQUENCY
50	15
55	20
60	35
65	20
70	10

14.32. NorthStar Airlines runs daily commuter flights from Washington, D.C., to Chicago. The planes hold 60 passengers and cater to the business traveler with comparable business rates. The recent economic downturn has reduced the occupancy rate of flights to such an extent that NorthStar would like to offer a set number of seats at discount rates to gain more passengers. The board of directors is worried that discounted seats will cut into profit margins and will upset the regular business traveler. The ticket price for a business traveler is $350. Discounted tickets would sell for $120. Assuming that empty seats can be sold if discounted, use the following data gathered from 100 flights to determine how many seats should be discounted.

NO. OF FULL-FARE PASSENGERS	FREQUENCY
10	15
20	25
30	25
40	20
50	10
60	5

14.33. The Forestry Club sells Christmas trees each year to raise money for club activities. The trees cost $10 to cut and are sold for $25. Unused trees are stripped of their limbs and sold as firewood for $1 apiece. Data on past sales appear below. How many trees should the forestry club cut this year?

NO. OF TREES SOLD	FREQUENCY
10	6
15	3
20	6
25	3
30	2

14.34. Pizza Pie runs the pizza concessions at the University basketball games. Personal-size pizzas are assembled two hours prior to the game and cooked throughout the night in a mobile oven outside of the coliseum. Pizza sells for $5 and costs approximately $2 to make. Unsold pizzas at the end of the game are given to nearby dormitory students for a nominal $1 per pizza. Having sold out of pizza during the past two games, Pizza Pie is reevaluating its planning policy. Use the past demand data given below to determine how many pizzas should be made for each game.

NO. OF PIZZAS SOLD	FREQUENCY
25	15
50	15
75	30
100	20
125	10
150	10

14.35. Tariott Hotel rents rooms for $125 a night that cost approximately $50 per day to maintain. Overbooking is a common practice in the industry. Customers whose rooms have been leased to someone else are put up in a nearby hotel for $100 a night. Records show that during the past month, there were 10 days with zero no-shows, 5 days with 1 no-show, 6 days with 2 no-shows, and 9 days with 3 no-shows.

a. What is the cost of overbooking?
b. What is the cost of underbooking?
c. What is the optimum probability of no-shows for Tariott?
d. How many rooms should Tariott overbook?

14-36. Amy and Matt are getting married in their hometown the same weekend as the Battle of Bristol, the largest college football game ever played. That's good news for the couple, but bad news for the Inn where the wedding is scheduled. A block of 50 of the hotel's 100 rooms have been reserved for wedding guests on Saturday night at a reduced wedding package rate of $95 a room. If those rooms had been available for football fans, both Friday and Saturday nights would have been booked for $300 a night. The Inn's manager is feeling the heat to overbook the hotel, given that wedding guests are known to cancel at the last minute, and football fans book rooms well in advance. Bianca, the event coordinator, has provided data on the number of no-shows or canceled rooms from past weddings at the Inn. She cautions that while overbooking is a sound business practice and would yield lucrative income for that particular weekend, if word gets around that blocked rooms are not really blocked, the future of their wedding business would be in jeopardy.

Use the data below to recommend an overbooking strategy for the Inn. Since fans would be looking for a 2-night package for the game, assume that the unavailability of a Saturday night room would result in lost revenue from an unsold Friday night room as well. Further assume that guests who are bumped will be moved to an expensive resort nearby for $450/night, paid for by the Inn.

NO-SHOWS	FREQUENCY
0	1
1	2
2	3
3	4

Case Problems

Case Problem 14.1 Seats for Sale

State's football program has risen to the ranks of the elite with postseason bowl games in each of the past 10 years, including a national championship game. The Bruins (as the fans are called) fill the stadium each game. Season tickets are increasingly difficult to find. In response to the outstanding fan support, State has decided to use its bowl revenues to expand the stadium to 75,000 seats.

The administration is confident that all 75,000 seats can be sold at the normal price of $40 per game ticket; however, Frank Pinto's job, as athletic director, is to get as much revenue out of the stadium expansion as possible. In addition to stadium boxes for wealthy alums, Frank would like to take this opportunity to repurpose existing seats. A certain number of seats (yet to be determined) would be set aside for premium ticket holders who would pay $200 per ticket for the privilege of 50-yard line seats with chair backs and access to indoor concessions. The question is, how many fans would be willing to pay such a premium? If too many seats are designated in the premium sections, they could remain vacant. Too few premium seats would lose potential revenue for the program.

Frank has decided that if the plan has any chance of success, unsold premium seats should not be sold at reduced rates. It would be better to donate them to local charities instead. Gathering data from his cohorts at peer institutions, Frank has put together the following probability distribution of premium ticket holders. The data begin with 1000 tickets since Frank already has requests for 999 tickets from alumni donors. He is asking for your help in performing the analysis.

NO. OF PREMIUM TICKETS	PROBABILITY
1,000	0.10
5,000	0.30
10,000	0.24
15,000	0.15
20,000	0.10
25,000	0.06
30,000	0.05

a. Using revenue management, determine how many seats should be reserved for premium ticket holders.

b. Considering your answer to part (a) and the possible outcomes listed above, how much total revenue (i.e., regular and premium) can be expected from ticket sales?

c. The administration is unsure about Frank's plan. The VP of Finance thinks an expected value of the number of premium seats would produce better results. How would the number of premium seats change using expected value? Considering the possible outcomes, which approach yields the most potential revenue?

Case Problem 14.2 Erin's Energy Plan

The discussion was getting heated. A brightly colored chart at the front of the room told the story all too well. At Waylan Industries sales were up, profits down.

"Larry, there's no way we can hit our profit objective with your high cost of production. You've got to cut back."

"Why pick on me? We're running bare bones as it is. Last winter's energy prices really killed us. How can you cut costs with a 250% increase in energy prices?"

Everyone stared at Erin, the newly appointed sustainability chief for the company. Erin stood up and walked to the front of the room, "I know you've talked about stockpiling fuel before. Perhaps it's time to look at that option. I've been collecting data. . . ."

"Well, let's see it then."

Erin projected an Excel chart on the screen. "Although it's not how we purchase energy, I've converted the prices to millions of BTUs for comparison. Coal costs $8 per million BTUs, but we can only burn 500 million per quarter to stay within our environmental air standards. Natural gas costs $32 per million BTUs, and petroleum $46. We can burn 1000 million BTUs of each per quarter. Coal and natural gas can be stored for later use at a holding cost of 30 percent of purchase price per quarter. The holding cost for petroleum is 20 percent. Electricity cannot be stored, but it can be reserved in advance. The cost of electricity also varies considerably by season of the year, as do our energy needs. The cost of electricity from the local utility is $20 per million BTUs in the spring, $40 in the summer, $24 in the fall, and $70 in the winter. These are averages from last year. A nearby utility quotes slightly higher prices at $22, $44, $26, and $75 for spring, summer, fall, and winter. As far as availability is concerned, 4000 million BTUs of electricity are available in the spring and fall, 5000 in the summer and winter. We can save some money by contracting with the utilities in advance of the season. I've summarized the options in the table here, along with our energy needs. . . ."

"Wow," interrupted Larry, "you have done your homework. I think your data would fit nicely into our aggregate production planning software. Do you want to try it?" Before Erin could answer, Tom spoke up. "Hey, that's a great idea. Why don't you two work on that and have it ready for our meeting on Thursday."

Source: This case was developed with the help of Richard Hirsh, Professor of Science and Technology at Virginia Tech.

	USED IN							
	SPRING		SUMMER		FALL		WINTER	
PURCHASED IN	UTILITY A	UTILITY B	UTILITY A	UTILITY B	UTILITY A	UTILITY B	UTILITY A	UTILITY B
Spring	$20	$22	$40	$44	$20	$22	$45	$50
Summer			$40	$44	$22	$24	$50	$60
Fall					$24	$26	$60	$65
Winter							$70	$75
Demand	1500		5000		5000		10,000	

Use Erin's data to develop an aggregate energy plan for Waylan Industries.

References

Bowman, E. H. "Production Planning by the Transportation Method of Linear Programming." *Journal of Operations Research Society* (February 1956), pp. 100–103.

Bowman, E. H. "Consistency and Optimality in Managerial Decision Making." *Management Science* (January 1963), pp. 310–321.

Buffa, E. S., and J. G. Miller. *Production-Inventory Systems: Planning and Control,* 3rd ed. Homewood, IL: Irwin, 1979.

Correll, J., and N. Edson. *Gaining Control.* New York: Wiley, 1998.

Haksever, C., B. Render, R. Russell and R. Murdick. *Service Operations and Management.* Upper Saddle River, NJ: Prentice Hall, 2000.

Holt, C., F. Modigliani, J. Muth, and H. Simon. *Planning Production, Inventories and Work Force.* Englewood Cliffs, NJ: Prentice Hall, 1960.

Jacobs, R., W. Berry, D. C. Whybark, and T. Vollmann. *Manufacturing Planning and Control Systems,* Homewood, IL: Irwin, 2011.

Palmatier, G. E., and C. Crum. *Enterprise Sales and Operations Planning.* Boca Raton: J. Ross Publishers, 2003.

SAP AG. "Global Available to Promise." December 1999. SAP AG 2000, APO ATP 3.0. http://www.sap.com/solutions/scm/apo/pdf/atp.pdf.

Taubert, W. "A Search Decision Rule for the Aggregate Scheduling Problem." *Management Science* (February 1968), pp. B343– 359.

Tersine, R. *Production/Operations Management: Concepts, Structure, and Analysis.* New York: Elsevier-North Holland, 1985.

Wallace, T. *Sales and Operations Planning—The How-to Handbook.* Columbus, OH: T. F. Wallace & Co., 2000.

SUPPLEMENT TO CHAPTER 14

Operational Decision-Making Tools: Linear Programming

IN THIS SUPPLEMENT, YOU WILL LEARN ABOUT . . .

- Model Formulation
- Graphical Solution Method
- Linear Programming Model Solution
- Solving Linear Programming Problems with Excel
- Sensitivity Analysis

One of the quantitative techniques used in Chapter 14 for operations planning and in Chapter 17 for scheduling is linear programming. Linear programming is one of the most widely used and powerful quantitative tools in operations management. It can be applied to a wide variety of different operational problems. Some of the more popular model types and their specific OM applications are described in Table S14.1.

Linear programming A model consisting of linear relationships representing a firm's objective and resource constraints.

Linear programming is a mathematical modeling technique used to determine a level of operational activity in order to achieve an objective, subject to restrictions called constraints. Many decisions faced by an operations manager are centered around the best way to achieve the objectives of the firm subject to the constraints of the operating environment. These constraints can be limited resources, such as time, labor, energy, materials, or money, or they can be restrictive guidelines, such as a recipe for making cereal, engineering specifications, or a blend for gasoline. The most frequent objective of business firms is to *maximize profit*—whereas the objective of individual operational units within a firm (such as a production or packaging department) is often to *minimize cost.*

A common linear programming problem is to determine the number of units to produce to maximize profit subject to resource constraints such as labor and materials. All these components of the decision situation—the decisions, objectives, and constraints—are expressed as mathematically linear relationships that together form a model.

TABLE S14.1 Types of Linear Programming Models and Applications

LINEAR PROGRAMMING MODEL TYPE	OM APPLICATION
Aggregate Production Planning	Determines the resource capacity needed to meet demand over an immediate time horizon, including units produced, workers hired and fired and inventory. (See Chapter 14.)
Product Mix	Mix of different products to produce that will maximize profit or minimize cost given resource constraints such as material, labor, budget, etc.
Transportation	Logistical flow of items (goods or services) from sources to destinations, for example, truckloads of goods from plants to warehouses. (See Supplement to Chapter 11.)
Transshipment	Flow of items from sources to destinations with intermediate points, for example, shipping from plant to distribution center and then to stores. (See Supplement to Chapter 11.)
Assignment	Assigns work to limited resources, called "Loading," for example, assigning jobs or workers to different machines. (See Chapter 17.)
Multiperiod Scheduling	Schedules regular and overtime production, plus inventory to carry over, to meet demand in future periods. (See Chapter 14.)
Blend	Determines "recipe" requirements, for example, how to blend different petroleum components to produce different grades of gasoline and other petroleum products.
Diet	Menu of food items that meets nutritional or other requirements, for example, hospital or school cafeteria menus.
Investment/Capital Budgeting	Financial model that determines amount to invest in different alternatives given return objectives and constraints for risk, diversity, etc., for example, how much to invest in new plant, facilities or equipment.
Data Envelopment Analysis (DEA)	Compares service units of the same type—banks, hospitals, schools—based on their resources and outputs to see which units are less productive or inefficient.
Shortest Route	Shortest routes from sources to destinations, for example, the shortest highway truck route from coast to coast.
Maximal Flow	Maximizes the amount of flow from sources to destinations, for example, the flow of work in process through an assembly operation.
Trim-Loss	Determines patterns to cut sheet items to minimize waste, for example, cutting lumber, film, cloth, glass, etc.
Facility Location	Selects facility locations based on constraints such as fixed, operating, and shipping costs, production capacity, etc.
Set Covering	Selection of facilities that can service a set of other facilities, for example, the selection of distribution hubs that will be able to deliver packages to a set of cities.

Model Formulation

A linear programming model consists of decision variables, an objective function, and model constraints. **Decision variables** are mathematical symbols that represent levels of activity of an operation. For example, an electrical manufacturing firm wants to produce radios, toasters, and clocks. The number of each item to produce is represented by symbols, x_1, x_2, and x_3. Thus, x_1 = the number of radios, x_2 = the number of toasters, and x_3 = the number of clocks. The final values of x_1, x_2, and x_3, as determined by the firm, constitute a *decision* (e.g., $x_1 = 10$ radios is a decision by the firm to produce 10 radios).

Decision variables Mathematical symbols representing levels of activity of an operation.

Objective function A linear relationship reflecting the objective of an operation.

The **objective function** is a linear mathematical relationship that describes the objective of an operation in terms of the decision variables. The objective function always either *maximizes* or *minimizes* some value (e.g., maximizing the profit or minimizing the cost of producing radios). For example, if the profit from a radio is \$6, the profit from a toaster is \$4, and the profit from a clock is \$2, then the total profit, Z, is $Z = \$6x_1 + 4x_2 + 2x_3$.

Constraint A linear relationship representing a restriction on decision making.

The model **constraints** are also linear relationships of the decision variables; they represent the restrictions placed on the decision situation by the operating environment. The restrictions can be in the form of limited resources or restrictive guidelines. For example, if it requires 2 hours of labor to produce a radio, 1 hour to produce a toaster, and 1.5 hours to produce a clock, and only 40 hours of labor are available, the constraint reflecting this is $2x_1 + 1x_2 + 1.5x_3 \leq 40$.

The general structure of a linear programming model is as follows:

$$\text{Maximize (or minimize) } Z = c_1x_1 + c_2x_2 + \cdots + c_nx_n$$

subject to

$$\begin{aligned} a_{11}x_1 + a_{12}x_2 + \cdots + a_{1n}x_n &(\leq, =, \geq) b_1 \\ a_{21}x_1 + a_{22}x_2 + \cdots + a_{2n}x_n &(\leq, =, \geq) b_2 \\ &\vdots \\ a_{n1}x_1 + a_{n2}x_2 + \ldots + a_{nn}x_n &(\leq, =, \geq) b_n \\ x_i &\geq 0 \end{aligned}$$

where

x_i = decision variables
b_i = constraint levels
c_j = objective function coefficients
a_{ij} = constraint coefficients

EXAMPLE S14.1 | Linear Programming Model Formulation

The Highlands Craft Store is a small craft operation that employs local artisans to produce clay bowls and mugs based on designs and colors from the 1700s and 1800s. The two primary resources used by the company are special pottery clay and skilled labor. Given these limited resources, the company wants to know how many bowls and mugs to produce each day to maximize profit.

The two products have the following resource requirements for production and selling price per item produced (i.e., the model parameters):

	RESOURCE REQUIREMENTS		
PRODUCT	*LABOR (HR/UNIT)*	*CLAY (LB/UNIT)*	*REVENUE (\$/UNIT)*
Bowl	1	4	40
Mug	2	3	50

There are 40 hours of labor and 120 pounds of clay available each day. Formulate this problem as a linear programming model.

Solution: Management's decision is how many bowls and mugs to produce represented by the following decision variables.

x_1 = number of bowls to produce
x_2 = number of mugs to produce

The objective of the company is to maximize total revenue computed as the sum of the individual profits gained from each bowl and mug:

$$\text{Maximize } Z = \$40x_1 + 50x_2$$

The model contains the constraints for labor and clay, which are

$$x_1 + 2x_2 \leq 40 \text{ hr}$$
$$4x_1 + 3x_2 \leq 120 \text{ lb}$$

The less than or equal to inequality ($\leq$) is used instead of an equality ($=$) because 40 hours of labor is a maximum that *can be used*, not an amount that *must be used*. However, constraints can be equalities ($=$), greater than or equal to inequalities ($\geq$), or less than or equal to inequalities ($\leq$).

The complete linear programming model for this problem can now be summarized as follows:

$$\text{Maximize } Z = \$40x_1 + \$50x_2$$
subject to
$$1x_1 + 2x_2 \leq 40$$
$$4x_1 + 3x_2 \leq 120$$
$$x_1, x_2 \geq 0$$

The solution of this model will result in numerical values for x_1 and x_2 that maximize total profit, Z, without violating the constraints. The solution that achieves this objective is $x_1 = 24$ bowls and $x_2 = 8$ mugs, with a corresponding revenue of \$1360. We will discuss how we determined these values next.

Graphical Solution Method

The linear programming model in the previous section has characteristics common to all linear programming models. The mathematical relationships are additive; the model parameters are assumed to be known with certainty; the variable values are continuous (not restricted to integers); and the relationships are linear. Because of linearity, models with two decision variables (corresponding to two dimensions) can be solved graphically. Although graphical solution is cumbersome, it is useful in that it provides a picture of how a solution is derived.

The basic steps in the **graphical solution method** are to plot the model constraints on a set of coordinates in a plane and identify the area on the graph that satisfies all the constraints simultaneously. The point on the boundary of this space that maximizes (or minimizes) the objective function is the solution. The following example illustrates these steps.

Graphical solution method A method for solving a linear programming problem using a graph.

EXAMPLE S14.2 | Graphical Solution

Determine the solution for Highlands Craft Store in Example S14.1:

$$\text{Maximize } Z = \$40x_1 + \$50x_2$$
subject to
$$x_1 + 2x_2 \leq 40$$
$$4x_1 + 3x_2 \leq 120$$
$$x_1, x_2 \geq 0$$

Solution: The graph of the model constraints is shown in the following figure of the feasible solution space. The graph is produced in the positive quadrant since both decision variables must be positive or zero; that is, $x_1, x_2 \geq 0$:

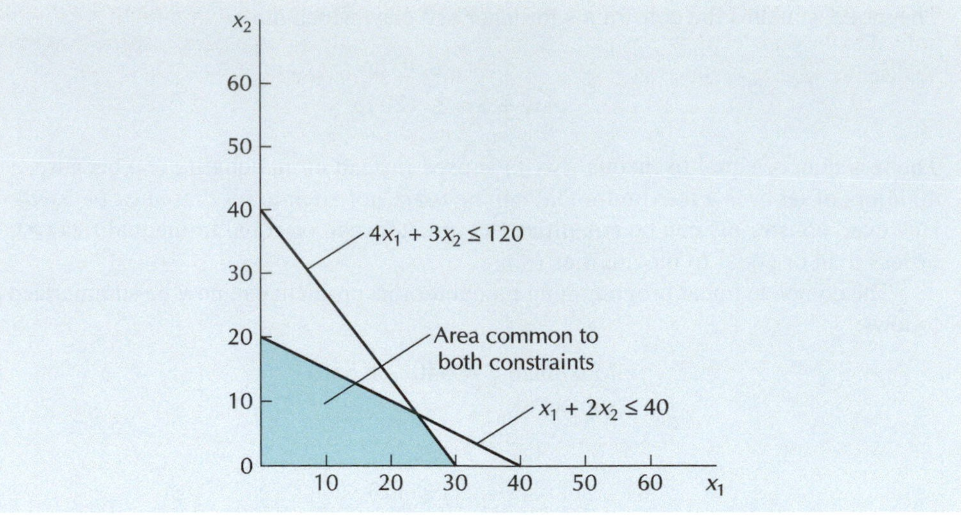

The first step is to plot the constraints on the graph. This is done by treating both constraints as equations (or straight lines) and plotting each line on the graph. A simple way to plot a line is to determine where it intersects the horizontal and vertical axes and draw a straight line connecting the points. The shaded area in the preceding figure is the area that is common to both model constraints. Therefore, this is the only area on the graph that contains points (i.e., values for x_1 and x_2) that will satisfy both constraints simultaneously. This area is the **feasible solution space**, because it is the only area that contains values for the variables that are feasible, or do not violate the constraints.

Feasible solution space An area that satisfies all constraints in a linear programming model simultaneously.

The second step in the graphical solution method is to locate the point in the feasible solution area that represents the greatest total revenue. We will plot the objective function line for an *arbitrarily* selected level of revenue. For example, if revenue, Z, is \$800, the objective function is

$$\$800 = 40x_1 + 50x_2$$

Plotting this line just as we plotted the constraint lines results in the graph showing the determination of the optimal point in the following figure. Every point on this line is in the feasible solution area and will result in a revenue of \$800 (i.e., every combination of x_1 and x_2 on this line will give a Z value of \$800). As the value of Z increases, the objective function line moves out through the feasible solution space away from the origin until it reaches the last feasible point on the boundary of the solution space and then leaves the solution space.

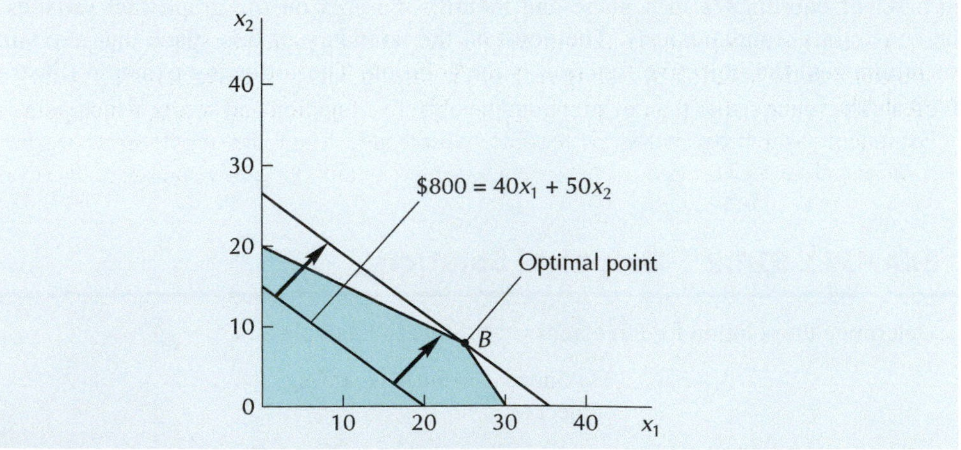

The solution point is always on this boundary, because the boundary contains the points farthest from the origin (i.e., the points corresponding to the greatest profit). Moreover, the solution point will not only be on the boundary of the feasible solution area, but it will be at one of the *corners* of the boundary where two constraint lines intersect. These corners (labeled *A*, *B*, and *C* in the following figure) are protrusions called **extreme points**. It has been proven mathematically that the optimal solution in a linear programming model will always

Extreme points Corner points on the boundary of the feasible solution space.

occur at an extreme point. Therefore, in our example problem, the possible solution points are limited to the three extreme points A, B, and C. The **optimal**, or "one best," **solution** point is B, since the objective function touches it last before it leaves the feasible solution area.

Optimal solution The single best solution to a problem.

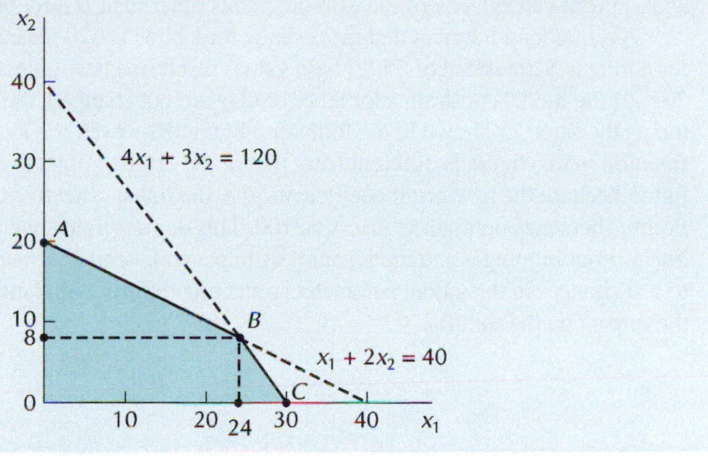

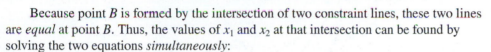

Because point B is formed by the intersection of two constraint lines, these two lines are *equal* at point B. Thus, the values of x_1 and x_2 at that intersection can be found by solving the two equations *simultaneously*:

$$\begin{array}{r} x_1 + 2x_2 = 40 \\ 4x_1 + 3x_2 = 120 \\ \hline 4x_1 + 8x_2 = 160 \\ -4x_1 - 3x_2 = -120 \\ \hline 5x_2 = 40 \\ x_2 = 8 \end{array}$$

Thus,

$$x_1 + 2(8) = 40$$
$$x_1 = 24$$

The optimal solution at point B in the preceding figure is $x_1 = 24$ bowls and $x_2 = 8$ mugs. Substituting these values into the objective function gives the maximum revenue,

$$Z = \$40(24) + \$50(8)$$
$$= \$1360$$

Given that the optimal solution will be at one of the extreme corner points A, B, or C, you can find the solution by testing each of the three points to see which results in the greatest revenue rather than by graphing the objective function and seeing which point it last touches as it moves out of the feasible solution area. The following figure shows the solution values for all three points A, B, and C and the amount of revenue, Z, at each point:

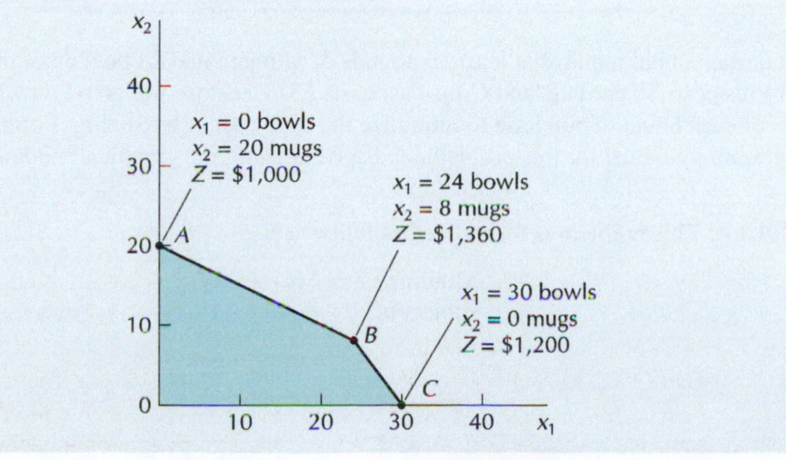

The objective function determines which extreme point is optimal, because the objective function designates the revenue that will accrue from each combination of x_1 and x_2 values at the extreme points. If the objective function had had different coefficients (i.e., different x_1 and x_2 profit values), one of the extreme points other than B might have been optimal.

Assume for a moment that the revenue for a bowl is \$70 instead of \$40 and the revenue for a mug is \$20 instead of \$50. These values result in a new objective function, $Z = \$70x_1 + 20x_2$. If the model constraints for labor or clay are not changed, the feasible solution area remains the same, as shown in the following figure. However, the location of the objective function in this figure is different from that of the original objective function in the previous figure because the new profit coefficients give the linear objective function a new *slope*. Point C becomes optimal, with $Z = \$2100$. This demonstrates one of the useful functions of linear programming—and model analysis in general—called *sensitivity analysis*: the ability to test changes in the model parameters reflecting different operating environments to analyze the impact on the solution.

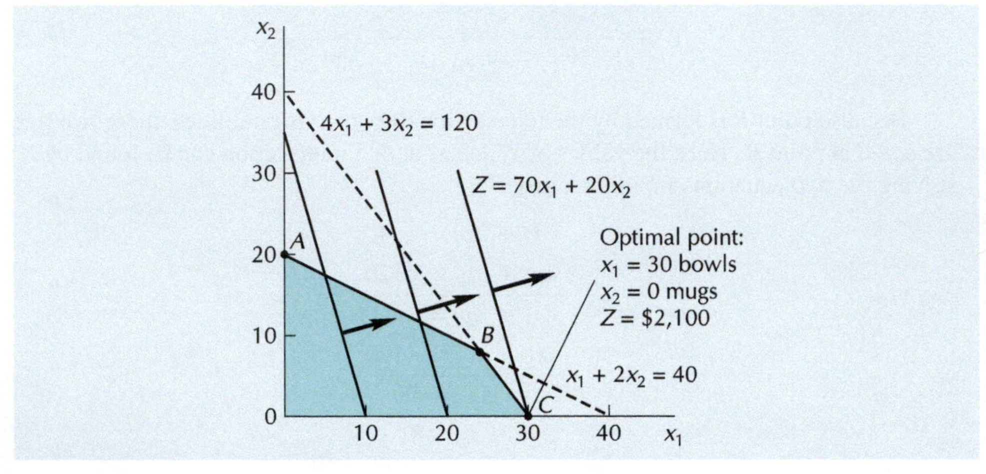

EXAMPLE S14.3 | A Minimization Linear Programming Model

The Farmer's Hardware and Feed Store is putting together a fertilizer mix for a farmer who is preparing a field to plant a crop. The store will use two brands of fertilizer, Gro-Plus and Crop-Fast, to make the proper mix for the farmer. Each brand yields a specific amount of nitrogen and phosphate, as follows:

	CHEMICAL CONTRIBUTION	
BRAND	*NITROGEN (LB/BAG)*	*PHOSPHATE (LB/BAG)*
Gro-Plus	2	4
Crop-Fast	4	3

The farmer's field requires at least 16 pounds of nitrogen and 24 pounds of phosphate. Gro-Plus costs \$6 per bag, and Crop-Fast costs \$3. The store wants to know how many bags of each brand to purchase to minimize the total cost of fertilizing. Formulate a linear programming model for this problem, and solve it using the graphical method.

Solution: This problem is formulated as follows:

$$\text{Minimize } Z = \$6x_1 + 3x_2$$
subject to

$$2x_1 + 4x_2 \geq 16 \text{ lb of nitrogen}$$
$$4x_1 + 3x_2 \geq 24 \text{ lb of phosphate}$$
$$x_1, x_2 \geq 0$$

The graphical solution of the problem is shown in the following figure. Notice that the optimal solution, point A, occurs at the last extreme point the objective function touches as it moves toward the origin (point 0,0).

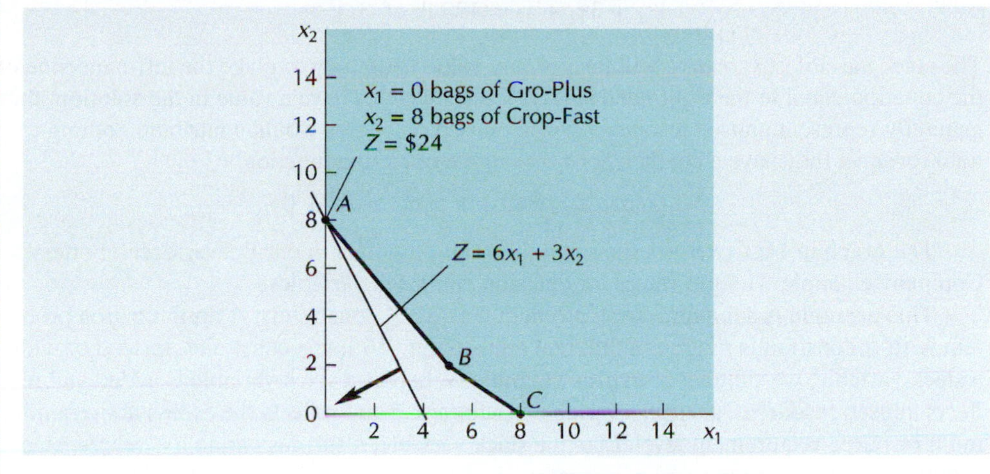

Linear Programming Model Solution

The Simplex Method

Graphically determining the solution to a linear programming model can provide insight into how a solution is derived, but it is not generally effective or efficient. The traditional mathematical approach for solving a linear programming problem is a mathematical procedure called the **simplex method**. In the simplex method, the model is put into the form of a table, and then a number of mathematical steps are performed on the table. These mathematical steps are the same as moving from one extreme point on the solution boundary to another. However, unlike the graphical method, in which we simply searched through *all* the solution points to find the best one, the simplex method moves from one *better* solution to another until the best one is found.

Simplex method A mathematical procedure for solving a linear programming problem according to a set of steps.

The simplex method for solving linear programming problems is based, at least partially, on the solution of simultaneous equations and matrix algebra. In this supplement on linear programming, we are not going to provide a detailed presentation of the simplex method. It is a mathematically cumbersome approach that is very time-consuming even for very small problems of two or three variables and a few constraints. It includes a number of mathematical steps and requires numerous arithmetic computations, which frequently result in simple arithmetic errors when done by hand. Instead, we will demonstrate how linear programming problems are solved on the computer. Depending on the software used, the computer solution to a linear programming problem may be in the same form as a simplex solution. Thus, we will review the procedures for setting up a linear programming model in the simplex format for solution.

Slack and Surplus Variables

Recall that the solution to a linear programming problem occurs at an extreme point where constraint equation lines intersect with each other or with the axis. Thus, the model constraints must all be in the form of equations (=) rather than inequalities ($\geq$ or $\leq$).

The procedure for transforming inequality constraints into equations is by adding a new variable, called a **slack variable**, to each constraint. For the Beaver Creek Pottery Company, the

Slack variable A variable added to a linear programming constraint to make it an equality.

addition of a unique slack variable (s_i) to each of the constraint inequalities results in the following equations:

$$x_1 + 2x_2 + s_1 = 40 \text{ hours of labor}$$
$$4x_1 + 3x_2 + s_2 = 120 \text{ lb of clay}$$

The slack variables, s_1 and s_2, will take on any value necessary to make the left-hand side of the equation equal to the right-hand side. If slack variables have a value in the solution, they generally represent unused resources. Since unused resources would contribute nothing to total revenue, they have a coefficient of zero in the objective function:

$$\text{Maximize } Z = \$40x_1 + 50x_2 + 0s_1 + 0s_2$$

The graph in Figure S14.1 shows all the solution points in our Beaver Creek Pottery Company example with the values for decision *and* slack variables.

This example is a maximization problem with all ≤ constraints. A minimization problem with ≥ constraints requires a different adjustment. With a ≥ constraint, instead of adding a slack variable, we subtract a **surplus variable**. Whereas a slack variable is added and reflects unused resources, a surplus variable is subtracted and reflects the excess above a minimum resource-requirement level. Like the slack variable, a surplus variable is represented symbolically by s_i and must be nonnegative. For example, consider the following constraint from our fertilizer mix problem in Example S14.3:

Surplus variable A variable subtracted from a linear programming constraint to make it an equality.

$$2x_1 + 4x_2 \geq 16$$

Subtracting a surplus variable results in

$$2x_1 + 4x_2 - s_1 = 16$$

The graph in Figure S14.2 shows all the solution points with the values for decision *and* surplus variables for the minimization problem in Example S14.3.

FIGURE S14.1 Solution Points with Slack Variables

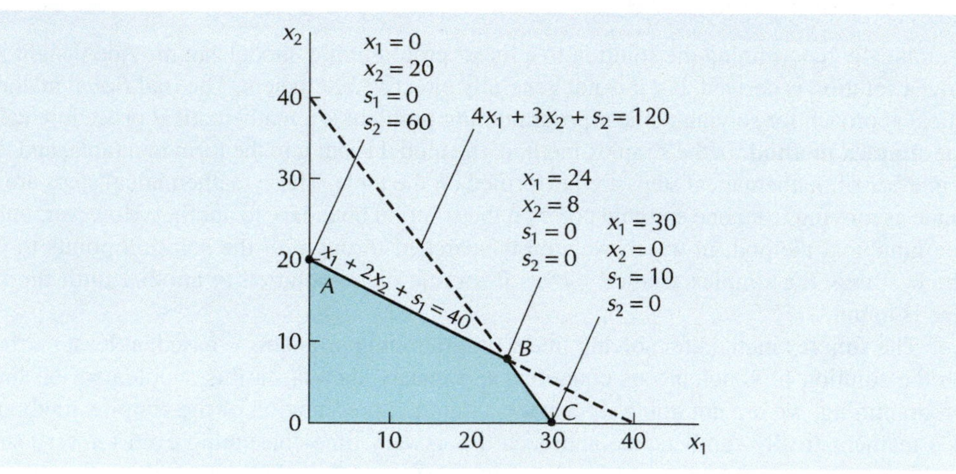

FIGURE S14.2 Solution Points with Slack Variables

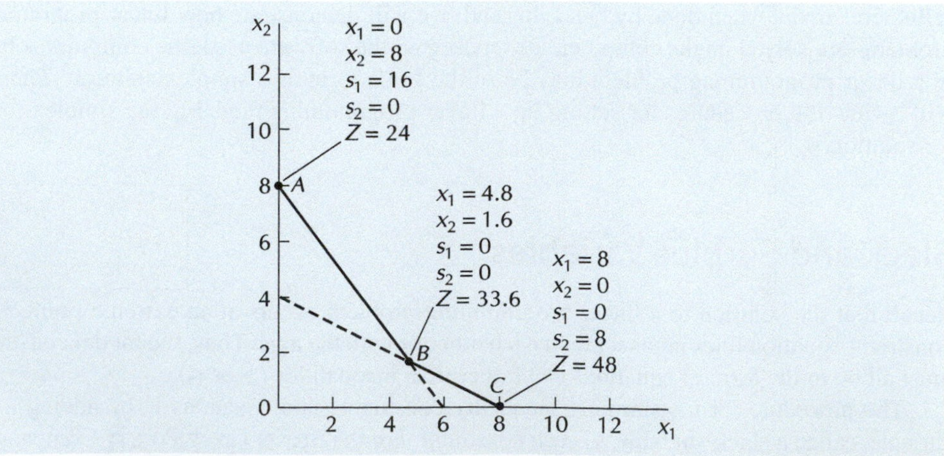

Solving Linear Programming Problems with Excel

In this section we will demonstrate how to use Excel to solve the Highlands Craft Store model from Example S14.1.

Exhibit S14.1 shows the Excel spreadsheet screen for Example S14.1 for the Highlands Craft Store. The values for bowls, mugs, and maximum profit are contained in cells B10, B11, and B12. They are currently empty since the problem has not yet been solved. The objective function for profit embedded in cell B12 is shown on the formula bar on the top of the screen. Similar formulas for the constraints for labor and clay are embedded in cells F6 and F7.

To solve this problem, first click on the "Data" tab from the toolbar at the top of the screen and then select "Solver" from the list of menu items. (If Solver is not shown on the Data menu, it can be activated by clicking on "Add-ins" on the Tools menu and then "Solver." If Solver is not available from the Add-ins menu, it must be installed on the Add-ins menu directly from the Office or Excel software.) The window for "Solver Parameters" will appear as shown in **Exhibit S14.2**.

EXHIBIT S14.1

Excel File

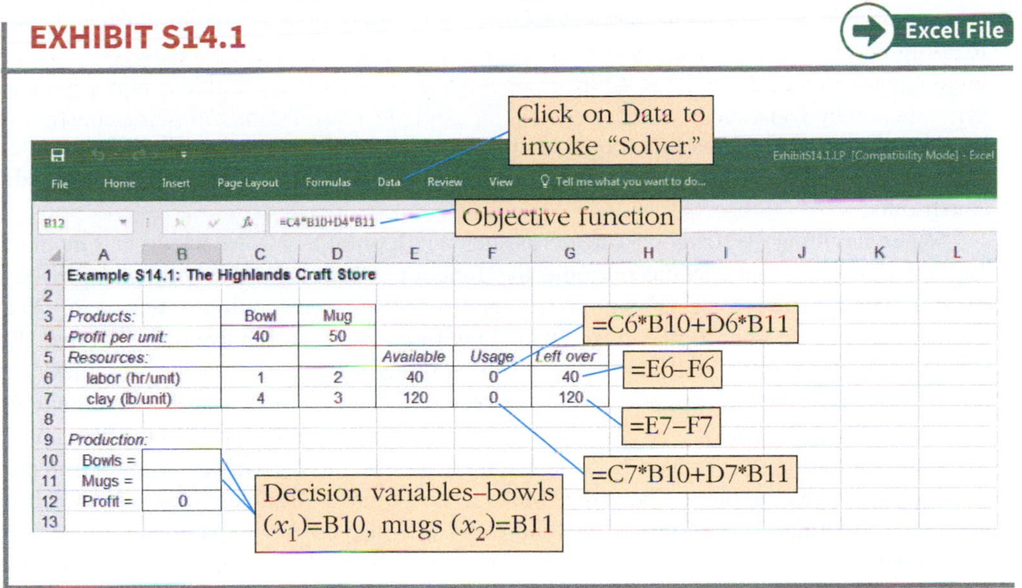

EXHIBIT S14.2

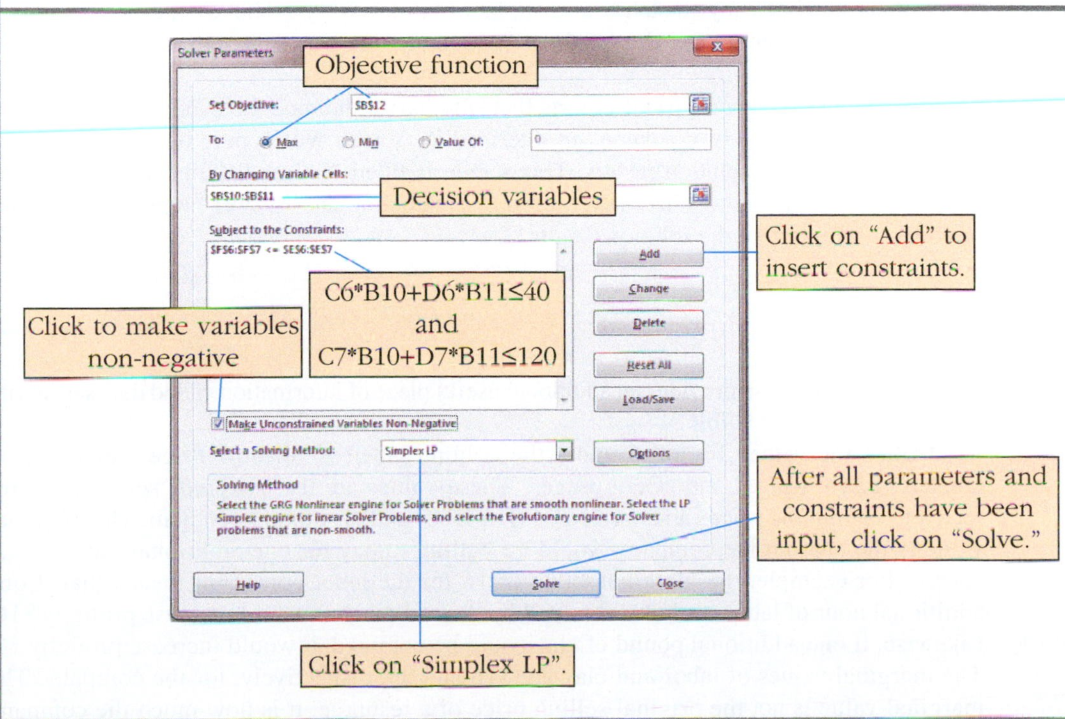

EXHIBIT S14.3

Excel File

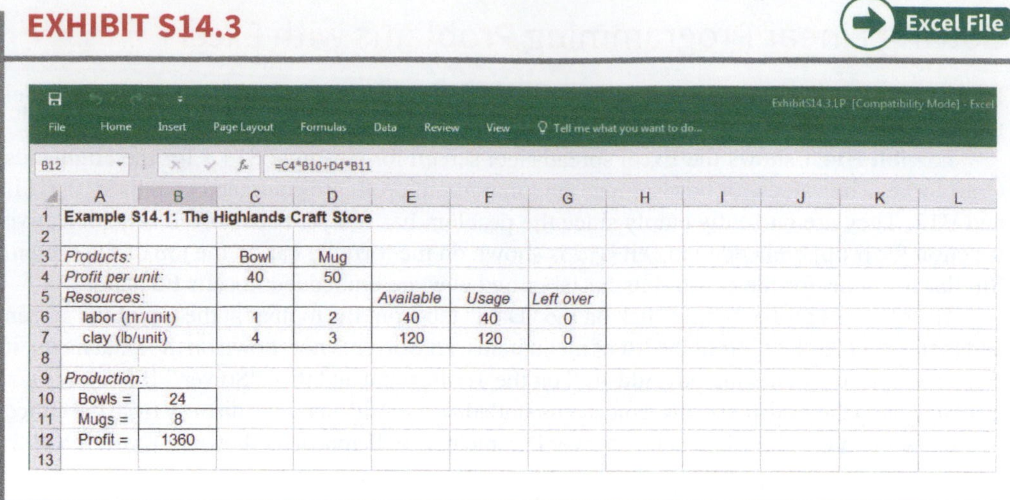

	A	B	C	D	E	F	G
1	**Example S14.1: The Highlands Craft Store**						
2							
3	*Products:*		Bowl	Mug			
4	*Profit per unit:*		40	50			
5	*Resources:*				*Available*	*Usage*	*Left over*
6	labor (hr/unit)		1	2	40	40	0
7	clay (lb/unit)		4	3	120	120	0
8							
9	*Production:*						
10	Bowls =	24					
11	Mugs =	8					
12	Profit =	1360					
13							

Initially all the windows on this screen are blank, and we must input the objective function cell, the cells representing the decision variables, and the cells that make up the model constraints.

When inputting the solver parameters as shown in Exhibit S14.2, we would first input the "set objective" cell that contains our objective function, which is B12 for our example. (Excel automatically inserts the "$" sign next to cell addresses; you should not type it in.) Next we indicate that we want to maximize by clicking on "Max." We achieve our objective "By Changing Variable Cells" B10 and B11, which represent our model decision variables. The designation "B10:B11" means all the cells between B10 and B11 inclusive. We next input our model constraints by clicking on "Add," which will access a window for adding constraints.

After all the constraints have been added, there are two more necessary steps before proceeding to solve the problem. Check the "Make Unconstrained Variables Non-Negative" box; and in the "Solving Method" box select "Simplex LP." Once the model parameters have been input, click on "Solve" in the upper right-hand corner of the "Solver Parameters" screen. First, a screen will appear entitled "Solver Results," which will provide you with the opportunity to select several different reports and then by clicking on "OK" the solution screen shown in **Exhibit S14.3** will appear.

If there had been any slack left over for labor or clay, it would have appeared in column G on our spreadsheet under the heading "Left Over." In this case there are no slack resources left over.

We can also generate several reports that summarize the model results. When you click on "OK" from the "Solver" screen, an intermediate screen will appear before the original spreadsheet with the solution results. This screen is titled "Solver Results" and it provides an opportunity for you to select several reports, including an "Answer" report. This report provides a summary of the solution results.

Sensitivity Analysis

The Excel solution also provides an additional useful piece of information called the "sensitivity report" as shown in **Exhibit S14.4**.

Notice the values 16 and 6 under the column labeled "Shadow Price" for the rows labeled "Labor usage" and "Clay usage." These values are the *marginal values* (also referred to as *shadow prices* and *dual values*) of labor and clay in our problem. The marginal value is the amount the company would be willing to pay for one additional unit of a resource. For example, the marginal value of 16 for the labor constraint means that if one additional hour of labor could be obtained by the company, it would increase profit by $16. Likewise, if one additional pound of clay could be obtained, it would increase profit by $6. The marginal values of labor and clay are $16 and $6, respectively, for the company. The marginal value is not the original selling price of a resource; it is how much the company

EXHIBIT S14.4 Excel File

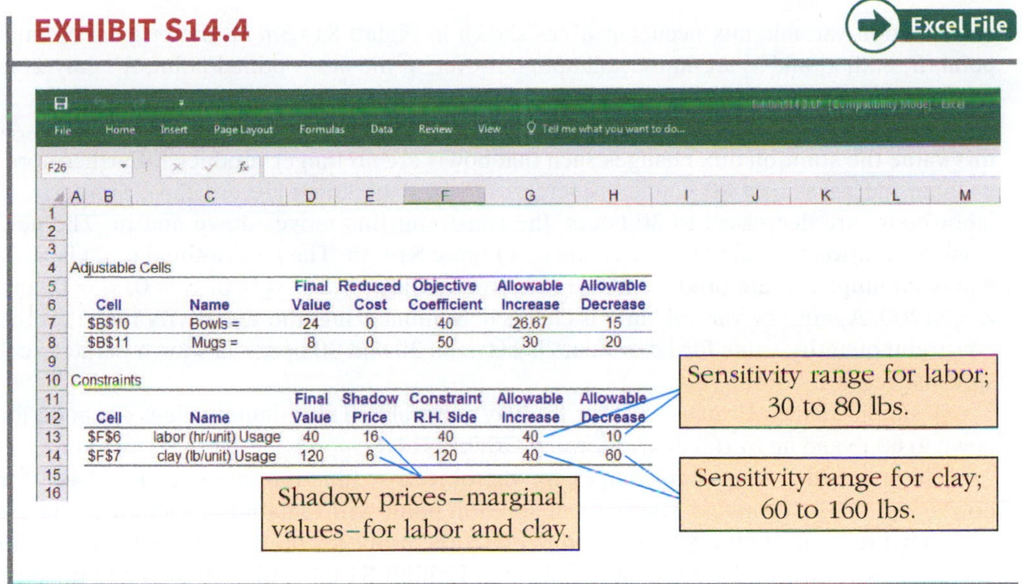

Adjustable Cells

Cell	Name	Final Value	Reduced Cost	Objective Coefficient	Allowable Increase	Allowable Decrease
$B$10	Bowls =	24	0	40	26.67	15
$B$11	Mugs =	8	0	50	30	20

Constraints

Cell	Name	Final Value	Shadow Price	Constraint R.H. Side	Allowable Increase	Allowable Decrease
$F$6	labor (hr/unit) Usage	40	16	40	40	10
$F$7	clay (lb/unit) Usage	120	6	120	40	60

should pay to get more of the resource. The store should not be willing to pay more than \$16 for an hour of labor because if it gets one more hour, profit will increase by only \$16. The marginal value is helpful to the company in pricing resources and making decisions about securing additional resources.

Sensitivity Ranges

The marginal, or dual values do not hold for an unlimited supply of labor and clay. As the store increases (or reduces) the amount of labor or clay it has, the constraints change, which will eventually change the solution to a new point. Thus, the dual values are only good within a range of consistent values. These ranges are given under the column labeled "Allowable Increase" and "Allowable Decrease" in Exhibit S14.4. For example, the original amount of labor available is 40 hours. The dual value of \$16 for one hour of labor holds if the available labor is between 30 and 80 hours. If there are more than 80 hours of labor, then a new solution point occurs and the dual value of \$16 is no longer valid. The problem would have to be solved again to see what the new solution is and the new dual value.

This can be observed graphically in Figure S14.3. If the labor hours are increased from 40 to 80 hours, the constraint line moves out and up. The new solution space is $OA'C$, and a

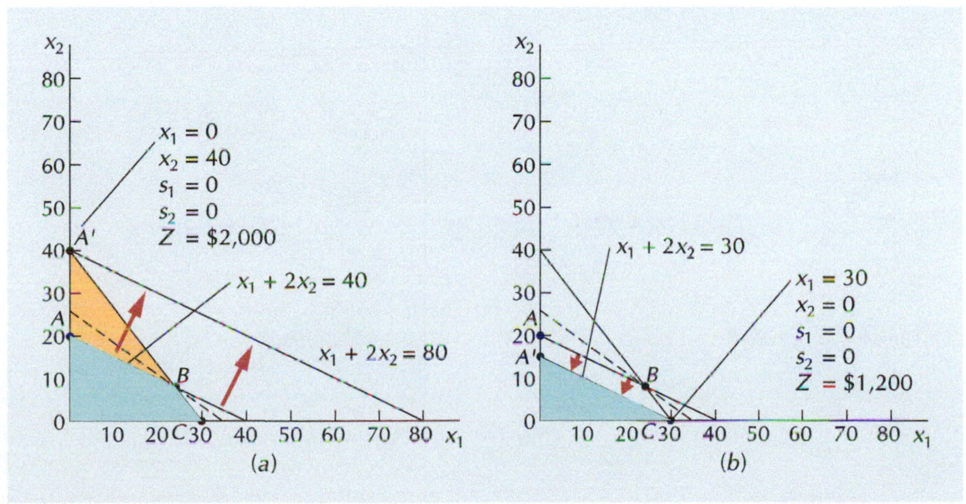

FIGURE S14.3 **The Sensitivity Range for Labor Hours**

new solution variable mix occurs at A', as shown in Figure S14.3*a*. At the original optimal point, B, both x_1 and x_2 are in the solution; however, at the new optimal point, A', only x_2 is produced (i.e., $x_1 = 0$, $x_2 = 40$, $s_1 = 0$, $s_2 = 0$).

Thus, the upper limit of the sensitivity range for the labor constraint is 80 hours. At this value the solution mix changes such that bowls are no longer produced. Furthermore, as labor increases past 80 hours, s_1 increases (i.e., slack hours are created). Similarly, if labor hours are decreased to 30 hours, the constraint line moves down and in. The new feasible solution space is $OA'C$, as shown in Figure S14.3*b*. The new optimal point is at C, where no mugs (x_2) are produced. The new solution is $x_1 = 30$, $x_2 = 0$, $s_1 = 0$, $s_2 = 0$, and $Z = \$1200$. Again, the variable mix is changed. Summarizing, the sensitivity range for the constraint quantity value for labor hours is between 30 and 80 hours as shown in the Excel spreadsheet in Exhibit S14.4.

A similar range of values exist for the clay constraint. The solution values are good for down to 60 lb and up to 160 lb, as shown in Exhibit S14.4.

There are also sensitivity ranges for the objective function coefficients: "\$40" for bowls and "\$50" for mugs. The optimal solution point will remain the same if the profit for a bowl remains within \$25 and \$66.67, or if the profit for mugs remains between \$30 and \$80, as shown in the Excel spreadsheet in Exhibit S14.4. This can also be observed graphically in **Figure S14.4**.

If the profit for a bowl increases from \$40 to \$66.67, the objective function line rotates to a new location where it is parallel with the constraint line for clay, as shown in Figure S14.4*a*. (At this new location, the objective function line and the constraint line for clay have the same slope.) Both points B and C are now optimal. If the profit for bowls is increased greater than \$66.67, then only point C will be optimal and we will have a new solution mix. Similarly, if the profit for a bowl is decreased to \$25, as shown in Figure S14.4*b*, points A and B are both optimal. If the profit for a bowl is decreased to less than \$25, only point A will be optimal and a new solution exists. Thus, the range for the profit for a bowl is between \$25 and \$66.67 as shown in the Excel spreadsheet in Exhibit S14.4. Over this range the current solution mix will remain optimal, and the marginal values are valid.

These sensitivity ranges for constraint values and objective function values provide managers with a convenient means for analyzing resource usage. The marginal value of resources lets managers know what their resources are worth as they make decisions, and the sensitivity ranges indicate the ranges over which the marginal values are valid. When using software like Excel, it is often just as easy to change different values in the linear programming model and see what happens. In either case, this points out a very useful feature of linear programming: it not only provides you with a possible solution or decision, but it also enables you to "experiment" with the model to test different operational scenarios.

FIGURE S14.4 The Sensitivity Range for Profit for Bowls

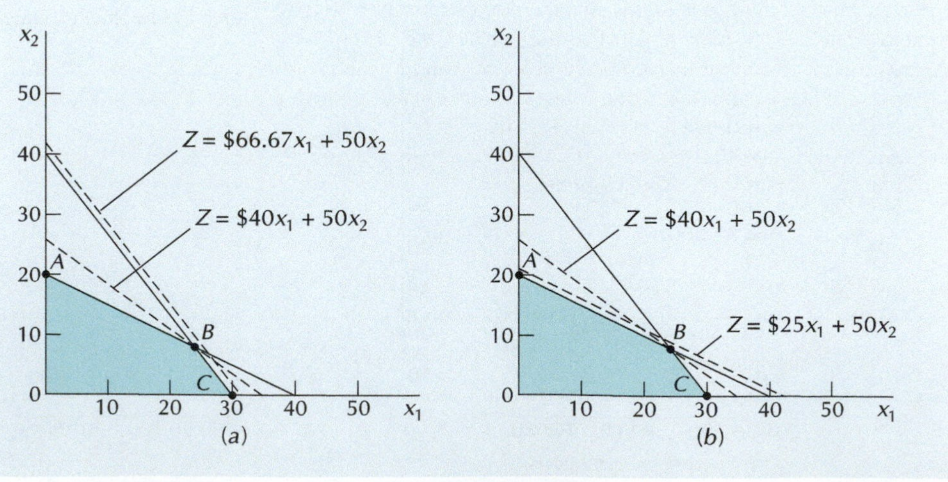

Summary

Linear programming is one of several related quantitative techniques that are generally classified as mathematical programming models. Other quantitative techniques that fall into this general category include integer programming, nonlinear programming, and goal or multiobjective programming. These modeling techniques are capable of addressing a large variety of complex operational decision-making problems, and they are used extensively to do so by businesses and companies around the world. Computer software packages are available to solve most of these types of models, which greatly promotes their use.

Key Terms

constraints Linear relationships of decision variables representing the restrictions placed on the decision situation by the operating environment.

decision variables Mathematical symbols that represent levels of activity of an operation.

extreme points Corner points, or protrusions, on the boundary of the feasible solution space in a linear programming model.

feasible solution space An area that satisfies all constraints in a linear programming model simultaneously.

graphical solution method A method for determining the solution of a linear programming problem using a two-dimensional graph of the model.

linear programming A technique for general decision situations in which the decision is to determine a level of operational activity in order to achieve an objective, subject to restrictions.

objective function A linear mathematical relationship that describes the objective of an operation in terms of decision variables.

optimal solution The single best solution to a problem.

simplex method A series of mathematical steps conducted within a tabular structure for solving a linear programming model.

slack variable A variable added to a linear programming ≤ constraint to make it an equality.

surplus variable A variable subtracted from a ≥ linear programming constraint to make it an equality.

Solved Problems

A leather shop makes custom-designed, hand-tooled briefcases and luggage. The shop makes a $400 profit from each briefcase and a $200 profit from each piece of luggage. (The profit for briefcases is higher because briefcases require more hand-tooling.) The shop has a contract to provide a store with exactly 30 items per month. A tannery supplies the shop with at least 80 square yards of leather per month. The shop must purchase at least this amount but can order more. Each briefcase requires 2 square yards of leather; each piece of luggage requires 8 square yards of leather. From past performance, the shop owners know they cannot make more than 20 briefcases per month. They want to know the number of briefcases and pieces of luggage to produce in order to maximize profit. Formulate a linear programming model for this problem and solve it graphically.

Solution

Step 1. Model formulation

$$\begin{aligned} &\text{Maximize } Z = \$400x_1 + 200x_2 \\ &\text{subject to} \\ &\quad x_1 + x_2 = 30 \text{ contracted items} \\ &\quad 2x_1 + 8x_2 \geq 80 \text{ yd}^2 \text{ of leather} \\ &\quad x_1 \leq 20 \text{ briefcases} \\ &\quad x_1, x_2 \geq 0 \end{aligned}$$

where

$$x_1 = \text{briefcases}$$
$$x_2 = \text{pieces of luggage}$$

Step 2. Graphical solution

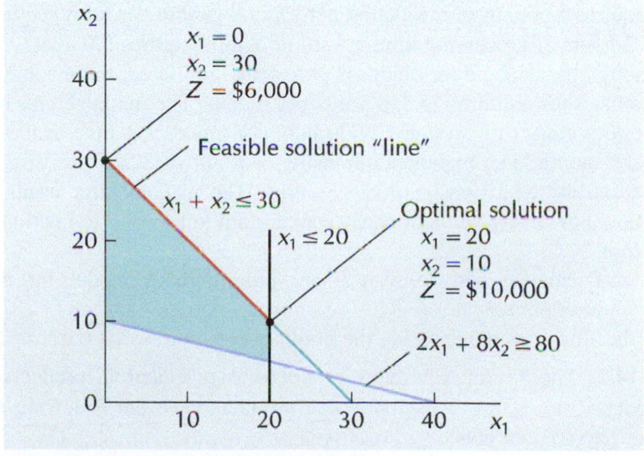

Step 3. Model solution

The model solution obtained with Excel is shown as follows:

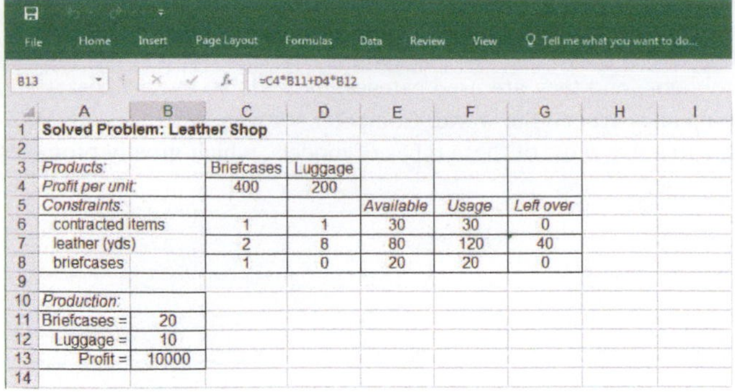

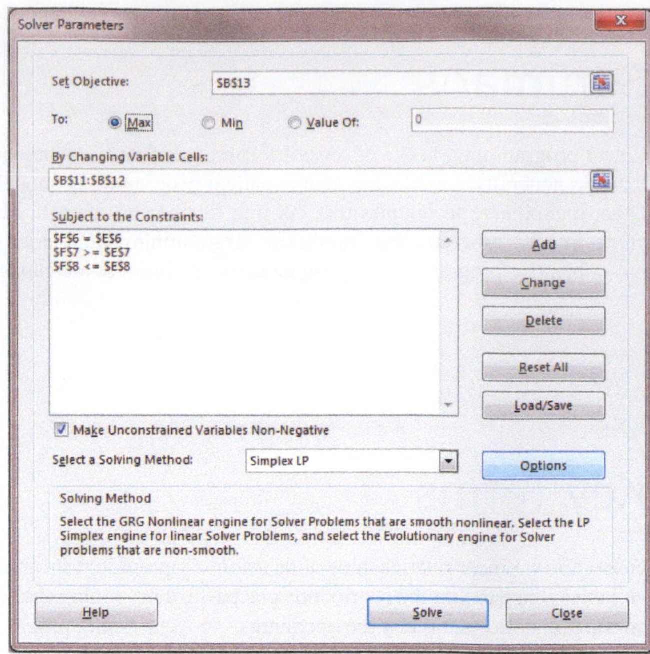

Questions

S14.1. Why is the term *linear* used in the name *linear programming*?

S14.2. Describe the steps one should follow in formulating a linear programming model.

S14.3. Summarize the steps for solving a linear programming model graphically.

S14.4. In the graphical analysis of a linear programming model, what occurs when the slope of the objective function is the same as the slope of one of the constraint equations?

S14.5. What are the benefits and limitations of the graphical method for solving linear programming problems?

S14.6. What constitutes the feasible solution area on the graph of a linear programming model?

S14.7. How is the optimal solution point identified on the graph of a linear programming model?

S14.8. Why does the coefficient of a slack variable equal zero in the objective function?

Problems

S14.1. Barrows Textile Mills produces two types of cotton cloth—denim and corduroy. Corduroy is a heavier grade of cotton cloth and, as such, requires 7.5 pounds of raw cotton per yard, whereas denim requires 5 pounds of raw cotton per yard. A yard of corduroy requires 3.2 hours of processing time; a yard of denim requires 3.0 hours. Although the demand for denim is practically unlimited, the maximum demand for corduroy is 510 yards per month. The manufacturer has 6500 pounds of cotton and 3000 hours of processing time available each month. The manufacturer makes a profit of $2.25 per yard of denim and $3.10 per yard of corduroy. The manufacturer wants to know how many yards of each type of cloth to produce to maximize profit.

a. Formulate and solve a linear programming model for this problem.

b. Solve this model using the graphical method.

S14.2. The Tycron Company produces three electrical products—clocks, radios, and toasters. These products have the following resource requirements:

	RESOURCE REQUIREMENTS	
PRODUCT	COST/UNIT	LABOR HOURS/UNIT
Clock	$ 7	2
Radio	10	3
Toaster	5	2

The manufacturer has a daily production budget of $2000 and a maximum of 660 hours of labor. Maximum daily customer demand is for 200 clocks, 300 radios, and 150 toasters. Clocks sell for $15, radios, for $20, and toasters, for $12. The company desires to know the optimal product mix that will maximize profit.

Formulate and solve a linear programming model for this problem.

S14.3. The Seaboard Trucking Company has expanded its shipping capacity by purchasing 120 trucks and trailers from a competitor that went bankrupt. The company subsequently located 40 of the purchased trucks at each of its shipping warehouses in Charlotte,

Memphis, and Louisville. The company makes shipments from each of these warehouses to terminals in St. Louis, Atlanta, and New York. Each truck is capable of making one shipment per week. The terminal managers have each indicated their capacity for extra shipments. The manager at St. Louis can accommodate 40 additional trucks per week, the manager at Atlanta can accommodate 60 additional trucks, and the manager at New York can accommodate 50 additional trucks. The company makes the following profit per truckload shipment from each warehouse to each terminal. The profits differ as a result of differences in products shipped, shipping costs, and transport rates.

	TERMINAL		
WAREHOUSE	ST. LOUIS	ATLANTA	NEW YORK
Charlotte	$1800	$2100	$1600
Memphis	1000	700	900
Louisville	1400	800	2200

The company wants to know how many trucks to assign to each route (i.e., warehouse to terminal) to maximize profit. Formulate a linear programming model for this problem and solve it.

S14.4. The Pinewood Cabinet and Furniture Company produces sofas, tables, and chairs at its plant in Greensboro, North Carolina. The plant uses three main resources to make furniture—wood, upholstery, and labor. The resource requirements for each piece of furniture and the total resources available weekly are as follows:

	RESOURCE REQUIREMENTS		
FURNITURE PRODUCT	WOOD (LB)	UPHOLSTERY (YD)	LABOR (HOUR)
Sofa	7	12	9
Table	5	—	7
Chair	4	7	5
Total available resources	2250	1000	240

The furniture is produced on a weekly basis and stored in a warehouse until the end of the week, when it is shipped out. The warehouse has a total capacity of 500 pieces of furniture; however, a sofa takes up twice as much space as a table or chair. Each sofa earns $320 in profit, each table, $275, and each chair, $190. The company wants to know how many pieces of each type of furniture to make per week in order to maximize profit.

Formulate and solve a linear programming model for this problem.

S14.5. The Mystic Coffee Shop blends coffee on the premises for its customers. It sells three basic blends in one-pound bags: Special, Mountain Dark, and Mill Regular. It uses four different types of coffee to produce the blends: Brazilian, mocha, Colombian, and mild. The shop used the following blend recipe requirements:

BLEND	MIX REQUIREMENTS	SELLING PRICE/LB
Special	At least 40% Colombian, at least 30% mocha	$6.50
Dark	At least 60% Brazilian, no more than 10% mild	5.25
Regular	No more than 60% mild, at least 30% Brazilian	3.75

The cost of Brazilian coffee is $2.00 per pound, the cost of mocha is $2.75 per pound, the cost of Colombian is $2.90 per pound, and the cost of mild is $1.70 per pound. The shop has 110 pounds of Brazilian coffee, 70 pounds of mocha, 80 pounds of Colombian, and 150 pounds of mild coffee available per week. The shop wants to know the amount of each blend it should prepare each week in order to maximize profit.

Formulate and solve a linear programming model for this problem.

S14.6. A small metal-parts shop contains three machines—a drill press, a lathe, and a grinder—and has three operators, each certified to work on all three machines. However, each operator performs better on some machines than on others. The shop has contracted to do a big job that requires all three machines. The times required by the various operators to perform the required operations on each machine are summarized as follows:

OPERATOR	DRILL PRESS (MIN)	LATHE (MIN)	GRINDER (MIN)
1	22	18	35
2	29	30	28
3	25	36	18

The shop manager wants to assign one operator to each machine so that the total operating time for all three operators is minimized. Formulate and solve a linear programming model for this problem.

S14.7. H&N stores in the United States stock a particular type of designer denim jeans that is manufactured in India and Bangladesh and imported to the H&N's distribution center in the United States. It orders 500 pairs of jeans each month from its two suppliers. The Indian supplier charges H&N $11 per pair of jeans and the Bangladesh supplier charges $16 per pair (and then H&N marks them up almost a thousand percent). Although the jeans from India are cheaper, they also have more defects than those from Bangladesh. Based on past data, H&N estimates that 7% of the Indian jeans will be defective, compared to only 2% from Bangladesh, and H&N does not want to import any more than 5% defective items. However, H&N also does not want to rely only on a single supplier, so it wants to order at least 20% from each supplier every month.

a. Formulate and solve a linear programming model for this problem.

b. If the Indian supplier was able to reduce its percentage of defective pairs of jeans from 7% to 5%, what would be the effect on the solution?

c. If H&N decided to minimize its defective items while budgeting $7,000 for purchasing the jeans, what would be the effect on the solution?

S14.8. A manufacturer of bathroom fixtures produces fiberglass bathtubs in an assembly operation consisting of three processes: molding, smoothing, and painting. The number of units that can be put through each process in an hour is as follows:

PROCESS	OUTPUT (UNITS/HR)
Molding	7
Smoothing	12
Painting	10

(*Note*: The three processes are continuous and sequential; thus, no more units can be smoothed or painted than have been molded.) The labor costs per hour are $8 for molding, $5 for smoothing, and $6.50 for painting. The company's labor budget is $3000 per week. A total of 120 hours of labor is available for all three processes per week. Each completed bathtub requires 90 pounds of fiberglass, and the company has a total of 10,000 pounds of fiberglass available each week. Each bathtub earns a profit of $175. The manager of the company wants to know how many hours per week to run each process in order to maximize profit. Formulate and solve a linear programming model for this problem.

S14.9. A refinery blends four petroleum components into three grades of gasoline—regular, premium, and super. The maximum quantities available of each component and the cost per barrel are as follows:

COMPONENT	MAXIMUM BARRELS AVAILABLE/DAY	COST (BARREL)
1	5000	$9.00
2	2400	7.00
3	4000	12.00
4	1500	6.00

To ensure that each gasoline grade retains certain essential characteristics, the refinery has put limits on the percentage of the components in each blend. The limits as well as the selling prices for the various grades are as follows:

GRADE	COMPONENT SPECIFICATIONS	SELLING PRICE (BARREL)
Super	Not less than 40% of 1	$12.00
	Not more than 20% of 2	
	Not less than 30% of 3	
Premium	Not less than 40% of 3	18.00
	Not more than 50% of 2	10.00
Regular	Not less than 10% of 1	

The refinery wants to produce at least 3000 barrels each of super and premium and 4000 barrels of regular. Management wishes to determine the optimal mix of the four components that will maximize profit. Formulate and solve a linear programming model for this problem.

S14.10. The Home Improvement Building Supply Company has received the following order for boards in three lengths:

LENGTH	ORDER (QUANTITY)
7 feet	700 boards
9 feet	1200 boards
10 feet	500 boards

The company has 25-foot standard-length boards in stock. Therefore, the standard-length boards must be cut into the lengths necessary to meet order requirements. Naturally, the company wishes to minimize the number of standard-length boards used. The company must, therefore, determine how to cut up the 25-foot boards in order to meet the order requirements and minimize the number of standard-length boards used.

a. Formulate and solve a linear programming model for this problem.
b. When a board is cut in a specific pattern, the amount of board left over is referred to as *trim loss*. Reformulate and solve the linear programming model for this problem, assuming that the objective is to minimize trim loss rather than to minimize the total number of boards used.

S14.11. IT Computer Services assembles its own brand of personal computers from component parts it purchases overseas and domestically. IT sells most of its computers locally to different departments at State University as well as to individuals and businesses in the immediate geographic region.

IT has enough regular production capacity to produce 160 computers per week. It can produce an additional 50 computers with overtime. The cost of assembly, inspecting, and packaging a computer during regular time is $190. Overtime production of a computer costs $260. Further, it costs $5 per computer per week to hold a computer in inventory for future delivery. IT wants to be able to meet all customer orders with no shortages in order to provide quality service. IT's order schedule for the next 6 weeks is as follows:

WEEK	COMPUTER ORDERS
1	105
2	170
3	230
4	180
5	150
6	250

IT Computers wants to determine a schedule that will indicate how much regular and overtime production it will need each week in order to meet its orders at the minimum cost. The company wants no inventory left over at the end of the six-week period. Formulate and solve a linear programming model for this problem.

S14.12 The manager of Biggs Department Store has four employees available to assign to three departments in the store: lamps, sporting goods, and linen. The manager wants each of these departments to have at least one employee but not more than two. Therefore, two departments will be assigned one employee, and one department will be assigned two. Each employee has different areas of expertise, which are reflected in the following average daily sales record for each employee from previous experience in each department:

EMPLOYEE	DEPARTMENT		
	LAMPS	SPORTING GOODS	LINEN
1	$130	$190	$ 90
2	275	300	100
3	180	225	140
4	200	120	160

The manager wishes to know which employee(s) to assign to each department in order to maximize expected sales. Formulate and solve a linear programming model for this problem.

S14.13. Dr. Beth McKenzie, the head administrator at Washington County Regional Hospital, must determine a schedule for nurses to make sure there are enough nurses on duty throughout the day. During the day, the demand for nurses varies. Beth has broken the day into twelve 2-hour periods. The slowest time of the day encompasses the three periods from 12:00 A.M. to 6:00 A.M., which, beginning at midnight, require a minimum of 30, 20, and 40 nurses, respectively. The demand for nurses steadily increases during the next four daytime periods. Beginning with the 6:00 A.M.–8:00 A.M. period, a minimum of 50, 60, 80, and 90 nurses are required for these four periods, respectively. After 2:00 P.M., the demand for nurses decreases during the afternoon and evening hours. For the five 2-hour periods beginning at 2:00 P.M., and ending at midnight, 70, 70, 60, 50, and 40 nurses are required, respectively. A nurse reports for duty at the beginning of one of the 2-hour periods and works 8 consecutive hours (as required in the nurses' contract).

Dr. McKenzie wants to determine a nursing schedule that will meet the hospital's minimum requirements throughout the day while using the minimum number of nurses. Formulate and solve a linear programming model for this problem.

S14.14. Grass Unlimited is a lawn care and maintenance company. One of its services is to seed new lawns as well as bare areas or damaged areas in established lawns. The company uses three basic grass seed mixes it calls Home 1, Home 2, and Commercial 3. It uses three kinds of grass seed—tall fescue, mustang fescue, and bluegrass. The requirements for each grass mix are as follows:

MIX	MIX REQUIREMENTS
Home 1	No more than 50% tall fescue
	At least 20% mustang fescue
Home 2	At least 30% bluegrass
	At least 30% mustang fescue
	No more than 20% tall fescue
Commercial 3	At least 50% but no more than 70% tall fescue
	At least 10% bluegrass

The company believes it needs to have at least 1500 pounds of Home 1 mix, 900 pounds of Home 2 mix, and 2400 pounds of Commercial 3 seed mix on hand. A pound of tall fescue costs the company $1.70, a pound of mustang fescue costs $2.80, and a pound of bluegrass costs $3.25. The company wants to know how many pounds of each type of grass seed to purchase in order to minimize cost. Formulate a linear programming model for this problem.

S14.15. A jewelry store makes necklaces and bracelets from gold and platinum. The store has developed the following linear programming model for determining the number of necklaces and bracelets (x_1 and x_2) to make in order to maximize profit:

Maximize $Z = 300x_1 + 400x_2$ (profit, \$)
subject to

$$\begin{aligned} 3x_1 + 2x_2 &\leq 18 \quad \text{(gold, oz)} \\ 2x_1 + 4x_2 &\leq 20 \quad \text{(platinum, oz)} \\ x_2 &\leq 4 \quad \text{(demand, bracelets)} \\ x_1, x_2 &\geq 0 \end{aligned}$$

a. Solve this model graphically.
b. The maximum demand for bracelets is 4. If the store produces the optimal number of bracelets and necklaces, will the maximum demand for bracelets be met? If not, by how much will it be missed?
c. What profit for a necklace would result in no bracelets being produced, and what would be the optimal solution for this problem?

S14.16. The Copperfield Mining Company owns two mines that produce three grades of ore: high, medium, and low. The company has a contract to supply a smelting company with 12 tons of high-grade ore, 8 tons of medium-grade ore, and 24 tons of low-grade ore. Each mine produces a certain amount of each type of ore each hour it is in operation. The company has developed the following linear programming model to determine the number of hours to operate each mine (x_1 and x_2) so that contracted obligations can be met at the lowest cost:

Minimize $Z = 200x_1 + 160x_2$(cost, \$)
subject to

$$\begin{aligned} 6x_1 + 2x_2 &\geq 12 \quad \text{(high-grade ore, tons)} \\ 2x_1 + 2x_2 &\geq 8 \quad \text{(medium-grade ore, tons)} \\ 4x_1 + 12x_2 &\geq 24 \quad \text{(low-grade ore, tons)} \\ x_1, x_2 &\geq 0 \end{aligned}$$

a. Solve this model graphically.
b. Solve the model using Excel.

S14.17. A manufacturing firm produces two products. Each product must go through an assembly process and a finishing process. The product is then transferred to the warehouse, which has space for only a limited number of items. The following linear programming model has been developed for determining the quantity of each product to produce in order to maximize profit:

Maximize $Z = 30x_1 + 70x_2$ (profit, \$)
subject to

$$\begin{aligned} 4x_1 + 10x_2 &\leq 80 \quad \text{(assembly, hours)} \\ 14x_1 + 8x_2 &\leq 112 \quad \text{(finishing, hours)} \\ x_1 + x_2 &\leq 10 \quad \text{(inventory, units)} \\ x_1, x_2 &\geq 0 \end{aligned}$$

a. Solve this model graphically.
b. Assume that the objective function has been changed to $Z = 90x_1 + 70x_2$. Determine the slope of each objective function and discuss what effect these slopes have on the optimal solution.

S14.18. The Admissions Office at Tech wants to determine how many in-state and out-of-state students to accept for next fall's entering freshman class. Tuition for an in-state student is $7600 per year while out-of-state tuition is $22,500 per year. A total of 12,800 in-state and 8100 out-of-state freshman have applied for next fall, and Tech does not want to accept more than 3500 students. However, since Tech is a state institution, the state mandates that it can accept no more than 40% out-of-state students. From past experience the admissions office knows that 12% of in-state students and 24% of out-of-state students will drop out during their first year. Tech wants to maximize total tuition while limiting the total attrition to 600 first-year students.

a. Formulate a linear programming model for this problem.
b. Solve this model using graphical analysis.
c. Solve this problem using Excel.

S14.19. Janet Lopez is establishing an investment portfolio that will include stock and bond funds. She has $720,000 to invest, and she does not want the portfolio to include more than 65% stocks. The average annual return for the stock fund she plans to invest in is 18%, while the average annual return for the bond fund is 6%. She further estimates that the most she could lose in the next year in the stock fund is 22%, while the most she could lose in the bond fund is 5%. To reduce her risk she wants to limit her potential maximum losses to $100,000.

a. Formulate a linear programming model for this problem.
b. Solve this model using graphical analysis.
c. Solve this problem using Excel.

S14.20. Professor Wang teaches two sections of operations management, which combined will result in 130 final exams to be graded. Professor Wang has two graduate assistants (GAs), James and Ann, who will grade the final exam. There is a 3-day period between the time the exam is administered and when final grades must be posted. During this period James has 14 hours available and Ann has 12 available hours to grade the exams. It takes James an average of 8.4 minutes to grade an exam, and it takes Sarah 15 minutes to grade an exam; however, James's exams will have errors that will require Professor Wang to ultimately regrade 12% of his exams, while only 5% of Ann's exams will require regrading. Professor Wang wants to know how many exams to assign to each GA to grade in order to get all of them graded, but she also wants to minimize the number of exams that she will be required to regrade.

a. Formulate a linear programming model for this problem.
b. Solve this model using graphical analysis.
c. Solve this model using Excel.
d. If Professor Wang could hire James or Ann to work one more hour, which should she choose? What would be the effect of hiring the selected GA for one additional hour?

S14.21. The Star City Café at the campus student center serves two coffee blends it brews daily, Morning Blend and Study Break. Each is a blend of three high-quality coffees from Brazil, Tanzania, and Guatemala. The Café has 5 lbs. of each of these coffees available each day. Each pound of coffee will produce sixteen 16-oz cups of coffee, and the Cafe has enough brewing capacity to brew 25 gl. of the two coffee blends each day. Morning Blend includes 25% Brazilian, 30% Tanzanian, and 45% Guatemalan, while Study Break is a blend of 55% Brazilian, 15% Tanzanian, and 30% Guatemalan. The shop sells one and a half times more Morning Blend than Study Break each day. Morning Blend sells for $1.95 per cup, and Study Break sells for $1.70 per cup. The manager wants to know the number of cups of each blend to sell each day in order to maximize sales.

a. Formulate a linear programming model for this problem.
b. Solve this model using graphical analysis.
c. Solve this model using Excel.
d. If the Café could get one more pound of coffee, which one should it be? What would be the effect on sales of getting one more pound of this coffee?
e. Would it benefit the shop to increases its brewing capacity from 25 gallons to 30 gallons?
f. Should the Cafe spend $25 per day on advertising if it would increase the relative demand for Morning Blend to twice that of Study Break?

S14.22. Inditek makes women's designer shirts and sells them in its chain of retail stores in the United States. The shirts are made in plants in the Dominican Republic and Panama. The shirts from the plant in the Dominican Republic cost $0.46 apiece, and 9% are defective and can't be sold at Inditek's stores (and are shipped to discounters), and while the shirts from Panama cost only $0.35 each, they have an 18% defective rate. Inditek needs 3500 shirts, and it wants to order at least 1000 from each plant and it would like at least 88% of the shirts to be salable in its stores.

Formulate and solve a linear programming model for this problem.

S14.23. In problem S14.22, if Inditek wants to minimize the defective shirts and keep costs below $2000, reformulate the problem and solve. How many fewer defective items resulted with this reformulation?

S14.24. Inditek imports designer-inspired women's apparel to the United States from suppliers in China and Argentina. It estimates that it will have 45 orders annually and it must arrange to transport their orders in container ships from Singapore and Buenos Aires. The shipping time from Singapore is 32 days and from Buenos Aires it is 14 days and Inditek wants its orders to have an average transport time of no more than 21 days. About 10% of the orders from Singapore and about 4% of the orders from Buenos Aires are damaged, and Inditek does not want to receive more than six damaged orders per year. Inditek wants to receive at least 25% of its orders from each supplier. The shipping cost from Singapore is $3700 and from Buenos Aires it is $5100. Inditek wants to know how many orders it should ship from each supplier in order to minimize shipping costs.

Formulate and solve a linear programming model for this problem.

S14.25. In problem S14.24 would Inditek give the Chinese supplier more orders if it reduced its shipping costs to $2500 per shipment? Would Inditek give the Chinese supplier more orders if it reduced its damaged orders to 5%? Would Inditek give the Chinese supplier more orders if it reduced the shipping time to 28 days?

S14.26. Breathtakers, a health and fitness center, operates a morning fitness program for senior citizens. The program includes aerobic exercise, either swimming or step exercise, followed by a healthy breakfast in its dining room. The dietitian of Breathtakers wants to develop a breakfast that will be high in calories, calcium, protein, and fiber, which are especially important to senior citizens, but low in fat and cholesterol. She also wants to minimize cost. She has selected the following possible food items, with individual nutrient contributions and cost from which to develop a standard breakfast menu.

BREAKFAST FOOD	CALORIES	FAT (G)	CHOLESTEROL (MG)	IRON (MG)	CALCIUM (MG)	PROTEIN (G)	FIBER (G)	COST ($)
1. Bran cereal (cup)	90	0	0	6	20	3	5	0.18
2. Dry cereal (cup)	110	2	0	4	48	4	2	0.22
3. Oatmeal (cup)	100	2	0	2	12	5	3	0.10
4. Oat bran (cup)	90	2	0	3	8	6	4	0.12
5. Egg	75	5	270	1	30	7	0	0.10
6. Bacon (slice)	35	3	8	0	0	2	0	0.09
7. Orange	65	0	0	1	52	1	1	0.40
8. Milk–2% (cup)	100	4	12	0	250	9	0	0.16
9. Orange juice (cup)	120	0	0	0	3	1	0	0.50
10. Wheat toast (slice)	65	1	0	1	26	3	3	0.07

The dietitian wants the breakfast to include at least 420 calories, 5 milligrams of iron, 400 milligrams of calcium, 20 grams of protein, and 12 grams of fiber. Furthermore, she wants to limit fat to no more than 20 grams and cholesterol to 30 milligrams. Formulate the linear programming model for this problem and solve.

S14.27. The Midland Tool Shop has four heavy presses it uses to stamp out prefabricated metal covers and housings for electronic consumer products. All four presses operate differently and are of different sizes. Currently, the firm has a contract to produce three products. The contract calls for 450 units of product 1; 600 units of product 2; and 320 units of product 3. The time (minutes) required for each product to be produced on each machine is as follows:

	MACHINE			
PRODUCT	*1*	*2*	*3*	*4*
1	35	41	34	39
2	40	36	32	43
3	38	37	33	40

Machine 1 is available for 150 hours, machine 2 for 240 hours, machine 3 for 200 hours, and machine 4 for 250 hours. The products also result in different profits according to the machine they are produced on because of time, waste, and operating cost. The profit per unit per machine for each product is summarized as follows:

	MACHINE			
PRODUCT	*1*	*2*	*3*	*4*
1	$7.8	7.8	8.2	7.9
2	6.7	8.9	9.2	6.3
3	8.4	8.1	9.0	5.8

The company wants to know how many units of each product to produce on each machine in order to maximize profit.

Formulate and solve a linear programming model for this problem.

S14.28. The Willow Run Coal Company operates three mines in Kentucky and West Virginia and supplies coal to four utility power plants along the East Coast. The cost of shipping coal from each mine to each plant, the capacity at each of the four mines, and demand at each plant are shown in the following table:

	PLANT				
MINE	*1*	*2*	*3*	*4*	MINE CAPACITY (TONS)
1	$7	9	10	12	220
2	9	7	8	12	190
3	11	14	5	7	280
Demand (tons)	110	160	90	180	

The cost of mining and processing coal is $62 per ton at mine 1, $67 per ton at mine 2, and $75 per ton at mine 3. The percentage of ash and sulfur content per ton of coal at each mine is as follows:

MINE	% ASH	% SULFUR
1	9	6
2	5	4
3	4	3

Each plant has different cleaning equipment. Plant 1 requires that the coal it receives can have no more than 6% ash and 5% sulfur; plant 2 coal can have no more than 5% ash and sulfur combined; plant 3 can have no more than 5% ash and 7% sulfur; and plant 4 can have no more than 6% ash and sulfur combined. The company wants to determine the amount of coal to produce at each mine and ship to its customers that will minimize its total cost.

Formulate and solve a linear programming model for this problem.

S14.29. Armco, Inc., is a manufacturing company that has a contract to supply a customer with parts from April through September. However, Armco does not have enough storage space to store the parts during this period, so it needs to lease extra warehouse space during the 6-month period. Following are Armco's space requirements:

MONTH	REQUIRED SPACE (FT^2)
April	47,000
May	35,000
June	52,000
July	27,000
August	19,000
September	15,000

The rental agent Armco is dealing with has provided it with the following cost schedule for warehouse space. This schedule shows that the longer the space is rented the cheaper it is. For example, if Armco rents space for all six months, it costs $1.00/ft^2 per month, whereas if it rents the same space for only one month, it costs $1.70/ft^2 per month.

RENTAL PERIOD (MONTHS)	$/FT^2/MO
6	1.00
5	1.05
4	1.10
3	1.20
2	1.40
1	1.70

Armco can rent any amount of warehouse space on a monthly basis at any time for any number of (whole) months. Armco wants to determine the least costly rental agreement that will exactly meet its space needs each month and avoid any unused space.

a. Formulate and solve a linear programming model for this problem.

b. Suppose that Armco decided to relax its restriction that is rent exactly the space it needs every month so that it would rent excess space if it were cheaper. How would this affect the optimal solution?

S14.30. Fun 'n Games is a large discount toy store in Fashion City Mall. The store typically has slow sales in the summer months that increase dramatically and rise to a peak at Christmas. However, during the summer and fall, the store must build up its inventory to have enough stock for the Christmas season. In order to purchase and build up its stock during the months when its revenues are low, the store borrows money.

Following is the store's projected revenue and liabilities schedule for July through December (where revenues are received and bills are paid at the first of each month).

MONTH	REVENUES	LIABILITIES
July	$20,000	$60,000
August	30,000	60,000
September	40,000	80,000
October	50,000	30,000
November	80,000	30,000
December	100,000	20,000

At the beginning of July the store can take out a six-month loan that carries an 11% interest rate and must be paid back at the end of December. (The store cannot reduce its interest payment by paying back the loan early.) The store can also borrow money monthly at a rate of 5% interest per month. Money borrowed on a monthly basis must be paid back at the beginning of the next month. The store wants to borrow enough money to meet its cash flow needs while minimizing its cost of borrowing.

a Formulate and solve a linear programming model for this problem.

b. What would be the effect on the optimal solution if the store could secure a 9% interest rate for a 6-month loan from another bank?

S14.31. The Bassone Boat Company manufactures the Water Wiz bass fishing boat. The company purchases the engines it installs in its boats from the Mar-gine Company that specializes in marine engines. Bassone has the following production scheduling for April, May, June, and July:

MONTH	PRODUCTION
April	60
May	85

MONTH	PRODUCTION
June	100
July	120

Mar-gine usually manufactures and ships engines to Bassone during the month the engines are due. However, from April through July Mar-gine has a large order with another boat customer and it can only manufacture 40 engines in April, 60 in May, 90 in June, and 50 in July. Mar-gine has several alternative ways to meet Bassone's production schedule. It can produce up to 30 engines in January, February, and March and carry them in inventory at a cost of $50 per engine per month until it ships them to Bassone. For example, Mar-gine could build an engine in January and ship it to Bassone in April incurring $150 in inventory charges. Mar-gine can also manufacture up to 20 engines in the month they are due on an overtime basis with an additional cost of $400 per engine. Mar-gine wants to determine the least costly production schedule that will meet Bassone's schedule.

a. Formulate and solve a linear programming model for this problem.
b. If Mar-gine is able to increase its production capacity in January, February, and March from 30 to 40 engines, what would be the effect on the optimal solution?

S14.32. Far North Outfitters is a retail phone-catalog company that specializes in outdoor clothing and equipment. A phone station at the company will be staffed with either full-time operators or temporary operators 8 hours per day. Full-time operators, because of their experience and training, process more orders and make fewer mistakes than temporary operators. However, temporary operators are cheaper because of a lower wage rate, and they are not paid benefits. A full-time operator can process about 360 orders per week, whereas a temporary operator can process about 270 orders per week. A full-time operator will average 1.1 defective orders per week, and a part-time operator will incur about 2.7 defective orders per week. The company wants to limit defective orders to 200 per week. The cost of staffing a station with full-time operators is $610 per week, and the cost of a station with part-time operators is $450 per week. Using historical data and forecasting techniques, the company has developed estimates of phone orders for an eight-week period as follows:

WEEKS	ORDERS	WEEKS	ORDERS
1	19,500	5	33,400
2	21,000	6	29,800
3	25,600	7	27,000
4	27,200	8	31,000

The company does not want to hire or dismiss full-time employees after the first week (i.e., the company wants a constant group of full-time operators over the eight-week period). The company wants to determine how many full-time operators it needs and how many temporary operators to hire each week in order to meet weekly demand while minimizing labor costs.

a. Formulate and solve a linear programming model for this problem.
b. Far North Outfitters is going to alter its staffing policy. Instead of hiring a constant group of full-time operators for the entire eight-week planning period, it has decided to hire and add full-time operators as the eight-week period progresses, although once it hires full-time operators it will not dismiss them. Reformulate the linear programming model to reflect this altered policy and solve to determine the cost savings (if any).

S14.33. The Big Max grocery store sells three brands of milk in half-gallon cartons—its own brand, a local dairy brand, and a national brand. The profit from its own brand is $0.97 a carton, the profit from the local dairy brand is $0.83 per carton, and the profit from the national brand is $0.69 per carton. The total refrigerated shelf space allotted to half-gallon cartons of milk is 36 square feet per week. A half-gallon carton takes up 16 square inches of shelf space. The store manager knows that they always sell more of the national brand than the local dairy brand and their own brand combined each week, and they always sell at least three times as much of the national brand as their own brand each week. In addition, the local dairy can supply only 10 dozen cartons per week. The store manager wants to know how many half-gallon cartons of each brand to stock each week in order to maximize profit.

Formulate and solve a linear programming model for this problem.

a. If Big Max could increase its shelf space for half-gallon cartons of milk, how much would profit increase per carton?
b. If Big Max could get the local dairy to increase the amount of milk it could supply each week, would it increase profit?
c. Big Max is considering discounting its own brand in order to increase sales. If it does so, it would decrease the profit margin for its own brand to $0.86 per carton but it would cut the demand for the national brand relative to its own brand in half. Discuss whether or not the store should implement the price discount.

S14.34. John Davis owns Eastcoasters, a bicycle shop in Millersville. Most of John's bicycle sales are customer orders; however, he also stocks bicycles for walk-in customers. He stocks three types of bicycles—road racing, cross country, and mountain. The cost of a road racing bike is $1200, a cross-country bike costs $1700, and a mountain bike costs $900. He sells road racing bikes for $1800, cross-country bikes for $2100, and mountain bikes for $1200. He has $12,000 available this month to purchase bikes. Each bike must be assembled; a road racing bike requires 8 hours to assemble, a cross-country bike requires 12 hours, and a mountain bike requires 16 hours. He estimates that he and his employees have 120 hours available to assemble bikes. He has enough space in his store to order 20 bikes this month. Based on past sales, John wants to stock at least twice as many mountain bikes as the other two combined because they sell better.

Formulate and solve a linear programming model for this problem.

a. Should John try to increase his budget for purchasing bikes, get more space to stock bikes, or get additional labor hours to assemble bikes? Why?
b. If, in (a), John hired an additional worker for 30 hours at $10/hr, how much additional profit would he make, if any?
c. If John purchased a cheaper cross-country bike for $1200 and sold it for $1900 would it affect the original solution?

S14.35. The Townside Food Services Company delivers fresh sandwiches each morning to vending machines throughout the city. Workers assemble sandwiches from previously prepared ingredients through the night for morning delivery. The company makes three kinds of sandwiches: ham and cheese, bologna, and chicken salad. A ham and cheese sandwich requires a worker 0.45 minute to assemble, a bologna sandwich requires 0.41 minute, and a chicken salad sandwich 0.50 minute to make. The company has 960 available minutes each night for sandwich assembly. The company has available vending machine capacity for 2000 sandwiches each day. The profit for a ham and cheese sandwich is $0.35, the profit for a bologna sandwich is $0.42, and the profit for a chicken salad sandwich is $0.37. The company knows from past sales records that their customers buy as many or more of the ham and cheese sandwiches than the other two sandwiches combined, but they need to have a variety of sandwiches available, so they stock at least 200 of each. Townside management wants to know how many of each sandwich it should stock in order to maximize profit.

Formulate and solve a linear programming model for this problem.

a. If Townside Food Service could hire another worker and increase its available assembly time by 480 minutes, or increase its vending machine capacity by 100 sandwiches, which should it do? Why? How much additional profit would your decision result in?

b. What would be the effect on the optimal solution if the requirement that at least 200 sandwiches of each kind be stocked was eliminated? Compare the profit between the optimal solution and this solution, and indicate which solution you would recommend.

c. What would be the effect on the optimal solution if the profit for a ham and cheese sandwich was increased to \$0.40? \$0.45?

S14.36. The admissions office at State University wants to develop a planning model for next year's entering freshman class. The university has 4500 available openings for freshman. Tuition is \$8600 for an in-state student and \$19,200 for an out-of-state student. The university wants to maximize the money it receives from tuition, but by state mandate it can admit no more than 47% out-of-state students. Also, each college in the university must have at least 30% in-state students in its freshman class. In order to be ranked in several national magazines, it wants the freshman class to have an average SAT score of 1150. Following are the average SAT scores for last year's freshman class for in-state and out-of-state students in each college in the university, plus the maximum size of the freshman class for each college.

	AVERAGE SAT SCARES		
COLLEGE	IN-STATE	OUT-OF-STATE	TOTAL CAPACITY
1. Architecture	1350	1460	470
2. Arts & Sciences	1010	1050	1300
3. Agriculture	1020	1110	240
4. Business	1090	1180	820
5. Engineering	1360	1420	1060
6. Human Resources	1000	1400	610

a. Formulate and solve a linear programming model that will determine the number of in-state and out-of-state students that should enter each college.

b. If the solution in part (a) does not achieve the maximum freshman class size, discuss how you might adjust the model to reach this class size.

S14.37. Vantage Systems is a consulting firm that develops e-commerce systems and websites for its clients. It has six available consultants and eight client projects under contract. The consultants have different technical abilities and experience, and as a result the company charges different hourly rates for their services. Also, the consultants' skills are more suited for some projects than for others, and clients sometimes prefer some consultants over others. The suitability of a consultant for a project is rated according to a five-point scale, where 1 is the worst and 5 is the best. The following table shows the rating for each consultant for each project as well as the hours available for each consultant, and the contracted hours and maximum budget for each project.

		PROJECT								
CONSULTANT	HOURLY RATE	*1*	*2*	*3*	*4*	*5*	*6*	*7*	*8*	AVAILABLE HOURS
A	\$155	3	3	5	5	3	3	3	3	450
B	140	3	3	7	5	5	5	3	3	600
C	165	2	1	3	3	2	1	5	3	500
D	300	1	3	1	1	2	2	5	1	300
E	270	3	1	1	2	2	1	3	3	710
F	150	4	5	3	2	3	5	4	3	860
Project Hour		500	240	400	475	350	460	290	200	
Contract Budget (\$1000s)		100	80	120	90	65	85	50	55	

The company wants to know how many hours to assign each consultant to each project that will best utilize the consultants' skills while meeting the clients' needs.

a. Formulate and solve a linear programming model for this problem.

b. If the company's objective is to maximize revenue while ignoring client preferences and consultant compatibility, will this change the solution in (b)?

S14.38. East Coast Airlines operates a hub at the Pittsburgh International Airport. During the summer, the airline schedules seven flights daily from Pittsburgh to Orlando and ten flights daily from Orlando to Pittsburgh according to the following schedule.

FLIGHT	LEAVE PITTSBURGH	ARRIVE ORLANDO	FLIGHT	LEAVE ORLANDO	ARRIVE PITTSBURGH
1	6 A.M.	9 A.M.	A	6 A.M.	9 A.M.
2	8 A.M.	11 A.M.	B	7 A.M.	10 A.M.
3	9 A.M.	Noon	C	8 A.M.	11 A.M.
4	3 P.M.	6 P.M.	D	10 A.M.	1 P.M.
5	5 P.M.	8 P.M.	E	Noon	3 P.M.
6	7 P.M.	10 P.M.	F	2 P.M.	5 P.M.
7	8 P.M.	11 P.M.	G	3 P.M.	6 P.M.
			H	6 P.M.	9 P.M.
			I	7 P.M.	10 P.M.
			J	9 P.M.	Midnight

The flight crews live in Pittsburgh or Orlando, and each day a new crew must fly one flight from Pittsburgh to Orlando and one flight from Orlando to Pittsburgh. A crew must return to its home city at the end of each day. For example, if a crew originates in Orlando and flies a flight to Pittsburgh, it must then be scheduled for a return flight from Pittsburgh back to Orlando. A crew must have at least one hour between flights at the city where it arrives. Some scheduling combinations are not possible; for example, a crew on flight 1 from Pittsburgh cannot return on flights A, B, or C from Orlando. It is also possible for a flight to ferry one additional crew to a city in order to fly a return flight, if there are not enough crews in that city.

The airline wants to schedule its crews in order to minimize the total amount of crew ground time (i.e., the time the crew is on the ground between flights). Excessive ground time for a crew lengthens its work day, is bad for crew morale, and is expensive for the airline. Formulate a linear programming model to determine a flight schedule for the airline and solve using Excel. How many crews need to be based in each city? How much ground time will each crew experience?

S14.39. The National Cereal Company produces a Light-Snak cereal package with a selection of small pouches of four different cereals—Crunchies, Toasties, Snakmix, and Granolies. Each cereal is produced at a single production facility and then shipped to three packaging facilities where the four different cereal pouches are combined into a single box. The boxes are then sent to one of three distribution centers where they are combined to fill customer orders and shipped. The diagram shows the weekly flow of the product through the production, packaging, and distribution facilities (referred to as a supply chain).

Ingredients capacities (per 1000 pouches) per week are shown along branches 1–2, 1–3, 1–4, and 1–5. For example, ingredients for 60,000 pouches are available at the production facility as shown on branch 1–2. The weekly production capacity at each plant (in 1000s of pouches) is shown at nodes 2, 3, 4, and 5. The packaging facilities at nodes 6, 7, and 8 and the distribution centers at nodes 9, 10, and 11 have capacities for boxes (1000s) as shown.

The various production, packaging and distribution costs per unit at each facility are shown in the following table.

FACILITY	2	3	4	5	6	7	8	9	10	11
Unit cost	$0.17	0.20	0.18	0.16	0.26	0.29	0.27	0.12	0.11	0.14

Weekly demand for the Light-Snak product is 37,000 boxes.

Formulate and solve a linear programming model that indicates how much product is produced at each facility that will meet weekly demand at the minimum cost.

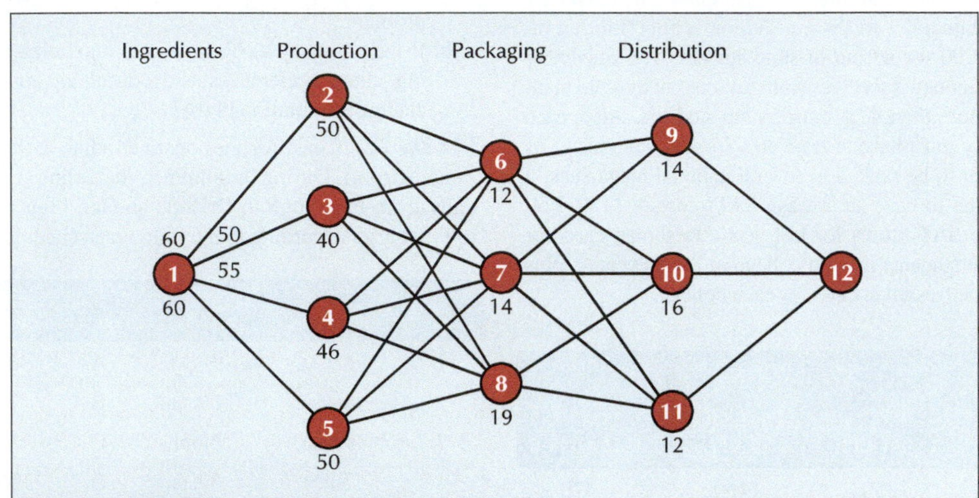

S14.40. Annie's Barbecue Restaurant prepares two primary food items fresh each morning, pulled pork barbecue and beef brisket barbecue, which are sold as a part of different menu items, including sandwiches and barbecue plates with a variety of different sides. The maximum amount of barbecue it has ever sold in a day is 250 lbs. and the least amount is 120 lbs. It generally sells twice as much pork barbecue as beef barbecue, and as little as 20% more pork than beef. The restaurant's meat supplier delivers 150 lbs. of pork and 110 lbs. of beef each daily. Regardless of how it is served on the menu, the restaurant makes a profit of about $8.65 per lb. of pork barbecue and $10.95 per pound for beef barbecue. The restaurant wants to know how many lbs. of each type of barbecue to cook each day in order to maximize profit.

a. Formulate and solve a linear programming model for this problem.

b. If Annie's could get additional pork or beef from the meat supplier, which should it get? Why?

c. If the restaurant orders 10 more lbs. of beef from its supplier, how much would this increase its profit? Is this something it should do?

d. If the restaurant reduces the price of its pork BBQ menu items such that the profit from pork BBQ is $7.50 per lb., it believes it could sell two and a half times more pork than beef BBQ. Is this something they should do?

S14.41. MidSouth Tool Company produces an aircraft part. The company can produce the part entirely at a flexible work center with computerized machines. The company has four work centers, all of which have different machines. Each work center has a single operator; however, the company's operators have different skill levels and levels of experience with the machines, resulting in different levels of daily output and product quality. The following tables show the average daily output and average number of defects per day for each of the company's five operators at each of the work centers.

	AVERAGE DAILY OUTPUT PER CENTER			
OPERATOR	A	B	C	D
1	18	20	21	17
2	19	15	22	18
3	20	20	17	19
4	24	21	16	23
5	22	19	21	21

	AVERAGE NUMBER OF DEFECTS DAILY PER CENTER			
OPERATOR	A	B	C	D
1	0.3	0.9	0.6	0.4
2	0.8	0.5	1.1	0.7
3	1.1	1.3	0.6	0.8
4	1.2	0.8	0.6	0.9
5	1.0	0.9	1.0	1.0

The company wants to determine which operator to assign to each machine to maximize daily output and keep the percentage of defects to less than 4%. Formulate and solve this problem.

S14.42. National Parcel Service (NPS) has determined that it needs to add several new package distribution hubs to service 12 Eastern U.S. cities. The company wants to construct the minimum set of new hubs so that there is a hub within 300 miles of each city.

CITY	CITIES WITHIN 300 MILES
1. Atlanta	Atlanta, Charlotte, Nashville
2. Boston	Boston, New York
3. Charlotte	Atlanta, Charlotte, Richmond
4. Cincinnati	Cincinnati, Detroit, Indianapolis, Nashville, Pittsburgh
5. Detroit	Cincinnati, Detroit, Indianapolis, Milwaukee, Pittsburgh
6. Indianapolis	Cincinnati, Detroit, Indianapolis, Milwaukee, Nashville, St. Louis
7. Milwaukee	Detroit, Indianapolis, Milwaukee
8. Nashville	Atlanta, Cincinnati, Indianapolis, Nashville, St. Louis
9. New York	Boston, New York, Richmond
10. Pittsburgh	Cincinnati, Detroit, Pittsburgh, Richmond
11. Richmond	Charlotte, New York, Pittsburgh, Richmond
12. St. Louis	Indianapolis, Nashville, St. Louis

Formulate and solve this problem.

S14.43. The Midlands Produce Company is a food distributor that wants to construct new warehouse-distribution centers in some of the cities where it has grocery store customers, which will also serve stores in the other cities where it doesn't have distribution centers. A distribution center can effectively service all stores within a 300-mile radius. The company also wants to limit its fixed annual costs to less than $900,000. The following table shows the cities within 300 miles of every city, and the projected fixed annual charge for a distribution center in each city.

CITY	ANNUAL FIXED CHARGE ($1,000s)	CITIES WITHIN 300 MILES
1. Atlanta	276	Atlanta, Charlotte, Nashville
2. Charlotte	253	Atlanta, Charlotte, Richmond
3. Cincinnati	394	Cincinnati, Cleveland, Indianapolis, Louisville, Nashville, Pittsburgh
4. Cleveland	408	Cincinnati, Cleveland, Indianapolis, Pittsburgh
5. Indianapolis	282	Cincinnati, Cleveland, Indianapolis, Louisville, Nashville, St. Louis
6. Louisville	365	Cincinnati, Indianapolis, Louisville, Nashville, St. Louis
7. Nashville	268	Atlanta, Cincinnati, Indianapolis, Louisville, Nashville, St. Louis
8. Pittsburgh	323	Cincinnati, Cleveland, Pittsburgh, Richmond
9. Richmond	385	Charlotte, Pittsburgh, Richmond
10. St. Louis	298	Indianapolis, Louisville, Nashville, St. Louis

a. Determine the locations of the minimum number of stores Midlands will have to build to serve all ten cities in its supply chain network.

b. What is the solution if the cost constraint is removed from the model formulation? What is the difference in cost?

S14.44. CableCast TV provides cable television and Internet service for a college town in Virginia. Its service staff is sufficient to handle installations and hookups for almost the entire year, except for the month-long period right before and during the beginning of fall semester in August, when all the students return. CableCast is overwhelmed and must bring in an additional 14 technicians from other company service areas. The following table shows the number of technicians who can be loaned from seven other service area offices; the mileages from the other service area cities to the town; and the cost for relocating a technician for one month, which includes monthly salary and a bonus. (The national CableCast office incurs this monthly cost).

CITY	RICHMOND	CHARLOTTE	ATLANTA	GREENSBORO	D.C.	NASHVILLE	NORFOLK
Available technicians	4	3	5	2	6	3	2
Mileage	211	173	410	152	263	414	302
Cost ($)	3400	3920	4760	3560	4980	4050	3240

Since most of the technicians will commute to their homes at least once a week for a few days, the company wants to minimize the total distance incurred by its employees, although it would also like to keep its labor costs to $60,000 or less.

a. Formulate and solve a linear programming model for this problem.

b. If CableCast wants to minimize its cost and not the mileage, how would it affect the solution?

S14.45. Ballmart is a retail store chain with 175 stores around the country. It is planning to undertake several sustainability (i.e., "green") projects; it has been shown that sustainability projects can have a positive impact on cost (especially energy) savings and can generate positive media exposure. The projects being considered include installing solar panels at some or all of its stores, or installing small wind turbines; replacing some or all of Ballmart's 165 trucks with more fuel-efficient hybrid trucks; waste reduction, including recycling; and the reduction of plastic bags in their stores. The costs for these projects, the resulting reduction in GHG emissions, the energy savings, and the annual costs savings are shown in the following table.

	SUSTAINABLE PROJECTS				
	SOLAR POWER	WIND POWER	SHIPPING/ VEHICLES	WASTE/ RECYCLING	PLASTIC BAGS
Media/ public relations score	3	2	1	1	2
Cost ($)	$2,600,000	950,000	38,000	365,000	175,000
GHG reductions (metric tons per year)	17,500	8,600	25	1,700	900
Cost savings ($)	220,000	125,000	26,000	75,000	45,000
Energy savings (kWh)	400,000	150,000	34,000	1,200	55,000
Units	75	75	165	75	75

The "media public/relations score" in this table designates the importance of a particular project relative to the other projects in generating public awareness and publicity. For example, a score of "3" indicates that the solar power project will have the greatest public impact. However, Ballmart believes it will require a threshold number of projects to make an impact; specifically, a solar power installation for at least one store, wind power projects at three stores, at least ten new trucks, at least two waste/recycling store projects, and at least six stores with plastic bag projects. $30 million has been budgeted for sustainable projects, and Ballmart wants to achieve GHG emission reductions of at least 250,000 metric tons per year; annual cost savings of at least $4 million; and annual energy savings of at least 5 million kilowatt hours (kWh); while maximizing the public relations impact of its sustainability program.

a. Formulate and solve a linear programming model to determine how many projects of each type should be undertaken.

b. Reformulate and solve the model to maximize savings and not consider the media/public relations impact at all.

S14.46. Grove Food Products Company has contracted with apple growers in Wisconsin, Iowa, and Virginia to purchase apples, which the company then ships to its plants in Ohio and Alabama where it is processed into apple juice. Each bushel of apples will produce two gallons of apple juice. The juice is canned and bottled at the plants and shipped by rail and truck to warehouse/distribution centers in Pennsylvania, Tennessee, and North Carolina. The shipping costs per bushel from the farms to the plants and the shipping costs per gallon from the plants to the distribution centers are summarized in the following tables.

	PLANT		
FARM	4. OHIO	5. ALABAMA	SUPPLY (BUSHELS)
1. Wisconsin	.42	.56	27,000
2. Iowa	.39	.44	16,000
3. Virginia	.52	.61	35,000
Plant Capacity	45,000	34,000	

PLANT	6. PENNSYLVANIA	7. TENNESSEE	8. NORTH CAROLINA
4. Ohio	.24	.12	.21
5. Alabama	.16	.18	.19
Demand (gals)	10,000	14,000	16,000

Formulate and solve a linear programming model to determine the optimal shipments from the farms to the plants and from the plants to the distribution centers that will minimize total shipping costs.

S14.47. Valley Electric Company generates electrical power at four coal-fired power plants in Pennsylvania, West Virginia, Kentucky, and Virginia. The company purchases coal from six producers in southwestern Virginia, West Virginia, and Kentucky. Valley Electric has fixed contracts for coal delivery from the following three coal producers:

COAL PRODUCER	TONS	COST ($/TON)	MILLION BTUs/TON
APCO	180,000	24	27.2
Balfour	315,000	27	28.1
Cannon	340,800	26	26.6

The power-producing capabilities of the coal produced by these suppliers differs according to the quality of the coal. For example, coal produced by APCO provides 27.2 million BTUs per ton while coal produced at Balfour provides 28.1 million BTUs per ton. Valley Electric also purchases coal from three back-up auxiliary suppliers as needed (i.e., it does not have fixed contracts with these producers). In general, the coal from these back-up suppliers is more costly and lower grade:

COAL PRODUCER	AVAILABLE TONS	COST ($/TON)	MILLION BTUs/TON
Denton	115,000	33	22.4
ESCO	105,000	28	19.7
Frampton	185,000	36	24.6

The demand for electricity at Valley Electric's four power plants is as follows. (Note that it requires approximately 10 million BTUs to generate 1 MW hr):

POWER PLANT	ELECTRICITY DEMAND (MILLION BTUs)
1. Alton	4,700,000
2. Sandstone	6,300,000
3. Devon	5,600,000
4. Baytown	7,400,000

For example, the Alton plant must produce at least 4,700,000 million BTUs next year, which translates to approximately 470,000 megawatt hours.

Coal is primarily transported from the producers to the power plants by rail and the cost of processing coal at each is different. Following are the combined transportation and processing costs for coal from each supplier to each plant.

	POWER PLANT			
COAL PRODUCER	1. ALTON	2. SANDSTONE	3. DEVON	4. BAYTOWN
APCO	$12.10	14.35	11.25	15.05
Balfour	10.95	13.75	11.65	14.55
Cannon	15.15	16.75	12.70	12.10
Denton	14.35	11.80	16.15	11.45
ESCO	12.75	9.85	10.25	9.75
Baytown	16.55	14.75	13.60	14.70

Formulate and solve a linear programming model to determine how much coal should be purchased and shipped from each supplier to each power plant in order to minimize cost.

S14.48. The Metro Soccer Club has 16 boys and girls travel soccer teams. The club has access to three town fields which its teams practice on in the fall during the season. Field 1 is large enough to accommodate two teams at one time, and field 3 can accommodate three teams, while field 2 only has enough room for one team. The teams practice twice per week, either on Monday and Wednesday from 3 to 5 or 5 to 7, or on Tuesday and Thursday from 3 to 5 or 5 to 7. Field 3 is in the worst condition of all the fields so teams generally prefer the other fields, and teams also do not like to practice there because it can get crowded with three teams. In general, the younger teams like to practice right after school while the older teams like to practice later in the day. In addition, some teams must practice later because their coaches are only available after work. Some teams may also prefer a specific field because it's closer to their player's homes. Each team has been asked by the club coordinator to select three practice locations and times in priority order, and they have responded as follows.

	PRIORITY		
TEAM	1	2	3
U11B	2, 3-5M	1, 3-5M	3, 3-5M
U11G	1, 3-5T	2, 3-5T	3, 3-5T
U12B	2, 3-5T	1, 3-5T	3, 3-5T
U12G	1, 3-5M	1, 3-5T	2, 3-5M
U13B	2, 3-5T	2, 3-5M	1, 3-5M
U13G	1, 3-5M	2, 3-5M	1, 3-5T
U14B	1, 5-7M	1, 5-7T	2, 5-7T
U14G	2, 3-5M	1, 3-5M	2, 3-5T
U15B	1, 5-7T	2, 5-7T	1, 5-7M
U15G	2, 5-7M	1, 5-7M	1, 5-7T
U16B	1, 5-7T	2, 5-7T	3, 5-7T
U16G	2, 5-7T	1, 5-7T	3, 5-7T
U17B	2, 5-7M	1, 5-7T	1, 5-7M
U17G	1, 5-7T	2, 5-7T	1, 5-7M
U18B	2, 5-7M	2, 5-7T	1, 5-7M
U18G	1, 5-7M	1, 5-7T	2, 5-7T

For example, the under-11 boys team has selected field 2 from 3 to 5 on Monday and Wednesday as their top priority, field 1 from 3 to 5 on Monday and Wednesday as their second priority, and so on.

Formulate and solve a linear programming model that will optimally assign the teams to fields and times according to their priorities. Were any of the teams not assigned to one of their top three selections? If not, how might you modify or use the model to assign these teams to the best possible and location? How could you make sure that the model does not assign teams to unacceptable locations and times—for example, a team whose coach can only be at practice at 5?

S14.49. The NetRoad Trucking Company participates in an Internet transportation exchange where customers advertise their shipments including load weight and volume and trip origin and destination. NetRoad then computes the cost and time of the trip and determines the bid it should make for the shipment to achieve a certain profit level. Twelve customers have posted shipments on the exchange and NetRoad has 3 trucks available for shipments. Each truck has a load capacity of 80,000 lbs. and 5,500 ft^3 and available driving time of 90 hours. The following table shows the load parameters (i.e., weight in lbs and volume in ft^3) for each customer shipment and the profit NetRoad would realize from each shipment.

CUSTOMER	PROFIT ($)	LOAD (LBS)	LOAD (FT^3)	TIME (HOURS)
1	20,000	44,000	1,600	51
2	17,000	39,000	2,100	22
3	15,000	24,000	3,200	45
4	7,000	33,000	3,700	36
5	18,000	18,000	4,400	110
6	12,000	21,000	2,900	105
7	5,000	15,000	1,100	44
8	4,600	19,000	1,600	56
9	11,000	23,000	800	60
10	6,200	36,000	1,800	25
11	14,000	55,000	3,700	37
12	9,000	45,000	2,900	41

Formulate and solve a linear programming model to determine which customer shipments NetRoad should bid on in order to maximize profit.

S14.50. The NetRoad Trucking Company based in Charlotte has 8 trucks located throughout the southeast that have delivered their loads and are available for shipments. Through their Internet logistics site NetRoad has received shipping requests from 12 customers. The following table shows the mileage for a truck to travel to a customer location, pick up the load, and deliver it.

TRUCK	A	B	C	D	E	F	G	H	I	J	K	L
1	500	730	620	410	550	600	390	480	670	710	440	590
2	900	570	820	770	910	660	650	780	840	950	590	670
3	630	660	750	540	680	750	810	560	710	1200	490	650
4	870	1200	810	670	710	820	1200	630	700	900	540	620
5	950	910	740	810	630	590	930	650	840	930	460	560
6	1100	860	800	590	570	550	780	610	1300	840	550	790
7	610	710	910	550	810	730	910	720	850	760	580	630
8	560	690	660	640	720	670	830	690	880	1000	710	680

Determine the optimal assignment of trucks to customers that will minimize the total mileage.

S14.51. In Problem S14.50, assume that the customers have the following truck capacity loads:

	CUSTOMER											
	A	B	C	D	E	F	G	H	I	J	K	L
Capacity	89	78	94	82	90	83	88	79	71	96	78	85

Determine the optimal assignment of trucks to customers that will minimize total mileage while also achieving at last an average truck load capacity of 85%. Does this load capacity requirement significantly increase the total mileage?

S14.52. Mill Mountain Coffee Company currently operates 12 coffee shops in downtown Charlotte. The company has been losing money and wants to downsize by closing some stores. Its policy has been to saturate the downtown area with stores so that one is virtually always in sight of a potential or current customer. However, the company's new policy is to have enough stores so that each is within 5 minutes' walking distance of another store. The company would also like to have annual operating costs of no more than $900,000.

The following table shows the coffee shops within 5 minutes' walking distance of another shop and the average annual cost of the existing stores:

STORE LOCATION	ANNUAL AVERAGE OPERATING COST ($)	STORES WITHIN 5 MINUTES' WALKING DISTANCE
1. 3rd Street	456	3rd Street, Rose Street
2. 10th Street	207	10th Street, South Street, Broad Street
3. South Street	139	South Street, Hill Street, 10th Street
4. Mulberry Avenue	246	Mulberry Avenue, Beamer Boulevard
5. Rose Street	177	Rose Street, 3rd Street, Church Street
6. Wisham Avenue	212	Wisham Avenue, Broad Street
7. Richmond Road	195	Richmond Road, Broad Street
8. Hill Street	170	Hill Street, South Street
9. 23rd Avenue	184	23rd Avenue, Wisham Avenue
10. Broad Street	163	Broad Street, Wisham Avenue, Richmond Road, 10th Street
11. Church Street	225	Church Street, Rose Street, Beamer Boulevard
12. Beamer Boulevard	236	Beamer Boulevard, Mulberry Avenue, Church Street

Formulate and solve a linear programming model that will select the minimum number of stores the company will need to achieve its new policy objective.

S14.53. The town of Burlington has recently purchased a 55-acre tract of farm land and it has $550,000 budgeted to develop recreational facilities. The impetus for the purchase was the need for soccer fields to meet the increasing demand of youth soccer in the area. However, once the land was purchased a number of other interest groups began to lobby the town council to develop other recreational facilities including rugby, football, softball and baseball fields, plus walking and running trails, a children's playground, and a dog park. The table below shows the amount of acreage required by each project, the annual expected usage for each facility, and the cost to construct each facility. Also included is a priority designation determined by the town's recreation committee based on several public hearings and their perceptions of the critical need of each facility.

a. Formulate and solve a linear programming model that will maximize annual usage and achieve an average priority level of no more than 1.75.

b. Reformulate the model such that the objective is to achieve the minimum average priority level while achieving an annual usage of at least 120,000.

c. What combination of facilities will use the maximum acreage available without exceeding the budget and achieving an average priority level of no more than 1.75? What is the annual usage with these facilities?

FACILITY	ANNUAL USAGE (PEOPLE)	ACRES	COST ($)	PRIORITY
Rugby fields	4700	7	75,000	3
Football fields	12,500	12	180,000	2
Soccer fields	32,000	20	350,000	1
Dog park	7500	6	45,000	3
Playground	41,000	3	120,000	2
Walking/Running trails	47,000	25	80,000	1
Softball fields	23,000	5	115,000	2
Baseball fields	16,000	8	210,000	3

S14.54. In the event of a disaster situation at State University from weather, an accident, or terrorism, victims will be transported by emergency vehicles to three area hospitals: County General, Memorial, and All Souls. County General is (on average) 10 minutes away from State, Memorial is 20 minutes away, and All Souls is 35 minutes away. State wants to analyze a hypothetical disaster situation in which there are 15 victims with different types of injuries. The emergency facilities at County General can accommodate, at most, 8 victims; Memorial can handle 10 victims; and All Souls can admit 7 victims. A priority has been assigned for each victim according to the hospital that would best treat that victim's type of injury, as shown in the following table (where 1 reflects the best treatment).

	PATIENT						
HOSPITAL	1	2	3	4	5	6	7
County General	1	1	2	2	2	1	3
Memorial	2	2	3	3	1	3	3
All Souls	3	3	1	1	3	2	1

	PATIENT							
HOSPITAL	8	9	10	11	12	13	14	15
County General	3	3	1	3	3	2	1	3
Memorial	1	1	1	3	3	2	2	3
All Souls	2	2	2	1	1	1	2	1

For example, for victim 1's type of injury, the best hospital is County General, the next best is Memorial, and All Souls is third best.

a. Formulate and solve a linear programming model that will send the victims to the hospital best suited to minister to their specific injuries while keeping the average transport time to 22 minutes or less.

b. Formulate and solve a linear programming model that will minimize the average transport time for victims while achieving an average hospital priority of at least 1.50.

S14.55. Each day Carolina Coastal Food Services makes deliveries to four restaurants it supplies in the metro D.C. area. The service uses one truck that starts at its warehouse and makes a delivery to each restaurant, and then returns to the warehouse. In the following table the warehouse is location 1, and the mileage is shown between it and the restaurants, which are locations 2 through 5.

	LOCATION				
LOCATION	1	2	3	4	5
1	—	10	15	20	40
2	10	—	12	16	24
3	15	12	—	10	20
4	20	16	10	—	16
5	40	24	20	16	—

Formulate and solve a model to determine the route (or tour) the truck should take that will start at the warehouse, visit each restaurant once, and return to the warehouse with the minimum total distance traveled.

Case Problems

Case Problem S14.1 Mosaic Tile Company

Gilbert Moss and Angela Pasaic spent several summers during their college years working at archaeological sites in the Southwest. While at these digs they learned from local artisans how to make ceramic tiles. After college they started a tile manufacturing firm called Mosaic Tiles, Ltd. They opened their plant in New Mexico, where they would have convenient access to a special clay to make a clay derivative for their tiles. Their manufacturing operation consists of a few simple but difficult steps, including molding the tiles, baking, and glazing.

Gilbert and Angela plan to produce two basic types of tile for use in home bathrooms, kitchens, sunrooms, and laundry rooms: a larger single-colored tile; and a smaller patterned tile. In the manufacturing process the color or pattern is added before a tile is glazed. Either a single color or a stenciled pattern is sprayed on the top of a newly baked set of tiles.

The tiles are produced in batches of 100. The first step is to pour the clay derivative into specially constructed molds. It takes 18 minutes to mold a batch of 100 larger tiles and 15 minutes to prepare a mold for a batch of 100 smaller tiles. The company has 60 hours available each week for molding. After the tiles are molded, they are baked in a kiln: 0.27 hour for a batch of 100 larger tiles and 0.58 hour for a batch of 100 smaller tiles. The company has 105 hours available each week for baking. After baking, the tiles are either colored or patterned and glazed. This process takes 0.16 hour for a batch of 100 larger tiles and 0.20 hour for a batch of 100 smaller tiles. Forty hours are available each week for the glazing process. Each batch of 100 large tiles requires 32.8 pounds of the clay derivative to produce, while each batch of smaller tiles requires 20 pounds. The company has 6000 pounds of the clay derivative available each week.

Mosaic Tile earns a profit of $190 for each batch of 100 of the larger tiles and $240 for each batch of 100 smaller patterned tiles. Angela and Gilbert want to know how many batches of each type of tile to produce each week in order to maximize profit. They also have some questions about resource usage they would like you to answer.

a. Formulate a linear programming model for the Mosaic Tile Company to determine the mix of the tiles it should manufacture each week.

b. Transform the model into standard form.

c. Solve the linear programming model graphically.

d. Determine the resources left over and not used at the optimal solution point.

e. For artistic reasons Gilbert and Angela like to produce the smaller patterned tiles best. They also believe in the long run the smaller tiles will be a more successful product. What must be the profit for the smaller tiles in order for the company to produce only the smaller tiles?

f. Solve the linear programming model using Excel.

g. Mosaic believes that it may be able to reduce the time required for molding to 16 minutes for a batch of larger tiles and 12 minutes for a batch of the smaller tiles. How will this affect the solution?

h. The company that provides Mosaic with clay has indicated that it can deliver an additional 100 pounds of clay each week. Should Mosaic agree to this offer?

i. Mosaic is considering adding capacity to one of its kilns to provide 20 additional glazing hours per week at a cost of $90,000. Should it make the investment?

j. The kiln for glazing had to be shut down for three hours, reducing the available kiln hours from 40 to 37. What effect will this have on the solution?

Case Problem S14.2 Summer Sports Camp at State University

Mary Kelly is a scholarship soccer player at State University. During the summer she works at a youth all-sports camp that several of the university's coaches operate. The sports camp runs for eight weeks during July and August. Campers come for a one-week period, during which time they live in the State dormitories and use the State athletic fields and facilities. At the end of a week a new group of kids comes in. Mary serves primarily as one of the camp soccer instructors. However, she has also been placed in charge of arranging for sheets for the beds the campers will sleep on in the dormitories. Mary has been instructed to develop a plan for purchasing and cleaning sheets each week of camp at the lowest possible cost.

Clean sheets are needed at the beginning of each week, and the campers use the sheets all week. At the end of the week the campers strip their beds and place the sheets in large bins. Mary must arrange either to purchase new sheets or clean old sheets. A set of new sheets costs $10. A local laundry has indicated that it will clean a set of sheets for $4. Also, a couple of Mary's friends have asked her to let them clean some of the sheets. They have told her they will charge only $2 for each set of sheets. However, while the laundry will provide cleaned sheets in a week, Mary's friends can only deliver cleaned sheets in two weeks. They are going to summer school and plan to launder the sheets at night at a neighborhood laundromat.

The following number of campers have registered during each of the eight weeks the camp will operate:

WEEK	REGISTERED CAMPERS
1	115
2	210
3	250
4	230
5	260
6	300
7	250
8	190

Based on discussions with camp administrators from previous summers and on some old camp records and receipts, Mary estimates that each week about 20% of the cleaned sheets that are returned will have to be discarded and replaced. The campers spill food and drinks on the sheets, and sometimes the stains will not come out during cleaning. Also, the campers occasionally tear the sheets or the sheets can get torn at the cleaners. In either case, when the sheets come back from the cleaners and are put on the beds, 20% are taken off and thrown away.

At the beginning of the summer, the camp has no sheets available, so initially sheets must be purchased. Sheets are thrown away at the end of the summer.

Mary's major at State is operations management, and she wants to develop a plan for purchasing and cleaning sheets using linear programming. Help Mary formulate a linear programming model for this problem, and solve it using Excel.

Case Problem S14.3 Spring Garden Tools

The Spring family has owned and operated a garden tool and implements manufacturing company since 1952. The company sells garden tools to distributors and also directly to hardware stores and home improvement discount chains. The Spring Company's four most popular small garden tools are a trowel, a hoe, a rake, and a shovel. Each of these tools is made from durable steel and has a wooden handle. The Spring family prides itself on its high-quality tools.

The manufacturing process encompasses two stages. The first stage includes two operations—stamping out the metal tool heads and drilling screw holes in them. The completed tool heads then flow to the second stage. The second stage includes an assembly operation, in which the handles are attached to the tool heads, a finishing step, and finally packaging. The processing times per tool for each operation are provided in the following table:

	TOOL (HOURS/UNIT)				TOTAL HOURS AVAILABLE
OPERATION	TROWEL	HOE	RAKE	SHOVEL	PER MONTH
Stamping	0.04	0.17	0.06	0.12	500
Drilling	0.05	0.14	—	0.14	400
Assembly	0.06	0.13	0.05	0.10	600
Finishing	0.05	0.21	0.02	0.10	550
Packaging	0.03	0.15	0.04	0.15	500

The steel the company uses is ordered from an iron and steel works in Japan. The company has 10,000 square feet of sheet steel available each month. The metal required for each tool and the monthly contracted production volume per tool are provided in the following table:

	SHEET METAL (FT^2)	MONTHLY CONTRACTED SALES
Trowel	1.2	1800
Hoe	1.6	1400
Rake	2.1	1600
Shovel	2.4	1800

The reasons the company has prospered are its ability to meet customer demand on time and its high quality. As a result, the Spring Company will produce on an overtime basis in order to meet its sales requirements, and it also has a longstanding arrangement with a local tool and die company to manufacture its tool heads. The Spring Company feels comfortable subcontracting the first-stage operations, since it is easier to detect defects prior to assembly and finishing. For the same reason, the company will not subcontract for the entire tool, since defects would be particularly hard to detect after the tool is finished and packaged. However, the company does have 100 hours of overtime available each month for each operation in both stages. The regular production and overtime costs per tool for both stages are provided in the following table:

	STAGE 1		STAGE 2	
	REGULAR COST ($)	OVERTIME COST ($)	REGULAR COST ($)	OVERTIME COST ($)
Trowel	6.00	6.20	3.00	3.10
Hoe	10.00	10.70	5.00	5.40
Rake	8.00	8.50	4.00	4.30
Shovel	10.00	10.70	5.00	5.40

The cost of subcontracting in stage 1 adds 20% to the regular production cost.

The Spring Company wants to establish a production schedule for regular and overtime production in each stage and for the number of tool heads subcontracted, at the minimum cost. Formulate a linear programming model for this problem and solve the model using Excel. Which resources appear to be most critical in the production process?

Case Problem S14.4 Walsh's Juice Company

Walsh's Juice Company produces three products from unprocessed grape juice—bottled juice, frozen juice concentrate, and jelly. It purchases grape juice from three vineyards near the Great Lakes. The climate in this area is good for growing the concord grapes necessary to produce grape juice products. The grapes are harvested at the vineyards and immediately converted into juice at plants at the vineyard sites and stored in refrigerated tanks. The juice is then transported to four different plants in Virginia, Michigan, Tennessee, and Indiana, where it is processed into bottled grape juice, frozen concentrated juice, and jelly. Vineyard output typically differs each month in the harvesting season and the plants have different processing capacity.

In a particular month the vineyard in New York has 1400 tons of unprocessed grape juice available, while the vineyard in Ohio has 1700 tons and the vineyard in Pennsylvania has 1100 tons. The processing capacity per month is 1200 tons of unprocessed juice at the plant in Virginia, 1100 tons of juice at the plant in Michigan, 1400 tons at the plant in Tennessee, and 1400 tons at the plant in Indiana. The cost per ton of transporting unprocessed juice from the vineyards to the plant is as follows:

	PLANT			
VINEYARD	VIRGINIA	MICHIGAN	TENNESSEE	INDIANA
New York	$850	720	910	750
Pennsylvania	970	790	1050	880
Ohio	900	830	780	820

The plants are different ages, have different equipment, and have different wage rates; thus, the cost of processing each product at each plant ($/ton) differs as follows:

	PLANT			
VINEYARD	VIRGINIA	MICHIGAN	TENNESSEE	INDIANA
Juice	$2100	2350	2200	1900
Concentrate	4100	4300	3950	3900
Jelly	2600	2300	2500	2800

This month the company needs to process a total of 1200 tons of bottled juice, 900 tons of frozen concentrate, and 700 tons of jelly at the four plants combined. However, the production process for frozen concentrate results in some juice dehydration, and the process for jelly includes a cooking stage that evaporates water content. To process 1 ton of frozen concentrate requires 2 tons of unprocessed juice; a ton of jelly requires 1.5 tons of unprocessed juice; and a ton of bottled juice requires 1 ton of unprocessed juice.

Walsh's management wants to determine how many tons of grape juice to ship from each of the vineyards to each of the plants, and the number of tons of each product to process at each plant. Thus, management needs a model that includes both the logistical aspects of this problem and the production processing aspects. It wants a solution that will minimize total costs, including the cost of transporting grape juice from the vineyards to the plants and the product processing costs. Help Walsh's solve this problem by formulating a linear programming model and solve it using Excel.

Case Problem S14.5 Julia's Food Booth

Julia Robertson is a senior at Tech, and she's investigating different ways to finance her final year at school. In her first three years at school she worked a part-time job at a local bar, but she wants more free time during the week in her senior year to interview for jobs after she graduates, to work on some senior projects, and to have some fun with her friends. She is considering leasing a food booth outside the stadium at the Tech home football games which Tech allows for selected students and student groups. Tech sells out every home game, and she knows from going to the games herself that everyone eats a lot of food. She has to pay \$1000 per game for a booth and the booths are not very large. Vendors can sell only food or drinks on Tech property but not both. Only the Tech athletic department concession stands can sell both inside the stadium. She thinks slices of cheese pizza, hot dogs, and barbecue sandwiches are the most popular food items among fans, so these are the items she would sell.

Most food items are sold during the hour before the game starts and during half time; thus, it will not be possible for Julia to prepare the food while she is selling it. She must prepare the food ahead of time and then store it in a warming oven. She can lease a warming oven for the home season, which includes six games, for \$600. The oven has 16 shelves, and each shelf is 3 ft by 4 ft. She plans to fill the oven with the three food items before the game and before half time.

Julia has negotiated with a local pizza delivery company to deliver 14-inch cheese pizzas twice each game: two hours before the game and right after the opening kickoff. Each pizza will cost her \$6 and will include eight slices. She estimates it will cost her \$0.45 for each hot dog and \$0.90 for each barbecue sandwich if she makes the barbecue herself the night before. She measured a hot dog and found it takes up about 16 in.^{2} of space, while a barbecue sandwich takes up about 25 in.^{2} She plans to sell a slice of pizza and a hot dog for \$1.50 apiece and a barbecue sandwich for \$2.25. She has \$1500 in cash available to purchase and prepare the food items for the first home game; for the remaining five games she will purchase her ingredients with money she has made from the previous game.

Julia has talked to some students and vendors who have sold food at previous football games at Tech as well as at other universities. From this she has discovered that she can expect to sell at least as many slices of pizza as hot dogs and barbecue sandwiches combined. She also anticipates that she will probably sell at least twice as many hot dogs as barbecue sandwiches. She believes that she will sell everything she can stock and develop a customer base for the season if she follows these general guidelines for demand.

If Julia clears at least \$1000 in profit for each game after paying all her expenses, she believes it will be worth leasing the booth.

a. Formulate and solve a linear programming model for Julia that will help you advise her if she should lease the booth.

b. If Julia can borrow some more money from a friend before the first game to purchase more ingredients, could she increase her profit? If so, how much should she borrow and how much additional profit would she make? What factor constrains her from borrowing even more money than this amount (indicated in your answer to the previous question)?

c. When Julia looked at the solution in (a), she realized that it would be physically difficult for her to prepare all the hot dogs and barbecue sandwiches indicated in this solution. She believes she can hire a friend of hers to help her for \$100 per game. Based on the results in (a) and (b), is this something you think she could reasonably do and should do?

d. Julia seems to be basing her analysis on "certain" assumptions that everything will go as she plans. What are some of the uncertain factors in the model that could go wrong and adversely affect Julia's analysis? Given these uncertainties and the results in (a), (b), and (c), what do you recommend that Julia do?

Case Problem S14.6 The Sea Village Amusement Park

Sea Village is a large amusement and water park located on the coast of South Carolina. The park hires high school and college students to work during the summer months of May, June, July, August, and September. The student employees operate virtually all of the highly mechanized, computerized rides; perform as entertainers; perform most of the custodial work during park hours; make up the work force for restaurants, food services, retail shops, and stores; drive trams; and park cars. Park management has assessed their monthly needs based on previous summers' attendance at the park and the expected available work force. Park attendance is relatively low in May until public schools are out, then it increases through June, July, and August, and decreases dramatically in September when schools reopen after Labor Day. The park is open seven days a week through the summer until September when it cuts back to weekends only. Management estimates that it will require 21,000 hours of labor in each of the first two weeks of May, 26,000 hours during the third week of May, and 32,000 hours during the last week in May. During the first two weeks of June, it will require at least 36,000 hours of labor and 41,000 hours during the last two weeks in June. In July, 46,000 hours will be required each week, and in August 47,000 hours will be needed each week. In September, they will only need 14,000 hours in the first week, 12,000 hours in each of the second and third weeks, and 9,000 hours the last week of September.

The park hires new employees each week from the first week in May through August. A new employee mostly trains the first week by observing and helping more experienced employees; however, they do work approximately 10 hours under the supervision of an experienced employee. An employee is considered experienced after completing one week on the job. Experienced employees are considered part-time and are scheduled to work 30 hours per week in order to eliminate overtime and reduce the cost of benefits, and to give more students the opportunity to work. However, no one is ever laid off or will be scheduled for less (or more) than 30 hours, even if more employees are available than needed. Management believes this is a necessary condition of employment because so many of the student employees move to the area during the summer just to work in the park and live near the beach nearby. If these employees were sporadically laid off and were stuck with lease payments and other expenses, it would be bad public relations and hurt employment efforts in future summers. Although no one is laid off, 15% of all experienced employees quit each week for a variety of reasons, including homesickness, illness, and other personal reasons, plus some are asked to leave because of very poor job performance.

Park management is able to start the first week in May with 800 experienced employees who worked in the Park in previous summers and live in the area. They are generally able to work a lot of hours on the weekends and then some during the week; however, in May, attendance is much heavier on the weekend so most of the labor hours are needed then. The park expects to have a pool of 1,600 available applicants to hire for the first week in May. After the first week, the pool is diminished by the number of new employees hired the previous week, but each week through June the park gets 210 new job applicants, which decreases to 120 new applicants each week for the rest of the summer. For example, the available applicant pool in the second week in May would be the previous week's pool, which in week 1 is 1,600, minus the number of new employees hired in week 1, plus 210 new applicants. At the end of the last week in August, 75% of all the experienced employees will quit to go back to school and the park will not hire any new employees in September. The park must operate in September using experienced employees who live in the area, but the weekly attrition rate for these employees in September drops to 12%.

Formulate and solve a linear programming model to assist the park's management to plan and schedule the number of new employees it hires each week that will minimize the total number of new employees it must hire during the summer.

References

Charnes, A., and W. W. Cooper. *Management Models and Industrial Applications of Linear Programming*. New York: John Wiley & Sons, 1961.

Dantzig, G. B. *Linear Programming and Extensions*. Princeton, NJ: Princeton University, 1963.

Gass, S. *Linear Programming*, 4th ed. New York: McGraw-Hill, 1975.

Moore, L. J., S. M. Lee, and B. W. Taylor. *Management Science*, 4th ed. Needham Heights, MA: Allyn and Bacon, 1993.

Taylor, B. W. *Introduction to Management Science*, 6th ed. Upper Saddle River, NJ: Prentice Hall, 1999.

Wagner, A. M. *Principles of Operations Research*, 2nd ed. Upper Saddle River, NJ: Prentice Hall, 1975.

CHAPTER 15

Resource Planning

ullstein bild/Getty Images, Inc.

LEARNING OBJECTIVES

After reading this chapter, you will be able to:

- Discuss the differences between independent and dependent demand systems.
- Describe the inputs and outputs to an MRP system, and execute the MRP process.
- Determine resource capacity and load percent, and perform load leveling on capacitated resources.
- Explain the hierarchical planning process for resources as a closed loop system, and discuss the assumptions on which this process is based.
- Describe basic ERP systems and the scope of their implementations, including the connection to SCM, CRM and PLM.
- Discuss the issues, advantages and drawbacks of the enterprise IT software systems that run today's global businesses.

High Tech Manufacturing Needs ERP

Electronics and high tech industries need sophisticated IT systems to run their businesses and manage their supply chains. Short product life-cycles and new technologies mean revamping processes and sourcing new materials on an ongoing basis. The IT system must keep track of all changes in design and workflow and be able to trace the source of materials, components, and assemblies to lots, locations, machines, and operators throughout the entire production and logistics process. Strict quality control standards are essential for several reasons. First, electronic system failures can have devastating effects on such products as automobiles, medical equipment, communications equipment (see photo), and industrial processes. Second, downtime in high volume manufacturing is costly, as are product recalls and product liability lawsuits. Thus, the IT system must be able to handle real-time defect analysis, the quarantining of defective parts or processes, and continuous vendor compliance.

The manufacturing processes themselves, whether internal or at a supplier's site, must meet strict regulatory requirements as well. Use of conflict materials, proper use and disposal of chemicals, and proper disposal of hazardous waste must be monitored closely. Automated equipment must be programmed to complete assemblies according to scheduled production plans and changing design parameters. Scheduling of customer orders, inventory control, procurement, material traceability, and production tracking must all be taken into account.

The type of IT system that can accomplish the myriad of tasks and assignments is called enterprise resource planning (ERP). ERP and related software systems are the topic of this chapter.

Sources: PLEX Systems, "7 Must-Have ERP Features for High Tech/Electronics Manufacturers," White paper, www.plex.com (accessed January 2, 2016); ABAS, "Why the fast-paced electronics industry relies on ERP systems," posted August 7, 2015, http://abas-erp.com/en/news/why-fast-paced-electronics-industry-relies-erp-systems (accessed January 3, 2016).

Enterprise resource planning (ERP) systems provide the information infrastructure for today's corporations. They bring functions, processes, and resources together to meet customer needs and provide value to shareholders. ERP evolved from more modest versions of manufacturing resource planning aimed at providing material resources and machine/labor resources to support production plans. We begin this chapter by describing the resource planning systems of material requirements planning (MRP) and capacity requirements planning (CRP), and we end with a discussion of the scope and impact of more elaborate ERP systems, with extensions to customers and suppliers.

As a framework for discussion, Figure 15.1 shows the resource planning process from the sales and operations plan to manufacture. Recall that the *sales and operations plan* is for families of items and the *master production schedule* is for individual products. The *material requirements plan* translates the master production schedule into requirements for components, subassemblies, and raw materials. The *capacity requirements plan* converts the material plan into labor and machine requirements. Once the plans have been approved, purchase orders are released to suppliers and work orders are released to the shop. Purchased parts and manufactured parts are assembled in manufacture.

FIGURE 15.1 Resource Planning for Manufacturing

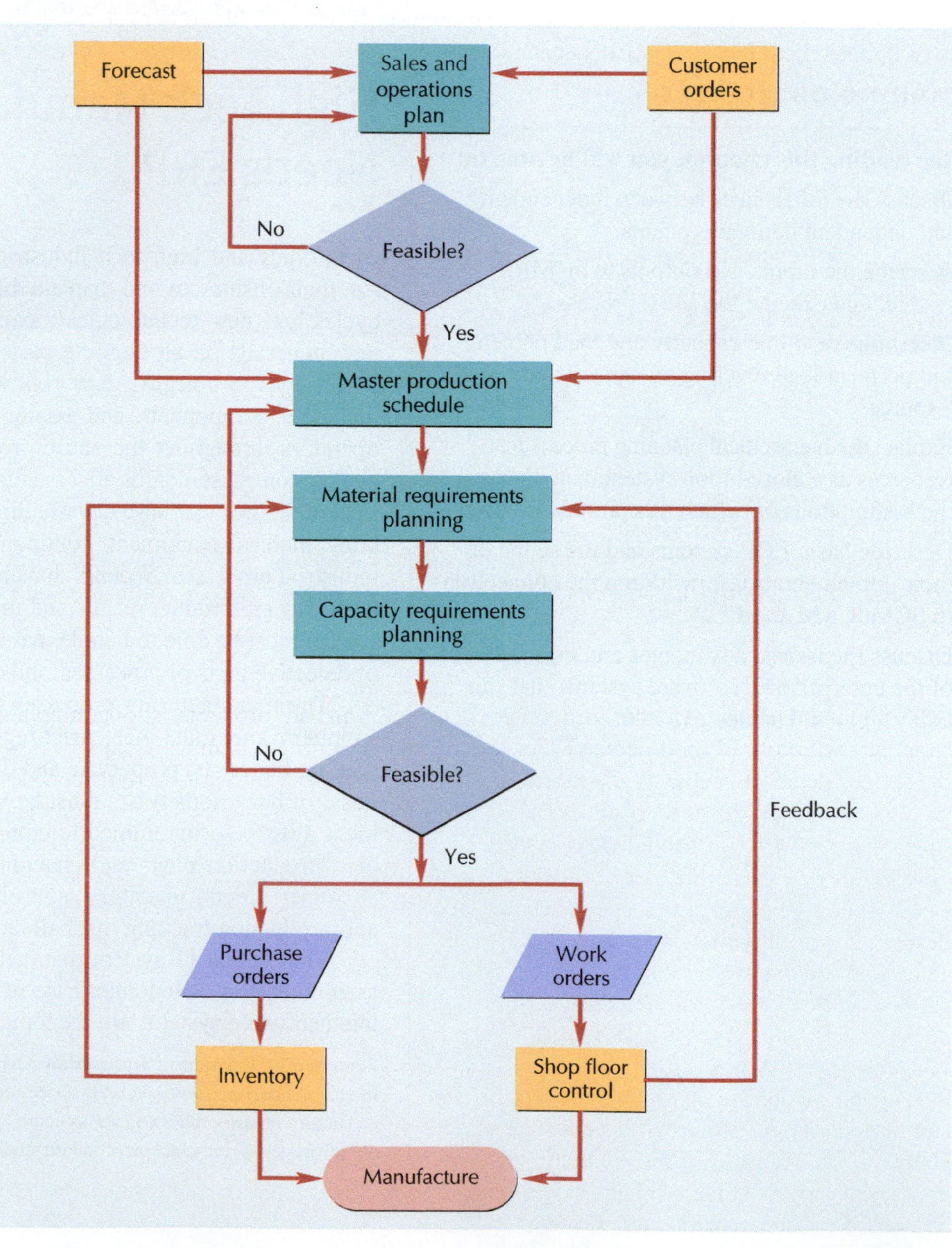

Material Requirements Planning (MRP)

Material requirements planning (MRP) is a computerized inventory control and production planning system. The main objective of any inventory system is to ensure that material is available when needed—which can easily lead to a tremendous investment of funds in unnecessary inventory. One objective of MRP is to maintain the lowest possible level of inventory. MRP does this by determining *when* component items are needed and scheduling them to be ready at that time, no earlier and no later.

Material requirements planning (MRP) A computerized inventory control and production planning system.

MRP was the first inventory system to recognize that inventories of raw materials, components, and finished goods may need to be handled differently. In the process of planning inventory levels for these various types of goods, the system also planned purchasing activities (for raw materials and purchased components), manufacturing activities (for component parts and assemblies), and delivery schedules (for finished products). Thus, the system was more than an inventory control system; it became a production scheduling system as well.

One of the few certainties in a manufacturing environment is that things rarely go as planned—orders arrive late, machines break down, workers are absent, designs are changed, and so on. With its computerized database, MRP is able to keep track of the relationship of job orders so that if a delay in one aspect of production is unavoidable, other related activities can be rescheduled, too. MRP systems have the ability to keep schedules valid and up to date.

When to Use MRP

MRP is useful for dependent and discrete demand items, complex products, job shop production, and assemble-to-order environments. Managing component demand inventory is different from managing finished goods inventory.

Dependent Demand For one thing, the demand for component parts does not have to be forecasted; it can be derived from the demand for the finished product. For example, suppose demand for a table, consisting of four legs and a tabletop, is 100 units per week. Then, demand for tabletops would also be 100 per week, and demand for table legs would be 400 per week. Demand for table legs is totally *dependent* on the demand for tables. The demand for tables may be forecasted, but the demand for table legs is calculated. The tables are an example of *independent demand*. The tabletop and table legs exhibit *dependent demand*.

Discrete Demand Another difference between finished products and component parts is the continuity of their demand. For the inventory control systems in Chapter 13, we assumed that demand occurred at a constant rate. The inventory systems were designed to keep some inventory on hand at all times, enough, we hoped, to meet each day's demand. With component items, demand does not necessarily occur on a continuous basis. Let us assume in our table example that table legs are the last items to be assembled onto the tables before shipping. Also assume that it takes one week to make a batch of tables and that table legs are assembled onto the tabletops every Friday. If we were to graph the demand for table legs, as shown in Figure 15.2, it would be zero for Monday, Tuesday, Wednesday, and Thursday, but on Friday the demand for table legs would jump to 400. The same pattern would repeat the following week. With this scenario, we do not need to keep an inventory of table legs available on Monday through Thursday of any week. We need table legs only on Fridays. Looking at our graph, demand for table legs occurs in *lumps;* it is *discrete*, not continuous. Using an inventory system such as economic order quantity (EOQ) for component items would result in inventory being held that we know will not be needed until a later date. The excess inventory takes up space, soaks up funds, and requires additional resources for counting, sorting, storing, and moving.

FIGURE 15.2 Demand Characteristics for Finished Products and Their Components

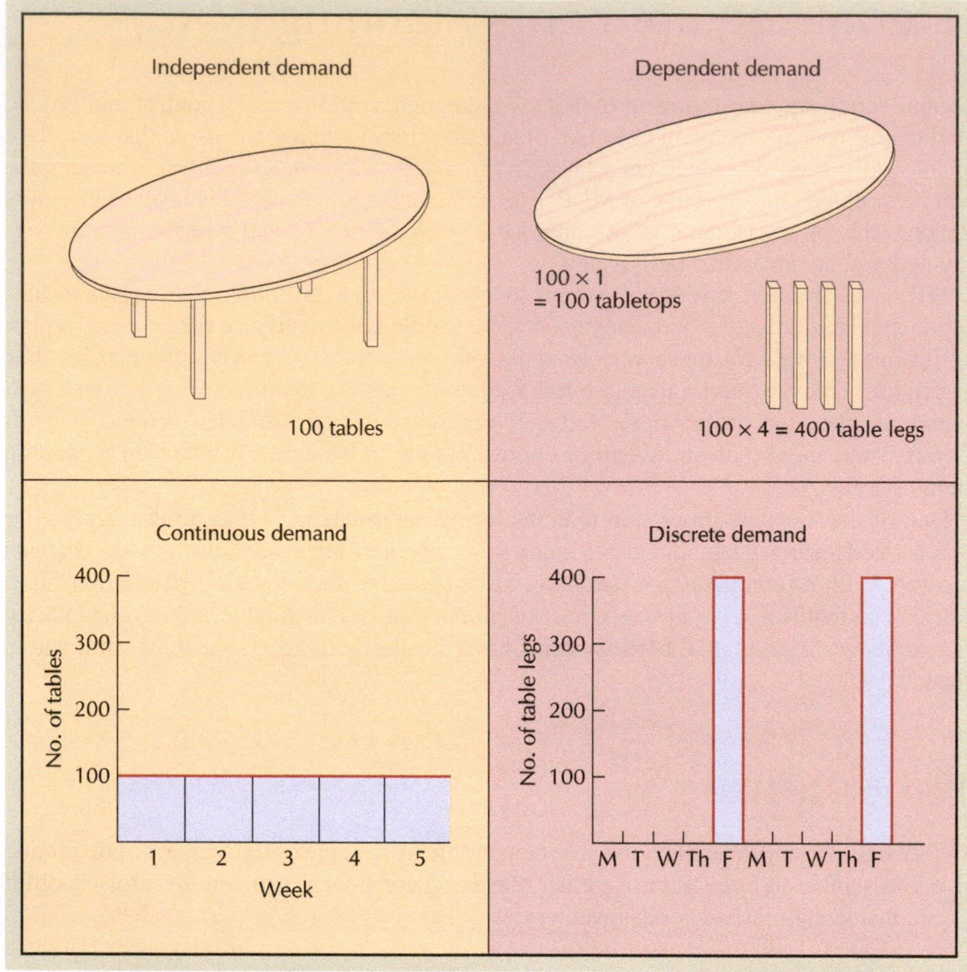

Complex Products Industries that manufacture complex products, requiring the coordination of component production, find MRP especially useful. A complex product may have hundreds of component parts, dozens of assemblies, and several levels of assembly. MRP tries to ensure that multiple components of an assembly are ready at the same time so that they can be assembled together. Products with simple structures do not need MRP to plan production or monitor inventory levels.

Erratic Orders The advantages of MRP are more evident when the manufacturing environment is complex and uncertain. Manufacturing environments in which customer orders are erratic, each job takes a different path through the system, lead time is uncertain, and due dates vary need an information system such as MRP to keep track of the different jobs and coordinate their schedules. The type of environment we are describing is characteristic of *batch*, or *job shop*, processes.[1] Although MRP is currently available for continuous and repetitive manufacturing, it was designed primarily for systems that produce goods in batches.

Assemble-to-Order Finally, MRP systems are very useful in industries in which the customer is allowed to choose among different options. These products have many common components that are inventoried in some form before the customer order is received. For example, customers of a well-known electronics firm routinely expect delivery in six weeks on goods that take 28 weeks to manufacture. The manufacturer copes with this seemingly unrealistic demand by producing major assemblies and subassemblies in advance of the customer order and then completing the product on receipt of the order. This type of operation is called **assemble-to-order** or *build-to-order*.

Assemble-to-order A manufacturing environment in which previously completed subassemblies are configured to order.

[1]For a more thorough discussion of types of processes, see Chapter 6.

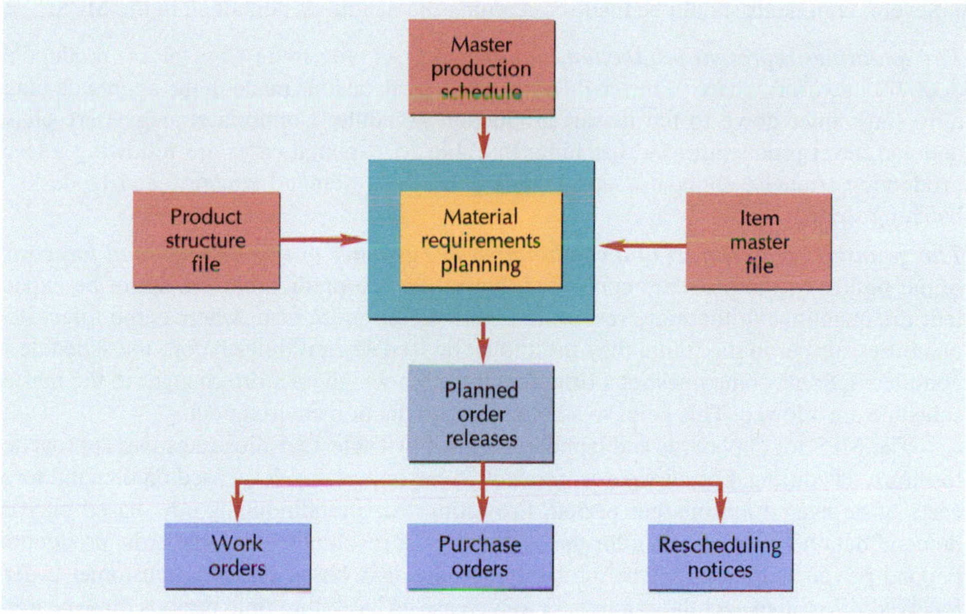

FIGURE 15.3 Material Requirements Planning

Figure 15.3 shows the inputs to and outputs from the MRP process. There are three major inputs:

- Master production schedule
- Product structure file
- Item master file

Master Production Schedule

The **master production schedule (MPS),** also called the *master schedule*, specifies which end items or finished products a firm is to produce, how many are needed, and when they are needed. Recall that the sales and operations plan is a similar schedule for product lines or families, given by months or quarters of a year. The master production schedule works within the constraints of the aggregate production plan but produces a more specific schedule by individual products. The time frame is more specific, too. An MPS is usually expressed in days or weeks and may extend over several months to cover the complete manufacture of the items contained in the MPS. The total length of time required to manufacture a product is called its **cumulative lead time**.

Master production schedule A schedule of finished products that drives the MRP process.

Cumulative lead time The total length of time needed to manufacture a product.

The master production schedule drives the MRP process. The schedule of finished products provided by the master schedule is needed before the MRP system can do its job of generating production schedules for component items. Table 15.1 shows a sample master production schedule consisting of four end items produced by a manufacturer of specialty writing accessories.

TABLE 15.1 Master Production Schedule (MPS)

	PERIOD				
MPS ITEM	1	2	3	4	5
Pencil case	125	125	125	125	125
Clipboard	85	95	120	100	100
Lapboard	75	120	47	20	17
Lapdesk	0	60	0	60	0

Several comments should be made concerning the quantities contained in the MPS:

- ***The quantities represent production, not demand.*** As we saw in Chapter 14, production does not necessarily have to match demand. Strategy decisions made in the aggregate planning stage filter down to the master production schedule. Common strategies are chase demand, level production, and batching. In Table 15.1, pencil cases are following a level production strategy, clipboards and lapboards a chase demand strategy, and lapdesks a batching strategy.
- ***The quantities may consist of a combination of customer orders and demand forecasts.*** Some figures in the MPS are confirmed, but others are predictions. As might be expected, the quantities in the more recent time periods are more firm, whereas the forecasted quantities further in the future may need to be revised several times before the schedule is completed. Some companies set a **time fence**, within which no more changes to the master schedule are allowed. This helps to stabilize the production environment.

Time fence A management-specified date within which no changes in the master schedule are allowed.

The MPS for clipboards and lapboards shown in Table 15.1 illustrates two approaches to future scheduling. For clipboards, production beyond period 3 is based on demand forecasts of an even 100 units per period. Projecting these requirements now based on past demand data helps in planning for the availability of resources. For lapboards, production beyond period 3 appears sparse, probably because it is based on actual customer orders received. We can expect those numbers to increase as the future time periods draw nearer.

- ***The quantities represent what needs to be produced, not what can be produced.*** Because the MPS is derived from the aggregate production plan, its requirements are probably "doable," but until the MRP system considers the specific resource needs and the timing of those needs, the feasibility of the MPS cannot be guaranteed. Thus, the MRP system is often used to *simulate* production to verify that the MPS is feasible or to confirm that a particular order can be completed by a certain date before the quote is given to the customer.
- ***The quantities represent end items that may or may not be finished products.*** The level of master scheduling can differ by type of production system. In make-to-stock companies, the MPS consists of finished products. In assemble-to-order companies, the MPS usually represents major subassemblies or modules. In make-to-order companies, the master schedule can consist of critical components, hard-to-get materials, and service parts. Separate final assembly schedules are then used for the finished product or customer order. As Figure 15.4 shows, companies usually master schedule at the smallest part of the product structure. To simplify discussions, we assume in this chapter that an end item is, in fact, the finished product.

Product Structure File

Product structure file A file that contains a computerized bill of material for every item produced.

Bill of material (BOM) A list of all the materials, parts, and assemblies that make up a product, including quantities, parent–component relationships, and order of assembly.

Once the MPS is set, the MRP system accesses the **product structure file** to determine which component items need to be scheduled. The product structure file contains a **bill of material (BOM)** for every item produced. The bill of material for a product lists the items that go into the product, includes a brief description of each item, and specifies when and in what quantity each item is needed in the assembly process.

When each item is needed can best be described in the form of a product structure diagram, shown in Figure 15.5 for a clipboard. An assembled item is sometimes referred to as a *parent*, and a component as a *child*. The number in parentheses with each item is the quantity of a given component needed to make *one* parent. Thus, one clip assembly, two rivets, and one

FIGURE 15.4 Master Schedule at the Smallest Part of the Product Structure

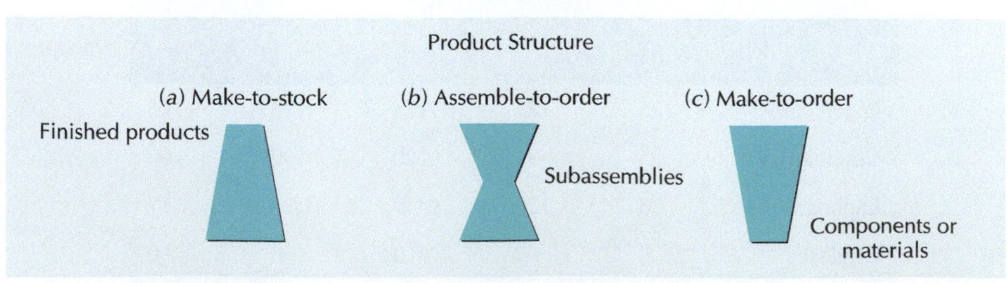

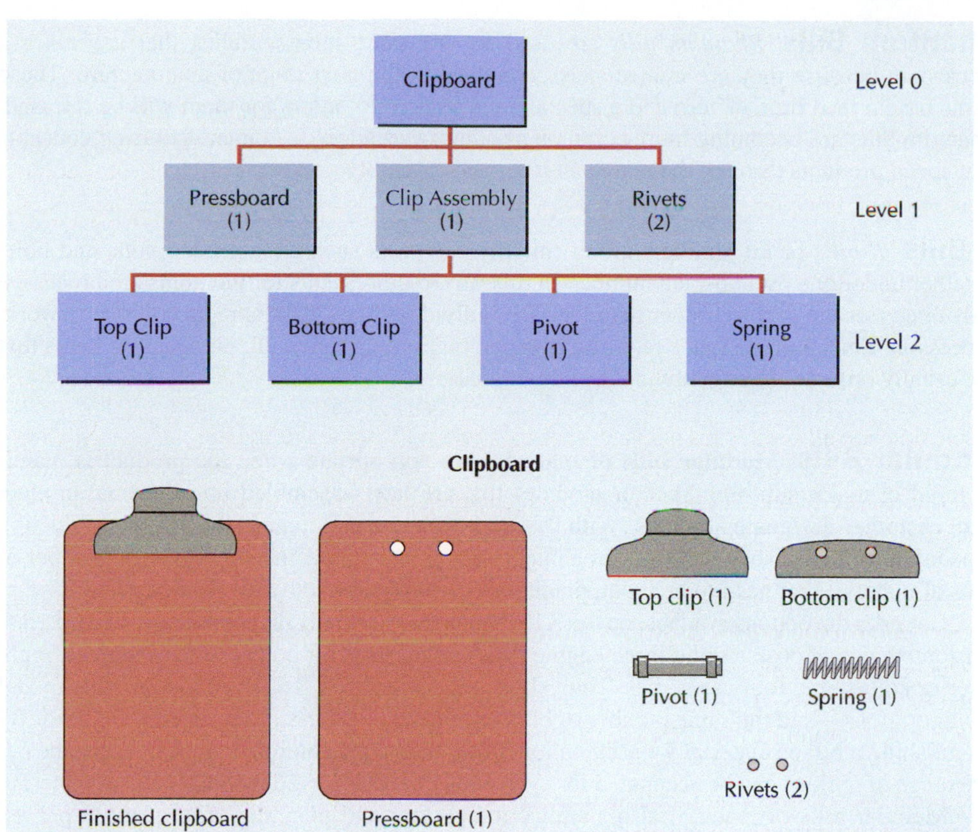

FIGURE 15.5 Product Structure Diagram for a Clipboard

pressboard are needed to make each clipboard. The clip assembly, rivets, and board appear at the same level of the product structure because they are to be assembled together.

A diagram can be converted to a computerized bill of material by labeling the levels in the product structure. The final product or end item at the top of the structure—in this case, the clipboard—is labeled level 0. The level number increases as we move down the product structure. The clipboard has three levels of assembly. The bill of material for the clipboard, listed in Table 15.2, shows some levels indented underneath others. This specifies which components belong to which parents and can easily be matched to the product structure diagram.

Several specialized bills of material have been designed to simplify information requirements, clarify relationships, and reduce computer processing time. They include phantom bills, K-bills, and modular bills.

TABLE 15.2 Multilevel Indented Bill of Material

LEVEL	ITEM	UNIT OF MEASURE	QUANTITY
0- - - -	Clipboard	ea	1
- 1- - -	Clip assembly	ea	1
- - 2- -	Top clip	ea	1
- - 2- -	Bottom clip	ea	1
- - 2- -	Pivot	ea	1
- - 2- -	Spring	ea	1
- 1- - -	Rivet	ea	2
- 1- - -	Pressboard	ea	1

Phantom Bills *Phantom bills* are used for transient subassemblies that never see a stockroom because they are immediately consumed in the next stage of manufacture. These items have a lead time of zero and a special code so that no orders for them will be released. Phantom bills are becoming more common as companies adopt lean manufacturing concepts that speed products through the manufacturing and assembly process.

K-Bills *K-bills* or kit numbers group small, loose parts such as fasteners, nuts, and bolts together under one pseudo-item number. In this way, requirements for the items are processed only once (for the group), rather than for each individual item. K-bills reduce the paperwork, processing time, and file space required in generating orders for small, inexpensive items that are usually ordered infrequently in large quantities.

Modular bills of material Bills used to plan the production of products with many optional features.

Modular Bills **Modular bills of material** are appropriate when the product is manufactured in major subassemblies or modules that are later assembled into the final product with customer-designated options. With this approach, the end item in the master production schedule is not a finished product, but a major option or module. This reduces the number of bills of material that need to be input, maintained, and processed by the MRP system.

Consider the options available on the X10 automobile, partially diagrammed in Figure 15.6. Customers can choose among three engine types, eight exterior colors, three interiors, eight interior colors, and four car bodies. Thus, there are $3 \times 8 \times 3 \times 8 \times 4 = 2304$ possible model configurations—and the same number of bills of material—unless modular bills are used. By establishing a bill of material for each option rather than each combination of options, the entire range of options can be accounted for by $3 + 8 + 3 + 8 + 4 = 26$ modular bills of material.

Modular bills of material also simplify forecasting and planning. The quantity per assembly for an option is given as a decimal figure, interpreted as a percentage of the requirements for the parent item. For example, from Figure 15.6, in preparation for an anticipated demand of 1000 X10 automobiles, 1000 engines are needed. Of those 1000 engines, the master production schedule would generate requirements for 400 four-cylinder engines, 500 six-cylinder engines, and 100 eight-cylinder engines.

The creation of a product structure file can take a considerable amount of time. Accurate bills of material are essential to an effective MRP system. The bill of material must specify how a product is actually manufactured rather than how it was *designed* to be manufactured. Redundant or obsolete part numbers must be purged from the system. This may not seem like a big task, but in some companies every time a part is purchased from a different supplier, it is assigned a different part number. One firm in the process of implementing MRP was able to eliminate 6000 extra part numbers from its database and dispose of thousands of dollars of obsolete inventory that had not previously been identified as such.

Time-phased bill of material An assembly chart shown against a time scale.

Time-Phased Bills A **time-phased bill of material**, also known as a *time-phased assembly chart*, is basically a horizontal product structure diagram that graphically shows the

FIGURE 15.6 **Modular Bills of Material**

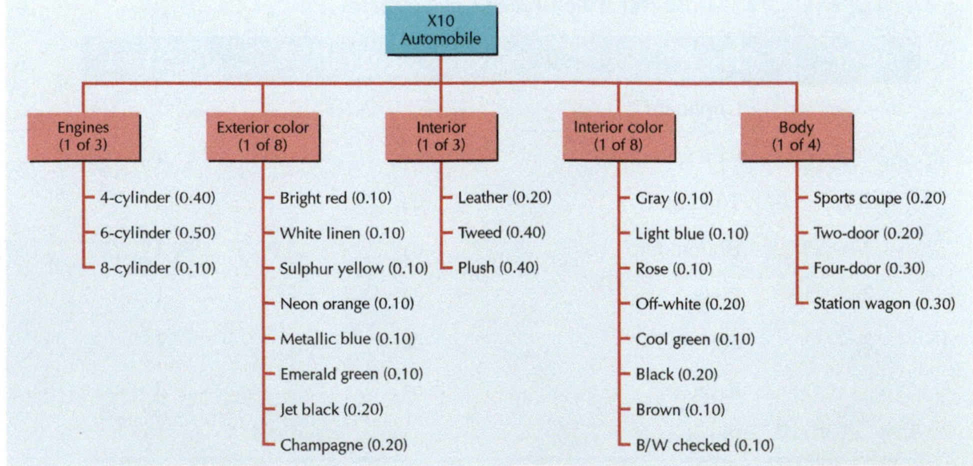

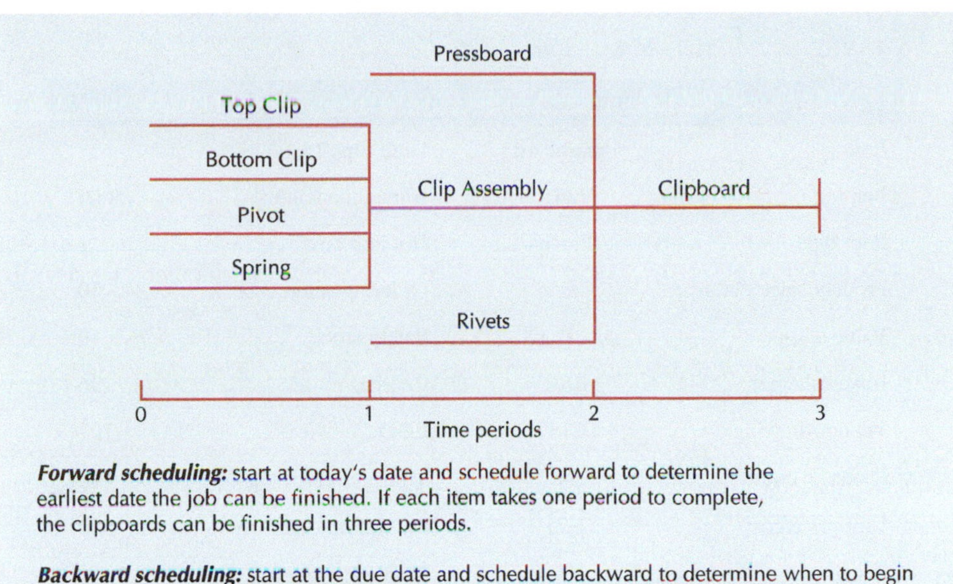
Pressboard
Top Clip
Bottom Clip
Clip Assembly
Clipboard
Pivot
Spring
Rivets
0
1
2
3
Time periods
Forward scheduling: start at today's date and schedule forward to determine the earliest date the job can be finished. If each item takes one period to complete, the clipboards can be finished in three periods.
Backward scheduling: start at the due date and schedule backward to determine when to begin work. If an order for clipboards is due by period three, we should start production now.

FIGURE 15.7 **Time-Phased Assembly Chart**

lead time required to purchase or manufacture an item. Assuming the lead time for each item in the bill of material for a clipboard is one week, Figure 15.7 shows how long it will take to assemble a clipboard from scratch. An MRP system can **forward schedule** or **backward schedule** production. Forward scheduling starts at today's date and schedules forward to determine the earliest date a job can be finished. In Figure 15.7, the clipboard can be finished by period 3. Backward scheduling starts at the due date and schedules backwards to determine when to begin work. In our example, if an order for clipboards is due by period 3, production should begin now.

Forward scheduling Schedules forward from today's date.

Backward scheduling Schedules backwards from the due date.

Item Master File

The **item master file,** or inventory file, contains an extensive amount of information on every item that is produced, ordered, or inventoried in the system. It includes such data as on-hand quantities, on-order quantities, lot sizes, safety stock, lead time, and past usage figures. Table 15.3 displays the item master file of the pressboard component from the clipboard example. It provides a detailed description of the item, specifies the inventory policy, updates

Item master file A database of information on every item produced, ordered, or inventoried.

iStockphoto

iStockphoto

MRP systems can be used for services, too. In renovating hotel rooms, Marriott develops a bill of material and a bill of labor for each room type and then "explodes" the bill throughout the facility to summarize its furniture and decorating needs. Menus in restaurants can be thought of as master schedules. Demand for menu items is forecasted and then multiplied by a bill of ingredients to ensure sufficient "material" is on hand for the chef to prepare what the customer orders. The bill of ingredients can also be used to accurately price menu items.

TABLE 15.3 Item Master File

DESCRIPTION		INVENTORY POLICY	
Item	Pressboard	Lead time (wks)	1
Item no.	7341	Annual demand	5000
Item type	Purch	Holding cost	1
Product/sales class	Comp	Ordering/setup cost	50
Value class	B	Safety stock	0
Buyer/planner	RSR	Reorder point	96
Vendor/drawing	07142	EOQ	707
Phantom code	N	Minimum order qty.	100
Unit price/cost	1.25	Maximum order qty.	500
Pegging	Y	Multiple order qty.	1
LLC	1	Policy code	3
PHYSICAL INVENTORY		**USAGE/SALES**	
On hand	150	YTD usage/sales	1100
Location	W142	MTD usage/sales	75
On order	100	YTD receipts	1200
Allocated	75	MTD receipts	0
Cycle	3	Last receipt	8/25
Last count	9/5	Last issue	10/5
Difference	–2		
		CODES	
		Cost acct.	00754
		Routing	00326
		Engr.	07142

the physical inventory count, summarizes the item's year-to-date or month-to-date usage, and provides internal codes to link this file with other related information in the MRP database.

The item master file is updated whenever items are withdrawn from or added to inventory or whenever an order is released, revised, or completed. Accuracy of inventory transactions is essential to MRP's ability to keep inventory levels at a minimum. It is estimated that 95% inventory accuracy is a prerequisite for an effective MRP system. Although technologies such as bar codes, voice-activated systems, and automated "picking" equipment can improve inventory accuracy considerably, a general overhaul of inventory procedures is often needed. This involves (1) maintaining orderly stockrooms; (2) establishing and enforcing procedures for inventory withdrawal; (3) ensuring prompt and accurate entry of inventory transactions; (4) taking physical inventory count on a regular basis; and (5) reconciling inventory discrepancies in a timely manner.

If you have ever taken part in an end-of-year inventory count, you can verify the wide discrepancies that are commonly found between what the records say is in inventory and what is physically there. Unfortunately, by the time the errors are discovered, it is too late to correct them or find out why they occurred. The slate is merely cleaned for next year's record, with the hope or promise that next time will be better.

Vignesh Ramachandran

Systems Auditor for a Big Four Accounting Firm

Roberta Russell

In today's regulatory environment, audits go far beyond the scope of traditional financial and regulatory compliance. With the Sarbanes-Oxley Act, PATRIOT Act, and revised Financial Modernization Act, it has become a requirement for all public corporations to document their business processes and verify them by external auditors. As a financial auditor and now a systems auditor (see photo), I interview various personnel at different stages of the production or service process, compare their activities with those documented, and point out inconsistencies, as well as inefficiencies. It takes about two months to thoroughly understand a process and about two weeks to audit it.

Corporations nowadays have complicated ERP and MRP systems whose methods of operation are not always evident to the people using the systems. These systems, though technologically advanced, rely on basic concepts in operations management. As an auditor, a complete understanding of the various processes and methodologies is very important, and my study of operations management has provided the groundwork for such knowledge.

Cycle counting involves taking physical count of at least some inventory items daily and reconciling differences as they occur. The system specifies which items are to be counted each day and may tie the frequency of the count to the frequency of orders for the item within the MRP system. Thus, items that are used more often are counted more often. The cycle counting system may also be related to the *ABC classification system* discussed in Chapter 13. *A* items would be counted more often than *B* items, perhaps weekly. *B* items would be counted monthly, and *C* items may still be counted only once a year. Approved cycle counting systems are accepted by the accounting standards boards as valid replacements for end-of-year physical inventories.

Cycle counting Taking physical count of inventory at various cycles during the year.

The MRP Process

The MRP system is responsible for scheduling the production of all items beneath the end item level. It recommends the release of work orders and purchase orders, and issues rescheduling notices when necessary.

The MRP process consists of four basic steps: (1) exploding the bill of material (see photo), (2) **netting** out inventory, (3) lot sizing, and (4) time-phasing requirements. The process is performed again and again, moving down the product structure until all items have been scheduled. An MRP matrix, as shown in Table 15.4, is completed for each item starting with level zero items. Identifying information at the top of the matrix includes the item name or number, the lowest level at which the item appears in the product structure (called *low level code* or LLC), the time required to make or purchase an item (called *lead time* or LT), and the quantities in which an item is usually made or purchased (called *lot size*).

Netting The process of subtracting on-hand quantities and scheduled receipts from gross requirements to produce net requirements.

TABLE 15.4 The MRP Matrix

		PERIOD				
ITEM LOT SIZE	LLC LT	1	2	3	4	5
Gross Requirements		*Derived from MPS or planned order releases of the parent*				
Scheduled Receipts		*On order and scheduled to be received*				
Projected on Hand	Beg. Inv	*Anticipated quantity on hand at the end of the period*				
Net Requirements		*Gross requirements net of inventory and scheduled receipts*				
Planned Order Receipts		*When orders need to be received*				
Planned Order Releases		*When orders need to be placed to be received on time*				

Entries in the matrix include gross requirements, scheduled receipts, projected on hand, net requirements, planned order receipts, and planned order releases. *Gross requirements* begin the MRP process. They are given in the master production schedule (MPS) for end items and derived from the parent for component items. *Scheduled receipts* are items on order that are scheduled to arrive in future time periods. *Projected on hand* is inventory currently on hand or projected to be on hand at the end of each time period as a result of the MRP schedule. *Net requirements* are what actually needs to be produced after on-hand and on-order quantities have been taken into account. *Planned order receipts* represent the quantities that will be ordered and when they must be received. These quantities differ from net requirements by **lot sizing** rules when production or purchasing is made in predetermined batches or lots. Common lot sizing rules include ordering in minimum or multiple quantities, using an EOQ or periodic order quantity, or ordering the exact quantities needed (called **lot-for-lot** or L4L). We discuss these techniques later in the chapter.

Lot sizing Determining the quantities in which items are usually made or purchased.

Lot-for-lot (L4L) Ordering in the exact quantities needed.

The last row of the matrix, *planned order releases*, determines when orders should be placed (i.e., released) so that they are received when needed. This involves offsetting or **time phasing** the planned order receipts by the item's lead time. Planned order releases at one level of a product structure generate gross requirements at the next lower level. When the MRP process is complete, the planned order releases are compiled in a planned order report.

Time phasing Subtracting an item's lead time from its due date to determine when to order an item.

Lot Sizing in MRP Systems

Example 15.1 illustrates the use of minimum order quantities, multiple order quantities, and lot-for-lot sizing rules. Although the L4L approach is most consistent with the objectives of MRP, in some circumstances it is useful to order an amount different from what is needed. For example, *minimum order quantities* are typically used to take advantage of quantity discounts or to conform to vendor requirements, *maximum order quantities* are used for large or expensive items when space or funds are limited, and *multiple order quantities* accommodate packaging restrictions (such as a set number in a box, gallon containers, bundles, or pallet loads). Several additional lot sizing techniques are available with most MRP systems. These include economic order quantity (EOQ) and **periodic order quantity (POQ)**.

Periodic order quantity (POQ) A lot sizing technique that orders at set time intervals.

EXAMPLE 15.1 | School Mate Products

School Mate offers a number of standard products to encourage writing outside of the classroom, including clipboards, lapdesks, lapboards, and pencil boxes. Rising costs and inventory levels have prompted the company to install a computerized planning and control system called MRP. The MPS and bill-of-material modules are up and running. Sample output follows. Before going live with the MRP module, School Mate has asked for a manual demonstration. Since manual calculations can be quite tedious, you have decided to prepare MRP matrices for only three items—the clipboard and lapdesk products, and a common component, pressboard. The master production schedule, abbreviated product structure diagrams, and inventory information are given below.

Master Production Schedule

	1	2	3	4	5
Clipboard	85	95	120	100	100
Lapdesk	0	60	0	60	0

Item Master File

	CLIPBOARD	LAPDESK	PRESSBOARD
On hand	25	20	150
On order (sch receipt)	175 (period 1)	0	0
LLC	0	0	1
Lot size	L4L	Mult 50	Min 100
Lead time	1	1	1

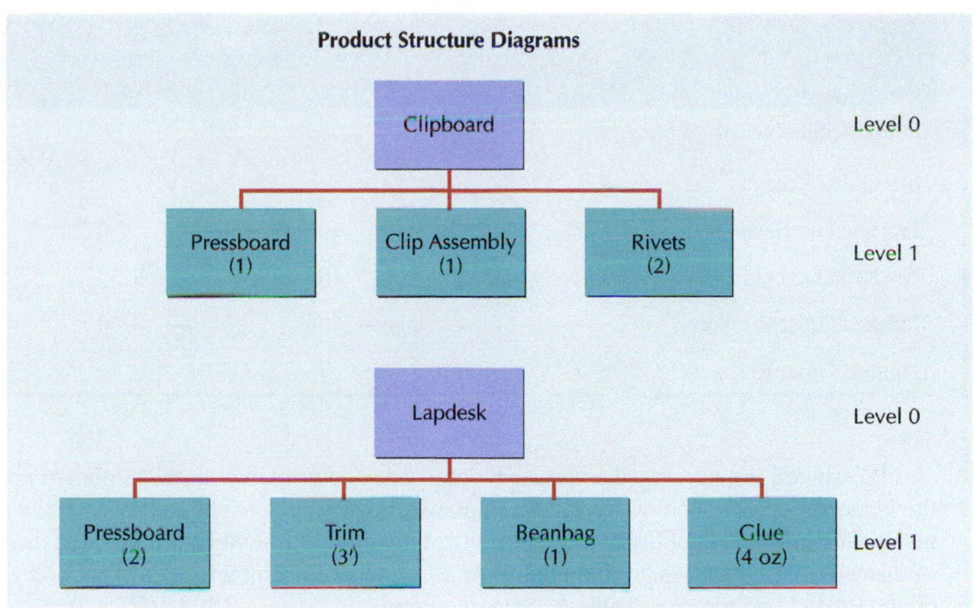

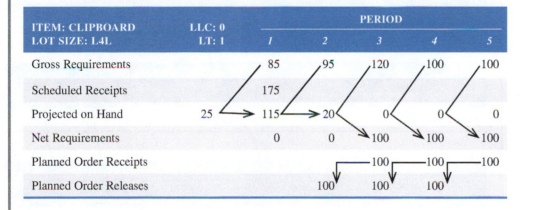

Solution: We begin with the level 0 items, the clipboard and lapdesk. Since these are finished products, the *gross requirements* row is simply copied from the master production schedule for those items. We'll begin with the clipboard.

ITEM: CLIPBOARD LOT SIZE: L4L	LLC: 0 LT: 1	PERIOD 1	 2	 3	 4	 5
Gross Requirements		85	95	120	100	100
Scheduled Receipts		175				
Projected on Hand	25	115	20	0	0	0
Net Requirements		0	0	100	100	100
Planned Order Receipts				100	100	100
Planned Order Releases			100	100	100	

In period 1 we have 25 units on hand and 175 scheduled to be received. That gives us (25 + 175) = 200 units available. We use 85 of them to satisfy demand, leaving (200 − 85) = 115 units in inventory at the end of period 1. In period 2, we can meet demand from stock, leaving (115 − 95) = 20 units in inventory at the end of the period. In period 3, the 20 units on hand is not enough to cover our demand of 120 units. We need to make 100 more. Thus, our *net requirements* are 100 units. Since our lot sizing rule is lot-for-lot, we order exactly what we need, 100 units. Recall that our lead time is one week. If we wish to *receive* our order for 100 units in period 3, we must *place* the order one week in advance, in period 2. To meet demand in periods 4 and 5, we order 100 units in weeks 3 and 4, one week in advance of when we need them.

The MRP matrix for lapdesks appears below. To meet our demand for 60 units in period 2, we'll use the 20 units in stock and make 40 more. Before we release our work order for production, we check our lot sizing rule. It says we should make 50 lapdesks at a time. If the 50 desks are to be ready by week 2, we need to start production in week 1. When the desks are completed, we'll use 40 of them to meet demand and place 10 back in inventory. Those 10 remain in inventory until period 4 when we use them to partially satisfy the demand for 60 desks. We'll need to make 50 more, and since 50 is our lot size quantity, that's what we make. If the desks are to be completed by week 4, we need to start production in week 3.

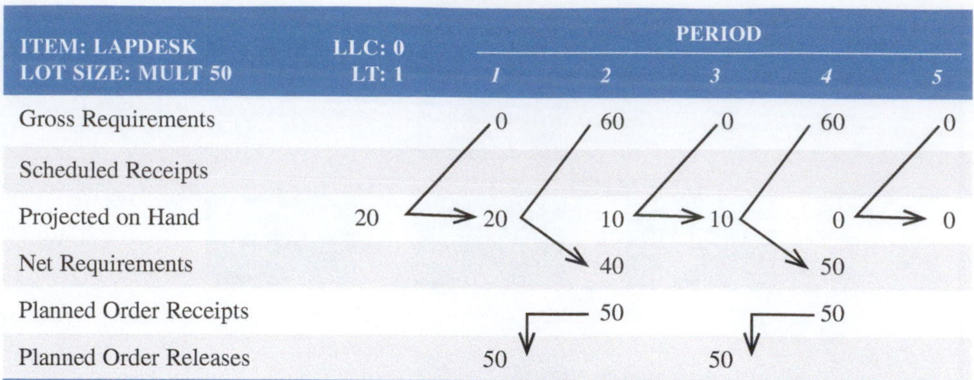

ITEM: LAPDESK LOT SIZE: MULT 50	LLC: 0 LT: 1	1	2	3	4	5
Gross Requirements		0	60	0	60	0
Scheduled Receipts						
Projected on Hand	20	20	10	10	0	0
Net Requirements			40		50	
Planned Order Receipts			50		50	
Planned Order Releases		50		50		

Pressboard is a purchased component cut to size and used in both the clipboard and the lapdesk. As shown below, its gross requirements are calculated by multiplying the planned order releases of each parent times the quantity per assembly contained in the bill of material. This process is called **explosion**. Since one pressboard is needed for every clipboard and two for every lapdesk, gross requirements for period 1 are $(50 \times 2) = 100$; period 2, $(100 \times 1 = 100)$; period 3, $(100 \times 1) + (50 \times 2) = 200$; and period 4, $(100 \times 1) = 100$.

Explosion The process of determining requirements for lower-level items.

ITEM: CLIPBOARD LOT SIZE: L4L	LLC: 0 LT: 1	1	2	3	4	5
Planned Order Releases			100	100	100	

100 × 1   *100 × 1*   *100 × 1*

ITEM: LAPDESK LOT SIZE: MULT 50	LLC: 0 LT: 1	1	2	3	4	5
Planned Order Releases		50		50		

50 × 2   *50 × 2*

ITEM: PRESSBOARD LOT SIZE: MIN 100	LLC: 1 LT: 1	1	2	3	4	5
Gross Requirement		100	100	200	100	0
Scheduled Receipts						
Projected on Hand	150	50	50	0	0	0
Net Requirements			50	150	100	
Planned Order Receipts			100	150	100	
Planned Order Releases		100	150	100		

With 150 units on hand, we can satisfy the demand in period 1 with 50 units left over. For period 2, we use the 50 in inventory and need 50 more. Because our lot sizing rule says we must order *at least* 100 units and it takes 1 week to process an order, we place an order for 100 pressboards in week 1. When the 100 boards come in, we use 50 of them and put 50 back in stock. To meet our demand in period 3, we use the 50 boards in stock and order 150 more. The order is placed in week 2 to arrive in week 3. To meet period 4's demand, we order 100 boards in week 3, one week in advance of delivery.

We have now completed the MRP calculations. To summarize the results, we construct a *planned order report* from the planned order release row of each matrix, as follows:

Planned Order Report

ITEM	PERIOD 1	2	3	4	5
Clipboard		100	100	100	
Lapdesk	50		50		
Pressboard	100	150	100		

Economic Order Quantity We discussed the economic order quantity for independent demand items in Chapter 13. The EOQ can be adapted for use with MRP if it is treated as a minimum order quantity. In addition, annual demand, D, is replaced with average demand per period, d, and carrying cost, C_c, is converted to a per-period amount. The EOQ is used only sparingly, usually at the finished product or raw material level, and does not perform well when demand is highly variable.

Periodic Order Quantity The periodic order quantity (POQ) was created as a variation of the EOQ more suited to variable demand. POQ is calculated by dividing the EOQ by average demand. It represents the number of demand periods covered by each order. Thus, if the POQ were three, an order would be placed for three weeks worth of demand.

Example 15.2 compares the L4L, EOQ, and POQ lot sizing techniques.

EXAMPLE 15.2 | Advanced Lot Sizing Rules

The Lifetime Sports Company has been using MRP to manufacture sports equipment for a number of years. Recently, Bob Sage, the operations manager, decided to investigate the use of lot sizing for MRP-generated orders. As a test case, Bob selected a typical product in their line of fishing rods and gathered weekly data over a month's time. Ordering costs are \$60 per order, and carrying costs are \$1 per unit per week. The beginning inventory is 30 units, and lead time is one week. Help Bob determine whether the L4L, EOQ, or POQ lot sizing technique is more appropriate.

PERIOD	1	2	3	4	5
Gross Requirements	30	50	20	10	40

a.

$$C_o = \$60$$
$$C_c = \$1$$
$$\bar{d} = (30 + 50 + 20 + 10 + 40)/5 = 30$$

With L4L, orders are placed for the exact amount needed. Total cost is calculated as (number of orders × ordering cost) + (total projected on hand × carrying cost). Beginning inventory that is used right away incurs no cost.

ITEM: ROD LOT SIZE: L4L	LLC: 0 LT: 1	PERIOD 1	2	3	4	5
Gross Requirements		30	50	20	10	40
Scheduled Receipts						
Projected on Hand	30	0	0	0	0	0
Net Requirements			50	20	10	40
Planned Order Receipts			50	20	10	40
Planned Order Releases		50	20	10	40	

$$\text{Total cost of L4L} = (4 \times \$60) + (0 \times \$1) = \$240$$

b. $EOQ = \sqrt{\dfrac{2(30)(60)}{1}} = 60$ Use as a minimum order quantity.

ITEM: ROD LOT SIZE: EOQ 60	LLC: 0 LT: 1	PERIOD 1	2	3	4	5
Gross Requirements		30	50	20	10	40
Scheduled Receipts						
Projected on Hand	30	0	10	50	40	0
Net Requirements			50	10		
Planned Order Receipts			60	60		
Planned Order Releases		60	60			

Total cost of EOQ = (2 × \$60) + [(10 + 50 + 40) × \$1] = \$220

c. $POQ = Q/\bar{d} = 60/30 = 2$ period's worth of requirements

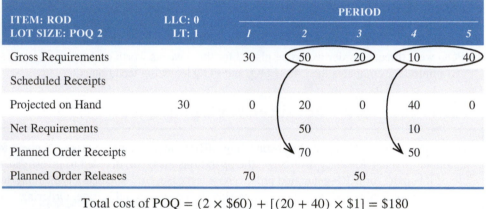

ITEM: ROD LOT SIZE: POQ 2	LLC: 0 LT: 1	PERIOD 1	2	3	4	5
Gross Requirements		30	50	20	10	40
Scheduled Receipts						
Projected on Hand	30	0	20	0	40	0
Net Requirements			50		10	
Planned Order Receipts			70		50	
Planned Order Releases		70		50		

Total cost of POQ = (2 × \$60) + [(20 + 40) × \$1] = \$180

POQ is the lowest cost lot sizing technique for this example.

MRP Outputs

The outputs of the MRP process are planned orders from the planned order release row of the MRP matrix. As shown in Figure 15.4, these can represent *work orders* to be released to the shop floor for in-house production or *purchase orders* to be sent to outside suppliers. MRP output can also recommend changes in previous plans or existing schedules. These *action notices,* or *rescheduling notices,* are issued for items that are no longer needed as soon as planned or for quantities that may have changed. One of the advantages of the MRP system is its ability to show the effect of change in one part of the production process on the rest of the system. It simulates the ordering, receiving, and use of raw materials, components, and assemblies into future time periods and issues warnings to the MRP planner of impending stockouts or missed due dates.

Table 15.5 shows a monthly *planned order report* for an individual item, in this case, item #2740. The report maps out the material orders planned and released orders scheduled to be completed in anticipation of demand. Notice that safety stock is treated as a quantity not to be used and that a problem exists on 10-01, when projected on hand first goes negative. To correct this, the system suggests that the scheduled receipt of 200 units due on 10-08 be moved forward to 10-01. The MRP system will not generate a new order if a deficit can be solved by expediting existing orders. It is up to the MRP planner to assess the feasibility of expediting the scheduled receipt and to take appropriate action.

Table 15.6 shows an *MRP action report* for a family of items for which a particular MRP planner is responsible. It summarizes the action messages that have been compiled for individual items. On 10-08, we see the action message for item #2740 that appeared on the previous report. Notice the variety of action messages listed. Some suggest that planned

TABLE 15.5 Planned Order Report

Item	#2740	Date	9-25
On hand	100	Lead time	2 weeks
On order	200	Lot size	200
Allocated	50	Safety stock	50

DATE	ORDER NO.	GROSS REQS.	SCHEDULED RECEIPTS	PROJECTED ON HAND	ACTION	
				50		
9–26	AL 4416	25		25		
9–30	AL 4174	25		0		
10–01	GR 6470	50		–50		
10–08	SR 7542		200	150	Expedite SR	10–01
10–10	CO 4471	75		75		
10–15	GR 6471	50		25		
10–23	GR 6471	25		0		
10–27	GR 6473	50		–50	Release PO	10–13

Key: AL = allocated WO = work order
CO = customer order SR = scheduled receipt
PO = purchase order GR = gross requirement

orders be moved forward or backward. Others suggest that scheduled receipts be expedited or de-expedited.

It is the planner's job to respond to the actions contained in the action report. If a planner decides to **expedite** an order—that is, have it completed in less than its normal lead time—he or she might call up a supplier or a shop supervisor and ask for priority treatment. Giving one job higher priority may involve reducing the priority of other jobs. This is possible if the MRP action report indicates that some jobs are not needed as early as anticipated. The process of moving some jobs *forward* in the schedule (expediting) and moving other jobs *backward* (de-expediting) allows the material planner, with the aid of the MRP system, to fine-tune the material plan. Temporary lead time adjustments through overtime or outside purchases of material can also fix a timing problem in the MRP plan, but at a cost. An MRP action report that is exceedingly long or does not strike a balance between speeding up some orders and slowing down others can signify trouble. Action messages that recommend only the expediting of orders indicate an overloaded master schedule and an ineffective MRP system.

Expedite To speed up an order so it is completed in less than its normal lead time.

TABLE 15.6 MRP Action Report

CURRENT DATE: 9-25						
ITEM	DATE	ORDER NO.	QTY.	ACTION		
#2740	10-08	7542	200	Expedite	SR	10-01
#3616	10-09			Move forward	PO	10-07
#2412	10-10			Move forward	PO	10-05
#3427	10-15			Move backward	PO	10-25
#2516	10-20	7648	100	De-expedite	SR	10-30
#2740	10-27		200	Release	PO	10-30
#3666	10-31		50	Release	WO	10-24

The MRP system, as the name implies, ensures that *material* requirements are met. However, material is not the only resource necessary to produce goods—a certain amount of labor and machine hours are also required. Thus, the next step in the planning process is to verify that the MRP plan is "feasible" by checking for the availability of labor and/or machine hours. This process is called *capacity requirements planning* and is similar to MRP.

Capacity Requirements Planning (CRP)

Capacity requirements planning (CRP) Creates a load profile that identifies underloads and overloads.

Capacity requirements planning (CRP) is a computerized system that projects the load from a given material plan onto the capacity of a system and identifies underloads and overloads. It is then up to the MRP planner to *level the load*—smooth out the resource requirements so that capacity constraints are not violated. This can be accomplished by shifting requirements, reducing requirements, or temporarily expanding capacity.

There are three major inputs to CRP, as shown in Figure 15.8:

- The *planned order* releases from the MRP process
- A *routing file,* which specifies which machines or workers are required to complete an order from the MRP plan, in what order the operations are to be conducted, and the length of time each operation should take
- An *open orders file*, which contains information on the status of jobs that have already been released but have not yet been completed

With this information, CRP can produce a load profile for each process or work center in the shop. The load profile compares released orders and planned orders with work center capacity.

Calculating Capacity

Capacity The maximum capability to produce.

Capacity is the maximum capability to produce. It can be measured as units of output, dollars of output, hours of work, or number of customers processed over a specified period of time. Capacity is affected by the mix of products and services, the choice of technology, the size of a facility, and the resources allocated.

Rated capacity is the theoretical output that could be attained if a process were operating at full speed without interruption, exceptions, or downtime. Effective capacity takes into account the efficiency with which a particular product or customer can be processed, and the

FIGURE 15.8 **Capacity Requirements Planning**

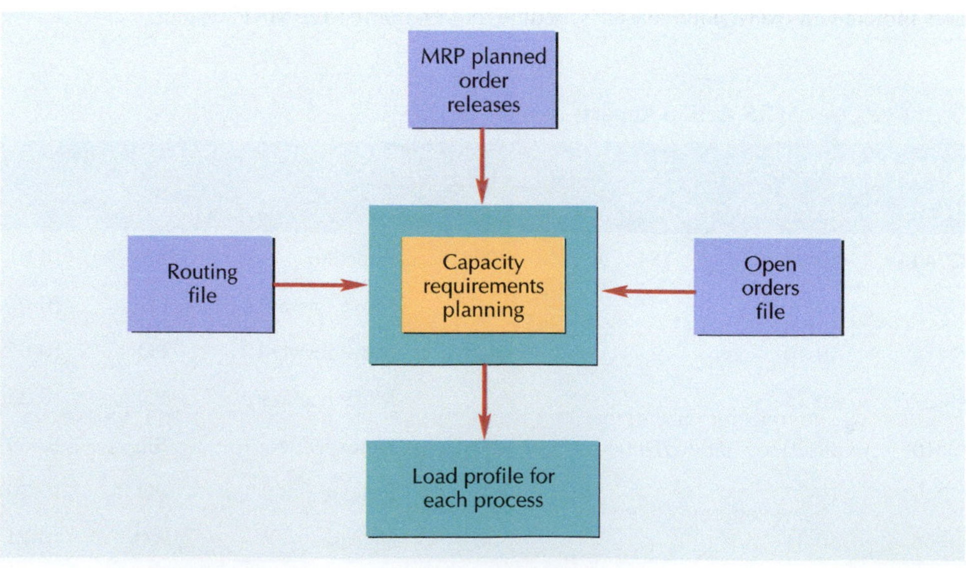

utilization of the scheduled hours or work. Effective capacity expressed in hours per day is calculated as:

$$\text{Effective daily capacity} = (\text{no. of machines or workers}) \times (\text{hours per shift}) \times (\text{no. of shifts}) \times (\text{utilization}) \times (\text{efficiency})$$

Utilization refers to the percentage of available working time that a worker actually works or a machine actually runs. Scheduled maintenance, lunch breaks, and setup time are examples of activities that reduce actual working time. **Efficiency** refers to how well a machine or worker performs compared to a standard output level. Standards can be based on past records of performance or can be developed from the work-measurement techniques discussed in Chapter S8. An efficiency of 100% is considered normal or standard performance, 125% is above normal, and 90% is below normal. Efficiency is also dependent on product mix. Some orders obviously will take longer than others to process, and some machines or workers may be better at processing certain types of orders.

Utilization The percent available time spent working.

Efficiency How well a machine or worker performs compared to a standard output level.

Load is the standard hours of work (or equivalent units of production) assigned to a production facility. After load and capacity have been determined, a **load percent** can be calculated as

Load The standard hours of work assigned to a facility.

Load percent The ratio of load to capacity.

$$\text{Load percent} = \frac{\text{load}}{\text{capacity}} \times 100\%$$

Centers loaded above 100% will not be able to complete the scheduled work without some adjustment in capacity or reduction in load.

EXAMPLE 15.3 | Determining Loads and Capacities

Copy Courier (CC) is a fledgling copy center in downtown Richmond run by two college students. Currently, the equipment consists of two high-speed copiers that can be operated by one operator. If the students work alone, it is conceivable that two shifts per day can be staffed. The students each work 8 hours a day, 5 days a week. They do not take breaks during the day, but they do allow themselves 30 minutes for lunch or dinner. In addition, they service the machines for about 30 minutes at the beginning of each shift. The time required to set up for each order varies by the type of paper, use of color, number of copies, and so on. Estimates of setup time are kept with each order. Since the machines are new, their efficiency is estimated at 90%.

Due to extensive advertising and new customer incentives, orders have been pouring in. The students need help determining the capacity of their operation and the current load on their facility. Use the following information to calculate the normal daily capacity of Copy Courier and to project next Monday's load and load percent.

JOB NO.	NO. OF COPIES	SETUP TIME (MIN)	RUN TIME (MIN/UNIT)
10	500	5.2	0.08
20	1000	10.6	0.10
30	5000	3.4	0.12
40	4500	11.2	0.14
50	2000	15.3	0.10

Solution: The machines and operators at Copy Courier are out of service for 1 hour each shift for maintenance and lunch. Utilization is thus 7/8, or 87.5%. Daily copy shop capacity is:

$$2 \text{ machines} \times 2 \text{ shifts} \times 8 \text{ hours/shift} \times 90\% \text{ efficiency} \times 87.5\% \text{ utilization} = 25.2 \text{ hours or } 1512 \text{ minutes}$$

The projected load for Monday of next week is as follows:

JOB NO.	TOTAL × TIME
10	$5.2 + (500 \times 0.08) = 45.20$
20	$10.6 + (1000 \times 0.10) = 110.60$
30	$3.4 + (5000 \times 0.12) = 603.40$
40	$11.2 + (4500 \times 0.14) = 641.20$
50	$15.3 + (2000 \times 0.10) = 215.30$
	1615.70 minutes

$$\text{Load percent} = \frac{1615.70}{1512} = 1.068 \times 100\% = 106.8\%$$

Copy Courier is overloaded 6.8%. Several options are available to alleviate the overload. If each worker extends his or her working day by approximately 36 minutes, the load percent will reduce to 99%. The same effect can be achieved by increasing efficiency to 97%. This may involve limiting the orders accepted to those that can be processed more efficiently, or grouping jobs by similar processing requirements so that setup time is reduced.

Load Profiles

Load profile A graphical comparison of load versus capacity.

Load profiles are a graphical comparison of load versus capacity. As shown in Figure 15.9, the normal capacity of Department A is 40 hours per week. We can see that the machine is *underloaded* in periods 1, 5, and 6, and *overloaded* in periods 2, 3, and 4. Underloaded conditions can be leveled by:

1. Acquiring more work;
2. *Pulling work ahead* that is scheduled for later periods; or
3. Reducing normal capacity.

Additional work can be acquired by transferring similar work from other machines in the same shop that are near or over capacity, by making components in-house that are normally purchased from outside suppliers, or by seeking work from outside sources. Pulling work ahead seems like a quick and easy alternative to alleviate both underloads and overloads. However, we must remember that the MRP plan was devised based on an interrelated product structure, so the feasibility of scheduling work in an earlier time period is contingent on the availability of required materials or components. In addition, work completed prior to its due date must be

FIGURE 15.9 **Initial Load Profile for Department A**

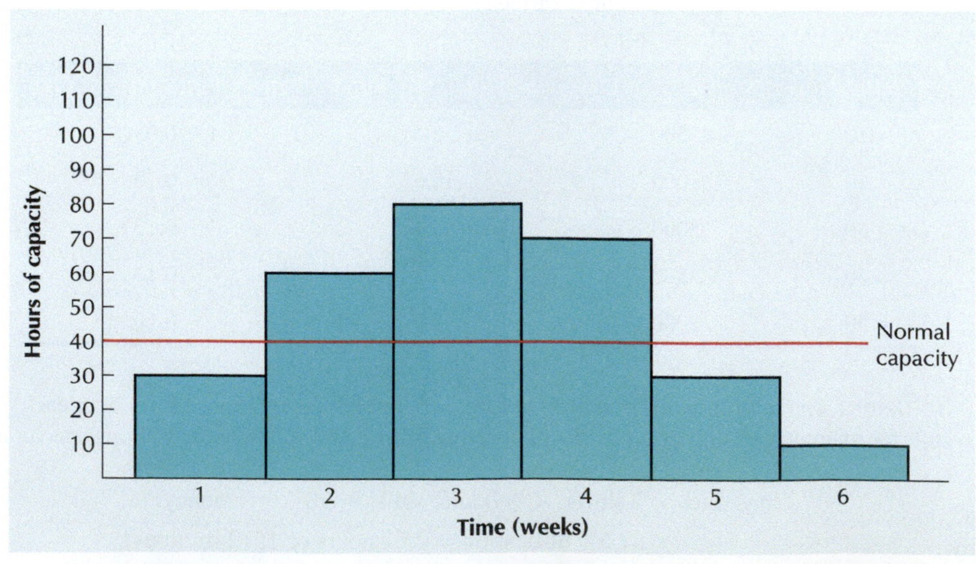

stored in inventory and thus incurs a holding cost. When work is shifted to other time periods, the MRP plan should be rerun to check the feasibility of the proposed schedule.

If an underloaded condition continues for some time, reducing the size of the workforce may be necessary. Smaller underloads can be handled by reducing the length of the working day or workweek, by scheduling idled workers for training sessions or vacations, or by transferring workers to other positions at machine centers or processes where overloads are occurring.

Overloads

Overloaded conditions are the primary concern of the MRP planner because an overloaded schedule left unchecked cannot possibly be completed as planned. Overloads can be reduced by:

1. Eliminating unnecessary requirements;
2. Rerouting jobs to alternative machines, workers, or work centers;
3. Splitting lots between two or more machines;
4. Increasing normal capacity;
5. Subcontracting;
6. Increasing the efficiency of the operation;
7. Pushing work back to later time periods; or
8. Revising the master schedule.

Some capacity problems are generated from an MRP plan that includes lot sizes, safety stock, and unsubstantiated requirements for service parts or forecasted demand. To verify that a capacity overload is caused by "real" need, the planner might examine the MRP matrices of the items assigned to a machine center during an overloaded period as well as the matrices of the parents of those items processed, all the way up the product structure to the master schedule. Or, the MRP system could be rerun with lot sizes temporarily set to one and safety stock to zero to see if the capacity problem is eliminated.

MRP systems assume that an entire lot of goods is processed by one machine or operator. Given the job shop environment in which most MRP systems are installed, there are usually several machines that can perform the same job (although perhaps not as efficiently). With CRP, load profiles are determined with jobs assigned to the preferred machine first, but when capacity problems occur, jobs can certainly be reassigned to alternate machines. In addition, if two or more similar machines are available at the same time, it may be possible to *split* a batch—that is, assign part of an order to one machine and the remainder to another machine.

Normal capacity can be increased by adding extra hours to the work day, extra days to the work week, or extra shifts. Temporary overloads are usually handled with overtime. More extensive overloads may require hiring additional workers. Work can also be outsourced.

Improving the efficiency of an operation increases its capacity. Assigning the most efficient workers to an overloaded machine, improving the operating procedures or tools, or decreasing the percentage of items that need to be reworked or scrapped increases efficiency and allows more items to be processed in the same amount of time. Because output increases with the same amount of input, *productivity* increases. This is especially useful for alleviating chronic overloads at bottleneck operations, but it does take time to put into effect.

If later time periods are underloaded, it may be possible to push work back to those periods so that the work is completed but later than originally scheduled. There are two problems with this approach. First, postponing some jobs could throw the entire schedule off, meaning customers will not receive the goods when promised. This could involve a penalty for late delivery, loss of an order, or loss of a customer. Second, filling up the later time periods may preclude accepting new orders during those periods. It is normal for time periods further in the future to be underloaded. As these periods draw nearer, customer orders accelerate and begin taking up more of the system's capacity.

If all the preceding approaches to remedying overloads have been tried, but an overload still exists, the only option is to revise the master schedule. That means some customers will not receive goods as previously promised. The planner, in conjunction with the sales manager and master scheduler, determines which customers have the lowest priority and whether their orders should be postponed or canceled.

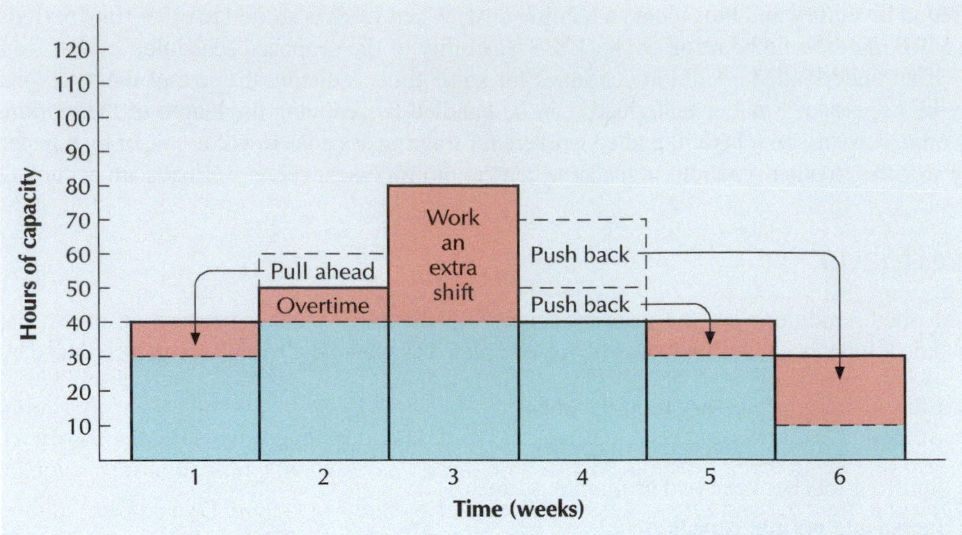

FIGURE 15.10 Adjusted Load Profile for Department A

There are cost consequences associated with each of these alternatives, but there is usually no attempt to derive an optimal solution. More than likely, the MRP planner will use the options that produce a feasible solution quickly. In many manufacturing environments, new customer orders arrive daily, and feasible MRP plans can become infeasible overnight.

Load Leveling

Figure 15.10 shows one possible remedy for the overloads shown in Figure 15.9. Ten hours of work are pulled ahead from period 2 to period 1. Ten hours of overtime are assigned in period 2. An entire 40-hour shift is added in period 3. Ten hours of work from period 4 are pushed back to period 5, and 20 hours are pushed back to period 6. This process of balancing underloads and overloads is called **load leveling**.

Load leveling The process of balancing underloads and overloads.

CRP *identifies* capacity problems, but the planner *solves* the problems. With experience, the task of shifting work and leveling loads is not as formidable as it appears. However, it is helpful if the initial load profile is as accurate as possible and if previous planning stages (i.e., sales and operations planning and master production scheduling) have considered capacity constraints. Some companies formalize capacity planning at each stage of production planning. *Resource requirements planning* is associated with the sales and operations plan, and *rough-cut capacity planning* is performed prior to the approval of a master schedule. Capacity requirements planning may still be performed on the material requirements plan, but its role is to fine-tune existing resources rather than to find or develop new resources.

Once the feasibility of an MRP plan has been verified by CRP, the plan can be executed by releasing orders in the time periods indicated. Normally, the ERP system automatically releases the orders. Work orders sent to the shop enter a shop floor control system, where daily scheduling and monitoring take place. When received, purchase orders are logged through the inventory system electronically before moving to manufacturing. Refer back to Figure 15.1. The figure shows the entire MRP process from the sales and operations plan to manufacture as a *closed-loop* system. The term is used to describe the numerous feedback loops between plans for production and available capacity.

Relaxing MRP Assumptions

The MRP process described in the previous sections and depicted in Figure 15.1 makes certain assumptions about production resources and how they should be allocated. Today's ERP technology allows us to relax some of the more restrictive assumptions of MRP. For example, we have learned the following:

- ***Material is not always the most constraining resource*.** The iterative procedure described in the previous section for determining material availability first, then verifying capacity may not be relevant to some industries. If there are particular processes that constrain the system or other capacity constraints that are difficult to relax, then they should drive the schedule rather than the availability of materials. Similarly, a bill of material may not be as important as a *bill of labor, a bill of resources, a bill of distribution,* or *a bill of information.*

- ***Lead times can vary.*** Fixed lead times assume that either lot sizes will continue unchanged or that they have no bearing on lead time. Under this assumption, the lead time necessary to process an order would remain the same whether that order consists of 1 unit or 100 units, and whether the shop is operating empty or at capacity. ERP processors today are able to handle variable lead times, but users must determine how sensitive the system should be to parameters that change.
- ***Not every transaction needs to be recorded.*** MRP tries to keep track of the status of all jobs in the system and reschedules jobs as problems occur. In a manufacturing environment of speed and small lot sizes, this is cumbersome. It might take as long to *record* the processing of an item at a workstation as it does to process the item. Managers must assess how much processing detail is really needed in the common database and how much control is enough.
- ***The shop floor may require a more sophisticated scheduling system.*** Dynamic scheduling environments require a level of sophistication not present in most MRP systems. Chapter 17 introduces more advanced planning and control techniques for detailed scheduling.
- ***Scheduling in advance may not be appropriate for on-demand production.*** Many companies today produce products on-demand from customers. The just-in-time or lean production environment, discussed in the next chapter, may produce better results under those circumstances. Whereas the master scheduling and bill-of-material explosion aspects of MRP are used in virtually all manufacturing environments, the MRP/CRP process may not be necessary in repetitive manufacturing driven by customer orders.

Enterprise Resource Planning (ERP)

Enterprise resource planning (ERP) is software that organizes and manages a company's business processes by sharing information across functional areas. It transforms transactional data like sales into useful information that supports business decisions in other parts of the company, such as manufacturing, inventory, procurement, invoicing, distribution, and accounting. In addition to managing all sorts of back-office functions, ERP connects with supply chain and customer management applications, helping businesses share information both inside and outside the company. Thus, ERP serves as the backbone for an organization's information needs, as well as its e-business initiatives.

Enterprise resource planning (ERP) Software that organizes and manages a company's business processes by sharing information across functional areas.

Prior to ERP, most companies supported a full staff of program developers, who wrote their business applications from scratch or developed complicated interfaces to allow prepackaged applications from several vendors to pass data back and forth as necessary to complete business transactions throughout the enterprise. This process was costly, time-consuming, and error-prone. Communication among various areas of the business was difficult, and managers could not get a comprehensive view of how the business was doing at any point in time.

SAP, a German software company, created a generic ERP software package to integrate all business processes together for use by any business in the world. Established first in a mainframe version, the software was updated to client-server architecture just as companies began replacing their old legacy systems in preparation for the Y2K problem. Sales were robust, and with essentially one product, SAP became the third largest software company in the world.

With ERP, companies can integrate their accounting, sales, distribution, manufacturing, planning, purchasing, human resources, and other transactions into one application software. This enables transactions to be synchronized throughout the entire system. For example, a customer order entered into an ERP system automatically updates inventory levels, parts supplies, accounting entries, production schedules, shipping schedules, and balance sheets.

ERP systems help companies manage their resources efficiently and, at the same time, better serve their customers. Owens Corning replaced over 200 legacy systems with one ERP system. By coordinating customer orders, financial reporting, and global procurement, the

John Snead

Senior Manager of Financial Planning and Analysis for Air Products

Roberta Russell

I began working at Air Products as a business analyst assessing the profitability of capital projects (see photo). Air Products spends between $700 and $800 million a year on capital projects, 25% of which support existing operations. The remaining 75% is invested in growth opportunities, predominantly building new or expanded production facilities. Our company was founded on the strength of a simple, yet revolutionary, idea—producing and selling industrial gases "on-site." That means building gas-generating facilities adjacent to customer sites to reduce distribution costs.

Air Products has since broadened its scope to include specialty gases and chemicals, but "on-sites," as we call them, remain a core business. Because we are investing a great deal of money in new plant and equipment to supply each customer, we negotiate 15-year contracts with minimum-volume commitments and cost pass-through provisions. Capital project analysis is more than "running the numbers." As a business analyst, I worked with operations, engineering, marketing, and sales to put together a thorough analysis of each investment opportunity.

My current job involves setting policies for financial analysis (such as worldwide hurdle rates and risk assessment) and developing the financial plan for the company using multiyear cash flow projections to make decisions on capital and acquisition spending, dividend policy, and debt restructuring. A portion of my time is spent monitoring working capital. By lowering inventories, purchasing costs, and receivables, we have more capital to invest in growth. Two corporate initiatives that are significantly reducing costs are e-procurement and ERP (enterprise resource planning.)

Implementation of SAP's ERP system has taken about five years. The system automates transactions, streamlines processes, and provides us with more useful information with which to make decisions. For example, we're getting a better handle on our costs through newly designed cost centers. SAP also helps us rationalize our facilities and make better sourcing decisions. Implementation has been going well. It's been more of a cultural and process change than a technical one. We can standardize processes, but getting people to follow them consistently is another matter.

We use APDirect, an Ariba product, for various e-procurement initiatives. For B2B, we are members of industry exchanges such as Elemica for the chemical industry and Rosetta Net for electronics. Many of our transactions take place over established EDI (electronic data interchange) systems. For strategic sourcing, we've joined a consortium called LSN (Leveraged Sourcing Network) consisting of 20 to 25 companies from a variety of industries who, when combined, represent the purchasing power of a Fortune 10 company. We also have a direct sourcing application that allows closed bids, forward and reverse auctions, and project workspaces for collaboration. We probably save $10 million annually in costs with our e-procurement initiatives.

In our company, like many others, most of our capital projects and costs savings opportunities involve operations. By streamlining our processes, automating and standardizing our systems, and working collaboratively across functional lines, we can increase our efficiency and profitability—not to mention "face time" with our customers. Air Products is successful today not only because of its operational excellence, but also because of the ability of its people to create lasting relationships built on understanding our customers' needs.

company was able to save over $65 million. IBM Storage Systems reduced the time required to reprice its line of products from 5 days to 5 minutes, the time to ship a replacement part from 22 days to 3 days, and the time to complete a credit check from 20 minutes to 3 seconds. Microsoft saved $12 million annually just in early-payment discounts from vendors when its ERP system went live. Monsanto cut its production planning from 6 weeks to 3, reduced working capital, and enhanced its bargaining position with suppliers, saving the company an estimated $200 million a year.

Global companies and those that share data regularly benefit the most from ERP. Nation-specific laws, currencies, and business practices embedded in the system enable it to translate sales transactions smoothly between business units in different countries—for example, a company in Taiwan and its customer in Brazil.

ERP simplifies customer interaction and speeds production with its configure-to-order capabilities. Customers ordering online or through a sales rep can quickly choose from a variety of options, for which a bill of material is automatically generated and sent to production. National Park Service employees log on to a special segment of VF Corporation's website to purchase their uniforms. VF's ERP system makes sure the items selected are approved and automatically debits their clothing allowance. Walmart's 5000 suppliers can link directly to a data warehouse to see how their products are selling and decide when to replenish the stock.

Data entered once into an ERP system, say from manufacturing, need not be reconciled with accounting or warehouse records because the records are all the same. With broader, more timely access to operating and financial data, ERP systems encourage flatter organizational structures and more decentralized decision making. At the same time, they centralize control over information and standardize processes. Standardized transactions make businesses more efficient; shared data helps solve problems.

ERP Modules

ERP systems consist of a series of application modules that can be used alone or in concert. The modules are fully integrated, use a common database, and support processes that extend across functional areas. Transactions in one module are immediately available to all other modules at all relevant sites—corporate headquarters, manufacturing plants, suppliers, sales offices, and subsidiaries.

Although ERP modules differ by vendor, they are typically grouped into four main categories: (1) finance and accounting, (2) sales and marketing, (3) production and materials management, and (4) human resources. Figure 15.11 shows the type of information that flows between customers, suppliers, and these various functional areas.

Finance/Accounting The *finance and accounting module* encompasses financial accounting, investment management, cost control, treasury management, asset management, and enterprise controlling. Included are cost centers, profit centers, activity-based costing, capital budgeting, and profitability analysis, as well as enterprise measures of performance. The finance module provides consistent financial data that is updated in real time and that links operational results with the financial effects of those results. For every physical transaction, the financial result is shown.

Sales/Marketing The *sales and marketing module* supports customer-related activities such as order processing, product configuration, and delivery quotations. Pricing, promotions, availability, and shipping options are determined as sales orders are entered. The sales module allows for profitability analyses based on different pricing strategies with discounts and rebates, and the projection of accurate delivery dates. It can also look into the company's finished goods and work-in-process inventories as well as material availability to determine how quickly an order can be filled. Managers can reserve inventory for specific customers, request certain supplier options, and customize orders. Distribution requirements, transportation management, shipping schedules, and export controls are included in the module, as are billing, invoicing, rebate processing, product registrations, and customer complaints. Distribution is coordinated more closely with manufacturing and sales in order to maintain customer delivery schedules.

Production/Materials Management The *production and materials management module* is set up to handle all types of manufacturing processes—make-to-order,

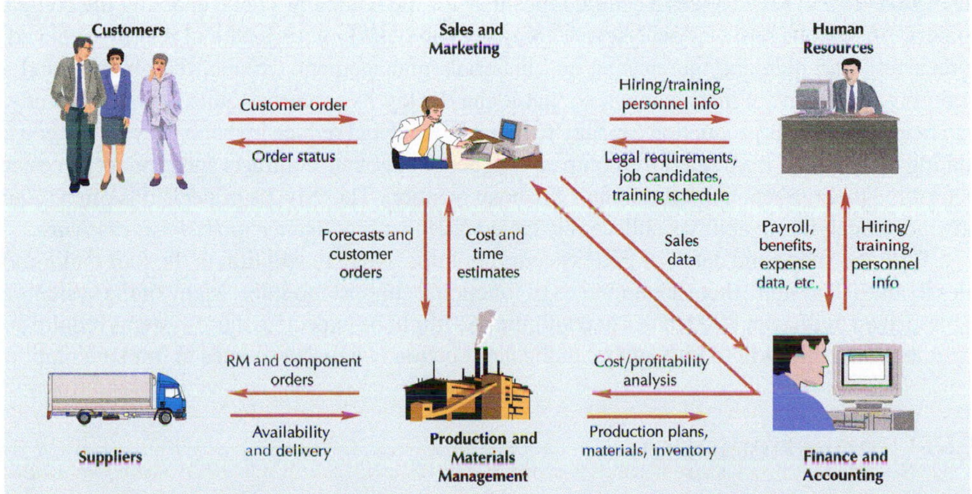

FIGURE 15.11 Organizational Data Flows

Source: Adapted from Joseph Brady, Ellen Monk, and Bret Wagner, *Concepts in Enterprise Resource Planning* (Boston: Course Technology, 2001), pp. 7–12. Note: The flow between HR and Production is similar to that between HR and Sales. It was eliminated from the figure to simplify the diagram.

FIGURE 15.12 **ERP's Central Database**

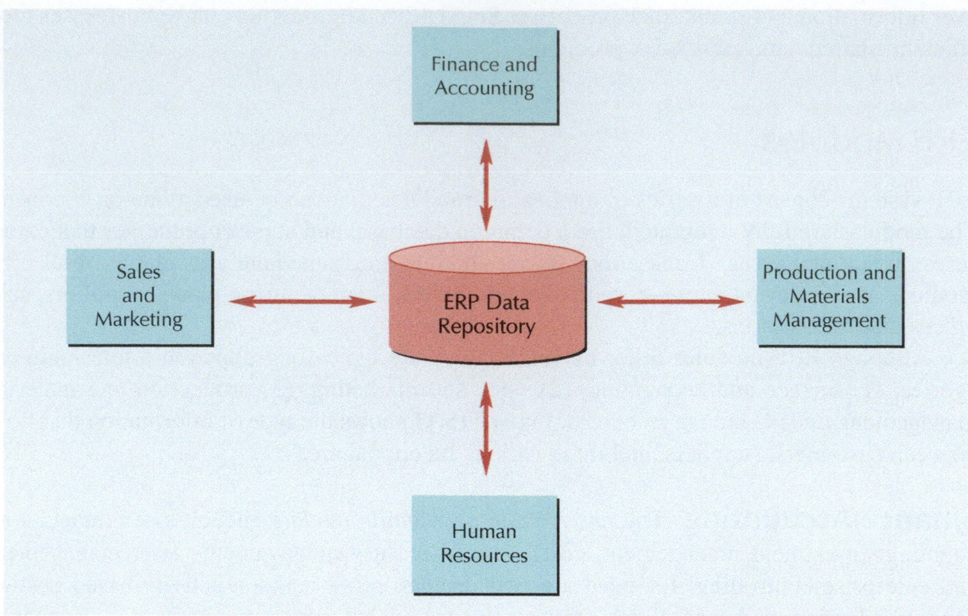

assemble-to-order, repetitive, and continuous. The module interfaces with CAD programs; performs process planning, bill-of-material processing, and product costing; processes engineering change orders; plans material requirements (MRP); allocates resources; and schedules and monitors production. Kanbans, Gantt charts, master schedules, and available-to-promise are all supported. It links sales and distribution to materials management, production planning, and financial effects in real time. Inventory is adjusted instantly and resource planning is done on a daily basis. Materials management refers to supply-chain-related activities such as purchasing, inventory and warehouse functions, supplier evaluations, just-in-time (JIT) deliveries, and invoice verification.

Human Resources The *human resources* module covers all personnel management tasks, including workforce planning, employee scheduling, training and development, payroll and benefits, travel expense reimbursement, applicant data, job descriptions, organization charts, and workflow analysis. It provides a database of personnel, maintains salary and benefits structures, and does payroll accounting as well.

Together, these modules form an integrated information technology strategy for effectively managing the entire enterprise. ERP connects processes that belong together, giving every employee fast, convenient access to the information required for their jobs. As shown in Figure 15.12, ERP creates a central repository for the company's data, enabling the company to perform various business analyses. A company can quickly access data in real time related to forecasting and planning, purchasing and materials management, product distribution, and accounting and financial management, so that it can deploy its resources quickly and efficiently. It can help schedule its production capacity to meet demand and reduce inventory levels. By consolidating information from sales, the company can better negotiate contracts and product prices, and determine their effect on the company's financial position. These types of decisions often require advanced analytic capabilities collectively called *business intelligence* or *business analytics.*

Both the scope and detail of ERP systems are impressive. In addition to the four major modules in an ERP system, there are hundreds of functional support modules. Many of the systems are table-driven, with over 8000 tables to configure. As might be expected, these systems require considerable time and skill to implement. In the next section, we discuss issues in implementation.

ERP Implementation

ERP implementation has a checkered history of mammoth projects over budget and out of control. Dow Chemical spent half a billion dollars and seven years implementing an ERP system that has since been overhauled. FoxMeyer Drug claims that ERP implementation sent it into bankruptcy.

TABLE 15.7 Selected Enterprise Software Vendors and Their Area of Expertise

VENDOR	SPECIALTY
1. SAP	Large enterprise manufacturing ERP/SCM; Big data
2. Oracle Corp.	Large enterprise discrete manufacturing and services
3. Oracle's PeopleSoft; Workday	Human resources and employee relationship management
4. Oracle's Siebel Systems	Customer relationship management (CRM)
5. Infor; JDA	Supply chain management (SCM); Retail
6. PTC, EDS, Dassault Systems	Product lifecycle management (PLM)
7. Siemens	Manufacturing execution systems (MES); energy
8. Ellucian	Public sector; education; financial services
9. QAD	Multinational midmarket manufacturing
10. Microsoft Dynamics	Small to midmarket ERP, CRM

ERP vendors and their customers have learned from these debacles, and the second-generation ERP systems are substantially different from the first generation, although they are still complex.

New ERP offerings sport stand-alone modules and open architecture. Companies can pick and choose the modules they want to install and can even choose a collection of modules from different vendors—the **best-of-breed** approach. While single-source ERP systems are easier to integrate, best-of-breed systems may provide a better match with organizational needs. Table 15.7 lists several enterprise software vendors and their area of expertise.

Best-of-breed Refers to the selection of ERP modules from different vendors.

ERP implementation involves: (1) analyzing business processes, (2) choosing the modules to implement, (3) aligning the level of sophistication, (4) finalizing delivery and access, and (5) linking with external partners.

Analyze Business Processes Analyzing business processes is the first step in implementation. Since ERP is an integrated technology that pervades and connects all parts of a company, it usually alters the way a company makes decisions; thus, its implementation typically requires major changes in a company's organizational structure and business processes. Companies that have had success with ERP have taken the time to think about how their processes work and how they can best be integrated before "automating" them. To guide companies in this massive project, ERP vendors have designed their software around best practices for specific industries. Solution maps and stories of successful implementations are available for such industries as aerospace and defense, apparel, automotive, chemicals, consumer products, engineering and construction, healthcare, high-tech industries, insurance, media, oil and gas, pharmaceuticals, the public sector, real estate, retail, telecommunications, and utilities. Companies can either use the software as a blueprint for how their processes should operate and adjust their processes, or they can map out their own business processes and customize the software accordingly. Most companies try a combination of these approaches.

Choose Modules to Implement Determining which ERP modules to implement and how they should be configured is a process-oriented (rather than technology-oriented) decision. The decision should be guided by questions such as: (1) Which processes have the biggest impact on customer relations? (2) Which processes would benefit the most from cross-functional or interorganizational integration? (3) Which processes should be standardized throughout the organization and which should be allowed to vary?

Small-market and midsize-market companies with time and budget constraints have an especially hard time implementing ERP. In response, software vendors like SAP have created a fast-track approach to ERP implementation. Based on the processes and applications that have proved most successful in the past, SAP has created 11 industry-specific best-practices templates designed to maximize efficiency and minimize customization. Plain vanilla,

Along the Supply Chain

SAP Powers NFL Fantasy Football and the NFL

What do business executives and fantasy football fans have in common? They both love performance dashboards. Since providing performance data is one of the services offered by ERP vendors, it should not come as a big surprise that the same software can be tailored to Fantasy Football players to help users create and maintain winning rosters. In North America, fantasy football now has over 57 million participants, a 72% increase over last year alone (see photo). The NFL, which actually collects player performance data, is not the top provider in the fantasy market. To gain traction in the burgeoning industry, the NFL employed SAP, the leading ERP vendor, to develop an online Player Comparison Tool that can handle 720 requests for information per second.

The Player Comparison Tool lets NFL fans and fantasy team owners instantly track and analyze more than 100 stats from each player and environmental conditions from competitor, to turf type and wind direction at kickoff. The statistical models reflect what a particular player is most likely to do in any situation. As a result, football fans can be as engaged in developing fantasy teams and players as they are watching real games during football season in the fall.

Of course, the NFL and all 32 professional teams actually use SAP, too, for the critical job of managing talent. SAP's SuccessFactors HRM suite provides a clear overview of team performance, evaluates individual player performance against measureable goals and objectives, and seeks to maximize individual contributions to the team. The HR platform is also a place for players and other employees to showcase achievements and adjust goals as new initiatives and opportunities arise. Currently, 99.5% of employees are using the system to track their own performance against goals. The software was implemented in three months' time, a performance that pleased everyone from fan to player to coach to commissioner.

Rawpixel.com/Shutterstock

Source: "National Football League: Scoring Big for Fans and Employees with Cloud Technology from SAP," SAP Business Transformation Study: Sports and Entertainment, 2014.

template-based modules chosen by the client are provided at a fixed price and implemented over a fixed timetable. The results are impressive. eCompany installed fully functional ERP modules for materials management, function planning, finance, and online retailing in three weeks for less than $200,000. Interactive Apparel implemented SAP's materials management, sales and distribution, warehouse management, and financial modules in nine weeks for less than $150,000.

Align Level of Sophistication Knowing the level of sophistication needed for your business is also key to effective ERP implementation. QAD, a midmarket ERP vendor, offers industry-specific software to manufacturing companies and international clients. QAD software can be directed with instructions much simpler than those of larger ERP vendors. Instead of deploying a single system to manage all of a company's plants, QAD tailors its software to individual plants, then links them with corporate financial, distribution, and support functions. Since 65% of QAD's customers are international, its software incorporates country-specific methods for invoicing, accounting, and amortization. For example, QAD uses a model to decide how an incoming order from a trading partner should be handled, automatically processing transactions across enterprises, languages, and customs. QAD is known for both its ease of implementation and ease of use.

Finalize Delivery and Access The Internet provides another aid to implementation. ERP vendors, including Oracle and SAP, now offer their products through portals. The vendor hosts the application, which the customer accesses over the Internet with their browser. Portals are less expensive, so they give midsize market and smaller clients access to the same services as larger corporations. ERP services can also be accessed through third-party application service providers (ASPs). Redback Networks, for example, uses Qwest CyberSolutions to access

Oracle's suite of enterprise solutions, including finance, order management, human resources, manufacturing, shipping, and inventory systems.

Link with External Partners The value of e-business relies on a company's ability to integrate its internal processes with external suppliers, customers, and companies. First-generation ERP systems lacked the ability to interact outside the organization with other ERP systems, with e-businesses, or directly with customers. By the second generation of ERP, vendors had learned to create web-centric systems by consolidating data and allowing dynamic access from various clients. Software vendors have developed powerful new analytic tools and applications that capitalize on ERP's infrastructure. Examples of such software systems are customer relationship management, supply chain management, and product lifecycle management.

Customer Relationship Management (CRM)

Perhaps no new application reinforces the changing focus of ERP better than customer relationship management. **Customer relationship management (CRM)** software plans and executes business processes that involve customer interaction, such as marketing, sales, fulfillment, and service. CRM changes the focus from managing products to managing customers. With the advent of e-commerce, companies have the opportunity to sell directly to the customer. Marketing can be personalized to individual preferences and behaviors. A wealth of data on customer buying behavior is available from records of purchases and analysis of clickstreams. Special events, such as holidays or product promotions, can trigger customer purchases. Point-of-sale data from physical stores, mail-order purchases, and online purchases are monitored. All of these data go into a data warehouse, where they are analyzed for patterns (called *data mining*) from which predictions of future behavior are made.

Customer relationship management (CRM) Software that plans and executes business processes involving customer interaction, such as sales, marketing, fulfillment, and customer service.

Prospect information, customer profiles, sales-force automation, and campaign modules for direct mail and special sales promotions are managed with CRM. In addition to collecting and analyzing customer data, CRM provides decision support for forecasting demand, demand management, pricing products and services, quoting order delivery dates, and planning for customer service needs. Customer service includes tracking and tracing orders, returns, repairs, service, and warranty management. CRM interacts with supply chain management (SCM) software and ERP to ensure prompt and accurate order fulfillment, and to plan for future requirements.

Supply Chain Management (SCM)

As discussed in Chapter 10, **supply chain management (SCM)** software includes supply chain planning, supply chain execution, and supplier relationship management. *Planning* involves designing the supply chain network, demand planning, and collaborative supply planning. *Execution* involves fulfillment, manufacturing, and delivery. *Relationship management* handles all the interactions with suppliers from supplier certification to quality assurance, contracts, and agreements.

Supply chain management (SCM) Software that plans and executes business processes related to supply chains.

From the above list you can see that the distinction between business software applications has become increasingly blurred as ERP vendors are adding more SCM functions, and SCM vendors are encroaching on ERP. SAP, whose ERP application runs most *Fortune* 500 companies, is now concentrating on a suite of new offerings in supply chain management, customer relationship management, and product lifecycle management. i2 technologies, now owned by JDA, has incorporated ERP functions into its TradeMatrix software. Oracle, known for its database management systems, emphasizes CRM, B2B, and business intelligence.

Along the Supply Chain

Roku Runs on NetSuite

Roku is a consumer electronics company that produces devices and software to stream movies, music, and games to TVs and other consumer electronic devices. To handle its explosive increase in demand, Roku implemented NetSuite's cloud-based ERP system, incorporating core financials, inventory management, order management, distribution, and procurement processes. After implementation, Roku was able to close the books 500% faster each month, optimize its stock levels across multiple locations, reduce both purchasing and IT costs, and automate 85% of its order management by revenue. The software also supported expansion into global markets with multi-subsidiary and multi-currency financials and sales.

In addition to providing a scalable foundation for growth, Roku's new ERP system streamlined transactions with more than 100 retailers and enabled the company to interact seamlessly with retail giants Walmart, Target, Amazon, and Best Buy through EDI, rapid fulfillment, and demand planning capabilities. Data visibility and analytics further enabled Roku to uncover growth opportunities, identify areas for improvement, and make better business decisions. Those skills are especially important in a highly competitive environment facing larger rivals Samsung, Sony, LG, Apple, and Google.

Nearly 24,000 businesses run NetSuite's ERP, CRM, and omnichannel software suite, including top innovators Airbnb, Jawbone, Uber, Warby Parker, Square, and App Annie. According to Gartner, NetSuite is the fastest growing financial management software vendor in the world.

1. What capabilities are important for a startup in a competitive environment dominated by larger firms?
2. What do NetSuite's clients have in common? Why would a company like NetSuite win out over larger ERP vendors SAP and Oracle?

Source: "World's Most Innovative Companies Run Business on NetSuite Cloud," Panorama Consulting, http://panorama-consulting.com, posted April 25, 2012 (accessed January 30, 2016); "Roku Uses NetSuite's Cloud Platform and the Skies the Limit," http://www.netsuite.com (accessed January 31, 2016).

Product Lifecycle Management (PLM)

Product lifecycle management (PLM) Software that manages the product development process, product lifecycles, and design collaboration with suppliers and customers.

A new entry into business application software is **product lifecycle management (PLM)**. PLM manages product data through the life of the product, coordinates product and processes redesign, and collaborates with suppliers and customers in the design process.

PLM, CRM, ERP, and SCM make a powerful combination. Figure 15.13 shows how these types of software systems can work together. Customer and supplier collaboration on

FIGURE 15.13 ERP and Related Software Systems

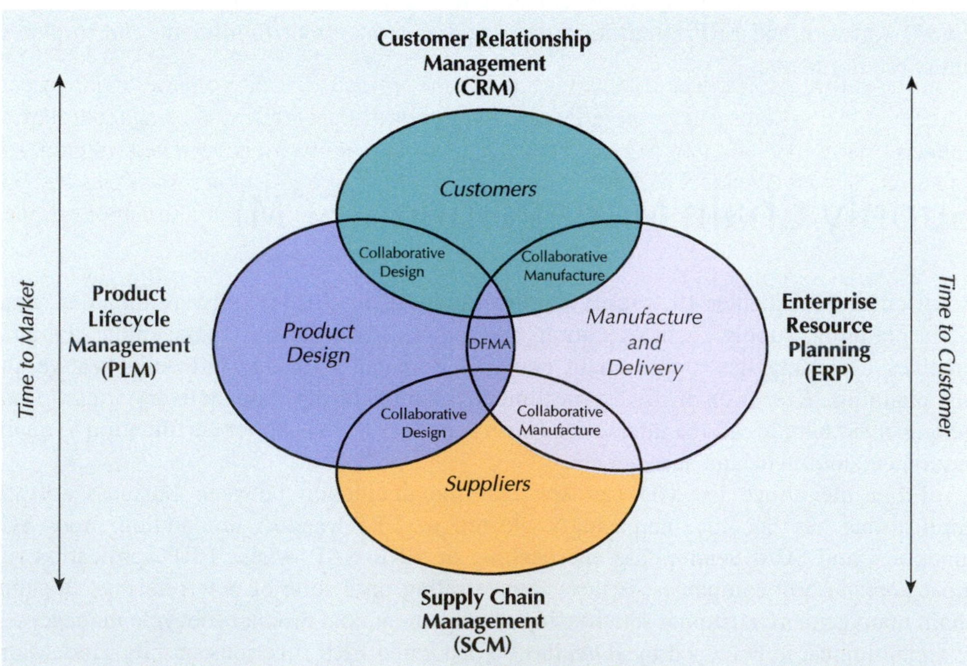

Source: Adapted from George Shaw, "Building the Lean Enterprise: Reducing Time to Market." *Industry Week* (Webcast, June 14, 2001), http://www.industryweek.com/Events/TimeToMarket/pent0614.html.

design with PLM can reduce time to market for new products and services. Similarly, customer and supplier collaboration in manufacturing via ERP helps speed the product to the customer. Design and manufacture collaborate in the DFMA (design for manufacture and assembly) process discussed in Chapter 4.

Connectivity, Integration, Big Data, and the Cloud

Getting ERP, PLM, CRM, and SCM systems talking to each other within a company is difficult. Getting them to communicate across hundreds of different companies and vendors is a daunting task. Using the same suite of products from one vendor facilitates integration, but most companies prefer a best-of-breed approach, buying the products or modules that best fit their business from a variety of vendors. It is common for e-business applications to come with application programming interfaces (APIs) that give other programs well-defined ways of speaking to them. But APIs that allow communication between application A and application B are overwhelmed when applications C, D, and E are added to the exchange. Enter third-party vendors that offer enterprise application integration (EAI). This software breaks down a complex business process into a series of transactions between applications. It then brokers those transactions in language each application can understand. That language is most likely **XML** (for extensible markup language); newer software uses XML extensively.

XML The business language of the Internet.

Electronic data interchange (EDI) used to be the language of business-to-business communication. While EDI is good at transmitting orders and invoices, it cannot change product descriptions, transmit product drawings, update in real time, or easily communicate with ERP systems. XML, on the other hand, was built for the Internet. Instead of downloading data from one system and reentering it into another, XML tags each chunk of data—such as part number, price, and delivery date—before sending it to a trading partner. The receiving XML-run system picks out the data by its tag and inserts it into the proper place in its ERP system. Thus, websites can communicate with websites, computers with computers.

For many companies, purchasing an ERP software package means paying too much money for features and functionality they will never use. Recent trends in software engineering, such as SOA, can provide relief. **Service-oriented architecture (SOA)** is a collection of "services" that communicate with each other within software or between software. Clients can bundle together the services that they need and do not need to purchase the entire software system. These systems can be more flexible and efficient than current offerings, but they can also cost more to customize. SOA radically changes how software is designed, offered, sold, and used. Software vendors like the ability to reuse and share services across clients and business services. SOA also provides a means to deploy and quickly reconfigure applications as business conditions change.

Service-oriented architecture (SOA) A software architecture that bundles together stand-alone services.

We have seen that ERP software can be quite expensive and time consuming to install, maintain, and operate. The decomposition of large software systems into services has prompted another revolution in the way software is delivered to customers. Many companies prefer storing their data or accessing business software, such as ERP or CRM, from the vendor's site or a third-party host site, instead of installing, running and maintaining it in-house. This approach, known as **software as a service (SaaS),** is gaining popularity in both large and small companies. In addition to providing the software on-demand to its clients, vendors or third-party providers also maintain and run the IT infrastructure, including the networks, servers, operating systems, and storage necessary to run the software. This broader view of on-demand IT services, usually delivered by a provider over the Internet, is known as **cloud computing**. Salesforce was the first business software vendor to successfully use cloud computing in the CRM market, followed by NetSuite for e-commerce and financials. Most ERP vendors today offer cloud services. For example, SAP offers *NetWeaver* as its technology platform for SOA and *Business ByDesign* for small to mid-sized businesses who are interested in SaaS.

Software as a service (SaaS) On-demand access of software from a provider site.

Cloud computing On-demand IT services housed on the Internet.

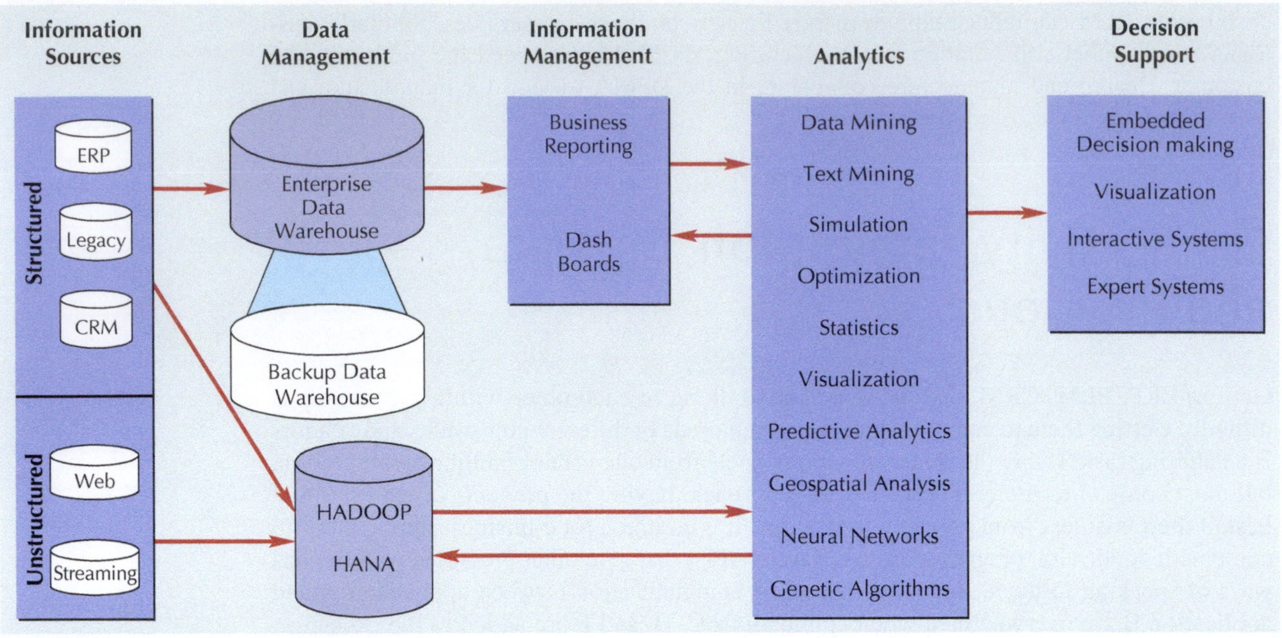

FIGURE 15.14 **Big Data and Analytics**

ERP systems are also challenged by new technologies in big data and analytics. The amount of data in the world is increasing at an unparalleled rate; 90% of the data in the world today was created in the past two years alone. These massive data streams containing both structured and unstructured data are known collectively as **big data**. Companies are challenged with where to store this amount of data, how to analyze it, and how to act on it.

Big data Large volumes of both structured and unstructured data

Unstructured data (video, images, texts, emails, logs, IoT output, etc.) is not represented in a form that can be stored or processed in a relational database, the type of database used by ERP systems. Google, P&G, Ancestry.com, and many other businesses with large data sets use Hadoop, an open-source software for storing and running applications in parallel across hundreds or thousands of machine clusters. While Hadoop is the most popular platform currently used for big data, new technologies for cluster computing are in development. There are also other approaches for big data processing, such as in-memory computing, represented by SAP's HANA platform. How do ERP systems interact with these new technologies? As shown in Figure 15.14, transactional data and other structured data from ERP and related CRM, SCM, and PLM systems are processed through a data warehouse but can also be added to the unstructured data sent to Hadoop or HANA for analysis. Business analytics of various types are applied, decisions are made, and the results sent back to enterprise systems for use in the next cycle. Enterprise systems continue to evolve in functionality, connectivity and integration with new technologies.

Summary

Material requirements planning (MRP) is a computerized inventory control and production planning system. It has enjoyed widespread use in industry, primarily for batch manufacturing, as an information system that improves manufacturing decision making. MRP began as a system for ensuring that sufficient *material* was available when needed. However, in application, it became clear that material was not the only resource in short supply. Planning capabilities for machine and labor resources were added to the system in the form of *capacity requirements planning* (CRP).

MRP requires input from other functional areas of a firm, such as marketing and finance. As these areas began to see the power of a common database system, they encouraged the expansion of MRP into areas such as demand forecasting, demand management, customer order entry, accounts payable, accounts receivable, budgets, and cash flow analysis. Clearly, this enhanced version was more powerful than the original MRP system that ordered material and scheduled production. It provided a common database that the entire company could use. Its what if? capability proved invaluable in evaluating tradeoffs, and the easy access to information encouraged more sophisticated planning. Thus, MRP evolved into a more comprehensive *enterprise resource planning system,* or ERP.

ERP is a powerful software system that organizes and manages business processes across functional areas. In addition to managing all sorts of back-office functions, ERP connects with supply chain and customer management applications, helping businesses share information both inside and outside the company. ERP is essential to related software systems, such as customer relationship management (CRM), supply chain management (SCM), and product lifecycle management (PLM). Connectivity, integration, big data and analytics, and the cloud are current issues in ERP implementation and success.

Key Terms

assemble-to-order A manufacturing environment in which major subassemblies are produced in advance of a customer's order and are then *configured to order.*

backward scheduling Scheduling backward from a due date to determine when to begin a job.

best-of-breed The selection of ERP modules from different vendors.

big data Very large volumes of both structured and unstructured data.

bill of material (BOM) A list of all the materials, parts, and assemblies that make up a product, including quantities, parent–component relationships, and order of assembly.

capacity The maximum capability to produce.

capacity requirements planning (CRP) A computerized system that projects the load from a given material plan onto the capacity of a system and identifies underloads and overloads.

cloud computing On-demand IT services usually delivered over the Internet; includes data storage as well as SaaS.

cumulative lead time The total length of time required to manufacture a product; also, the longest path through a product structure.

customer relationship management (CRM) Software that plans and executes business processes that involve customer interaction, such as sales, marketing, fulfillment, and customer service.

cycle counting A method for auditing inventory accuracy that counts inventory and reconciles errors on a cyclical schedule rather than once a year.

efficiency How well a machine or worker performs compared to a standard output level.

enterprise resource planning (ERP) Software that organizes and manages a company's business processes by sharing information across functional areas.

expedite To speed up orders so that they are completed in less than their normal lead time.

explosion The process of determining requirements for lower-level items by multiplying the planned orders of parent items by the quantity per assembly of component items.

forward scheduling Scheduling forward from today's date to determine the earliest time a job can be completed.

item master file A file that contains inventory status and descriptive information on every item in inventory.

load The standard hours of work assigned to a facility.

load leveling The process of balancing underloads and overloads.

load percent The ratio of load to capacity.

load profile A chart that compares released orders and planned orders with the capacity of a facility.

lot-for-lot (L4L) Ordering in the exact quantities needed.

lot sizing Determining the quantities in which items are usually made or purchased.

master production schedule (MPS) A schedule for the production of end items (usually final products). It drives the MRP process that schedules the production of component parts.

material requirements planning (MRP) A computerized inventory control and production planning system for generating purchase orders and work orders of materials, components, and assemblies.

modular bill of material A special bill of material used to plan the production of products with many optional features.

netting The process of subtracting on-hand quantities and scheduled receipts from gross requirements to produce net requirements.

periodic order quantity A lot sizing technique that orders at set time intervals.

product lifecycle management (PLM) Software that manages the product development process, product lifecycles, and design collaboration with suppliers and customers.

product structure file A file that contains computerized bills of material for all products.

SaaS Software as a service; on-demand access of software from a provider's site.

SOA Service-oriented architecture; a software architecture that bundles together stand-alone services.

supply chain management (SCM) Software that plans and executes business processes related to supply chains.

time fence A date specified by management beyond which no changes in the master schedule are allowed.

time-phased bill of material An assembly chart shown against a time scale.

time phasing The process of subtracting an item's lead time from its due date to determine when an order should be released.

utilization The percentage of available working time that a worker spends working or a machine operating.

XML Extensible markup language; used to help different ERP systems communicate over the Internet.

Solved Problems

Complete the following MRP matrix for item X.

ITEM: X	LLC: 0	PERIOD							
LOT SIZE: MIN 50	**LT: 2**	*1*	*2*	*3*	*4*	*5*	*6*	*7*	*8*
Gross Requirements		20	30	50	50	60	90	40	60
Scheduled Receipts			50						
Projected on Hand	40								
Net Requirements									
Planned Order Receipts									
Planned Order Releases									

a. In what periods should orders be released, and what should be the size of those orders?

b. How would your answer change if the cost of ordering item X were \$100, the cost of carrying were \$2 a week, and the POQ lot sizing technique were used?

c. Which lot sizing technique yields the lowest total cost?

Solution

a.

ITEM: X	LLC: 0	PERIOD							
LOT SIZE: MIN 50	**LT: 2**	*1*	*2*	*3*	*4*	*5*	*6*	*7*	*8*
Gross Requirements		20	30	50	50	60	90	40	60
Scheduled Receipts			50						
Projected on Hand	40	20	40	40	40	30	0	10	0
Net Requirements				10	10	20	60	40	50
Planned Order Receipts				50	50	50	60	50	50
Planned Order Releases		50	50	50	60	50	50		

b. $\bar{d} = 50$ $\quad Q = \sqrt{\dfrac{2(50)(100)}{2}} = 70.711$

$C_o = \$100$

$C_c = \$2$

$POQ = Q/\bar{d} = 1.41 \text{ or } 2 \text{ periods}$

ITEM: X	LLC: 0	PERIOD							
LOT SIZE: POQ 2	**LT: 2**	*1*	*2*	*3*	*4*	*5*	*6*	*7*	*8*
Gross Requirements		20	30	50	50	60	90	40	60
Scheduled Receipts			50						
Projected on Hand	40	20	40	50	0	90	0	60	0
Net Requirements				10		60		40	
Planned Order Receipts				60		150		100	
Planned Order Releases		60		150		100			

c. $TC_{MIN50} = (6 \times \$100) + (180 \times \$2) = \$960$

$TC_{POQ2} = (3 \times \$100) + (260 \times \$2) = \$820$

Choose the POQ lot-sizing technique.

Questions

15.1. Describe a production environment in which MRP would be useful. Describe a production environment in which MRP would *not* be useful.

15.2. Explain with an example the difference between dependent and independent demand.

15.3. What are the objectives, inputs, and outputs of an MRP system?

15.4. How is a master production schedule created, and how is it used?

15.5. What is the purpose of phantom bills, K-bills, and modular bills of material?

15.6. What type of information is included in the item master file?

15.7. Describe cycle counting. How does it improve inventory performance?

15.8. Describe the MRP process, including netting, explosion, lot sizing, and time phasing.

15.9. What are the inputs to capacity requirements planning? Discuss several alternatives for leveling the load on a facility.

15.10. Discuss several assumptions of MRP and how they are being relaxed with new technology.

15.11. Explain how MRP could be applied to (a) the surgery suite of a hospital, (b) scheduling university classes, (c) a chain of restaurants, and (d) hotel renovations.

15.12. How does MRP differ from ERP? Find a description of an MRP module from a software vendor.

15.13. Access the website of an ERP vendor such as Oracle, SAP, Infor, or QAD. Make a list of the modules available. Choose one module to describe in detail.

15.14. What are the capabilities of customer relationship management software? How do ERP and CRM relate?

15.15. What are the capabilities of supply chain management software? How do ERP and SCM relate?

15.16. Compare the ERP/CRM/SCM offerings of two different software vendors.

15.17. What is PLM? How does it relate to other business software?

15.18. Describe how the ERP systems from two different companies can converse.

15.19. While there are numerous ERP software vendors, the two largest are SAP and Oracle. Find out how these two companies compete, and compare their customers and product offerings.

15.20. Discuss the scope of ERP and difficulties in implementation.

15.21. Interview managers at three companies in your area about their use of ERP. How have their experiences been similar? What accounts for the similarities and differences?

15.22. APICS is a professional organization for operations and supply chain management. Find out if there is a local APICS chapter in your area. Attend a meeting and write a summary of the speaker's comments, or access *www.APICS.org* and read one of its online articles.

15.23. From articles in recent business magazines, describe the newest trends in big data, business analytics software, cloud computing and in-memory computing.

15.24. Research the new types of databases and platforms needed to process big data and analytics, such as SAP's HANA and Apache's Hadoop or Spark. What new capabilities do these system bring? How do the approaches differ?

Problems

15.1. Referring to the product structure diagram for product A, determine:

a. how many Ks are needed for each A.

b. how many Es are needed for each A.

c. the low-level code for item E.

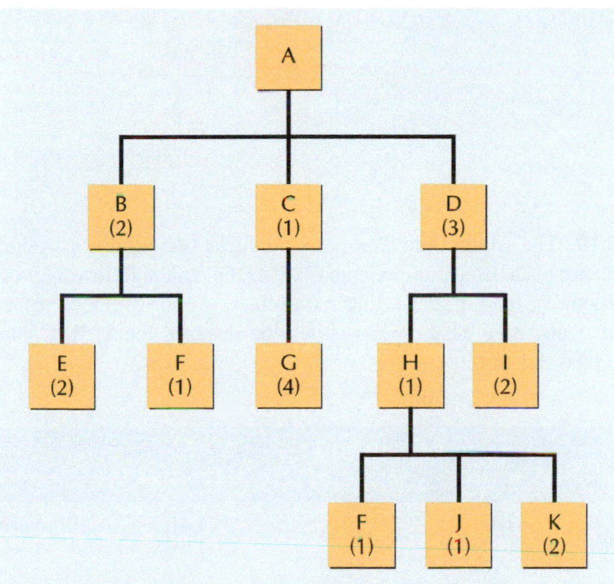

15.2. Construct a multilevel bill of material for product Z. How many Us are needed to make each Z? How many Ws are needed to make each Z?

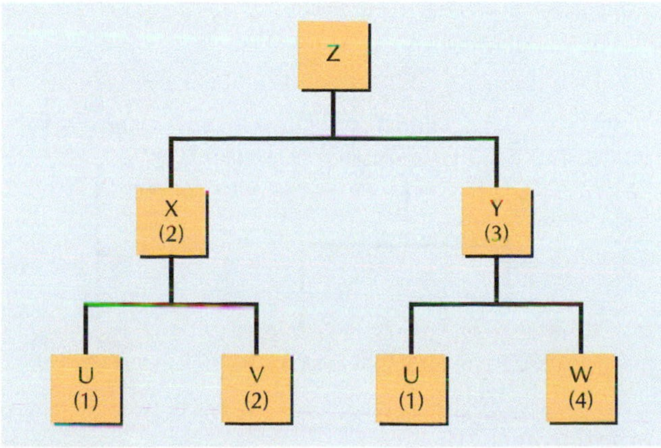

15.3. The classic One-Step step stool shown in the next column is assembled from a prefabricated seat (with bolts attached), one bottom leg, one top leg, five nuts, and four leg tips. Construct a product structure diagram for the One-Step step stool. Be sure to include subassemblies that are formed as part of the assembly process.

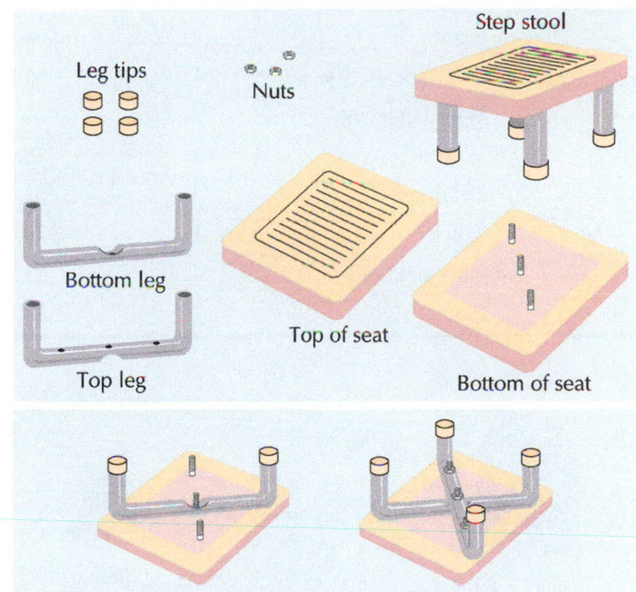

15.4. Draw a product structure diagram from the following bill of materials and calculate how many Ds are needed for each A.

LEVEL	ITEM	QUANTITY
0- - - -	A	1
- 1- - -	B	2
- - 2- -	D	3
- - 2- -	E	2
- 1- - -	C	4
- - 2- -	D	3
- - 2- -	F	1

15.5. Product A is assembled from two units of S1 and three units of S2. S1 is made of one unit of C1, four units of C2, and one unit of C3. S2 is made of three units of C2 and two units of C3.

a. Draw a product structure diagram for product A.

b. How many C3s are needed to fill an order for 100 As?

c. Assume no inventory on hand, products take one day to assemble, subassemblies take two days and components take three days. When should an order be released for C3 if the 100 As are needed by day 7?

15.6. The popular Racer Scooter comes in a variety of colors with lots of options. The customer can choose one of four color wheels, one of three sizes (small, medium, or large), and whether or not to have shocks, a wheelie bar, foam handles, racing stripes, lights, sound effects, a carrying strap, or a carrying bag.

How many different scooters can be made from the various options? Construct a modular bill of material for the Racer Scooter. How many items are in the modular bill? What are the pros and cons of giving the customer so many choices?

15.7. Draw a product structure diagram from the bill of material for an Xavier skateboard shown below. Assuming a 10% profit margin, how should the Xavier be priced?

LEVEL	ITEM	QUANTITY	PRICE
0- - - -	Skateboard	1	
- 1- - -	Deck	1	$54.90
- 1- - -	Grip tape	1	$4.95
- 1- - -	Wheel assembly	2	—
- - 2- -	Wheels	2	$8.95
- - 2- -	Bearings	4	$4.95
- - 2- -	Truck	1	$33.90
- 1- - -	Nuts and bolts	4	$1.99
- 1- - -	Riser	2	$3.95

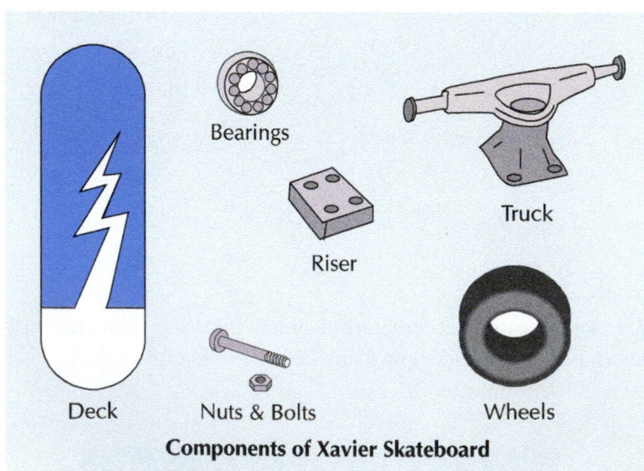

Components of Xavier Skateboard

15.8. The Best Wheels Bicycle Company produces bicycles in different styles for boys and girls, in heights of 26 inches or 20 inches, and with 10 speeds, 3 speeds, or 1 speed.

a. How many different kinds of bicycles does Best Wheels make?

b. Construct a modular bill of material for Best Wheels (one level). Assume that bike sales are equally split between boys and girls, 26-inch bikes are preferred two-to-one to 20-inch bikes, and 3-speed bikes account for only 20% of sales. The remaining sales are divided equally between 10-speed and 1-speed bikes.

c. If bicycle sales are expected to reach 10,000 over the holiday shopping season, how many 26-inch bikes should Best Wheels plan to produce? How many 10-speed bikes?

15.9. Use the product structure diagram for item X shown below to determine:

a. how many E's are needed for each X.

b. how many F's are needed for each X.

c. the LLC for item E.

d. the LLC for item F.

e. how many of each lower-level items (B through I) are needed to fill an order for 50 Xs.

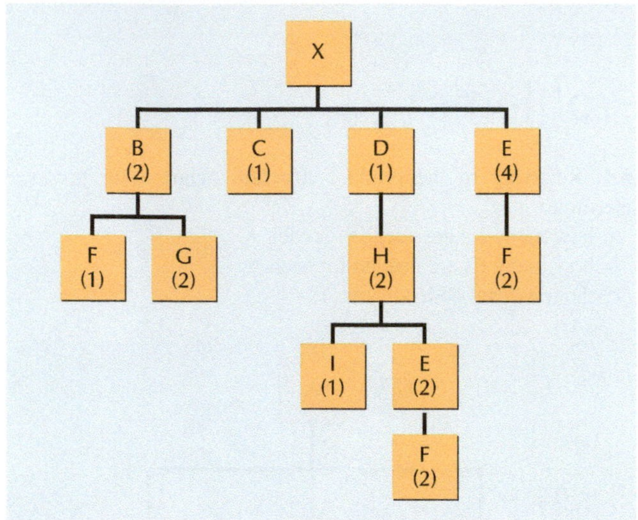

15.10. The Alpha Beta Company produces two products, A and B, that are made from components C and D. Given the following product structures, master scheduling requirements, and inventory information, determine when orders should be released for A, B, C, and D and the size of those orders.

	ON HAND	SCHEDULED RECEIPTS	LOT SIZE	MPS
A	10	0	L4L	100, period 8
B	5	0	L4L	200, period 6
C	140	0	Min 50	—
D	200	250, period 2	Mult 250	—

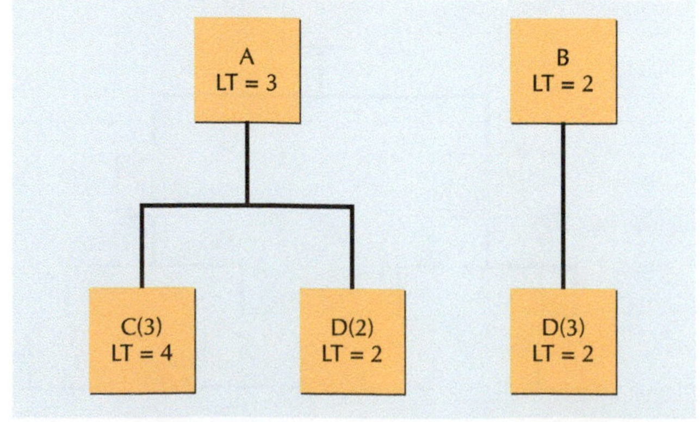

15.11. Kid's World sells outdoor play equipment for children. One of its most popular items is a 5-foot by 7-foot wooden sandbox shown below. General assembly instructions follow.

Assembly Instructions: The wood pieces for the sandbox are ordered precut and treated. Kid's World sands the wood, drills several holes in each piece as required for assembly, and coats each piece with 2 ounces of water sealer. The sides are then assembled one corner at a time by attaching a 1-foot wood strip cater-corner between a 5-foot and 7-foot side. Four bolts are inserted through the predrilled holes and secured with nuts. After the left and right corners of the sandbox have been assembled, the two pieces are joined in a similar manner to form the box assembly. A triangular-shaped wooden seat is attached to each corner of the box assembly with four flat-headed nails for each seat. The sandbox is now complete.

Construct a multilevel bill of material for the sandbox.

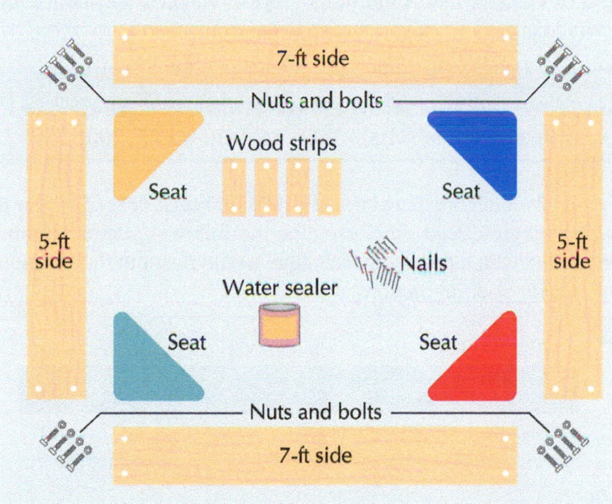

15.12. Complete the following MRP matrix for item A:

ITEM: A	LLC: 1	PERIOD							
LOT SIZE: MULT 50	LT: 2	1	2	3	4	5	6	7	8
Gross Requirements		10	15	25	75	60	85	45	60
Scheduled Receipts									
Projected on Hand	50								
Net Requirements									
Planned Order Receipts									
Planned Order Releases									

15.13. Complete the following MRP matrix for Item X. Determine when orders should be released and the size of those orders.

ITEM: X	LLC: 0	PERIOD							
LOT SIZE: MIN 50	LT: 2	1	2	3	4	5	6	7	8
Gross Requirements		25	30	56	25	100	40	30	20
Scheduled Receipts			50						
Projected on Hand	30								
Net Requirements									
Planned Order Receipts									
Planned Order Releases									

15.14. Complete the MRP matrix below, then answer the questions that follow.

ITEM: D	LLC: 1	PERIOD						
LOT SIZE: MIN 100	LT: 2	1	2	3	4	5	6	7
Gross Requirements		60	90	150	50	180	270	120
Scheduled Receipts			150					
Projected on Hand	120							
Net Requirements								
Planned Order Receipts								
Planned Order Releases								

a. In what periods should orders be released for item D?
b. What is the projected on hand at the end of period 6?
c. What is the size of the order in period 3?
d. How would the periods in which orders are released change if the lot size were L4L?
e. How would the size and timing of the orders released change if the lot size were Mult 100?

15.15. Alpha Corp. (a spinoff of Alpha Beta) makes Product X, which is composed of two Part Ys. Complete the following MRP matrices for X and Y, and construct a planned order report. When are orders placed for items X and Y, and what are the size of those orders?

ITEM: X	LLC: 0	PERIOD							
LOT SIZE: MULT 25	LT: 1	1	2	3	4	5	6	7	8
Gross Requirements					54	75	50	80	100
Scheduled Receipts			150						
Projected on Hand	10								
Net Requirements									
Planned Order Receipts									
Planned Order Releases									

ITEM: Y	LLC: 0	PERIOD							
LOT SIZE: MULT 100	LT: 1	1	2	3	4	5	6	7	8
Gross Requirements									
Scheduled Receipts									
Projected on Hand	25								
Net Requirements									
Planned Order Receipts									
Planned Order Releases									

15.16. Files & More (F&M), a manufacturer of office equipment, is introducing a new product, the BUNGEE desk chair, made from elastic webbing that provides both comfort and support. The materials that go into the chair are shown below.

a. Construct a product structure diagram that reflects how the product is assembled.
b. Convert the product structure diagram into a multi-level indented bill of material.
c. F&M is trying to decide how much of the chair to assemble for the customer prior to shipping. Recommend a pre-assembly

strategy that would allow easy assembly for the customer, and document it with a revised multi-level indented bill of material.

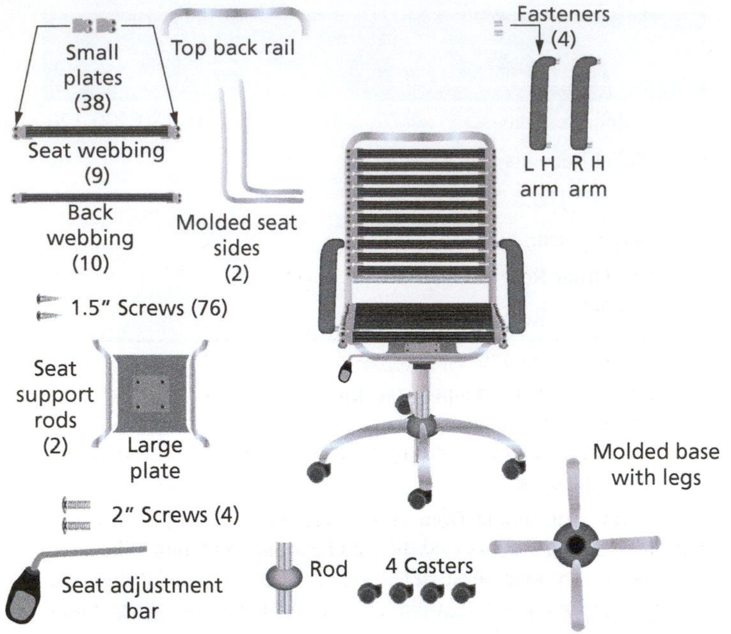

15.17. F&M's best-selling item is a standard office desk. The desk consists of four legs, one top, one drawer, two side panels, one back panel, and two drawer guides, as shown in the next column. Each side is assembled from a side panel, two legs, and a drawer guide. The base is formed from the back panel and two sides. In final assembly, the top is attached to the base and the drawer is slid into place. Lead times are two days for purchased items and one day for assembled items.

a. Construct a time-phased assembly chart for the desk.

b. With no inventory on hand, how long would it take to complete a customer order?

c. The desk sides, back, and drawer are metal. The top is woodgrain. F&M is considering making the desk top in its own factory. The top would take four days to manufacture. Would making the desk top in-house affect the time required to fill a customer order?

d. F&M's customers like the desk and its price, but would like to be able to get desks in three days. Which items should F&M keep in inventory to fill an order in three days?

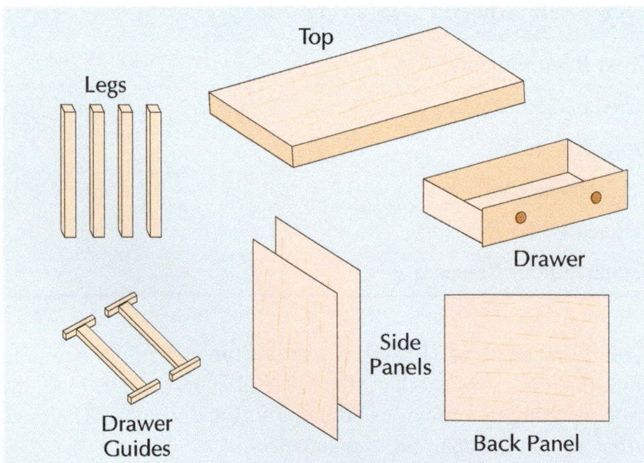

15.18. F&M uses MRP to schedule its production. Because of the current recession and the need to cut costs, F&M has targeted inventory as a prime area for cost reduction. However, the company does not want to reduce its customer service level in the process. Demand and inventory data for a two-drawer file cabinet are given in the following table. Complete an MRP matrix for the file cabinet using: (a) L4L, (b) EOQ, and (c) POQ lot sizing. Which lot-sizing rule do you recommend?

PERIOD	1	2	3	4	5
Demand	20	40	30	10	45

Ordering cost = \$100 per order
Holding cost = \$1 per cabinet per period
Lead time = 1 period
Beginning inventory = 25

15.19. Given 150 units of beginning inventory, a lead time of one period, an ordering cost of \$400 per order, and a holding cost of \$2 per unit per period, determine which lot sizing technique (L4L, EOQ or POQ) would result in the lowest total cost for the following demand data.

PERIOD	1	2	3	4	5	6	7	8
Gross Requirements	100	90	85	70	150	200	300	250

15.20. Given an ordering cost of \$200, a holding cost of \$2 per unit, and a negligible lead time, examine the following demand patterns and predict which lot-sizing technique would result in the lowest total cost. Verify your predictions.

a.

PERIOD	1	2	3	4
Gross Requirements	50	50	50	50

b.

PERIOD	1	2	3	4
Gross Requirements	50	10	50	10

c.

PERIOD	1	2	3	4
Gross Requirements	50	50	10	10

d.

PERIOD	1	2	3	4
Gross Requirements	50	10	10	50

15.21. Daily demand for an item is shown here. Assume a holding cost of \$0.50 per unit per day, a setup cost of \$100 per setup, a lead time of one day and 70 units on hand. Determine when a work order should be released for the item and the size of the order using the L4L, EOQ, and POQ lot sizing techniques. Which technique produces the lowest total cost?

PERIOD	1	2	3	4	5	6	7	8	9	10
Gross Requirements	50	30	25	35	40	50	35	45	70	75

15.22. Product A is assembled from one B and two Cs. Each item requires one or more operations, as indicated by the circles in the product structure diagram. Assume lead time is negligible. From the information given:

a. Develop a load profile chart for each of the three work centers.
b. Level the loads. Discuss possible consequences of shifting work to other periods.

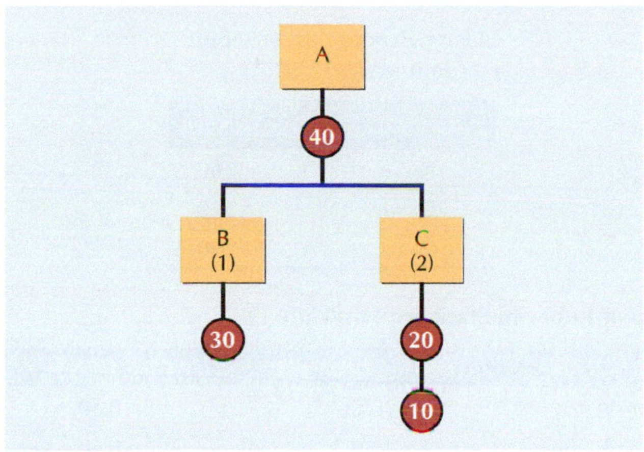

Master Production Schedule

PERIOD	1	2	3	4	5	6
Product A	100	150	100	200	100	100

Routing and Work Standards File

OPERATION	ITEM	WORK CENTER	STANDARD TIME PER UNIT (HR)
10	C	Machining	0.50
20	C	Heat treat	2.00
30	B	Machining	1.00
40	A	Assembly	0.40

15.23. Sitting on Maggie Brumfield's desk is the latest planned order report (shown below) from the company's MRP system. Maggie's job is to determine if there is enough capacity to handle the workload and to level the load if it's uneven. She gathers the latest cost figures and gets to work. Subcontracting and hiring extra workers are not options at this point, but overtime, pulling work ahead, and postponing work are. Regular production costs $10 an hour and is limited to 40 hours a week. Overtime costs $15 an hour and cannot exceed 40 extra hours (i.e., a double shift). An inventory cost of $3 per period is assessed for each hour's worth of work performed in advance. Postponing work costs $20 per period for each hour of work postponed.

a. Completely level the load by working the same number of hours each period (fractions of an hour are acceptable).
b. Economically level the load by assigning work that meets demand at the lowest possible cost. How much money is saved by economically leveling the load?

Planned Order Report

	WEEK			
ITEM	1	2	3	4
A	90			
B	100		250	
C		600		160
D	60			

Processing Times

ITEM	SETUP TIME (MIN)	RUN TIME (MIN PER UNIT)
A	15	3
B	30	15
C	50	10
D	45	4

15.24. Pizza Express offers large pepperoni pizzas for $5 on Tuesdays from 5:00 to 9:00 in the evening. Three cooks are on duty during that time. The fixed cost for the four-hour period is $100. The variable cost is $2 per pizza.

a. If it takes 10 minutes to prepare each pizza, worker efficiency is approximately 95% and employees get a 10-minute break each hour, how many pepperoni pizzas can Pizza Express produce during its four-hour special?
b. Assuming all pizzas produced can be sold, is the promotion worth the effort?

15.25. Amy gets home from classes around 5 P.M. each day and can only reasonably work on her studies until midnight. She usually watches an hour of Netflix to relax, works out for 30 minutes, and takes 30 minutes to eat dinner. She has found that if she takes a 5-minute break each hour, she can remain more focused. Today she feels 80% on task. Homework for the evening includes two critical analyses for Government, one essay for American Lit, and three Spanish translations. Estimated processing times are shown below. Setup time includes time spent online gathering resources and finding reference books around the apartment.

a. What is Amy's effective capacity to do work this evening?
b. What is her load percent?
c. How would you suggest she adjust her capacity to complete her tasks on time?

TASKS	SETUP TIME	PROCESSING TIME PER TASK
Government	15 minutes	40 minutes
American Lit	30 minutes	120 minutes
Spanish	10 minutes	30 minutes

15.26. The Best Wheels Bicycle Company has scheduled the production of the following bicycles this month.

		WEEK			
	MODEL	1	2	3	4
[B2610]	26-inch 10-speed	50	100	195	150
[B2003]	20-inch 3-speed	15	30	65	45
[B2001]	20-inch 1-speed	20	40	80	60

The two critical work centers for producing these bikes are welding and assembly. Welding has an efficiency of 95% and a utilization of 90%. Assembly has an efficiency of 90% and a utilization of 92%. The time required (in hours) by each bike in the two work centers is as follows:

	WELDING	ASSEMBLY
B2610	0.20	0.18
B2003	0.15	0.15
B2001	0.07	0.10

Assume 40 hours is available per week for each work center. Calculate the capacity and load percent per work center per week.

15.27. Bryan is Professor Russell's graduate assistant. He would like to leave for Spring Break tomorrow, but first he has to grade the midterm exams from four classes. These classes are new for Bryan, so he estimates his grading efficiency to be 80%. Professor Russell has estimated the time required to create the key and the time to grade each paper as shown below. Bryan anticipates that he'll need five hours of sleep, an hour to pack, an hour to get to the airport, an hour to post the grades, and three 20-minute breaks during the day for meals. Can Bryan finish his work and make it to the airport on time in a 24-hour day?

CLASS	TIME TO CREATE	TIME TO GRADE EACH PAPER (MINS)	# PAPERS
1	10	2	35
2	15	5	50
3	5	1	60
4	20	10	25

15.28. Given the following information for products A, B, and C, determine the work load in work centers 1 and 2 for January, and the number of workers to assign to each work center. Assume full-time workers work a 40-hour week, 4 weeks per month, and part-time workers are available.

Master Production Schedule For January

PRODUCT	UNITS
A	60
B	220
C	140

Bill of Labor in Standard Hrs/Unit

PRODUCT	WORK CENTER 1	WORK CENTER 2
A	1.70	0.50
B	1.30	0.90
C	1.80	0.66

Case Problems

Case Problem 15.1 Just ERP

Just Sofas (JS) had begun the year full of promise with a new facility, restructured manufacturing process, and high hopes for its new ERP system. Most of the domestic furniture manufacturers had long since gone overseas, but JS believed being close to the customer gave it a competitive edge. The workers had rallied behind President Ruffner's idea of guaranteed four-day deliveries on customer orders. And for a while, the promo had worked. Then orders began pouring in and the scheduling system imploded.

It was for just such a case that Ruffner had sought out an ERP system—to automatically handle customer orders, factory schedules, and supply chain coordination as demand varied. Ruffner had carefully chosen the ERP software package used by all the large corporations he knew of, reasoning that if successful companies had chosen this vendor, who was he to choose otherwise? Implementation had proceeded carefully as well, one might say painstakingly slow, as the IT staff started with the finance module and worked down through sales and marketing, order fulfillment, production planning, MRP, capacity planning, and finally scheduling. Actually, the scheduling module was still having the kinks worked out and the bill of materials file had not been updated to the current catalog offerings, but everything else seemed to be working fine.

Ruffner had included statements about the ERP system in his earnings reports for the past three quarters, noting that "productivity wanes as new IT system is being implemented," "earnings down as company adjusts to new ordering system," and "scheduling glitch causes backlog of customer orders." For this quarter, he was trying to put a more positive spin on "only 5% of orders shipped on time due to incomplete jobs waiting for materials that were not ordered as they should have been." He supposed a more innocuous "new scheduling system still not up to speed" would suffice. What Ruffner really wondered was if the company could survive another year like this one.

1. What capabilities of an ERP system would be useful for a company like Just Sofas?
2. Describe the environment under which the ERP system was being implemented. Was due diligence conducted in choosing the ERP vendor?
3. Does Ruffner understand the relationships between strategy and operations? Why or why not?
4. What problems contributed to the disappointing results of the ERP system? How would you suggest that Just Sofa proceed next year?

Case Problem 15.2 It's Snowing Again!

Gastonia, North Carolina, is not accustomed to significant snowfalls. In the past few years, however, the snow has been relentless. Determined to be prepared this year, the city manager has requested a capacity plan from GDOT (Gastonia Department of Transportation). The roads for which the city is responsible include 10 miles of 6-lane highways, 25 miles of 4-lane primary roads, and 50 miles of 2-lane secondary roads. The standard coverage for keeping roads clear during inclement weather is three passes over highways during a 12-hour time period, two passes over primary roads, and one pass over secondary roads. Gastonia has 10 snowplows with a maximum speed of 35 mph that can clear a width of one lane at a time. During a 3-in. snowfall, the plows are running at 90% efficiency. The efficiency (measured by speed) decreases with the amount of snowfall to 75% during a 6-in. snowfall, 50% for a 1-ft snowfall, and 30% for a 2-ft or greater snowfall. During a normal 8-hour day, workers take one hour total for breaks and lunch. The same ratio is used for 12-hour shifts. This downtime is especially important during inclement weather, as the drivers need to warm up and refocus, and excess snow and salt needs to be removed from the equipment.

Prepare a snow removal capacity plan for Gastonia roads that includes:

a. An estimate of the *capacity* to clear roads in a 12-hour period expressed in miles per type of snowfall (3 in, 6 in., 1 ft, and 2 ft or greater).

b. An estimate of the total work *load* (in miles traveled) over a 12-hour period to keep roadways clear, and per type of road (highway, primary, and secondary).

c. An estimate of the current *load percent*, and a recommendation for adjusting the work load when load percent exceeds 100%.

d. Three alternative recommendations for improving service by expanding capacity and/or reducing the workload. (Budget limitations would allow *at most* the purchase of five extra snowplows). What additional information would you need to make an informed decision?

Case Problem 15.3 Hosuki

Hosuki, a small car maker, competes with larger manufacturers by building cars to order. The company has invested heavily in technology and close partnerships with suppliers. Customers enter their orders and choose their options on the company website. Hosuki's ERP system responds with an estimated cost and completion date. After the customer approves the order, Hosuki sets to work.

Quick response for Hosuki is dependent on collaborative manufacturing with its trading partners. A virtual bill of material for a typical car appears below. Notice each item is color-coded to its supplier and indented beneath its parent assembly. Hosuki has full visibility into its suppliers' ERP systems to check on-hand quantities and order progress. These data are essential in quoting accurate due dates. Most of the car's components are purchased. Hosuki makes the car body, assembles major subassemblies, and completes final assembly and testing. The body stamping machine operates eight hours a day; setup times per item and run times per unit are given in the next column.

Since the suppliers produce in high volume, the lead time for an order is the same regardless of the quantity of the order. In contrast, with limited sales volume and limited space, Hosuki assembles its cars in batches of 10. Each assembly process takes half a day.

Hosuki has just received its first corporate order—for 10 midsized vehicles. The customer would like delivery as soon as possible.

1. Create a time-phased assembly chart to determine when the 10 cars can be delivered.
2. What adjustments are needed in inventory levels, lead times, and batch sizes to fill an additional customer order for five custom cars in five days?

Virtual Bill of Material

Item	Qty
Midsize car	1
Chassis Assembly	1
Frame	1
Power Train Subassembly	1
Engine	1
Transmission	1
Radiator	1
Battery	1
Suspension Subassembly	1
Shocks	2
Brakes	1
Body Assembly	1
Windshield	1
Seats	4
Tire Assembly	4
Wheels	1
Rims	1
Tires	1

Supplier

A	B	C	D	E	F	Hosuki

Supplier lead time is given in days

Supplier A	OH	LT
Shocks	20	1
Brakes	2	4

Supplier D	OH	LT
Frame	10	2
Windshield	5	4

Supplier B	OH	LT
Seats	6	2

Supplier E	OH	LT
Engine	5	5
Transmission	10	6

Supplier C	OH	LT
Wheels	20	1
Rims	2	2
Tires	10	5

Supplier F	OH	LT
Radiator	10	1
Battery	5	3

Hosuki's Body Stamping Machine

	Qty	Setup (hrs)	Runtime (hrs/unit)
Qtr Panel	4	2	0.5
Hood	1	1	0.3
Fender	2	2	0.3
Roof	1	2	0.2
Doors (LH, RH)	4	2	0.2

key: OH = on hand quantity
LT = lead time
Qty = quantity per next level of assembly

References

Bancroft, N., H. Seip, and A. Spungel. *Implementing SAP R/3*. Greenwich, CT: Manning, 1998.

Bond, B., Y. Genovese, et al. "ERP Is Dead—Long Live ERP II." *Gartner Advisory Research Note* (October 4, 2000) http://www.gartner.com.

Bylinsky, G. "Heroes of U.S. Manufacturing." *Fortune* (March 19, 2001). http://www.fortune.com.

Curran, T., and G. Keller. *SAP/3 Business Blueprint*. Upper Saddle River, NJ: Prentice Hall, 1998.

Davenport, T. "Putting the Enterprise into the Enterprise System." *Harvard Business Review* (July/August 1998), pp. 121–131.

Davenport, T. *Mission Critical: Realizing the Promise of Enterprise Systems*. Boston: Harvard Business School Press, 2000.

ERP software vendors: www.sap.com, www.i2.com, www.oracle.com, www.QAD.com.

Jacobs, F.R., W.L. Berry, D.C. Whybark, and T.E. Vollman, *Manufacturing Planning and Control for Supply Chain Management*. New York: McGraw-Hill, 2010.

Kerstetter, J. "When Machines Chat." *BusinessWeek* (July 23, 2001), pp. 76–77.

Michel, R. "ERP Gets Redefined." *MSI Magazine* (February 1, 2001). http://www.manufacturingsystems.com.

Miller, D. "Tying It All Together." *The Industry Standard Magazine* (July 2, 2001). http://www.thestandard.net.

Monk, E. and B. Wagner. *Concepts in Enterprise Resource Planning*. Boston: Course Technology, 2013.

Pender, L. "Faster, Cheaper ERP." *CIO Magazine* (May 15, 2001). http://www.cio.com.

Peterson, K., K. Brant, et al. "Manufacturing Imperatives in Collaborative Commerce." *Gartner Advisory Research Note* (July 31, 2000). http://www.gartner.com.

Phillips, S. *Control Your ERP Destiny*. Street Smarts ERP. 2012.

Ptak, Carol, and Chad Smith, *Orlicky's Material Requirements Planning*. New York: McGraw Hill, 2011.

Savitz, E. "The End of ERP," *Forbes* (February 9, 2012).

Wight, O. *Production Planning and Inverntory Control in the Computer Age*. Boston: Cahners Books International., 1974.

Word, J. *SAP Hana Essentials*. Epistemy Press. 2012.

CHAPTER **16**

Lean Systems

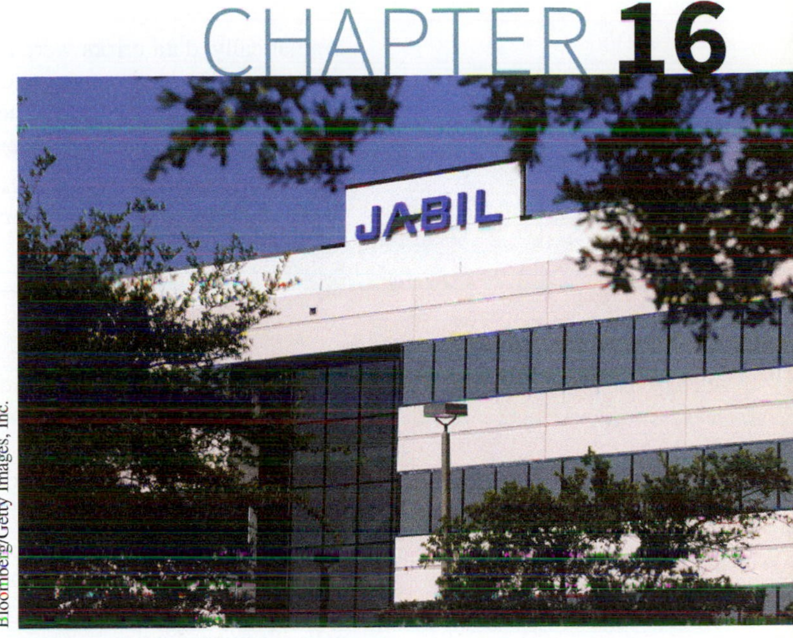

Bloomberg/Getty Images, Inc.

LEARNING OBJECTIVES

After reading this chapter, you will be able to:

- Explain how the basic elements of lean eliminate waste, create flow, and continuously improve operations.
- Assess the benefits of lean, as well as the difficulties in implementing lean systems.
- Explain how the complementary concepts of lean and six sigma work together for process improvement.
- Construct and interpret a value stream map.
- Use lean concepts and techniques to enhance environmental initiatives.
- Create strategies for implementing lean in service industries.

Lean at Jabil

Jabil, like Foxconn, is an electronics manufacturing services (EMS) provider. That means product companies such as Cisco, IBM, and HP will contract out their manufacturing and related services (such as design or testing or servicing) to Jabil to complete. With headquarters in St. Petersburg, Florida (see photo), Jabil employs 180,000 workers at 101 locations in 26 countries, all of whom receive continuous improvement training.

Having a culture of continuous improvement has helped to unify the diverse organization and keep it focused on common goals and practices. Employees can receive a bronze certification for exhibiting knowledge of Lean Six Sigma principles and systems and tools for eliminating waste; a Silver certification for leadership skills and more advanced knowledge of lean principles and tools; a Champion certification for senior leaders who facilitate change management within the company, and a Black Belt certification for in-depth knowledge of Six Sigma principles that lead to variation reduction. A "Deliver Best Practices" event is held annually to reward, recognize, and disseminate innovative process improvements. Teams use the DMAIC methodology to present their improvement projects. This year, 952 teams from 60 sites participated in the competition.

Being able to identify and eliminate waste on a continual basis is a mindset Jabil instills throughout the company into its operations worldwide. In one year, the company conducted more than 71,000 kaizen events. At Jabil Chihuahua, improvement teams used value stream mapping to analyze process flows and redesign the factory floor layout for increased production, cost savings, and less waste. At Jabil Tainjin, a materials team identified the five most costly and least productive manufacturing steps, and proceeded to find a semi-automatic or fully automatic solution to improve each of them. At Jabil Shanghai, a cross-functional team evaluated the inbound customs process to reduce the number of steps, enhance compliance, and convert product data to required customs formats. As a result of their efforts, engineering change notices improved dramatically, data errors were reduced, and inspection rates neared zero. Inbound lead time fell by two days and numerous customs fees and other costs were eliminated.

In this chapter, we study the principles of lean systems and learn how they are applied in both manufacturing and service settings.

Source: Steve Minter, "2014 IW 1000: Jabil Circuit—The Manufacturer's Manufacturer," *Industry Week* (September 8, 2014); Jabil corporate website, http://www.jabil.com/solutions/lean-six-sigma.html (accessed January 19, 2016).

Shortened product lifecycles, demanding customers, globalization, and e-commerce have placed intense pressure on companies for quicker response and shorter cycle times. One way to ensure a quick turnaround is by holding inventory. But inventory costs can easily become prohibitive, especially when product obsolescence is considered. A wiser approach is to make your operating system lean and agile, able to adapt to changing customer demands. We have talked extensively in this book about supply chains. Collaboration along a supply chain can work only if the participants coordinate their production and operate under the same rhythm. Companies have found this rhythm in a well-respected but difficult to implement philosophy called lean production.

Lean production An integrated management system that emphasizes the elimination of waste and the continuous improvement of operations.

Just-in-time (JIT) Smoothing the flow of material to arrive just as it is needed.

Lean production means doing more with less—less inventory, fewer workers, less space. The term was coined by James Womack and Daniel Jones[1] to describe the Toyota Production System, widely recognized as the most efficient manufacturing system in the world.

The Toyota Production System evolved slowly over a span of 20 years. Initially known as **just-in-time (JIT)**, it emphasized minimizing inventory and smoothing the flow of materials so that material arrived just as it was needed or "just-in-time." As the concept widened in scope, the term *lean production* became more prevalent. Now the terms are often used interchangeably.

Taiichi Ohno, a former shop manager and later vice president of Toyota Motor Company, is the individual generally credited with the development of lean production. The idea of producing only what you need when you need it hardly seems the basis of a revolution in manufacturing, but the concept is deceptively simple. If you produce only what you need when you need it, there is no room for error. For lean production to work well, many fundamental elements must be in place—steady production, flexible resources, extremely high quality, reliable equipment, reliable suppliers, quick setups, and the discipline to maintain these elements.

In this chapter, we explore the elements of lean production and try to discover how they became part of Ohno's integrated management system, known as the *Toyota Production System*. We also explore the benefits and drawbacks of lean production and its implementation. We conclude with a discussion of lean services.

The Basic Elements of Lean Production

In the 1950s, the entire Japanese automobile industry produced 30,000 vehicles, fewer than a half day's production for U.S. automakers. With such low levels of demand, the principles of mass production that worked so well for U.S. manufacturers could not be applied in Japan. Furthermore, the Japanese were short on capital and storage space. So it seems natural that efforts to improve performance (and stay solvent) would center on reducing the asset that soaks up both funds and space—inventory. What is significant is that a system originally designed to reduce inventory levels eventually became a system for continually improving all aspects of operations. The stage was set for this evolution by the president of Toyota, Eiji Toyoda, who gave a mandate to his people to "eliminate waste." Waste, or **muda**, was defined as "anything other than the minimum amount of equipment, materials, parts, space, and time which are absolutely essential to add value to the product."[2] Examples of the seven wastes in operations are shown in **Figure 16.1**.

Muda Waste, anything other than that which adds value to the product or service.

[1]J. Womack and D. Jones, *The Machine that Changed the World* (New York: Macmillan, 1990).
[2]Ibid., pp. 8–9.

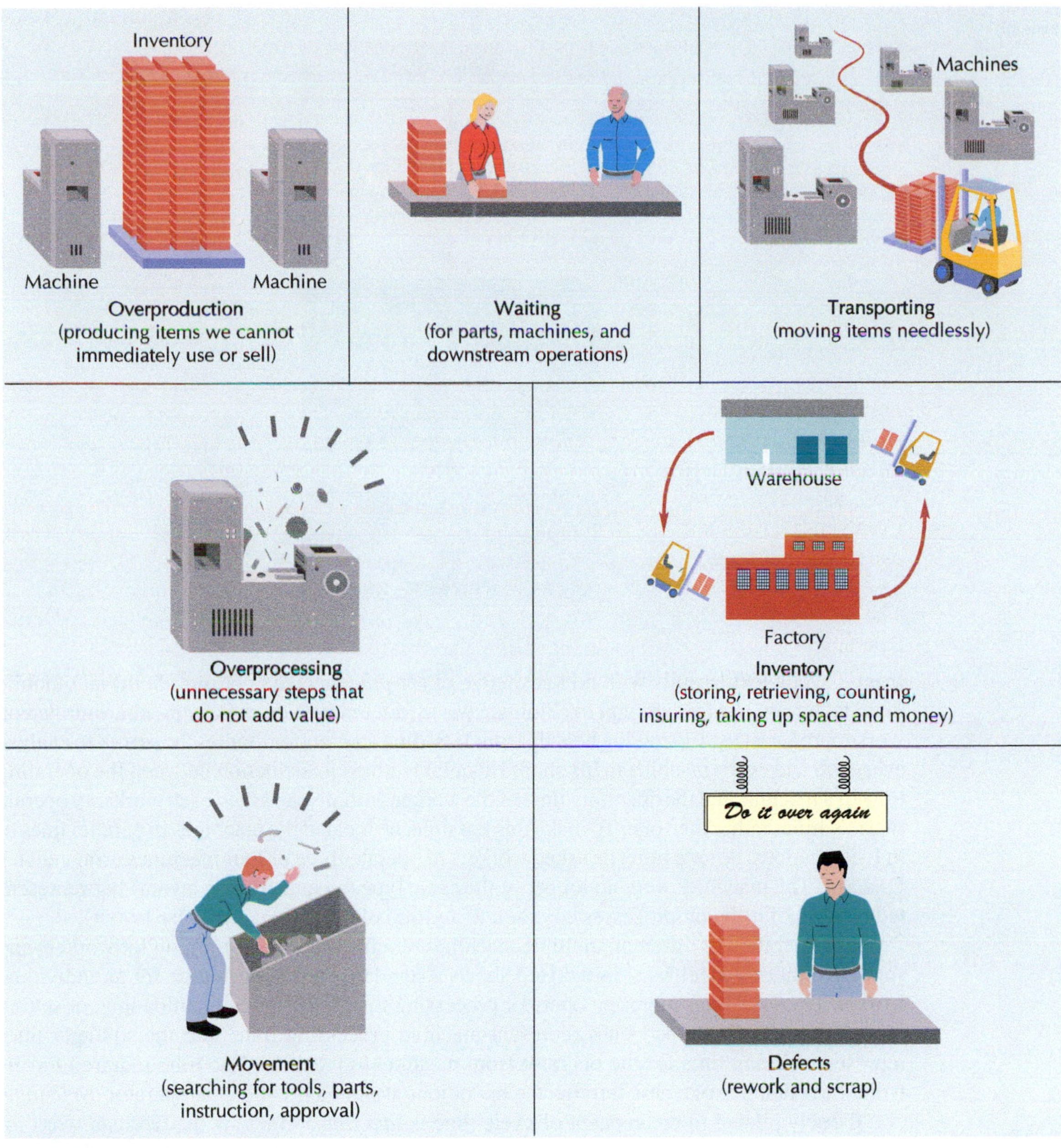

FIGURE 16.1 **The Seven Wastes**

Lean production is the result of the mandate to eliminate waste. It is composed of ten elements:

1. Flexible resources
2. Cellular layouts
3. Pull system
4. Kanbans
5. Small lots
6. Quick setups
7. Uniform production levels
8. Quality at the source
9. Total productive maintenance
10. Supplier networks

These elements can be loosely organized into three phases, as shown in Figure 16.2. Let's explore each of these elements and determine how they work in concert.[3]

Flexible Resources

Multifunctional workers Perform more than one job.

General-purpose machines Perform several basic functions.

The concept of flexible resources, in the form of **multifunctional workers** and **general-purpose machines**, is recognized as a key element of lean production, but most people do not realize that it was the first element to fall into place. Taiichi Ohno had transferred to Toyota

[3]Much of the material in these sections is adapted from Chapter 5 in Michael Cusomano's book, *The Japanese Automobile Industry* (Cambridge, MA: Harvard University Press), 1985.

FIGURE 16.2 **Elements of Lean Production**

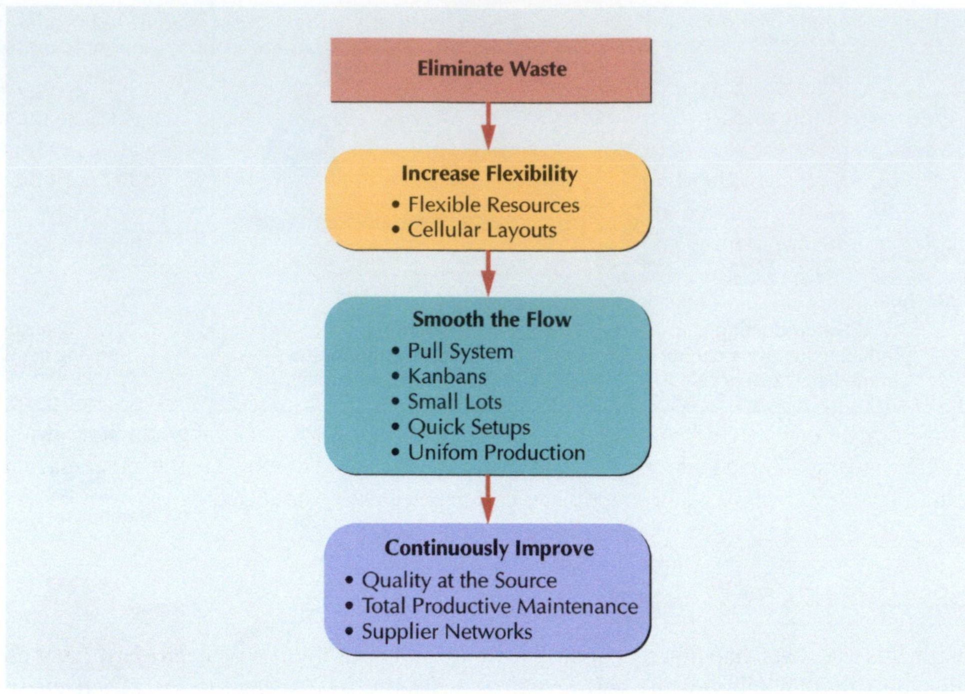

from Toyoda textile mills with no knowledge of (or preconceived notions about) automobile manufacturing. His first attempt to eliminate waste (not unlike U.S. managers) concentrated on worker productivity. Borrowing heavily from U.S. time and motion studies, he set out to analyze every job and every machine in his shop. He quickly noted a distinction between the operating time of a machine and the operating time of the worker. Initially, he asked each worker to operate two machines rather than one. To make this possible, he located the machines in parallel lines or in L-formations. After a time, he asked workers to operate three or four machines arranged in a U-shape. The machines were no longer of the same type (as in a process layout) but represented a series of different processes common to a group of parts (i.e., a cellular layout).

The operation of different, multiple machines required additional training for workers and specific rotation schedules. Figure 16.3 shows a standard operating routine for an individual worker. The solid lines represent operator processing time (e.g., loading, unloading, or setting up a machine), the dashed lines represent machine processing time, and the squiggly lines represent walking time for the operator from machine to machine. The time required for the worker to complete one pass through the operations assigned is called the operator *cycle time.*

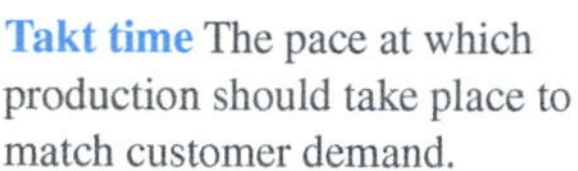

Takt time The pace at which production should take place to match customer demand.

Closely related to the concept of cycle time is *takt time*. "Takt" is the German word for baton, such as an orchestra leader would use to signal the timing at which musicians play. **Takt time**, then, is the pace at which production should take place to match the rate of

FIGURE 16.3 **Standard Operating Routine for a Worker**

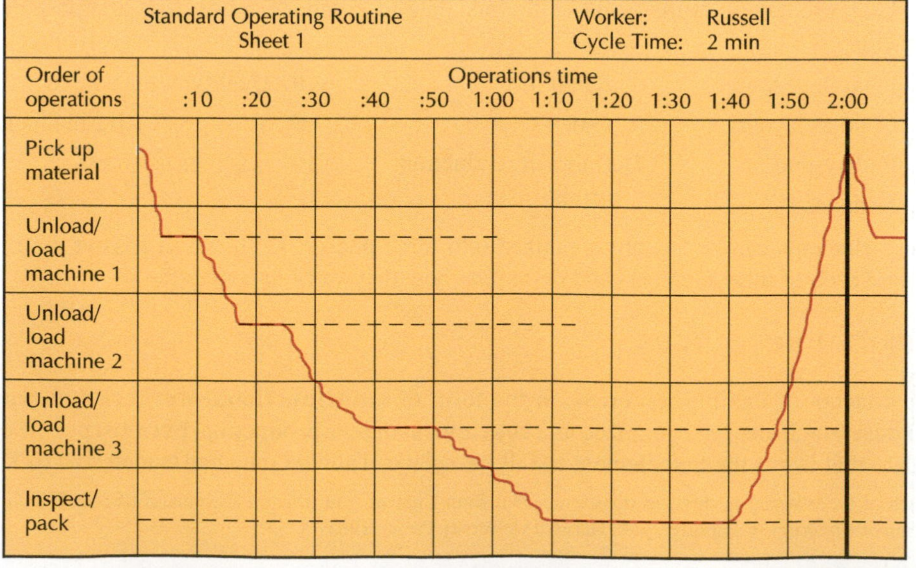

customer demand. An operator's cycle time is coordinated with the takt time of the product or service being produced.

With single workers operating multiple machines, the machines themselves also required some adjustments. Limit switches were installed to turn off machines automatically after each operation was completed. Changes in jigs and fixtures allowed machines to hold a workpiece in place, rather than rely on the presence of an operator. Extra tools and fixtures were purchased and placed at their point of use so that operators did not have to leave their stations to retrieve them when needed. By the time Ohno was finished with this phase of his improvement efforts, it was possible for one worker to operate as many as 17 machines (the average was 5 to 10).

The flexibility of labor brought about by Ohno's changes prompted a switch to more flexible machines. Thus, although other manufacturers were interested in purchasing more specialized automated equipment, Toyota preferred small, general-purpose machines. A general-purpose lathe, for example, might be used to bore holes in an engine block and then do other drilling, milling, and threading operations at the same station. The waste of movement to other machines, setting up other machines, and waiting at other machines was eliminated.

Cellular Layouts

While it is true that Ohno first reorganized his shop into **manufacturing cells** to use labor more efficiently, the flexibility of the new layout proved to be fundamental to the effectiveness of the system as a whole. The concept of cellular layouts did not originate with Ohno. It was first described by a U.S. engineer in the 1920s, but it was Ohno's inspired application of the idea that brought it to the attention of the world. We discussed cellular layouts (and the concept of group technology on which it is based) in Chapter 7. Let us review some of that material here.

Manufacturing cells Dissimilar machines brought together to manufacture a family of parts.

Cells group dissimilar machines together to process a family of parts with similar shapes or processing requirements. The layout of machines within the cell resembles a small assembly line and is usually U-shaped. Work is moved within the cell, ideally one unit at a time, from one process to the next by a worker as he or she walks around the cell in a prescribed path. Figure 16.4 shows a typical manufacturing cell with worker routes.

Work normally flows through the cell in one direction and experiences little waiting. In a one-person cell, the cycle time of the cell is determined by the time it takes for the worker to complete his or her path through the cell. This means that, although different items produced in the cell may take different amounts of time to complete, the time between successive items

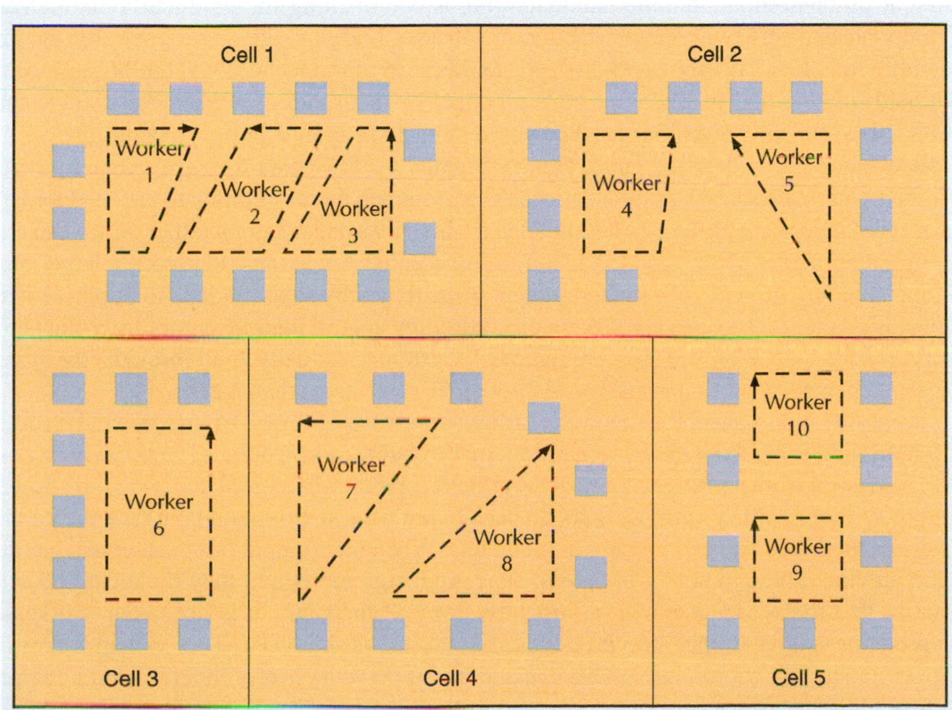

FIGURE 16.4 Cells with Worker Routes

FIGURE 16.5 **Worker Routes Lengthen as Volume Decreases**

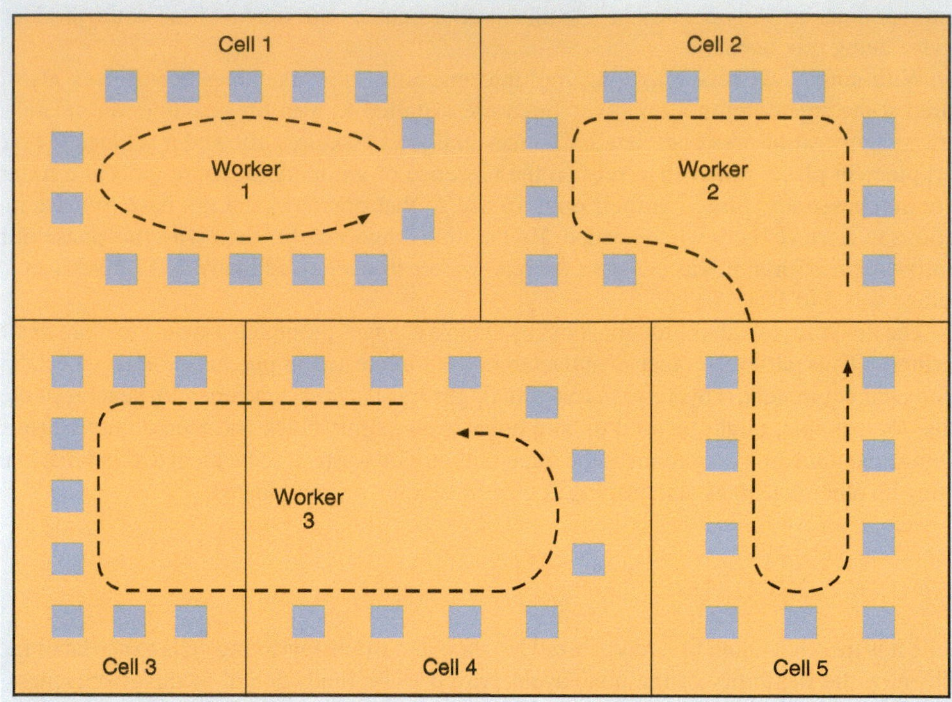

leaving the cell remains virtually the same because the worker's path remains the same. Thus, changes of product mix within the cell are easy to accommodate. Changes in volume or takt time can be handled by adding workers to or subtracting workers from the cell and adjusting their walking routes accordingly as shown in Figure 16.5.

Because cells produce similar items, setup time requirements are low and lot sizes can be reduced. Movement of output from the cells to subassembly or assembly lines occurs in small lots and is controlled by kanbans (which we discuss later). Cellular layouts, because of their manageable size, workflow, and flexibility, facilitate another element of lean production, the *pull system*.

The Pull System

A major problem in automobile manufacturing is coordinating the production and delivery of materials and parts with the production of subassemblies and the requirements of the final assembly line. It is a complicated process, not because of the technology, but because of the thousands of large and small components produced by thousands of workers for a single automobile. Traditionally, inventory has been used to cushion against lapses in coordination, and these inventories can be quite large. Ohno struggled for five years trying to come up with a system to improve the coordination between processes and thereby eliminate the need for large amounts of inventory. He finally got the idea for his *pull* system from another American classic, the supermarket. Ohno read (and later observed) that Americans do not keep large stocks of food at home. Instead, they make frequent visits to nearby supermarkets to purchase items as they need them. The supermarkets, in turn, carefully control their inventory by replenishing items on their shelves only as they are removed. Customers actually "pull through" the system the items they need, and supermarkets do not order more items than can be sold.

Push systems Rely on a predetermined schedule.

Pull systems Rely on customer requests.

Applying this concept to manufacturing requires a reversal of the normal process/information flow, called a *push* system. In a **push system**, a schedule is prepared in advance for a series of workstations, and each workstation pushes its completed work to the next station. With the **pull system**, workers go back to previous stations and take only the parts or materials they need and can process immediately. When their output has been taken, workers at the previous station know it is time to start producing more, and they replenish the exact quantity that the subsequent station just took away. If their output is not taken, workers at the previous station simply stop production; no excess is produced. This system forces operations to work in coordination with one another. It prevents overproduction and underproduction; only necessary quantities are produced. "Necessary" is not defined by a schedule

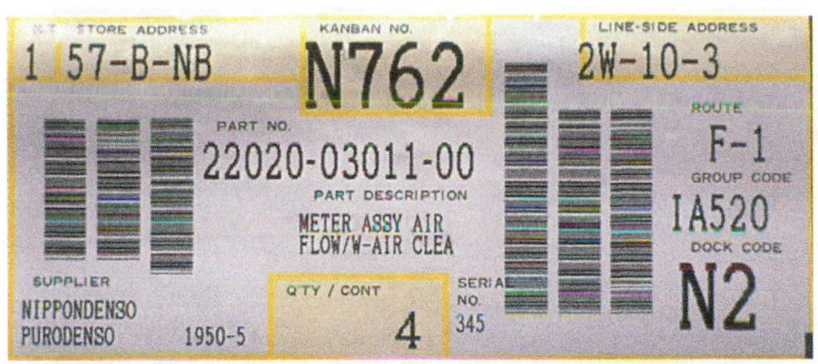

Photo Courtesy Toyota Motor Manufacturing, Kentucky, Inc. Georgetown, Kentucky, and Purodenso

This supplier kanban attached to a container rotates between Purodenso Manufacturing and a Toyota assembly plant. The part number, description, and quantity per container appear in the center of the card, directly beneath the kanban number. Notice the container holds four air flow meter assemblies. The store address in the upper left-hand corner specifies where the full container is to be delivered. The line-side address in the upper right-hand corner specifies where the empty container is to be picked up. The lower left-hand corner identifies the preceding process (the assemblies come from Purodenso), and the lower right-hand corner identifies the subsequent process (N2). Barcoding the information on the card speeds processing and increases the accuracy of production and financial records.

that specifies what ought to be needed; rather, it is defined by the operation of the shop floor, complete with unanticipated occurrences and variations in performance.

Although the concept of pull production seems simple, it can be difficult to implement because it is so different from normal scheduling procedures. After several years of experimenting with the pull system, Ohno found it necessary to introduce *kanbans* to exercise more control over the pull process on the shop floor.

Kanbans

Kanban is the Japanese word for card. In the pull system, each kanban corresponds to a standard quantity of production or size of container. A kanban contains basic information such as part number, brief description, type of container, unit load (i.e., quantity per container), preceding station (where it came from), and subsequent station (where it goes to), as shown in the photo. Sometimes the kanban is color-coded to indicate raw materials or other stages of manufacturing. The information on the kanban does not change during production. The same kanban can rotate back and forth between preceding and subsequent workstations.

Kanban A card that corresponds to a standard quantity of production (usually a container size).

Kanbans are closely associated with the fixed-quantity inventory system we discussed in Chapter 13. Recall that in the fixed-quantity system, a certain quantity, Q, is ordered whenever the stock on hand falls below a reorder point. The reorder point is determined so that demand can be met while an order for new material is being processed. Thus, the reorder point corresponds to demand during lead time. A visual fixed-quantity system, called the *two-bin system*, illustrates the concept nicely. Referring to **Figure 16.6*a***, two bins are maintained for each item. The first (and usually larger) bin contains the order quantity minus the reorder point, and the second bin contains the reorder point quantity. At the bottom of the first bin is an order card that describes the item and specifies the supplier and the quantity that is to be ordered. When the first bin is empty, the card is removed and sent to the supplier as a new order. While the order is being filled, the quantity in the second bin is used. If everything goes as planned, when the second bin is empty, the new order will arrive and both bins will be filled again.

Ohno looked at this system and liked its simplicity, but he could not understand the purpose of the first bin. As shown in Figure 16.6*b*, by eliminating the first bin and placing the order card (which he called a *kanban*) at the top of the second bin, $(Q - R)$ inventory could be eliminated. In this system, an order is continually in transit. When the new order arrives, the supplier is reissued the same kanban to fill the order again. The only inventory that is maintained is the amount needed to cover usage until the next order can be processed. This concept is the basis for the kanban system.

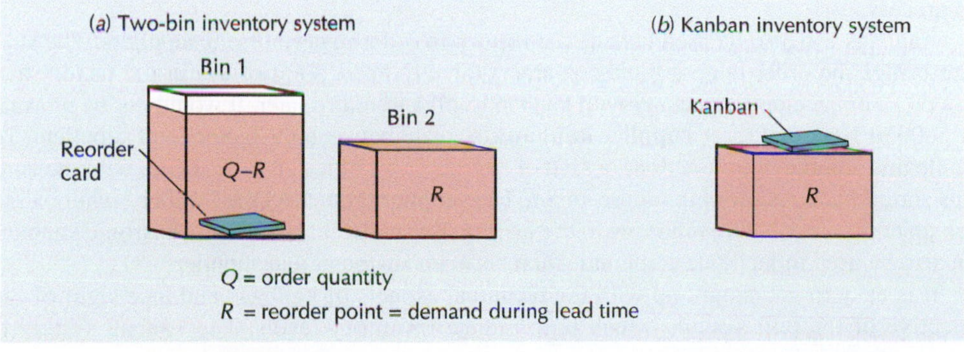

FIGURE 16.6 **The Origin of Kanban**

FIGURE 16.7 **Dual Kanbans**

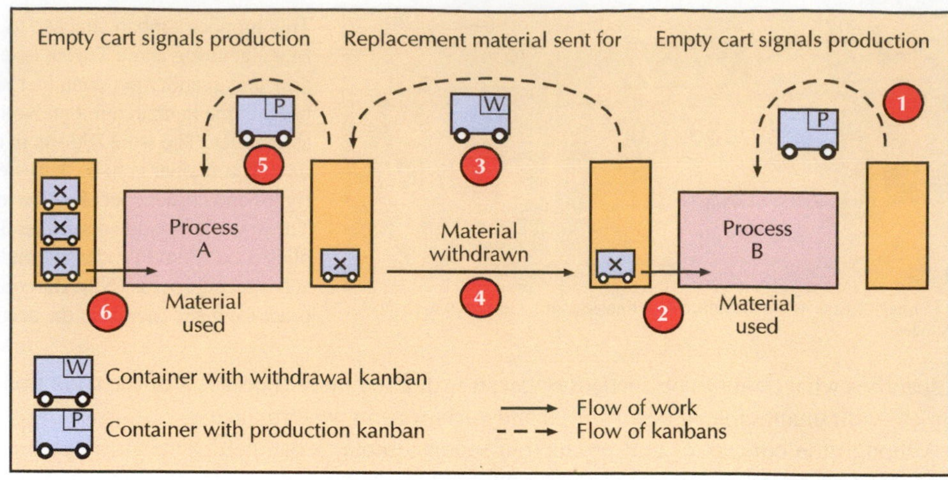

Kanbans do not make the schedule of production; they maintain the discipline of pull production by authorizing the production and movement of materials. If there is no kanban, there is no production. If there is no kanban, there is no movement of material. There are many different types and variations of kanbans. The most sophisticated is probably the dual kanban system used by Toyota, which uses two types of kanbans: *production kanbans* and *withdrawal kanbans*. As their names imply, a **production kanban** is a card authorizing production of goods, and a **withdrawal kanban** is a card authorizing the movement of goods. Each kanban is physically attached to a container or cart. As shown in Figure 16.7, an empty cart signals production or withdrawal of goods. Kanbans are exchanged between containers as needed to support the pull process.

Production kanban A card authorizing production of goods.

Withdrawal kanban A card authorizing the movement of goods.

The dual kanban approach is used when material is not necessarily moving between two consecutive processes, or when there is more than one input to a process and the inputs are dispersed throughout the facility (as for an assembly process). If the processes are tightly linked, other types of kanbans can be used.

Figure 16.8*a* shows the use of kanban squares placed between successive workstations. A **kanban square** is a marked area that will hold a certain number of output items (usually one or two). If the kanban square following his or her process is empty, the worker knows it is time to begin production again. *Kanban racks*, also known as *supermarkets*, are illustrated in Figure 16.8*b*. When the allocated slots on a rack or shelf are empty, workers know it is time to begin a new round of production to fill up the slots. Often, these racks or shelves will be open-backed and placed between two operations with the operator on one side using the material on the racks and the operator on the other side replenishing the material. If the distance between stations prohibits the use of kanban squares or racks, the signal for production can be a colored golf ball rolled down a tube, a flag on a post, a light flashing on a board, or an electronic or verbal message requesting more.

Kanban square A marked area designated to hold items.

Signal kanbans are used when inventory between processes is still necessary. It closely resembles the reorder point system. As shown in Figure 16.8*c*, a triangular marker is placed at a certain level of inventory. When the marker is reached (a visual reorder point), it is removed from the stack of goods and placed on a kanban post, thereby generating a replenishment order for the item. The rectangular-shaped kanban in the diagram is called a **material kanban**. In some cases it is necessary to order the *material* for a process in advance of the initiation of the process.

Signal kanban A triangular kanban used to signal production at the previous workstation.

Material kanban A rectangular kanban used to order material in advance of a process.

Kanbans can also be used outside the factory to order material from suppliers. The supplier brings the order (e.g., a filled container) directly to its point of use in the factory and then picks up an empty container with kanban to fill and return later. It would not be unusual for 5000 to 10,000 of these **supplier kanbans** to rotate between the factory and suppliers. To handle this volume of transactions, a kind of kanban "post office" can be set up, with the kanbans sorted by supplier, as in Figure 16.8*d*. The supplier then checks his or her "mailbox" to pick up new orders before returning to the factory. Bar-coded kanbans and electronic kanbans can also be used to facilitate communication between customer and supplier.

Supplier kanbans Rotate between the factory and suppliers.

It is easy to get caught up with the technical aspects of kanbans and lose sight of the objective of the pull system, which is to reduce inventory levels. The kanban system is

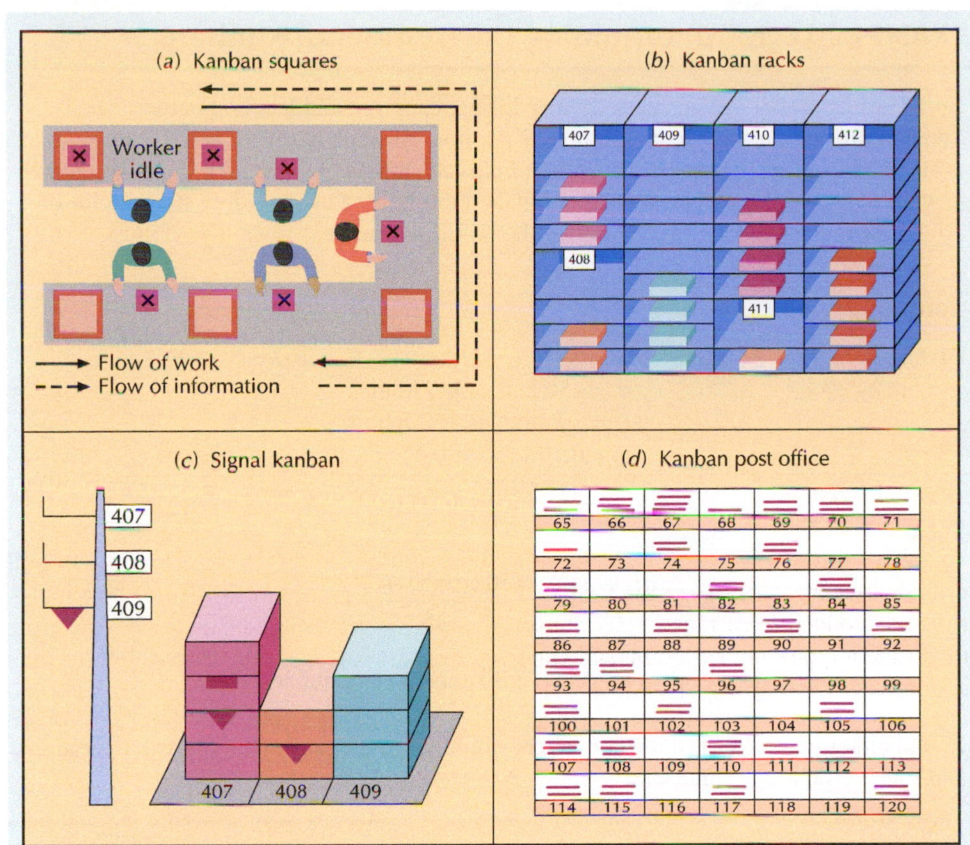

FIGURE 16.8 Other Types of Kanbans

actually very similar to the reorder point system. The difference is in application. The reorder point system attempts to create a permanent ordering policy, whereas the kanban system encourages the continual reduction of inventory. We can see how that occurs by examining the formula for determining the number of kanbans needed to control the production of a particular item.

$$\text{No. of kanbans} = \frac{\text{average demand during lead time} + \text{safety stock}}{\text{container size}}$$

$$N = \frac{\bar{d}L + S}{C}$$

where

N = number of kanbans or containers
$\bar{d}$ = average number of units demanded over some time period
L = lead time; the time it takes to replenish an order (expressed in the same terms as demand)
S = safety stock; usually given as a percentage of demand during lead time but can be based on service level, lead time and the standard deviation of demand during lead time (as in Chapter 13)
C = container size

To force the improvement process, the container size is usually much smaller than the demand during lead time. At Toyota, containers can hold at most 10% of a day's demand. This allows the number of kanbans (i.e., containers) to be reduced one at a time. The smaller number of kanbans (and corresponding lower level of inventory) causes problems in the system to become visible. Workers and managers then attempt to solve the problems that have been identified.

EXAMPLE 16.1 | Determining the Number of Kanbans

Julie Hurling works in a cosmetic factory filling, capping, and labeling bottles. She is asked to process an average of 150 bottles per hour through her work cell. If one kanban is attached to every container, a container holds 25 bottles, it takes 30 minutes to receive new bottles from the previous workstation, and the factory uses a safety stock factor of 10%, how many kanbans are needed for the bottling process?

Solution:

Given:

$$\bar{d} = 150 \text{ bottles per hour}$$
$$L = 30 \text{ minutes} = 0.5 \text{ hour}$$
$$S = 0.10\,(150 \times 0.5) = 7.5$$
$$C = 25 \text{ bottles}$$

Then,

$$N = \frac{dL + S}{C} = \frac{(150 \times 0.5) + 7.5}{25}$$
$$= \frac{75 + 7.5}{25} = 3.3 \text{ kanbans or containers}$$

Round either up or down (three containers would force the factory to improve operations, and four would allow some slack).

Small Lots

Small-lot production requires less space and capital investment than systems that incur large inventories. By producing small amounts at a time, processes can be physically moved closer together and transportation between stations can be simplified. In small-lot production, quality problems are easier to detect and workers show less tendency to let poor quality pass (as they might in a system that is producing huge amounts of an item anyway). Lower inventory levels make processes more dependent on each other. This is beneficial because it reveals errors and bottlenecks more quickly and gives workers an opportunity to solve them.

The analogy of water flowing over a bed of rocks is useful here. As shown in **Figure 16.9**, the inventory level is like the level of water. It hides problems but allows for smooth sailing. When the inventory level is reduced, the problems (or rocks) are exposed. After the exposed rocks are removed from the river, the boat can again progress, this time more quickly than before.

Although it is true that a company can produce in small lot sizes without using the pull system or kanbans, from experience we know that small-lot production in a push system is difficult to coordinate. Similarly, using large lot sizes with a pull system and kanbans would not be advisable. Let's look more closely at the relationship between small lot sizes, the pull system, and kanbans.

From the kanban formula, it becomes clear that a reduction in the number of kanbans (given a constant container size) requires a corresponding reduction in safety stock or in lead time itself. The need for safety stock can be reduced by making demand and supply more certain. Flexible resources allow the system to adapt more readily to unanticipated changes in demand. Demand fluctuations can also be controlled through closer contact with customers and better forecasting systems. Deficiencies in supply can be controlled through eliminating mistakes, producing only good units, and reducing or eliminating machine breakdowns.

Lead time is typically made up of four components:

- Processing time
- Move time
- Waiting time
- Setup time

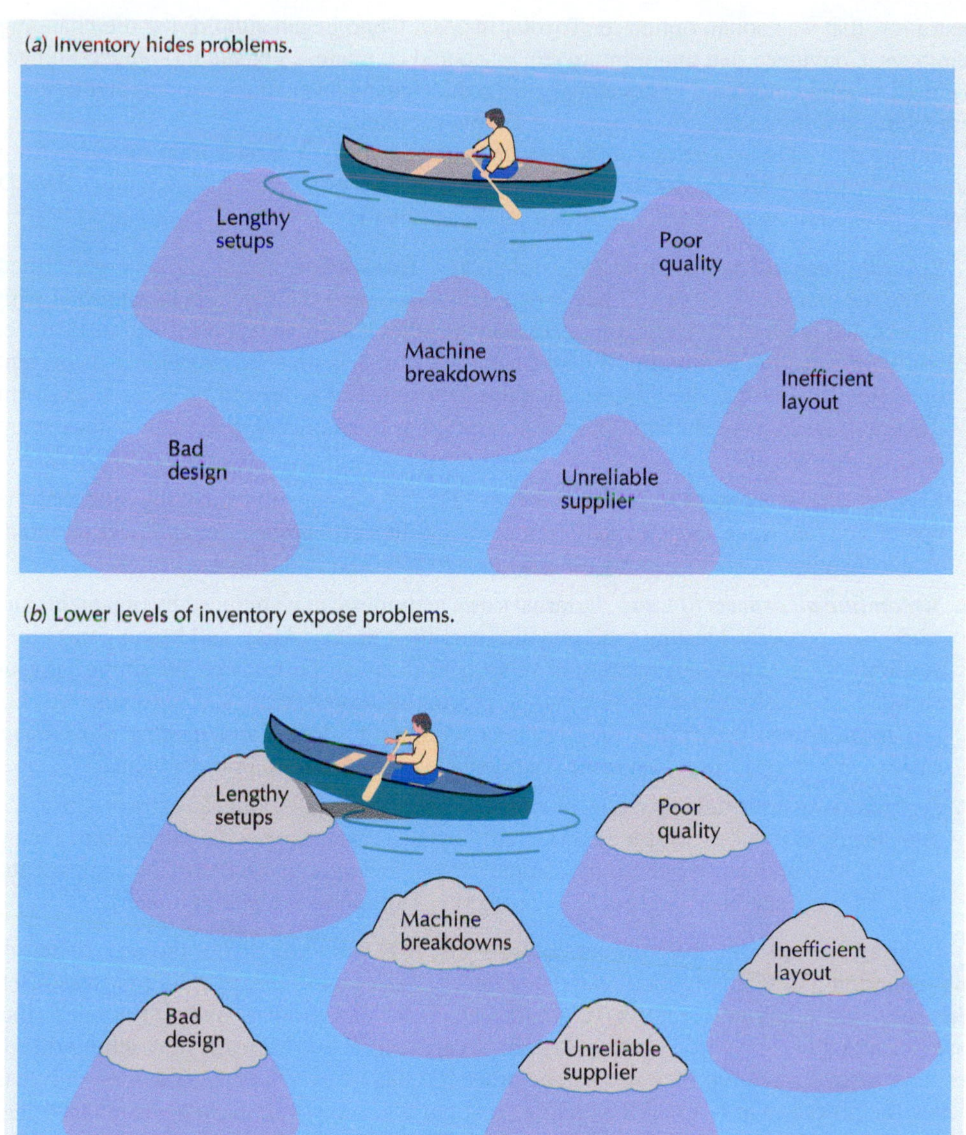

FIGURE 16.9 Reduced Inventory Makes Problems Visible

Processing time can be reduced by reducing the number of items processed and the efficiency or speed of the machine or worker. *Move time* can be decreased if machines are moved closer together, the method of movement is simplified, routings are standardized, or the need for movement is eliminated. *Waiting time* can be reduced through better scheduling of materials, workers and machines, and sufficient capacity. In many companies, however, lengthy *setup times* are the biggest bottleneck. Reduction of setup time is an important part of lean production.

Quick Setups

Several processes in automobile manufacturing defy production in small lots because of the enormous amount of time required to set up the machines. Stamping is a good example. First, a large roll of sheet steel is run through a blanking press to produce stacks of flat blanks slightly larger than the size of the desired parts. Then, the blanks are inserted into huge stamping presses that contain a matched set of upper and lower dies. When the dies are held together under thousands of pounds of pressure, a three-dimensional shape emerges, such as a car door or fender. Because the dies weigh several tons each and have to be aligned with exact precision, die changes typically take an entire day to complete.

Obviously, manufacturers are reluctant to change dies often. Ford, for example, might produce 500,000 right door panels and store them in inventory before switching dies to produce left door panels. Some manufacturers have found it easier to purchase several sets of presses and dedicate them to stamping out a specific part for months or years. Due to capital constraints, that was not an option for Toyota. Instead, Ohno began simplifying die-changing techniques. Convinced that major improvements could be made, a consultant, Shigeo Shingo, was hired to study die setup systematically, to reduce changeover times further, and to teach these techniques to production workers and Toyota suppliers.

SMED Single minute exchange of dies

Internal setups Setup activities that can be performed only when a process is stopped.

External setups Setup activities that can be performed in advance.

Shingo proved to be a genius at the task. He reduced setup time on a 1000-ton press from 6 hours to 3 minutes using a system he called **SMED** (single-minute exchange of dies). SMED is based on the following principles, which can be applied to any type of setup:

1. ***Separate internal setups from external setups.*** **Internal setups** have to be performed while the machine is stopped; they cannot take place until the machine has finished with the previous operation. **External setups**, on the other hand, can be performed in advance, while the machine is running. By the time a machine has finished processing its current operation, the worker should have completed the external setup and be ready to perform the internal setup for the next operation. Applying this concept alone can reduce setup time by 30% to 50%.
2. ***Convert internal setups to external setups***. This process involves making sure that the operating conditions, such as gathering tools and fixtures, preheating an injection mold, centering a die, or standardizing die heights, are prepared in advance.
3. ***Streamline all aspects of setup***. External setup activities can be reduced by organizing the workplace properly, locating tools and dies near their points of use, and keeping machines and fixtures in good repair. Internal setup activities can be reduced by simplifying or eliminating adjustments. Examples include precoding desired settings, using quick fasteners and locator pins, preventing misalignment, eliminating tools, and making movements easier. Figure 16.10 provides some common analogies for these improvements.
4. ***Perform setup activities in parallel or eliminate them entirely***. Adding an extra person to the setup team can reduce setup time considerably. In most cases, two people can perform a setup in less than half the time needed by a single person. In addition, standardizing components, parts, and raw materials can reduce and sometimes eliminate setup requirements.

In order to view the setup process objectively, it is useful to assign the task of setup-time reduction to a team of workers and engineers. Videotaping the setup in progress often helps the team generate ideas for improvement. Time and motion study principles (like those discussed in the Supplement to Chapter 8) can be applied. After the new setup procedures have been agreed on, they need to be practiced until they are perfected. One only has to view the pit crews at NASCAR to realize that quick changeovers have to be orchestrated and practiced.

Reducing setup time requires teamwork, practice, and a careful coordination of activities, not unlike the precision pit crews in auto racing.

Kevin Fleming/Corbis/VCG/Getty Images, Inc.

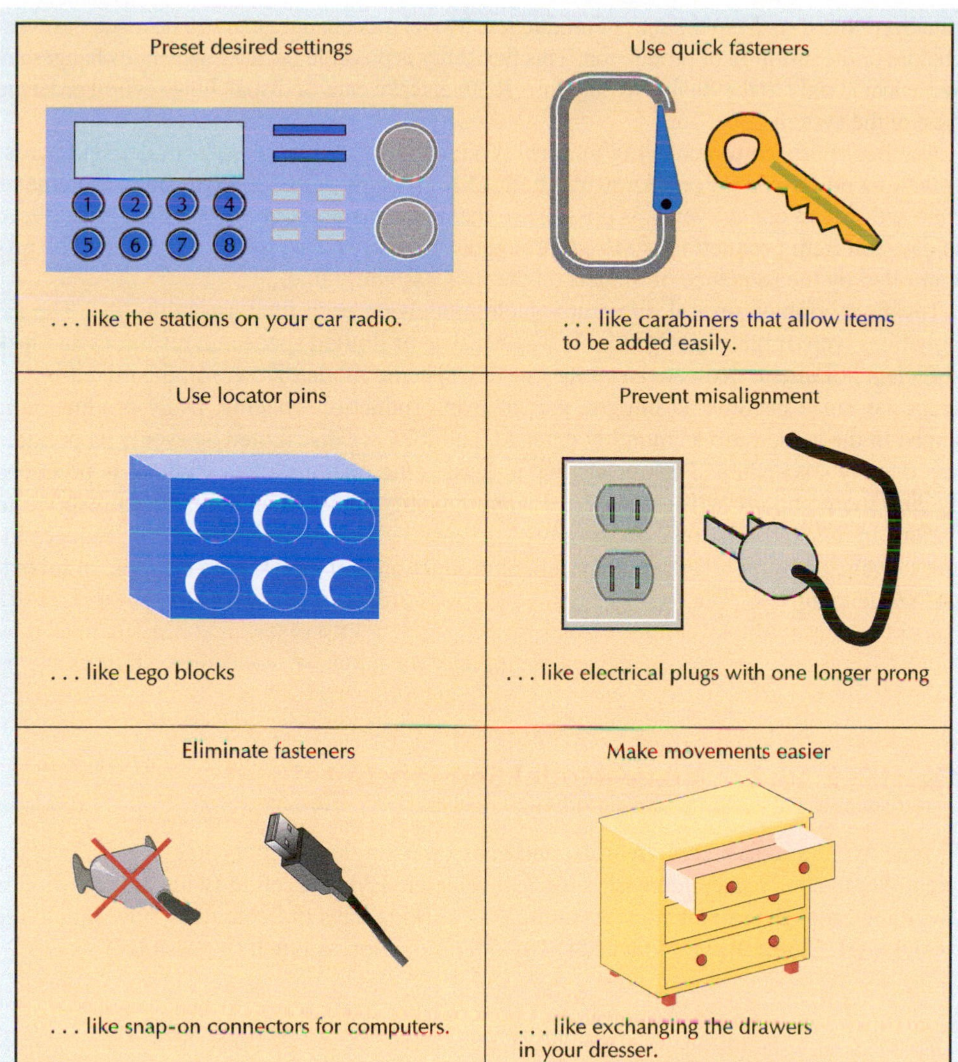

FIGURE 16.10 **Some Common Techniques for Reducing Setup Time**

Uniform Production Levels

The flow of production created by the pull system, kanbans, small lots, and quick setups can only be maintained if production is relatively steady. Lean production systems attempt to maintain **uniform production levels** by smoothing the production requirements on the final assembly line. Changes in final assembly often have dramatic effects on component production upstream. When this happens in a kanban system, kanbans for certain parts will circulate very quickly at some times and very slowly at others. Adjustments of plus or minus 10% in monthly demand can be absorbed by the kanban system, but wider demand fluctuations cannot be handled without substantially increasing inventory levels or scheduling large amounts of overtime.[4]

Uniform production levels The result from smoothing production requirements on the final assembly line.

One way to reduce variability in production is to guard against unexpected demand through more accurate forecasts. To accomplish this, the sales division of Toyota takes the lead in production planning. Toyota Motor Sales conducts surveys of tens of thousands of people twice a year to estimate demand for Toyota cars and trucks. Monthly production schedules are drawn up from the forecasts two months in advance. The plans are reviewed one month in advance and then again 10 days in advance. Daily production schedules, which by then include firm orders from dealers,

[4]P. Y. Huang, L. P. Rees, and B. W. Taylor, "A Simulation Analysis of the Just-in-Time Technique (with Kanbans) for a Multiline, Multistage Production System," *Decision Sciences* (July 1983), pp. 326–345.

are finalized four days from the start of production. Model mix changes can still be made the evening before or the morning of production. This flexibility is possible because schedule changes are communicated only to the final assembly line. Kanbans take care of dispatching revised orders to the rest of the system.

Heijunka The process of smoothing demand across the planning horizon.

Another approach to achieving uniform production is to *level* or smooth demand across the planning horizon, a process known as **heijunka**. Demand is divided into small increments of time and spread out as evenly as possible so that the same amount of each item is produced each day, and item production is *mixed* throughout the day in very small quantities. The mix is controlled by the sequence of models on the final assembly line.

Toyota assembles several different vehicle models on each final assembly line. The assembly lines were initially designed this way because of limited space and resources and lack of sufficient volume to dedicate an entire line to a specific model. However, the mixed-model concept has since become an integral part of lean production systems. Daily production is arranged in the same ratio as monthly demand, and jobs are distributed as evenly as possible across the day's schedule. This means that at least some quantity of every item is produced daily, and the company will always have some quantity of an item available to respond to variations in demand. The mix of assembly also steadies component production, reduces inventory levels, and supports the pull system of production. Let's look at an example of mixed-model sequencing.

EXAMPLE 16.2 | Mixed-Model Sequencing

Tyrone Motors makes cars, hybrids, and vans on a single assembly line at its Cleveland plant. September's sales forecast is for 220 vehicles. Hybrids sell at twice the rate of cars and three times the rate of vans. Assuming 20 working days in September, how should the vehicles (H, C, and V) be produced to smooth production as much as possible?

Solution:

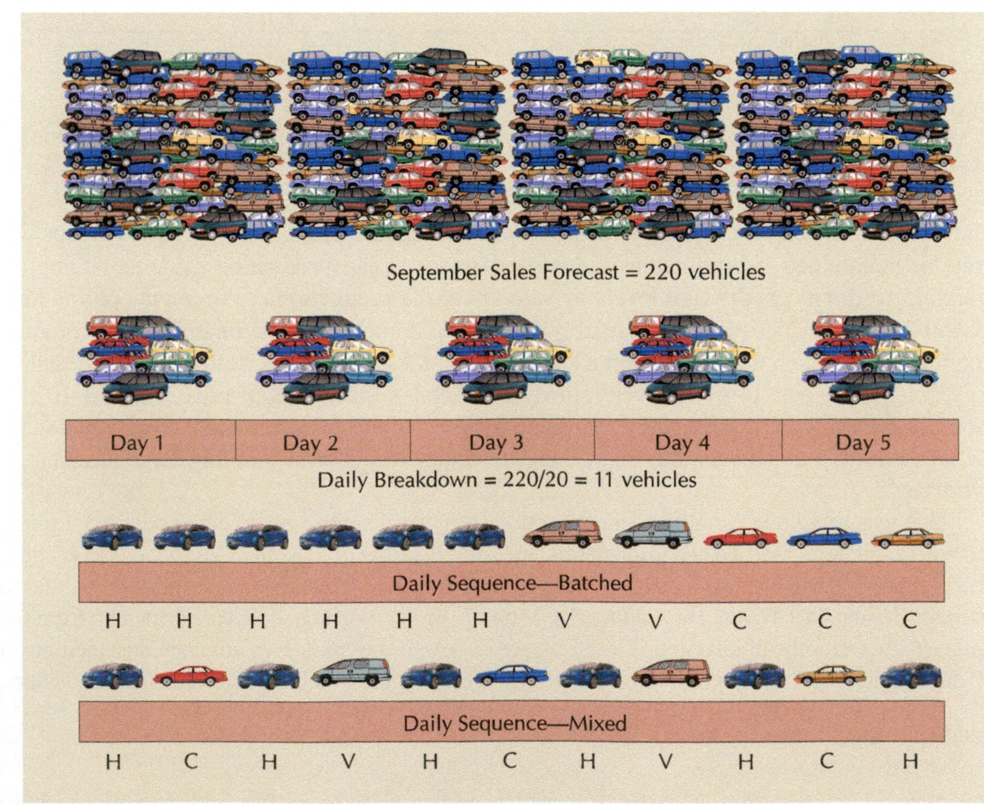

Along the Supply Chain

Lean R&D

It's surprising that a discussion of the "Most Innovative Companies" would include lean practices, but it's true; companies that value innovation also value speed, technology, exploration, and lean processes. For the first time, the annual BCG innovation survey asked respondents to rate their company's participation in a dozen lean practices, and the results were compelling. Companies classified as "strong innovators" were two to three times more likely to engage in lean practices than other companies, and that held true for every single lean dimension. Further, those companies engaged in lean R&D developed higher quality products up to six months earlier than their counterparts.

When we think of research and development, we think of creativity and innovation, not processes or efficiency. So what is it about lean that enables effective R&D? Try modular product design, parallel development, and transparent product requirements. Add a strong project manager, meaningful KPIs, acceptance of failures, and a global knowledge management system. The result is an R&D process that models and tests prototypes quickly, integrates across functions, standardizes subprocesses, shortens the iterative design cycle, and develops an intelligent launch plan. Lean and creativity? You bet.

Source: M. Ringel, A. Taylor, and H. Zablit, "Strong Innovators are Lean Innovators," *The Most Innovative Companies 2015*, Boston Consulting Group: December, 2015.

If the preceding example sounds extreme, it is not. Toyota assembles three models in 100 variations on a single assembly line at its Tahara plant, and the mix is juggled daily with almost no warning. The plant is highly automated, and each model carries with it a small yellow disc that transmits instructions to the next workstation. Cars roll off the final assembly line in what looks like unit production—a black Lexus sedan, a blue Camry, a red Lexus sports coupe, a white Corolla, and so on.

This is in sharp contrast to the large lots of similar items produced by mass production factories, in which luxury cars might be produced the first week and a half of the month, mid-size cars the second week and a half, and small cars the final week. Under mass production, it's difficult to change product mix midway through the month, and small-car customers would have to wait three to four weeks before their orders would be available.

Quality at the Source

For lean systems to work well, quality has to be extremely high. There is no extra inventory to buffer against defective units. Producing poor-quality items and then having to rework or reject them is a waste that should be eliminated. Producing in smaller lots encourages better quality. Workers can observe quality problems more easily; when problems are detected, they can be traced to their source and remedied without reworking too many units. Also, by inspecting the first and the last unit in a small batch or by having a worker make a part and then use the part, virtually 100% inspection can be achieved.

Visual Control Quality improves when problems are made visible and workers have clear expectations of performance. Production systems designed with quality in mind include visible instructions for worker or machine action, and direct feedback on the results of that action. This is known as **visual control**. Examples include kanbans, standard operation sheets, andons, process control charts, and tool boards. A factory with visual control will look different from other factories. You may find machines or stockpoints in each section painted different colors, material-handling routes marked clearly on the floor, demonstration stands and instructional photographs placed near machines, graphs of quality or performance data displayed at each workstation, and explanations and pictures of recent improvement efforts posted by work teams. Figure 16.11 shows several examples of visual control.

Visual control Procedures or mechanisms that make problems visible.

Visual control of quality often leads to what the Japanese call a **poka-yoke**. A poka-yoke is any foolproof device or mechanism that prevents defects from occurring. For example, a dial on which desired ranges are marked in different colors is an example of visual control. A dial that shuts off a machine whenever the instrument needle falls above or below the desired range is a poka-yoke. Machines set to stop after a certain amount of production are poka-yokes, as are sensors that prevent the addition of too many items into a package or the misalignment of components for an assembly.

Poka-yoke A foolproof device that prevents defects from occurring.

FIGURE 16.11 Examples of Visual Control

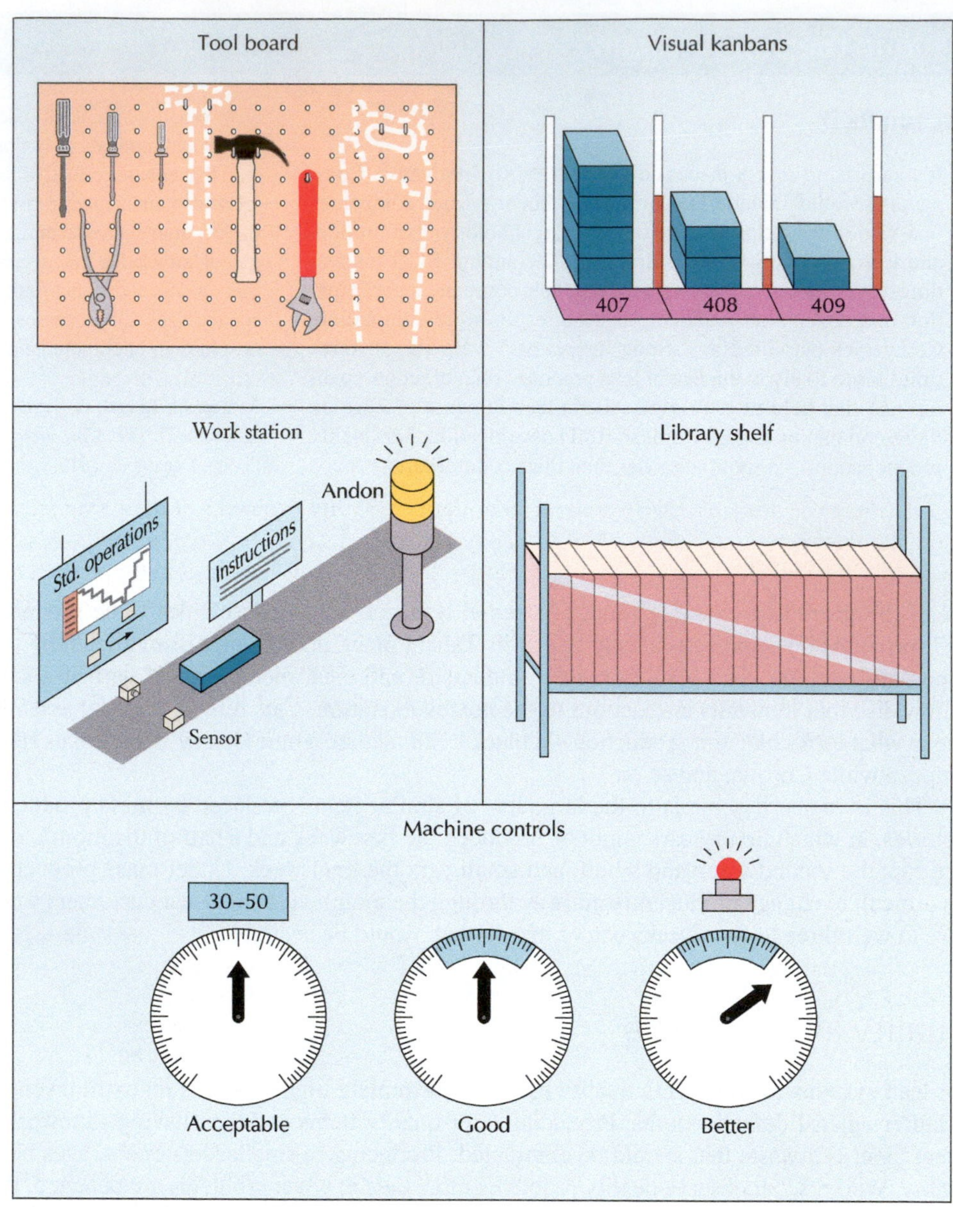

Kaizen A system of continuous improvement; "change for the good of all."

Kaizen

Quality in lean systems is based on **kaizen**, the Japanese term for "change for the good of all" or *continuous improvement*. Recall, we discussed kaizen earlier in Chapter 2. As a practical management system based on trial-and-error experiences in eliminating waste and simplifying operations, lean was created and is sustained through kaizen. Continuous improvement is not something that can be delegated to a department or a staff of experts. It is a monumental undertaking that requires the participation of every employee at every level. The essence of lean success is the willingness of workers to spot quality problems, halt operations when necessary, generate ideas for improvement, analyze processes, perform different functions, and adjust their working routines. In one year alone workers at Toyota's Georgetown, Kentucky, plant suggested 500 kaizens, 99.8% of which were implemented. Team member ideas helped the plant install the first assembly line shared by a sedan and a minivan.

5 Why's Repeatedly asking "why?" until a root cause is identified.

One of the keys to an effective kaizen is finding the *root cause* of a problem and eliminating it so that the problem does not reoccur. A simple, yet powerful, technique for finding the root cause is the **5 Why's**, a practice of asking "why?" repeatedly until the underlying cause is identified (usually requiring five questions). An often-cited example follows.[5]

[5]This example appears in the isixsigma dictionary, *http://www.isixsigma.com*, accessed May 5, 2007.

5 Why's Example

Problem: The Washington Monument is deteriorating.

1. Why is the monument deteriorating? Because harsh chemicals are used to clean the monument.
2. Why are harsh chemicals used to clean the monument? Because there are a lot of birds in the area that deposit their droppings on the monument.
3. Why are there a lot of birds in the area? Because birds eat spiders, and there are a lot of spiders.
4. Why are there a lot of spiders? Because spiders eat gnats, and there are a lot of gnats.
5. Why are there a lot of gnats? Because they are attracted to bright lights at dusk.

Solution: Turn on the monument lights a half hour later.

Jidoka It was the idea that workers could identify quality problems at their source, solve them, and never pass on a defective item that led Ohno to believe in zero defects. To that end, Ohno was determined that the workers, not inspectors, should be responsible for product quality. To go along with this responsibility, he also gave workers the unprecedented authority of **jidoka**—the authority to stop the production line if quality problems were encountered.

Jidoka Authority to stop the production line.

Andons Call lights that signal quality problems.

To encourage jidoka, each worker is given access to a switch that can be used to activate call lights or to halt production. The call lights, called **andons,** flash above the workstation and at several andon boards throughout the plant. Green lights indicate normal operation, yellow

Nicole Sanders

Commodity Manager for Danaher Motion

Roberta Russell

Danaher Motion is a leading global manufacturer of motion control products that improve the efficiency and productivity of complex manufacturing operations. I am a commodity manager at Danaher, responsible for sourcing, purchasing, and e-procurement of all the electronics components that go into our products. I locate suppliers, negotiate contracts, manage supplier relations, and supervise the work of four buyers.

The job has changed quite a bit since I started working here. Until a year ago, we used forecasts from our material requirements planning (MRP) system to generate purchase orders. It would not be uncommon to purchase the same item from eight different vendors over the course of a year. Today our core supplier base has been reduced from 400 vendors to 10, and most of our parts (3000 to 4000 of them) use kanbans to generate replenishment orders. We provide our suppliers with a six-month forecast of demand with weekly, then daily, updates. A supplier must be able to fill an order within five days with 100% good quality. We are in the process of moving 40% of our dollar spend to low-cost regions, such as China and Malaysia. The logistics of global supply is not as difficult for small products such as electronics. Shipments can be air freighted from China in a week's time, versus five weeks by ship. Increased moisture content of the product is a bigger problem than long lead times.

New suppliers submit bids to our RFQ (request for quote). Then we conduct site audits on probably three suppliers that had reasonable bids. We look at their business processes, their production operations, their bottlenecks, workflow, quality systems, and capability to deliver. A typical contract is for three to five years with built-in price reductions of 5% a year. The contract is very explicit, including not only the negotiated price, but also required finished goods, raw material and work-in-process stocking levels, liability issues, forecasts of demand, logistics, inventory review cycles, kanban procedures (such as quantities per container), policies on rejects, repairs, and corrective action, air freighting, and dock dates. For the first few months, we'll perform 100% incoming inspection on goods from new suppliers and ask them to submit statistical process control data (which we call *part qualifying checksheets*). For the next few months, we'll sample, say, 100 pieces of a 500-piece shipment. If all goes well, after six months we accept the supplier shipments *dock to stock*.

Danaher is passionate about continually improving its operations and eliminating waste. We use kaizen teams for continuous improvement and policy deployment to focus our improvements on break-through achievements. Every year we have policy goals for *Quality, Delivery, Cost, and Innovation* (QDCI) that cascade down from corporate to department levels. I'm at level six, after the CEO, vice president of operations, global supply chain manager, plant manager, and purchasing manager. My buyers are at level seven. This year our quality objectives refer to reducing the number of returns and the efficient processing of those returns. On-time delivery goals are 85% to voice of the customer (i.e., to customer request, not our promise dates). Our purchase price reduction goal is $2 million for the year, and employees must participate in a number of kaizen events. Each of my buyers, for example, will be members of five kaizen teams and leader of one of them. My goal is to attain a Black Belt in Materials Kaizen.

You know, when I look back at what I learned in my operations management class, it's amazing how much what we talked about is actually used in the business world.

lights are a call for help, and red lights indicate a line stoppage. Supervisors, maintenance personnel, and engineers are summoned to troubled workstations quickly by flashing lights on the andon board. At Toyota, the assembly line is stopped for an average of 20 minutes a day because of jidoka. Each jidoka drill is recorded on easels kept at the work area. A block of time is reserved at the end of the day for workers to go over the list and work on solving the problems raised. For example, an eight-hour day might consist of seven hours of production and one hour of problem solving.

Undercapacity scheduling Extra time built into a schedule for planning, problem solving, and maintenance.

This concept of allocating extra time to a schedule for nonproductive tasks is called **undercapacity scheduling**. Another example of undercapacity scheduling is producing for two shifts each day and reserving the third shift for preventive maintenance activities. Making time to plan, train, solve problems, and maintain the work environment is an important part of lean's success.

Total Productive Maintenance

Breakdown maintenance Repairs needed to make a failed machine operational.

Preventive maintenance A system of periodic inspection and maintenance designed to keep a machine in operation.

Machines cannot operate continuously without some attention. Maintenance activities can be performed when a machine breaks down to restore the machine to its original operating condition, or at different times during regular operation of the machine in an attempt to prevent a breakdown from occurring. The first type of activity is referred to as **breakdown maintenance**; the second is called **preventive maintenance**.

Breakdowns seldom occur at convenient times. Lost production, poor quality, and missed deadlines from an inefficient or broken-down machine can represent a significant expense. In addition, the cost of breakdown maintenance is usually much greater than preventive maintenance. (Most of us know that to be true from our own experience at maintaining an automobile. Regular oil changes cost pennies compared to replacing a car engine.) For these reasons, most companies do not find it cost-effective to rely solely on breakdown maintenance. The question then becomes, how much preventive maintenance is necessary and when should it be performed?

With accurate records on the time between breakdowns, the frequency of breakdowns, and the cost of breakdown and preventive maintenance, we can mathematically determine the best preventive maintenance schedule. But even with this degree of precision, breakdowns can still occur. Lean production requires more than preventive maintenance—it requires *total productive maintenance*.

This lighted board shows where an andon cord has been pulled to signal a problem on the line at Toyota Motor Corp.'s plant in Georgetown, Kentucky. If the issue is not fixed before the car reaches the next stage of assembly, the line stops.

Bloomberg/Getty Images, Inc.

TABLE 16.1 5S Workplace Scan

5S's	GOAL	ELIMINATE OR CORRECT
1. Seiri (*sort*)	Keep only what you need	Unneeded equipment, tools, furniture; unneeded items on walls or bulletin boards, items blocking aisles or stacked in corners; unneeded inventory, supplies or parts; safety hazards
2. Seiton (*set in order*)	A place for everything and everything in its place	Items not in their correct places; correct places not obvious; aisles, workstations, and equipment locations not indicated; items not put away immediately after use
3. Seiso (*shine*)	Cleaning, and looking for ways to keep clean and organized	Floors, walls, stairs, equipment, and surfaces not clean; cleaning materials not easily accessible; lines, labels, or signs broken or unclean; other cleaning problems
4. Seiketsu (*standardize*)	Maintaining and monitoring the first three categories	Necessary information not visible; standards not known; checklists missing; quantities and limits not easily recognizable; items can't be located within 30 seconds
5. Shitsuke (*sustain*)	Sticking to the rules	Number of workers without 5S training; number of daily 5S inspections not performed; number of personal items not stored; number of times job instructions not available or up-to-date

Total productive maintenance (TPM) combines the practice of preventive maintenance with the concepts of total quality—employee involvement, decisions based on data, zero defects, and a strategic focus. Machine operators maintain their own machines with daily care, periodic inspections, and preventive repair activities. They compile and interpret maintenance and operating data on their machines, identifying signs of deterioration prior to failure.[6] They also scrupulously clean equipment, tools, and workspaces to make unusual occurrences more noticeable. Oil spots on a clean floor may indicate a machine problem, whereas oil spots on a dirty floor would go unnoticed. In Japan this is known as the **5 S**—*seiri, seiton, seiso, seiketsu,* and *shitsuke*—roughly translated as sort, set, shine, standardize, and sustain. Table 16.1 explains the 5 S in more detail.

Total productive maintenance (TPM) A system that combines the practice of preventive maintenance with the concepts of total quality.

5 S A set of processes for workplace organization

In addition to operator involvement and attention to detail, TPM requires management to take a broader, strategic view of maintenance. That means:

- Designing products that can easily be produced on existing machines;
- Designing machines for easier operation, changeover, and maintenance;
- Training and retraining workers to operate and maintain machines properly;
- Purchasing machines that maximize productive potential; and
- Designing a preventive maintenance plan that spans the entire life of each machine.

Supplier Networks

Supplier support is essential to the success of lean production. Not only do suppliers need to be reliable, their production needs to be synchronized to the needs of the customer they are supplying. Toyota understood this and developed strong long-term working relationships with a select group of suppliers. Supplier plants encircled the 50-mile radius around Toyota City, making deliveries several times a day. Bulky parts such as engines and transmissions were delivered every 15 to 30 minutes. Suppliers who met stringent quality standards could forgo inspection of incoming goods. That meant goods could be brought right to the assembly line or area of use without being counted, inspected, tagged, or stocked.

Suppliers who try to meet the increasing demands of a lean customer without being lean themselves are overrun with inventory and exorbitantly high production and distribution costs. Lean supply involves:

1. ***Long-term supplier contracts.*** Suppliers are chosen on the basis of their ability to meet delivery schedules with high quality at a reasonable cost, and their willingness to adapt their production system to meet increasingly stringent customer requirements. Typical contracts are for three to five years, although some companies will choose a supplier for the life of the product.

[6]Maintaining and repairing your own machine is called *autonomous maintenance*. Collecting data and designing maintenance remedies based on the data collected is referred to as *predictive maintenance*.

2. ***Synchronized production.*** With longer-term contracts, suppliers are able to concentrate on fewer customers. Guaranteed, steady demand with advanced notice of volume changes allows the supplier to synchronize their production with that of the customer. Engineering and quality management assistance may also be provided to the supplier.
3. ***Supplier certification.*** Suppliers go through several stages before certification. Typically, their products undergo quality tests, their production facilities and quality systems are examined, and statistical measures of quality are sent with each shipment. After six months or so with no complications, a certification is issued that exempts the supplier from incoming quality and quantity inspections. In spite of certification, many companies bill their suppliers for the damage incurred by a defective part, such as the cost of a line shutdown or product recall.
4. ***Mixed loads and frequent deliveries.*** A lean supplier is an extension of the customer's assembly line. Small quantities may be delivered several times a day (or even hourly) directly to their point of use in the customer's factory. This usually involves smaller trucks containing a mixed load of goods. Different suppliers often join together to consolidate deliveries or share local warehouses.
5. ***Precise delivery schedules.*** Delivery windows to specific locations (docks, bays, or areas along an assembly line) can be as short as 15 minutes. Penalties for missing delivery times are high. One automobile company penalizes its suppliers $32,000 for each hour a delivery is late. With such tight schedules, signing for and paying for a shipment at the time of delivery is too time-consuming. Paying at regular intervals for shipments documented with bar codes or RFID[7] tags is more in tune with lean.
6. ***Standardized, sequenced delivery.*** Using standardized containers and exchanging full containers for empty ones upon delivery also speeds the delivery and replenishment process. In some cases, deliveries made directly to the manufacturer are sequenced in the order of assembly. Nissan, for example, receives deliveries of vehicle seats four times an hour and notifies the supplier two hours in advance with the exact sequence (size and color) in which seats are to be unloaded.
7. ***Locating in close proximity to the customer.*** With the increased number of deliveries in lean production, it is imperative that the source of supply be located close to the customer. When geographic distances between supplier and customer prohibit daily deliveries, suppliers may need to establish small warehouses near to the customer or consolidate warehouses with other suppliers. Trucking firms increasingly use consolidation warehouses as load-switching points for JIT delivery to various customers. Maintaining close proximity can mean relocating around the world, as shown by the number of suppliers who have moved to China and other Asian countries in support of their customers.

Implementing Lean Systems

Firms that have tried to implement lean by slashing inventory and demanding that their suppliers make frequent deliveries have missed the power of the system. Supplier deliveries and kanbans are some of the last elements of lean production to implement. Today, globalization and tough times have brought a new generation of manufacturers and suppliers into the lean fold.

The firms that are most successful in implementing lean production understand the breadth and interrelatedness of the concepts and have adapted them to their own particular environment. This makes sense when you consider the essence of lean—eliminate waste, speed up changeovers, work closely with suppliers, streamline the flow of work, use flexible resources, pay attention to quality, expose problems, and use worker teams to solve problems. None of these concepts or techniques are new or particularly revolutionary. How they are applied can differ considerably from company to company. What is unique and remarkable is how the pieces are tied together into a finely tuned operating system and how synchronized that system can be with both the external and internal business environments.

Lean applications on U.S. soil, whether in Japanese or U.S. run plants, differ somewhat from the original Japanese versions. Lean U.S. plants are typically larger, deliveries

[7]RFID tags are radio frequency IDs that can store updated information on an item.

Along the Supply Chain

Nike's Lean Philosophy

Paul Joseph Brown/Seattle Post-Intelligencer

Nike, well known for its sweatshop labor problems in the 1990s, has transformed its approach to contract manufacturing, not by reducing outsourcing, but by working more closely with its suppliers to improve working conditions and develop best practices in sustainable manufacturing. Over the past 15 years, Nike has evolved from approaching sustainability reactively as a reputation management issue to "embracing it as a key driver of innovation and an important source of competitive advantage."

We discussed Nike's achievements in sustainable design and manufacturing in Chapter 4. What we have not addressed so far is the vital role of lean in Nike's success. A recent corporate responsibility report by the company describes a strategic shift away from the prior compliance-based audit relationship with contract manufacturers toward cooperation around lean principles as the driver toward sustainable manufacturing in all its forms. Nike believes that lean can empower workers and teams, and that an engaged workforce is the fastest and most sustainable path to innovation and lasting improvements.

More than 2.5 million people work at various stages throughout Nike's supply chain, including more than 1 million in the factories with whom they contract directly. Pilot studies of lean manufacturing implementations found that lean can benefit both factory owners and workers by increasing productivity, reducing environmental impacts, eliminating excessive overtime, and improving working conditions. Nike is now requiring a commitment to lean manufacturing and demonstrated progress toward a lean culture for contract factories by the end of FY15. As of FY13, 85% of Nike brand footwear and 76% of Nike brand apparel (by product volume) was made on lean-certified lines.

1. What does Nike mean by "sustainable manufacturing in all its forms"?
2. Why would lean principles be an effective means of driving innovation and sustainability?
3. Visit the Nike Responsibility website and examine their supplier scorecards (gold, silver, bronze, etc.). On what factors are suppliers evaluated? How is performance measured? What penalties are assessed for noncompliance?

Source: Nike, Inc., "Sustainable Business Performance FY 12/13," available online at http://www.nikeresponsibility.com/report/ (accessed January 22, 2016).

from suppliers are less frequent, more buffer inventory is held (because of the longer delivery lead times), and kanbans are very simple compared to lean plants in Japan. Worker-designed feedback systems are different, too. At the Nissan plant in Tennessee, workers are reminded to change workstations along an S-shaped assembly line by the changing tempo of piped-in music (from country to rock). Morning calisthenics are out for most U.S. plants, but the placement of ping-pong tables and basketball hoops alongside the assembly line for exercise during worker-designated breaks is popular. The slow pace of continuous improvement is hard to maintain for American workers. Thus, *kaizen blitzes*, intense process improvement over a week's time with immediate results, are easier and more energizing to conduct.

The Benefits of Lean Production

A study of the average benefits accrued to U.S. manufacturers over a five-year period from implementing lean production are impressive: 90% reductions in manufacturing cycle time, 70% reductions in inventory, 50% reductions in labor costs, and 80% reductions in space requirements.

While not every company can achieve results at this level, lean production does provide a wide range of benefits, including:

1. Reduced inventory
2. Improved quality
3. Lower costs
4. Reduced space requirements
5. Shorter lead time

6. Increased productivity
7. Greater flexibility
8. Better relations with suppliers
9. Simplified scheduling and control activities
10. Increased capacity
11. Better use of human resources
12. More product variety

The Drawbacks of Lean Production

Lean production is not appropriate for every type of organization. Professor Rajan Suri, author of *Quick Response Manufacturing*, notes that the key to lean production is creating flow. To do this, lean manufacturers determine takt times, create a level schedule, and use kanbans to control production. This approach starts to have serious deficiencies when applied to companies that have high variability in demand (takt time breaks down), or large variety of low-volume products (too many kanbans in the system), or custom-engineered products (there are no kanbans for something that is yet to be designed).

Nor is lean production the best choice for high-volume repetitive items where mass production is more common. Even Toyota produces high-demand components (typically, small

Along the Supply Chain

Kata at La-Z-Boy

Lean principles are not difficult to understand, but they are difficult to implement and sustain. Toyota's ability to sustain its continuous improvement focus for decades is remarkable (and enviable). Stories abound of companies implementing lean with great success, then facing a stalemate, and finally reverting to old ways. La-Z-Boy, a well-known manufacturer of recliners and other types of upholstered furniture, is one example. The company began its lean journey in 2005 and by 2011 had reached a plateau; that is, until it tried a lean learning technique called *kata*.

Kata is a Japanese word that means "way of doing." Originating with the martial arts, it refers to a form or pattern that can be practiced to develop particular skills and mindsets. In terms of lean, think of it as developing "muscle memory" for continuous improvement. The human brain is wired to fill-in-the blanks in the face of incomplete information. Stated another way, people have a natural tendency to jump to conclusions, although it is so natural that we tend not to see this about ourselves. Improvement katas make the scientific method of problem solving a habit, to help us and our colleagues make better decisions.

The kata process starts by identifying the challenge or future state, that is, what you are trying to accomplish. The next step is to understand the current state by seeing, sketching, and measuring the current pattern of activity and studying the data. The third step is to describe where you want to be next, the target condition. This is an incremental step, not a leap to the final condition. The fourth step is to iterate toward the target using something like the PDCA cycle (discussed in Chapter 2). The process repeats until the future state is reached. Each learner has a coach who helps him or her practice and move to the next step or target. The coach has a vested interest in their partner's development, which "leads to a better leader, better problem-solver, and overall higher performance." Kata involve activities that are practiced daily.

La-Z-Boy began using kata at its Dayton, Tennessee, plant in 2012. Daily coaching katas averaged 64% at the end of the first quarter of 2015, and are expected to exceed 75% by 2016. That translates to 75% of the time, a coach and/or second-level coach will be participating in daily kata coaching activities with a learner. For a 1200 person factory with team members paid on an incentive system, that in itself is quite an accomplishment. Although kata emphasizes the learner, rather than the process or project, improvements in processes are expected. At La-Z-Boy, over a two year period, cell productivity increased by 10% to 28% and defect levels decreased by 20% to 50%.

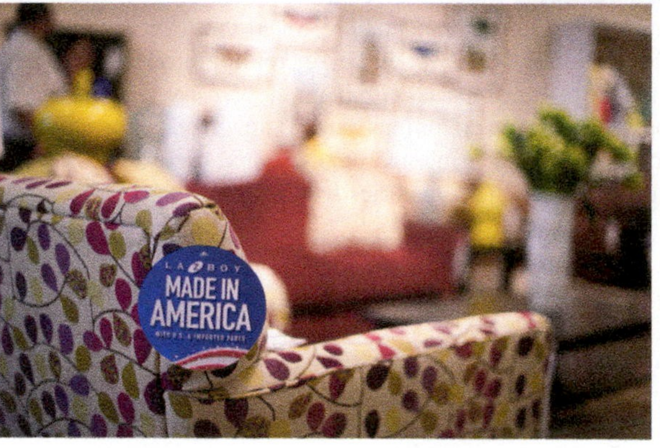

Jeff Swensen/Getty Images, Inc.

1. For what kinds of activities have you practiced daily, today or in the past? Describe how kata can be used to develop expertise and maintain skill levels.
2. Kata are used in many different kinds of professions. Search the web for kata related to your chosen career. For those of you who are programmers, try CodeKata.
3. Aristotle said, "*We are what we repeatedly do. Excellence, then, is not an act, but a habit.*" Do you believe this? How does this relate to kata?

Source: Jill Jusko, "Toyota Kata Delivers Lean Improvements at La-Z-Boy," *Industry Week*, (July 30, 2013).

items that require stamping and forging) in lots as large as 10,000 units, sending them to subsequent processes in small batches only when requested.

Lean production can also present problems when unexpected changes in demand or supply occur. For example, a fire at one supplier's brake factory shut down three Toyota plants one year, and the Japanese tsunami delayed production of GM cars and Apple iPads for months. Add to that possible epidemics, natural disasters, financial meltdowns, terrorist attacks, and armed conflicts, and being completely lean is risky.

Thus, lean production must be compatible with a company's products, processes, and customers. Companies must also assess risk and uncertainty in their business environment, and adapt lean practices accordingly. Even with these drawbacks, however, we have found that most types of businesses can find some parts or processes that can benefit from lean concepts.

Lean Six Sigma

Lean and **Six Sigma** are natural partners for process improvement. The predominance of both techniques in today's corporate environment reinforces the value of both continuous and breakthrough improvements. Lean concentrates on eliminating waste and creating flow while Six Sigma reduces variability and enhances process capabilities. Lean is associated more with continuous improvement, whereas Six Sigma quality often requires breakthrough improvements.

Lean Six Sigma A combination of lean's principles for eliminating waste with Six Sigma's reduction of variability.

Lean's kaizen initiatives enable Six Sigma by streamlining processes and empowering workers with teamwork and problem-solving skills. Six Sigma provides sophisticated statistical techniques to solve the more complex problems uncovered by lean systems. Together they accelerate the rate of process improvement and help sustain the results. An important tool in Lean Six Sigma projects is value stream mapping, discussed in the next section.

Value Stream Mapping (VSM)

Value stream mapping (VSM) is a tool for analyzing process flow and eliminating waste. Maps of the current state and the future state of a system are created. VSM has several special icons, as shown in Exhibit 16.1, that differ from traditional flowcharts. These

EXHIBIT 16.1 | Value Stream Mapping Symbols in Microsoft Visio

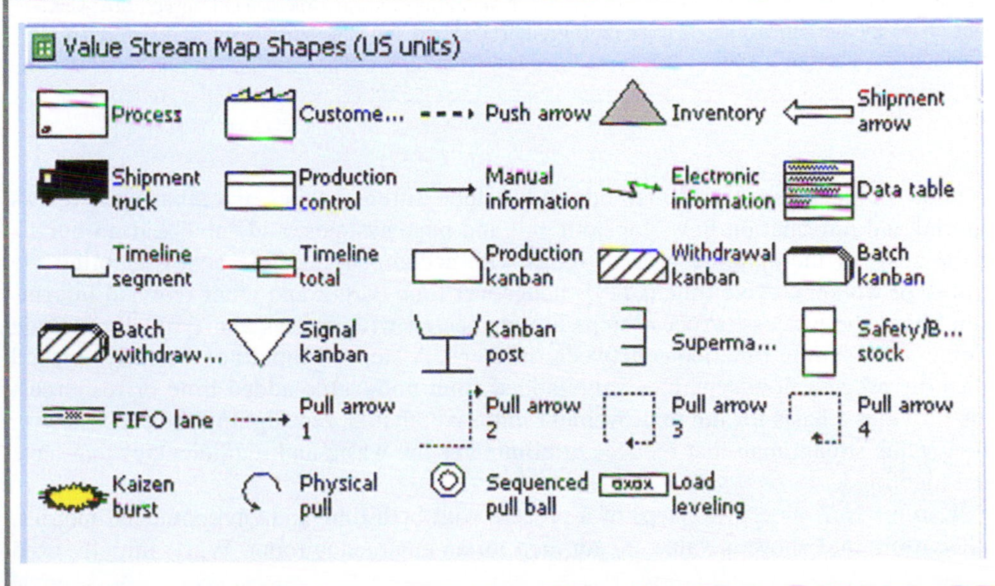

Along the Supply Chain

Lean at Virginia Mason Healthcare Center

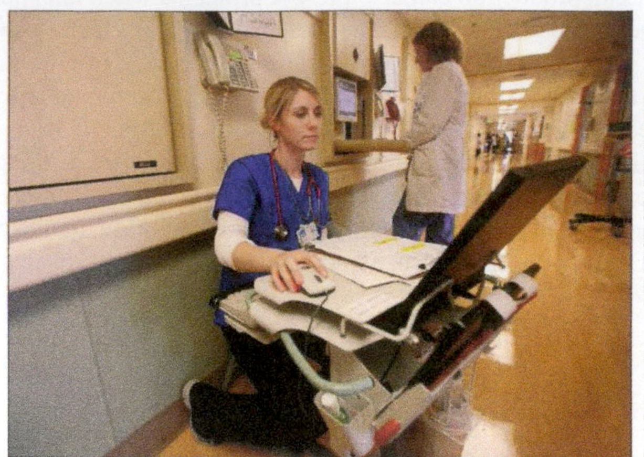
Paul Joseph Brown/HEARST SEATTLE MEDIA, LLC

Virginia Mason Healthcare Center, located in Seattle, Washington and pictured in the photo, has received numerous accolades, including "Hospital of the Decade" for patient safety. The hospital is known for applying the Toyota Production System to healthcare, and shares that experience through the Virginia Mason Institute. Its management system, called Virginia Mason Production System (VMPS), uses many of Toyota's principles to redesign basic services, improve the quality of healthcare, and enhance patient safety. Over the years, VMPS has held over 850 Rapid Process Improvement Workshops (RPIW), kaizen events, and 3P training exercises with staff, patients, and guests at its facilities. A sampling of the results of these improvements is given here.

VMPS uses a patient safety alert (PSA) system that requires all staff who encounter patients in potentially harmful situations to cease the activity and make an immediate report. The hospital receives about 2000 PSAs a year, and most are processed within 24 hours. Since the implementation of this system, hospital liability claims have been reduced by 60%.

Primary care teams at eight Virginia Mason locations used VMPS to analyze patient, staff, and material flow through the system. Teams standardized patient rooms and the inventory of materials in each room, revised lab procedures and indirect patient-care activities, and changed the appointment schedule to same-day visits. The size of the waiting room was reduced in all of the primary care locations, and entirely eliminated in some so that arriving patients go directly into examining rooms. These clinics have a medical assistant in charge of patient flow who monitors activities and directs patients, staff, and resources where and when they are needed.

Emergency departments are major bottlenecks in patient care, usually with longer wait times, limited capacity, and expensive resources. A team-sort process using standard clinical assessment tools was implemented to identify patients who could be treated quickly and released, thereby freeing up time and beds for more serious cases. The result was a 90% improvement in throughput.

Using 3P (i.e., a production preparation process), facility redesign at the Cancer Institute brought all of the activities for chemotherapy patients into one area, including a laboratory and pharmacy, so that patient time in the system was reduced from 10 hours to 2 hours. Hyperbaric Medicine increased capacity (in the same space) from treating two or three patients at a time, to as many as 20 patients.

In most hospitals, nurses spend only 35% of their time directly caring for patients. Using VWPS, nurses at Virginia Mason were reallocated to work as a team with a patient-care technician to monitor a pod (or cell) of patients, rather than an entire unit. Supplies were removed from a central location and distributed to patient rooms. The cell model allowed nurses to be more responsive to patient needs and increased the percent of a nurse's time spent on direct patient care to 90%. The steps walked per day were reduced, as well, from 10,000 to 1200.

1. Match the VMPS improvements with the lean principles and techniques discussed in the chapter.
2. Discuss the advantages and disadvantages of lean healthcare. What do you think are the major barriers to implementing this approach?

Sources: Based on "Rooting Out Waste in Health Care by Taking Cue from Toyota Assembly Lines," PBS News Hour (October 24, 2012); Charles Kenney, *Transforming Health Care: Virginia Mason Medical Center's Pursuit of the Perfect Patient Experience*, Danvers, MA: CRC Press, 2010; Virginia Mason Institute, https://www.virginiamason.org/VMPS, accessed January 8, 2013.

are related to lean production methods and include different types of kanbans, as well as material and information flows for both pull and push systems, and "aha" kaizen bursts. At the heart of the map are process icons with accompanying data boxes denoting the number of workers, cycle time (C/T), changeover time (C/O), and other relevant information about the process. Process steps are connected with arrows and typically include inventory or waiting time icons between the steps. A stepped timeline of metrics placed under the process flow separates value-added from non–value-added time or resources. This provides a basis for the improvement initiative, that is, redesigning the process with a new value stream map that reduces or eliminates the waste and inefficiencies that have been identified.

Exhibit 16.2 shows two steps of a process with both time and environmental metrics, and **Exhibit 16.3** shows a value stream map for an emergency room. While initially used

EXHIBIT 16.2 | A Simple Value Stream Map

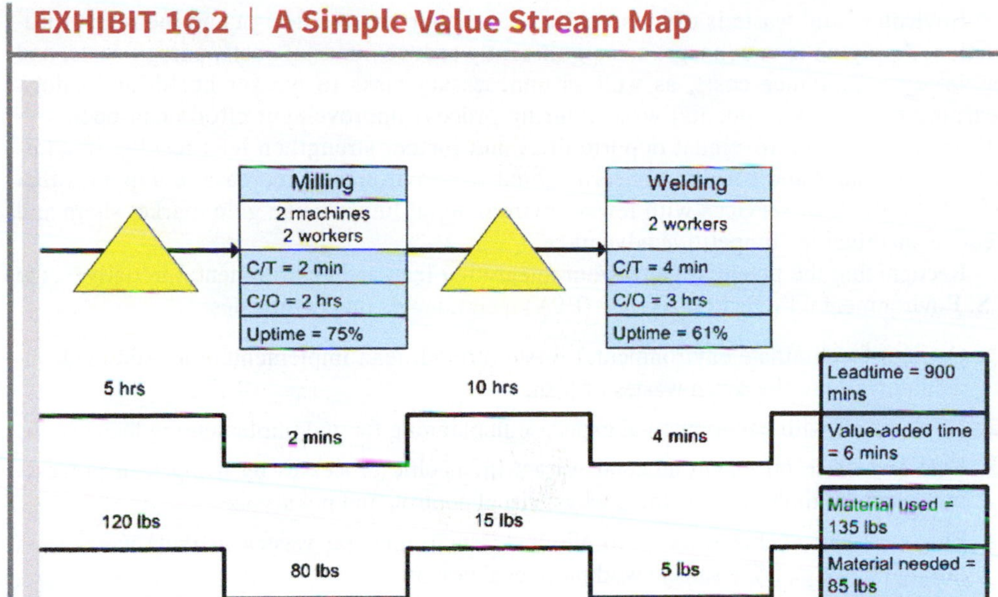

Key: C/T = cycle time
C/O = change over time

Source: Adapted from Environment Protection Agency, "Value Stream Mapping," *Lean and the Environment Toolkit*, retrieved from http://www.epa.gov/lean/toolkit/ch3.htm.

EXHIBIT 16.3 | Emergency Room Value Stream Map

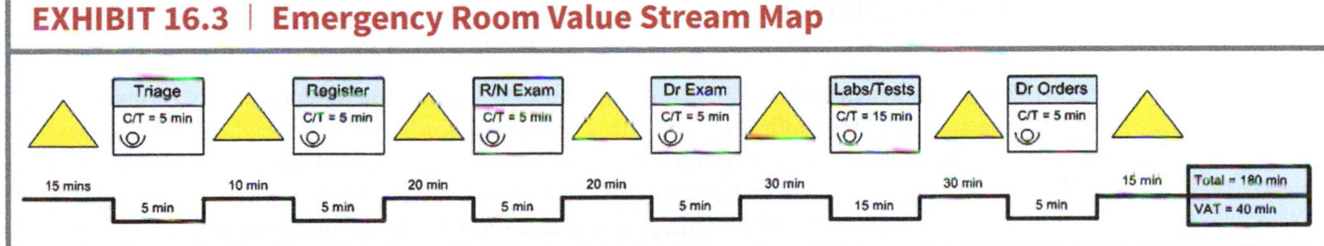

Key: C/T = cycle time
VAT = value added time

Source: Adapted from E. Dickson, S. Singh, D. Cheung, C. Wyatt, and A. Nugent, "Application of Lean Manufacturing Techniques in the Emergency Department," *The Journal of Emergency Medicine*, Volume 37, Issue 2, p. 177–182.

primarily in manufacturing, value stream maps have become an essential tool for improvements in the service sector. Creating the maps with a group of stakeholders helps create buy-in when process changes are proposed. The maps are created by "going to see" the process in action, rather than from memory.

Value stream maps are also important tools for reducing energy and material consumption in a company's sustainability efforts. The next section describes the partnership between lean and the environment.

Lean and the Environment

Lean's mandate to eliminate waste and operate only with those resources that are absolutely necessary aligns well with environmental initiatives. Managers and workers can be trained to identify environmental wastes and improvement opportunities alongside the many other wastes and improvement opportunities uncovered by lean. This provides several benefits to business, industry, and consumers.

Environmental waste is often an indicator of poor process design and inefficient production. Applying lean concepts can significantly reduce material costs, energy costs, and regulatory compliance costs, as well as unnecessary risks to worker health and safety. Learning to see environmental wastes during process improvement efforts can open significant business improvement opportunities and further strengthen lean results. In addition, as consumer and societal concerns about the environment increase, companies that provide products or services with fewer environmental impacts can gain market share and create a sustainable competitive advantage.

Recognizing the potential gains from integrating lean and environmental initiatives, the U.S. Environmental Protection Agency (EPA) recommends that companies:

1. Commit to eliminate environmental waste through lean implementation. Add environmental waste to the seven wastes of lean.
2. Involve staff with environmental expertise in planning for and implementing lean events.
3. Find and drive out environmental wastes in specific processes by using lean process-improvement tools, such as the 5 whys, visual control, and poka-yokes.
4. Empower and enable workers to eliminate environmental wastes in their work areas through 6S (e.g., 5S + safety) workplace evaluations.
5. Recognize new improvement opportunities by incorporating environmental, health, and safety icons and data into value stream maps. Include environmental metrics in the lean metrics of a process.[8]

As you can see, lean has many applications in the environment. We discuss lean in the service section next.

Lean Services

Most people who think of lean production as a system for reducing inventory do not consider the system to be applicable to services. However, you know from reading this chapter that lean production consists of more than low inventory levels. It eliminates waste, streamlines operations, promotes fast changeovers and close supplier relations, and adjusts quickly to changes in demand. As a result, products and services can be provided quickly, at less cost, and in more variety. Thus, we can readily observe the basic elements of lean production in service operations. Think about:

- McDonald's, Domino's, and FedEx, who compete on speed and still provide their products and services at low cost and with increasing variety;
- Construction firms that coordinate the arrival of materials "just as needed" instead of stockpiling them at the site;
- Multifunctional workers in department stores who work the cash register, stock goods, arrange displays, and make sales;
- Level selling with "everyday low prices" at Walmart and Food Lion;
- Work cells at fast-food restaurants that allow workers to be added during peak times and reduced during slow times;
- "Dollar" stores that price everything the same and simply count the number of items purchased as the customer leaves;
- Process mapping that has streamlined operations and eliminated waste in many services (especially in processing information);
- Medical facilities that have the flexibility to fill prescriptions, perform tests, and treat patients without routing them from one end of the building to another;
- JIT publishing that allows professors to choose material from a variety of sources and construct a custom-made book in the same amount of time off-the-shelf books can be ordered and at competitive prices;

[8]U.S. Environmental Protection Agency, *Lean and the Environment Toolkit*, retrieved from http://www.epa.gov/lean.

- Lens providers, cleaners, and car-repair services that can turn around customer orders in an hour;
- Cleaning teams that follow standard operating routines in quickly performing their tasks;
- Supermarkets that replenish their shelves according to what the customer withdraws; and
- Retailers who introduce dozens of new clothing lines each year in smaller quantities.

In addition to these incidences of lean, entire service systems have been redesigned around lean principles. The most prevalent applications are lean retailing, lean banking, and lean healthcare. We also discuss leaning the supply chain.

Lean Retailing

Retail stores provide customers with more choices faster than ever before. *Lean retailing*, like lean production, involves smaller, more frequent orders and rapid replenishment of stock. For example, Zara, a Spanish fashion chain, ships new products to its stores around the world every few days, not once a season. The company produces over 11,000 different stock items per year, instead of several hundred. Time-to-market (from design to store) is less than 10 days. That means Zara can keep up with fashion trends and adjust its merchandise accordingly.

Lean Banking

Lean banking is practiced by Bank of America, Citibank, Capital One, Jefferson Pilot, and Progressive Insurance, among others. The banking and insurance industries are particularly well suited to lean techniques because of their repetitive processes. Significant savings in both time and money can be achieved through differentiating processes, rationalizing decision approvals, simplifying service offerings, designing services in modules, and standardizing processes.

Lean Healthcare

Lean concepts are popular in the healthcare industry. One reason is the interest of corporations in keeping the cost of healthcare down. Pella Corporation loans its employees to a regional health center for "hot teams" to scrutinize medical operations. It was Boeing who convinced

97/E+/Getty Images

The supermarket represents a pull system of production where goods are replenished after a customer buys them. The space on the shelf allocated to each item serves as the maximum inventory level. Supermarket icons are used in value stream maps (see Exhibit 16.1).

30 executives from Seattle's Virginia Mason Medical Center to spend two weeks in Japan studying Toyota's methods.

In Iowa, a group of manufacturers, including Maytag, formed a task force to facilitate lean best practices in their local healthcare systems. People from hospitals, healthcare providers, third-party insurance providers, and manufacturing executives met together to identify waste and map out the way money and information flows through the healthcare system. The group discovered that every insurance company and employer had specific plans and rules for processing employee healthcare claims, requiring different information on a multitude of forms. The forms were so confusing that much of the processor's time was spent calling the provider for clarifications and reworking returned claims.

At ThedaCare in Wisconsin, a dozen doctors, nurses, and staffers brainstormed ways of cutting a typical hour-long office visit to 30 minutes or less. They constructed a 25-foot process map of a pneumonia patient's office visit, concluding that 17 steps were useful and 51 were not. At the end of the session, the team concluded that doctor's assistants should be assigned to a pool rather than individual doctors and that lab tests should be performed in examining rooms rather than at a central location.

Flowcharts, mistake-proofing, flow management, quick setups, and kaizen are just a few of the lean healthcare tools.

Leaning the Supply Chain

One of the first elements of lean production to receive widespread acclaim among manufacturers was just-in-time inventory. Too often, companies pushed back inventory onto their suppliers in the name of just-in-time. While dominant companies in an industry sought lean objectives within their four walls, outside suppliers suffered. A number of suppliers in the U.S. auto industry were bankrupted by this approach. In the end, the need to hold excess inventory to fulfill a customer's just-in-time mandate resulted in a higher *total* supply chain cost.

Leaning a supply chain means "pulling" a smooth flow of material through a series of suppliers to support frequent replenishment orders and changes in customer demand. To accomplish this, firms need to share information and coordinate demand forecasts, production planning, and inventory replenishment with suppliers and their supplier's suppliers throughout the supply chain.

Developing and maintaining a lean production system within a firm is difficult enough; coordinating a lean supply chain across hundreds of different companies with different goals and cost structures is extremely challenging. The first step is to build a highly collaborative business environment that ensures all of the participants in the supply chain reap the rewards of a leaner system. Adopting the technology to support such a system is purely secondary.

Time, as well as cost, is reduced in a lean supply chain; however, recent trends toward outsourcing great distances lengthen supply chain time and make it more difficult not only to coordinate suppliers but also to ensure their commitment to lean goals. In response, some companies are *nearshoring* products that have volatile demand. Nike, for example, outsources the production of shoes to Asia, but locally produces personalized items such as bags.

Summary

Lean production has truly changed the face of manufacturing and transformed the global economy. Originally known as just-in-time (JIT), it began at Toyota Motor Company as an effort to eliminate waste (particularly inventories), but evolved into a system for the continuous improvement of all aspects of manufacturing operations. *Lean production* is both a philosophy and a collection of management methods and techniques. The main advantage of the system is derived from the integration of the techniques into a focused, smooth-running management system.

In lean systems, workers are multifunctional and are required to perform different tasks, as well as aid in the improvement process. Machines are also multifunctional and are arranged in small, U-shaped work cells that enable parts to be processed in a continuous flow through the cell. Workers produce parts one at a time within the cells and transport parts between cells in small lots as called for by subassembly lines, assembly lines, or other work cells. The environment is kept clean, orderly, and free of waste so that unusual occurrences are visible.

Schedules are prepared only for the final assembly line, in which several different models are assembled on the same line. Requirements for component parts and subassemblies are then pulled through the system with kanbans. The principle of the pull system is not to make anything until requested to do so by the next station. The "pull" system will not work unless production is uniform, setups are quick, and lot sizes are low.

The pull system and kanbans are also used to order materials from outside suppliers. Suppliers are fewer in number and must be very reliable. They may be requested to make multiple deliveries of the same item in the same day, so their manufacturing system must be flexible, too. Deliveries are made directly to the factory floor, eliminating stockrooms and the waste of counting, inspecting, recording, storing, and transporting.

Lean production does not produce in anticipation of need. It produces only necessary items in necessary quantities at necessary times. Inventory is viewed as a waste of resources and an obstacle to improvement. Because there is little buffer inventory between workstations, quality must be extremely high, and every effort is made to prevent machine breakdowns.

When all these elements are in place, lean systems produce high-quality goods, quickly and at low cost. These systems also are able to respond to changes in customer demand. Lean production systems are most effective in repetitive environments, but elements of lean can be applied to almost any operation, including service operations. Lean retailing, lean banking, and lean healthcare are good examples.

Key Terms

andons Call lights installed at workstations to notify management and other workers of a quality problem in production.

breakdown maintenance A maintenance activity that involves repairs needed to make a failed machine operational.

external setup Setup activities that can be performed in advance while the machine is operating.

5 S A set of processes for workplace organization.

5 Why's Repeatedly asking "why?" until a root cause is identified.

general-purpose machines Perform several basic functions.

heijunka The process of smoothing demand across a planning horizon.

internal setup Setup activities that can be performed only when the machine is stopped.

jidoka Authority given to the workers to stop the assembly line when quality problems are encountered.

just-in-time (JIT) Smoothing the flow of material to arrive just as it is needed; evolved into a system for eliminating waste.

kaizen A Japanese term for a system of continuous improvement.

kanban A card corresponding to a standard quantity of production (or size container) used in the pull system to authorize the production or withdrawal of goods.

kanban square A marked area designated to hold a certain amount of items; an empty square is the signal to produce more items.

lean production Both a philosophy and an integrated system of management that emphasizes the elimination of waste and the continuous improvement of operations.

lean six sigma A combination of lean's principles for eliminating waste with Six Sigma's reduction of variability.

manufacturing cell A group of dissimilar machines brought together to manufacture a family of parts with similar shapes or processing requirements.

material kanban A rectangular-shaped kanban used to order material in advance of a process.

muda Anything other than the minimum amount of equipment, materials, parts, space, and time that are absolutely essential to add value to the product.

multifunctional workers Workers who have been trained to perform more than one job or function.

poka-yoke Any foolproof device or mechanism that prevents defects from occurring.

preventive maintenance A system of daily maintenance, periodic inspection, and preventive repairs designed to reduce the probability of machine breakdown.

production kanban A card authorizing the production of a container of goods.

pull system A production system in which items are manufactured only when called for by the users of those items.

push system A production system in which items are manufactured according to a schedule prepared in advance.

signal kanban A triangular kanban used as a reorder point to signal production at the previous workstation.

SMED Single minute exchange of die, a setup time reduction procedure.

supplier kanban A kanban that rotates between a factory and its supplier.

takt time The cycle time of an operation paced to the rate of customer demand.

total productive maintenance (TPM) An approach to machine maintenance that combines the practice of preventive maintenance with the concepts of total quality and employer involvement.

undercapacity scheduling The allocation of extra time in a schedule for nonproductive tasks such as problem solving or maintenance.

uniform production levels The result of smoothing production requirements on the final assembly line.

visual control Procedures and mechanisms for making problems visible.

withdrawal kanban A card authorizing the withdrawal and movement of a container of goods.

Key Formulas

Determining the number of kanbans

$$N = \frac{\bar{d}L + S}{C}$$

Questions

16.1. What is the purpose of lean production?

16.2. How did lean production evolve into a system of continuous improvement?

16.3. Why are flexible resources essential to lean production?

16.4. What does a cellular layout contribute to lean production?

16.5. Differentiate between a push and a pull production system.

16.6. How was the concept of kanban developed from the two-bin inventory system?

16.7. How are the kanban system and the reorder point system similar? How are they different?

16.8. Describe how the following kanbans operate:

a. Production and withdrawal kanbans
b. Kanban squares
c. Signal kanbans
d. Material kanbans
e. Supplier kanbans

16.9. What are the advantages of small-lot sizes?

16.10. Why do large-lot sizes not work well with pull systems?

16.11. Why are small-lot sizes not as effective in a push system?

16.12. Explain the principles of SMED. What does SMED try to achieve?

16.13. Why is uniform production important to lean? How is it achieved?

16.14. What are the advantages of mixed-model sequencing?

16.15. How are lean production and quality related? What is Lean Six Sigma?

16.16. How can a balance be struck between the cost of breakdown maintenance and the cost of preventive maintenance?

16.17. Explain the concept of total productive maintenance (TPM).

16.18. What role does the equipment operator play in TPM?

16.19. Preventive maintenance can be viewed as the process of maintaining the "health" of a machine. Using healthcare as an analogy, explain the differences and tradeoffs between breakdown maintenance, preventive maintenance, and total productive maintenance.

16.20. How are suppliers affected by lean production?

16.21. Suggest several ways that lean requirements can be made easier for suppliers.

16.22. Give examples of visual control. How does visual control affect quality?

16.23. What is a poka-yoke? Give an example.

16.24. Why is worker involvement important to kaizen? Find the Kaizen Institute on the Web and walk through the site. Summarize what you learned.

16.25. What are some typical benefits from implementing lean?

16.26. Which elements of lean are the most difficult to implement? Why?

16.27. In what type of environment is lean production most successful?

16.28. Give examples of lean services.

16.29. Lean has been applied extensively in the automobile industry. Report on other industries who use lean production.

16.30. Explain how lean and concern for the environment are related.

16.31. Discuss the problems of implementing lean production a) in an extended global supply chain, b) during periods of uncertainty or disruption, c) when managers make decisions solely based on cost.

Problems

16.1. Demand for the popular water toy Sudsy Soaker has far exceeded expectations. In order to increase the availability of different models of the toy, the manufacturer has decided to begin producing its most popular models as often as possible on its one assembly line. Given monthly requirements of 7200, 3600, and 3600 units for Sudsy Soaker 50, Sudsy Soaker 100, and Sudsy Soaker 200, respectively, determine a model sequence for the final assembly line that will smooth out the production of each model. (Assume 30 working days per month and eight working hours per day. Also assume that the time required to assemble each model is approximately the same.)

16.2. As local developers prepare for an increase in housing starts, they must anticipate their demand for various materials. One such material is tile. Used in bathrooms, kitchens, and for decoration, tiles come in many shapes, colors, and sizes. In order to accommodate the varying needs, the tile manufacturer must schedule its production efficiently. Each month developers order 30,000 boxes of quarry tile, 15,000 boxes of Italian mosaic tile, and 45,000 boxes of 4-inch bathroom tile. Determine a mixed-model sequence that will efficiently meet these needs. Assume 30 days per month.

16.3. An assembly station is asked to process 100 circuit boards per hour. It takes 20 minutes to receive the necessary components from the previous workstation. Completed circuit boards are placed in a rack that will hold 10 boards. The rack must be full before it is sent on to the next workstation. If the factory uses a safety factor of 10%, how many kanbans are needed for the circuit board assembly process?

16.4. Referring to Problem 16.3, how many kanbans would be needed in each case?

a. Demand is increased to 200 circuit boards per hour.
b. The lead time for components is increased to 30 minutes.
c. The rack size is halved.
d. The safety factor is increased to 20%.

16.5. It takes Aaron 15 minutes to produce 10 widgets to fill a container and 5 minutes to transport the container to the next station, where Maria works. Maria's process takes about 30 minutes. The factory uses a safety factor of 20%. Currently, five kanbans rotate between Aaron and Maria's stations. What is the approximate demand for widgets?

16.6. Stan Weakly can sort a bin of 100 letters in 10 minutes. He typically receives 600 letters an hour. A truck arrives with more bins every 30 minutes. The office uses a safety factor of 10%. How many kanbans are needed for the letter-sorting process?

16.7. The office administrator wishes to decrease the number of kanbans in the letter-sorting process described in Problem 16.6. Which of the following alternatives has the greatest effect on reducing the number of kanbans?

a. Eliminating the safety factor.

b. Receiving truck deliveries every 15 minutes.

c. Increasing the bin capacity to 300 letters.

What is the effect on inventory levels of decreasing the number of kanbans?

16.8. Sandy is asked to produce 250 squidgets an hour. It takes 30 minutes to receive the necessary material from the previous workstation. Each output container holds 25 squidgets. The factory currently works with a safety factor of 10%. How many kanbans should be circulating between Sandy's process and the previous process?

16.9. Referring to Problem 16.8, what happens to the number of kanbans and to inventory levels in each case?

a. The time required to receive material is increased to 45 minutes.

b. Output expectations decrease to 125 squidgets an hour.

c. The size of the container is cut to 10 squidgets.

16.10. In a large microelectronics plant, the assembly cell for circuit boards has a demand for 200 units an hour. Two feeder cells supply parts A and B to the assembly cell (one A and one B for each board). Standard containers that look like divided trays are used. A container will hold 20 As or 10 Bs. It takes 10 minutes to fill up a container with As and 20 minutes to fill up a container with Bs. Transit time to the assembly cell is 5 minutes for both A and B. No safety factor is used. Set up a kanban control system for the assembly process.

16.11. Universal Motors installed a mixed model assembly line at its Huntsville plant last year when demand for SUVs was still strong. With the rising gas prices, however, SUV and van sales have plummeted, and demand for smaller, more fuel-efficient cars has surged. The plant has the capacity to produce 200 vehicles per day. Monthly demand for cars is estimated at 2000 per month, vans at 1000 per month and SUVs at 500 per month. The plant is operating at a slow-down schedule of 20 days per month.

a. Design a production sequence that will meet demand and level production of the various models.

b. How many times will that sequence be repeated per day?

c. Explain how the sequence you propose allows quicker adjustments to demand changes. What impact does it have on component demand?

16.12. Solvo produces three types of trucks on one assembly line: the long-haul (L), the short-haul (S) and the vocational truck (V). Next month the company has orders for 500 long-haul trucks, 750 short-haul trucks, and 250 vocational trucks. Chris Riggs, the production manager for Solvo, wants to try uniform production and mixed-model sequencing. Assuming 25 working days per month, what assembly sequence would you recommend and how many times per day should the sequence be repeated?

16.13. Backyard Equipment manufactures garden tillers, leaf blowers, and lawn mowers for home use in a mixed model assembly line. Annual demand is estimated as 4500 for garden tillers, 3000 for leaf blowers, and 9000 for lawn mowers. The plant is currently operating one shift at an overtime schedule of 25 days per month. Backyard is pursuing the lean principles of uniform production and mixed model assembly.

a. Determine a mixed model production sequence that satisfies the goals of smoothing component production and assembling a variety of products each sequence.

b. How many times would the designed sequence be repeated per day to meet demand?

Case Problems

Case Problem 16.1 The Blitz Is On

Tina Rossi had been preparing for her company's first kaizen blitz and wondered if she had thought of everything. The process they had chosen to kaizen had been the subject of numerous customer complaints and employee grumblings. Tina's list of reported problems, goals for the kaizen process, and team objectives were stated in the team charter. Tina had planned for the group to review the charter first, then tour the process, measure overall cycle time, and complete a process map. From there the team would break up into four subgroups to perform a muda walk and 5S scan, conduct gripe interviews, and analyze process flow. Tina provided forms for each activity and a digital camera for visually documenting the current process and future improvements.

The second day of the blitz was less directed. Team members would regroup to go over the data collected in the previous day and suggest improvements to be tried out on the third day. This is when Tina would have to prod the team to take action—to transform the process or the layout, to improve quality or safety—to make a change and analyze the results. On day four, the team would observe the new process in action, review cycle times, identify problems, and make adjustments. After agreeing on the parameters of the new process, the team would record their kaizen results by drawing standard operation sheets, training operators, and establishing visual control tools.

All those things in one week. Tina was ready and anxious to begin.

Take Tina's challenge and perform a kaizen blitz at your school or work. An excel file with kaizen blitz worksheets is provided on the text website.

Case Problem 16.2 Where's My Cart?

The Senior Seminar at Allegheny State requires students to complete a process improvement project with local industry. Jim Davis and Leanna Hearn have been assigned to Wiley Construction. Here is their report.

Wiley Construction

Company History

Founded in 1975, Wiley Construction was one of the first designers and builders of wooden roof trusses. Over the past 40 years Wiley has prospered, and it now has office and manufacturing space of approximately 132,200 square feet and additional lumber storage facilities of about 22,300 square feet, on a 60-acre site near the Monongahela River in Pittsburgh, Pennsylvania. Utilization of this space has never been difficult, and in the fall of 2000 Wiley proudly opened a new 6000-square-foot showroom, which serves as an educational building center and showcase for many of the products it builds and/or sells. In addition to its core roof truss business, Wiley now has over 200 employees designing and building floor truss systems and preconstructed interior and exterior wall systems.

Joseph Wiley, the founder and chairman of Wiley Construction, not only wanted to build superior roofing systems, he also envisioned the idea of prepackaging an entire house. The package of materials, from foundation blocks to roofing shingles, would be available through one source. This idea soon led to a custom-designed line of homes, called Wiley Homes. The key selling point to these "prepackaged" homes, besides convenience and accuracy, was that, while the interior layout was universally applicable, the exterior of the home was designed with a very local flavor.

The exemplary reputation of the Wiley Home program as well as attention to customer service, prompt delivery times, and accurate product specifications allowed Wiley to become an international supplier of quality building products. Their products have been shipped to dozens of countries, including Russia, Germany, Spain, Japan, Korea, China, Greece, Turkey, Mexico, and Chile.

Gary Cox replaced Joe Wiley as president of Wiley Construction in January 2013. Executive Vice President Ciro Alvarez is one of the many highly skilled and motivated Wiley professional management employees. To accomplish its diverse objectives, the company has assembled a team of employees with degrees in Architecture, Building Construction, Civil Engineering, Math, Forestry, Wood Science, Accounting, Business, International Relations, Computer Science, Architectural Technology, and Biological Systems Engineering.

Technology

From the days of hand drafting and manually designed framing layouts, Wiley now utilizes highly automated methods of production as well as completely computerized design programs. These technologies have resulted in annual sales approaching $25 million. The most automated piece of equipment at their Pittsburgh facility is a Uni-saw, a highly sophisticated machine capable of simultaneously making the necessary angle adjustments on four circular saw blades. One of Wiley's newest endeavors is the construction of prefabricated wall panels, for which it now has a new wall panel machine to more efficiently construct a higher quality wall panel. The new partially computer-controlled machine was designed especially for Wiley and is one of the best in the industry. In order to maximize the utility of its automated capabilities, Wiley employs nearly 50 computer operators and programmers experienced in engineering, design, export, sales, and accounting software systems. Central to the operation is the highly specialized wooden-truss design program used by the engineering staff. To ensure that all of this technology results in the highest quality products, the Wiley production facility is one of a very small percentage of facilities that opens their doors to the rigid quality-control specifications of the Pre-Fab Construction Industry.

Current Production Process

Wiley Housing Systems, Inc., is a batch production company that specializes in make-to-order timber housing systems. The manufacturing facility is over 100,000 square feet in size (see the accompanying figure) and is sectioned off into different areas such as wall, floor, and roof truss assembly; raw material cutting; and metal storage. Each of the assembly lines is fed by a common 26,000 square foot on-site supply point. The only required materials are common-sized lumber (i.e., 2 × 4, 2 × 6, etc.), aluminum connecting plates, and nails. However, each of the processes is tailored to meet customer demands and specifications.

All of Wiley's products are constructed of standard dimensional lumber that arrives via truck or train and is stockpiled in its lumber yard. Typically, Wiley has enough lumber on site for two weeks of continuous operation without replenishment. All other inventory, work-in-process, and common materials are stored inside the production facility. Once an order is received, the staff engineers design the truss system and electronically queue the order for manufacture. The production foreman then assigns the order to a cutting team. This team consists of two men—the sawer and the tailor. The sawer is responsible for saw setup, as well as lumber retrieval and optimization, while the tailor stacks and labels the cut lumber for assembly. Mr. Alvarez explained that his major concern was the amount of setup time required by the cutting teams. He said that up to 45% of production time was spent adjusting the saws for each job, a very typical problem in batch production. This is where Wiley's problem and our challenge began.

Process Improvement

After our initial plant tour, where we noted the large amount of work-in-process inventory waiting in carts between the saws and the assembly stations, we spent a day interviewing workers on the assembly teams. It was brought to our attention that at certain points during the day the backup of WIP carts was in fact problematic, from the standpoint of worker safety and from the ability to locate the required cart quickly and easily. There are approximately 80 to 90 carts in use at any given time, which are loaded with raw materials on a per-job basis and are tagged with a work order. After the carts are loaded and tagged, they are placed in front of the assembly workstations. Copies of the work orders are taken to the plant control office. The plant supervisor then assigns the jobs to assembly stations by placing the work order copy in assigned bins located on the plant control office wall. The assembly employees will go to their assigned bin, pick their next job ticket, and then locate the corresponding cart for that job. Mr. Alvarez mentioned that locating the cart required for the next job could take anywhere from one to ten minutes depending on the assembly backup (number of full carts used that day) and the location of the cart within the facility. The manufacturing employees are tracked on a 100th-of-the-hour time basis for work, which means that there should, in theory, be very little unproductive time during the day, with the exception of break periods. This also reduces socialization of employees.

We decided to narrow our analysis to the immediate problem of locating the correct cart. After brainstorming possible solutions, we have concluded that Wiley should use an electronic paging system similar to what restaurants use to notify customers that their table is ready. We recommend that the carts be outfitted with long-life, durable, and replaceable lithium battery-powered strobe lights that are activated by a keypad located on the plant control office wall beside the pending job order bins. Each light would have a unique

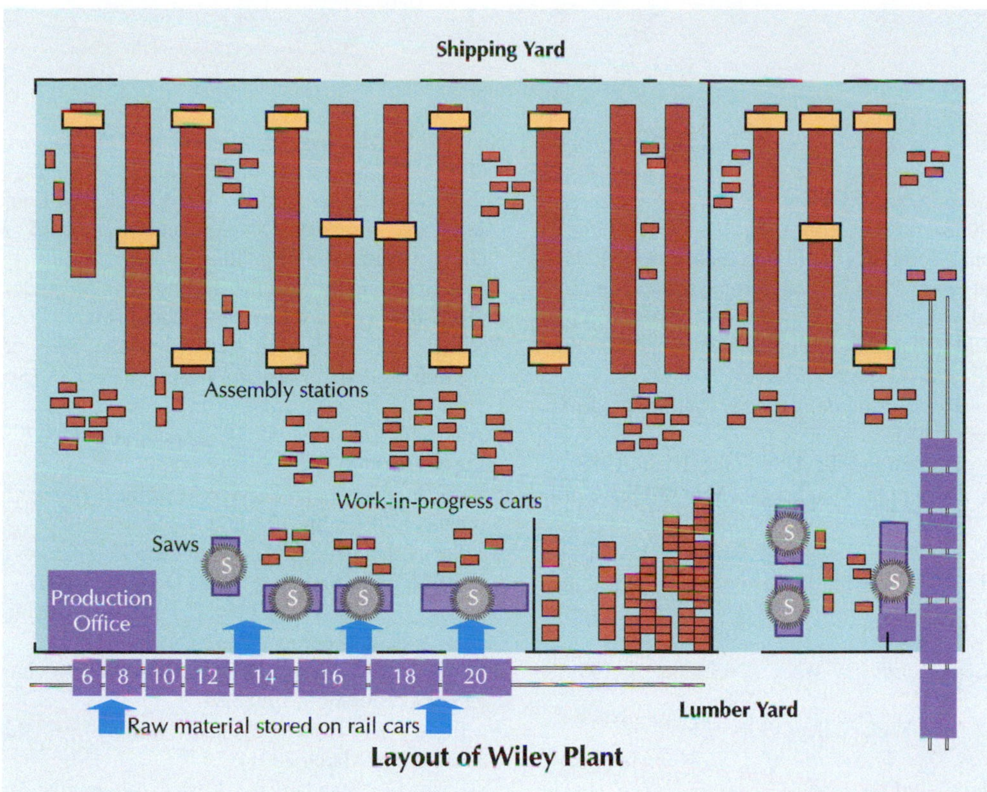

Layout of Wiley Plant

three-digit number assigned to it. These numbers would be hand-written on the work order, by the individual who loads the cart, before it is given to the plant supervisor to be assigned. There is a chance of multiple carts being needed for the same job, but each cart has its own individual work order and therefore would have its own three-digit identification number and light. This is no deviation from the current process. The assembly workers would walk to the plant control office, retrieve their next job from the bin, type the three-digit code into the keypad, and then find the cart that has the strobe light turned on. This process would eliminate all of the guessing currently required to locate the cart with the raw materials and should reduce the overall average time needed to locate a cart. This would also allow remote storage of the carts, rather than stacking as many as 30 carts at the top of the assembly line, a hindrance to traffic flow and safety.

1. Identify waste in the current production process.
2. How does the pager suggestion eliminate waste?
3. Have the students and Mr. Alvarez found the root cause of the cart problem? Why or why not?
4. How would you apply the principles of lean production to improve Wiley's situation?

Case Problem 16.3 Leaning the Warehouse

"We are interested in lean training for our distribution center workers. Can you provide that for us, Professor Warren?" the (DC) manager inquired.

"Yes, we have training material on lean systems and would be happy to facilitate a series of workshops for you and your employees. We usually start with a week of manager or supervisor training and then move on to front-line employee workshops one day a week for about two months. As your workers gain experience participating in improvement teams, we would return for day-long workshops once a month for six months after that. The entire process takes about a year, after which time your facility would have its own lean trainers certified to . . ."

"Actually," interrupted the manager, "we don't need to educate our supervisors on lean—just our hourly workers, and I think that could be done in about two days, one day for each shift."

"I see," replied Professor Warren. "Perhaps you could tell me more about what your lean objectives are and why you're seeking lean training at this time."

"Sure. We're implementing a new performance-based pay system from corporate in which our industrial engineering staff has determined how long workers should take to complete a task and what a day's output should be. We'll be recording task completion times and daily throughput with scanners and comparing those with the standards that have been developed. Those workers who beat the standard receive bonus pay; those who do not risk losing their position. Our pilot project at the Atlanta DC didn't go very well. None of the workers met standard and they didn't seem to get how important this is. For example, they'd be running off looking for tools, or moving the same merchandise several times to get an aisle clear or to reach a pallet in back, or *picking* what they'd just *put away*, or stopping one task to work on another more urgent one. So we thought if we taught them lean principles for eliminating waste, it'd be easier to get the job done, and performance against standard would improve."

1. Explain the different views of lean in this case. What might Professor Warren include in his more extensive training program?
2. What elements of lean would be most useful to the DC manager and his staff?
3. Are the manager's views of lean realistic? What is the best he can hope to achieve in the time allotted?
4. What might be some drawbacks in approaching lean implementation in this way? What might be some advantages? Does warehouse work lend itself to lean?

References

Black, J. T. *The Design of the Factory with a Future*. New York: McGraw-Hill, 1991.

Bremner, B., and C. Dawson. "Can Anything Stop Toyota?" *BusinessWeek* (November 17, 2003), pp. 114–118.

Brown, S. "Toyota's Global Body Shop." *Fortune* (February 9, 2004), Industrial Edition, http://www.fortune.com/fortune/subs/columnist/0,15704,581557,00.html.

Bylinsky, G. "Heroes of Manufacturing." *Fortune* (March 20, 2000), pp. 192A–205A.

Cusomano, M. *The Japanese Automobile Industry*. Cambridge, MA: Harvard University Press, 1985.

Hall, R. *Zero Inventories*. Homewood, IL: Dow Jones-Irwin, 1983.

Hirano, H. *JIT Factory Revolution*. Cambridge, MA: Productivity Press, 1988.

Huang, P. Y., L. P. Rees, and B. W. Taylor. "A Simulation Analysis of the Just-in-Time Technique (with Kanbans) for a Multiline, Multistage Production System." *Decision Sciences* (July 1983), pp. 326–345.

Jusko, J. "A Look at Lean." *Industry Week* (December 6, 1999), pp. 88–91.

Kinni, T. *America's Best*. New York: Wiley, 1996.

Liker, J. *Becoming Lean: Inside Stories of U.S. Manufacturers*. Cambridge, MA: Productivity Press, 1998.

Monden, Y., ed. *Applying Just-In-Time: The American/Japanese Experience*. Atlanta: Industrial Engineering and Management Press, 1986.

Monden, Y. *Toyota Production System: An Integrated Approach to Just-in-Time*, 3rd ed. Atlanta: Industrial Engineering and Management Press, 1986.

Panchak, P. "Lean Health Care? It Works!" *Industry Week* (November 1, 2003).

Phillips, T. "Building the Lean Machine." *Advanced Manufacturing* (January 1, 2000). http://www.advancedmanufacturing.com.

Sepehri, M. *Just-in-Time, Not Just in Japan*. Falls Church, VA: American Production and Inventory Control Society, 1986.

Shingo, S. *Modern Approaches to Manufacturing Improvement*. Cambridge, MA: Productivity Press, 1990.

Sobek, D., J. Liker, and A. Ward. "Another Look at How Toyota Integrates Product Development." *Harvard Business Review* (July–August 1998), pp. 36–49.

Spear, S. "Comments on the Second Toyota Paradox." Teaching Note 9-602-035, Harvard Business School (March 2003).

Spear, S., and K. Bowen. "Decoding the DNA of the Toyota Production System." *Harvard Business Review* (September–October 1999), pp. 96–106.

Suzaki, K. *The New Manufacturing Challenge*. New York: Free Press, 1985.

Swank, C. "The Lean Service Machine." *Harvard Business Review* (October 2003), pp. 123–131.

Tagliabue, J. "Spanish Clothing Chain Zara Grows by Being Fast and Flexible." *The New York Times* (May 30, 2003).

Tierney, C. "Big Three Play Catch-Up to Toyota Plant Prowess." *Detroit News* (February 22, 2004).

The Toyota Production System. Company brochure. Japan: Toyota Motor Corporation, 1998.

Vasilash, G. "Lean Lessons." *Automotive Manufacturing and Production* (March 2001).

Vasilash, G. "Standardized Lean." *Automotive Manufacturing and Production* (February 2000). http://www.automfg.com.

Ward, A., J. Liker, J. Cristiano, and Durward Sobek II. "The Second Toyota Paradox: How Delaying Decisions Can Make Better Cars Faster." *Sloan Management Review* (Spring 1995), pp. 43–62.

Womack, J., D. Jones, and D. Roos. *The Machine That Changed the World*. New York: Macmillan, 1990.

Womack, J., and D. Jones. *Lean Thinking*. New York: Simon & Schuster, 1996.

Wysocki, B. "Industrial Strength: To Fix Health Care, Hospitals Take Tips from Factory Floor," *The Wall Street Journal* (April 9, 2004), p. A1.

CHAPTER 17

Scheduling

Mike Fuentes/Bloomberg/Getty Images, Inc.

LEARNING OBJECTIVES

After reading this chapter, you will be able to:

- Explain the multiple dimensions of a good schedule, and determine which type of schedule is appropriate for different types of productive systems.
- Use several different quantitative techniques for loading, sequencing, and monitoring work.
- Discuss advanced planning and scheduling systems, and contrast finite and infinite scheduling.
- Use the theory of constraints to identify the bottleneck and pace a system to the bottleneck operation.
- Create efficient and equitable employee schedules.

Scheduling Electronics Production

Innovation in the world of electronics brings new products to the consumer market at a rapid pace. Customers want the latest and greatest technology in an array of options. As a result, those manufacturers who build the circuitry inside these products receive orders for an increasingly diverse and complicated mix of items in lower volumes with abbreviated lead times. Scheduling such varied production on automated equipment requires frequent changeovers, which can be extremely inefficient if changeover times are high. In addition, profit margins in the industry are slim and controlling cost while satisfying customer requirements is a challenge.

An advanced scheduling system can help alleviate these problems (see photo). One such system, Optimized Dynamic Scheduling, matches detailed production information with customer orders in an integrated database. The system selects which work orders and quantities to schedule first based on specified priorities and parameters. Line fit and verification of assemblies is automatically performed. Optimization of the schedule is then performed using three levels of advanced scheduling algorithms: (1) a heuristic greedy algorithm that groups work orders based on component commonality and similar setups; (2) an advanced genetic algorithm that sequences work within the groups to maximize fixed feeder placements, and (3) additional genetic algorithms to reduce setup time and minimize component placement time for SMT (surface mount technology) robots. The schedule can also be dynamically adjusted and re-optimized as new work orders are received.

In this chapter, we examine different types of scheduling systems and introduce several advanced scheduling techniques.

Source: Optimal Electronic Corporation, "How to Increase Production and Reduce Costs Through Optimized Dynamic Scheduling," Whitepaper, http://optelco.com/pdf/ods_white_paper.pdf (accessed December 31, 2015).

Scheduling The last stage of planning before production.

Scheduling specifies *when* labor, equipment, and facilities are needed to produce a product or provide a service. It is the last stage of planning before production takes place. The scheduling function differs considerably based on the type of operation:

- In *process industries*, such as chemicals and pharmaceuticals, scheduling might consist of determining the mix of ingredients that goes into a vat or when the system should stop producing one type of mixture, clean out the vat, and start producing another. Linear programming can find the lowest-cost mix of ingredients, and the production order quantity can determine the optimal length of a production run. These techniques are described in detail in Chapter 14 Supplement and Chapter 13, respectively.
- For *mass production*, the schedule of production is pretty much determined when the assembly line is laid out. Products simply flow down the assembly line from one station to the next in the same prescribed, nondeviating order every time. Day-to-day scheduling decisions consist of determining how fast to feed items into the line and how many hours per day to run the line. On a mixed-model assembly line, the *order* of products assembled also has to be determined. We discuss these issues in Chapters 7 and 16.
- For *projects*, the scheduling decisions are so numerous and interrelated that specialized project-scheduling techniques such as PERT and CPM have been devised. Chapter 9 is devoted to these planning and control tools for project management.
- For *batch or job shop production*, scheduling decisions can be quite complex. In previous chapters, we discussed *sales and operations planning*, which plans for the production of product lines or families; *master scheduling*, which plans for the production of individual end items or finished goods; and *material requirements planning* (MRP) and *capacity requirements planning* (CRP), which plan for the production of components and assemblies. Scheduling determines to which machine a part will be routed for processing, which worker will operate a machine that produces a part, and the order in which the parts are to be processed. Scheduling also determines which patient to assign to an operating room, which doctors and nurses are to care for a patient during certain hours of the day, the order in which a doctor is to see patients, and when meals should be delivered or medications dispensed.

What makes scheduling so difficult in a job shop is the variety of jobs (or patients) that are processed, each with distinctive routing and processing requirements. In addition, although the volume of each customer order may be small, there are probably a great number of different orders in the shop at any one time. This necessitates planning for the production of each job as it arrives, scheduling its use of limited resources, and monitoring its progress through the system.

This chapter concentrates on scheduling issues for job shop production. We also examine one of the most difficult scheduling problems for services—employee scheduling.

Objectives in Scheduling

There are many possible objectives in constructing a schedule, including

- Meeting customer due dates;
- Minimizing job lateness;
- Minimizing response time;
- Minimizing completion time;
- Minimizing time in the system;
- Minimizing overtime;
- Maximizing machine or labor utilization;
- Minimizing idle time; and
- Minimizing work-in-process inventory.

Production control The scheduling and monitoring of day-to-day production in a job shop.

Job shop scheduling is also known as **production control**, *shop floor control* (SFC), *and production activity control* (PAC). Regardless of their primary scheduling objective, manufacturers typically have a *production control department* whose responsibilities consist of three activities:

1. ***Loading**—checking the availability of material, machines, and labor.* The MRP system plans for material availability. CRP converts the material plan into machine and labor requirements, and projects resource overloads and underloads. Production control assigns work to individual workers or machines, and then attempts to smooth out the load to make the MRP schedule "doable." Smoothing the load is called **load leveling**.
2. ***Sequencing**—releasing work orders to the shop and issuing dispatch lists for individual machines.* MRP recommends when orders should be released (hence the name *planned* order releases). After verifying their feasibility, production control actually releases the orders. When several orders are released to one machine center, they must be prioritized so that the worker will know which ones to do first. The **dispatch list** contains the sequence in which jobs should be processed. This sequence is often based on certain *sequencing rules*.
3. ***Monitoring**—maintaining progress reports on each job until it is completed.* This is important because items may need to be rescheduled as changes occur in the system. In addition to timely data collection, it involves the use of Gantt charts and input/output control charts.

Load leveling The process of smoothing out the work assigned.

Dispatch list A list of orders released to the shop that specifies the sequence in which jobs should be processed.

Loading

Loading is the process of assigning work to limited resources. Many times an operation can be performed by various persons, machines, or work centers but with varying efficiencies. If there is enough capacity, each worker should be assigned to the task that he or she performs best, and each job to the machine that can process it most efficiently. In effect, that is what happens when CRP generates a load profile for each machine center. The routing file used by CRP lists the machine that can perform the job most efficiently first. If no overloads appear in the load profile, then production control can proceed to the next task of sequencing the work at each center. However, when resource constraints produce overloads in the load profile, production control must examine the list of jobs initially assigned and decide which jobs to reassign elsewhere. The problem of determining how best to allocate jobs to machines or workers to tasks can be solved with the *assignment method* of linear programming.

Loading The process of assigning work to limited resources.

The Assignment Method

The *assignment method* is a specialized linear programming solution procedure for deciding which worker to assign to a task, or which job to assign to a machine. (See Supplement 14 for linear programming.) Given a table of tasks and resources, the procedure creates an *opportunity cost matrix* and selects the best assignment in consideration of tradeoffs among alternatives. With this technique, only one job may be assigned to each worker or machine. The procedure for a minimization problem is outlined as follows:

1. Perform *row reductions* by subtracting the minimum value in each row from all other row values.
2. Perform *column reductions* by subtracting the minimum value in each column from all other column values.
3. The resulting table is an *opportunity cost matrix*. Cross out all zeros in the matrix using the minimum number of horizontal or vertical lines.
4. If the number of lines equals the number of rows in the matrix, an optimal solution has been reached and assignments can be made where the zeros appear. Otherwise, *modify the matrix* by subtracting the minimum uncrossed value from all other uncrossed values and adding this same amount to all cells where two lines intersect. All other values in the matrix remain unchanged.
5. Repeat steps 3 and 4 until an optimal solution is reached.

EXAMPLE 17.1 | Assigning Work at WebStar

WebStar, Inc. has four web projects to complete and four workers with varying degrees of expertise in web development for particular industries. Estimates of processing times (in hours) for each project by each worker are shown below. Development time costs an average of $100 an hour. Assign each worker to a project so that cost is minimized.

INITIAL MATRIX	PROJECT 1	PROJECT 2	PROJECT 3	PROJECT 4
Bryan	10	5	6	10
Kari	6	2	4	6
Noah	7	6	5	6
Chris	9	5	4	10

Solution:

1. ***Row reduction***—*Find the best assignment in each row. Subtract the smallest value in each row from all other row values*. The resulting number is the opportunity cost of assigning a worker to that project. For example, the best assignment for Bryan would be project 2. Thus, its value in the following matrix is zero. However, if Bryan were assigned to project 1 or 4, it would take (10 − 5) = 5 hours longer to complete, and if assigned to project 3, one hour longer.

ROW REDUCTION	PROJECT 1	PROJECT 2	PROJECT 3	PROJECT 4
Bryan	5	0	1	5
Kari	4	0	2	4
Noah	2	1	0	1
Chris	5	1	0	6

2. ***Column reduction***—*Find the best assignment in each column. Subtract the smallest value in each column from all other values in the column.* For example, project 1 can be completed the fastest with Noah as project leader, so it has an opportunity cost of zero. Assigning Bryan to project 1 would require 3 more hours of processing; thus, its opportunity cost is 3.

COLUMN REDUCTION	PROJECT 1	PROJECT 2	PROJECT 3	PROJECT 4
Bryan	3	0	1	4
Kari	2	0	2	3
Noah	0	1	0	0
Chris	3	1	0	5

3. ***Look for unique assignments***—*Examine the matrix and cover all zeros*. Remember that each person can only be assigned to one project and each project can only have one leader. A problem occurs when project 2 is the best for both Bryan and Kari, and project 3 is best for both Noah and Chris. In the following matrix, rows or columns containing optimal assignments are highlighted. This is called "covering all zeros." If the number of lines (or highlighting) is less than the number of rows, the matrix needs to be modified.

INITIAL ASSIGNMENT	PROJECT 1	PROJECT 2	PROJECT 3	PROJECT 4
Bryan	3	0	1	4
Kari	2	0	2	3
Noah	0	1	0	0
Chris	3	1	0	5

4. ***Modify the matrix****—Find the smallest value of the entries that are not highlighted. Subtract that value from all other non-highlighted entries, and add it to the entries where the lines intersect*. Below we have subtracted 2 from the noncovered entries and added it to the intersection points (i.e., Noah's project 2 and project 3 values).

MODIFIED MATRIX	PROJECT 1	PROJECT 2	PROJECT 3	PROJECT 4
Bryan	1	0	1	2
Kari	0	0	2	1
Noah	0	3	2	0
Chris	1	1	0	3

5. ***Look for unique assignments****—Assign each worker to the best project available*. Bryan is assigned to project 2. With project 2 eliminated, Kari is assigned to project 1. Since project 1 has been eliminated, Noah is assigned to project 4. That leaves Chris for project 3.

FINAL ASSIGNMENT	PROJECT 1	PROJECT 2	PROJECT 3	PROJECT 4
Bryan	1	0	1	2
Kari	0	0	2	1
Noah	0	3	2	0
Chris	1	1	0	3

6. ***Calculate performance***—Refer back to the original assignment matrix to find the times required to finish each project by the assigned worker. At a cost of \$100 hour, the projects will cost $(5 + 6 + 4 + 6) \times \$100 = \$2100$ to complete.

FINAL MATRIX	PROJECT 1	PROJECT 2	PROJECT 3	PROJECT 4
Bryan	10	5	6	10
Kari	6	2	4	6
Noah	7	6	5	6
Chris	9	5	4	10

Smaller assignment problems, such as our example, are usually solved by hand. Larger ones can be solved in Excel with Solver, as shown in Exhibit 17.1. Assignment problems may also involve maximizing profit or customer satisfaction. When solving maximization problems by hand, each entry in the initial matrix should be subtracted from the largest matrix value before proceeding as a minimization problem. When solving with Excel, simply change the Solver objective function from min to max.

EXHIBIT 17.1 | The Assignment Method

Excel File

(a) Setup

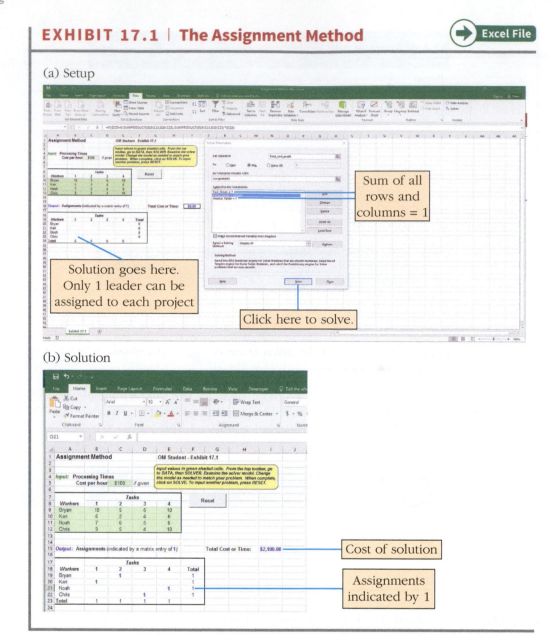

Sum of all rows and columns = 1

Solution goes here. Only 1 leader can be assigned to each project

Click here to solve.

(b) Solution

Assignment Method — OM Student - Exhibit 17.1

Input values in green shaded cells. From the top toolbar, go to DATA, then SOLVER. Examine the solver model. Change the model as needed to match your problem. When complete, click on SOLVE. To input another problem, press RESET.

Input: Processing Times
Cost per hour $100 if given

Workers	Tasks 1	2	3	4
Bryan	10	5	6	10
Kari	6	2	4	6
Noah	7	6	5	6
Chris	9	5	4	10

Output: Assignments (indicated by a matrix entry of 1) — Total Cost or Time: $2,100.00

Workers	Tasks 1	2	3	4	Total
Bryan		1			1
Kari	1				1
Noah				1	1
Chris			1		1
Total	1	1	1	1	

Cost of solution

Assignments indicated by 1

Along the Supply Chain

Scheduling Major League Baseball Umpires

Perspectives/Jeff Smith/Shutterstock

It used to be that major league baseball (MLB) umpires were scheduled on an Excel spreadsheet. The task took several weeks and had to be revised often. Now they use a scheduling system developed by researchers at the University of Miami, Carnegie Mellon, and Michigan State University. A variant of the classic *Traveling Salesman* problem, umpires, as shown in the photo, are assigned to crews that must visit all ballparks at least once during the year. Of course, there are many more constraints.

MLB teams play 2430 games in a two- to four-game series during a six-month season. Each game requires a crew of four umpires. There are currently 70 umpires on MLB staff, and 22 AAA umpires who may be called up as needed to fill in for games. A typical umpire will handle 142 games a year. Unlike football referees, umpires are full-time employees of MLB. Umpires are normally assigned to crews, but the content of these crews can change during the year. Constraints to umpire crew scheduling include mandated vacations, overexposure to individual teams, prohibition to refereeing at home, and minimizing coast-to-coast travel. Examples of MLB rules used to enforce these constraints are:

- Crews should travel to all 30 ballparks at least once during a season.
- Crews should not umpire the same team's series of games more than once every 18 days.
- Crews must not travel from the West Coast to the East Coast without an intermediate day off.
- Crews must not umpire consecutive series more than 1700 miles apart without an intermediate day off.
- Crews must not travel more than 300 miles preceding a series whose first game is a day game.
- Crews should not work more than 21 days without a day off.
- Crews should see each team at home and on the road at least once.
- Crews should have balanced schedules (i.e., travel approximately the same number of miles, umpire the same number of games, and have the same number of days off).

Real-life scheduling problems, like umpire scheduling, can be quite complex. The general solution approach is similar to the assignment method of linear programming described in this chapter. There is an objective function of minimizing distance traveled subject to a number of constraints, as listed earlier. The variables are (0,1) meaning an umpire is either assigned to a game slot (i.e., 1), or not (i.e., 0), and the game slots are numerous (2430 × 4 = 9720). While this can be solved as an integer linear programming (LP) problem, the length of time to do so and the inability to relax constraints make it difficult to find a feasible solution.

Academics use heuristics, or rules of thumb, to solve these types of problems. Heuristics do not necessarily satisfy all constraints and do not guarantee an optimal solution, but they can give satisficing or "good enough" solutions. The heuristics are evaluated against performance metrics, previous solutions, and "optimal" solutions (from mathematical programming such as LP). The heuristics are usually improved on with use until users accept them. Many are then coded into software and sold as scheduling systems for particular applications.

1. Search the Internet for scheduling software specific to sports teams or referees. What functionality does the software promise?
2. Approximate the number of possible solutions for this problem. With computer systems able to process huge amounts of data quickly, would it be possible to enumerate all possible schedules and choose the best? Investigate.

Source: Based on Michael Trick, Hakan Yildiz, and Tallys Yunes, "Scheduling Major League Baseball Umpires and the Traveling Umpire Problem," *Interfaces*, 42 (3) (May/June 2012), pp. 232–244.

Sequencing

When more than one job is assigned to a machine or activity, the operator needs to know the order in which to process the jobs. The process of prioritizing jobs is called **sequencing**. If no particular order is specified, the operator would probably process the job that arrived first. This default sequence is called *first-come, first-served* (FCFS). If jobs are stacked on arrival to a machine, it might be easier to process the job first that arrived last and is now on top of the stack. This is called *last-come, first-served* (LCFS) sequencing.

Sequencing Prioritizes jobs that have been assigned to a resource.

Another common approach is to process the job first that is due the soonest or the job that has the highest customer priority. These are known as *earliest due date* (DDATE) and *highest customer priority* (CUSTPR) sequencing. Operators may also look through a stack of jobs to find one with a *similar setup* to the job that is currently being processed (SETUP). That would minimize the downtime of the machine and make the operator's job easier.

Variations on the DDATE rule include *minimum slack* (SLACK) and *smallest critical ratio* (CR). SLACK considers the work remaining to be performed on a job as well as the time remaining (until the due date) to perform that work. Jobs are processed first that have the least difference (or slack) between the two, as follows:

$$\text{SLACK} = (\text{due date} - \text{today's date}) - (\text{processing time})$$

The critical ratio uses the same information as SLACK, but recalculates the sequence as processing continues and arranges the information in ratio form. Mathematically, the CR is calculated as follows:

$$\text{CR} = \frac{\text{time remaining}}{\text{work remaining}} = \frac{\text{due date} - \text{today's date}}{\text{remaining processing time}}$$

If the work remaining is greater than the time remaining, the critical ratio will be less than 1. If the time remaining is greater than the work remaining, the critical ratio will be greater than 1.

If the time remaining equals work remaining, the critical ratio exactly equals 1. The critical ratio allows us to make the following statements about our schedule:

If CR > 1, then the job is *ahead of schedule*

If CR < 1, then the job is *behind schedule*

If CR = 1, then the job is exactly *on schedule*

Other sequencing rules examine processing time at a particular operation and order the work either by shortest processing time (SPT) or longest processing time (LPT). LPT assumes long jobs are important jobs and is analogous to the strategy of doing larger tasks first to get them out of the way. SPT focuses instead on shorter jobs and is able to complete many more jobs earlier than LPT. With either rule, some jobs may be inordinately late because they are always put at the back of a queue.

All these "rules" for arranging jobs in a certain order for processing seem reasonable. We might wonder which methods are best or if it really matters which jobs are processed first anyway. Perhaps a few examples will help answer those questions.

Sequencing Jobs Through One Process

Flow time The time it takes a job to flow through the system.

Makespan The time it takes for a group of jobs to be completed.

Tardiness The difference between the late job's due date and its completion time.

The simplest sequencing problem consists of a queue of jobs at one machine or process. No new jobs arrive to the machine during the analysis, processing times and due dates are fixed, and setup time is considered negligible. For this scenario, the *completion time* (also called **flow time**) of each job will differ depending on its place in the sequence, but the overall completion time for the set of jobs (called the **makespan**) will not change. **Tardiness** is the difference between a late job's due date and its completion time. Even in this simple case, there is no sequencing rule that optimizes both processing efficiency and due date performance. Let's consider an example.

EXAMPLE 17.2 | Simple Sequencing Rules

Because of the approaching holiday season, Joe Palotty is scheduled to work seven days a week for the next two months. October's work for Joe consists of five jobs, A, B, C, D, and E. Job A takes five days to complete and is due on day 10, job B takes ten days to complete and is due on day 15, job C takes two days to process and is due on day 5, job D takes eight days to process and is due on day 12, and job E, which takes six days to process, is due on day 8.

There are 120 possible sequences for the five jobs. Clearly, enumeration is impossible. Let's try some simple sequencing rules. Sequence the jobs by (a) first-come, first-served (FCFS), (b) earliest due date (DDATE), (c) minimum slack (SLACK), and (d) shortest processing time (SPT). Determine the completion time and tardiness of each job under each sequencing rule. Should Joe process his work as is—first-come, first-served? If not, what sequencing rule would you recommend to Joe?

Solution:

Prepare a table for each sequencing rule. Start the first job at time 0. (When today's date is not given, assume it is day 0.) Completion time is the sum of the start time and the processing time. The start time of the next job is the completion time of the previous job.

(a) FCFS: Process the jobs in order of their arrival, A, B, C, D, E.

FCFS SEQUENCE	START TIME	PROCESSING TIME	COMPLETION TIME	DUE DATE	TARDINESS
A	0	5	5	10	0
B	5	10	15	15	0
C	15	2	17	5	12
D	17	8	25	12	13
E	25	6	31	8	23
Total			93		48
Average			93/5 = 18.60		48/5 = 9.6

(b) DDATE: Sequence the jobs by earliest due date.

DDATE SEQUENCE	START TIME	PROCESSING TIME	COMPLETION TIME	DUE DATE	TARDINESS
C	0	2	2	5	0
E	2	6	8	8	0
A	8	5	13	10	3
D	13	8	21	12	9
B	21	10	31	15	16
Total			75		28
Average			75/5 = 15.00		28/5 = 5.6

(c) SLACK: Sequence the jobs by minimum slack. The slack for each job is calculated as: (due date − today's date) − remaining processing time.

Job A (10 − 0) − 5 = 5*
B (15 − 0) − 10 = 5*
C (5 − 0) − 2 = 3
D (12 − 0) − 8 = 4
E (8 − 0) − 6 = 2

*break the tie arbitrarily with FCFS

SLACK SEQUENCE	START TIME	PROCESSING TIME	COMPLETION TIME	DUE DATE	TARDINESS
E	0	6	6	8	0
C	6	2	8	5	3
D	8	8	16	12	4
A	16	5	21	10	11
B	21	10	31	15	16
Total			82		34
Average			82/5 = 16.40		34/5 = 6.8

(d) SPT: Sequence the jobs by smallest processing time.

SPT SEQUENCE	START TIME	PROCESSING TIME	COMPLETION TIME	DUE DATE	TARDINESS
C	0	2	2	5	0
A	2	5	7	10	0
E	7	6	13	8	5
D	13	8	21	12	9
B	21	10	31	15	16
Total			74		30
Average			74/5 = 14.80		30/5 = 6

Summary

RULE	AVERAGE COMPLETION TIME	AVERAGE TARDINESS	NO. OF JOBS TARDY	MAXIMUM TARDINESS
FCFS	18.60	9.6	3*	23
DDATE	15.00	5.6*	3*	16*
SLACK	16.40	6.8	4	16*
SPT	14.80*	6.0	3*	16*

*Best Value

All the sequencing rules complete the month's work by day 31, as planned. However, no sequencing rule is able to complete *all* jobs on time. The performance of FCFS is either met or exceeded by DDATE and SPT. Thus, Joe should take the time to sequence this month's work.

Whether Joe sequences his work by DDATE or SPT depends on the objectives of the company for whom he works. The particular jobs that are tardy may also make a difference.

The Excel solution to this problem is shown in **Exhibit 17.2**.

Are the preceding results a function of this particular example, or are they indicative of the types of results we will get whenever these rules are applied? Analytically, we can prove that for a set number of jobs to be processed on *one* machine, the SPT sequencing rule will minimize mean job completion time (also known as *flowtime*) and minimize mean number of jobs in the system. On the other hand, the DDATE sequencing rule will minimize mean tardiness. No definitive statements can be made concerning the performance of the other sequencing rules.

EXHIBIT 17.2 | Using Excel for Sequencing Rules

Excel File

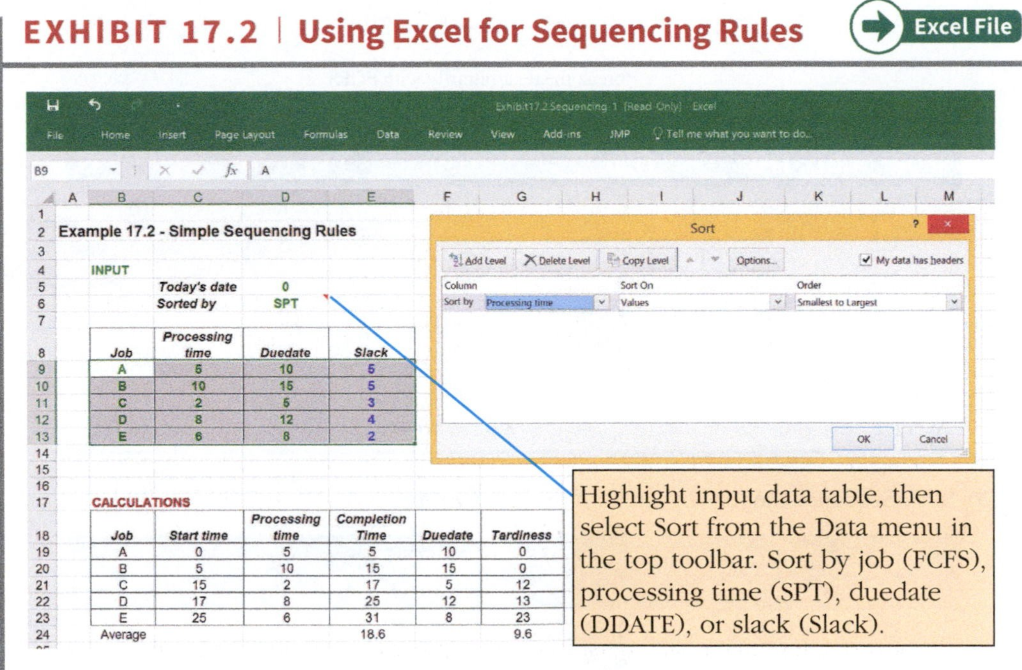

Sequencing Jobs Through Two Serial Processes

Johnson's rule Gives an optimal sequence for jobs processed serially through two processes.

Since few factories consist of just one process, we might wonder if techniques exist that will produce an optimal sequence for any number of jobs processed through more than one machine or process. **Johnson's rule** finds the fastest way to process a series of jobs through a two-step system in which every job follows the same sequence through two processes. Based on a variation of the SPT rule, it requires that the sequence be "mapped out" to determine the final completion time, or *makespan*, for the set of jobs. The procedure is as follows:

1. List the time required to complete each job at each process. Set up a one-dimensional matrix to represent the desired sequence with the number of slots equal to the number of jobs.
2. Select the smallest processing time at either process. If that time occurs at process 1, put the associated job as near to the *beginning* of the sequence as possible.

3. If the smallest time occurs at process 2, put the associated job as near to the *end* of the sequence as possible.
4. Remove the job from the list.
5. Repeat steps 2–4 until all slots in the matrix have been filled or all jobs have been sequenced.

EXAMPLE 17.3 | Johnson's Rule

Johnson's Fine Restorations has received a rush order to refinish five carousel animals—an alligator, a bear, a cat, a deer, and an elephant. The restoration involves two major processes: sanding and painting. Mr. Johnson takes care of the sanding; his son does the painting. The time required for each refinishing job differs with the state of disrepair and degree of detail of each animal. Given the following processing times (in hours), determine the order in which the jobs should be processed so that the rush order can be completed as soon as possible.

JOB	PROCESS 1	PROCESS 2
A	6	8
B	11	6
C	7	3
D	9	7
E	5	10

Solution:

The smallest processing time, three hours, occurs at process 2 for job C, so we place job C as near to the end of the sequence as possible. C is now eliminated from the job list.

The next smallest time is five hours. It occurs at process 1 for job E, so we place job E as near to the beginning of the sequence as possible. Job E is eliminated from the job list.

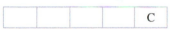

The next smallest time is six hours. It occurs at process 1 for job A and at process 2 for job B. Thus, we place job A as near to the beginning of the sequence as possible and job B as near to the end of the sequence as possible. Jobs A and B are eliminated from the job list.

E	A		B	C

The only job remaining is job D. It is placed in the only available slot, in the middle of the sequence.

E	A	D	B	C

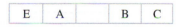

This sequence will complete these jobs faster than any other sequence. The following bar charts (called *Gantt charts*) are used to determine the makespan or final completion time for the set of five jobs. Notice that the sequence of jobs (E, A, D, B, C) is the same for both processes and that a job cannot begin at process 2 until it has been completed at process 1. Also, a job cannot begin at process 2 if another job is currently in process. Time periods during which a job is being processed are labeled with the job's letter. The gray shaded areas represent idle time.

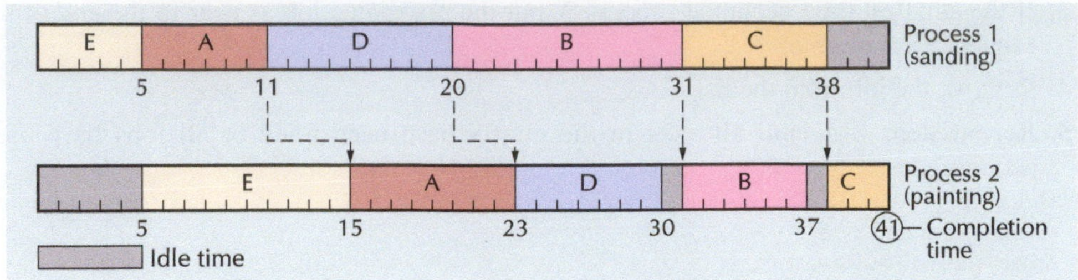

The completion time for the set of five jobs is 41 hours. Note that although Johnson's rule minimizes makespan and idle time, it does not consider job due dates in constructing a sequence, so there is no attempt to minimize job tardiness.

The Excel solution to this problem is shown in Exhibit 17.3.

EXHIBIT 17.3 | Using Excel for Johnson's Rule

Excel File

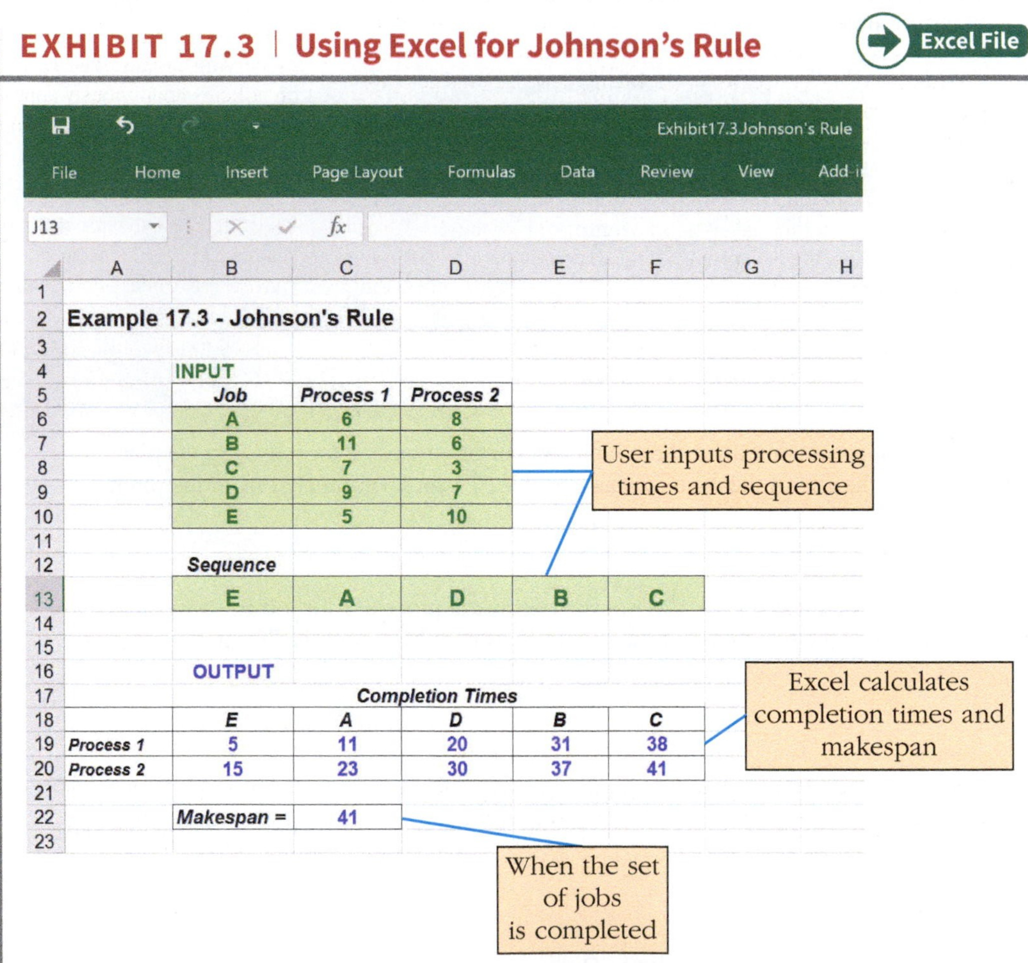

Along the Supply Chain

Solving Tough Scheduling Problems in Healthcare

There are many scheduling problems in the healthcare arena, from scheduling nurses and OR rooms, to scheduling doctor's appointments with no-shows, to triaging patients and doling out vaccinations; but one of the most critical scheduling problems involves organ transplants. A husband and wife team of surgeon (Segev) and mathematician (Gentry) have studied both kidney and liver transplant allocation and have made some groundbreaking recommendations.

For kidney transplants, finding an appropriate match is sometimes difficult. Waiting for a kidney from someone who is deceased can take too long. Unfortunately, even though a person can function with only one kidney, donating the other kidney to a loved one may not be possible if the blood type and other antibodies do not match. One solution is to pair two such incompatible couples so that the donors' kidneys do not help their loved one directly but do allow them to receive a transplant more quickly. This is known as the Kidney Paired Donation (KPD) program, and before Gentry and Segev completed their research, perhaps 60 such exchanges took place each year. After applying a new matching algorithm to a nationwide set of donors/recipients, more than 600 exchange transplants were occurring each year, saving lives and over $750 million annually in healthcare costs.

Livers come from deceased donors and have a short shelf life of less than four hours, eliminating the possibility of lengthy transit times between donor and transplant center. In the United States, a recipient waiting list used to be divided into 11 geographic districts, and available livers were allocated within the same district (perhaps because of the limited transit time). This led to a disparity in service, with some districts having more need and less availability than others. Desperate patients were known to move into a more receptive district to await transplant. Gentry and Sedev sought to redraw the district boundaries to minimize disparity in access to livers.

Redistricting is a class of problems that uses integer programming (similar to linear programming) to design geographic boundaries between units, and is usually applied to school districts or voting districts. The integer programming model proposed by Gentry and Segev is designed specifically for liver transplant redistricting and is more transparent to the user than previous models. As is common with practical models, the liver committee had some design constraints in mind that reduced the size of the problem. The districts should be adjoining, the number of districts should be at least four and no more than eight, the maximum transport time should be three hours, and each district should have a minimum of six transplant centers. Gentry and Segev added the ranking of patients by need, called the MELD index, to the analysis. MELD prioritizes candidates based on the risk of death while awaiting liver transplantation.

A simulation model was built to test out the proposed 4-district, 6-district, and 8-district models over a five year time frame. The

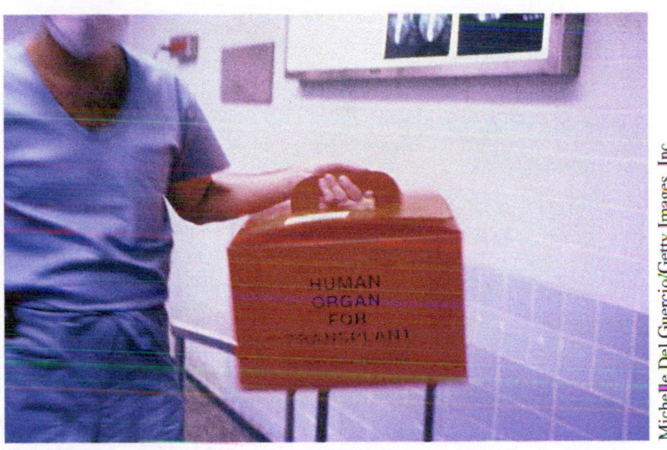

Michelle Del Guercio/Getty Images, Inc.

recommended 4-district plan would save 554 lives, cost $25,000 less than other plans, and eliminate the disparity between districts in receiving organs. The Liver Committee that manages allocation policies unanimously approved the 4-district plan (even when transplant centers in their own district would see a reduction in allocations).

1. For more details about Gentry and Segev's transplant models, search YouTube for the video, "The Right Match: A Short Documentary." Comment on the process of discovery and the cross-functional interaction of the two researchers.
2. Saving lives is an incredible payout for implementing a new scheduling or allocation model. What other kinds of major scheduling/allocation problems do you see in society that could be improved with careful analysis?

Sources: Mary Carole McCauley, "Genius pair rewrite rules of organ transplants, among other interests," *The Baltimore Sun* (November 14, 2012); S. Gentry, E.K.H. Chow, A.B. Massie, and D.L. Segev, "Gerrymandering for justice: redistricting U.S. liver allocation," *Interfaces* (September 2015).

Guidelines for Selecting a Sequencing Rule

In a real-world job shop, jobs follow different routes through a facility that consists of many different machine centers or departments. A small job shop may have three or four departments; a large job shop may have 50 or more. From several to several hundred jobs may be circulating the shop at any given time. New jobs are released into the shop daily and placed in competition with existing jobs for priority in processing. Queues form and dissipate as jobs move through the system. A dispatch list that shows the sequence in which jobs are to be processed at a particular machine may be valid at the beginning of a day or week but become outdated as new jobs arrive in the system. Some jobs may have to wait to be assembled with others before continuing to be processed. Delays in completing operations can cause due dates to be revised and schedules changed.

The complexity and dynamic nature of most scheduling environments precludes the use of analytical solution techniques. The most popular form of analysis for these systems is *simulation*. Academia has especially enjoyed creating and testing sequencing rules in simulations of hypothetical job shops. One early simulation study alone examined 92 different sequencing rules. Although no optimal solutions have been identified in these simulation studies, they have produced some general guidelines for *when* certain sequencing rules may be appropriate. Here are a few of their suggestions:

1. ***SPT is most useful when the shop is highly congested.*** SPT tends to minimize mean flow time, mean number of jobs in the system (and thus work-in-process inventory), and

percent of jobs tardy. By completing more jobs quickly, it theoretically satisfies a greater number of customers than the other rules. However, with SPT some long jobs may be completed *very* late, resulting in a small number of very unsatisfied customers.

For this reason, when SPT is used in practice, it is usually truncated (or stopped), depending on the amount of time a job has been waiting or the nearness of its due date. For example, many shared computer services process jobs by SPT. Jobs that are submitted are placed in several categories (A, B, or C) based on expected CPU time. The shorter jobs, or A jobs, are processed first, but every couple of hours the system stops processing A jobs and picks the first job from the B stack to run. After the B job is finished, the system returns to the A stack and continues processing. C jobs may be processed only once a day. Other systems that have access to due date information will keep a long job waiting until its SLACK is zero or its due date is within a certain range.

2. ***Use SLACK for periods of normal activity***. When capacity is not severely restrained, a SLACK-oriented rule that takes into account both due date and processing time will produce good results.
3. ***Use DDATE when only small tardiness values can be tolerated***. DDATE tends to minimize mean tardiness and maximum tardiness. Although more jobs will be tardy under DDATE than SPT, the degree of tardiness will be much less.
4. ***Use LPT if subcontracting is anticipated*** so that larger jobs are completed in-house, and smaller jobs are sent out as their due date draws near.
5. ***Use FCFS when operating at low-capacity levels.*** FCFS allows the shop to operate essentially without sequencing jobs. When the workload at a facility is light, any sequencing rule will do, and FCFS is certainly the easiest to apply.
6. ***Do not use SPT to sequence jobs that have to be assembled with other jobs at a later date***. For assembly jobs, a sequencing rule that gives a common priority to the processing of different components in an assembly, such as *assembly DDATE*, produces a more effective schedule.

Monitoring

In a job shop environment, where jobs follow different paths through the shop, visit many different machine centers, and compete for similar resources, it is not always easy to keep track of the status of a job. When jobs are first released to the shop, it is relatively easy to observe the queue that they join and predict when their initial operations might be completed. As the job progresses, however, or the shop becomes more congested, it becomes increasingly difficult to follow the job through the system. Competition for resources (resulting in long queues), machine breakdowns, quality problems, and setup requirements are just a few of the things that can delay a job's progress.

Work package Shop paperwork that travels with a job.

Shop paperwork, sometimes called a **work package**, travels with a job to specify what work needs to be done at a particular work center and where the item should be routed next. Workers are usually required to sign off on a job, indicating the work they have performed, either manually on the work package or electronically through a PC located on the shop floor. Bar code technology and RFID tags have made this task easier by eliminating much of the tedium and errors of entering the information by computer keyboard. In its simplest form, the bar code is attached to the work package, which the worker reads with a wand at the beginning and end of his or her work on the job. In other cases, an RFID tag is attached to the pallet or crate that carries the items from work center to work center. The tag is read automatically as it enters and leaves the work area. The time a worker spends on each job, the results of quality checks or inspections, and the utilization of resources can also be recorded in a similar fashion.

For the information gathered at each work center to be valuable, it must be up-to-date, accurate, and accessible to operations personnel. The monitoring function performed by production control takes this information and transforms it into various reports for workers and managers to use. Progress reports can be generated to show the status of individual jobs, the

FIGURE 17.1 A Gantt Chart

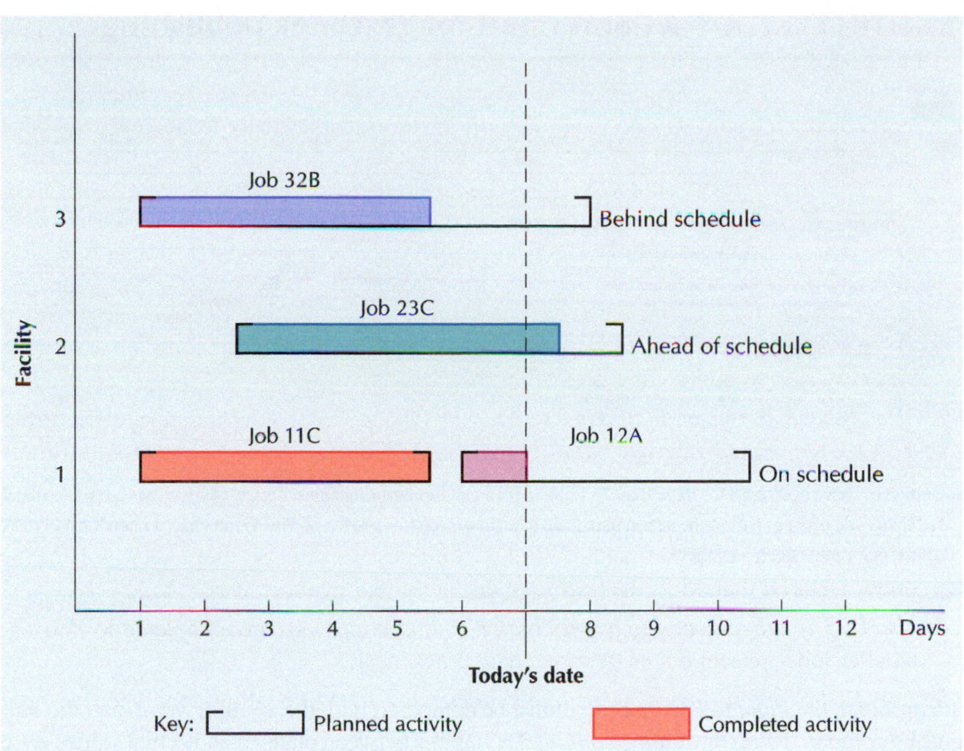

availability or utilization of certain resources, and the performance of individual workers or work centers. Exception reports may be generated to highlight deficiencies in certain areas, such as scrap, rework, shortages, anticipated delays, and unfilled orders. *Hot lists* show which jobs receive the highest priority and must be done immediately. A well-run facility will produce fewer *exception reports* and more *progress reports*. In the next two sections we describe two such progress reports, the Gantt chart and the input/output control chart.

Gantt Charts

Gantt charts, used to plan or map out work activities, can also be used to monitor a job's progress against the plan. As shown in Figure 17.1, Gantt charts can display both planned and completed activities against a time scale. In this figure, the dashed line indicating today's date crosses over the schedules for job 12A, job 23C, and job 32B.

Gantt charts Show both planned and completed activities against a time scale

From the chart we can quickly see that job 12A is exactly on schedule because the bar monitoring its completion exactly meets the line for the current date. Job 23C is ahead of schedule and job 32B is behind schedule.

Gantt charts have been used since the early 1900s and are still popular today. They may be created and maintained digitally or by hand. In some facilities, Gantt charts consist of large scheduling boards (the size of several bulletin boards) with magnetic strips, pegs, or string of different colors that mark job schedules and job progress for everyone to see. Gantt charts are a common feature of project management software, such as Microsoft Project, as seen in Exhibit 17.4.

Input/Output Control

Input/output (I/O) control monitors the input to and output from each work center. Prior to such analysis, it was common to examine only the output from a work center and to compare the actual output with the output planned in the shop schedule. Using that approach in a job shop environment in which the performance of different work centers is interrelated may result in erroneous conclusions about the source of a problem. Reduced output at one point in the production process may be caused by problems at the current work center, but it may also be caused by problems at previous work centers that *feed* the current work center. Thus, to identify more clearly the source

Input/output (I/O) control Monitors the input and output from each work center.

EXHIBIT 17.4 | A Gantt Chart for Textbook publishing

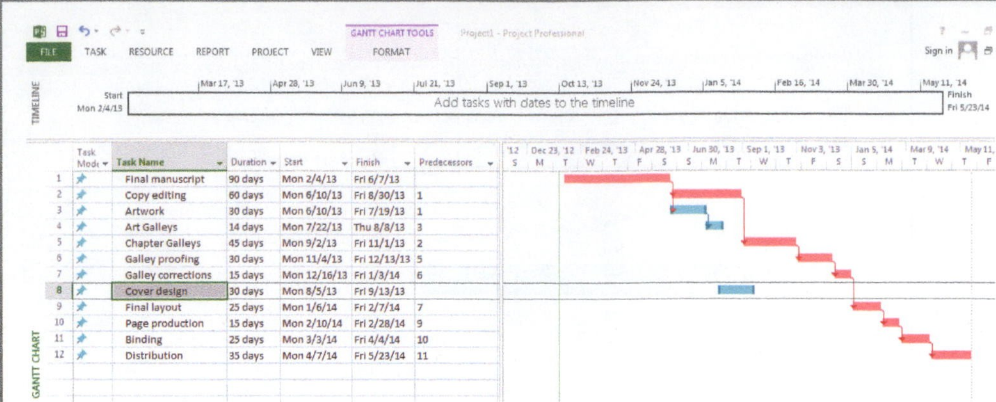

	Task Name	Duration	Start	Finish	Predecessors
1	Final manuscript	90 days	Mon 2/4/13	Fri 6/7/13	
2	Copy editing	60 days	Mon 6/10/13	Fri 8/30/13	1
3	Artwork	30 days	Mon 6/10/13	Fri 7/19/13	1
4	Art Galleys	14 days	Mon 7/22/13	Thu 8/8/13	3
5	Chapter Galleys	45 days	Mon 9/2/13	Fri 11/1/13	2
6	Galley proofing	30 days	Mon 11/4/13	Fri 12/13/13	5
7	Galley corrections	15 days	Mon 12/16/13	Fri 1/3/14	6
8	Cover design	30 days	Mon 8/5/13	Fri 9/13/13	
9	Final layout	25 days	Mon 1/6/14	Fri 2/7/14	7
10	Page production	15 days	Mon 2/10/14	Fri 2/28/14	9
11	Binding	25 days	Mon 3/3/14	Fri 4/4/14	10
12	Distribution	35 days	Mon 4/7/14	Fri 5/23/14	11

Gantt charts have been used for more than 75 years to plan and monitor schedules. Today, Gantt charts are more widely used than ever, often as part of the action plan from a quality-improvement team. This Gantt chart, created in Microsoft Project, is for publishing a textbook.

of a problem, the *input* to a work center must be compared with the *planned input*, and the *output* must be compared with the *planned output*. Deviations between planned and actual values are calculated, and their cumulative effects are observed. The resulting backlog or waiting line of work to be completed is monitored to ensure that it stays within a manageable range.

The input rate to a work center can be controlled only for the initial operations of a job. These first work centers are often called *gateway* work centers, because the majority of jobs must pass through them before subsequent operations are performed. Input to later operations, performed at *downstream* work centers, is difficult to control because it is a function of how well the rest of the shop is operating—that is, where queues are forming and how smoothly jobs are progressing through the system. The deviation of planned to actual input for downstream work centers can be minimized by controlling the output rates of feeding work centers. The use of input/output reports can best be illustrated with an example.

EXAMPLE 17.4 | Input/Output Control

Hall Industries has begun input/output planning for its work centers. Below are the planned inputs and outputs for Work Center 5.

(a) If production proceeds as planned, what will be the backlog at the end of period 4?

(b) If actual input values are 60, 60, 65, 65 for periods 1 through 4, respectively, and output values cannot exceed 75, how much output can be expected from Work Center 5?

(c) Is there a problem with production at Work Center 5?

Input/Output Report for Work Center 5

PERIOD		1	2	3	4	TOTAL
Planned input		65	65	70	70	270
Actual input						0
Deviation						0
Planned output		75	75	75	75	300
Actual output						0
Deviation						0
Backlog	30					

Solution:

(a)

PERIOD		1	2	3	4	TOTAL
Planned input		65	65	70	70	270
Actual input						0
Deviation						0
Planned output		75	75	75	75	300
Actual output						0
Deviation						0
Backlog	30	20	10	5	0	

If everything goes as planned, the backlog will be zero by period 4.

(b)

PERIOD		1	2	3	4	TOTAL
Planned input		65	65	70	70	270
Actual input		60	60	65	65	250
Deviation		–5	–5	–5	–5	–20
Planned output		75	75	75	75	300
Actual output		75	75	65	65	280
Deviation		0	0	–10	–10	–20
Backlog	30	15	0	0	0	

With the reduced input, the backlog is worked off sooner, but the total production cannot keep pace with what was planned.

(c) Although Work Center 5 has produced only 280 units instead of the planned 300, the problem appears to be with the process that feeds Work Center 5. Notice the deviations from planned are the same for both the input and output values. An Excel solution to this example is shown in Exhibit 17.5.

EXHIBIT 17.5 | Using Excel for Input/Output Control

	A	B	C	D	E	F	G	H
1								
2		**Example 17.4 - Input / Output Control**						
3								
4								
5		*Period*		1	2	3	4	*Total*
6		Planned input		65	65	70	70	270
7		Actual input		60	60	65	65	250
8		Deviation		-5	-5	-5	-5	-20
9		Planned output		75	75	75	75	300
10		Actual output		75	75	65	65	280
11		Deviation		0	0	-10	-10	-20
12		Backlog	30	15	0	0	0	

User inputs planned and actual values

Excel calculates deviations and backlog

Margie Deck

Plant Manager

Roberta Russell

I began working for a manufacturing company as a third-shift supervisor 15 years ago, straight out of grad school. I had no desire to work in a factory and just took the job to gain what I thought would be useful experience for pursuing a career in Human Resources. But I loved it from the start—manufacturing is fast-paced and exciting. There are deadlines to meet and real work to be done. No sitting behind a computer all day writing reports. Nothing is routine. We are always trying to get work done better or faster or cheaper than before. Our customers are demanding, and so are our stockholders.

We make engine bearings at this plant—lots of them, 88 million bearings a year—for a total of six customers in the automotive and industrial machinery industry. We use so many of the things you learn in an operations class—scheduling, lean production, theory of constraints, and tons of quality tools, like Pareto charts, root cause analysis, process improvement teams, and SPC. Quality and safety are our biggest concerns. You'll hear your professor talk about Six Sigma quality. Well, *our* defect rate is even better, at 2 parts per million. But if even one bad part goes to a customer's plant, it could cause a line shutdown and we'd be charged $500 a minute until the line is up and running again!

We have a very close relationship with our customers. They each have their own personality and ways of doing business. These are longstanding customers. If we get the bid for an engine program, we have it for the life of the product. The contract might say that we should be capable of producing 100,000 bearings per day. We'll be given a three-month forecast of usage that we use for manpower planning, and a two-week forecast for material planning. But day-to-day usage can vary significantly. Every morning at 2 A.M. our customers send us their orders for the day and tell us when a truck will be arriving to pick them up. We check the EDI system when we get in and start to work putting together the day's schedule. There's always a challenge, always something new.

Input/output control provides the information necessary to regulate the flow of work to and from a network of work centers. Increasing the capacity of a work center that is processing all the work available to it will not increase output. The source of the problem needs to be identified. Excessive queues, or *backlogs*, are one indication that *bottlenecks* exist. To alleviate bottleneck work centers, the problem causing the backlog can be worked on, the capacity of the work center can be adjusted, or input to the work center can be reduced. Increasing the input to a bottleneck work center will not increase the center's output. It will merely clog the system further and create longer queues of work-in-process.

Advanced Planning and Scheduling Systems

The process for scheduling that we have described thus far in this chapter, loading work into work centers, leveling the load, sequencing the work, and monitoring its progress, is called **infinite scheduling**. The term *infinite* is used because the initial loading process assumes infinite capacity. Leveling and sequencing decisions are made after overloads or underloads have been identified. This iterative process is time-consuming and not very efficient.

Infinite scheduling Loads without regard to capacity, then levels the load and sequences the jobs.

Finite scheduling Sequences jobs as part of the loading decision. Resources are never loaded beyond capacity.

An alternative approach to scheduling called **finite scheduling** assumes a fixed maximum capacity and will not load the resource beyond its capacity. Loading and sequencing decisions are made at the same time, so that the first jobs loaded onto a work center are of highest priority. Any jobs remaining after the capacity of the work center or resource has been reached are of lower priority and are scheduled for later time periods. This approach is easier than the infinite scheduling approach, but it will be successful only if the criteria for choosing the work to be performed, as well as capacity limitations, can be expressed accurately and concisely.

Finite scheduling systems use a variety of methods to develop their schedules, including mathematical programming, network analysis, simulation, constraint-based programming, genetic algorithms, neural networks, and expert systems. Because the scheduling system, not the human scheduler, makes most of the decisions, considerable time is spent incorporating the special characteristics and requirements of the production system into the database and knowledge base of the scheduling software. While some companies will develop their own finite scheduling software, most will purchase generic or industry-specific scheduling software as an

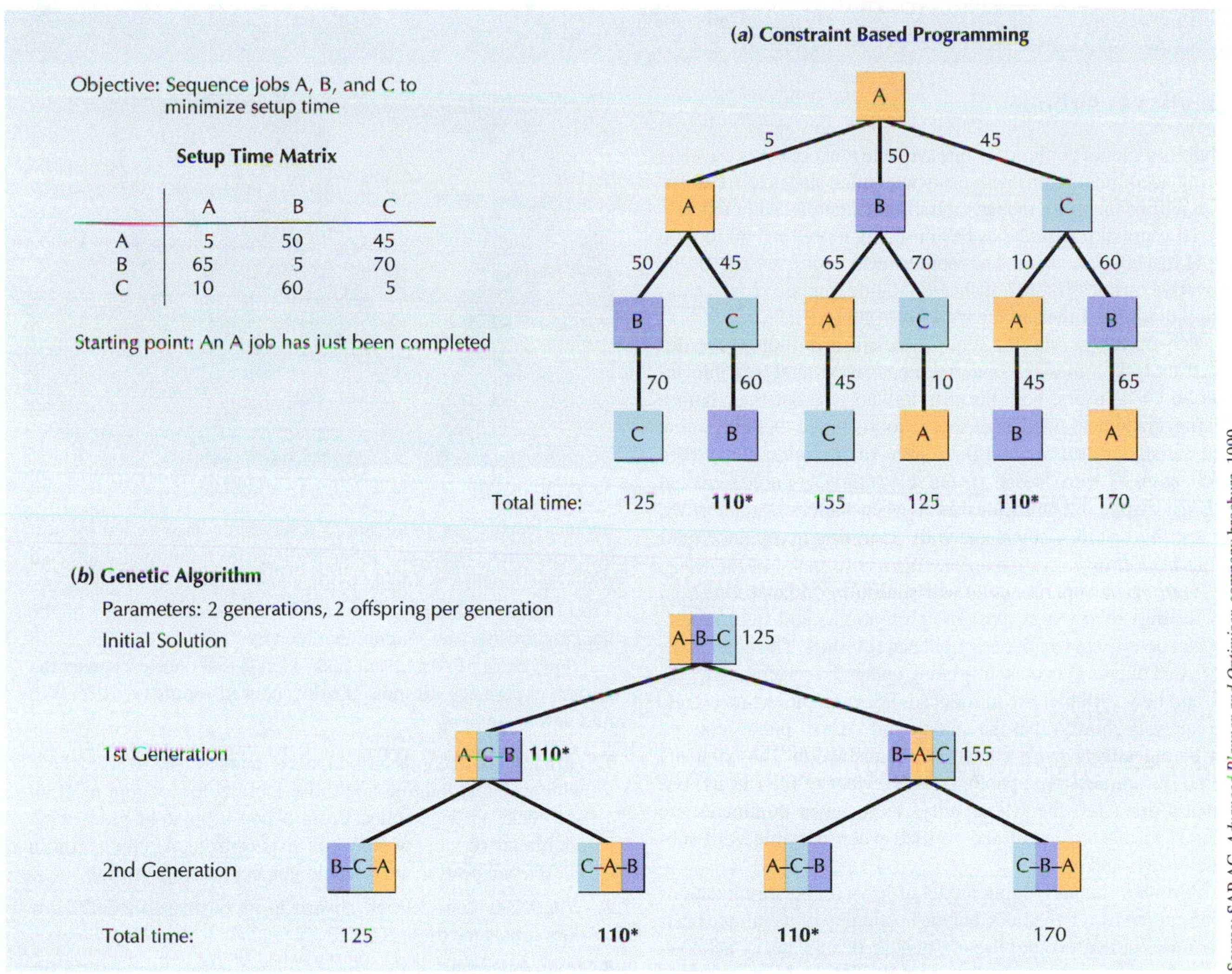

FIGURE 17.2 **Advanced Planning and Scheduling Techniques**

add-on to their ERP system. This class of scheduling software, with libraries of algorithms and heuristics from which to choose, has become known as **advanced planning and scheduling (APS)**. SAP's APS system is called the Advanced Planner and Optimizer (APO), and JDA's is called Factory Planner. These systems also support collaborative planning and scheduling with trading partners. Both APO and Factory Planner use constraint-based programming and genetic algorithms to develop schedules. Figure 17.2 applies these techniques to sequence a set of jobs so that setup time is minimized.

Advanced planning and scheduling (APS) A software system that uses intelligent analytical tools and techniques to develop realistic schedules.

Scheduling problems can be enormous in size, especially as the number of product options proliferate and linked schedules along a supply chain are considered. Some relief has come from the availability of more powerful computers and the use of artificial intelligence techniques. But the biggest impact has come from altered views of the production system. By grouping parts or products into families and scheduling bottleneck resources first, the scheduling problem is sufficiently reduced so that sophisticated solutions are feasible. In the next section, we present a common precept of today's scheduling systems, the *theory of constraints.*

Theory of Constraints

In the 1970s, an Israeli physicist named Eliyahu Goldratt responded to a friend's request for help in scheduling his chicken coop business. Lacking a background in manufacturing or production theory, Dr. Goldratt took a commonsense, intuitive approach to the

Along the Supply Chain

Analytics at Airbnb

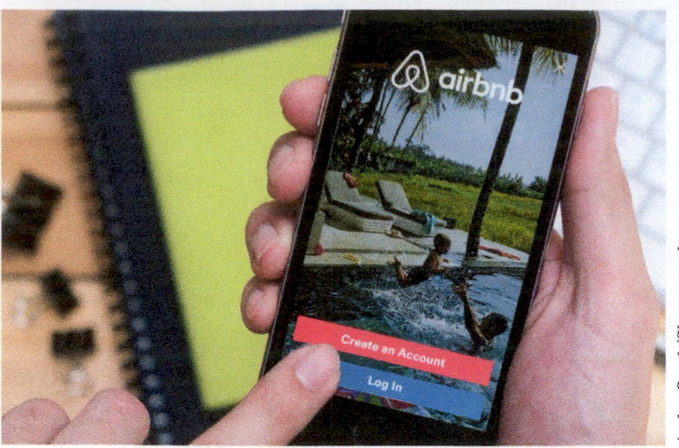

ArthurStock/Shutterstock

Airbnb is a global community marketplace that connects travelers seeking accommodations with hosts who offer places to stay, usually at a price one sixth the rate of traditional hotels. Although less than 10 years old, Airbnb has been used by more than 60 million people in 190+ countries. The rapid growth is due not only to its innovative business model of shared lodging, but also to the technology that makes the service work (see photo).

Scheduling guests into more than half a million properties posted daily is a massive undertaking. Airbnb analyzes information about its users, both the people who rent out their homes and the customers who stay there, to facilitate bookings that yield satisfied customers on both sides of the table. They then match "guests" with "hosts" *(using a variation of the assignment method)*, display recommended sites to customers in rank order, and test the results of their match by analyzing acceptance rates and user reviews.

Further, by experimenting with multiple configurations (i.e., A/B testing) of postings, designs, promotions, and information, they can determine which ones yield better results. The algorithms that match clients are constantly being updated, services are modified, and new variables are introduced. For example, when regression analysis showed that the quality and type of photo attached to a listing affects guest choices and satisfaction, the company offered free professional photography services to their hosts. But numbers don't tell the whole story, so reviewer comments are "mined" to discern intent and verified when possible with subsequent stays and reviews.

Airbnb's shared lodging model of low-cost accommodations can be copied by competitors, but the hospitality of its unique hosts is far more difficult to duplicate. Founder Brian Chesky acknowledges that the success of his business is first and foremost about the hosts. With satisfied hosts, satisfied guests will follow. Determining what factors are important to hosts is a first step to providing them with the tools to help them succeed. Data scientists at Airbnb have created a model that learns host preferences for accepting accommodation requests based on past behavior. For example, an analysis found that hosts located in larger markets tend to accept guest requests that maximize occupancy, while hosts in smaller markets like a few days between bookings. Preferences for "last minute" versus "far in advance" reservations also varied by host characteristics. These and other findings from the model affected the order in which available listings were presented to guests. As a result, both the booking conversion rate and satisfaction with the booking process saw a significant increase.

One mark of Airbnb success? Hotels that once eschewed the Airbnb experience are now posting unused rooms on Airbnb to find new customers.

1. Airbnb has been described as a marketplace where those with available lodging and those looking for lodging meet up and make arrangements. From a host's point of view, what additional services would you expect from Airbnb? From a guest's perspective what would you expect from Airbnb?
2. What risks does Airbnb absorb in its business model? How does it balance these risks?
3. How important is the use of data for the business? How important is the sense of community? Can the collection and processing of too much data affect community? Explain.
4. What advanced forms of scheduling presented in this chapter would be useful for Airbnb?

Source: Eugene Kim, "Airbnb: how it does data analysis," *Business Insider* (February 11, 2015); Bar Ifrach, "How Airbnb uses machine learning to detect host preferences," *Data* (April 14, 2015).

scheduling problem. He developed a software system that used mathematical programming and simulation to create a schedule that realistically considered the constraints of the manufacturing system. The software produced good schedules quickly and was marketed in the early 1980s in the United States. After more than 100 firms had successfully used the scheduling system (called OPT), the creator sold the rights to the software and began marketing the theory behind the software instead. He called his approach to scheduling the **theory of constraints (TOC)**. General Motors and other manufacturers call its application *synchronous manufacturing*.

Theory of constraints (TOC) A finite scheduling approach that concentrates on scheduling the bottleneck resource.

Decision making in manufacturing is often difficult because of the size and complexity of the problems faced. Dr. Goldratt's first insight into the scheduling problem led him to simplify the number of variables considered. He learned early that manufacturing resources typically are not used evenly. Instead of trying to balance the capacity of the manufacturing system, he decided that most systems are inherently unbalanced and that he would try to balance the *flow* of work through the system instead. He identified resources as bottleneck or nonbottleneck and observed that the flow through the system is controlled by the bottleneck resource. This resource should always have material to work on, should spend as little time as possible on nonproductive activities (e.g., setups, waiting for work), should be fully staffed, and should be the focus of improvement or automation efforts. Goldratt pointed out that an hour's worth of production lost at a bottleneck reduces the output of the system by the same amount of time, whereas an hour lost at a nonbottleneck may have no effect on system output.

From this realization, Goldratt was able to simplify the scheduling problem significantly. He concentrated initially on scheduling production at the bottleneck resource and then scheduling the nonbottleneck resources to support the bottleneck activities. Thus, production is synchronized, or "in sync," with the needs of the bottleneck and the system as a whole.

Drum-Buffer-Rope

To maintain this synchronization, Goldratt introduced the concept of **drum-buffer-rope (DBR)**. The *drum* is the bottleneck, beating to set the pace of production for the rest of the system. The *buffer* is inventory placed in front of the bottleneck to ensure it is always kept busy. This is necessary because output from the bottleneck determines the output or *throughput* of the system. The *rope* is the communication signal that tells the processes upstream from the bottleneck when they should begin production (similar to a kanban).

Drum-buffer-rope The *drum* sets the pace for the production, a *buffer* is placed before the bottleneck, and a *rope* communicates changes.

This idea of scheduling the bottleneck first and supporting its schedule with production at nonbottleneck operations is the basis for virtually all scheduling software on the market today.

Process vs. Transfer Batch Sizes

Goldratt's second insight into manufacturing concerned the concept of lot sizes or batch sizes. Goldratt saw no reason for fixed lot sizes. He differentiated between the quantity in which items are produced, called the *process batch*, and the quantity in which the items are transported, called the *transfer batch*. Ideally, items should be transferred in lot sizes of one. The process batch size for bottlenecks should be large, to eliminate the need for setups. The process batch size for nonbottlenecks can be small because time spent in setups for nonbottlenecks does not affect the rest of the system.

The TOC scheduling procedure, illustrated in Example 17.5, follows these steps:

1. Identify the bottleneck.
2. Schedule the job first whose lead time to the bottleneck is less than or equal to the bottleneck processing time.
3. Forward schedule the bottleneck machine.
4. Backward schedule the other machines to sustain the bottleneck schedule.
5. Transfer in batch sizes smaller than the process batch size.

EXAMPLE 17.5 | Synchronous Manufacturing

The following diagram contains the product structure, routing, and processing time information for product A. The process flows from the bottom of the diagram upward. Assume one unit of items B, C, and D are needed to make each A. The manufacture of each item requires three operations at machine centers 1, 2, or 3. Each machine center contains only one machine. A machine setup time of 60 minutes occurs whenever a machine is switched from one operation to another (within the same item or between items).

Design a schedule of production for each machine center that will produce 100 A's as quickly as possible. Show the schedule on a Gantt chart of each machine center.

Solution: The bottleneck machine is identified by summing the processing times of all operations to be performed at a machine.

MACHINE 1		MACHINE 2		MACHINE 3	
B1	5	B2	3	C1	2
B3	7	C3	15	D3	5
C2	10	D2	8	D1	10
Sum	22		26*		17

*Bottleneck

- ***Identify the bottleneck:*** Machine 2 is identified as the bottleneck, so we schedule machine 2 first. From the product structure diagram, we see that three operations are performed at machine 2—B2, C3, and D2. If we schedule item B first, B will reach machine 2 every five minutes (since B has to be processed through machine 1 first), but each B takes only three minutes to process at machine 2, so the bottleneck will be idle for two minutes of every five minutes. A similar result occurs if we schedule item D first on machine 2. The bottleneck will be idle for two minutes of every ten until D has finished processing. The best alternative is to schedule item C first. The first C will not reach machine 2 until time 12, but after that the bottleneck machine will remain busy.

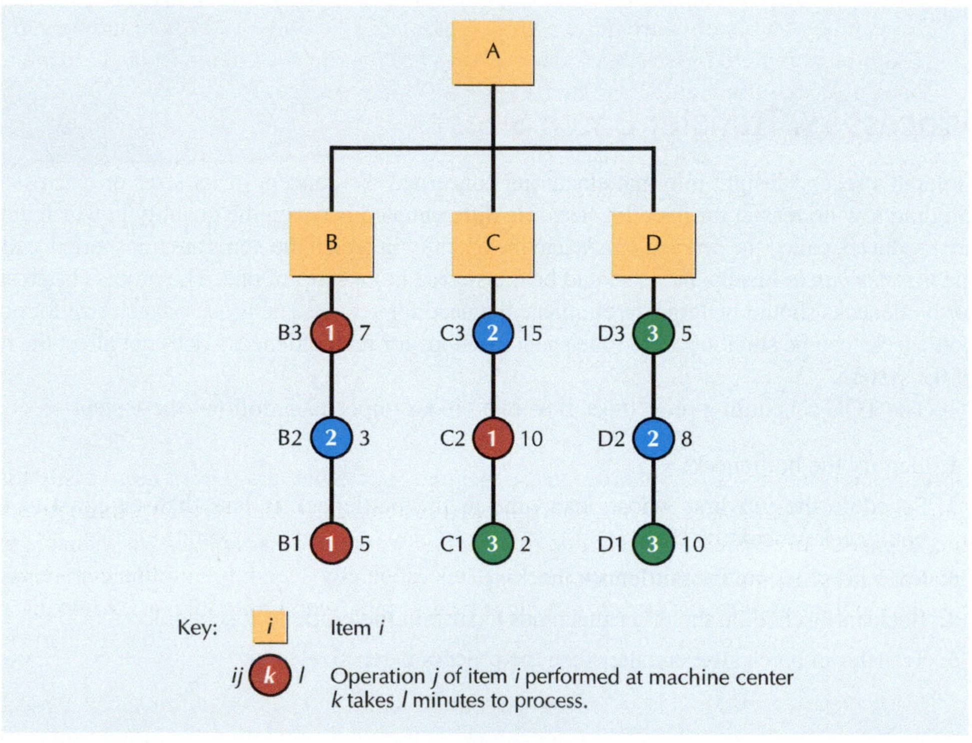

- ***Process in batches of 100, transfer one-at-a-time:*** We begin our Gantt charts by processing item C through the three machine centers. As shown in Figure 17.3, the Gantt charts look different from our earlier examples because we allow each item to be transferred to the next operation immediately after it is completed at the current operation (i.e., the transfer batch size is 1). We will still process the items in batches of 100 to match our demand requirements. The gray shaded areas represent idle time between operations due to setup time requirements or because a feeding operation has not yet been completed.
- ***Sustain the bottleneck:*** C3 is completed at machine center 2 at time 1512. After setup, it is ready for a new item at time 1572. We have a choice between B2 and D2,

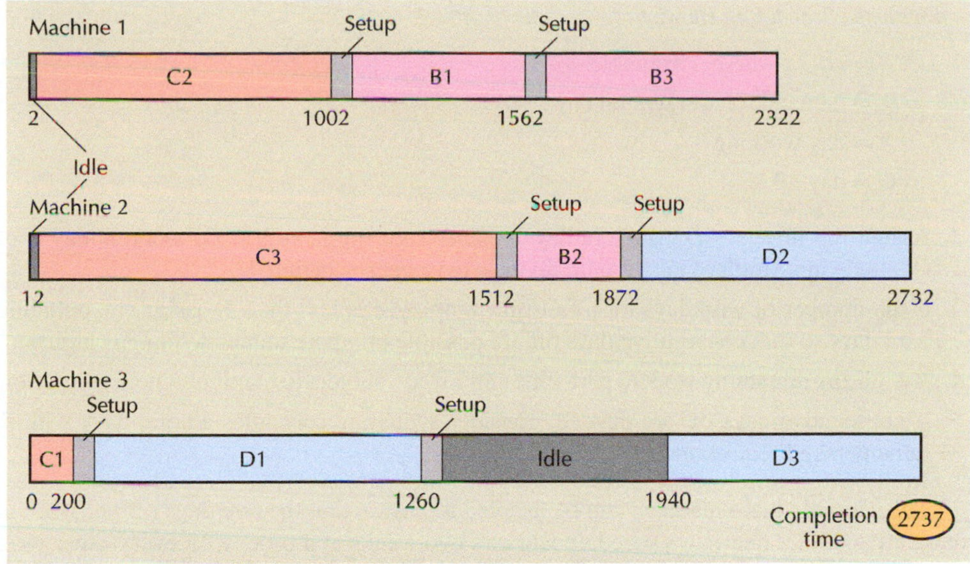

FIGURE 17.3 **Gantt Chart Solution to Example 17.5**

since both B1 and D1 can be completed by 1572. Completion time at machine center 2 will be the same regardless of whether B2 or D2 is processed first; however, the completion time at the other machine centers (and thus for product A) will be affected by the bottleneck sequence. From the product structure diagram, we note that B3 can be completed more quickly than D3 because D3 must wait three minutes for D2 to be completed, whereas B3 will always have a queue of items from B2 to work on. Thus, we schedule B2 and then D2 on machine center 2.

- ***Sequence the other machines to support the bottleneck sequence:*** With the bottleneck sequence of C3, B2, D2 established, we can now schedule machine center 1 (C2, B1, B3) and machine center 3 (C1, D1, D3) in the same general order as the bottleneck sequence. The completion time for producing 100 As is 2737 minutes. The total idle time at the three machine centers is 994 minutes.

Employee Scheduling

Labor is one of the most flexible resources. Workers can be hired and fired more easily than equipment can be purchased or sold. Labor-limited systems can expand capacity through overtime, expanded workweeks, extra shifts, or part-time workers. This flexibility is valuable but it tends to make scheduling difficult. Service firms especially spend an inordinate amount of time developing employee schedules. A supervisor might spend an entire week making up the next month's employee schedule. The task becomes even more daunting for facilities that operate on a 24-hour basis with multiple shifts.

The assignment method of linear programming discussed earlier in this chapter can be used to assign workers with different performance ratings to available jobs. Large-scale linear programming is currently used by McDonald's to schedule its large part-time workforce. American Airlines uses a combination of integer linear programming and expert systems for scheduling ticket agents to coincide with peak and slack demand periods and for the complicated scheduling of flight crews. Although mathematical programming certainly has found application in employee scheduling, most scheduling problems are solved by heuristics (i.e., rules of thumb) that develop a repeating pattern of work assignments. Often heuristics are imbedded in a decision support system to facilitate their use and increase their flexibility. One such heuristic[1] used for scheduling full-time workers with two days off per week, is given next.

[1]Kenneth R. Baker and Michael J. Magazine, "Workforce Scheduling with Cyclic Demands and Days-off Constraints." *Management Science* 24(2; October 1977), pp. 161–167.

Employee Scheduling Heuristic:

1. Let N = no. of workers available

   D_i = demand for workers on day i

   X = day working

   O = day off

2. Assign the first $N - D_1$ workers day 1 off. Assign the next $N - D_2$ workers day 2 off. Continue in a similar manner until all days have been scheduled.
3. If the number of workdays for a full-time employee is less than 5, assign the remaining workdays so that consecutive days off are possible or where unmet demand is highest.
4. Assign any remaining work to part-time employees, subject to maximum hour restrictions.
5. If consecutive days off are desired, consider switching schedules among days with the same demand requirements.

The heuristic just illustrated can be adapted to ensure that the two days off per week are consecutive. Other heuristics schedule workers two weeks at a time, with every other weekend off.

EXAMPLE 17.6 | Employee Scheduling

Diet-Tech employs five workers to operate its weight-reduction facility. Demand for service each week (in terms of minimum number of workers required) is given in the following table. Create an employee schedule that will meet the demand requirements and guarantee each worker two days off per week. Use O for day off and X for working.

DAY OF WEEK	M	T	W	TH	F	SA	SU
NO. OF WORKERS	3	3	4	3	4	5	3
Taylor							
Smith							
Simpson							
Allen							
Dickerson							

Solution: The completed employee schedule matrix is shown next.

DAY OF WEEK	M	T	W	TH	F	SA	SU
NO. OF WORKERS	3	3	4	3	4	5	3
Taylor	O	X	X	O	X	X	X
Smith	O	X	X	O	X	X	X
Simpson	X	O	X	X	O	X	X
Allen	X	O	X	X	X	X	O
Dickerson	X	X	O	X	X	X	O

Following the heuristic, the first (5 – 3) = 2 workers, Taylor and Smith, are assigned Monday off. The next (5 – 3) = 2 workers, Simpson and Allen, are assigned Tuesday off. The next (5 – 4) = 1 worker, Dickerson, is assigned Wednesday off. Returning to the top of the roster, the next (5 – 3) = 2 workers, Taylor and Smith, are assigned Thursday off. The next (5 – 4) = 1 worker, Simpson, is assigned Friday off. Everyone works on Saturday, and the next (5 – 3) = 2 workers, Allen and Dickerson, get Sunday off.

The resulting schedule meets demand and has every employee working 5 days a week with 2 days off. Unfortunately, none of the days off are consecutive. By switching the initial schedules for Tuesday and Thursday (both with a demand of 3) and the schedules for Wednesday and Friday (both with a demand of 4), the following schedule results:

DAY OF WEEK	M	T	W	TH	F	SA	SU
NO. OF WORKERS	3	3	4	3	4	5	3
Taylor	O	O	X	X	X	X	X
Smith	O	O	X	X	X	X	X
Simpson	X	X	O	O	X	X	X
Allen	X	X	X	O	X	X	O
Dickerson	X	X	X	X	O	X	O

In this revised schedule, the first three workers have consecutive days off. The last two workers have one weekend day off and one day off during the week.

Automated Scheduling Systems

Scheduling large numbers of workers at numerous locations requires a computerized scheduling system. Sophisticated employee scheduling software is available as a stand-alone system or as part of an ERP package. For example, Infor's Workforce Labor Scheduler system provides:

- **Staff scheduling** assigns qualified workers to standardized shift patterns, taking into account leave requests and scheduling conflicts. The solutions consider legal and social constraints such as labor laws for minors, overtime payment regulations, and legal or religious holidays that may differ by global location.
- **Schedule bidding** puts certain shift positions or schedule assignments up for bid and allows workers to post and trade schedules with others as long as coverage and skill criteria are met.
- **Schedule optimization** creates demand-driven forecasts of labor requirements and assigns workers to variable schedules (in some cases, as small as 15-minute blocks of time) that change dynamically with demand. The optimization is based on mathematical programming and artificial intelligence techniques.

Summary

Scheduling techniques vary by type of production process. Scheduling in a job shop environment is difficult because jobs arrive at varying time intervals, require different resources and sequences of operations, and are due at different times. This lowest level of scheduling is referred to as shop floor control or production control. It involves assigning jobs to machines or workers (called loading), specifying the order in which operations are to be performed, and monitoring the work as it progresses. Techniques such as the assignment method are used for *loading*, various rules whose performance varies according to the scheduling objective are used for *sequencing*, and Gantt charts and input/output control charts are used for *monitoring*.

Realistic schedules must reflect capacity limitations. *Infinite scheduling* initially assumes infinite capacity and then manually "levels the load" of resources that have exceeded capacity. *Finite scheduling* loads jobs in priority order and delays those jobs for which current capacity is exceeded. The *theory of constraints* is a finite scheduling approach that schedules bottleneck resources first and then schedules other resources to support the bottleneck schedule. It also allows items to be transferred between resources in lot sizes that differ from the lot size in which the item is produced. Other advanced planning and scheduling techniques include mathematical programming, genetic algorithms, and simulation.

Employee scheduling is often difficult because of the variety of options available and the special requirements for individual workers. Scheduling heuristics are typically used to develop patterns of worker assignment. Automated workforce scheduling systems are becoming more commonplace.

Key Terms

advanced planning and scheduling (APS) A software system that uses intelligent analytical tools and techniques to develop realistic schedules.

dispatch list A shop paper that specifies the sequence in which jobs should be processed; it is often derived from specific sequencing rules.

drum-buffer-rope A concept in theory of constraints where the *drum* sets the pace of production, *buffer* is placed in front of the bottleneck, and *rope* communicates changes.

finite scheduling An approach to scheduling that loads jobs in priority order and delays those jobs for which current capacity is exceeded.

flow time The time that it takes for a job to "flow" through the system; that is, its completion time.

Gantt chart A bar chart that shows a job's progress graphically or compares actual against planned performance.

infinite scheduling An approach to scheduling that initially assumes infinite capacity and then manually "levels the load" of resources that have exceeded capacity.

input/output (I/O) control A procedure for monitoring the input to and output from a work center to regulate the flow of work through a system.

Johnson's rule An algorithm for sequencing any number of jobs through two serial operations to minimize makespan.

load leveling The process of smoothing out the work assigned across time and the available resources.

loading The process of assigning work to individual workers or machines.

makespan The time that it takes for a group of jobs to be completed—that is, the completion time of the last job in a group.

production control Scheduling and monitoring day-to-day production in a job shop.

scheduling The determination of *when* labor, equipment, and facilities are needed to produce a product or provide a service.

sequencing The process of assigning priorities to jobs so that they are processed in a particular order.

tardiness The difference between a job's due date and its completion time for jobs completed after their due date.

theory of constraints A finite scheduling approach that differentiates between bottleneck and nonbottleneck resources and between transfer batches and process batches.

work package Shop paperwork that travels with a job to specify what work needs to be done at a particular machine center and where the item should be routed next.

Key Formulas

Minimum Slack

$$\text{SLACK} = (\text{due date} - \text{today's date}) - (\text{processing time})$$

Critical Ratio

$$\text{CR} = \frac{\text{time remaining}}{\text{work remaining}} = \frac{\text{due date} - \text{today's date}}{\text{remaining processing time}}$$

Solved Problems

1. Assignment Problem

Wilkerson Printing has four jobs waiting to be run this morning. Fortunately, four printing presses are available. However, the presses are of different vintage and operate at different speeds. The approximate times (in minutes) required to process each job on each press are given next. Assign jobs to presses to minimize the press running times.

	PRESS			
JOB	*1*	*2*	*3*	*4*
A	20	90	40	10
B	40	45	50	35
C	30	70	35	25
D	60	45	70	40

Solution

Row reduction:

10	80	30	0
5	10	15	0
5	45	10	0
20	5	30	0

Column reduction:

5	75	20	0
0	5	5	0
0	40	0	0
15	0	20	0

Cover all zeros:

5	75	20	0
0	5	5	0
0	40	0	0
15	0	20	0

The number of lines equals the number of rows, so this is the final solution. Make assignments:

5	75	20	0
0	5	5	0
0	40	0	0
15	0	20	0

Assign job A to press 4, job B to press 1, job C to press 3, and job D to press 2. Refer to the original matrix for actual processing times. The total machining time required is (10 + 40 + 35 + 45) = 130 minutes.

2. Johnson's Rule

Clean and Shine Car Service has five cars waiting to be washed and waxed. The time required (in minutes) for each activity is given next. In what order should the cars be processed through the facility? When will the batch of cars be completed?

CAR	WASH	WAX
1	5	0
2	7	2
3	10	5
4	8	6
5	3	5

Solution

Use Johnson's rule to sequence the cars. The lowest processing time is two minutes for waxing car 2. Since waxing is the second operation, we place car 2 as near to the end of the sequence as possible, in last place. The next-lowest time is three minutes for washing car 5. Since washing is the first operation, we place car 5 as near to the front of the sequence as possible, in first place. The next-lowest time is five minutes for washing car 1 and waxing car 3. Car 1 is scheduled in second place, and car 3 is put in next-to-last place (i.e., fourth). That leaves car 4 for third place.

The completion time for washing and waxing the five cars is 35 minutes. The washing facility is idle for two minutes at the end of the cycle. The waxing facility is idle for three minutes at the beginning of the cycle and four minutes during the cycle.

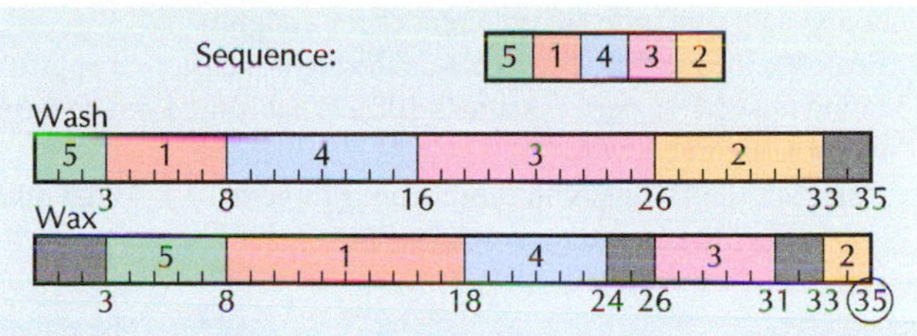

Questions

17.1. How do scheduling activities differ for projects, mass production, and process industries?

17.2. Why is scheduling a job shop so difficult?

17.3. What three functions are typically performed by a production control department?

17.4. Give examples of four types of operations (manufacturing or service) and suggest which scheduling objectives might be appropriate for each.

17.5. How can the success of a scheduling system be measured?

17.6. Describe the process of loading and load leveling. What quantitative techniques are available to help in this process?

17.7. What is the purpose of dispatch lists? How are they usually constructed?

17.8. When should the following sequencing rules be used? (a) SPT; (b) Johnson's rule; (c) DDATE; (d) FCFS.

17.9. Give examples of sequencing rules you use to prioritize work.

17.10. What information is provided by the critical ratio sequencing rule? How does it differ from SLACK?

17.11. How are work packages, hot lists, and exception reports used in a job shop?

17.12. What are Gantt charts, and why are they used so often?

17.13. Explain the concept behind input/output control. Describe how gateway work centers, downstream work centers, and backlogs affect shop performance.

17.14. Explain the difference between infinite and finite scheduling.

17.15. How does theory of constraints differ from traditional scheduling? How should bottleneck resources and nonbottleneck resources be scheduled? Why should transfer batches and process batches be treated differently?

17.16. Explain the drum-buffer-rope concept.

17.17. Discuss the similarities and differences between theory of constraints and lean production.

17.18. What are some typical issues involved in employee scheduling?

17.19. What quantitative techniques are available to help develop employee schedules? What quantitative techniques are available for advanced planning and scheduling systems?

17.20. Look for advanced planning and scheduling software on the Internet. Write a summary of the techniques presented.

Problems

17.1. At Valley Hospital, nurses beginning a new shift report to a central area to receive their primary patient assignments. Not every nurse is as efficient as another with particular kinds of patients. Given the following patient roster, care levels, and time estimates, assign nurses to patients to optimize efficiency. Also, determine how long it will take for the nurses to complete their routine tasks on this shift.

PATIENT	CARE LEVEL	TIME REQUIRED (HOURS) TO COMPLETE ROUTINE TASKS			
		NURSE 1	*NURSE 2*	*NURSE 3*	*NURSE 4*
A. Jones	A2	3	5	4	3
B. Hathaway	B2	2	1	3	2
C. Bryant	B1	3	4	2	2
D. Sweeney	A1	4	3	3	4

17.2. Valley Hospital (from Problem 17.1) wants to focus on customer perceptions of quality, so it has asked its patients to evaluate the nursing staff and indicate preferences for assignment.

a. Reassign the nursing staff to obtain the highest customer approval rating possible (a perfect score is 100). What is the average rating of the assignment?

b. Compare the results with those from Problem 17.1. What other criteria could be used to assign nurses?

PATIENT	RATING			
	NURSE 1	*NURSE 2*	*NURSE 3*	*NURSE 4*
A. Jones	89	95	83	84
B. Hathaway	88	80	96	85
C. Bryant	87	92	82	84
D. Sweeney	93	82	36	94

17.3. Fibrous Incorporated makes products from rough tree fibers. Its product line consists of five items processed through one of five machines. The machines are not identical, and some products are better suited to some machines. Given the following production time in minutes per unit, determine an optimal assignment of product to machine:

PRODUCT	MACHINE				
	A	*B*	*C*	*D*	*E*
1	17	10	15	16	20
2	12	9	16	9	14
3	11	16	14	15	12
4	14	10	10	18	17
5	13	12	9	15	11

17.4. Sunshine House received a contract this year as a supplier of Girl Scout cookies. Sunshine currently has five production lines, each of which will be dedicated to a particular kind of cookie. The production lines differ by sophistication of machines, site, and experience of personnel. Given the following estimates of processing times (in hours), assign cookies to lines to minimize the sum of completion times:

COOKIES	PRODUCTION LINE				
	1	*2*	*3*	*4*	*5*
Chocolate Mint	30	18	26	17	15
Peanut Butter	23	22	32	25	30
Shortbread	17	31	24	22	29
Fudge Delight	28	19	13	18	23
Macaroons	23	14	16	20	27

17.5. Karina Nieto works for New Products Inc., and one of her many tasks is assigning new workers to departments. The company recently hired six new employees and would like each one to be assigned to a different department. The employees have completed a two-month training session in each of the six departments from which they received the evaluations shown below (higher numbers are better). Determine how the new employees should be assigned to departments so that overall performance is maximized.

EMPLOYEES	DEPARTMENTS					
	SALES	FINANCE	LOGISTICS	MARKETING RESEARCH	PRODUCTION	CUSTOMER SERVICE
Albertson	18	17	14	19	19	18
Bunch	17	15	12	14	20	17
Carson	15	15	13	17	20	18
Denali	19	16	18	18	18	20
Ebersole	18	15	12	17	19	17
Finch	16	16	16	18	20	17

17.6. Decenture has four new IT hires available for assignment to ERP implementation projects. Their expertise varies across platforms and technologies, resulting in different time estimates for completing project tasks. Given the expected time to completion (in weeks) for the list of project tasks below, determine the project assignment that will ensure the tasks are completed in the shortest amount of time.

HIRES	PROJECT 1	PROJECT 2	PROJECT 3	PROJECT 4
Alex	8	10	17	9
Bhavna	3	8	5	6
Chen	10	12	11	9
Denise	6	13	9	7

17.7. Blue Jeans Modeling Agency specializes in providing wholesome youthful models for top women's magazines. Blue Jeans assigns models to clients with an understanding of client philosophies, target markets and product characteristics. The company rates its models on a scale of 1 to 5 (with 5 being best) as to how close they are to the client's ideal model. For a given month's issue, only one model can be assigned to each client, and models cannot appear in more than one magazine. Given the ratings below, assign models to clients so that total client satisfaction is maximized. What is the total client satisfaction score?

MODEL	CLIENT				
	MON AMI	*SIXTEEN*	*TITLE NINE*	*ELOQUENCE*	*CLAIRE*
Anita	1	2	1	4	5
Bella	5	4	3	2	1
Christy	4	1	2	3	5
Danielle	4	2	2	1	3
Elise	2	4	4	4	1

17.8. Evan Schwartz has six jobs waiting to be processed through his machine. Processing time (in days) and due date information for each job are as follows:

JOB	PROCESSING TIME	DUE DATE
A	2	3
B	1	2
C	4	12
D	3	4
E	4	8
F	5	10

Sequence the jobs by FCFS, SPT, SLACK, and DDATE. Calculate the mean flow time and mean tardiness of the six jobs under each sequencing rule. Which rule would you recommend?

17.9. College students always have a lot of work to do, but this semester, Katie Lawrence is overwhelmed. Following are the assignments she faces (listed in the order in which they were received), the estimated completion times (in days), and due dates. Today is November 2.

ASSIGNMENT	ESTIMATED COMPLETION TIME	DUE DATE
1. Management case	5	11-20
2. Marketing survey	10	12-3
3. Financial analysis	4	11-25
4. Term project	21	12-15
5. Computer program	14	12-2

Help Katie prioritize her work so that she completes as many assignments on time as possible. Use the SPT, DDATE and FCFS sequencing rule. Which rule would you recommend? How would your sequence of assignments change if Katie were interested in minimizing the mean tardiness of her assignments?

17.10. Today is day 4 of the planning cycle. Sequence the following jobs by FCFS, SPT, SLACK, and DDATE. Calculate the mean flow time and mean tardiness for each sequencing rule. Which rule would you recommend?

JOB	PROCESSING TIME (IN DAYS)	DUE DATE
A	3	10
B	10	12
C	2	25
D	4	8
E	5	15
F	8	18
G	7	20

17.11. Alice's Alterations has eight jobs to be completed and only one sewing machine (and sewing machine operator). Given the processing times and due dates as shown here, prioritize the jobs by SPT, DDATE, and SLACK. Today is day 5.

TASK	PROCESSING TIME (IN DAYS)	DUE DATE
A	5	10
B	8	15
C	6	15
D	3	20
E	10	25
F	14	40
G	7	45
H	3	50

Calculate mean flow time, mean tardiness, maximum tardiness, and number of jobs tardy for each sequence. Which sequencing rule would you recommend? Why?

17.12. Jobs A, B, C, and D must be processed through the same machine center. Sequence the following jobs by (a) SPT and (b) SLACK. Calculate mean flow time, mean tardiness, and maximum tardiness. Which sequencing rule would you recommend? Why?

JOB	PROCESSING TIME	DUE DATE
A	20	20
B	10	15
C	30	50
D	15	30

17.13. Sequence the following jobs by (a) SPT, (b) DDATE, and (c) SLACK. Calculate mean flow time, mean tardiness, and maximum tardiness. Which sequencing rule would you recommend? Why?

JOB	PROCESSING TIME	DUE DATE
A	5	8
B	3	5
C	9	18
D	6	7

17.14. Price's Fork Body Shop has four jobs queued up for work, with processing times and due dates listed below. Tremaine Thomas, the new hire, is taking classes at the local university and thought he'd look at how to sequence the set of jobs. Price's normally uses FCFS, but that doesn't always lead to happy customers.

JOB	PROCESSING TIME	DUE DATE
A	2	7
B	5	8
C	1	15
D	8	9

a. Sequence the jobs by FCFS and calculate mean job flowtime and mean job tardiness.
b. Sequence the jobs by SLACK and calculate mean job flowtime and mean job tardiness.
c. Sequence the jobs by SPT and calculate mean job flowtime and mean job tardiness.
d. Help Tremaine explain which sequence is best for the shop and why.

17.15. Claims received by Healthwise Insurance Company are entered into the database at one station, and sent to another station for review. The processing time (in minutes) required for each general type of claim is shown here. Currently, Bill Frazier has a backlog of 10 claims. In what order should he process the claims so that the entire batch is finished as soon as possible? How long will it take to completely process the 10 claims?

	PROCESSING TIME	
CLASSIFICATION	DATE ENTRY	REVIEW
1. Medicare I	8	6
2. Physician 24	15	9
3. Medicare II	6	5
4. Physician 4	5	10
5. HM0 I	17	15
6. Physician 17	9	10
7. Emergency II	5	3
8. HM0 II	4	15
9. Physician 37	12	10
10. Emergency I	20	4

17.16. Jobs processed through Percy's machine shop pass through milling first, and then turning. The current backlog of jobs and hours required at each machine follow.

JOB	MILLING	TURNING
A	5	4
B	2	5
C	3	1
D	1	0
E	4	2

Sequence the jobs so that the entire set of jobs is completed as soon as possible. Make a Gantt chart to map out the schedule on each machine and determine the makespan for the set of jobs.

17.17. The Blue Plate Special restaurant, famous for its slow-cooked stews and meats, serves one meal a day family style. Sous Chef Lisle marinates the meat, fish, and vegetables for the five different dishes on the menu, while Chef Graham handles the cooking. The time required for marinating and cooking can vary, depending on the complexity of the dish and the spiciness desired, as shown below. Assuming only one dish can be marinating and one dish cooking at a time, determine in what order the dishes should be fixed to minimize the total preparation time. When will the entire menu be completed?

DISH	MARINATING	COOKING
Irish Stew	7	8
Barbeque Pork	3	6
Creamy Herb Roast	8	4
Smoked Turkey	6	5
Parrot Isle Salmon	3	2

17.18. Sassy U makes fashion jeans out of a variety of denim materials that differ in thickness, stiffness, drape, and weave. Customers receive a sampling of product in each type of material before final orders are placed. Each day, bolts of denim cloth received from suppliers wait their turn in the cutting department. The cutting sequence is developed from an algorithm called *Johnson's Rule* which examines the time required for *spreading* the cloth on a cutting table (plus marking the pattern) and the time required for *cutting* it into pattern pieces that will later be sewn together. These times can vary considerably due to number of pattern pieces, pattern placement (matching stripes, for example), cloth thickness, and whether the cutting is to be performed by hand (with an electric knife) or by a CNC textile-cutting machine.

a. Given the time data below, determine the optimal sequence of denim cloth through the cutting room so that makespan is minimized.
b. Map out the spreading and cutting processes on a Gantt chart and calculate the makespan.
c. Using the sequence determined above, when will the stretch denim material leave the cutting room?

CLOTH	CODE	SPREADING (HRS)	CUTTING (HRS)
Organic Denim	O	2	6
Poly Denim	P	4	2
Quilted Denim	Q	6	3
Ramie Denim	R	2	1
Stretch Denim	S	3	5
Twill Denim	T	1	4

17.19. Restore is a small repair shop that makes customized parts for old equipment. All customer orders must be machined first, then polished. Determine a sequence that will minimize the time required to process all six jobs. Chart the schedule on a Gantt chart and indicate the makespan.

JOBS	MACHINING	POLISHING
A	5.0	4.0
B	7.0	3.0
C	3.0	2.0
D	4.0	1.0
E	1.0	2.0
F	3.0	4.0

17.20. Precision Painters, Inc., has five house painting jobs in one neighborhood. The houses differ in size, state of repair, and painting requirements, but each house must be prepped (cleaned, old paint chipped off, primed) first, then painted.

a. In what sequence should the houses be worked on in order to finish all five houses as soon as possible? Chart out your sequences on Gantt charts and calculate the makespan.

b. Use LPT to sequence the houses for prep work. Paint will follow in same sequence. Calculate makespan. How much time is saved with Johnson's rule?

	DAYS	
HOUSES	*PREP*	*PAINT*
Addison	4	2
Brown	3	6
Clayton	6	4
Daniels	5	6
Ebersole	1	4

17.21. Tracy has six chapters on her desk that must be typed and proofed as soon as possible. Tracy does the typing; the author does the proofing. Some chapters are easy to type but more difficult to proof. The estimated time (in minutes) for each activity is given here. In what order should Tracy type the chapters so that the entire batch can be finished as soon as possible? When will the chapters be completed?

CHAPTER	TYPING	PROOFING
1	30	20
2	90	25
3	60	15
4	45	30
5	75	60
6	20	30

17.22. Updike Upholstery cuts and sews fabric for custom ordered chairs, ottomans, and sofas. Often, the more complicated patterns are for the smaller pieces, where cutting is more time consuming than sewing. Thus, cutting and sewing times vary. Today's list of jobs, shown below, are for an important customer who needs them shipped out (in one shipment) as soon as possible. Determine the sequence of jobs that will complete the customer's order as quickly as possible, and notify the customer when the order is expected to ship.

JOBS	CUTTING	SEWING
A	4	2
B	6	3
C	1	3
D	2	4
E	3	1

17.23. The following data have been compiled for an input/output report at Work Center 7. Complete the report and analyze the results.

PERIOD		1	2	3	4	5	TOTAL
Planned input		50	55	60	65	65	
Actual input		50	50	55	60	65	
Deviation							
Planned output		65	65	65	65	65	
Actual output		60	60	60	60	60	
Deviation							
Backlog	30						

17.24. The input/output report for Work Center 6 is as follows. Complete the report and comment on the results.

PERIOD		1	2	3	4	5	TOTAL
Planned input		50	55	60	65	65	
Actual input		40	50	55	60	65	
Deviation							
Planned output		50	55	60	65	65	
Actual output		50	50	55	60	65	
Deviation							
Backlog	10						

17.25. Kim Johnson, R.N., the charge nurse of the antepartum ward of City Hospital in Burtonsville, Maryland, needs help in scheduling the nurse workforce for next week.

a. Create an employee schedule that will meet the demand requirements and guarantee each nurse two days off per week.

b. Revise the schedule so that the two days off are consecutive.

DAYS OF WEEK	M	T	W	TH	F	SA	SU
NO. OF NURSES	3	3	4	5	4	3	3
Kim Johnson							
Tom Swann							
Flo Coligny							
Shelly Belts							
Phuong Truong							

17.26. Rosemary Hanes needs help in scheduling volunteers at the local crisis pregnancy center. Create a work schedule that will meet the demand requirements, given that volunteers can only work four days per week.

DAYS OF WEEK	M	T	W	TH	F	SA	SU
VOLUNTEERS NEEDED	4	3	2	3	6	4	2
Rosemary Hanes							
Alicia Tagliero							
Rashona White							
Gail Cooke							
Shelly Black							
Karen Romero							

17.27. Schedule the wait staff at Vincent's Restaurant based on the following estimates of demand. Each employee should have two or more days off per week.

DAYS OF THE WEEK	M	T	W	TH	F	SA	SU
EMPLOYEES NEEDED	2	3	4	4	5	5	4
Amy Russell							
Shannon Hiller							
Jessica Jones							
Tom Turner							
Evalin Trice							
Pierre Dubois							

17.28. Mr. Baskins, manager of Tom and Jerry's Ice Cream Shoppe, needs help scheduling servers for next week. Create a schedule that will meet the demand requirements given below and guarantee each server two days off per week.

DAILY REQUIREMENTS	M 1	T 3	W 3	TH 5	F 4	SA 5	SU 4
Anna							
Brent							
Caleb							
David							
Edhas							

17.29. Casey Belzer runs a machine shop that fabricates parts for sprayers used in foam insulation equipment. Due to increasing interest in green building practices and high energy costs, demand for his products has increased dramatically. The shop has three CNC machines that can serve a variety of purposes. As customer orders come in, a routing sheet is developed and the order is diagrammed in Figure 17.4. When demand was low, it didn't really matter how the jobs were scheduled. Now, Casey wants to finish each job as quickly as possible so he can move on to the next one. Help Casey develop a schedule that would finish a customer order for 200 units of part A as soon as possible. Assume one B, C, and D are needed for each A.

a. Find the bottleneck process.

b. According to the theory of constraints, which component (i.e., B, C, or D) should be scheduled first on the bottleneck process?

c. Which component should be scheduled last?

d. Map out the optimum schedule on a Gantt chart and calculate the completion time. Assume that the process batch size is 200 and the transfer batch size is one.

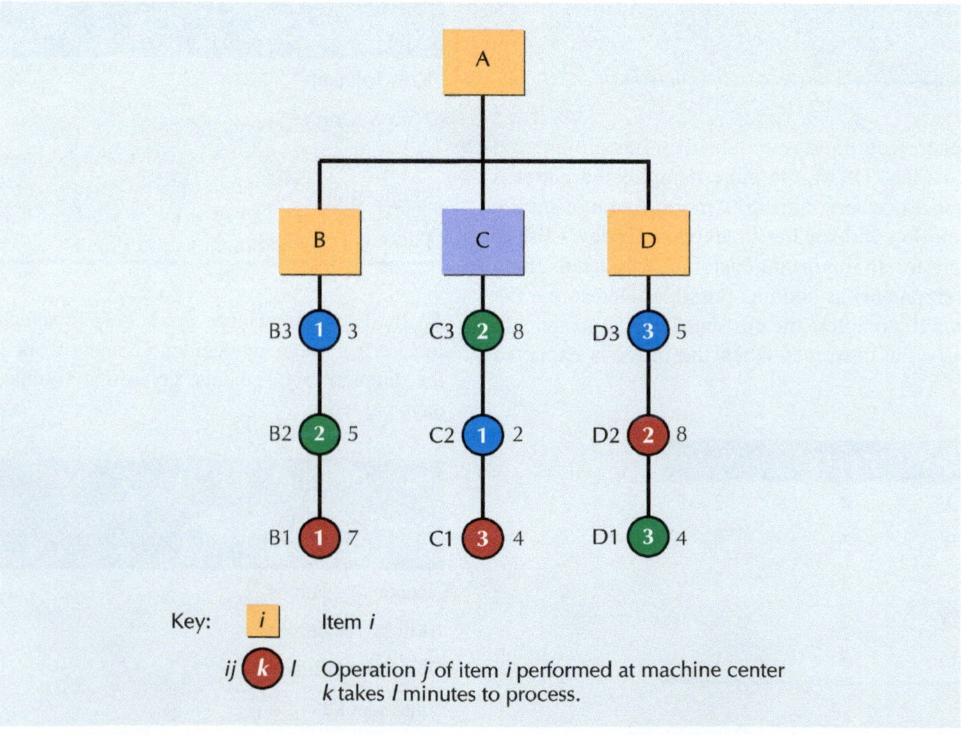

FIGURE 17.4

Case Problems

Case Problem 17.1 America Reads & America Counts

America Reads & America Counts (ARC) is a nonprofit organization that matches college students with public schools who need support in developing literacy and math skills in the classroom. University students receive federal work study funds for working one-on-one with at-risk children, normally for 10 hours a week in 2-hour increments. The program is most popular in urban areas where there is a large concentration of college and university students. For one university alone in the New York city area, 1000 students are placed each semester in more than 100 elementary and secondary schools.

Placement must consider the academic calendar, changing class schedules, travel distances from schools, student skills (e.g., bilingual) and preferences (grade levels, etc.), and school needs. The process of matching students with schools can take one to two months, by which time applicants may have found other employment and the process must be repeated. Currently the administrator uses an Excel spreadsheet to organize the relevant data, but the assignment process is basically manual. ARC would like you to review their scheduling process and develop a quantitative model that would improve both the speed and quality of assignments. Sample data is given below for your analysis. Assign one student to each school.

1. Assign students to schools such that travel time is minimized.
2. Assign students to schools such that preferences are maximized.
3. Assign students to schools such that both travel time and preferences are considered.
4. How would you incorporate different priorities on needs or preferences?

Distance to School (in minutes)

	SCHOOL					
STUDENT	1	2	3	4	5	6
Amy	15	30	60	30	45	20
Brent	10	30	45	20	45	10
Calvin	30	45	20	60	20	30
Deidre	20	30	45	15	10	45
Elena	45	20	15	45	15	30
Franklin	15	45	30	15	20	60

Student Preferences

STUDENT	TYPE	LEVEL	TIME	DAYS	SKILL
Amy	Math	Primary	Morning	MWF	Spanish
Brent	Math	Primary	Afternoon	T TH	Mandarin
Calvin	Reading	Primary	Afternoon	T TH	Spanish
Deidre	Math	Secondary	Afternoon	MWF	ASL*
Elena	Reading	Secondary	Morning	T TH	Spanish
Franklin	Reading	Secondary	Morning	MWF	ASL

*ASL is American Sign Language.

School Needs

SCHOOL	TYPE	LEVEL	TIME	DAYS	SKILL
1	Math	Primary	Morning	MWF	Spanish
2	Reading	Secondary	Morning	T Th	Spanish
3	Reading	Primary	Afternoon	T Th	Mandarin
4	Reading	Secondary	Afternoon	MWF	Spanish
5	Math	Primary	Morning	MWF	Mandarin
6	Math	Secondary	Afternoon	T Th	ASL

Case Problem 17.2 From a Different Perspective

"And do you have the answer to Problem 6, Pete?" asked Professor Grasso.

"Yes sir, I have the answer according to the textbook, but I'm not sure I get it," replied Pete.

"You don't understand how to get the solution?"

"Oh, I understand the numbers, but I don't know what they're good for. Where I work, nobody ever 'sequences' anything. You don't have time to calculate things like slack and critical ratio. You do what's next in line or on top of the stack, unless you see a red tag on something that needs to be rushed through. Or maybe you run what's most like what you've just finished working on so the machine doesn't have to be changed. Or you run what can get done the fastest because when you produce more you get paid more."

"Pete, it sounds to me like you are using sequencing rules—FCFS, highest priority, minimum setup, and SPT."

Pete hesitated. "Maybe you're right, but there's still something that bothers me. If you're going to go to all the trouble to rearrange a stack of jobs, you'd want more information than what we're working with."

"What do you mean?"

"I mean, there's no use rushing a job at one station to let it sit and wait at the next. It's like those maniacs who break their neck to pass you on the road, but they never get anywhere. A few minutes later you're right behind them at a stoplight."

"I see."

"You need some way of looking at the entire job, where it's going next, what resources it's going to use, if it has to be assembled with something else, things like that."

"You've got a point, Pete. Why don't you give us a 'real' example we can work with? You talk, I'll write it on the board."

Pete talked for about 10 more minutes, and when he was finished, Professor Grasso had the following diagram on the board.

"Okay, class, let's take this home and work on it. A, B, C, and D are products that comprise a customer's order. They must all be completed before the order can be shipped. The circles represent operations that must be performed to make each product. We've labeled them A1 for the first operation of product A, A2 for the second operation, and so on. The numbers inside the circles are the machines, that are used to perform each operation. We have only three machines 1, 2, and 3. Your job is to decide the sequence in which the products should be processed on each machine. There is no setup time between processes, no inventory on hand, and nothing on order. Assume the customer has ordered 50 units of each product. We'll use a process batch of 100 units and a transfer batch of one. Make a Gantt chart for each machine to show us how quickly you can ship the customer's order. Earliest shipment gets 5 extra points on the final exam."

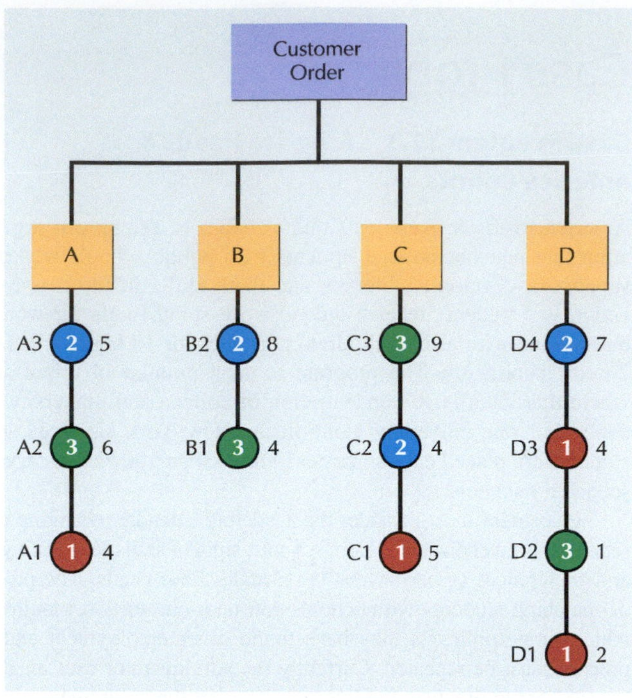

References

Baker, K., and M. Magazine. "Workforce Scheduling with Cyclic Demands and Days-Off Constraints." *Management Science* 24(2; October 1977), pp. 161–167.

Conway, R., W. Maxwell, and L. Miller. *Theory of Scheduling*. Reading, MA: Addison-Wesley, 1967.

Goldratt, E. *What Is This Thing Called Theory of Constraints and How Should It Be Implemented?* Croton-on-Hudson, NY: North River Press, 1990.

Goldratt, E., and J. Cox. *The Goal: Excellence in Manufacturing*. Croton-on-Hudson, NY: North River Press, 1984.

Gupta, J. N. D. "An Excursion in Scheduling Theory." *Production Planning and Control* 13(2; 2002), pp. 105–116.

Huang, P., L. Moore, and R. Russell. "Workload versus Scheduling Policies in a Dual-Resource Constrained Job Shop." *Computers and Operations Research* 11(1; 1984), pp. 37–47.

Jacobs, R, W. Berry, and D. C. Whybark and T. Vollman. *Manufacturing Planning and Control Systems for Supply Chain Management*. New York: McGraw Hill, 2011.

Langevin, A., D. Riopel, and K. Stecke. "Transfer Batch Sizes in Flexible Manufacturing Systems." *Journal of Manufacturing Systems* (March–April 1999), pp. 140–151.

Pinedo, M. *Scheduling: Theory, Algorithms and Systems*. New York: Springer, 2008.

Russell, R., and B. W. Taylor. "An Evaluation of Sequencing Rules for an Assembly Shop." *Decision Sciences* 16(2; 1985), pp. 196–212.

SAP AG. "Production Planning and Detailed Scheduling." Company brochure (December 1999).

Smith, K. A., and J. N. D. Gupta. "Neural Networks in Business." *Computers and Operations Research* 27(1; 2000), pp. 1023–1044.

Umble, M., and M. L. Srikanth. *Synchronous Manufacturing: Principles for World Class Excellence*. Cincinnati: South-Western, 1990.

Xudong, H., R. Russell, and J. Dickey. "Workload Analysis Expert System and Optimizer." *Proceedings of the Seventh International Congress of Cybernetics and Systems,* Vol. 1, London (September 1987), pp. 68–72.

Appendix A

Normal Curve Areas

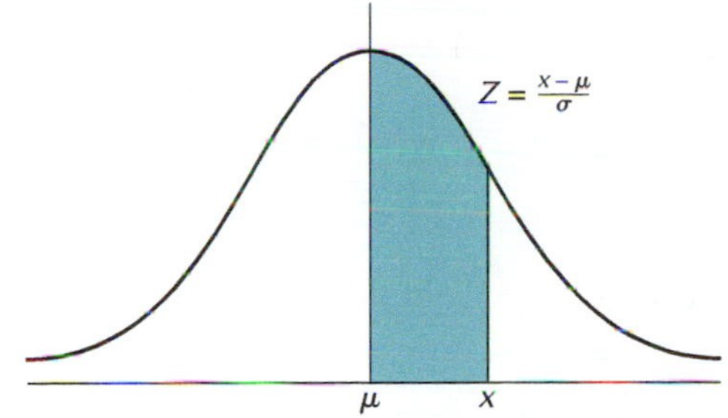

TABLE A.1 Normal Curve Areas

Z	0.00	0.01	0.02	0.03	0.04	0.05	0.06	0.07	0.08	0.09
0.0	0.0000	0.0040	0.0080	0.0120	0.0160	0.0199	0.0239	0.0279	0.0319	0.0359
0.1	0.0398	0.0438	0.0478	0.0517	0.0557	0.0596	0.0636	0.0675	0.0714	0.0753
0.2	0.0793	0.0832	0.0871	0.0910	0.0948	0.0987	0.1026	0.1064	0.1103	0.1141
0.3	0.1179	0.1217	0.1255	0.1293	0.1331	0.1368	0.1406	0.1443	0.1480	0.1517
0.4	0.1554	0.1591	0.1628	0.1664	0.1700	0.1736	0.1772	0.1808	0.1844	0.1879
0.5	0.1915	0.1950	0.1985	0.2019	0.2054	0.2088	0.2123	0.2157	0.2190	0.2224
0.6	0.2257	0.2291	0.2324	0.2357	0.2389	0.2422	0.2454	0.2486	0.2517	0.2549
0.7	0.2580	0.2611	0.2642	0.2673	0.2704	0.2734	0.2764	0.2794	0.2823	0.2852
0.8	0.2881	0.2910	0.2939	0.2967	0.2995	0.3023	0.3051	0.3078	0.3106	0.3133
0.9	0.3159	0.3186	0.3212	0.3238	0.3264	0.3289	0.3315	0.3340	0.3365	0.3389
1.0	0.3413	0.3438	0.3461	0.3485	0.3508	0.3531	0.3554	0.3577	0.3599	0.3621
1.1	0.3643	0.3665	0.3686	0.3708	0.3729	0.3749	0.3770	0.3790	0.3810	0.3830
1.2	0.3849	0.3869	0.3888	0.3907	0.3925	0.3944	0.3962	0.3980	0.3997	0.4015
1.3	0.4032	0.4049	0.4066	0.4082	0.4099	0.4115	0.4131	0.4147	0.4162	0.4177
1.4	0.4192	0.4207	0.4222	0.4236	0.4251	0.4265	0.4279	0.4292	0.4306	0.4319
1.5	0.4332	0.4345	0.4357	0.4370	0.4382	0.4394	0.4406	0.4418	0.4429	0.4441
1.6	0.4452	0.4463	0.4474	0.4484	0.4495	0.4505	0.4515	0.4525	0.4535	0.4545
1.7	0.4554	0.4564	0.4573	0.4582	0.4591	0.4599	0.4608	0.4616	0.4625	0.4633
1.8	0.4641	0.4649	0.4656	0.4664	0.4671	0.4678	0.4686	0.4693	0.4699	0.4706
1.9	0.4713	0.4719	0.4726	0.4732	0.4738	0.4744	0.4750	0.4756	0.4761	0.4767
2.0	0.4772	0.4778	0.4783	0.4788	0.4793	0.4798	0.4803	0.4808	0.4812	0.4817
2.1	0.4821	0.4826	0.4830	0.4834	0.4838	0.4842	0.4846	0.4850	0.4854	0.4857
2.2	0.4861	0.4864	0.4868	0.4871	0.4875	0.4878	0.4881	0.4884	0.4887	0.4890
2.3	0.4893	0.4896	0.4898	0.4901	0.4904	0.4906	0.4909	0.4911	0.4913	0.4916
2.4	0.4918	0.4920	0.4922	0.4925	0.4927	0.4929	0.4931	0.4932	0.4934	0.4936
2.5	0.4938	0.4940	0.4941	0.4943	0.4945	0.4946	0.4948	0.4949	0.4951	0.4952
2.6	0.4953	0.4955	0.4956	0.4957	0.4959	0.4960	0.4961	0.4962	0.4963	0.4964
2.7	0.4965	0.4966	0.4967	0.4968	0.4969	0.4970	0.4971	0.4972	0.4973	0.4974
2.8	0.4974	0.4975	0.4976	0.4977	0.4977	0.4978	0.4979	0.4979	0.4980	0.4981
2.9	0.4981	0.4982	0.4982	0.4983	0.4984	0.4984	0.4985	0.4985	0.4986	0.4986
3.0	0.4987	0.4987	0.4987	0.4988	0.4988	0.4989	0.4989	0.4989	0.4990	0.4990

Appendix B

Answers to Selected Odd-Numbered Problems

Chapter 1

1. Blacksburg

3. last year; yes

5. United States

7. Henry; Fournette

9. **a.** 15.38, 26.67, 40.54; **b.** decreases; **c.** yes

11. John

13. **a.** 10, **b.** 13.33, **c.** .014, **d.** .016

15. Most productive — Taiwan, China, Poland, Czech Republic, Singapore. Least productive — Norway, Germany, Belgium, Sweden, Switzerland.

Supplement 1

1. **a.** Mexico; **b.** China; **c.** Taiwan; **d.** Taiwan

3. **a.** office building; **b.** parking lot; **c.** parking lot or shopping mall; **d.** parking lot

5. **a.** risk fund; **b.** savings bond; **c.** bond fund

7. **a.** Philippines; **b.** Mexico; **c.** Philippines; **d.** Philippines

9. **a.** Thailand; **b.** India; **c.** India; **d.** Philippines

11. **a.** Widget; **b.** EVPI = $24,000; **c.** maximax-widget, maximin-nimnot, regret-widget, equal likelihood-widget

13. major content revision; EVPI = $85,080

15. **a.** Singapore; **b.** Singapore

17. $237,740

19. lockers and showers

21. **a.** stock 28 boxes, $53.50; **b.** EV = $54.90, EVPI = $1.60

23. **a.** Manila, **b.** Veracruz, **c.** Manila, **d.** Manila

25. EVPI = $543,000

29. **a.** Real Estate, **b.** Nursing, **c.** Real Estate, **d.** Nursing

31. **a.** Ramon, **b.** Rodriguez, **c.** Ramon, **d.** Rodriguez

33. **a.** Pusan, **b.** Pusan, **c.** Hong Kong, **d.** Shanghai

35. $101.10; don't purchase the snowblower

37. change oil regularly; EV = $98.80

39. **a.** go for 2; **b.** 0.0306

41. Plan 2

43. conduct test market

Chapter 2

1. **a.** 2012: 84.24%, 2013: 80.22%, 2014: 72.28%, 2015: 65.6%, 2016: 58.3%, decreasing trend; **b.** 2012: 1.71% and 14.05%, 2013: 5.3% and 14.48%, 2014: 13.32% and 14.4%, 2015: 21.97% and 12.43%, 2016. 29.96% and 11.74%; **c.** 2012; 6.93 and 44.48, 2013: 7.50 and 47.64, 2014: 7.85 and 50.04, 2015: 6.90 and 44.46, 2016: 5.79 and 38.32

3. **a.** 139.8; **b.** good = 91.67%

5. 2014: $10.54, 2015: $9.74, 2016: $9.34; 2014–15: −8.21%, 2015–16: −4.22%

7. a. alternative 2, 204; b. alternative 2

9. a. 5.11; b. 5.11; c. 5.58; d. 5.24

11. a. 6.39; b. $31,982.26

13. with defects = 875 units; without defects = 761 units

Chapter 3

1. $\bar{p} = 0.151$, UCL = 0.258, LCL = 0.044; out of control

3. $\bar{p} = 0.053$, UCL = 0.100, LCL = 0.005; in control

5. $\bar{c} = 24.73$, UCL = 39.65, LCL = 9.81; out of control

7. $\bar{c} = 4.167$, UCL = 8.249, LCL = 0.084; out of control

9. $\bar{c} = 12.75$, UCL = 23.46, LCL = 2.04; in control

11. $\bar{R} = 3.17$, UCL = 6.69, LCL = 0; $\bar{\bar{x}} = 3.00$, UCL = 4.83, LCL = 1.18; in control

13. $\bar{p} = 0.097$, UCL = 0.186, LCL = 0.008; in control

15. $\bar{P} = 0.091$, UCL = 0.213, LCL = 0; in control

17. $\bar{R} = 0.57$, UCL = 1.21, LCL = 0; in control

19. a. $\bar{R} = 2$, UCL = 4.56, LCL = 0; b. out of control

21. $\bar{\bar{x}} = 39.7$, UCL = 43.31, LCL = 36.12; out of control

23. no pattern

25. pattern may exist

27. patterns exist

29. $\bar{\bar{x}} = 3.25$, UCL = 5.50, LCL = 1.00; in control

31. $\bar{c} = 16.3$, UCL = 28.41, LCL = 4.19; in control

33. $\bar{\bar{x}} = 7.28$, UCL = 9.73, LCL = 0; in control

35. $\bar{c} = 10.1$, UCL = 19.6, LCL = 0.57; in control

37. $\bar{\bar{x}} = 3.17$; $\bar{R} = 3.25$; $C_p = .53$; $C_{pk} = 0.44$; not capable

39. $\bar{\bar{x}} = 9$; $\bar{R} = 0.57$; $C_p = 1.52$; $C_{pk} = 1.52$; capable

41. $C_p = 1$, $C_{pk} = 0.75$

43. 1: $C_p = 1.25$, $C_{pk} = 1.04$; 2: $C_p = 0.56$, $C_{pk} = .44$; 3: $C_p = 1$, $C_{pk} = 0.87$

45. $\bar{p} = 0.48$, UCL = 0.60, LCL = 0.36; not in control

47. process mean = 145.5 gms, UCL = 147.25, LCL = 143.75

49. a. $\bar{R}$-chart, $\bar{R} = 16.4$, UCL = 34.69, LCL = 0; $\bar{x}$-chart, $\bar{\bar{x}} = 25.54$, UCL = 34.05, LCL = 15.03, in control; b. $C_p = 0.52$, $C_{pk} = 0.48$, not capable

51. $\bar{c} = 2.667$, UCL = 7.57, LCL = 0

53. a. $\bar{R} = 47.47$, $\bar{\bar{x}} = 146.79$, UCL = 122.18, LCL = 0, in control; $\bar{x}$-chart, UCL = 195.35, LCL = 98.23; b. $C_p = 0.31$, $C_{pk} = -0.024$, not capable

Supplement 3

1. a. $n = 131$, $c = 5$, $\alpha = .0049$, $\beta = .095$

3. no; $n = 208$, $c \leq 18$

5. $n = 131$, $c = 5$

Chapter 4

3. 0.934

5. 0.994

7. a. no; b. 0.992

9. a. professional; b. standard

11. a. 0.422, b. 0.347, c. 0.470

13. a. 0.804, 0.656; b. 0.961, 0.959; c. when replacement workers are used

15. a. 0.839, b. 0.966

17. Able Copy

19. JCN

Chapter 5

1. $L_q = 1.33$, $W_q = 4.80$ min; not good service
3. **a.** $L_q = 0.5$, $W = 0.20$ hr, $W_q = 0.10$ hr; **b.** $\lambda > \mu$
5. $\lambda = 9$/hr
7. no
9. **a.** $L_q = 5.14$ trucks, $W = 0.05$ day, $W_q = 0.03$ day; **b.** yes
11. $L = 1.01$, Lq = 0.177, $W = 0.101$ hr, $W_q = 0.0175$ hr; yes
13. Yes, assign an operator
15. $P_0 = 0.005$, $L = 7.94$, $L_q = 2.938$, $W_q = 0.783$, $W = 2.11$
17. Yes, hire a third doctor
19. 3 servers should be sufficient
21. Add more employees; expected savings = \$25.50/day
23. $L_q = 1.94$, $W_q = 0.176$ hr
25. $P_{n \geq 10} = 0.4182$
27. 7:00 A.M. – 9:00 A.M. = 4, 9:00 A.M. – noon = 2, noon – 2:00 P.M. = 6, 2:00 P.M. – 5:00 P.M. = 4
29. $L = 0.1476$ car out of service, $W = 13.52$ hr.
31. Select new service agreement, savings = \$1813.50
33. $L_q = 16.35$ manuscripts, $L = 27.78$ manuscripts, $W_q = 2.09$ weeks, $W = 3.47$ weeks, $U = 0.952$
35. high-speed copier
37. **a.** $W_q = 17.34$ min.; **b.** $P(x \geq 6) = 0.0006$
39. 4 registers
41. $W_q = 0.31$ hr, $W = 0.81$ hr, system adequate
43. **a.** $L_q = 1.177$, $W_q = 2.33$ hr, $W = 3.82$ hr, $U = 0.7551$; not effective; reduce athletes to 6.
45. 4 cranes
47. **a.** 5, **b.** 2.25, **c.** 4.5, **d.** 0.75
49. **a.** 4; **b.** 16 mins; **c.** 20%; **d.** 41%

Chapter 6

3. 500; \$7500
5. 625; \$31,250
7. **a.** 18,118; **b.** 363 days, 91 days; **c.** 84 days, yes
9. choose supplier if demand <800; choose process B if demand >2000; choose process A otherwise
11. **a.** 2, **b.** 1, **c.** below 100 units choose 3; above 250 units choose 1; otherwise choose 2.
13. choose provider 1 if claims >10; choose provider 2 if claims <5; otherwise, choose provider 3
15. choose labor-intensive if units <6667; choose fully automated if units >41,666; otherwise, choose automated
17. choose A if demand <2400; choose C if demand >20,000; otherwise, choose B
19. choose A if <20 movies; choose C if >40 movies; choose B otherwise
21. choose A > 2000; C < 1000; B otherwise
23. **a.** 10 **b.** \$9075 **c.** 1072 **d.** 24,952 **e.** basic **f.** deluxe **g.** >163

Chapter 7

1.

3	1	2
4	6	5

3.

1	3	2
	5	4

5.

2	1	3
4	5	

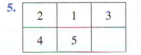

7. a. 135; **b.** 70; **c.** switch 4 and 5, or 1 and 3;

9.

1	3	2
4	5	6

90 nonadjacent loads

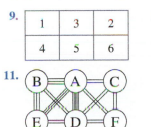

11.

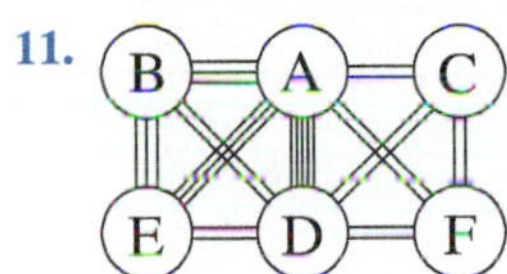

13. A, B → D → C, E; 85.19%, 53.33

15. a. A → B, C, D → E, F, G → H, I, J (multiple solutions); 4 workers; 77.5%;
b. A, B, C, D → E, F, G → H, I, J (multiple solutions); 3 workers, 93.94%

17. $C_d = 4$ min; N = 4; A, E → B, C → D → F; 100%

19. 4 students; A, B → C → D, E → F (multiple solutions); no, students would have to work more than 5 days a week

21. A, B, C, D, E → F, G, H → I, J → K (multiple solutions); 75%

23. Multiple solutions; A, B, D → E, F, C → G, H, I → J, K; 34 beds; or A, B, D → E, F, H → G, I, J → C, K; 36 beds

25. A, D, F → E, H → B, C, G → I, J, K; 95.8%; 40 units

27. Assign jobs A, C, D, G, I, M to Cell 1 which contains processes 1, 2, 3, 7, 9, 12, 14; Assign jobs H, K, N, O to Cell 2 which contains processes 5, 10, 15, 16; Assign jobs B, E, F, J, L, P, Q to Cell 3 which contains processes 4, 6, 8, 11, 13.

Supplement 7

1. Mall 1 = 62.75, mall 2 = 73.50, mall 3 = 79.50, mall 4 = 67.00; select mall 3

3. South = 73.80, West A = 74.50, West B = 67.25, East = 73.90; select West A

5. C = 76, E = 75, D = 74, B = 70, A = 69; select C

7. A = 77.5, B = 75.5, C = 74.25, D = 78.75 select Dowling.

11. varies based on student-defined weights

13. a. $x = 253.36$; $y = 238.70$

15. $x = 935.71$, $y = 971.27$

17. $x = 1665.4$, $y = 1562.9$

19. $x = 78.8$, $y = 106$

21. $x = 265.23$, $y = 363.84$

23. $x = 1559.8$, $y = 1766.8$

25. $x = 271$, $y = 893$

27. $x = 635.1$, $y = 441.4$

Chapter 8

1. $t_{100} = 20.5$ min; 16,424.1 min per week

3. $t_{60} = 48.89$ hr, $t_{120} = 44.98$ hr

5. $t_{30} = 807.88$ hr, $t_{60} = 702.86$ hr

7. 0.9024

9. $t_{80} = 45.1$ sec

11. $t_{136,000} = 3$ min per line; 250 lines

Supplement 8

1. 4.163 min

3. **a.** 2.39 min; **b.** avg. = \$4.52/hr, subject = \$4.82/hr

5. **a.** 4.52 min; **b.** $n = 31$

7. $n = 12.2$ or 13 cycles

9. **a.** 1.383 min; **b.** $n = 7.7$ or 8 cycles; **c.** poorer quality

11. $n = 683$

13. **a.** 88.8%; **b.** 151 more observations

15. 3.946 min

17. **a.** $n = 271$

19. **a.** 347 additional observations; **b.** 69%

Chapter 9

1. Time = 10 weeks

3. **a.** 23 weeks; $s_1 = 0, s_2 = 1, s_3 = 0, s_4 = 10, s_5 = 1, s_6 = 0, s_7 = 9, s_8 = 0, s_9 = 11$; **b.** 1-3-6-8

5. 1: ES = 0, EF = 7, LS = 2, LF = 9, S = 2; 2: ES = 0, EF = 10, LS = 0, LF = 10, S = 0; 3: ES = 7, EF = 13, LS = 9, LF = 15, S = 2; 4: ES = 10, EF = 15, LS = 10, LF = 15, S = 0; 5: ES = 10, EF = 14, LS = 14, LF = 18, S = 4; 6: ES = 15, EF = 18, LS = 15, LF = 18, S = 0; 7: ES = 18, EF = 20, LS = 18, LF = 20, S = 0; CP = 2-4-6-7

7. 1: ES = 0, EF = 10, LS = 0, LF = 10, S = 0; 2: ES = 0, EF = 7, LS = 5, LF = 12, S = 5; 4: ES = 10, EF = 14, LS = 14, LF = 18, S = 4; 3: ES = 10, EF = 25, LS = 10, LF = 25, S = 0; 5: ES = 7, EF = 13, LS = 12, LF = 18, S = 5; 6: ES = 7, EF = 19, LS = 13, LF = 25, S = 6; 7: ES = 14, EF = 21, LS = 18, LF = 25, S = 4; 8: ES = 25, EF = 34, LS = 25, LF = 34, S = 0; CP = 1-3-8 = 34

9. CP = 1-3-7-8 10-12 = 15 days

11. CP = a-b-f-h = 15 wk

13. CP = a-d-g-k = 33 wk, $\sigma = 3.87$, $P(x \leq 40) = .9649$

15. CP = a-b-d-g-k = 33 hours

17. **e.** CP = 1-3-7-8-10-12; **f.** 18 months

19. **c.** CP = b-f-j-k; **d.** 28.17 wk; **e.** 0.0113

21. 57.33 days $P(x \leq 67) = .9535$

23. CP = a-c-d-h-l-o-q = 118.67; $P(x \leq 120) = .59$

25. crash cost = \$23.250

27. CP = a-d-g-k, crashing cost = \$5100

29. CP = a-b-e-f-g-h-i-j-k = 104.83

31. CP = 2-5-9-11-15-16 = 85.66; $P(x \leq 96) = .947$

33. CP = a-b-e-g-i-j-k-l-m-n = 71.17; $P(x \leq 76) = .9147$

35. CP = a-h-l-m-n-o-s-w = 126.67; $P(x \leq 150) = .9974$

Chapter 10

1. Inventory turns = 14.2; days of supply = 25.94

3. Inventory turns = 10.17; weeks of supply = 35.88

5. Inventory turns = 2.72, days of supply = 134.22

7. Supplier 1: inventory turns = 22.6, weeks of supply = 2.3; Supplier 2: inventory turns = 9.25, weeks of supply = 5.6

9. $\bar{c} = 12.75$, UCL = 23.46, LCL = 2.04, in control

11. $\bar{\bar{x}} = 3.01$, UCL = 4.85, LCL = 1.17; $\bar{R} = 3.17$, UCL = 6.69, LCL = 0; in control

Supplement 11

1. Bethlehem – Detroit = 130, Bethlehem – St. Louis = 50, Birmingham – Detroit = 30, Birmingham – Norfolk = 220, Gary – St. Louis = 70, Gary – Chicago = 170; \$84,100.

3. T – NY = 160, T – C = 130, M – P = 140, F – P = 70, F – B = 180; \$6220

5. P – L = 10, S – L = 5, St.L. – C = 15, D – G = 10, D – C = 5; \$215,000

7. A – B = 25, A – P = 25, St.L. – B = 25, St.L. – D = 90; $10,500

9. No change

11. Alternative 1 = $28,920, alternative 2 = $25,600; select 2

13. 1 – 1 = 27, 1 – 2 = 5, 1 – 4 = 10, 2 – 2 = 21, 3 – 3 = 18, 4 – 4 = 23, 5 – 4 = 4, 5 – 5 = 31, 6 – 3 = 4, 6 – 4 = 7, 6 – 6 = 16; 467 miles

15. A – 3 = 1, C – 1 = 1, D – 1 = 1, E – 3 = 1, F – 2 = 1, G – 2 = 1, H – 1 = 1; 1070

17. N – Addison = 270, S – Beeks = 120, S – Canfield = 190,E – Addison = 130, E – Canfield = 190, W – Daley = 220, C – Beeks = 280; 20,550 minutes

19. A – 3 = 8, A – 4 = 18, B – 3 = 13, B – 5 = 27, D – 3 = 5, D – 6 = 35, E – 1 = 25, E – 2 = 15, E – 3 = 4; $1528

21. 1 – E = 8, 2 – C = 12, 3 – E = 2, 4 – D = 8, 5 – A = 9, 6 – B = 6; 1263 hrs.

23. Sac. – St Paul = 15, Sac. – Topeka = 1, Bak. – Denver = 10, S.A – Topeka = 12, Mont. – Denver = 10, Jack. – Akron = 15, Jack. – Topeka = 7, Ocala – Louisville = 15; $276,200

25. L.A. – Singapore = 150, L.A. – Taipei = 300, Savannah – H.K. = 400, Savannah – Taipei = 200, Galv. – Singapore = 350, Shortages – H.K. = 200; $723,500; penalties = $160,000

27. 1 – G = 1, 2 – B = 1, 3 – H = 1, 4 – L = 1, 5 – K = 1, 6 – F = 1, 7 – D = 1, 8 – A = 1; $4260.

29. x_{1C} = 11,200; x_{2A} = 2400; x_{2B} = 8100; x_{4B} = 1900; x_{4C} = 2800; x_{6A} = 9600; y_1 = 1, y_2 = 1, y_4 = 1, y_6 = 1, Z = $2,082,300

31. Houston – Singapore = 26,000, Savannah – Singapore = 8000, Savannah – Karachi = 10,000, Savannah – Mumbai = 1000, New Orleans – Mumbai = 14,000, Charleston – Karachi = 12,000; Z = $1,748,000

33. China – Philadelphia = 3,149,000, China – New Orleans = 468,000, India – Philadelphia = 3,978,000, India – Rotterdam = 255,000, Japan – London = 368,000, Japan – New Orleans = 1,932,000, Turkey – Rotterdam = 3,167,000, Italy – London = 2,067,000; Z = $6,850,280

35. Hamburg – Norfolk = 42, NY – Chicago = 50, Marseilles – Savannah = 63, Liverpool – NY = 37, Norfolk – St. Louis = 42, Hamburg – NY = 13, Savannah – Dallas = 60, Savannah – St. Louis = 3; Z = $77,362

37. **a.** OH – IN = 72, PA – GA = 105, NY – IN = 83, IN – VA = 75, IN – KY = 80, GA – VA = 15, GA – LA = 90, Z = $10,043,000; **b.** OH – IN = 72, PA – GA = 105, NY – IN = 48, NY – GA = 35, IN – VA = 40, IN – KY = 80, GA – VA = 50, GA – KY = 90, Z = $10,043,000

39. Italy – TX = 2.1, Germany – Mexico = 5.2, Belgium – Panama = 6.3, Mexico – OH = 5.2, Panama – VA = 3.7, Panama – OH = 2.6, Z = $27.12 million

41. Antwerp – Boston = 85, Antwerp – Savannah = 40, Barcelona – Savannah = 70, Barcelona – Mobile = 15, Barcelona – Houston = 125, Cherbourg – Mobile = 85, Boston – NC = 85, Savannah –TX = 55, Savannah – NC = 55, Mobile – OH = 100, Houston –OH = 70, Houston – TX = 55, OH – Phoenix = 85, OH – KC = 35, OH – Louisville = 90, TX – Columbus = 40, TX – KC = 70, NC – Phoenix = 20, NC – Memphis = 120; Z = $1,179.400

43. Antwerp = 1, Bremen = 1, Valencia = 1, Hong Kong – Antwerp = 235, Antwerp – Miami = 190, Shanghai – Bremen = 170, Antwerp – New Orleans = 330, Busan – Valencia = 165, Bremen – New York = 165, Mumbai – Antwerp = 285, Bremen – Savannah = 305, Mumbai – Valencia = 40, Valencia – New York = 275, Kaoshiung – Bremen = 300, Valencia – New Orleans = 35, Kaoshiung – Valencia = 105, Z = $47,986,050, Shipping cost = $6,215,050

45. Louisiana – Charleston = 12,000, Mississippi – Savannah = 19,000, Mississippi – New Orleans = 14,000, Texas – Houston = 26,000, Houston – Singapore = 26,000, Savannah – Singapore = 8000, Savannah – Karachi = 10,000, Savannah – Mumbai = 1000, New Orleans – Mumbai = 14,000, Charleston – Karachi = 12,000; Z = $2,945,000

Chapter 12

1. **a.** Apr = 8.67, May = 8.33, Jun = 8.33, Jul = 9.00, Aug = 9.67, Sep = 11.0, Oct = 11.00, Nov = 11.00, Dec = 12.00, Jan = 13.33; **b.** Jun = 8.20, Jul = 8.80, Aug = 9.40, Sep = 9.60, Oct = 10.40, Nov = 11.00, Dec = 11.40, Jan = 12.60; **c.** MAD(3) = 1.89, MAD(5) = 2.43

3. **a.** F_4 = 116.00, F_5 = 121.33, F_6 = 118.00, F_7 = 143.67, F_8 = 138.33, F_9 = 141.67, F_{10} = 135.00, F_{11} = 156.67, F_{12} = 143.33, F_{13} = 136.67; **b.** F_6 = 121.80, F_7 = 134.80, F_8 = 125.80, F_9 = 137.20, F_{10} = 143.00, F_{11} = 149.00, F_{12} = 137.00, F_{13} = 142.00; **c.** F_4 = 113.95, F_5 = 116.69, F_6 = 125.74, F_7 = 151.77, F_8 = 132.4, F_9 = 138.55, F_{10} = 142.35, F_{11} = 160.00, F_{12} = 136.69, F_{13} = 130.20; **d.** 3-qtr MA: E = 32.0, 5-qtr MA: E = 36.4, weighted MA: E = 28.05

5. **a.** F_4 = 276.67, F_5 = 283.32, F_6 = 303.33, F_7 = 356.67, F_8 = 393.33, F_9 = 420.00, **b.** F_2 = 270.00, F_3 = 278.00, F_4 = 272.40, F_5 = 275.92, F_6 = 294.74, F_7 = 317.79, F_8 = 334.23, F_9 = 357.38; **c.** 3-sem MAD = 61.33, exp. smooth MAD = 70.42

7. F_{11} (exp. smooth) = 68.6, F_{11} (adjusted) = 69.17, F_{11} (linear trend) = 70.22; exp. smooth: $E = 14.75$, MAD = 1.89; adjusted: $E = 10.73$, MAD = 1.72; linear trend: MAD = 1.09

9. a. MAD = 3.12; **b.** MAD = 2.98; **c.** MAD = 2.87

11. $F_{13} = 631.22$, $\overline{E} = 26.30$, $E = 289.33$, biased low

13. SF1 = 154.2, SF2 = 191.3, SF3 = 120.3, SF4 = 156.6.

15. F_9 (adjusted) = 3,313.19, F_9 (linear trend) = 2,785.00; adjusted: MAD = 431.71, $E = -2522$; linear trend: MAD = 166.25

17. $y = 195.55 + 2.39x$; fall = 44.61 winter = 40.13, spring = 52.38, summer = 70.34

19. $F_9 = 492.31$, F_9 (adjusted) = 503.27; MAD = 49.36

21. $y = 347.33 + 3.856x$, $F_{37} = 490.01$, MAD = 65.48; $F_{37} = 460.56$, MAD = 74.92; $F_{37} = 467.80$, MAD = 65.75; 5 – mo. moving avg.

23. $E = 86.00$, $\overline{E} = 8.60$, MAD = 15.00, MAPD = 0.08

25. UCL = 718.14, LCL = −718.84, no apparent bias

27. a. $\overline{E} = 10.73$, MAD = 16.76, MAPD = 0.1038, $E = 75.10$; **b.** $\overline{E} = 8.00$, MAD = 12.67, MAPD = 0.08, $E = 39.99$; **c.** biased low

29. MAD = 1.78, $E = 12.36$, biased high; MAD (linear trend) = 0.688

31. $y = 3643.35 - 15.67x$; $y(115) = 1841.78$; $r = -0.655$.

33. a. $y = 0.51 + 0.403x$, $y(x = 25) = 10.57$; **b.** r = 0.914

35. 0.694

37. $y = 15.864 - 0.575x$; $r^2 = 0.616$; $y(23) = 2.64\%$

39. $y = 6253.33 - 183.606x$; **a.** MAD (linear regression) = 310, MAD (linear trend) = 256; **b.** −0.850

41. a. $y = 380.93 + 16.03x$ ($y = 557.26$); **b.** $y = -22.07 + 41x$ ($y = 594.10$): **c.** "b" best

43. a. $SF_1 = 62.78$, $SF_2 = 68.53$, $SF_3 = 82.89$, $SF_4 = 71.40$; **b.** Q1 = 60.64, Q2 = 65.94, Q3 = 80.86, Q4 = 69.39.

45. Exponential smoothing models appear to be most accurate

49. $y = 28{,}923.02 + 3{,}715.9x$, $y(3) = 40{,}070.74$

51. a. $y = 37.72 + 247x$, 65.15%; **b.** $y(11) = 64.54\%$

53. a. $y = 219.27 + 12.28x$, $y = 415.67$; **b.** $y = -5349.77 + .147x$, $r = 0.966$, $y = 541.41$.

55. $y = 1.704 + 0.269x$, $r^2 = 0.546$

57. a. $y = 745.91 - 2.226x_1 + 0.163x_2$; **b.** $r^2 = 0.992$; c. $y = 7{,}186.91$

59. a. $y = 219.67 - 0.027x_1 + 233.871x_2$; **b.** $r^2 = 0.956$; **c.** $y = \$882.82$

61. a. $y = 43.09 + .0007x_1 + 1.397x_2$; **b.** $r^2 = 0.696$; **c.** $y = 76.66$

Chapter 13

1. a. $Q = 120.1$; **b.** TC = \$15,612.49; **c.** 12.49 orders; **d.** 29.14 days

3. a. $Q = 292.5$; **b.** TC = \$7,897.47; **c.** 56.41 orders; **d.** 5.67 days

5. a. $Q = 278{,}971.3$; **b.** TC = \$22,317.71; **c.** 5.07 orders; **d.** 72 days

7. a. $Q = 79$, TC = \$5,924.53

9. a. $Q = 1{,}264.9$; **b.** TC = \$632.46; **c.** $R = 54.79$

11. $Q = 20{,}263.88$; TC = \$486,333.22

13. a. $Q = 2{,}529.8$; **b.** TC = \$12,648; **c.** 63.2 days; **d.** 42.2 days

15. a. $Q = 90{,}137.52$; TC = \$3,020.45 **b.** no

17. a. $Q = 9.1$; TC = \$1,095.45; **b.** $Q = 6$, TC = \$1,193.33

19. $Q = 70{,}000$; TC = \$56,000; 4 orders

21. $Q = 52.3$, TC = \$19,595.92, Time between orders = 119.2, orders = 3.06, $R = 13.33$

23. $Q = 2346.59$; TC = 162,486.91, Max. inventory level = 2,346, $R = 2{,}008.9$

25. $Q = 603{,}008$; TC = \$9,497,381; 2.06 shipments; Time between shipments = 176.8 days

27. $Q = 5000$; TC = \$68,725

29. $Q = 500$; TC = \$64,704

31. $Q = 6000$; TC = \$87,030.33

33. $Q = 20{,}000$; TC = \$893,368

35. $R = 30{,}603.42$; safety stock = 2,603.42

37. $R = 83{,}016.7$

39. $R = 259.2$; safety stock = 46.67

41. $R = 32.38$

43. $Q = 122$ pizzas; 117 pizzas

47. $R = 9.22$

Supplement 13

1. **b.** $\mu = 3.48$, EV = 3.65, not enough simulations; **c.** 21 calls, no, repeat simulation

3. $\mu = \$251$

5. reorder at 5-car level

7. avg. waiting time = 22 min

11. avg. rating of Salem dates: 2.92

Chapter 14

1. **a.** \$9,024,500; **b.** \$9,403,500

3. **a.** \$3,812,000; **b.** \$3,780,000; **c.** \$3,770,000; **d.** \$3,800,000

5. **a.** \$1,232,000; **b.** \$1,560,000; **c.** \$1,267,000

7. **a.** \$421,800; **b.** \$335,750; **c.** \$334,400; **d.** \$314,000

9. \$1,432,600

11. \$1,210,000

13. \$45,900

15. \$1,800,000

17. \$451,500

19. \$144,700

21. \$683,000

23. 5; 105

25. 16, 0, 0, 0, 55, 27

27. 85, 13, 0, 28, 77, 95; 13; 6 weeks

29. 2 seats; 1 seat

31. 55 seats

33. 20 trees

35. **a.** 100; **b.** 75; **c.** 43; **d.** 1

Supplement 14

1. **a.** Maximize $Z = \$2.25x_1 + 3.10x_2$; s.t. $5.0x_1 + 7.5x_2 \le 6500$, $3.0x_1 + 3.2x_2 \le 3000$, $x_2 \le 510$, $x_1 \ge 0$, $x_2 \ge 0$; **b.** and c. $x_1 = 456$, $x_2 = 510$, $Z = \$2{,}607$

3. Maximize $Z = 1800x_{1a} + 2100x_{1b} + 1600x_{1c} + 1000x_{2a} + 700x_{2b} + 900x_{2c} + 1400x_{3a} + 800x_{3b} + 2200x_{3c}$; s.t. $x_{1a} + x_{1b} + x_{1c} = 40$, $x_{2a} + x_{2b} + x_{2c} = 40$, $x_{3a} + x_{3b} + x_{3c} = 40$, $x_{1a} + x_{2a} + x_{3a} \le 40$, $x_{1b} + x_{2b} + x_{3b} \le 60$, $x_{1c} + x_{2c} + x_{3c} \le 50$, $x_{ij} \ge 0$; $x_{1b} = 40$, $x_{2a} = 40$, $x_{3c} = 40$, $Z = \$212{,}000$

5. Maximize $Z = 4.5x_{bs} + 3.75x_{os} + 3.60x_{cs} + 4.8x_{ms} + 3.25x_{bd} + 2.5x_{od} + 2.35x_{cd} + 3.55x_{md} + 1.75x_{br} + 1.00x_{or} + 0.85x_{cr} + 2.05x_{mr}$; s.t. $0.6x_{cs} - 0.4x_{bs} - 0.4x_{os} - 0.4x_{ms} \ge 0$, $-0.3x_{bs} + 0.7x_{os} - 0.3x_{cs} - 0.3x_{ms} \ge 0$, $0.4x_{bd} - 0.6x_{od} - 0.6x_{cd} - 0.6x_{md} \ge 0$, $-0.1x_{bd} - 0.1x_{od} - 0.1x_{cd} + 0.9x_{md} \le 0$, $-0.6x_{br} - 0.6x_{or} - 0.6x_{cr} + 0.4x_{mr} \le 0$, $0.7x_{br} - 0.3x_{or} - 0.3x_{cr} - 0.3x_{mr} \ge 0$, $x_{bs} + x_{bd} + x_{br} \le 110$, $x_{os} + x_{od} + x_{or} \le 80 < x_{cs} + x_{cd} + x_{cr} \le 70 < x_{ms} + x_{md} + x_{mr} \le 150$, $x_{ij} \ge 0$

b. $x_{os} = 52.5$, $x_{cs} = 70$, $x_{ms} = 52.5$, $x_{bd} = 52.2$, $x_{md} = 8.7$, $x_{br} = 57.8$, $x_{or} = 1.4$, $x_{mr} = 88.8$, $x_{od} = 26.1$, $Z = \$1251$

7. **a.** Maximize $Z = 8x_1 + 10x_2$; s.t. $x_1 + x_2 \ge 400$, $x_1 \ge 0.4(x_1 + x_2)$, $x_2 \le 250 < x_1 = 2x_{2,}$ $x_1 + x_2 \le 500$, $x_i \ge 0$; **b.** $x_1 = 333.3$, $x_2 = 166.6$, $Z = 4332.4$

9. Maximize $Z = 3x_{1s} + 5x_{2s} + 6x_{4s} + 9x_{1P} + 11x_{2P} + 6x_{3P} + 12x_{4P} + 1x_{1R} + 3x_{2R} + 4x_{4R} - 2x_{3R}$; s.t. $x_{1S} + x_{2S} + x_{3S} + x_{4s} \ge 3000$, $x_{1P} + x_{2P} + x_{3P} + x_{4P} \ge 3000$, $x_{1R} + x_{2R} + x_{3R} + x_{4R} \ge 4000$, $x_{1S} + x_{1P} + x_{1R} \le 5000$, $x_{2S} + x_{2P} + x_{2R} \le 2400$, $x_{3S} + x_{3P} + x_{3R} \le 4000$, $x_{4s} + x_{4P} + x_{4R} \le 1500$, $0.6x_{1S} - 0.4x_{2S} - 0.4x_{3S} - 0.4x_{4S} \ge 0$, $-0.2x_{1S} + 0.8x_{2S} - 0.2x_{3S} - 0.2x_{4S} \le \phi \ge \ge 11 < -0.3x_{1S} - 0.3x_{2S} + 0.7x_{3S} - 0.3x_{4S} \ge 0$, $-0.4x_{1P} - 0.4x_{2P} + 0.6x_{3P} - 0.4x_{4P} \ge 0$, $-0.5x_{1R} + 0.5x_{2R} - 0.5x_{3R} - 0.5x_{4R} \le 0$, $0.9x_{1R} - 0.1x_{2R} - 0.1x_{3R} - 0.1x_{4R} \ge 0$, $x_{ij} \ge 0$; $x_{1s} = 1200$, $x_{1R} = 3800$, $x_{2P} = 2200$, $x_{2R} = 200$, $x_{3S} = 900$, $x_{3P} = 3100$, $x_{4S} = 900$, $x_{4P} = 600$, $Z = \$63{,}400$

11. Minimize $Z = 190\ Sr_j + 260\ SO_j + 5\ Si_j$; s.t. $r_j \leq 160$, $O_j \leq 50$, $r_1 + O_1 - i_1 \geq 105$, $r_2 + O_2 + i_1 - i_2 \geq 170$, $r_3 + O_3 + i_2 - i_3 \geq 230$, $r_4 + O_4 + i_3 - i_4 \geq 180$, $r_5 + O_5 + i_4 - i_5 \geq 150$, $r_6 + O_6 + i_5 \geq 250$, $Z =$ \$215,600

13. $x_1 = 12$ A.M. – 2 A.M. $= 40$, $x_4 = 20$, $x_5 = 40$, $x_6 = 20$, $x_7 = 10$, $x_9 = 40$, $x_{10} = 10$, $Z = 180$

15. $x_{t1} = 750$, $x_{t2} = 180$, $x_{t3} = 1680$, $x_{m1} = 750$, $x_{m2} = 450$, $x_{m3} = 480$, $x_{b2} = 270$, $x_{b3} = 240$, $Z = 10{,}798.50$

17. $x_1 = 3.3$, $x_2 = 6.7$, $Z = 566.67$

19. $x_1 = 376{,}470.59$; $x_2 = 343{,}526.41$; $Z = 88{,}376.47$

21. b. $x_1 = 120$ cups, $x = 80$ cups, $z = \$370$; **d.** does not affect solution; **e.** $x_1 = 123.1$ cups, $x_2 = 82.1$ cups, $Z = \$379.53$; **f.** not spend

23. $x_1 = 2945$, $x_2 = 1000$, $Z = 445$; 32 fewer defective items

25. Stays same; stays same; changes to $x_1 = 22.5$, $x_2 = 22.5$, $Z = \$198{,}000$

27. b. $x_{11} = 65.385$, $x_{14} = 384.615$, $x_{22} = 400$, $x_{23} = 170$, $x_{31} = 150.3$, $x_{33} = 169.7$; $Z = \$11{,}738.28$

29. $x_{13} = 25{,}000$, $x_{14} = 8000$, $x_{16} = 2000$, $x_{24} = 4000$, $x_{25} = 8000$, $x_{34} = 5000$, $Z = \$59{,}100$; **b.** $Z =$ \$52,000

31. a. $x_{14} = 20$, $x_{44} = 40$, $x_{35} = 20$, $x_{55} = 60$, $x_{66} = 90$, $x_{17} = 20$, $x_{27} = 30$, $x_{77} = 50$, $y_5 = 5$, $y_6 = 10$, $y_7 = 20$, $Z = \$31{,}500$; **b.** $x_{34} = 20$, $x_{44} = 40$, $x_{25} = 5$, $x_{35} = 20$, $x_{55} = 60$, $x_{26} = 10$, $x_{66} = 90$, $x_{17} = 40$, $x_{27} = 25$, $x_{77} = 50$, $y_7 = 5$, $Z = \$26{,}000$

33. $x_1 = 54$, $x_2 = 108$, $x_3 = 162$, $Z = \$253.80$; **a.** \$0.78; **b.** \$0; **c.** $x_1 = 108$, $x_2 = 104$, $x_3 = 162$, $Z = \$249.48$

35. $x_1 = 1000$, $x_2 = 800$, $x_3 = 200$, $Z = \$760$; **a.** \$38; **b.** $x_1 = 1000$, $x_2 = 1000$, $Z = \$770$; **c.** $x_1 = 1600$, $x_2 = 200$, $x_3 = 200$

37. $x_{A3} = 400$, $x_{A4} = 50$, $x_{B4} = 250$, $x_{B5} = 350$, $x_{C4} = 175$, $x_{C7} = 274.1$, $x_{C8} = 50.93$, $x_{D2} = 131.7$, $x_{D7} = 15.93$, $x_{E1} = 208.33$, $x_{E8} = 149.07$, $x_{F1} = 291.67$, $x_{F2} = 108.3$, $x_{F6} = 460$; $Z = 12{,}853.33$

39. $x_{12} = x_{13} = x_{14} = x_{15} = 37{,}000$; $x_{26} = x_{36} = x_{46} = x_{56} = 12{,}000$; $x_{27} = x_{37} = x_{47} = x_{57} = 6{,}000$; $x_{28} = x_{38} = x_{48} = x_{58} = 19{,}000$; $x_{69} = 5000$; $x_{79} = 6000$; $x_{89} = 3000$; $x_{810} = 16{,}000$; $x_{611} = 7000$; $x_{912} = 14{,}000$; $x_{1012} = 16{,}000$; $x_{1112} = 7000$; $Z = \$40{,}680$

41. $x_{1C} = 1$, $x_{3D} = 1$, $x_{AB} = 1$, $x_{5A} = 1$, $Z = 83$

43. a. Atlanta = 1, Nashville = 1, Pittsburgh = 1, $Z = 3$; **b.** Cleveland = 1, Nashville = 1, Richmond = 1, $Z = 3$, TC = \$1061 million

45. a. $y_1, y_2, y_3, y_4, y_5 = 1$, $x_1 = 1$, $x_2 = 26$, $x_3 = 10$, $x_4 = 2$, $x_6 = 7$, $Z = 9$; **b.** $y_2 = 1$, $y_3 = 1$, $x_2 = 29$, $x_3 = 64$, $Z = \$5{,}289{,}000$

47. $x_{A2} = 34{,}558.82$; $x_{A3} = 145{,}441.18$; $x_{B1} = 167{,}259.79$; $x_{B2} = 147{,}740.21$; $x_{C3} = 61{,}804.51$; $x_{C4} = 278{,}195.49$; $x_{E2} = 61{,}345.18$; $Z = \$34{,}133{,}052.63$

49. $x_{1B} = 1$, $x_{2A} = 1$, $x_{3A} = 1$, $x_{4B} = 1$, $x_{7C} = 1$, $x_{11C} = 1$, $Z = \$79{,}000$

51. $x_{1G} = 1$, $x_{2B} = 1$, $x_{3D} = 1$, $x_{4L} = 1$, $x_{5K} = 1$, $x_{6E} = 1$, $x_{7A} = 1$, $x_{8C} = 1$, $z = 4.420$

53. a. football fields, playgrounds, walking/running trails, softball fields, $z = 123{,}500$; **b.** soccer fields, playgrounds, walking/running trails; $z = 4.0$ or 1.33 avg. priority.

55. 1 – 3 – 4 – 5 – 2 – 1, z = 75 miles

Chapter 15

1. a. 6; **b.** 7; **c.** 3

5. b. 800; **c.** day 1

7. \$240.80

9. 100 B's, 50 C's, 50 D's, 400 E's, 900 F's, 200 G's, 100 H's, 100 I's

13. order in periods 1–5 for quantities 50, 50, 56, 50, 50

15. Order 25, 75 and 100 product X in periods 5, 6, and 7. Order 100, 100, and 200 part Y in periods 3, 4, and 5.

17. b. 5 days; **c.** no; **d.** back panel, drawer guide, side panel, legs

19. L4L = \$2900; EOQ = \$4220; POQ = \$2770

21. L4L = \$910; EOQ = \$632.50; POQ = 527.50

23. a. 56.68 hours each period; **b.** 55.83, 80, 63, and 27.5 hours in periods 1–4; \$480 is saved

25. a. 3.53 hours; **b.** 163%

27. 94% load; yes

Chapter 16

1. SS50—SS100—SS50—SS200

3. 4 (these answers are rounded up)

5. 125/hr

7. c; decreases

9. **a.** 9 kanbans, inventory increases; **b.** 3 kanbans, inventory halved; **c.** 14 kanbans, no change in inventory

11. **a.** C-V-C-S-C-V-C; **b.** 25

13. **a.** M-T-M-B-M-T-M-B-M-T-M; **b.** 5

Chapter 17

1. Jones to Nurse 1, Hathaway to Nurse 2, Sweeney to Nurse 3, Bryant to Nurse 4

3. Product 1 to machine B, product 2 to machine D, product 3 to machine A, product 4 to machine C, product 5 to machine E

5. A to Finance, B to Production, C to Customer Service, D to Logistics, E to Sales, F to Marketing Research

7. 21

9. FCFS; DDATE; Point value of assignment, grade in class, major

11. SPT: 23.88, 9.75, 22, 5; DDATE: 30.75, 8.25, 13, 7; SLACK: 31.63, 9.13, 17, 7; depends on criteria

13. **a.** 12, 3, 7; **b.** 12.25, 3.25, 6; **c.** 13, 3.75, 6; depends on criteria

15. 8-4-6-5-9-2-1-3-10-7; 104 mins

17. **a.** T, O, S, Q, P, R; **b.** 22 hrs; **c.** 16 hrs

19. E-F-A-B-C-D; 24 hrs

21. 6, 5, 4, 2, 1, 3; 335 mins

23. Backlog = 20, 10, 5, 5, 10

25. **b.**

	M	T	W	Th	F	Sa	Sn
K.J.	0	X	X	X	X	X	0
T.S.	0	0	X	X	X	X	X
F.C.	X	X	X	X	0	0	X
S.B.	X	X	X	X	X	0	0
P.T.	X	0	0	X	X	X	X

27.

	M	T	W	Th	F	Sa	Sn
A.R.	0	0	X	X	X	0	X
S.H.	0	X	0	X	X	X	0
J.J.	0	X	0	X	X	X	0
T.T.	0	X	X	0	X	X	X
E.T.	X	0	X	0	X	X	X
P.D.	X	0	X	X	0	X	X

29. **d.** 5201

Index

Note: Page numbers followed by a "*t*" indicate the entry may be found within a table. Page numbers followed by an "*f*" may be found within a figure.

Q

R

T